श्रीगङ्गेशोपाध्यायकृतः

तत्त्वचिन्तामणिः

श्रीगङ्गेशोपाध्यायकृतः

तत्त्वचिन्तामणिः

प्रथमो भागः

प्रत्यक्षखण्डम्

श्रीकामाख्यानाथतर्कवागीशेन परिशोधितम्

श्रीमथुरानाथतर्कवागीशविरचितया
रहस्याख्यया टीकया सहितः

मोतीलाल बनारसीदास
दिल्ली • मुम्बई • चेन्नई • कोलकाता • बंगलौर
वाराणसी • पुणे • पटना

Reissued in 2013
Reprint: Delhi, 1974
First Edition: Calcutta, 1897
(The Asiatic Society of Bengal)

ISBN: 978-81-208-2549-9

MOTILAL BANARSIDASS
41 U.A. Bungalow Road, Jawahar Nagar, Delhi 110 007
8 Mahalaxmi Chamber, 22 Bhulabhai Desai Road, Mumbai 400 026
203 Royapettah High Road, Mylapore, Chennai 600 004
236, 9th Main III Block, Jayanagar, Bengaluru 560 011
Sanas Plaza, 1302 Baji Rao Road, Pune 411 002
8 Camac Street, Kolkata 700 017
Ashok Rajpath, Patna 800 004
Chowk, Varanasi 221 001

Printed in India
by RP Jain at NAB Printing Unit,
A-44, Naraina Industrial Area, Phase I, New Delhi–110028
and published by JP Jain for Motilal Banarsidass Publishers (P) Ltd,
41 U.A. Bungalow Road, Jawahar Nagar, Delhi-110007

INTRODUCTION*

39. Importance of Tattva-cintāmaṇi.

The **Tattva-cintāmaṇi** ("a thought-jewel of truth"), otherwise known as **Pramāṇa-cintāmāṇi** ("a thought-jewel of valid knowledge"), of which a short summary in English is given in the following pages, was written by a Brāhmaṇa logician of Mithilā named Gaṅgeśa Upādhyāya. It introduces a new era in the development of Logic in India and is justly reckoned as the first work on the Modern School of Hindu Logic. In modern India Sanskrit scholarship is not considered of any worth unless it is accompanied by a knowledge of the Tattva-cintāmaṇi or at least a portion of it. The study of this work develops to an enormous extent the discursive faculty in the reader and enables him to argue with hair-splitting distinctions and subtleties.

The book, since its first composition in the 12th century A.D., has been a subject of close study by the Paṇḍits of Mithilā, and about the middle of the 15th century its study was introduced into Bengal by Vāsudeva Sārvabhauma, who had been educated in the academies of Mithilā. Since 1503 A.D., when the university of Navadvīpa was established, the Tattva-cintāmaṇi was much popularised in Bengal through the endeavours of the famous Raghunātha Śiromaṇi and others. Gradually the book was introduced into Madras, Mahārāṣṭra and Kāśmīra, and in a couple of centuries it became known all over India. The influence of this epoch-making book can be traced in the works on almost all the branches of Sanskrit learning that have appeared during the last five hundred years. Unfortunately no attempt has yet been made to present the contents of the work in English, Bengali, Hindi or any other modern language, perhaps on account of the bewildering abstruseness of its style and thought.

40. Gaṅgeśa—the Author of the Tattva-cintāmaṇi. (1200 A.D.).

The **Tattva-cintāmāṇi** is the immortal work of Gaṅgeśa, also called Gaṅgeśvara, surnamed Upādhyāya, who was a Maithila Brāhmaṇa. He was born in a village named Karion on the banks of the river Kamalā, twelve miles south-east of Darbhanga. It is said that Gaṅgeśa while young was altogether illiterate. He propitiated the goddess Kālī, on the cremation ground adjacent to

*Reproduced from *History of Indian Logic* by Satis Chandra Vidyabhushana

his uncle's house, and acquired from her, as a boon, deep erudition in the science of Logic.

Gaṅgeśa mentions the name of Śivāditya Miśra,[1] the well-known author of Saptapadārthī, and makes frequent quotations from Ratna-kośa,[2] which is a work on the Vaiśeṣika philosophy. Nothing is definitely known about the Gauḍa Mīmāṁsaka[3] or Śrīkara[4] mentioned by him. Gaṅgeśa must have flourished after 1093-1150 A.D., the period when Ānanda Sūri and Amaracandra Sūri,[5] whose opinions he has quoted, flourished. As he criticises the Khaṇḍana-khaṇḍa-khādya, he must have been posterior also to Śrī Harṣa who lived in Kanauj in the Court of King Jayacandra in 1186 A.D.[6] The earliest date that has been assigned to Gaṅgeśa is before the first quarter of the 13th century A.D., when his son Vardhamāna Upādhyāya lived, in other words Gaṅgeśa is assigned to the last quarter of the 12th century A.D.[7]

---

1 *Vide* Tattva-cintāmaṇi, pratyakṣa-khaṇḍa, p. 830.

2 The Ratnakośa, a work on Vaiśeṣika philosophy, has been quoted not only by Gaṅgeśa in the Tattva-cintāmaṇi (śabda-khaṇḍa, ākhyāta-vāda, p. 830, and anumāna-khaṇḍa, p. 885), but also by Vardhamāna in the Nyāya-kusumāñjali and by Raghunātha Śiromaṇi in the Anumāna-dīdhiti. Glosses on Ratnakośa are said to have been written both by Harirāma and Gadādhara. This Ratnakośa is different from the Advaita-ratna-kośa—a work on the Vedānta philosophy by Akhaṇḍānanda—as well as from the Prameya-ratna-kośa, a work on Jaina philosophy by Candraprabha Sūri (1102 A.D.).

3 *Vide* Tattva-cintāmaṇi, śabda-khaṇḍa, śabda-prāmāṇya-vāda, p. 88.

4 *Vide* Tattva-cintāmaṇi, śabda-khaṇḍa, jāti-śakti-vāda, p. 569.

5 *Vide* S. C. Vidyabhuṣaṇa's 'Indian Logic: Mediæval School', pp. 47-48. Ānanda and Amaracandra, nicknamed respectively Vyāghraśiśuka and Siṁhaśiśuka, have been referred to by Gaṅgeśa in the Tattva-cintāmaṇi under *siṁha-vyāghrokta-lakṣaṇa* of *vyāpti*. (*Vide* p. 396 above.)

6 Khaṇḍana-khaṇḍa-khādya is quoted in the Tattva-cintāmaṇi, anumāna-khaṇḍa, p. 233, Bibliotheca Indica Series. For Śrī Harṣa and Jayacandra, see the Indian Antiquary, 1911-12; Prācīna-lekha-mālā, nos. 22-23; and B.B.R.A.S. of 1875, p. 279. Jayacandra was killed by Sahabuddin Ghori in 1194 A.D.

7 According to the Dhanukhā inscription Maheśa Ṭhakkura, brother of Bhagīratha Ṭhakkura, the well-known author of a sub-commentary on the Tattva-cintāmaṇi, lived in 1556 A.D. Considering that in the succession of the generations of pupils Bhagīratha Ṭhakkura was seventh in descent from Gaṅgeśa Upādhyāya, and allowing an average life of thirty years for each generation, we may assume that Gaṅgeśa lived 180 years before Bhagīratha, that is, about the year 1376 A.D.

The succession of pupils from Gaṅgeśa is as follows:—

1. Gaṅgeśa; 2. Vardhamāna; 3. Yajñapati; 4. Hari Miśra; 5. Pakṣadhara; 6. (*a*) Vāsudeva, (*b*) Rucidatta, (*c*) Candrapati (?); 7. (*a*) Maheśa Thakkura, (*b*) Bhagīratha Ṭhakkura; 8. A pupil; 9. Bhavanātha; 10. Śaṅkara Miśra.

The inscription is found on a stone-slab attached to a well at the village Dhanukhā near Janakapura in Darbhanga. It runs thus:—

आसीत् पश्चिम[illegible]विदितो [illegible],
[illegible] गिरि[illegible] महेशः [illegible]।
शाके [illegible] संवत्सरे [illegible],
[illegible]।

[Those who maintain that Gaṅgeśa lived in the fourth quarter of the 12th century A.D.[1] base their contention on the mention of Vardhamāna, son of Gaṅgeśa, in the Sarvadarśana-saṁgraha in the 14th century A.D.[2] and upon an interpretation of the expression *śakābdā la saṁ 1509*, occurring in a manuscript of Pakṣadhara Miśra's commentary on Gaṅgeśa's Tattva-cintāmaṇi, as equivalent to 1278 A.D.[3] Now the verse on the authority of which Vardhamāna is supposed to have been mentioned in the Sarvadarśana-saṁgraha is obviously an interpolation, and the expression *śakābdā la saṁ 1509*, written in very modern characters, refers in my opinion *not* to Lakṣmaṇa saṁvat 159, corresponding to 1278 A.D., but to *śaka* year 1509 corresponding to 1587 A.D., the word *la saṁ* being either redundant or signifying simply a year. In fact, if Gaṅgeśa had been older than the author of the Sarvadarśana-saṁgraha, his work would have been reviewed, or at any rate referred to, in it.]

41. The Text of Tattva-cintāmaṇi.

Book I.—Perception—*Pratyakṣa-khaṇḍa*.

The Tattva-cintāmaṇi is divided into four books dealing respectively with (1) Perception (*pratyakṣa*), (2) Inference (*anumāna*), (3) Comparison (*upamāna*), and (4) Verbal testimony (*śabda*), which are the four means of deriving valid knowledge. The first book, which treats of perception, opens with stanzas saluting God Śiva.[4]

The śaka 1478 referred to here corresponds to 1556 A.D. That Maheśa Ṭhakkura was a brother of Bhagīratha Ṭhakkura appears from the opening lines of the Dravya-prakāśikā by the latter.

[1] *Vide* M. M. Chakravarti's History of Navya-nyāya, J.A.S.B. for 1915, p. 265; Rājendra Nath Ghose's Vyāpti-pañcaka, Introduction, p. 33.

[2] *Vide* Sarvadarśana-saṁgraha, Pāṇiniya-darśana.

[3] प्रत्यक्षालोक (Pratyakṣāloka), which is a commentary on Gaṅgeśa's Tattva-cintāmaṇi by Pakṣadhara Miśra, was, according to its colophon, copied in the Śaka year 1509 (corresponding to 1587 A.D.) and *not* in the Lakṣmaṇa saṁvat 159 (corresponding to 1278 A.D.), as the date contained in the colophon runs thus :—

शुभमस्तु श्रीरस्तु शकाब्दा ॥ ल सं १५०९ तें श्रावणस ६ ॥

गुणातीतोऽपीशस्त्रिगुणसचिवस्त्र्यक्षरमयः
त्रिमूर्त्तिर्यः सर्गस्थितिविलयकर्माणि तनुते ।
कृपापारावारः परममतिरेकस्त्रिजगतां
नमस्तस्मै कस्मैचिदमितमहिम्ने पुरभिदे ॥ १ ॥
अन्वीक्षानयमाकलय्य गुरुभिर्ज्ञात्वा गुरूणां मतं
चिन्तादिव्यविलोचनेन च तयोः सारं विलोक्याखिलम्
तन्त्रे दोषगणेन दुर्गमतरे सिद्धान्तदीक्षागुरु
र्गङ्गेशस्तनुते मितेन वचसा श्रीतत्त्वचिन्तामणिम् ॥ २ ॥

Invocation of Blessings—*Maṅgala-vāda*.

Salutation is offered to Śiva to invoke his blessings. The invocation is of three kinds, *viz*. bodily, vocal, and mental. The bodily invocation consists in saluting a deity, the vocal in reciting the eulogy of the deity, and the mental in meditating on him. "All polite people," says Gaṅgeśa, "must observe the decorum of invoking blessings if they wish to bring their work to a successful completion." Though we do not find any explicit text in the Veda enjoining invocation of blessings, yet from the laudable practice of good people we can easily infer the implicit existence of such a text. It should be stated that the invocation of blessings is not the immediate cause of the completion of a work but is the means of removing obstacles which beset the work. In the case of an atheist finishing his work successfully without any invocation of blessings, we are to suppose that there were no obstacles in his way, or that he performed the invocation in his previous life. The case of a theist invoking blessings and yet failing to finish his work, is explained on the supposition that he encountered enormous obstacles which his feeble invocation could not remove. The Kādambarī, which opens with a profuse invocation of blessings, furnishes an illustration of a work remaining unfinished, owing to the excess of obstacles in its way.

The Validity of Knowledge—*Prāmāṇya-vāda*.

Pramā or valid knowledge.

In determining the true meaning of *pramāṇa* (the means of valid knowledge) one must understand the true meaning of the word *pramā* (valid knowledge). *Pramā* or valid knowledge is the knowledge of a thing as it is,—it is the knowledge of the generic nature as abiding in its own subject, that is, abiding in every one of its individual embodiments. For instance, to know a piece of silver to be as such, is valid knowledge inasmuch as "silverness," which is a generic nature, really abides in the individual silver which is its subject.

How is valid knowledge derived and known?

Two questions arise here: (1) whence is the validity of knowledge derived, and (2) how are we conscious of the validity? To the first question the Mīmāṁsakas (*Prāabhākaras*) reply by saying that knowledge derives its validity from its own general grounds (or causes). As to the second question they say that knowledge is self-evident, that is, the very grounds, out of which arises consciousness of knowledge, produce also the consciousness of its validity, and this consciousness of validity prompts us to activity.

Gaṅgeśa opposes the first reply by saying that if the validity of knowledge were derived from the general grounds of knowledge itself, then invalid knowledge would have been identical with valid knowledge. The second reply is also opposed on the ground that if we were conscious of the validity of knowledge along with our consciousness of knowledge itself, there could not have arisen in us doubt with regard to the validity of any kind of knowledge specially in the unhabitual condition. But there often arises in us knowledge of a dubious character, and the Mīmāṁsakas cannot satisfactorily explain the production of this dubious knowledge or doubt. If there is consciousness of knowledge, there is, according to them, along with it a consciousness of its validity which leaves no room for doubt, and if, on the other hand, there is no consciousness of knowledge, there cannot arise any consciousness of its dubiousness. Hence Gaṅgeśa concludes that the validity of knowledge is not derived from its general grounds (or causes). It is, according to him, derived through its special cause called instrument. The general grounds of knowledge are the union of the tactual surface with the mind and that of the latter with the soul, while the special causes are different. The special cause of perception is the intercourse of a sense-organ with its object without any hindrance, that of inference is consideration (or the knowledge of premisses), that of comparison is the knowledge of similarity, and that of verbal testimony is the knowledge of consistency. Our knowledge of colour, for instance, is valid if there is the contact of our eye with the colour without any hindrance. Gaṅgeśa further observes that our consciousness of the validity of a particular knowledge does not arise from our consciousness of the particular knowledge itself, but from a different source, *viz* inference from the fruitful correspondence between our knowledge (idea) and the activity prompted by it. "This knowledge (idea)," says he, "is valid because it is conducive to activity which is fruitful; whatever is not conducive to activity which is fruitful, is not valid knowledge." Suppose, for instance, a person cognises from distance a white thing to be a piece of silver. His knowledge will be valid if it harmonises with his actual experience when he approaches the piece of silver. Our consciousness of the validity of a particular knowledge arises therefore from our consciousness of the fruitful correspondence or harmony between the particular knowledge (idea) and the activity which it leads to.

Invalid Knowledge—*Anyathākhyāti*.

apramā, anyathākhyāti, bhrama, or invalid knowledge.

Gaṅgeśa says that invalid knowledge or error, in Sanskrit *apramā*, *anyāthā-khyāti* or *bhrama*, is the knowledge (experience) of a thing as it is not,—it is the knowledge (experience) of a generic nature, which does not abide in its own subject, but which abides in the subject of another generic nature. For instance, to know a pearl to be a piece of silver is invalid knowledge, inasmuch as the generic nature "silverness" does not abide here in the piece of silver which is its own subject, but abides in a pearl which is the subject of another generic nature, *viz.* "pearlness."

How is activity, *pravṛtti*, caused?

The Mīmāṁsakas (*Prābhākaras*) do not admit invalid knowledge or error. All knowledge, according to them, is valid and, as such, prompts us to activity. In the case of a person who takes a pearl to be a piece of silver by saying "this is silver," we should bear in mind that he acquires the knowledge of "this" (pearl) through perception and that of "silver" through recollection. But he, owing to some defect, is not conscious of the distinction between "this" (pearl) and "silver," that is, between "perception" and "recollection"; and this non-consciousness of distinction leads him to activity.

Gaṅgeśa opposes the Mīmāṁsakas by saying that the non-consciousness of distinction cannot account for the activity to which the person is prompted. There are here, according to the Mīmāṁsakas, grounds for activity, counter-activity and non-activity. The knowledge of "silver," for which the person is solicitous, must cause in him an activity, while the knowledge of "this" (pearl), for which he is not solicitous, must cause in him a counter-activity, and the non-consciousness of distinction (which is absence of knowledge) causes in him neither activity nor counter-activity, but leaves him in non-activity. The non-consciousness of distinction is not therefore the cause which leads him to activity.

According to Gaṅgeśa, when a person takes a pearl to be a piece of silver by saying "this is silver," he acquires the knowledge of both "this" (pearl) and "silver" by means of perception (the first through the ordinary intercourse between the sense-organ and its object, and the second through the transcendent intercourse whose character is knowledge). He, through some defect (of his eye, etc.), identifies "this" (pearl) with "silver," that is, becomes conscious of the generic nature "silverness" as abiding in "this" (pearl), which is not its own subject. Here his knowledge is invalid, or, in other words, he commits an error. When a person, on the other hand, takes a piece of silver to be silver by saying "this is silver," he identifies "this" with "silver," or, in other words, becomes conscious of the generic nature "silverness" as abiding in "silver" which is its own subject. His knowledge is valid.

Whether a particular knowledge is valid or invalid, it must be of a determinate character, if it is to lead us to activity. Determinate knowledge is the knowledge of a generic nature as abiding in a subject. As already stated, when the generic nature abides in its own subject, the knowledge is valid: but when it abides in the subject of another generic nature, the knowledge is invalid. A valid determinate knowledge (*pramā*) leads us to activity which is fruitful, while an invalid determinate knowledge (*apramā*) leads us to activity which does not end in fruition. In explaining the cause of activity, whether fruitful or fruitless, we must assume determinate knowledge, and in accounting for fruitless activity we must assume error. Moreover, it is a matter of experience that in our consciousness, valid or invalid, of the form "this is silver," there is only one kind of knowledge, *viz.* determinate knowledge, and it will be cumbrous to assume two kinds, *viz.* perception and recollection.

Intercourse between Senses and their Objects—*Sannikarṣa.*

Ordinary Preception (*laukika-pratyakṣa*).

Perceptual knowledge, or, more simply, perception, has been defined (by Akṣapāda) as knowledge which arises from the intercourse of a sense with its object, and which is non-erratic, being either reflective (mediate) or non-reflective (immediate). This definition, according to Gaṅgeśa, is too wide in so far as it includes recollection and inference of the soul, and is also too narrow in so far as it excludes perception by God. To avoid such defects Gaṅgeśa proposes to define perception as a direct apprehension. When, for instance, a visual perception takes place, there arises in us a corresponding knowledge of the form "I apprehend direct." Perception is further defined by Gaṅgeśa as knowledge whose intrumental cause is not knowledge. The instrumental causes of inference, comparison and verbal testimony are respectively the knowledge of premisses, the knowledge of similarity and the knowledge of consistency; but the instrumental cause of the perception is a sense-organ which is not knowledge.

Perceptual knowledge, (*pratyakṣa*).

The word perception, which ordinarily signifies perceptual knowledge or rather the means by which we derive perceptual knowledge, does sometimes stand for the whole process in which a sense in intercourse with its object produces knowledge. The senses are six, *viz.* (1) the eye, (2) the ear, (3) the nose, (4) the tongue, (5) the tactual surface, and (6) the mind. Their objects are respectively the following:—(1) colour, (2) sound, (3) odour, (4) savour, (5) touch (of warmth, coldness, hardness, softness, etc.), and (6) feeling (of pleasure, pain, etc.). Correspondent with the senses there are six kinds of knowledge (perception), *viz.* the visual, auditory, olfactory, gustatory, tactual and mental (internal).

The intercourse, or rather the ordinary intercourse, which is the connection of a sense with its object, is of six kinds as mentioned below :—

(1) *Union* (*saṁyoga*), *e.g.* in the visual perception of a jar there is a union of our eye with the jar.

(2) *United-inherence* (*saṁyukta-samavāya*), that is, inherence in that which is in union, *e.g.* in the visual perception of the colour of a jar there is a union of our eye with the jar in which colour inheres.

(3) *United-inherent-inherence* (*saṁyukta-samaveta-samavāya*), that is, inherence in that which inheres in what is in union, *e.g.* in the visual perception of the "colourness" (the generic nature of colour) of a jar there is a union of our eye with the jar in which inheres colour wherein again abides "colourness" in the relation of inherence.

(4) *Inherence* (*samavāya*), *e.g.* in the auditory perception of sound there is the inherence of sound in the ether which pervades the cavity of our ear.

(5) *Inherent-inherence* (*samaveta-samavāya*), that is, inherence in that which inheres, *e.g.* in the auditory perception of "soundness" (the generic nature of sound), there is the inherence of "soundness" in sound which again inheres in the ether of our ear-cavity.

(6) *Particularity* (*viśeṣaṇatā*), *e.g.* in the perception of non-existence of a jar on a ground, there is a union of our eye with the ground which is possessed of non-existence of the jar.

Transcendent Perception (*alaukika-pratyakṣa*).

The supersensuous or transcendent perception does not take place through any of the six kinds of ordinary intercourse described above But it is produced through an intercourse which is transcendent. The transcendent intercourse is of three kinds, *viz.* (1) the intercourse whose character is general (*sāmānya-lakṣaṇa*); (2) the intercourse whose character is knowledge (*jñāna lakṣaṇa*); and (3) the intercourse which is produced by meditation (*yogaja*).

Intercourse (*perception*) *whose character is general.*—In the perception of all individuals possessing a generic nature, the knowledge of the generic nature constitutes the intercourse. This is a transcendent intercourse whose character is general. When, for instance, there is an intercourse of our eye with a case of smoke, there arises in us a perception of smoke of all times and all places. The process by which this perception takes place is as follows :—

The intercourse between our eye and the case of smoke is an ordinary one called union (*saṁyoga*) and that between our eye and "smokeness" (the generic nature of smoke) is also an ordinary one which is called united-inherence (*saṁyukta-samavāya*). But the intercourse between our eye and all cases of smoke is not an ordinary one. It is a transcendent intercourse, as there is no ordinary union of our eye with all cases of smoke of all times and all places. The intercourse consists here of the knowledge of "smokeness", a generic nature which is possessed by all cases of smoke of all times and all places. This sort of intercourse which consists of the knowledge of a generic nature, is called a transcendent intercourse whose character is general. The objection that if there were a transcendent intercourse (perception) whose character is general, we could become omniscient, inasmuch as in perceiving an object of knowledge we could perceive all objects of knowledge, is untenable because, though we can perceive all objects of knowledge comprehended under a generic nature, we cannot perceive their mutual differences, and as such cannot be omniscient.

Intercourse (perception) whose character is knowledge.—If in the perception of a thing the knowledge of the thing itself constitutes the intercourse, it is called an intercourse whose character is knowledge. On seeing a piece of sandal-wood we often say that it is fragrant. How does this visual perception of fragrance take place? The answer is that when the eye comes in union with the piece of sandal-wood, there arises within us a kind of knowledge (recollection) of fragrance which serves as the intercourse for our perception of the same. This is an instance of what is called in Western Psychology an "indirect perception"

Some say that the case cited above may be explained by the intercourse whose character is general, and there is no necessity for our assuming another intercourse whose character is knowledge. On seeing a piece of sandal-wood there arises in us the recollection of fragrance and "fragrancy" (the generic nature of fragrance), which abide in sandal-wood in the relations of inherence (*samavāya*) and inherent-inherence (*samaveta-samavāya*) respectively. From the recollection of "fragrancy", through the intercourse whose character is general, there arises in us the perception of all individual fragrances including the fragrance of this particular piece of sandal-wood.

In reply Gaṅgeśa says that, though, through the intercourse whose character is general, we can somehow explain the perception of fragrance, we cannot through this intercourse explain the perception of "fragrancy". Had there been a "fragranciness" (which is the generic nature of *fragrancy*), we could have, through the intercourse whose character is general, derived the perception of "fragrancy". But there is no generic nature of "fragrancy", which is itself the generic nature of fragrance. We cannot therefore perceive "fragrancy" through the intercourse whose character is general. It is through the intercourse whose character is knowledge that we can perceive "fragrancy", the recollection of which serves as the intercourse for such perception.

Intercourse (perception) produced by meditation.—It is of two kinds, *viz.* (1) the intercourse (perception) of an ascetic who has attained union with the Supreme Being, and (2) that of an ascetic who is endeavouring to attain such union. The first ascetic enjoys a constant perception of all things, while the second ascetic can secure perception only when he is attended with mediation.

Inherence—*Samavāya-vāda.*

In the visual perception of the colour of a jar, the intercourse that exists between our eye and the colour has been designated as united-inherence. It is not possible to understand the meaning of this term unless we understand the meaning of inherence. Inherence (*samavāya*) is an intimate relation between two things which cannot exist separately. Of the two things one exists only as lodged in the other. Such things are the whole and its parts, the substance and its qualities or action, the community and individuals, and the eternal substances and their final particulars. The relation that exists between these things is called inherence, *e.g.* threads inhere in the cloth, colour inheres in the jar, and so on. The knowledge of a whole as composed of parts, or of a substance as possessing qualities, etc. is determinate knowledge. In such knowledge we have to consider three things, *viz.* the subject, the predicate, and the relation that exists between them. For instance, in our determinate knowledge of the form "the man has a stick," the man is the subject and the stick is the predicate, while the relation that exists between them is union. Similarly in our determinate knowledge of the form "the flower has colour," the flower is the subject and the colour is the predicate, but the relation that exists between them is not union but inherence. When two things can be separated from each other, the relation between them is union, but when they cannot be mutually separated their relation is inherence. In fact colour is not united with flower but inheres in it.

The Invalidity of Non-perception—*Anupalabdhyaprāmāṇya-vāda.*

Some say that non-existence is not perceptible by any of our senses and that the knowledge of non-existence of a thing arises through non-perception of the thing itself. For instance, the way in which the knowledge of non-existence of a pot arises is as follows: Had there been a pot here, it would have been perceived: since it is not perceived, there is no pot here. The non-perception of a pot is therefore the means of knowing the non-existence of the pot. Gaṅgeśa does not admit non-perception to be a means of knowledge. Non-existence, according to him, is perceived by our senses through the intercourse of particularity. For instance, in the perception of non-existence of a pot on the floor, there is the union of our eye with the floor in which abides non-existence of the pot as a particularity, that is, there is perception of the floor as possessed of the non-existence of the pot. The sense employed in the perception of a thing is the same as that which is employed in the perception of its non-existence. Whatever thing is perceptible by a sense, the non-existence of that thing is also perceptible by the same sense, *e.g.* a colour and its non-existence are both perceived by the eye, a sound and its non-existence by the ear, an odour and its non-existence by the nose, a savour and its non-existence by the tongue, warmth and its non-existence by the tactual surface, and pleasure and its non-existence by the mind.

Non-existence (or negation)—*Abhāva-vāda*.

Some say that there is no separate entity called non-existence (*abhāva*), that perception of what is ordinarily called the "non-existence of a thing" depends upon the locus (*adhikaraṇa*) of non-existence of the thing, and that the intercourse through which we perceive the thing, must be the same as that through which we perceive its non-existence, *viz.* union, etc. For instance, our perception of the non-existence of a pot (in the form "there is no pot on the floor") does not presuppose a separate entity called "non-existence", but rests entirely on "the floor" which is the locus of the non-existence of the pot, and is carried on through the intercourse of union.

Gaṅgeśa opposes the above view by saying that we must admit a separate entity called non-existence, that our perception of what is ordinarily called the non-existence of a thing, does not rest entirely on the locus of the non-existence of the thing, and that the intercourse through which we perceive the non-existence of the thing is not union etc., but particularity (*viśeṣaṇatā*). In the instance cited above our perception of the non-existence of the pot does not rest on "the floor", that is, the non-existence of the pot is not identical with the floor. Had the one rested on the other, or had the two been identical, there would have been perception of the non-existence of the pot even when the pot was on the floor, and further there would have been a disturbance of the relation of container and contained that exists between the two. Since this contingency is disastrous, we must admit that there is something on the ground which operates in our failure to perceive the pot. This something is "non-existence" which is a separate entity lying over and above the floor. Our failure to perceive a thing does not therefore rest on the mere locus of the thing, but on the locus as possessed of this something or "non-existence." The relation that exists between the locus and non-existence is that of particularity (*viśeṣaṇatā*). When we perceive the non-existence of a pot on the floor our eye comes in union with the floor on which abides the non-existence of the pot in the relation of particularity. The intercourse in this case is, therefore, of united particularity (*saṁyukta-viśeṣaṇatā*). Similarly the relation of particularity is to be associated with inherence, united-inherence, etc.

Every non-existence has a counterpart, *e.g.* with reference to the non-existence of a pot and that of a piece of cloth, the pot and the piece of cloth are respectively the counterparts. The perception of a non-existence is subject to that of its counterpart. The process, by which we perceive non-existence through the relation of particularity, involves knowledge of its counterpart which is produced through memory or from any other source. In our perception of the non-existence of a pot on the floor, there arises in us first of all recollection of the pot, and as soon as our eye comes in union with the floor we perceive the non-existence of the pot on the same.

Non-existence is of two kinds: (1) universal, and (2) reciprocal. The universal non-existence is sub-divided into (*a*) the antecedent, (*b*) the subsequent, and (*c*) the absolute. The antecedent non-existence is that which has no beginning but has an end, *e.g.* a jar is in antecedent non-existence before it is made up. The subsequent non-existence has a beginning but no end, *e.g.* a jar is in subsequent non-existence after it is destroyed. The absolute non-existence is that whose counterpart is viewed in relation to all the three times—past, present, and future, *e.g.* there is no jar on the floor. The reciprocal non-existence is the non-existence of identity, *e.g.* a jar is not a pot.

Causes of Perception—*Pratyakṣa-kāraṇa-vāda*.

The causes of perception are the following:—

(1) A union of the mind with the tactual surface and the soul.

Causes of knowledge in general.

While a person is in deep sleep there is produced in him no knowledge, as there is then a union of his mind with the soul alone but not with the tactual surface. The mind abides at that time near the heart in a *nāḍī* called pericardium which is without a tactual surface. In recollecting a thing our mind is in union with both the tactual surface and the soul.

(2) A union of the mind with the senses and an intercourse of

the senses with their objects, *e.g.* in the perception of a colour there is a union of our mind with the eye which is in intercourse with the colour.

(3) Proportionate extension of the objects of sense, that is, the objects must not be of infinite extension as ether, or of no extension as atoms. The ether and atoms are not perceived but inferred, the former being the locus of sound, and the latter the final particulars of things.

Special causes of perception.

(4) An obviousness or manifest form of an object of sense, *e.g.* a colour, if it is to be perceptible, must possess obviousness. A meteor, which is obscured in the midday blaze, cannot be perceived. Similarly, a fire which exists in the latent condition in a heated frying-pan, is not perceptible.

(5) A special connection of light with the object of sense, *e.g.* a pot, if it is to be perceptible, must have sufficient light on its front rather than on its back.

Special causes of visual perception.

(6) Absence of obstacles, *e.g.* too much proxmity or too much distance, is often obstructive to our perception.

The Atomic Nature of the Mind—*Manoṇutva-vāda*.

The senses through the instrumentality of which we perceive colour, sound, odour, savour and touch, are the eye, ear, nose, tongue and tactual surface respectively. The sense which operates as an instrument in our perception of pleasure, pain, desire, aversion, intellect and volition, is the mind, which is called the internal sense in contrast to the other five senses which are external.

The mind is atomic in extension, inasmuch as we cannot perceive various objects at one and the same time. Although there may exist intercourse of our external senses with their corresponding objects, no perception will be produced until the mind comes in union with them. Had the mind been of infinite extension, or even of proportionate extension, it could have come into union with all the five external senses at once so as to give rise to the five kinds of perception simultaneously. But everybody is aware that it is impossible for more than one kind of perception to arise at one and the same time. This shows that the mind can come into union with only *one* external sense at a time, or in other words, the mind is atomic in extension.

Those who deny the atomic nature of the mind on the ground that sometimes, *e.g.* in eating a large cake soaked in milk and sugar, we find the operations of the mind united with several senses simultaneously, should be told that the operations, which they suppose to be simultaneous, do really take place in succession, as the hundred leaves of a lotus are pierced one after another by a needle.

The Doctrine of Self-consciousness—*Anu-vyavasāya-vāda.*

Some philosophers maintain that any particular kind of knowledge performs by itself all its practical functions and does not depend upon another knowledge for the same. For instance, all practical functions connected with a pot can, according to them, be performed when there is knowledge of the pot, but we cannot perform those functions when there is no such knowledge. It is therefore knowledge which performs all its practical functions. We must not however suppose that all practical functions are performed by all kinds of knowledge promiscuously. In fact each kind of knowledge is, by its very nature, related to a particular object which enables us to perform its corresponding functions.

Some others, who hold the doctrine of triangular perception (*tripuṭī-pratyakṣa-vādinaḥ*), say that each kind of knowledge is self-manifest and that it manifests itself in the form "I know this," which involves an assumption of a knower (the soul), a knowable (the object), and knowledge (the act), and as such performs all its practical functions.

Gaṅgeśa, in opposing the above views, says that a particular kind of knowledge cannot by itself perform its practical functions, but is dependent upon another sort called self-consciousness (*anuvyavasāya*) which enables it to perform the same. Our knowledge, continues Gaṅgeśa, arises in the form "this" or "pot," but not in the form "I know this" or "I know the pot"; and until it assumes the latter form no practical functions can be performed. He therefore lays down that after the origination of knowledge of the form "this" or "pot," there arises another knowledge called self-consciousness of the form "I know this" or "I know the pot," which performs all practical functions. This latter variety, called self-consciousness, arises through the intercourse of the previous knowledge with our mind. The intercourse is united-inherence (*saṁyukta-samavāya*), inasmuch as there is a union of the mind with the soul in which resided the previous knowledge in the relation of inherence. In fact the latter knowledge or self-consciousness is the mental (or internal) perception of the previous knowledge.

Immediate Perception—*Nirvikalpaka-vāda.*

Perception is of two kinds, *viz.* (1) the immediate, non-reflective or abstract (*nirvikalpaka*) and (2) the mediate, reflective or concrete (*savikalpaka*). The immediate is perception of an indeterminate character. It is perception of a subject and its generic nature as separate from each other, *e.g.* the perception of a mere "pot" or mere "potness" without any mutual connection.

Even the mere "pot" or mere "potness" is of the form "something" of which it is absurd to talk as a "pot" or "potness." On the intercourse of a sense with its object the first perception that takes place is immediate or non-reflective. It is supersensuous, that is, not cognisable by any of our senses, not even by the mind. It has been defined as knowledge which is devoid of all connection with name, generic nature, etc., which indicates no relation and involves no specification.

Mediate Perception—*Savikalpaka-vāda.*

The mediate or reflective perception is of a determinate character. It indicates a subject and its generic nature through their relation to each other, *e.g.* "this is a pot" where "potness" (the generic nature) abides in "this" (the subject) in the relation of inherence. The perception of the form "this is a pot" is therefore mediate or reflective.

The doctrine of mediate or reflective perception may be set forth as follows :—

Immediate perception—the perception of "pot" and "potness" as separate from each other.

Mediate perception—the perception of "potness" as abiding in "this" in the form "this is a pot."

Self-consciousness—the mental perception of the knowledge of "potness" as abiding in "this," in the form "I know this is a pot."

Book II.—Inference—*Anumāna-khaṇḍa.*

THE DETERMINATION OF INFERENTIAL KNOWLEDGE—*Anumiti-nirūpaṇa.*

Inferential knowledge (*anumiti*) is that knowledge which is derived through another kind of knowledge, *viz.* that the middle term, in invariable concomitance with the major term, abides in the minor term, *e.g.*

The hill is full of fire,
because it is full of smoke.

Here "hill" is the minor term which is also called the subject, locus or side; "fire" is the major term, also called the predicate or probandum; and "smoke" is the middle term, also called the reason or mark. The knowledge of the form "the hill is full of smoke" is inferential knowledge inasmuch as it is derived through another kind of knowledge, *viz.* that of the smoke which, as being in invariable concomitance with fire, abides in the hill. This other knowledge, *viz.* that smoke, in invariable concomitance with fire, abides in the hill, is an instance of what is called *consideration, knowledge of premises* or *inference* (*parāmarśa* or *anumāna*). It is the intercourse or operation through which we arrive at the inferential knowledge. The whole process of arriving at that knowledge is also sometimes called inference.

Inference distinct from Perception.

Some say that perception is the only means of knowledge and that there is no separate means of knowledge called inference. Their reasons are as follows :—

(1) There cannot be any knowledge of the invariable concomitance between the middle term and the major term ;

(2) The middle term may be erratic owing to its connection with a condition accepted or disputed ; and

(3) We often associate the middle term with the major term through a mere probability which involves no certainty.

Gaṅgeśa sets aside the above view by saying that there are other means of knowledge over and above perception, and that inference is at any rate one means of knowledge. The doctrine of invariable concomitance, etc., will be treated later. In support of inference as a means of knowledge it will suffice at present to observe the following arguments :—

1. One cannot establish the invalidity of an inference unless one *infers* the invalidity from the similarity of the inference with things previously known as invalid. This process presupposes inference as a means of knowledge.

2. The statement that " inference is not a means of knowledge " is of no use to an expert who is aware of the invalidity of inference. It may be advanced usefully before a suspicious or an erring person. Now, how are we to know that the person is in suspicion or error ? It is certainly not through perception but through inference.

3. " Inference is not a means of knowledge " : is this statement valid or invalid ? If it is valid, we must admit verbal testimony to be a means of knowledge. If on the other hand it is invalid, inference is to be admitted as a means of knowledge. Both the alternatives are incompatible with the opponent's view.

4. Moreover if inference is not valid, perception, too, cannot be valid. The validity being an object of inference, how can we, in the absence of inference, ascertain the validity of perception ? If again perception were by itself valid, then there could not arise any doubt about its validity.

Perception is, therefore, not the only means of knowledge. but inference also is one of the means.

Inferential knowledge having been based upon an invariable concomitance of the middle term with the major term. it is necessary to define the phrase "invariable concomitance." In Sanskrit it is called *vyāpti* which is rendered by such expressions as pervasion, inseparable connection, perpetual attendance, constant co-presence, etc.

Five Provisional Definitions of Invariable Concomitance—*Vyāpti-pañcakam.*

1. Invariable concomitance is the non-presence of the middle term in the locus of the non-existence of the major term, *e.g.*

The hill is full of fire,
because it is full of smoke.

Diagram I.

Diagram II.

Here smoke (the middle term) is absent from all regions outside the region of fire (the major term) as shown in diagram I. Gaṅgeśa observes that the definition is defective inasmuch as it does not apply to an exclusively affirmative inference, such as "all are nameable, because they are knowable", illustrated in diagram II, in which outside the region of the nameable there is nothing from which the knowable may be absent.

Diagram III.

2. Invariable concomitance is the non-presence of the middle term in that locus of the non-existence of the major term which is not the locus of the major term itself, *e.g.*

This is occupied by the ape, because it is the tree.

Here "the tree" is the middle term, and "occupied by the ape" is the major term. In diagram III the tree is totally absent from the region not occupied by the ape. The part of the tree not occupied by the ape is excluded from the locus of the non-existence of the major term by the clause "which is not the locus of the major term itself." This definition too is defective, because it, like the previous one, does not apply to an exclusively affirmative inference.

3. Invariable concomitance is the non-co-presence of the middle term with that reciprocal non-existence whose counterpart abides in the locus of the major term, *e.g.*

> The hill is full of fire,
> because it is full of smoke.

In diagram I. we find that smoke is not co-present with anything which is non-existent in reciprocity to fire. Water, book, cloth, table, etc., are all non-existent in their reciprocal relation to fire, that is, they are not fire.

Gaṅgeśa observes that this definition too is defective, as it does not cover the case of an exclusively affirmative inference. In diagram II. we find that there is no reciprocal non-existence whose counterpart is the region of the nameable.

4. Invariable concomitance is the state in which the middle term forms the counterpart of that non-existence which abides in the locus of the non-existence of the entire major term, *e.g.*

> The hill is full of fire,
> because it is full of smoke.

Here smoke forms the counterpart of the non-existence of smoke which abides in the region of the non-existence of entire fire.

According to Gaṅgeśa this definition is defective, as it fails to explain the case of an exclusively affirmative inference. In diagram II. we find that there is no non-existence of the knowable which abides in the region of the non-existence of the nameable.

5. Invariable concomitance is the non-presence of the middle term in what is not the locus of the major term, *e.g.*

> The hill is full of fire.
> because it is full of smoke.

Here smoke is not present in anything which is not the abode of fire. This definition too, according to Gaṅgeśa, is defective, as it does not meet the case of an exclusively affirmative inference. In diagram II. we find that there is no non-presence of the knowable in what is not included in the region of the nameable.

Definition of Invariable Concomitance given by "Lion" and "Tiger"—*Siṁha-vyāghrokta-vyāptilakṣaṇa*.

1. Invariable concomitance is the state in which the middle term has not a locus in which there is the non-co-presence of the major term, *e.g.*

The hill is full of fire,
because it is full of smoke.

Here fire is always co-present with smoke in the locus of the latter. It never occurs that in the locus of smoke there is no fire.

2. Invariable concomitance is the state in which the middle term has not a locus which is different from the locus of the major term, *e.g.*

The hill is full of fire,
because it is full of smoke.

The locus of smoke is never different from that of fire, that is, the former never extends beyond the latter.

Gaṅgeśa observes that both these definitions are defective, inasmuch as their import is to show that the middle term has not a locus which is also not the locus of the major term. On the contrary we find that the middle term has often a locus which is not the locus of the major term. For instance, smoke on a hill has a locus which is not the locus of fire in a kitchen.

Non-existence whose Counterpart is Qualified by a Nature abiding in a Different Locus—*Vyadhikaraṇa-dharmāvacchinnābhāvaḥ*.

Most of the definitions of invariable concomitance given above were defective inasmuch as they did not cover the case of an exclusively affirmative inference. They involved such phrases as "non-existence of the major term" and "difference of locus of the major term" which could not apply to an exclusively affirmative inference in which the major term was all-pervading. To make the "non-existence of the major term" and "difference of locus of the major term" possible, even in an exclusively affirmative inference, some logicians assume a non-existence whose counterpart is qualified by a nature abiding in a locus different from the counterpart. The expression "there is no fire possessing the nature of a pot" signifies that "there is non-existence of a fire as qualified by the nature of a pot" which, according to them, is quite correct inasmuch as the nature of a pot abides in the relation of inherence in a pot and not in fire. Similarly "there is no nameableness possessing the nature of a pot" signifies that "there is non existence of nameableness as qualified by the nature of a pot." Though nameableness (major term) is all-pervading we have, they say, been able to talk of its non-existence by assuming the nature of a pot to abide in it (instead of it in the pot).

Gaṅgeśa opposes the above view in four ways:—(1) On the assumption of a non-existence of this form, invariable concomitance has to be defined as the state in which the middle term has not the co-presence with a non-existence whose counterpart is qualified by a nature which is the nature of the major term. This definition, in which the counterpart and the major term are identical, does not involve a non-existence of the form proposed. The definitions already condemned cannot also be defended by the assumption of this non-existence. (2) This sort of non-existence is not well known and cannot be established by any evidence. (3) The counterpart of the non-existence is said to be qualified by a quality which does not abide in it. This is impossible because our knowledge of non-existence depends on that of its counterpart as possessed of the nature. (4) And to assert a non-existence of this form is as absurd as to say that there is no hare-horn (*śaśa-śṛṅga*) in a cow.

Other Objectionable Definitions of Invariable Concomitance—*Pūrvapakṣaḥ*.

Gaṅgeśa examines and condemns twelve other definitions of invariable concomitance called objectionable definitions given by previous logicians.

The Conclusive Definition of Invariable Concomitance—*Siddhānta-lakṣaṇam*.

Invariable concomitance is the co-presence of the middle term with the major term which is not qualified by the nature of the counterpart of that absolute non-existence, which abides in the same locus with the middle term, but abides in a different locus in respect of that counterpart, *e.g*

The hill is full of fire,
because it is full of smoke.

Diagram IV

Diagram V.

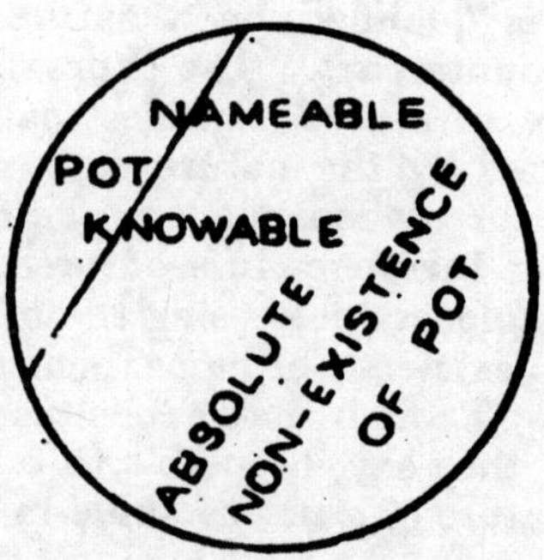

Here there is co-presence of smoke (the middle term) with fire (the major term) which is not qualified by the nature of a pot, and the absolute non-existence, whose counterpart is the pot, abides in the same locus with smoke, but abides in a different locus in respect of the pot.

This definition covers the case of an exclusively affirmative inference inasmuch as it does not involve a non-existence of the major term, and the major term is not the counterpart of that non-existence which abides in the same locus with the middle term. Looking at diagram V, we find that there is co-presence of the knowable with the nameable which is not qualified by the nature of a pot (though the pot is qualified by the nature of the nameable), and the absolute non-existence, whose counterpart is the pot, abides in the same locus with the knowable, but in a different locus in respect of the pot.

Non-existence of the General Form—*Sāmānyābhāvaḥ*.

Some say that even the conclusive definition given above is defective inasmuch as in seeking to establish the invariable concomitance of smoke with fire we notice that fires are manifold owing to the difference of their loci, *e.g.* the fire of a kitchen, of a sacrificial ground, and so on. There is non-existence of these fires, except one, in the locus of a particular case of smoke. This, by making fire the counterpart of that non-existence which abides in the same locus with smoke, altogether upsets the conclusive definition.

Gaṅgeśa in reply says that though in the locus of smoke there is the non-existence of various fires, the natures which qualify the counterparts of those non-existences are not one and the same, *viz.* the nature of fire in general. They are different, that is, particular fires have particular natures, as for instance, the nature of the fire of a kitchen is different from that of the fire of a sacrificial ground, and so on. It is therefore necessary to admit a non-existence of fire of the general form—such as 'there is no fire' distinguished from non-existences of particular forms as 'there are not such and such fires.' A non-existence of the general form is the non-existence whose counterpart is not of a particular nature. Had the non-existence of the general form been a name merely for the sum total of particular non-existences then there would not have arisen in us a doubt of the form—'is not there a colour in air?' It is perfectly known to us that in air there are no particular colours as red, yellow, etc.; yet we entertain a doubt in our mind as to whether there is not in air a non-existence of colour of the general form.

Invariable Concomitance of Special Forms—*Viśeṣa-vyāptiḥ.*

It is to be admitted that there is non-existence of the fire of a hill in the locus of smoke of a sacrificial ground, and there is non-existence of the fire of a sacrifical ground, in the locus of smoke of a hill. There is no invariable concomitance of smoke with fire if the two occupy different loci, that is, if the locus of smoke is different from that of the fire. But nobody can deny the invariable concomitance of smoke with fire if the two occupy the same locus, *e.g.* there is an invariable concomitance of smoke of a hill with the fire of the same. Though there is no invariable concomitance of all cases of smoke with all cases of fire, there is the concomitance of particular cases of smoke with their corresponding fires. The comprehensive connection of smoke with fire is not, by this particular concomitance, disturbed, for there is no smoke without fire.

This sort of invariable concomitance, called the invariable concomitance of special forms, may be defined as follows:—

1. Invariable concomitance is the co-presence of the middle term with the major term which is different from the counterpart of that absolute non-existence which does not abide in the locus of that counterpart, but abides with the middle term in the latter's own locus.

2. Invariable concomitance is the co-presence of the middle term with the major term, the locus of which is different from that of the counterpart of the reciprocal non-existence which abides in the locus of the middle term.

3. Invariable concomitance is the connection of the middle term with the major term which is different from the counterpart of that reciprocal non-existence which abides in the same locus with the middle term.

4. Invariable concomitance may also be defined as the co-presence of the middle term with the major term when there is no condition attached to the middle term.

5. Invariable concomitance is the co-presence of the middle term with the major term which co-abides with that absolute existence whose counterpart is that which is qualified by the nature of the counterpart of the absolute non-existence abiding in the same locus with the middle term.

6. Invariable concomitance is the possession of that nature which establishes the connection (that is, brings about the co-presence) of the middle term with the major term.

The Means of Apprehending Invariable Concomitance—*Vyāpti-grahopāyaḥ.*

Some logicians maintain that repeated observations of one thing as accompanying another thing are the means of apprehending invariable concomitance of the one with the other, *e.g.* we apprehend the invariable concomitance of smoke with fire after we have observed repeatedly that the one accompanies the other.

Gaṅgeśa opposes the above view on the following grounds :—

(1) Of the repeated observations each one separately cannot be the cause of apprehension of invariable concomitance owing to lack of unity among the observations. As the successive observations perish quickly there is nothing which unites them together to cause in us an apprehension of invariable concomitance. The impression left in our mind by the past observations are no doubt competent to produce recollection and recognition of equal things, but they cannot produce apprehension of invariable concomitance which involves unequal things such as occurrence of smoke in a kitchen, a sacrificial ground, a hill, etc.

(2) What again is the meaning of repeated observations ? Does it mean observation in numerous places, or observation of numerous instances, or observation of the same instance numerous times ? None of these alternatives are of any help to us in apprehending invariable concomitance. Can we establish invariable concomitance of colour with savour, even if we have observed them together in numerous places ? Can numerous instances of colour observed along with savour in the same place (as a pot) entitle us to establish invariable concomitance between them ? As regards the observation of an instance numerous times, it may be asked how many times ? There is certainly no fixity as to the number of times There cannot in fact be an invariable concomitance of a pen with the floor even if they have been observed together a hundred times.

2. Some other logicians say that a reasoning (*tarka*) coupled with the observation of co-accompaniment (*sahacāra*) is the means of our apprehending invariable concomitance. For instance, smoke is in invariable concomitance with fire inasmuch as we observe the former co-accompanied by the latter ; and by applying our reasoning we further find that had there been no inseparable connection between smoke and fire, we could have seen the former without the latter, but as such a contingency is an absurdity, there is certainly an invariable concomitance of smoke with fire.

According to Gaṅgeśa the above view is untenable inasmuch as a reasoning, being itself based on an apprehension of invariable concomitance, cannot be the cause of the same. Unless a person apprehends the invariable concomitance of one thing with another thing, his reasoning, which is to reveal the absurdity of all contrary apprehensions, cannot come into operation. We could argue *ad infinitum* without being able to ascertain whether reasoning preceded the apprehension of invariable concomitance, or the latter preceded the former.

Conclusion as to the Means of Apprehending Invariable Concomitance—*Vyāptigrahopāya-siddhānta.*

The observation of co-accompaniment attended with the absence of knowledge of exceptions is the means of apprehending invariable concomitance, *e.g.* there is invariable concomitance of smoke with fire as the former constantly accompanies the latter without any exceptions.

The knowledge of exceptions may assume the form of a certainty or doubt. In the former alternative we cannot at all apprehend invariable concomitance, and in the latter there is great difficulty in apprehending it. Doubt arises from two sources, *viz.* sometimes from the suspicion of a condition (*upādhi*) and sometimes from the recognition of common properties and non-recognition of special properties. As an instance of the latter source we may point out a tall object which in the twilight produces in us a doubt as to whether it is a man or a post, because we recognize in it tallness which is the common property of a man and a post without the recognition of locomotion, etc., which are the special properties of a man. As an instance of the former source, we may cite the case of a fire which, if wet fuel is attached to it as a condition, may be inseparably connected with smoke. In asserting the invariable concomitance of smoke with fire [1] we are therefore in doubt as to whether wet fuel is not a condition.

In certain instances the doubt does not arise at all on account of absence of such defects as myopia, long distance, etc. In certain other instances the doubt is removed by the employment of reasoning. For instance, our doubt as to whether there is invariable concomitance of fire with smoke, is removed by reasoning as follows: Had fire constantly accompanied smoke there would have been smoke in a red-hot iron-ball; but in it there is fire and no smoke; so there is no invariable concomitance of fire with smoke (but there is that of smoke with fire).

The reasoning which is to remove doubt, is to be carried on only as long as the doubt is not removed. The charge of *regressus ad infinitum* brought against the reasoning employed to establish invariable concomitance, does not apply to the present case, in which reasoning ceases with the disappearance of doubt and does not continue up to the commencement of the processes establishing invariable concomitance.

---

[1] There is invariable concomitance of smoke with fire but not of fire with smoke; that is, wherever there is smoke there is fire, but not *vice versa*

Reasoning (or Confutation)—*Tarka.*

The processes of reasoning (or confutation) may be illustrated as follows :--

Interrogation.—Can smoke abide without fire ?

Reasoning.—If smoke could abide without fire, it would not have been a product of fire

Re-interrogation.—Is smoke a product of fire ?

Reasoning.—If smoke were produced neither from fire nor from non-fire, then it would have been a non-product. But it is not so.

Doubt.—Smoke then may have been produced either from fire or without a cause.

Incompatibility.—Why a person, who thus indulges in doubt, is nevertheless led on to activity ? If he doubts whether an effect may or may not be produced without a cause, why does he seek for a fire to obtain smoke, and for food to get satisfaction ? His own activity indicates that he is well aware of the connection between a cause and its effect. Why does he then entertain doubt ? It is incompatible with his own activity. There is no doubt that smoke as an effect cannot be produced without a cause. Smoke is in fact a product of fire without which it cannot abide.

Comprehensiveness of Invariable Concomitance—*Vyāptyanugamaḥ.*

Comprehensiveness (*anugama*) is the nature which exhibits in one form all the various kinds of invariable concomitance previously defined. The invariable concomitance involving reciprocal non-existence is a comprehensive one, and is on account of shortness to be accepted as the cause of inference. Of the five provisional definitions of invariable concomitance the third and the fifth, and of those of the invariable concomitance of a special form, the second and the third involve reciprocal non-existence. The conclusive definition of invariable concomitance may also be so modified as to involve reciprocal non-existence. Of these the third definition of the invariable concomitance of a special form is very short by far.

Intercourse whose Character is General—*Sāmānya-lakṣaṇa.*

We observed that there is invariable concomitance of smoke of a kitchen with fire of the same, and similarly there is invariable concomitance of smoke of a sacrifical ground with fire of the same. Though we thus observe that there is invariable concomitance of particular cases of smoke with particular cases of fire, we cannot infer fire on a hill by seeing smoke there, until we can establish the invariable concomitance of all cases of smoke with all cases of fire. We can establish the invariable concomitance of all cases of smoke with all cases of fire, if we assume the knowledge of "smokeness" (the generic nature of smoke) as the intercourse for our perception of all cases of smoke, and the knowledge of "fireness" (the generic nature of fire) as the intercourse for our perception of all cases of fire. This sort of intercourse which consists of the knowledge of a generic nature is called an intercourse whose character is general. It is described by some logicians as an ordinary intercourse of particularity, while others describe it as a transcendent intercourse. The logicians, who hold the first view, say that in perceiving a particular smoke by means of our eye there is the intercourse of union, while in perceiving "smokeness" there is the intercourse of united-inherence, and in perceiving all cases of smoke (at all times and in all places) through the knowledge of "smokeness" there is the intercourse of particularity. All these cases of intercourse are ordinary ones.

The logicians, who hold the second view, say that in the perception as a particular smoke and "smokeness" there are no doubt ordinary intercourses of union and united-inherence respectively, but in the perception of all cases of smoke through the knowledge of "smokeness" the intercourse is a transcendent one. It cannot be an ordinary intercourse because of all cases of smoke the present ones can be perceived by our eyes independent of the knowledge of "smokeness," while the past and future cases of smoke with which our eyes are not connected, cannot be perceived at all through any of the six ordinary intercourses. Therefore the intercourse, *viz.* the knowledge of "smokeness", through which we perceive all cases of smoke, is a transcendent one whose character is general. Hence the apprehension of invariable concomitance of a particular case of smoke with a particular case of fire refers through the intercourse whose character is general to all cases of smoke and all cases of fire.

Conclusion about the Intercourse whose Character is General.—*Sāmānya-lakṣaṇa-siddhāntaḥ.*

If the intercourse, whose character is general, were not accepted, there could not arise any doubt as to whether there were instances in which smoke (the middle term) did not accompany fire (the major term). As to the cases of smoke which were present, we could perceive their co-accompaniment with cases of fire, and they could leave no room for doubt regarding any case of exception. As for the past and future cases of smoke, or the cases of smoke of distant places, we could not know them as they were beyond the range of our eyes. In the absence of knowledge of those cases of smoke it would be impossible for us to entertain any doubt as to whether they constantly accompanied fire. Doubt being impossible, there could not be any reasoning employed to remove it. Hence we could not apprehend an invariable concomitance. But if the intercourse whose character is general, is admitted, we can explain the perception of all cases of smoke through the intercourse of "smokeness." It is possible for doubt to arise in respect of some of these cases of smoke through non-recognition of their special properties. We must therefore admit intercourse whose character is general.

The Conditional Middle Term—*Upādhi-vādaḥ*.

The middle term, if it is to be in invariable concomitance with the major, should be devoid of condition, that is, should be unconditional. A condition (*upādhi*) is that which constantly accompanies the major term, but does not always accompany the middle term, *e.g.*

The hill is full of smoke,
because it is full of fire (nourished by wet fuel).

Diagram VI.

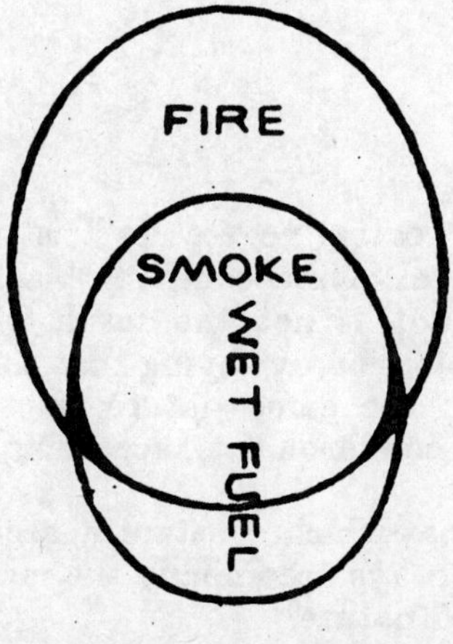

Here smoke is the major term, fire is the middle term and wet fuel is a condition. The wet fuel constantly accompanies smoke, but does not always accompany fire. For instance, the fire in an ignited iron-ball is not accompanied by wet fuel at all.

"Accompanying the major term" signifies the state of not being the counterpart of that absolute non-existence which abides in the locus of the major term, that is, the state of not being absent from the locus of the major term. "Not accompanying the middle term" is the state of being the counterpart of that absolute non-existence which abides in the locus of the middle term, that is, the state of being absent from the locus of the middle term. In diagram VI. "wet fuel" is not absent from the region of smoke, but it is present in some regions of fire and absent from the remaining regions of the same.

"Mitrā has many sons of whom one is black, and the rest fair-complexioned. The son conceived at a time when Mitrā ate vegetables, is black, but other sons that were conceived while she did not eat vegetables but drank milk, are fair-complexioned." In diagram VII. we find that "eating vegetable" is a condition which accompanies Mitrā's black son, but does not accompany her fair-complexioned sons.

Diagram VII.

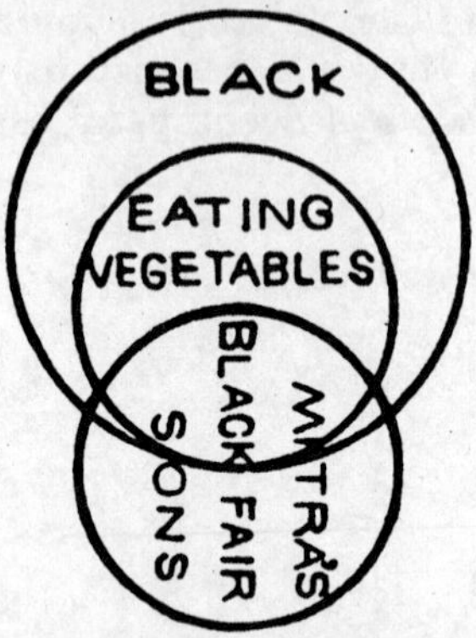

He is black,
because he is a son of Mitrā
(who eats vegetables).

Some say that "eating vegetables" is not a condition inasmuch as it does not always accompany blackness; for instance, the blackness of a pot is not the result of eating vegetables. Gaṅgeśa meets the objection by saying that the blackness marking Mitrā's son is not of the same nature as the blackness which abides in a pot. A "condition" is, according to him, to be clearly defined as follows:—

A condition is that which constantly accompanies the major term, but does not always accompany the middle term, in respect of an entity of a fixed nature.

Condition is of two kinds, *viz.* (1) sure, and (2) suspected. A condition is said to be "sure" when we know with certainty that it constantly accompanies the major term, but does not always accompany the middle term; and it is said to be "suspected" when there is doubt as to its accompanying the major term or as to its not accompanying the middle term. An instance of a suspected condition is given below:—

The earth has a maker,
because it is a product (caused by a body).

Here "caused by a body" is a condition which constantly accompanies a maker (if the maker is a person, but not if the maker is a collection of atoms), but does not always accompany a product (for instance, a product like a pot is caused by a body, but a product like a lightning is not so caused). The condition, *viz.* "causing by a body", is therefore a suspected one.

A condition is not in itself a defect, but its attachment to the middle term indicates that that term is erratic and the conclusion drawn therefrom wrong.

The State of Being the Locus or Minor Term—*Pakṣatā*.

The state of being the locus or the minor term (*pakṣatā*) has been defined by some logicians as the state in which it is doubtful whether the major term abides in it or not. Seeing that the connection of the major term with the locus or minor term, may not necessarily involve a doubt, Gaṅgeśa prefers to define the minor term as that whose connection with the major term is not known with certainty in consequence of the absence of a desire to know the connection. *E.g.* in the proposition "the hill is full of fire", the hill is the minor term whose connection with fire was hitherto neither investigated nor known. The minor term is so named not merely if there is an absence of knowledge of its connection with the major term, but also if the absence of knowledge is due to the absence of a desire to arrive at the knowledge. We cannot treat the minor term as such merely by establishing with it a connection of the major term if that connection has already been known, but we shall be justified in treating it as the minor term if there is in us a desire again to establish the connection.

A homologue, a similar locus, a homogeneous affirmative or positive example (*sapakṣa*), is that in which the major term is known with certainty to abide, *e.g.* the hill is full of fire, because it is full of smoke, as *a kitchen*.

A heterologue, a dissimilar locus, a heterogeneous or negative example (*vipakṣa*), is that in which the major term is known not to abide, *e.g.* the hill is full of fire, because it is full of smoke; where there is no fire, there is no smoke, as *a lake*.

Consideration or Knowledge of Premises—*Parāmarśaḥ*.

Consideration (*parāmarśaḥ*) is the knowledge that the middle term, in invariable concomitance with the major term, abides in the minor, *e.g.*

The hill is full of fire,
because it is full of smoke.

Here consideration consists of the knowledge that in the hill abides smoke which is in invariable concomitance with fire. This knowledge (consideration) is the cause of inference.

The ancients held that smoke actually perceived together with the knowledge that it is in invariable concomitance with fire was the cause of inference. But Gaṅgeśa opposes this view by saying that if smoke actually perceived were the cause, then inference could not take place from smoke that had been destroyed or that had not yet arisen. On hearing that there *will be* smoke here, a person can at once infer that there *will be* fire here, although he does not actually perceive the smoke which is not present. It is therefore not smoke itself but the knowledge of it that is the cause of the inference. In other words, the middle term actually perceived together with the knowledge that it is in invariable concomitance with fire, is not the cause of inference, but consideration or knowledge that in the minor term abides the middle term which is, in invariable concomitance with the major term, such a cause.

An Exclusively Affirmative Inference—*Kevalānvayyanumānam.*

Inference is of three kinds, *viz.* (1) an exclusively affirmative inference (*kevalānvayyanumānam*), (2) an exclusively negative inference (*kevalavyatirekyanumānam*), and (3) an affirmative negative inference (*anvaya-vyatirekyanumānam*).

The exclusively affirmative is an inference in which there is no negative example. It may also be defined as an inference in which the major term is not the counterpart of that absolute non-existence which has an abode; or, as an inference in which there is no non-presence of the major term, *e.g.*

This is nameable,
because it is knowable—(*vide* diagram II).

An Exclusively Negative Inference—*Kevalavyatirekyanumānam.*

An exclusively negative inference is the inference in which the major term has no affirmative example. It may also be defined as the inference in which the major term does not abide in anything else but in the minor term, *e.g.*

Diagram VIII.

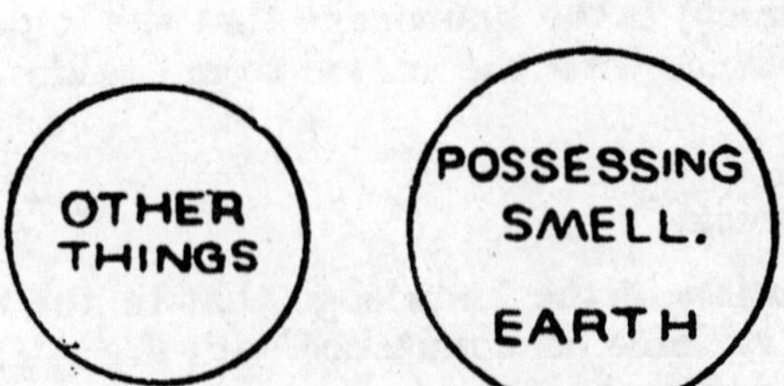

The earth is different from other things,
because it possesses smell.

An Affirmative-Negative Inference.

The affirmative-negative is an inference in which the major term has both affirmative and negative examples, *e.g.*

The hill is full of fire,
because it is full of smoke,
as a kitchen and not as a lake.

Presumption—*Arthāpatti.*

The Mīmāṁsakas say that presumption (*arthāpatti*) is a separate means of knowledge. On hearing that "Devadatta, who is fat, does not eat in the day", we at once conclude that he eats in the night. Since a person cannot become fat unless he eats either in the day or in the night, and, since he does not eat in the day, it follows by presumption that he eats in the night.

Gaṅgeśa does not admit presumption to be a separate means of knowledge, but includes it in the negative inference [1] which establishes the absence of the middle term through the absence of the major term. Here the absence of eating in the night would have been followed by the absence of that fatness which is attended with non-eating in the day.

Inference for One's Self—*Svārthānumāna.*

Inference is of two kinds: (1) inference for one's self (*svārthānumāna*) and (2) inference for the sake of others (*parārthānumāna*). A person having himself repeatedly observed in the kitchen and other places the invariable concomitance of smoke with fire, goes near a hill and sees smoke on it. He recollects that, wherever there is smoke, there is fire, and thereupon knowledge arises in him that "this hill has smoke which is in invariable concomitance with fire." This knowledge is called "consideration of the sign" (*liṅgaparāmarśa*) or simply "consideration" (*parāmarśa*), from which follows the knowledge that "this hill has fire", which is called inferential conclusion (*anumiti*). This is the process of inference for one's self.

Inference for the sake of Others—*Parārthānumāna.*

When a person, having inferred fire from smoke, demonstrates it to others by the employment of a syllogism, it is called "an inference for the sake of others." The process of this inference is as follows :-

---

[1] A person to be fat must take his food either in the day or in the night—(A proposition).
Devadatta, who is fat, does not take his food in the day—(E proposition).
Therefore Devadatta must take his food in the night. (This is a disjunctive categorical syllogism.)

(1) The hill is full of fire,
(2) Because it is full of smoke,
(3) All that is full of smoke is full of fire, as a kitchen,
(4) This hill is full of smoke,
(5) Therefore this hill is full of fire.

The demonstration given above produces in other people "consideration of the sign", which necessarily makes them admit that the hill has fire.

Syllogism—*Nyāyaḥ*.

Syllogism (*nyāya*) is the name for a collection of five sentences which give rise to knowledge that produces consideration. It is set forth as follows:—

(1) This hill is full of fire—*Proposition.*
(2) Because it is full of smoke—*Reason.*
(3) All that is full of smoke is full of fire, as a kitchen—*Example.*
(4) This hill is full of smoke—*Application.*
(5) Therefore this hill is full of fire—*Conclusion.*

After these five sentences have been employed there arises in the mind of the listener consideration of the form, 'this hill is full of smoke, which is in invariable concomitance with fire", from which follows the conclusion, "this hill is full of fire." Syllogism is therefore the name for the entire collection of these five sentences, each of which is called a part or member.

Parts of a Syllogism—*Avayavaḥ*.

A part or member (*avayavaḥ*) is a sentence that gives rise to knowledge which contributes to the production of an entire knowledge which produces consideration. On the employment of the five sentences there arises, at first, knowledge from each of them separately. Then arises collective knowledge from the five sentences combined together. This collective knowledge which produces consideration is based on each of the five sentences called a part or member. The parts are five, *viz.* (1) the proposition, (2) the reason, (3) the example, (4) the application, and (5) the conclusion.

The Proposition—*Pratijñā*.

The proposition (*pratijñā*) is a sentence which causes knowledge, whose object is the same as that of the conclusion and which contributes to the production of the entire knowledge which produces consideration, *e.g.*

This hill is full of fire.

It may also be defined as a sentence which gives rise to an inquiry necessitating the mention of the reason, *e.g.* this hill is full of fire. (Why so ? because it is smoky.)

The Reason or Middle Term—*Hetuḥ.*

The reason or middle term (*hetuḥ*) is a word, with the instrumental or ablative suffix attached to it, which produces knowledge whose object is not the *probandum* (major term) but which contributes to the production of the entire knowledge that gives rise to consideration, *e.g.* because it is full of smoke (*i.e.* by or from smokiness).

The reason is of two kinds : (1) the affirmative (*anvayi*) and (2) the negative (*vyatireki*). The affirmative reason is a member with the instrumental or ablative suffix attached to it, which produces knowledge that necessitates the mention of the member expressive of an affirmative invariable concomitance, *e.g.* because it has smoke (*i.e.* by or from "smokiness"), all that has smoke has fire, as a kitchen. The negative reason is a member with the instrumental or ablative suffix attached to it, which produces knowledge that necessitates the mention of the member expressive of a negative invariable concomitance, *e.g.* because it has smoke, (*i.e.* by or from "smokiness"), all that has no fire has no smoke, as a lake.

Example—*udāharaṇam.*

The example (*udāharaṇam*) is a word which, while producing knowledge of connection of the form that the locus of the middle term is constantly occupied by the major term, causes another knowledge which proceeds from the sentence expressive of consideration,[1] *e.g.*

All that has smoke has fire, as a kitchen,
[So this hill has smoke].

Application—*upanayaḥ.*

The application (*upanayaḥ*) is a member which produces consideration, *e.g.* All that has smoke has fire, this hill too has smoke.

Conclusion—*Nigamanam.*

Conclusion (*nigamanam*) is a sentence which, while causing the knowledge which gives rise to consideration, produces knowledge of the major term as indicated by that of the middle term through its invariable concomitance with the major term and

---

1 *i.e.* application (*upanayaḥ*), the sentence expressive of consideration.

its nature of abiding in the minor term, *e.g.* In this hill there is smoke, which is in invariable concomitance with fire. Therefore in this hill there is fire, or therefore this hill is full of fire.

Fallacies—*Hetvābhāsāḥ*.

A General Definition of Fallacy—*Hetvābhāsa-sāmānya-niruktiḥ*.

A person can ascertain truths and achieve victory by exposing fallacies in the argument of his opponent. It is therefore necessary to define a fallacy, which in Sanskrit is called ***hetvābhāsa***, a semblance of reason, a fallacy of reason or a fallacious reason.

A fallacy is an object of knowledge which obstructs an inference. It is in brief a defective reason. There are five kinds of fallacy or defective reason, viz. (1) the erratic or uncertain (*savyabhicāra* or *anaikānta*), (2) the contradictory (*viruddha*), (3) the counterbalanced (*satpratipakṣita*), (4) the unproved or inconclusive (*asiddha*), and (5) the incompatible (*bādhita*). The defects involved in the above reasons are respectively the following:—(1) the erraticalness or uncertainty (*vyabhicāra*), (2) contradiction (*virodha*), (3) counterbalance (*satpratipakṣa*), (4) absence of proof or inclusiveness (*asiddhi*), and (5) incompatibility, (*bādhā*).

The Erratic Reason—*Savyabhicāraḥ*.

The erratic (*savyabhicāra*) is a reason or middle term in which abides a character, the possession of which causes that presence of two alternatives which produces doubt in the *probandum* or major term. The nature refers to the constant accompaniment with, or absence from, both the major term and its non-existence. The erratic reason is subdivided into (1) that which is too general (*sādhāraṇa*), (2) that which is non-general or not general enough (*asādhāraṇa*), and (3) that which is non-exclusive (*anupasaṁhārī*).

A reason is said to be *too general*, if it abides in the locus of the major term as well as in that of its absence, *e.g.*

This hill is full of smoke,
because it is full of fire.

Here the reason "fire" abides in the region of smoke (as in a kitchen) as well as in the region of the absence of smoke (as in an ignited iron-ball).

A reason is said to be *non-general* or *not general enough*, if it abides neither in the locus of the major term nor in that of its absence, *e.g.*

This hill is full of smoke,
because it is full of ether.

Here the reason is ether, which has no locus. Ether abides neither in the locus of fire nor in that of the absence of fire.

A reason is said to be *non-exclusive*, if it is destitute of an example, whether affirmative or negative, *e.g.*

All things are impermanent,
because they are knowable.

Here we cannot cite any example, as "all things" is the subject.

The Contradictory Reason—*Viruddhaḥ*.

The contradictory (*viruddhaḥ*) is a reason which is the counterpart of that non-existence which constantly accompanies the major term, *e.g.*

This hill is full of fire,
because it is full of water.

Here the reason is contradictory, inasmuch as water is the counterpart of the *non-existence of water*, which constantly accompanies fire.

The contradictory may also be defined as a reason (middle term) which is constantly accompanied by the absence of the *probandum*, major term.

The Counterbalanced Reason—*Satpratipakṣitaḥ*

If, at the time of the consideration of a reason which seeks to establish the *existence* of the *probandum* or major term, there occurs the consideration of another reason which seeks to establish the *non-existence* of that term, the first reason is a counterbalanced one,—in fact, *both* the reasons are counterbalanced, *e.g.*

One reason—Sound is eternal, because it is audible.
Opposite reason—Sound is non-eternal, because it is a product.

In the above instances, as consideration of both the sides prevails, there is no real inference. The inference from one reason being of as much force as that from the other reason, the two inferences neutralize each other.

The Unproved Reason—*Asiddhaḥ*.

The unproved (*asiddhaḥ*) reason is of three kinds: (1) unproved on the part of its locus or the subject (*āśrayāsiddhaḥ*), (2) unproved with regard to its own nature (*svarūpāsiddhaḥ*), and (3) unproved in respect of accompaniment (*vyāpyatvāsiddhaḥ*).

(1) A reason is said to be unproved on the part of its locus, if the characteristic distinguishing the locus does not belong to it, *e.g.*

This golden hill is full of fire,
because it is full of smoke.

Here the reason "smoke" is unproved, as its locus is unreal, on account of the "goldenness" not belonging to a hill.

(2) A reason is said to be unproved with regard to its own nature, if it does not abide in the locus or minor term, *e.g.*

The lake is full of fire,
because it is full of smoke.

Here the reason is unproved, as smoke from its very nature does not abide in a lake.

(3) A reason is said to be unproved in respect of constant accompaniment, if its generic nature is not useful in establishing its invariable concomitance with the major term. It is subdivided as follows:—

(*a*) Unproved on the part of the major term (*sādhyāsiddhi*) which occurs when there is a useless adjective appended to that term, *e.g.*

This hill is full of golden fire,
because it is full of smoke.

"Golden" is useless.

(*b*) Unproved on the part of the reason (*hetvasiddhi*) which occurs when there is a useless adjective appended to it, *e.g.*

This hill is full of fire,
because it is full of blue smoke.

"Blue" is useless.

(*c*) Unproved in respect of invariable concomitance (*vyāptyasiddhi*) which occurs when there is a condition attached to the reason, *e.g.*

This hill is full of smoke,
because it is full of fire nourished by wet fuel (which is a condition attached to the reason).

The Incompatible Reason—*Bādhitaḥ*.

An incompatible reason (*bādhitaḥ*) occurs when there is the knowledge that the major term, which is assigned to the minor term, does not really abide in it, *e.g.*

Fire is cold,
because it is a substance.

The incompatible reason, which is of ten kinds, occurs under the following circumstances:—

(1) The minor term being incompatible with perception (*pakṣaḥ pratyakṣa-bādhitaḥ*), *e.g.*

A pot is all-pervading,
because it is existent.

(2) The minor term being incompatible with inference (*pakṣaḥ anumāna-bādhitaḥ*), *e.g.*

An atom has parts,
because it has a shape.

An atom has in fact no shape and no parts.

(3) The minor term being incompatible with verbal testimony (*pakṣaḥ śabda-bādhitaḥ*), *e.g.*

The golden mountain (Meru) is stony,
because it is a mountain.

(4) The minor term being incompatible with perception which establishes the counterpart of the major term (*pakṣaḥ sādhya-pratiyogi-pratyakṣa-bādhitaḥ*), *e.g.*

Fire is non-warm,
because it is a product.

(5) The minor term being incompatible with the inference which establishes the counterpart of the major term (*pakṣaḥ sādhya-pratiyogyanumāna-bādhitaḥ*), *e.g.*

Sound is inaudible,
because it is a quality (of ether).

(6) The minor term being incompatible with comparison which establishes the counterpart of the major term (*pakṣaḥ sādhya-pratiyogyupamāna-bādhitaḥ*), *e.g.*

Bos-gavaeus-ness is not the connotation of the term *bos-gavaeus*,
because it is a general notion.

(7) The minor term being incompatible with the evidence which is analogous to the evidence that establishes the major term *pakṣaḥ sādhya-grāhaka-pramāṇa-jātīya-pramāṇa-viruddhaḥ*), *e.g.*

The skull of a deceased person is pure,
because it is the limb of a being that had life, as a conch-shell.

[The scripture declares a conch-shell to be pure but not the skull of a deceased person.]

(8) The minor term being incompatible with perception which establishes the middle term (*pakṣaḥ hetu-grāhaka-pratyakṣa-bādhitaḥ*), *e.g.*

Water and air are warm,
because they are possessed of touch, unlike that of the earth.

(9) The minor term being incompatible with inference which establishes the middle term (*pakṣaḥ hetu-grāhakānumāna-bādhitaḥ*), *e.g.*

The mind is all-pervading,
because it is a seat of union which is a non-coexistent cause of knowledge.

(10) The minor term being incompatible with verbal testimony which establishes the middle term (*pakṣaḥ hetu-grāhaka-śabda-bādhitaḥ*), *e.g.*

The Rājasūya sacrifice should be celebrated by Brāhmaṇas,
because it is the means of conquering heaven.

[From verbal testimony the Rājasūya sacrifice is ascertained to be a duty of the Kṣatriyas and not of the Brāhmaṇas].

Fallacies are serviceable as they point out Inefficiency—*Hetvābhāsānām-asādhakatā-sādhakatva-nirūpaṇam.*

A fallacy when exposed is a good reply to an opponent, whose argument is thus pointed out to be inefficient. Quibbles and far-fetched analogies are not good replies as they are of no use in this respect. Far-fetched analogies are moreover self-destructive.

Inference of God—*Īśvarānumānam.*

By inference we can prove the existence of God, the Maker of the universe. The inference employed for this purpose is as follows :—

The universe has a maker,
because it is a product, as a pot.

The causes which operate in the case of a product may be stated thus :—

There must be (1) a direct knowledge (perception) by an agent himself of the materials which constitute a product, (2) a desire on the part of the agent to make it, and (3) an act of making it.

For instance, in making a product called a pot there are in the potter, (1) a perception of the pieces that constitute a pot, (2) a desire on his part to make it, and (3) his actual making of it.

Similarly in the case of a product called a binary atomic compound (*dvyaṇuka*) there must be (1) perception by an agent of the atoms which constitute the compound, (2) a desire in him to make it, (3) and his actual making of it. Now atoms are supersensuous, and, as such, cannot be perceived by man. Hence the maker of the binary atomic compound is an agent, who is not man but God.

Book III. Comparison—*Upamāna-khaṇḍa.*

How knowledge is derived through comparison.

A man, who does not know the signification of the word *bos-gavaeus*, hearing from an elder that the word *bos-gavaeus* signifies an animal which is like a cow, goes into a forest where he sees an animal like a cow. Recollecting the instructive assertion of the elder, he institutes a comparison by which he arrives at the conclusion that the animal which he sees is the thing signified by the word *bos-gavaeus*. The means by which this conclusion has been arrived at is called comparison (*upamāna*). This means is the knowledge of likeness between a cow and a bos-gavaeus The word comparison is ordinarily taken to signify the whole process.

The intercourse or operation (*vyāpāra*), in the case of comparison, consists in the recollection of the instructive assertion of the elder, *viz.* that the word *bos-gavaeus* signifies an animal which is like a cow. The result of comparison (*upamiti*) is the knowledge of the relation of a name to something so named.

Likeness explained.

The Mīmāṁsakas maintain that likeness (*sādṛśya*) is a distinct object which is not included in the seven categories of the Vaiśeṣikas. The signification of the word *bos-gavaeus* is, according to them, an animal which possesses likeness to a cow. Gaṅgeśa opposes this view by saying that it is cumbersome. A thing is said to bear likeness to another thing, if it, while possessing the special property of the latter thing, is different from the same in the generic nature. Such being the definition of likeness, we have to admit an infinite number of likenesses corresponding to the thing to which they refer. The real signification of the word *bos-gavaeus*, according to Gaṅgeśa, is not an animal which possesses likeness to a cow but an animal which possesses the generic nature of a bos-gavaeus (that is, which is a type of all *bos-gavaeus*). Hence the result of comparison consists of knowledge of the relation between the word *bos-gavaeus* and the animal which possesses the generic nature of a bos-gavaeus.

Comparison is not perception.

Some say that the knowledge of the signification of the word *bos-gavaeus* is derived through perception. This is absurd. Though the relation between the word *bos-gavaeus* and the animal called bos-gavaeus may be perceived in a particular case with which our eyes are in union, it is impossible for us to perceive such a relation in other cases which are beyond our eyes. Therefore the knowledge of signification of the word *bos-gavaeus* is not derived through perception, but through a separate means of knowledge, called comparison.

Neither can the knowledge of signification of the word *bos-gavaeus* be derived through inference, inasmuch as in the case of comparison knowledge is derived through the knowledge of likeness, independent of knowledge of invariable concomitance which is indispensable to an inference. Moreover in the case of knowledge derived through comparison there is in us a self-consciousness of the form "I *compare*", but not of the form "I infer."

Comparison is not inference.

Book IV. Verbal Testimony—*Śabda-khaṇḍa.*

Definition of Verbal Testimony—*Śabda-nirūpaṇam*

Speech [1] (*śabda*) is a means of valid knowledge if it is uttered by a person as an outcome of the true knowledge of its meaning, *e.g.* the speech, the *horse runs*, is a means of valid knowledge if it has been uttered by a person who knows its meaning. The means by which or the process through which the valid knowledge is derived is called verbal testimony (*śabda-pramāṇam*). A speech uttered by a person who does not know its meaning may produce knowledge the validity of which is uncertain.

Verbal Knowledge—*Śabda-bodhaḥ.*

Any knowledge derived from a speech is called verbal knowledge (*śabda-bodhaḥ*). It is the knowledge of the mutual connection of things signified by words which possess expectancy, consistency, contiguity and potentiality, and convey intention. The process through which verbal knowledge is produced is described as follows:—

In a speech—*ghaṭaḥ asti* (there is a pot)—are to be noted the following:

(i) At first there is the *hearing* [2] *of* (*śabdasya śravaṇam*) *words* in the speech, *viz. ghaṭa* + *ḥ* + *as* + *ti* (there + is + a + pot).

(ii) Then there is the *recollection of things* (*arthasya smaraṇam*) signified by the words, *viz.* the recollection of "pot" signified by the word *ghaṭa*, of "one" signified by *ḥ* (a modification of the first-case-ending *su*), of "existing" signified by *as* and of "the state of abiding" signified by *ti*, (a verbal termination of the third person, singular number, present tense).

(iii) Afterwards there is the knowledge of the *mutual connection of things* thus recollected (*saṁsarga-bodhaḥ*), that is, the knowledge that 'pot' as qualified by oneness is an abode

---

[1] "Speech" signifies "the knowledge of speech."

[2] The words need not always be actually *heard*, for sometimes we may recollect them from a written statement.

of existence. The knowledge in this third step is specially called a verbal knowledge.

(iv) Lastly there is *self-conciousness* (*anuvyavasāya*) of the knowledge in the following form: "I am the possessor of the knowledge of pot which as qualified by oneness is an abode of existence."

Speech as a means of Valid Knowledge—*Śabda-prāmāṇyavādaḥ*.

(*a*) *Can it be denied that speech is a means of valid knowledge?*

A means, otherwise called an instrument (*karaṇa*), is that cause which, when brought into operation, necessarily produces its effect. Speech is not, according to the Buddhists, such a means, inasmuch as it does not, even when uttered by a person who knows its meaning, produce knowledge, unless it is attended with expectancy, consistency, etc. Therefore "speech is not," say the Buddhists, "a means of valid knowledge."

Speech is indeed a means of valid knowledge, and Gaṅgeśa opposes the above view by asking whence, if the Buddhists do not admit speech to be a means of valid knowledge, they derive the validity of their own speech, *viz.* "speech is not a means of valid knowledge." The verbal testimony being denied, their speech cannot be proved as valid, and as such cannot be advanced against any party. On the contrary if their speech is admitted as valid, they will have to abandom their contention that "speech is not a means of valid knowledge." The contention of the Buddhists is therefore baseless, and speech is indeed a means of valid knowledge. But speech, if it is to be a means of valid knowledge, must not be a bare one: it should be attended with expectancy, consistency, etc.

Speech is mentioned as the means or instrument because it is the main cause in the production of valid knowledge, while expectancy, consistency, etc., are mere attendant causes or conditions. It should be stated here that only one cause without attendant conditions cannot produce any effect.

(*b*) *Is verbal testimony included in perception?*

The Buddhists, while not claiming their speech to be valid, say that it serves at any rate to produce in us a mental perception of the form "speech is not a means of valid knowledge" by causing the recollection of things signified by it. When we hear the speech, *viz.* "speech is not a means of valid knowledge," there arises in us a knowledge (recollection) of the things signified by it, and, through the intercourse whose character is knowledge, we actually perceive the thing in our mind. The function of verbal testimony being thus performed by mental perception, there is no necessity for assuming the former as a distinct means of valid knowledge.

(*c*) *Verbal testimony is not included in perception.*

Gaṅgeśa holds that speech which is attended with expectancy, etc., and produces recollection of things signified by it, must be accepted as a means of valid knowledge quite distinct from perception. Just as in the perception of a colour our eye is the means or instrument, its union with the colour is the intercourse and the perceptual knowledge is the result, so in verbal testimony, speech is the means or instrument, the recollection of things signified by it is the intercourse and the verbal knowledge is the result. Speech therefore serves the same purpose in verbal testimony as the sense-organs do in perception, in other words, speech is the means of verbal knowledge, and considering the distinct nature of this means we must admit verbal testimony to be a distinct means of valid knowledge.

(*d*) *Is verbal testimony included in inference?*

The Vaiśeṣikas maintain that verbal testimony is not a distinct means of valid knowledge but is included in inference. In deriving knowledge from speech we first hear the words constituting the speech and then recollect the things signified by the words. The knowledge of the mutual connection of things thus recollected, which is designated as verbal knowledge, is, according to the Vaiśeṣikas, derived from inference. Suppose one utters a speech thus: "he beat the cow with a stick." On hearing this speech the listener may, say the Vaiśeṣikas, infer as follows:—

(1) The words constituting this speech must have been preceded by knowledge of the mutual connection of things as intended by the speaker and recollected by his words,—*proposition*.

(2) Because they are possessed of expectancy, etc., and convey the intention of the speaker,—*reason*.

(3) The words of all speeches possessing expectancy, etc. and conveying the intention of a speaker are preceded by the knowledge of the mutual connection of things as intended by the speaker and recollected by his words, just as the words of a speech, *viz*, "bring a pot" uttered by me (the listener),—*example*.

If we can thus derive knowledge of the speech by means of inference, there is, according to the Vaiśeṣikas, no necessity for admitting a separate means of knowledge called verbal testimony.

(*e*) *Verbal knowledge is not included in inference.*

Gaṅgeśa opposes the above view as follows:

The inference as shown above is not valid, inasmuch as it does not involve knowledge (recollection) of actual things as in the case of verbal testimony, but the knowledge of things recollected, *i.e.* the knowledge of knowledge (recollection) of the things. This is not only cumbersome but also fallacious. Our activity in respect of a thing arises from our knowledge of the thing itself, but not from our knowledge of knowledge of the thing, which, as in the case of knowledge of error, may not contain in itself the cause of activity. Moreover, verbal knowledge is not, like inferential knowledge, dependent on the knowledge of invariable concomitance between the words of a speech and knowledge of the mutual connection of things signified by them, but results immediately from the words as soon as expectancy, consistency, etc., existing among them have been known. Again, after verbal knowledge has been produced, there arises self-consciousness of the form "I know from *the speech*" but not of the form "I know through *inference*."

It has already been observed that a speech cannot produce verbal knowledge unless the words composing it possess expectancy, consistency, contiguity and potentiality and convey intention.

Expectancy—*Ākāṅkṣā-vādaḥ*.

A word is said to bear the relation of expectancy (*ākāṅkṣā*) to another word if it cannot without the latter produce knowledge of its interconnection in a speech. For instance. *Devadattaḥ grāmaṁ gacchati* (Devadatta goes to the village) is a speech in which the word *Devadattaḥ* (in the nominative case) is expectant for the word *gacchati* ('goes', the verb), and this latter in its turn is expectant for *grāmaṁ* ('village,' in the objective case). In the same way the crude word *Devadatta* is expectant for *ḥ* (the same as *su,* the first-case-ending), the crude word *grāma* for *am* (the second-case-ending) and *gaṁ* (the root) for *ti* (the verbal suffix). A crude word (*nāma*) and a case-ending (*vibhakti*), a root (*dhātu*) and a verbal suffix (*ākhyāta*), and a verb (*kriyā*) and a case (*kāraka*) are expectant for each other.

Consistency—*Yogyatā*.

Consistency (*yogyatā*) consists in a word not bearing a meaning which is incompatible with the meanings of other words in a speech. For instance, no verbal knowledge is derived from such a speech as *agninā siñca* (sprinkle with fire) because it is incompatible with fire being an instrument in the act of sprinkling. Consistency may be certain or doubtful, but in either case there will be verbal knowledge.

Contiguity—*Āsattiḥ*.

Contiguity (*āsattiḥ*) consists in the enunciation of words, which are connected with each other, without a long pause between them, *e.g.* the speech, *viz.* "bring water", will convey no meaning if one utters the word "bring" now, and the word "water" after an hour.

Intention—*Tātparyam*.

Intention (*tātparyam*), which indicates the wish of a speaker, consists in the utterance of a word to convey knowledge of a special thing. If at the time of eating a meal, one says "bring *saindhava*" we are to understand by the word *saindhava* a quantity of salt and not a horse.

The Non-eternity of Sound—*Śabdānityatā-vādaḥ*.

Sounds (*śabda*) such as *k*, etc., are multifarious, inasmuch as we find that a sound uttered by a man is different from the corresponding sound uttered by a parrot. On the ground that sounds are many, each of which is produced and destroyed, we must admit them to be non-eternal. In fact such an expression as 'the uproar that arose in the market has now ceased' proves beyond a doubt that sound is liable to destruction.

Sound destroyed and not concealed—*Ucchanna-pracchanna-vādaḥ*.

If sounds are destructible, their aggregates, the speeches, must also be so. The Veda, a collection of speeches, is consequently non-eternal. The Mīmāṁsakas say that, though the Veda as a collection of speeches is liable to destruction, as it has come down through succession of teachers, its continuity is uninterrupted. Gaṅgeśa opposes the above view by saying that from allusions occurring in the socio-religious institutes (*smṛti*) and from usages that have prevailed from olden times we can infer that once there existed certain branches of the Vedas which have since disappeared. Therefore the Veda is non-eternal.

The Veda is defined by Gaṅgeśa as a collection of valid speeches which are not the outcome of knowledge of things signified by words, and the things signified by which are not the objects of those kinds of knowledge which are derived from means other than verbal testimony.

Injunction—*Vidhi-vādaḥ*.

The Veda is the foundation of our good customs inasmuch as it is the source of all injunctions. An injunction (*vidhi*) is a speech which produces in a person such conviction as induces him to perform or desist from performing the act signified by the speech, *e.g.* "Let a person, who wishes to go to heaven, perform a horse-sacrifice" is an injunction. "Let not a man drink wine" is another injunction.

According to Kumārila the conviction, which in an ordinary speech represents the purpose of the speaker, and in the case of the Vedic speech (not emanating from any person) the potentiality of the speech itself, consists of an idea of the form: "this speech directs me to perform or to desist from performing the act signified by it."

Prabhākara says that the conviction consists of the belief that merit or demerit that accrues from the act signified by the speech, is capable of being earned by our efforts.

Gaṅgeśa, who is not satisfied with any of the above explanations, maintains that the conviction produced in the person consists of the consciousness (*a*) that the act signified by the speech is capable of being performed by him, (*b*) that the performance of it will fulfil the object of his desire, and (*c*) that no serious inconvenience will accompany the performance.

All logicians agree, however, in holding that the conviction is produced by the potentiality of the hortative particle *liṅ* (corresponding to the English word "let") in the speech itself.

Merit and Demerit—*Apūrva-vādaḥ*.

Prabhākara says that the conviction produced by a Vedic speech, consists first of the belief that the merit or demerit that accrues from the act signified by the speech, is capable of being acquired by our efforts. This belief is followed by the presumption that the act from which merit or demerit accrues, is such as can be performed by us. Gradually there arise two other beliefs. *viz.* (1) that the act, if performed, will fulfil the object of our desire, and (2) that there is no serious inconvenience involved in the act.

Gaṅgeśa opposes the above view by saying that it is cumbersome to assume that so many kinds of belief are produced from a speech to induce us to perform or desist from performing the act signified by it. Let us, for the sake of brevity, assume that the conviction produced by a speech consists merely of the belief that the act signified by the speech is such as can be performed by us. This belief in the theory of Gaṅgeśa includes in it two other beliefs, *viz.* that the act is capable of fulfilling our desire and that there is no serious inconvenience involved in it.

Potentiality—*Śakti-vādaḥ*.

The relation that exists between a word and the thing referred to by it is a special relation[1] called *indication* (*vṛtti*). It

[1] The relation is not an ordinary one, *e.g.* the word (sound) jar does not produce in us the recollection of either although the former abides in the latter in the relation of inherence (*samavāya*).

is on account of this special relation that we are, on hearing the word *pot*, able to recollect the thing known as a pot. This special relation possessed by a word is generally called its *potentiality* (*śakti*). Nice distinctions are however often made in this matter. The special relation is described as being of two kinds, viz. (1) signification (*saṁketa*) and (2) implication (*lakṣaṇā*). The signification is again subdivided into, (*a*) permanent and (*b*) occasional. The permanent signification which a word bears is called specially its *potentiality* (*śakti*). This potentiality, which is the capacity of a word to refer to (*i.e.* produce recollection of) a particular thing, depends upon the will of God manifesting itself in the form: "let such and such a thing be understood by such and such a word." For instance the potentiality of the word *pot* consists in its producing the recollection of an earthen vessel. The occasional signification is called *technicality* (*paribhāṣā*) which depends upon the will of man manifesting itself in the form: "such and such a thing is to be understood by such and such a word." A word is said to be *technical* if it produces recollection of a particular thing as desired by man. For instance *nadī* is a technical word for nouns ending in *ī* or *ū*. The distinction between the permanent and occasional significations is overlooked by those logicians who maintain that words derive their signification, or rather potentiality, not from the will of God but from the will of man. There is according to them as much potentiality in an ordinary word as in a technical one. The potentiality of a word is ascertained from the following sources:—

(1) *Grammar* (*vyākaraṇa*), *e.g.* in the sentence: *Caitraḥ pacati* (Caitra cooks), the potentiality of the crude word *Caitra*, the nominative case-ending *ḥ*, the root *pac* and the verbal suffix *ti* is ascertained from grammar.

(2) *Comparison* (*upamāna*), *e.g.* in the sentence: "a bos-gavaeus is like a cow," the potentiality of "bos-gavaeus" is ascertained through comparison.

(3) *Dictionary* (*koṣa*), *e.g.* the potentiality of the word *pika* to refer to the quality of blueness is ascertained from dictionary.

(4) *Reliable assertion* (*āpta-vākya*), *e.g* that the word *pika* signifies a black cuckoo is ascertained from the word of a competent scholar.

(5) *Usage* (*vyavahāra*), *e.g.* on hearing "bring a table," "take away a table," etc., and on seeing the table brought and taken away, one understands the potentiality of the word "table."

(6) *Context* (*vākya-śeṣa*), *e.g.* if in a sentence the meaning of the word *yava* (which may refer to a barley-corn or a panic seed) is not clear, we can ascertain its true meaning (as a barley-corn) by a reference to the remaining sentences in which it is spoken of as having ears.

(7) *Description* (*vivṛti*), *e.g.* when we describe a belligerent nation as a warlike one, we can understand the potentiality of the word "belligerent."

(8) *Association* with well-known words, *e.g.* the potentiality of the word *pika* to refer to a bird is easily understood when the word is associated with some well-known words such as : "in this mango-tree the *pika* sings sweetly."

We have seen that each word possesses the potentiality of producing the recollection of a thing dependent upon the will of God or man. Now the question arises as to whether the potentiality refers to the genus of the thing or to the thing as an individual. If we suppose that the potentiality refers to an individual, we shall have to assume, say the Mīmāṁsakas, an infinite number of potentialities corresponding to the individuals to which they refer. If, on the other hand, we assume that the potentiality refers to a genus, we shall have to assume only one potentiality corresponding to the genus which will also include individuals without which it cannot stand.

Gaṅgeśa opposes the above view by saying that we could not recollect individuals unless the potentiality resided in them. On the supposition of the potentiality referring to an individual, it is not, continues he, necessary to assume an infinite number of potentialities, as one and the same potentiality refers to all the individuals which are comprehended under one genus. Hence, he concludes that the potentiality really refers to the individuals coming under a genus and possessing a form.

Words possessed of potentiality may be specified as follows :—

(1) The *etymological* (*yaugika*) is a word which is understood by the potentiality of its component parts alone, *e.g.* the word *dātā* (giver) refers to the agent of giving.

(2) The *conventional* (*rūḍha*) is a word which is understood by the potentiality of its entirety independently of that of its parts, *e.g.* the word *go* signifies a cow (and not 'the agent of going' which is the meaning of its parts).

(3) The *etymologo-conventional* (*yoga-rūḍha*) is a word which is understood by the potentiality of the whole harmoniously with the potentiality of its parts, *e.g.* the word *paṅkaja* signifies a water-lily, which is born in the mud.

(4) The *etymological-conventional* (*yaugika-rūḍha*) is a word which is understood either by the power of its entirety or by that of its parts, *e.g.* the word *udbhid* signifies a germ, the sprouting of a seed or a sacrifice.

Implication—*Lakṣaṇā*.

By implication (*lakṣaṇā*) a word refers to a thing which is related to another thing which is the signification of the word, but which does not signify the intention of the speaker, *e.g.* the word 'Ganges' in the sentence, 'the cow-keeper dwells on the Ganges,' does not signify the current which is referred to by the potentiality of the word but signifies the bank which bears to the current the relation of proximity. Similarly the word 'crow' in the sentence, 'protect the curd from the crow' signifies by implication any thing that injures the curd.

Compound Words—*Samāsa-vādaḥ*.

In Sanskrit the compound word (*sāmasa*) is of six kinds, *viz.*: (1) an ***attributive compound*** (*bahuvrīhi*), (2) a ***determinative compound*** (*tatpuruṣa*) including the negative determinative compound (*nañ-tatpuruṣa*)), (3) a ***descriptive compound*** (*karmadhāraya*), (4) a ***numeral compound*** (*dvigu*) including the ***unified numeral compound*** (*samāhāra*), (5) an ***aggregative compound*** (*dvandva*) comprising the ***mutually aggregative compound*** (*itaretara*), the ***unified aggregative compound*** (*samāhāra*), and the ***residual aggregative compound*** (*ekaśeṣa*) and (6) an ***indeclinable compound*** (*avyayībhāva*).

In the attributive compound the first word possesses its fixed potentiality and the second word, which through its potentiality points out a thing, refers also by implication to another thing, *e.g* *citragum ānaya* (lit. bring the brindled-cow-man) signifies "bring the man having a brindled-cow." The first word *citra* (brindled) refers through its potentiality to the quality of "brindledness" while the second word *go* (cow) besides pointing out, through its potentiality, the thing called "cow" refers also by implication to its owner.

Grammarians maintain that, when two words are combined together to form an attributive compound, the combination possesses the potentiality of referring to a thing which is connected with but lies beyond the things signified by its component words, *e.g.* *citra-gu* (brindled-cow) refers to "ownership" over and above the quality of being "brindled" and the "cow." Gaṅgeśa holds that in an attributive compound all potentialities lie in the words which are combined together to form the compound, and there is no potentiality in the combination itself.

In the determinative compound the second word possesses its fixed potentiality while in the first word there are both potentiality and implication, *e.g.* *rāja-puruśaḥ* (a "king-officer", that is, an officer of the king) signifies an officer belonging to the king in which the word *rāja* refers to a "king" as well as to "connection with him."

In the descriptive compound in which the component words stand to each other in the relation of identity, there is no special rule for the possession of potentialities by them, *e.g.* *nīlotpalam* (blue-lotus). The same is the case with the numeral compound, *e.g.* *pañca-guvam* (five cows).

In the aggregative compound there is no special rule for the assumption of potentiality or implication by the component words, *e.g. yama-varuṇau* (Yama and Varuṇa).

In an indeclinable compound there are both potentiality and implication in the last word, *e.g. upakumbham* (near the jar).

Verbal Suffixes—*Ākhyāta-vādaḥ*.

A verbal suffix (*ākhyāta—ti, tas, anti*, etc.) used after a root, refers to the effort favourable to what is signified by the root, *e.g. Caitraḥ pacati* (Caitra cooks) signifies that Caitra is possessed of efforts favourable to cooking. If the agent is an inanimate thing the verbal suffix refers by implication to the operation favourable to what is signified by the root, *e.g, ratho gacchati* (a chariot moves) signifies that the chariot is possessed of the operation favourable to moving.

The Roots—*Dhātu vādaḥ*.

The root (*dhātu*) of a verb refers to the operation favourable to the effect of what is signified by the verb, *e.g.* the root *gam* (going) in the sentence, *viz. sa grāmaṁ gacchati* (he goes to the village) refers to moving, which is favourable to his connection with the village, which is the effect of his going. In the case of an intransitive verb the root refers merely to the operation, *e.g. sa tiṣṭhati* (he stays) in which *sthā* signifies merely 'staying.'

Prefixes—*Upasarga-vādaḥ*.

The prefix (*upasarga*) by itself does not bear any meaning but points out the speciality of meaning borne by the root that follows, *e.g. vi* in *vijayate* (completely conquers) signifies a completeness of conquest.

Validity of the Four Means of Knowledge—*Pramāṇa-catuṣṭaya-prāmāṇya-vādaḥ*.

Some say that a gesture (*ceṣṭā*) is a means of valid knowledge. But this is absurd, inasmuch as a gesture merely reminds us of words which produce knowledge. That a deaf person is sometimes prompted to activity by a gesture, must be due to the fact that he infers the desire of the man who makes the gesture. So a gesture is included in either verbal testimony or inference. Similarly tradition (*aitihya*) and rumour (*janaśruti*) are not distinct from verbal testimony while presumption (*arthāpatti*) and non-perception (*anupalabdhi*) are comprised in inference.

तत्त्वचिन्तामणौ प्रत्यक्षखण्डे सूचीपत्रम् ।

शुद्धिपत्रम्।

अशुद्धं		शुद्धं		पृष्ठं		पङ्क्तिः
सर्ग	…	सर्ग	…	१	…	४
न्योन्याश्रेया	…	न्योन्याश्रया	…	८	…	१२
अनलताड़ना	…	अलतताड़ना	…	९।१०।११	…	१४।१०।१
अन्यत्म	…	अन्यत्व	…	१५	…	१०
'शिष्टेति'	…	'शिष्टेति,	…	१७	…	८
आरम्द	…	आरब्ध	…	२०	…	१६
भिस्थाना	…	भिधाना	…	२२	…	११
कारयन्त्रा-	…	कारयत्ना-	…	२२	…	१२
विषयविषया-	…	विषयविषया-	…	२४	…	१२
अन्य	…	अन्य	…	२६	…	१४
मतृप्रति	…	मत्प्रति	…	२९	…	६
सुन	…	स्तून	…	२९	…	१०
निष्वाचात्	…	निर्व्वाचात्	…	३१	…	२
यपारः	…	व्यापारः	…	३२	…	४
पत्या	…	पथ्या	…	३५	…	१५
इत्युद्देश्य	…	इत्युद्दिश्य	…	३५	…	१७
कल्पिना	…	कल्पना	…	३६	…	१९
मथात्मात	…	मथात्मात्	…	४०	…	२०
फलषिति	…	फलमिति	…	४८	…	८
मञ्जुते	…	मङ्क्ते	…	५२	…	१५
नध्वंस	…	नवंस	…	५७	…	६
सिद्धतः	…	सिध्यतः	…	५८	…	१०
तार्ष्र्वता	…	कार्ष्र्वता	…	६०	…	१६

अशुद्ध		शुद्धं		पृष्ठं		पङ्क्तिः
प्रधान	...	प्रधाने	...	६२	...	१२
एकत्राहपि	...	एकत्राहपि	...	६७	...	१५
वैशिष्ट्यस्य	...	वैशिष्ट्यस्य	...	७१	...	१९
सर्वोत्पत्त्या	...	सर्वोत्पत्त्या	...	७२	...	१८
तदुपजिवि	...	तदुपजीवि	...	७९	...	१२
एतद्विवेन	...	पक्षविवेन	...	८२	...	११
गुपधायक	...	गुपधायक	...	८५	...	११
गोमर	...	गोचर	...	९०	...	१०
चिमकाला	...	चिरकाला	...	९०	...	१५
हृत्नय	...	हृन्मय	...	९०	...	१८
प्रकारत्वेन	...	प्रकारेणैव	...	९९	...	१२
मनस	...	मनसा	...	१०१	...	१९
महना	...	मन्दना	...	१०७	...	४
तौर्थिकत्वापीति-	...	तौर्थिकत्वापीति	...	११२	...	१०
विवेपि	...	विनापि	...	११७	...	२२
चेतुन	...	चेतुन	...	१२२	...	१४
भावात	...	भावात्	...	१२२	...	२२
प्रामाण्य-	...	प्रमाण्य-	...	१२४	...	१९
यद्विशेषत	...	यद्विशेषण	...	१२५	...	१९
विशेषणसम्बन्धेन	...	विशेषणसम्बन्धेन	...	१२६	...	१०
प्रामाण्याभावा	...	प्रामाण्याभावा	...	१२६	...	२२
मायस्य	...	मानस्य	...	१४२	...	२
प्रामाण्य पक्षीभवे	...	प्रामाण्ये पक्षीभवते	...	१४२	...	१९
विशिष्ट-	...	विशिष्ट-	...	१५७	...	५
वैशिष्ट्य	...	वैशिष्ट्य	...	१६१	...	२२
व्याप्यनु	...	व्याप्यनु	...	१६६	...	१४
वय	...	वम	...	१६८	...	५

अशुद्धं	शुद्धं	पृष्ठं	पङ्क्तिः
सन्देक	... सन्देहक	... १७२	... ५
रूपनायक	... रूपनाशक	... १७६	... ११
विशेयक	... विशेषक	... १८४	... ७
चतुर्था	... चतुर्थी	... १८५	... २
सौकार्य्यात्	... सौकर्य्यात्	... १८५	... ८
नार्भावेन	... नाभावेन	... १८६	... १२
निश्चयात्मककत्वे	... निश्चयात्मकत्वे	... १९१	... १४
ग्रहण	... चतुष्टय	... १९२	... १।६।१०
तथापीद	... तथापीदं	... १९३	... १८
संशयस्य । न	... संशयस्य न	... १९३	... १९
न्यायनय	... न्यायनये	... १९३	... १९
भावोभावो	... भावाभावो	... २०३	... २०
सिद्ध्य	... सिद्धत्व	... २०९	... ८
विपर्य्यस्य	... विपर्य्ययस्य	... २१०	... २
उद्भावा	... तद्भावा	... २१६	... १३
निष्यकारक	... निष्प्रकारक	... २२२	... १०
निर्व्विकल्पकं	... निर्व्विकल्पकत्वं	... २२२	... २०
प्रामाण्याभावे	... प्रामाण्याभावे	... २२३	... १४
येन	... यत्	... २२३	... १२
प्राशस्यात्	... प्राशस्त्यात्	... २२५	... २
प्रत्यक	... प्रत्येक	... २२९	... १४
यावतीन्यायेन	... यावतीन्यायेन	... २४१	... १२
संशयवार्थं	... संशयसार्थं	... २४४	... १९
प्रामण्यं	... प्रामाण्यं	... २५१	... ११
साधन	... साधना	... २५१	... १२
विशेषण	... विशेषण	... २५५	... १४
द्वित्वन	... द्वित्वेन	... २६२	... २०

अशुद्धं	शुद्धं	पृष्ठं	पङ्क्तिः
विरहाच	ह्रि	१९४	१९
समर्थं		१७०	५
गुमित्यर	अर्थंमकार-	१८४	११
गुणा-	गुणत्व	१८४	१२
मन्वक्षते	मन्वक्षतै	१८९	११
वैचित्यात्	वैचित्र्यात्	१८८	४
गुणादोष-	गुणदोष	१८८	५
एतेन	एतेन	१९९	२
दृष्टान्तत	दृष्टान्ते	१९८	२
प्रतिबन्धककानुभव	प्रतिबन्धकानुभव	२०२	१९
व्यभिचार-	व्यभिचार-	२०२	२०
व्याप्यतया	व्याप्युतया	२०३	४
सामेग्री	सामग्री	२०३	१०
अनलं	अनकलं	२०९	२
वक्ष्योरेव	वक्ष्योरेव	२०८	४
चाक्षष	चाक्षुष	२१२	३
यावच्चमात्	यावर्च्चमात्	२१५	२
भागाङ्गीकारा-	भागाङ्गीकारा-	२१७	१४
सदृश	सदृशं	२१८	२
त्वात्	त्वात्	२२०	७
दर्शनमेव	दर्शनमेव	२२४	२१
बलक्षेन	बलक्षेन	२२९	१५
दर्शनमेव	दर्शनमेव	२२८	२
केवलान्वायमि	केवलान्वयिनि	२२२	२
विशेषित	विशेषपदित	२२५	८
रोधात	रोधात्	२२५	१०
तज्जन्य	तज्जन्य	२५०	९

अशुद्धं	शुद्धं	पृष्ठं	पङ्क्तिः
वेद्दाथ	वेद्दार्थे	२५२	९
सान्यय	सामर्थ्य	२५४	७
अप्रमाणत्व	अप्रामाणत्व	२५६	१०
दूषयितृत्वमाव	दूषयितृत्वमाव	२५६	१२
किन्चति	किञ्चिति	२५८	१२
सामथ्या	सामर्थ्या	२५९	२
प्रामाण्येति	प्रामण्यमाण्येति	२५९	१८
मित्यर्थ,	मित्यर्थः,	२६२	२०
प्रथायां	प्रमायां	२७६	१८
तथवाप्ति	तथाव्याप्ति	२८२	१९
धमाप्रकार	धर्माप्रकार-	२८५	२
सवपतो	सकपतो	२८८	१९
याधिकरणेति	यधिकरणेति	२८९	५
वैशिष्ट्यांश	वैशिष्ट्यांश	२९८	११
वैशिष्ट्यावा-	वैशिष्ट्यावा-	२९८	११
सत्तावान	सत्तावान्	४०४	९
यवमाणेते	यवमाणते	४१२	१०।१२
मर्थः	मर्थः	४१४	२१
षिकर्ष	षिकरण	४२४	१८
यङ्गुलक	यङ्गुलक	४२६	१०
मेवं	मेवे	४२६	२२
इति	इति	४२२	२
यद्दापाद्दाम	यद्दोपाद्दाम	४३५	१५
त्विम	वच्छिन्न	४४८	१५
भेद्दायत्व	भेद्दायत्व	४४८	१६
प्रत्यव	प्रत्यक्षेव	४५८	१०
एक भेद्दा	एकभेद्दा	४५९	५

अशुद्धं	शुद्धं	पृष्ठं	पङ्क्तिः
खातन्त्र्य	... स्वातन्त्र्य	... ४५९	... ६
भयक	... भमक	... ४६०	... ६
इसुमिनो	... इनुमिनो	... ४६२	... ११
यथा	... यथा	... ४७२	... ७
प्राकार	... प्रकार	... ४७४	... ६
मन इहात्मक	... म इहात्मक	... ४७४	... १५
सुवम	... सुषम	... ४७४	... १६
पद्दात्मक	... पाद्दात्मक	... ४७७	... ७
वज्ञककला-	... वज्ञकला-	... ४७९	... २
ववक्षाध्यमाण	... ववक्षाध्यमाण	... ४८०	... १२
निर्घर्षिता	... निर्घंर्षिता	... ४८१	... २।११
ममनयाश्रित	... ममन्नयाश्रित	... ४८३	... ६
रजोतोपादानव	... रजतोपादानः	... ४८५	... ५
कदाचिदा	... कदाचिद्दिदा	... ४८७	... ८
स्वाख्येत्रा	... स्वाक्षेत्रा	... ४८८	... २
रजत-रज्जवा	... रजत-रज्जवो	... ४८८	... १५
राग-द्वेषवो	... राग-द्वेषवो	... ४८८	... १७
जिम्बा	... जिह्वा	... ४८८	... १९
नत	... नतु	... ४८८	... २१
गोर	... गोचर	... ४८९	... ६
संपयः	... संशयः	... ४९३	... १०
हिजितया	... हिद्दजितया	... ४९५	... ११
पुरोवर्ति	... पुरोवर्ति	... ४९८	... २
समभ्ये	... समभ्येव	... ५००	... ९
तद्दपि	... तद्दद्दपि	... ५०२	... २१
विविद	... विविद्द	... ५०७	... १७
वये	... वर्ये	... ५०९	... ३

अशुद्धं		शुद्धं		पृष्ठं		पङ्क्तिः
काय्या	...	कार्य्या	...	५१०	...	२
रूपासिद्धे:	...	स्वरूपासिद्धेः	...	५१०	...	११
संसगा	...	असंसर्गा	...	५१४	...	५
संसगस्य	...	संसर्गस्य	...	५१५	...	४
तव्यये	...	तन्नये	...	५२०	...	१०
विधानत्यिन	...	विधानमित्यन	...	५२२	...	१०
रू	...	रत्र	...	५२२	...	९
अन्यस्येव	...	अन्यस्यैव	...	५२४	...	११
संन्निकर्षात्	...	सन्निकर्षात्	...	५२५	...	२
मेवेभयत्र	...	मेवोभयत्र	...	५२५	...	८
मूलेवा-	...	मूलेर्वा	...	५२९	...	२
गौकार्य्या	...	सौकर्य्या	...	५२७	...	११
सायस्य	...	व्यवसायस्य	...	५३०	...	१०
यौत्सगिक	...	मित्यौत्सर्गिक	...	५३४	...	२
षयेपदसना	...	विशेषदर्शना	...	५३४	...	६
माण्य	...	प्रामाण्ये	...	५३४	...	७
षयत्वपि	...	विषयत्वेपि	...	५३९	...	४
'विव्याप्ति	...	व्यतिव्याप्ति	...	५६०	...	७
शषेण	...	विशेषण	...	५६७	...	१८
मवायत्वेति	...	समवायत्वेति	...	५७३	...	८
त्कूत	...	उत्कूत	...	५८७	...	६
मवायस्य	...	स्वसमवायस्य	...	५६८	...	५
द्धजाति	...	बुद्धेर्जाति	...	६००	...	३
न्द्रियत्वत्व	...	तौन्द्रियत्वमेव	...	६०२	...	२
निते	...	तत्त्वते	...	६०२	...	५
वैक	...	येकैक	...	६०३	...	२
वेक	...	व्यापक	...	६०७	...	६

अशुद्ध	शुद्ध	पृष्ठं	पंक्तिः
संकुर ...	अङ्कुर ...	६१० ...	२०
विव ...	विवे ...	६११ ...	५
प्रेहक ...	मनोहक ...	६११ ...	१२
निर्बंधा ...	निबाधा ...	६१५ ...	१९
मोत्वाहक ...	मोत्वाहक ...	६१९ ...	३
मन्द ...	मन्दे ...	६२० ...	८
सयोगा ...	संयोगा ...	६२१ ...	६
मन्नाना ...	ममन्नाना ...	६२२ ...	२२
त्वस्तु ...	स्तिन्तु ...	६७० ...	१२
अनुपस्थ्या ...	अनुपसस्थ्या ...	६७९ ...	२
हता ...	हतो ...	६८२ ...	२१
प्रमिती ...	प्रतीति ...	७०१ ...	१५
कुमति ...	कुमति ...	७११ ...	२
सामथ्यात् ...	सामर्थ्यात् ...	७१६ ...	४
मुन्वन ...	सुन्वन ...	७२५ ...	१८
कमज ...	कमंज ...	७२६ ...	१४
सम ...	सम्म ...	७२७ ...	५
नोक्कन ...	नोक्कुंल ...	७३० ...	५
कमबा ...	कर्मबां ...	७३७ ...	३
उक्कन ...	उक्कुल ...	७३९ ...	१५
प्रभावन ...	प्रभावत् ...	७४३ ...	१६
नैमिताक ...	नैमित्तिक ...	७५३ ...	१७
वच ...	वचु ...	७७३ ...	९
अनुमीत ...	अनुमितो ...	८०८ ...	२

तत्त्वचिन्तामणिः ।

प्रत्यक्षखण्डे मङ्गलवादरहस्यं ।

गुणातीतोऽपीशस्त्रिगुणसचिवस्त्र्यक्षरमयः
त्रिमूर्त्तिर्यः स्वर्ग-स्थिति-विलयकर्म्माणि तनुते ।
कृपापारावारः परमगतिरेकस्त्रिजगतां
नमस्तस्मै कस्मैचिदमितमहिम्ने पुरभिदे ॥ १ ॥

न्यायाम्बुधिकृतसेतुं हेतुं श्रीरामभखिलसम्पत्तेः ।
तातं त्रिभुवनगीतं तर्कालङ्कारमादरान्नत्वा ॥१॥
श्रीमता मथुरानाथतर्कवागीशधीमता ।
विषदीकृत्य दर्श्यन्ते प्रत्यक्षमणिफक्किकाः ॥२॥

निर्विघ्नं प्रारिप्सिततत्त्वचिन्तामणिनामग्रन्थसमाप्तिकामनया कृतं महादेवनमस्काररूपं मङ्गलं शिष्यशिक्षार्थमादौ निबध्नाति 'गुणातीतः' इति। 'तस्मै नमः', तस्मै कस्मै इत्यपेक्षायामाह 'गुणातीतः' इति। 'यः', 'गुणातीतोऽपि' समवायसम्बन्धेन गुणसामान्याभाववानपि, 'ईशः' अप्रतिहतेच्छः, अप्रतिहतत्व अविसम्वादित्वं। 'अपि', सर्व्वत्र विरोधाभाससूचनाय। निर्गुणत्वस्य इच्छाविरोधात् गुणपदस्य साङ्ख्यमतसिद्ध-सत्त्व-रजस्तमोलक्षणगुणपरतया हि विरोधपरीहारसम्भवात् विरोधाभासत्वं। सत्त्वादयस्च न्यायनये सृष्टि-स्थिति-प्रलयोत्पादकाः अदृष्टभेदा

एवेति नाप्रसिद्धिः[१]। 'योगुणातीतोऽपि', त्रिगुणस्य चेव:' स्वनिष्ठज्ञानेच्छा-कृतिसहकारेण कार्य्यमात्रहेतुः। स्वनिष्ठत्वप्रवेशाद्विरोधः एवं 'योगुणातीतोऽपि', इत्यस्य सर्व्वत्रान्वयः। 'अक्षरमयः' 'क्षर ज्ञानेच्छा-प्रयत्नाः, 'अक्षराः' अविनाशिनः, यत्र 'तन्मयः' तदात्मकः केचित्तु 'अक्षरमयः' 'त्रयः' अकारोकार-मकाररूपवर्णत्रयघटितौ-ङ्कारपदाभिधेयः, सङ्केतसम्बन्धेन ॐकाररूपशब्दवानिति यावत्। गुणातीतपदेन सम्बन्धसामान्यावच्छिन्नगुणसामान्याभाववतो विवक्षितत्वात्[२] विरोधः। समवायसम्बन्धावच्छिन्नगुणसामान्याभावपरतया सत्त्वादिलक्षणगुणाभावपरतया वा विरोधपरीहार इत्याहुः। 'त्रि-मूर्त्तिः' इति। सन्निति शेषः; ब्रह्म-विष्णु-शिवात्मकशरीरत्रयवान्सन् सृष्टि-स्थिति-प्रलयकर्म्माणि 'तनुते', इत्यर्थः। 'तनुते' वि-स्तारानुकूलयत्नवान्, अतो विरोधः। एतेन सर्गादिरेव ईश्वरे प्रमाणमिति सूचितं। 'कृपापारावारः' निरुपधिपरदुःखप्रहाणेच्छा[३] 'कृपा', तस्या असाधारणाधिकरणमित्यर्थः। अत्रापि इच्छाया गुणत्वाद्विरोधः। 'त्रिजगतां', 'परमगतिः' परमहितकर्त्ता, कर्त्तृ-त्वस्य[४] गुणत्वाद्विरोधः[५]। 'एकः' अद्वितीयः, नित्यकृतिमद्वृत्तिभेद-

---

(१) सत्त्वादयश्च न्यायमते अदृष्टविशेष एव स च ईश्वरे नास्तीति न विरोध इति भावः।

(२) सम्बन्धत्वावच्छिन्नसंसर्गकप्रतियोगिताकगुणसामान्याभाववतो विवक्षितत्वादिति ग०।

(३) निरुपधिपरदुःखप्रहरणेच्छेति ग०।

(४) कृतिरूपस्येत्यर्थः।

(५) पूर्व्वोक्तगुणातीतोऽपीत्यनेन विरोध इति भावः।

अन्वीक्षानयमाकलय्य गुरुभिर्ज्ञात्वा गुरूणां मतं
चिन्तादिव्यविलोचनेन च तयोः सारं विलोक्याखिलं।
तन्त्रे दोषगणेन दुर्गमतरे सिद्धान्तदीक्षागुरु-
र्गङ्गेशस्तनुते मितेन वचसा श्रीतत्त्वचिन्तामणिं ॥२॥

प्रतियोगितानवच्छेदकैकत्ववानिति यावत्[(१)] । एकत्वस्य गुणत्वाद्विरोधः । तस्मै किम्भूताय इत्यपेक्षायामाह 'कस्मैचित्' इति विशिष्यानिर्व्वचनीयगुणग्रामायेत्यर्थः । पुनः किम्भूताय 'अमितमहिम्ने' 'महिमा' सौन्दर्य्य-करुणादयः । पुनः किम्भूताय 'पुरभिदे' एकदा पुरत्रयभेदनकर्त्रे । पुरभिदित्यनेन एकदा पुरत्रयभेदनसमर्थस्य सुतरां विघ्नवारणक्षमत्वं सूचितं ॥१॥

प्रेक्षावत्प्रवृत्त्यर्थं ग्रन्थान्तरापेक्षया स्वीयग्रन्थस्योत्कर्षं दर्शयन् स्वकीर्त्त्यनुवृत्तये स्वनाम ग्रन्थनाम च दर्शयति 'अन्वीक्षेति' । 'गङ्गेशः' 'अन्वीक्षानयं' न्यायशास्त्रं, 'गुरुभिः', 'आकलय्य' ज्ञात्वा, 'गुरूणां' प्राभाकराणां, 'मतं', च गुरुभिर्ज्ञात्वा, 'चिन्तादिव्यविलोचनेन च'[(२)] चिन्तारूपदिव्यचक्षुषा, 'तयोः' न्याय-गुरुमतयोः, 'अखिलं' निःशेषं, 'सारं' अभिप्रायं, 'विलोक्य', 'मितेन वचसा श्रीतत्त्वचिन्तामणिं', 'तनुते', इत्यन्वयः । अन्योऽपि 'गङ्गेशः' समुद्रः, 'मितेन वचसा' स्तवादिना, 'चिन्तामणिं तनुते', इत्युपमालङ्कारो व्यक्तः । गुरुमतस्य

---

(१) ननु अद्वितीय इत्यस्य स्वजातीयद्वितीयरहित इत्यर्थस्तथा च प्रतियोग्यप्रसिद्धिः राहित्यस्य अभावत्वेन गुणरूपत्वाभावाद्विरोधासङ्गतिश्चेत्तत आह नित्येति ।

(२) चिन्तादिव्यविलोकनेनेति ग० ।

यतो मणेः पण्डितमण्डनक्रिया
प्रचण्डपाषण्डतमस्तिरस्क्रिया ।
विपक्षपक्षे न विचारचातुरी
न च स्वसिद्धान्तवचोदरिद्रता ॥ ३ ॥

प्रायशः निरस्ततया विशिष्य तदुल्लेखः । गङ्गेशः किम्भूतः 'दोषगणेन' दोषसमूहेन, 'दुर्गमतरे' अत्यन्तदुर्गमे, 'तत्त्वे' सूत्रादौ, 'सिद्धान्तदीक्षागुरुः' सिद्धान्तोपदेशगुरुः ॥ २ ॥

ग्रन्थस्य चिन्तामणिनामकरणे बीजभूतं मणेः सादृश्यं(१) दर्शयति । 'यतो मणे'रिति । इदञ्च सर्व्वत्र सम्बध्यते । 'प्रचण्डे'ति, 'प्रचण्डाः' पाषण्डाः बौद्धाः, त एव तमांसि तेषां 'तिरस्क्रिया' । मणिपक्षे प्रचण्डपाषण्डीभूतानि यानि तमांसि तेषां तिरस्क्रियेत्युन्नेयं । 'विपक्षे'ति 'विपक्षाः' ये बौद्धादयः, तेषां यः 'पक्षः' सिद्धान्तः, तत्र 'न विचारचातुरी' न व्यवस्थानकौशलं(२) । मणिपक्षे तु 'विपक्षपक्षे' चौरादिपक्षे, न विलक्षणचरणचातुरी । मणिप्रभया तमोनिवृत्तेरिति भावः । 'न चे'ति । 'स्वस्य' न्यायदर्शनस्य, यानि सिद्धान्तवचांसि तेषां 'न दरिद्रता' । मणिपक्षे 'स्वस्य' धनस्य, सिद्धः 'अन्तः' अवसानं, वृत्तमिति वचसोऽदरिद्रता न चेत्यर्थः, अकारप्रश्लेषात् । 'दरिद्रता' च प्रयोगाभावः, अनन्तं धनं भवतीत्यर्थः(३) । केचित्तु मणिपक्षे विशेषणत्वस्य 'विपक्षपक्षेशस्य' विपक्षपक्षश्रेष्ठस्य, 'विचारचातुरी' विल-

---

(१) मणिसादृश्यमिति ख० ।
(२) न व्यवस्थापनकौशलमिति ख० ।
(३) भवतीत्यभिप्राय इति ख० ।

इह खलु सकलशिष्टैकवाक्यतया अभिमतकर्म्मारम्भसमये तत्समाप्तिकामा मङ्गलमाचरन्ति। तत्र यद्यपि मङ्गलस्य कारणता नान्वयव्यतिरेकगम्या विनापि मङ्गलं प्रमत्तानुष्ठितसमाप्तेः। न च तत्र[१] जन्मान्तरीयतत्कल्पनं, अन्योन्याश्रयात् लोकावगतकारणेनान्यथासिद्धेश्च।

लक्षणचरणचातुरी, न चेत्यन्वयः। स्वसिद्धेत्यस्य 'स्वस्य' साधनस्य, सिद्धः 'अन्तः' अवसानं, वृत्तमिति वचसा दर्शितेत्यर्थः इत्याहुः। एतन्मते नाकारप्रश्लेषः ॥३॥

एवं कृतस्य मङ्गलस्य कदाचित् केनचित् निरर्थकत्वमाशङ्क्येतेत्यतो मङ्गलस्य सफलत्वं व्यवस्थापयितुं प्रथमतो मीमांसकसम्प्रदायमतमुपदर्शयति 'इह'इत्यादिना सम्प्रदायविद इत्यन्तेन[२]। 'इह' अस्मिन् लोके, मनुष्यलोक इति यावत्। 'खलु' अवश्यं, 'सकलशिष्टैकवाक्यतया' मङ्गलस्य समाप्तिहेतुत्वेन सकलशिष्टसम्मततया, एतेन[३] भ्रममूलकता निराकृता[४]। 'आरम्भसमये' तत्पूर्व्वसमये, 'तत्समाप्तिकामाः' अभिमतकर्म्मसमाप्तिकामाः। ननु समाप्तिहेतुताया मङ्गलवृत्तित्वे किं मानं, न तावत् प्रत्यक्षं, यस्य पुरुषस्य प्रमत्तकर्तृकसमाप्तिस्थले ऐहिकमङ्गलविरहनिश्चयो मङ्गले लोकावगतकारणेन समाप्तिं प्रति अन्यथासिद्धत्वग्रहश्च विद्यमानः तेन पुरुषेण

---

(१) नापीति ख०।

(२) सम्प्रदाय इत्यन्तेनेति ग०।

(३) एतेन मङ्गलस्य समाप्तिहेतुत्वेन सकलशिष्टसम्मतत्वकथनेनेत्यर्थः।

(४) सर्व्वेषामेकदा भ्रमो न सम्भवतीति भावः।

तदानीं मङ्गलवृत्तितया तस्याः प्रत्यक्षतो निश्चेतुमशक्यत्वात्। अतएव नानुमानाद्यपि, तादृशपुरुषविशेषेण तदानीं तस्य अनुमानादिनापि ग्रहासम्भवात् इत्यत आह 'तत्र यद्यपीति। 'तत्र' आचारे, सप्तम्यर्थो-निमित्तत्वं तच्च प्रयोजकत्वं अन्वयश्चास्य कारणतायां, तथा च तदा-चारप्रयोजकीभूता समाप्तिकारणता यद्यपि तादृशपुरुषविशेषेण तादृशकालविशेषे न मङ्गलस्यान्वयव्यतिरेकगम्येति योजना। एतेन मङ्गलवृत्तिसमाप्तिकारणतात्वेन पक्षत्वे तादृशकारणतायां सिद्धायां विवादाभावः। असिद्धायामाश्रयासिद्धिः। न च मङ्गलवृत्तिकारणता-त्वेन पक्षता न तु समाप्त्यन्तर्भावः, समाप्त्यन्वयव्यतिरेकगम्यत्वाभावस्य साध्यः, कारणतात्वस्य कारणपदप्रवृत्तिनिमित्तत्वं[१] तेन कारणतात्वस्य कार्य्यभेदेन विभिन्नतया प्रकृतकारणतात्वेन पक्षत्वे नाश्रयासिद्धिः कारणतान्तरत्वेन पक्षत्वे चार्थान्तरमिति दोषस्य नावकाश इति वाच्यं। तत्रेत्यस्यानन्वयापत्तेः मङ्गलवृत्तिकारणतायास्तादृशाचारविषयत्वा-सिद्धेरिति दूषणं प्रत्युक्तं, समाप्तिकारणतात्वेन पक्षत्वात्। तादृश-पुरुषविशेषस्य तादृशकालविशेषे मङ्गलान्वय-व्यतिरेकगम्यत्वञ्च मङ्गलान्वयव्यतिरेकसहचारज्ञानजन्यमङ्गलवृत्तिताप्रकारकप्रत्यक्षनिश्चय-विषयत्वं तथा च समाप्तिकारणता न मङ्गलान्वयव्यतिरेकसहचार-ज्ञानजन्यतत्कालीन-तत्पुरुषीयमङ्गलवृत्तिताप्रकारकप्रत्यक्षनिश्चयवि-षय इति फलितं। अखण्डाभावस्य साध्यत्वान्न अन्यान्तभागवैयर्थ्यं[२]

---

(१) कारणपदशक्यतावच्छेदकत्वमित्यर्थः।

(२) तत्कालीन-तत्पुरुषीय-मङ्गलवृत्तिताप्रकारकनिश्चयविषयत्वाभा-वस्य अभावान्तरत्वेन साध्यानन्तर्गतत्वात् न साध्यस्य व्यर्थविशेषणघटितत्व-मिति भावः।

पक्षतावच्छेदकावच्छेदेन साध्यसिद्धेरुद्देश्यतया च नांशतः सिद्धसाधनं[१]। नन्वनन्यथासिद्धनियतपूर्ववर्त्तिता कारणता, तच्चानन्यथासिद्धत्वज्ञाने न सहचारज्ञानापेक्षा न वा नियमांशज्ञानेपि, व्यापकताग्रहे सहचारग्रहस्याहेतुत्वात्। धूमत्वादिघटितव्याप्तिग्रह एवान्वयसहचारग्रहस्य हेतुत्वेन व्यवस्थापितत्वात्। अतएवान्वयोऽन्वयसहचारधीः, व्यतिरेकश्च व्यभिचारज्ञानव्यतिरेकः, तदुभयजन्यतादृशप्रत्यक्षनिश्चयविषयो नेत्यर्थः इत्यपि निरस्तं। व्यतिरेकसहचारज्ञानवदन्वयसहचारज्ञानस्याप्यहेतुत्वात्। अत्राहुः तदितरयावत्कारणसत्त्वे तत्सत्त्वेऽवश्यं कार्य्यं, तदभावे च कार्य्याभाव इत्यन्वयसहचारव्यतिरेकसहचारग्रहो विशिष्टकारणतासाक्षात्कारहेतुः तथैवान्वयव्यतिरेकात्। न त्वंशभेदव्यवस्था। नव्यास्तु अन्वयो हेत्वभाववति कार्य्यान्वयज्ञानं व्यभिचारज्ञानमिति यावत्। तद्व्यतिरेकजन्यतादृशनिश्चयविषयो नेत्यर्थः इति प्रोचुः[२]। हेतुमाह 'विनापीति। तदानीं तत्पुरुषेण विनापि मङ्गलं प्रमत्तानुष्ठितसमाप्त्युत्पत्तिदर्शनादित्यर्थः। तथा च तत्कालीन-तत्पुरुषीयमङ्गलव्यतिरेकव्यभिचारग्रहविषयनिरूपितकारणतात्वादितिहेतुर्नातो वैयधिकरण्यं[३]। केचित्तु मङ्गलं

(१ समाप्तिकारणतात्वसामानाधिकरण्येन पक्षत्वे मङ्गलार्थत्तिसमाप्तिकारणतात्वांशे न सिद्धसाधनं स्यादिति भावः।

(२) इति प्राहुरिति ख०।

(३) पक्षतावच्छेदकेन साद्धं हेतोरसामानाधिकरण्यमित्यर्थः। तथा च समाप्तिकारणता न मङ्गलान्वयव्यतिरेकसहचारज्ञानजन्य-तत्कालीन-तत्पुरुषीय-मङ्गलाद्वृत्तितावप्रकारक-प्रत्यक्षनिश्चयविषयः तत्कालीन-तत्पुरुषीय-मङ्गलव्यतिरेकव्यभिचारज्ञानविषयनिरूपितकारणतात्वात् इत्यभिप्रायः।

न समाप्त्यन्वयव्यतिरेकज्ञानजन्य तत्कालीन-तत्पुरुषीय-समाप्तिकारणत्वप्रकारकप्रत्यक्षनिरूपितविषय: तत्कालीन-तत्पुरुषीय-समाप्तिव्यभिचारित्वग्रहविषयत्वादिति समुदितार्थः इत्याहु:। नन्वुक्तहेतुरसिद्ध:, तस्य हि पुरुषस्य तदानीं प्रमत्तानुष्ठितसमाप्ताविष्टकमङ्गलव्यभिचारित्वग्रहेऽपि न तत्र मङ्गलसामान्यव्यतिरेकव्यभिचारित्वग्रहः, तदानीं तेन पुरुषेण प्रमत्तानुष्ठितसमाप्तिपूर्वं जन्मान्तरीयमङ्गलानुमानादित्यभिप्रायेणाशङ्कते 'न च तत्रेति। 'तत्र' प्रमत्तानुष्ठितसमाप्तिपूर्वं, 'जन्मान्तरीय-तत्कल्पनं' तेन पुरुषेण तदानीं जन्मान्तरीयमङ्गलानुमानं, इयं समाप्तिर्मङ्गलपूर्व्विका समाप्तित्वात् शिष्टानुष्ठितसमाप्तिवदित्येवंरूपेणेति भाव:। 'अन्योन्याश्रयादिति' सिद्धे जन्मान्तरीणमङ्गले व्यभिचारज्ञानाभावे हेतुताग्रह:, हेतुताग्रहे च समाप्तित्वेन जन्मान्तरीयमङ्गलानुमानमन्यथा त्वप्रयोजकमित्यन्योन्याश्रयादित्यर्थः। नन्वऽनुकूलतर्को न व्याप्तिग्रहहेतु:, किन्तु क्वचिद्व्यभिचारज्ञाननिवर्त्तकतया तस्योपयोग: तथा च कारणत्वग्रहं विनापि व्यभिचारज्ञानसामग्र्या असार्व्वदिकत्वेन समाप्तित्वे स्वत:सिद्धमङ्गलपूर्व्वकत्वव्यभिचारज्ञानाभावादेव जन्मान्तरीयमङ्गलानुमानसम्भव इत्यस्वरसादुक्तान्तरमाह 'लोकावगतकारणेनेति। कण्ठ-ताल्वाद्यभिघातादिनेत्यर्थः। 'अन्यथासिद्धेश्च' तस्य पुरुषस्य तदानीं मङ्गले समाप्तिं प्रति अन्यथासिद्धत्वज्ञानाच्च। तथा च तत्कालीन-तत्पुरुषीय-मङ्गलनिष्ठान्यथासिद्धत्वज्ञानविषयनिरूपितकारणतात्वादिति हेतु:।

नापि मङ्गलं सफलं अविगीतशिष्टाचारविषयत्वात् दर्शवदिति फलसिद्धौ[१] प्रारिप्सितसमाप्तेस्तदानीमपेक्षितत्वेन नियमेनोपस्थितत्वात् फलान्तरस्यातथाभावात् विश्वजिन्न्यायेन फलकल्पने गौरवात् परिशेषानुमानेन तत्कारणताग्रहः।

तस्य पुरुषस्य तदानीमनुमानेनापि मङ्गले न समाप्तिकारणताग्रहसम्भव इत्याह 'नापीत्यादिना 'कारणताग्रहः' इत्यन्तेन। 'मङ्गलमिति नमस्कारादिकमित्यर्थः। नतिस्तुत्यादिसाधारणस्य मङ्गलत्वस्यैकस्याभावात् मङ्गलपदस्य नानार्थत्वात्। 'सफलमिति अभीष्टफलजनकमित्यर्थः। अभीष्टत्वञ्च[२] स्वकर्त्तव्यताप्रयोजकेच्छाविषयत्वं। 'अविगीतशिष्टाचारविषयत्वादिति। अविगीतो यः शिष्टाचारस्तद्विषयत्वादित्यर्थः। 'आचारः' प्रवृत्तिः, न तु क्रिया, विषयत्वासम्भवात्। शिष्टकृते निष्फलजनताड़नादौ व्यभिचारवारणायाविगीतेत्याचारविशेषणं, 'अविगीतत्वं' वेदनिषिद्धाविषयकत्वं, पापाजनकत्वं वा। शिष्टकृतनिष्फलस्य न तथा[३]। "नित्य-नैमित्तिकैश्चैव काम्यैरन्यैरगर्हितैः। कर्म्मभिस्तु नयेत् कालं न विप्रः क्षणिको भवेत्" इत्यनेन, "वृथाचेष्टां न कुर्वीत" इति, "निष्फलानि च कर्म्माणि नारभेत विचक्षणः" इत्यादिना च तन्निषेधात्[४]। तथापि पश्वादिकृतनि-

---

(१) सफलत्वसिद्धाविति ख०, ग०, घ।

(२) अभीष्टफलत्वञ्चेति ख०।

(३) न पापाजनकमित्यर्थः।

(४) तन्न निषेधादिति ख० :

ष्फलचेष्टायां व्यभिचारः । "नित्य-नैमित्तिकैरित्यादिनिषेधविधीना-मुपक्रमानुरोधेनाधिकारिमात्रपरतया तदीयस्याचेष्टाया अनिषिद्धत्वादतः 'शिष्टेति, 'शिष्टत्वं' च बालक-पतितान्यजात्यतिरिक्तत्वे सति वेदप्रामाण्याभ्युपगन्तृत्वं । न च तथापि भोगे व्यभिचारः तस्याप्युद्देश्यतया कृतिविषयत्वादिति वाच्यं । साध्यत्वेन प्रवृत्तिविषयतायाः फलव्यावृत्ताया अत्र प्रवेशात् । एतेन[१] नान्तरीयकस्य प्रवृत्तिविषयत्वाभ्युपगमेपि निष्फले[२] भोजनादि-नान्तरीयके न व्यभिचारः, तत्र तादृशविषयत्वाभावात् । परमेश्वरकृतेरपि तादृशविषयत्वाभावात्[३] तादृशविषयत्वाभ्युपगमेपि प्रवृत्तित्वादिजातेस्तत्राभावाच्च न तामादाय निष्फले जनताड़नादौ[४] व्यभिचारस्तदवस्थः । न च तथापि कीर्त्तनादिना फलाजनके शिष्टकृतयागे व्यभिचार इति वाच्यं । स्वरूपयोग्यत्वरूपस्य फलजनकत्वस्य विवक्षितत्वात् तस्य च तत्रापि सत्त्वात् ।

यद्वा आचारस्यात्र कृतिमात्रं, तथा च बौद्धकृते निष्फलजनताड़नादौ व्यभिचारवारणाय शिष्टेत्याचारविशेषणं, 'शिष्टत्वं' भ्रमाजन्यत्वं, परमेश्वरकृतेरपि निष्फलविषयत्वात्तामादाय निष्फले व्यभिचारवारणायाविगीतेत्याचारविशेषणं, 'अविगीतत्वं' अनित्यत्वं ।

केचित्तु अविगीताचारविषयत्वाच्छिष्टाचारविषयत्वादितिहेतुद्वये तात्पर्यं, निष्फले चैत्यवन्दनादौ व्यभिचारवारणाय प्रथमहेतावविः

---

(१) साध्यत्वाख्यविषयत्वप्रवेशेनेत्यर्थः ।

(२) स्वकर्त्तव्यताप्रयोजकेच्छाविषयाजनके इत्यर्थः ।

(३) साध्यत्वेन प्रवृत्तिविषयत्वाभावादित्यर्थः ।

(४) पश्वादिकृत इति शेषः अन्यथा अविगीतपदेनैव वारणसम्भवात् ।

गीतत्वं, द्वितीयहेतौ च शिष्टत्वमाचारविशेषणं। 'अविगीतत्वं' च दृष्टोत्पत्तिनान्तरीयकदुःखेतरदुःखाजनकत्वं, बलवदनिष्टाननुबन्धित्वे सति इष्टसाधनत्वं वा तद्ग्रहस्य शिष्टैकवाक्यतया, जनताड़नादिकन्तु नैतादृशं निष्फलत्वात् कर्म्ममात्रस्यैव कष्टत्वाच्च। न तु वेदनिषिद्धाविषयकत्वं, पापाजनकत्वं वा 'अविगीतत्वं', तावता वैदिककर्म्माधिकारिणा कृते निष्फले व्यभिचारवारणसम्भवेपि पश्वादिकृतरथ्याचेष्टायां व्यभिचारस्य दुर्व्वारत्वात्। "नित्य-नैमित्तिकैरित्यादिना च निषेधविधीनामधिकारिमात्रपरत्वात्। द्वितीयहेतौ च 'शिष्टत्वं' भ्रमाजन्यत्वं। अन्यत् सर्व्वं पूर्व्ववदित्याहुः।

केचित्तु सफलमित्यस्य पापाजनकत्वे सतीष्टसाधनमित्यर्थः। तथा च श्येनयागागम्यागमनादौ व्यभिचारवारणायाविगीतेत्याचारविशेषणं, 'अविगीतत्वं' पापाजनकत्वं, निष्फले चैत्यवन्दनादौ व्यभिचारवारणाय शिष्टेति 'शिष्टत्वं' च इष्टसाधनताभ्रमाजन्यत्वं, न तु भ्रमाजन्यत्वमात्रं तथा सति अगम्यागमनाद्याचारस्यापि बलवदनिष्टाननुबन्धित्वभ्रमजन्यतया ऽतावविगीतपदवैयर्थ्यापत्तेः। बलवदनिष्टाननुबन्धित्वज्ञानस्य प्रवृत्त्यजनकत्वनये च भ्रमाजन्यत्वमात्रमेव तत्। न च "कष्टं कर्म्म" इतिन्यायात् "रथ्याचेष्टां न कुर्व्वीत" इत्यादिस्मृतेश्च[१] चैत्यवन्दनादावपि पापजनकत्वाच्छिष्टपदवैयर्थ्यमिति वाच्यं। तद्विलक्षणपापस्यैवात्र प्रवेशात् पश्वादिकृतरथ्याचेष्टाया अप्युक्तक्रमेण पापाजनकतया तत्रैव व्यभिचारवारकत्वेन पापसामान्यप्रवेशेपि साार्थ-

---

(१) श्रुतेश्चेति ख०, ग०, च।

कत्वसम्भवाच्चेत्याहुः । तदसत् । समाप्तिफलकत्वविचारे विशिष्टसा-ध्यकरणे अर्थान्तरत्वापत्तेरिति संक्षेपः ।

'इति फलसिद्धौ' 'इति' इत्यनुमानेन, सफलत्वसिद्धौ, जातायां, 'परिशेषानुमानेन तत्कारणताग्रहः' 'तस्य' पुरुषस्य, तदानीं मङ्गले समाप्तिकारणताग्रहः, इति योजना । 'परिशेषानुमानं' च मङ्गलं समाप्तिजनकं समाप्त्यन्यफलाजनकत्वे सति सफलत्वादित्याकारकं । 'फलत्वं' च स्वकर्त्तव्यताप्रयोजकेच्छाविषयत्वं, तेन मङ्गलस्य स्वध्वंस-विघ्नध्वंसादिजनकत्वेपि न सत्यन्तविशेषणासिद्धिः[१] । एतदनुमाने च पूर्व्वानुमानं[२] विशेष्यदलसाधकतया[३] उपयुक्तमिति भावः ।

ननु मङ्गलं न समाप्तिजनकं समाप्तिविषयककामनावत्पुरुषाक-र्त्तृकत्वात् घटादिविषयककामनावत्पुरुषाकर्त्तृको यागादिर्यथा न घटादिजनक इति सामान्यतोदृष्टानुमानेन[४] मङ्गले समाप्तिजनक-त्वाभावग्रहणात् कथमिदं समाप्तिजनकत्वानुमानमित्यत आह 'प्रारि-प्सितेति, 'नियमेनापेक्षितत्वेन' नियमेन मङ्गलकर्तुः कामनाविषय-त्वेन, 'उपस्थितत्वात्' अनुमातुस्तादृशपुरुषस्योपस्थितत्वात्, तथा च समाप्तिजनकत्वाभावसाधकोक्तहेतोरप्रामाण्यसिद्धिरिति भावः ।

---

(१) अन्यथा स्वध्वंसं प्रति स्वस्य कारणत्वेन मङ्गलस्य मङ्गलध्वंसं प्रति-कारणत्वात् विघ्नध्वंसादिकं प्रति कारणत्वाच्च समाप्त्यन्यफलाजनकत्वे सति इति विशेषणासिद्धिः स्यादिति भावः ।

(२) मङ्गलं सफलं अविगीतशिष्टाचारविषयत्वादित्यनुमानमित्यर्थः ।

(३) सफलत्वादितिदलसाधकतयेत्यर्थः ।

(४) यो यद्विषयककामनावत्पुरुषाकर्तृकः स न तज्जनकः इत्यनु-मानेनेत्यर्थः ।

ननु तथापि समाप्तिभिन्नस्य ग्राम-पशु-हिरण्यादेरपि फलत्व-ज्ञानसम्भवात् सत्यन्तविशेषणज्ञानमेव नास्ति कुतोऽनुमानमिदमित्यत आह 'फलान्तरस्येति समाप्तिभिन्नस्य ग्राम-पशु-हिरण्यादेरित्यर्थः। 'अतथाभावात्' अतथाभूतत्वेनोपस्थितत्वात्, मङ्गलकर्तुस्तदानीं काम-नाया अविषयत्वेनोपस्थितत्वादिति यावत्। तथा च हेतुज्ञान-सत्त्वान्मङ्गलं न समाप्तिभिन्नग्रामादिफलकं ग्रामादिविषयककामना-वत्पुरुषाकर्तृकत्वात् घटादिविषयककामनावत्पुरुषाकर्तृको यागादि-र्यथा न घटादिफलक इति सामान्यतोदृष्टानुमानेन ग्रामादिफल-कत्वाभावज्ञानमिति भावः।

नन्वेतादृशानुमानेन समाप्तिभिन्नग्रामादिफलकत्वाभावज्ञानसम्भ-वेपि विश्वजिन्न्यायेन समाप्तिभिन्नस्वर्गफलकत्वज्ञाने बाधकाभावात् कुतः सत्यन्तविशेषणज्ञानं, स्वर्गकामनां विना समाप्तिकामनाया एवानुपपन्नतया मङ्गलकर्तुस्तदानीं स्वर्गकामनाया अप्यावश्यकत्वेन उक्तहेतुना स्वर्गफलकत्वाभावज्ञानसम्भवादित्यत आह 'विश्वजिदिति। यथा विश्वजिद्यागस्य स्वर्गरूपफलाश्रवणेऽपि स्वर्गफकत्वज्ञानं तथे-त्यर्थः। 'फलकल्पने' समाप्तिभिन्नस्वर्गफलकत्वज्ञाने, 'गौरवादिति, अनन्तस्वर्गव्यक्तिकल्पनारूपगौरवज्ञानस्य प्रतिबन्धकत्वादित्यर्थः। न च समाप्तित्वापेक्षया लघुतया स्वर्गत्वावान्तरवैजात्यस्य कार्य्यतावच्छेदकस्य कल्पनेऽनन्तस्वर्गव्यक्तिकल्पनं फलमुखतया न दोषायेति वाच्यं। फलमुखगौरवस्यापि दोषत्वादिति भावः।

यद्वा स्वर्गमात्रस्य फलत्वे नियमतः समाप्तिकामनया शिष्टानां मङ्गलानुष्ठानानुपपत्त्या समाप्ति-स्वर्गयोरुभयोः फलत्वकल्पने गौरव-

व्यभिचारेण कारणत्वस्याभावात् उपायसहस्रेणापि ग्रहीतुमशक्यत्वात् ।

मिति गौरवज्ञानस्य प्रतिबन्धकत्वादित्यर्थः । स्वर्गकामना च समाप्तिकामनोपपादकतया उपपन्नेति भावः ।

नव्यास्तु 'इतिफलसिद्धाविति, तस्य पुरुषस्य तदानीं आयमानायामिति शेषः । तथा चैतदनुमानेन नस्य पुरुषस्य तदानीं सफलत्वसिद्धौ आयमानायां 'परिशेषानुमानेन' समाप्त्यन्यफलजनकत्वबाधज्ञानसहकारेण, 'तत्कारणताग्रहः' समाप्तिकारणताग्रहः, इति योजना प्रारिप्सितेत्यादिग्रन्थस्तु पूर्ववदिति व्याचक्षुः ।

'व्यभिचारेण' व्यभिचारज्ञानेन, अन्यथासिद्धत्वग्रहेण चेति शेषः । 'कारणत्वस्याभावात्' कारणत्वाभावज्ञानात्, तथा च बाध इति भावः । 'उपायसहस्रेण' हेतुसहस्रेण, 'ग्रहीतुमशक्यत्वादिति । न च प्रमत्तानुष्ठितसमाप्तिस्थले जन्मान्तरीयमङ्गलसंशयेन व्यभिचारसंशयादन्यथासिद्धत्वसंशयाच्च बाधसंशय एव न तु बाधनिश्चयः, स चानुमानप्रवृत्तावनुकूल एव[१] न तु प्रतिबन्धक इति वाच्यं । प्रमत्तानुष्ठितसमाप्तिस्थले जन्मान्तरमङ्गलस्य साधकाभावेन व्यतिरेकनिर्णये व्यभिचारनिर्णयस्यैव सत्त्वात् अन्यथासिद्धत्वस्यापि निर्णयसत्त्वाच्च । न चैवंसिद्धान्ते वेदोऽपि कथं बोधकः[२] स्यात् बाधनिश्चयसत्त्वेन योग्यताज्ञानविरहादिति वाच्यं । मीमांसकनयेऽन्वयप्रयोजकरूपवत्त्व-

---

(१) संशयस्य पक्षतात्वादिति भावः ।

(२) मङ्गले समाप्तिसाधनताया इत्यादिः ।

तथापि तथाविधशिष्टाचारानुमितश्रुतिरेव मङ्गलस्याभिमतहेतुत्वे मानं।

स्यैव योग्यतात्वेन बाधनिश्चयसत्त्वेऽपि योग्यताज्ञानसम्भवाद्बाधनिश्चयस्य शाब्दबोधाप्रतिबन्धकत्वादिति भावः।

केचित्तु 'गृहीतुमशक्यत्वादित्यस्य अप्रामाण्यज्ञानानास्कन्दितनिश्चयस्याशक्यत्वादित्यर्थः। व्यभिचारान्यथासिद्धत्वयोः संशयसत्त्वादुत्पन्नानामप्यनुमितानामप्रामाण्यसंशयादितिभावः। न चैवंसिद्धान्ते वेदस्यापि तादृशनिश्चयजनकत्वासम्भवः, व्यभिचारादिसंशयसत्त्वेन तत्राप्यप्रामाण्यसंशयसम्भवादिति वाच्यं। वेदजन्यत्वज्ञानादेव तत्र नाप्रामाण्यसंशय इत्यभिप्रायादित्याहुः। तदसत् तथा सति वेदानुमाने अप्रामाण्यसंशयस्य दुर्वारत्वादिति ध्येयं।

यद्यपि तत्पुरुषस्य तदानीं प्रत्यक्षादितो मङ्गले समाप्तिकारणत्वग्रहासम्भवेऽपि पुरुषान्तरस्य कालान्तरे तस्यैव पुरुषस्य च मङ्गले समाप्तिकारणत्वप्रत्यक्षानुमानसम्भवात् प्रत्यक्षानुमानमपि तत्र प्रमाणं सम्भवति, अन्यथा दण्डादावपि प्रत्यक्षादितो घटादिकारणत्वासिद्धिप्रसङ्गात्, कस्यचित् पुरुषस्य कदाचित्तत्रापि व्यभिचारादिज्ञानसत्त्वात्, तथापि प्रौढ़िवादेन तादृशपुरुषस्यापि तस्मिन्काले समाप्तिकारणत्वग्रहमुपपादयति 'तथापीति, 'तथाविधशिष्टाचारानुमितेति अविगीतशिष्टाचारानुमितेत्यर्थः। 'मानमिति तस्य पुरुषस्य तदानीं' प्रमाजनकमित्यर्थः। न चानुमितवेदः आनुपूर्वीविशेषानिश्चयेन

नार्थप्रत्ययेऽ[१] क्षम इति वाच्यं। विनाप्यानुपूर्वीज्ञानं तदर्थबोधकत्वेन[२] ज्ञातादेव शब्दात्तदर्थबोधादिति भावः। श्रुत्यनुमानञ्च, नमस्कारादिकं वेदबोधितसमाप्तिसाधनताकं समाप्त्युद्देश्यकाविगीतशिष्टाचारविषयत्वात्। साध्ये विशिष्य समाप्तेः प्रवेशादविगीतशिष्टाचारविषयत्वे सामान्यतो हेतूकृते दर्शादावेव व्यभिचार इति हेतौ समाप्त्युद्देश्यकेत्याचारविशेषणं। उद्देश्यत्वञ्च विषयताविशेषः। तथा च यो यदुद्देश्यकाविगीतशिष्टाचारविषयः, स वेदबोधिततत्साधनताकः यथा दर्शः, इति सामान्यतोव्याप्तिः[३] शिष्टकृते निष्फले चैत्यवन्दनादौ व्यभिचारवारणायाविगीतेति, 'अविगीतत्वं' वेदनिषिद्धाविषयकत्वं, शिष्टकृतनिष्फलस्य "वृथाचेष्टां न कुर्व्वीतेत्यादिवेदनिषिद्धमेव। पश्वादिकृते निष्फले व्यभिचारवारणाय शिष्टेति, 'शिष्टत्वं' च बालकपतिताद्यजाद्यतिरिक्तत्वे सति वेदप्रामाण्याभ्युपगमविशिष्टत्वं[४] अभ्युपगमो निश्चयः। न च तथापि वेदप्रामाण्याभ्युपगन्तुर्भोजनादौ व्यभिचार इति वाच्यं। अलौकिकत्वे सतीत्यनेनापि विशेषणीयत्वात्। अलौकिकत्वञ्च लोकावगतेष्टसाधनताश्रयान्यत्वं। वेद-तदुपजीविप्रमाणातिरिक्तप्रमाणं लोकः, दर्शादेरिष्टसाधनत्वस्य वेदेन तदुपजीविना यागः स्वर्गसाधनं स्वर्गसाधनत्वेन वेदबोधितत्वादित्यनुमानेनैव वा बोधनात्र दृष्टान्तासिद्ध्यादिः। तावत्पदार्थोपस्थितिसहकृतमनोजन्य-

(१) नार्थप्रत्यायन इति ग०।
(२) तदर्थज्ञापकत्वेनेति ग०।
(३) इत्युदाहरणवाक्यप्रतिपाद्या सामान्यमुखी व्याप्तिरित्यर्थः।
(४) वेदप्रामाण्याभ्युपगन्तृत्वमिति ग०।

विशिष्टज्ञानमादाय यथा न दृष्टान्तासिद्ध्यादिः तथा वेदलक्षण एव स्फुटीभविष्यति । न च तथापि भ्रान्तया स्वर्गफलान्यफलमुद्दिश्य यथोक्त-शिष्टकृतयागादौ व्यभिचारः, तस्य तत्साधनत्वेन वेदाबोधितत्वादिति वाच्यं। चैत्यवन्दनादिवत्तस्यापि वृथाचेष्टात्वेन वेदनिषिद्धत्वात्(१) स्वकर्त्तव्यतप्रयोजकेच्छाविषयस्वरूपायोग्यकर्म्मण एव वृथाचेष्टात्वात् । वस्तुतस्तु पश्वादि-तदितरसाधारणकृते चैत्यवन्दनादिनिष्फलसामान्ये स्वःफलान्यफलमुद्दिश्य कृते यागादौ च व्यभिचारवारणाय 'शिष्टेति' 'शिष्टत्वं' भ्रमाजन्यत्वं। भोजनादौ लौकिककर्म्मणि व्यभिचारवारणाया-विगीतेति, 'अविगीतत्वं' लौकिकाविषयकत्वं, तच्च निरुक्तमेव । न च तथापि उत्पन्नतत्त्वज्ञानिकृते चैत्यवन्दनादौ व्यभिचारस्तस्यापि भ्रमा-जन्यत्वादिति वाच्यं । चैत्यवन्दनादेस्तत्त्वज्ञानिकर्तृकत्वे मानाभावात् तत्सत्त्वे प्रवृत्त्यन्यथानुपपत्त्या भ्रमस्याप्यावश्यकत्वाच्च । तदुद्देश्य त्वेना-प्याचारो विशेषणीयः तेन दर्शादौ वेदबोधितसमाप्तिसाधनत्वाभावे-ऽपि न व्यभिचार इति तत्त्वम् ।

उपाध्यायास्तु भोजनादौ व्यभिचारवारणायालौकिकत्वे सतीति पूरणीयम् । अलौकिकत्वञ्च लोकावगतबलवदनिष्टाननुबन्धित्ववि-शिष्टेष्टसाधनताश्रयान्यत्वं, अविगीतपदसार्थक्याय बलवदनिष्टाननुब-न्धित्वमखण्डभेदघटकं । इत्यञ्चागम्यागमनादौ व्यभिचारवारणायावि-गीतेति, 'अविगीतत्वं' बलवदनिष्टाननुबन्धित्वं, अत्र निष्फलजन्या-निष्टव्यावृत्तानिष्टस्य प्रविष्टतया चैत्यवन्दनादौ धात्र्या स्वःफलान्य-

(१) तथाचाविगीतत्वाभावात्तद्घटितहेत्वभावादेव न तत्र व्यभिचार इति भावः ।

फलमुद्दिश्य कृते यागादौ च व्यभिचारवारणाय शिष्टेति। बलवद-निष्टसामान्यप्रवेशेऽपि पश्वादिकृतस्वर्गाचेष्टायां व्यभिचारवारणाय शिष्टेति, 'शिष्टत्वं' इष्टसाधनत्वभ्रमाजन्यत्वं, न तु भ्रमाजन्यत्वमात्रं, अगम्यागमनाचारस्यापि[१] बलवदनिष्टाननुबन्धित्वभ्रमजन्यतया अवि-गीतपदवैयर्थ्यापत्तेः[२] बलवदनिष्टाननुबन्धित्वज्ञानस्य प्रवृत्त्यहेतुत्वनये तु[३] भ्रमाजन्यत्वमेव शिष्टत्वमित्यप्याहुः।

अन्ये तु नमस्कारादिर्वेदबोधितबलवदनिष्टाननुबन्धित्वविशिष्टस-माप्तिसाधनताकः समाप्त्युद्देश्यकाविगीतशिष्टाचारविषयत्वादित्यनुमानं, व्याप्तिश्च पूर्ववत्। हेतावगीतत्वविशेषणसार्थक्याय साध्ये बलवदि-त्यादि[४]। तथा सति[५] हेतावविगीतविशेषणानुपादाने इष्टानिष्टो-भयजनके श्येनादौ व्यभिचारापत्तेः। 'अविगीतत्वं' च पापाजनकत्वं। रात्रिश्राद्धादिवारणाय शिष्टेति, 'शिष्टत्वं' इष्टसाधनत्वांशे अभ्रान्तत्वं, न त्वभ्रान्तत्वमात्रं, अविगीतपदवैयर्थ्यापत्तेः, श्येनादेरपि बलवदनिष्टा-ननुबन्धित्वभ्रमेणाचारात्। तथा चेष्टसाधनत्वांशे भ्रमाजन्येति फलि-तार्थः[६]। बलवदनिष्टाननुबन्धित्वज्ञानस्य हेतुत्वे च भ्रमाजन्यत्वमात्रं

---

(१) अगम्यागमनप्रवृत्तेरपीत्यर्थः।

(२) शिष्टपदेनैव वारणसम्भवादिति भावः।

(३) इष्टसाधनत्वज्ञानमेव प्रवृत्तौ हेतुः न तु बलवदनिष्टाननुबन्धित्वज्ञान-मिति भावः।

(४) साध्ये बलवदितीति ग०।

(५) साध्यस्य बलवदित्यादिविशेषणघटितत्वे सतीत्यर्थः।

(६) इष्टसाधनत्वांशे भ्रमाजन्यत्वं ईश्वरज्ञानावृत्ति इष्टसाधनत्वविषयत्वा-वच्छिन्नविषयताविशिष्टज्ञानाजन्यत्वमित्यर्थः ईश्वरज्ञानस्य सर्वांशे प्रमात्वेन भ्रमविषयताया ईश्वरज्ञानावृत्तित्वादिति भावः।

न च व्यभिचारः। निष्परिपन्थिश्रुत्या मङ्गलं समाप्तिसाधनमिति प्रमापिते तत्रापि तयैव लिङ्गेन जन्मान्तरीयतदनुमानात्। तच्चेदमारब्धकर्म्माङ्गं कर्म्मार्थितया शिष्टैस्तत्पूर्व्वं क्रियमाणत्वात् फलान्तराभावे सति फलवत्कर्म्मारिप्समानेन नियमतस्तत्पूर्व्वं क्रियमाणत्वाच्च दर्शे प्रयाजादिवत्।

वक्तव्यं। लौकिकभोजनादौ व्यभिचारवारणायालौकिकत्वे सतीत्यनेनापि विशेषणीयं, तत्त्वञ्च[१] इष्टसाधनत्वेन लोकावगतान्यत्वं, लोकश्च वेद-तदुजीविप्रमाणातिरिक्तप्रमाणमेव। यदि च श्राद्धत्वेनामावास्याश्राद्धत्वेन वा रात्रिश्राद्धमपि पितृतृप्तिस्वरूपयोग्यतया वेदबोधितमिति साध्यसत्त्वादन्यथा तु चैत्यवन्दनादिवन्निष्फलत्वेन पापजनकतया हेत्वसत्त्वादेव न तत्र व्यभिचार इति विभाव्यते, तदा तु लोकावगतेष्टसाधनताश्रयान्यत्वमलौकिकत्वं, तथा च पश्वादिप्रातस्याचेष्टायां व्यभिचारवारणायैव शिष्टेति तत्र निरुक्तमेवेत्याहुः। तदुभयमपि 'स्वीकृतवेदप्रमाणभावः शिष्टः' इत्यग्रिममूलविरुद्धत्वादश्रद्धेयम्।

'न च व्यभिचारः' इति प्रमत्तानुष्ठितसमाप्तौ व्यभिचार इत्यर्थः। तथा च विषयबाधेन वेदजन्यज्ञानस्य भ्रमतया कुतो वेदस्य तत्र प्रमाणत्वमिति भावः। 'निष्परिपन्थीति शाब्दबोधविघटकासमव-

---

(१) अलौकिकत्वस्येत्यर्थः।

ष्ठितेत्यर्थः। बाधसंशय-तन्निश्चययोः शाब्दबोधाप्रतिबन्धकत्वादन्वय-प्रयोजकरूपवत्त्वस्यैव योग्यतात्वेन बाधनिश्चयसत्त्वेपि योग्यताज्ञान-सम्भवाच्चेति भावः। 'प्रमापिते' ज्ञापिते, 'तथापि' नास्तिक-समाप्तावपि, 'तथैव' समाप्त्यैव, प्रमत्तानुष्ठितसमाप्तिर्मङ्गलजन्या समाप्तित्वात् शिष्टानुष्ठितसमाप्तिवदित्यनुमानप्रकारः[1]। तथा च तत्रापि मङ्गलस्य प्रमाणसिद्धत्वात्[2] न व्यभिचारः। यद्यपि स्वजन्यविघ्नध्वंसोत्पत्त्यवच्छेदकत्वसम्बन्धेन फलीभूतसमाप्तिकर्तृशरीरनि-ष्ठतया मङ्गलस्य, स्वोत्पत्त्यवच्छेदकत्वसम्बन्धेन तादृशशरीरनिष्ठतया मङ्गलजन्यविघ्नध्वंसस्य वा समाप्तिहेतुत्वं वक्ष्यमाणयुक्तेः, तथा च जन्मान्तरीयमङ्गलसत्त्वेपि व्यभिचारो दुर्वारः, नास्तिकशरीरे जन्मा-न्तरीयमङ्गलजन्यविघ्नध्वंसोत्पत्त्यभावात्। तथापि स्वजन्यविघ्नध्वंस-वत्त्वसम्बन्धेन मङ्गलस्य, विशेषणताविशेषसम्बन्धेन तज्जन्यविघ्नध्वंसस्य चात्मनिष्ठतयैव समाप्तिहेतुत्वमित्येकदेशिमतमाश्रित्यैतत्समाधानं। यथोक्तहेतुत्वपक्षे च व्यभिचारोऽग्रे निरसनीयः।

यद्यपि मङ्गलस्य आरब्धकर्मभिन्नस्य एतावता प्रबन्धेन वस्तुगत्या आरब्धकर्मजन्या या समाप्तिस्तज्जनकत्वं सिद्धं[3]। तथापि आरब्ध-कर्माङ्गत्वरूपेण आरब्धकर्माङ्गत्वं न सिद्धं[4] अतः प्रसङ्गात्तदपि

(१) अपरसमाप्तिवदित्यनुमानप्रकार इति ग०।

(२) मङ्गले समाप्तिसाधनत्वस्य प्रमाणसिद्धत्वादिति ग०।

(३) मङ्गले आरब्धकर्मभिन्नत्वमेतावता प्रबन्धेन वस्तुगत्या आरब्धकर्म-जन्या या समाप्तिः तज्जनकत्वञ्च सिद्धमिति ख०, ग० च।

(४) आरब्धकर्माङ्गत्वं विशिष्टं न सिद्धमिति ख०, ग० च।

साधयति 'तच्चेदमिति, 'आरब्धकर्म्माङ्गं' आरब्धकर्म्मभिन्नत्वे सति आरब्धकर्म्मजन्यफलजनकं। नचैवं तद्भिन्नत्वे सति तज्जन्यफलजनकत्वस्य तदङ्गत्वरूपत्वे आरब्धकर्म्मणोपि मङ्गलाङ्गत्वापत्तिः दर्शस्य प्रयाजाद्यङ्गत्वापत्तिश्चेति वाच्यं। सहकारित्वरूपस्याङ्गत्वस्य तत्रेष्टत्वात्। मुख्यफलाजनकत्वे सति मुख्यफलजनकव्यापारजनकत्वरूपं लौकिकाङ्गव्यावृत्तपारिभाषिकाङ्गत्वमेव हि न दर्शादौ किन्तु प्रयाजादावेव, प्रयाजादेरङ्गापूर्व्वद्वारा परमापूर्व्वमात्रं प्रत्येव जनकत्वेन स्वर्गं प्रत्यजनकत्वात्। परमापूर्व्वसाधनताज्ञानात् स्वर्गप्रयोजकताज्ञानाद्वा तत्र प्रवृत्तेः। अङ्ग-प्रधानव्यवस्थान्यथानुपपत्त्या तथैव कल्पनात्। तदुक्तं "यागे रागादङ्गे वैधी" इति 'रागात्' मुख्यफलेच्छातः[१] प्रवृत्तिरिति शेषः, 'वैधीति 'विधिः' अपूर्व्वं, तदिच्छा, प्रवर्त्तिकेति शेषः। अथैवं "फलवत्सन्निधावफलं तदङ्गं" इति जैमिनिसूत्रस्य[२] का गतिरिति चेत् तत्रारम्भणीयादावतिव्याप्तिवारणाय सप्तम्यन्तं, फलवान् यः सन्निधिस्तदीयमुख्यफलजनको यो व्यापारः तत्रेति तदर्थः। जनकत्वं सप्तम्यर्थः, अन्वयश्चास्याफलमित्यनेन। 'अफलत्वं' च तदीयमुख्यफलाजनकत्वं, एतच्च स्वस्य स्वाङ्गत्ववारणाय, दर्शादेः प्रयाजाद्यङ्गत्ववारणाय च। तदीयमुख्यफलजनकजनकत्वे सति तदीयमुख्यफलाजनकत्वं तदङ्गत्वमित्येव फलितं। न च प्रायश्चित्तादेर्दक्षिणादानादिचरमाङ्गेऽव्याप्तिः तस्य साक्षादेव पापनाशरूपमुख्यफलजनकत्वादिति वाच्यम्। अङ्गत्वान्यथानुपपत्त्या तत्राप्यङ्गापूर्वाद्युपगमात्। न चाङ्गाङ्गेऽतिव्याप्तिः,

---

(१) रागो मुख्यफलेच्छा ततः इति क०।

(२) जैमिनेरङ्गलक्षणसूत्रस्येति ख०, ग० घ।

तस्याप्यङ्गत्वस्येष्टत्वात्, अङ्गाङ्गस्य अङ्गाङ्गापूर्वजनकतयैवान्यथासिद्धतयाऽङ्गापूर्वजनकत्वे मानाभावाच्च। 'मुख्यफलत्वं' च वैधफलत्वं। न च मीमांसकमते अपूर्वस्यापि विध्यर्थत्वादङ्गस्य च तज्जनकत्वादसम्भव इति वाच्यम्। अङ्गस्याङ्गापूर्वजनकतयैवान्यथासिद्धतया स्वर्गादिमुख्यफलमिव परमापूर्वं प्रत्यजनकत्वात् अङ्गापूर्व्वजनकतामादायैव च सर्व्वत्र लक्षणसम्भवात्, प्रायश्चित्तस्थलवत् यागादिस्थलेप्यङ्गत्वान्यथानुपपत्त्या दक्षिणादानादेश्चरमाङ्गस्यापूर्व्वजनकत्वाभ्युपगमात्।

यद्वा यत्कामनात्वेन तदीयफलं प्रति जनकता तत्त्वं तदीयमुख्यफलत्वं, भवति च स्वर्गादिकामना स्वप्रयोज्यदर्शादिसम्बन्धेन दर्शादिफलस्वर्गादिकं प्रति जनिका, अन्यथा भ्रान्त्या स्वर्गफलान्यफलकामनया कृतादपि दर्शात् स्वर्गोत्पत्त्यापत्तेः, अपूर्व्वकामना च न तत्त्वेन दर्शादिजन्यस्वर्गजनिका मानाभावात्। पुत्रादिफलान्तरकामनावत् केवलापूर्व्वकामनया कृतादपि दर्शात् स्वर्गानुत्पत्तेः सकलमीमांसकसिद्धत्वात्।

यत्तु अफलत्वं फलान्तराभाववत्त्वं तदीयफलातिरिक्तफलकत्वमिति यावत्। फलत्वञ्च स्वकर्त्तव्यताप्रयोजकेच्छाविषयत्वमिति। तन्न अङ्ग-प्रधानोभयरूपे शिखादावव्याप्तेः। न च शिखाया न द्वैरूप्यं किन्तु "विशिखो व्युपवीतश्च यत्करोति न तत्कृतं" इतिवचनादङ्गत्वमेवेति वाच्यं। "सदोपवीतिना भाव्यं सदा बद्धशिखेन तु" इतिवचनात् प्रधानत्वस्यापि तत्र सत्त्वात्। न चैकस्याः शिखाव्यक्तेर्नोभयरूपत्वं किन्तु व्यक्तिभेदेनेति वाच्यं। तथा सति कर्म्मापूर्व्वं नियमतः शिखाद्वयानुष्ठानापत्तेः प्रधानफलकामनाकृतशिखादिव्यक्तित एव प्रसङ्गाद-

ङ्गस्यापि निर्व्वाह इति सकलशिष्टसम्मतत्वाच्च। न च शिखा प्रधानं, तद्बन्धनश्चाङ्गं बन्धनस्य क्रियाविशेषरूपस्याऽस्थिरत्वेपि तज्जन्याङ्गापूर्व्व-सत्त्वादेव दिनान्तरबद्धशिखातोप्यङ्गनिर्व्वाह इति वाच्यं। शिखां बध्नीयात् इतिश्रवणेन शिखाया एवाङ्गत्वप्रतीतेः। लौकिकस्थले च सहकारित्वमेवाङ्गत्वं न त्वन्यत् दुर्व्वचत्वात्।

ननु तथापि किं? तावदारब्धं कर्म्म। न च उपान्त्यवर्णपर्य्यन्त-वर्णसमूहरूपो ग्रन्थ एवारब्धं कर्म्म, चरमवर्णस्य समाप्तिः तस्य चास-मवायिकारणविधया उपान्त्यवर्णजन्यत्वेन समाप्तेरारब्धकर्म्मजन्यत्वमिति वाच्यम्। उपान्त्यवर्णस्य चरमवर्णविजातीयतया तदसमवायिकारण-त्वासम्भवात्(१)। सजातीयस्थलेपि कण्ठताल्वाद्यभिघातादिजन्ये चरम-वर्णे तस्याऽसमवायिकारणत्वासम्भवाच्च(२) इति चेन्न। प्रकृते चरम-वर्णपर्य्यन्तवर्णसमूहरूपो ग्रन्थ एवारब्धं कर्म्म। चरमवर्णजन्यं तद्-द्वितीयक्षणोत्पन्नतत्सजातीयं वर्णान्तरं चरमवर्णध्वंसो वा(३) समाप्तिः। न चैवं समाप्तेरारब्धकर्म्मजन्यत्वमनुपपन्नं, चरमवर्णस्याऽसमवायिकारण-तया प्रतियोगितया वा(४) यथोक्तसमाप्तिफलकत्वेपि(५) तत्पूर्व्वपूर्व्व-

---

(१) सजातीयशब्दस्यैव सजातीयशब्दासमवायिकारणत्वनियमादिति भावः।

(२) उपान्त्यवर्णस्य शब्दात्मकत्वेन द्विक्षणस्थायितया चरमवर्णकारणीभूत-कण्ठताल्वाद्यभिघातादिना नाशात् कारणत्वासम्भव इति भावः।

(३) ननु यत्र चरमवर्णनाशानन्तरमेव तत्सजातीयवर्णान्तरोत्पत्तिः तत्र न चरमवर्णस्याप्यसमवायिकारणत्वमत आह चरमेति।

(४) चरमवर्णसजातीयवर्णान्तरस्य समाप्तित्वे असमवायिकारणतया, चरमवर्णध्वंसस्य समाप्तित्वे च प्रतियोगितया समाप्तिजनकत्वमिति भावः।

(५) समाप्तिजनकत्वेपीति ग॰।

वर्णानां तथाजनकत्वादिति वाच्यं। पूर्व्वपूर्व्ववर्णाजन्यत्वेपि चरमवर्ण-जन्यतयैव ग्रन्थत्वाश्रयजन्यतानिर्व्वाहात् ग्रन्थत्वपर्य्याप्त्यधिकरणजन्यत्वस्य प्रकृते अविवक्षितत्वात्। घटादिस्थले च तत्सामग्रीसम्पादनमेवारब्धं कर्म्म, घटादिरेव समाप्तिः।

केचित्तु ग्रन्थादिस्थलेपि कण्ठताल्वाद्यभिघात-दृष्टप्रतिबन्धका-भावादिरेव पुरुषप्रयत्नसाध्यतया आरब्धं कर्म्म, चरमवर्णपर्य्यन्तवर्ण-समूहरूपग्रन्थादिरेव समाप्तिः।

अन्ये तु चरमवर्णपर्य्यन्तवर्णसमूहरूपो ग्रन्थ एवारब्धं कर्म्म, चरमवर्णांशे लौकिकप्रत्यक्षात्मकं आनुपूर्व्वीविशेषविशिष्टतावद्वर्णवि-षयकसमूहालम्बनानुसन्धानं समाप्तिः, तस्य च विषयविषया चरम-वर्णजन्यत्वेन ग्रन्थत्वाश्रयजन्यत्वमित्याहुः।

'कर्म्मार्थितयेति आरब्धकर्म्मजन्यफलेच्छयेत्यर्थः, न तु आरब्धकर्म्म-निष्पत्तीच्छयेत्यर्थः। 'दर्शे प्रयाजादिवत्', इतिदृष्टान्तासङ्गतेः, प्रया-जस्य दर्शानिष्पादकत्वात्। 'शिष्टैः' अभ्रान्तैः, 'तत्पूर्व्वम्' आरब्धकर्म्म-पूर्व्वं। तथा च तद्विषयककृतिपूर्व्वकालीनभ्रमाजन्यताफलेच्छाजन्य-कृतिविषयत्वादिति हेतुः। यत् तद्विषयककृतिपूर्व्वकालीनभ्रमाजन्य-यत्फलेच्छाजन्यकृतिविषयो भवति तत् तदङ्गं भवतीति सामान्यतो व्याप्तिः। दर्शप्राक्क्रियमाणायामारम्भनीयायां, समिदाहरणादौ च व्यभिचारवारणाय तत्फलेच्छाजन्येति तत्र तत्फलार्थितया अप्रवृत्तेः। दर्शादिफलसाधनताभ्रमेण तत्प्राक्कृते तदनङ्गे व्यभिचारवारणाय भ्रमाजन्येति। प्रधानस्यापि प्रधानफलेच्छया क्रियमाणत्वमिति तत्र व्यभिचारवारणाय कालीनान्तं। न चैवमैन्द्र-दधि-पयोयागचितया-

त्मकस्य दर्शस्य पूर्व्वप्रतीके व्यभिचारः। यत् फलजनकतावच्छेदकपर्य्याप्त्यधिकरणयद्विषयककृतिपूर्व्वकालीनभ्रमाजन्यतत्फलेच्छाजन्यकृतिविषयो भवति तत् तदङ्गं भवतीतिविवक्षितत्वात्। ऐन्द्रादिप्रत्येकयागस्तु न फलजनकतावच्छेदकधर्म्मत्वपर्याप्त्यधिकरणः, तस्य चितयनिष्ठत्वादिति न व्यभिचारः। फलत्वञ्च स्वकर्त्तव्यताप्रयोजकेच्छाविषयत्वमिति। हेत्वन्तरमाह 'फलान्तराभावे सतीति, दर्शप्राक्क्रियमाणारम्भणीयायां व्यभिचारवारणाय सत्यन्तं, तदजन्यफलजनकान्यत्वे सतीति तदर्थः। न चेदमसिद्धं नमस्कारादेरपि फलान्तरस्य स्वध्वंसविघ्नध्वंसादेर्जनकत्वादिति वाच्यं। फलपदस्य स्वकर्त्तव्यताप्रयोजकेच्छाविषयपरत्वात्। अतएव नमस्कारस्यानुषङ्गिकफलान्तरसत्त्वेपि नासिद्धिः। नियमतश्चैत्यवन्दनादिनिष्फलप्राक्क्रियमाणे केशोल्लुञ्चनादौ न तदङ्गत्वमिति तत्र व्यभिचारवारणाय तत्पूर्व्वमित्युक्त तत्पदार्थस्य फलवत्त्वविशेषणलाभार्थं 'फलवत्कर्म्मारिप्समानेनेति फलवत्कर्म्मेच्छावतेत्यर्थकं। तथा च तदजन्यफलाजनकत्वे सति नियमतः फलवत्तत्पूर्व्वं क्रियमाणत्वादिति समुदितार्थः। फलत्वञ्च स्वकर्त्तव्यताप्रयोजकेच्छाविषयत्वं, अन्यथा चैत्यवन्दनादेरपि ध्वंसादिलक्षणफलसत्त्वेन व्यभिचारतादवस्थ्यात्। प्रधानत्वाभिमतपूर्व्वं कदाचित् क्रियमाणे निष्फले कर्मणि अनैकान्तवारणाय(१) 'नियमत इति। प्रधानकर्म्मणि व्यभिचारवारणाय 'तत्पूर्व्वमिति।

ननु नियमतो यत्किञ्चित्प्रधानव्यक्तिप्राक्कृते प्रतारकशिष्टचिते-

---

(१) व्यभिचारवारणायेत्यर्थः।

आचारमूलकश्रुत्यनुमानाभ्यां(१) तदर्थितया तत्कर्त्तव्यत्वबोधनात् तत्फलकत्वबोधनाच्च। दर्शारम्भसमये नियमेन क्रियमाणाया अप्यारम्भनीयायास्तदर्थितया अक्रियमाणत्वात् फलान्तरश्रवणाच्च प्रधानत्वमिति न तया व्यभिचारः।

ऽङ्गभूते निष्फले व्यभिचारः। न च तद्व्यक्तित्वफलजनकतावच्छेदकाश्रयफलोपहितसकलकर्मव्यक्तिप्राक्क्रियमाणत्वं विवक्षितं प्रयाजं विनापि केनचिद् भ्रान्त्यादिना दर्शानुष्ठानादृष्टान्तासिद्धिवारणाय फलोपहितेति कर्मविशेषणमिति वाच्यं। तथा सति सत्यन्तवैयर्थ्यात् आरम्भणीयामन्तरापि कस्यचिद्दर्शकरणसम्भवेन तत्र उक्तहेतोरभावात् कस्यापि मङ्गलस्य न तादृशसकलव्यक्तिप्राक्क्रियमाणत्वमित्यसिद्धेश्च। अत आह: 'नियमतः' इत्यस्य भ्रमं विनेत्यर्थः, अन्वयश्चास्य प्रधानत्वर्थहेतौ। न चैवं 'फलवत्कर्मारिप्समानेनेति व्यर्थं केनोनुष्ठानादेर्भ्रमजन्यकृतिविषयत्वादिति वाच्यं। फलजनकतावच्छेदकपर्याप्त्यधिकरणतद्व्यक्तिपूर्वत्वलाभार्थं तदुपादानात् अन्यथा ऐन्द्राग्न्येकदेशे व्यभिचारापत्तेः फलवत्त्वं पूर्ववत्। न च तथाप्यङ्गाङ्गे व्यभिचार इति वाच्यं। अङ्गापूर्वस्यैव तत्फलत्वेन फलान्तराभाववत्त्वस्यैव तत्राभावादिति संक्षेपः।

प्रथमहेतौ 'कर्मार्थितये'ति विशेषणस्य द्वितीयहेतौ 'फलान्तराभावे सती'ति विशेषणस्य चासिद्धिं परिहरति 'आचारमूलकश्रुत्यनुमानाभ्या-

(१) आचारश्रुत्यनुमानाभ्यामिति क०।

ननु मङ्गलमलौकिकं लौकिके नाङ्गं भवति लोकावगतकारणत एव तदुपपत्तेः। अतएव गृहरथादावारे

मिति, एतद्द्वयं यथासङ्ख्येन 'तदर्थितया तत्कर्त्तव्यत्वबोधने', 'तत्फलकत्वबोधने' चान्वितम्, 'आचारमूलकत्वं' समाप्त्युद्देश्यकाविगीतशिष्टाचारानुमितत्वं, 'तदर्थितया' तत्कर्मजन्यफलार्थितया(१)। यद्यपि वेदोऽपि विवक्षितफलार्थिकर्त्तव्यत्वं न बोधयति, तथापि समाप्तिसाधनतायां बोधितायामर्थात्तत्सिद्धिरिति भावः। 'तत्फलकत्वबोधनात्' तत्फलमात्रफलकत्वबोधनात् तत्फलान्याफलकत्वबोधनादिति यावत्। यथाश्रुते फलान्तराभावस्यैव हेतुघटकतया 'तत्फलकत्वबोधनस्यानुपयुक्तत्वापत्तेः। तत्फलान्याफलकत्वानुमानञ्च मङ्गलं नारम्भकर्म्माजन्यफलजनकं समाप्त्युद्देश्यकशिष्टाचारविषयत्वादारम्भकर्म्मवदित्याकारकं, फलत्वञ्च निरुक्तमेव। उभयहेतौ प्रथमविशेषणप्रयोजनमाह 'दर्शेति, 'दर्शारम्भसमये' दर्शारम्भपूर्व्वसमये,(२) 'आरम्भणीयायाः' यागस्य, "आग्नेयाष्टाकपालं चरुं निर्व्वपेत् दर्श-पौर्णमासावारिप्समानः" इतिश्रुतिवचनेन दर्श-पौर्णमासपूर्व्वकाले क्रियमाणत्वं न तु तदर्थितया(३)। न वा फलान्तराभाव इति भावः।

मङ्गलस्य समाप्तिजनकत्वे "अलौकिकं लौकिके नाङ्ग" इति तद्ग्रन्थं बाधकमाशङ्कते 'नन्विति, 'अलौकिकं मङ्गलं लौकिकेऽङ्गं न भवति' इति योजना 'भवति' सम्भवति, "अलौकिकं लौकिके नाङ्गं"

---

(१) तज्जन्यफलार्थितयेति ग०।

(२) दर्शपूर्व्वसमये इति ख०, ग० च।

(३) क्रियमाणत्वमिति पूर्व्वेणान्वयः।

भग्ने इन्द्रबाहुर्बद्धव्यः, पायसं ब्राह्मणो भोजयितव्य इत्यत्र तदुभयं नाङ्गं, किन्तु नैमित्तिकं, तद्वदिदमप्यारम्भसमय-निमित्तकमस्तु विश्वजिन्न्यायात् स्वर्गफलमिति चेत्। न।

भवति" इति तत्सूत्रविरोधापत्तेः। तत्सूत्रेणालौकिकत्वस्यालौकिकानङ्गत्वव्याप्यत्वबोधनात्। 'अलौकिकत्वं' च वेदबोधितेष्टसाधनताककर्मत्वं, लौकिकानङ्गत्वञ्च न लौकिककर्मजन्यफलाजनकत्वं, यागादेरपि शरीरात्मादिसहकारेण चन्दनसंयोगादिसहकारेण च स्वर्गादिफलजनकतया तत्रैव व्यभिचारापत्तेः, किन्तु लौकिकफलाजनकत्वं, फलनिष्ठलौकिकत्वञ्च मानसेतरलौकिकसाक्षात्कारविषयत्वं, समाप्तिश्च तथा। घटादिजनकादृष्टजनककर्मणश्च न घटादिजनकत्वं मानाभावात्। नापि यागादेः स्वर्गादिजनकशरीर-तच्चन्दनसंयोगादिजनकत्वं, तेन न तेषु व्यभिचारः। न च तथापि वृष्टि-पुत्रादिरूपलौकिकफलजनके कारीरी-पुत्रेष्ट्यादौ, रोगनाशादिरूपलौकिकफलजनके भेषजपानाभिमन्त्रणादौ[१] व्यभिचार इति वाच्यं। व्यापारीभूतावग्रहनिवृत्त्यादेरलौकिकस्यैव[२] तेषां फलत्वात् न तु वृष्ट्यादेः, "वृष्टिकामो यजेत" इत्यादौ च वृष्ट्यादिप्रयोजकत्वस्यैव विध्यर्थत्वात्। एवं यत्र यत्र लौकिकं फलं श्रूयते तत्रैव प्रयोजकत्वं विध्यर्थः, तज्जनकव्यापार एव फलमिति न क्वापि व्यभिचारः। 'फलत्वं' तु स्वकर्त्तव्यताप्रयोजकेच्छाविषयत्वमिति भावः।

---

(१) भेषजाभिमन्त्रणादाविति ख०, ग० च।

(२) अवग्रहस्य वृष्टिप्रतिबन्धकीभूतदुरदृष्टविशेषः।

केचित्तु 'तच्चेदमारम्भकर्म्माङ्गमिति'पूर्व्वोक्तानुमाने बाधकमाशङ्कते 'ननु मङ्गलमिति 'मङ्गलं', यतः 'अलौकिकं', अतो लौकिकफलजनकं न भवतीत्यर्थः । तथा चालौकिकत्वेन हेतुना लौकिकफलजनकत्वाभावसिद्धौ तेनैव हेतुना आरम्भकर्म्माङ्गत्वाभावसिद्धेः पूर्व्वोक्तानुमाने बाध इत्याहुः । तदसत् समानबलतया तत्प्रतिपक्षत्वेन बाधासम्भवात् । न च वक्ष्यमाणस्टहरयाद्यधिकरणविरोधप्रसङ्गलक्षणानुकूलतर्केणाध्याधिकबलत्वमिति वाच्यं । तावता लौकिकफलजनकत्वाभावसाधकहेतावधिकबलत्वेऽपि आरम्भकर्म्माङ्गत्वाभावसाधकहेतावधिकबलत्वाभावात् । नन्वेवं कुतः समाप्तिरित्यत आह 'लोकेति, ननु तत्सुखमप्रयोजकमित्यत आह 'अत एवेति अलौकिकस्य लौकिकफलाजनकत्वादेवेत्यर्थः । 'आरः' लौहकीलः, स्टहरयादिचक्रमित्यन्ये । 'इन्द्रबाहुः' लौहकाकः, 'तदुभयमिति लौहकाकबन्धन-ब्राह्मणभोजने इत्यर्थः । 'नैमित्तिकमिति अपूर्व्वद्वारा आरम्भनिमित्तकपापनाशजनकमित्यर्थः । तच्च पापमनिष्टान्तरजनकं । न च तस्य पापनाशफलत्वे प्रायश्चित्तवत् साक्षादेव तन्नाशसम्भवेनापूर्व्वद्वारत्वाभ्युपगमो व्यर्थ इति वाच्यं । क्रियाविशेषरूपस्य बन्धनादेराशुविनाशितया दक्षिणादानाद्युत्तराङ्गपर्य्यन्तमवस्थानासम्भवेनापूर्व्वस्य व्यापारत्वावश्यकत्वात् अतएव प्रायश्चित्तस्थलेऽपि पापनाशार्थमपूर्व्वमावश्यकमिति भावः । नन्वेवं प्रकृतानुपयोगित्वे आरम्भसमये नियमतः शिष्टैर्नानुष्ठीयेत इत्यत आह । 'तद्वदिति इन्द्रबाहुबन्धनादिकं यथा आरम्भोत्तरकालसहकारेणैव स्वर्गफलजनकव्यापारजनकं तथा मङ्गलमपि आरम्भसमयसहकारेणैव स्वर्गफलजनकव्यापारजनकमित्यर्थः । 'आरम्भसमयः' कर्त्तव्य-

तस्यापूर्व्वरूपोपकारजनकाङ्गविषयत्वात् । अयन्तु प्रतिबन्धकाभावरूप उपकारः, तस्य च लोकावगतकारण-सहकारितैव, प्रतिबन्धके सति तस्मात्तदनुत्पत्तेः । अपूर्वन्तु न तथा, विघ्नध्वंसद्वारा चेदमङ्गं, न त्विष्टो यजतीत्यादिविधिबोधितप्रयाजाद्यङ्गयागवददृष्टद्वारा, मङ्गल-

---

कर्म्मचिकीर्षासमयः । ननु मङ्गलस्य समाप्तिजनकत्वे तस्य किं फलं को वा व्यापार इत्यत आह 'विश्वजिदिति, अपूर्वञ्च व्यापारः, अन्यथानुपपत्त्या(१) तथैव कल्पनादिति भावः ।

'तस्येति "अलौकिकं लौकिके नाङ्गं" इति तत्सूत्रस्येत्यर्थः । 'अपूर्व्वरूपेति, 'उपकारः' व्यापारः, अपूर्व्वद्वारा स्वफलजनककर्म्म-विषयत्वादित्यर्थः । स्वफलत्वं स्वकर्त्तव्यताप्रयोजकेच्छाविषयत्वं, तेन समाप्तिमुद्दिश्य कृतस्य दक्षिणादानाद्यङ्गकस्य कस्यचिन्मङ्गलस्या-पूर्व्वद्वारा विघ्नध्वंसजनकत्वेऽपि न क्षतिः, समाप्तेरेव निरुक्ततत्फलत्वात् तत्र च अपूर्व्वस्याद्वारत्वात् । न च तत्सूत्रस्य तादृशकर्म्मविशेषपरत्वे मानाभाव इति वाच्यं । तस्यालौकिककर्म्ममात्रपरत्वे "वृष्टिकामो यजेत" इत्यादि विधीनामप्रामाण्यापत्तेः, समभिव्याहृतफलजनकत्वस्यैव(२) विध्यर्थतायाः सकलमीमांसकसिद्धत्वादिति भावः ।

---

(१) ननु प्रागुक्तबाधकसत्त्वात् कथं स्वर्गस्य फलत्वकल्पनमतआहान्यथेति ।

(२) ननु तत्र वृष्टिप्रयोजकत्वस्यैव विध्यर्थत्वमुक्तमेवेति कथमप्रामाण्यापत्तिरित्यत आह समभिव्याहृतेति ।

जन्यादृष्टं विनापि स्वतःसिद्धविघ्नविरहवत आरब्धनिर्व्वाहात् । न चैवं विघ्नध्वंसद्वारापि नेदमङ्गं तत्रैव व्यभिचारादिति वाच्यं । सति विघ्ने तद्ध्वंसद्वारा तस्याङ्गत्वात् । न चैवं प्रयाजादेरपि दुरितध्वंस एव द्वारं । कल्प्यदुरितध्वंसतः अपूर्व्वस्य लघुत्वात् ।

ननु तथापि मङ्गलस्य लौकिकसमाप्तिं जनकत्वासम्भव एव मङ्गलस्याशुविनाशितया चिरकालानन्तरभाविसमाप्तिं प्रति साक्षाज्जनकत्वासम्भवेनापूर्व्वद्वारजनकताया वाच्यत्वात्[१] इत्यत आह 'अयन्त्विति'[२] मङ्गलजन्यस्त्वित्यर्थः । 'प्रतिबन्धकाभावरूपः' विघ्नाभावरूपः, प्रतिबन्धपदस्य विघ्नेपि प्रयोगात्, न तु कारणीभूताभावप्रतियोगित्वमत्र प्रतिबन्धकत्वं, 'तस्य चे'त्यादिग्रन्थानुत्थितेः । ननु विघ्नाभावस्य कुतो व्यापारत्वं समाप्तौ तस्याजनकत्वादित्यत आह 'तस्य चेति विघ्नाभावस्य चेत्यर्थः । 'सहकारिता' समाप्तिजनने सहकारिता, कॢप्तैव । 'प्रतिबन्धके सति' विघ्ने सति, विघ्नत्वञ्च मङ्गलनाश्यतावच्छेदकोऽदृष्टनिष्ठो जातिविशेषः[३] । नन्वेवं यत्र लौकिकं फलं श्रूयते तत्रापि तज्जनकत्वमेव विध्यर्थः अन्यथा सूत्रस्य विशेषपरत्वे मानाभावात् तथा च "पुत्रकामो यजेत" इत्यादिपुत्रेष्ट्यादिविधीनामप्रामाण्यापत्तिः

---

(१) अपूर्व्वस्य द्वारताया अवश्यवाच्यत्वादिति ख० ।

(२) अयन्त्वितीति ग० ।

(३) धर्म्मविशेष इति ग० ।

तस्यापूर्व्वद्वारकत्वेन भवन्मतेऽपि पुत्रादिलौकिकफलजनकत्वासम्भवादित्यत आह 'अपूर्व्वन्त्विति, 'न तथेति न लौकिकफलजनने यागादेर्व्यापारः किन्तु प्रतिबन्धकीभूतपापध्वंस एव तस्य व्यापार इत्यर्थः। तथा च यत्र यत्र लौकिकं फलं श्रूयते तत्रैव तत्प्रतिबन्धकपापनाशो व्यापारः इति भावः। ननु विघ्नाभावस्य कुतो मङ्गलव्यापारत्वमत्यन्ताभावरूपस्य तस्य नित्यत्वात्(१) इत्यत आह 'विघ्नध्वंसेति, 'अङ्गं' समाप्तिकारणं। मङ्गलस्यापूर्व्वविशेष एव समाप्तिजनने व्यापारः न तु विघ्नध्वंसः, विघ्नध्वंसत्वमपेक्ष्यापूर्व्वविशेषत्वस्य लघुत्वात्, विघ्नध्वंसस्य व्यापारत्वे विघ्नानुरोधेन मङ्गलकर्तुस्तज्जनककर्मकल्पनापत्तेः अपूर्व्वविशेषस्य व्यापारत्वे मङ्गलकर्तुर्विघ्नसत्त्वे मानाभावेन तज्जनककर्मणोऽप्यकल्पनादिति केचिन्मीमांसका वदन्ति तन्मतं दूषयति 'न त्विति न तु मङ्गलमलौकिकं लौकिके नाङ्गं इति पूर्व्वपक्षिणामपूर्व्वद्वारकत्वाशङ्कायामेतद्ग्रन्थावतारः, 'अपूर्व्वद्वारकत्वे लौकिकाङ्गत्वविरोधः' इत्यग्रिमदूषणासङ्गतेः, तेन लौकिकानङ्गत्वस्यैवाभ्युपगमात्। 'इड़ः' इति द्वितीयाबहुवचनं, इड़ादयो देवताभेदाः। 'मङ्गलजन्यादृष्टं विनाप्नोति'। यद्यपि जन्मान्तरीयमङ्गलजन्यादृष्टस्यैव सुवचत्वात् कुतोऽस्य दोषः, तथापि जन्मान्तरकृतमङ्गलस्यापि अदृष्टद्वारा जन्मान्तरीयसमाप्त्युपधायकत्वे जन्मान्तरीयग्रन्थसमाप्तिमुद्दिश्यापि मङ्गले शिष्टप्रवृत्तिप्रसङ्ग इतिवक्ष्यमाणदोषापत्तिरतो जन्मान्तरीयमङ्गलस्य जन्मान्तरीयसमाप्त्युपधायकतावारणाय स्वोत्प-

---

(१) जन्यत्वगर्भस्य व्यापारत्वस्य नित्ये असम्भवादिति भावः।

च्छवच्छेदकतासम्बन्धेन समाप्तिकर्तृशरीरनिष्ठतयैव मङ्गलजन्यादृष्टस्य समाप्तिहेतुत्वं वाच्यं, स्वोत्पत्त्यवच्छेदकत्वञ्च स्वोत्पत्तिसमानाधिकरणं स्वावच्छेदकत्वमित्यभिप्रायेणायं दोषः, जन्मान्तरीयमङ्गलजन्यादृष्टस्य नास्तिकशरीरे स्वोत्पत्त्यवच्छेदकतासम्बन्धेनाभावात् एवञ्च 'मङ्गलजन्यादृष्टं विनापि' मङ्गलजन्यादृष्टस्य स्वोत्पत्त्यवच्छेदकतासम्बन्धेनाभावेपि, 'स्वतःसिद्धविघ्नविरहवतः' स्वावच्छेदेन मङ्गलानुष्ठानं विनापि सिद्धविघ्नाभावकस्य नास्तिकशरीरस्य, 'स्वं' नास्तिकशरीरं, 'आरब्धनिर्व्वाहात्' आरब्धकर्म्मसमाप्तेरिति ग्रन्थार्थः। इदमुपलक्षणं युवादिशरीरे मङ्गलानुष्ठानाद्वृद्धादिशरीरे यत्र समाप्तिस्तत्रापि व्यभिचारो बोध्यः। 'दुरितध्वंसद्वारापीति विघ्नध्वंसद्वारापि, 'इदं' मङ्गलं, 'साङ्गं' न समाप्तिजनकमित्यर्थः। 'तत्रैव' स्वतःसिद्धविघ्नविरहवतो नास्तिकशरीरस्य समाप्तावेव, 'व्यभिचारात्' स्वोत्पत्त्यवच्छेदकतासम्बन्धेन विघ्नध्वंसस्य व्यभिचारात्, उक्तातिप्रसङ्गवारणाय(१) तथापि स्वोत्पत्त्यवच्छेदकतासम्बन्धेन फलीभूतसमाप्तिकर्तृशरीरनिष्ठतयैव मङ्गलजन्यविघ्नध्वंसस्य समाप्तिहेतुताया वाच्यत्वादिति भावः। 'सति विघ्ने' इति विघ्नस्खलीयसमाप्तावित्यर्थः। 'तस्य' मङ्गलस्य, 'अङ्गत्वात्' विघ्नध्वंसद्वाराऽङ्गत्वात्। प्रमत्तादिशरीरकर्तृकसमाप्तिश्च न विघ्नस्खलीया, विघ्नस्य फलाभावोन्नेयतया विघ्नस्खलीयत्वस्य तत्र विरहात्। भवन्मते तु विघ्नस्खलीयत्वस्य न कार्य्यतावच्छेदकत्वसम्भवः, त्वया कर्तुर्विघ्नाख्यादृष्टविशेषानभ्युपगमात्। विघ्नस्खलीयत्वञ्च विघ्नविशिष्टत्वं, वैशिष्ट्यञ्च स्वोत्तरत्वे सति स्वाश्रयशरीर-

(१) जन्मान्तरकृतमङ्गलजन्यविघ्नध्वंसस्य जन्मान्तरीयसमाप्त्युपधायकत्ववारणायेत्यर्थः।

कर्तृकत्वं तत्र संसर्गविधया प्रविष्टमतः स्वत्वस्याननुगततयाऽननुगतत्वेपि न क्षतिः[१]। यत्रैकस्मिन्नेव शरीरे पूर्व्वाह्णे मङ्गलं विनापि प्रारब्धकर्म्मसमाप्तिः मध्याह्नोत्पन्नविघ्नेन प्रतिबन्धाच्चापराह्णे न प्रारब्धकर्म्मसमाप्तिस्तत्र भाविविघ्नवच्छरीरकर्तृकपूर्व्वाह्णजातसमाप्तौ व्यभिचारवारणाय सत्यन्तं। वस्तुतस्तु तत्रापराह्णे प्रारब्धकर्म्मसमाप्त्यभावस्य लोकावगतकारणाभावादेव सुवचतया तस्य विघ्नप्रयुक्तत्वे मानाभावात् सत्यन्तमनुपादेयमेव। न चैवं मङ्गलस्यापि किं समाप्तिहेतुत्वेन, मङ्गलविरहस्थलेपि लोकावगतकारणाभावादेव समाप्त्यभावस्य सुवचत्वादिति वाच्यं। शिष्टाचारतः कल्पितविध्यन्यथानुपपत्त्या एव मङ्गलस्य हेतुत्वकल्पनात्। तथा च विघ्नवच्छरीरकर्तृकत्वमेव विघ्नस्थलीयत्वं, न तु स्वत्वघटितमिति भावः।

केचित्तु विघ्नध्वंसजन्यत्वं विघ्नस्थलीयत्वं, नास्तिकादिकर्तृकसमाप्तिश्च न विघ्नध्वंसजन्या, तत्त्वस्य फलबलकल्प्यत्वादित्याहुः। तदसत् प्रतिबन्धकीभूतविघ्नाभावस्य यदि विघ्नसामान्यात्यन्ताभावत्वेन हेतुत्वं तदा समाप्तेर्विघ्नध्वंसजन्यत्वस्यैवासिद्धेः, अथ विघ्नसंसर्गाभावत्वेन तथा[२] तदा नास्तिककर्तृकसमाप्तेरपि जन्मान्तरोत्पन्नविघ्नध्वंसजन्यतया व्यभिचारतादवस्थ्यादिति ध्येयम्।

'न चैवमिति 'एवं' ध्वंसस्यापि व्यापारत्वे। 'कल्प्ये'ति दर्शजन्यपरमापूर्व्वं प्रति कारणत्वेन कल्पनीयो यो दुरितध्वंसस्तमपेक्ष्येत्यर्थः। तस्य कारणत्वेन क्लृप्तत्वे तदेव विनिगमकं स्यादिति हृदयम्। 'लघुत्वा-

(१) स्वान्तरत्व-स्वाश्रयशरीरकर्तृकत्वोभयसम्बन्धेन विघ्नविशिष्टसमाप्तित्वमेव कार्य्यतावच्छेदकमिति भावः।

(२) हेतुत्वमित्यर्थः।

वस्तुतस्तु प्रायशो विघ्नसंशये तन्निश्चये वा नियमेन शिष्टानां मङ्गलाचरणे विघ्नाभाव एव द्वारत्वेनाभिमतः[१]। निर्विघ्नं समाप्यतामितिकामनया तत्करणपक्षे श्रुतित एव द्वारत्वनिर्णयः।

दिति लघुशरीरत्वादित्यर्थः। प्रकृते चापूर्व्वस्य द्वारत्वासम्भवादनायत्या गुरुरपि व्यापारः स्वीक्रियत इति भावः। इदमुपलक्षणं प्रयाजादिस्थले विघ्नध्वंसस्य व्यापारत्वे स्वतःसिद्धविघ्नाभावस्थले प्रयाजादिकं विनापि कर्म्मसाङ्गतापत्तेः, प्रकृते च नेदृशी क्षतिरित्यपि बोध्यम्।

ननु मयाप्यनायत्या मङ्गलकर्तुर्व्विघ्नोऽभ्युपेयस्तथा च तत्स्थलीयसमाप्तावेव फलीभूतसमाप्तिकर्त्तृशरीरनिष्ठतया मङ्गलजन्यमपूर्व्वं कारणमतो नोक्तव्यभिचार इत्यस्वरसादाह 'वस्तुतस्त्विति, 'अभिमतः' अनुमितः, 'आकाङ्क्षितः' इतिपाठेऽप्ययमेवार्थः। अनुमानञ्च मङ्गलं विघ्नध्वंसजनकं विघ्नाजनकत्वे सति विघ्नज्ञानवतामेव श्रमाजन्यतत्प्रवृत्तिविषयत्वादित्याकारकं. समाप्त्युद्देश्यकप्रवृत्त्यनुपपत्त्या विघ्नाजनकत्वस्य सिद्धत्वात्। सिद्धे विघ्नध्वंसे फले समाप्त्युद्देश्यकप्रवृत्त्यनुपपत्त्यैव तस्य मुख्यफलत्वे निरस्ते परिशेषाद्द्वारत्वनिर्णय इति भावः। 'इतिकामनया' इत्युद्देश्य, 'तत्करणपक्षे' तस्य शिष्टाचारविषयत्वपक्षे, 'श्रुतितः' इति निर्व्विघ्नसमाप्तिकामो मङ्गलमाचरेदितितादृशाचारानुमितविघ्नध्वंसविशिष्टसमाप्तिजनकताबोधकवेदादेवेत्यर्थः। न च तज्जन्यत्वे सति तज्जन्यजनकत्वस्य द्वारत्वस्य न वेदादुपस्थितिः निर्व्विघ्नपदस्य

---

(१) आकाङ्क्षितः इति ख०।

किञ्चापूर्व्वंद्वारत्वे लौकिकाङ्गत्वविरोधः, क्लृप्तकारणादेव तदुत्पत्तेरिन्द्रबाहुबन्धनवत्। ननु विघ्नसन्देहे कथं तन्नाशार्थं प्रवृत्तिः दुरितध्वंसार्थिप्रवृत्तौ तन्निश्चयस्य हेतुत्वात् प्रायश्चित्तवदिति चेत्। न।

अन्यतासम्बन्धेन विघ्नध्वंसविशिष्टार्थकतया समाप्तौ विघ्नध्वंसजन्यत्वस्य मङ्गले तद्विशिष्टसमाप्तिजनकत्वस्यैव च तस्मात् प्रतीतेरिति वाच्यं। विशिष्टनिरूपितकारणताग्राहकमानेन विशेषणं प्रत्यपि कारणताग्रहनियमाद्विघ्नध्वंसं प्रत्यपि मङ्गलस्य तेन कारणताग्रहादितिभावः।

ननु नियमतो विघ्नज्ञानसत्त्व एव शिष्टैस्तत्करणं निर्विघ्नं समाप्यतामिति कामनया शिष्टैस्तत्करणस्यासिद्धमित्यरुचेराह 'किञ्चेति, 'अपूर्व्वद्वारत्वे' अपूर्व्वद्वारा फलजनकत्वे, 'लौकिकाङ्गत्वविरोधः' लौकिकफलजनकत्वाभावप्रसङ्गः, 'क्लृप्तकारणादेव' अपूर्व्वद्वारकफलजनककारणातिरिक्तकारणादेव, 'तदुत्पत्तेः' तदुत्पत्तिनियमात्, लौकिकफलोत्पत्तिनियमादिति यावत्। "अलौकिकं लौकिके नाङ्गं" इति तत्रस्थत्वस्यापूर्व्वद्वारा स्वफलजनककर्म्मविषयत्वादिति भावः। 'इन्द्रबाहुबन्धनवदिति तादृशनियमादिन्द्रबाहुबन्धनस्य यथा लौकिकफलजनकत्वाभाव इत्यर्थः। इदमुपलक्षणं अपूर्व्वधर्म्मिकल्पनां तस्य समाप्तिकारणत्वकल्पनाञ्चापेक्ष्य प्रतिबन्धकाभावतया समाप्तिकारणत्वेन क्लृप्तस्य विघ्नध्वंसस्य मङ्गलजन्यत्वमात्रकल्पने लाघवात् नाप्यकान्तरकल्पने गौरवात्तस्य समाप्तिजनकताया अपि क्लृप्तत्वाच्चेत्यपि बोध्यं।

विघ्नसंशये निश्चये वा नियमेन शिष्टानां मङ्गलाचारात् विघ्नध्वंसज्ञानं प्रवर्त्तकं। तादृशाचारानुमितविधिनापि विघ्नध्वंसवानारब्धसमाप्तिकामोऽधिकारी बोध्यते। प्रा-

विघ्नध्वंसविशिष्टसमाप्तेर्मङ्गलाचारोद्देश्यत्वमते[१] बाधकमाशङ्कते 'नन्विति, 'तन्नाशार्थं' तन्नाशमुद्दिश्य, दुरितध्वंसार्थिप्रवृत्ताविति दुरितध्वंसोद्देश्यकप्रवृत्तावित्यर्थः। 'तन्निश्चयस्य' दुरितनिश्चयस्य, 'प्रायश्चित्तवत्' प्रायश्चित्तप्रवृत्तिवत्। ननु "दुरितध्वंसार्थिप्रवृत्तावित्यादेः कतमोऽर्थः किं पापध्वंसार्थिप्रवृत्तौ पापनिश्चयो हेतुः, किं वा सामान्यतोऽनिष्टध्वंसार्थिप्रवृत्तावनिष्टनिश्चयो हेतुः, किं वा तदुद्देश्यकप्रवृत्तौ तदुपधायकत्वनिश्चयो हेतुः, प्रकृते च विघ्नसन्देहेन विघ्नध्वंसोपधायकत्वसन्देहात् कथं तदर्थिप्रवृत्तिरिति तत्र नाद्य इत्याह 'विघ्नसंशय इति, 'विघ्नध्वंसज्ञानं' विघ्नध्वंसज्ञानसामान्यं, 'प्रवर्त्तकं' मङ्गले प्रवर्त्तकं, तथा च पापध्वंसार्थिप्रवृत्तौ पापनिश्चयो हेतुरिति व्याप्तिरप्रयोजिकेति भावः[२]। इदमुपलक्षणं "संवत्सरस्यैकमपि[३] चरेत् कृच्छ्रं द्विजोत्तमः। अज्ञातभुक्तशुद्ध्यर्थं ज्ञातस्य च विशेषतः"॥ इत्येतद्वचनबोधितपापसंशयजन्यप्रायश्चित्तविशेषप्रवृत्तौ शौचाचमनादिलक्षणदुरितध्वंसहेतुक्रियाविशेषप्रवृत्तौ च व्यभिचारोऽपि बोध्यः।

नन्वेवं विधिनापि विघ्नध्वंसवन्मात्रकर्त्तव्यत्वेन बोध्येतेत्यनिष्टापत्तिमाह, 'तादृशाचारेति विघ्नस्य संशये निश्चये च शिष्टाचारेत्यर्थः।

(१) मङ्गलोद्देश्यत्वमते इति ख०।

(२) अप्रयोजिका अनुकूलतर्कशून्येत्यर्थः।

(३) प्रतिसंवत्सरस्यैकमिति क०।

यश्चित्ते तु तन्निश्चयवान्[१] तथैव विधिबोधनात्। अत एवाधिकारिविशेषणं विघ्न इति तत्सन्देहे कथंप्रवृत्तिः वैदिके अधिकारनिश्चयादेव प्रवृत्तेरित्यपास्तं[२]। यतः प्रधानाधिकारिण एवाङ्गेऽधिकारो न स्वतन्त्रः अङ्गत्वभङ्गप्रसङ्गात्।

अनुमानञ्च मङ्गलं विघ्नज्ञानवन्मात्रकर्त्तव्यत्वेन[३] वेदबोधितं विघ्नस्य संशये निश्चये च शिष्टाचरणात्[४] इत्याकारकमिति भावः। 'अधिकारी', 'बोध्यते' कर्त्तृत्वेन बोध्यते, तत्कर्त्तव्यत्वेन मङ्गलं बोध्यते इति यावत्, "विघ्नज्ञानवान् समाप्तिकामो मङ्गलं कुर्य्यात्" इत्येवानुमितवेदशरीरमिति भावः। 'प्रायश्चित्ते तु' प्रायश्चित्तविशेषे तु, 'तन्निश्चयवानिति पापनिश्चयवानित्यर्थः, कर्त्तेति शेषः। तथा च विधिना यत्र पापनिश्चयमात्रवत्कर्त्तव्यत्वं बोध्यते तत्रैव पापनिश्चयो हेतुरन्यत्र पापज्ञानसामान्यमेवेति भावः। 'अत एवेति 'इत्यपास्तं' इत्यनेनान्वितम्, 'अधिकारिविशेषणमिति अधिकार इत्यर्थः। यत् प्रवर्त्तमानपुरुषनिष्ठतया ज्ञायमानं सत्प्रवृत्तिहेतुः सोऽधिकारः यथा शौचतत्कालजीवित्वादि। शौचभ्रमाद्यत्र[५] प्रवृत्तिस्तत्रापि भ्रमविषयी-

---

(१) तन्निश्चयज्ञानवानिति क०।

(२) इति परास्तमिति क०।

(३) विघ्नज्ञानमात्रवत्कर्त्तव्यत्वेनेति क०, ग० च०।

(४) विघ्नसंशय-निश्चयकालीनालौकिकशिष्टाचारविषयत्वामिति ख०। विघ्नसंशयनिश्चयकालीनशिष्टाचारविषयत्वादिति ग०!

(५) अधिकारिविशेषणमिति यथाश्रुते अक्षरसं प्रकाशयति शौचेति।

भूतं व्यधिकरणशौचमेव प्रवृत्तिहेतुरिति भावः। विघ्नस्य मङ्गलेऽधिकारत्वमेव नास्तीत्याह 'यतः' इति, 'प्रधानाधिकारिण एव' प्रधानाधिकारस्यैवेति यावत्। 'अङ्गेऽधिकारः' तदीयवैदिकाङ्गेऽधिकारत्वं, तदीयवैदिकाङ्गत्वञ्च तज्जन्यफलजनकत्वप्रकारेण वेदबोधितत्वं भवति च प्रयाजादिस्तथा। अङ्गविधयो हि तावत् प्रधानसहका-र्य्याकाङ्क्षायां प्रवर्त्तन्ते न तु फलजनकत्वमात्राकाङ्क्षायां, प्रधानविधितः प्रधानस्यानादेव तदुच्छेदात्, तथा च यदाकाङ्क्षया यत्प्रवर्त्तते स तस्यार्थ इति सकलमीमांसकमतसिद्धतया दर्शादिसहकारित्वस्या-प्यङ्गविध्यर्थत्वात्। न च "विधौ न परः शब्दार्थः" इतिन्याया-दङ्गविधेरपीष्टसाधनत्वमेवार्थ इति वाच्यं। शाब्दबोधस्याकाङ्क्षा-नुरोधितया "न विधौ" इत्यस्य प्रधानविधिपरत्वात् तथैव मी-मांसकैरभ्युपगमादिति भावः। 'न स्वतन्त्रः' न तदधिकारातिरिक्तः तदीयवैदिकाङ्गेऽधिकारः, अङ्गत्वभङ्गप्रसङ्गादिति वैदिकाङ्गत्वभङ्ग-प्रसङ्गादित्यर्थः। तदधिकारातिरिक्तानधिकारकत्वस्य निरुक्ततदीय-वैदिकाङ्गत्वव्यापकत्वादिति भावः[१]। यद्यपि प्रारब्धकर्म्मण्यनधिकार-स्यापि शौचादेर्मङ्गलेऽधिकारत्वान्नायं नियमः, तथापि तदति-रिक्ताधिकारेऽयं नियमो बोध्यः।

नन्वेतावता प्रकृतेपि किमायातमित्यत आह 'न चेति 'प्रधाने' स्वजन्यफलजनकत्वेन वेदबोधितमङ्गलके, स्वपदं प्रारिप्सितकर्म्म-परं, 'अधिकारिविशेषणं' अधिकारः, 'विरोधादिति अधिकारत्व-फलप्रतिबन्धकत्वयोर्व्विरोधस्य सर्व्वसिद्धत्वादित्यर्थः। तथा च तदी-

(८) तथाच व्यापकाभावेन व्याप्याभावसिद्धिरिति भावः।

न च प्रधाने प्रारिप्सिते दुरितमधिकारिविशेषणं, विरोधात् । किन्तु समाप्तिकामना सा तु[१] निश्चितैव ।

यद्वैदिकाङ्गे मङ्गले कुतोविघ्नस्याधिकारत्वमिति भावः । न च समाप्तिकामो मङ्गलमाचरेदित्याकारकः, निर्विघ्नसमाप्तिकामो मङ्गलमाचरेदित्याकारको वा विधिः, तथा च प्रारब्धकर्मजन्यफलजनकत्वप्रकारेण वेदबोधितत्वरूपं तदीयवैदिकाङ्गत्वं कुतोमङ्गल इति वाच्यं । प्रारब्धकर्मजन्यसमाप्तिर्मे जायतामित्युद्दिश्य शिष्टप्रवृत्तेर्निर्विघ्नप्रारब्धकर्मजन्यसमाप्तिकामो मङ्गलमाचरेदित्याकारकस्यैव विधेरुन्नयनात्, विधेः समाप्तिकामो मङ्गलमाचरेदित्याकारकत्वेपि प्रारब्धकर्मोपकार्य्याकाङ्क्षयैव तत्प्रवृत्तेः प्रारब्धकर्मोपकारित्वस्य तदर्थत्वाच्च । मीमांसकनये आकाङ्क्षानुरोधित्वाच्छाब्दानामिति भावः ।

ननु कस्तर्ह्यधिकार इत्यत आह 'किन्त्विति, 'सान्विति, स्वर्गकामस्याग्निष्टोमः कार्य्यः अहमपि तथेति[२] प्रतिसन्धानेन प्रवृत्तेः कामनाज्ञानमपि प्रवृत्तिहेतुरित्यभिमानेनेदं । वस्तुतस्तु कामनाफलं प्रति प्रवृत्तिं प्रति च स्वरूपसत्येव हेतुः, न तु ज्ञाता मानाभावात् । न चैवमधिकारित्वानुपपत्तिः यत् स्वनिष्ठतया ज्ञातं सत्पुरुषं प्रवर्त्तयति तस्याधिकारित्वादिति वाच्यं । यद्धर्मविशिष्टेन कृतस्य कर्मणः फलजनकत्वं सोऽधिकार इति तल्लक्षणात् । न चाधिकारनिश्चयः फलाङ्गमिति वाच्यं । स्वरूपसत एव तस्य तथात्वात अन्यथा मौचादिभ्रमात्

---

(१) सा चेति क० ।

(२) तथा स्वर्गकामः इत्यर्थः ।

यस्त्वन्यत्र निश्चिताधिकारकर्तृकत्वेपि मङ्गलं सन्दिग्धाधिकारकर्तृकमेव विघ्नसन्देहवतां शिष्टानामाचारानुमितवेदेन तथैव बोधनादिति। तन्न। विघ्नवत्त्वेनाधिकाराभावात् क्वचित्तन्निश्चयेऽपि प्रवृत्तेश्च।

कृतमपि सुकृतमर्ज्जयेत्, न च तत्प्रमा तथा, मानाभावात्। न चैवं प्रायश्चित्तविशेषादौ पापानिश्चयेऽपि प्रवृत्तिः स्यात् स्याच्च तन्निश्चयं विना कृतादपि तस्मात् फलोत्पाद इति वाच्यं। तत्र पापनिश्चयवत्त्वस्याधिकारत्वात् निश्चितपापकर्तृकत्वेन वेदबोधनात्। न च कामनाभिलापं विना काम्यकर्म्मणः फलानिष्पत्तेः कामनाज्ञानमपि प्रवर्त्तकमिति वाच्यं। तावता फलं प्रति तस्य हेतुत्वेपि प्रवृत्तिं प्रति तस्य हेतुत्वे मानाभावात्। न हि काम्यकर्म्मप्रवृत्तिं प्रति कामनाभिलापो हेतुः, भ्रान्त्या[१] अभिलापमकृत्वा केनचित् काम्यकर्म्मानुष्ठानात् फलं प्रति कामनाभिलापस्यैव हेतुतया कामनाज्ञानस्य हेतुत्वे मानाभावाच्च। वाक्यप्रयोगं प्रति वाक्यार्थज्ञानस्याहेतुतया प्रयोजकत्वस्याप्यसम्भावितत्वादित्यन्यत्र विस्तरः।

'अन्यत्र' प्रायश्चित्तविशेषादौ, 'निश्चिताधिकारकर्तृकत्वेपीति' अधिकारनिश्चयस्यैव प्रवर्त्तकत्वेऽपीत्यर्थः। 'मङ्गलं सन्दिग्धाधिकारकर्तृकमेव' इति मङ्गले विघ्नरूपाधिकारसंशय एव प्रवर्त्तक इत्यर्थः। विघ्नवत्त्वेनेति विघ्नस्याधिकारत्वाभावादित्यर्थः। अभ्युपगम्याह, 'क्वचिदिति, तथा च विघ्नसंशय एव प्रवर्त्तक इति नियमोऽसिद्ध इति भावः।

---

(१) अहेतुत्वे हेतुमाह भ्रान्त्येत्यादि।

अपिच शङ्कितानिष्टवारणार्थमपि प्रवर्त्तन्ते परीक्षकाः, यथा सर्पादिदंशजन्यविषसंशये तन्नाशाय भेषजपानादौ। किञ्च फलस्य संशयेप्युपायत्वनिश्चयाद् यथा कृष्यादौ प्रवृत्तिः तथा मङ्गलेपि। यदि च वृष्ट्यादौ सति कृष्यादितोऽवश्यं फलमिति तर्कात्तत्र प्रवृत्तिस्तदा सति विघ्ने मङ्गलादवश्यं फलमिति तर्कादत्रापि प्रवृत्तिः।

द्वितीयविकल्पे व्यभिचारमाह,'अपि चेति, यथाश्रुते दुरितध्वंसार्थिप्रवृत्तावेव दुरितनिश्चयहेतुतायाः पूर्वं शङ्कितत्वादनिष्टध्वंसार्थिप्रवृत्तावनिष्टनिश्चयव्यभिचाराभिधानस्यासङ्गतत्वापत्तेः।

केचित्तु पूर्व्वत्रैव[१] दुरितध्वंसार्थिप्रवृत्तावित्यादौ दुरितपदमनिष्टसामान्यपरमतो नासङ्गतिरित्याहुः। तदसत् तथापि 'किञ्चेत्यादिवक्ष्यमाणदोषासङ्गतेः। इदमुपलक्षणं एतत्कल्पेपि "संवत्सरेणैकमपीत्यादिवचनबोधितप्रायश्चित्तप्रवृत्त्यादौ व्यभिचारोऽपि बोध्यः।

तृतीयकल्पमभिप्रेत्याह, 'किञ्चेति, 'फलस्य' फलोपधायकत्वस्य, 'उपायत्वनिश्चयात्' स्वरूपयोग्यत्वनिश्चयात्, 'कृष्यादौ,' इत्यादिपदात् कृतप्रायश्चित्तविप्रवादिपरिग्रहः। 'तथा मङ्गलेपीति विघ्नध्वंसरूपफलोपधायकत्वसंशयेपि, प्रवृत्तिरिति शेषः।

ननु सति वृष्ट्यादौ कृष्यादावपि सामान्यतः फलावश्यम्भावनिश्चयोऽस्त्येवेत्यत आह 'यदि चेति, 'तर्कात्' निश्चयात्, 'सति विघ्ने' इति विघ्नसमवहितमङ्गलमवश्यं विघ्नध्वंसोपधायकमिति निश्चयादित्यर्थः।

---

(१) सर्व्वत्रैवेति ख०।

ननु स्फ्यस्य भक्ताश्लेषनिमित्तकेज्यायामिष्टत्वेन दर्श-धर्म्मत्वे[१] सत्यतिदेशागतपूर्व्वदिनकर्त्तव्यदेवतावाहन-स्याङ्गस्य स्फ्याश्लेषद्वारसंशयेऽननुष्ठानमुक्तं यथा कृष्णाले द्वारबाधे । अतोविघ्नसंशयात्तद्ध्वंसद्वारसंशये कथं

न च कृष्यादौ सामान्यतो निश्चयस्य हेतुत्वेपि वैदिके विशिष्य तन्नि-श्चयो हेतुरिति वाच्यं। अन्तरा कर्म्मन्याशालस्पर्श-करतोयापार-गमनादिशङ्कया तत्रापि[२] विशिष्य तत्संशयात्[३]। न च व्यापारवति वैदिके व्यापारावश्यम्भावनिश्चयस्तथा, तत्राप्युक्तराङ्गनिर्व्वाहसंशयेन संशयादिति भावः ।

ननु वैदिके द्वारवैपरीत्यज्ञाने न प्रवृत्तिः अतएव "यत्स्फ्या चाश्लि-षेत् तदधोऽपमृज्यात् विष्णवे उरुविक्रमाय चरुं[४] निर्व्वपेत्" इत्यनेन विहितस्य स्फ्यस्य भक्ताश्लेषनिमित्तकस्य यागस्य इष्टित्वेन दर्शप्रकृति-कत्वात् प्रकृतिवद्विकृतिरितिन्यायेन दर्शधर्म्मकत्वेपि पूर्व्वदिने देवतावा-हनस्य दर्शधर्म्मस्य स्फ्याश्लेषरूपद्वारसंशयादननुष्ठानमुक्तं, तथा च मङ्गले दुरितध्वंसरूपसंशयात् कथं प्रवृत्तिरित्याशङ्कते, 'नन्विति, 'स्फ्यः' खदिर-काष्ठनिर्म्मितः खड्गः[५], 'इज्या' यागः, 'दर्शधर्म्मत्वे सति' दर्शप्रकृतिकत्वे सत्यपि, 'दर्शधर्म्मग्रहे सतीति पाठेप्ययमेवार्थः। 'अतिदेशेति प्रकृति-

---

(१) दर्शधर्म्मग्रहे इति क० ।

(२) वैदिकेपीत्यर्थः ।

(३) फलोपधायकत्वसंशयादित्यर्थः ।

(४) द्वादशकपालं चरुमिति ग० ।

(५) खदिरकाष्ठनिर्म्मितखड्गरूपकरणविशेष इति ख०, ग० च ।

मङ्गलानुष्ठानमिति चेत्। न। नैमित्तिके हि निमित्तवानधिकारी[1] यथा भिन्ने जुहोतीत्यत्र पात्रभेदवान्, तथेहाश्लेषवानधिकारीति पूर्व्वदिने आश्लेषनिश्चयाभावात् युक्तमननुष्ठानं।

वह्निरुत्तिरित्यतिदेशेत्यर्थः। स्फ्याश्लेषेज्यायां देवतावाहनस्याननुष्ठाने दृष्टान्तमाह,' यथेति, 'कृष्णलः' सुवर्णकलायः, 'द्वारबाधे' वैतुष्यरूपद्वाराभावनिश्चये, अवघाताननुष्ठानमिति शेषः। "व्रीहीन् प्रोक्षति व्रीहीनवहन्ति" इत्यत्र यवादिसाधारणार्थं व्रीहिपदस्याजहत्स्वार्थलक्षणया घृतादिव्यावृत्तनियोगसाधनताश्रयद्रव्यमात्रपरत्वेन[2] "कृष्णलं श्रपयेत्" इति श्रुत्या तादृशनियोगसाधनत्वेन बोधिते कृष्णलेऽप्यवघातप्राप्तावपि वैतुष्यद्वारबाधाद् यथाननुष्ठानमित्यर्थः। 'अत इति द्वारसंशयेऽननुष्ठानवचनाद्वैदिकप्रवृत्तौ द्वारसंशयस्य प्रतिबन्धकत्वकल्पनादिति भावः।

'यथावेति वाकारसम्वलितपाठपक्षे विघ्नध्वंससन्देहे मङ्गलानुष्ठानानुपपत्तौ हेत्वन्तरमाह, 'यथावेति, 'यथा वा' येन वा यतो वेति यावत्। यथाश्रुते यत इत्यनेनानन्वयापत्तेः। शेषस्तु पूर्व्ववत्। 'अत इति द्वारस्य संशये व्यतिरेकनिश्चये वाननुष्ठानात् द्वारवैपरीत्यज्ञानमात्रस्यैव प्रतिबन्धकत्वकल्पनादिति भावः। वस्तुतः मूले

---

(१) निमित्तनिश्चयवानिति क०।

(२) व्रीहिपदस्य इतावृत्तिप्रयोगसाधनत्वावच्छिन्ने लक्षणा, इयं लक्षणा अजहत्स्वार्थरूपा अजहत्स्वार्थलक्षणात्वञ्च शक्य-लक्ष्योभयवृत्तिधर्म्मावच्छिन्नलक्षणात्वं इति भावः।

वाकारः प्रामादिक इति ध्येयं । स्पर्शाश्लेषो हि निमित्तमतो निमित्तनिश्चयाभावादेव तत्र न प्रवृत्तिः, न तु द्वारसन्देहात् स्पर्शाश्लेषस्य द्वारत्वाभावादित्याशयेन सिद्धान्तयति, 'नैमित्तिके हीति, 'निमित्तवान्' निमित्तनिश्चयवान्, 'अधिकारी' अनुष्ठाता, निमित्तनिश्चयः निष्कम्पप्रवृत्तिहेतुरित्यर्थः । 'पात्रभेदवान्' पात्रभेदनिश्चयवान्, पात्रभेदनिमित्तकहोमे पात्रभेदनिश्चयो यथा निष्कम्पप्रवृत्तिहेतुरित्यर्थः । 'इह' स्पर्शाश्लेषनिमित्तकेज्यायां, 'आश्लेषवान्' आश्लेषनिश्चयवान्, 'अधिकारी' अनुष्ठाता, आश्लेषनिश्चयो निष्कम्पप्रवृत्तिहेतुरित्यर्थः । आश्लेषस्य निमित्तत्वादिति भावः । 'युक्तमननुष्ठानमिति युक्तं पूर्व्वदिने देवतावाहनाननुष्ठानमित्यर्थः । स्पर्शाश्लेषनिमित्तनिश्चयस्य प्रधाने प्रवर्त्तकत्वेनाङ्गेपि प्रवर्त्तकत्वात् । तत्र प्रवर्त्तकस्य तदीयवैदिकाङ्गेपि प्रवर्त्तकत्वनियमात् । अतएव प्रधानचिकीर्षया एव वैदिकाङ्गे प्रवर्त्तकत्वं, प्रकृते च विघ्नध्वंसो न निमित्तं किन्तु व्यापार एवातस्तत्सन्देहे अनुष्ठाने न किञ्चिद्बाधकमिति भावः ।

ननु यत्राप्तवाक्यादिना पूर्व्वदिने भक्ताश्लेषनिश्चयस्तत्रावाहनप्रसङ्गः, न च निमित्तस्य स्वरूपसतो हेतुत्वेन तत्रापि न तदनुष्ठानमिति(१) वाच्यं । तथा सति त्र्याहनिमित्तकश्राद्धादौ पूर्व्वदिने त्र्याहाभावात् तदङ्गनिरामिषभोजनाद्यकरणापत्तेरिति चेत् । न । यत्र पूर्व्वदिने भक्ताश्लेषनिश्चयस्तत्र पूर्व्वदिने देवतावाहनस्येष्टत्वात् ।

प्रकारान्तरेणापि पूर्व्वदिने देवतावाहनाननुष्ठानमुपपादयति, 'अपि चेति,'तदङ्गानुष्ठानं' तदीयवैदिकाङ्गस्य देवतावाहनस्यानुष्ठानं,

(१) तादृशानुष्ठानमिति घ० ।

अपि चेज्याकर्त्तव्यतानिश्चये तदङ्गानुष्ठानं । न चाश्लेषसंशये तन्निश्चयः पूर्व्वदिने । अतः प्रधानेऽधिका-

---

प्रधानकर्त्तव्यतानिश्चयस्य वैदिकाङ्गे निष्कम्पं प्रवर्त्तकत्वात् "कर्त्तव्य-मितिनिश्चित्य" इत्यादिस्मृतेरिति भावः । 'तन्निश्चयः' इज्या-कर्त्तव्यतानिश्चयः, न चैवं चयाहनिमित्तकश्राद्धादावपि अशौचादि-सन्देहेन कर्त्तव्यतासन्देहात् पूर्व्वदिने तदङ्गनिरामिषभोजनाद्यकर-णापत्तिरिति वाच्यम्। तत्रापि तर्कादिना मानसकर्त्तव्यतानिश्चयात् अन्यथा न निष्कम्पं क्रियत एव। यद्वा सकलशिष्टाचारान्यथानुप-पत्त्या तत्र उत्कटकोटिककर्त्तव्यतासंशयस्यैव प्रवर्त्तकत्वं तदतिरक्त-स्थले च तन्निश्चयो हेतुरिति। वस्तुतस्तु इदमभ्युपगमवादेन, प्रधान-कर्त्तव्यतानिश्चयस्य वैदिकाङ्गप्रवृत्तौ तदङ्गफले वा कारणत्वे माना-भावादतः प्रथमपक्षमेवोपसंहरति, 'अत इति, 'प्रधाने' स्फराश्लेषे-ज्यायां, यः 'अधिकारः' निष्कम्पं प्रवर्त्तकः स्फराश्लेषनिमित्तनिश्चयः, तस्य पूर्व्वदिने ऽभावात् न तदीयवैदिकाङ्गे देवतावाहने 'अधिकारः' निष्कम्पं प्रवर्त्तक इत्यर्थः ।

यद्वा अधिक्रियते अनेन इत्यधिकारः कर्त्तव्यतानिश्चयः, तेन प्रधाने कर्त्तव्यतानिश्चयाभावात् न अङ्गे देवतावाहने 'अधिकारः' निष्कम्पं प्रवर्त्तकः इत्यर्थः। तथा च चरमपक्षस्यैवायमुपसंहार इति ध्येयम्।

ननु तथापि स्फाश्लेषरूपनिमित्तनिश्चयाभावेऽपि "यदि न स्या-त्ततः किं स्यात्" इतिन्यायेन सकम्पप्रवृत्तौ बाधकाभावेन तादृशप्रवृत्त्या

राभावान्नाङ्गेऽधिकार इति नावाहनं पूर्व्वदिने । यदि च यदि न स्यादितिन्यायेन कुर्य्यात्तदा अनधिकृतकर्तृकत्वेन निष्फलं स्यात् । स्पर्शाश्लेषे सतीज्याकर्त्तव्यतानिश्चयेपि नावाहनं, पूर्व्वदिनस्याङ्गस्याभावादिती-

---

पूर्व्वदिनजनितदेवतावाहनात् फलोत्पत्तिप्रसङ्ग इत्यत आह, 'यदीत्यादि, "सन्दिग्धे परलोकेऽपि त्याज्यमेवाशुभं नरैः(१) । यदि न स्यात्ततः किं स्यादस्ति चेन्नास्तिको हतः" इति न्यायेनेत्यर्थः । 'कुर्य्यात्' पूर्व्वदिने सङ्कल्पं करोति, 'तदा' तथापि, 'अनधिकृतकर्तृकत्वेन' निष्कम्पप्रवृत्तिजनकनिमित्तनिश्चयाभाववत्कर्तृकत्वेन, 'निष्फलं स्यादिति निष्फलं भवतीत्यर्थः । निमित्तनिश्चयस्य स्वप्रयोज्यनैमित्तिकेज्याद्वारा तज्जन्यव्यापारं प्रति हेतुत्ववत्तदीयवैदिकाङ्गजन्यव्यापारं प्रत्यपि स्वप्रयोज्यतदङ्गद्वारा हेतुत्वात् । न चैवमुपरागश्राद्धादावपि निमित्तीभूतोपरागादिसंशयात् कृतस्य तद्वैदिकाङ्गपूर्व्वदिननिरामिषभोजनस्य निष्फलत्वापत्तिरिति वाच्यं । इष्टत्वात् ।

यदा तत्रोपरागसंशयेपि शिष्टाचारादुत्कटकोटिकनिमित्तज्ञानमेव हेतुः, तदतिरिक्तस्थल एव निमित्तनिश्चयो हेतुरिति भावः ।

ननु तथाप्युत्तरदिने स्पर्शाश्लेषेज्याकर्त्तव्यतानिश्चये जाते देवतावाहनकरणसम्भवात्तदपि देवतावाहनं फलजनकं स्यादित्यत आह, 'स्पर्शाश्लेष इति, 'निश्चयेपीति, सतीति शेषः । 'नावाहनं' नोत्तर-

---

(१) बुधैरिति ख॰ ।

ज्यायां आवाहनबाध एव। मङ्गले तु विघ्नध्वंसवानधि-कारीत्युक्तं तच्च संशयेऽप्यस्ति। प्रधाने कर्त्तव्यतानिश्चये-ऽस्त्येवेति द्वारसन्देहेऽपि युक्तमनुष्ठानं।

दिनकृतमात्रावाहनं, फलजनकमिति शेषः। 'अङ्गस्य' तज्जनिताङ्गा-पूर्व्वजनकस्य 'आवाहनबाध एव' आवाहनस्य सफलत्वबाध एव।

ननु पूर्व्वदिने देवतावाहनाकरणे स्फ्याश्लेषज्यातः कथं फलसिद्धिः अङ्गहानेर्न भवत्येव फलमिति चेत्। न। सकलवैदिकमीमांसकैः पूर्व्वदिने तदकृत्वापि तद्यागानुष्ठानात्। न चातएव न तच्च तस्याङ्गत्वमिति वाच्यं। प्रकृतिवद्विकृतिरितिन्यायेन तदङ्गत्वस्यावश्यकत्वात्, न्यायलब्धसहकारित्वस्यापि मीमांसकैर्विधौ भानाभ्युपगमात्। न च नित्यवन्नैमित्तिकेपि किञ्चिदङ्गहानावपि फलसिद्धिरिति वाच्यं। तर्हि पूर्व्वदिनस्याङ्गस्य बाधेप्युत्तरदिने देवतावाहनापत्तेः किञ्चिदङ्ग-हानावपि कर्म्मनिष्पत्त्यभ्युपगमे ततएव यागनिष्पत्तिसम्भवेन प्रयत्नगौ-रवादङ्गाननुष्ठानापत्तेश्चेति। मैवं। स्फ्याश्लेषसंशयस्थले तस्याङ्गत्वात् प्रकृतिवद्विकृतिरितिन्यायेनाङ्गत्वे कल्प्यमाने यत्र न बाधकं तत्रैव कल्पनात्। अत्र तु अधिकाराभावस्यैव बाधकत्वात्। यत्र तु आप्तवा-क्यादिना स्फ्याश्लेषनिश्चयस्तत्र पूर्व्वदिने तत्कर्त्तव्यमेवान्यथाङ्गबाधात्। अतएवैकादश्याहक्रियमाणेऽधिवासाङ्गकगोयागविकृतीभूते वृषोत्सर्गे-ऽधिवासो नाङ्गं, कार्त्तिक्यादिक्रियमाणे त्वङ्गमेव। एवमशौचमध्य-क्रियमाणे कर्म्मणि सन्ध्याया नाङ्गत्वं तदतिरिक्तस्थले त्वङ्गमेव। प्रकृति-विकृतिन्यायेनाङ्गत्वे कल्प्यमाने यत्राशौचादि बाधकान्तरं वा न वर्त्तते

भविष्यद्विवाहादावाभ्युदयिकेऽपि तज्ज्ञानवानधिकारी तथैवाचारात्। नन्वङ्गानां प्रधानविधिविधेयत्वं। न च ग्रन्थादिसमाप्तौ प्रधानविधिरस्ति। न च तत्-

---

तत्रैवाङ्गत्वस्य कल्पनादिति दिक्। प्रकृतेऽनुष्ठानमुपपादयति,'मङ्गलेत्विति, 'विघ्नज्ञानवानिति विघ्नज्ञानमात्रं कारणमित्यर्थः। न चैवं द्वाराभावनिश्चयत्वेन प्रतिबन्धकत्वे गौरवं लाघवात् तज्ज्ञानत्वेनैव प्रतिबन्धकत्वस्यैवोचितत्वादिति वाच्यम्। आचारानुमितश्रुत्या विघ्नज्ञानमात्रस्य कारणत्वे बोधिते प्रामाणिकगौरवस्यादोषत्वादिति भावः।

ननु नैमित्तिके निमित्तनिश्चयवानधिकारीत्युक्तं तत् कथं विवाहादिनिमित्तसंशयेपि नैमित्तकश्राद्धानुष्ठानमित्यत आह 'भविष्यदिति, तत्राचारबलात् निमित्तज्ञानमात्रमेवाधिकार इत्यर्थः। नैमित्तिके निमित्तनिश्चयवानधिकारीति नियमो रुषोत्सर्गादाविति भावः। न च विवाहो न निमित्तं किन्तु सीमन्तोन्नयनादिवद्विवाहे श्राद्धमङ्गमेव, तथा च तत्सन्देहेपि तत्र प्रवृत्तौ न किञ्चिद्बाधकमिति कथं 'भविष्यदितिग्रन्थोत्थितिरिति वाच्यं। नूतनगृहप्रवेशादौ लौकिकविवाहादौ च वृद्धिश्राद्धं नाङ्गम, "दृष्टे पुंसवने चैव सीमन्तोन्नयने तथा। एतेष्वेव प्रधानेषु श्राद्धकर्म्माङ्गमिष्यते" ॥ इति वचनान्नैमित्तिकमेवेत्यभिप्रायात्।

अन्ये तु ननु दृज्याकर्त्तव्यतानिश्चयाभावात् पूर्व्वादने तदङ्गानुष्ठानमित्ययुक्तं विवाहसन्देहेपि तदङ्गाभ्युदयिकाचरणादित्यत आह

कर्त्तव्यताबोधकस्य लौकिकप्रमाणस्य शास्त्रमेकदेशो युज्यते । तस्य तन्निरपेक्षत्वादिति चेत् । न । अपूर्व-जनकाङ्गानां तथात्वात् आचारानुमितस्मृत्या प्रधान-विधिं विनापि तदङ्गत्वविधानाच्च ।

'भविष्यदितीत्याहुः । मङ्गले व्यापकाभावात् प्रारब्धकर्म्मीयवैदि-काङ्गत्वासम्भवमाशङ्कते 'नन्विति, 'अङ्गानां' तदीयवैदिकाङ्गानां, तदीयवैदिकाङ्गत्वस्य प्राङ्निरुक्तमेव[१] यथाश्रुते लौकिकाङ्गे[२] व्यभि-चारापत्तेः, यागादेरपि शरीरात्मादेः यत्नादेश्च सहकारिताख्यपा-ङ्गत्वाश्रयतया तत्रापि व्यभिचारापत्तेश्च । 'ग्रन्थादिसमाप्तौ' ग्रन्थादि-समाप्तित्वले, 'प्रधाने विधिरस्ति' 'प्रधाने' मङ्गलविधिप्रकारीभूत-मङ्गलनिष्ठफलसहकारिताके प्रारब्धकर्म्मणि,[३] 'विधिरस्ति', तथाच तत्कर्त्तव्यताबोधकविधिसाकाङ्क्षविधिबोधितत्वस्य तदीयवैदिकाङ्गत्व-व्यापकतया व्यापकाभावान्मङ्गले प्रारब्धकर्म्मवैदिकाङ्गत्वासम्भव इति भावः ।

ननु प्राथमिकं विधित्वमतन्त्रं गौरवात् किन्तु तद्बोधक[४]प्रमाण-साकाङ्क्षविधिविधेयत्वमेव तदीयवैदिकाङ्गत्वव्यापकं लाघवात् तथानु-

---

(१) प्रधानफलातिरिक्तफलाजनकत्वे सति प्रधानजनकव्यापारजनकत्वेन वेदबोधितत्वमित्यर्थः ।

(२) नैमित्तिकाङ्गे इति क० ।

(३) प्रधानकर्म्मणीति क० ।

(४) प्रधानकर्तव्यताबोधकेत्यर्थः ।

अपि च प्रधानकर्त्तव्यताबोधकबोध्यकर्त्तव्यताकत्वं प्रयोजकं तच्चेहाप्यस्ति, प्रतिबन्धकाभावस्य सकल-

---

मानादिलौकिकप्रमाणादावपि सम्भवत्येवेत्यत आह 'न चेति नचेत्यर्थः । 'शास्त्रं' मङ्गलबोधकवेदः, 'एकदेशः' साकाङ्क्षः, 'तस्य' लौकिकप्रमाणस्य, 'निरपेक्षत्वादिति आकाङ्क्षायाः शब्दमात्रधर्म्मतया आकाङ्क्षाया अनिरूपकत्वादित्यर्थः । तथा चैतदपि मङ्गले नास्तीति भावः । 'अपूर्व्वजनकाङ्गानां' अपूर्व्वद्वारा तदीयवैदिकाङ्गानां, 'तथात्वात्' तद्विधिविधेयत्वनियमात्[१] तथा चोक्तनियमोऽप्रयोजक इति भावः ।

केचित्तु तथा चापूर्व्वद्वारकत्वं[२] उपाधिरिति भावः इत्याहुः । तदसत् योगाङ्गप्राणायामादौ भेषजपानाङ्गभेषजाभिमन्त्रणादौ च साध्याव्यापकत्वात् तेषां पापनाशादिद्वारैवाङ्गत्वात् ।

व्यभिचारमप्याह, 'आचारेति, 'प्रधानविधिं विनापि' प्रारब्धकर्म्मविधिं विनापि, 'तदङ्गत्वविधानाच्च' तथाविधाचारानुमितश्रुत्या मङ्गलस्य प्रारब्धकर्म्मजन्यसमाप्तिजनकत्वप्रकारेण बोधनाच्च तथा च साध्याभाववतो मङ्गलस्यैव निश्चितहेतुमत्त्वात्तत्रैव व्यभिचार इति भावः । यथा च मङ्गलविधेः प्रारब्धकर्म्मजन्यसमाप्तिजनकत्वप्रकारेण बोधजनकत्वं तथोपपादितमधस्तात् ।

---

(१) प्रधानविधिविधेयत्वनियमादित्यर्थः ।
(२) अपूर्व्वजनकत्वमिति ख०, ग० च ।

कार्य्यहेतुत्वेन लौकिकप्रमाणस्यापि तत्सापेक्षत्वात्। ननु यागादिवत् प्रधानदेश-कालान्वयस्तदङ्गे मङ्गले स्यादिति चेत्। न। असाधारणेऽपूर्व्वजनके चाङ्गे तदन्वयात्।

उभयत्रैव त्रिधिलमतन्त्रं गौरवादित्याशयेनाह, 'अपि चेति' 'प्रधानेति, प्रधानकर्त्तव्यताबोधकापेक्षणीयबोध्यकर्त्तव्यताकत्वमित्यर्थः। 'प्रयोजकं' वैदिकाङ्गत्वव्यापकं, 'इहापि' मङ्गलेपि, 'प्रतिबन्धकाभावस्य' मङ्गलजन्यविघ्नध्वंसस्य, 'सकलकार्य्यहेतुत्वेन' सकलप्रारब्धकर्म्मजन्यसमाप्तिहेतुत्वेन, 'लौकिकप्रमणस्यापि' प्रारब्धकर्म्मकर्त्तव्यताबोधकलौकिकप्रमाणस्यापि, 'तत्सापेक्षत्वात्' मङ्गलकर्त्तव्यताबोधकसापेक्षत्वात्। एतच्चापाततः अपेक्षाया दुर्व्वचत्वात्। ननु तद्देश-कालसहकारेणैव व्यापारजनकत्वस्य तदीयवैदिकाङ्गत्वव्यापकतया मङ्गलस्य प्रारब्धकर्म्मवैदिकाङ्गत्वे[१] तद्देश-कालसहकारेणैव विघ्नध्वंसजनकत्वं स्यात्। न चेष्टापत्तिः, देशान्तरे कालान्तरेपि शिष्टैर्मङ्गलाचरणादित्याशङ्कते, 'यागादिवदिति अङ्गयागादिवदित्यर्थः। 'प्रधानदेश-कालान्वयः' प्रारब्धकर्म्मदेश-कालसहकारेणैव व्यापारजनकत्वं, 'तदङ्गे' तदीयवैदिकाङ्गे, क्वचित्तु वतिप्रत्ययशून्यः पाठः, तत्र यागादि यत्प्रधानं तद्देश-कालान्वयः यागाद्यङ्गे स्यादित्यर्थः। यद्यपि स्थूलदेश-कालावादाय मङ्गलस्यापि तदुभयान्वयसम्भवः, सूक्ष्मदेश-कालावादाय प्रयाजादेरप्यसम्भवस्तथापि

---

(१) प्रारब्धकर्म्माङ्गत्वे इति क०।

अतएव बद्धशिखत्वादौ न प्रधानदेशकालान्वयः। न च दुरिताभावे स्वतः सिद्धे साङ्गमङ्गलानुष्ठानं निष्फल-

---

प्रधानकर्त्तव्यताबोधकप्रमाणेन यादृशापराह्णादिकाले दक्षिणाप्लवनादिदेशे प्रधानानुष्ठानं बोधितं तदीयवैदिकाङ्गानां तथाविधदेशकालसहकारेणैव व्यापारजनकत्वनियम इत्यर्थः। लौकिकस्य प्रधानत्वे तु देश-कालनियमः केनापि न बोधित इति भावः।

'असाधारणस्य' इति, 'अङ्गे' वैदिकाङ्गे, 'तदन्वयात्' प्रधानदेशकालसहकारेणैव व्यापारजनकत्वनियमात्, अत्रापूर्व्वजनकाङ्गत्वमात्रं शिखाबन्धने व्यभिचारीति तद्वारणाय 'असाधारणे'ति, 'असाधारणत्वञ्च न यावद्वैधकर्म्माङ्गान्यत्वं, शिखाबन्धनस्यापि वामागमबोधिताद्यनङ्गत्वेन तथात्वात् किन्तु वैधफलजनकतावच्छेदकयावदवच्छिन्नस्यानङ्गत्वं। न च शिखाबन्धनं तथा, बहुतरकर्म्माङ्गत्वात्। दक्षिणागमबोधितयावत्कर्म्मानङ्गत्वं वा तत्[1]। शिखाङ्गकयावत्कर्म्माङ्गान्यत्वं तदिति केचित्। असाधारणत्वमात्रं पापक्षयद्वारा यागाङ्गभूते आसनप्राणायामादौ व्यभिचारीति तद्वारणाय 'अपूर्व्वजनके'ति, अपूर्व्वजनकाङ्गत्वञ्च अपूर्व्वद्वाराङ्गत्वं, अन्यथा समाप्तिकामनया दिनान्तरक्रियमाणे शिवपूजादिरूपमङ्गले[2] आनुषङ्गिकादृष्टजनके व्यभिचारापत्तेः। न च पूर्व्वदिनविहिताधिवासाश्वमेधाङ्गभूताश्वरक्षण-लक्ष्मीपूजा-

---

(१) असाधारणत्वमित्यर्थः।

(२) शिवनमस्कारादिरूपमङ्गले इति ख०, ग० च।

मिति तद्वेदाप्रामाण्यं। शोकावगतकारणे हि दुरिते सति वेदेन तस्य तद्ध्वंसजनकत्वं बोध्यते, न तु तदुत्सङ्गः।

कृष्णचतुर्दश्यादीपदानादौ[१] व्यभिचार इति वाच्यं। विशेषविधिं विनेति विशेषणात्।

ननु केशस्य चिरन्तनसंयोगविशेषः शिखा तद्बन्धनस्य तदनुकूलक्रिया सा च नाङ्गं किन्तु शिखैव विशिष्य इति श्रवणात् तस्याश्च नापूर्व्वद्वाराङ्गत्वं स्थिरत्वेन परमापूर्व्वकालपर्य्यन्तस्थायित्वात् तथाच किमसाधारणत्वविशेषणेनापूर्व्वजनकत्वदानेनैव वारणात्। न च शौचादिहेतुमृद्ग्रहणादौ व्यभिचारवारणाय तदिति वाच्यं। तस्याप्यपूर्व्वाजनकत्वात् अशुद्ध्यात्मकवैधकर्म्मप्रतिबन्धकादृष्टध्वंसरूपत्वात्[२] शौचपदार्थस्येति, मैवं शिखामात्रं हि नाङ्गं, किन्तु मन्त्रविशेषविशिष्टैव, अन्यथा मन्त्रोपदेशवैयर्थ्यात् विशिष्टा च न परमापूर्व्वपर्य्यन्तस्थायिनी मन्त्रस्यास्थिरत्वात् अतोऽदृष्टं द्वारमावश्यकं। न च विशिष्टस्य तावत्कालानवस्थायित्वेपि न क्षतिः कारणतावच्छेदकपूर्व्वमत्त्वस्यानपेक्षितत्वादिति वाच्यं। तत्पूर्व्वसत्त्वमप्यपेक्षितमित्यन्यत्र व्यवस्थापितत्वात् अन्यथा व्यभिचारात्। मास्तु वा कारणतावच्छेदकपूर्व्वसत्त्वमपेक्षितं तथापि मन्त्रपूर्व्वकशिखाबन्धनानन्तरं त्रुटिकाबन्धनादिकाले कराभिघातादिना मन्त्रपूर्व्वकसंयोगविशेषात्मकशिखानाशेपि कर्म्मणोऽङ्गवैगुण्यवारणायादृष्टं द्वारमावश्यकं। न चादृष्टस्य द्वारत्वेऽदृष्टोत्पत्त्यनन्तरं शिखामोक्षणेपि कर्म्म साङ्गं स्यादिति वाच्यं। मोक्षणस्य स्वप्रतियोगिजन्यत्वसम्बन्धेनादृष्टनाशकत्वात्।

(१) कृष्णचतुर्दश्यादाविति ख०, ग० च।

(२) अशुद्ध्यात्मकप्रतिबन्धकाधर्म्मध्वंसरूपत्वादिति क०।

अतएव तत्त्वज्ञानवतो भोगार्थं निषिद्धानुष्ठानं दोषाभावान्नाधर्म्मजनकमिति न तद्वेदाप्रामाण्यं। प्रमाणा-

---

मोक्षणञ्च न मन्त्रपूर्वकतत्संयोगविशेषध्वंसमात्रं, तथा सति त्रुटिकाबन्धनादिकाले कराभिघातादिना तादृशसंयोगविशेषनाशे अदृष्टनाशात् कर्म्मणो निष्फलत्वापत्तितादवस्थ्य(१) किन्तु तादृशसंयोगविशेषनाशमव्यवहितोत्पत्तिकमन्त्रपूर्वकतत्संयोगविशेषनाश एव मोक्षणमिति भावः। तन्मतानुयायिनस्तु निरुक्तमोक्षणं न तददृष्टनाशकं किन्त्वङ्गपूर्व्ववत् स्वजन्यपरमापूर्व्वान्तरमेव तददृष्टनाशकं मोक्षणेपि कर्म्म साङ्गं भवत्येव, किन्तु "सदोपवीतिना भाव्यं सदा बद्धशिखेन तु" इत्यनेन सार्व्वकालिकशिखाधारणस्यापि विहिततया तदकरणात् पुरुषस्य प्रत्यवायमात्रं, न च स्वजन्यपरमापूर्व्वस्य तदपूर्व्वनाशकत्वे यत्र एकयैव शिखया नानाकर्म्मानुष्ठानं तत्र प्रथमकर्म्मजन्यपरमापूर्व्वेणैव तज्जन्यापूर्व्वनाशात् द्वितीयादिकर्म्मणोऽङ्गवैगुण्यापत्तिरिति वाच्यं। प्रथमकर्म्मजन्यपरमापूर्व्वेण तदपूर्व्वनाशेप्यवस्थितशिखया पुनरपूर्व्वान्तरजननात्। न च मन्त्रपूर्व्वकशिखाया उत्पत्तिसम्बन्धेनैवापूर्व्वजनकत्वमन्यथा धारावाहिकापूर्व्वोत्पत्तिप्रसङ्गादिति कथमवस्थितशिखयाऽपूर्व्वान्तरोत्पत्तिरिति वाच्यम्। शिखाजन्याङ्गापूर्व्वं प्रति शिखाजन्याङ्गापूर्व्वस्य प्रतिबन्धकत्वादेव धारावाहिकापूर्वानुत्पत्तेः क्रमिकशिखाद्वयस्थले द्वितीयशिखयाऽपूर्व्वजननेपि क्षतिविरहात् प्राथमिकशिखाजन्यापूर्व्वत एव कर्म्मसाङ्गतोपपत्तेरित्याहुः।

---

(१) कर्म्मणोऽङ्गवैगुण्यतादवस्थ्यादिति ख०, ग० च।

न्तरात् स्वतःसिद्धदुरितभावावगतौ मङ्गलाकरणे नित्यवदनुष्ठानं शिष्टानां भज्येतेति चेत्। न। विघ्नशङ्कावतो नित्यवदनुष्ठानादिति सम्प्रदायः[१] ॥ १ ॥

'बहुशिखत्वादाविति शिखाबन्धनादावित्यर्थः। यद्वा बहुशिखा-दावित्यर्थः, तेन बन्धनस्थानकृत्वेपि न क्षतिः। 'न प्रधानदेश-कालान्वयः' न प्रधानदेश-कालसहकारेणैवाङ्गापूर्वजनकत्वनियमः। 'न चेति, 'स्वतःसिद्धे' दुरितकारणाभावप्रयुक्ते, 'निष्फलं' विघ्नध्वंसानुपधायकं, ध्वंसं प्रति प्रतियोगिनोपि हेतुत्वादिति भावः। 'तद्वेदाप्रामाण्य-मिति विशेषणीभूतविघ्नध्वंसं प्रत्यपि जनकताबोधकस्य "निर्विघ्न-समाप्तिकामो मङ्गलमाचरेत्" इति विशिष्टसमाप्तिकारणताबोधक-वेदस्याप्रामाण्यमित्यर्थः। यद्यपि फलोपधायकत्वं न विध्यर्थः, किन्तु स्वरूपयोग्यत्वं तस्य च सहकारिविरहेण क्वचित् फलानुप-धानेपि सम्भवात् कुतोऽप्रामाण्यं तथापि साङ्गवैदिककर्मत्वव्यापकं फलोपधानमतस्तदभावेन साङ्गे तस्मिन् साङ्गवेदबोधितकर्मत्वाभावः सिध्यन् तद्बोधकविधेः वेदत्वाभावमादाय[२] सिध्यति, वेदत्वाभावश्च सिध्यन् शब्द-तदुपजीविप्रमाणातिरिक्तप्रमाणजन्यप्रमित्यविषयार्थके तस्मिन् प्रमाणत्वाभावमादायैव पर्य्यवस्यतीतिक्रमेण प्रामाण्यं स्यादिति भावः। 'लोकावगतकारणे हीति, 'हि' यस्मात्, 'लोकावगतकारणे दुरिते सतीति योजना, 'वेदेन' वेदसहकृतप्रामाणान्तरेण, वेदस्य

---

(१) सम्प्रदायविद इति ख०।

(२) वेदत्वञ्च शब्द-तदुपजीविप्रमाणातिरिक्तप्रमाणजन्यप्रमित्यविषयार्थकप्रमाणशब्दत्वम्।

मैवम् मङ्गलं विनापि प्रमत्तानुष्ठितसमाप्तेः। न च तेन विनापि सिध्यतस्तदङ्गम्। न च जन्मान्तरीयं तत्, जन्मान्तरीयग्रन्थादिकमुद्दिश्य शिष्टैस्तदकरणात्। ननु यथा पुत्रेष्टौ कर्मसाङ्गुण्ये ऐहिकफलाभावे आमु-

---

फलोपधायकत्वाबोधकत्वाद्यथाश्रुतासङ्गतेः। 'तस्य' मङ्गलस्य, 'तद्ध्वंस-जनकत्वं' दुरितध्वंसोपधायकत्वं, 'न तु तदुपलब्ध्यु' न लोकावगतकारण-दुरितं विना, तथा च दुरितध्वंसजनने दुरितस्याप्यङ्गतया साङ्ग-त्वाभावादेव तत्र विशिष्टाभावसिद्धिः, न तु वेदस्य प्रामाण्याभावादिति भावः। एतदेव दृष्टान्तेन द्रढयति, 'अतएवेति, 'निषिद्धानुष्ठानं, इत्युपलक्षणं विहितानुष्ठानमपि न धर्म्मजनकमित्यपि बोध्यम्। 'मङ्ग-लाकरणे इति, निष्फलत्वादिति[१] भावः। 'विघ्नध्वानवत इति, तथा च सर्व्वेषां शिष्टानां नित्यवदनुष्ठानमेवासिद्धमिति भावः। 'सम्प्रदायः' मीमांसकसम्प्रदायः ॥ १ ॥

इह खलु सकलशिष्टैकवाक्यतयेत्यारभ्य सम्प्रदायमतं,[२] तत् दूषयति 'मैवमिति, मङ्गलव्यापारीभूतस्य तज्जन्यविघ्नध्वंसस्य स्वोत्प-त्त्यवच्छेदकजातीयतासम्बन्धेन फलीभूतसमाप्तिकर्त्तृशरीरनिष्ठतया समाप्तिकारणत्वं, उत आश्रयतासम्बन्धेन तादृशात्मनिष्ठतया[३] वा, आद्ये व्यभिचारमाह, 'मङ्गलं विनापीत्यादिना, 'मङ्गलं विनापि'

---

(१) कर्त्तैकफलत्वादितीति ग०।
(२) सम्प्रदायविदां मतं इति ख०।
(३) फलीभूतसमाप्तिकर्त्तृनिष्ठतयेत्यर्थः।

ष्मिकं फलं तथा साङ्गेऽपि मङ्गले यत्र न फलं तत्रामुष्मिकफलमिति चेत्। न। तत्र पुत्रमात्रस्य कामनाश्रवणात्।

ऐहिकमङ्गलं विनापि, 'प्रमत्तानुष्ठितेति, प्रमत्तनास्तिकशरीरे कर्तृतासम्बन्धेन समाप्त्युत्पत्तेरित्यर्थः। तथा च ऐहिकमङ्गलाभावेन समाप्तिकर्त्तरि तच्छरीरे वा विघ्नध्वंसस्योत्पत्तेरसम्भवात् स्वोत्पत्त्यवच्छेदकजातीयत्वसम्बन्धेन विघ्नध्वंसो व्यभिचारीति भावः।

ननु जन्मान्तरीयशरीरकृतमङ्गलादेव प्रमत्तादिशरीरे विघ्नध्वंसोत्पत्तिरित्यतो न व्यभिचार इत्यत आह, 'न चेति, 'तेन विनापि' अव्यवहितपूर्व्वक्षणे तेन विनापि, 'सिद्धतः' उत्पद्यमानस्य, 'तदङ्गं' तत्कारणं, तथा च जन्मान्तरकृतमङ्गलान्नास्तिकशरीरे विघ्नध्वंसोत्पादे विघ्नध्वंसं प्रति मङ्गलं कारणमेव न स्यात् अव्यवहितपूर्व्ववर्त्तित्वस्य कारणताशरीरत्वादिति भावः। अन्यमभिप्रेत्य शङ्कते, 'न चेति, 'जन्मान्तरीयमिति जन्मान्तरीयमङ्गलाज्जन्मान्तरोत्पन्नं विघ्नध्वंसवत्त्वमित्यर्थः। 'तत्' प्रमत्तकर्तृकसमाप्तौ कारणं, 'जन्मान्तरीयग्रन्थमुद्दिश्येति[१] जन्मान्तरीयग्रन्थसमाप्तिमुद्दिश्येत्यर्थः। तथा च जन्मान्तरीयग्रन्थसमाप्तिमुद्दिश्य मङ्गले शिष्टप्रवृत्त्यापत्त्या यथोक्तस्यैव मङ्गलस्य[२] न समाप्तिकारणत्वमिति भावः।

पुत्रेष्टिरपि जन्मान्तरीयपुत्रमुद्दिश्य न क्रियत इति भ्रमेणाशङ्कते, 'पुत्रेति तथा च तत्र यथा जन्मान्तरीयपुत्रमुद्दिश्य शिष्टैः करणप्रव-

---

(१) जन्मान्तरीयग्रन्थादिकमुद्दिश्येतीति ग०।
(२) मङ्गलजन्यविघ्नध्वंसस्येति ख०।

इह तु प्रारिप्सितसमाप्तिकामनया मङ्गलाचार इति तथैव वेदानुमानात् कारीरीवदासन्नसमयारब्धसमाप्तिः फलम्। नन्वासन्नसमयस्तत्सम्बन्धो वा न मङ्गलजन्य इति समाप्तिमात्रं जन्यं तच्चैहिकामुष्मिकसाधारणमिति चेत्। न। आसन्नसमयस्य स्ववृत्तिसमाप्त्युप

ङ्गरूपबाधकसत्त्वेप्यात्मनिष्ठतया व्यापारीभूतस्यादृष्टस्य हेतुत्वं तथाचापि विघ्नध्वंसस्यात्मनिष्ठतयैव हेतुत्वमिति भावः। भ्रमं निराकृत्य दूषयति, 'तत्रेति, 'कामनाश्रवणादित्यस्य जन्मान्तरीयपुत्रमुद्दिश्यापि श्रिष्टैः करणादिति शेषः। 'इह त्विति 'फलमित्यन्तमेको ग्रन्थः, 'प्रारिप्सितसमाप्तिकामनया मङ्गलाचारः' प्ररिप्सितसमाप्तिकामनयैव मङ्गलाचारः, जन्मान्तरीयग्रन्थसमाप्तिमुद्दिश्य[१] न मङ्गलाचार इति यावत्। 'तथैव' स्वोत्पत्त्यवच्छेदकजातीयत्वसम्बन्धेन फलीभूतसमाप्तिकर्तृशरीरनिष्ठतया मङ्गलजन्यविघ्नध्वंसस्य समाप्तिकारणताबोधकत्वेनैव, 'वेदानुमा.ात्' वेदस्यानुमेयत्वात्, 'आसन्नसमयेति मङ्गलानुष्ठानसन्निहितसमयेत्यर्थः। 'फलं' फलोपधानात्मकमङ्गलजन्यताश्रयः। आसन्नसमयस्य विशेषणत्वमभिप्रेत्य शङ्कते, 'नन्विति, 'स्ववृत्तीति, आधेयतया मङ्गलफलीभूतसमाप्तीनां परिचायकत्वादित्यर्थः। तथा च तत्र[२] मङ्गलकार्य्यत्वाभ्युपगमेपि न क्षतिरिति भावः। 'तस्मादिति, 'व्यभिचारात्' नास्तिकसमाप्तौ स्वोत्पत्त्यवच्छेदकजातीयत्वसम्बन्धेन

---

(१) स्वोक्तैतत्कारव्यवच्छेद्यमाह जन्मान्तरीयेति।
(२) आसन्नसमयादाविन्वयः।

लक्षकत्वात्। अन्यथा कारीर्य्यपि नासन्नसमयफला स्यात्। तस्माद्व्यभिचाराच्च तदङ्गमिति। अन्ये तु मङ्गलं प्रधानं अदृष्टद्वारा आरब्धकर्मसमाप्तिः फलं तत्कामो-

---

मङ्गलजन्यविघ्नध्वंसस्य व्यभिचारात्, 'न तदङ्गमिति न स्वोत्पत्त्यवच्छेदकजातीयत्वसम्बन्धेन फलीभूतसमाप्तिकर्तृशरीरनिष्ठतया समाप्तिजनकीभूतं विघ्नध्वंसं द्वारीकृत्य मङ्गलं समाप्तिजनकमित्यर्थः। यद्यपि सति विघ्ने तद्ध्वंसद्वारा तस्याङ्गत्वादिति पूर्व्वमभिधानात् विघ्नस्थलीयसमाप्तित्वमेव कार्य्यतावच्छेदकं तथा च नास्तिकशरीरकर्तृकसमाप्तौ व्यभिचारेऽपि न क्षतिः तत्कर्तृकसमाप्तेः कार्य्यतावच्छेदकानाक्रान्तत्वात्। न च तादृशसमाप्तित्वस्य कार्य्यतावच्छेदकत्वं वेदेन न बोध्यत इति वाच्यं। कारणतामात्रं हि वेदो बोधयति कार्य्यतावच्छेदकस्योत्तरकालकल्प्यं, तथापि विघ्नस्थलीयत्वं विघ्नवज्जातीयशरीरकर्तृकत्वं तच्च तादृशशरीरनिष्ठकृतिजन्यत्वं तथाच कृतौ समाप्तिजनकतायां गृहीतायामेव मङ्गले समाप्तिकारणताग्रहसम्भवादन्यथासिद्धिरतो न तत् कार्य्यतावच्छेदकं किन्तु समाप्तित्वमात्रं अतो नास्तिकसमाप्तिरपि कार्य्यतावच्छेदकाक्रान्तेति भावः। एतच्चोपलक्षणं। विघ्नवज्जातीयशरीरनिष्ठकृतिजन्यत्वस्य चानुगतस्य(१) अभावादनन्तकार्य्यकारणभावापत्तेश्चेत्यपि बोध्यम्।

मीमांसकैकदेशिमतमाह, 'अन्ये त्विति। 'प्रधानं' आरब्धकर्म्मणो नाङ्गं नारब्धकर्म्मजन्यसमाप्तिजनकमिति यावत्। आरब्धकर्म्मजन्य-

---

(१) मृति-मत्वादिनाशस्य विघ्नस्य नानात्वादिति भावः।

ऽधिकारी क्वचित्तु फलाभावः कर्म्मादिवैकल्यात्कारीरीवत्। न चान्यदापि करणम्। नियतकालीनताहृशाचारेण फलवत्कर्मारिप्समानस्तत्समाप्तिकामो मङ्गलमाचरेदिति श्रुत्या आरम्भसमयकर्त्तव्यताबोधनात्। यथा अग्नावैष्णवमेकादशकपालं चरुं निर्वपेद्दर्शपूर्णमा-

---

समाप्तिश्च चरमवर्णरूपा तद्ध्वंसरूपा वा एतच्चापूर्व्वद्वारकत्वे लौकिकफलाङ्गत्वविरोध इति पूर्व्वोक्तदोषवारणायाभिहितं। 'आरब्धकर्म्मसमाप्तिः' आरब्धकर्म्मोत्पत्तिः, 'फलं' तस्य फलं, सा चातीन्द्रियत्वेनालौकिकी एवेति भावः।

नन्वेवं विघ्नध्वंसकामनया मङ्गले शिष्टप्रवृत्तिर्न स्यादित्यत्रेष्टापत्तिमाह, 'तत्कामः' इति आरब्धकर्म्मोत्पत्तिकामनैव मङ्गले शिष्टप्रवृत्तिजनिका न तु विघ्नध्वंसकामनेत्यर्थः। तथा च श्रुतिरपि तथैवोन्नेया, न तु "निर्व्विघ्नसमाप्तिकामो मङ्गलमाचरेत्" इत्याकारिकेति भावः। 'कर्म्मादीत्यादिपदात् कर्त्तृ-साधनयोः परिग्रहः। 'अन्यदापि' आरब्धकर्म्मप्राक्कालातिरिक्तकालेपि, 'करणमिति, अपूर्व्वं जनयत्विति शेषः। 'आरम्भसमयकर्त्तव्यताबोधनादिति आरब्धकर्म्मपूर्व्वसमयकर्त्तव्यताबोधनादित्यर्थः। तथा च तज्जन्यापूर्व्वं प्रति तादृशसमयस्यापि हेतुत्वात् अन्यदा तत्करणान्नापूर्व्वमिति भावः। 'अग्नावैष्णवमिति छान्दसः, अग्नौ वैष्णवमेकादशकपालं चरुं निर्व्वपेदित्यर्थः। यद्वा अग्निदेवताकविष्णुदेवताकमेकादशकपालं तच्च संस्कृतं चरुं निर्व्वपेदित्यर्थः। अग्निश्च विष्णुश्च अग्नाविष्णू तौ देवतेऽस्येति व्युत्पत्तेः। 'प्रधानायाः'

साधारिष्समान इति श्रुत्याऽऽरम्भणीयेष्टेः प्रधानायाः दर्शारम्भसमयकर्त्तव्यत्वम् कामनोपाधिकार्यत्वेप्यारम्भसमये[१] नियतमनुष्ठानम् आरब्धकर्मसमाप्त्यर्थिनोपायत्वेनावश्यन्तदनुष्ठानात् । न च काम्यत्वे परि-

---

दर्शजन्यफलाजनिकायाः, 'कर्त्तव्यत्वमिति, बोध्यत इति शेषः । ननु मङ्गलस्याङ्गत्वेऽङ्गवैगुण्यभिया अनायत्या आरम्भसमयेऽवश्यं तत्करणं घटते अनङ्गत्वे त्वारम्भसमयेऽवश्यं कथं तत्करणं, न ह्यारम्भणीया दर्शसमयेऽवश्यं क्रियत इति नियमः, इत्यत आह, 'कामनोपाधिकार्य्यत्वेपीति फलान्तरकामनाधीनेच्छाजन्यकृतिविषयत्वेपीत्यर्थः । 'आरम्भसमये' आरब्धकर्म्मपूर्व्वसमये, 'आरब्धकर्म्मसमाप्त्यर्थिना' आरब्धकर्म्मोत्पत्त्यर्थिना आरब्धकर्म्मकर्त्त्रा, 'उपायत्वेन' तादृशोत्पत्तिरूपेष्टसाधनत्वेन, 'अवश्यं तदनुष्ठानादिति अवश्यमारब्धकर्म्मपूर्व्वसमये तस्य ज्ञानादित्यर्थः । तथा चेष्टसाधनताज्ञाननियमेन इच्छानियमात् प्रवृत्तिनियम इति भावः । नन्वेवं यत्रोत्पत्तिकामनां विनैव कर्म्मारब्धं तत्र मङ्गलं नानुष्ठीयेतेत्याशङ्कते, 'न चेति, 'काम्यत्वे' आरब्धकर्म्मोत्पत्तिकामनाधीनकामनाविषयत्वे, 'परिसमाप्तिकामनां विना' आरब्धकर्म्मोत्पत्तिकामनाविरहेण, 'समाप्तं कर्म्म' उत्पन्नं कर्म्म, 'अलं' समर्थं, 'फलार्थिनः' ग्रन्थप्रयोजनकीर्त्त्यर्थिनः, 'समाप्तौ' उत्पत्तौ, 'अवश्यम्भावादिति तदभावेऽननुष्ठानमिष्टमेवेति भावः । 'विहितेति विहितजन्यप्रधानापूर्व्वत्वादित्यर्थः । विहितजन्यप्रधानापूर्व्वस्य फल-

---

(१) आरम्भकाले इति क० ।

समाप्तिकामनां विना फलवत्कर्मारम्भेऽपि तदनुष्ठानं न स्यादिति वाच्यम्। समाप्तं कर्म फलायालमिति फलार्थिनः समाप्तौ कामनावश्यंभावादिति। तन्न। कारीरीजन्यातिशयवद्विहितप्रधानजन्यातिशयत्वात् मङ्गलजन्यापूर्वस्यापि फलसम्पादकाशेषकारणसम्पादकतया आरब्धकर्मसमाप्त्यवश्यम्भावापत्तेः फलावश्यम्भावनिश्चयं विना वैदिककर्माननुष्ठानात्। न चैवं, भूयसि

सम्पादकाशेषकारणसम्पादकत्वनियमादिति भावः। अत्र फलपदस्येष्टपरतया पापे व्यभिचारवारणाय विहितजन्येति, विहितत्वं बलवदनिष्टाननुबन्धित्वेन वेदबोधितत्वं, तेन श्येनजन्यपापे न व्यभिचारः। विहितजन्यत्वमात्रोक्तौ फले व्यभिचार इत्यतः प्रधानापूर्व्वेति, अजनितप्रधानापूर्व्वाङ्गापूर्व्वे व्यभिचारवारणायप्रधनेत्यपूर्व्वविशेषणं, प्रधानेत्यस्य विहितेन सहान्वयेऽङ्गप्रधानोभयरूपशिखादिना[१] अङ्गविधया जनितेऽपूर्व्वे व्यभिचारापत्तेः। फलशिरस्कापूर्व्वमेव प्रधानापूर्व्वं तेन दक्षिणादानादिविनाकृतप्रधानजन्यापूर्व्वे न व्यभिचारः। कीर्त्तनाद्यनाश्यत्वमप्यपूर्व्वविशेषणं तेन तन्नाश्ये न व्यभिचारः। फलोपधायकत्वस्य साध्यत्वात् स्वरूपयोग्यत्वस्य मङ्गलजन्यादृष्टेऽपि सत्त्वात्। यदि च सत्यपि अपूर्व्वे सत्प्रतिपक्षवत् प्रतिकृत्याप्रतिबन्धात्[२] न फलोदय इत्युपगम्यते तदा तदप्रतिरुद्धत्वेनाप्यपूर्व्वं विशेषणीय-

(१) आदिना उपवीतिपरिग्रहः।

(२) प्रतिकृत्याप्रतिरोधादिति ख॰। सतप्रतिपक्षरूपदुरितेन प्रतिबन्धादिति क॰।

साङ्गेऽपि मङ्गले क्वचिदारब्धसमाप्त्यभावात्। न च तच्चामुष्मिकं फलम् ऐहिकमात्रफलत्वात् वैदिककर्मणः फलावश्यम्भावेनागन्तुकदुरितेनाप्यप्रतिबन्धात्। किञ्च यथा कारीर्य्यादिकमग्निमपुरुषव्यापारं विनैव फलहेतुः तथा मङ्गलमपि तेन विनैव हेतुः स्यात्।

मिति। न च मङ्गलजन्यापूर्व्वाप्रसिद्ध्या पक्षाप्रसिद्धेः कथमिदमापादनमिति वाच्यं। मङ्गलं यदि विहितत्वे सति प्रधानापूर्व्वजनकं स्यात्तदा फलसम्पादकाशेषकारणसम्पादकापूर्व्वजनकं स्यादित्यापादनात्। पापजनके कर्म्मणि व्यभिचारवारणाय सत्यन्तं पक्षतावच्छेदकावच्छेदेनापाद्यसिद्धेरुद्देश्यत्वादिति दिक्। 'आरब्धकर्म्मसमाप्त्यवश्यम्भावापत्तेरिति मङ्गले कृते सर्व्वत्रैवारब्धकर्म्मोत्पत्त्यापत्तेरित्यर्थः। नन्विदमप्रयोजकमित्यत आह, 'फलावश्यम्भावेति, तन्निश्चयश्च नोक्तनियमं विनेति भावः। इष्टापत्तिमाशङ्क्याह, 'न चैवमिति। न च मङ्गले कृतेऽवश्यमारब्धकर्म्मोत्पत्तिरित्यर्थः। 'भूयमीति प्रौढ्या, 'समाप्त्यभावात्' उत्पत्त्यभावात्,(१) 'ऐहिकमात्रेति स्वोत्पत्त्यवच्छेदकजातीयत्वसम्बन्धेन फलीभूतारब्धकर्म्मोत्पत्तिजनककर्तृशरीरनिष्ठतयैव मङ्गलजन्यापूर्व्वस्यारब्धकर्म्मोत्पत्तिहेतुत्वाभ्युपगमादित्यर्थः। अन्यथा स्वावच्छेदकत्वसम्बन्धेन शरीरनिष्ठतया समवायसम्बन्धेन तादृशात्मनिष्ठतया वा आरब्धकर्म्मोत्पत्तिजनकत्वे ः जन्मान्तरीयग्रन्थोत्पत्तिमुद्दिश्यापि मङ्गले शिष्टप्रवृत्त्यापत्तेरिति भावः। ननु मङ्गलपूर्व्वोत्पन्नेन मङ्ग-

---

(१) प्रारब्धसमाप्त्यभावात् तदुत्पत्त्यभावादिति क०।

न चैवं। लोकावगतकारणत्वात्तदपेक्षेति चेत्तर्हि स एव हेतुरस्तु किमनेन। आरब्धकर्म्मजनकादृष्टकारण-

---

सामन्तरोत्पन्नेन वा दुरितेन प्रतिबन्धान्न फलं प्रथमनये मङ्गलस्य दुरितानाशकतया तत्पूर्व्वोत्पन्नेनापि प्रतिबन्धसम्भवादित्यत आह, 'वैदिकेति, 'फलावश्यम्भावेन' फलावश्यम्भावनियमेन, 'आगन्तुकेति मङ्गलपूर्व्वोत्तरोत्पन्नेत्यर्थः। ननूक्तनियमोऽप्रयोजकः इतरसकलकारण-सत्त्वे फलावश्यम्भावनिश्चयरूपायाः श्रद्धाया एव वैदिककर्म्मप्रवृत्तौ हेतुत्वादित्यस्वरसादाह, 'किञ्चेति, 'यथेति, कारीर्य्यपि अदृष्टद्वारा हेतुरितिमते नेदं। वस्तुतस्तु अवग्रहनिवृत्तिरेव तत्फलमित्यन्यत्र सुव्यक्तं। 'हेतुः स्यादिति, प्रधानापूर्व्वजनकविहितकर्म्मणोऽग्रिमपुरुष-व्यापारानपेक्ष्यफलजनकत्वनियमादितिभावः। 'नचैवमिति छेदः। शङ्कते 'लोकेति, 'तदपेक्षा' कण्ठाभिघातादेरारब्धकर्म्मजनकत्वे कण्ठा-दिक्रियाद्यपेक्षा, तथा च प्रधानापूर्वजनकविहितकर्मत्वं लोकाव-गतकारणेतराग्रिमपुरुषव्यापारानपेक्ष्यफलजनकत्वस्यैव व्याप्यमन्यथा पुत्रेष्टौ भोजनादिद्वारा भोगजनकादृष्टजनककर्म्मणि च व्यभिचारा-दितिभावः। 'स एवेति कण्ठाभिघातादिरेवेत्यर्थः। 'किमनेन' किं मङ्गलेन, दृष्टकारणसाकल्येऽदृष्टविलम्बेन कार्य्यविलम्बाभावा-दितिभावः। 'तत्समाप्तिसाधनत्वमिति मङ्गलस्य तदुत्पत्तिजनकत्व-मित्यर्थः। 'कर्मनिर्वाहे' कर्मोत्पत्तौ, 'येनेति, तथाच बाधेन तादृशश्रुतिरप्यसिद्धैवेतिभावः। 'मङ्गलं विनापि' ऐहिकमङ्गलं विनापि, 'प्रमत्तनास्तिकेति प्रमत्तनास्तिकशरीरकर्तृकप्रारब्धकर्मोत्पत्तेरित्यर्थः।

सम्पत्तौ पुत्रेष्टिवत्तत्समाप्तिसाधनत्वं(१) श्रुत्या बोध्यत इति चेत् । न । तत्र दृष्टकारणसम्पत्तौ पुत्रानुत्पादाद-

---

तथा च ऐहिकमङ्गलाभावेन स्वोत्पत्त्यवच्छेदकजातीयतासम्बन्धेन मङ्गलजन्यापूर्वासम्भवेऽपि प्रारब्धकर्मोत्पत्तेस्तेन सम्बन्धेन मङ्गलजन्यापूर्वं तत्र व्यभिचारीतिभावः । 'न तत्कारणमिति न तादृशसम्बन्धेन फलीभूतकर्मोत्पत्त्यवच्छेदकशरीरनिष्ठतया मङ्गलजन्यादृष्टं कर्मोत्पत्तिकारणमित्यर्थः । प्रकृते, 'जन्मान्तरीयेति, 'पुण्यसम्पत्तिः' प्रारब्धकर्मसमाप्तिकामनाकृतमहादेवपूजादिजन्यपुण्यसम्पत्तिः, 'तथापि व्यभिचारादिति स्वोत्पत्त्यवच्छेदकत्वसम्बन्धेन मङ्गलजन्यादृष्टस्य व्यभिचारादित्यर्थः । प्रकृते, 'क्वचिदिति, विघ्नस्थलीयेतरारब्धकर्मोत्पत्तौ कर्मान्तरजन्यपुण्यविशेषसम्पत्तिर्हेतुः, विघ्नस्थलीयारब्धकर्मोत्पत्तौ मङ्गलजन्यमदृष्टं स्वोत्पत्त्यवच्छेदकजातीयत्वसम्बन्धेन फलीभूतारब्धकर्मोत्पत्त्यधिकरणशरीरनिष्ठतया हेतुरित्यर्थः । शिष्टाचारानुरोधादिति भावः । नन्वेवं येन तत्कर्मान्तरं मङ्गलञ्चोभयमेव कृतं तस्य विनिगमकाभावात् परस्परविरुद्धकार्यद्वयप्रसङ्गः द्वयोरेव कारणसत्त्वादित्यत आह, 'व्रीहि-यववदिति तत्र यथा परस्पराभावविशिष्टत्वेन व्रीहिकरणक-यवकरणकयागयोः कारणत्वं तथा प्रकृतेऽपि विघ्नस्थलीयेतरसमाप्तौ स्वोत्पत्त्यवच्छेदकजातीयत्वसम्बन्धावच्छिन्नप्रतियोगिताकमङ्गलजन्यपुण्यविशेषाभावविशिष्टकर्मान्तरजन्यपुण्यविशेषत्वेन कारणत्वं, विघ्नस्थलीयसमाप्तौ च कर्मान्तर-

---

(१) तत्समाप्तिकारणत्वमिति ख० ।

दृष्टद्वारा पुण्येष्टेस्तज्जनकत्वमस्तु। न च कर्म्मनिर्व्वाहे दृष्टसकलहेतुसम्पत्तौ विलम्बो येन मङ्गलजन्यादृष्टा-

---

जन्यपुण्यविशेषाभावविशिष्टमङ्गलजन्यपुण्यविशेषत्वेन कारणत्वं वैशिष्ट्यञ्च एककालावच्छेदेन एकशरीरवृत्तित्वमित्यर्थः। अतएव कृतेपि साङ्गे मङ्गले क्वचित् फलाभावस्तत्र फलबलेन कर्म्मान्तरजन्यपुण्यविशेषस्य कल्पनादिति भावः। 'तत्सत्त्वसम्भावनयेति जन्मान्तरीयकर्म्मान्तरजन्यपुण्यसत्त्वसम्भावनयेत्यर्थः। एकाभावविशिष्टापरस्यैव फलजनकत्वादिति भावः। 'यत्रप्रयोगे' यवकरणकयागे, 'उभयस्य' मिलितस्य, 'अशास्त्रार्थत्वात्' शास्त्रबोधितफलाजनकत्वात्, एतच्चोपलक्षणं शिवपूजादिकर्म्मान्तरमङ्गलोभयकरणादपि समाप्तिदर्शनात् विघ्नस्थलीयत्वस्योक्तक्रमेणान्यथासिद्धिसम्पादकतया अननुगततया च कार्य्यतावच्छेदकत्वासम्भवाच्चेत्यपि बोद्धव्यं। ननु व्रीहि-यवादिविकल्पस्थले कथं कार्य्यकारणभावः एकजातीयदर्शजन्यापूर्व्वविशेषे तज्जन्यस्वर्गविशेषे चोभयोः प्रत्येकं कारणत्वे व्यभिचारात् एकस्मादपि तादृशकार्य्यविशेषोत्पत्तेः। न चोभयत्र दर्शजन्यतावच्छेदकं वैजात्यद्वयमस्ति तदवच्छिन्नं प्रत्येव प्रत्येकं हेतुत्वं तृणादिवदिति वाच्यं। उभयकरणकयागादेरपि फलोत्पत्त्यापत्तेः। न चेष्टापत्तिः, अशास्त्रार्थत्वात्। भिन्नभिन्नावच्छिन्नं प्रति कारणतापि यदि वैकल्पिकी तदा अश्वमेधवाजपेययोः स्वर्गजनकताया अपि तथात्वापत्तेः। अथ व्रीहिकरणकयवकरणकयोरुभयोरेव दर्शात्मकत्वादपूर्व्वविशेषं प्रति स्वर्गविशेषं प्रति च दर्शत्वेनैवोभयोरनुगतहेतुता दर्शत्वञ्च जातिविशेषः। न चैवं

पेक्षा स्यात्। अपि च मङ्गलं विनापि प्रमत्तनास्तिकानुष्ठितसमाप्तेर्न तत्तच कारणम्। अन्मान्तरीय-

---

उभयकरणकदर्शादपि फलोदयप्रसङ्ग इति वाच्यं। जनकतावच्छेदकदर्शत्वस्य तद्व्यावृत्तत्वात्। एकधर्मावच्छिन्नं प्रत्युभयोर्जनकत्वमेव वैकल्पिककारणता अतएव अश्वमेध-वाजपेययोर्न विकल्प इति चेत्। न। उभयकरणकेपि दर्शव्यवहारात् तत्रापि दर्शत्वसत्त्वात्। न च दर्शत्वेन न कारणता किन्तु उभयकरणकदर्शव्यावृत्तेन दर्शत्वव्याप्यजातिविशेषेण, न हि दर्शत्वस्य कारणतावच्छेदकत्वपर्य्यन्तं वेदो बोधयतीति वाच्यं। कारणतावच्छेदकैक्येपि यदि वैकल्पिककारणता तदा दण्डयोर्घटजनकत्वस्यापि तथात्वप्रसङ्गात् परस्परविरुद्धवैजात्याश्रययोर्द्वयोर्वैकल्पिककारणतास्थले एकरूपेण कारणत्वस्य वक्तुमशक्यत्वाच्च। अत्राहुः व्रीहिकरणकयाग-यवकरणकयागयोरुभयोर्जन्यतावच्छेदकमपूर्व्वनिष्ठवैजात्यद्वयमस्ति अतो न परस्परं व्यभिचारः। कारणत्वञ्च तदुभयावच्छिन्नं प्रति प्रत्येकं व्रीहिकरणकयागाभावविशिष्टयवकरणकयागत्व-यवकरणकयागाभावविशिष्टव्रीहिकरणकयागत्वाभ्यां अतो नोभयकरणकयागादपूर्व्वोत्पत्तिः, न वाश्वमेध-वाजपेययोः कारणतापि वैकल्पिकी एकाभावविशिष्टापरत्वेन कारणताया एव तथात्वात्। व्रीहि-यवकरणकत्वञ्च तज्जन्यपुरोडाशविषयकत्वं तच्च दर्शनिष्ठपरस्परव्यावृत्तजातिद्वयपरिचायकं। न च परस्पराभावविशिष्टत्वेन कारणत्वे व्रीहिकरणकदर्शाव्यवधानकृतयवकरणकदर्शादपूर्व्वानुत्पत्तिप्रसङ्गः उत्पत्तिसम्बन्धेन यागादेरदृष्टजनक-

पुण्यसम्पत्तिस्तत्र हेतुरिति चेत्। न। तथापि व्यभिचारात्। क्वचित् पुण्यसम्पत्तिः क्वचिन्मङ्गलं हेतुरिति

तथा क्षणविलम्बस्य वक्तुमशक्यत्वादिति वाच्यं। बहुतरव्यापारसाध्यतया अव्यवधानेन तादृशदर्शद्वयोत्पत्तेरसम्भवात्। न च विशिष्टस्य कारणतावच्छेदकत्वे विशेष्यविशेषणभावे विनिगमकाभावेन गुरुतरकार्य्यकारणभावचतुष्टयापत्तिरिति वाच्यं। "व्रीहिभिर्यजेत" इत्यादिश्रुतेरेव विनिगमकत्वात्। तादृशश्रुत्या यागस्यैव कारणत्वबोधनात् न त्वभावस्य। न च तथापि व्रीहिकरणकयागाभावादिविशिष्टत्व-यवकरणकयागत्वयोर्धर्म्मयोर्विशेष्यविशेषणभावे विनिगमकाभाव इति वाच्यं। लाघवात्तयोरेव एकत्र द्वयमिति न्यायेनैव यागनिष्ठतया व्यासज्यवृत्त्यवच्छेदकत्वाभ्युपगमात्। न च परस्परव्यावृत्तवैजात्यद्वयस्य कार्य्यतावच्छेदकत्वे वाजपेयाश्वमेधयोरिव व्रीहिकरणक-यवकरणकयोरुभयोरेव तुल्यवदनुष्ठानापत्तिरिति वाच्यं। तादृशापूर्व्वयोर्गेरेव कामनासत्त्वे इष्टापत्तेः।

केचित् तादृशवैजात्यद्वयावच्छिन्नं प्रति प्रत्येकं लाघवात् व्रीहिकरणकयागत्व-यवकरणकयागत्वाभ्यामेव कारणत्वं न तु परस्पराभावविशिष्टत्वेन व्यासज्यवृत्त्यवच्छेदकतायाः सिद्धान्तासिद्धत्वात् गौरवाच्च। परस्परकार्य्यतावच्छेदकावच्छिन्नापूर्व्वं प्रति परस्परस्य प्रतिबन्धकतया च नोभयकरणकदर्शादपूर्व्वोत्पत्तिः। न चैवमतिरिक्तप्रतिबध्य-प्रतिबन्धकभावान्तरकल्पने गौरवमिति वाच्यं। तस्य कार्य्यकारणभावग्रहोत्तरकल्प्यत्वेन फलमुखत्वात्। यत्र परस्परं परस्परकार्य्यतावच्छे-

व्रीहि-यववद्विकल्प एवेति चेन्नहिं तत्सम्भावनया नियतं मङ्गलानुष्ठानं न स्यात् यवप्रयोगे व्रीहेरिव विकल्पे

दकावच्छिन्नं प्रति प्रतिबन्धकं तत्रैव वैकल्पिकी कारणता । तेनाश्वमेध-वाजपेययोर्जनकता न वैकल्पिकी । न चैवं तत्तदभावव्याप्यपरामर्शयोरप्यनुमितिं प्रति कारणतापि वैकल्पिकी स्यादिति वाच्यं । तयोः परस्परकार्य्यतावच्छेदकावच्छिन्नं प्रति अप्रतिबन्धकत्वात् विशिष्टबुद्धित्वेनैव तयोः प्रतिबध्यतावच्छेदकत्वादित्याहुः ।

यत्तु दर्शजन्यस्वर्गविशेषनिष्ठमेवोभयजन्यतावच्छेदकं जातिद्वयं, परस्परस्य परस्परकार्य्यतावच्छेदकावच्छिन्नस्वर्गं प्रति प्रतिबन्धकत्वान्नोभयकरणकदर्शात् स्वर्गोत्पत्तिरिति वदन्ति । तदसत् । उभयकरणकदर्शादपि स्वर्गोत्पत्त्यापत्तेः यागस्याशुविनाशितया स्वर्गोत्पत्तिसमये प्रतिबन्धकासत्त्वात् । परस्परजन्यापूर्व्वस्य प्रतिबन्धकत्वे च व्रीहिकरणकदर्शान्तरकृतयवकरणकदर्शात् स्वर्गानुत्पत्तिप्रसङ्गात् ।

अन्ये तु सामान्यतो दर्शत्वेनैव व्रीहिकरणकदर्श-यवकरणकदर्शयोरुभयोरपूर्व्वविशेषं प्रति स्वर्गविशेषं प्रति च हेतुत्वं न तु तयोर्विशेषतोपि हेतुत्वं किन्तु दर्शसामान्यजन्यतावच्छेदकापूर्व्वनिष्ठवैजात्यव्याप्यं व्रीहिकरणकदर्श-यवकरणकदर्शयोः प्रतिबध्यतावच्छेदकं परस्परव्यावृत्तवैजात्यद्वयं तेन सामान्यसामग्रीसत्त्वेपि प्रतिबन्धकाभावरूपविशेषसामग्र्यभावादेव नोभयकरणकदर्शात् फलावाप्तिः । वस्तुतस्तु प्रत्येकं व्रीहिकरणकदर्शत्व-यवकरणकदर्शत्वाभ्यां प्रतिबन्धकतापि न वाच्या प्रतिबध्यतावच्छेदकवैजात्यद्वयकल्पने प्रतिबध्य-प्रतिबन्धकभावद्वयकल्पने

वोभयस्याशास्त्रार्थत्वात् । ननु विधिवाक्यं न फलनियतपूर्व्वसत्त्वं बोधयति किन्तु मङ्गलात् फलावश्यम्भा-

---

च महागौरवात् । परन्तु दर्शसामान्यजन्यतावच्छेदकापूर्व्वनिष्ठवैजात्यावच्छिन्नं प्रत्येव व्रीहियवोभयकरणकदर्शत्वेन प्रतिबन्धकत्वं । अतएवाव्यवधानेन व्रीहियवप्रत्येकमात्रकरणकयागद्वयसम्भवेपि द्वितीयादपूर्व्वोत्पत्तौ न बाधकं । न च तत्रापि व्रीहि-यवोभयकरणकयागाव्यवहितोत्पन्नप्रत्येकमात्रकरणकयागान्नापूर्व्वोत्पत्तिः स्यात् उत्पत्तिसम्बन्धेन यागादेरपूर्व्वजनकतया क्षणविलम्बस्यापि वक्तुमशक्यत्वादिति वाच्यं । इष्टत्वात् । उभयकरणकयागानन्तरं क्षणैकविलम्बोत्पन्नप्रत्येकमात्रकरणकयागादेवापूर्व्वोत्पादादित्याहुः ।

यत्तु यागं प्रत्येव व्रीहियवयोर्वैकल्पिकी कारणतेति । तदसत् स्वत्वध्वंसजनिकाया अनेन देवताप्रीतिर्भवत्वित्याकारिकाया इदं द्रव्यं देवताया भवत्वित्याकारिकाया वा इच्छाया यागत्वेन तत्र व्रीह्यादेर्हेतुत्वे मानाभावात् "व्रीहिभिर्यजेत" इत्यादौ व्रीह्यादिजन्यपुरोडाशविषयकत्वस्यैव तृतीयार्थत्वात् कृतावेव तृतीयाविभक्तेः शक्ततया अन्यत्वार्थकत्वेपि लाक्षणिकत्वाविशेषात् । यागं प्रति व्रीह्यभावविशिष्टयवत्वादिना कारणत्वस्य व्रीहित्वादिना प्रतिबन्धकत्वस्य वा वक्तुमशक्यत्वाच्च । अनुगतानतिप्रसक्तवैशिष्ट्यस्य प्रतिबन्धकतावच्छेदकसम्बन्धस्य च दुर्वचत्वादिति संक्षेपः ।

'नन्विति, 'विधिवाक्यं' मङ्गलबोधकविधिवाक्यं, 'फलं' समाप्तिः, 'किन्त्विति. 'मङ्गलात्' स्वजन्यादृष्टोत्पत्त्यवच्छेदकत्वसम्बन्धेन मङ्गल-

वमिति चेत् । न । इष्टसाधनत्वस्य विध्यर्थत्वात् । अथान्वयव्यतिरेकाभ्यां तद्ग्रहे व्यभिचारो दोषाय, न त्वागमेन तद्ग्रहे । तदुक्तमागममूलत्वाच्चास्यार्थस्य व्यभिचारो न दोषायेति । अतएव यागादेः स्वर्गसाधनतेति चेत् । न । नियतपूर्व्वसत्त्वस्य ग्राह्यस्याभावादागमेनापि बोधयितुमशक्यत्वात् यागजनितस्वर्गे कारीरीजनितवृष्टौ च जातिविशेष एवास्ति । अपरे तु मङ्गलस्यारब्धनिर्व्वाहकत्वं विघ्नसंसर्गाभावद्वारा,

---

सत्त्वात् । यद्वा स्वोत्पत्त्यवच्छेदकत्वसम्बन्धेन मङ्गलजन्यादृष्टसत्त्वात् । 'फलावश्यम्भावं' तदितरसकलकारणसमवधाने सति फलावश्यम्भावं । तथाच व्यतिरेकव्यभिचारो न दोषायेतिभावः । 'तद्ग्रहे' कारणताग्रहे, 'व्यभिचार व्यतिरेकव्यभिचारज्ञानं, 'आगमेन' वेदेन, 'तदुक्तमिति, द्रव्यकिरणावल्यामाचार्य्यचरणैरितिशेषः । 'आगममूलत्वादिति, 'अस्यार्थस्य' मङ्गले समाप्तिकारणत्वग्रहस्य, 'आगममूलत्वात्' आगमजन्यत्वात्, 'व्यभिचारः' व्यभिचारज्ञानं, 'न दोषायेति तदर्थ इत्यभिमानः । 'स्वर्गसाधनता' वेदेन स्वर्गसाधनताग्रहः, अन्यथा गङ्गास्नानादितोऽपि स्वर्गोत्पत्त्या व्यभिचारेण कारणताग्रहो न स्यादितिभावः । 'आगमेन बोधयितुमशक्यत्वात्' आगमेन प्रमापयितुमशक्यत्वात्, आगमजन्यज्ञानस्याप्रमात्वापातादिति यावत् । नन्वेवं यागादौ कथं वेदेन स्वर्गसाधनताप्रमा[१] इत्यत आह, 'यागजनितेति,

---

(१) स्वर्गसाधनताग्रह इति ख० ।

तथैव प्रतिबन्धकाभावस्य हेतुत्वात्[१] स चाभावः सतो विघ्नस्य ध्वंसोऽनागतस्यानुत्पादश्च कर्मनिर्व्वाहसमयस्थायी। विघ्नकारणविनाशद्वारा प्रागभावस्य साध्यत्वं,

'कारीरीति, इदं परमतेन। वस्तुतस्तु अवग्रहनिवृत्तेरेव तत्फलत्वादिति बोध्यम्।

मङ्गलमपूर्व्वं जनयति तेन चापूर्व्वेण विघ्नसंसर्गाभावो जायते विघ्नसंसर्गाभावाच्च समाप्तिरिति क्रमेण स्वजन्यापूर्व्वजनितविघ्नसंसर्गाभावद्वारा मङ्गलस्य समाप्तिहेतुत्वमिति केचिन्मीमांसका वदन्ति तन्मतमुपन्यस्यति, 'अपरे त्विति, 'निर्व्वाहकत्वं' समापकत्वं, 'विघ्नसंसर्गाभावेति स्वजन्यापूर्व्वजनितविघ्नसंसर्गाभावद्वारेत्यर्थः। 'तथैव' विघ्नसंसर्गाभावत्वेनैव, 'प्रतिबन्धकाभावस्य' विघ्नाभावस्य, 'अनुत्पादः' प्रागभावः, 'कर्मनिर्व्वाहसमयस्थायी' कर्मसमाप्तिकालस्थायी। ननु विघ्नप्रागभावस्य किंविधया मङ्गलजन्यत्वमित्यत आह, 'विघ्नकारणेति 'विघ्नकारणं' मङ्गलप्रागभावः, तद्ध्वंसविधयेत्यर्थः। 'प्रागभावस्य' विघ्नप्रागभावस्य, 'साध्यत्वं' मङ्गलजन्यत्वं, यथाश्रुते विघ्नकारणस्य निषिद्धकर्मणो मङ्गलेन नाशाऽसम्भवादसङ्गतापत्तेः। ननु तथापि प्रागभावस्य अन्यत्वात् कथं मङ्गलजन्यत्वमित्यत आह, 'यस्मिन् सतीति, 'असत्वं' व्यतिरेकः, एवञ्च मङ्गलसत्त्वे विघ्नप्रागभावसत्त्वं विघ्नप्रतिबन्धकसत्त्वेन विघ्नानुत्पत्तेः, मङ्गलव्यतिरेके च विघ्नप्रागभावव्यतिरेकः प्रतिबन्धका-

(१) कारणत्वादिति ख०।

यस्मिन् सत्यग्रिमक्षणे यस्य सत्त्वं यद्व्यतिरेके चासत्त्वं तदेव तस्य तज्जन्यत्वं न त्वसतः सत्त्वं गौरवात्। अस्ति च विघ्नकारणनाशे सति विघ्नप्रागभावस्य तथात्वम्।

भावसत्त्वेन विघ्नोत्पत्तेरिति विघ्नप्रागभावस्तज्जन्य इति भावः। ननु यस्मिन् सत्यग्रिमक्षणे यस्य सत्त्वं इत्यत्र यद्व्यतिरेके यस्यासत्त्वमित्यत्र च सतिसप्तम्याः सामानाधिकरण्यमात्रमर्थः व्यापकत्वं वा नाद्यः अतिप्रसङ्गात् सामग्रीक्षणे उदासीनसत्त्वेपि कार्य्यसत्त्वात् यत्किञ्चित्कारणाभावस्थले उदासीनाभावादपि कार्य्याभावात्। न च स्व-स्वव्याप्येतरयावत्कारणसमवधाने यत्सत्त्वे यत्सत्त्वं यद्व्यतिरेके यद्व्यतिरेक इति वक्तव्यं स्वपदञ्च कारणत्वाभिमतपरमिति वाच्यं। विघ्नप्रागभावादेः कारणाभावेनाव्याप्त्यापत्तेः यत्सत्त्वे यत्सत्त्वमित्यन्वयदलस्य व्यर्थतापत्तेश्च। न हि अकारणस्य स्वेतरयावत्कारणकाले स्वाभावेन कार्य्याभावः। नान्त्यः विघ्नप्रागभावादेर्मङ्गलाद्यजन्यत्वापत्तेः तद्व्यतिरेकेपि तस्यानादित्वेन पूर्व्वक्षणे सत्त्वात्, घटाद्यव्याप्त्यापत्तेश्च दण्डादिविरहेपि घटाद्यनुवृत्तेः। न च व्यतिरेकः प्रागभावः, ज्ञानादेरात्माद्यजन्यत्वापत्तेः प्रागभावेऽव्याप्त्यापत्तेश्च। अतएवासत्त्वमुत्पत्तिव्यतिरेक इति परास्तम्। किञ्च यथातथास्तु व्यतिरेकपदार्थोऽसत्त्वपदार्थश्च सर्व्वथैव युगपदुत्पन्नविनष्टेष्वन्यथासिद्धेषु च अतिव्याप्तिः स्वस्य स्वजन्यतापत्तिश्च अन्वयदलव्यर्थतापत्तिश्च।

अत्राहुः यदधीनो यस्य समयसम्बन्धः यद्व्यतिरेकप्रयुक्तो यद्व्यतिरेकस्तदेव तज्जन्यमित्यर्थः अधीनत्वञ्च घटस्यैतत्समयसम्बन्धो

तावति समये दुरितानुत्पादस्य न साक्षान्मङ्गलजन्य इत्यदृष्टद्वारा तथा। एवं निर्व्विघ्नं समाप्यतामिति कामनया तदाचारोऽपि सङ्गच्छते। अतएव यत्र विघ्ना-

---

दण्डाधीन इत्यादिविलक्षणप्रतीतिसाक्षिकः स्वरूपसम्बन्धविशेषः, प्रयुक्तत्वमपि दण्डाभावाद्घटाभाव इत्यादिप्रतीतिसाक्षिकः स्वरूपसम्बन्धविशेषः। न चान्यतरदलवैयर्थ्यं न ह्यकारणाधीनं कार्य्यसत्त्वं अकारणाभावप्रयुक्तो वा कार्य्याभाव इति वाच्यं। लक्षणद्वये तात्पर्य्यात्। वस्तुतस्तु स्व-स्वव्याप्येतरप्रागभावनाशकसकलसमवधाने सति यद्व्यतिरेके अग्रिमक्षणे यस्य व्यतिरेकः यस्य सत्त्वे अग्रिमक्षणे यस्य सत्त्वं तत्तज्जन्यमित्यर्थः। स्वपदं कारणत्वेनाभिमतपरं, अस्ति च कश्चिद्दण्ड-दण्डव्याप्येतरघटप्रागभावनाशकसाकल्ये दण्डव्यतिरेके अग्रे घटव्यतिरेकः दण्डसत्त्वे च घटसत्त्वमिति स तत्साध्यः, रासभादौ तु नैवं, रासभ-तद्व्याप्येतरसकलघटप्रागभावनाशकस्य यावद्घटोत्पादकस्य समवधाने सति कश्चिदपि रासभव्यतिरेकेण घटव्यतिरेकासिद्धेः। अत्र प्रागभावपदं न साध्यत्वेनाभिमतप्रागभावपरं विघ्नप्रागभावादावव्याप्त्यापत्तेः प्रागभावस्य प्रागभावाभावात्। न वा यत्किञ्चित्प्रागभावपरं उदासीनेऽप्यतिव्याप्तेः घटसामग्र्यभावस्थले पटप्रागभावनाशकसकलसमधाने उदासीनव्यतिरेकेणापि घटव्यतिरेकात्। न वा प्रागभावसामान्यपरम्, असम्भवात् कुत्रापि तन्नाशकसकलसमवधानाभावात्। किन्तु साध्यत्वेनाभिमतं यत्तदितरतदीयभिन्नप्रागभावान्यप्रागभावपरं घटादिस्थले साध्यत्वाभिमतो घटादिस्तदितरस्तदीयभिन्नप्रागभावः पटादिप्राग-

भावः स्वतः सिद्धः तच्च मङ्गलस्याकिञ्चित्करत्वेन वेदाप्रामाण्यमिति निरस्तम् । अनागतविघ्नाभावस्य[१]

भावः तदन्यो घटप्रागभाव एव, विघ्नप्रागभावस्थले तु साध्यत्वाभिमतो विघ्नप्रागभावस्तदितरस्तदीयभिन्नप्रागभावः पटादिप्रागभावः तदन्यप्रागभावो विघ्नप्रागभाव एव। यद्वा साध्यत्वाभिमतं यत्तन्निष्ठत्व-तन्निरूपितत्वयोरन्यतराश्रयस्य प्रतियोगित्वस्य निरूपको यः प्रागभावस्तत्परं घटादिस्थले साध्यत्वाभिमतो घटादिः तन्निष्ठत्व-तन्निरूपितत्वयोरन्यतराश्रयप्रतियोगित्वं घटादिनिष्ठप्रतियोगित्वमेव तन्निरूपकप्रागभावो घटादिप्रागभावः। विघ्नप्रागभावस्थले तु साध्यत्वाभिमतो विघ्नप्रागभावस्तन्निष्ठत्व-तन्निरूपितत्वयोरन्यतराश्रयप्रतियोगित्वं विघ्नप्रागभावनिरूपितप्रतियोगित्वमेव तन्निरूपकप्रागभावो विघ्नप्रागभाव एव। घटप्रागभावनाशकसकलसमवधाने दण्डव्यतिरेक एवासिद्धः दण्डस्यापि यावन्मध्यपातित्वादतः स्वेतरेति घटप्रागभावनाशकचक्रभ्रम्यादिरूपदण्डव्यापारचक्रादिसकलकारणसमवधाने दण्डव्यतिरेके घटव्यतिरेकोऽसिद्धः भ्रम्यादिसत्त्वे दण्डासत्त्वेप्यवश्यं घटोत्पत्तेरतः स्वव्याप्येतरेति। न च मङ्गल-तद्व्याप्येतरविघ्नप्रागभावनाशकसकलसमवधाने मङ्गलसत्त्वे इति विरुद्धं मङ्गलाभावस्यापि विघ्नप्रागभावनाशकयावन्मध्यपातित्वात् मङ्गलस्य विघ्नप्रतिबन्धकतया तदभावस्य विघ्नोत्पादकत्वेन तत्प्रागभावनाशकत्वादिति वाच्यं स्वाभावेतरत्वेनापि तद्विशेषणात् मङ्गल-तद्व्याप्य-तदभावेतरविघ्न-

---

(१) अनागतविघ्नानुत्पादस्येति ख०। अनागतविघ्नप्रागभावस्येति ग०।

तथापि साध्यत्वात्। सर्व्वे विघ्नाः क्षयं यान्तीति यत्र विनायकस्तवपाठादौ श्रुतमस्ति तत्र तत एव

प्रागभावनाशकसकलसमवधानदशायां मङ्गलव्यतिरेके विघ्नप्रागभावव्यतिरेको विरुद्धः विघ्नप्रागभावस्यापि विघ्नप्रागभावनाशकयावन्मध्यपातित्वात्। एवं तादृशप्रागभावनाशकसकलसमवधानदशायां दण्डसत्त्वे घटसत्त्वमपि विरुद्धं घटप्रागभावस्यापि घटप्रागभावनाशकयावदन्तर्गतत्वादतोऽग्रिमक्षण इति, अन्वयदलमात्रोपादाने उदासीनजन्यतापि घटे स्यात् घटप्रागभावनाशकसकलसमवधाने उदासीनसत्त्वेपि घटसत्त्वादतो व्यतिरेकदलं, व्यतिरेकदलमात्रोपादाने रासभादिसाध्यत्वमपि विघ्नप्रागभावे स्यात् विघ्नप्रागभावनाशकसकलसमवधाने रासभव्यतिरेके सति तदनन्तरं विघ्नोत्पादेन तत्प्रागभावव्यतिरेकावश्यम्भावात् अन्वयदलोपादानं तदुपादाने च यथोक्तसकलसमवधाने रासभसत्त्वेपि विघ्नस्यैवोत्पादेन विघ्नप्रागभावासत्त्वान्नातिप्रसङ्गः। न च घटादेर्दण्डावयव-चक्रावयवादिजन्यत्वापत्तिरिति वाच्यं। अनन्यथासिद्धयद्व्यतिरेक इति विवक्षितत्वात्। इदञ्चानित्यानां जन्यताया लक्षणमतो घटादेर्नेश्वरबुद्ध्याद्यजन्यत्वापत्तिरिति सङ्क्षेपः।

ननु यस्मिन् सत्यग्रिमक्षणे यस्योत्पत्तिः यद्व्यतिरेके चानुत्पत्तिः तत्तज्जन्यमित्येव जन्यतालक्षणं न तु यथोक्तं तथा च विघ्नप्रागभावस्योत्पत्तिविरहात् कथं मङ्गलजन्यत्वमित्यत आह, 'न त्विति, 'असतः सत्त्वं' असतः सत्त्वघटितं, उत्पत्तिघटितमिति यावत्। विघ्न-

प्रमत्तानुष्ठितसमाप्तेः अनादौ संसारेऽवश्यं तदाचारात् तथा च तेन समं मङ्गलस्य विकल्प एव। यच्च साङ्गे मङ्गले सत्यपि न फलं तत्र विघ्नभूयस्त्वादिति।

प्रागभावेऽन्वयदलं सङ्गमयति, 'अस्ति चेति, 'विघ्नकारणेति, 'विघ्नकारणं' मङ्गलप्रागभावः, तद्ध्वंसो मङ्गलं तस्मिन् सतीत्यर्थः। 'तथात्वं' सत्त्वं, 'तावति समयइति, आरम्भानन्तरं यावता कालेन समाप्तिः तावत्समयवृत्तित्वविशिष्टविघ्नप्रागभावस्येत्यर्थः। 'न साक्षादिति, मङ्गलस्याशुतरविनाशित्वेन तावत्कालानवस्थायित्वादिति भावः। 'तथा' विघ्नसंसर्गाभावस्य द्वारता। नन्वदृष्टाभ्युपगमे तदेव साक्षात् समाप्तिजनकमस्तु किं विघ्नसंसर्गाभावस्य द्वारत्वेनेत्यत आह, 'एवमिति संसर्गाभावस्य द्वारत्वेनेत्यर्थः। 'निर्व्विघ्नमिति, 'इतिकामनया' इत्युद्दिश्य, 'आचारोपि' मङ्गले शिष्टप्रवृत्तिरपि, तथा च विघ्नसंसर्गाभावविशिष्टसमाप्त्युद्देश्यकमङ्गलगोचरशिष्टप्रवृत्तिरपीत्यर्थः। शिष्टत्वं भ्रमाजन्यत्वं, 'सङ्गच्छत इति, अन्यथा विघ्नसंसर्गाभावस्य मङ्गलाजन्यत्वे विशिष्टसमाप्त्युद्देश्यकप्रवृत्तौ विशेषणीभूतविघ्नसंसर्गाभावस्याप्युद्देश्यतया तत्प्रवृत्तेर्नियमतोऽशिष्टत्वापत्तेः तदुद्देश्यकतत्प्रवृत्तौ तत्साधनताज्ञानस्य हेतुतया भ्रमरूपस्य विघ्नसंसर्गाभावसाधनताज्ञानस्य तत्र हेतुत्वादिति भावः। ननु तथापि विघ्नध्वंस एव व्यापारोऽस्तु किमजन्यस्य विघ्नप्रागभावस्य व्यापारत्वेन विशिष्टसमाप्त्युद्देश्यकप्रवृत्तौ विघ्नप्रागभावस्योद्देश्यत्वे मानाभावादित्यत आह, 'अतएवेति यत एव विघ्नप्रागभावस्यापि व्यापारत्वम् अतएवेत्यर्थः।

तत्र। विघ्नानुत्पादस्य व्यापारत्वे मानाभावात् संसर्गाभावत्वेन हेतुत्वात्। तथैव व्यापारत्वं तच्च प्राग-

---

'अकिञ्चित्करत्वेन' विघ्नसंसर्गाभावरूपव्यापारानुपधायकत्वेन, 'वेदाप्रामाण्यमिति विशेषणीभूतविघ्नसंसर्गाभावस्यापि मङ्गले कारणताग्राहकस्य "निर्व्विघ्नसमाप्तिकामो मङ्गलमाचरेत्" इति मङ्गले विशिष्टसमाप्तिसाधनताबोधकवेदस्याप्रामाण्यमित्यर्थः। यद्यपि फलोपधायकत्वं न वेदार्थः किन्तु स्वरूपयोग्यत्वं तच्च क्वचित् फलानुपधानेपि सम्भवति कुतो वेदस्याप्रामाण्यं, तथापि साङ्गवेदबोधितकर्म्मत्वव्यापकं फलोपधानमतस्तदभावेन साङ्गे तस्मिन् साङ्गवेदबोधितकर्म्मत्वाभावः सिध्यन् तद्बोधकविधेर्व्वेदत्वाभावमादाय सिध्यति, वेदत्वाभावः सिध्यन् शब्द-तदुपजीविप्रमाणातिरिक्तप्रमाणजन्यप्रमित्यविषयार्थके तस्मिन् प्रमाणत्वाभावमादायैव पर्य्यवस्यतीतिक्रमेण वेदस्याप्रामाण्यमितिभावः। 'अनागतविघ्नाभावस्य'(१) अनागतविघ्नप्रागभावोपधायकत्वस्य, 'तथापि' मङ्गलेपि, 'साध्यत्वात्' वेदबोधितत्वात्। ननु मङ्गलजन्यापूर्व्वस्य स्वोत्पत्त्यवच्छेदकजातीयत्वसम्बन्धेन मङ्गलकर्तृशरीरनिष्ठतयैव कारणत्वं वाच्यम् अन्यथा समवायसम्बन्धेनात्मनिष्ठतया कारणत्वे जन्मान्तरीयग्रन्थसमाप्तिमुद्दिश्यापि मङ्गले शिष्टप्रवृत्त्यापत्तेः तथा च प्रमत्तशरीरानुष्ठितसमाप्तिः कथं स्यात् तच्छरीरे तेन सम्बन्धेन मङ्गलजन्यापूर्व्वविरहादित्यत आह, 'सर्व्वे

---

(१) अनागतविघ्नप्रागभावस्येति ग०।

भावेप्यस्तीति चेत्। न। अत्यन्ताभावस्यापि व्यापारत्वापत्तेः। स्वतः सिद्धस्य न हेतुत्वं यदि तदा प्रागभावेपि तुल्यम्। किञ्च यच्च मङ्गलं न तत्र नियमेन विघ्नकारणमस्ति, येन तन्नाशद्वारा प्रागभावस्य सा-

---

विघ्ना इति, 'पाठः' तदनुकूलकण्ठाभिघातादिः, 'तत एव' तज्जन्यापूर्व्वत एव, 'तदाचारात्' जन्मान्तरे तदाचरणात्। नन्वेवं यथोक्तसम्बन्धेन मङ्गलजन्यादृष्टं व्यभिचार्य्येवेत्यत आह, 'तथा चेति, 'मङ्गलस्य' मङ्गलजन्यापूर्व्वस्य, 'विकल्प एवेति मङ्गलनाश्यतावच्छेदकवैजात्याक्रान्तविघ्नध्वंसीयसमाप्तिं प्रति मङ्गलजन्यापूर्व्वं हेतुः, तादृशध्वंसीयेतरसमाप्तिं प्रति च विनायकस्तवपाठादिजन्यमपूर्व्वं हेतुः, कारणत्वञ्च व्रीहि-यवकरणकयागवत् परस्पराभावविशिष्टत्वेन तेन नोभयोरनुष्ठाने परस्परविरुद्धतत्कार्य्यद्वयप्रसङ्ग इत्यर्थः। न च विनायकस्तवपाठादिजन्यापूर्व्वस्य सामान्यतः समाप्तिमात्रं प्रत्येव हेतुत्वमस्तु सर्व्वत्रान्ततो जन्मान्तरीयस्यैव तस्य सुवचत्वात् एवञ्च व्रीहि-यववत् परस्पराभावविशिष्टत्वेन कारणत्वानभ्युपगमेपि न क्षतिरिति वाच्यं। सर्व्वत्र विनायकादिस्तवपाठादिजन्यापूर्व्वकल्पने गौरवात् फलमुखगौरवस्यापि दोषत्वादिति भावः। समाप्तिं प्रत्यन्वयव्यभिचारमुद्धरति, 'यच्चेति, 'साङ्गे' सकलवैदिकाङ्गसम्पन्ने, 'न फलं' न समाप्तिः, 'विघ्नभूयस्त्वात्' भूयोजातीयविघ्नसत्त्वात्, यन्मङ्गलं कृतं तन्नाश्यजातीयविघ्नसत्त्वादिति यावत्। नति-स्तुत्यादिभेदेन मङ्गलस्य विभिन्नतया मङ्गलत्वस्य सर्व्वसाधारणस्यैकस्य दुर्व्वचतया परस्परव्यावृत्तविघ्ननिष्ठवैजात्यानामेव

ध्यत्वम्। एवमपि यत्र विघ्नानुत्पादेऽपि स्वतः सिद्धस्तत्र मङ्गलमकिञ्चित्करमेव, विघ्नध्वंसानुत्पादयोरारब्धनिर्व्वाहकालावस्थायिनोर्मङ्गलादेवोत्पत्तेर्न तदर्थ-

---

प्रत्येकं नाश्यतावच्छेदकत्वादिति भावः। न चैवं कारणान्तराभावेन कश्चित् फलानुपधाने समाप्तिसाधनताबोधकवेदस्योक्तक्रमेणाप्रामाण्यसिद्धिप्रसङ्गः(१) इति वाच्यम्। समाप्तिजनने विघ्नसामान्याभावस्याप्यङ्गतया साङ्गत्वाभावादेव साङ्गवेदबोधितकर्म्मत्वाभावसिद्धिसम्भवेनाप्रामाण्यासिद्धेरिति हृदयम्।

प्राञ्चस्तु 'विघ्नभूयस्त्वादित्यस्य कृतमङ्गलमपेक्ष्य विघ्नानां भूयस्त्वादित्यर्थः। तथा च विघ्नसमसङ्ख्यमङ्गलत्वेन विघ्ननाशकतया कृतमङ्गलतत्समसङ्ख्यविघ्ननाशेऽपि विघ्नान्तरसत्त्वान्न समाप्तिः, मङ्गलस्य च शक्तिविशेषसम्बन्धेन मङ्गलपदवाच्यं विघ्नत्वञ्च मङ्गलनाश्यतावच्छेदकतया सिद्धा नति-स्तुत्यादिनाश्यसकलादृष्टसाधारण्येकैव जातिरितिभावः इत्याहुः। तदसत्। सामान्यतो विघ्नसमसङ्ख्यमङ्गलत्वेन नाशकत्वेप्येकमङ्गलतः सर्व्वविघ्ननाशस्य दुर्व्वारत्वात् एकमङ्गलस्याप्येकविघ्नसमसङ्ख्यत्वात्। न चैकविघ्ननाशं प्रति एकमङ्गलत्वेन, विघ्नद्वयनाशं प्रति मङ्गलद्वयत्वेन विघ्नत्रयनाशं प्रति मङ्गलत्रयत्वेनेत्यादि प्रातिस्विकरूपेण नाश्य-नाशकभाव इति वाच्यं। तथापि भूयोविघ्नस्थले एक-द्व्यादिमङ्गलतः एक-द्व्यादिविघ्ननाशो भवन् विनिगमनाविरहेण सर्व्वेषामेव विघ्नानां नाशस्य दुर्व्वारत्वात्।

---

(१) प्रामाण्यासिद्धिप्रसङ्ग इति ख०।

महदृष्टद्वारता। मङ्गलस्य विकल्पेनान्वये शिष्टैर्नियमतो मङ्गलानुष्ठानं न स्यादित्युक्तम्। किञ्च प्रधानत्वे साङ्ग-मङ्गलमात्रं[१] न समाप्तिहेतुः तस्मिन् सत्यपि तदभा-

केचित्तु मङ्गलत्वेन विघ्नत्वेनैव नाश्य-नाशकभावः, कार्य्य-कारण-भावस्तु[२] एकविघ्नस्थलीयसमाप्तौ एकमङ्गलत्वेन, विघ्नद्वयस्थलीय-समाप्तौ मङ्गलद्वयत्वेन, विघ्नत्रयस्थलीयसमाप्तौ मङ्गलत्रयत्वेनेत्यादि-प्रातिस्विकरूपेण, विघ्नस्थलीयत्वञ्च प्राङ्निरुक्तमेव, तेन कृतेपि मङ्गले विघ्नस्य ततो भूयस्त्वान्न सिद्धिः[३] इत्याहुः। तदप्यसत्। विघ्नभूयस्त्वेपि एक-द्व्यादिमङ्गलादेक-द्व्यादिविघ्नस्थलीयसमाप्त्यापत्तेर्दुर्व्वारत्वात् कारणसत्त्वादिति कृतं पल्लवितेन।

'विघ्नानुत्पादस्येति विघ्नप्रागभावस्येत्यर्थः। 'व्यापारत्वे' मङ्गल-जन्यत्वे, 'मानाभावादिति विघ्नप्रागभावं प्रति मङ्गलस्यानन्यथा-सिद्धत्वे मानाभावात्। यथोक्तजन्यताया अपि अनन्यथासिद्ध-त्वघटितत्वात् यथोक्तरूपमपेक्ष्य लाघवेन तत्कारणत्वस्यैव तज्ज-न्यतात्मकत्वाच। न च यत्र स्वतः सिद्धो विघ्नाभावस्तत्रत्यमङ्ग-लपक्षकफलोपधायकाभावहेतुकसाङ्गवेदबोधितकर्म्मत्वाभावानुमानादुप-क्रमेण "निर्व्विघ्नसमाप्तिकामो मङ्गलमाचरेत्" इतिवेदाप्रामाण्य-सिद्धिप्रसङ्ग एव विघ्नप्रागभावस्य मङ्गलजन्यत्वे मानम्, अतएव

(१) मङ्गलमात्रमिति ख०।

(२) मङ्गल-समाप्त्योरित्यादिः।

(३) न समाप्तिरिति क०।

वात्। प्रचितं तथेति चेत्। न। अप्रचितादपि फलसत्त्वात्[१]। नोभयम् अननुगमात्। गुरुकर्म्मारम्भे प्रचितमल्पकर्म्मारम्भेऽल्पमिति चेत्। न। क्वचित्ताद्दशादपि

यथोक्तरूपस्य गुरुत्वेपि तदेव जन्यत्वं प्रामाणिकगौरवस्यादोषत्वादिति वाच्यं। विघ्नध्वंसजनने विघ्नस्याप्यङ्गतया साङ्गत्वाभावादेव तत्र साङ्गवेदबोधितकर्मत्वाभावसिद्धि सम्भवेनाप्रामाण्यसिद्धिप्रसङ्गविरहात्। अन्यथा नास्तिकेपि यत्र कृतेपि मङ्गले न समाप्तिस्तत्र समाप्त्युपधायकत्वाभावेन वेदाप्रामाण्यसिद्धिप्रसङ्गस्य दुर्व्वारत्वात्। यत्र विघ्नस्य प्रागभावो नास्ति तत्र वेदाप्रामाण्यसिद्धिप्रसङ्गस्य दुर्व्वारत्वाच्चेति भावः।

विघ्नध्वंसस्य व्यापारतया उभयसिद्धत्वाभिमानेन प्रकृते, 'संसर्गाभावत्वेनेति विघ्नसंसर्गाभावत्वेनेत्यर्थः। 'हेतुत्वात्' मङ्गलजन्यविघ्नध्वंसस्य समाप्तौ हेतुत्वात्। 'तथैव' विघ्नसंसर्गाभावत्वेनैव, 'व्यापारत्वं' विघ्नध्वंसस्य मङ्गलजन्यत्वं, व्यापारस्य फलं प्रति येन रूपेण कारणत्वं तेनैव रूपेण करणजन्यत्वस्यौत्सर्गिकत्वात् ज्ञानसंस्कारादिस्थले तथा दृष्टत्वादिति भावः। 'तत्र' विघ्नसंसर्गाभावत्वस्य, 'अत्यन्ताभावस्यापीति, तत्रापि विघ्नसंसर्गाभावत्वसत्त्वादिति भावः। 'स्वतःसिद्धस्येति नित्यस्येत्यर्थः, 'तस्य' विघ्नात्यन्ताभावस्य,[२] 'हेतुत्वं'

(१) फलनिष्पत्तेरिति ख०

(२) कस्मिंश्चिन्मूले 'स्वतःसिद्धस्य' इत्यनन्तरं 'तस्य' इत्यधिकपाठो वर्त्तते तादृशमूलमवलम्ब्यैव टीकाकृता 'तस्य' इति पाठो धृतः विघ्नात्यन्ताभावस्येति व्याख्यातञ्च। मदवलम्बितमूलादर्शपुस्तकद्वये स च पाठो नास्ति अतस्तादृशः पाठो मूले मया नोद्धृतः इति।

फलासत्त्वात् वैपरीत्येऽपि फलसत्त्वाच्च। एतेन बहुविघ्नशङ्कया बहुतरं अल्पविघ्नशङ्कया अल्पतरञ्च हेतुतादृशाचारेण तादृशश्रुत्युन्नयनादिति[१] निरस्तम्।

समाप्तिहेतुत्वमेव, न तु यथोक्तमङ्गलजन्यत्वं अतो न व्यापारत्वमितिभावः। 'प्रागभावेऽपि तुल्यमिति विघ्नप्रागभावस्यापि समाप्तिहेतुत्वमेव न तु यथोक्तमङ्गलजन्यत्वं तत्र मङ्गलस्यानन्यथासिद्धत्वे मानाभावात् यथोक्तजन्यतायामपि अनन्यथासिद्धत्वप्रवेशस्यावश्यकत्वादित्यर्थः।

ननु यथा प्रत्यवायानुत्पादमुद्दिश्य सन्ध्यावन्दनादौ शिष्टप्रवृत्तेः प्रत्यवायानुत्पादस्य सन्ध्यावन्दनादिजन्यत्व तथा विघ्नानुत्पादमुद्दिश्यापि मङ्गले शिष्टप्रवृत्तेः विघ्नप्रागभावस्यापि मङ्गलजन्यत्वम् आवश्यकम् अतएव यथोक्तरूपस्य गुरुत्वेऽपि तदेव जन्यत्वं प्रामाणिकगौरवस्यादोषत्वादित्यनुशयादाह, 'किञ्चेति। 'विघ्नकारणं' मङ्गलाभावेतरविघ्नोत्पादककारणकलापः, मङ्गलाभावेतरविघ्नप्रागभावनाशककारणकलाप इति यावत्। 'तन्नाशद्वारेति[२] विघ्नकारणं मङ्गलजादृष्टप्रागभावः तन्नाशोऽदृष्टं तद्द्वारेत्यर्थः। 'प्रागभावस्य' विघ्नप्रागभावस्य[३] 'साध्यत्वं' सर्वत्र मङ्गलसाध्यत्वं, तथा च यन्मङ्गल-

---

(१) तादृशश्रुत्यनुमानादितीति क०।

(२) तद्ध्वंसद्वारेतीति क०, ग०, घ०, च।

(३) प्रागभावस्यापि विघ्न प्रागभावस्यापीति क०, एतेन 'प्रागभावस्यापि' इति कस्यचिन्मूलपुस्तकस्य पाठ इत्यनुमितः।

तादृशादपि प्रारिप्सितासमाप्तेः वैपरीत्येपि समाप्तेश्च बहुत्वस्य त्रि-चतुरादिभावेन अल्पत्वस्य चैक द्व्यादिरू-

व्यक्तेरनन्तरं समाप्तिपर्य्यन्तं मध्ये विघ्नप्रागभावनाशकान्तरसमवधानमेव न जातं तन्मङ्गलव्यक्तेरेवोक्तरूपजन्यत्वं न विघ्नप्रागभावस्येति भावः। ननु मास्तु तन्मङ्गलव्यक्तिजन्यत्वं विघ्नभागभावस्य किन्त्वस्ति च्छिन्नमित्यत आह 'एवमपीति एवञ्चेत्यर्थः,'विघ्नानुत्पादोपीति, अपिना विघ्नध्वंस-समुच्चयः विघ्नानुत्पादस्य स्वतःसिद्धत्वं विघ्नप्रागभावनाशकान्तराभावा-धीनत्वं विघ्नध्वंसस्य स्वतःसिद्धत्वं जन्मान्तरार्जितमङ्गलात् सिद्धत्वम्। 'अकिञ्चित्करमेव' व्यापारीभूतविघ्नसंसर्गाभावानुपधायकमेव। ननु तत्र तदनुपधायकत्वेपि न क्षतिर्वेदाप्रामाण्यसिद्धिप्रसङ्गनिरासस्य त्वदुक्त-रीत्यैव सुकरत्वादित्यस्वरसात्तावतीत्याद्युक्तं(१) दूषयति, 'विघ्नध्वंसेति, 'स्थायिनोः' स्थायित्वविशिष्टयोः, विशिष्टस्यानतिरिक्तत्वादिति भावः। 'तदर्थं' तावत्समयवृत्तित्वविशिष्टविघ्नप्रागभावार्थं। न च मङ्गलस्या-शुविनाशितया तावतां समयानां तेन जननासम्भवादपूर्व्वस्वीकार इति वाच्यं। समयानां मङ्गलजन्यत्वे मानाभावादिति भावः। ननु मङ्गलानन्तरं समाप्तिपूर्व्वं मध्ये विघ्नजनककर्म्मानुष्ठाने विघ्नोत्पत्ति-प्रतिबन्धार्थमदृष्टाभ्युपगमः मङ्गलस्याशुविनाशितया तेन तावत्-कालं साक्षाद्विघ्नोत्पत्तिप्रतिबन्धासम्भवादित्यरुचेराह, 'मङ्गलस्येति मङ्गलजन्यापूर्व्वस्येत्यर्थः, 'अन्वये' कारणत्वे, 'न स्यादिति गणेशस्तव-पाठादिजन्यादृष्टसत्त्वसम्भावनया न स्यादित्यर्थः। एकाभावविशिष्टा-

(१) 'तावति समये दुरितानुत्पादस्य' इत्यादिमूलोक्तमित्यर्थः।

पतया अननुगमेन तादृशशिष्टाचारेण तादृशश्रुत्या

परस्यैव जनकत्वादिति भावः। इदमुपलक्षणं गणेशस्तवपाठ-मङ्गलयो-रुभयोरनुष्ठानेपि समाप्तिर्दृश्यते तदपि न स्यादित्यपि बोध्यम्।

ननु गणेशस्तवपाठजन्यापूर्व्व-मङ्गलजन्यापूर्व्वयोर्न विकल्पेन कार-णत्वं किन्तु तृणारणि-मणिन्यायेन यत्र गणेशस्तवपाठ-मङ्गलयो-रनुष्ठानं तत्र मङ्गलनाश्यविघ्नस्थलीयाद्स्थलीयसमाप्तिद्वयानुत्पादस्य भूयोजातीयविघ्नसत्त्वात्। यद्वा मङ्गलजन्यापूर्व्वस्य तन्नाश्यजातीय-विघ्नस्थलीयसमाप्तित्वं कार्य्यतावच्छेदकं, गणेशस्तवपाठादिजन्यापूर्व्वस्य तत्तत्पाठादिनाश्यजातीयविघ्नस्थलीयसमाप्तित्वं, न तु मङ्गलजन्या-पूर्व्वनाश्यजातीयविघ्नस्थलीयेतरसमाप्तित्वम् अतएव उभयोरनुष्ठानेपि क्वचित् फलदर्शनं नानुपपन्नमित्यरुचेराह, 'किञ्चेति, 'प्रधानत्वे' अपूर्व्वद्वारा समाप्तिरूपप्रधानफलजनकत्वे, 'तस्मिन् सत्यपीति सर्व्व-जातीयेषु एकैकमङ्गलेषु कृतेष्वपीत्यर्थः, 'तदभावात्' समाप्तेरभा-वात्। तथा च तत्र समाप्त्यापत्तिरिति भावः। न च तत्र मङ्गला-नन्तरोत्पन्नविघ्नेन प्रतिबन्धान्न समाप्त्युदय इति वाच्यं। मङ्गलज-न्यादृष्टस्य विघ्नप्रतिबन्धकतया मङ्गलानन्तरं समाप्तिपर्य्यन्तं विघ्ना-न्तरोत्पत्तेरसम्भवादिति हृदयं। 'प्रचितमिति बहुतरं तत्तज्जातीय-मङ्गलमित्यर्थः, 'फलमत्त्वात्' फलोदयात्, प्रचितस्यैव हेतुत्वे ततः फलानुदयः स्यादितिभावः। अप्रचितात् फलानुदयप्रसङ्गमुद्धरति, 'नोभयमिति 'उभयं' प्रचितमप्रचितञ्च, 'अननुगमादिति यत्र सर्व्वजातीयेषु एकैकमङ्गलेषु कृतेष्वपि न समाप्तिः तत्स्थलीयाप्रचि-

बोधयितुमशक्यत्वाच्च । तस्मान्मङ्गलं नाङ्गं न वा प्रधानमिति पूर्व्वपक्षसंक्षेपः ।

तनमस्कारादिव्याहत्तस्य प्रचितमङ्गलनिष्ठानुगतकारणतावच्छेदकस्याभावादित्यर्थः । तथा च तत्र कार्य्योपपत्तितादवस्थ्यमिति भावः । इदमुपलक्षणं यत्राप्रचितात् समाप्तिस्तत्र प्रचितस्य व्यतिरेकव्यभिचार इत्यपि बोध्यम् ।

'गुरुकर्म्मारम्भे' गुरुतरारब्धकर्म्मसमाप्तौ, 'प्रचितं' बहुतरं नमस्कारादिकमित्यर्थः । 'अल्पकर्म्मारम्भे' अल्पतरारब्धकर्म्मसमाप्तौ, 'अल्पं' नमस्कारत्रयाभावविशिष्टनमस्कारादिकं, 'तादृशादपीति, यत्र सर्व्वजातीयान्येव त्रीणि त्रीणि मङ्गलानि कृतानि तत्रापि गुरुकर्म्मासमाप्तेर्यत्र सर्व्वजातीयान्येव एकैकमङ्गलानि कृतानि तत्राप्यल्पतरकर्म्मसमाप्तेश्चेत्यर्थः । 'वैपरीत्येपीति, प्रचितादप्यल्पतरकर्म्मसमाप्तेरप्रचितादपि गुरुतरकर्म्मसमाप्तेश्चेत्यर्थः । 'बहुविघ्नेति शङ्कितबहुतरविघ्नसमाप्तौ बहुतरं शङ्किताल्पतरविघ्नसमाप्तौ अल्पतरं मङ्गलं हेतुरित्यर्थः । 'तादृशश्रुतीति अल्पविघ्नज्ञानवान् अल्पमङ्गलं बहुतरविघ्नज्ञानवान् बहुतरमङ्गलमाचरेदित्याकारकश्रुतीत्यर्थः । 'तादृशादपीति बहुतरमङ्गले कृतेपि शङ्कितबहुतरविघ्नसमाप्तेरनुदयात् अल्पतरमङ्गले कृतेपि शङ्किताल्पतरविघ्नसमाप्तेरनुदयादित्यर्थः । 'वैपरीत्येपीति बहुतरविघ्नज्ञानवतोप्यल्पमङ्गलात् समाप्तेः अल्पविघ्नज्ञानवतोपि बहुतरमङ्गलात् समाप्तेरित्यर्थः । तथा च व्यतिरेकव्यभिचार इति भावः । 'त्रि-चतुरादिभावेनेति त्रित्व-चतुष्ट्वादिरूपत्वेनेत्यर्थः,

सिद्धान्तस्तु। आरब्धकर्म्मसमाप्तौ मङ्गलं नाङ्गं न वा प्रधानमहेतुत्वात्। किन्तु प्रायश्चित्तवत् प्रधानं विघ्नध्वंसः फलम्। आरब्धकर्म्मनिर्व्वाहे विघ्नो माभूदिति-कामनया तदनुष्ठानात् विघ्नसंशये निश्चये वा शिष्टानां

'एक-द्व्यादिरूपतया' एकत्व-द्वित्वरूपतया। न च द्वित्वैकत्वभिन्न-सङ्ख्यात्वेन त्रित्वत्वेन वाऽनुगमः चतुरादिस्थलेऽपि त्रयाणां सत्त्वादिति वाच्यं। मङ्गलस्याद्रव्यतया तद्वृत्तित्रित्वादेः सङ्ख्यानात्मकत्वेन तद्वृत्ति-त्रित्वत्वादेरप्यननुगतत्वादिति भावः। 'नाङ्गं न वा प्रधानमिति नारब्ध-कर्म्मजन्यसमाप्तिजनकं न वा तदजन्यतदुत्पत्तिजनकमित्यर्थः।

इति मङ्गलवादपूर्व्वपक्षरहस्यम्।

अथ मङ्गलवादसिद्धान्तरहस्यं।

'आरब्धकर्म्मसमाप्ताविति आरब्धकर्म्मजन्यसमाप्तावित्यर्थः। 'नाङ्गं' नारब्धकर्म्मजन्यसमाप्तेरुपधायकं, 'न वा प्रधानमिति न वा आरब्ध-कर्म्माजन्यारब्धकर्म्मोत्पत्तेरुपधायकमित्यर्थः। 'अहेतुत्वादिति मङ्गले तदुभयस्वरूपयोग्यत्वस्यैवाभावादित्यर्थः। 'प्रधानमिति आरब्धकर्म्मा-जन्यफलान्तरजनकमित्यर्थः। तदेव फलान्तरमाह, 'विघ्नध्वंस इति। ननु तस्य मङ्गलफलत्वे किं मानमित्यत आह, 'आरब्धकर्म्मनिर्व्वाह इति 'निर्व्वाहः' समाप्तिः, प्रतिबन्धकत्वं सप्तम्यर्थः, अन्वयश्चास्य विघ्न इत्यनेन, 'माभूत्' मा वर्त्ततां, यथाश्रुते विघ्नप्रागभावस्यैवो-

तदाचरणाद्विघ्नाभावस्याकाङ्क्षितत्वाच्च । यदि च निर्व्विघ्नं समाप्यतामितिकामनया तदाचरणं तदापि नागृहीतविशेषणान्यायेनाहं स्वर्गी स्यामित्यत्र स्वर्ग-

---

द्देश्यत्वलाभात् । 'इतिकामनया' इत्युद्दिश्य, 'तदनुष्ठानादिति मत्र शिष्टप्रवृत्तेरित्यर्थः । तथा च मङ्गलं विघ्नध्वंसजनकं विघ्नध्वंसोद्देश्यक-शिष्टप्रवृत्तिविषयत्वादित्यनुमानमेव मानं शिष्टत्वं भ्रमाजन्यत्वं । न चेदमप्रयोजकं, तदुद्देश्यकप्रवृत्तौ तत्साधनताज्ञानस्य हेतुत्वादिति भावः ।

केचित्तु 'इतिकामनयेति यथाश्रुतमूलानुरोधात् मङ्गलं विघ्न-ध्वंसजनकं विघ्नध्वंसकामनाजन्यशिष्टप्रवृत्तिविषयत्वादित्यनुमानं मान-मित्याहुः । तदसत् । विघ्नध्वंस-स्वर्गोभयोद्देश्यकसमूहालम्बनफलका-मनासहकृतस्वर्गसाधनतामात्रविषयकप्रमाजन्यप्रवृत्तिविषये यागादौ व्यभिचारापत्तेरिति ध्येयं ।

हेत्वन्तरमाह, 'विघ्नसंशयेति, तथा च मङ्गलं विघ्नध्वंसजनकं विघ्नाजनकत्वे सति(१) विघ्नज्ञानवतामेव शिष्टप्रवृत्तिविषयत्वादित्य-नुमेयमितिभावः । हेत्वन्तरमप्याह, 'विघ्नाभावस्येति, 'आकाङ्क्षित-त्वात्' मङ्गलगोचरकामनायाः फलत्वेनोद्देश्यत्वात्, तथा च मङ्गलं विघ्नध्वंसजनकं विघ्नध्वंसोद्देश्यकशिष्टकामनाविषयत्वादित्यनुमेयं । शिष्टत्वं भ्रमाजन्यत्वं । न चेदमप्रयोजकं, तदुद्देश्यककामनां प्रति तत्सा-धनताज्ञानस्य हेतुत्वादिति भावः । नन्वेवं निर्व्विघ्नं समाप्यतामित्यु-

---

(१) विघ्नकारणे व्यभिचारवारणाय सत्यन्तं ।

इव विघ्नाभाव एव फलम् । न समाप्तिरुभयतोव्यभिचा-
रात् । समाप्तिस्तु विघ्नरूपप्रतिबन्धकाभावे सति लोका-
वगतस्वकारणादेव । प्रचिताप्रचितदेवतास्तुत्यादिसा-

द्दिश्यापि मङ्गले शिष्टप्रवृत्तेः समाप्तेरपि फलत्वमावश्यकं तदुद्देश्य-
कप्रवृत्तौ तत्साधनताज्ञानस्य, हेतुत्वादित्यत आह, 'यदि' चेति, 'इतिकामनया' इत्युद्दिश्य, 'तदाचरणं' तत्र शिष्टप्रवृत्तिः, 'नागृहीत-
विशेषणान्यायेन' नागृहीतविशेषणा बुद्धिर्विशेष्ये चोपजायतइतिन्या-
येन, भवन्मतेपि विघ्नध्वंसस्य तत्रोद्देश्यतावश्यकतयेति शेषः । 'इत्यत्र' इत्याकारकोद्देश्यताशालियागादिगोचरप्रवृत्तौ, 'स्वर्गइव' स्ववृत्तित्वो-
पलक्षितस्वर्गइव, 'विघ्नाभाव एव फलं' समाप्त्यव्यवहितपूर्व्ववर्त्तित्वोप-
लक्षितविघ्नध्वंस एव तादृशप्रवृत्तावुद्देश्यः, 'उभयतो व्यभिचारादिति
शरीरनिष्ठसम्बन्धेनात्मनिष्ठसम्बन्धेन च मङ्गलस्य समाप्तिं प्रति व्यति-
रेकव्यभिचारादित्यर्थः । मङ्गलस्याशुविनाशितया[१]चिरकालानन्तर-
भाविसमाप्त्यव्यवहितपूर्व्वं तदनवस्थानात् । न च विघ्नध्वंसद्वारा तस्य
हेतुत्वान्न व्यभिचार इति वाच्यं । तथा सति जन्मान्तरीयग्रन्थ-
समाप्तिमुद्दिश्यापि तत्र शिष्टप्रवृत्तिप्रसङ्ग इत्युक्तत्वात् । न च तज्जन्य-
विघ्नध्वंसस्य स्वोत्पत्त्यवच्छेदकजातीयत्वसम्बन्धेन शरीरनिष्ठतया हेतु-
त्वान्नायमतिप्रसङ्ग इति वाच्यं । तर्हि तज्जन्यविघ्नध्वंसस्य प्रमत्तानु-
ष्ठितसमाप्तावेव व्यभिचारात् विघ्नस्थलीयत्वस्योक्तक्रमेण कार्य्य-

---

(१) व्यतिरेकव्यभिचारमाह मङ्गलस्येत्यादि ।

ङ्गमङ्गलात् प्रत्येकं विघ्नध्वंसो भवत्येव । अतो वैदिके फलनिश्चयान्मङ्गले प्रवृत्तिः । न च वेदाप्रामाण्यम् । समाप्त्यभावस्य क्वचित् प्राचीनविघ्नभूयस्त्वात् क्वचिन्मङ्ग-

तावच्छेदकत्वाम्भवादिति भावः । एतच्चोपलक्षणं समाप्तित्वस्य विघ्नध्वंसत्वापेक्षया गुरुत्वात् अनुगतस्य तस्य दुर्व्वचत्वाच्च । विघ्न-ध्वंसत्वन्तु विजातीयादृष्टध्वंसत्वमेव वैजात्यञ्च प्रायश्चित्तादिनाश्यादृष्ट-व्यावृत्तो नत्यादिनाश्यतावच्छेदकतया सिद्धोऽदृष्टनिष्ठो जातिवि-शेषः नत्यादिभेदेन कार्य्य-कारणभावश्चिन्त्यत एव[१] अतएव नाना-विधमङ्गलाचरणं नानाविधविघ्नशङ्कया । न चैवमेकनमस्कारादित एव तत्पूर्व्वोत्पन्नतन्नाश्यसजातीयसकलविघ्ननाशापत्तिरिति वाच्यम् । दृष्टत्वात् । एकजातीयनानामङ्गलाचरणन्तु पूर्व्वमङ्गलस्याङ्गवैगुण्यश-ङ्कया । किञ्च समाप्तौ मङ्गलस्य हेतुत्वेपि विघ्नध्वंसं प्रति हेतुत्वमावश्यकं तथा चावश्यकत्वात् तदेवास्तु किं समाप्तिहेतुत्वेन । न च व्यापारेण व्यापारिणो नान्यथासिद्धिरिति वाच्यम् । विघ्नस्य प्रतिबन्धकतया तदत्यन्ताभावस्यैव समाप्तिहेतुत्वेन विघ्नध्वंसे व्यापारत्वस्यैवासिद्धेः । विघ्नध्वंसस्यापि समाप्तौ पृथक् कारणत्वकल्पने च महागौरवापत्तेः । समाप्तौ विघ्नध्वंस-तत्सामान्यात्यन्ताभाव-मङ्गलानां त्रयाणां कारण-त्वस्य विघ्नध्वंसं प्रति मङ्गलकारणत्वस्य च कल्पनीयत्वादित्यपि बोध्यम् ।

(१) ननु मङ्गलत्वस्यैकस्याभावात् नतित्वादिनैव हेतुत्वं वाच्यं । तथा च व्यभिचार इत्यत आह, नत्यादीति । तथा च सा जातिरपि भिन्नेति भावः ।

स्यानन्तरोत्पन्नविघ्नात् क्वचिल्लोकावगतकारणाभावात्। प्रारिप्सितविघ्नध्वंसस्य न मङ्गलं विना। न च प्रायश्चित्तेन शङ्कितविघ्नविनाशः। विघ्नसंशये तदनुपदेशात्।

केचित्तु 'उभयतो व्यभिचारादित्यस्य अन्वयतो व्यतिरेकतश्च मङ्गलस्य समाप्तिं प्रति व्यभिचारित्वादित्यर्थ इत्याहुः।

नन्वेवं समाप्तिः किंहेतुका स्यादित्यत आह, 'समाप्तिस्त्विति। अत्र आचार्य्यानुयायिनः विघ्नध्वंसमिव समाप्तिर्मे जायतामिति समाप्तिमुद्दिश्यापि मङ्गले शिष्टप्रवृत्तः विघ्नध्वंसवत् समाप्तिरपि मङ्गलफलं। न च समाप्तिमुद्दिश्य मङ्गलाचरणमेवासिद्धमिति वाच्यम्। असङ्ख्यसंसारे मणिकृन्मतेऽपि अवश्यं केनचित्तामुद्दिश्य मङ्गलानुष्ठानात्। न च तामुद्दिश्य मङ्गलाचरणं मङ्गले समाप्तिसाधनताभ्रमजन्यं लाघवात् तथैव कल्पनादिति वाच्यम्। तर्हि विघ्नध्वंसमुद्दिश्य मङ्गलाचरणमपि भ्रमजन्यं लाघवादिति निष्फलमेव मङ्गलाचरणमिति जितं चार्व्वाकैः। यदि च तदाचारस्य भ्रमाजन्यत्वं तज्जनकविघ्नध्वंसजनकताज्ञानस्य भ्रमेतरत्वस्यानुभवसिद्धमिति गौरवं प्रामाणिकं तदा प्रकृतेऽपि तुल्यं। न च मङ्गलं न साक्षात् समाप्तिहेतुरस्थिरत्वात् न वा विघ्नध्वंसद्वारा विघ्नात्यन्ताभावस्यैवं समाप्तिहेतुत्वात् अत्यन्ताभावस्तु न द्वारं अजन्यत्वात् इत्यगत्या विघ्नध्वंसजनकत्वमेव तस्येति वाच्यम्। समाप्तिहेतुतायां प्रमाणसिद्धायामगत्या अपूर्व्वस्यैव द्वारत्वकल्पनात विघ्नध्वंससम्बन्धेनैव साक्षाद्धेतुत्वस्यापि सुवचत्वाच। अन्वयव्यभिचारस्य चानुपदं

न च कामनोपाधिकर्त्तव्यत्वे नियतमनुष्ठानं न स्यादिति वाच्यं। आरब्धकर्म्मकारणप्रतिबन्धकाभावोपायत्वेनावश्यं तदनुष्ठानात्। तेन विना प्रतिबन्धकाभावे-

---

ग्रन्थकृतैव निराकरिष्यमाणत्वात्। न चैवं जन्मान्तरीयग्रन्थसमाप्तिमुद्दिश्यापि मङ्गले शिष्टप्रवृत्तिप्रसङ्ग इति वाच्यम्। इष्टत्वात् अनादिसंसारे सर्व्वैरेव जन्मान्तरीयग्रन्थसमाप्तिमुद्दिश्य केनचिन्मङ्गलाचरणात् तस्य च भ्रमजन्यत्वे मानाभावात्। न च तथापि समाप्तित्वस्यैकस्यानुगतस्याभावात् कार्य्यतावच्छेदकं दुर्व्वचमिति वाच्यम्। कारणत्वे प्रमाणसिद्धे अनायत्या अननुगतस्यैव कार्य्यतावच्छेदकत्वात्। न चैवं विघ्नसत्त्वेपि समाप्त्युत्पादापत्तिः अनादौ संसारे अवश्यं जन्मान्तरोत्पन्नविघ्नध्वंससमन्वेन मङ्गलसत्त्वादिति वाच्यम्। विघ्नस्य प्रतिबन्धकतया तत्सामान्याभावस्यापि हेतुत्वात् केवलमाचारानुरोधेनैव मङ्गलस्य हेतुत्वकल्पनादित्याहुः। तदसत्। तथा सति यदुद्दिश्य यत्क्रियते तस्यैव तद्धेतुतया चैत्यवन्दनादेरपि स्वर्गादिहेतुत्वापत्तेः तत्रापि तज्जनकीभूतज्ञानस्य भ्रमत्वमादाय विवादसम्भवादिति दिक्।

ननु मङ्गले सति यत्र समाप्त्यनुदयस्तत्र कृतेपि साङ्गमङ्गले विघ्नध्वंसानुदयादन्वयव्यभिचार इत्यत आह, 'प्रचितेति। 'प्रत्येकमिति स्तुतिनाम्नानां सर्व्वेषां स्तुतितो नाशः नत्यादिनाश्यानां नत्यादितो-नाशो भवत्येवेत्यर्थः। स्वतःसिद्धविघ्नासत्त्वस्थले च मङ्गलस्य साङ्गत्वमेव नास्ति विघ्नस्याप्यङ्गत्वात् मङ्गलकर्त्तुर्व्विघ्नासत्त्वे मानाभावाच्चेति भावः। 'अत इति, 'फलनिश्चयात्' सकलाङ्गसम्पत्तौ फलावश्यम्भाव-

ऽसति कर्म्मानुत्पत्तेः। न च प्रधानत्वे नान्यदापि तत्करणम्। नियतसमयशिष्टाचारानुमितश्रुत्या कर्म्मारम्भसमये तत्कर्त्तव्यत्वबोधनात् दर्शारम्भसमये आर-

---

निश्चयात्, 'वैदिके मङ्गले प्रवृत्तिरिति योजना, 'प्रवृत्तिः' निष्कम्पप्रवृत्तिः, 'प्राचीनविघ्नभूयस्त्वादिति प्राचीनानां विघ्नानां भूयोजातीयत्वादित्यर्थः। तथा च यन्मङ्गलं कृतं तदनाश्यजातीयसत्त्वादिति फलितम्।

ननु यत्र सर्व्वजातीयान्येव मङ्गलानि कृतानि तत्र समाप्त्यभावो न स्यादित्यत आह, 'क्वचिन्मङ्गलानन्तरेति। पापोत्पादककारणानां यत्र बाधः तत्राह, 'क्वचिल्लोकावगतेति। ननु तथापि यत्र प्रायश्चित्तादितो विघ्ननाशस्तत्र व्यतिरेकव्यभिचार इत्यत आह, 'प्रारिप्सितेति मङ्गलनाश्यजातीयविघ्ननाशस्येत्यर्थः। ननु यथा विघ्नसंशयान्मङ्गलाचरणेपि फलं एवं ब्रह्मवधादिप्रायश्चित्तेपि स्यादित्यत आह, 'न चेति नहीत्यर्थः, 'प्रायश्चित्तेन' ब्रह्मवधादिप्रायश्चित्तेन, 'शङ्कितविघ्ननाशः' शङ्कितदुरितनाशः, 'विघ्नसंशये' दुरितसंशये, 'कामनोपाधिकर्त्तव्यत्वे' विघ्नध्वंसकामनाधीनप्रवृत्तिविषयत्वे, 'नियतमनुष्ठानं न स्यादिति यस्य विघ्नज्ञानं नास्ति तस्यानुष्ठानं न स्यादित्यर्थः। अत्रेष्टापत्तिमाह, 'आरब्धकर्म्मकारणेति आरब्धकर्म्मसमाप्तिकारणस्येत्यर्थः, 'प्रतिबन्धकाभावोपायत्वेन' तत्प्रतिबन्धकध्वंसोपायत्वज्ञानेन, 'अवश्यं तदनुष्ठानादिति विघ्नज्ञानवतैवावश्यं तदनुष्ठानादित्यर्थः। ननु मङ्गलस्य समाप्तिजनकत्वे यत्र मङ्गलं न

भ्मणीयावत्। विघ्नसंसर्गाभावश्च समाप्तिहेतुः। स च क्वचित् स्वतःसिद्धः क्वचिन्मङ्गलसाध्यः। अतएव मङ्गलं

कृतं तत्र विघ्नध्वंसो मास्तु समाप्तिस्तु स्यादेवेत्यत आह, 'तेन विनेति, 'प्रतिबन्धकाभावाभावे' प्रतिबन्धकीभूतविघ्नसत्त्वे, 'प्रतिबन्धकभावे असतीति पाठेप्ययमेवार्थः(१) 'कर्म्मानुत्पत्तेः' कर्म्मासमाप्तेः। 'न चेति, 'प्रधानत्वे' विघ्नध्वंसमात्रजनकत्वे, समाप्त्यजनकत्व इति यावत्। 'अन्यदापि' कर्त्तव्यकर्म्मचिकीर्षाकालातिरिक्तकालेपि, 'तत्करणमिति, फलजनकं स्यादिति शेषः। 'नियतसमयेति तादृश-चिकीर्षाकालनियतेत्यर्थः, 'कर्म्मारम्भसमयेति कर्त्तव्यकर्म्मचिकीर्षाकाल इत्यर्थः, 'दर्शारम्भसमये' दर्शचिकीर्षासमये, तथा च मङ्गलेन विघ्नध्वंसजनने कर्त्तव्यकर्म्मप्रतिबन्धकीभूतविघ्नध्वंसगोचरेच्छादिजनन-क्रमेण मङ्गलजननद्वारा कर्त्तव्यकर्म्मचिकीर्षापयङ्गं अन्यथा समाप्तेः फलत्वेपि भ्रान्त्या फलान्तरकामनया अन्यदा कृतान्मङ्गलाद्विघ्नध्वंसो-त्पत्तेर्दुर्व्वारत्वादिति भावः। ननु भवन्मते मङ्गलस्य विघ्नध्वंसद्वारा समाप्त्यजनकत्वेपि तज्जन्यविघ्नध्वंसस्य प्रतिबन्धकाभावतया समाप्ति-कारणत्वमस्त्येव तस्य कारणत्वञ्च किं स्वोत्पत्त्यवच्छेदकत्वसम्बन्धेन फलीभूतसमाप्तिकर्तृशरीरनिष्ठतया विशेषणताविशेषसम्बन्धेन तादृ-शात्मनिष्ठतया वा, आद्ये नास्तिकादिशरीरकर्तृकसमाप्तौ व्यभिचारः, अन्त्ये जनकत्वमपेक्ष्य कारणतत्कारणसाधारणप्रयोजकत्वस्य लघुतया तादृशतत्प्रयोजकताज्ञानस्यैव तदुद्देश्यकप्रवृत्तौ हेतुत्वमते जन्मा-

---

(१) 'विघ्नाभावेऽसति' इति पाठान्तरं।

विनापि जन्मान्तरानुवर्त्तमानविघ्नात्यन्ताभावात् प्रमत्तनास्तिकानुष्ठितसमाप्तिः। न चानध्यवसायः। शङ्कितविघ्नवारणार्थं प्रवृत्तिरतो यावद्विघ्नशङ्कं तदाचरणात्।

न्तरीयग्रन्थसमाप्तिमुद्दिश्यापि मङ्गले शिष्टप्रवृत्त्यापत्तिरित्यत आह, 'विघ्नसंसर्गाभावस्येति समवायसंसर्गावच्छिन्नतत्तद्विजातीयविघ्नसामान्याभावकूटस्येत्यर्थः। तथा च मङ्गलवत् तज्जन्यविघ्नध्वंसोपि न समाप्तिहेतुरित्यर्थः। 'स्वतःसिद्धः' विघ्नकारणाभावप्रयुक्तः, 'क्वचिदिति यत्र मङ्गलेन विघ्ननाश इति समाप्तिस्तत्रेत्यर्थः। 'मङ्गलसाध्यः' मङ्गलाधीनः, 'अतएवेति यत एव स्वोत्पत्त्यवच्छेदकत्वसम्बन्धेन शरीरनिष्ठतया विघ्नध्वंसो न हेतुः अपि तु विघ्नात्यन्ताभाव एव हेतुरत एवेत्यर्थः, 'मङ्गलं विनापि' ऐहिकमङ्गलं विनापि। न चैवं विघ्नध्वंसे कथं कामना सुखत्व-दुःखाभावत्वप्रकारकेच्छां प्रति तत्प्रकारज्ञानस्य तदन्येच्छां प्रति इष्टसाधनताज्ञानस्य हेतुत्वात् विघ्नात्यन्ताभावस्यैव समाप्तिरूपेष्टसाधनत्वेन विघ्नध्वंसस्येष्टसाधनत्वाभावादिति वाच्यं। सुखत्व-दुःखाभावत्वेष्टसाधनत्वप्रकारकज्ञानवत् यत्र द्वेषस्तदभावत्वप्रकारकज्ञानस्यापि पृथगिच्छाहेतुतया विघ्ने द्वेषसत्त्वेन विघ्नाभावत्वप्रकारकज्ञानादेव विघ्नध्वंसे कामनोत्पत्तेः अन्यथा प्रायश्चित्तादिजन्यपापनाशेपि कामनानुपपत्तेः। न च विघ्ने द्वेष एवकथं स्यात् सुखाभावत्व-दुःखत्वप्रकारकद्वेषं प्रति तत्प्रकारकज्ञानस्य तदन्यद्वेषञ्च प्रति अनिष्टसाधनताज्ञानस्य हेतुत्वादिति वाच्यं। यद्धर्म्मावच्छिन्नाभावे इच्छा तद्धर्म्मप्रकारकज्ञानस्यापि पृथक् द्वेषहेतुतया समाप्तिरूपेष्टसाधनतया

अतएव तच्छङ्कया मध्येपि तदाचरन्ति । गुर्व्वारम्भेपि बहुविघ्नशङ्कया बहुमङ्गलाचरणम् । यथा च विघ्न संशयेपि प्रवृत्तिस्तथोक्तमेव । स्यादेतत् मङ्गलमाच-

---

दुच्छासत्त्वेन विघ्नत्वप्रकारकज्ञानादेव द्वेषोत्पत्तेः, अन्यथा दाहार्थिनस्तत्-प्रतिबन्धके मणौ द्वेषानुपपत्तेः(१) अतएव च समाप्तिकामनापि परम्परया मङ्गलाचारप्रयोजिकेति भावः । 'न चानध्यवसाय इति कियन्ति मङ्गलानि कर्त्तव्यानि कीदृशं वा मङ्गलं कर्त्तव्यम् इत्यत्र नियामका-भाव इत्यर्थः । 'यावद्विघ्नशङ्कं' यावज्जातीयविघ्नशङ्कं, 'तदाचारात्' तज्जातीयमङ्गलाचारात् । 'अतएवेति यतः शङ्कितविघ्नवारणार्थं मङ्गल-करणम् अतएवेत्यर्थः । 'तच्छङ्कया' परकाले यत्कर्त्तव्यं तत्प्रति-बन्धकीभूतविघ्नान्तरोत्पत्तिशङ्कया, 'मध्येपीति आरब्धकर्म्ममध्यकाले-पीत्यर्थः । न चारब्धकर्म्मचिकीर्षाकालस्याङ्गतया कथं तदा तदनु-ष्ठानात् शङ्कितविघ्ननाश इति वाच्यम् । तच परकालकर्त्तव्य-भागस्यैवारब्धकर्म्मतया तच्चिकीर्षाकालस्यैवाङ्गत्वात् इति भावः ।

ननु समाप्तौ चेन्मङ्गलं न हेतुस्तदा गुरुतरकर्म्मारम्भे बहुतर-मङ्गलाचरणं न स्यात् अस्मन्मये तु गुरुतरकर्म्मसमाप्तौ बहुतरमङ्गलस्य हेतुत्वात् तदनुष्ठानमित्यत आह, 'गुर्व्वारम्भेपीति, 'बहुविघ्नशङ्कया' बहुविघ्नशङ्कयैव, न तु गुरुकर्म्मसमाप्तौ बहुतरमङ्गलस्य हेतुतये-त्यर्थः । 'तथोक्तमिति, तादृशाचारानुमितश्रुत्या तथैव बोधनादिति भावः । 'इतिविधाविति इतिविधिप्रतिपाद्यं मङ्गलत्वं किमित्यर्थः । 'अननुगमादिति आदित्वस्य चानुगतस्यैकस्य दुर्व्वचत्वादिति भावः ।

---

(१) द्वेषानुत्पत्तेरिति क० ।

रेदिति विधौ किं मङ्गलत्वं न तावद्देवतास्तुत्यादित्वम् अननुगमात्। नापि प्रारिप्सितप्रतिबन्धकविघ्नोपशम-हेतुक्रियात्वम् विघ्नोत्सारणासाधारणकारणत्वं वा,

'नापी'त्यादि, 'विघ्नः' दुरितं, अन्यथा प्रारिप्सितसमाप्तिप्रतिबन्धकस्यैव विघ्नपदार्थतया प्रतिबन्धकान्तवैयर्थ्यापातात्। अत्र प्रायश्चित्ते-ऽतिव्याप्तिवारणाय प्रतिबन्धकान्तं, कारीर्यां श्येनादिहेतुक्रियाया-श्चातिप्रसङ्गवारणाय 'प्रारिप्सिते'ति प्रारब्धसमाप्तीत्यर्थः। नाशकृति-दुरिते प्रतियोगितया ध्वंसजनकेऽतिव्याप्तिवारणाय 'क्रिये'ति, 'क्रियात्वं' प्रवृत्तिविषयत्वं, प्रवृत्तित्वञ्च चिकीर्षाजन्यतावच्छेदको-जातिविशेषः एतच्च विनायकस्तवपाठेऽतिप्रसक्तं गणेशस्तवस्य मङ्गल-त्वेपि तदनुकूलकण्ठाभिघातात्मकस्य तत्पाठस्यामङ्गलत्वात्। न च पाठकतासम्बन्धेन विनायकस्तव एव तन्नाशको न तु निरुक्त-तत्पाठः स्तवस्य मङ्गलत्वमेवेति वाच्यं। "सर्व्वे विघ्नाः शमं यान्ति" इति श्रुत्या तत्पाठस्यापि विघ्ननाशकत्वबोधनादित्यतो लक्षणान्तर-माह, 'विघ्ने'ति विघ्नध्वंसासाधारणकारणत्वमित्यर्थः। 'विघ्नः' मङ्गल-नाश्यतावच्छेदकवैजात्याश्रयो दुरितं, तेन विनायकस्तवपाठे प्राय-श्चित्ते कारीर्य्यादौ च नातिव्याप्तिः, तेषाञ्च शक्तिविशेषसम्बन्धेन विघ्नपदवत्त्वेनानुगमान्नाननुगमः। प्रतियोगिविधया कारणतामादाय विघ्नेऽतिव्याप्तिवारणाय, 'असाधारणे'ति 'असाधारणकारणत्वं' च विघ्ननाशमात्रवृत्तिध्वंसत्वावच्छिन्नकार्य्यतानिरूपितकारणताश्रयत्वं(१) विघ्ने

(१) कार्य्यताप्रतियोगिककारणताश्रयत्वं इति क॰ पुस्तकपाठः तत्रापि प्रतियोगिकत्वं निरूपितत्वमेव न त्वन्यदिति।

क्रियाविशेषस्य तदसाधारणकारणस्य वा स्तुत्यादेर्वेदा-द्विशिष्टापरिचये[१] प्रवृत्तिविषयालाभात्। नापि निर्विघ्नं समाप्यतामिति कामनया शिष्टाचारविषयत्वम्, वेदस्याचारानुपजीवकत्वात्, वेदादाद्याचारानुपपत्तेश्च अन्योन्याश्रयात्। नापि तत्कामनया वेदविहितत्वम्, प्रारिप्सितकर्म्मविघ्नध्वंसकत्वे सति कर्म्मारम्भकाले वि-

---

ऽतिव्याप्तिवारणाय वृत्त्यन्तं कार्य्यताविशेषणं, ध्वंसं प्रति च सामान्यतः सत्त्वेनैव हेतुत्वान्नोक्तातिव्याप्तिः, ध्वंस-प्रतियोगिनोस्तत्तद्व्यक्तित्वेनापि हेतु-हेतुमद्भावे तादृशकारणतामादायातिव्याप्तिवारणाय ध्वंसत्वावच्छिन्नेति, ध्वंसत्वावच्छिन्ना, स्त न ध्वंसत्वपर्य्याप्तावच्छेदकताकत्वं किन्तु तद्वृत्त्यवच्छेदकताकत्वमात्रं तेन नासम्भव इति भावः।

निरुक्तधर्म्मप्रकारेणैव विधिना बोधने अन्योन्याश्रयमाह, 'क्रियाविशेषस्येत्यादि। 'विशिष्टापरिचये' निरुक्तधर्म्मप्रकारेण पूर्व्वं ज्ञानं विना, 'प्रवृत्तिविषयालाभादिति निरुक्तधर्म्मप्रकारेण प्रथमं विशेषतो ज्ञानासम्भवादित्यर्थः। स्तुत्यादेर्व्विघ्नध्वंसजनकत्वस्य वेदमात्रवेद्यत्वादिति भावः। 'शिष्टाचारेति भ्रमाजन्याचारेत्यर्थः, तेन भ्रमात्तादृशकामनया प्रवृत्तिविषये नातिप्रसङ्ग इति भावः। 'आचारानुपजीवकत्वादिति आचारविषयकज्ञानाधीनशाब्दबोधाजनकत्वादित्यर्थः। नन्विदमप्रयोजकमित्यत आह, 'वेदादिति, 'आद्याचारेति पुरुषान्त-

---

(१) विशिष्यापरिचये इति ख॰।

हितवैदिककर्म्मत्वं वा, तादृशवेदान्तराभावात्। नापि स्मृत्यादौ मङ्गलत्वेनोत्कीर्त्तितत्वम्। वेदस्य स्मृत्यनुपजीवकत्वात् स्मृतिकर्तुरेव वेदाद्याचारानुपपत्तेश्च। उच्यते[१]। मङ्गलमाचरेदिति न विधिः किन्तु निर्व्विघ्नसमाप्तिकामो देवतास्तुतिमाचरेदित्यादिप्रत्येकमेव विधिः। तथैव शिष्टाचारात्। तदुपजीव्य निर्व्विघ्न-

---

राचारविषयत्वस्य स्वीयकालान्तरीयाचारविषयत्वस्य वा ज्ञानं विना प्रवृत्त्यनुपपत्तेश्चेत्यर्थः। अनुपपत्तौ हेतुमाह, 'अन्योन्याश्रयादिति वेदात् स्वस्याचारे जाते तद्विषयत्वप्रकारकशक्तिग्रहाद् वेदाच्छाब्दधीर्वेदाच्छाब्दबोधे एव च स्वस्याचार इत्यन्योन्याश्रयप्रसङ्गादित्यर्थः। यद्यपि पदान्तरशक्तिग्रहवत् प्रथममीश्वराचारदर्शनादेव शक्तिग्रहः सम्भवत्येव, तथापि यद्धर्म्मावच्छेदेन भगवदाचारदर्शनं तेनैव रूपेण शक्तिग्रहः स्यात् स च मतित्वादिरेव न त्वाचारविषयत्वमिति भावः। 'तत्कामतया' तत्काममताप्रकारेण, तत्कामिकर्त्तव्यत्वप्रकारेणेति यावत्। तेन कामनाया विधिजन्यशाब्दबोधाजनकत्वेपि न क्षतिः। 'प्रारिप्सितेति आरम्भणीयादावतिव्याप्तिवारणाय सत्यन्तं प्रारब्धकर्म्मसमाप्तिप्रयोजकत्वे सतीत्यर्थः। मङ्गलस्य समाप्त्यजनकतया जनकत्वमपहाय प्रयोजकत्वप्रवेशः प्रयोजकत्वञ्च कारण-तत्कारणसाधारणं, अतएवादृष्टद्वारा समाप्तिप्रयोजककर्म्मान्तरेऽतिव्याप्तिवारणाय विहितान्तं कर्म्मपूर्व्व-

---

(१) अत्रोच्यत इति ख०।

मारब्धं परिसमाप्यतामिति कामनया तद्विघ्नोपशम-हेतुत्वेन वा वेदविहितत्वं मङ्गलत्वमित्यधिगम्य देवता-स्तुति-नमस्कारादिषु मङ्गलव्यवहारः शिष्टानामिति। अतएव दुरितनाशकमपि गङ्गास्नानादि न मङ्गलम् तथाऽविधानात्। "मङ्गलाचारयुक्तानां नित्यञ्च प्रयता-

---

कालकर्त्तव्यतया विहितत्वार्थकं, असम्भववारणाय पूर्व्वत्वप्रवेशः। वैदिकपदं विहितान्तेन तादृशकालकर्त्तव्यतया वेदविहितत्वलाभाय अन्यथा कल्पितव्रतादिप्राक्कालकर्त्तव्यत्वेन लौकिककल्पितविधि-विषयेऽदृष्टद्वारा तत्समाप्तिजनके होमादावतिव्याप्त्यापत्तेः। 'तादृश-वेदान्तराभावादिति, इदमुपलक्षणं द्वितीयेऽदृष्टद्वारा प्रारब्धकर्म्म-समाप्तिप्रयोजके आरम्भनीयादावतिव्याप्तेः विघ्नध्वंसस्य समाप्त्यजनक-तया मङ्गलस्य प्रारब्धकर्म्मसमाप्तिं प्रति प्रयोजकत्वस्याप्यभावेनासम्भ-वापत्तेश्चेत्यपि बोध्यं। 'निर्व्विघ्नसमाप्तिकाम इति, एतच्च सम्प्रदायम-यमाश्रित्य, स्वनये तु प्रारिप्सितविघ्नोपशमनकाम इति बोध्यं। 'तथैव' स्तुतित्वादिनैव, 'शिष्टाचारात्' शिष्टप्रवृत्तिविषयत्वात्, 'तदुपजीव्येति तत्तद्विधिजन्यज्ञानसहकारेणेत्यर्थः। 'तद्विघ्नेति प्रारब्धकर्म्मविघ्नेत्यर्थः। लक्षणद्वयं मतभेदेन। नन्वेतल्लक्षणद्वयमादर्शदर्शनादावव्यापकमित्या-शङ्क्याह, 'मङ्गलचारेति 'मङ्गलाचारः' आदर्शदर्शनादि, 'विनिपातः' दुरितं, 'न विद्यते' नोत्पद्यते, 'मङ्गलत्वं' मङ्गलपदशक्यत्वं, 'तच्च' नानार्थतैवेति, अत इत्यादिः, 'तच्च' मङ्गलपदे। ननु नानार्थताया अन्याय्यतया 'विनिपातपदं प्रारिप्सितपरमेवास्तु 'न विद्यत इत्यपि

त्मनाम्। जपतां जुह्वताञ्चैव विनिपातो न विद्यते” इत्यनेन बोधितादर्शदर्शनादेः पृथगेव मङ्गलत्वं न तु विघ्ननिवर्तकतया तच्च नानार्थतैव। अन्यथा ग्रन्थारम्भे नमस्कारतुल्यतया तत्करणप्रसङ्गः। अथशब्दो विघ्ननिवर्तकत्वान्मङ्गलमेव “ओङ्कारश्चाथशब्दश्च द्वावेतौ ब्रह्मणः पुरा। कण्ठं भित्त्वा तु निर्यातौ तेन माङ्गलि-

---

विनाशपरमस्तु तथा चादर्शदर्शनादेरपि नत्यादिवदेव मङ्गलत्वं। न च 'जुह्वतामिति न होमान्तरविधिः किन्तु अग्निहोत्रस्यैवानुवादः तथा च तस्य नित्यतया विघ्नेतरपापानुत्पत्तिफलकत्वेन प्राप्तत्वात् 'विनिपातपदस्य विघ्नपरत्वं 'न विद्यत इत्यस्य विनाशपरत्वञ्च न सम्भवति अग्निहोत्रानुरोधेन 'विनिपातो न विद्यत इत्यस्य पापानुत्पादपरत्वं मङ्गलानुरोधाच्च विघ्ननाशपरत्वमित्युपगमे च वाक्यभेद इति वाच्यं। तथापि पापसंसर्गाभावत्वसामानाधिकरण्येन सर्व्वेषां जन्यतान्वयसम्भवात् कार्य्यतावच्छेदककल्पना च यथायोग्यमौत्तरकालिकीत्यत आह, अन्यथेति।

ननु तथाप्यथशब्देऽतिव्याप्तिः ग्रन्थारम्भप्राक्काले तदुच्चारणस्यापि शिष्टैः करणादित्यत इष्टापत्तिमाह, 'अथशब्द इति, 'पुरा' सृष्ट्यारम्भकाले, 'कण्ठं भित्त्वा' कण्ठ्यवर्णघटितत्वात् कण्ठाभिहतवायुना, 'विनिर्यातौ',(१) 'तेन' तादृशविघ्नोपशमनकामशिष्टाचारविषयत्वेन, 'माङ्गलिकौ' मङ्गलस्वरूपौ, स्वार्थे इकण् प्रत्ययात्। एवञ्च ग्रन्थसन्दर्भि-

---

(१) 'विनिर्जातौ' जातौ, इति क०, ख०, ग०, घ।

काबुभौ" इति स्मृतेः। न च शुभसूचकत्वमेव तस्य, शास्त्रारम्भे महर्षिणा तदनुपादानप्रसङ्गात्। गुणवत्तया ज्ञापनं स्तुतिः, यमुद्दिश्य यस्य स्वापकर्षबोधनानुकूलो व्यापारविशेषः स तस्य नमस्कारः। व्यापारे च कायिक-वाचिक-मानसिकरूपे विशेषो जातिविशेष

षेण, ग्रन्थस्य तदघटितत्वे प्राक्काले अनुष्ठानविषयत्वासम्भवादिति बोध्यम्[१]। ननु यथा यात्रापूर्व्वकालेपि शुभसूचकतया आदर्श-दर्शनादि क्रियते तथैव ग्रन्थशब्दोपि शुभसूचकः स्यादित्याशङ्कां निराकरोति, 'न चेति, 'शास्त्रारम्भसमये' शास्त्रारम्भसमय एव, तथा यात्रादर्शदर्शनादिवदन्यदापि तदनुष्ठानापत्तिरिति भावः।

ननु स्तुतिमाचरेदित्यादौ का स्तुतिरित्यत आह, 'गुणवत्तयेति उत्कर्षवत्तयेत्यर्थः। तेनाधार्म्मिकत्वास्पृश्यसंयोगित्वादेर्व्युदासः[२] उत्कर्षत्वञ्च शक्तिविशेषसम्बन्धेनोत्कर्षपदवत्त्वमतो नाननुगमः, 'ज्ञापनं' ज्ञानानुकूलः शब्दः, तेन व्यापारान्तरे तादृशि नाति प्रसङ्गः। न च तथापि उत्कर्षस्य जातिविशेषरूपतया त्वं दयाशीलस्त्वं दाता पुत्री त्वमेवेत्यादावव्याप्तिरिति वाच्यम्। दयादिष्वप्युत्कर्षव्यवहारेण तेषामप्युत्कर्षपदवाच्यत्वात्। न च तथापि तादृशि स्वरूपाख्यानेऽतिव्याप्तिः तस्यापि स्तुतित्वे भवतां स्वरूपं कथयामो न तु स्तुम इति सकलप्रामाणिकव्यवहारासङ्गतेरिति वाच्यं। ज्ञानपदेन भ्रम-

---

(१) ध्येयं इति क०।

(२) तेनाधार्म्मिकत्वमस्पृश्यसंयोगी त्वमित्यादेर्व्युदासः इति ख०।

एवानुभवसाक्षिकः करशिरःसंयोगमात्रे तदव्यवहारात् भवतोऽहमपकृष्ट इत्यादिवचने तदव्यवहाराच्च। यद्वा। कायिकादौ प्रत्येकमेव विधिकल्पनं अतो नानार्थतैव। यत्तु। बुद्धिविशेषपूर्वकत्वज्ञानं विना कायिकादौ न तद्व्यवहार इति स एव वाच्योऽन्यच्च लक्षणेति। तन्न।

रूपज्ञानस्य विवक्षितत्वात्। अतएवारोप्यगुणकथनं स्तुतिरिति प्रामाणिकाः, भगवत्स्तुत्यादिषु तत्प्रयोगो भाक्तः।

नव्यास्तु ज्ञानवि[illegible]धायकः शब्दः स्तुतिः ज्ञाननिष्ठो विशेषस्य शाब्दत्वव्याप्यो जातिविशेषः, उपधायकत्वञ्च ज्ञानविशेषशब्दयोः संसर्गमर्य्यादया प्रविष्टमतो नाननुगमो दोषाय। न च स्तुतिनिन्दार्थोभयविषयकसमूहालम्बनज्ञाने साङ्कर्य्यापत्तिः विनिगमनाविरहेण निन्दापदशक्यतावच्छेदकस्यापि जातित्वस्य दुर्व्वारत्वादिति वाच्यम्। तदुभयजातेः समूहालम्बनज्ञानव्यावृत्तत्वाभ्युपगमात् समूहालम्बनमात्रजनकस्तुत्यादौ च मानाभावात् तत्सत्त्वे च तत्र स्तुतिव्यवहारस्य भाक्तत्वादित्याहुः।

'यमुद्दिश्येति यदवधिकेत्यर्थः, तथा च स्वापकर्षबोधजनकतावच्छेदकजातिसत्त्वमेव लक्षणं, को व्यापारः कस्य नमस्कार इत्याकाङ्क्षायां 'यमुद्दिश्येति, स्वत्वघटितत्वेनाननुगममाशङ्क्याह, 'यद्वेति, 'नानार्थतैवेति कायिकादिप्रत्येकवृत्तिजातिविशेषा एव नमस्कारपदशक्यतावच्छेदका इत्यर्थः। ननु करशिरःसंयोगादिः कायिकनमस्कारस्तत्र कथं जातिविशेषः नोदनत्वाभिघातत्व-संयोगजत्वादिना

कायिकादिव्यापारविशेषमनवगम्य बुद्धिविशेषपूर्व्वक-

साङ्कर्य्यात्। न च संयोगत्वादिजातयो नाना कार्य्यतावच्छेदका-ननुगमश्चादोषत्वात् नमस्कारपदशक्यतावच्छेदकजातिस्त्वेका विघ्न-विशेषनाशकतावच्छेदकतया सिद्धा तन्नानात्वे व्यभिचारापत्तेरिति वाच्यम्। तथापि शब्दविशेषजनकतावच्छेदकाभिघातत्वमादाय साङ्कर्य्यस्य दुर्व्वारत्वात् उभयोरेव जनकतावच्छेदकतया नानात्वे विनिगमकाभावादिति चेत्। न। करशिरःसंयोगाद्यनुकूलचेष्टाविशेष-स्यैव कायिकनमस्कारत्वाच्चेष्टानिष्ठविशेषस्तु चेष्टात्वव्याप्यो जाति-विशेषः स च विघ्नविशेषनाशकतावच्छेदकतया सिद्धः। ननु तथापि यत्र नमःपदादिरेव वाचनिकनमस्कारः तत्र कथं जातिविशेषः नत्वादिना साङ्कर्य्यात्। न च मकारादिचरमवर्णवृत्तिनत्वादिव्याप्यो नानाजातिविशेष एव वाचनिकत्वं नोत्तरमकारविशेषादिरेव वाच-निकनमस्कारः, पूर्व्वपूर्व्ववर्णज्ञानन्तु तद्व्यञ्जकमतश्चरमवर्णमात्रश्रवणे न तज्जातिसाक्षात्कार इति वाच्यम्। विनिगमनाविरहेण नपूर्व्व-मकारविशेषस्यापि वाचनिकत्वस्य दुर्व्वारत्वादिति चेत्। न। विनि-गमनाविरहान्नत्व-मत्वादिव्याप्या नानाजातय एव वाचनिकत्वमि-त्यभिप्रायात्।

नव्यास्तु शब्दबोधवृत्तिशब्दत्वव्याप्यजातिविशेष एव वाचनिकत्व-मत एव वाचनिक इत्युच्यते न तु वचनमित्याहुः।

मानसिकत्वन्तु मानसत्वव्याप्यो जातिविशेष एव। न च स्वप्नत्व-मादाय साङ्कर्य्यमिति वाच्यं। तस्य स्वप्नत्वविरुद्धत्वादिति ध्येयम्।

त्वाम्नानात् । स्वीकृतवेदप्रमाणभावः शिष्टः । आचारे च वेदानिषिद्धत्वमविगीतत्वं विशेषणं(१) देयं । यद्वा

प्राभाकरमतमाह, 'यत्त्विति, 'बुद्धिविशेषेति ज्ञानविशेषजन्यत्वस्यैव कायिकादिनिष्ठजातिविशेषव्यञ्जकत्वादित्यभिमानः । 'स एवेति मानसज्ञानविशेष एवेत्यर्थः । 'अन्यत्र' कायिकादौ, 'कायिकादीति, तं प्रति तस्य लिङ्गत्वात् तथा च ज्ञानविशेषजन्यत्वग्रहो न तादृशजातिविशेषव्यञ्जक इति भावः । न च तथापि चेष्टात्व-मानसत्वव्याप्यजातिविशेष एव शक्यतावच्छेदकः न तु वाचनिकत्वं तस्य नानादिव्याप्यनानात्वाभ्युपगमादिति वाच्यम् । तस्याप्युक्तक्रमेणैकत्वात् नानात्वेऽपि प्रत्येकमादाय विनिगमनाविरहेण शक्यतावच्छेदकत्वस्य दुर्वारत्वाचेति हृदयं ।

ननु मङ्गलं वेदबोधितसमाप्तिसाधनताकं समाप्त्युद्देश्यकाविगीतशिष्टाचारविषयत्वादिति साम्प्रदायिकानां प्रागुक्तवेदानुमाने किन्तावत् शिष्टत्वमित्यत आह, 'स्वीकृतेति वेदविशेष्यकप्रामाण्याभ्युपगमवानित्यर्थः । अभ्युपगमः निश्चयः, तावतैव यत्तज्ञौ सामान्यतो व्याप्तौ पशु-पक्ष्यादिकृतकृपाचेष्टायां व्यभिचारवारणादिति भावः । वाचकपतितान्यजात्यतिरिक्तत्वे सतीत्यनेनापि विशेषणीयं तेन तदीयकृपाचेष्टायां पश्वादिकृपाचेष्टावद्वेदानिषिद्धायां न व्यभिचारः ।

(१) आचारे च वेदानिषिद्धत्वमलौकिकत्वञ्च विशेषणं इति क० पुस्तकपाठः न समीचीनः अलौकिकत्वे सतीत्यनेनापि विशेषणीयमिति मथुरानाथोक्तस्वरसभङ्गापत्तेः ।

अलौकिकविषयशिष्टाचारत्वमेव हेतुः। शिष्टाचारत्वञ्च भ्रमाजन्याचारत्वं। आस्तिक-नास्तिकयोरगम्यागमन-चैत्यवदनादावाचारजनकज्ञानस्य भ्रमत्वात् बलवद-

---

नन्वेवं वेदप्रामाण्याभ्युपगन्त्रा भ्रान्त्या क्रियमाणे चैत्यवन्दनादौ व्यभिचार इत्यत आह, 'आचारे चेति आचारे अविगीतत्त्वं यद्वि-शेषणं दत्तं तद्वेदानिषिद्धत्वरूपमित्यर्थः। प्रामाणिककृतचैत्यवन्दना-दिकञ्च न तथा तस्य पूर्व्वलिखितवेदनिषिद्धत्वादिति भावः। अलौकिकत्वे सतीत्यनेनापि विशेषणीयं तेन शिष्टकृतभोजनादौ न व्यभिचारः, अलौकिकत्वञ्च प्राङ्निरुक्तमेव। न च तथापि भ्रान्त्या स्वःफलान्यफलमुद्दिश्य कृते यागादौ व्यभिचारः तत्साधनत्वेन तस्य वेदबोधितत्वाभावादिति वाच्यं। चैत्यवन्दनादिवत् तस्यापि वृथा-चेष्टात्वेन वेदनिषिद्धत्वात्।

लाघवादाह, 'यद्वेति, 'अलौकिकविषयेति अलौकिकविषयकेत्यर्थः, 'हेतुः' पूर्व्वोक्तहेत्वर्थः, तथा चाविगीतपदस्यैव लौकिकाविषयक-त्वमर्थः, तच्च भोजनादौ लौकिककर्म्मणि व्यभिचारवारणायेति भावः। लौकिकाविषयकत्वन्तु प्राङ्निरुक्तमेव। नन्वेवं शिष्टकृतचैत्य-वन्दनादौ व्यभिचार इत्यत आह, 'शिष्टत्वञ्चेति। 'अगम्यागमनेति अगम्या गमनायोग्या या भूमिस्तत्र तीर्थत्वभ्रान्त्या कृतं यद्गमन-मित्यर्थः। यथाश्रुतन्तु न सङ्गच्छते अलौकिकविषयकत्वविशेषणेनैव तद्वारणात्।

निष्टानुबन्धित्वादिष्टासाधनत्वाच्च। लोके च पाषण्डव्यावृत्तशिष्टव्यवहारो वेदप्रामाण्याभ्युपगमनिबन्धनः। नैयिकत्वेपि शिष्टाशिष्टव्यवहारो वेदनिषिद्धाकर्तृत्व-तत्कर्तृत्वनिबन्धनः। यद्वा वेदप्रामाण्याभ्युपगन्तृत्वे सति यो यदा वेदनिषिद्धाकर्त्ता स तदा शिष्टः

केचित्तु अगम्यागमनस्योभयविशेषणेनैव वारणं सम्भवति इति-सूचनाय तदभिधानमित्याहुः।

'बलवदनिष्टेति, निष्फलत्वादिति भावः तदुद्देश्यकत्वेनाप्याचारो विशेषणीयः प्रयोजनस्योक्तमेव, नन्वेवं भ्रमाजन्यः शिष्ट इति फलितं तथा च घट-पटादौ गगनादौ पाषण्डे च शिष्टव्यवहारापत्तिरित्यत आह, 'लोके चेति, 'वेदप्रामाण्याभ्युपगमेति, तथा च सर्व्वे वेदाः स्वस्वतात्पर्य्यविषयार्थे प्रमाणमित्याकारकयावद्वेदविशेष्यकानाहार्य्यनिश्चयवत्त्वं शिष्टपदशक्यतावच्छेदकं, प्रकृते च शिष्टपदं भाक्तं। एवं वेदो न प्रमाणमिति यत्किञ्चिद्वेदविशेष्यकानाहार्य्यनिश्चयवत्त्वमेव बौद्धत्वमिति भावः। बौद्धस्यापि "मा हिंस्यात् सर्व्वा भूतानि" इत्यादियत्किञ्चिद्वेदप्रामाण्याभ्युपगन्तृत्वात् वेदत्वावच्छेदेनैवाहार्य्यप्रामाण्याभ्युपगमवत्त्वाच्च यावत्त्वानाहार्य्यत्वयोरुपादानं। नन्वच तादृशनिश्चयो विशेषणमुपलक्षणं वा नाद्यः सुसुप्त्यादिदशायामशिष्टत्वापत्तेः, न चेष्टापत्तिः, तदानीमपि शिष्टव्यवहारात्। नान्त्यः बौद्धातिव्याप्तेः, अनादौ संसारे कदाचित्तेनापि तदभ्युपगमात्। न च तच्छरीरावच्छेदेन तदभ्युपगमो विवक्षितः, एकस्मिन्नेव शरीरे काल-

तत्कर्त्ता त्वशिष्टः। अतएव वेदानिषिद्धाकर्तृत्वेपि बौद्धो न शिष्टः। पापजनकत्वज्ञानं विना वेदनिषिद्धकर्तृत्वं यस्य नास्ति स शिष्ट इति तु न तैर्थिकस्यापि[(१)] कस्यचित् पापजनकत्वज्ञानं विना वेदनिषिद्धकर्तृत्वात्।

भेदेन शिष्टता-बौद्धतोभयदर्शनाद्बौद्धतादशायामतिव्याप्तेः तदानीं शिष्टव्यवहाराभावात् अन्यथा अनादौ संसारे सर्व्वस्यैवात्मनो यदा कदाचिच्छिष्टत्वेनात्मत्वस्यैव तथात्वस्य सुवचत्वात्। अथ तत्पुरुषीयतादृशनिश्चयसमानकालीना यावन्तस्तत्पुरुषीयास्तादृशविरोधिनिश्चयाभावास्तद्वत्त्वं तत्पुरुषीयशिष्टत्वं शिष्टतोत्तरबौद्धतादशायां तादृशनिश्चयसमानकालीनस्य बौद्धताकालीनविरोधिनिश्चयव्यक्तेः प्रागभावस्य यावदन्तर्गतस्यासत्त्वान्नातिप्रसङ्ग इति चेत्। न। यस्य पुरुषस्य शिष्टतोत्तरं बौद्धता तदनन्तरं पुनः शिष्टता च तत्र पूर्व्वशिष्टतादशायामव्याप्तिः मध्यवर्त्तिबौद्धताकालीनविरोधिनिश्चयव्यक्तिध्वंसस्यापि तादृशयावदभावान्तर्गतस्य तदानीमभावात्, तदुत्तरशिष्टतादशायामप्यव्याप्तिः मध्यवर्त्तिबौद्धताकालीनविरोधिनिश्चयव्यक्तिप्रागभावस्यापि तादृशयावदभावान्तर्गतस्य तदानीमसत्त्वादिति। मैवं। यावतीस्तादृशनिश्चयव्यक्तीः प्रातिस्विकरूपेणोपादाय तत्तन्निश्चयव्यक्तिसमानाधिकरणत्वे सति तत्तद्व्यक्तिसमानकालीना यावन्तस्तत्तद्व्यक्तिविरोधिनिश्चयाभावास्तद्वत्त्वे सति तत्तद्व्यक्त्यपूर्व्वकालाव-

---

(१) तीर्थिकस्यापि इति पाठान्तरम्।

यत्तु रागद्वेषहीनः शिष्टः स च सर्व्वज्ञत्वान्मन्वादिरेव, अविगीततदाचारादेव वेदानुमानमिति। तन्न। एवं हि मन्वाद्याचारादर्शिनामाधुनिकानां मङ्गले प्रवृत्तिर्न स्यात् आधुनिकानामाचारेण मन्वाद्याचार-

---

च्छिन्नत्वं शिष्टत्वमिति विवक्षितत्वात्। पुरुषान्तरवृत्तिविरोधिनिश्चयप्रागभावमादायासम्भववारणाय समानाधिकरणत्वोपादानं, स्वीयपूर्व्वजन्मीयविरोधिनिश्चयप्रागभावमादायासम्भववारणाय समानकालीनत्वोपादानं, वेदा न प्रमाणमिति निश्चयनाशोत्तरं वेदाः प्रमाणमिति निश्चयानुत्पादकाले शिष्टतावारणाय विशेष्यदलं। यदि च वेदाप्रामाण्याभ्युपगमाव्यवहितोत्तरक्षणे तत्प्रामाण्याभ्युपगमस्ततस्तृतीयक्षणे तदप्रामाण्याभ्युपगमव्यक्तिनाशः सम्भाव्यते तदा तत्समानकालीनत्वं तदुत्पत्तिसमानकालीनत्वं वा वाच्यम्, अभावो वा अनादिर्व्वाच्यः, अन्यथा तत्र तादृशनाशस्य यावदन्तर्गतस्य वेदप्रामाण्याभ्युपगमव्यक्त्युत्पत्तिकाले असत्त्वादव्याप्त्यापत्तेः। न च यस्यैतज्जन्मनि वेदप्रामाण्याप्रामाण्ययोरुभयोरेवानभ्युपगमः पूर्वजन्मनि तु प्रामाण्यमात्रमभ्युपेत्यैव मरणं तस्यैतज्जन्मनि शिष्टत्वापत्तिरिति वाच्यं। इष्टापत्तेः। एवं यस्यैतज्जन्मनि प्रामाण्याप्रामाण्ययोरुभयोरेवानभ्युपगमः पूर्वजन्मनि चाप्रामाण्यमभ्युपेत्यैव मरणं तस्यैतज्जन्मन्यप्यशिष्टत्वे इष्टापत्तिः। जन्मान्तरीणप्रामाण्याभ्युपगमानन्तरकाकादिशरीरावच्छिन्नवारणाय परं प्रकृष्टचैतन्यावच्छेदकावच्छिन्नत्वेनापि विशेष्यं। यद्वा तत्तद्व्यक्त्यपूर्वकालावच्छिन्नत्वपदेन तत्तद्व्यक्त्यवच्छेदकजन्मान्त-

मनुमाय तेन च वेदमनुमाय बालः प्रवर्त्तत इति चेत् तर्हि यादृशाचारेण मन्वाद्याचारानुमानं स एव वेदानुमापकोऽस्तु किमनुमितानुमानेन आधुनिकानामपि शिष्टत्वेन व्यवह्रियमाणत्वाच्च। तथा च स्मृतिः "यस्मिन्

रावच्छिन्नत्वविशिष्टतत्तद्व्यक्तिपूर्वकालावच्छिन्नत्वं विवक्षितं, उभयाभ्युपगमक्षणेऽपि शिष्टाशिष्टबहिर्भूत एव। एवञ्च यथोक्तकाकादिशरीरावच्छिन्नेऽपि नातिव्याप्तिः। न चैवं तत्तच्छिष्टव्यक्तेः प्रातिस्विकरूपेणोपादानादननुगम इति वाच्यं। शिष्टपदस्य नानार्थत्वेनाननुगमस्यादोषत्वात्। अस्तु वा तावदभावकूटाभावघटितान्यत्वं तावदन्यतमधर्मवत्त्वं वा तत्त्वं।

केचित्तु तादृशवेदप्रामाण्याभ्युपगमजन्यसंस्कारवत्त्वं शिष्टत्वं तदभ्युपगमोत्पत्तिक्षणे च न शिष्टः, स च संस्कारो विरोध्यभ्युपगमनाश्य इति शिष्टतोत्तरं बौद्धनादशायां नातिव्याप्तिः। संस्कारस्याविनश्यदवस्थत्वेन विशेषणीयः तेन तत्प्रामाण्याभ्युपगमोत्पत्तिक्षणे नातिप्रसङ्गः। न च घटविषयकतादृशसमूहालम्बनसंस्कारस्य विरोध्यभ्युपगमेन नाशे घटस्मृतिरपि न स्यादिति वाच्यं। तादृशसमूहालम्बनसंस्कारस्य विरोध्यभ्युपगमोत्तरं घटस्मृतिजनकत्वे मानाभावात् स्मृतिनाश्यतावच्छेदकवैजात्यस्य तद्व्याप्यतया घटस्मृति-घटसंस्कारयोर्नाश्यनाशकभावे न व्यभिचार इत्याहुः।

नन्वेवं निरुक्ताभ्युपगमाभाववत्यपि कदाचित् शिष्टव्यवहारस्तद्वत्यपि कदाचिदशिष्टव्यवहारो दृश्यते स कथं स्यादित्यत आह, 'तैर्थि-

देशे य आचारः पारम्पर्य्यक्रमागतः। श्रुति-स्मृत्यविरोधेन सदाचारः स उच्यते"॥ सर्व्वज्ञस्य मङ्गलाचारे मानाभावाच्च। मन्वादिप्रणीतस्मृतौ मङ्गलं दृश्यते इति चेत्। तन्न। स्मृतिकर्तुरसर्व्वज्ञत्वेपि वेदादर्थं

कत्वेपीति निरुक्ताभ्युपगमाभावनिरुक्ताभ्युपगमयोः सत्त्वेपीत्यर्थः। तथा च तादृशे शिष्टाशिष्टव्यवहारो भाक्त इति भावः। तत्रापि शिष्टाशिष्टव्यवहारयोर्मुख्यत्वमेवेत्यभिप्रायेणाह, 'यद्वेति, अत्यन्तं निरुक्तार्थकं, अत्यन्तविशेषणस्य प्रयोजनं दर्शयति, 'अतएवेति, 'वेदानिषिद्धकर्तृत्वेपि वेदनिषिद्धाकर्तृत्वेपि। कस्यचिल्लक्षणं दूषयति, 'पापजनकत्वेति पापजनकत्वज्ञानाभावविशिष्टवेदनिषिद्धकर्तृत्वाभाववत्त्वमित्यर्थः। बौद्धस्य तु वेदनिषिद्धकर्म्मणि पापजनकत्वज्ञानमेव नास्तीति भावः। अत्र रागौत्कट्यात् पापजनकत्वज्ञानसत्त्वेपि वेदनिषिद्धकर्त्तरि शिष्टेऽव्याप्तिवारणाय विशिष्टान्तं कर्तृत्वविशेषणं, वैशिष्ट्यञ्चैककालावच्छेदेनैकात्मवृत्तित्वं विशेषणाभाववत्त्वमात्रोक्तौ पापजनकत्वज्ञानशून्ये वेदानिषिद्धकर्त्तरि शिष्टेऽव्याप्तिरतो विशिष्टाभावानुधावनं। मूर्च्छादिदशायां शिष्टेऽव्याप्तिमाह, 'तीर्थिकस्यापीति शिष्टस्यापीत्यर्थः। 'रागद्वेषहीन इति आत्यन्तिकराग-द्वेषध्वंसवत्त्वमित्यर्थः। यथाश्रुते घटादावतिव्याप्तेः। पाषण्डेऽतिव्याप्तिवारणायात्यन्तिकत्वं ध्वंसविशेषणं, तच्च मिथ्याज्ञानप्रागभावविशिष्टभिन्नत्वं मिथ्याज्ञानविशिष्टभिन्नत्वं वा वैशिष्ट्यञ्चैककालावच्छेदेनैकात्मवृत्तित्वं। आत्यन्तिकध्वंसवत्त्वमात्रोक्तौ घटादावतिव्याप्तिनादवस्थमतो रागद्वेषयोर्वैकल्पिकमुपादानं तथा च

प्रतीत्य स्मृतिप्रणयनसम्भवात्। यत्तु शिष्टाचारत्वेन कर्त्तव्यतैवानुमीयतां किं वेदेनेति तत्र वक्ष्यामः।

लक्षणद्वये तात्पर्य्यं। मन्वादेस्तथात्वे हेतुः 'सर्व्वज्ञत्वादिति तत्त्वज्ञत्वादित्यर्थः। 'तदाचारेति तादृशशिष्टत्वविशिष्टाचारेत्यर्थः। वैशिष्ट्यञ्चैककालावच्छेदेनैकात्मवृत्तित्वं तेन बाल्यदशायां तादृशशिष्टेन कृते चैत्यवन्दनादौ न व्यभिचारः। न वा तादृशशिष्टत्वानुत्पत्तिदशायां भ्रान्त्या स्वःफलान्यफलमुद्दिश्य तादृशशिष्टेन कृते तत्फलजनकत्वेन वेदबोधिते यागादौ व्यभिचारः। कर्म्मक्षयार्थं तादृशशिष्टेन कृते निषिद्धकर्म्मणि व्यभिचारवारणायाविगीतत्वमाचारविशेषणं तच्च वेदानिषिद्धत्वं, अलौकिकत्वमपि वाच्यं तेन तत्कृतभोजनादौ न व्यभिचारः। 'स एवेति, व्याप्यव्याप्यस्य सुतरां व्याप्यत्वादिति भावः।

ननु तथाप्यनुष्ठानोपयोगि मास्तु व्यवहारोपयोगि तु स्यादित्यत आह,'आधुनिकानामपीति, 'सदाचारः' यथोक्तमविगीततदाचारादेव वेदानुमानं। तत्र दोषान्तरमाह, 'सर्व्वज्ञस्येति 'तत्त्वज्ञस्येत्यर्थः। अत्रैव प्रकृते, 'मन्वादिस्मृताविति भारत-पुराणादावित्यर्थः। भारतादिकर्तुर्यथोक्तशिष्टत्वमेव नास्तीत्याह, 'स्मृतिकर्तुरिति भारतादिकर्तुरित्यर्थः। 'असर्व्वज्ञत्वेपि' अतत्त्वज्ञत्वेऽपि, 'शिष्टाचारत्वेन' समाप्त्युद्देश्यकशिष्टाचारविषयत्वेन, शिष्टत्वं भ्रमाजन्यत्वं 'कर्त्तव्यतैवानुमीयतामिति इष्टसाधनत्वे सति कृतिसाध्यतामनुमायैव सर्व्वे मङ्गले प्रवर्त्तन्तां किं मङ्गले तादृशकृतिसाध्यताबोधकवेदेनेत्यर्थः। 'तत्र वक्ष्यामः' अलौकिकत्वे सति शिष्टाचारविषयत्वस्य वेदबोधितत्वव्याप्यतया अलौकिके मङ्गले शिष्टाचारविषयत्वस्य च व्यापकीभूतवेद-

इति श्रीमहोपाध्यायश्रीमद्गङ्गेश्वरविरचिते तत्त्वचिन्तामणौ प्रत्यक्षखण्डे मङ्गलवादः समाप्तः ॥

बोधितत्वं विना अनुपपन्नत्वात् वेदस्यापि आवश्यकत्वं। न च तादृशव्याप्तौ मानाभावः। अबाधितसर्व्वजनानुभवसिद्धत्वादित्युच्छन्नप्रच्छन्नवादे शब्दखण्डे वक्ष्याम इत्यर्थः ॥०॥

इति श्रीमथुरानाथतर्कवागीश-विरचितं तत्त्वचिन्तामणौ प्रत्यक्षखण्डे मङ्गलवादरहस्यं सम्पूर्णम् ॥०॥

अथ प्रामाण्यवादः।

अथ जगदेव दुःखपङ्कनिमग्नमुद्दिधीर्षुरष्टादशविद्यास्थानेष्वभ्यर्हिततमामान्वीक्षिकीं परमकारुणिको मुनिः

अथ प्रामाण्यवादरहस्यम्।

मङ्गलस्य सफलत्वं व्यवस्थाप्य मोक्षसाधनीभूततत्त्वज्ञानचिकीर्षावतां स्वीयग्रन्थोपादानकप्रवृत्तये मोक्षसाधनीभूततत्त्वज्ञानरूपफलवदान्वीक्षिकीप्रतिपादितप्रतिपादकत्वेन हेतुना मोक्षसाधनीभूततत्त्वज्ञानजनकतां स्वीयग्रन्थस्य प्रतिपादयितुं तादृशहेतुमत्त्वं स्वीयग्रन्थस्य दर्शयति 'अथेत्यादिना 'विविच्यते' इत्यन्तेन, 'अथ' मङ्गलस्य सफलत्वव्यवस्थापनानन्तरं, 'जगदेवेति जगत्पदं बहुत्वविशिष्टपरं, एव-

प्रणिनाय । तच्च प्रेक्षावत्प्रवृत्त्यर्थं प्रमाणादिषोडश-पदार्थानां तत्त्वज्ञानान्निःश्रेयसाधिगमः इत्यादावसूत्र-

कारस्तु यावदर्थकः, तथा च 'दुःखपङ्कनिमग्नं' तदानीं दुःखसमूहाधिकरणं यावद्वस्तु, 'उद्दिधीर्षुः' तदात्यन्तिकदुःखध्वंसविशिष्टं चिकीर्षुः, 'परमकारुणिकोमुनिः', 'अष्टादशविद्यास्थानेषु' "अङ्गानि वेदाश्चत्वारो मीमांसा न्यायविस्तरः । धर्म्मशास्त्रं पुराणञ्च विद्या ह्येताश्चतुर्दश" ॥ "आयुर्व्वेदो धनुर्व्वेदो गान्धर्व्वश्चेति ते त्रयः । अर्थशास्त्रञ्च विज्ञेयं विद्या ह्यष्टादशैव तु" ॥ इति परिगणितेषु विद्यास्थानेषु, 'अभ्यर्हिततमां' प्रकृष्टतमां, 'आन्वीक्षिकीं'(१) न्यायशास्त्रं, 'प्रणिनाय'ेति योजना । वस्तुत्वसामानाधिकरण्येन दुःखपङ्कमग्नत्वस्यान्वयात् घटादिस्वरूपे वस्तुनि दुःखपङ्कमग्नत्वस्य बाधितत्वेऽपि न क्षतिः । मुक्तात्मनोऽपि यदा कदाचित् दुःखपङ्कमग्नत्वात् तदुद्धारणेच्छायां मुनेरप्रामाणिकत्वापत्तिरतस्तदानीमिति ।

दीधितिकृतस्तु जगत्पदं तदानीं संसारविशिष्टात्मपरं तथा च अन्वयितावच्छेदकावच्छेदेनैव दुःखपङ्कमग्नत्वस्य दुःखसमूहाधिकरणत्वस्यान्वयः । भगवदात्मनो मुक्तात्मनश्च व्यवच्छेदाय विशिष्टान्तमित्याहुः ।

'तच्चेति 'तच्च' न्यायशास्त्रं, 'प्रेक्षावत्प्रवृत्त्यर्थमिति 'प्रेक्षावतां' मोक्ष-

(१) 'अनु' श्रवणादनु, 'ईक्षा' मननं, तन्निर्वाहिकां 'आन्वीक्षिकीं' "श्रोतव्यो मन्तव्यः" इति श्रुतेः मननस्य श्रवणानन्तरकर्त्तव्यत्वात् ।

यत्, तेष्वपि प्रमाणाधीना सर्व्वेषां व्यवस्थितिरिति प्रमाणतत्त्वमत्र विविच्यते। ननु प्रमाणादीनां तत्त्वं प्रतिपादयच्छास्त्रं परम्परया निःश्रेयसेन सम्बध्यते

साधनीभूततत्त्वज्ञानचिकीर्षावतां, तद्ग्रन्थोपादानकप्रवृत्त्यर्थमित्यर्थः। 'तत्त्वज्ञानादिति तत्त्वेन प्रमाणत्वादिरूपेण ज्ञायतेऽनेनेति व्युत्पत्त्या प्रमाणादिषोडशपदार्थविशेष्यकप्रमाकरणत्वादिषोडशधर्मप्रकारकज्ञान-जनकादेतच्छास्त्रादित्यर्थः। 'निःश्रेयसाधिगमः' इति निःश्रेयसाय योऽधिगम इति व्युत्पत्त्या निःश्रेयससाधनीभूतं तत्त्वज्ञानमित्यर्थः, 'इतीति एतदर्थकमित्यर्थः, 'आदौ' प्रथमतः, 'अक्षचरणः' शास्त्रस्य तत्त्वज्ञानसाधनताप्रतिपादकं सूत्रं[१] कृतवान्। 'तेष्विति 'तेषु' शास्त्रो-द्दिष्टप्रमाणादिषोडशपदार्थेषु मध्ये, 'प्रमाणतत्त्वमत्र विविच्यते' इति योजना। 'प्रमाणतत्त्वं' प्रमाणस्य लक्षण-स्वरूपादिकं, 'अत्र चिन्तामणौ। एतेन मोक्षसाधनीभूततत्त्वज्ञानरूपफलवत्त्वशास्त्रीयचिकीर्षितप्रतिपादितप्रति-पादकत्वमत्रास्तीति प्रतिपादितमिति ध्येयम्।

ननु षोडशपदार्थेषु सत्सु प्रमाणतत्त्वस्यैव कुतो विवेचनमित्या-शङ्कां निराकर्तुमाह, 'प्रमाणाधीनेति, 'व्यवस्थितिः' व्यवस्था निश्चयः। तथा च प्रमाणाधीनतद्ग्रहादेव प्रमाणस्य प्रकृष्टत्वे तस्यैवात्र निरू-पणमिति भावः। माध्यमकः प्रत्यवतिष्ठते, 'नन्विति, एतन्मते शास्त्र-

---

(१) प्रमाण-प्रमेय-संशय-प्रयोजन-दृष्टान्त-सिद्धान्तावयव-तर्क-निर्णय-वाद-जल्प-वितण्डा-हेत्वाभास-छल-जाति-निग्रहस्थानानां तत्त्वज्ञानान्निःश्रेयसाधि-गमः इति गौतमसूत्रम्।

इति न युक्तं प्रमाणतत्त्वावधारणस्याशक्यत्वात्। तद्धि प्रमातत्त्वावधारणाधीनं तच्च स्वतः परतो वा न सम्भवति वक्ष्यमाणदूषणगणग्रासात्। अथ किं प्रामा-

---

मात्रस्यैव तद्वति तत्प्रकारकत्वरूपं न प्रमात्वं तच्च तस्य निश्चेतुमशक्य-त्वेन तत्र तत्सत्त्वे मानाभावादिति ध्येयम्। 'तत्त्वं प्रतिपादयदिति 'तत्त्वं' प्रमाकरणत्वादिकं, प्रकारिता द्वितीयार्थः। तथा च प्रमा-णादीनां प्रमाकरणत्वादिप्रकारेण ज्ञानं जनयदित्यर्थः। 'परम्पर-येति मोक्षसाधनीभूततत्त्वज्ञानद्वारा इत्यर्थः। 'इति न युक्तमिति सूचकतोऽभिप्रेतं न युक्तमित्यर्थः। 'प्रमाणतत्त्वेति प्रमाकरणानां प्रमाकरणत्वप्रकारकावधारणस्येत्यर्थः। 'तद्धि' तादृशावधारणं हि, 'प्रमातत्त्वावधारणेति प्रमायाः प्रमात्वप्रकारकावधारणस्याधीनमि-त्यर्थः, विशेषणतावच्छेदकप्रकारकज्ञानं विना विशिष्टवैशिष्ट्यबोधा-सम्भवादिति भावः। 'तच्च' प्रमातत्त्वावधारणञ्च, 'स्वतः' स्वाश्रय-जनकसामग्रीतः, स्वं प्रमात्वं, एतच्च गुरुमते, 'परतः' तदन्यसामग्रीतः, एतच्च मिश्रमत-भट्टमत-न्यायमतेषु। न च प्रमापदादेव प्रमात्वप्रकार-कोपस्थितिसम्भव इति वाच्यं। मानान्तरेण प्रमात्वप्रकारकज्ञानं विना प्रमापदशक्तिग्रहस्यैवासम्भवादिति भावः। 'वक्ष्यमाणेति गुरुमते प्रामाण्यसंशयानुपपत्तिरूपं, नैयायिकमते चानवस्थारूपं। 'प्रामा-ण्यज्ञानेनेति प्रमात्वनिश्चयेनेत्यर्थः। 'तस्य व्यभिचारादिति प्रवर्त्त-केष्टसाधनतादिज्ञाननिष्ठप्रमात्वनिश्चयस्य व्यभिचारादित्यर्थः, सकम्प-प्रवृत्तेस्तेन विनापि दर्शनादिति भावः। सकम्पत्वं निष्कम्पत्वञ्च प्रवृ-

ण्यज्ञानेन प्रवृत्तिमात्रे तस्य व्यभिचारात् बहुवित्त-व्ययायाससाध्ये प्रवृत्तिश्चावश्यकार्थनिश्चयादेव। न च यत्संशय-व्यतिरेकनिश्चयौ यस्य प्रवृत्तिप्रतिबन्धकौ

त्तिनिष्ठो विषयिताविशेषः न तु जातिरांशिकत्वापत्तेरिति ध्येयम्[१]।

ननु मास्तु प्रवृत्तिमात्रे तस्य हेतुत्वं तथापि निष्कम्पप्रवृत्तौ तस्य हेतुत्वेन जनकज्ञाने प्रामाण्यनिश्चयोऽवश्यमपेक्षितः इत्यत आह, 'बहुवित्तेति निष्कम्पप्रवृत्तिरित्यर्थः। 'अर्थनिश्चयादेवेति इदमिष्टसाधनमेव इत्यवधारणात्मकज्ञानादेवेत्यर्थः। अवधारणत्वञ्च निश्चयनिष्ठो विषयिताविशेषः, तथा च निष्कम्पप्रवृत्तावपि तस्यान्यथासिद्धत्वान्न हेतुत्वमिति भावः। यद्यपि किं प्रामाण्यज्ञानेनेति ग्रन्थोऽसङ्गतः प्रवृत्त्यर्थं प्रवर्त्तकेष्टसाधनतादिज्ञाननिष्ठप्रमात्वनिश्चयापेक्षायाः पूर्व्वमनुक्तत्वेन तस्य प्रवृत्तिहेतुत्वनिराकरणद्वारा तदनपेक्षाकथनस्य सन्दर्भविरुद्धत्वात्, तथापि 'नन्वित्यादिमाध्यमकशङ्कोत्सारको नायं ग्रन्थः, परन्तु शास्त्रस्य मननादिनिष्ठनिःश्रेयससाधनताज्ञाने प्रमात्वनिश्चयजननद्वारा मननादौ निःश्रेयसार्थिप्रवृत्तिप्रयोजकत्वेन निःश्रेयसोपयोगित्वमिति सूत्रकर्तुराशय इति भ्रमेणान्तरा तटस्थो नैयायिकोपरि शङ्कां कुरुते, 'अथ किमिति, 'किं प्रामाण्यज्ञानेनेत्यस्य च मननादिनिष्ठमोक्षसाधनतादिज्ञाने प्रमात्वनिश्चयेन किमित्यर्थः, तथा च निष्फलं तन्निश्चायकं शास्त्रमित्यभिप्रायः। सूत्रकर्तुस्तादृशाभिप्राय-

---

(१) सकम्पत्वस्य निष्कम्पत्वस्य च जातित्वे कस्मिंश्चिदंशे सकम्पायां कस्मिंश्चिदंशे च निष्कम्पायां समूहालम्बनप्रवृत्तौ सकम्पत्व-निष्कम्पत्वयोर्जात्योरांशिकत्वं स्यादिति भावः।

तन्निश्चयस्तद्धेतुरनुमितौ व्याप्तेरिवेति वाच्यम्। तत्स-न्देहे सत्यर्थसन्देहेनार्थानिश्चयादेवाप्रवृत्तेः तच्च तयो-

---

रभिप्रेत्यैव 'प्रामाण्यसंशयानन्तरमिदं' इत्यादिना नैयायिकस्तन्निरा-करिष्यतीति न कश्चिद्दोषः ।

केचित्तु ननु ग्रन्थकर्तुः शास्त्रानुकूलप्रवृत्त्यनन्तरं शास्त्रे जाते ततः प्रमाणादीनां प्रमाकरणत्वादिप्रकारकज्ञानं भविष्यति शास्त्रानुकूल-प्रवृत्तिश्च विना प्रवर्त्तकशास्त्रनिष्ठेष्टसाधनताज्ञानादेः प्रमात्वावधारणं तव नये न सम्भवति तव प्रमात्वनिश्चयस्य प्रवर्त्तकत्वात्, प्रमात्व-निश्चयश्च न सम्भवति उपायाभावादित्याशयेन माध्यमकः शङ्कते, 'ननु प्रमाणादीनामिति 'अशक्यत्वात्' शास्त्रादशक्यत्वादित्यर्थः । 'तद्धि' शास्त्रं हि, तवेतिशेषः, 'प्रमातत्त्वेति शास्त्रानुकूलप्रवृत्तिजनकज्ञा-नस्य प्रमात्वनिश्चयाधीनमित्यर्थः, 'तच्च' प्रमातत्त्वावधारणञ्च, अत्रैवा-न्तरा समाधत्ते, 'अथेति, 'प्रामाण्यज्ञानेनेति प्रवर्त्तकशास्त्रनिष्ठेष्ट-साधनताज्ञानादेः प्रमात्वनिश्चयेनेत्यर्थः । तथा च प्रमात्वनिश्चयं विनापि शास्त्रानुकूलप्रवृत्तिसम्भवेन शास्त्रोत्पत्तिसम्भवान्न ततः प्रमा-णतत्त्वावधारणमशक्यमिति भावः । अग्रे च 'प्रामाण्यनिश्चयाधीनत्वा-दित्यस्य तव मते प्रमात्वनिश्चयाधीनत्वादित्यर्थ इत्याहुः ।

अन्ये तु प्रमातत्त्वावधारणं विना प्रमाणानां प्रमाकरणत्वरूपेणा-वधारणासम्भवात् तेन रूपेण तदवधारणं मास्तु इन्द्रियत्वज्ञानजन-कत्वादिनैव तदवधारणं शास्त्रात् स्यादित्याशयेन माध्यमकशङ्कापर्य्यैव शङ्कते, 'अथेति, 'प्रामाण्यज्ञानेनेति प्रमाकरणत्वरूपेणावधारणेनेत्यर्थः। ननु तथापि तव नये प्रवर्त्तकज्ञाने प्रमात्वनिश्चयस्य प्रवृत्ति-

रप्रतिबन्धकत्वादिति चेत् । न । प्रामाण्यसंशयानन्तरं इदं इत्थमेवेत्यवधारणस्य[१] निष्कम्पप्रवृत्त्यङ्गस्य

प्रयोजकतया प्रमात्वनिश्चयोऽवश्यमपेक्षितः स च न सम्भवति उपायाभावादित्यत आह, 'प्रवृत्तिमात्र इति, 'तस्य' प्रमात्वनिश्चयस्य, अग्रे च 'प्रामाण्यनिश्चयाधीनत्वादित्यस्य तत्र मते प्रमात्वनिश्चयाधीनत्वादित्यर्थः । यथाश्रुते प्रमात्वानभ्युपगन्त्रा माध्यमकेन तन्निश्चयकारणत्वव्यवस्थापनस्यासङ्गतत्वापत्तेरित्याहुः ।

नव्यास्तु नन्वेवं तत्रापि प्रवृत्त्यर्थं प्रवर्त्तकज्ञानोत्पत्त्यनन्तरं तत्र ज्ञाने प्रमात्वनिश्चयोऽपेक्षितः स कथं स्यादुपायाभावादित्याशङ्कायां माध्यमकः समाधत्ते, 'अथ किं प्रामाण्यज्ञानेनेति 'अथ' प्रवर्त्तकज्ञानोत्पत्त्यनन्तरं, तत्र ज्ञाने प्रामाण्यनिश्चयेन मम किमित्यर्थः । 'तस्य' प्रवर्त्तकज्ञाननिष्ठप्रमात्वनिश्चयस्य, इत्यस्य 'ननु प्रमाणादीनामित्यारभ्य 'तयोरप्रतिबन्धकत्वादित्यन्तं माध्यमकपूर्व्वपक्षः, तत्र नैयायिकः समाधास्यति, 'प्रामाण्यसंशयानन्तरमित्यादिना । 'प्रामाण्यनिश्चयाधीनत्वादित्यस्य च अवश्यं प्रमात्वनिश्चयाधीनत्वेन स्वीकर्त्तव्यत्वादित्यर्थः । तथा च प्रमात्वनिश्चयार्थं कश्चिदुपायस्त्वयाप्यवश्यं परिचिन्तनीय इति सिद्धान्तयितुराशयः । इत्थं निरस्ते माध्यमके मीमांसकः नैयायिकैः समं विवादमवतारयति, 'ननु स्वत एवेत्यादिना, इति प्राहुः ।

प्रामाण्यसंशय-प्रामाण्यव्यतिरेकनिश्चययोर्निष्कम्पप्रवृत्तिप्रतिबन्धकत्वात् प्रामाण्यनिश्चयस्तद्धेतुरित्याशङ्कते, 'न च यस्येति यस्य संशयो यस्य व्यतिरेकनिश्चयस्य इत्यर्थः । 'प्रवृत्तिप्रतिबन्धकाविति

(१) इदं रजतमित्थमेवेत्यवधारणस्येति क० ।

प्रामाण्यनिश्चयाधीनत्वात्। ननु स्वत एवास्तु तन्निरूपणं। तथाहि तत्र विप्रतिपत्तयः। ज्ञानप्रामाण्यं तद-

'प्रवृत्तिः' उत्पत्तिः, 'यस्येत्यनुषज्यते। अग्रेऽपि प्रवृत्तिपदं तदुत्पत्तिपरं, तथा च यस्य संशयो यस्य व्यतिरेकनिश्चयश्च यदुत्पत्ति-प्रतिबन्धकस्तन्निश्चयस्तद्धेतुरित्यर्थः। अन्यथा प्रवृत्तिपदस्य प्रयत्नपरत्वे 'अनुमितौ व्याप्तेरिवेति दृष्टान्तासङ्गतेः। न च तथापि व्याप्तिसंशयादेरनुमित्यप्रतिबन्धकत्वे(१) दृष्टान्तासङ्गतिः प्रयोजकीभूताभाव प्रतियोगित्वरूपप्रतिबन्धकत्वनिवेशे(२) च तत्र तयोरप्रतिबन्धकत्वादिति वक्ष्यमाणदूषणासङ्गतिरिति वाच्यम्। व्याप्तिसंशयादेरप्यनुमितिप्रतिबन्धकत्वमिति मतेनैतदभिधानात्(३)। अत्र तन्निश्चयत्वेन तन्निश्चये हेतुत्वमेव साध्यम्, अन्यथा ज्ञानत्वादिना भगवत्प्रामाण्यनिश्चयनिष्ठहेतुत्वमादाय सिद्धसाधनापत्तेः। एवञ्च ग्राह्यव्यतिरेकनिश्चयप्रतिबध्ये ग्राह्यविशिष्टज्ञाने ग्राह्यनिश्चयत्वेनाहेतुत्वाद्व्यभिचारापत्तिरतो 'यत्संशय इति, घटाभावनिश्चयात्मकपटादिसंशयप्रतिबध्ये घटविशिष्टज्ञाने पटादिनिश्चयत्वेनाहेतुत्वात् व्यभिचार इति 'यद्व्यतिरेकनिश्चय इति, तथा च संशयनिश्चयसाधारणं यद्व्यतिरेकज्ञानत्वं यत्र प्रतिबन्धकतावच्छेदकं इत्यर्थः। अन्यथा व्यतिरेकनिश्चयोपादानेऽपि

(१) व्याप्तिसंशयादेरनुमितिप्रतिबन्धकत्वे मानाभावादिति ध०।

(२) व्याप्तिसंशयाभावस्य अनुमित्यकारणत्वेपि कथञ्चित् प्रयोजकत्वं सम्भवतीति भावः।

(३) अनुमितिप्रतिबन्धकत्वाभिमानेनैव तदभिधानादिति ध०।

प्रामाण्याग्राहकयावज्ज्ञानग्राहकसामग्रीग्राह्यं न वा। तज्ज्ञानविषयकज्ञानाजन्यज्ञानग्राह्यं न वा। परतः पक्षे ज्ञातएव ज्ञाने प्रामाण्यग्रहः स्वतस्त्वे प्रामाण्यवत

घटविशिष्टज्ञानस्य घटाभावनिश्चयात्मकपटादिव्यतिरेकनिश्चयस्यापि प्रतिबध्यत्वेन उक्तव्यभिचारतादवस्थ्यात्। इत्यस्य यत् यद्व्यतिरेकज्ञानत्वावच्छिन्नप्रतिबन्धकतानिरूपितप्रतिबध्यतावत् तत् तन्निश्चयत्वाच्छिन्नकारणतानिरूपितकार्य्यतावत् व्याप्तिनिश्चयजन्यानुमितिवदिति व्याप्तिशरीरं, नातो वैयधिकरण्यं। ग्राह्याभावान्तरसंशयवद्व्यभिचाराभावाभावसंशयस्यापि व्याप्तिनिश्चयाप्रतिबन्धकत्वात् अव्यभिचारव्यतिरेकज्ञानमादाय व्याप्तिज्ञाने न व्यभिचारः। न च यद्व्यतिरेकज्ञानत्वावच्छिन्नत्वं तत्पर्य्याप्तावच्छेदकताकत्वं तद्वृत्त्यवच्छेदकताकत्वं वा आद्ये दृष्टान्तासिद्धि-स्वरूपासिद्धी अनिश्चिताप्रामाण्यकव्याप्तिव्यतिरेकज्ञानत्वादिनैव प्रतिबन्धकत्वात्। द्वितीये ग्राह्याभावनिश्चयत्वस्य ग्राह्याभावज्ञानत्वघटिततया ग्राह्याभावनिश्चयप्रतिबध्ये ग्राह्यविशिष्टज्ञाने व्यभिचार इति वाच्यम्। यत् अनिश्चिताप्रामाण्यकयद्धर्म्मितावच्छेदककयद्धर्म्मावच्छिन्नव्यतिरेकज्ञानत्वपर्य्याप्तावच्छेदकताकप्रतिबन्धकताकं तत् तद्धर्म्मितावच्छेदककतद्धर्म्मावच्छिन्नप्रकारकज्ञाननिष्ठतद्धर्म्मिविशिष्टनिश्चयत्वावच्छिन्नकारणताकमिति विवक्षितत्वात्। साध्ये च तद्धर्म्मविशिष्टनिश्चयत्वावच्छिन्नत्वं तादृशनिश्चयत्ववृत्त्यवच्छेदकताकत्वमात्रं न तु पर्य्याप्तिपर्य्यन्तं विवक्षणीयं प्रयोजनाभावात् दृष्टान्तस्य साध्यविकलत्वापत्तेश्च, तथाऽगृहीताप्रामाण्यकव्याप्तिनिश्चयत्वेनैव हेतु-

एव ज्ञानस्य ग्रहात्। स्वाश्रयग्राहकेण गृह्यत एव न वा, स्वाश्रयेण गृह्यत एव न वेति प्रत्येकमेव वा। यत्तु योग-

---

त्वात्। अथ तथाप्यनुमितौ व्याप्तिविरहज्ञानस्य प्रतिबन्धकत्वोपगमे लाघवाद्व्याप्तिज्ञानत्वेनैव तत्र हेतुत्वं प्रतिबन्धकसत्त्वादेव व्याप्तिसंशयादनुमित्यनुत्पादसम्भवात् तथा च साध्यविकलो दृष्टान्तो व्यभिचारश्च। न च तज्ज्ञानत्वेन तज्ज्ञानहेतुत्वमेव साध्यमिति वाच्यं। निश्चयपदोपादानानुपपत्तेरिति चेत्। न। धूमो वह्निव्याप्यो न वेति संशयसत्त्वेऽपि रूपान्तरधर्मितावच्छेदकव्याप्तिनिश्चयादनुमित्युत्पत्त्या धूमत्वावच्छिन्नलिङ्गकवह्न्यनुमितिं प्रत्येव धूमत्वावच्छिन्नविशेष्यकव्याप्तिविरहज्ञानस्य प्रतिबन्धकतया धूमो वह्निव्याप्यो न वेति संशयसत्त्वे धूमत्वावच्छिन्नलिङ्गकानुमित्यनुत्पादेऽपि धूमलिङ्गकानुमितिसामान्यवारणाय धूमलिङ्गकानुमितिसामान्यं प्रति धूमलिङ्गकवह्निव्याप्तिनिश्चयत्वेनैव हेतुत्वस्यावश्यकत्वात्। वस्तुतस्तु स्वसमानाधिकरणतादृशनिश्चयाव्यवहितोत्तरक्षणोत्पत्तिकत्वादिरूपं फलोपधानघटितजन्यत्वमेवात्र साध्यं तावतापि भगवत्प्रामाण्यनिश्चयमादाय सिद्धसाधनाभावात्। न चैवमपि प्रामाण्यविषयकदृष्टसाधनतादिनिश्चयजन्यप्रवृत्तिव्यक्त्यावंशतः सिद्धसाधनमिति वाच्यम्। पक्षतावच्छेदकावच्छेदेन साध्यसिद्धेरुद्देश्यत्वात्। एतेन निष्कम्पप्रवृत्तिं प्रति प्रामाण्यज्ञानत्वेनैव हेतुत्वं न तु तन्निश्चयत्वेन प्रामाण्यसंशये तदनुत्पादस्य पृथक्प्रामाण्याभावज्ञानप्रतिबन्धकत्वेनैवोपपत्तेः। निश्चयत्वघटकदलद्वयस्य विशेष्य-विशेषणभावे विनिगमकाभावात निश्चयत्वेन

जधर्म्मसामान्यलक्षणप्रत्यसत्त्या स्वाश्रयप्रामाण्यं तेनैव गृह्यत इत्यंशतः सिद्धसाधनमतो योगजधर्म्माद्यजन्यत्वं विशेषणमिति। तन्न। परं प्रत्यसत्तेः प्रामाण्यमात्र-

---

हेतुत्वोपगमेऽपि गुरुतरकार्य्य-कारणभावद्वयस्यावश्यकत्वात् तथा च निश्चयत्वेन हेतुत्वस्य साध्यत्वे बाधः। एवं अनुमितिं प्रत्यपि व्याप्ति-ज्ञानत्वेनैव हेतुत्वं न तु व्याप्तिनिश्चयत्वेन व्याप्तिसंशयादनुमित्यनु-त्पादस्य लाघवाद्व्याप्तिविशिष्टवैशिष्ट्यावगाहिज्ञानस्यैवानुमितिहेतुतया तदभावादेव सम्भवात्, तत्सत्त्वे चानुमितेः सर्व्वसिद्धात् व्याप्त्यंशे संशया-त्मकपरामर्शस्य च व्याप्तिविशिष्टवैशिष्ट्यावगाहित्वाभावात्[१] इत्यपि निरस्तं इति।

हेतोः स्वरूपासिद्धिमाह, 'तत्सन्देहे सतीति इष्टसाधनतादि-निश्चये प्रामाण्यसन्देहे सतीत्यर्थः। 'अर्थसन्देहेनेति तदनन्तरमिष्ट-साधनतादिसन्देहस्यैव उत्पादेनेत्यर्थः। 'अर्थानिश्चयादेव' इति इद-मिष्टसाधनमेव इत्यवधारणात्मकनिश्चयविरहादेवेत्यर्थः। पूर्व्वोत्पन्न-निश्चयस्तु नावधारणात्मक इति भावः। 'अप्रवृत्तेरिति निष्कम्प-प्रवृत्तिविरहोपपत्तेरित्यर्थः। निष्कम्पप्रवृत्ताववधारणात्मकनिश्चयस्यैव हेतुत्वादिति भावः। 'तच्च' निष्कम्पप्रवृत्तौ, 'तयोः' प्रामाण्यसंशय-तद्-व्यतिरेकनिश्चययोः।

---

(१) विशिष्टवैशिष्ट्यावगाहिबुद्धिं प्रति विशेषणतावच्छेदक-प्रकारक-नि-श्चयस्य हेतुत्वादिति भावः।

पक्षत्वे प्रामाण्यं स्वाश्रयेण गृह्यत एवेत्युद्देश्यप्रतीतेरसिद्धेश्च नांशतः सिद्धसाधनम्। यद्वा घटोऽयमिति

ननु यत्रावधारणात्मकज्ञान एवाप्रामाण्यग्रहो जातस्तत्र निष्कम्पप्रवृत्तिवारणाय प्रामाण्याभावज्ञानस्य प्रतिबन्धकत्वमावश्यकं । न च तत्र प्रवृत्तिवारणाय अप्रामाण्यज्ञानविरहविशिष्टावधारणत्वेनैव हेतुत्वं न तु प्रामाण्याभावज्ञानं प्रतिबन्धकमिति वाच्यम्। अप्रामाण्यज्ञानविरहावधारणत्वयोर्विशेष्य-विशेषणभावे विनिगमकाभावेन तदपेक्ष्य लाघवादप्रामाण्यग्रहस्यैव प्रतिबन्धकत्वौचित्यादिति चेत्। न। अवधारणत्वात्मकविषयिताविशेषस्य स्वरूपसत एव स्वाश्रये प्रामाण्याभावग्रहप्रतिबन्धकतया तत्राप्रामाण्यग्रहस्यैवानुत्पत्तेरित्यभिमानः। वस्तुतस्तु व्याप्त्यभावज्ञानस्यानुमितिप्रतिबन्धकत्वे मानाभावात् दृष्टान्तासिद्धिः। न च प्रयोजकीभूताभावप्रतियोगित्वरूपं प्रतिबन्धकत्वं हेतौ निवेशनीयमिति वाच्यम्। तथाप्यप्रयोजकत्वात् यत्तदर्थयोरननुगतत्वेन दृष्टान्ताभावाच्च। न च व्यतिरेकेण सुलभो दृष्टान्तः इति वाच्यम्। प्रामाण्यनिश्चयत्वेन हेतुत्वस्य क्वाप्यसिद्ध्या साध्यप्रसिद्ध्यभावेन व्यतिरेकदृष्टान्तस्याप्यसम्भवादित्येव दूषणं सारं। 'प्रामाण्यसंशयानन्तरमिति पूर्वोत्पन्नेष्टसाधनतानिश्चये प्रामाण्यनिश्चयाभावेतरप्रामाण्यसंशयजनकसकलकारणसमवधानानन्तरमित्यर्थः। 'इत्थमेव' इष्टसाधनमेव, 'प्रामाण्यनिश्चयाधीनत्वादिति प्रामाण्यसंशयनिवृत्तिद्वारा प्रामाण्यनिश्चयाधीनत्वादित्यर्थः। तथा च इष्टसाधनताद्यवधारणं प्रति पूर्वोत्पन्नेष्टसाधनतादिनिश्चये प्रामाण्याभावज्ञानस्य प्रतिबन्धकतया तन्निवृत्तये क्वचित् प्रामाण्यनिश्चयोऽपेक्षितः इति भावः।

ज्ञानप्रामाण्यं एतज्ज्ञानग्राह्यं न वा। एतज्ज्ञानग्राह्यकमात्रग्राह्यं न वेति। तत्र यद्यपि विशेष्यावृत्त्यप्रकारकत्वमगृहीतग्राहित्वं वा, सर्व्वधीयथार्थत्वपक्षेऽनुभव-

---

मीमांसकद्वारा माध्यमकमतं निराकर्त्तुं मीमांसकमतमुत्थापयति, 'नन्विति, 'स्वतएव' स्वकीयेभ्य एव, स्वजनकसामग्री-स्वजन्यस्वप्रत्यक्षसामग्री-स्वजन्यज्ञाततालिङ्गकानुमितिसामग्र्यन्यतमेभ्य इति यावत्। स्वजन्येति स्वप्रत्यक्ष-ज्ञाततयोर्विशेषणं। पञ्चम्या जन्यत्वमर्थः। 'तन्निरूपणं' स्वस्मिन् प्रामाण्यनिरूपणं, स्वस्मिन् प्रामाण्यनिश्चय इति यावत्। अत्र स्वस्यैव स्वप्रामाण्यविषयकतया स्वजनकसामग्र्येव स्वनिष्ठप्रामाण्यनिश्चायिका इति गुरवः। स्वोत्तरवर्त्तिस्वविषयकलौकिकप्रत्यक्षस्य स्वनिष्ठप्रामाण्यविषयकतया स्वजन्यस्वविषयकप्रत्यक्षसामग्री स्वनिष्ठप्रामाण्यनिश्चायिका इति मिश्राः। ज्ञानस्यातीन्द्रियतया प्रत्यक्षासम्भवेन स्वजन्यज्ञाततालिङ्गकानुमितिसामग्री स्वनिष्ठप्रामाण्यनिश्चायिका इति भट्टाः। ज्ञातता च ज्ञात इति प्रतीतिसिद्धो ज्ञानजन्यो विषयसमवेतः प्राकट्यापरनामातिरिक्तपदार्थविशेषः। तल्लिङ्गेन प्रामाण्यानुमितिप्रकारस्तु अग्रे विवेचयिष्यामः। संवादिप्रवृत्तिजनकत्वादिहेतुना प्रामाण्यग्रह इति तु नैयायिकाः। तद्धेतुकप्रामाण्यग्रहस्तु सकलमीमांसकानामपि सम्मतः इति मतभेदो द्रष्टव्यः। केचित्तु 'स्वत एव' स्वकीयेनैव, स्व-स्वजन्यप्रत्यक्ष-स्वजन्यज्ञाततालिङ्गकानुमित्यन्यतमेनैव इति यावत्। स्वस्यापि तादात्म्यसम्बन्धेन स्वकीयत्वं, जन्यत्वं तृतीयार्थः। 'तन्निरूपणं इत्यस्य स्वनिष्ठप्रामाण्य-

त्वजातेरभावेन स्मरणान्यज्ञानत्वं विशिष्टज्ञानत्वं वा प्रामाण्यं स्वस्य न तेनैव न वा अनुव्यवसायेन ग्रहण-योग्यम्। विशेष्यावृत्त्यप्रकारकत्वादेर्विशेषणस्य प्रागनु-

---

व्यवहार इत्यर्थः। यद्वा तृतीयार्थोऽभेदः, 'तन्निरूपणं' इत्यस्य च स्वनिष्ठप्रामाण्यविषयकनिश्चय इत्यर्थ इत्याहुः।

नन्वत्र प्रामाण्यं तादृशान्यतमग्राह्यं न वेति न विप्रतिपत्तिः। नैयायिकमते गुरु-मिश्रमते च ज्ञाततायाऽनभ्युपगमेन विधिकोटेरप्रसिद्धत्वात्। एवं भट्टनयेपि ज्ञानस्यातीन्द्रियतया स्वजन्यस्वप्रत्यक्षाप्रसिद्ध्या न विधिकोटिप्रसिद्धिः, तथा च विप्रतिपत्त्यसम्भवेन कथं विवादप्रसक्तिरत आह,(१) 'तत्र विप्रतिपत्तयः' इति 'तत्र' मतत्रयसाधारणस्वकीयग्राह्यत्वे, व्यापारानुबन्धि विषयत्वं सप्तम्यर्थः। ज्ञान'प्रामाण्यमित्यादि, ज्ञानप्रामाण्यं तदप्रामाण्याग्राहिका यावती ज्ञानग्राहिका सामग्री तज्जन्यग्रहविषयो न वेत्यर्थः। विधिकोटिर्मीमांसकानां(२) निषेधकोटिश्च नैयायिकानां। विधिप्रसिद्धिस्तु वक्ष्यमाणक्रमेण तत्तज्ज्ञाने तत्तज्ज्ञानविषये घटत्वादौ ज्ञानत्वे वा। अत्र प्रामाण्यमात्रस्य पक्षत्वे इच्छादिवृत्तितद्वतितत्प्रकारकत्वादिरूपप्रामाण्येऽंशतोबाध इति पक्षे ज्ञानपदं। तथा च ज्ञाननिष्ठप्रामाण्यस्य पक्षत्वान्न बाधः। यद्यपि तस्य पक्षत्वेऽपि प्रशब्दसमभिव्याहृतेन माधातुना तद्वति

---

(१) विवादप्रवृत्तिरित्यत आहेति घ०।

(२) मीमांसकानां त्रयाणामिति घ०।

पस्थितौ तद्वैशिष्ट्यस्य ज्ञातुमशक्यत्वात्। नापि ज्ञानातीन्द्रियत्वे ज्ञानानुमित्या तद्गृह्यते। ज्ञानमात्रवि-

---

तत्प्रकारकत्वादिरूपप्रकर्षविशेषविशिष्टं ज्ञानं प्रत्याय्यते, भावल्युडुत्तरतद्धितप्रत्ययेन तादृशज्ञानत्वं प्रत्याय्यते इति प्रामाण्यपदेनैव तद्वति तत्प्रकारकत्वविशिष्टज्ञानत्वलाभादिच्छादिवृत्तितद्वतितत्प्रकारकत्वे बाधाभावेन ज्ञानपदमत्र व्यर्थं, तथापि तद्वति तत्प्रकारकत्वविशिष्टज्ञानत्वमत्र न प्रामाण्यपदार्थः, ज्ञानत्वभागस्य व्यर्थत्वात्। तद्वति तत्प्रकारकत्वस्य तत्पदार्थभेदेन ज्ञानभेदेन च भिन्नतया केनापि तद्वति तत्प्रकारकत्वेन विशिष्टस्य ज्ञानत्वस्य यावज्ज्ञानग्राहकसामग्रीग्राह्यत्वाभावेन बाधापत्त्या साध्ये ज्ञानपदस्य तज्ज्ञानपरत्वावश्यकत्वेन ज्ञानत्वांशोपादानेऽपि ज्ञानान्तरवृत्ति तद्वति तत्प्रकारकत्वमादाय अंशतो बाधतादवस्थ्यात्। तन्मतेऽप्यनुव्यवसायादौ तद्वतितत्प्रकारकत्वज्ञानत्वयोः स्वातन्त्र्येण विशिष्टे वैशिष्ट्यमितिन्यायेन ज्ञाने प्रकारतया तद्वति तत्प्रकारकत्वस्य वैशिष्ट्यसम्बन्धेन ज्ञानत्वेऽप्रकारत्वाद्बाधापत्तेश्च। ज्ञानत्वघटितप्रामाण्यस्य पक्षत्वे विवक्षणीयेषु सर्व्वेष्वेव विशेषणेषु ज्ञानत्वघटितप्रामाण्यस्यैव निवेशनीयतया गौरवापत्तेश्च। किन्तु प्रसमभिव्याहृतमाधातोस्तद्वति तत्प्रकारकपरतया तद्वति तत्प्रकारकत्वमात्रं तदर्थः, तथा च इच्छादिवृत्तितद्वतितत्प्रकारकत्वे ज्ञानान्तरवृत्तितद्वतितत्प्रकारत्वे चांशतो बाधवारणाय ज्ञानपदं तज्ज्ञाननिष्ठार्थकं, तथा च तज्ज्ञाननिष्ठघटत्ववतिघटत्वप्रकारकत्वं यावत्तज्ज्ञान-

ग्राहकसामग्रीग्राह्यं न वा, इत्यादिक्रमेण तत्तज्ज्ञानस्य तत्तत्प्रामाण्य-मादाय विप्रतिपत्तिः। न च तद्वति तत्प्रकारकत्वमेव तत्त्वेनोपादीयतां किं ज्ञाननिष्ठत्वोपादानेन इति वाच्यं। तद्वति तत्प्रकारकत्वनिष्ठतत्त्व-स्याज्ञाप्रवेशेन यथासन्निवेशे वैयर्थ्याभावात्। यदि च ज्ञानव्यक्ति-भेदेऽपि घटत्ववति घटत्वप्रकारकत्वादेर्न भेदस्तदा ज्ञानपदं तज्ज्ञान-परमपि न, किन्तु सामान्यतः ज्ञानवृत्तिघटत्ववतिघटत्वप्रकारकत्वत्वादि-मेव पक्षत्वम्, इच्छादिवृत्तिघटत्ववति घटत्वप्रकारकत्वादौ बाधवारणाय ज्ञानवृत्तित्वप्रवेशः,घटत्ववति घटत्वप्रकारकत्वादेरेकस्यैव ज्ञानेच्छादि-सकलसाधारणत्वे तु ज्ञानवृत्तित्वमपि नोपादेयं। घटत्ववति घटत्व-प्रकारत्वादिकमेव पक्षः पक्षे ज्ञानपदन्तु प्रामाण्यपदेन क्वचित् प्रमाक-रणत्वस्यापि बोधनात् घटत्ववति घटत्वप्रकारकत्वरूपप्रामाण्ये(१) प्रामा-ण्यपदस्य तात्पर्य्यग्राहकं चित्रगुरित्यादौ चित्रादिपदमिव। साध्ये ज्ञान-पदं घटत्ववति घटत्वप्रकारकत्वाद्याश्रयज्ञानपरं अन्यथा घटत्ववति घटत्वप्रकारकत्वादेः पटादिज्ञानग्राहकसामग्रीग्राह्यत्वाभावेन बाधा-पत्तेः। तथा च तज्ज्ञानवृत्तिघटत्ववतिघटत्वप्रकारकत्वं घटत्ववति घटत्वप्रकारकत्वं वा यावत्स्वाश्रयज्ञानग्राहकसामग्रीग्राह्यं न वेत्यादि-विप्रतिपत्तिशरीरं, स्वपदं पक्षीभूतघटत्ववतिघटत्वप्रकारकत्वादि-परं। न च ज्ञानपदसमभिव्याहृतप्रामाण्यपदेनापि क्वचित् व्याप्ति-ज्ञानादिवृत्तिप्रमाकरणत्वादिबोधनात् कुतस्तस्य तादृशप्रमात्वतात्प-र्य्यग्राहकत्वमिति वाच्यं। सामान्यतो ज्ञानपदसमभिव्याहारस्य तादृश-प्रमात्वतात्पर्य्यकत्वव्यभिचारित्वेऽपि व्यभिचारास्फूर्त्तिदशायां तत्तत्पद-

(१) घटत्ववति घटत्वप्रकारकत्वादिरूपप्रमात्वे इति ख०।

त्वेन वा तादृशप्रमात्वे तात्पर्य्यग्राहकत्वसम्भवात्। अन्यथा पित्रादि-पदादेर्भोजनादिप्रकरणादेश्चापि तात्पर्य्यग्राहकत्वानुपपत्तिरिति न काप्यनुपपत्तिः। वस्तुतस्तु घटत्ववति घटत्वप्रकारकत्वादेर्ज्ञानेच्छादि-साधारणस्य एकत्वेऽपि ज्ञाननिष्ठघटत्ववतिघटत्वप्रकारकत्वत्वादिना सा-ध्यसिद्धेरुद्देश्यतया न पक्षे ज्ञानपदवैयर्थ्यम् इत्येव तत्त्वं।

केचित्तु तद्वति तत्प्रकारकत्वविशिष्टज्ञानत्वत्वेन न पक्षता तच्छ-ब्दार्थस्य प्रकारभेदेन भिन्नतया सर्व्वेषां विशिष्योपादानस्याशक्यत्वात् किन्तु प्रामाण्यपदार्थत्वेनैव पक्षत्वं तथा च प्रमाकरणत्वस्यापि प्रामा-ण्यपदार्थत्वेन तदंशतो बाधवारणाय ज्ञानपदं, तदुपादाने च ज्ञान-निष्ठप्रामाण्यपदार्थस्य पक्षत्वात् प्रमाकरणत्वस्य ज्ञाननिष्ठत्वाभावान्न-बाधः। साध्ये ज्ञानपदं स्वाश्रयज्ञानपरमित्याहुः।

तदसत् प्रमाकरणत्वस्यापि व्याप्तिज्ञानादिवृत्तित्वेन ज्ञाननिष्ठ-त्वात् विशेष्यावृत्त्यप्रकारकत्वादेरपि ज्ञाननिष्ठप्रमाण्यपदार्थत्वात् तदं-शतो बाधस्य दुर्व्वारत्वाच्च। न च ज्ञाननिष्ठत्वं ज्ञानमात्रनिष्ठत्वं प्रमा-करणत्वादिकञ्च न तथा तस्य मनःप्रभृतिवृत्तित्वात् इति वाच्यं। व्याप्तिज्ञानादिनिष्ठानुमित्यादिरूपप्रमाकरणत्वव्यक्तेः स्वविशेष्यावृत्त्य-प्रकारकज्ञानत्वस्य च ज्ञानमात्रनिष्ठत्वेन तत्र बाधस्य दुर्व्वारत्वात् स्वत्वस्याननुगतस्याभावात् साध्ये स्वपदेन घटत्ववतिघटत्वप्रकारक-त्वाद्येकैकोपादानेऽपरत्रांशतो बाधस्य दुर्व्वारत्वाच्च। अतएव प्रामाण्य-पदार्थत्वेनैवात्र पक्षत्वात् प्रमाकरणत्व-विशेष्यावृत्त्यप्रकारकत्वादौ बाध वारणाय ज्ञानपदं प्रवृत्तिहेतुज्ञानविषयपरं[१] प्रमाकरणत्व-विशेष्या-

(१) प्रवृत्तिहेतुज्ञानपरमिति क०।

वृत्त्यप्रकारकत्वादिकन्तु न तथा[१], लाघवात् तद्वतितत्प्रकारकज्ञानत्वज्ञानस्यैव प्रवृत्तिहेतुत्वात्। साध्ये च ज्ञानपदं स्वाश्रयपरमेवेति कस्यचित् प्रलपितमप्यपास्तं, स्वत्वस्यानुगतस्याभावेनांशतो बाधस्य दुर्व्वारत्वादिति दिक्।

इदं ज्ञानं प्रमेत्यनुमितिसामग्रीग्राह्यत्वमादाय विधौ सिद्धसाधनवारणाय निषेधकोटौ बाधस्य च वारणाय यावदिति सामग्रीविशेषणं। न च तादृशयावत्सामग्रीजन्यग्रहोऽप्रसिद्धः शाब्दानुमित्यादिसामग्रीजन्यत्वस्य कुत्रचिद्ग्रहेऽभावादिति वाच्यम्। तादृशसामग्रीत्वव्यापकस्वग्राहकताकत्वस्य विवक्षितत्वादिति प्राञ्चः।

तदसत् स्वत्वस्यानुगतस्याभावात् स्वपदस्य दृष्टान्तपरत्वे बाधात् पक्षीभूतप्रामाण्यपरत्वे साध्याप्रसिद्धेः तादृशग्राहकत्वव्यापकत्वस्यैव सम्यक्त्वेन सामग्रीपदवैयर्थ्यापत्तेश्च। एतेन प्रामाण्यग्राहकत्वं तज्ज्ञानग्राहकसामग्रीत्वव्यापकं न वेत्यत्र तात्पर्य्यमित्यपि निरस्तं। सामग्रीपदवैयर्थ्यापत्तेः पक्षे तज्ज्ञानवृत्तित्वविशेषणवैयर्थ्यापत्तेश्च। न च तज्ज्ञानग्राहकसामग्रीत्वव्यापकजनकतानिरूपकग्रहविषयत्वमर्थ इति वाच्यं। तज्ज्ञानग्राहकसामग्रीत्वस्य शाब्दानुमित्यादिसकलसामग्रीनिष्ठत्वेन तादृशग्रहाप्रसिद्धितादवस्थ्यात्।

दीधितिकृतस्तु यावदिति चरमग्रहविशेषणं तथा च तदप्रामाण्याग्राहकतज्ज्ञानग्राहकसामग्रीजन्ययावद्ग्रहविषयो न वेत्यर्थः। तद्ग्राहकात्मादिजन्ययावद्ग्रहविषयत्वाप्रसिद्धेः सामग्रीति। न चैक

---

(१) प्रवृत्तिहेतुज्ञानविषय इत्यर्थः।

एव यत्र ज्ञानग्राहकसामग्रीजन्योग्रहस्तत्र साध्याप्रसिद्धेर्यावत्त्वमपि दुर्लक्षमिति वाच्यम्। यावत्पदस्य व्यापकतापरत्वात्। तथा च विषयितासम्बन्धेन तादृशसामग्रीजन्यग्रहत्वव्यापक न वेत्यर्थः। व्यापकत्वञ्च विषयितासम्बन्धसामान्यावच्छिन्ना या तद्दन्निष्ठान्योन्याभावप्रतियोगितावच्छेदकता तच्छून्यत्वम्। अथ सामग्रीपदस्य यावत्कारणवाचितया तज्ज्ञानग्राहकसामग्रीजन्यग्रहस्याप्यक्रमेणाप्रसिद्धिः। न च सामग्रीपदं प्रागभावपरं इति वाच्यम्। प्रागभावस्य परैरनभ्युपगमात् इति चेत्। न। तज्ज्ञानग्राहकसामग्रीजन्यग्रहत्वपदेन तज्ज्ञानग्रहमात्रवृत्तिकार्य्यताप्रतियोगिककारणतानिरूपितकार्य्यताश्रयग्रहत्वस्य विवक्षितत्वात्। तादृशी च कारणता विषयादेस्तत्तद्व्यक्तित्वेन कारणतामादायैव प्रसिद्धा। नचैवं तज्ज्ञानमात्रवृत्तिकार्य्यताश्रयग्रहत्वमेव सम्यक् व्यर्थमधिकमिति वाच्यं। यथासन्निवेशे वैयर्थ्याभावादन्यथा तज्ज्ञानग्राहकसामग्रीजन्यग्रहस्य तज्ज्ञानग्रहरूपतया यावत्तज्ज्ञानग्रहविषयत्वस्यैव सम्यक्त्वेन सामग्रीजन्यत्वविशेषणस्यापि वैयर्थ्यापातादिति प्राहुः(१)।

केचित्तु यावत्त्वं तज्ज्ञानग्राहकेत्यत्र ग्रहधात्वर्थस्य तज्ज्ञानविषयकग्रहस्य विशेषणं तथा च यावानेव तज्ज्ञानग्रहस्तत्प्रत्येकजनकसामग्रीजन्यग्रहविषयो न वेत्यर्थः। तत्प्रत्येकजनकात्मादिजन्यग्रहविषयत्वमादाय विधौ सिद्धसाधनस्य निषेधेऽप्रसिद्धेश्च वारणाय सामग्रीति। न च योगिज्ञानानङ्गीकर्तृनये यत्र एक एव तज्ज्ञानग्रह-

---

(१) वैयर्थ्यापातादिति भाव इति ख०, ग० च।

त्तच साध्याप्रसिद्धिः[१] इति वाच्यं। तज्ज्ञानप्रामाण्यपक्षीकरणे यावत्-पदस्य वैयर्थ्येनानुपादेयत्वात्। न च यावान् तज्ज्ञानग्रहस्तद्विषयत्वमेवास्तु किं तत्प्रत्येकसामग्रीजन्यग्रहप्रवेशेनेति वाच्यम्। यथासन्निवेशे वैयर्थ्याभावादित्याहुः।

इदं ज्ञानं घटत्ववति घटत्वप्रकारकत्वाभाववदित्यादिपक्षीभूत-प्रमात्वाभावभ्रमात्मकतज्ज्ञानग्रहसामग्र्या यावदन्तर्गततया प्रतिबन्धकवशेन प्रामाण्यग्रहाद्बाधवारणाय 'तदप्रामाण्याग्राहकेति, एतच्च यावत्पदस्य सामग्रीविशेषणत्वपक्षे सामग्रीविशेषणमेव। तथा च तदप्रामाण्यग्रहाजनकेत्यर्थः। यावत्त्वस्य प्रथमग्रहधात्वर्थे चरमग्रहधात्वर्थे वा विशेषणत्वपक्षे तु प्रथमग्रहधात्वर्थस्यैव विशेषणं, तथा च तदप्रामाण्याविषयकेत्यर्थः। तत्पदं विशिष्य पक्षीभूतप्रामाण्याभावपरिचयाय, तदप्रामाण्येत्यस्य तत्प्रामाण्याभावेत्यर्थः, अन्यथा प्रामाण्यैकस्याभावादितरप्रामाण्याभावपरतायां यथोक्तबाधतादवस्थ्यात्। न च तथापि प्रमात्वाभावभ्रमोत्तरोत्पन्नतज्ज्ञानग्रहजनकसामग्रीं तादृशतज्ज्ञानग्रहं वा आदाय बाधो दुर्वार इति वाच्यं। पूर्वं प्रमात्वाभावभ्रमसत्त्वे तदुत्तरोत्पन्नतज्ज्ञानग्रहस्यापि प्रमात्वाभावविषयकत्वावश्यकत्वेन तदप्रामाण्याग्राहकपदेनैव वारणात्। तज्ज्ञानग्रहपदेन तज्ज्ञानग्रहविशेषस्यैवात्र विवक्षणीयतया प्रमात्वाभावभ्रमोत्तरोत्पन्नानुमित्याद्यात्मकतज्ज्ञानग्रहमादाय दोषाभावात्। अथ वा तदप्रामाण्याग्राहकत्वं तदप्रामाण्यग्रहाभावविशिष्टत्वं वैशिष्ट्यञ्च सामग्रीविशेषणत्वपक्षे स्वक्षण-स्वाव्यवहितोत्तरक्षणान्यतरक्षणावच्छेदेन एकाधिकर-

(१) यावत्त्वघटितसाध्याप्रसिद्धिरित्यर्थः।

णस्थत्तित्वं स्वपदं सामग्रीपरं, प्रथमग्रहधात्वर्थविशेषणत्वपक्षे तु स्वक्षणस्वाव्यवहितपूर्व्वक्षणान्यतरक्षणावच्छेदेन एकात्मवृत्तित्वमिति यथाश्रुतानुयायिनः।

तदसत् इदं ज्ञानं घटत्ववति घटत्वप्रकारकत्वाभाववदित्यादिभ्रमात्मकज्ञानग्राहकसामग्र्यापि प्रतियोगिविधया प्रामाण्यग्रहजननात्तामादाय बाधाभावात्। न च प्रामाण्याभावग्रहस्य(१) प्रतियोगिविधया प्रामाण्यविषयकत्वेऽपि इदं ज्ञानं भ्रम इति ज्ञानग्रहस्य प्रमात्वाविषयकत्वात् तत्सामग्रीमादाय बाधवारणायाप्रामाण्याग्राहकपदं अप्रामाण्यपदस्य भ्रमत्वपरत्वादिति वाच्यं। स्वरूपतो भ्रमत्वग्रहस्य प्रमात्वग्रहाविरोधित्वेन तत्सामग्र्या प्रमात्वग्रहजनने बाधकाभावात्। प्रमात्वविरोधित्वेन प्रामात्वाभावावच्छेदकत्वेन च भ्रमत्वग्रहस्य प्रमात्वविषयकत्वनियमेन तत्सामग्रीमादायापि बाधकाभावात्। किञ्च तद्विशेषणोपादानेपि इदं ज्ञानं निष्प्रकारकं इदं ज्ञानं निर्व्विशेष्यकमित्यादिज्ञानग्राहकसामग्र्या प्रतियोगिविधयापि प्रामाण्यग्रहाद्बाधस्यैव दुर्व्वारत्वात्।

साम्प्रदायिकास्तु इदं ज्ञानं निर्व्विशेष्यकमिदं ज्ञानं निष्प्रकारकमित्यादिज्ञानग्रहसामग्र्या प्रतियोगिविधयापि प्रामाण्याग्रहाद्बाधः, एवं गुरुनये इदं ज्ञानं न प्रमा इति प्रमात्वाभावभ्रमात्मकतज्ज्ञानग्रहसामग्रीमादायापि बाधः तन्मते प्रमात्वाभावभ्रमस्येदंज्ञानानुभव-प्रामाण्याभावस्मरणोभयरूपत्वात्(२) इदंज्ञानानु-

---

(१) प्रामाण्याभावभ्रमस्येति क०।

(२) गुरुमते अन्यथाख्यात्यस्वीकारादिति भावः।

भवसामग्र्या यावदन्तर्गतायाः प्रतियोगिविधयापि प्रामाण्याग्राहकत्वा-
दतः 'तदप्रामाण्याग्राहकेति सामग्र्याः प्रथमग्रहधात्वर्थस्य वा विशेषणं।
अप्रामाण्यपदस्य पक्षीभूतप्रामाण्यविरोधिपरं, तेन इदं निष्प्रकारक-
मित्यादिज्ञानग्राहकसामग्रीमादाय न बाधतादवस्थ्यं, निष्प्रकारक-
त्वादेरपि पक्षीभूतप्रामाण्यविरोधित्वात्। तद्विरोधित्वञ्च न तज्ज्ञान-
प्रतिबन्धकग्रहविषयत्वं, प्रामाण्यस्यापि प्रामाण्यग्रहप्रतिबन्धकग्रहविषय-
तया तदग्राहकतज्ज्ञानग्रहजनकसामग्रीजन्यग्रहविषयत्वस्य बाधापत्तेः।
अपि तु तदवच्छेदकतानिरूपकसम्बन्धेन तदवच्छेदकावच्छिन्नं विशे-
षणताविशेषसम्बन्धेन तदधिकरणवृत्तित्वं तच्छून्यत्वं, तेन प्रामाण्या-
धिकरणेऽपि किञ्चिदंशे निष्प्रकारकत्वादिसत्त्वेऽपि न विरोधित्वानुप-
पत्तिः। जातित्ववति जातित्वप्रकारकत्वरूपप्रामाण्यस्य पक्षतायां जाति-
मान् घट इत्यादावेकस्मिन्नेव घटत्वांशे जातित्ववति जातित्वप्रकारकत्व-
निष्प्रकारकत्वयोरुभयोरेव सत्त्वेन निष्प्रकारकत्वस्य पक्षीभूतप्रामा-
ण्यस्य विरोधित्वासम्भवात् तदवच्छेदकतानिरूपकसम्बन्धेनेत्युक्तं, जाति-
मान् घट इति ज्ञाने च घटत्वं निरवच्छिन्नप्रकारिताव्यक्तिसम्बन्धेन नि-
ष्प्रकारकत्वावच्छेदकं जातित्वावच्छिन्नविषयिताव्यक्तिसम्बन्धेन जाति-
त्ववति जातित्वप्रकारकत्वावच्छेदकमिति नैकसम्बन्धेन द्वयोरवच्छेदकं।
तदवच्छेदकतापर्य्याप्त्यधिकरणपर्य्याप्तावच्छेदकताकं यद्विशेषणताविशे-
षेण तदधिकरणवृत्तित्वं तच्छून्यत्वं वा वक्तव्यं। जातिमान् घट इति ज्ञाने
च स्वरूपतो घटत्वं निष्प्रकारकतावच्छेदकतापर्य्याप्त्यधिकरणं जातित्व-
विशिष्टं सज्जातित्ववतिजातित्वप्रकारकतावच्छेदकतापर्य्याप्त्यधिकरण-
मिति न दोषः। न चाप्रामाण्यपदस्य यथोक्तप्रामाण्यविरोधिपरत्वे

अनुव्यवसायादिसामग्र्यामनुव्यवसायादौ वा तद्ग्राहकत्वमप्रसिद्धं, प्रा-
माण्यभाने प्रामाण्यविरोधिनो घटत्वादेरवश्यं भानादिति वाच्यं ।
तदप्रामाण्येत्यत्र तदिति लुप्तसप्तमीकं, तथा च सामग्रीविशेषणत्व-
पक्षे तस्मिन् ज्ञाने विशेषणतासम्बन्धेन तत्प्रामाण्यविरोधिप्रकारक-
ग्रहाजनकेत्यर्थः । अनुव्यवसायादिसामग्री च न ज्ञाने विशेषणतावि-
शेषणसम्बन्धेन प्रामाण्यविरोधिनो घटत्वादेर्ग्रहजनिकेति नाप्रसिद्धिः ।
प्रथमग्रहविशेषणत्वपक्षे तु तस्मिन् ज्ञाने विशेषणताविशेषसम्बन्धेन
तत्प्रामाण्यविरोधिप्रकारकग्रहभिन्नेत्यर्थः । अनुव्यवसायादिर्न विशे-
षणताविशेषसम्बन्धेन ज्ञाने प्रामाण्यविरोधिघटत्वादिप्रकारक इति
नाप्रसिद्धिः । अनुव्यवसायादौ समवायादिसम्बन्धेन निरुक्तप्रामाण्य-
विरोधिनो ज्ञानत्वस्य प्रकारत्वात् विशेषणताविशेषसम्बन्धेनेति । न
च तथापि तज्ज्ञाने घटत्ववतिघटत्वप्रकारकत्वादिविरोधित्वेन तद-
भावावच्छेदकत्वेन वा तज्ज्ञानीयघटविषयकत्वघटत्वप्रकारकत्वादि-
भ्रमात्मकतज्ज्ञानग्रहजनकसामग्र्या तज्ज्ञाननिष्ठप्रामाण्यग्रहाद्बाधः,
तज्ज्ञानीयघटविषयकत्वादेर्वस्तुगत्या प्रामाण्यविरोधित्वाभावेन तत्र
ज्ञाने प्रामाण्यविरोध्यग्राहकत्वस्य तत्रापि सत्त्वादिति वाच्यम् ।
तत्रापि प्रतियोगिविधया प्रामाण्यभाने बाधकाभावात् तत्र ज्ञाने
प्रामाण्याभाववत्त्वभाने बाधकाभावेन तज्ज्ञानप्रामाण्यविरोध्यग्राहक-
त्वस्यासत्त्वाच्च । एतेनोक्तज्ञाने निष्प्रकारकत्व-निर्विशेष्यकत्वादिव्याप्य-
त्वेन तदवच्छेदकत्वेन वा तज्ज्ञानीयघटविषयकत्व-घटत्वप्रकारक-
त्वादिभ्रमात्मकतज्ज्ञानग्रहसामग्र्या तज्ज्ञाननिष्ठप्रामाण्याग्रहाद्बाधः
तत्र प्रतियोगिविधयापि प्रामाण्यभानादित्यपि निरस्तं । तत्र ज्ञाने

निष्प्रकारकत्वादेरपि भाने बाधकाभावेन तज्ज्ञाने प्रामाण्यविरोध्य-ग्राहकत्वस्यैवासत्त्वात्। न च घटत्वप्रकारकत्वं न घटत्ववद्विशेष्यकत्वावच्छिन्नमित्यादिभ्रमात्मकतज्ज्ञानग्रहजनकसामग्रीमादाय बाधः तज्ज्ञाने प्रामाण्यविरोध्यग्राहकत्वस्य तत्रापि सत्त्वादिति वाच्यम्। तादृशज्ञानप्रामाण्यस्यापक्षत्वात् तज्ज्ञानव्यक्तिनिष्ठप्रामाण्यत्वेनैव पक्षत्वात्। अतएव यत्र ज्ञाने कदाचिदपि न प्रामाण्यविरोधिग्रहस्तज्ज्ञाननिष्ठप्रामाण्यविरोधिग्रहाप्रसिद्ध्या तदग्राहकाप्रसिद्धिरित्यपि निरस्तम्। तज्ज्ञानप्रामाण्यपक्षीकरणे तदप्रामाण्याग्राहकत्वविशेषणस्य साध्येऽनुपादेयत्वात् पक्षभेदेनैव साध्यभेदात्। न चैवं यत्र ज्ञाने प्रामाण्यविरोधिग्रहस्तज्ज्ञाननिष्ठप्रामाण्यस्यापक्षत्वमेवास्तु किं तदप्रामाण्याग्राहकत्वविशेषणेनेति वाच्यम्। पक्षत्वेन संग्रहसम्भवे संग्रहाकरणस्यान्याय्यत्वात्।

ननु तथापि गुरुनये इदं ज्ञानं निष्प्रकारकमिदं ज्ञानं निर्विशेष्यकमित्यादिभ्रमात्मकज्ञानग्रहसामग्रीमादाय बाधस्तदवस्थः तन्मते निष्प्रकारकत्वादिभ्रमस्येदंज्ञानानुभव-निष्प्रकारकत्वादिस्मरणोभयरूपतया तत्सामग्र्या अपि तज्ज्ञाने प्रामाण्यविरोध्यग्राहकत्वादेव तन्नये इदं ज्ञानं न प्रमा इदं ज्ञानं प्रमात्वाभावव्याप्यवदित्यादिभ्रमात्मकतज्ज्ञानग्रहसामग्रीमादायापि बाधस्तदवस्थः। तन्मते प्रमात्वाभावादिभ्रमस्येदंज्ञानानुभव-प्रामाण्याभावादिस्मरणोभयरूपतया तत्सामग्र्या अपि ज्ञाने प्रामाण्यविरोध्यग्राहकत्वादिदंज्ञानानुभवसामग्रीरूपायास्तज्ज्ञानग्राहकसामग्र्याः प्रतियोगिविधयापि प्रामाण्याग्राहकत्वादप्रामाण्यस्मृतिसामग्र्या एव तथात्वादिति चेत्। न। तज-

ज्ञाननिष्ठप्रामाण्यविरोधिप्रकारकग्रहपदेन तज्ज्ञानविशेष्यकप्रमात्वविरोधिप्रकारकव्यवहारजनकग्रहस्योक्तत्वात्। स च गुरुनये भ्रमस्थलाभिषिक्तज्ञानद्वयमेवेति न बाधः, व्यवहारस्य तादृशेच्छादिरेव। न च तथापि यत्र तज्ज्ञाने प्रामाण्यविरोधिप्रकारकग्रहो जातस्तज्जन्यव्यवहारस्तु न जातस्तज्ज्ञानप्रामाण्यस्य पक्षीकरणे साध्येऽग्राहकान्तविशेषणोपादानेऽप्रसिद्धिः, तदनुपादाने च बाधः-इति वाच्यम्। तज्ज्ञानप्रामाण्यस्यापक्षत्वादित्याहुः।

तदप्यसत्। इदं निष्प्रकारकमित्यादभ्रमात्मकतज्ज्ञानग्रहस्यापि निर्द्धर्मितावच्छेदकप्रामाण्यविषयकत्वे बाधकाभावेन तदप्रामाण्याग्राहकत्वविशेषणानुपादानेपि बाधाभावात् बहूनां तज्ज्ञानप्रामाण्यानां पक्षबहिर्भावप्रसङ्गाच्च सामान्यतः पक्ष-साध्यमते तु पक्षबहिर्भावस्यैवासम्भवाच्च।

नव्यास्तु तादृशसामग्रीजन्यग्रहविषयत्वमात्रमत्र न साध्यं तथा सति प्रमात्वकालीनत्वादिविषयकत्वेन कालिकादियत्किञ्चित्सम्बन्धेन तत्प्रकारकत्वादियत्किञ्चिद्रूपेण वा ज्ञाने प्रमात्वप्रकारकत्वेन चार्थान्तरापत्तेः घटत्ववद्विशेष्यकत्वावच्छिन्नघटत्वप्रकारकत्वस्य घटत्वप्रकारकत्वानतिरिक्ततया सिद्धसाधनापत्तेश्च। न्यायनयेप्यनुव्यवसाये घटत्वादिप्रकारकत्वभानाभ्युपगमात् अग्रे इदं ज्ञानं प्रमा न वेति संशयानुपपत्त्या विधिकोटिनिराकरणानुपपत्तेश्च। यथाकथञ्चित्प्रमात्वज्ञानसत्त्वेऽपि तादृशसंशयसम्भवात्। किन्तु तज्ज्ञानत्वविशिष्टविशेष्यतानिरूपिता विशेषणताविशेषसम्बन्धावच्छिन्ना या विशिष्टप्रामाण्यीयप्रकारिता या च ज्ञानत्वीयप्रकारिता तदन्यतरप्रकारितासम्बन्धेन

तादृशसामग्रीजन्यग्रहत्वव्यापकत्वमेव साध्यं, विधिप्रसिद्ध्यर्थं ज्ञान-त्वीयप्रकारित्वान्तर्भावः, ज्ञानत्वीयप्रकारितासम्बन्धेन प्रामाण्यस्य व्यापकत्वासम्भवात् पक्षधर्मताबलेन तादृशविशिष्टप्रामाण्यीयप्रकारिता-सम्बन्धेनैव प्रामाण्यस्य व्यापकत्वसिद्धिः । यदि तु साध्ये ज्ञानपदं सामान्यतो घटत्ववतिघटत्वप्रकारकत्वाद्याश्रयज्ञानपरं तदा तदाश्रयी-भूतानि यावन्ति ज्ञानानि तत्तज्ज्ञानत्वविशिष्टतत्तज्ज्ञानविशेष्य-तानिरूपिता विशेषणताविशेषसम्बन्धावच्छिन्ना या या विशिष्टप्रामा-ण्यीयप्रकारिता या च ज्ञानत्वीयप्रकारिता तदन्यतमप्रकारितासम्ब-न्धेन स्वाश्रयज्ञानग्राहकसामग्रीजन्यग्रहत्वव्यापकत्वमेव साध्यम् ।

यद्वा ज्ञानत्वविशिष्टविशेष्यतानिरूपितविशेषणताविशेषसम्बन्धाव-च्छिन्नविशिष्टप्रामाण्यीयप्रकारिता-ज्ञानत्वीयप्रकारितान्यतरप्रकारिता-सम्बन्धेन व्यापकत्वमेव साध्यम । अग्रे च ज्ञानं प्रमा न वेति संशया-नुपपत्त्यैव विधिकोटिर्निराकरणीया । तथा च इदं ज्ञानं निष्प्र-कारकं इदं ज्ञानं निर्विशेष्यकमित्यादिभ्रमात्मकतज्ज्ञानग्रहं इदं ज्ञानं प्रमात्वाभाववत् इदं ज्ञानं प्रमात्वाभावव्याप्यवत् इत्यादि-भ्रमात्मकतज्ज्ञानग्रहमादाय बाधः । तत्र धर्मितावच्छेदकविधया प्रतियोगिविधया वा प्रामाण्यस्य विषयत्वेऽपि इदंज्ञानत्वावच्छिन्ने ज्ञानत्वावच्छिन्ने वा प्रामाण्यस्याविशेषणत्वात् अतस्तदप्रामाण्यग्राह-केति, तदर्थश्च तत्प्रामाण्यग्रहप्रतिबन्धकीभूताप्रामाण्याश्रयविषयक-ग्रहासमवहितत्वं तेन इदं ज्ञानं निष्प्रकारकमित्यादिज्ञानग्रहमा-दाय न बाधतादवस्थ्यं, न वा तज्ज्ञाने निष्प्रकारकत्व-निर्विशेष्यक-त्वादिव्याप्यत्वेन तदवच्छेदकत्वेन वा घटविषयकत्व-घटत्वप्रकारक-

त्वादिभ्रमात्मकतज्ज्ञानपरं घटत्वप्रकारकत्वं घटत्ववद्विशेष्यकत्वान-वच्छिन्नं इत्यादिभ्रमात्मकतज्ज्ञानपरं वा समादाय बाधः। गुरुनये च भ्रमस्याभिषिक्तज्ञानद्वयस्यैव प्रामाण्यग्रहप्रतिबन्धकतया तत्-समवहितत्वादेव न बाधः। तत्पदस्य विशिष्य पक्षीभूतप्रामाण्यपरि-चयाय अन्यथा प्रामाण्यत्वस्यानुगतस्याभावात् इतरप्रामाण्यपरतायां यथोक्तबाधनादवस्थरात् इत्युक्तमेव। तादृशग्रहासमवहितत्वञ्च तादृश-ग्रहाभावविशिष्टत्वं वैशिष्ट्यञ्च सामग्रीविशेषणत्वपक्षे स्वक्षण-स्वाव्यवहि-तोत्तरक्षणान्यतरक्षणावच्छेदेनैकाधिकरणवृत्तित्वं स्वपदं सामग्रीपरं, प्रथमग्रहविशेषणत्वपक्षे तु स्वक्षण-स्वाव्यवहितपूर्वक्षणान्यतरक्षणावच्छे-देनैकात्मवृत्तित्वं स्वपदं ग्रहपरमिति प्राहुः।

ननु तदप्रामाण्याग्राहकत्वविशेषणोपादानेपि ज्ञानपदादिजन्य-ज्ञानशाब्दबोधमादाय बाधः। न च विषयविशिष्टज्ञानग्राहकसाम-ग्रीति विवक्षणीयमतो नायं दोष इति वाच्यं। तथापि घटज्ञा-नपदादिजन्यशाब्दबोध-घटज्ञानवानित्याद्यनुमिति-स्मृत्यादिकमादाय बाधस्य दुर्वारत्वात्। न च गुरुमते स्वप्रामाण्यमवश्यं ज्ञानं गृह्णाति इति नियमः, भवति चेयमनुमितिः शाब्दादिमितिश्च घटत्ववति घटत्वप्रकारिका इति तत्त्वमपि गृह्णातीति न बाध इति वाच्यम्। घटत्ववति घटत्वप्रकारकत्वस्य प्रतिज्ञानं विभिन्नत्वेन अनुमित्यादिवृत्ति तद्ग्रहेपि अनुमित्यादिविषयीभूतज्ञानवृत्तेस्तस्याग्रहेण बाधतादव-स्थ्यात् भट्ट-मिश्रमते बाधस्य दुर्वारत्वाच्च। न च घटत्वादिप्रकारकत्वेन सविशेष्यकत्वेन च तज्ज्ञानग्राहकत्वं विवक्षणीयं अतो यथोक्तशाब्द-बोधादिकमादाय न बाधः इति वाच्यम्। तथापि इदं ज्ञानं घटत्व-

प्रकारकं सविशेष्यकञ्च इत्याद्यनुमित्यादिमादाय बाधस्य दुर्वारत्वात्। न च घटत्वादिविशिष्टविशेष्यकत्वेन घटत्वादिप्रकारकत्वेन च तज्ज्ञानग्राहकत्वं विवक्षणीयमतो न बाधः इति वाच्यम्। तथापि इदं घटविशेष्यकं घटत्वप्रकारकञ्च इत्यादिशाब्दादिकमामाय बाधस्य दुर्वारत्वात् घटत्वादिविशिष्टविशेष्यकत्वावच्छिन्नघटत्वादिप्रकारकत्वेन तज्ज्ञानग्राहकत्वविवक्षणे च सिद्धसाधनापत्तेः। न हि तादृश्यपि सामग्री प्रामाण्यं न गृह्णाति इति नैयायिकानामभ्युपगमः। किन्तु अनुव्यवसायादिसामग्री तादृश्येव न इत्यभ्युपगमः।

मैवं। ज्ञानग्राहकेत्यत्र ग्रहपदेन तज्ज्ञाननिष्ठप्रामाण्याविषयकपरोक्षभिन्नतज्ज्ञानग्रहस्य विवक्षितत्वात्। परोक्षत्वं साक्षात्कारेतरज्ञानत्वं, तादृशस्य ग्रहः तज्ज्ञानसाक्षात्कारः तज्ज्ञाननिष्ठप्रामाण्यानुमित्यादिश्च इति न कश्चिद्दोषः। सिद्धसाधनवारणाय परोक्षेति। अतएव तदप्रामाण्याग्राहकपदमपि सार्थकम्। अप्रामाण्यादिविषयकतज्ज्ञानलौकिकप्रत्यक्षवारणाय तस्यावश्यकत्वात्। भट्टमतसाधारण्याय तज्ज्ञाननिष्ठप्रामाण्याविषयकेति परोक्षविशेषणं। एवं तज्ज्ञानांशे संयुक्तसमवायेतरप्रत्यासत्तिजन्यत्वाभाववत्त्वेन तज्ज्ञानांशे लौकिकविषयत्वशून्यत्व-साक्षात्कारत्वविशिष्टविषयित्वोभयाभाववत्त्वेन वा तज्ज्ञानग्रहो विशेषणीयः। तज्ज्ञानांशे इत्युभयत्रैवाभावान्वयि, नातः प्रामाण्याविषयकज्ञानोपनीतभानमादाय बाधः। न च गुरुनये एतद्विशेषणवैयर्थ्यं तेन उपनीतभानानङ्गीकारात् भट्टनये च तदप्रामाण्याग्राहकत्वविशेषणवैयर्थ्यं तन्नये ज्ञानस्यातीन्द्रियतयाऽप्रामाण्यादिविषयकतज्ज्ञानलौकिकप्रत्यक्षाभावादिति वाच्यम्। सर्व्वमते सर्व्व-

विशेषणसार्थक्याभावेऽपि क्षतिविरहात्। यत्किञ्चिन्मते सार्थकत्वमात्रस्य कर्त्तव्यत्वात्। यावत्त्वस्य सामग्रीविशेषणत्वपक्षे सामग्र्येव वा तज्ज्ञाननिष्ठप्रामाण्यग्राहकपरोक्षभिन्नत्वेन विशेषणीया, परोक्षत्वञ्च साक्षात्कारजनकेतरत्वं, तादृशी च सामग्री तज्ज्ञानसाक्षात्कारजनकसामग्री तज्ज्ञाननिष्ठप्रामाण्यानुमित्यादिसामग्री च। ज्ञानांशे संयुक्तसमवायेतरप्रत्यासत्त्यजन्यत्वादिना तज्ज्ञानग्रहविशेषणादेव प्रामाण्याविषयकतज्ज्ञानोपनीतभानसामग्रीमादाय न बाधः। न चैवं चरमग्रह एव तज्ज्ञाननिष्ठप्रामाण्याविषयकपरोक्षभिन्नत्वेन तज्ज्ञानांशे संयुक्तसमवायेतरप्रत्यासत्त्यजन्यत्वादिना च विशेष्यतां किं तज्ज्ञानग्राहकेति विशेषणेनेति तदप्रामाण्यग्राहकसामग्रीजन्यतादृशयावद्ग्रहविषयत्वस्य तदप्रामाण्यग्राहकतादृशयावद्ग्रहविषयत्वस्य वा सम्यक्त्वात् तज्ज्ञानविषयकज्ञानस्य तज्ज्ञानांशे तादृशप्रत्यासत्त्यजन्यत्वाद्यभावादेव वारणादिति वाच्यम्। यथासन्निवेशे वैयर्थ्याभावात्। न च तथापि यत्र घटः पटश्च द्रव्यमित्यादेरेकस्मिन्नेव ज्ञाने विशेष्यतावच्छेदकभेदेन द्रव्यत्ववति द्रव्यत्वप्रकारकत्वादिद्वयं समूहालम्बनानुमित्यादिना मिलित्वापि गृहीतं परस्पराग्राहकतज्ज्ञानग्राहकानुमित्यादिना पृथक् पृथगपि गृहीतं तज्ज्ञानवृत्तिद्रव्यत्ववतिद्रव्यत्वप्रकारकत्वादिपक्षीकरणे प्रत्येकमात्रविषयकानुमित्यादिमादाय बाधो दुर्वार इति वाच्यम्। तज्ज्ञाननिष्ठयावत्प्रामाण्याविषयकपरोक्षेतरत्वस्य विवक्षितत्वात् प्रत्येकमात्रविषयकानुमित्यादिषु न तथा। न चैवं यत्रैकस्मिन्नेव ज्ञाने विशेष्यतावच्छेदकभेदेन प्रामाण्यद्वयमिच्छादिसामग्र्या अनुमित्यादिसामग्र्या वा प्रतिबन्धाच्च न ज्ञानज्ञानानुव-

साय: परन्तु परस्पराग्राह्यकतज्ज्ञानग्राह्यकानुमित्यादिना पृथक् पृथगेव गृहीतं समूहालम्बनानुमित्यादिश्च न जात: तज्ज्ञानवृत्तिप्रामाण्यस्य पक्षीकरणे तज्ज्ञानवृत्तियावत्प्रामाण्याविषयकपरोक्षेतरतज्ज्ञानग्रहो-ऽप्रसिद्ध इति वाच्यम्। तज्ज्ञानवृत्तिप्रामण्यस्यापक्षत्वात्।

यद्वा तत्र तत्तत्प्रामाण्यव्यक्तित्वेनैव पक्ष: करणीय: न तु सामान्यतस्तज्ज्ञानवृत्तिप्रामाण्यत्वेन पक्षत्वं साध्येऽपि तज्ज्ञाननिष्ठतत्प्रामाण्यव्यक्त्यविषयकपरोक्षेतरतज्ज्ञानग्रहो विवक्षणीय इति न काप्यनुपपत्ति:। विधिप्रसिद्धिस्तु तज्ज्ञाने तज्ज्ञानविषयीभूते घटत्वादौ च, निरुक्तान्यतरप्रकारितासम्बन्धेन व्यापकत्वविधिकोटिहेतुप्रसिद्ध्यर्थं ज्ञानत्वविशिष्टतज्ज्ञानग्राह्यकत्वविवक्षणाज्ज्ञानत्वे तत्प्रसिद्धिरिति सर्वं चतुरस्रम।

मतत्रयसाधारणं विप्रतिपत्त्यन्तरमाह, 'तज्ज्ञानविषयकेति। विधिकोटि: परेषां निषेधकोटिश्च नैयायिकानाम्। अत्र ज्ञानग्राह्यं न वेत्येतावन्मात्रे कृते विधौ सिद्धसाधनं निषेधे चाप्रसिद्धिरत: 'अजन्यान्तं ज्ञानविशेषणं। ज्ञानाजन्यज्ञानग्राह्यं न वेत्युक्तौ मिश्रभट्टयोर्मते विधिकोटौ बाध:। अनुव्यवसाय-ज्ञातता-लिङ्गकामित्योरपि व्यवसायव्याप्ति-ज्ञानजन्यत्वात्। गुरुमतेप्यनुमिति-शाब्दज्ञानादिमात्रनिष्ठे मनस्त्ववति मनस्त्वप्रकारकत्वादावतीन्द्रियघटितप्रामाण्यपक्षीकृते बाध: तत्रानुमित्यादिरूपस्य व्यवसायस्यापि परामर्शयोग्यतादिज्ञानजन्यत्वनियमादत: 'तज्ज्ञानविषयकेति ज्ञानविशेषणं। तज्ज्ञानविषयकत्वञ्च न पक्षीकृतघटत्ववतिघटत्वप्रकारकत्वाद्याश्रयज्ञानविषयकत्वं तथा सति घटविशेष्यकघटत्ववद्विशेष्यकत्वावच्छिन्नघटत्वप्रकारकत्वरूप-

प्रमात्वात्मकसामान्यलक्षणप्रत्यासत्तिजन्यं तादृशोपनयसन्निकर्षजन्यं वा ज्ञानविशेष्यकघटत्ववतिघटत्वप्रकारकत्वप्रकारकप्रत्यक्षमादाय विधौ सिद्धसाधनस्य निषेधे बाधस्य प्रसङ्गात्। किन्तु तत्र ज्ञानविषयो ज्ञानानुवन्धिविषयताश्रयो यस्य ज्ञानस्येति बहुव्रीहिः। तत्पदं पक्षी-भूतघटत्ववतिघटत्वप्रकारकत्वादिपरं। तथा च घटत्ववतिघटत्वप्रका-रकत्वंप्रतिपत्त्यनुवन्धिघटत्ववतिघटत्वप्रकारकत्वविषयिताऽश्रयज्ञानाजन्य-ज्ञानविषयो न वेत्यादिप्रातिस्विकरूपेण विप्रतिपत्तिशरीरं। मिश्र-मते व्यापारानुवन्धिविषयतामादाय व्यवसायस्यापि घटत्ववतीत्यादि-प्रामाण्यविषयकत्वात् तस्य च विषयविधया विशेषणज्ञानादिविधया चानुव्यवसायहेतुत्वात्। तन्नये बाधवारणाय प्रतिपत्त्यनुवन्धित्वं विष-यताविशेषणं। द्वितीयज्ञानपदञ्च स्वरूपकथनं। न्यायनये च घटत्व-वतिघटत्वप्रकारकत्वादिरूपप्रामाण्योपस्थितिं विना कदाचिदपि न तादृशप्रामाण्यविशिष्टग्रह इति विधौ सिद्धसाधनस्य निषेधे बाधस्य च न सम्भावनापि। न च तथापि भट्टमते विधौ बाधः तन्नये इयं ज्ञातता घटत्ववतिघटत्वप्रकारकज्ञानजन्या घटत्ववतिघटत्वप्रकारक-ज्ञाततात्वादित्यनुमानेन प्रामाण्यग्रहात्तस्य च घटत्ववतिघटत्वप्रका-रकत्वविषयकव्याप्तिज्ञानादिजन्यत्वादिति वाच्यम्। तन्नये अहं ज्ञान-वान् ज्ञाततावत्त्वादित्यनुमानस्य सर्वत्र प्रामाण्यग्राहकत्वात्। तत्र प्रामा-ण्यभानप्रकारस्याग्रे स्फुटीभविष्यति। न च तथापि घटमहं जाना-मीत्यनुव्यवसायस्यापि घटत्वरूपेण घटविषयकतया तद्वृत्तिघटत्व-वतिघटत्वप्रकारकत्वव्यक्तौ मिश्रनये अंशतो बाधः। तदनुव्यवसायानु-व्यवसायस्य घटत्ववतिघटत्वप्रकारकत्वविषयिनोऽनुव्यवसायस्यैव विषय

विधया विशेषणज्ञानादिविधया वा जन्यत्वादिति वाच्यम् । ज्ञानभेदेन घटत्ववतिघटत्वप्रकारकत्वादीनां भेदानभ्युपगमात् । ज्ञानभेदेन तद्भेदाभ्युपगमेऽपि घटत्ववतिघटत्वप्रकारकत्वत्वादेर्निखिलघटत्ववतिघटत्वप्रकारकत्वादिव्यक्तिसाधारणस्यैकस्य पक्षतावच्छेदकस्याभ्युपगमात् पक्षतावच्छेदकसामानाधिकरण्येन विधिकोटिसिद्धेरुद्देश्यत्वे तयैवांशतो बाधनिराससम्भवाच्च । न च पक्षतावच्छेदकसामानाधिकरण्येन विधिसिद्धेरुद्देश्यत्वे प्रामाण्यमात्रस्य मानुव्यवसायग्राह्यत्वसिद्धिरिति वाच्यम् । एतद्धि साक्षात्स्वानुव्यवसायग्राह्यत्वसाधकमपि तु विशिष्टप्रामाण्योपस्थितेः प्रामाण्यप्रत्यक्षं प्रति कारणत्वस्य नैयायिकाभिमतस्याभावसाधकं, सिद्धे च तस्मिन् सामग्रीबलादेव प्रामाण्यमात्रस्यानुव्यवसायग्राह्यत्वसिद्धिः । निषेधकोटिसिद्धिः पक्षतावच्छेदकावच्छेदेनोद्देश्या नातोऽनुव्यवसायनिष्ठघटत्ववतिघटत्वप्रकारकत्वादिव्यक्त्यनुक्रमेणांशतः सिद्धसाधनं ।

नन्वेवं गुरुमते घटत्ववतिघटत्वप्रकारकत्वादावैन्द्रियकघटितप्रामाण्ये पक्षीकृते तत्रत्यविप्रतिपत्तौ तज्ज्ञानविषयकेति ज्ञानविशेषणं व्यर्थं सामान्यतो ज्ञानाजन्यज्ञानविषयत्वस्यैव कोटित्वस्य सुवचत्वात्तन्मते विशेषणज्ञानस्य विशिष्टबुद्धावहेतुतयाऽयं घट इतिसाक्षात्कारात्मकव्यवसायस्यैव ज्ञानाजन्यज्ञानत्वेन तद्विषयत्वमादायैव तत्र विधिकोटिसम्भवात् । न च तस्मिन् पक्षीकृतेऽप्यनुमिति-शाब्दात्मकव्यवसायनिष्ठघटत्ववतीत्यादिव्यक्त्यंशतो बाधवारणाय गुरुमतेऽपि तदुपादानमावश्यकमनुमित्यादेर्व्याप्तिज्ञानादिजन्यत्वनियमादिति वाच्यम् । उक्तव्यक्त्यनुक्रमेणैवांशतो बाधनिरासम्भवात् । न च तादृशप्रामाण्ये

पक्षीकृते नोपादेयमेव तदिति वाच्यं। भट्ट-मिश्रमते बाधापत्ते-रिति चेत्। न। तस्मिन् पक्षीकृतेऽप्यखण्डाभावघटकतया गुरुमते वैयर्थ्याभावात्मतत्रयसाधारणविप्रतिपत्तौ सर्वमते सर्वविशेषणानां सार्थकत्वविरहेऽपि क्षतिविरहाच्च। न च न्यायनये व्यवसायविरहदशायां खण्डशः प्रामाण्यघटकपदार्थानामुपस्थितिसहकारेण मनसा विशेष्ये विशेषणमितिन्यायेन तादृशप्रामाण्यप्रकारकमुपनीतव्यवसायविशेष्यकप्रत्यक्षं जन्यते तदादायैव विधौ सिद्धसाधनं निषेधे च बाध इति वाच्यं। न्यायनये प्रामाण्यानुपस्थितिदशायामनुव्यवसायादिना प्रामाण्यग्रहवारणाय प्रामाण्यप्रत्यक्षे विशिष्टप्रामाण्योपस्थितेर्हेतुत्वात् अभावादिप्रत्यक्षवत्, विशेष्ये विशेषणमितिन्यायेन प्रामाण्यप्रत्यक्षस्यानभ्युपगमात्। अन्यथा विशिष्टप्रामाण्योपस्थितेः प्रामाण्यप्रत्यक्षं प्रति तत्रैव व्यभिचारापत्तेः। न चैवमनवस्थेति वाच्यं। बीजाङ्कुरवदनादित्वात्। न च तथापि गवादिविशेष्यकप्रकारितात्वाभिधेयत्व-घटभिन्नत्वादिप्रकारकज्ञानात्मकसामान्यलक्षणप्रत्यासत्तिजन्यप्रामाण्यविशेष्यकप्रत्यक्षमादाय सिद्धसाधनमिति वाच्यम्। विषयतापदेन प्रकारताया विवक्षितत्वात्। ननु तथापि अभिधेयत्वादिरूपेण घटादित्वलक्षणयत्किञ्चिदभिधेयप्रकारकज्ञानादभिधेयसामान्यलक्षणप्रत्यासत्त्या घटत्ववतिघटत्वप्रकारकत्वादिनिखिलाभिधेयप्रकारकतदाश्रयसाक्षात्कारमादाय सिद्धसाधनम्। न च न्यायनये विशिष्टबुद्धौ विशेषणज्ञानस्य हेतुतया कथमज्ञातघटत्ववद्विशेष्यकत्वावच्छिन्नघटत्वप्रकारकत्वादेः प्रकारतया भानमिति वाच्यम्। विशिष्टवैशिष्ट्यबोधं प्रति विशेषणतावच्छेदकप्रकारकज्ञानस्य हेतुत्वं न तु विशिष्टबुद्धौ

विशेषणज्ञानमपीति नैयायिकैकदेशिमते सिद्धसाधनस्य दुर्वारत्वात् नैयायिकैस्तथाज्ञानानभ्युपगमेपि तादृशज्ञानमादायार्थान्तरापत्ते-र्दुर्वारत्वाच्च। किञ्च घटत्ववद्विशेष्यकत्वावच्छिन्नघटत्वप्रकारकत्वस्य घटत्वप्रकारकत्वानतिरिक्ततयाऽनुव्यवसायमादायैव सिद्धसाधनं न्याय-नयेऽनुव्यवसाये घटत्वप्रकारकत्वादिभानाभ्युपगमादिति चेत्। न। घटत्ववद्विशेष्यकत्वावच्छिन्नघटत्वप्रकारकत्वत्वाद्यतिरिक्तानवच्छिन्नप्रका-रताया विवक्षितत्वात्। निरवच्छिन्नप्रकारतामादाय सत्ता-गुणत्व-ज्ञानत्व-घटत्वादौ विधिकोटिप्रसिद्धिसम्पादनायाभावद्वयगर्भता, नि-षेधकोटिप्रसिद्धिश्च प्रामाण्यातिरिक्तजात्यखण्डोपाध्यतिरिक्तपदार्थ-मात्र एव सुलभा जात्यखण्डोपाध्यतिरिक्तपदार्थस्य किञ्चिद्धर्मप्रका-रेणैव भाननियमात्(१)। घटत्ववद्विशेष्यकत्वावच्छिन्नघटत्वप्रकारक-त्वत्वातिरिक्तानवच्छिन्नत्वन्तु तादृशघटत्वप्रकारकत्वत्वपर्याप्तावच्छेद-कताकान्यत्वे सति यदवच्छिन्नं तद्भिन्नत्वं, तेन घटत्वप्रकारकत्वत्वस्य घटत्ववद्विशेष्यकत्वावच्छिन्नघटत्वप्रकारत्वत्वानतिरिक्तत्वेपि नानुव्यव-सायमादाय सिद्धसाधनतादवस्थ्यं। घटत्वप्रकारकत्वस्य स्वरूपतो नानुव्यवसाये प्रकारः किन्तु प्रकारकत्वत्व-घटनिरूपितत्वादिरूपे-णैव तेन प्रकारकत्वस्य निरवच्छिन्नव्यवसायप्रकारतामादाय न सिद्धसाधनम्।

वस्तुतस्तु यथाकथञ्चित्तादृशज्ञानप्रकारत्वैव विधिकोटिः, परन्तु

---

(१) अनन्तर्भूतजात्यखण्डोपाध्यतिरिक्तपदार्थस्य स्वरूपतो भानानभ्यु-पगमादिति नियमः।

मूलावच्छिन्नस्तु च: कपिसंयोगीत्यादाविव स्वरूपसम्बन्धरूपपक्षतावच्छेदकावच्छिन्नत्वविशिष्टसाध्यतावच्छेदकसम्बन्धेन विधिकोटिसिद्धिरुद्देश्या तेन नोक्तक्रमेणार्थान्तरं सिद्धसाधनं वा। न च तथापि निषेधकोटिसाधने बाधस्तदवस्थ: घटत्वप्रकारकत्वादेरनुव्यवसाये भानस्य न्यायनयेऽभ्युपगमात् घटत्ववद्विशेष्यकत्वावच्छिन्नघटत्वप्रकारकत्वस्य घटत्वप्रकारकत्वानतिरिक्तत्वादिति वाच्यम्। घटत्ववतिघटत्वप्रकारकत्वत्वावच्छिन्नत्वविशिष्टविशेषणताविशेषसम्बन्धावच्छिन्नप्रतियोगिताकतादृशज्ञानप्रकारत्वाभावस्य निषेधकोटित्वात् तस्य च न्यायनयेऽपि घटत्वादावेव प्रसिद्धिसौलभ्यात् घटत्ववतिघटत्वप्रकारकत्वत्वरूपेण घटत्वादीनां सर्व्वेषां पदार्थानां भ्रमे मानाभावात् तादृशभ्रमस्य घटत्ववतिघटत्वप्रकारकत्वत्वघटकतया घटत्ववतिघटत्वप्रकारत्वज्ञानजन्यत्वनियमाच्च। न च विधिकोटौ विशेषणतासामान्यं साध्यतावच्छेदकसम्बन्ध: निषेधकोटिस्तु निरुक्तविशेषणताविशेषसम्बन्धावच्छिन्नप्रतियोगिताकाभाव इति फलितं तथासङ्गतं विशेषणतासामान्येन तादृशज्ञानप्रकारकत्वस्य निरुक्तविशेषणताविशेषावच्छिन्नतादृशज्ञानप्रकारकत्वाभावेन समं विरोधाभावेन विप्रतिपत्तिजन्यसंशयकोटित्वासम्भवात्[१] इति वाच्यम्। विधिकोटौ विशेषणतासामान्यस्य साध्यतावच्छेदकसम्बन्धत्वेऽपि विप्रतिपत्तिजन्यसंशये[२] विशेष्यतावच्छेदकावच्छिन्नत्वविशिष्टविशेषणतासम्बन्धे-

(१) विप्रतिपत्तिजन्यसंशयकोटित्वादिति ग०।

(२) विप्रतिपत्तिवाक्यजन्यकोट्युपस्थितिजन्यसंशये इत्यर्थः।

नैव विधिकोटेः प्रकारतया भानादेव विरोधसम्भवात्। अनुमिताविव विशिष्टबुद्धिमात्र एवासति बाधके विशेष्यतावच्छेदकावच्छिन्नत्वविशिष्टविधेयतावच्छेदकसम्बन्धेन विधेयभानाभ्युपगमात्।

यद्वा घटत्ववतिघटत्वप्रकारकत्वत्वावच्छिन्नत्वविशिष्टघटत्ववतिघटत्वप्रकारकत्वनिष्ठविशेषणतासम्बन्धेनैव तादृशज्ञानप्रकारकत्वं विधिकोटिः, न तु विशेषणतासामान्येन तादृशसम्बन्धावच्छिन्नप्रतियोगिताकतादृशज्ञानप्रकारत्वाभाव एव निषेधकोटिः, स च न्यायनयेपि संयोगादिरूपव्यधिकरणसम्बन्धावच्छिन्नगुणाद्यभाववत् केवलान्वयितया घटत्वादावेव प्रसिद्धः। न च तादृशसम्बन्धविशेषेण विधिकोटिर्न्यायनये त्वप्रसिद्ध इति वाच्यम्। निषेधकोटेः प्रतियोगिप्रसिद्ध्यर्थमुभयमते विधिकोटिप्रसिद्धेरपेक्षितत्वेपि साध्यतावच्छेदकसम्बन्धेनोभयमते विधिकोटिप्रसिद्धेरनपेक्षितत्वात्। परनये च पक्ष एव तेन सम्बन्धेन तत्प्रसिद्धिसौलभ्यात् साध्यतावच्छेदकसम्बन्धेन साध्यप्रसिद्धेरनङ्गतया परनयेपि तेन सम्बन्धेन विधिकोटिप्रसिद्धिविरहेपि क्षतिविरहाच्च। अन्यथा संयोगादिसम्बन्धेन गुणादेरनुमित्यनुपपत्तेः। न च तथापि परेण विधिकोटिसाधने दृष्टान्तस्थलाभाव इति वाच्यम्। दृष्टान्तोपन्यासस्य समयबन्धाधीनतया तदसिद्धेरपि क्षतिविरहात् कम्बुग्रीवादिमद्विशेष्यकत्वावच्छिन्नघटत्वप्रकारकत्वादेः पक्षमात्रवृत्तेर्धर्मस्य हेतुतया व्यतिरेकेन दृष्टान्तस्य सुलभत्वाच्च। व्यतिरेकसहचारेणैवान्वयव्याप्तिधीसम्भवेन परनये व्यतिरेकव्याप्तिज्ञानस्यानुमितिहेतुत्वाभावेपि क्षतिविरहात्। न च तथापि इदं ज्ञानं घटत्ववति घटत्वप्रकारकं तादृशप्रवृत्तिजनकत्वादित्य-

नुमित्या पक्षधर्मताबलात् पूर्व्वोपस्थितघटत्ववति घटत्वप्रकारकत्वव्याप्ति-ग्राहिण्याऽर्थान्तरमिति वाच्यम्। तदनुमितेः स्वविषयीभूतघटत्व-वतिघटत्वप्रकारकत्वव्याप्तिज्ञानाजन्यत्वेपि घटत्ववतिघटत्वप्रकारकत्वत्व-रूपेण तादृशघटत्वप्रकारकत्वव्यक्त्यन्तरज्ञानजन्यतया घटत्ववतिघटत्व-प्रकारकत्वज्ञानजन्यत्वसामान्याभावस्य तत्राभावात्[१]। न च तथापि योगजधर्मजन्यनिखिलप्रामाण्यप्रकारकनिखिलप्रमाविशेष्यकमानसान्का-रमादाय सिद्धसाधनमिति वाच्यम्। योगजधर्मस्य निर्व्विकल्पकजनक-तया विश्वगोचरनिर्व्विकल्पकादेव तादृशज्ञानोत्पत्तेः तत्र प्रामाण्य-विषयकज्ञानाजन्यत्वं नास्तीति न दोषः। न चेश्वरीयज्ञानस्य नित्य-तया प्रामाण्यविषयकज्ञानाजन्यत्वात्तदादाय[२] विधौ सिद्धसाधनं निषेधे च बाध इति वाच्यम्। अनित्यत्वेन चरमज्ञानविशेषणात्[३] नैयायिकेऽङ्गीकरणीयसिद्धसाधनवारकत्वेन परमतेपि वैयर्थ्याभावात्। न च परनये व्यावर्त्त्याप्रसिद्धिः, सिद्धसाधनवारकतया उपरञ्जकविशे-षणस्यापि अदोषत्वात्। जैत्रीयत्वेन वा चरमज्ञानं विशेषणीयं तथा च परमतेपि न व्यावर्त्त्याप्रसिद्धिः। अतएव योगजधर्मजन्यविशिष्टबुद्धे-र्विशेषणज्ञानाहेतुकत्वेपि न क्षतिः। एवञ्च समवायघटितसामा-नाधिकरण्यप्रत्यासत्त्या तद्विषयकज्ञानजन्यत्वं विवक्षितं, नातोऽनित्य-

---

(१) घटत्ववतिघटत्वप्रकारकत्वत्वावच्छिन्नज्ञानजन्यत्वसामान्याभावस्य तत्रासत्त्वादिति क०।

(२) तादृशज्ञानाजन्यभगवज्ज्ञानमादायेति ध०।

(३) अनित्यत्वेन चरमज्ञानविशेषणादित्यनन्तरं अनित्यत्वस्य प्रतियोगि-तासम्बन्धेन ध्वंसवत्त्वं इत्यधिकः पाठो धचिह्नितपुस्तके वर्त्तते।

ज्ञानमात्रस्य प्रामाण्यविषयकपरमेश्वरज्ञानजन्यत्वेन तादृशज्ञानाजन्य-ज्ञानाप्रसिद्धिः।

केचित्तु तज्ज्ञानविषयकेत्यत्र तस्य ज्ञानं तज्ज्ञानं तदेव विषयो यस्येति षष्ठीतत्पुरुषगर्भबहुव्रीहिः, आश्रयत्वं षष्ठ्यर्थः, तत्पदं पक्षीभूतघटत्ववद्विशेष्यकत्वावच्छिन्नघटत्वप्रकारकत्वादिपरं तथा च घटत्ववद्विशेष्यकत्वावच्छिन्नघटत्वप्रकारकत्वाश्रयज्ञानविषयकज्ञानाजन्यज्ञानविषयो न वेति विप्रतिपत्तिः विधिकोटिः परेषां, तादृशाश्रयविषयकं ज्ञानं गुरुमतेऽयं घट इति व्यवसाय एव, मिश्रमते प्रथमानुव्यवसाय एव, भट्टमते ज्ञाततालिङ्गकानुमितिः, तदजन्यं ज्ञानं तान्येव, तद्विषयत्वस्य घटत्ववतिघटत्वप्रकारकत्वे सत्त्वात्। निषेधकोटिश्च नैयायिकानां तन्मये इदं ज्ञानं घटत्ववतिघटत्वप्रकारकं तादृशप्रवृत्तिप्रयोजकत्वात् इत्यनुमानादेरेव प्रामाण्यग्राहकत्वात्, तस्य च पक्षादिज्ञानविधया तादृशाश्रयविषयकज्ञानजन्यत्वनियमात् अन्यत् सर्व्वं पूर्व्ववत्[१]। इयांस्तु विशेषो यदेतन्मते प्रथमज्ञानपदमेव स्वरूपकथनं न तु ज्ञानत्वेन निविष्टं वैयर्थ्यात्। द्वितीयज्ञानपदञ्च प्रतिपत्त्यनुबन्धिविषयतालाभाय। न च ज्ञानविषयकज्ञानाजन्येत्येवास्तु कथं तादृशप्रकारकत्वाश्रयत्वरूपेण प्रवेश इति वाच्यं। भट्टमते बाधापत्तेः, अहं ज्ञानवान् ज्ञाततावत्त्वादित्यादिज्ञाततालिङ्गकानुमितेर्ज्ञानविषयकज्ञानजन्यत्वनियमात्। एवं मिश्रमते ज्ञानत्ववतीत्यादिप्रामाण्ये पक्षीकृते बाधापत्तेः ज्ञानमहं जानामी-

---

(१) प्रत्येकदानव्यावृत्तिस्तु पूर्व्ववत्, भगवज्ज्ञानवारणमपि पूर्व्ववदिति ध०।

त्यनुव्यवसायस्य ज्ञानविषयकज्ञानजन्यत्वनियमात्। गुरुमतेऽपि प्रा-माण्यानुमिति—शाब्दमात्रग्राह्यप्रामाण्यघटितप्रामाण्ये पक्षीकृते बा-धापत्तेश्च प्रामाण्यानुमित्यादेर्ज्ञानविषयकज्ञानजन्यत्वनियमात्। अयं घट इतिव्यवसायस्य स्वनिष्ठघटत्ववन्निघटत्वप्रकारकत्वरूपप्रामाण्याव-गाहित्वाभ्युपगमेपि विषयानवस्थाभयात् तादृशप्रामाण्यवतितादृश-प्रामाण्यप्रकारकत्वानभ्युपगमात् तत्रापि गुरुमते बाधः। एतद-तिरिक्तप्रामाण्यपक्षीकरणे गुरु—मिश्रयोर्मते व्यर्थत्वेऽपि भट्टमत-साधारण्याय तस्यावश्यकत्वात्। न हि सर्व्वमते सर्व्वविशेषणसार्थक्य-मिति प्रागुक्तमेव।

ननु घटत्ववतीत्यादिप्रामाण्यविषयकज्ञानाजन्यत्वमेवास्तु किं तदाश्रयत्वान्तर्भावेण अजन्यत्वपदेन तादृशज्ञानजन्यत्वसामान्याभावस्य विवक्षितत्वादेव पक्षधर्मताबलात् पूर्व्वाज्ञातघटत्ववतिघटत्वप्रकारकत्व-व्यक्तिघटितस्य ज्ञानपक्षकप्रामाण्यानुमित्यार्थान्तरवारणसम्भवात्। तद-नुमितेरपि घटत्ववतीत्यादियत्किञ्चिद्व्यक्तिज्ञानजन्यत्वात्। अन्यथा आ-श्रयत्वान्तर्भावेऽपि पक्षधर्मताबलात् पूर्व्वाज्ञातघटत्वप्रमाव्यक्तिघटितस्य पुरुषादिपक्षकघटत्वप्रमासाध्यकानुमित्याऽर्थान्तरप्रसङ्गस्य दुर्व्वारत्वा-दिति चेत्। न। यथा सन्निवेशे वैयर्थ्याभावात्। न च घटादिवि-शेष्यकघटत्ववद्विशेष्यकत्वावच्छिन्नघटत्वप्रकारकत्वप्रकारकभ्रमात्मक-सामान्यप्रत्यासत्तिजन्यं तादृशज्ञानलक्षणसन्निकर्षजन्यं वा ज्ञानविशे-ष्यकघटत्ववतीत्यादिप्रकारकप्रत्यक्षमादाय विधौ सिद्धसाधनं निषेधे च बाध इति वाच्यं। घटत्ववतिघटत्वप्रकारकत्वविशिष्टज्ञानत्वस्य पक्षत्वात्, वैशिष्ट्यञ्च सामानाधिकरण्यतया, तदाश्रयगर्भमतः सामान्यलक्षणादि

न्यतत्-प्रकारकप्रत्यक्षेऽपि वैशिष्ट्यघटकतया घटत्ववतीत्याद्याश्रयज्ञानं कारणमतो नोक्तसिद्धसाधनाद्यवकाशः। ज्ञानत्वस्यानुपस्थितस्यापि प्रकारतया भानाभ्युपगमात् मिश्रमते प्रथमानुव्यवसाये प्रकारतया भानसम्भवः।

ननु तथापि घटत्ववतिघटत्वप्रकारकत्वभ्रमात्मकज्ञानसन्निकर्षजन्यं ज्ञानांशे प्रकारीभूतज्ञानत्वे सामानाधिकरण्यसम्बन्धेन घटत्ववतिघटत्व-प्रकारकत्वप्रकारकप्रत्यक्षमादाय विधौ सिद्धसाधनं निषेधे च बाधः। विशिष्टज्ञानत्वस्य पक्षत्वेऽपि प्रकारत्वसामान्यस्यैव कोटित्वात्। तादृश-विशिष्टज्ञानत्वनिष्ठतादृशप्रकारत्वस्य कोटित्वे साध्याप्रसिद्धेः। एवं विशेष्ये विशेषणमितिन्यायेन प्रामाण्यप्रत्यक्षाभ्युपगमे खण्डशः प्रामा-ण्यघटकपदार्थोपस्थितिसहकारेण मनसा जनितं विशेष्ये विशेषणमिति न्यायेन तादृशविशिष्टज्ञानत्वप्रकारकप्रत्यक्षमादाय विधौ सिद्धसाधनं निषेधे च बाधः। सम्बन्धज्ञानस्य विशिष्टबुद्धावहेतुतया तस्यापि घटत्व-वतिघटत्वप्रकारकत्वाश्रयविषयकज्ञानाजन्यत्वात्। किञ्च घटत्ववति-घटत्वप्रकारकत्वविशिष्टज्ञानत्वस्य ज्ञानत्वानतिरेकेण ज्ञानत्वप्रकारक-त्वकृशादिज्ञानानुव्यवसायमादायैव विधौ सिद्धसाधनं निषेधे च बाधः। न च मूलावच्छिन्नो वृक्षः कपिसंयोगीत्यादौ पक्षतावच्छेदक-मूलावच्छिन्नत्वविशिष्टसमवायसम्बन्धेन कपिसंयोगसिद्धिवदत्रापि घट-त्ववतिघटत्वप्रकारकत्वत्वरूपविशिष्टपक्षतावच्छेदकावच्छिन्नत्वविशिष्टवि-शेषणतासम्बन्धेन विधिकोटेरुद्देश्यतया न तादृशज्ञानान्यादाय सिद्ध-साधनावकाशः। तादृशज्ञानेषु घटत्वप्रकारकत्वप्रकारेण ज्ञानत्वस्य प्रका-रत्वेऽपि घटत्ववतिघटत्वप्रकारकत्वत्वरूपविशिष्टतद्धर्मावच्छिन्नप्रकारिता-

विरहात् घटत्ववतिघटत्वप्रकारकत्वविशिष्टज्ञानत्वनिरूपितवैशिष्ट्यबुद्धावेव ज्ञानत्वस्य तादृशप्रकारतामत्त्वादिति वाच्यम्। तथापि तादृशज्ञानान्यादाय निषेधे बाधस्य दुर्व्वारत्वादिति चेत्। न। घटत्ववतिघटत्वप्रकारकत्वत्वरूपविशिष्टधर्म्मावच्छिन्नत्वविशिष्टविशेषणतासम्बन्धेन तादृशज्ञानप्रकारत्वस्य विधिकोटित्वात् तादृशविशेषणताविशेषावच्छिन्नप्रतियोगिताकतादृशज्ञानप्रकारकत्वाभावस्य च निषेधकोटित्वात् तादृशाभावस्य न्यायनयेपि संयोगादिसम्बन्धेन गुणाद्यभाववत् केवलान्वयित्वात् घटत्वादावेव प्रसिद्धेः। न च तादृशसम्बन्धविशेषेण विधिकोटिर्न्यायनये त्वप्रसिद्ध इति वाच्यम्। निषेधकोटेः प्रतियोगिप्रसिद्ध्यर्थमुभयमते यथाकथञ्चित् विधिकोटिप्रसिद्धेरपेक्षितत्वेपि साध्यतावच्छेदकसम्बन्धेनोभयमते प्रमात्मकविधिकोटिप्रसिद्धेरनपेक्षितत्वात्। परनये च पक्ष एव तेन सम्बन्धेन तत्प्रसिद्धिसौलभ्यात् केवलसाध्यप्रसिद्धैव विशिष्टे विशेषणमितिन्यायेन सहचारग्रहसम्भवात साध्यतावच्छेदकसम्बन्धेन प्रसिद्धेरनङ्गतया परनयेपि तेन सम्बन्धेन विधिकोटिप्रसिद्धिविरहेपि क्षतिविरहाच्च। न च तथापि विधिकोटिसाधने दृष्टान्तस्थलाभाव इतिवाच्यम्। दृष्टान्तस्य[१] समयबन्धाधीनतया तद्विरहेपि क्षतिविरहात् ज्ञानत्वादेः पक्षमात्रवृत्तिधर्म्मस्य हेतुतया व्यतिरेकदृष्टान्तस्य[२] सुलभत्वाच्च। न च तथापि घटमहं जानामीत्यनुव्यवसायस्यापि घटत्वरूपेण घटविषयकतया तद्वृत्तिघटत्ववतिघटत्वप्रकारकत्वव्यक्तिविशिष्टज्ञानत्वे भिन्नमते तेन सम्बन्धेन

(१) दृष्टान्तोपन्यासस्येति ख०।

(२) व्यतिरेकेण दृष्टान्तस्येति ख०।

विधिकोटेरंशतो बाधः तदनुव्यवसायानुव्यवसायस्य घटत्ववतिघटत्व-प्रकारकत्वाश्रयविषयिणोऽनुव्यवसायस्यैव विशेषणज्ञानादिविधया जन्यत्वादिति वाच्यम्। ज्ञानभेदेन घटत्ववतीत्यादेर्भेदानभ्युपगमात् अनुव्यवसायनिष्ठघटत्ववतिघटत्वप्रकारकत्वविशिष्टज्ञानत्वस्य व्यवसायनिष्ठ घटत्ववतिघटत्वप्रकारत्वव्यक्तिविशिष्टज्ञानत्वानतिरिक्ततया ज्ञानभेदेन घटत्ववतीत्यादेर्भेदाभ्युपगमेऽपि तेन सम्बन्धेन विधिकोटौ बाधविरहाच्च। अनुव्यवसायानुव्यवसायस्य तदाश्रयविषयकज्ञानजन्यत्वेऽप्यनुव्यवसायस्य तदजन्यतया तमादायैव तेन सम्बन्धेन तत्र विधिकोटिसाम्राज्यात्। न च तथापि भट्टमते विधौ बाधः अहं ज्ञानवान् ज्ञाततावत्वादित्यनुमितेरपि ज्ञानत्वरूपेण घटत्वप्रमात्वाश्रयविषयकंव्याप्तिज्ञानादिजन्यत्वादिति वाच्यम्। तन्नये पक्षधर्मताबललभ्यसाध्यप्रसिद्धेरनङ्गतया ज्ञानत्वरूपेण घटत्ववतिघटत्वप्रकारकत्वानाश्रयीभूतज्ञानान्तरविषयकज्ञानादपि घटत्ववतिघटत्वप्रकारकत्वविशिष्टज्ञानत्वावच्छिन्नज्ञानानुमितिसम्भवेन तदनुमितिमादायैव[1] निरुक्तसम्बन्धेन विधिकोटिसम्भवात्। न च[2] सर्व्वविषयकत्ववतिसर्व्वविषयकत्वप्रकारकत्वविशिष्टज्ञानत्वरूपे प्रामाण्ये पक्षीकृते मिश्रनये बाधः सर्व्वविषयकमहं जानामीत्यनुव्यवसायस्य सर्व्वसम्मततया तादृशप्रामाण्याश्रयविषयकज्ञानजन्यत्वनियमादिति वाच्यं। तादृशस्याप्रसिद्धत्वादित्याहुः।

नव्यास्तु ज्ञानभेदेन घटत्ववतीत्यादेः[3] भिन्नत्वमतेनैवेयं विप्रति-

(१) घटत्ववतीत्याद्यनाश्रयीभूतज्ञानान्तरविषयकादपि घटत्ववतीत्यादिप्रकारेण ज्ञानानुमितिसम्भवे तामादायैवेति क० ।

(२) न च तथापीति ख० ।

(३) घटत्ववतिघटत्वप्रकारकत्वादेः इति ख० ।

पत्तिः तथा च तज्ज्ञाननिष्ठं घटत्ववतिघटत्वप्रकारकत्वं तज्ज्ञानविषयकज्ञानाजन्यज्ञानप्रकारो न वेति शृङ्गग्राहिकान्यायेन तत्तज्ज्ञानमादाय विप्रतिपत्तिः। विधिकोटिः परेषां, तज्ज्ञानविषयकज्ञानाजन्यं गुरुमते तज्ज्ञानमेव, मिश्रमते प्रथमानुव्यवसायः, भट्टमते ज्ञाततालिङ्गकानुमितिः, तत्प्रकारत्वस्य तज्ज्ञानवृत्तिघटत्ववतिघटत्वप्रकारकत्वे सत्त्वात्। निषेधकोटिश्च नैयायिकानां, तन्मते इदं ज्ञानं घटत्ववति घटत्वप्रकारकं तादृशप्रवृत्तिजनकत्वादित्यनुमित्यादेरेव प्रामाण्यग्राहकत्वात् तस्य च पक्षादिज्ञानविधया तज्ज्ञानविषयकज्ञानजन्यत्वनियमात् प्रथमज्ञानपदस्य स्वरूपकथनं न तु ज्ञानत्वेन प्रवेशः तद्विषयकेत्यस्यैव सम्यक्त्वात्। तज्ज्ञानसमानाधिकरणत्वेन चरमं ज्ञानं विशेषणीयं तेन भगवज्ज्ञानमादाय न विधिकोटि-निषेधकोट्योः सिद्धसाधन-बाधावकाशः, तज्ज्ञानपदेन योगिभिन्नपुरुषीयज्ञानस्य ग्रहणात्[१] नैयायिकसिद्धप्रामाण्यानुमितिमादाय सिद्धसाधनवारणायाजन्यान्तं ज्ञानविशेषणं, पदान्तरव्यावृत्तिस्तु पूर्ववत्[२]। न च तज्ज्ञानपूर्वोत्पन्नघटत्ववतिघटत्वप्रकारकत्वप्रकारकनिखिलघटत्ववतिघटत्वप्रकारकत्वव्यक्तिविषयकस्मरण-तदिन्द्रियसन्निकर्षाभ्यां तज्ज्ञानोत्पत्तिद्वितीयक्षणजनितज्ञानविशेष्यकतज्ज्ञानवृत्तिप्रामाण्यप्रकारकप्रथमानुव्यवसायमादाय विधि-निषेधकोट्योः सिद्धसाधन-बाधाविति वाच्यम्। स्वसमानाधिकरणघटत्ववतिघटत्वप्रकारकत्वानुपस्थितिकालोत्पन्नतज्ज्ञानव्यक्तिप्रामाण्यस्य पक्षत्वात्।

---

(१) तेन न योगिज्ञानमादाय सिद्धसाधनमिति भावः।

(२) दलान्तरव्यावृत्तिस्त्विति ख०।

त्वपदं तज्ज्ञानव्यक्तिपरं, उत्पन्नान्तं व्यक्तिविशेषपरिचायकं न तु पक्षतावच्छेदकघटकम्।

ननु तथापीयं प्रवृत्तिः घटत्वप्रमाजन्या यथार्थघटत्वप्रकारक-प्रवृत्तित्वादित्यनुमित्या पक्षधर्मताबलाद्घटत्वप्रमात्वविशिष्टपूर्व्वानुपस्थित-तज्ज्ञानव्यक्तिग्राहिण्या प्रामाण्यमादायार्थान्तरं परनये सामान्य-लक्षणाविरहेण पक्षधर्मताबललभ्यसाध्यतावच्छेदकव्यक्तिज्ञानस्यानुमि-त्यनङ्गत्वात्। न च तज्ज्ञानविषयकज्ञानजन्यत्वेन यन्नैयायिकसिद्धं तद्भिन्नमजन्यान्तेन विवक्षितमिति वाच्यम्। तथापि तज्ज्ञानोत्पत्ति-द्वितीयक्षणादिजातघटत्ववति घटत्वप्रकारकत्वप्रकारकनिखिलघटत्व-वतिघटत्वप्रकारकत्वव्यक्ति विशेषणक-घटादिविशेष्यकप्रमात्मकस्मरणल-क्षणसामान्यप्रत्यासत्तिजन्यतज्ज्ञानविशेष्यकप्रामाण्यप्रकारकप्रत्यक्षमा-दाय विधि-निषेधकोट्योः सिद्धसाधन-बाधापत्तेर्दुर्व्वारत्वादिति चेत्। न। तज्ज्ञानं विषयः पुरोवर्त्ति यस्येति व्युत्पत्त्या तज्ज्ञानविषयक-ज्ञानपदेन तज्ज्ञानाधिकरणकालोत्तरकालोत्पन्नज्ञानस्य विवक्षित-त्वात् विषयपदस्य कारणवाचकस्यात्र पुरोवर्त्तिमात्रपरत्वात् तथा च तज्ज्ञानाधिकरणकालोत्तरोत्पन्नज्ञानाजन्येत्यजन्यान्तार्थः। व्यवसाया-व्यवहितोत्तरोत्पन्नमेव ज्ञानं मिश्रमते प्रामाण्यग्राहकं। तज्ज्ञाना-धिकरणकालोत्तरवर्त्तित्वेनापि चरमज्ञानं विशेष्यं तेन तज्ज्ञानपूर्व्वो-त्पन्नतादृशसामान्यप्रत्यासत्तिजन्यप्रत्यक्षमादाय न सिद्धसाधनावव-काशः। व्यवसायस्यापि व्यवसायाधिकरणकालोत्तरवर्त्तित्वात् न गुरुमतापरिग्रहः। न च तथापि भट्टमतापरिग्रहः तन्मये तज्ज्ञानो-त्पत्तिः, ततस्तज्ज्ञानजन्यज्ञाततोत्पत्तिः, ततः तज्ज्ञाततप्रत्यक्षं, तत-

स्तज्ज्ञातताविशेष्यकपरामर्शोत्पत्तिः, तदनन्तरमियं ज्ञातता घटत्ववतिघटत्वप्रकारकज्ञानजन्या ज्ञाततात्वादित्यनुमित्या प्रामाण्यग्रहात्तदनुमितेश्च तज्ज्ञानोत्तरोत्पन्नज्ञानजन्यत्वनियमादिति वाच्यम्। भट्टैरपि व्यवसायपूर्वोत्पन्नेन व्यवसायसमकालोत्पन्नेन वा स्मरणाद्यात्मकपरामर्शेन व्यवसायोत्पत्तिद्वितीयक्षणे जनितया अहं ज्ञानवान् ज्ञाततावत्त्वादित्यनुमित्यैव प्रामाण्यग्रहाभ्युपगमात् व्यवसायोत्पत्त्यव्यवहितोत्तरक्षणेनोत्पन्नानुव्यवसायव्यक्तेरेव भट्टैः ज्ञाततालिङ्गकानुमितित्वेन मिश्रादिभिश्च साक्षात्कारत्वेनाभ्युपगमात्। अन्यथा व्यवसायोत्पत्तिद्वितीयक्षणे तदनुव्यवसायस्य मीमांसक-नैयायिकानुभवसिद्धस्य तन्मते अपलापापत्तेः स्वाश्रयनिश्चयव्यक्त्युत्तरतृतीयक्षणवृत्तिसंशयविषयत्वादिति वक्ष्यमाणहेतोस्तन्मतेऽसिद्ध्यापत्तेश्च। तच्चाग्रे स्फुटीभविष्यति।

यद्वा प्रथमं मतत्रयसाधारणी विप्रतिपत्तिरभिहिता, इयञ्च गुरुमिश्रोभयमतसाधारणी, अग्रिमाश्च प्रत्येकमतसाधारण्यः इति भेदादेव भट्टमतापरिग्रहेऽपि क्षतिविरहात्। न च कालिकविशेषणतया तज्ज्ञानवृत्तित्वेनैव चरमज्ञानं विशेष्यतां किमजन्यान्तविशेषणेन उत्तरवर्त्तित्वान्तरविशेषणेन वा, तज्ज्ञाननिष्ठं घटत्ववतिघटत्वप्रकारकत्वं तज्ज्ञानवृत्तितज्ज्ञानसमानाधिकरणज्ञानप्रकारो न वेत्यस्यैव सम्यक्त्वात्, तज्ज्ञानपदेन प्रामाण्यानुपस्थितिकालोत्पन्नतज्ज्ञानग्रहणादेव तज्ज्ञानोत्पत्तिद्वितीयक्षणवर्त्तितज्ज्ञानविशेष्यकप्रामाण्यानुमित्यादिमादाय सिद्धसाधनाद्यनवकाशादिति वाच्यम्। अपेक्षाबुद्ध्यात्मकव्यवसायव्यक्तिनिष्ठप्रामाण्ये पक्षीकृते व्यवसायोत्पत्तिद्वितीयक्षणजातयथोक्तसामान्यप्रत्यासत्त्या तत्तृतीयक्षणे जनितं प्रत्यक्षमादाय

सिद्धसाधनादिप्रसङ्गात् ज्ञानान्तरप्रामाण्ये पक्षीकृतेपि यथासन्निवेशे वैयर्थ्याभावाच्च। एतेन तज्ज्ञानोत्पत्तिद्वितीयक्षणवृत्तित्वेनैव तज्ज्ञानसमानाधिकरणं ज्ञानं विशेष्यतां किमजन्यत्वादिविशेषणेन, एवमपेक्षाबुद्ध्यात्मकव्यवसायव्यक्तिप्रामाण्ये पक्षीकृतेऽपि न सिद्धसाधनाद्यवकाशः इति निरस्तम्। यथासन्निवेशे वैयर्थ्याभावात्।

ननु तथापि घटत्ववतिघटत्वप्रकारकत्वस्य घटत्वप्रकारकत्वानतिरिक्ततया प्रथमानुव्यवसायमादायैव विधौ सिद्धसाधनं निषेधे च बाधः न्यायनयेपि प्रथमनुव्यवसाये घटत्वप्रकारकत्वादिभानाभ्युपगमात्। किञ्च विशेष्ये विशेषणमितिन्यायेन प्रामाण्यप्रत्यक्षाभ्युपगमे तज्ज्ञानपूर्व्वोत्पन्नखण्डशःप्रामाण्यघटकपदार्थोपस्थिति-तज्ज्ञानेन्द्रियसन्निकर्षाभ्यां तज्ज्ञानोत्पत्तिद्वितीयक्षणे जनितं विशेष्ये विशेषणमिति न्यायेन तज्ज्ञानविशेष्यकप्रामाण्यप्रकारकप्रत्यक्षमादाय विधौ सिद्धसाधनं निषेधे च बाधः। न च मूलावच्छिन्नो वृक्षः कपिसंयोगीत्यादौ पक्षतावच्छेदकमूलावच्छिन्नत्वविशिष्टसमवायसंसर्गेण कपिसंयोगसिद्धिवदत्रापि घटत्ववतिघटत्वप्रकारकत्वत्वरूपविशिष्टपक्षतावच्छेदकावच्छिन्नत्वविशिष्टविशेषणतासम्बन्धेन विधिकोटिसिद्धेरुद्देश्यतया सिद्धसाधनानवकाश इति वाच्यं। तथापि निषेधे बाधस्य दुर्व्वारत्वात् इति चेत्। न। घटत्ववद्विशेष्यकत्वावच्छिन्नघटत्वप्रकारकत्वत्वातिरिक्तानवच्छिन्नतादृशज्ञानप्रकारत्व-तदभावयोः कोटित्वात्, अनवच्छिन्नान्तार्थस्तु पूर्व्ववत्। निरवच्छिन्नप्रकारतामादाय सत्त्व-गुणत्व-घटत्वादौ विधिकोटिप्रसिद्धिसम्पादनायाभावद्वयगर्भता, निषेधसिद्धिस्तु तज्ज्ञाने तज्ज्ञानानुव्यवसायाविषयआत्यखण्डोपाध्यतिरिक्तपदार्थमात्रे च बोध्या

त्यखण्डोपाध्यतिरिक्तपदार्थस्य किञ्चिद्धर्मप्रकारेणैव भाननियमात्।

वस्तुतस्तु यथाकथञ्चिज्ज्ञानप्रकारत्वमेव विधिकोटिः, परन्तु घटत्ववतिघटत्वप्रकारकत्वत्वावच्छिन्नत्वविशिष्टघटत्वप्रकारतानिष्ठविशेषणताविशेषः कोटितावच्छेदकसम्बन्धः, तादृशविशेषणताविशेषावच्छिन्नप्रतियोगिताकतादृशज्ञानप्रकारत्वाभावः निषेधकोटिः शेषञ्च दर्शितदिशावसेयमिति प्राहुः।

नैयायिकमते निषेधकोटिमुपपादयति। 'परतः पत्र इति नैयायिकमत इत्यर्थः। 'ज्ञात एवेति, विशिष्टप्रामाण्यस्येति शेषः। 'ज्ञाने प्रामाण्यग्रहः' ज्ञानविशेष्यकप्रामाण्यग्रहः। मीमांसकमते विधिकोटिमुपपादयति, 'स्वतस्त्व इति मीमांसकमत इत्यर्थः। विशिष्टप्रामाण्योपस्थितिं विनापीतिशेषः। द्वितीयमते 'ज्ञात एव ज्ञाने' इत्यत्र ज्ञात एव प्रामाण्याश्रय इत्यर्थः, 'स्वतस्त्व इत्यस्य प्रामाण्योपस्थितिं विनापीति शेषः। नव्यमते तु 'ज्ञात एवेत्यस्य तज्ज्ञानाधिकरणकालोत्तरोत्पन्नज्ञानजन्य एवेत्यर्थः। 'ज्ञाने' तज्ज्ञानसमानाधिकरणतज्ज्ञानाधिकरणकालोत्तरवर्त्तिज्ञाने, 'प्रामाण्यग्रहः' प्रामाण्यविषयकत्वं, 'स्वतस्त्व इत्यस्य तज्ज्ञानसमानाधिकरणतज्ज्ञानाधिकरणकालोत्तरोत्पन्नज्ञानं विनापि तज्ज्ञानाधिकरणकालोत्तरकालमिति शेषः।

मतत्रयसाधारणं लघुविप्रतिपत्त्यन्तरमाह, 'स्वाश्रयेति। स्वाश्रयज्ञानविषयकग्रहेणैव विषयीक्रियते न वेत्यत्रकारव्यत्यासेन योजना, एवकारस्य यावदर्थकः, स्वपदं सामान्यतः पक्षीभूतघटत्ववतीत्यादिपरं(१)

(१) पक्षीभूतघटत्ववतिघटत्वप्रकारकत्वादिपरमिति ख०।

तथा च तज्ज्ञानवृत्तिघटत्ववतिघटत्वप्रकारकत्वं स्वाश्रयज्ञानविषयकयावद्ग्रहप्रकारो न वेति[1] फलितं, ज्ञानभेदेन घटत्ववतिघटत्वप्रकारकत्वादेर्विभिन्नत्वे तु स्वाश्रयपदं पक्षीभूतप्रामाण्यव्यक्त्याश्रयपरं, तथा च तज्ज्ञानवृत्ति घटत्ववतिघटत्वप्रकारकत्वं तज्ज्ञानविषयकयावद्ग्रहप्रकारो न वेति फलितं, इदं ज्ञानं प्रमा समर्थप्रवृत्तिजनकत्वादित्यादिनैयायिकसिद्धप्रामाण्यानुमितिमादाय विधौ सिद्धसाधनवारणाय यावदिति ग्रहविशेषणं, तदर्थश्च दीधितिकृन्मतोक्तरीत्या प्रथमविप्रतिपत्त्यनुसारेण बोध्यः[2], प्रकारता[3] प्रथमविप्रतिपत्तौ सर्व्वोक्तान्यतररूपा[4] ग्राह्या नातस्तत्रोक्तार्थान्तरावकाशः । एवं इदं ज्ञानं निष्प्रकारकं, इदं ज्ञानं निर्विशेष्यकं, इदं ज्ञानं प्रमात्वाभाववदित्यादिज्ञानलौकिकप्रत्यक्षमादाय गुरु-मिश्रयोर्मते विधौ बाधवारणाय तत्प्रामाण्यग्रहप्रतिबन्धकीभूततत्प्रामाण्याश्रयविषयकग्रहाविशिष्टत्वेन ग्रहो विशेषणीयः, तत्पदं विशिष्यपक्षीभूतप्रामाण्यपरिचयाय, वैशिष्ट्यञ्च स्वजन्य-स्वाव्यवहितोत्तरक्षणान्यतरक्षणावच्छेदेन एकात्मवृत्तित्वं,[5] स्वपदञ्च ग्रहपरं, घटत्ववतिघटत्व-

---

(१) घटत्ववतिघटत्वप्रकारकत्वाश्रयज्ञानविषयकयावद्ग्रहप्रकारो न वेतीति ख० ।

(२) तदर्थश्च प्रथमविप्रतिपत्तौ दीधितिकृन्मतोक्तरीत्या बोध्यः इति ख० ।

(३) बोधप्रकारता चेति क० ।

(४) पूर्व्वोक्तरूपेति क० ।

(५) इदं ज्ञानं निष्प्रकारकमित्यादिज्ञानोत्तरवर्त्तितज्ज्ञानविषयकज्ञानमादाय बाधवारणाय अन्यतरक्षणस्य वैशिष्ट्यघटकत्वमिति भावः ।

प्रकारकत्वाश्रयज्ञानविषयकत्वस्य तादृशज्ञानांशे लौकिकविषयताशून्यत्व-साक्षात्कारत्वविशिष्टविषयत्वोभयाभाववत्त्वं एवं पक्षे तज्ज्ञानविषयकत्वमपि तज्ज्ञानांशे तादृशोभयाभाववत्त्वं तेन प्रामाण्यविषयकज्ञानस्योपनीतचाक्षुषादिमादाय न बाधः, भट्टमतसाधारणाय उभयाभावानुधावनम्। न च गुरुनये तादृशविवक्षणं व्यर्थं तेनोपनीतचाक्षुषादेरनभ्युपगमादिति वाच्यम्। सर्व्वमते सर्व्वविवक्षासाफल्याभावेऽपि क्षतिविरहात् यत्किञ्चिन्मते सार्थकत्वस्य कर्त्तव्यत्वात् गुरुमतेऽप्युपनीतभानस्य लाघवेन ग्रहण-स्मरणात्मकैकज्ञानरूपतया तद्विवक्षणस्यावश्यकत्वाच्च। अतएव तन्मते लौकिकविषयत्वस्यापि नाप्रसिद्धिः। सुरभि चन्दनमित्यादेः लाघवेन ग्रहण-स्मरणात्मकैकज्ञानरूपतया तत्र सौरभं पश्यामीत्यनुव्यवसायवारणाय वह्न्याद्यनुमितेरपि स्वांशे मानससाक्षात्काररूपतया तत्रापि वह्निं साक्षात्करोमीत्याद्यनुव्यवसायवारणाय तदभ्युपगमस्यावश्यकत्वात्। परन्तु तदेतन्मते साक्षात्कारत्वमिति परं विवादः। तादृशज्ञानांशे इत्यभावान्वयि तेन तज्ज्ञानविषयकज्ञानस्य व्युदासः तत्र च तादृशज्ञानांशे तादृशोभयाभाववत्त्वविरहात्

ननु प्रथमविप्रतिपत्त्युक्तरीत्या ज्ञानपदजन्यशाब्दबोधं ज्ञानवानित्यनुमिति-स्मृत्यादिकं घटज्ञानपदादिजन्यशाब्दबोधं घटज्ञानवानित्याद्यनुमिति-स्मृत्यादिकञ्चादाय बाधो दुर्व्वार इति चेत्। न। घटत्ववतिघटत्वप्रकारकज्ञाननिष्ठप्रामाण्याविषयकपरोक्षभिन्नत्वेन ग्रहविशेषणात् तादृशग्रहस्य तादृशज्ञानसाक्षात्कारः तादृशज्ञानविषयकप्रामाण्यानुमित्यादिश्च। सिद्धसाधनवारणाय परोक्षेति,

परोक्षत्वञ्च चाक्षुषादिभेदपञ्चकजन्यज्ञानत्वं," भट्टमतसाधारण्यायाविषय-कान्तं परोक्षविशेषणं, शेषं प्रथमविप्रतिपत्तौ नव्यमतोक्तरीत्याव-सेयं।

वस्तुतस्तु न ह्येकदा त्रिभिर्द्वाभ्यां वा विवादः, अतः प्रत्येकमत-मात्रसाधारणं विप्रतिपत्तिद्वयमाह, 'स्वाश्रयग्राहकेणेत्यादि, इदन्तु मिश्रमते। 'स्वाश्रयग्राहकेण' स्वाश्रयविषयकसाक्षात्कारेण, 'गृह्यत एव न वा' प्रकारीक्रियत एव न वेत्यर्थः। भिन्नक्रमस्यैवकारः स्वाश्रयविषयकसाक्षात्कारस्य यावत्त्वलाभाय। अन्यथा प्रामाण्यस्तत्या-दिकालीनेनानुव्यवसायेन नैयायिकमतेपि प्रामाण्यग्रहात् सिद्धसा-धनापत्तेः, तथा च स्वाश्रयविषयकयावत्साक्षात्कारप्रकारतावन्न वेति फलितं। साक्षात्कारश्च स्वाश्रयांशे संयुक्तसमवायजन्यत्वेन लौकिकत्वेन वा विशेषणीयः तेन प्रामाण्याविषयकोपनीतभानमादाय न बाधः। तत्प्रामाण्यग्रहप्रतिबन्धकासमवहितत्वेन साक्षात्कारो विशेषणीयः तेनेदं निष्प्रकारकं इत्यादिज्ञानलौकिकप्रत्यक्षमादाय न बाधः। अनुव्यवसी-यमानज्ञानप्रामाण्यमेव पक्षः नातो बाधः। प्रकारता च ज्ञानत्वावच्छि-न्नविशेष्यतानिरूपितत्वविशिष्टप्रामाण्यत्वावच्छिन्नप्रकारता-घटत्वादिनि-ष्ठप्रकारतानिरूपितप्रकारतयोरन्यतरप्रकारतारूपा ग्राह्या। अन्यथा प्रमात्व-कालीनत्वादिविषयकत्वेन कालिकादियत्किञ्चित्सम्बन्धेन प्र-कारत्वत्वादियत्किञ्चिद्रुपेण वा प्रमात्वप्रकारकत्वेन स्वार्थान्तरापत्तेः घटत्ववद्विशेष्यकत्वावच्छिन्नघटत्वप्रकारकत्वस्य केवलघटत्वप्रकारकत्वान-तिरिक्ततया सिद्धसाधनापत्तेश्च, न्यायनयेप्यनुव्यवसाये घटत्वप्रकारक-त्वादिभानाभ्युपगमात् इदं ज्ञानं प्रमा न वेति संशयोत्पत्त्या विधि-

कोटिनिराकरणानुपपत्तेश्च यथाकथञ्चित् तत्सत्त्वेऽपि[१] तादृशसंशय-प्रसङ्गात्। एवमग्रिमविप्रतिपत्तिष्वपि बोध्यमित्येव सारम्।

गुरुमतमात्रसाधारणविप्रतिपत्त्यन्तरमाह, 'स्वाश्रयेणेति 'स्वाश्र-येण प्रकारीक्रियत एव न वेत्यर्थः। ज्ञानभेदेन घटत्ववतीत्यादेः[२] भिन्नत्वमतेनाद्यं, सामान्यतो घटत्ववतिघटत्वप्रकारत्वत्वादिना च पक्षत्वं न तु तज्ज्ञानवृत्तिप्रामाण्यत्वेन, तज्ज्ञानवृत्तिप्रामाण्यत्वेन पक्षत्वे स्वाश्र-यपदस्य तज्ज्ञानपरत्वे च 'प्रामाण्यमात्रस्य पक्षत्वादित्युत्तरग्रन्थासङ्गतेः यद्वेत्यादिना वक्ष्यमाणेन पौनरुक्त्यापत्तेश्च। साध्ये च स्वपदस्य सम-भिव्याहृतपरतया स्वाश्रयपदं यदा यत्र साध्यं ग्राह्यं तदाश्रयपरं न तु सामान्यतो घटत्ववतिघटत्वप्रकारकत्वाश्रयपरं भगवज्ज्ञानमादाय पक्षतावच्छेदकावच्छेदेनैव सिद्धसाधनापत्तेः। एवकारस्य पक्षतावच्छे-दकावच्छेदेन साध्यसिद्धेरुद्देश्यत्वलाभाय अन्यथा योगिज्ञान-भगवज्ज्ञा-नयोः सर्व्वविषयकत्वेन सकलपदार्थघटितप्रामाण्याश्रयतया तद्वृत्ति-घटत्ववतिघटत्वप्रकारकत्वव्यक्त्यावच्छिन्नतः सिद्धसाधनापत्तेः सर्व्वं ज्ञानं प्रमेत्यनुमितिनिष्ठघटत्ववतिघटत्वप्रकारकत्वव्यक्त्यावच्छिन्नतः सिद्धसाधनाप-त्तेश्च। न च क्रियासङ्गतैवकारस्यान्वयितावच्छेदकसामानाधिकरण्येन व्यवच्छेदबोधकत्वस्वाभाव्यात् कथं तल्लाभ इति वाच्यं। ज्ञानं रजतं गृह्णात्येवेत्याद्यप्रयोगात् ग्रहादिधातुयोग्यैवकारस्यान्वयितावच्छेदकाव-च्छेदेनैवायोगव्यवच्छेदस्य लक्षणयोपस्थितस्य धर्म्मिणोऽन्ययोगव्यवच्छे-दस्य बोधकत्वात्, यावद्घटज्ञानप्रामाण्यानामैक्ये तु पूर्व्ववद्विकल्प-

---

(१) प्रमात्वज्ञानसत्त्वेपीति ख० घ०, च।
(२) घटत्ववतिघटत्वप्रारत्वादेरिति ख०।

स्यैवकारः स्वाश्रययावत्त्वस्याभावान्यथा योगिज्ञानेश्वरज्ञानयोः सर्व्वविषयकत्वेन सकलप्रामाण्याश्रयतया तद्ग्राह्यत्वेन सिद्धसाधनापत्तेः । साध्येऽपि स्वाश्रयपदं सामान्यतो घटत्ववतीत्याद्याश्रयपरं[(१)] परन्तु ग्रन्थो नैतदभिप्रायकः उक्तग्रन्थासङ्गतेरिति । 'प्रत्येकमेवेति एवम्प्रकारेण प्रत्येकमेवेत्यर्थः । यद्यपि मिश्रमते उक्तैव विप्रतिपत्तिः, भट्टमते च किमनुमितिग्राह्यत्व-तदभावौ कोटी. यावदनुमितिग्राह्यत्व-तदभावौ वा, ज्ञाततालिङ्गकानुमितिग्राह्यत्व-तदभावौ वा आद्ये सिद्धसाधनं, द्वितीये सर्व्वमतएवाप्रसिद्धिः, तृतीये न्यायनयेऽप्रसिद्धिः तन्मते ज्ञाततायाः शशविषाणकल्पत्वात् । तथापि तन्मते घटत्ववतिघटत्वप्रकारकत्वं घटवृत्तिज्ञाततापक्षकघटावृत्तिजन्यतासंसर्गकभ्रमभिन्नानुमितिविधेयतावच्छेदकं न वेति विप्रतिपत्तिः, तन्मते इयं ज्ञातता घटविशेष्यकघटत्वप्रकारकज्ञानवती घटविशेष्यकघटत्वप्रकारकज्ञाततात्वात् इति अन्यतासंसर्गकानुमित्या, इयं ज्ञातता घटविशेष्यकघटत्वप्रकारकज्ञानजन्या ज्ञाततात्वादिति अन्यताविधेयकानुमित्या वा प्रामाण्यग्रहात् । न च न्यायनये ज्ञाततायाः शशविषाणकल्पत्वेनाप्रसिद्धिरिति वाच्यम् । गुणेतरपदार्थस्यैव प्रकृते ज्ञाततापदेन विवक्षितत्वात् । भट्टेन द्वित्वादेरपेक्षाबुद्धिजन्यत्वानभ्युपगमेपि न्यायनये घटवृत्तिद्वित्वादिपक्षकापेक्षाबुद्ध्यात्मकघटत्वप्रमाजन्यत्वानुमितिमादाय सिद्धसाधनवारणाय गुणेतरत्वं पदार्थविशेषणं, घटवृत्तित्वञ्च समवायेन विवक्षितं, समवायानभ्युपगमे विशेषणताविशेषेणैव वृत्तित्वं विवक्षणीयं, तथा च गुणेतरत्वं नोपादेयं, ज्ञानस्य साधारणजन्यतामादाय सिद्धसाधनवारणाय

(१) घटत्ववतिघटत्वप्रकारकत्वाश्रयपरमिति ख० ।

घटावृत्तित्वं जन्यतःविशेषणं, पक्षतावच्छेदकसमानाधिकरणेन विधेस्तदवच्छेदेन च निषेधस्य च उद्देश्यतया ज्ञानभेदेन प्रकारत्वादेर्भेदनयेपि नांशतः सिद्धसाधन-बाधयोरवकाशः, यावद्घटज्ञाननिष्ठप्रमात्वस्यैक्यमते तु नानुपपत्तिगन्धोपि। भट्टेन नैयायिकेन वा ख्यात्यतिरिक्तपदार्थत्वाभ्युपगमे क्रय-प्रतिग्रहादीतरत्वेन विधेयता विशेषणीया नातस्तत्पक्षकानुमितिमादायार्थान्तरं सिद्धसाधनं वा। यदि च भ्रमव्यावृत्तं स्वतोग्राह्यत्वं निर्वाच्यं तदा घटत्वप्रमावृत्तित्वेनाप्यनुमितिविधेयता विशेषणीयेति भावः।

वस्तुतस्तु ज्ञाननिष्ठं घटत्ववतिघटत्वप्रकारकत्वं लौकिकसाक्षात्काराग्राह्यत्वे सति ग्राह्यं न वेति तन्मते विप्रतिपत्तिः, तन्मते ज्ञानस्यातीन्द्रियतया तद्वृत्तिविशेष्यकत्व-प्रकारकत्वादेरप्यतीन्द्रियत्वात्, न्यायनये विशिष्टस्यानतिरिक्ततया केवलघटत्वप्रकारकत्व-घटविशेष्यकत्वयोरनुव्यवसायग्राह्यत्वादेव विशिष्टस्यान्यनुव्यवसायग्राह्यत्वात् विशिष्टप्रामाण्योपस्थितिदशायां विशिष्टत्वरूपेणाप्यनुव्यवसायग्राह्यत्वाच्च। न च सिद्धसाधनावकाशः, पक्षतावच्छेदकावच्छेदेन विधिकोटिसिद्धेरुद्देश्यतया ज्ञानभेदेन प्रकारत्वादेर्भेदेपि नांशतः सिद्धसाधनं। न चैवं लौकिकसाक्षात्काराग्राह्यत्वे सति ग्राह्यत्वमेव तन्मते स्वतोग्राह्यत्वमितिफलितं तथा च प्रामाण्यवदप्रामाण्यस्यापि स्वतोग्राह्यत्वापत्तिरिति वाच्यम्। तादृशस्वतोग्राह्यत्वस्याप्रामाण्येपीष्टत्वात्, प्रामाण्यं स्वतोग्राह्यं नाप्रामाण्यमिति प्रवादस्य च मतत्रयसाधारणविप्रतिपत्त्युपवर्णितविधिकोटिरूपस्वतोग्राह्यत्वपरत्वादित्येव तत्त्वम्।

भट्टाचार्यास्तु प्रामाण्याश्रयविषयकत्वेन भट्टमतसिद्धं यत् तद्-

भिन्नयावद्ग्रहविषयो न वेति भट्टमते विप्रतिपत्तिः। नैयायिकसिद्धप्रामाण्यानुमितिमादाय सिद्धसाधनवारणाय यावत्त्वं ग्रहविशेषणं। इत्यस्यानुव्यवसायस्य भट्टमते शशविषाणकल्पतया यावद्ग्रहान्तर्गतत्वात् तद्ग्राह्यत्वाभावेन सिद्धसाधनस्य नावकाशः। सिद्धान्तश्च भेदकूटप्रतियोगिपरिचायकं न तु तस्य कोटितावच्छेदकेऽन्तर्भावः, प्रातिस्विकरूपेण तत्तद्व्यक्तिभेदकूटस्यैव कोटितावच्छेदकत्वात्, तेन सिद्धसाधनत्वस्यानुगतानतिप्रसक्तस्य दुर्वचत्वेऽपि न क्षतिः। न च तत्प्रामाण्यविषयकत्वेन न्यायनयसिद्धा या अनुमितिस्तद्भिन्नग्राह्यं न वेति सम्यगिति वाच्यम्। स्वप्रकाशमर्य्यादयाऽयं घट इत्याद्यनुमित्यात्मकव्यवसायग्राह्यत्वमादायार्थान्तरापत्तेरित्याहुः।

मिश्रास्तु भट्टमते ज्ञानत्वावच्छिन्नव्यापकताज्ञानजन्य-तदितरव्यापकताज्ञानाद्यजन्यानुमितिव्यापकतावच्छेदकं न वेति विप्रतिपत्तिः, आदिपदाद्बाधज्ञान-लाघवज्ञानपरिग्रहः। भट्टमते अयं ज्ञानवान् ज्ञाततावत्त्वादियं ज्ञातता ज्ञानजन्या ज्ञाततात्वादित्यनुमितावेव बाधादिप्रतिसन्धानं विनापि वक्ष्यमाणरीत्या घटत्ववतिघटत्वप्रकारकत्वादिरूपेण ज्ञानस्य सिद्धेरित्याहुः।

अत्र केचित् योगजधर्मजन्ययोगिप्रत्यक्षेण सर्वविषयकेन ज्ञानत्वादिसामान्यलक्षणयोपस्थिते सर्वस्मिन्नेव ज्ञाने घटत्ववतिघटत्वप्रकारकत्वसामान्यलक्षणोपनीतघटत्ववतीत्यादिप्रकारकप्रत्यक्षेण च[1] स्वनिष्ठघटत्ववतिघटत्वप्रकारकत्वव्यक्तेरपि घटत्ववतिघटत्वप्रकारत्वत्वरूपेण स्वस्मिन्नेव प्रकारतया विषयीकरणात्तयोः प्रामाण्ये चतुर्थविप्रति-

(१) निखिलघटत्ववतिघटत्वप्रकारकत्वप्रकारकप्रत्यक्षेण चेति ख०।

पक्षतावंशतः सिद्धसाधनमतस्तदुद्धारणाय तत्र योगजधर्म्माद्यजन्यत्वेन पक्षघटकं ज्ञानं विशेषणीयमित्याऽऽहुस्तन्मतमुपन्यस्य दूषयति, 'यत्त्वित्यादिना 'सामान्यलक्षणप्रत्यासत्त्येति सामान्यं लक्षणं प्रयोजकं यस्यास्तादृशप्रत्यासत्त्येति व्युत्पत्त्या घटत्ववतिघटत्वप्रकारकत्वत्वादिरूपसामान्यलक्षणप्रत्यासत्तिजन्यघटत्ववतिघटत्वप्रकारकत्वत्वादिप्रकारकनिखिलघटत्ववतिघटत्वप्रकारकत्वादिविषयकज्ञानलक्षणप्रत्यासत्त्येत्यर्थः । 'तेनैव' स्वेनैव, 'गृह्यते' ज्ञानत्वसामान्यलक्षणोपस्थिते स्वस्मिन् प्रकारतया गृह्यते, 'अंशतः सिद्धसाधनमिति, घटत्ववति घटत्वप्रकारकत्वादेः प्रतिज्ञानं विभिन्नतया पक्षतावच्छेदकावच्छेदेन स्वाश्रयघटितसाध्यस्य सिद्धसाधनासम्भवादंशत इत्युक्तं । 'योगजधर्म्माद्यजन्यत्वमिति योगजधर्म्माद्यजन्यत्वे सति जन्यत्वमित्यर्थः । अन्यथेश्वरज्ञानस्य सर्व्वविषयकतया तत्प्रामाण्येऽंशतः सिद्धसाधनतादवस्थ्यात् । आदिपदात् प्रमाणज्ञानपरिग्रहः, 'विशेषणं' पक्षघटकज्ञाने विशेषणं, न तु साध्यघटकज्ञानेऽंशतः साध्याप्रसिद्ध्यापत्तेः । तथा च योगजधर्म्माद्यजन्यज्ञानप्रामाण्यं पक्ष इति भावः । योगजधर्म्माद्यजन्यत्वञ्च प्रत्यक्षमात्रवृत्तिधर्म्मावच्छिन्नयोगजधर्म्मादिजन्यतानाश्रयत्वं, अन्यथा ज्ञानादृष्टादेः कार्य्यमात्रजनकतया तदजन्यज्ञानाप्रसिद्धेः, अतएव दूषयति, 'परम्प्रत्यसिद्धेरिति प्रतियोगिनस्तादृशजन्यत्वस्याप्रसिद्धा तदनाश्रयत्वस्याप्रसिद्धेरित्यर्थः । कथं तर्हि सिद्धसाधनोद्धार इत्यत आह, 'प्रामाण्यमात्रस्येति[१] घटत्ववतिघटत्वप्रकारकत्वत्वादिरूपेण पक्षतयेत्यर्थः । 'प्रामाण्यं स्वाश्रयेण गृह्यत एवेतीति प्रामाण्यं स्वाश्रयेण

(१) "प्रामाण्यमात्रस्य पक्षत्वे" इति कस्यचिन्मूलपुस्तकस्य पाठः तदनुसारेण "प्रामाण्यमात्रस्येतीत्यनेन मूलपाठो धृतः मथुरानाथेन ।

ग्राह्यत एवेत्याकारिकाया घटत्ववतिघटत्वप्रकारकत्वादिरूपोद्देश्यता-वच्छेदकावच्छेदेन फलीभूतानुमितेरित्यर्थः। 'असिद्धेः' पक्षताव-च्छेदकसामानाधिकरण्येन साध्यविषयकत्वासिद्धेः, 'नांशतः सिद्धसा-धनमिति, दोषः इति शेषः। न च तथापि यावद्घटज्ञानप्रामा-ण्यानामैक्येन सिद्धसाधनं दुर्वारमिति वाच्यम्। तन्मते यावत्त्वस्य स्वाश्रयविशेषणत्वादेव वारणसम्भवादिति भावः। नन्विदमयुक्तं यदि ज्ञानव्यक्तिभेदेन प्रामाण्यभेदः तदा साध्ये स्वपदस्य तत्तत्प्रामाण्य-व्यक्तिपरत्वे कस्यापि साध्यस्य पक्षतावच्छेदकावच्छेदेनासत्तेरंशतोबाधा-पत्तेः सामान्यतो घटत्ववतिघटत्वप्रकारकत्वादिपरतायां तदाश्रय-विषयकयावत्प्रत्यक्षविषयत्वस्य कुत्राप्यभावाद्बाधापत्तिरित्यस्वरसादाह, 'यद्वेति, 'घटोयमिति, 'ज्ञानप्रामाण्यमिति, एतज्ज्ञानवृत्तिप्रामाण्य-मित्यर्थः। 'एतज्ज्ञानग्राहकमात्रेति मात्रपदं कृत्स्नार्थकं, तथाचैत-ज्ज्ञानविषयकयावल्लौकिकप्रत्यक्षप्रकारो न वेत्यर्थः, व्याख्याततत्त्वमेतत्।

ननु मीमांसकैः प्रामाण्यमेव स्वतो ग्राह्यमुच्यते, प्रामाण्यस्य न तद्वतितत्प्रकारकत्वादिकमपि तु विशेष्यावृत्त्यप्रकारकत्वादिकं तच्च वक्ष्यमाणरीत्या न स्वतोग्राह्यं सम्भवतीत्याह, 'यद्यपीति, 'विशेष्या-वृत्तीति स्वाधिकरणावृत्तिधर्म्मानिरूपितविशेष्यताकत्वमित्यर्थः। तेन वह्निगुञ्जयोर्गुञ्जावह्नी इति विपरीतभ्रमे(१) नातिव्याप्तिः स्वपदं भेदप्रतियोगिविशेष्यतापरं(२) इदं रजतमित्यादिभ्रमो धर्म्मितावच्छेद-

---

(१) गुञ्जायां वह्नित्वस्य वह्नौ गुञ्जात्वस्य भ्रम इत्यर्थः।

(२) तथा च स्वाधिकरणावृत्तिधर्म्मनिरूपितविशेष्यताभिन्नविशेष्यताशा-लित्वमित्यर्थः।

ज्ञस्य प्राकव्यादेस्तद्व्यभिचारात्। नापि प्रमाहितज्ञाततावि्शेषात्, तस्य प्रथमं दुर्निरूपत्वात्। अन्यथा अप्रमाहितज्ञाततया अप्रामाण्यस्यापि स्वतोग्रहापत्तिरिति। तथापि तद्वति तत्प्रकारकज्ञानत्वं तद्वतितद्वैशिष्ट्यज्ञानत्वं वा प्रामाण्यं। तन्निश्चयादेव निष्कम्पव्यवहारात् लाघवात् नान्यद्गौरवात्। तच्च ज्ञानग्राहकसामग्री-

---

कांशे प्रमापि प्रमुक्तत्ताकस्मरणवन्न लक्ष्यः। स्वाधिकरणवृत्तिधर्म्मनिष्ठविशेष्यतावच्छेदकत्वातिरिक्तप्रकारतानिरूपितविशेष्यताकत्वमात्रस्यैव[१] सम्यक्त्वेऽप्यनुगमार्थं निषेधद्वयगर्भता। 'अगृहीतग्राहित्वमिति स्वसमानाधिकरणस्वाव्यवहितपूर्ववर्त्तिस्वसमानाकारनिश्चयाविषयविषयकत्वमित्यर्थः। धारावाहिकज्ञानस्य न प्रमेत्यभिमानः। 'सर्वेति[२], निर्विकल्पक-व्यधिकरणप्रकारकज्ञानयोरनभ्युपगमादिति भावः। 'स्मृत्यन्येति[३], स्मृतौ प्रमाव्यवहारविरहात् तत्परित्यागः। 'विशिष्टज्ञानत्वमिति। यद्यपि विशिष्टज्ञानत्वं न तत्प्रकारकज्ञानत्वं, 'प्रागनुपस्थितेः' इत्यग्रिमदूषणासङ्गतेः ज्ञानत्व-प्रकारत्वादेरनुपस्थितस्यैव प्रकारत्वाभ्युपगमात् अन्यथा सिद्धान्तेऽपि तद्दोषापरीहारात्। तथाप्यगृहीतासंसर्गकतदुभयविषयकज्ञानत्वं परस्परं तदुभयविशिष्टज्ञानत्वं, न

---

(१) प्रकारतायां विशेष्यतावच्छेदकत्वातिरिक्तत्वविशेषणात् ह्रदो वह्निमानित्यादिभ्रमे ह्रदत्वनिष्ठावच्छेदकत्वात्मकप्रकारतामादाय नातिव्याप्तिः।

(२) सर्व्वधीतीति ख०।

(३) "स्मृत्यन्यज्ञानत्वं" इति कस्यचिन्मूलपुस्तकस्य पाठमनुसृत्य स्मृत्यन्येतीत्यनेन मूलपाठो धृतो मथुरानाथेन।

ग्राह्यमेव। तथा हि विशेष्ये तद्धर्म्मवत्त्वं तद्धर्म्मप्रकारकत्वञ्च व्यवसायस्यानुव्यवसायेनानुमित्या स्वप्रकाशेन वा गृह्यते विषयनिरूप्यं हि ज्ञानमतो ज्ञानवित्तिवेद्यो विषय इति व्यवसाये भासमाने धर्म्म-धर्म्मिवत्तद्वैशिष्ट्य-

---

तत्प्रकारज्ञानत्वं, परस्परं तदुभयप्रमात्वमपि तदैवेत्यर्थः। असंसर्गाग्रह-कालीनसमूहालम्बनज्ञानमपि परस्परमुभयप्रमेति भावः। 'प्रामाण्यं' प्रामाण्यव्यवहारास्पदं, निरूढ़लक्षणया प्रोपसंहितमाधातुप्रतिपाद्यतावच्छेदकमितियावत्[१] 'ज्ञानातीन्द्रियत्व इति ज्ञानातीन्द्रियत्वमत इत्यर्थः। 'ज्ञानानुमित्येति तत्तज्ज्ञाततापक्षकजन्यतासंसर्गकज्ञानानुमित्येत्यर्थः। 'तत्' विशेष्यावृत्त्यप्रकारकत्वादिकं, 'गृह्यते' ग्रहीतुं शक्यते,'ज्ञानमात्रलिङ्गस्येति तादात्म्यादिसम्बन्धेन भ्रम-प्रमासाधारण-निखिलज्ञानजन्यस्य ज्ञाततालिङ्गस्येत्यर्थः। 'प्राकट्यादेः' इत्यादिपदात् प्राकट्यत्वपरिग्रहः। तथा च तादात्म्यसम्बन्धेन प्राकट्यमाश्रयता-सम्बन्धेन प्राकट्यत्वस्य न तदनुमापकं सम्भवतीति भावः।

ननु प्रमाजन्यज्ञाततात्वं हेतुरित्यत आह, 'नापीति। 'प्रमाहित-ज्ञातताविशेषात्' प्रमाहितज्ञाततानिष्ठो यो विशेषः प्रमाजन्यज्ञात-तात्वं तस्मात्, 'तस्य' ज्ञाततानिष्ठप्रमाजन्यत्वस्य, 'प्रथमं' कारणीभूत-व्यवसाये प्रमात्वज्ञानं विना। ननु प्रमाजन्यज्ञाततात्वं न हेतुरपि तु प्रमाजन्यतावच्छेदकं ज्ञाततानिष्ठं वैजात्यमस्ति तेन रूपेण

---

(१) 'प्रोपसंहितमांधातुप्रतिपाद्यतावच्छेदकं' प्रकृष्टोपसर्गयुक्तमाधातुप्रतिपाद्यतावच्छेदकमित्यर्थः।

तादात्म्यसम्बन्धेन ज्ञाततैव हेतुरित्यत आह, 'अन्यथेति यदि प्रमोत्पत्त्यनन्तरं तज्जन्यतावच्छेदकवैजात्यरूपेण ज्ञाततया हेतुना प्रामाण्यमनुमेयं तदेत्यर्थः। 'अप्रमाहितज्ञाततयेति अप्रमाजन्यतावच्छेदकवैजात्यरूपेण ज्ञाततया हेतुनेत्यर्थः। तुल्यन्यायतया अप्रमाजन्यतावच्छेदकवैजात्यस्यापि तत्र सुवचत्वादिति भावः। 'स्वतोग्रहापत्तिरिति स्वात्मकव्यवसायोत्तरं ग्रहापत्तिरित्यर्थः। 'तद्वतितद्वैशिष्ट्यज्ञानत्वं वा' तद्वतितद्वैशिष्ट्यज्ञानत्वं वापि[१], तद्वतितद्वैशिष्ट्यज्ञानत्वञ्च तद्वन्निष्ठविषयतानिरूपिततद्विषयताकज्ञानत्वं तद्वति संसर्गमर्य्यादया तद्धर्म्मताविषयकत्वं वा, प्रथमे प्रकारित्वं विषयिताविशेष इति नाभेदः।

नन्वस्तु तदपि प्रामाण्यं, तथापि निष्कम्पप्रवृत्त्युपयोगि यत्प्रामाण्यं तदेव स्वतोग्राह्यं परैरुपेयते तच्च न तथेत्यत आह, 'तन्निरूपणादेवेति। 'लाघवादिति पाठः, 'लाघवाच्चेति पाठस्त्वप्रामाणिकः[२], तस्यापि प्रामाणिकत्वे तु 'निष्कम्पव्यवहारात्' निष्कम्पस्य व्यवहारात्, निष्कम्पप्रवृत्तेरनुभवासंकुलत्वादिति यावत्, 'लाघवाच्चेत्यस्य तदेव निष्कम्पप्रवृत्त्युपयोगीति शेषः।

ननु भवतु तदेव निष्कम्पप्रवृत्त्युपयोगि प्रामाण्यं तथापि तस्य स्वतोग्राह्यत्वं कथमित्यत आह, 'तच्चेति। 'विशेष्ये' व्यवसायविशेष्ये, 'तद्धर्म्मप्रकारकत्वमिति तद्विशेष्यकत्वे सति तद्धर्म्मप्रकारकत्वमित्यर्थः। अनुव्यवसायेन तद्ग्रहमुपपादयति, 'विषयनिरूप्यमिति विषयाविषयकलौकिकसाक्षात्काराविषय इत्यर्थः।

(१) तथा च मूलस्योवाकारो व्यवस्थितविकल्पार्थः।
(२) लाघवाच्चेति ख॰ चिह्नितमूलपुस्तकपाठः।

मपि विषयः व्यवसायरूपप्रत्यासत्तेस्तुल्यत्वात् सम्बन्धितावच्छेदकरूपवत्तया ज्ञायमाने सम्बन्धिनि ससम्बन्धिकपदार्थनिरूपणमित्यनुव्यवसायस्य रजतत्वावच्छिन्नत्वेन पुरोवर्त्तिविषयत्वाच्च । अन्यथा पुरोवर्त्तिनं रज-

---

ननु तद्विषयकव्यवसायस्य तद्विषयकव्यवसायत्वे तद्भानप्रतिबन्धकत्वाज्ज्ञानानुव्यवसाये वैशिष्ट्यभानसम्भव इत्यत आह, 'व्यवसायेति, 'व्यवसायरूपप्रत्यासत्तेः' व्यवसायनिरूपितसम्बन्धस्य व्यवसायविषयत्वस्येति यावत्, 'तुल्यत्वात्' वैशिष्ट्यवद्धर्म-धर्मिणोरपि सत्त्वात् । तथा च तादृशप्रतिबध्य-प्रतिबन्धकभावे धर्म-धर्मिणोरपि भानं न स्यादिति भावः ।

नन्वेतावतापि समूहालम्बनसाधारणमनुव्यवसायस्य वैशिष्ट्यविषयकत्वं सिद्धं न तु रजतविशेष्यकरजतत्वप्रकारकत्वं तस्यैव च प्रकृते उद्देश्यत्वादित्यतस्तदप्युपपादयति, 'सम्बन्धितेति सम्बन्धितावच्छेदकरूपेण सम्बन्धिनं स्पृशदेव प्रत्यक्षं ससम्बन्धिकपदार्थं स्पृशतीत्यर्थः । यथाश्रुते फलीभूतज्ञाने तद्विषयत्वासिद्धेः । 'अनुव्यवसायस्य' इदं रजतमिति ज्ञानानुव्यवसायस्य ।

मिश्रास्तु 'अनुव्यवसायस्येत्यस्य, इदंविशेष्यकरजतत्वप्रकारकधीजन्यतयेति शेषः । 'रजतत्वावच्छिन्नत्वेनेति, यद्विशेष्यकयत्प्रकारकधीजन्यं यत्प्रत्यक्षं बाधकं विना तत्तद्विशेष्यक-तत्प्रकारकमिति नियमादिति भावः । एवञ्च 'सम्बन्धितेत्यादिग्रन्थो यथाश्रुत एव साधुरित्याहुः ।

तच्च जानामीति तदाकारः स्यान्न तु रजतत्वेन पुरोवर्तिनमिति। अत एवाप्रमापि प्रमेत्येव गृह्यते, अनुव्यवसायस्य भ्रमविषयवैशिष्ट्यविषयत्वात्। न च न प्रामाण्यं प्रथमतो ज्ञातमिति न तदारोपः स्यादिति

'अन्यथा' अनुव्यवसायस्य प्रकारीभूतधर्मवैशिष्ट्यानवगाहित्वे, 'पुरोवर्त्तिनं' इमं, 'रजतञ्च', रजतञ्च, 'रजतत्वेनेति, वैशिष्ट्यं तृतीयार्थः अन्वयश्चास्य पुरोवर्त्तिनि तथा च रजतत्वविशिष्टं पुरोवर्त्तिनमित्यर्थः। 'अतएवेति उक्तनियमद्वयादेवेत्यर्थः। 'प्रमेत्येवेति, एवशब्दस्तुल्यार्थे[१] प्रमेत्याकारकज्ञानजन्यो योऽनुव्यवसायस्तद्विषय इत्यर्थः। तुल्यतामेवोपपादयति, 'अनुव्यवसायस्येति, तथा च तज्ज्ञाने यथा विषयीभूतव्यवसायविशेष्ये तत्प्रकारीभूतधर्मवैशिष्ट्यं भासते तथा भ्रमानुव्यवसायेपि भ्रमविशेष्ये तत्प्रकारीभूतवैशिष्ट्यं भासत इति तुल्यतेति भावः।

प्राञ्चस्तु 'प्रमेत्येव गृह्यते' प्रमात्वप्रकारेण गृह्यते इत्यर्थः इत्याहुः। तदसत् अप्रमानुव्यवसायेन प्रमात्वपदस्याशक्यत्वात् प्रमात्वघटकस्य तद्वतोऽनुपस्थितेः 'अनुव्यवसायस्येत्यग्रिमग्रन्थासङ्गतेश्च।

'प्रथमतोऽज्ञातमिति तद्घटकयोः प्रकारित्व-विशेष्यकत्वयोर्व्यवसायाविशेष्यत्वादिति भावः। 'न तदारोप इति न तादृशविशिष्टबुद्धिरित्यर्थः, विशेषणज्ञानस्य विशिष्टानुभवहेतुत्वादिति भावः। 'ज्ञानग्राहकसामग्रीग्राह्यत्वेनेति ज्ञानसाक्षात्कारमात्रस्यैव ग्राह्यत्वेनेत्यर्थः। अनुपस्थितस्या-

---

(१) इवार्थे इति ख०।

वाच्यम्। प्रामाण्यस्य ज्ञानग्राहकसामग्रीग्राह्यत्वेन ज्ञानवित्तिवेद्यत्वात् अभावप्रतीतौ[१] प्रतियोगित्वाभावत्वयोरिव। तदभाववति तत्प्रकारकज्ञानत्वमप्रामाण्यं

पीति शेषः। 'अभावप्रतीताविति यथा घटप्रतियोगिकोऽभाव इत्यादिप्रत्यक्षे प्रतियोगित्वमभावत्वञ्चानुपस्थितमपि प्रकारः तथेहापि प्रामाण्यमित्यर्थः। अभावत्वञ्च भावव्यावृत्ताखण्डो धर्मविशेषः तथा प्रतियोगित्वमपि, न तु द्रव्यादिषट्कान्योन्याभाववत्त्वमभावत्वं अभावाभावत्वञ्च प्रतियोगित्वं[२] तस्य द्रव्यादिघटितत्वेनानुपस्थितस्य प्रकारत्वासम्भवात्। एतच्च सम्प्रदायमतमाश्रित्य उक्तं। वस्तुतस्तु विशेष्यितासम्बन्धेन तद्धर्मवदवच्छिन्नं प्रकारितासम्बन्धेन तद्धर्मवत्त्वमपि प्रामाण्यं, विशेष्यिता-प्रकारितयोरिव विशेष्यिता-प्रकारितासम्बन्धेन विशेष्य-विशेषणयोरपि परस्परमवच्छेद्यावच्छेदकभावाभ्युपगमात्, घटविशेष्यकत्वावच्छेदेन घटत्वप्रकारकमिति प्रतीतिवदिदं ज्ञानं घटांशे प्रकारितासम्बन्धेन घटत्ववदित्यादिप्रतीतेरपि सत्त्वात्तथा च तादृशप्रामाण्यमेव परनये अनुव्यवसायग्राह्यं तस्य प्रकारित्व-विशेष्यित्वयोः प्रागनुपस्थितावपि विशिष्टबुद्धिसम्भवात् प्रकारित्व-विशेष्यित्वयोः संसर्गमर्य्यादयैव तत्र घटकत्वात विशेष्य-विशेषणयोर्व्यवसायत एवोपस्थितेरित्येव तत्त्वम्।

---

(१) अभावप्रतिपत्ताविति ख०।

(२) अभावाभावत्वस्य प्रतियोगित्वरूपत्वं आचार्य्यसम्मतं, 'अभावविरहात्मत्वं वस्तुनः प्रतियोगितेति लक्षणस्य तैरुक्तत्वात्।

परतो ज्ञायते तदभाववत्त्वस्य भ्रमानुल्लिखितत्वेना-नुव्यवसायाविषयत्वात्। नचैवमनुव्यवसायस्य यावद्-व्यवसायविषयविषयकत्वे भ्रान्त-भ्रान्तिज्ञसङ्कर इति वाच्यम्। बाधानवतारदशायां तस्येष्टत्वात्। तदवतारे तस्यैव प्रतिबन्धकत्वात् उपनायकभ्रान्तेरभावाच्च। अतएवान्यभ्रान्तिज्ञस्य न भ्रमः।

नन्वेवं तदभाववति तत्प्रकारकत्वरूपाप्रामाण्यस्याप्यनुव्यवसायग्राह्यत्वापत्तिरित्यत आह, 'तदभाववतीति, 'परतो ज्ञायते', न तु भ्रमानुव्यवसायेन गृह्यते, 'अनुव्यवसायाविषयत्वात्' भ्रमानुव्यवसायविषयत्वासम्भवात्। 'यावद्व्यवसायविषयविषयकत्व इति व्यवसायो यद्यद्विशेष्यक-यद्यत्प्रकारकस्तत्तद्विशेष्यकस्तत्तत्प्रकारकत्व इत्यर्थः। 'भ्रान्त-भ्रान्तिज्ञेति 'भ्रान्तं' भ्रमः, 'भ्रान्तिज्ञं' भ्रमविषयकप्रत्यक्षं, तयोः, 'सङ्करः' सङ्करप्रसङ्गः, प्रवर्त्तकत्वरूपेणाभेदप्रसङ्ग इति यावत्, तथा च भ्रमवत् तदनुव्यवसायस्यापि पुरोवर्त्तिनि रजतत्वप्रकारकतया प्रवर्त्तकत्वप्रसङ्ग इत्यर्थः। यद्वा 'सङ्करः' सङ्करप्रसङ्गः, भ्रमत्वरूपेणाभेदप्रसङ्ग इति यावत्। तथा च भ्रमवत् तदनुव्यवसायस्यापि भ्रमत्वप्रसङ्ग इत्यर्थः। 'तस्य' प्रवर्त्तकत्वस्य भ्रमत्वस्य वा। 'तदवतार इति अलौकिकप्रत्यक्षात्मकं लौकिकप्रत्यक्षात्मकबाधावतारे लौकिकप्रत्यक्षाद्यात्मकभ्रमपूर्वमनुमित्यात्मकबाधावतारे वेत्यर्थः। 'प्रतिबन्धकत्वात्' प्रतिबन्धकतया, 'उपनायकभ्रान्तेरभावात्' भ्रान्तेरुपनायकत्वासम्भवात् भ्रान्तेरनुव्यवसाये पुरोवर्त्तिनि रजतत्वादिवैशिष्ट्यभासकत्वासम्भवादिति यावत्।

अथ तद्वत्त्वं न धर्म्म-धर्म्मिवैशिष्ट्यमात्रं किन्तु तस्य विशेषणताविशेषः, स च व्यवसाये भासते नानुव्यवसाये मनसो बहिरस्वातन्त्र्यादिति चेत् । न । व्यवसायोपनीतत्वेन विशेषण-विशेष्ययोरिव विशेषणता-

---

न च द्वितीयव्याख्यायां[१] इदमसङ्गतं बाधावतारेऽपि निर्द्धर्म्मितावच्छेदकभ्रमोत्पत्तौ बाधकाभावादिति वाच्यं । संशयवदनुभवात्मकभ्रमस्यापि[२] सधर्म्मितावच्छेदकत्वनियमेनानुव्यवसायस्यापि निर्द्धर्म्मितावच्छेदकत्वासम्भवादिति निगर्व्वात्[३] । 'अतएव' पुरोवर्त्तिनि रजतत्वादिवैशिष्ट्यभासकाभावादेव, 'अन्यभ्रान्तिग्रस्य' अनुमानादिनाऽन्यपुरुषीयभ्रान्तिग्रस्य । 'तद्वत्त्वमिति प्रामाण्यघटकीभूतरजतत्वादिमत्त्वमित्यर्थः, 'धर्म्म-धर्म्मिवैशिष्ट्यमात्रमिति रजतत्वादि-पुरोवर्त्तिनोः समवाय एवेत्यर्थः, समवायस्यातिप्रसक्तत्वादितिभावः । 'तस्य' रजतत्वादेः, 'विशेषणताविशेषः' समवायसम्बन्धनिरूपिताधारताख्यव्या-

---

(१) द्वितीयविवक्षायामिति ख० ।

(२) किञ्चिन्निष्ठधर्म्मितावच्छेदकत्वाख्यविषयत्वानिरूपिता या घटत्वप्रकारतानिरूपितविशेष्यता तया सम्बन्धेनानुभवं प्रति स्वविषयीभूतघटत्ववत्त्वसम्बन्धेन घटत्वप्रमा हेतुरतो निर्द्धर्म्मितावच्छेदककभ्रम-संशययोर्निरासः प्रमुक्तत्ताकसंस्कारसादौ व्यभिचारवारणाय कार्य्यतावच्छेदकेऽनुभवत्वनिवेश इति ।

(३) समानविषयत्वेन विरोधित्वात् पुरोवर्त्तिनि रजतत्वाभावभाने निर्द्धर्म्मितावच्छेदकतयापि तत्र रजते न रजतत्वं भासते इति केचित्'

विशेषस्यापि तद्विषयत्वात् विशेषणताया निराकरिष्यमाणत्वाच्च। एतेनास्वप्रकाशे न स्वतः प्रामाण्यग्रहः धर्म्यग्रहे तद्धर्म्माग्रहात्। शब्द-गन्धवत् योग्यत्वात्तद्ग्रहेऽपि

वृत्त्यातिरिक्तविशेषणताविशेषः(१) 'व्यवसाये' अनुमित्यात्मकव्यवसाये, 'मनसो वहिरस्वातन्त्र्यात्' मनसश्चक्षुराद्यसहकारेण वहिर्विषयकप्रत्यक्षाजनकत्वात् चक्षुराद्यजन्यमनोजन्यप्रत्यक्षे वहिर्विषयकत्वाभावादिति यावत्, समवायस्य वह्निस्वाभावेऽपि तन्निरूपिताधारताया वह्निस्वादिति भावः। चक्षुराद्यजन्यमनोजन्यप्रत्यक्षे वाह्यार्थस्य लौकिकविषयतानभ्युपगमेऽपि तदतिरिक्तविषयत्वमभ्युपेयत एवान्यथा धर्म्म-धर्म्मिविषयकत्वस्याप्यनुपपत्तेरित्यभिप्रायेण समाधत्ते,'व्यवसायोपनीतत्वेनेति वैशिष्ट्ये तृतीया अन्वयश्चास्य विशेषण-विशेष्ययोरित्यत्र, व्यवसायविषयीभूतयोर्धर्म्म-धर्म्मिणोरित्यर्थः। वैशिष्ट्यांशे प्रत्यासत्तेरप्रयोजकत्वादाधारत्वस्येदं रजतमितिव्यवसायाविषयत्वाच्च हेतुत्वस्य तृतीयार्थत्वासम्भवात् गुरुमते तस्य हेतुत्वासम्भवाच्च।

ननु चक्षुराद्यजन्यमनोजन्यप्रत्यक्षे मुख्यविशेष्यतातिरिक्तरूपेण पूर्व्वानुपस्थितस्य वहिरर्थस्य विषयित्वं नाभ्युपेयते इत्यत आह, 'विशेषणताया इति धर्म्म-धर्म्म्यतिरिक्तविशेषणताया इत्यर्थः। तथा च पूर्व्वानुपस्थितत्वमेव तत्र नास्तीति भावः। 'एतेनेति वक्ष्यमाणरीत्येत्यर्थः(२)।

---

(१) गुरुमते समवायस्यातीन्द्रियतया तद्घटिताधारत्वस्यापि तत्त्वेन तन्मतसाधारण्यार्थमाह।

(२) चक्षुरादिजन्यघटादिज्ञानं स्वप्रामाण्यं प्रकाशाति न तु स्वं इति प्राचीन गुरुमतं तन्नैव मध्यगुरुमते प्रक्रिया।

ज्ञानं प्रमाणमितिधीन स्यात्। स्वप्रकाशेपि स्वमात्र-साक्षिणः स्वधर्मग्रहेऽसामर्थ्यात्। सामर्थ्ये वा अप्रा-माण्यमपि गृह्णीयात्। परप्रकाशे लिङ्गेन मनसा वा जायमानं ज्ञानं न भ्रमव्यावृत्तं प्रामाण्यं गृह्णीयात्

ननु यथा शब्द-गन्धविषयप्रत्यक्षं स्वाश्रयमविषयीकृत्यापि शब्द-गन्धौ विषयीकरोति तथा व्यवसायोऽपि स्वमविषयीकृत्यापि स्ववृत्तिप्रामाण्यं विषयीकरिष्यति। न च तथापि स्वाश्रयग्राहकग्राह्यत्व-रूपस्य मतत्रयसाधारणस्य स्वतस्त्वस्य नोपपत्तिरिति वाच्यं। तादृश-मतत्रयसाधारणस्य स्वतस्त्वस्याभावेपि तज्ज्ञानविषयकज्ञानाजन्य-ज्ञानविषयत्वरूपग्राह्यत्वस्य मतत्रयसाधारणस्वतस्त्वस्य सम्भवादित्यत आह,'शब्द-गन्धवदिति,'तद्ग्रहेपीति स्वाश्रयमविषयीकृत्यापि तद्वि-षयीकरणेपीत्यर्थः। 'ज्ञानं प्रमाणमिति ज्ञानत्वावच्छिन्नविशेष्यता-निरूपितविशिष्टप्रामाण्यत्वावच्छिन्नप्रकारताशालिज्ञानमित्यर्थः, एतादृ-शप्रकारताया एव भवता प्रामाण्येऽभ्युपगमादत एव विप्रतिप-त्तावपि यथाकथञ्चित् प्रामाण्यविषयतामादायार्थान्तरवारणाय तादृशप्रकारत्वस्य ग्राह्यत्वपदार्थे प्रवेश इति भावः। 'स्वप्रकाशेपीति स्वस्यापि विषयीकरणेपीत्यर्थः, 'स्वमात्रसाक्षिण इति ज्ञानत्वेतरस्ववृ-त्तिधर्माविषयकत्वस्वभाविन इत्यर्थः, 'स्वधर्मग्रह इति ज्ञानत्वेतर-स्ववृत्तिधर्मस्य विषयीकरण इत्यर्थः। एतेन स्वधर्मग्रहासामर्थ्ये ज्ञानत्वेन विना कथं ज्ञानग्रहः जातिव्यक्त्योः प्रत्यक्षतुल्यवित्तिवेद्यता-नियमादिति निरस्तं।

व्यभिचारात्। न च यच यदस्ति तच तद्गृह्यते। अप्रामाण्यस्यापि स्वतोग्रहापत्तेः अनुव्यवसायस्यानुमितेर्वा विषयाजन्यत्वाच्चेति निरस्तं। तद्वति तत्प्रका-

---

'अस्वप्रकाशे' स्वस्य स्वाविषयकत्वे, 'न स्वतः प्रामाण्यग्रहः' न स्वस्य स्वनिष्ठप्रामाण्यविषयकत्वं, 'धर्म्यग्रहे' धर्म्यविषयकत्वे, 'तद्धर्म्माग्रहात्' तद्धर्म्मविषयकत्वासम्भवात्।

ननु तादृशधर्मग्रहेपि सामर्थ्यं कथमन्यथा ज्ञानेच्छान्यतरवानहमित्यादि प्रत्यक्षेण तादृशधर्मस्यान्यतरत्वादेर्ग्रह इत्यत आह, 'सामर्थ्ये वेति।

गुरुमतं दूषयित्वा भट्ट-मिश्रमतं दूषयति, 'परप्रकाश इति 'परप्रकाशे' परप्रकाशमते भट्ट-मिश्रमते इति यावत्। 'जायमानं ज्ञानं' इति जायमानं ज्ञानविषयकं ज्ञानं इत्यर्थः। क्वचित् 'ज्ञायमानं ज्ञानमिति पाठः तत्र ज्ञानं ज्ञायमानमिति योजना, 'ज्ञायमानमिति भावसाधनं 'ज्ञानमिति कर्मपदं, न निष्ठादिष्वित्यनेन निषेधादनभिहितेपि कर्मणि न षष्ठी। 'लिङ्गेनेत्यादौ जन्यत्वं तृतीयार्थः, तथा च लिङ्गजन्यं मनोजन्यं वा ज्ञानविषयकं ज्ञानमिति समुदायार्थः,'न भ्रमव्यावृत्तमिति वस्तुगत्या भ्रमव्यावृत्तं यत्प्रामाण्यं तन्न गृह्णीयादित्यर्थः, भ्रमव्यावृत्तमित्यनेन तत्प्रकारकज्ञानत्वरूपप्रामाण्यव्यवच्छेदः। ननु अनुव्यवसायादिसामग्र्येव प्रामाण्यग्रहसामग्रीति कथं न गृह्णीयादित्यत आह, 'व्यभिचारादिति अनुव्यवसायादिसामग्र्याः पुरोवर्त्तिनि रज-

एकज्ञानत्वं तद्वति तद्वैशिष्ट्यज्ञानत्वं वा प्रामाण्यं व्यवसायस्येति स्वेनानुव्यवसायेनानुमित्या वा तद्ग्रहात् ।

तत्वादिमत्ताग्रहं प्रत्यन्वयव्यभिचारादित्यर्थः । तत्सत्त्वेपि भ्रमानुव्यवसाये तत्र तद्ग्रहान्न हि तादृश्यपि सामग्रीति भावः । ज्ञानमितिशेषः। 'भ्रमव्यावृत्तमिति 'गृह्णीयादितिक्रियाविशेषणं, ग्रहधातोरर्थे विषयित्वे तदर्थस्याभेदेनान्वयः, 'प्राभाण्यं' पुरोवर्त्तिविशेष्यत्वादिकं, तथा च मनसा ज्ञाततया लिङ्गेन वा जायमानं भ्रमविषयकं ज्ञानं भ्रमावृत्ति-पुरोवर्त्तिविशेष्यकत्वादिविषयिताश्रयो न स्यात् तुल्यन्यायतया प्रमानुव्यवसायादाविव भ्रमानुव्यवसायादावपि तद्विषये पुरोवर्त्तिनि रजतत्वादिमत्त्वभानादित्यर्थः । 'व्यभिचारादिति अन्यथानुव्यवसायादिसामग्र्याः पुरोवर्त्तिनि रजतत्वादिमत्त्वग्रहं प्रत्यन्वयव्यभिचारप्रसङ्गादित्यर्थः । न च पूर्व्वोक्तसङ्करापादनेनास्य ग्रन्थस्य पुनरुक्तत्वमिति वाच्यम् । प्रकारभेदात् पूर्व्वोक्तसङ्करापादनस्य प्रवर्त्तकत्वेन सङ्करापादनरूपत्वाच्चेति प्राञ्चः ।

ननु न केवलमनुव्यवसायादिसामग्री पुरोवर्त्तिनि रजतत्वादिमत्त्वग्रहजनिका किन्तु सामान्यतो ज्ञानविषयकतत्प्रकारकप्रत्यक्षे ज्ञाततालिङ्गकज्ञानसाध्यकतत्प्रकारकानुमितौ वा प्रकारतानियामकसम्बन्धेन विशेष्यनिष्ठतया तद्वत्त्वस्यापि हेतुत्वेन पुरोवर्त्तिनि रजतत्वादिमत्तापि तज्जनिका, सा च भ्रमविषये पुरोवर्त्तिनि नास्तीति केवलतादृशसामग्र्या अन्वयव्यभिचारो न दोषायेत्यभिप्रायेण शङ्कते, 'न चेति, 'गृह्यते' अनुव्यवसायादिसामग्र्या गृह्यते, 'अप्रामाण्यस्या-

तद्विषयत्वस्य तत्प्रकारत्वस्य च ज्ञानग्राहकसामग्रीग्राह्यत्वात्। यदि च प्रामाण्यं परतो ज्ञायेत तदा प्रामाण्यज्ञानेपि तदनुमापकलिङ्ग-पक्ष-व्याप्त्यादिज्ञानेषु च

पीति तथापीत्यादिः, 'स्वतोग्रहापत्तेः' नियमतोभ्रमानुव्यवसायग्राह्यत्वापत्तेः।

ननु प्रमात्वघटकतदभाववत्त्वस्य पूर्व्वानुपस्थित्या कारणान्तराभावादेव नियमतो न तद्भानमित्यरुचेराह, 'अनुव्यवसायस्येति, अतीतादिगोचरप्रमाया इत्यादिः, 'विषयाजन्यत्वाच्चेति पुरोवर्त्तिनि प्रमीयमानधर्म्मविरहदशायामपि ज्ञायमानत्वाच्चेत्यर्थः। तत्रापि पुरोवर्त्तिन्युपनीततद्वत्ताभानस्य त्वयाभ्युपगमादिति भावः।

अप्रामाण्यस्यापि स्वतोग्राह्यत्वमुद्धरति, 'तद्वतीति, 'तद्विषयत्वस्येति तद्विशेष्यकत्वस्येत्यर्थः। 'ज्ञानग्राहकेति स्वाश्रयज्ञानग्राहकसामग्रीमात्रस्यैव ग्राह्यत्वादिति भावः। अप्रामाण्यञ्च न तादृशसामग्रीमात्रस्य ग्राह्यं तदभावग्राहकसामग्रीविलम्बेन तद्ग्रहविलम्बात्। न च तथापि न भ्रमव्यावृत्तं प्रामाण्यं गृह्णीयादिति दोषस्तदवस्थ इति वाच्यम्। बाधानवतारे इष्टत्वात् तदवतारे तस्यैव प्रतिबन्धकत्वादिति प्रागेवाभिधानादिति भावः।

गुरुः स्वमतमुपपाद्य न्यायमते बाधकमाह, 'यदि चेति। 'परतो ज्ञायेत' परत एव ज्ञायेत न स्वतो ज्ञायेतेति यावत्। 'प्रामाण्यज्ञानेपि' प्रामाण्यानुमितावपि, 'ज्ञानेषु च' ज्ञानेष्वपि च, 'स्वविषयनिश्चयार्थमिति स्वविशेष्यकप्रामाण्यानुमित्यर्थमित्यर्थः। 'प्रामाण्यस्य

स्वविषयनिश्चयार्थं प्रामाण्यस्य परतो ज्ञेयत्वे फल-मुखी कारणमुखी चानवस्था स्यादिति प्रामाण्यं न ज्ञायेतैवेति परिशेषादपि स्वतः प्रामाण्यग्रहः इति पूर्वः

परतो ज्ञेयत्वे' इति प्रामाण्यविषयकानुमिति-परामर्शधाराया आवश्यकत्व इत्यर्थः। 'फलमुखीति प्रामाण्यानुमिति-परामर्शयोरनवस्थापत्तेरित्यर्थः। 'प्रामाण्यं न ज्ञायेतैवेति किञ्चिज्ज्ञाननिष्ठं प्रामाण्यमज्ञातमेव स्यादित्यर्थः। न चेष्टापत्तिः, तथा सति तस्य प्रामाण्ये एव मानाभावप्रसङ्गादिति भावः। 'परिशेषादिति स्वाश्रयभिन्नाग्राह्यत्वे सति ग्राह्यत्वादित्यर्थः। किञ्चिज्ज्ञाननिष्ठप्रामाण्यस्य स्वाश्रयग्राह्यत्वे सिद्ध इति शेषः। 'स्वतः प्रामाण्यग्रह इति सर्व्वेषामेव प्रामाण्यानां स्वाश्रयाद्ग्रह इत्यर्थः, तुल्यन्यायादिति भावः।

ननु भवतु गुरुमते स्वाश्रयजनकसामग्र्या मिश्रमते चानुव्यवसायसामग्र्या प्रामाण्यग्रहः, भट्टमते तु ज्ञाततालिङ्गेन कथं प्रामाण्यानुमानमिति चेदित्थं, आदावयं घट इति प्रत्यक्षमथ ज्ञाततोत्पत्तिः घटविशेष्यक-घटत्वप्रकारकज्ञानजन्यत्वव्याप्या घटविशेष्यक-घटत्वप्रकारकज्ञाततेति व्याप्तिस्मरणसेत्येकः कालः, फलबलेन सर्व्वत्र तथैव कल्पमात्। तत इन्द्रियसम्बद्धविशेषणतात्मकज्ञाततेन्द्रियसन्निकर्ष-व्याप्तिस्मरणाभ्यां तादृशज्ञानजन्यत्वव्याप्यघटविशेष्यकघटत्वप्रकारकज्ञाततावतीयमिति तादात्म्यसम्बन्धेन व्याप्यवत्तापरामर्शः, तदिन्द्रिययोग्यव्यक्तिज्ञाततायाः एव तदिन्द्रिययोग्यत्वात् अन्यथाख्यातिवादिना भट्टेनोपनीतभानस्याभ्युपगमात्। अन्यत्र विशिष्टविशेष्यकवैशिष्ट्यबुद्धौ

पक्षः। सिद्धान्तस्तु प्रामाण्यस्य स्वतो ग्रहेऽनभ्यासदशोत्पन्नज्ञाने तत्संशयो न स्यात्। ज्ञानग्रहे प्रामाण्यनिश्चयात्। अनिश्चये वा न स्वतः प्रामाण्यग्रहः। ज्ञाना-

---

विशेष्यतावच्छेदकप्रकारकनिश्चयस्य हेतुत्वेपीदन्त्वविशिष्टविशेष्यकवैशिष्ट्यबुद्धाविदन्त्वप्रकारकज्ञानस्याहेतुत्वात्। तदनन्तरमियं ज्ञातता घटविशेष्यक-घटत्वप्रकारकज्ञानजन्या घटविशेष्यक-घटत्वप्रकारकज्ञाततान्तरवदित्यनुमित्या पक्षधर्म्मताबलात् प्रकृतज्ञाने घटत्ववतिघटत्वप्रकारकत्वसिद्धिः। न च ज्ञानस्यातीन्द्रियत्वेन घटत्ववतिघटत्वप्रकारकत्वस्यातीन्द्रियत्वेन प्राथमिकानुमानस्थले साध्याप्रसिद्ध्या कथं व्याप्तिग्रह इति वाच्यम्। या यद्वृत्तियंत्प्रकारिका ज्ञातता सा तद्विशेष्यक-तत्प्रकारकज्ञानजन्या यथा पटवृत्तिपटत्वप्रकारकज्ञानजन्यज्ञाततेति यत्तद्भ्यां सामान्यतो व्याप्तिग्रहसम्भवात्। न च व्याप्तिग्रहेपि घटवृत्तिघटत्वप्रकारकज्ञाततात्वेन प्रकृतहेतोरज्ञानात् कथमनुमितिरितिवाच्यम्। ज्ञातताप्रत्यक्षेण ज्ञाततायामिन्द्रियसम्बद्धविशेषणताप्रत्यासत्त्या घटत्वप्रकारकत्वस्योपनयादिसन्निकर्षवशादाधेयतासम्बन्धेन घटस्य च ग्रहात् सामान्यतो व्याप्तेरनभ्युपगमे जन्मान्तरसंस्कारात् साध्यादिप्रसिद्ध्या विशेषत एव व्याप्तिग्रहसम्भवाच्च। न चैवं 'तद्विषयकज्ञानाजन्येत्यादिद्वितीयविप्रतिपत्त्युपदर्शितविधिकोटिरूपस्य स्वतोग्राह्यत्वस्य न प्रामाण्ये निर्व्वाह इति वाच्यम्। तस्य गुरुमत-मिश्रमतोभयसाधारणस्वतस्त्वरूपतया भट्टमते तदनिर्व्वाहेपि क्षतिविरहात्। प्रथमविप्रतिपत्तिर्मतत्रयसाधारणी, द्वितीयविप्रतिपत्तिर्गुरुमि-

ओभयमतसाधारणी, तृतीया मिश्रमतमात्रसाधारणी, चतुर्थी च गुरुमतमात्रसाधारणी, एवमेव पूर्व्वं व्याख्यातत्वात्।

अथाप्येवं रीत्या ज्ञाततालिङ्गेन प्रामाण्यानुमाने रजतत्वाभाववतीति विशेषणं प्रक्षिप्याप्रमोत्पत्त्यनन्तरमप्रामाण्यस्यापि ज्ञाततालिङ्गेन ग्रहापत्तिः, इयं ज्ञातता रजतत्वाभाववद्विशेष्यकरजतत्वप्रकारकज्ञानजन्या रजतत्वाभाववद्वृत्तिरजतत्वप्रकारकज्ञाततात्वात् इत्यनुमानसौकर्य्यात्। न च साध्य-हेतुभेदेन परामर्शानुमित्योः कार्य्य-कारणभावभेदादप्रमाजन्यत्वव्याप्यतया ज्ञाततापरामर्शो नानुमितिहेतुरिति वाच्यम्। साध्याभाववदवृत्तित्वरूपव्याप्तिज्ञानस्यैव तन्मते हेतुतया[१] हेतुभेदेन कार्य्य-कारणभावभेदाभावादिति चेत्। न। शुक्ताविदं रजतमित्यादिप्रत्यक्षभ्रमजन्यज्ञाततप्रत्यक्षेण ज्ञाततायां रजतत्वाभाववद्वृत्तित्वग्रहासम्भवेन हेतुज्ञानाभावात्। व्यवसाये रजतत्वाभावभानप्रतिबन्धकदोषस्य फलबलात् तदानीमपि सत्त्वकल्पनेन तेनैव प्रतिबन्धात्। यत्र च हेतुज्ञानं तत्र तथा रीत्याऽप्रामाण्यस्यापि ग्रहस्येष्टत्वात्। तावतापि भट्टमतसाधारणविप्रतिपत्त्युपवर्णितविधिकोटिरूपस्य प्रामाण्यादिघटितपारिभाषिकस्वतोग्राह्यत्वस्य तत्रासत्त्वादेव प्रामाण्यं स्वतोग्राह्यं नाप्रामाण्यमिति प्रवादाविरोधात्। न च तथापि घटमहं जानामीत्यात्मविशेष्यकज्ञानज्ञानस्य सर्व्वसिद्धस्योक्तानुमानान्न निर्व्वाह इति वाच्यम्। तथा सत्यहं घटविशेष्यकघटत्वप्रकारकज्ञानवान् घटवृत्तिघटत्वप्रकारकज्ञाततावत्त्वादित्यात्मविशेष्यकज्ञानप्रकारकानुमानस्यैवानुसरणीयत्वात्। ज्ञाततावत्त्वञ्च आत्मनस्तदी-

(१) साध्याभाववदवृत्तित्वरूपव्याप्तेः हेत्वघटितत्वादिति भावः।

यतानियामकस्वरूपसम्बन्धविशेषेण । घटो मया ज्ञात इत्यनुभवात् । न चातीन्द्रियामन्निकृष्टस्थले कथमनुमित्यादिजनितज्ञातताया: प्रत्यक्षं तन्निष्ठतद्वृत्तित्व-तत्प्रकारकत्वज्ञानं वा तद्धेतोरिन्द्रियसन्निकर्षादेरभावादिति वाच्यम्। तत्रेच्छादिकं पक्षीकृत्य तद्विशेष्यक-तत्प्रकारकेच्छादिहेतुनैव उक्तरूपेण प्रामाण्यग्रहसम्भवात् । न हि ज्ञाततापक्षकज्ञातताlिङ्गकानुमित्यैव प्रामाण्यग्रहो नान्यथेति तेषामभ्युपगमः। तत्राप्यात्मघटितमनःसंयुक्तविशेषणतोपनयसन्निकर्षाभ्यां मनसैव तेन रूपेण ज्ञातताया: प्रत्यक्षसम्भवाच्च । बहिरर्थस्यापि ज्ञातताया: सत्तादिवन्मानसत्वाविरोधात्। वस्तुतस्तु गुरुमते ज्ञानस्येव भट्टमते ज्ञातताया अपि स्वप्रकाशत्वोपगमात् उत्पन्नाया एव तस्यास्तन्निष्ठघटवृत्तित्वादेः प्रामाण्यव्याप्यत्वादेश्च भानं ज्ञानत्व-ज्ञातताlत्वयोरेकत्र सत्त्वेपि क्षतिविरहात्। ज्ञाततेतरज्ञानस्यैव तेन स्वप्रकाशत्वानभ्युपगमात् । ज्ञातताlत्मकज्ञानस्य प्रत्यक्षविजातीयं किन्तु केवलज्ञानत्वाश्रयः।

यद्वा विनैव सन्निकर्षादिकं गुरूणां ज्ञानस्य स्वविषयत्ववत् भट्टमतेपि स्वस्मिन्नेव स्वजन्यज्ञातताlयास्तद्वृत्तिघटवृत्तित्वादेश्च भानं किन्तु तदंशे उपदर्शितव्यवसायस्य ज्ञानत्वमात्रं न प्रत्यक्षत्वादि। अस्तु वा प्रामाण्यव्याप्यघटवृत्तित्वादिप्रकारेण ज्ञातताप्रत्यक्षं प्रति ज्ञाततैव कारणं न तु नियतमिन्द्रियसन्निकर्षादि, नच ज्ञातताप्रत्यक्षं, यत्र चाक्षुषादिसामग्री तिष्ठति तत्र चाक्षुषादिरूपमन्यत्र तु चाक्षुषत्वादिकं तत्र नास्ति भगवत्साक्षात्कार इव केवलं प्रत्यक्षत्वं। अस्तु वा अव्यवहितोत्तरत्वान्तर्भावेन परामर्शस्य कार्य्यतया ज्ञातताlिङ्गकप्रामाण्यानुमितौ स्वरूपसती तद्वृत्तितत्प्रकारकज्ञाततैवानुमितिहेतुः न तु

व्याप्यत्वादिना तज्ज्ञानं, इत्यस्य प्राथमिकानुमानस्थले साध्यप्रसिद्धि-विरहेपि न क्षतिः। निरूपितत्वादिसम्बन्धेन घटत्वादिविशिष्टवैशिष्ठ्य-प्रत्यक्षं प्रत्येव तेन सम्बन्धेन घटत्वादिप्रकारकज्ञानस्य हेतुत्वात्। न च तथाप्यतीतादिव्यवसायस्थले[१] उपादानकारणाभावेन[२] ज्ञात-तानुत्पादात् कथं प्रामाण्यग्रह इति वाच्यं। तत्रापि तादृशेच्छादिनैव प्रामाण्यग्रहसम्भवात्।

वस्तुतस्तु ज्ञाततायां उपादानकारणं न विषयः, किन्तु मैव, तस्या उपादानतातिरिक्तविशेषणताविशेषः सम्बन्धः, स चातीताद्यधिकरणे अभावीयविशेषणताविशेषवदतीतादिविषयेपि वर्त्तते इत्यतीतादि-विषयकधीस्थले[३] ज्ञाततायां नासम्भव इति तत्त्वं।

मिश्रानुयायिनस्तु इयं ज्ञातता ज्ञानीया ज्ञाततात्वा इत्यनुमानादेव जन्यतासम्बन्धेन घटविशेष्यक-घटत्वप्रकारकत्वादिरूपेण प्रकृतज्ञानसि-द्धिः। ज्ञानव्याप्यज्ञाततावत्तापरामर्शस्य फलबलेन तथैव हेतु-हेतुमद्भाव-कल्पनात्। निरूपितत्वादिसम्बन्धेन घटत्वादिविशिष्टवैशिष्ठ्यप्रत्यक्षं प्रत्येव तेन सम्बन्धेन घटत्वादिप्रकारकज्ञानस्य हेतुतया विशिष्टप्रामाण्योपस्थितिं विनापि विशिष्टवैशिष्ट्यधीसम्भवात्। ईश्वरानुमाने ज्ञाननित्यत्वव्याप्-कतानवच्छेदकस्यापि तस्य विधेयतावच्छेदकतया भानात्। लाघवाद्य-प्रतिसन्धाने व्यापकतावच्छेदकप्रकारेणानुमितिनियमस्य सार्व्वत्रिकत्वे मानाभावात्। हेतु-साध्यभेदेन व्यापकताभेदात्। अतीन्द्रियासन्निकृष्ट-

(१) अतीतादिविषयस्थले इति ग०।

(२) उपादानहेत्वभावेनेति ग०।

(३) इत्यतीतादिविषयकज्ञानस्थले इति ख०, ग० च।

स्थलेपि ज्ञाततात्वरूपेण ज्ञातताज्ञानं सुलभं आत्मघटितमनःसंयुक्तविशेषणताविशेषप्रत्यासत्त्या मनसैव तादृशग्रहसम्भवात् आत्मन्यपि ज्ञाततायास्तदीयतानियामकस्वरूपसम्बन्धविशेषसत्त्वात् । अतीतादिविषयस्थले ज्ञाततानुत्पादेपि तद्भ्रमादेवानुमितिः, दोषबलात् तदभावग्रहेपि तद्ग्रहोत्पत्तौ बाधकाभावात् फलबलेन तथैव कल्पनात् । अप्रामाण्यस्य विना लाघवज्ञानादिसहकारेण तादृशानुमानान्न गृह्यते ज्ञानत्वावच्छिन्नव्याप्यत्वरूपेण ज्ञाततापरामर्शस्याप्रामाण्यप्रकारकानुमितावहेतुत्वात् । तेन प्रामाण्यं स्वतोग्राह्यं नाप्रामाण्यमिति विवादोपपत्तिः । ज्ञानत्वावच्छिन्नव्यापकता ज्ञानमात्रजन्यानुमितिविधेयतावच्छेदकत्वस्य भट्टमते स्वतोग्राह्यत्वपदार्थत्वात् । यदि चात्मविशेष्यकज्ञानमपेक्षितं तदाऽहं ज्ञानवान् ज्ञाततावत्त्वादित्यात्मपक्षकानुमानमेवानुसरणीयं । न चैवं स्वव्यक्तिवर्त्तमानज्ञानवदतीतादिज्ञानानामप्युक्तान्यतरप्रकारेण स्वतोग्रहापत्तिरिति वाच्यं । इष्टत्वादिति प्राञ्चः ।

इति प्रामाण्यवादे पूर्व्वपक्षरहस्यम् ।

अथ प्रामाण्यवादे सिद्धान्तरहस्यं।

ग्रहे धर्म्मिज्ञानाभावात् न संशयः। ननु कोटिस्मरणादिना संशयपूर्व्वक्षणे व्यवसायविनाशान्न तद्विशेष्यको मानसः संशय इति चेत्। न। ज्ञानेपनीते व्यव-

---

'अनभ्यासदेशोत्पन्नेति प्रामाण्यव्याप्यवत्तानिश्चयाकालीनेत्यर्थः। 'तत्संशय इति इदं प्रमा न वेतिप्रामाण्यसंशयो न स्यादित्यर्थः। 'अनिश्चये वेति संशयस्थले ज्ञानग्रहेपि प्रामाण्यस्यानिश्चये वेत्यर्थः। 'न स्वतः प्रामाण्यग्रह इति अन्यत्रापि न स्वतः प्रामाण्यग्रह इत्यर्थः, अविशेषादिति भावः। 'धर्म्मिज्ञानाभावादिति धर्म्मितावच्छेदकेदन्त्वादिप्रकारकधर्म्मिज्ञानाभावादित्यर्थः। ज्ञाननिष्ठेदन्त्वविशिष्टबुद्धौ विशेषणज्ञानस्याहेतुत्ववत् ज्ञाननिष्ठेदन्त्वविशिष्टविशेष्यकबुद्धिसामान्यं प्रति विशेष्यतावच्छेदकेदन्त्वप्रकारकज्ञानस्याहेतुत्वेपि ज्ञाननिष्ठेदन्त्वधर्मितावच्छेदकसंशयं प्रति तदिदन्त्वप्रकारकधर्म्मिज्ञानस्य वक्ष्यमाणयुक्त्या हेतुत्वावश्यकत्वादिति भावः। ज्ञाननिष्ठेदन्त्वञ्च स्वरूपतस्तत्प्रकारिताव्यक्तिः तत्तत्प्रकारिताव्यक्तिसम्बन्धेन प्रकारितात्वयक्तिर्वा ज्ञानत्वस्याप्यनुपस्थितस्य प्रकारत्वाभ्युपगमात् तज्ज्ञानव्यक्तिसम्बन्धेन ज्ञानत्वमेव वा। एतच्चोपलक्षणं धर्म्मितावच्छेदकविशिष्टधर्म्मिज्ञानस्याहेतुत्वमतेऽनुव्यवसायस्याहेतुत्वेपि अनुव्यवसायानन्तरमिदं ज्ञानं प्रमा न वेति संशयोऽनुभवसिद्धः स न स्यात् अनुव्यवसायेन प्रामाण्यनिश्चयादित्यपि

बोध्यं[१]। न चेदं प्रमा न वेति संशये इदन्त्वावच्छिन्ने प्रामाण्यनिश्चयस्यैव प्रतिबन्धकतया अनुव्यवसायस्य प्रामाण्यविषयकत्वेऽपि इदन्त्वावच्छिन्ने तदनवगाहित्वात् संशयो नानुपपन्नः[२] इति वाच्यम्। अनुव्यवसायस्य प्रामाण्यग्राहकत्वे इदन्त्वावच्छिन्ने तदवगाहित्वे बाधकाभावात्। न चेदन्त्वप्रकारकज्ञानाभावात नेदन्त्वावच्छिन्ने प्रमानुव्यवसायेन[३] प्रामाण्यग्रहसम्भव इति वाच्यम्। अन्यत्र विशिष्टविशेष्यकवैशिष्ट्यबुद्धौ विशेष्यतावच्छेदकप्रकारकनिश्चयस्य हेतुत्वेऽपि इदन्त्वविशिष्टविशेष्यक-वैशिष्ट्यबुद्धाविदन्त्वप्रकारकज्ञानस्याहेतुत्वात्। अन्यथा रजतत्वप्रका-रकत्व-पुरोवर्त्तिविशेष्यकत्वयोरपीदन्त्वावच्छेदेन तत्र भानानुपपत्तेः। न च तयोरपि न तदवच्छेदेन तत्र भानमिति वाच्यम्। तर्हि तदनन्तरं इदं रजतत्वप्रकारकं न वा इदं विशेष्यकं न वेत्यादि-संशयस्यापि दुर्व्वारतापत्तेः। किञ्च प्रथमानुव्यवसायानन्तरमिदं प्रमा न वेति संशयोपपादनेऽपि यत्र घटविशेष्यकं ज्ञानं स घट इति समूहालम्बनस्मरणात्मको व्यवसायस्तत्रानुव्यवसायानन्तरं घटविशेष्यक-ज्ञानं प्रमा न वेति संशयस्यानुभवसिद्धस्य नोपपत्तिः। पूर्वं घटविशे-ष्यकज्ञानत्वप्रकारकज्ञानसत्त्वेन घटविषयकज्ञानत्वावच्छिन्ने प्रथमानु-व्यवसायेनापि प्रामाण्यग्रहे बाधकाभावात्।

ननु व्यवसाये प्रामाण्यसंशयाभावः, कदा आपाद्यते न तावद्व्यव-सायोत्पत्तेस्तृतीयक्षणे अनुव्यवसायोत्पत्तेः द्वितीयक्षणे तदापादनं

---

(१) इत्यपि द्रष्टव्यमिति ख०।
(२) संशयोपपत्तिरिति ख०।
(३) प्रथमानुव्यवसायेनेति ख०।

न्यायनयेपि तदानीं संशयानुत्पत्तेरिदन्त्वादेरनुपस्थितस्यापि प्रकारतया अनुव्यवसायात्मकधर्म्मितावच्छेदकेदन्त्वविशिष्टधर्म्मिधीसत्त्वेपि प्रामाण्याप्रामाण्यकोट्युपस्थितिविरहात् । न च यत्र प्रामाण्याप्रामाण्यकोट्युपस्थित्यात्मा स घट इत्यादिस्मरणात्मको व्यवसायः ततोऽनुव्यवसायः तत्रैव व्यवसायोत्पत्तितृतीयक्षणे संशयाभावापादनसम्भवस्तत्र न्यायनये संशयोत्पादे प्रत्यूहविरहादिति वाच्यम्। तत्र प्रथमं कोटिद्वयोपस्थितिसत्त्वेनानुव्यवसायस्य प्रामाण्यांशे संशयात्मकतया तृतीयक्षणे प्रामाण्यसंशयान्तरोत्पत्तौ तन्मतेपि बाधकाभावात्। यदि तज्ज्ञाननिष्ठेदन्त्वविशिष्टविशेष्यकवैशिष्ट्यबुद्धिसामान्ये तदिदन्त्वादिप्रकारकज्ञानस्य हेतुत्वेपि तादृशेदन्त्वधर्म्मितावच्छेदककभ्रमे तादृशेदन्त्वप्रकारकधर्म्मिज्ञानस्य हेतुतया तदभावादनुव्यवसायस्य नाप्रामाण्यसंशयात्मकत्वसम्भव इत्युच्यते तदा तु न्यायनयेपि प्रामाण्योपस्थितिसत्त्वेनानुव्यवसायस्य प्रामाण्यनिश्चयात्मकत्वे बाधकाभावात् तृतीयक्षणे संशयोत्पत्तेरसम्भवादिति चेत्। न। व्यवसायोत्पत्तेश्चतुर्थक्षणे अनुव्यवसायोत्पत्तेश्च तृतीयक्षणे संशयाभावापादनात् अनुव्यवसायानन्तरोत्पन्नप्रामाण्याप्रामाण्यकोट्युपस्थित्या चतुर्थक्षणे न्यायनये प्रामाण्यसंशयसम्भवात्। न च क्षणिकापलापस्यादोषतयाऽनुव्यवसायानन्तरं पञ्चमक्षण एव तत्र संशय इति वाच्यम्। अनुव्यवसायनाशे धर्म्मिज्ञानाभावेन संशयासम्भवात्। धर्म्मिज्ञानस्य पृथगहेतुत्वमतेपि सन्निकर्षविधया तदावश्यकत्वात्। न चानुव्यवसायजन्यसंस्कारात् प्रामाण्यांशमोषेण चतुर्थक्षणे धर्म्मिस्मरणमिति वाच्यम्। अनन्तस्मृति-संस्कार-तत्कार्य्य-कारणभावादिकल्पने गौरवात् यत्रापेक्षाबुद्ध्यात्मकोऽनुव्यवसा-

यस्तत्र क्षणद्वयापलापप्रसङ्गाच्च । किञ्च यत्र व्यवसायोत्पत्त्यनन्तरमुत्कट-कोटिकप्रामाण्याप्रामाण्यविषयकोऽनुव्यवसायस्तत्र व्यवसायोत्पत्तितृतीय-क्षणे चतुर्थक्षणे वा इदं प्रमा न वेति संशयाभावापादनसम्भवः तत्र न्यायनये संशयोत्पादे प्रत्यूहविरहात् तत्रापि पञ्चमक्षण एव संशया-भ्युपगमे क्षणद्वयापलापापत्तेः । न च तत्रापि व्यवसायोत्पत्तिक्षणे प्रामाण्याप्रामाण्यज्ञानं विना उत्कटकोटिकप्रामाण्याप्रामाण्यविषयकत्वा-सम्भवेन तत्सत्त्वावश्यकत्वादुक्तक्रमेण संशयाभावापादनासम्भव इति वाच्यम् । विशिष्टप्रामाण्याप्रामाण्यज्ञानं विनापि खण्डशः प्रामाण्या-प्रामाण्यघटकपदार्थोपस्थित्या विशेष्ये विशेषणमितिन्यायेनानुव्यवसा-यस्योत्कटकोटिकप्रामाण्याप्रामाण्यविषयकत्वसम्भवात् । न चैवं तत्र न्याय-नयेऽपि विशेष्ये विशेषणमिति न्यायेन व्यवसाये प्रामाण्यनिश्चयसम्भवान्न संशयसम्भव इति वाच्यम् । न्यायनये प्रामाण्यानुपस्थितिविशिष्ट-व्यवसायस्य प्रामाण्यप्रत्यक्षप्रतिबन्धकतया विशेष्ये विशेषणमितिन्यायेन प्रामाण्यनिश्चयासम्भवात् धर्मिज्ञानस्य भ्रमहेतुतया तदभावादेवोभय-मते विशेष्ये विशेषणमिति न्यायेन प्रामाण्यविशिष्टबुद्ध्यसम्भवाच्च ।

ननु तथापि गुरुमते न चतुर्थक्षणे प्रामाण्यसंशयाभावापत्ति-सम्भवः तृतीयक्षणे प्रामाण्यनिश्चयात्मकव्यवसायनाशेन चतुर्थक्षणे तन्मतेऽपि संशयोत्पत्तौ बाधकाभावात् । न च तन्मते संशयस्य धर्मि-ज्ञान-कोटिद्वयस्मरणात्मकतया स्वप्रकाशात्मकव्यवसायनाशे धर्मि-ज्ञानस्यैवाभावान्न संशयसम्भव इति वाच्यं । स्वप्रकाशात्मकधर्मिज्ञान-जनितसंस्कारेण चतुर्थक्षणे प्रामाण्यांशमोषेण संशयस्थानाभिषिक्तस्य धर्मिस्मरणस्य सम्भवात् तावतापि धर्मिज्ञानाभावस्यैव संशयाभावापा-

दकतया प्रामाण्यनिश्चयस्य तदभापादकत्वेन प्रामाण्यस्य स्वतोग्रहे बाधकाप्राप्तेश्चेति चेत्। न। तन्मते चतुर्थक्षणे संशयाभावापत्त्यसम्भवेपि व्यवसायोत्पत्तितृतीयक्षणे तद्द्वितीयक्षणे वा संशयाभावापादनसम्भवात्। न च न्यायनयेपि तदानीं न संशयसम्भव इति वाच्यम्। यत्र स घटः प्रामाण्याप्रामाण्ये चेति समूहालम्बनस्मरणात्मको व्यवसायः ततो घटविदयकं ज्ञानमिति स्मरणरूपधर्म्मिज्ञानं तत्र तृतीयक्षणे घटविषयकं ज्ञानं प्रमा न वेति संशयस्य सम्भवात् यत्र च घटविषयकं ज्ञानं स घटः प्रामाण्याप्रामाण्ये चेति समूहालम्बनरूपो धर्म्मिज्ञानात्मको व्यवसायस्तत्र घटविषयकं ज्ञानं प्रमा न वेति संशयस्य द्वितीयक्षणे सम्भवात्। न चैतद्गुरुमतेपि सम्भवति, स्मरणात्मकव्यवसायेन स्वप्रामाण्यनिश्चयात्। न च व्यवसायेन प्रामाण्यनिश्चयेऽपि घटविषयकज्ञानत्वधर्मितावच्छेदकप्रामाण्यनिश्चयाभावाद्गुरुमतेऽपि तादृशप्रामाण्यसंशयो नानुपपन्न इति वाच्यम्। गुरुमते विशेष्यतावच्छेदकप्रकारकज्ञानस्य विशिष्टाधिकरणकवैशिष्ट्यबुद्धावहेतुतया व्यवसायस्य घटविषयकज्ञानत्वावच्छेदेन प्रामाण्यविषयकत्वेऽपि बाधकाभावात् यत्र तादृशस्मरणात्मकव्यवसायपूर्व्वमपि घटविषयकं ज्ञानमिति स्मरणं तत्र विशेष्यतावच्छेदकप्रकारकज्ञानस्यापि सम्भवाच्च। न च तथापीदं प्रमा न वेति इदन्त्वधर्मितावच्छेदकप्रामाण्यसंशयस्य। न न्यायनये तृतीये द्वितीये वा क्षणे सम्भवः धर्मितावच्छेदकेदन्त्वप्रकारकज्ञानाभावात् इदन्त्वरूपेणैतद्व्यवसायव्यक्तेः पूर्व्वमनुभवाभावेन स्मरणासम्भवादिति वाच्यम्। ज्ञाननिष्ठेदन्त्वं हि तत्तत्प्रकारिताव्यक्तिसम्बन्धेन प्रकारितात्ववत्त्वं तथाच यत्किञ्चित्प्रकारिताव्यक्तिसम्बन्धेन यत्किञ्चिज्-

सार्थे प्रामाण्यसंशयात्। ननु धर्मिज्ञानं न संशयहेतुः, कोटिज्ञान-विशेषादर्शन-धर्मीन्द्रियसन्निकर्षात् प्रामा-

---

ज्ञानव्यक्तौ प्रकारितात्वप्रकारकज्ञानात्मकसामान्यप्रत्यासत्त्या सर्व्वस्यैव तत्तत्प्रकारितासम्बन्धेन प्रकारितात्ववतो व्यवसायस्य न्यायनये पूर्व्व-मनुभवसम्भवात् ज्ञाननिष्ठेदन्त्वधर्मितावच्छेदककवैशिष्ट्यबुद्धिसामान्ये विशेष्यतावच्छेदकप्रकारकज्ञानस्य हेतुतया पूर्व्वमिदन्त्वप्रकारकज्ञाना-भावेऽपि सामान्यलक्षणानङ्गीकर्तृगुरुनये इदन्त्वावच्छेदेन व्यवसाये प्रामाण्यनिश्चये बाधकाभावादिति दिक्।

न्यायनयेऽपि संशयासम्भवमाशङ्कते, 'नन्विति, 'कोटिस्मरणादिनेति कोटिस्मरणादिरनुव्यवसायस्तेनेत्यर्थः।

केचित्तु मानससामग्र्यपेक्षया स्मृतिसामग्र्या बलवत्त्वात् यत्र कोटि-स्मरणानन्तरमनुव्यवसायस्तदभिप्रायेणेदं, तत्रादिपदाद् यत्रोद्बोधकमहि-म्नाऽनुव्यवसायानन्तरं कोटिस्मरणं तत्रानुव्यवसायपरिग्रह इत्याहुः। तदसत् यत्रानुव्यवसायानन्तरं कोट्युपस्थितिः तत्रैव नैयायिकैः संशयाभावापादनात्।

'स तद्विशेष्यक इति न भवन्मतेऽपि व्यवसायविशेष्यको मानसः संशय इत्यर्थः, विशेष्येन्द्रियसन्निकर्षविरहादिदं ज्ञानं प्रमा न वेति संशयस्य धर्म्यंशे लौकिकप्रत्यक्षरूपत्वेन विषयविधया व्यवसायरूपस्य धर्मिणस्तत्र हेतुत्वाच्चेति भावः। 'ज्ञानोपनीत इति अनुव्यवसायोप-नीत इत्यर्थः, उपनीतभाने च न विषयो हेतुरिति भावः। 'धर्मी-न्द्रियसन्निकर्षादिति ज्ञानेन्द्रियसन्निकर्षादित्यर्थः, 'प्रामाण्यसंशयरूप

ण्यसंशयरूप एव ज्ञानग्रह उत्पद्यत इति चेत् । न ज्ञानातीन्द्रियत्वे तज्ज्ञानं विना तद्धर्मिकमानससंशया-

---

एवेति प्रामाण्यसंशयात्मक एवेत्यर्थः, 'ज्ञानग्रहः' प्राथमिकज्ञानग्रहः, एतदाशङ्का तु भट्ट-मिश्रयोरेव न तु गुरोस्तन्मते ज्ञानेन्द्रियसन्निकर्षस्य ज्ञानहेतुत्वाभावात् संशयस्य कोटिस्मरणरूपतया संशये कोटिस्मरणस्याहेतुत्वाच्च । यद्यपि यत्रानुव्यवसायानन्तरमनुव्यवसायसमकालं वा कोट्युपस्थितिस्तत्रैव संशयाभावापत्तिः कृता तत्र च ज्ञानग्रहस्य न प्रामाण्यसंशयरूपत्वसम्भवः पूर्वं कोट्युपस्थितेः। तथाप्यभ्युपेत्य स्फुटतरं दोषमाह, 'ज्ञानातीन्द्रियत्व इति ज्ञानातीन्द्रियत्वमत इत्यर्थः, 'तज्ज्ञानं विनेति ज्ञानज्ञानं विनेत्यर्थः, ज्ञानस्यातीन्द्रियतया तदंशे लौकिकसंशयासम्भवेन तदंशे उपनीतभानात्मकत्वनियमादुपनयसन्निकर्षार्थं ज्ञानज्ञानस्यापेक्षितत्वादिति भावः ।

ननु साक्षात्कारसंशय एव सन्निकर्षोऽपेक्षितः न तु लैङ्गिके, तथाचाहं ज्ञानवान् ज्ञाततावत्त्वादित्यनुमानादेव ज्ञानग्रहो भवन् प्रामाण्यसंशयात्मक एव जायते । न च साध्यप्रसिद्ध्यर्थं तत्रापि ज्ञानग्रहोऽपेक्षित इति वाच्यं । तन्नये पक्षधर्मताबललभ्यसाध्यप्रसिद्धेरनङ्गतया ज्ञानत्वरूपेण प्रकृतप्रामाण्यानाश्रयीभूतज्ञानान्तरज्ञानादेव प्रकृतज्ञानानुमितिसम्भवादित्यत आह,'लिङ्गस्येति निश्चितं लिङ्गस्येत्यर्थः, तेन लिङ्गसन्देहस्य क्वचिल्लौकिकसंशयजनकत्वेपि न क्षतिः । 'तस्येति निश्चितस्य लिङ्गस्य निश्चयमात्रजनकत्वादित्यर्थः । न च लिङ्गसन्देह एव प्रामाण्यसंशयात्मकज्ञानग्रहजनक इति वाच्यं । लिङ्गनिश्चयस्यानु-

नुपपत्तिः, लिङ्गञ्च न संशयजनकं तस्य निश्चायकत्वात्। ज्ञानस्य मानसत्वे च प्रामाण्यज्ञानवत्तत्सामग्य्रपि संशयप्रतिबन्धिका तन्निश्चायकत्वात्। अन्यथा विशेष-

---

मितिहेतुतया लिङ्गसन्देहादनुमितिरूपसंशयासम्भवादिति[१] भावः। इदमुपलक्षणं अनुमितेर्व्यापकतावच्छेदकमात्रप्रकारकत्वनियमेन संश-यात्मकप्रामाण्यभानासम्भवाच्चेत्यपि बोध्यं।

मिश्रमते दोषमाह, 'ज्ञानस्य मानसत्वे चेति ज्ञानस्य लौकिक-मानसप्रत्यक्षत्वमते चेत्यर्थः। 'प्रामाण्यज्ञानवदिति प्रामाण्यनिश्चयव-दित्यर्थः, 'तत्सामग्य्रपीति ज्ञानलौकिकमानससामग्य्रपीत्यर्थः, 'प्रति-बन्धिका' प्रामाण्याभाववैशिष्टबुद्धित्वावच्छिन्नं प्रति प्रतिबन्धिका, 'तन्निश्चायकत्वादिति तन्मते ज्ञानलौकिकप्रत्यक्षसामग्य्रा एव प्रामाण्य-निश्चयोपधायकत्वादित्यर्थः, तथा च तन्मत्त्वे कथं तत्संशय इति भावः। न चोभयकोटिविशिष्टबुद्धिसामग्रीसत्त्वाद्य प्रामाण्यनिश्चयो-पधायकत्वमेव नास्तीति वाच्यं। 'अथेत्यादिना आशङ्कानुपदं स्वयमेव समाधास्यमानत्वात्। यद्यपि प्रामाण्यनिश्चयोपधाने प्रामाण्यनिश्च-यस्यैव कार्य्यसहभावेन प्रतिबन्धकत्वसम्भवात् सामग्य्राः प्रतिबन्धकत्व-पर्य्यन्तानुधावनमयुक्तं, तथापि ज्ञानरूपप्रतिबन्धकाभावः कार्य्यसह-भावेन[२] न हेतुः किन्तु पूर्व्ववर्त्त्यैव[३] हेतुरन्यथा सिषाधयिषा

---

(१) उपनयाभावात् नोपनीतभानसम्भव इति भावः।

(२) कार्य्यसहभूत इति ग०।

(३) नियतपूर्व्ववर्त्त्यैवेति ग०।

विना व्याप्त्यनुमितिर्न स्यात् स्वोत्पत्तिकाले स्वात्मकसिद्धिसत्त्वादित्यभिप्रायेण तदनुधावनं। नन्वप्रामाण्यनिश्चयोपधायकज्ञानग्रहसामग्र्याः प्रामाण्यसंशयप्रतिबन्धकत्वे मानाभावः, यस्य निश्चयोऽनुमितित्वानवच्छिन्नप्रतिबध्यताप्रतियोगिकयत्प्रतिबन्धकताश्रयस्तन्निश्चयोपधायकसामग्र्यपि तत्प्रतिबन्धिकेति व्याप्तेरभावादित्यत आह, 'अन्यथेति यन्निश्चयो यस्य नादृशप्रतिबन्धकताश्रयः[1] तन्निश्चयसामग्र्यास्तत्राप्रतिबन्धकत्वे इत्यर्थः, 'विशेषदर्शनकालेऽपीति तदभावव्याप्यवत्तानिश्चयोत्पत्तिकालेऽपीत्यर्थः, 'संशयापत्तेरिति, तदभावत्वप्रकारकज्ञानं विना तदभावनिश्चयासम्भवेन तदभावज्ञानस्यैव तत्तदभावोभयज्ञानरूपत्वादिति भावः। न च तदभावादिनिश्चयस्य कार्य्यकालवृत्तित्वेन प्रतिबन्धकत्वादेव न तदा संशय इति वाच्यं। ज्ञानरूपप्रतिबन्धकाभावः पूर्व्ववर्त्त्येव हेतुरिति ग्रन्थकर्त्तुराशयादन्यथा प्रकृते सामग्रीप्रतिबन्धकत्वानुधावनस्यासम्भवापत्तेः।

केचित्तु ननु तन्निश्चयोपधायकसामग्र्यास्तदभावज्ञानप्रतिबन्धकत्वे मानाभाव इत्यत आह, 'अन्यथेति तन्निश्चयोपधायकसामग्र्यास्तदभावज्ञानाप्रतिबन्धकत्वे इत्यर्थः, 'विशेषदर्शनकालेऽपीति अन्धकारे घटादिसंशयोत्तरमालोकादिसमवधाने सति घटादिचाक्षुषनिश्चयोत्पत्तिकाले, शब्दो नित्यो न वेत्यादिसंशये नित्यत्वादिशाब्दनिश्चयोत्पत्तिकाले चेत्यर्थः, 'संशयापत्तेरिति घटाद्यभावप्रत्यक्ष-नित्यत्वाभावादिशाब्दबोधापत्तेरित्यर्थः, इत्याहुः।

ननु निश्चयसामग्र्याः केन रूपेण प्रतिबन्धकत्वं न तावत्तदभाव-

---

(१) यो यस्य यादृशप्रतिबन्धकताश्रय इति ख०।

निश्चयजनकसामग्रीत्वेन तद्विशिष्टबुद्धिं प्रति प्रतिबन्धकत्वं सामग्री हि न तदीययावत्कारणं तदीयकारणतावच्छेदकानां यावतां प्रत्येकाश्रयसमवधानं वा अनुमिति-शाब्दबोधादिसकलनिश्चयकारणस्य काप्यसम्भवात्। नापि तदभावनिश्चयजनकत्वेन प्रतिबन्धकत्वं सामग्रीत्वस्याविवक्षितत्वादिति वाच्यं, कालादेरपि प्रतिबन्धकत्वापातात् स्थाण्वादीन्द्रियसन्निकर्षस्यापि पुरुषत्वादिसंशयप्रतिबन्धकत्वापाताच्च तस्यापि पुरुषत्वाभावादिनिश्चयस्वरूपयोग्यत्वात् कदाचित् पुरुषत्वाभावादिनिश्चयफलोपधायकत्वाच्च। नापि तदभावनिश्चयमात्रवृत्तिधर्मावच्छिन्नकार्य्यतानिरूपितकारणताश्रयत्वेन प्रतिबन्धकत्वं, व्याप्यदर्शनाद्यनुत्तरतदभावप्रत्यक्षनिश्चयोत्पत्तिकाले तत्संशयापत्तेस्तादवस्थ्यात् तदभावीयप्रत्यक्षतानुद्बुद्धसंस्कारयोग्यतासन्देहादिसत्त्वेपि तद्विशिष्टबुद्ध्यभावापत्तेश्च कार्य्यतावच्छेदकावच्छिन्ननिरूपितायाः कारणतायास्तदननुगमेनाननुगमाच्चेति चेत्। न। तदभावनिश्चयोपधायकसामग्रीत्वेनैव प्रतिबन्धकत्वात् तदुपधायकसामग्रीत्वञ्च स्वसमानाधिकरणत्वे सति स्वाव्यवहितपूर्व्वक्षणवृत्तित्वसम्बन्धेन तद्विशिष्टत्वं सामग्रीत्वं न निवेशनीयं, स्वं तदभावादिनिश्चयः। न चैवं तदभावव्याप्यदर्शन-तदभावावच्छेदकधर्म्मदर्शनादेः पृथक् प्रतिबन्धकत्वव्याघातः तदुत्तरं अन्ततो मानसस्यापि तदभावनिश्चयस्यावश्यकत्वात्तन्निश्चयसामग्र्यामेव तदन्तर्भावादिति वाच्यं। सत्प्रतिपक्षस्थले तत्तदभावोभयावच्छेदकादिधर्म्मदर्शनस्थले च तत्संशयापत्तेः तत्तदभावोभयानुमित्यापत्तेश्च तत्र परस्परविरोधेन कस्यापि निश्चयानुत्पत्त्या यथोक्तनिश्चयसामग्रीविरहादिति निगर्व्वः।

दर्शनकालेऽपि संशयापत्तेः। अथ धर्म्मिणि विशेषादर्शनदशायां एककोटिस्मरणे तदारोपः कोटिद्वयस्मरणे

अत्रेदमवधेयं तदभावादिनिश्चयसामग्री न तद्विशिष्टबुद्धिप्रतिबन्धिका तदभावादिनिश्चयस्य कार्य्यसहवर्त्तित्वेन प्रतिबन्धकत्वादेव तदुत्पत्तिकाले तद्विशिष्टबुद्ध्यभावसम्भवेन[१] अतिरिक्तप्रतिबध्य-प्रतिबन्धकभावकल्पने गौरवान्मानाभावाच्च। न च ज्ञानरूपप्रतिबन्धकस्यापि कार्य्यसहवर्त्तित्वेन प्रतिबन्धकत्वे विना सिषाधयिषां क्वाप्यनुमितिः न स्यादिति वाच्यं। प्रतिबध्य-प्रतिबन्धकभावस्य सकलसाधारणस्यानुगतस्याभावात् सिद्धेः फलबलेन पूर्व्ववर्त्तितामात्रेण प्रतिबन्धकत्वेपीह लाघवात् कार्य्यसहवर्त्तित्वेनैव प्रतिबन्धकत्वकल्पनात्। अत एव निश्चयसामग्र्यपि न तदभावविशिष्टबुद्धिप्रतिबन्धिका तन्निश्चयस्य कार्य्यसहवर्त्तित्वेन प्रतिबन्धकत्वादेवान्धकारे घटादिसंशयोत्तरमालोकसमवधानेपि तदुत्तरं घटाभावादिसंशयाभावोपपत्तेः तत्राप्यव्यवहितपूर्व्ववर्त्तितासम्बन्धेन घटादिनिश्चयस्यैव तत्र संशयाभावप्रयोजकत्वात्। एवं नित्यत्वादिशाब्दनिश्चयस्यैव कार्य्यसहभावेन प्रतिबन्धकत्वादेवानित्यत्वादिशाब्दसंशयस्याप्यभावः। न चान्धकारे घटसंशयाद्युत्तरमालोकसंयोगाद्युत्पत्तिकालेपि घटादिसंशयापत्तिवारणाय निश्चयसामग्र्याः कार्य्यसहभावेन प्रतिबन्धकत्वमावश्यकमिति वाच्यं। तदानीं संशयोत्पत्त्याविष्टापत्तेः। अथ कार्य्य-पहवर्त्तित्वेन तदभावादिनिश्चयस्य प्रतिबन्धकत्वमित्यस्य कोऽर्थः। न च

---

(१) वद्विशिष्टबुद्ध्यनुत्पादसम्भवेनेति ग०।

संशय इति निश्चयसामग्रीतः संशयसामग्री बलवतीति कोटिद्वयस्मरणे संशय एव स्यात् न तु निश्चय इति चेत्।

कार्य्योत्पत्तिकालीनतदभावादिनिश्चयत्वावच्छिन्नाभावो हेतुरित्यर्थः, तादृशाभावस्य पूर्व्वकाले सत्त्वादुक्तातिप्रसङ्गस्य दुर्व्वारत्वात्। नापि कार्य्योत्पत्तिकालीनो यस्तदभावादिनिश्चयाभावस्तत्त्वं कारणतावच्छेदकमित्यर्थः, कार्य्यपदं हि कार्य्यसामान्यपरं फलीभूततत्तद्विशिष्टबुद्धिव्यक्तिपरं वा नाद्यः अव्यावर्त्तकत्वात्, नान्त्यः अनन्तकार्य्यकारणभावकल्पनाप्रसङ्गात् कारणतावच्छेदकविशिष्टस्य पूर्व्वसत्ताया अपेक्षितत्वमते कार्य्यप्राक्काले तादृशकालीनत्वविशिष्टस्यासम्भवाच्च। अत एव तत्तत्कार्य्यकालसम्बन्धः कारणतावच्छेदकसंसर्गः, सम्बन्धाननुगमश्च न दोषायेत्यपि निरस्तं। तेन सम्बन्धेनाभावस्य कार्य्यप्राक्काले सत्त्वाद्व्यभिचारापत्तेः कारणतायाः पूर्व्ववर्त्तिताघटितत्वात्। न च प्रतिबन्धकाभावस्थले स्वरूपसम्बन्धेन कार्य्यकालवृत्तिताघटितैव कारणतेति वाच्यं। विनश्यदवस्थप्रतिबन्धकसत्त्वेऽपि तदुत्तरं कार्य्योत्पत्त्यापत्तेः। न च प्रतिबन्धकाभावस्थले स्वरूपसम्बन्धेन कार्य्यकालवृत्तित्वघटिता तेन सम्बन्धेन तत्पूर्व्वकालवृत्तित्वघटिता च कारणतेति वाच्यं। कारणताद्वयकल्पनापत्तेः। न चैवं कल्पे मण्यादेरपि कार्य्यसहभावेन प्रतिबन्धकत्वविलोपापत्तिरसमवायिकारणादेः कार्य्यसहभावेन हेतुत्वविलोपापत्तिश्चेति वाच्यं। इष्टत्वात् मण्युपधायकसामग्र्याः प्रतिबन्धकत्वादेव मण्युत्पत्तिकाले दाहाभावसम्भवात्। असमवायिकारणनाशकसामग्र्याः प्रतिबन्धकत्वादेव विनश्यदवस्थासमवायिकारणात्

कार्य्यानुत्पादसम्भवादिति चेत्। न। स्वोत्पत्ति-तदव्यवहितपूर्व्वत्वा-न्यतरसम्बन्धेन यदा कार्य्यं तदा प्रतिबन्धकाभावादिरिति प्रत्यासत्त्या कारणत्वस्यैव कार्य्यसहभावेन प्रतिबन्धकत्वादिपदार्थत्वात्।

केचित्तु सामग्र्या उत्तरक्षणे कार्य्यमिति व्याप्तौ प्रतिबन्धकाभावा-दिरूपतत्तत्कारणाधिकरणक्षणत्वविशिष्टसामग्र्यव्यवहितोत्तरक्षणत्वमेव व्यापककोटौ निविष्टमित्यत्र कार्य्यकालवृत्तित्वेन कारणत्वमित्यस्यार्थः, तावतैव प्रतिबन्धकोत्पत्तिक्षणे असमवायिकारणादिनाशक्षणे वा कार्य्योत्पत्त्यापादनासम्भवात्। न तु कार्य्योत्पत्तिकालेऽपि स्वातन्त्र्येण कारणतावच्छेदकसम्बन्धघटकतया कारणताप्रविष्ट इत्याहुः। तदसत् कारणताघटकव्यापकतावैलक्षण्येनैव कार्य्यातिप्रसङ्गः[१] वार्य्यत इति सकलप्रामाणिकसिद्धत्वादन्यथा कालिकसामानाधिकरण्यापेक्षया यत्र दैशिकसामानाधिकरण्यं गुरु तत्र दैशिकसामानाधिकरण्यस्यापि कार-णत्वानन्तर्भावप्रसङ्गात् सामग्र्या उत्तरक्षणे कार्य्यमिति व्याप्तौ दैशिक-सामानाधिकरण्यान्तर्भावादेवातिप्रसङ्गवारणसम्भवात् पूर्व्ववर्त्तित्वादेरपि कारणत्वानन्तर्भावप्रसङ्गाच्चेत्यास्तां विस्तरः।

नन्वत्र प्रामाण्यनिश्चयोपधायकसामाग्र्येव नास्ति प्रामाण्य-तद-भावोभयकोट्युपस्थितिसत्त्वेनोभयकोटिविशिष्टबुद्धेरेवोत्पादात्, न हि तन्मते ज्ञानेन्द्रियसन्निधेः प्रामाण्यनिश्चयत्वं कार्य्यतावच्छेदकं येनो-भयविशिष्टबुद्धिसामग्रीसत्त्वे प्रामाण्यनिश्चयः स्यादित्याशङ्कते, 'अथेति, 'एककोटिस्मरणे' एककोटिमात्रस्मरणे,'तदारोपः' तन्निश्चयः, 'इतीति इत्यनुभवादित्यर्थः, 'निश्चयसामग्रीत इत्यादि, उभयकोटिविशिष्ट-

(१) कार्य्योत्पत्तिप्रसङ्ग इति ख०।

।'न। विरुद्धोभयारोपसामग्रीद्वयसमाजादुभयारोप एक एव भवति स एव संशयः, न त्वेकारोपसामग्र्या अप-

---

बुद्धिसामग्रीरूपसंशयसामग्र्यां सत्यां नैककोटिनिश्चयोत्पत्तिरित्यर्थः। 'इतीति, प्रकृत इतिशेषः। 'कोटिद्वयस्मरणे' प्रामाण्याप्रामाण्योभयकोटिस्मरणे। दोषाभावात् कोटिद्वयविशिष्टबुद्धिसामग्रीसत्त्वेपि प्रामाण्यनिश्चय इति समाधत्ते, 'विरुद्धोभयारोपेति दोषसमवहितविरुद्धभावाभावोभयविशिष्टबुद्धिसामग्रीसमाजादेवेत्यर्थः, 'एक एवे-त्यग्रिमैवकारस्यात्रैवान्वयात्। आरोप इत्युपादानं दोषलाभाय। 'उभयारोपः' विरुद्धभावाभावोभयविषयकारोपः, यत्र तु न दोषस्तत्र कोटिद्वयविशिष्टबुद्धिसामग्रीसत्त्वेपि वास्तवकोटिनिश्चयः, अन्यथा विना विशेषदर्शनादिकं घटाभाववदिदमित्यादिप्रात्यचिकनिश्चयः क्वापि न स्यात्, घट-तदभावोभयोपस्थितिसत्त्वेन संशयस्यैवोत्पत्त्या कार्य्यसहभावेन घटाभावनिश्चयस्य, पूर्व्ववर्त्तितया तत्सामग्र्या वा प्रतिबन्धकत्वस्य वक्तुमशक्यत्वात्। न च दोषस्य भ्रमजनकत्वे मानाभावाद्दोषाभावे कोटिद्वयविशिष्टबुद्धिसामग्रीसत्त्वेपि वास्तवकोटेर्निश्चय इत्यत्र किं बीजमिति वाच्यं। तथैवानुभवात्। न च तथानुभवेपि कार्य्याभावस्य विना कारणाभावमनभ्युपगमादवास्तवकोटिविशिष्टबुद्ध्यभावः कथं स्यादिति वाच्यं। वास्तवकोटिनिश्चयस्य प्रामाणिकत्वे कार्य्यकालवृत्तितया तस्य, पूर्व्ववर्त्तितया तदुपधायकसामग्र्या वा प्रतिबन्धकत्वात्। अत एव दोषस्य संशयाजनकत्वेपि संशयप्रयोजकत्वप्रवादः। अनुभवबलेन दोषाभावविशिष्ट-

रारोपसामग्रीप्रतिबन्धः अविरोधात्। न चोभयारोपसामग्र्या एकनिश्चयसामग्रीप्रतिबन्ध इति वाच्यम्।

कोटिद्वयोपस्थित्यादेर्वास्तवकोटिनिश्चयव्याप्यतया दोषस्य संशयव्यापकत्वादिति भावः।

ननु कोटिद्वयविशिष्टबुद्धिसामग्रीसत्त्वेपि वास्तवकोटिनिश्चयस्योत्पादे संशय एव न स्यात् सर्व्वत्र वास्तवकोटिनिश्चयोत्पत्त्या तत्सामग्र्याः प्रतिबन्धकत्वादित्यत आह, 'स एवेति दोषकालीनविरुद्धभावाभावोभयारोप एवेत्यर्थः। 'न त्विति न हीत्यर्थः, तदानीमितिशेषः, 'एकारोपसामग्र्याः' वास्तवकोटिनिश्चयसामग्र्याः, 'अपरारोपेति अपरकोटिविशिष्टबुद्धिसामग्र्याः कार्य्योपधायकत्वे प्रतिबन्ध इत्यर्थः, 'अविरोधादिति विरोधितावच्छेदकस्य वास्तवकोटिनिश्चयोपधायकत्वस्य वस्तुगत्या तदानीमभावादित्यर्थः। न च वास्तवकोटिनिश्चय एवं कथं तत्र न जायते दोषस्य निश्चयप्रतिबन्धकत्वे मानाभावादिति वाच्यं। निश्चयत्वस्यार्थसमाजग्रस्तत्वेन कार्य्यतानवच्छेदकतया(१) तदवच्छिन्नापादकाभावादिति भावः।

ननु यत्र न दोषस्तत्र कोटिद्वयोपस्थित्यादिसत्त्वेपि वास्तवकोटिनिश्चय इत्यसिद्धं विरुद्धभावाभावोभयविशिष्टबुद्धिसामग्र्याः सत्प्रतिपक्षवत्परस्परनिश्चयप्रतिबन्धकत्वादित्याशङ्कते, 'न चेति, 'उभयारोपसामग्र्याः' विरुद्धभावोभावोभयविषयकारोपसामग्र्याः, 'एकनिश्चय-

---

(१) अर्थसमाजग्रस्तत्वं कार्य्यतावच्छेदकत्वे बाधकमिति भावः।

सामग्रीप्रतिबन्धः' परस्परनिश्चयोत्पत्तिप्रतिबन्धः । सामग्र्याः कारणकलापरूपतया दोषसत्त्वे उभयविषयकारोपसामाग्र्येव नास्तीति समाधत्ते, 'प्रत्यकेति प्रत्येककोटिविशिष्टबुद्धिसामग्रीद्वयभिन्नाया उभयविषयकारोपसामग्र्या अभावादित्यर्थः, प्रत्येककोटिविशिष्टबुद्धिसामग्रीद्वयञ्च तत्र नास्ति तत्र वास्तवकोटिनिश्चयस्यानुभविकत्वेन तत्सामग्र्या अवास्तवकोटिविशिष्टबुद्धिप्रतिबन्धकतया प्रतिबन्धकाभावरूपकारणस्यैवाभावादिति भावः । 'न चेति, प्रत्येककोटिविशिष्टबुद्धिसामग्रीद्वयभिन्नायाः कोटिद्वयविषयकारोपसामग्र्या विरह इति शेषः, 'कार्य्यद्वयमिति संशयस्थले कार्य्यद्वयं स्यादित्यर्थः, 'उपपत्तेरिति सामग्रीद्वयादपि कार्य्यैक्योपपत्तेरित्यर्थः(१)। 'प्रामाण्यनिश्चयसामग्रीसत्त्वादिति प्रामाण्यनिश्चयोपधायकसामग्रीसत्त्वादित्यर्थः । न च दोषाभावादेव संशयाभावस्य सुवचतया प्रामाण्यनिश्चयसामग्रीप्रतिबन्धकत्वानुधावनमफलमिति वाच्यं । दोषस्य संशयव्यापकत्वेपि संशयाजनकतया तदभावेन संशयाभावासम्भवः, विना कारणाभावं कार्य्याभावस्यानभ्युपगमादित्यभिप्रायात् ।

ननु दोषस्य फलोन्नेयतया यत्र प्रामाण्यसंशयोऽनुभवसिद्धस्तत्र व्यवसायोत्पत्तिप्राक्काले द्वि-त्रिक्षणस्थायिदोषोपि फलबलात्कल्प्यते तथापि प्रामाण्यसंशयार्थं तदुत्तरं दोषकल्पनादित्यरुचेर्दूषणान्तरमाह, 'धर्म्मिज्ञानस्येति ।

मिश्रास्तु अत्र निश्चयसामग्र्यास्तयानभ्युपगमात्तस्याः प्रतिबन्धकत्वस्य वक्तुमशक्यत्वेपि संशयं प्रति धर्म्मिज्ञानस्यापि हेतुतया तदभावे कथं

---

(१) कार्य्यस्योपपत्तेरित्यर्थ इति ख० ।

प्रत्येकारोपसामग्र्यतिरिक्तायास्तस्या अभावात्। न च सामग्रीद्वयात् कार्यद्वयं समूहालम्बनवदुपपत्तेः। तस्मात् प्रामाण्यनिश्चयसामग्रीसत्त्वात् न तत्संशयः स्यात्।

संशय इत्यभिप्रायेण समाधत्ते, 'विरुद्धोभयारोपेति, ज्ञानपदं विहायारोपपदोपादानं धर्म्मिज्ञानसाहित्यलाभाय, तथा च धर्म्मिज्ञानसहितविरुद्धोभयविशिष्टबुद्धिसामग्रीसमाजादेवोभयविषयकारोप एको भवति स एव संशय इति योजना। प्रकृते च धर्म्मिज्ञानाभावात् कथं प्रामाण्यसंशयात्मको ज्ञानग्रह इति भावः। ननु विरुद्धोभयविषयकैकारोप एव संशय इत्ययुक्तं सत्प्रतिपक्ष इव विरुद्धोभयविशिष्टबुद्धिसामग्र्याः परस्परं कार्य्यजनने प्रतिबन्धकत्वादित्यत आह, 'न त्विति न हीत्यर्थः, 'एकारोपसामग्र्याः' एककोटिविशिष्टबुद्धिसामग्र्याः, 'अपरारोपेति अपरकोटिविशिष्टबुद्धिसामग्रीजन्यकार्य्यप्रतिबन्ध इत्यर्थः, 'अविरोधादिति विरोधित्वे मानाभावादित्यर्थः, संशयस्यानुभवसिद्धत्वादिति भावः। ननु प्रथमं प्रामाण्यमविषयीकृत्यैव ज्ञानधर्म्मिग्रहः ततः प्रामाण्यसंशयः। न च तव मये प्रामाण्यस्य ज्ञानग्राहकसामग्रीग्राह्यत्वात् ज्ञानग्रहे कुतो न प्रामाण्यग्रहः इति वाच्यं। प्रामाण्य-तदभावोभयविषयकारोपसामग्र्याः प्रामाण्यनिश्चयप्रतिबन्धकत्वात्। न चैवं ज्ञानग्राहकयावत्सामग्रीग्राह्यत्वं त्वदभ्युपगतं बाधितमिति वाच्यं। अप्रामाण्यग्रहासमवहितयावत्सामग्रीग्राह्यत्वस्यैवाभ्युपगमादित्यभिप्रायेनाशङ्कते, 'न चेति, 'एकनिश्चयसामग्रीति एकनिश्चयोत्पत्तीत्यर्थः, सामग्र्याः कारणकलापरूपत्वादुभयविषयका-

रोपसामग्र्येव तत्र नास्तीत्याशयेन समाधत्ते, 'प्रत्येकेति प्रत्येककोटिविशिष्टबुद्धिसामग्रीदयभिन्नाया उभयविषयकारोपसामग्र्या अभावादित्यर्थः, प्रत्येककोटिविशिष्टबुद्धिसामग्रीदयस्थात्र नास्ति धर्म्मिज्ञानस्यारोपहेतुतया तदभावेन प्रामाण्याभावविशिष्टबुद्धिसामग्रीविरहादिति भावः । 'न चेत्यादिग्रन्थस्तु पूर्ववत् । उपसंहरति, 'तस्मादिति, 'प्रामाण्यनिश्चयसामग्रीसत्त्वात्' प्रामाण्यनिश्चयमात्रसामग्रीसत्त्वात्, प्रामाण्यसंशयसामग्र्यसत्त्वादिति यावत् । ननु लाघवाद्धर्म्मीन्द्रियसन्निकर्षादिरेव भ्रमहेतुः न तु धर्म्मिज्ञानमपीति पूर्व्वमुक्तत्वादिदमसङ्गतमित्यत आह, 'धर्म्मिज्ञानस्येतीति प्राञ्चः ।

'संशयहेतुरिति, 'संशयेति प्रकृताभिप्रायं आरोपमात्र एव तद्धेतुत्वमिति सिद्धान्तात् । कार्य्य-कारणभावस्तु तद्धर्म्मितावच्छेदकक-तद्धर्म्मिकभ्रमत्वेन तद्धर्म्मिणि तद्धर्म्मितावच्छेदकप्रकारकनिश्चयत्वेन(१) अतो धर्म्मितावच्छेदक-धर्म्मिणोर्निर्व्विकल्पकाद्रूपान्तरेण धर्म्मिज्ञानाद्वा न संशयः । दण्डो रक्तो न वेति संशयानन्तरं रक्तदण्डो द्रव्यं न वेत्यादिसंशयानुदयान्निश्चयत्वप्रवेशः । न च संसर्ग-प्रकारभेदेन भ्रमत्वस्य विभिन्नत्वात् कथमनुगतं कार्य्यतावच्छेदकमिति वाच्यं । तत्तत्संसर्गक-तत्तत्प्रकारकज्ञानत्वस्याननुगतस्यैव कार्य्यतावच्छेदकत्वात् कार्य्यतावच्छेदकाननुगमस्यादोषत्वात् । तदभाववद्विशेष्यकत्वं तु भ्रमत्वघटकं न निविशते, तत्त्वस्यानुगतस्याभावात् । यत्र धर्म्मिणि वस्तुगत्या बाधितो यो विषयस्तस्यैव विशिष्य तद्धर्म्मितावच्छेदक-

(१) तथाच तद्धर्म्मितावच्छेदकक-तद्धर्म्मिकभ्रमत्वावच्छिन्नं प्रति तद्धर्म्मिणि तद्धर्म्मितावच्छेदकप्रकारकनिश्चयत्वेन कारणत्वं इति फलितार्थः ।

धर्म्मिज्ञानं च संशयहेतुः, अन्यथा संशये धर्म्मिनियमः कोट्युत्कटत्वञ्च न स्यात्। अथ पीतः शङ्ख आदर्शे मुख-

---

विशिष्टतद्धर्म्मिज्ञानकार्य्यतावच्छेदकघटकत्वेनातिप्रसङ्गविरहात्। यद्वा विशिष्य तत्तत्प्रकारोपि नान्तर्भाવनीयः किन्तु तत्तत्संसर्गमात्रं, तथा च तद्धर्म्मितावच्छेदकक-तद्धर्म्मिक-संयोगसंसर्गक-तद्धर्म्मसंयुक्तधर्म्मप्रकारकज्ञानत्व-तद्धर्म्मितावच्छेदकक-तद्धर्म्मिक-समवायसंसर्गक-तद्धर्म्मसमवेतधर्म्मप्रकारकज्ञानत्वादिकमेव कार्य्यतावच्छेदकं, सामान्यादौ समवायादिसंसर्गेण सत्तादिभ्रमस्थले तु सामान्यादिविशेष्यक-समवायादिसंसर्गकज्ञानत्वमेव कार्य्यतावच्छेदकं तेन तदसमवेतत्वाप्रसिद्धावपि न क्षतिः। न चैवं वृक्षः संयोगी न वेत्यादौ यत्र कोटिद्वयांशे नारोपः किन्तु विरोधांश एवारोपस्तत्र संशये वृक्षादिरूपधर्म्मिधियो हेतुत्वं न स्यात् तत्र विरोधसंसर्गेण संयोगाभावांश एव संयोगस्य प्रकारतया तेन संसर्गेण वृक्षादावप्रकारत्वादिति वाच्यं। तत्राभावरूपधर्म्मिज्ञानस्यैव हेतुत्वेन वृक्षादिरूपधर्म्मिज्ञानस्याहेतुत्वे इष्टापत्तेः। वस्तुतस्तु[१] तद्धर्म्मावच्छिन्नतद्धर्म्मिविशिष्टज्ञानत्वमेव कार्य्यतावच्छेदकं वैशिष्ट्यञ्च स्वव्यधिकरणधर्म्मानिरूपित-तद्धर्म्मावच्छिन्नस्वनि-

---

(१) तद्धर्म्मितावच्छेदकावच्छिन्नविशेष्यताविशिष्टप्रकारताशालिज्ञानत्वरूपकार्य्यतावच्छेदके अनुगमस्य तात्पर्य्यं अतः यथाश्रुतानुगमे जातिर्द्रव्यमित्याकारकसमवायावच्छिन्नद्रव्यत्वनिष्ठप्रकारताक-जातिविशेष्यकभ्रमे स्वावच्छेदकसम्बन्धेन विशेष्यताधिकरणजातौ समवायेन वृत्तेरप्रसिद्धावपि न क्षतिः। प्रकारतायां विशेष्यतावैशिष्ट्यं स्वनिरूपितत्व-स्वाश्रयनिरूपितवृत्तितावत्त्वसम्बन्धावच्छिन्नस्वनिष्ठावच्छेदकताकभेदवत्त्वोभयसम्बन्धेन वृत्तितावत्त्वञ्च स्वाश्रयनिष्ठत्व-स्वावच्छेदकसम्बन्धावच्छिन्नत्वोभयसम्बन्धेन इति हृदयं।

मित्यादिभ्रमो विशेषदर्शनेपि यथा दोषान्तरात् तथा निश्चितेपि प्रामाण्ये दोषान्तरात् तत्संशय इति चेत्।

इविशेष्यताप्रतियोगित्वसम्बन्धेन(१) प्रथमं स्वपदं विशेष्यतापरं, द्वितीयस्वपदं धर्म्मिपरं, स्वव्यधिकरणत्वञ्च स्वावच्छेदकसम्बन्धेन(२) स्वाधिकरणावृत्तित्वं, स्वपदद्वयमेव विशेष्यतापरं, सम्बन्धाननुगमस्यादोषतया स्वत्वस्याननुगतत्वेपि न क्षतिः। वृक्षः संयोगी न वेत्यादावभावज्ञानमेव हेतुर्न तु वृक्षादिज्ञानमित्युक्तमेव। न चारोपमात्रं प्रत्येव धर्म्मिज्ञानस्य हेतुत्वे यत्र प्रमेयत्वं प्रति घटत्वादेर्व्यापकत्वग्रहे घटत्वाभावादिहेतुना अप्रसिद्ध एवाभावः प्रमेयत्वप्रकारेण विशेष्यतयानुमितौ भाषते तत्रारोपे धर्म्मिज्ञानस्य व्यभिचार इति वाच्यं। विशिष्टोद्देश्यकवैशिष्ट्यबुद्धौ विशेष्यतावच्छेदकप्रकारकविशेष्यज्ञानस्य हेतुतया तदभावेन व्यभिचाराभावात्। तत्राभावत्वस्य धर्म्मितानवच्छेदकत्वात्।

केचित्तु व्याप्तिघटकतयावगतस्यैवाभावस्य प्रमेयत्वीयत्वेन तत्र भानमित्याहुः।

यद्यप्येतावतानुव्यवसायपूर्व्वं धर्म्मितावच्छेदकविशिष्टधर्म्मिज्ञानाभावात्र तस्य प्रामाण्यसंशयरूपत्वसम्भवः अपि तु प्रामाण्यनिश्चयरूपत्वं अतो न तदुत्तरं प्रामाण्यसंशय इति फलितं तथापि तत्रमेव अनुव्यवसायात् पूर्व्वं धर्म्मितावच्छेदकविशिष्टधर्म्मिज्ञानाभावेनानुव्यव-

---

(१) 'विशेष्यताप्रतियोगित्वं' विशेष्यतानिरूपकत्वमित्यर्थः।

(२) 'स्वावच्छेदकसम्बन्धेन' स्वनिरूपितप्रकारतावच्छेदकसम्बन्धेनेत्यर्थः, अतः विशेष्यतायाः किञ्चित्संसर्गानवच्छिन्नत्वेपि न क्षतिः।

साये प्रामाण्यभानेपि संशयसमानधर्म्मितावच्छेदकप्रामाण्यनिश्चयाभावादेव तदुत्तरं तन्मतेपि प्रामाण्यसंशयसम्भवः विशेष्यतावच्छेदकप्रकारकज्ञानस्य विशिष्टाधिकरणकवैशिष्ट्यबुद्धिसामान्यहेतुतया धर्म्मितावच्छेदकप्रकारकज्ञानं विना समानधर्म्मितावच्छेदकप्रामाण्यनिश्चयस्याप्यसम्भवात् तथापि ज्ञाननिष्ठेदन्त्वविशिष्टबुद्धौ विशेषणज्ञानस्याहेतुत्ववत्तद्विशिष्टाधिकरणकवैशिष्ट्यबुद्धिसामान्येपि विशेष्यतावच्छेदकप्रकारकज्ञानं न हेतुरतः प्रथममिदन्त्वप्रकारकज्ञानाभावेपि तदवच्छेदेनानुव्यवसाये प्रामाण्यनिश्चयत्वसम्भवान्न तदुत्तरमिदं प्रमा न वेति संशयसम्भवः ज्ञाननिष्ठेदन्त्वधर्म्मितावच्छेदकसंशय-विपर्य्ययोस्तु धर्म्मितावच्छेदकप्रकारकज्ञानं हेतुरेवेत्यनुव्यवसायस्य न तदवच्छेदेन प्रामाण्यसंशयरूपत्वसम्भव इति मणिकृतो निगर्व्वः।

धर्म्मिज्ञानस्य भ्रमहेतुत्वे युक्तिमाह, 'अन्यथेति, 'धर्म्मिनियम इति तुरगादिमारुह्य वेगेन गच्छतोऽनन्तधर्म्मीन्द्रियसन्निकर्षेऽपि यस्यैव धर्म्मिणो ज्ञानं तस्यैव संशयो विपर्य्ययो वा, यस्य तु न ज्ञानं न तस्येति नियमो न स्यादित्यर्थः। न च तद्धेतोरेवेतिन्यायाद्धर्म्मिज्ञानोपधायकसामग्रीत्वेन धर्म्मिज्ञानसामग्र्येव हेतुरिति वाच्यं। धर्म्मिज्ञानसामग्रीत्वमपेक्ष्य धर्म्मिज्ञानत्वस्य लघुत्वादित भावः। ननु तत्र येषां धर्म्मिणां न ज्ञानं तेषामिन्द्रियसन्निकृष्टत्वेपि मानाभावः, किञ्च तत्तद्धर्म्मीन्द्रियसन्निकर्षसत्त्वे तत्तद्धर्म्मिणां ज्ञानमेव कुतो न जायते, दोषविशेष एव तत्तद्धर्म्मिज्ञानप्रतिबन्धक इति चेत तर्हि तत्तद्धर्म्मिकसंशयं प्रत्यपि स एव प्रतिबन्धकः संशयस्यापि तत्तद्धर्म्मिज्ञानरूपत्वादिति किं धर्म्मिज्ञानस्य पृथक् हेतुत्वेनेत्यरुचेराह,

'कोट्यनुत्कटत्वञ्चेति धर्म्मिज्ञानस्य भ्रमाहेतुत्वे संशयस्य विपर्य्यस्य वा किञ्चिदंशे उत्कटत्वं किञ्चिदंशेऽनुत्कटत्वञ्चेति न स्यादित्यर्थः। तेन तद्धर्म्मितावच्छेदकक-तद्धर्म्मिकतदुत्कटकोटिकभ्रमं प्रति तत्कोटि-सहचरितभूयोधर्म्मवत्तया तद्धर्म्मितावच्छेदकविशिष्टतद्धर्म्मिधीरवश्यं हेतुः, तच्च धर्म्मिज्ञानहेतुत्वं विना न सम्भवति। उत्कटत्वञ्च विषयताविशेषः न तु जातिः चाक्षुषत्वादिना सङ्करात् आंशिकत्वाच्च[१]। न च प्रमात्ववत् भ्रमत्वमर्थसमाजग्रस्ततया न कार्य्यतावच्छेदकमिति वाच्यं। तादृशभ्रमस्य तादृशधर्म्मिज्ञानं विनानुपपन्नत्वेनार्थसमाज-ग्रस्तत्वस्यैवासिद्धेः तत्त्वस्य[२] अनुगतस्याभावाद् यत्र धर्म्मिणि वस्तुगत्या बाधितो यो विषयस्तद्धर्म्मिक-तदुत्कटकोटिकज्ञानत्वस्यैव कार्य्यता-वच्छेदकत्वेन भ्रमत्वस्य कार्य्यतावच्छेदकेऽप्रवेशाच्च। न चैतावता तादृशसंशये तादृशविपर्य्यये च तादृशधर्म्मिज्ञानस्य हेतुत्वेपि संशय-सामान्ये विपर्य्ययसामान्ये च धर्म्मिज्ञानसामान्यस्य हेतुता नायातीति वाच्यं। तादृशभाने तादृशधर्म्मिज्ञानस्य हेतुत्वसिद्धौ यद्विशेषयोरि-तिव्याप्त्या[३] तद्धर्म्मितावच्छेदकक-तद्धर्म्मिकभ्रममात्र एव तद्धर्म्मिताव-च्छेदकप्रकारकतद्धर्म्मिनिश्चयस्य हेतुत्वसिद्धेरिति भावः। इदमप्या-पाततः उत्कटत्वं हि न विषयिताविशेषोमानाभावात् किन्तु तत्को-

---

(१) उत्कटत्वस्य जातित्वे जातेरांशिकत्वाभावेन उत्कटत्वस्यापि आंशिकत्वं न स्यादिति भावः।

(२) 'तत्त्वस्य' भ्रमत्वस्य, तदभाववद्विशेष्यक-तत्प्रकारकज्ञानत्वरूपभ्रमत्वस्य विषयविशेषघटितत्वेन विषयभेदेन भिन्नत्वादिति भावः।

(३) यद्विशेषयोः कार्य्य-कारणभावः तत्सामान्ययोरपीति न्यायेनेत्यर्थः।

टिसहचरितभूयोधर्म्मवद्धर्म्मिज्ञानकालीनत्वमेवोत्कटत्वं तच्च न कार्य्यतावच्छेदकमर्थसमाजग्रस्तत्वात्। किञ्च तत्कोटिसहचरितभूयोधर्म्मवद्धर्म्मिज्ञानत्वं कारणतावच्छेदकमपि नानुगतं सहचरितत्वस्य सम्बन्धभेदेनाननुगतत्वात् भूयस्त्वस्य द्वित्व-त्रित्वादिरूपत्वेनाननुगतत्वाच्च। न च सहचरितत्वं विशेषणताविशेषसम्बन्धेन वक्तव्यं भूयस्त्वन्तु त्रित्वमिति वाच्यं। समवायादिसम्बन्धेन तत्कोटिसहचरितभूयोधर्म्माणां ज्ञानकाले संशयस्य उत्कटकोटित्वानुपपत्तेः यत्र धर्म्मिण्येकधर्म्मसहचरितधर्म्मद्वयवत्ताज्ञानमन्यधर्म्मसहचरितैकधर्म्मवत्त्वज्ञानं। तत्रोत्कटत्वानुत्कटत्वानुपपत्तेश्च यत्रैकधर्म्मसहचरितधर्म्मपञ्चकज्ञानमन्यधर्म्मसहचरिततादृशधर्म्मत्रयवत्त्वज्ञानं तत्रोभयांशे उत्कटत्वापत्तेश्च। अपि च यद्विशेषयोरिति व्याप्त्या ज्ञानत्वादिनैव हेतुता सिद्ध्यतु न तु धर्म्मिज्ञानत्वेन गौरवात्। अतएव समानधर्म्मवद्धर्म्मिज्ञानमवश्यं संशयहेतुरन्यथा अगृह्यमाणसमानधर्म्मवद्धर्म्मिण्यपि संशयापत्तेः तथा च यद्विशेषयोरिति व्याप्त्या आरोपमात्र एव धर्म्मिज्ञानं हेतुः। न च संशयत्वमर्थसमाजग्रस्ततया कुतो जन्यतावच्छेदकमिति वाच्यं। तादृशधर्म्मिज्ञानं विना संशयस्यानुत्पादनियमेन अर्थसमाजग्रस्तत्वस्यैवासिद्धेरिति कस्यचित् प्रलपितमप्यपास्तं। तादृशव्याप्त्या ज्ञानत्वादिना हेतुत्वसिद्धेरेवोचितत्वात् असति प्रतिबन्धके साधारणधर्म्मवत्ताधीविलम्बेन संशयविलम्बासिद्धेश्च। क्वचित्तु कोटिस्मारकतया साधारणधर्म्मज्ञानोपयोगात्। अथ धर्म्मितावच्छेदकप्रकारकनिश्चयस्याहेतुत्वे दण्ड-दण्डत्वादिनिर्व्विकल्पकानन्तरमपि दण्डो गुणो न वा दण्डो गुण इत्यादिसंशय-विपर्य्ययोरुत्पत्त्यापत्तिः दण्डोरक्तो न

वेति संशयानन्तरमपि रक्तदण्डो द्रव्यं न वा रक्तदण्डो द्रव्यं नेत्यादि संशय-विपर्य्ययोरुत्पत्त्यापत्तिश्च । किञ्च धर्म्मितावच्छेदकप्रकारकधर्म्मिनिश्चयस्याहेतुत्वे घटो न वेत्यादिनिर्द्धर्म्मितावच्छेदककोपि संशयः स्यात् । न च धर्म्मितावच्छेदकप्रकारकधर्म्मिनिश्चयस्य तत्तद्धर्म्मितावच्छेदकक-तत्तद्धर्म्मिकसंशयं प्रत्येव हेतुतया तवाप्येष दोषोदुर्व्वार इति वाच्यं । तत्तद्धर्म्मितावच्छेदकक-तत्तद्धर्म्मिकसंशयातिरिक्तसंशयस्यालीकतया तत्तद्धर्म्मितावच्छेदकप्रकारकनिश्चयविरहादेव निर्द्धर्म्मितावच्छेदककसंशयानुत्पत्तेरिति चेत् । न । दण्डो गुणः रक्तदण्डो द्रव्यं नेत्यादिविपर्य्ययस्य विशिष्टाधिकरणकवैशिष्ट्यबुद्धिरूपतया विशेष्यतावच्छेदकप्रकारकविशेष्यनिश्चयरूपविशिष्टाधिकरणकवैशिष्ट्यबुद्धिसामग्रीविरहादेव निर्व्विकल्पकादितस्तादृशविपर्य्ययानुत्पत्तेः । एकत्र द्वयमिति न्यायेन तादृशविपर्य्यये चेष्टापत्तेः । अन्यथा एकत्र द्वयमिति न्यायेन तादृशभ्रमप्रसङ्गस्य तवापि दुर्व्वारत्वात् । निर्द्धर्म्मितावच्छेदककसंशयानभ्युपगमेऽपि निर्द्धर्म्मितावच्छेदककविपर्य्ययाभ्युपगमात् । एवं दण्डो गुणो न वा रक्तदण्डो द्रव्यं न वेत्यादिसंशयस्यापि विशिष्टाधिकरणकवैशिष्ट्यबुद्धिरूपतया विशेष्यतावच्छेदकप्रकारकनिश्चयरूपविशिष्टाधिकरणकवैशिष्ट्यबुद्धिसामान्यसामग्रीविरहादेव निर्व्विकल्पकादितोऽनुपपत्तिः । अतएव निर्व्विकल्पकादित एकत्र द्वयमिति न्यायेन तादृशसंशयो घटो न वेत्यादिनिर्द्धर्म्मितावच्छेदककसंशयोपि च नापादयितुं शक्यते तत्तद्धर्म्मितावच्छेदकविशिष्टतत्तद्धर्म्म्यधिकरणकवैशिष्ट्यबुद्धिभिन्नस्य संशयस्यालीकतया तत्तद्धर्म्मितावच्छेदकप्रकारकतत्तद्धर्म्मिनिश्चयरूपविशिष्टाधिकरणकवैशिष्ट्यबुद्धिसामान्यसामग्रीविर-

त्वादेव तदसम्भवात्तस्माद्धर्म्मितावच्छेदकप्रकारकधर्म्मिनिश्चयस्य पृथक् संशयादिहेतुत्वे मानाभावः ।

वस्तुतस्तु धर्म्मितावच्छेदकप्रकारकधर्म्मिनिश्चयस्य पृथक् संशयाद्य-हेतुत्वेपि संशयस्य विशिष्टाधिकरणकवैशिष्ट्यबुद्धिरूपतया नियमेन विशिष्टाधिकरणकवैशिष्ट्यबुद्धिसामान्यसामग्रीमर्य्यादयैव धर्म्मितावच्छे-दकप्रकारकधर्म्मिज्ञानस्य हेतुत्वमवर्जनीयमित्येव तत्त्वं ।

'विशेषदर्शनेपीति शङ्को न पीतः नादर्शे मुखमित्याद्यानुमानि-कादिविपरीतनिश्चयेऽपीत्यर्थः, 'दोषान्तरादिति दोषविशेषादित्यर्थः, दोषविशेषाजन्यतद्विशिष्टबुद्धेरेव तद्विपरीतनिश्चयप्रतिबध्यत्वादिति भावः । 'दोषान्तरात्तत्संशय इति दोषविशेषजन्यप्रामाण्यसंशय इत्यर्थः, 'तद्वदेवेति[१] प्रवृत्तिपदं व्यवहारपरं, तथा च तत्र यथा पीतत्वादिभ्रमेपि पूर्व्वोत्पन्नपीतत्वाद्यभावानुमित्या पीतत्वाद्यभाव-प्रकारकव्यवहारस्तथाऽत्रापि प्रामाण्यसंशयोत्तरं प्रामाण्यनिश्चयाधीनः प्रमाव्यवहारः स्यादित्यर्थः । प्रवृत्तिपदन्तु यथाश्रुतं न सङ्गच्छते प्रकृते पूर्व्वोत्पन्नप्रामाण्यनिश्चयस्य प्रत्यक्षरूपतया प्रमागोचरप्रवृत्ति-जनकत्वसम्भवेपि दृष्टान्तासङ्गतेः आनुमानिकपीतत्वाद्यभावनिश्चयस्य सिद्धशङ्खादिगोचरप्रवृत्तिजनकत्वासम्भवात् । तादृशव्यवहारे कदाचि-दिष्टापत्तेः सम्भवाद्दोषान्तरमाह, 'साक्षात्कारिभ्रमे चेति दोषवि-शेषजन्याजन्यसाधारणतदिन्द्रियजन्यसाक्षात्कारिभ्रममात्रे चेत्यर्थः,

---

(१) 'तद्वदत्रापीति।ख॰पुस्तकपाठदर्शनेन क्वचिन्मूलपुस्तके एतादृश एव पाठो वर्त्तत इत्यनुमीयते ।

न। तद्वदेवात्रापि प्रवृत्तिप्रसङ्गात् साक्षात्कारिभ्रमे साक्षात्कारिविशेषदर्शनं विरोधि दिङ्मोहादौ तथादर्श-

'भ्रमेति प्रकृताभिप्रायं विशिष्टसाक्षात्कारमात्रे इति बोध्यं, 'साक्षात्कारिविशेषदर्शनमिति तदिन्द्रियजन्यलौकिकविपरीतनिश्चय इत्यर्थः, लौकिकप्रत्यक्षं प्रति विपरीतनिश्चयस्य प्रतिबध्य-प्रतिबन्धकभावे दोषविशेषाजन्यत्वस्य प्रतिबध्यतावच्छेदकदिशि प्रवेशे प्रयोजनविरहाद्गौरवाच्चेति भावः। नन्वेवं दिङ्मोहादावपि तदिन्द्रियजन्यलौकिकविपरीतनिश्चयस्य प्रतिबन्धकत्वापत्तिः लौकिकप्रत्यक्षं प्रति विपरीतनिश्चयस्य प्रतिबध्य-प्रतिबन्धकभावे प्रतिबध्यतावच्छेदकदिशि लौकिकत्वस्य वैयर्थ्येनानुपादेयत्वात् उपनीतभानं प्रत्यपि अधिकन्त्विति न्यायेन सामानेन्द्रियजन्यविपरीतनिश्चयस्यापि प्रतिबन्धकत्वादित्यत आह, 'दिङ्मोहादाविति, 'तथा अदर्शनादित्यकारप्रश्लेषः तदिन्द्रियजन्यलौकिकविपरीतनिश्चयस्यैवाप्रसिद्धत्वादित्यर्थः।

नन्वेवं शङ्खो न पीतः अयं नोरग इत्यादिलौकिकचाक्षुषविपरीतनिश्चयोत्तरं शङ्खः पीतः अयमुरग इत्यादिदोषविशेषजन्यचाक्षुषभ्रमः कथं स्यात् दोषविशेषाजन्यत्वस्य प्रतिबध्यतावच्छेदकेऽप्रवेशादित्यत आह, 'तथेति शङ्खो न पीतः अयं नोरग इत्यादिलौकिकचाक्षुषविपरीतदर्शनस्येत्यर्थः, शङ्खः पीतः अयमुरग इत्यादिचाक्षुषभ्रमस्थल इति शेषः। 'पित्तादिना प्रतिबन्धादिति पित्तादेर्दोषविशेषस्य कार्य्यसहभावेन प्रतिबन्धकत्वादित्यर्थः, तेन[१] दोषविशेषोत्पत्तिकालेपि न लौकिकचाक्षुषविपरीतदर्शनोत्पत्तिसम्भवः। तथा च

(१) दोषविशेषस्य कार्य्यसहभावेन प्रतिबन्धकत्वकल्पनेनेत्यर्थः।

नात्। तच्च न, पित्तादिना प्रतिबन्धात्। न च जात्यैव कश्चिद्दोषोऽस्ति।

दोषविशेषजन्यभ्रमस्थले समानेन्द्रियजन्यलौकिकविपरीतनिश्चय एव न सम्भवति किमर्थं प्रतिबध्यतावच्छेदके दोषविशेषाजन्यत्वमुपादेयमिति भावः।

ननु तथापि यत्र चक्षुषा शङ्खो न पीतः अयं नोरगः स्फटिको न रक्त इत्यादिलौकिकविपरीतनिश्चयोत्तरं पित्त-मण्डूकवसाञ्जन-यवाकुसुमसान्निध्याद्यात्मकदोषविशेषोत्पत्तिस्तत्र तदग्रिमक्षणे शङ्खः पीतः अयमुरगः रक्तः स्फटिक इत्यादिदोषविशेषजन्यचाक्षुषभ्रमोदयात् लौकिकप्रत्यक्षं प्रति विपरीतनिश्चयस्य प्रतिबध्य-प्रतिबन्धकभावेपि दोषविशेषाजन्यत्वमवश्यं प्रतिबध्यतावच्छेदकप्रवेशनीयमिति चेत्। न। तत्र फलबलात् क्षणैकविलम्बेनैव दोषविशेषोत्पत्तिकल्पनात् क्षणैकविलम्बाभावस्य शपथनिर्णेयत्वात्। न च शङ्खो न पीत इत्यादिलौकिकप्रत्यक्षं प्रत्यनन्तदोषविशेषाणां प्रतिबन्धकत्वकल्पनामपेक्ष्य दोषविशेषाजन्यत्वस्य प्रतिबध्यतावच्छेदके प्रवेश एव लघीयानिति वाच्यं। पीतः शङ्ख इत्यादिभ्रमोत्पत्तिकाले निर्द्धर्मितावच्छेदककपीतत्वाभावादिलौकिकप्रत्यक्षस्याप्रामाण्यज्ञानास्कन्दितपीतत्वभ्रमोत्पत्तिकाले तदुत्तरकाले वा सधर्मितावच्छेदककपीतत्वाभावादिलौकिकप्रत्यक्षस्य च वारणाय तत्रापि दोषविशेषाणां प्रतिबन्धकत्वावश्यकत्वात् दोषविशेषाजन्यत्वस्य भेदकूटरूपतया विशेषण-विशेष्यभावे विनिगमकाभावेन तत्र गुरुतरानन्तप्रतिबध्य-प्रतिब

न्धकभावप्रसङ्गाच्च[१]। किञ्च दोषविशेषविरहस्थले विपरीतनिश्चयसत्त्वे दोषविशेषाजन्यविशिष्टप्रत्यक्षानुत्पादेऽपि दोषविशेषजन्यविशिष्टप्रत्यक्षवारणाय दोषविशेषाणामपि तादृशप्रत्यक्षं प्रति विशिष्य हेतुत्वं वाच्यमिति महद्गौरवं। न च दोषविशेषाजन्यत्वं प्रतिबध्यतावच्छेदके न प्रवेशनीयमपि तु तेषामु .जकत्वमिति वाच्यं। तथापि विशेष्य-विशेषणभावभेदेन गुरुतरानन्तप्रतिबध्य-प्रतिबन्धकभावस्य दुर्व्वारत्वादिति निगर्व्वः।

ननु यत्रायं नोरग इत्याद्यपेक्षाबुद्ध्यात्मकालौकिकविपरीतनिश्चयानन्तरं मण्डूकवसाञ्जनाद्यात्मकदोषोत्पत्तिस्तत्र तद्द्वितीयक्षणे ऽयमुरग इत्यादिदोषविशेषजन्यभ्रमोत्पत्तये दोषविशेषाजन्यत्वस्य प्रतिबध्यतावच्छेदकत्वं दोषविशेषाणामुत्तेजकत्वं वा ऽवश्यं वक्तव्यं तत्र क्षणविलम्बेन दोषोत्पादाभ्युपगमेऽपि भ्रमोत्पादनासम्भवात् तत्रापि चतुर्थक्षणे दोषोत्पादाभ्युपगमे च क्षणद्वयापलापप्रसङ्गात्। किञ्च भट्टमते प्रामाण्यनिश्चयस्यानुमितिरूपतया तत्सत्त्वेऽपि दोषविशेषजन्यप्रामाण्यसंशयोत्पत्तौ बाधकाभावः। लौकिकप्रत्यक्षनिश्चयान्यतद्विशिष्टबुद्धौ तद्विपरीतनिश्चयसामान्यस्य प्रतिबध्य-प्रतिबन्धकभावे प्रतिबध्यतावच्छेदककोटौ दोषविशेषाजन्यत्वस्य दोषविशेषाणामुत्तेजकत्वस्य वा आवश्यकत्वात् अन्यथा आनुमानिकादिविपरीतनिश्चयसत्त्वे दोषविशेषजन्यदिङ्मोहाद्युपनीतभानानुपपत्तेः दोषविशेषस्यानुमा-

---

(१) दोषत्वस्यानुगतस्यैकस्याभावात् तत्तत्दोषजन्यं यद् यत् तत्तद्भेदकूटस्य दोषविशेषाजन्यत्वपदेन विवक्षणीयतया भेदकूटानां विशेषणविशेष्यभावे विनिगमकाभावेन अनन्तप्रतिबध्य-प्रतिबन्धकभावप्रसङ्ग इति भावः।

निकादिज्ञानप्रतिबन्धकत्वाभावादित्यरुचेराह, 'न चेति न वेत्यर्थः, जात्यैवेति विशेषणे तृतीया, न वा उभयवादिसिद्धदोषविशेषजन्यप्रामाण्यसंशयस्थलीयदोषसाधारणदोषत्वरूपानुगतैकजातिविशिष्टः प्रकृते कश्चिद्दोषोऽस्तीत्यर्थः। तथा च दोषत्वस्यानुगतस्यैकस्याभावात् प्रकृते प्रामाण्यसंशयस्थलीयतत्तत्सम्बन्धादिकं दोषत्वेनाभ्युपेत्य प्रतिबध्यतावच्छेदके तत्तद्जन्यत्वस्य तेषामुत्तेजकत्वस्य वाभ्युपगमे महद्गौरवं। न च संशयान्यथानुपपत्त्या प्रामाणिकं गौरवं न दोषायेति वाच्यं। अनुव्यवसायादेः प्रामाण्याग्राहकत्वकल्पनयैव प्रामाण्यसंशयसम्भवात्। न च सामग्रीसत्त्वात्तदसम्भवः, तस्याये निरसनीयत्वादिति भावः।

साम्प्रदायिकास्तु प्रत्यक्षनिश्चये च समानेन्द्रियजन्यप्रत्यक्षरूपस्यैव विपरीतनिश्चयस्य प्रतिबन्धकत्वनियमेन तद्विरहाच्छङ्खो न पीत इत्याद्यानुमानिकादिविपरीतनिश्चयसत्त्वेपि पीतः शङ्ख इत्यादिभ्रमः न तु दोषविशेषाजन्यत्वमपि प्रतिबध्यतावच्छेदकं, प्रकृते च न तथा सुवचं प्रत्यक्षनिश्चयं प्रत्येव तथा नियमात् गुरु-मिश्रयोर्मते तदिन्द्रियजन्यप्रामाण्यनिश्चयस्यैव सत्त्वाच्चेत्यभिप्रेत्य दूषणान्तरमाह, 'साक्षात्कारिभ्रमे चेति प्रत्यक्षनिश्चये चेत्यर्थः। 'साक्षात्कारिविशेषदर्शनमिति समानेन्द्रियजन्यप्रत्यक्षरूप एव विपरीतनिश्चयो विरोधीत्यर्थः। 'दिङ्मोहादाविति दोषविशेषजन्ये इयं दिक् प्राचीत्यादिदिग्भ्रमादौ इयं दिक् न प्राचीत्याद्यानुमानिकादिविपरीतनिश्चयस्य प्रतिबन्धकत्वाभावदर्शनादित्यर्थः।

यद्वा तथादर्शनादित्यकारप्रश्लेषादियं दिक् न प्राचीत्याद्यानुमानिकादिज्ञानस्य प्रतिबन्धकत्वादर्शनादित्यर्थः। 'तच्चेति साक्षात्कारि-

विपरीतदर्शनश्चेत्यर्थः, शङ्खः पीत इत्यादिभ्रमस्थल इति शेषः। तथा च दोषविशेषाजन्यत्वं विपरीतनिश्चयप्रतिबध्यतावच्छेदके कथं प्रवेश-नीयमिति भावः[१]। ननु यथा सत्यपीन्द्रियसन्निकर्षादौ दोषान्न पीतत्वाभावग्रहस्तथा सत्यपि व्यवसायादौ दोषान्न प्रामाण्यनिश्चय इत्यत आह, 'न चेति न ह्रीत्यर्थः, 'आत्येति विशेषणे तृतीया, 'कश्चित्' कियान्, न हि प्रामाण्यनिश्चयप्रतिबन्धकतावच्छेदकदोषत्व-रूपानुगतजातिमान् कियान् दोषोऽस्तीत्यर्थः। तथा च दोषत्वस्यै-कस्यानुगतस्य प्रतिबन्धकतावच्छेदकस्याभावात् प्रामाण्यसंशयस्थलीयतत्तत्क्षणसम्बन्धादीनां विशिष्य प्रतिबन्धकत्वाभिधाने महद्गौरव-मिति भावः। इति यथाश्रुतग्रन्थं योजयन्ति। तदसत्। इदं रजतं सुरभि चन्दनमित्यादिदोषविशेषाजन्योपनीतभाने आनुमानिकादि-विपरीतनिश्चयस्य भिन्नेन्द्रियजन्यविपरीतनिश्चयस्य च प्रतिबन्धकताया अनुभवसिद्धत्वेन यथोक्तनियमस्य व्यभिचारात् साक्षात्कारिभ्रमपदस्य लौकिकसाक्षात्कारनिश्चयपरत्वे दिग्भ्रमादावित्यसङ्गतेः लौकिकप्र-त्यक्षनिश्चये तथा नियमेपि दिग्भ्रमादौ व्यभिचारवारणाय लौकिक-प्रत्यक्षनिश्चयान्यतद्विशिष्टबुद्धौ तदभावनिश्चयसामान्यस्य प्रतिबध्य-प्र-तिबन्धकभावे दोषविशेषाजन्यत्वस्य प्रतिबध्यतावच्छेदकत्वावश्यकतया प्रामाण्यनिश्चयसत्त्वेपि दोषविशेषात् प्रामाण्यसंशये बाधकाभावाच्च।

केचित्तु इदं रजतं सुरभि चन्दनमित्याद्युपनीतप्रत्यक्षे उक्तनियमो व्यभिचारीत्यस्वरसादाह, 'न च जात्येवेति, 'न चेत्यस्य नवेत्यर्थः, शेषं पूर्ववदित्याहुः।

---

(१) तत्त्वमिति ख०।

उच्छृङ्खलास्तु साक्षात्कारत्वनिरूपितविषयताशालिप्रत्यक्षे समानेन्द्रियजन्यलौकिकप्रत्यक्षरूपस्यैव विपरीतनिश्चयस्य प्रतिबन्धकतया तद्विरहाच्छङ्खो न पीत इत्याद्यानुमानिकादिविपरीतनिश्चयेऽपि पीतः शङ्ख इत्यादिलौकिकभ्रमः सम्भवति, प्रकृते च न तथा, लौकिकप्रत्यक्षनिश्चयं प्रत्येव तथा नियमात् गुरु-मिश्रयोर्मते तदिन्द्रियजन्यप्रामाण्यनिश्चयस्यैव सत्त्वाच्चेत्यभिप्रेत्य दूषणान्तरमाह, 'साक्षात्कारिभ्रमे चेति साक्षात्कारत्वनिरूपितविषयिताशालिनिश्चये चेत्यर्थः। 'साक्षात्कारिविशेषदर्शनमिति समानेन्द्रियजन्यलौकिकप्रत्यक्षरूप एव विपरीतनिश्चयो विरोधीत्यर्थः। सुरभि चन्दनमित्यादिदोषविशेषाजन्योपनीतभानं प्रत्यानुमानिकादिविपरीतनिश्चयस्य भिन्नेन्द्रियजन्यविपरीतनिश्चयस्य च प्रतिबन्धकताया अनुभवसिद्धत्वात् प्रतिबध्यदिशि विषयिताविशेषप्रवेशः, संशये व्यभिचारवारणाय प्रतिबध्यदिशि निश्चयत्वप्रवेशः, तच्च नियम एव प्रवेश्यते न तु प्रतिबध्यतावच्छेदकेऽपि, संशयं प्रत्यपि समानेन्द्रियजन्यलौकिकविपरीतनिश्चयस्य विरोधित्वेन व्यर्थत्वादर्थसमाजग्रस्तत्वाच्च। विषयिताविशेषोऽपि नियम एव प्रविष्टः न तु प्रतिबध्यतावच्छेदकेऽपि तत्प्रवेशः व्यर्थत्वात् प्रत्यक्षत्वमात्रस्यैव सम्यक्त्वादिति ध्येयं। 'दिङ्मोहादाविति दोषविशेषजन्ये इयं दिक्प्राचीत्यादिभ्रमादावित्यर्थः, आदिपदात् मण्डूकवसाञ्जनादिदोषविशेषजन्य-वंशे उरगत्वादिभ्रमपरिग्रहः। 'तथा दर्शनादिति इयं दिक् न प्राची अयं नोरग इत्याद्यानुमानिकादिविपरीतनिश्चयस्य प्रतिबन्धकत्वाभावदर्शनादित्यर्थः। यद्वा तथादर्शनादित्यकारप्रश्लेषादियं दिक् न प्राचीत्याद्यानुमानिकादिज्ञानस्य प्रतिबन्धकत्वादर्शना-

दित्यर्थः । तथा च दोषविशेषाजन्यत्वं विपरीतनिश्चयप्रतिबध्यताव- च्छेदके न विशेषणीयमिति भावः । यद्यपि चक्षुषा समं गोलकस्य- पित्तद्रव्यमपि बहिरागच्छतीति सिद्धान्तात् स्वच्छद्रव्याभिघातेन चक्षुषो विपरीतक्रियया मुखादिसम्बन्ध इति सिद्धान्ताच पीतः शङ्खः आदर्शे मुखमित्यादिभ्रमस्य तादृशविषयितासम्भवेपि दोष- विशेषजन्यदिग्भ्रम-वंशोरगत्वभ्रमादेरुपनीतभानतया तादृशविषयि- ताभावादिदमसङ्गतं, अतएव तत्रैव व्यभिचारवारणाय लौकिक- प्रत्यक्षनिश्चयान्यतद्विशिष्टबुद्धौ तद्विपरीतनिश्चयसामान्यस्य प्रति- बध्य-प्रतिबन्धकभावे दोषविशेषाजन्यत्वमपि प्रतिबध्यतावच्छेदके आवश्यकं तथापि लौकिकत्वरूपविषयिताविशेषस्य व्यापकीभूतदिगु- रगज्ञानसाधारणसाक्षात्कारत्वनिरूपितविषयिताविशेषो लौकिकप्रत्यक्ष इव दोषविशेषजन्योपनीतभानेप्यस्ति, प्राचीत्वं साक्षात्करोमि उरगत्वं साक्षात्करोमीत्याद्यनुभवाद्विपरीतनिश्चयसामान्यप्रतिबध्यतावच्छेदके- ऽपि तादृशविषयिताविशेषशालिप्रत्यक्षनिश्चयान्यत्वमेव घटकं न तु लौकिकप्रत्यक्षनिश्चयान्यत्वं, तेन तत्र दोषविशेषजन्यप्रत्यक्षस्य न संग्रहः । लौकिकसन्निकर्षजन्यतावच्छेदकस्तु इदं पश्यामीत्याद्यनुभवसिद्धस्तद्व्या- प्यीभूतो लौकिकत्वरूपविषयिताविशेषः तेन दोषविशेषजन्योपनीत- भाने लौकिकसन्निकर्षस्य न व्यभिचारः । न चेदं रजतमित्यादि- दोषविशेषाजन्योपनीतभ्रमेपि रजतत्वं साक्षात्करोमीत्याद्यनुव्यवसाय- सत्त्वेन तादृशविषयितासत्त्वात्तत्राप्यानुमानिकादिविपरीतनिश्चयस्या- प्रतिबन्धकत्वापत्तिरिति वाच्यं । तत्र रजतत्वं पश्यामीत्यनुव्यवसायस्य लौकिकविषयत्वांशे भ्रमत्वमत्र रजतत्वं साक्षात्करोमीत्यनुव्यवसाय-

न च प्रामाण्यसंशयाद्विषयसंशयवत् प्रामाण्यज्ञाने प्रामाण्यसंशयात् प्रामाण्यसंशय इति वाच्यम्।

स्यापि साक्षात्कारत्वनिरूपितविषयत्वांशे भ्रमत्वादिति मथिरूतो निगर्व्वः। ननु शङ्खो न पीत इत्यादिलौकिकचाक्षुषसत्त्वेपि पीतः शङ्ख इत्यादिचाक्षुषभ्रमोदयाद्दोषविशेषाजन्यत्वमवश्यं प्रतिबध्यतावच्छेदके निवेशनीयमित्यत आह, 'तथेति साक्षात्कारिविपरीतदर्शनस्येत्यर्थः, शङ्खः पीत इत्यादिभ्रमस्येत्य इति शेषः। ननु यथा सत्यपीन्द्रियसन्निकर्षादौ दोषान्न पीतत्वाभावग्रहस्तथा सत्यपि व्यवसायादौ दोषान्न प्रामाण्यनिश्चयः, किन्तु शङ्खो न पीत इत्याद्यपेक्षाबुद्ध्यात्मकलौकिकचाक्षुषनिश्चयसत्त्वेपि तदग्रिमक्षणोत्पन्नापित्तात्मकदोषात् पीतः शङ्ख इत्यादिभ्रमोदयात् लौकिकप्रत्यक्षं प्रति विपरीतनिश्चयस्य प्रतिबध्य-प्रतिबन्धकभावे दोषविशेषाजन्यत्वमवश्यं प्रतिबध्यतावच्छेदके प्रवेशनीयमित्यत आह, 'न चेति न वेत्यर्थः, 'आत्यैवेति अभेदे तृतीया, 'दोषः' दोषत्वरूपो धर्म्मः, न दोषत्वमनुगतैकजातिरस्तीति समुदितार्थः। तथा च प्रामाण्यसंशयसत्त्वीयसकलदोषसाधारणस्य दोषत्वस्यैकस्यानुगतस्याभावात् तत्तत्सम्बन्धानामेव प्रातिस्विकरूपेण प्रतिबन्धकत्वं तदजन्यत्वस्य प्रतिबध्यतावच्छेदकत्वं वा वक्तव्यं, एवञ्च तदपेक्ष्यानुव्यवसायादेः प्रामाण्यग्राहकत्वकल्पनैवोचिता लाघवादिति भावः, इति ग्रन्थं योजयन्ति।

'प्रामाण्यसंशयादिति घटवद्भूतलमित्यादिनिश्चये प्रामाण्यसंशयाद् भूतलं घटवन्न वेत्यादिसंशयवदित्यर्थः, 'प्रामाण्यज्ञाने' व्यवसायस्य

प्रामाण्यग्रहेऽपि स्वतः प्रामाण्याग्रहे तत्संशयानुपपत्तेः। ननु ज्ञानमात्रं न विरोधिबुद्धिनिवर्त्तकं भ्रमोत्तरं बाधकज्ञानोदयात्, किन्त्वनन्यथासिद्धं। अतएव तेन विनापि तज्ज्ञानं सम्भवतीति अन्यथासिद्धतया शङ्कितं तन्निश्चयं परिभूय ज्ञानविषयत्वाद्विषये यथा संशयस्तथा प्रामाण्ये तन्निश्चयस्यान्यथासिद्धिशङ्कया सं

प्रामाण्यनिश्चये, 'प्रामाण्यसंशयः' व्यवसाये प्रामाण्यसंशयः। ननु यथा घटवद्भूतलमित्यादिनिश्चये भ्रमत्वसंशयाद्भूतलं घटवन्न वेत्यादिविषयसंशयस्तथा व्यवसायनिष्ठप्रामाण्यनिश्चयेपि भ्रमत्वसंशयाद्व्यवसाये प्रामाण्यसंशयः स्यात् प्रामाण्यनिश्चये स्वतः प्रामाण्यग्रहेपि भ्रमत्वाभावस्य स्वतो ग्रहाभावाद्भ्रमत्वसंशये बाधकाभावादित्याशयेनाशङ्कते, 'नन्विति, 'ज्ञानमात्रं' तन्निश्चयमात्रं, 'विरोधिबुद्धीति तदभावविशिष्टबुद्धीत्यर्थः, 'भ्रमोत्तरमिति भ्रमत्वेन गृहीततन्निश्चयोत्तरमित्यर्थः, 'बाधकज्ञानेति तदभावविशिष्टज्ञानेत्यर्थः, 'अनन्यथासिद्धं' अन्यथासिद्धत्वेन भ्रमत्वेनागृहीतं, 'तेन विनापीति तदभाववत्यपीत्यर्थः, 'तज्ज्ञानं' तत्प्रकारकज्ञानं, 'इतीति, तत्प्रकारकज्ञानत्वरूपसाधारणधर्म्मदर्शनादितिशेषः। 'अन्यथासिद्धतया' भ्रमतया, 'तन्निश्चयं' घटादिनिश्चयं, 'परिभूय' स्वकार्य्याक्षमीकृत्य, 'ज्ञानविषयत्वादिति तत्प्रकारकज्ञानविषयत्वरूपसाधारणधर्म्मदर्शनादित्यर्थः, 'विषये' घटादौ, 'तथा प्रमाण्ये इति संशय इत्यग्रेतनेन सम्बन्धः, 'अन्यथासिद्धिशङ्कयेति भ्रमत्वशङ्कयेत्यर्थः, 'व्यवसायस्येति अनुव्यवसायेन निश्चित-

परिभूय भवति संशयः। न च व्यवसायस्य ज्ञानत्वे घटविषयकत्वे च यथानुव्यवसायविषयत्वान्न संशयस्तथा प्रामाण्येऽपि न स्यात् अनुव्यवसायस्य प्रमात्वनियमादिति वाच्यं। अज्ञाने अविषये च ज्ञानत्व-विषयत्वयोरनुव्यवसायेनाग्रहणनियमात् तद्विषयत्वमनन्यथासिद्धं प्रामाण्यविषयत्वञ्च तेन विनापि सम्भवतीति

इति शेषः, 'घटविषयकत्वे चेति सविषयकत्वे चेत्यर्थः, 'अनुव्यवसायविषयत्वादिति अनुव्यवसायस्य ज्ञानत्व-सविषयकत्वप्रकारकानुव्यवसायस्य विषयत्वादित्यर्थः, 'न संशय इति ज्ञानत्व-सविषयकत्वप्रकारकानुव्यवसायस्य ज्ञानत्व-सविषयकत्वांशे भ्रमत्वसंशयाधीनो न संशय इत्यर्थः, ज्ञानत्व-सविषयकत्वप्रकारकानुव्यवसायत्वस्य ज्ञानत्व-सविषयकत्वांशे भ्रमत्वाभावावच्छेदकतया तादृशानुव्यवसायत्वग्रहसत्त्वेन व्यवसायस्य ज्ञानत्व-सविषयकत्वग्राहकानुव्यवसाये ज्ञानत्व-सविषयकत्वांशे भ्रमत्वसंशयस्यैवासम्भवादिति भावः[१]। 'न स्यादिति प्रामाण्यप्रकारकानुव्यवसाये प्रामाण्यांशे भ्रमत्वसंशयाधीनः संशयो न स्यादित्यर्थः, 'अनुव्यवसायस्येति प्रामाण्यप्रकारकानुव्यवसायस्येत्यर्थः, 'प्रमात्वनियमादिति प्रामाण्यांशे भ्रमत्वाभावावच्छेदकत्वादित्यर्थः, तथा च प्रकृ-

(१) अनुव्यवसायत्वस्य ज्ञानत्वाभाववद्विशेष्यकत्वावच्छिन्न-ज्ञानत्वप्रकारकत्वरूपभ्रमत्वाभावावच्छेदकत्वात् न तत्र ज्ञानत्व-सविषयकत्वांशे भ्रमत्वसंशयस्ततस्तद्विषयत्वसाधारणधर्म्मदर्शनादपि न व्यवसाये ज्ञानत्वसंशयः, एवं पुरोवर्त्तिविशेष्यकत्वेपि बोध्यं तथाच तव मते प्रामाण्यांशे भ्रमत्वाभावव्याप्यमनुव्यवसायत्वमपीति भावः।

तत्र संशय इति चेत्। नैवं। भ्रमत्वमन्यथासिद्धत्वं। ततश्च प्रामाण्यनिश्चये भ्रमत्वसंशयेन तद्विषये प्रामाण्यसंशय इति फलितोऽर्थः। भ्रमत्वसंशयश्च तज्ज्ञानाज्ञानाभ्यां न सम्भवतीत्युक्तत्वात्। एवमन्यथापि भ्रमत्वसंशयात् न विषये संशयः स्वतः प्रामाण्यग्रहे भ्रमत्वसंशयाभावात्।

तेऽपि प्रामाण्यांशे भ्रमत्वाभावावच्छेदकीभूतस्य प्रामाण्यप्रकारकानुव्यवसायत्वस्य ग्रहसत्त्वेनानुव्यवसाये प्रामाण्यांशे भ्रमत्वसंशयस्यैवासम्भवान्न तदधीनप्रामाण्यसंशयसम्भव इति भावः। 'अविषये' निर्विषयके. 'ज्ञानत्व-विषयत्वयोरिति ज्ञानत्व-सविषयकत्वयोरित्यर्थः, 'तद्विषयत्वमिति ज्ञानत्व-सविषयकत्वप्रकारकानुव्यवसायत्वमित्यर्थः, 'अनन्यथासिद्धमिति ज्ञानत्व-सविषयकत्वांशे भ्रमत्वाभावावच्छेदकमित्यर्थः, 'तेन विनापीति प्रामाण्याभाववत्यपीत्यर्थः, 'सम्भवति' अनुव्यवसायस्य सम्भवति, 'तत्र संशय इति अनुव्यवसायस्य प्रामाण्यांशे भ्रमत्वसंशयाधीनो व्यवसायस्य प्रामाण्यसंशय इत्यर्थः, प्रामाण्यप्रकारकानुव्यवसायत्वस्य प्रामाण्यांशे भ्रमत्वाभावानवच्छेदकत्वादिति भावः। पूर्वपक्षमनूद्य दूषयति, 'भ्रमत्वमिति, 'अन्यथासिद्धत्वं भ्रमत्वमिति योजना। 'ततश्च' तथा च, 'भ्रमत्वसंशयस्येति अनुव्यवसाये प्रामाण्यांशे भ्रमत्वसंशयस्येत्यर्थः, 'तज्ज्ञानाज्ञानाभ्यामिति अनुव्यवसायस्य प्रामाण्यांशे प्रामाण्यनिश्चयानिश्चयाभ्यामित्यर्थः, अनुव्यवसाये प्रामाण्यांशे प्रामाण्यनिश्चयसत्त्वे तस्यैव प्रतिबन्धकत्वात्तदनिश्चये च भ्रमत्वसंशय-

न च वाच्यम् प्रामाण्यसंशयान्न विषये संशयोमानाभावात् ज्ञानविषयत्वात् समानधर्म्मादेव तदुपपत्तेः। न चैवं सर्व्वत्र विषयसंशये तन्निश्चयोच्छेदः, प्रामाण्यसंशयेऽपि तुल्यत्वादिति। तस्यासार्व्वत्रिकत्वात् भ्रमत्वसंशयं विना निश्चिते विषये संशयानुत्पत्तेरानुभविक-

---

धर्म्मिणोऽनुव्यवसायस्यैवाज्ञानादिति भावः। यद्यपि प्रमात्वनिश्चयस्य कुतो भ्रमत्वसंशयविरोधित्वं परस्परभावरूपत्वाभावात्। न च प्रमात्वस्य भ्रमत्वाभावव्याप्यतया विशेषदर्शनविधयैव तन्निश्चयस्य भ्रमत्वसंशयविरोधित्वं प्रमात्व-भ्रमत्वयोर्विशेष्यभेदेनैकत्र सत्त्वेऽपि[१] निरवच्छिन्नभ्रमत्वाभावाभावाधिकरणताश्रयावृत्तित्वरूपभ्रमत्वाभावव्याप्यत्वस्य प्रमात्वे सत्त्वादिति वाच्यम्। अनुव्यवसायादिना स्वगतप्रमात्वनिश्चयेऽपि भ्रमत्वाभावव्याप्यतया तदनिश्चयात्[२]। न च पुरोवर्त्तिनि प्रमात्वघटकतया तद्वत्त्वग्रहे तदभाववत्त्वग्रहासम्भवात् भ्रमत्वग्रहासम्भवः भ्रमत्वस्य तदभाववत्त्वघटितत्वादिति वाच्यम्। भ्रमत्वस्य तदभाववत्त्वांशे निर्द्धर्म्मितावच्छेदकतया तद्वत्त्वग्रहसत्त्वेऽपि तद्ग्रहसम्भवात्[३]। न च तदभावव्याप्यदर्शनमिव तदभावावच्छेदकीभूत

---

(१) समूहालम्बनज्ञाने इति भावः।

(२) तद्विशिष्टबुद्धिं प्रति तदभावव्याप्यवत्तानिश्चयस्य प्रतिबन्धकत्वेऽपि वस्तुतः तदभावव्याप्यीभूतः तस्य निश्चयस्य न प्रतिबन्धकत्वं किन्तु तदभावव्याप्यत्वेन निश्चयस्यैवेति भावः।

(३) सधर्म्मितावच्छेदककतद्वत्त्वग्रहं प्रत्येव सधर्म्मितावच्छेदककतदभाववत्त्वनिश्चयस्य प्रतिबन्धकत्वादिति भावः।

त्वाच्च। अथ तद्वति तत्प्रकारकज्ञानत्वं प्रामाण्यं तच्च ज्ञानग्राहकेण गृहीतमेवेति न तत्संशयः। न चास्मिन् निश्चितेऽपि प्रामाण्यसंशयात् न तत्प्रामाण्यमिति वाच्यम्। एतन्निश्चयादेव निष्कम्पव्यवहारादिति चेत् अस्तु तावदिदं प्रामाण्यम् तथाप्यनुव्यवसायानन्तरं व्यवसायस्य

धर्मदर्शनमपि तद्विशिष्टबुद्धिविरोधि तथा च भ्रमत्वाभावावच्छेदकीभूतधर्मदर्शनविधया प्रमात्वनिश्चयो भ्रमत्वसंशयविरोधीति वाच्यम्। तदभावावच्छेदकीभूतधर्मस्यापि स्वरूपतो निश्चयो न विरोधी किन्तु तदभावावच्छेदकत्वेन, तच्च प्रकृते नास्ति, अनुव्यवसायादिना स्वरूपत एव प्रामाण्यनिश्चयात्। तदभावावच्छेदकत्वन्तु व्याप्यतासम्बन्धेन तदभाववत्त्वं संसर्ग-प्रकारभेदेन व्याप्यदर्शनावच्छेदकधर्मदर्शनयोर्भेदः[१], स्वव्यापकतदभावकत्वं वा तदभावावच्छेदकत्वं व्याप्तिभेदाच्च व्याप्यदर्शनावच्छेदकधर्मदर्शनयोर्भेदः व्याप्यदर्शने तदभाववद्वृत्तित्वरूपव्याप्यत्वस्य प्रकारत्वात्[२]। तथापि प्राचां नये यद्धर्मावच्छेदेन तदभावो निश्चितः स्वरूपतस्तद्धर्मनिश्चयोऽपि तद्विशिष्टबुद्धिविरोधी तथा च येन पुरुषेण प्रमात्वावच्छेदेन भ्रमत्वाभावो निश्चितः तस्यापि प्रामाण्यसंशयान्न भ्रमत्वसंशयाधीनः प्रमात्वसंशयसम्भव इति मणिकृतो निगर्वः।

---

(१) अवच्छेदकधर्मदर्शने संसर्गविधया व्याप्यदर्शने प्रकारविधया व्याप्यत्वं भासते अतस्तयोर्भेद इति भावः।

(२) अवच्छेदकधर्मदर्शने तु व्यापकसामानाधिकरण्यरूपव्याप्तेर्विषयत्वादिति बोध्यम्॥

प्रामाण्येऽर्थस्य तद्वत्त्वे च संशयस्यानुभवसिद्धत्वान्नार्थतद्वत्त्वं तस्य विषयः। ननु व्यवसायस्येदन्त्व-रजतत्वविशिष्टेदंविषयत्वे अनुव्यवसाय एव मानं, तथा च यावद्व्यवसा-

---

वस्तुतस्तु भ्रमत्वादिसंशयं विनापि प्रामाण्यसंशयस्यानुभवसिद्धत्वान्न प्रामाण्यस्य स्वतस्त्वमभ्यव इत्येव तत्त्वम्।

प्रामाण्यस्य स्वतस्त्वे प्रामाण्यसंशयानुपपत्तिरूपं बाधकमभिधाय घटवद्भूतलमित्यादौ भ्रमत्वसंशयाद्घटादिसंशयानुपपत्तिबाधकमाह, 'एवमिति, 'अन्यत्रापि' घटवद्भूतलमित्यादौ प्रामाण्यनिश्चयातिरिक्तस्थलेपि' 'न विषये संशय इति न घटादौ संशय इत्यर्थः, तव मते स्यादिति शेषः। सन्निहितं बाधकमुद्धर्तुं शङ्कते, 'न च वाच्यमिति तुल्यत्वादितीत्यन्तेनान्वितं, 'प्रामाण्यसंशयात्' भ्रमत्वाभावसंशयात्, 'न विषये संशयः' न घटादौ संशयः, 'मानाभावादिति निश्चयोत्तरकालीनविषयसंशयपूर्व्वं भ्रमत्वसंशयस्यावश्यकत्वे मानाभावादित्यर्थः, 'सर्व्वत्रेति, विषयनिश्चयसत्त्वेपीति शेषः, 'संशये' संशयसम्भवे, 'तन्निश्चयोच्छेद इति क्वचिद्विषयनिश्चयसत्त्वेपि विषयसंशयानुत्पादस्यानुभवसिद्धस्योच्छेद इत्यर्थः, 'प्रामाण्यसंशयेपीति प्रामाण्यसंशयोत्तरं निश्चितविषये विषयसंशयाभ्युपगमेपीत्यर्थः, तस्येति प्रामाण्यसंशयस्येत्यर्थः।

ननु ममापि साधारणधर्म्मवत्ताज्ञानं न सार्व्वत्रिकमित्यत आह, 'भ्रमत्वसंशयमिति भ्रमत्वादिसंशयमित्यर्थः, आदिपदात् प्रमात्वपरिग्रहः। ननु निश्चिते विषये भ्रमत्वादिसंशयं विना कथं न संशयोत्पादः

येाल्लिखितप्रकारविशिष्ट एव धर्म्म्यनुव्यवसाये भासते। अन्यथा विषयांशे तस्य निर्विकल्पकत्वे इदं रजतं जानामीति तदाकारो न स्यात्। अतो धर्म्मिणीदन्त्व-रज-

---

विना कारणाभावं कार्याभावस्यासम्भवात्। न च तदभावविशिष्टबुद्धौ तन्निश्चयस्य प्रतिबन्धकतया निश्चयसत्त्वादेव संशयानुत्पाद इति वाच्यं। तर्हि भ्रमत्वादिसंशयेऽपि निश्चयसत्त्वे संशयोत्पादस्यासम्भवात् प्रतिबन्धकसद्भावादिति चेत्। न। भ्रमत्वादिज्ञानाभावविशिष्टतद्विपरीतनिश्चयस्य तद्विशिष्टबुद्धिप्रतिबन्धकतया भ्रमत्वादिसंशयं विना निश्चिते विषये संशयानुत्पादात् भ्रमत्वादिसंशये च तन्निश्चयसत्त्वेऽपि भ्रमत्वादिज्ञानाभावविशिष्टतन्निश्चयस्य प्रतिबन्धकस्याभावात् संशयोत्पादात्।

ननु भ्रमत्वादिज्ञानस्योत्तेजकत्वे मानाभावः लाघवाद्विपरीतनिश्चयत्वेनैव प्रतिबन्धकत्वात्। न च विपरीतनिश्चयसत्त्वेऽपि भ्रमत्वादिसंशये विषयसंशयस्यानुभवसिद्धतया प्रामाणिकं गौरवमिति वाच्यम्। तादृशस्थलाभावात् यत्र प्रथमतोऽयं घट इति निश्चयस्ततस्तदनुव्यवसायः ततः प्रामाण्याप्रामाण्यकोट्युपस्थितिस्ततः प्रामाण्यादिसंशयस्ततो विषयसंशयः तत्र प्रामाण्याप्रामाण्यकोट्युपस्थितिकाले निश्चयविनाशात् संशयपूर्व्वकाले विषयनिश्चयस्यैवाभावात्। एवं यत्रानुव्यवसायो मानसोच्छृङ्खलप्रामाण्याप्रामाण्यविषयकस्तदभावोपस्थितिरूपः तत्रापि चतुर्थक्षणे विषयसंशयोत्पादे न बाधकं तत्पूर्व्वं विषयनिश्चयासत्त्वात्। न च यत्रापेक्षाबुद्ध्यात्मकोऽयं घट इति निश्चयः ततो मानसोच्छृङ्खलप्रामाण्याप्रामाण्योपस्थितिरूपोऽनुव्यवसायः ततः

तत्ववैशिष्ट्यमनुव्यवसायेन गृहीतमिति धर्मिणि स्वतः प्रामाण्यग्रहवद्रजतत्ववैशिष्ट्येऽपि स्वतः प्रामाण्यज्ञानमवर्जनीयं (१) अतएव धर्म्यंशे न कदापि प्रामाण्यसंशय

प्रामाण्यादिसंशयः ततो विषयसन्देहस्तत्र यत्र वाऽपेक्षाबुद्ध्यात्मको-द्भूतप्रामाण्याप्रामाण्योपस्थितिरूपः सः घट इति स्मरणात्मको निश्चयः ततस्तदनुव्यवसायः ततः प्रामाण्यादिसंशयस्ततो विषयसंशय-स्तत्र च विषयनिश्चयस्य विषयसंशयपूर्व्वं सत्त्वसम्भव इति वाच्यम्। तत्र क्षणविलम्बेन संशयाभ्युपगमेऽपि क्षतिविरहात् क्षणैकविलम्बस्य अपथनिर्णेयत्वात्। एतेन यत्र तद्विशेष्यकघटप्रकारकं ज्ञानं स घटवान् प्रामाण्याप्रामाण्ये घट-तदभावौ चेत्येकं स्मरणं ततस्तस्यां घटस्तौ प्रामाण्यसंशयोऽनन्तरं स घटवान्नवेत्यादिसंशयस्त स्मरणरूपस्य निश्च-यस्य पूर्व्ववर्त्तित्वसम्भव इति निरस्तं। तत्रापि क्षणविलम्बेन संशया-भ्युपगमे क्षतिविरहात् क्षणैकापलापस्यादोषत्वादिति चेत्। न। प्रामा-ण्यादिसंशयस्यानुत्तेजकत्वे यत्रापेक्षाबुद्ध्यात्मक एव निरुक्तसमूहालम्बन-स्मरणरूपो निश्चयस्तत्र क्षणद्वयापलापापत्तेः। किञ्च यत्र भाविन्येव स घट इत्यादिनिश्चये प्रथमतोऽपेक्षाबुद्ध्यात्मकाऽप्रामाण्यसंशयस्ततः स घट इत्यादिनिश्चयोत्पत्तिः ततो द्वितीयक्षण एव स घटो न वेत्या-दिसंशयस्तत्र यत्र वा तद्विशेष्यकघटत्वादिप्रकारकज्ञानं प्रमा न वा स घट इत्यादिप्रामाण्यसमूहालम्बनानिश्चयः ततो द्वितीयक्षण एव स घटो न वेत्यादिसंशयस्तत्र च क्षणद्वयापलापापत्तिः तत्रैव निश्चय-स्यापेक्षाबुद्धिरूपत्वे क्षणत्रयापलापापत्तिश्चेति भावः।

---

(१) प्रामाण्यग्रहोऽवर्जनीय इति ख०।

इति चेत्। मैवं। इदं रजतञ्च जानामीति नानुव्यवसायः बहिर्विशेष्यके मनसोऽस्वातन्त्र्यात्। किन्त्विदं इदन्त्वेन रजतत्वेन जानामीति। तच्चेदन्त्व-रजतत्वे प्रकारकत्वेन भासेते तत्प्रकारकज्ञानवत्त्वञ्चात्मनि भासते। अन्यथा

प्राञ्चस्तु विपरीतनिश्चयोत्तरानाहार्य्यदोषविशेषाजन्यतद्विशिष्ट-बुद्धौ भ्रमत्वादिज्ञानस्य हेतुतया निश्चिते विषये भ्रमत्वादिसंशयं विना न विषयसंशयोत्पादः। न च क्वचित्प्रामाण्याभावज्ञानं हेतुः क्वचिच्च भ्रमत्वज्ञानमित्यननुगम इति वाच्यं। प्रामाण्यनिश्चयविरोधिज्ञान-त्वेनानुगमादित्याहुः। तदसत् भ्रमत्वज्ञानानास्कन्दितविरोधिनिश्च-यस्य संशय-निश्चयसाधारणविशिष्टबुद्धिप्रतिबन्धकत्वादेव भ्रमत्वादि-संशयं विना निश्चयसत्त्वे संशयानुत्पादसम्भवेन तादृशविशेषकारणत्व-कल्पने मानाभावात्। सति विरोधिनिश्चये भ्रमत्वादिज्ञानरूपविशेष-कारणाभावे विपरीतनिश्चयोत्तरतद्विशिष्टबुद्ध्यनुत्पादेऽपि विशिष्टबुद्धि-सामान्योत्पादस्य दुर्व्वारतया विरोधिनिश्चयस्य प्रतिबन्धकत्वावश्यक-त्वात् भ्रमत्वादिज्ञानस्याप्युत्तेजकत्वावश्यकत्वाच्च। अन्यथा विरोधिनिश्च-यसत्त्वे भ्रमत्वादिसंशयादप्यर्थसंशयानुपपत्तेः प्रतिबन्धकसत्त्वे कारणसह-स्राणामप्यकिञ्चित्करत्वात्। किञ्च प्रामाण्यनिश्चयविरोधित्वेनाप्यनु-गमासम्भवः विरोधित्वस्य प्रतिबध्य-प्रतिबन्धकतावच्छेदकभेदेन भेदात् स्वरूपतो भ्रमत्वज्ञानस्य प्रामाण्यनिश्चयप्रतिबन्धकत्वे मानाभावाच्च। नचैवं भ्रमत्वादिज्ञानानामननुगमादुत्तेजकत्वमपि कथमिति वाच्यं। उत्तेजकाननुगमस्यादोषत्वादिति दिक्।

'अथेति, 'प्रामाण्यं' प्रमापदप्रवृत्तिनिमित्तं, 'न तत्संशय इति,

प्रकारत्वाच्च तृतीयार्थासम्भवः। रजतत्ववैशिष्ट्यस्य तदर्थत्वे व्यवसायेऽपि तृतीयार्थोल्लेखापत्तिः। तथा च धर्मिणीदन्त्वरजतत्वप्रकारकज्ञानविषयत्वे तादृशज्ञानवत्त्वे

किन्तु स्मृत्यन्यज्ञानत्व-विशिष्टज्ञानत्वादौ संशय इति भावः। 'प्रामाण्यसंशयादिति इदं ज्ञानं प्रमा न वेत्याकारकसंशयादित्यर्थः, 'न तत्प्रामाण्यमिति, तादृशसंशयविषयस्यैव प्रामाण्यत्वमुचितं तद्वति तत्प्रकारकत्वन्तु निश्चितं न तथा संशयविषय इति नैतस्य प्रामाण्यत्वमिति भावः। 'एतन्निश्चयादिति, निष्कम्पप्रवृत्त्युपयुक्तस्यैव प्रामाण्यत्वादितिभावः। ननु भवतु एतस्यैव प्रामाण्यत्व तथाप्येतस्यापि संशय आनुभविकः स चानुव्यवसायेन तस्य निश्चये कथं स्यादित्याह, 'अस्तु तावदिति, 'इदं' तद्वति तत्प्रकारकत्वं, 'प्रामाण्ये' तद्वतीत्यादिरूपे, 'नार्थतद्वत्त्वमिति[१] प्रामाण्यमिति शेषः। 'तथा चेति, 'अन्यथा' अनुव्यवसायेन व्यवसायस्य इदन्त्व-रजतत्वविशिष्टविषयत्वाविषयीकरणे, तत्र[२] प्रमात्वानुपपत्तेरिति भावः। युक्त्यन्तरमाह, 'अत इति, 'धर्मिणीति धर्मितावच्छेदकांशे स्वतः प्रामाण्यग्रहत्वादित्यर्थः, अयञ्च प्रसाध्याङ्गको दृष्टान्तः[३] 'अवर्जनीयमिति, रजतत्वप्रकारकत्वं गृह्यत एव रजतत्वविशिष्टविशेषकत्वमपि चेद्गृहीतं तदा प्रामाण्यग्रहे विशेषाभावादिति भावः। दृष्टान्तासिद्धिं परिहरति, 'अत एवेति, 'धर्म्यंशे'

---

(१) अर्थे विशेष्ये भूतलादौ तद्वत्त्वं घटादिमत्त्वमित्यर्थः।

(२) तत्र व्यवसायगततादृशधर्म्मे इत्यर्थः।

(३) धर्म्मितावच्छेदकांशे प्रामाण्यस्यापि न्यायनये स्वतस्त्वाभावादिति दृष्टान्तस्य प्रसाध्याङ्गकत्वमुक्तं।

चात्मनोऽनुव्यवसाय एव मानमिति न विषये तस्य निर्विकल्पकत्वं। अत इदन्त्व-रजतत्ववैशिष्ट्यं पुरोवर्त्तिनि नानुव्यवसायविषय इति न स्वतः प्रामाण्यग्रहः। तस्मा-

---

धर्मितावच्छेदकांशे। अनुभवास्वीकारेण दृष्टान्त-दार्ष्टान्तोभयमेव दूषयति, 'मैवमिति, 'किन्त्विदमिति, अत्र स्वरूपेणेदंव्यक्तिविषयो बोध्यः न तु तत्र इदन्त्वमपि प्रकारः, तथा सति तदंशे स्वतः प्रामाण्यप्रसङ्गात् 'अत इदन्त्व रजतत्ववैशिष्ट्यं पुरोवर्त्तिनो नानुव्यवसायविषयः' इत्यग्रिमग्रन्थासङ्गतेश्च। 'प्रकारकत्वेनेति प्रकारिताविशेषणत्वेनेत्यर्थः। यद्वा 'प्रकारकत्वेन' प्रकारितासंसर्गेण, ज्ञान इति शेषः। ननु अनुव्यवसाये प्रकारिताभाने किम्मानमिति तटस्थाशङ्कां निराकरोति, 'अन्यथेति प्रकारित्वस्यानुव्यवसायाविषयत्व इत्यर्थः, 'प्रकारवाचीति प्रकारितावाचीत्यर्थः, 'रजतत्ववैशिष्ट्यस्य' पुरोवर्त्त्यन्वितरजतत्वसमवायस्य, 'तदर्थत्वे' तृतीयार्थत्वे, 'तृतीयार्थेति इदं रजतत्वेनेत्युल्लेखापत्तिरित्यर्थः। नन्वनुव्यवसायस्येदन्त्व-रजतत्वादिविशिष्टेदंविषयकत्वाभावे व्यवसायस्य धर्मिणि रजतत्वेदन्त्वादिप्रकारकत्वे मानाभावात् तस्य धर्म्यंशे निष्प्रकारकत्वापत्तिरित्यत आह, 'तथा चेति अनुव्यवसायस्य रजतत्वेदन्त्वादिप्रकारकत्वाभावे चेत्यर्थः, 'धर्मिणीति धर्म्यंशे व्यवसायस्येदन्त्व-रजतत्वप्रकारकत्व इत्यर्थः, 'विषये' धर्मिणि, 'तस्य' व्यवसायस्य, 'निर्विकल्पत्वं' निष्प्रकारकत्वं। उपसंहरति, 'अत इति, वहिर्विशेष्यकज्ञाने मनसोऽस्वातन्त्र्यादिति भावः।

ननु वहिर्विशेष्यके ज्ञाने मनसोऽस्वातन्त्र्यादित्यत्र किम्मानम् अस्वा-

दनभ्यासदशापन्नज्ञानप्रामाण्यं परतो ज्ञायते सांश-यिकत्वादप्रामाण्यवदित्याचार्य्याः। ननु स्वग्राह्यत्वेपि

तन्त्र्यं न तावच्चक्षुरादिरूपप्रमाणान्तरासहकारेणाजनकत्वं, कविका-व्यादिमूलभूतज्ञानस्य बहिरर्थविषयकस्य प्रमाणान्तरासहकारेणापि खण्डशस्तत्तदर्थोपस्थितिसहकारेण मनसा जननात् परमाणू रूपवन्न-वेत्यादिसंशयस्य प्रमाणान्तरं विनापि कोट्युपस्थिति-धर्म्मिज्ञान-सहकारेण जननाच्च। न वा ज्ञानाद्यसहकारेणाजनकत्वं, तर्हि प्रकृते व्यवसायरूपोपनयसहकारेण बहिर्विशेष्यकज्ञानजनने बाधकाभावात्। न च मनो बहिरान्तरोभयविशेष्यकज्ञाने प्रमाणान्तरमन्तरेणासमर्थं परमाणू रूपवन्न वेति संशयस्तु नोभयविशेष्यक इति वाच्यम्। गौरोऽहं सुखीत्यादिशरीराभेदबुद्धिविलयापत्तेः। न च मनो बहिरान्तरोभय-मुख्यविशेष्यकेऽसमर्थमिति वाच्यं। तादृशनियमे मानाभावात् प्रकृतेपि क्षतिविरहाच्च। प्रमाण्यभाने रजतत्वादिविशिष्टस्य धर्म्मिणो विशेष्यतांशे विशेषणतयैव भानात्। अस्तु वा बहिरर्थघटितो यथा तथा नियम-स्तथापि सुखत्वादिमतिसुखत्वादिप्रकारकत्वरूपान्तरार्थघटितप्रामाण्य-ज्ञाने बाधकाभावः।

अथ 'बहिर्विशेष्यक इत्यस्य पुरोवर्त्तिविशेष्यकत्वादावित्यर्थः, आदिपदाद्रजतत्वादिप्रकारकत्वपरिग्रहः, 'अस्वातन्त्र्यादित्यस्य विशे-ष्यकत्व-प्रकारकत्वयोरुपस्थितिं विना ज्ञानजनकत्वासम्भवादित्यर्थः। विशेषणज्ञानस्य विशिष्टबुद्धौ हेतुत्वादिति मणिकृतो निगर्व्वः इति चेत। न। प्रतियोगित्वाभावत्वयोरिव विशेष्यित्व-प्रकारित्वयोरप्यनु-

पस्थितयोरेव प्रकारत्वमिति नैयायिकस्यापि सिद्धान्तात्। अन्यथा पुरोवर्त्तिविशेष्यकत्व-रजतत्वप्रकारकत्वयोरपि भानानुपपत्तेः न्याय-मते प्रामाण्यभानानभ्युपगमेऽपि तयोर्भानाभ्युपगमात्। किञ्च तद्वद्विशेष्यकत्वे सति तत्प्रकारकत्वं न प्रामाण्यं किन्तु विशेष्यितासम्बन्धेन तद्विशिष्टवत्त्वे सति प्रकारितासम्बन्धेन तद्वत्त्वमेव प्रामाण्यं लाघवात्। तज्ज्ञानञ्च विशेष्यित्वादेः पूर्व्वमनुपस्थितावपि सम्भवति तत्र विशेष्यित्वादेः संसर्गतया विशेषणत्वाभावादिति। अत्रोच्यते। प्रामाण्यसंशयान्यथानुपपत्त्या प्रामाण्यनिश्चयविसामग्रीकल्पनावश्यकत्वेऽनायत्या तद्वति तत्प्रकारकत्वानुपस्थितिविशिष्टतत्प्रकारकज्ञानमेव ज्ञाने तद्वद्विशेष्यकत्वप्रत्यक्षं प्रति प्रतिबन्धकं कल्प्यते, स्वरूपेणेदं विशेष्यकत्वं रजतत्वादिप्रकारकत्वं ज्ञाने गृह्यत एव इदं रजतत्वेन जानामीत्यनुभवस्य दुरपह्नवतयारजतत्वादिविशिष्टविशेष्यकत्वप्रत्यक्षं प्रत्येव तादृशरजतत्वादिप्रकारकज्ञानस्य प्रतिबन्धकत्वात्। एतेनानभ्यासदशापन्नेऽपि न सर्व्वत्र प्रामाण्यसंशयः किन्तु क्वचिदेव, तथा च यत्र न प्रामाण्यसंशयस्तत्र प्रामाण्यनिश्चये किं बाधकमिति निरस्तं। प्रामाण्यग्रहाभावविशिष्टस्य व्यवसायस्य सामान्यत एव तद्वद्विशेष्यकत्वप्रत्यक्षप्रतिबन्धकत्वात्।

अथैवं तत्तत्संशयान्यप्रामाण्याभावविशिष्टबुद्धावेव प्रामाण्यनिश्चयो विरोधीत्येव कल्प्यतां प्रतिबध्य-प्रतिबन्धकभावान्तरकल्पनामपेक्ष्य कॢप्तप्रतिबध्यतावच्छेदककोटौ[१] विशेषणप्रक्षेपस्यैव लघुत्वादितिचेत्। न। अन्यदा प्रामाण्यनिश्चये तदुत्तरमप्रतिबध्यतत्तत्संशयात्मकप्रामाण्या-

(१) कॢप्तप्रतिबध्य-प्रतिबन्धकभावे अवच्छेदककोटाविति ख०।

कदाचित्परग्राह्यत्वात् स्वस्याप्यन्यापेक्षया परत्वात् भट्टमते च परग्राह्यत्वात्सिद्धसाधनं। न च ग्राह्यप्रा-

भावविशिष्टबुद्ध्यनुत्पादाय तत्र तत्रोपस्थितिविशेषस्य हेतुत्वमपि त्वया वक्तव्यमिति महद्गौरवापत्तेः तत्तत्संशयान्यत्वस्य तत्तत्संशयभेदकूट-रूपस्य परस्परं विशेषण-विशेष्यभावेन[१] अनन्तप्रतिबध्य-प्रतिबन्धक-भावप्रसङ्गाच्च। एतेन तत्तन्निश्चयान्यप्रामाण्यनिश्चयस्यैव प्रतिबन्धकत्वं कल्प्यतां लाघवात् प्रतिबन्धकान्तरकल्पनामपेक्ष्य क्लृप्तप्रतिबन्धकता-वच्छेदकसङ्कोचस्योचितत्वादिति परास्तं। भेदकूटस्य परस्परं विशेषण-विशेष्यभावे विनिगमकाभावेनानन्तप्रतिबध्य-प्रतिबन्धकभावप्रसङ्गात्। न चानभ्यासदशापन्नज्ञानेपि सर्व्वत्र न प्रामाण्यसंशयः किन्तु क्वचिदेव, तथा च यत्र प्रामाण्यसंशयस्तत्र प्रामाण्यसंशयहेतुत्वेन क्लृप्तदोषस्यैव प्रामाण्यनिश्चयप्रतिबन्धकत्वं कल्प्यतामन्यत्र तु स्वतः प्रामाण्यग्रह एवास्त्विति वाच्यं। दोषाणामननुगतत्वादिति ग्रन्थानुयायिनः। तदसत्। इदं रजतमिति व्यवसायानन्तरमिदं रजतत्वेन जानामीत्यनुव्यवसा-यानुपपत्तेः प्रतिबन्धकीभूतस्येदन्त्वप्रकारकव्यवसायस्य सत्त्वेन इदन्त्व-विशिष्टविशेष्यकत्वग्रहासम्भवात्। न च तस्येदमंशे निर्व्विकल्पकत्वमेवेति वाच्यं। जात्यतिरिक्तपदार्थस्य किञ्चिद्धर्म्मप्रकारेणैव प्रकारत्वनियमात्। न च तद्वद्विशेष्यकत्व-तत्प्रकारकत्वोभयविषयकप्रत्ययत्वं प्रतिबध्यता-वच्छेदकमत एव प्रत्येकं भासत एव न तु इदं इदन्त्वेन जानामीति वाच्यं। इदं रजतत्वेन जानामीत्यनुव्यवसायकाले तदुभयविषयकप्रत्य-

(१) विनिगमनाविरहादिति भावः।

यस्य प्रतिबन्धकसत्त्वेपि रजतत्वप्रकारकत्वभानवद्रजतत्वविशिष्टविशेष्यकत्वभानस्यापि दुर्व्वारत्वापत्तेः। किञ्च ज्ञाने तद्वद्विशेष्यकत्वभानं माभूत् प्रामाण्यभाने च किं बाधकं। न हि[१] तद्वद्विशेष्यकत्वतत्प्रकारकत्वमात्रं प्रामाण्यं, रजत-रङ्गयोरिमे रङ्ग-रजते इति विपरीतभ्रमेऽतिव्याप्तेः। किन्तु तद्विशिष्टविशेष्यकत्वावच्छिन्नतत्प्रकारकत्वं, अवच्छिन्नत्वञ्च इदमेतद्विशिष्टे एतत्प्रकारकमिति प्रतीतिसाक्षिकः स्वरूपसम्बन्धविशेषः, स च संसर्गमर्य्यादया प्रविष्ट इति।

नव्यास्तु पुरोवर्त्तिनि रजतत्वादिमत्त्वज्ञानेपि रजतत्वादिविशिष्टविशेष्यकत्वं रजतत्वादिप्रकारकत्वं अनुव्यवसाये भासत एव, एवं रजतत्वादिप्रकारकत्वे पुरोवर्त्तिविशेष्यकत्वावच्छिन्नत्वमपि भासते परन्तु रजतत्वादिप्रकारकत्वे रजतत्वादिविशिष्टविशेष्यकत्वावच्छिन्नत्वं न भासते, अवच्छिन्नत्वसम्बन्धेन तत्प्रकारकत्वविशेष्यक-तद्वद्विशेष्यकत्वप्रकारकप्रत्यक्षं प्रति तादृशविशिष्टप्रामाण्यानुपस्थितिकालीनव्यवसायस्य प्रतिबन्धकत्वात्। न च व्यवसायत्वस्यानुगतस्याभावात् कथमनुगतरूपेण प्रतिबन्धकत्वमननुगतानामेव प्रतिबन्धकत्वे तन्मतेपि प्रामाण्यसंशयस्थलीयतत्तद्व्यवसायव्यक्तेः प्रामाण्यसंशयानुकूलतत्तद्दोषव्यक्तेर्व्वा प्रतिबन्धकत्वस्य सुवचतयाऽन्यत्र स्वतः प्रामाण्यनिश्चये बाधकाभाव इति वाच्यं। तद्वति तत्प्रकारकज्ञानत्वेनानुगमात्।

अथैवं द्वितीयानुव्यवसाय एव न्यायनये कथं प्रामाण्यस्य भानं। न च विशिष्टप्रामाण्योपस्थितिवत् द्वितीयानुव्यवसायसामग्र्युत्तेजि-

---

(१) तत्प्रकारकत्वे अवच्छिन्नत्वसंसर्गेण तद्वद्विशेष्यकत्वं प्रकारः न तु ज्ञाने एतदेवोपपादयन्ति न हीति।

माण्यापेक्षया परत्वं, ग्राहकस्यापि ग्राह्यप्रामाण्यत्वेन तदपेक्षया परत्वाभावात्, स्वग्राह्यप्रामाण्यापेक्षया

केति वाच्यं। द्वितीयानुव्यवसायसामग्रीत्वस्यानुगतस्याभावात् तत्तत्कारणविशेषव्यक्तीनां प्रातिस्विकरूपेणोत्तेजकत्वे तदभावानां परस्परं विशेषणविशेष्यभावे विनिगमकाभावेनानन्तप्रतिबध्य-प्रतिबन्धकभावापत्तेः। न च अनायत्या अनन्तप्रतिबध्य-प्रतिबन्धकभावोऽभ्युपेयत इति वाच्यं। तथासति तदपेक्ष्य लाघवात् प्रामाण्यसंशयस्थलीयतत्तद्व्यवसायव्यक्तेस्तत्तद्दोषव्यक्तेर्व्वा प्रतिबन्धकत्वस्यैवोचिततया अन्यत्र स्वतः प्रामाण्यग्रहस्य दुर्व्वारत्वादिति चेत्। न। द्वितीयानुव्यवसायेपि प्रामाण्यभानस्यानभ्युपगमात्। अग्रे तत्र प्रामाण्यभानाभिधानमेकदेशिमते। न च तथापि गुरुमते व्यवसाये स्वतः प्रामाण्यभाने बाधकाभावः तादृशविशिष्टव्यवसायस्य प्रतिबन्धकस्य पूर्व्वमभावात् इति वाच्यं। प्रामाण्यसंशयान्यथानुपपत्त्या कार्य्यसहभावेन तादृशविशिष्टव्यवसायस्यानुगतस्य प्रतिबन्धकत्वकल्पनात्। किञ्च गुरुमते व्यवसाये व्यवसायनिष्ठतया प्रामाण्यभानमेव न सम्भवति लौकिकविषयत्व-तादात्म्यघटितसामानाधिकरण्यप्रत्यासत्त्या[1] प्रत्यक्षं प्रति विषयस्य हेतुतया विशेषणत्व-लौकिकविषयत्वघटितसामानाधिकरण्यप्रत्यासत्त्या[2] मनःसंयुक्तसमवायस्यात्मसमवेतमानसप्रत्यक्षहेतुतया च व्यवसाये व्यवसायभानसम्भवात् व्यवसायोत्पत्तिप्राक्काले व्यवसायरूपविषय-

---

(१) कार्य्यस्य लौकिकविषयत्वं कारणस्य तादात्म्यं प्रत्यासत्तिः।

(२) कारणस्य विशेषणत्वं कार्य्यस्य लौकिकविषयत्वं प्रत्यासत्तिः।

लौकिकसन्निकर्षयोरभावात् प्रामाण्येपि लौकिकसन्निकर्षाभावाच्च । न च ज्ञानेतरविषयकलौकिकप्रत्यक्षं प्रत्येव विषयादेर्हेतुत्वमिति वाच्यं ज्ञानेतरत्वप्रवेशे गौरवादिति प्राहुः ।

अन्ये तु प्रामाण्यसंशयान्यथानुपपत्त्या सामान्यतः प्रामाण्यप्रत्यक्षे विशिष्टप्रामाण्योपस्थितेर्हेतुत्वं कल्प्यते तेन प्रामाण्योपस्थितिं विना अनुव्यवसायादिना न प्रामाण्यग्रहः अग्रे च द्वितीयानुव्यवसायेन प्रामाण्यग्रहाभिधानमेकदेशिमताभिप्रायेण । ननु विशिष्टप्रामाण्योपस्थितेः प्रामाण्यप्रत्यक्षत्वावच्छिन्नं प्रति हेतुत्वे व्यवसायविरहदशायामपि खण्डशः प्रामाण्यघटकपदार्थानामुपस्थित्या विशेष्ये विशेषणमिति न्यायेन मानसप्रामाण्यप्रत्यक्षं न स्यादिष्टापत्तौ च विशेष्ये विशेषणमिति न्यायेन प्रामाण्यप्रत्यक्षस्यैवासिद्ध्यापत्तेः । अथ विशेष्यांशे लौकिकप्रामाण्यप्रत्यक्षत्वं कार्य्यतावच्छेदकं द्वितीयानुव्यवसाये प्रथमानुव्यवसायोपनीतविशेष्यित्वादिविषयकप्रामाण्यभानस्य चेष्टत्वात् । अत एवाग्रे द्वितीयानुव्यवसायेन प्रामाण्यग्रहाभिधानमपि साधु सङ्गच्छते इति चेत् । न । तथा सति विशिष्टप्रामाण्योपस्थितिं विनापि विशेष्यितासम्बन्धेन रजतत्वादिविशिष्टवत्त्वे सति प्रकारितासम्बन्धेन रजतत्वादिमत्त्वरूपस्य प्रामाण्यस्य प्रथमानुव्यवसाये उपनीतभाने बाधकाभावात् अत्र विशेष्यित्वादेः संसर्गत्वात् लाघवात्तस्यैव प्रामाण्यत्वात् । न च ज्ञानांशे लौकिकप्रत्यक्षात्मकप्रामाण्यप्रत्यक्षत्वं कार्य्यतावच्छेदकं प्रथमानुव्यवसाये उच्छृङ्खलप्रामाण्यभानस्य चेष्टत्वादिति वाच्यं । व्यवसायोत्पत्तिकाले ज्ञानोपस्थितिसत्त्वे प्रथमानुव्यवसाये उपनीतज्ञानविशेष्यकप्रामाण्यभानस्य दुर्वारत्वापत्तेः प्रथमानुव्यवसाये उच्छृ-

परत्वे[१] अप्रामाण्यप्रसङ्गात्। उच्यते। अनभ्यासदशाप-न्नज्ञानप्रामाण्यं न स्वाश्रयग्राह्यं स्वाश्रयातिरिक्तग्राह्यं

ज्ञत्वप्रामाण्यभानाभ्युपगमे तदनन्तरं रजतत्वप्रकारकत्वं रजतत्ववद्वि-शेष्यकत्वावच्छिन्नं न वेत्यादिसंशयानुपपत्तेश्चेति। मैवं। विशेष्ये विशेषणमिति न्यायेनाभावादिप्रत्यक्षवत् प्रामाण्यप्रत्यक्षस्यानभ्युपग-मात्। न चैवमनवस्थेति वाच्यं। वीजाङ्कुरवदनादित्वादित्याहुरिति संक्षेपः।

उक्तमेवार्थं प्रयोगारूढमाह, 'तस्मादिति, 'अनभ्यासदशेति अन-भ्यासदशापन्नं स्वाश्रयोत्पत्तिक्षणावधिकतृतीयक्षणवृत्तिसंशयविषयी-भूतं यज्ज्ञानप्रामाण्यं यद्घटत्वादिमति घटत्वादिप्रकारकत्वमित्यर्थः। प्रत्येकदलव्यावृत्तिस्तु अनुपदमेव विवेचनीया। 'सांशयिकत्वादिति स्वा-श्रयोत्पत्तिक्षणावधिकतृतीयक्षण वृत्तिसंशयविषयत्वादित्यर्थः, अत्रापि प्रत्यकदलव्यावृत्तिरनुपदं विवेचनीया। 'परग्राह्यत्वादिति 'सिद्धसाध-नमित्यग्रेतनेनान्वयः। ननु परमात्रग्राह्यत्वं वक्तव्यं तत्राह, 'स्वस्यापीति तथा च मात्रपदव्यवच्छेद्याप्रसिद्धेरिति भावः। ननु घटत्ववति घटत्वप्रकारकत्वं यावत्स्वाश्रयाग्राह्यत्वे सति ग्राह्यमिति साधनीयं तत्राह, 'भट्टमत इति, मिश्रमते चेत्यपि बोध्यं। 'स्वस्यापीत्यत्र शङ्कते, 'न चेति, 'ग्राह्यप्रामाण्येति ग्राह्यं प्रामाण्यं यस्येत्यर्थः, 'ग्राह-कस्यापीति ग्राहकत्वेन नैयायिकाभिमतस्यापीत्यर्थः, 'तदपेक्षया' ग्राह्यप्रामाण्यापेक्षया, 'परत्वाभावात्' भिन्नत्वाभावात्, 'स्वग्राह्येति

(१) अग्राह्यप्रामाण्यापेक्षया परत्व इति पाठान्तरं।

स्वग्राह्यप्रामाण्यं स्वग्राह्यत्वेन पराभ्युपगतस्य प्रामाण्यस्य घटत्ववति घटत्वप्रकारकत्वादेराश्रयस्तदन्यमात्रग्राह्यत्वं साध्ये इत्यर्थः, 'अप्रामाण्येति तादृशप्रामाण्याश्रयस्यापि प्रामाण्यानुमितीश्वरज्ञानादेस्तद्ग्राहकत्वेन विषयबाधादनुमितेरप्रामाण्यं स्यादित्यर्थः, प्रामाण्यानुमितेरपि प्रामाण्यघटकतया घटत्वविशिष्टाद्यवगाहित्वेन घटत्ववतीत्यादिप्रामाण्याश्रयत्वादिति भावः। 'अग्राह्यप्रामाण्यापेक्षयेति पाठे अग्राह्यप्रामाण्यं अग्राह्यत्वेन नैयायिकाभिमतस्य घटत्ववतीत्यादेराश्रयः तथा च पूर्वोक्त एवार्थ इति। 'अनभ्यासदशापन्नेति अनभ्यासदशापन्नं स्वाश्रयोत्पत्तिक्षणावधिकतृतीयक्षणवृत्तिसंशयविषयीभूतं, यज्ज्ञानप्रामाण्यं यद्घटत्वादिमति घटत्वादिप्रकारकत्वमित्यर्थः, पक्षे हेतोः सत्त्वप्रदर्शनाय भूतान्तार्थकमनभ्यासदशापन्नपदं स्वरूपकथनं न तु पक्षतावच्छेदकप्रविष्टार्थकं विप्रतिपत्तौ तस्य पक्षतावच्छेदकाघटकतया अत्र तेन रूपेण पक्षत्वे अर्थान्तरापत्तेः ज्ञानभेदेऽपि घटत्ववति घटत्वप्रकारकत्वादेरभिन्नत्वेनाव्यावर्त्तकत्वाच्च। न च यस्य विषयविशेषघटितप्रामाण्यस्य स्वाश्रयोत्पत्तितृतीयक्षणे संशय एव न जातस्तत्र स्वरूपासिद्धिवारणाय तस्य पक्षतावच्छेदकघटकत्वमावश्यकमिति वाच्यं। घटत्ववति घटत्वप्रकारकत्वादेः प्रातिस्विकरूपेणैव पक्षतया तस्य पक्षत्वाद्बहिर्भावादेव स्वरूपासिद्धिविरहात्। अन्यथा तस्य पक्षत्वे घटत्ववति घटत्वप्रकारकत्वादौ तद्विशेषणोपादानेऽपि तत्र स्वरूपासिद्धेर्दुर्व्वारत्वात्। न च तत्रैव तद्विशेषणमिति वाच्यं। काञ्चनमयः पर्व्वतो वह्निमानित्यादाविवाश्रयासिद्ध्यापत्तेः। न च घटत्ववति घटत्व प्रकारकत्वादिना प्रातिस्विकरूपेण न पक्षत्वमपि तु

वा। स्वाश्रये सत्यपि तदुत्तरतृतीयक्षणवृत्तिसंशयविष-
यत्वात् अप्रामाण्यसंशयाजन्यसंशयविषयत्वाद्वा अप्रा-
माण्यवत्। अर्थे निश्चितेऽपि न तन्निश्चयानन्तरतृतीय-

सामान्यतः प्रमापदप्रवृत्तिनिमित्तत्वेन तथा च यस्य विषयविशेषघ-
टितप्रमापदप्रवृत्तिनिमित्तस्य तृतीयक्षणे न संशयस्तत्र भागासिद्धि-
वारणाय तस्य पक्षतावच्छेदकघटकत्वमात्रप्रदर्शकमिति वाच्यं। प्रमाप-
दप्रवृत्तिनिमित्तत्वेन पक्षत्वे साध्येऽपि स्वपदस्य सामान्यतः प्रमापद-
प्रवृत्तिनिमित्तपरत्वे तदाश्रययावद्व्यक्तित्वस्य प्रतियोगिनो न्यायनये
अप्रसिद्ध्या साध्याप्रसिद्ध्यापत्तेः। विशिष्य घटत्ववति घटत्वप्रकारकत्वा-
द्येकैकपरत्वे पटत्ववति पटत्वप्रकारकत्वादौ प्रमापदप्रवृत्तिनिमित्तान्तरे
अंशतः सिद्धसाधनापत्तेः। न च पक्षतावच्छेदकावच्छेदेन साध्य-
सिद्धिरुद्देश्येति वाच्यं। साध्ये स्वपदस्य प्रामाण्यवति प्रामाण्यप्रकार-
कत्वपरतादशायां तद्घटकीभूतप्रामाण्ये अंशतो बाधापत्तेः विप्रतिपत्तौ
घटत्ववति घटत्वप्रकारकत्वत्वादिरूपेण पक्षतया प्रमापदप्रवृत्तिनिमि-
त्तत्वेनाच पक्षत्वेऽर्थान्तरापत्तेश्च। एतेन ज्ञानभेदेन घटत्ववति घट-
त्वप्रकारकत्वादेर्भिन्नत्वाद् यस्या घटत्ववति घटत्वप्रकारकत्वव्यक्तेस्तृती-
यक्षणे न संशयः तत्र भागासिद्धिवारणाय तस्य पक्षतावच्छेदकघट-
कत्वमात्रप्रदर्शकं, साध्ये च स्वाश्रयपदं तत्तज्ज्ञानपरं, पक्षतावच्छेद-
कावच्छेदेन साध्यसिद्धेरुद्देश्यत्वान्नांशतः सिद्धसाधनमन्यथा स्वाश्र-
यपदस्य सामान्यतः पक्षीकृतघटत्ववति घटत्वप्रकारकत्वाद्याश्रयपरत्वे
त्वात्तद्व्याप्यत्वाभावस्य चानमीन्यायेन सर्वत्र सत्त्वात् सिद्धसा-

क्षणेऽर्थसंशयो न वा प्रामाण्यसंशयं विनेति नार्थे व्यभिचारः। विवादपदं न यावत्स्वाश्रयग्राहकग्राह्यं स्वाश्रयनिश्चये सति तदुत्तरतृतीयक्षणेऽप्रामाण्यसंशयं

धनापत्तिरिति कस्यचित् प्रलपितमप्यपास्तं। तस्य पक्षतावच्छेदक-घटकत्वे विप्रतिपत्तौ तेन रूपेणापक्षत्वादर्थान्तरापत्तेः, किन्तु ज्ञानभेदेन प्रामाण्यभेदमते वस्तुगत्या यद् यज्ज्ञानव्यक्तेरुत्तरतृतीय-क्षणे तत्र प्रामाण्यसंशयः प्रातिस्विकरूपेण तत्तज्ज्ञानवृत्तिघटत्ववति-घटत्वप्रकारकत्वत्वादिना पक्षीकृत्य तत्तज्ज्ञानग्राह्यत्वाभावः साधनीय इति दिक्।

'न स्वाश्रयग्राह्यमिति, ज्ञानभेदेपि घटत्ववतिघटत्वप्रकारकत्वादे-रभेदनये स्वपदं सामान्यतः पक्षीकृतघटत्ववतिघटत्वप्रकारकत्वादि-परं, यावत्त्वेन चाश्रयो विशेषणीयः, अन्यथा सकलप्रामाण्याश्रयसर्व्व-विषयकेश्वरादिज्ञानग्राह्यतया प्रामाण्यानुमितेरपि प्रामाण्यघटकत्वेन घटत्ववतिघटत्वप्रकारकत्वाद्याश्रयत्वात्तद्ग्राह्यतया च बाधापत्तेः। न च तथापि सर्व्वविषयकत्ववतिसर्व्वविषयत्वप्रकारकत्वादौ सर्व्वान्तर्गत-त्वेन यावत्स्वाश्रयग्राह्ये बाध इति वाच्यं। तस्यापक्षत्वात्। घटत्ववति-घटत्वप्रकारकत्वादिकं प्रतिज्ञानमन्यदिति मते तु स्वाश्रयपदं तज्ज्ञान-व्यक्तिपरं पक्षतापि तत्तज्ज्ञानवृत्ति घटत्ववतिघटत्वप्रकारकत्वत्वादि-नेत्युक्तमेव, तथाचैतज्ज्ञानवृत्ति घटत्ववतिघटत्वप्रकारकत्वं नैतज्ज्ञान-ग्राह्यमिति फलितं, अन्यथा सामान्यतो घटत्ववतिघटत्वप्रकारकत्वा-द्याश्रयपरत्वे यावत्त्वविशेषणस्याप्युक्तक्रमेणावश्यकतया क्वापि घटत्व-

षिना वा सन्दिह्यमानत्वात् अप्रामाण्यवत्। यद्वा अनभ्यासदशापन्नैतज्ज्ञानप्रामाण्यं एतत्प्रामाण्यसंशयपूर्वकालीनैतज्ज्ञाननिश्चयाविषयः एतज्ज्ञाननिश्च-

---

वतिघटत्वप्रकारकत्वव्यक्तौ यावद्घटत्ववतिघटत्वप्रकारकत्वाश्रयग्राह्यत्वा-सत्त्वेन सिद्धसाधनापत्तेः।

ननु स्वाश्रयग्राह्यत्वाभावसिद्धावपि परतो ग्राह्यत्वं न सिद्धं अग्राह्यत्वेपि तदुपपत्तेरित्यतः साध्यान्तरमाह, 'स्वाश्रयातिरिक्तेति, नन्वत्र बाधः नैयायिकसिद्धप्रामाण्यानुमित्यादेरपि प्रामाण्यघटकतया घटत्वादिमत्त्वावगाहित्वेन घटत्ववतिघटत्वप्रकारकत्वाश्रयतया स्वाश्रयातिरिक्तत्वाभावात्। न च स्वाश्रयपदं सामान्यतो न घटत्ववतिघटत्वप्रकारकत्वाद्याश्रयपरमपि तु तदाश्रयत्वोपलक्षिततत्तद्व्यवसायव्यक्तिपरमिति वाच्यं। सिद्धसाधनापत्तेः गुरुणा नैयायिकसिद्धप्रामाण्यानुमित्यादिनापि प्रामाण्यग्रहस्वीकारादिति चेत्। न। स्वाश्रयातिरिक्तमात्रग्राह्यत्वस्य साध्यत्वात्। स्वाश्रयातिरिक्तमात्रग्राह्यत्वञ्च यावत्स्वाश्रयाग्राह्यत्वे सति ग्राह्यत्वं नातो बाधतादवस्थ्यं, स्वपदं पूर्ववत् पक्षीकृतघटत्ववतिघटत्वप्रकारकत्वादिपरं, निखिलप्रामाण्याश्रयसर्वविषयकभगवज्ज्ञानादिमादाय प्रामाण्यानुमितिमादाय च बाधवारणाय यावत्त्वोपादानं, परन्तु यदि ज्ञानभेदेन घटत्ववतिघटत्वप्रकारकत्वादिकं विभिन्नं तदा स्वाश्रयपदं तत्तद्व्यवसायव्यक्तिपरं यावत्त्वञ्च नोपादेयं तथा चैतज्ज्ञानवृत्ति घटत्ववतिघटत्वप्रकारकत्वमेतज्ज्ञानाग्राह्यत्वे सति ग्राह्यमिति फलितमिति दिक्।

यानन्तरं सन्दिग्धप्रामाण्यवत्त्वात् अप्रामाण्यवत् । न च स्वपदस्य प्रामाण्यमात्रपरत्वात्तदाश्रयाग्राह्यत्वे न बाधः स्वपदस्य सम्बन्धिपरत्वेन समभिव्याहृतपरत्वात् ।

'स्वाश्रये सतीति सतिसप्तमीमहिम्ना स्वाश्रयसामानाधिकरण्यं संशयविशेषणं लभ्यते तथा च स्वाश्रयसमानाधिकरणो यस्तदुत्तरतृतीयक्षणवृत्तिसंशयस्तद्विषयत्वादित्यर्थः, स्वपदं पक्षीभूतप्रामाण्यपरं । नन्विदं स्वरूपासिद्धं व्यवसायोत्पत्तिस्ततोऽनुव्यवसायस्ततः प्रामाण्याप्रामाण्यकोट्युपस्थितिः ततः प्रामाण्यसंशय इतिक्रमेण व्यवसायचतुर्थक्षण एव प्रामाण्यसंशयोत्पत्तेः । न च स्थितिक्षणापेक्षया तृतीयत्वं विवक्षितं तच्च चतुर्थक्षणेऽप्यस्तीति वाच्यं । गुरुमते अप्रयोजकत्वापत्तेः प्रामाण्यनिश्चयात्मकव्यवसायस्य तृतीयक्षण एव विनष्टतया निश्चयसत्त्वे संशयासम्भवरूपस्यानुकूलतर्कस्यासम्भवादिति चेत् । न । यत्र स घटः प्रामाण्याप्रामाण्ये चेति समूहालम्बनस्मरणात्मको व्यवसायः ततो घटविषयकं ज्ञानमिति स्मरणरूपं धर्मिज्ञानं तत्र तृतीयक्षणे घटविषयकं ज्ञानं प्रमा न वेति प्रामाण्यसंशयसम्भवादिति भावः । अत्र संशयविषयत्वमात्रोक्तावयं घटो न वेत्यादिसंशयविषये घटत्वादौ व्यभिचारः तत्र घटत्ववतीत्यादिप्रामाण्याश्रयत्वाभाववत्त्वादतः तदुत्तरतृतीयक्षणवृत्तीति, अयं घटो न वेत्यादिसंशयस्यायं घट इत्यादिव्यवसायोत्तरतृतीयक्षणवृत्तित्वमेव नेति न व्यभिचारः । तदुत्तरक्षणवृत्तिसंशयविषयत्वोक्तावपि अयं घट इति निश्चये प्रामाण्यसंशयाधीनार्थसंशयविषये घटत्वादौ व्यभिचारोऽतः 'तृतीयेति' प्रामाण्य-

अन्यथा स्वस्य परत्वात्परस्य च स्वत्वात् तदेतत्त्वस्य तदेतदन्यत्वस्य च स्व-परसाधारणत्वात् स्वतः परतो वेति संशयो न स्यात् । प्रामाण्यस्य स्वग्राह्यत्वे बाधा-

---

संशयाधीनार्थसंशयस्य चतुर्थक्षणादिवृत्तिरेवेति न व्यभिचारः । तृतीयक्षणवृत्तिसंशयविषयत्वादित्युक्तौ यत्र स्थाणुर्न वेति संशयस्ततो विशेषदर्शनं ततः अयं स्थाणुरिति निश्चयस्तत्र पूर्व्वतृतीयक्षणवृत्ति-संशयविषयत्वमादाय स्थाणुत्वे व्यभिचारोऽतो ध्वंसघटिततृतीयत्वला-भाय 'उत्तरेति, ध्वंसघटिततृतीयत्वञ्च तद्ध्वंसाधिकरणकालध्वंसान-धिकरणत्वे सति तद्ध्वंसाधिकरणत्वं तत्पदद्वयञ्च यद्व्यवसायव्यक्तेस्तृती-यक्षणे प्रामाण्यसंशयोऽनुभवसिद्धः तादृशयत्किञ्चिदेकव्यक्तिव्यवसायपरं न तु स्वाश्रयसामान्यपरं तथासत्यनादौ संसारे सर्व्वस्मिन्नेव क्षणे घटत्ववतीत्यादिप्रामाण्याश्रयज्ञानध्वंससत्त्वेन तद्ध्वंसाधिकरणकालध्वंसा-नधिकरणक्षणस्यैवाप्रसिद्धेः(१) । तद्व्यक्तितृतीयक्षणवृत्तिपुरुषान्तरीयसंश-यमादाय घटत्वादावर्थे व्यभिचार इति स्वाश्रयसमानाधिकरणेति संशयविशेषणं । न च पुरुषान्तरीयसंशयोपि तत्पुरुषीयस्वाश्रयसमा-नाधिकरण एवेति तद्दोषतादवस्थ्यमिति वाच्यं । स्वाश्रयपदस्य तद्व्यक्तिपरत्वात् तथा च तद्व्यक्तिसमानाधिकरणतद्व्यक्त्युत्तरतृतीय-क्षणवृत्तिसंशयविषयत्वादित्यर्थः, विषयत्वञ्च कोटित्वपर्य्याप्त्यधिकरणत्वं नातः प्रामाण्यसंशयमादाय प्रामाण्यघटकार्थे व्यभिचारः । अथ यत्र

---

(१) तद्ध्वंसाधिकरणकालध्वंसानधिकरणकालस्यैवाप्रसिद्धेः इति ख० ।

त्यविशेषेणान्यथाग्राह्यत्वं परतो ग्राह्यत्वमिति कश्चित्। प्रथमं च प्रामाण्यज्ञानं व्यतिरेकिणा। ननु प्रामाण्यप्रसिद्धिं विना व्याप्त्यग्रहात् कथमनुमानं, अथ

घटविषयकं ज्ञानं स घटः प्रामाण्याप्रामाण्ये चेति समूहालम्बनात्मको व्यवसायस्ततस्तस्मिन् व्यवसाये प्रामाण्यसंशयोऽनन्तरं स घटो न वेति संशयस्तत्र च तद्विषयत्वमादाय घटत्वादौ व्यभिचारः, एवं यत्रायं घटः पटश्चेति ज्ञानानन्तरं घटत्व-तदभावोपस्थितिः ततः पटो घटो न वेति संशयस्तत्र तद्विषयत्वमादाय घटत्वे व्यभिचारः, एवं यत्रादौ अयं घट इति ज्ञानं ततः समवाय-तदभावोपस्थितिः ततो घटः समवायवान्न वेति संशयस्तत्र तद्विषयत्वमादाय समवाये व्यभिचारः तत्र प्रामाण्याश्रयग्राह्यत्वाभावाभावादिति चेत्। न। तदुत्तरेत्यत्र तत्पदेन पक्षीभूतप्रामाण्याश्रययद्व्यक्त्युत्तरवृतीयत्वेन तस्य पुंसः प्रामाण्य एव संशयो न तद्धर्मादिषु तद्व्यक्तेरुक्तत्वात्। संशयपदस्य कोटिताख्यविषयताविशेषलाभाय प्रतिबध्य-प्रतिबन्धकभावात्मकानुकूलतर्कस्फोरणाय वा, न तु संशयत्वं हेतुघटकं पक्षदृष्टान्तसाधारणस्य न्यायमत-गुरुमतोभयसाधारणस्य च संशयत्वस्यानुगतस्यैकस्य दुर्व्वचत्वात् प्रयोजनविरहाच्च। एतेन संशयपदवाच्यत्वं संशयत्वं सर्व्वसाधारणमनुगतं सुवचमित्यपि निरस्तं। तथापि व्यर्थविशेषणत्वादिति न काप्यनुपपत्तिः। 'अप्रामाण्येति। न चाप्रामाण्यसंशयाजन्यस्वारसिकसंशयविषयघटत्वादौ व्यभिचार इति वाच्यं। मन्त्र्यत्यासेनाप्रामाण्यसंशयजन्यसंशयाविषयत्वस्य विवक्षितत्वात्। न चैवं प्रामाण्य-

व्याघातदण्डभयेन प्रमा-तद्विषयसिद्धौ तद्दृष्टान्तेन ज्ञेयत्वादिना वह्नेः प्रमाविषयत्वमनुमेयं, ततश्च सामान्यतस्तत्सिद्धौ न साध्याप्रसिद्धिः, विशिष्यानिर्णयाच्चा-

---

स्यापि प्रामाण्यवतिप्रामाण्यप्रकारकत्वरूपप्रामाण्यज्ञानप्रामाण्यसंशयाधीनसंशयविषयतया स्वरूपासिद्धिरिति वाच्यं। अप्रामाण्यपदेन पक्षीभूतघटत्ववतिघटत्वप्रकारकत्वादिरूपप्रामाण्यविरोधिनो घटत्ववतिघटत्वप्रकारकत्वाभावस्य घटत्वाभाववतिघटत्वप्रकारकत्वरूपभ्रमत्वस्य चोक्तत्वात्। न च यत्रार्थविशेषे अप्रामाण्यसंशयाहितसंशयः कदापि न वृत्तस्तत्रार्थे व्यभिचार इति वाच्यं। तद्घटितप्रामाण्यं पक्षीकृत्य तदाश्रयग्राह्यत्वाभावस्य असाधनीयत्वादिति। नन्वेवमपि स्वरूपासिद्धिः धारावाहिकाप्रामाण्यसंशयस्थले उत्तरोत्तरसंशयस्य विशेषणज्ञानविधया पूर्वपूर्वतत्संशयजन्यत्वात् तत्संशयस्य विषयत्वात् तादृशप्रामाण्यतदीयज्ञानप्रामाण्योभयसमूहालम्बनजन्यसंशयस्य विषयत्वाच्च। न च तत्तदप्रामाण्यसंशयत्वेन जनकत्वं विवक्षितमिति वाच्यं। क्वचिदपि तथा जनकत्वाभावात् अप्रामाण्यसंशयस्य निश्चयप्रतिबन्धकतायामुत्तेजकत्वादिति चेत्। न। जन्यत्वं हि उत्तेजकतया प्रयोज्यत्वं तथा च प्रकृतप्रामाण्यविरोधिविषयकबुद्ध्यनाक्रान्तत्वविशिष्टधर्मावच्छिन्नस्वप्रतिबन्धकताकसंशयाविषयत्वं हेतुरिति न कोपि दोषः, 'स्वपदं संशयपरमिति भावः। हेतुद्वय एव घटत्वादावर्थे व्यभिचारमुद्धरति, 'अर्थे निश्चितेपीति अर्थे घटत्वादौ, 'अर्थसंशयः' घटत्वादौ संशयः, 'प्रामाण्यसंशयं विनेति, अर्थे निश्चिते अर्थसंशय इत्यनुषज्यते। गुरु-

न्वयित्वासाधारण्ये। न च प्रामाण्यं नानुगतं किन्तु प्रतिज्ञानं विषय-प्रकारभेदाद्भिन्नं तथा च वह्निज्ञानस्य वह्निवृत्तिप्रकारानवच्छिन्नत्वादिकं साध्यं तच्चाप्रसिद्ध-मिति वाच्यं।

मतं निराकृत्य भट्ट-मिश्रौ निराकर्त्तुं तन्मतसिद्धस्वतस्त्वव्यतिरेकं साधयति, 'विवादेति 'ग्राहकं' ग्रहः, 'ग्राह्यं' विषयः, तथा च स्वाश्रय-विषयकयावद्ग्रहविषय इत्यर्थः, स्वपदं पक्षीभूतघटत्ववतिघटत्वप्रका-रकत्वादिपरं, प्रकृतप्रामाण्यग्रहप्रतिबन्धकाप्रमत्वविरहितत्वेन च ग्रहो विशेषणीयः तेन न सिद्धसाधनं। एवं तृतीयविप्रतिपत्तौ साध्ये यद्यद्विवक्षितं तत्सर्व्वमत्रापि बोध्यं, हेतौ च तदन्तरेत्यत्र तच्छब्देन यावत्त्वाविशेषितस्वाश्रयग्रहस्य परामर्शनीयः(१) 'सन्दिह्यमानत्वञ्च तत्र सन्दिह्यमानत्वं बोध्यं, तेन धर्म्मान्तरसन्दिह्यमाने ज्ञानत्वादौ न व्यभिचारः, अन्यत् सर्व्वं पूर्व्ववदिति। ज्ञानभेदेन प्रामाण्यभेदमते प्रकारान्तरेणानुमानमाह, 'यद्वेति, अत्र झटितिति एतत्पदार्थपरि-चयार्थमनभ्यासदशापन्नेत्यादि विशेषणं न तु व्यावर्त्तकं एतत्पदेनैव विशेषलाभात्। प्रामाण्यानुमित्यात्मकएतज्ज्ञाननिश्चयस्य तदुत्तरं प्रमावानहमित्यादिनिश्चयस्य च विषयत्वाद्बाधवारणाय साध्ये 'कालीनान्तं निश्चयविशेषणं, पूर्व्वकालीनत्वं पूर्व्वतृतीयक्षणवृत्तित्वं, नातो बाधतादवस्थ्यं। 'एतज्ज्ञाननिश्चयानन्तरमिति, तृतीयक्षण

(१) यावत्त्वविशेषितपरामर्शे अप्रसिद्धिरितिभावः।

इति शेषः, नातो ज्ञानत्वादौ व्यभिचारः, 'सन्दिह्यमानत्वादित्यस्य अत्र ज्ञाने इत्यादिः, अन्यथा धर्म्मान्तरसन्दिह्यमानज्ञानत्वादौ व्यभिचारापत्तेः । एवञ्च साध्येऽपि अत्र ज्ञाने इति पूरणीयं, अन्यथा तृतीयक्षणे ज्ञाने सन्दिह्यमानघटत्वादौ व्यभिचारापत्तेरिति दिक् । 'तदाश्रयाग्राह्यत्व इति, साध्ये इति शेषः । 'बाध इति अप्रसिद्धिरित्यर्थः, सर्व्वस्यैव प्रमाविषयत्वादिति भावः । 'समभिव्याहृतेति तथा च पक्षीकृतप्रामाण्यपरमिति भावः(१) । 'अन्यथा' समभिव्याहृतपरत्वाभावे । ननु तत्त्वमेतत्त्वं वा स्वत्वं, तदन्यत्वमेतदन्यत्वं वा परत्वमित्यत आह, 'तदिति, 'स्वग्राह्यत्वे' स्वाश्रयग्राह्यत्वे, 'परिशेषेण' स्वाश्रयाग्राह्यत्वेन, 'अन्यथा ग्राह्यत्वमित्यस्य विवरणं 'परतो ग्राह्यत्वमिति स्वाश्रयातिरिक्तमात्रग्राह्यत्वमित्यर्थः, 'कश्चिदित्यनेनास्वरसो दर्शितः, तद्बीजन्तु पूर्व्वोक्तक्रमेण स्वतोग्राह्यत्वाभावं प्रसाध्य पश्चात्तेनैव हेतुना स्वाश्रयातिरिक्तमात्रग्राह्यत्वरूपं परतो ग्राह्यत्वं साध्यमित्यनुमानद्वयकल्पने गौरवमिति ।

ननु प्रामाण्यस्य स्वतोग्राह्यत्वाभावे प्राथमिकप्रामाण्यग्रहः कथं स्यादित्यतः स्वमते प्रामाण्यज्ञानप्रकारमाह, 'प्रथमस्येति, 'व्यतिरेकिणेति वह्निविशेष्यकज्ञानमिदं वह्नित्वप्रकारानवच्छिन्नं दाहसमर्थविशेष्यकप्रवृत्तिजनकत्वादिति व्यतिरेकिणेत्यर्थः, 'व्याघातरक्षभयेनेति

---

(१) 'समभिव्याहृतेति तथाच पक्षीकृतप्रामाण्यपरमिति भावः' इत्यत्र सम्बन्धिपदत्वेन समभिव्याहृतपदत्वेन समभिव्याहृतपरत्वात् पक्षीकृतप्रामाण्यपरत्वादिति ख० ।

प्रमा नास्तीति शब्दरूपो यः परकीयव्याघातः स एव प्रतिवादिदुः-खहेतुत्वाद्दण्डः तस्य भयेन तस्य प्रतियोगिज्ञानं विनानुपपत्त्येत्यर्थः, तथा च इदं वाक्यं प्रतियोगिज्ञानपूर्व्वकं अभावज्ञानपूर्व्वकत्वात् इत्यनुमानेन प्रतियोगिज्ञानं विना अभावज्ञानासम्भवादिति तर्कसह-कृतेन प्रमासिद्धिरिति भावः। 'तद्विषयेति प्रमासिद्धौ प्रमा सविषया ज्ञानत्वादित्यनुमानात् प्रमाविषयसिद्धिरित्यर्थः, 'तद्दृष्टान्तेनेति सामान्यतः सिद्धप्रमाविषयदृष्टान्तेनेत्यर्थः, 'ज्ञेयत्वादिनेति वह्निर्वि-शेष्यावृत्त्यप्रकारकज्ञानविषयो ज्ञेयत्वादित्यनुमानेनेत्यर्थः। इदञ्च प्रामाण्यविशेषस्योक्तव्यतिरेकिसाध्यस्य प्रसिद्धये, अत्र तल्लाभश्च पक्ष-धर्म्मताबलादित्याकर एवाग्रे स्फुटं। न च व्याघातदण्डभयेन प्रमासिद्धौ वह्निज्ञानं प्रमा समर्थप्रवृत्तिजनकत्वादिति व्यतिरेकिणैव पक्षधर्म्मताबलात् प्रामाण्यविशेषलाभोऽस्तु किमनेनानुमानेनेति वाच्यं। एतस्याप्युपायान्तरत्वादिति भावः। 'सामान्यत इति ज्ञानत्वरूपेण यत्र कुत्रचिद्वह्निज्ञाने इत्यर्थः, 'तत्सिद्धौ' वक्ष्यवृत्तिप्रकारानवच्छिन्न-त्वसिद्धौ, 'न साध्याप्रसिद्धिरिति वह्निविशेष्यकज्ञानमिदं वक्ष्यवृत्ति-प्रकारानवच्छिन्नं दाहसमर्थविषयकप्रवृत्तिजनकत्वादिति व्यतिरेकिणि न साध्याप्रसिद्धिरित्यर्थः। न च पूर्व्वान्वयिनैव पक्षधर्म्मताबलाद्वह्नि-ज्ञानस्य प्रामाण्यविशेषसिद्धौ किमनेन व्यतिरेकिणेति वाच्यं। ज्ञानत्व-रूपेण यत्र कुत्रचिद्वह्निज्ञाने प्रमात्वे ज्ञातेपि प्रवृत्तिजनकवह्निज्ञाने इदं वह्निविशेष्यकं ज्ञानं वक्ष्यवृत्तिप्रकारानवच्छिन्नमित्याकारकस्य निष्कम्पप्रवृत्त्युपयुक्तस्यासिद्धेः, अतएवोक्तं 'सामान्यत इति। 'विशेष्येति हेतुसामानाधिकरण्येन हेत्वभावसामानाधिकरण्येन वा अनिश्चया-

वह्निज्ञानस्य विशेष्याद्वृत्तिप्रकारानवच्छिन्नत्वादिकं साध्यमानं पक्षधर्म्मताबलेन वह्निविषयकप्रमात्वे पर्य्यवस्यतीति चेत् तर्हि प्रथमं कस्यापि स्वार्थं प्रामाण्यानुमानं न स्यात् प्रामाण्यनिषेधरूपस्य परकीयव्याघातस्य तदा अनुपस्थितेः स्वयं प्रामाण्यनिषेधस्य तज्ज्ञोपूर्व्वकत्वात् प्रामाण्यमपरिज्ञाय प्रामाण्यनिषेधेन परकीय-

---

दित्यर्थः[१]। ननु व्यतिरेकिणा वह्न्यवृत्तिप्रकारानवच्छिन्नत्वं साध्यं तच्च न ज्ञेयत्वहेतुकानुमानेन प्रसिद्धं, न हि वह्निः वह्न्यवृत्तिप्रकारानवच्छिन्नज्ञानविषयः ज्ञेयत्वादिति साधनीयं, व्यभिचाराद्व्याघातादपि तादृशसाध्याप्रसिद्धेश्च। सिद्धौ वा किं ज्ञेयत्वहेतुकानुमानेनेत्याशङ्क्य निराकरोति, 'न वेति, 'साध्यं' व्यतिरेकिणा साध्यं, 'तच्चाप्रसिद्धमिति, ज्ञेयत्वहेतुकानुमानेन सामान्यतः प्रमेयत्वस्यैव सिद्धेरिति भावः।

'वह्निज्ञानस्येति वह्नेर्व्विशेष्याद्वृत्तिप्रकारानवच्छिन्नज्ञानविषयत्वं साध्यमानमित्यर्थः, 'वह्निविषयकप्रमात्व इति वह्न्यवृत्तिप्रकारानवच्छिन्नत्व इत्यर्थः। यद्यपीदमयुक्तं ज्ञेयत्वहेतुकानुमानेन पक्षधर्म्मताबलाद्वास्तविकवह्नित्वप्रमासिद्धावपि वह्न्यवृत्तिप्रकारानवच्छिन्नत्वरूपेणासिद्धेः अनुमितेर्व्यापकतावच्छेदकप्रकारकत्वनियमात्तस्यानुपस्थितत्वाच्च उपस्थितौ प्रथमं तदनुमानस्य व्यर्थत्वात्। तथापि स्फुटत्वादिदमुपेक्ष्य दूषणान्तरमाह, 'तर्हीति, ननु परकीयव्याघा-

---

(१) साध्यवन्निष्ठाभावप्रतियोगित्वमसाधारण्यमिति भावः।

व्याघातस्याप्यज्ञानाच्च । प्रवृत्तिसंवाद-विसंवादाभ्यां तद्धेतुज्ञानवैचित्र्यानुमानेऽपि यथोक्तरूपप्रामाण्यस्य विशेष्याप्रतीतेरिति उच्यते । प्राग्भवीयसंस्काराद्विशेष्यावृत्त्यप्रकारकत्वं तद्वति तत्प्रकारकज्ञानत्वं वा प्रामाण्यमात्रं स्मृतं वह्निज्ञानादौ साध्यमानं सर्व्वनाममहिम्ना पक्षधर्म्मताबलाद्वह्निज्ञानस्य विशेष्यावृत्त्यप्रकारकत्वादौ

ज्ञानवत्तायामपि स्वीयप्रामाण्यनिषेधानुपपत्त्यैव प्रामाण्यप्रसिद्धिरिष्टव्येत्यत आह, 'स्वयमिति । ननु प्रामाण्यमज्ञात्वापि प्रामाण्यं निषिध्यतामित्यत आह, 'प्रामाण्यमिति, 'अज्ञानात्' अज्ञापकत्वात्, अपिना स्वीयनिषेधः समुच्चितः । इदमुपलक्षणं परवाक्ये आचाप्रमात्वेन प्रतियोगित्वेन वा प्रमानुमेया आद्ये अप्रसिद्धिः, द्वितीये प्रमात्वप्रकारकव्यतिरेकिण्यनुपयोग इत्यपि द्रष्टव्यं । ननु संवादिप्रवृत्तिर्विसंवादिप्रवृत्तिकारणविचित्रकारणजन्या तद्विलक्षणकार्य्यत्वात् घटवदित्यनुमानादेव पक्षधर्म्मताबलात् प्रामाण्यात्मकं वैचित्र्यं सेत्स्यतीत्यत आह, 'प्रवृत्तीति प्रवृत्तिनिष्ठसंवादित्वप्रकारेणेत्यर्थः, 'तद्धेतुज्ञानेति संवादिप्रवृत्तिहेतुज्ञानेत्यर्थः, 'उक्तरूपप्रामाण्यस्येति, उक्तरूपप्रामाण्यत्वेनेति शेषः, विचित्रत्वेनैव तस्य भानादिति भावः । 'प्राग्भवीयेति जन्मान्तरीयेत्यर्थः, 'सर्व्वनामेति सामान्यतः सर्व्वविषयकस्मरणसहकारेणेत्यर्थः । 'विशेष्यावृत्त्यप्रकारकत्वादौ' वह्न्यवृत्त्यप्रकारकत्वादौ, आदिपदाद्वह्नित्ववति वह्नित्वप्रकारत्वपरिग्रहः, 'स्वतः प्रामाण्येति प्रामाण्यस्य स्वतस्त्वनिषेधे इत्यर्थः, 'सम्प्रदायविद इति, अत्रेदमस्वारसबीजं विशेष्यतया तद्वत्त्वस्य

पर्य्यवस्यति। स्वतः प्रामाण्यनिषेधे प्राथमिकप्रामाण्य-ज्ञानस्यान्यथोपपादयितुमशक्यत्वादिति संप्रदायविदः। वयन्तु ब्रूमः। प्रथममप्रामाण्याभाव एव प्रामाण्यं व्यतिरेकिणा साध्यम् तत एव निष्कम्पप्रवृत्तेरुपपत्तेः, तदेव वा सिध्यत् पक्षधर्म्मताबलेन तद्वति तत्प्रकारकत्वा-दिकमादाय सिध्यति, तदनन्तरं अर्थाद्वा सिध्यतीति

वैकल्याभावात् कथं सामान्यतः स्मरणं। न च विशिष्यैव स्मरणीयं घटत्ववतीत्यादिप्रामाण्यस्य पूर्व्वजन्मन्यप्यनुभवादिति वाच्यं। अपूर्व्व-वैचित्र्यादिज्ञानप्रामाण्ये तथात्वासम्भवादिति। नन्वेतस्य सुग्रहत्वेपि प्रवृ-त्त्यौपयिकं प्रामाण्यं दुर्ग्रहमेवेत्यत आह, 'तत एवेति अप्रामाण्यग्रहा-विधूननस्य ततोपि भावादिति भावः[१]। लाघवात्तद्वतीत्यादिज्ञानं प्रवृत्तिहेतुरिति यो ब्रूयात्तं प्रति तुष्यत्विति[२] न्यायेनाह,'तदेव वेति। ननु पक्षधर्म्मताबलादपि व्यापकतावच्छेदकावच्छिन्नमेव सिध्यति तद्व-तीत्यादिकं तु न तथा अप्रामाण्याभाव-प्रामाण्ययोर्भेदादित्यत आह, 'तदनन्तरमिति 'अर्थात्' व्यतिरेक्यनुमानात्,'अर्थमिति दाहसमर्थवि-शेषक इत्यर्थः, इदन्त्व वह्नित्वभ्रमे अंशतोबाधवारणाय, वह्न्यावद्वह्नित्व-भ्रमे भागासिद्धिवारणाय 'वह्नित्वेनेति, 'अनुभवः' निश्चयात्मकोऽनु-भवः, नातः अनिश्चये भागासिद्धिः, अनुभवत्वघटितत्वाच्च हेतु-पक्ष-तावच्छेदकयोरभेदः। 'तदभाववतीति वह्नित्वाभाववद्विशेष्यकत्वाव-

---

(१) अत्रापि भावादिति भाव इति ख०।

(२) तुष्यतु दुर्ज्जन इति न्यायेनेत्यर्थः।

वक्ष्यते, तथा हि अयं वह्नित्वेनानुभवो वह्नित्वाभाववति[१] वह्नित्वप्रकारको न, अवह्निवृत्तिप्रकारको न, विशेष्यावृत्तिप्रकारको न, वह्नित्वप्रकारकत्वे सति वह्निविशेष्यको न, वह्नित्वव्यधिकरणप्रकारावच्छिन्नो न, वह्न्यवृत्तिप्रकारको न वा दाहसमर्थविषयकप्रयत्नजनकत्वे सति वह्नित्वप्रकारकनिश्चयत्वात् दाहसमर्थविशेष्यक-

च्छिन्नवह्नित्वप्रकारकताश्रयो नेत्यर्थः, 'अवह्नीति अवह्निवृत्तिर्या वह्नित्वप्रकारता तदाश्रयो नेत्यर्थः, वृत्तित्वमच्छेदकतासम्बन्धेन तथा चावह्न्यवच्छिन्नवह्नित्वप्रकारकताश्रयो नेति फलितार्थः। न तु यथाश्रुतं तत् प्रतियोगिनो वह्नित्वभ्रमत्वरूपलाभाभावात् प्रमुष्टतत्ताकवह्नित्वभ्रमाव्याप्तेः इदं जलमित्यादिबुद्धावतिव्याप्तेश्च। किञ्च यथाश्रुते बाध एव स्यात् अवह्निवृत्तिसत्तादेरपि तत्र प्रकारत्वात्। न च विवक्षिते पूर्व्वाभेदः, वह्नित्वात्यन्ताभाव-वह्न्यन्योन्याभावाभ्यां भेदात्। 'विशेष्यावृत्तीति स्वविशेष्यावृत्तीत्यर्थः। ननु स्वविशेष्यावृत्तिप्रकारकत्वं नाप्रामाण्यं वह्नि-गुञ्जयोर्गुञ्जा-वह्नी इति भ्रमे अव्याप्तेः। न च यत्किञ्चित्स्वविशेष्यावृत्तिप्रकारकत्वं वक्तव्यमिति वाच्यं। वह्नि-गुञ्जे इति समूहालम्बनप्रमायामतिव्याप्तेः प्रकृते बाधापत्तेश्च इदन्त्वांशे परिमाणत्वादेरपि प्रकारत्वात्। न च वह्नौ वह्न्यवृत्तिप्रकारकत्वं

(१) 'वह्नित्वाभाववति' इत्यत्र 'तदभाववति' इत्ययं कस्यचिन्मूलपुस्तकस्य पाठः, तादृशं पाठमवलम्ब्य तदभाववतीतीत्यनेन पाठोऽयं मथुरानाथेन।

वह्नित्वप्रकारकनिश्चयत्वाद्वा यन्नैवं तन्नैवं यथा वह्न्यप्रमा । तत्र बाधानन्तरं स्मृत्युपनीते भ्रमे वह्नित्वाभाववति वह्नित्वेन मम ज्ञानं वृत्तमित्यप्रामाण्यं मनसैव परिच्छिद्यते मानान्तरेण वेति सर्व्वसिद्धम्[१] । एवं वह्न्यप्रमायां वह्नित्वाभाववति वह्नित्वप्रकारकत्वादिसमर्थ

विवक्षितमिति वाच्यं । अत्रापि वह्नित्वप्रामाण्याभावानात्मकत्वात् लोहितो वह्निरित्यत्रापि तत्सत्त्वात् वह्नित्वप्रकारकप्रवृत्त्युपयुक्तत्वेन तदभावस्यैव च सिषाधयिषितत्वादिति चेत् । न । वह्न्यवृत्तिर्या वह्नित्वप्रकारिता तद्वत्त्वेत्यर्थः । तदवृत्तिता च इहैतत्प्रकारकं ज्ञानमिति प्रतीतिसिद्धावच्छेदकतासम्बन्धेन बोध्येति दिक् । 'वह्न्यविशेष्यको नेति अवह्निविशेष्यको नेत्यर्थः । न तु यथाश्रुतं, तत्प्रतियोगिनो वह्नित्वाप्रामाण्यानात्मकत्वात् वह्नि-गुञ्जयोर्गुञ्जा-वह्नी इति भ्रमाव्याप्तेः । न च प्रथमाभेदः, विशेषण-विशेष्यभावभेदेन भेदात् । 'वह्नित्वेति वह्नित्वानधिकरणे तत्प्रकारको नेत्यर्थः । न च प्रथमाभेदः, इहाधिकरणत्वाभावप्रवेशात् । 'वह्न्यवृत्तीति वह्न्यवृत्तिर्या वह्नित्वप्रकारता तद्वत्त्वेत्यर्थः । न च तृतीयाभेदः, वृत्तित्वात्यन्ताभाव-तदन्योन्याभावभेदाभ्यां भेदादिति दिक् । 'दाहसमर्थेति दाहसमर्थतेजोविशेष्यकप्रवृत्तिजनकतांशे वह्नित्वप्रकारनिश्चयत्वादित्यर्थः । तेन वह्निगुञ्जयोर्गुञ्जावह्नी इति विपरीतभ्रमे दाहजनकेन्धनविशेष्यक-

---

(१) सर्व्वजनसिद्धमिति ख० ।

प्रवृत्तिजनकत्वाभावयोर्व्याप्तिग्रहेऽप्रामाण्यव्यापकहेत्व-भावाभावरूपाद्धेतोरप्रामाण्याभावरूपं साध्यं सिध्यति। यद्व्यापकतया हेत्वभावो गृहीतस्तदभाव एव हेतुना साध्यते। यत्र त्वभावस्य व्यापकता हेत्वभावस्य ज्ञायते तत्र साध्यप्रसिद्धिरङ्गं तां विना तदज्ञानात्।

वह्नित्वभ्रमे च न व्यभिचारः। न वा चन्द्रादितेजोविशेष्यकवह्नित्वभ्रमे व्यभिचारः। अत्र तादृशप्रयत्नफलोपधानं न सार्व्वत्रिकं दुर्ज्ञेयञ्च, अगृहीतप्रयत्नज्ञानकार्य्यकारणभावे तत्स्वरूपयोग्यत्वमपि स्वरूपयो-ग्यतावच्छेदकापरिचये दुर्ज्ञेयं गुरुतरञ्चेत्यतस्तदुपेक्ष्य हेत्वन्तरमाह, 'दाहसमर्थेति, अत्र प्रथमे साध्ये दाहसमर्थविशेष्यकत्वावच्छिन्नवह्नित्व-प्रकारताकनिश्चयत्वादित्यर्थः, तेन वह्नि-गुञ्जयोर्गुञ्जा-वह्नी इति ज्ञाने न व्यभिचारः। वह्न्यवह्न्योर्वह्नित्वज्ञाने व्यभिचारवारणाय 'निश्चयेति निश्चयत्वञ्च दाहसमर्थासमर्थयोर्व्वह्नित्वप्रकारकान्यत्वमिति। एवं द्वि-तीयसाध्येऽपि। तृतीये च निश्चयत्वं नोपादेयं व्यर्थत्वात्। एवं षष्ठेऽपि। चतुर्थ-पञ्चमयोस्तु प्रथमवदित्यलं विस्तरेणेति। 'यदेवं नन्वेवमित्येव पाठः, वह्नित्वाभाववति वह्नित्वप्रकारकत्वरूपप्रतियोगि-हेत्वभावयोरेव व्याप्तेरत्राभिमतत्वात् 'यन्वेवमिति पाठस्तु प्रामादिकः, साध्याप्रसिद्धौ तदभावाप्रसिद्धेरिति ध्येयं।

ननु प्रामाण्यवदप्रामाण्यमपि प्रथमतो दुर्ज्ञेयमिति कथं तदभा-वोऽनुमेय इत्यत आह, 'तत्रेति 'तत्र' अप्रमायां, 'परिच्छिद्यते' इत्यन्वयः। 'बाधावतारेति विषयबाधनिश्चयानन्तरमित्यर्थः। 'सत्यु-

यत्र तु भावव्यापकता हेत्वभावस्य तत्र न तदङ्गं, तेन विनापि व्यतिरेकव्याप्तेर्ग्रहात् । अतएवेतरव्यापकता आकाशत्वाभावस्य गृहीतेत्याकाशत्वेनाप्रसिद्ध एवेतरान्योन्याभावः सिध्यति। विशेषणज्ञानं विना कथं प्रामाण्यविशिष्टानुमितिरिति चेत्, प्रथमं न कथञ्चित् ।

पनीत इति भ्रमे स्मृत्युपनीते सतीत्यर्थः । यत्र च मनसा न तज्ज्ञानं तत्राप्यनुमानादेव तज्ज्ञानमित्याह, 'मानान्तरेण वेति । न चाप्रामाण्याप्रसिद्धौ कथमनुमानात् तद्ग्रह इति वाच्यं । वह्नित्वप्रकारकत्वेन ज्ञानं पक्षीकृत्य वह्नित्वाभाववद्विशेष्यक प्रवृत्तिजनकत्वहेतुना वह्नित्वाभाववद्विशेष्यकत्वसाधने अर्थादप्रामाण्यसिद्धेरिति भावः । 'सर्व्वसिद्धमिति, अप्रामाण्यस्य परतस्त्वे मीमांसकस्याप्यविवादादिति भावः । 'वह्नित्वप्रकारकत्वादीति प्रकृतसाध्याभावरूपेत्यर्थः । 'यद्व्यापकतयेति यत इत्यादिः । नन्वप्रामाण्याप्रसिद्धावपि तदभावरूपसाध्याप्रसिद्ध्या कथं व्याप्तिग्रह इत्यत आह, 'यत्र त्वभावेति भावभिन्नसाध्याभावेत्यर्थः, 'तां विनेति प्रतियोगिनः साध्यस्य ज्ञानं विना तदभावज्ञानासम्भवादिति भावः। 'भावव्यापकतेति भावरूपसाध्याभावेत्यर्थः। 'तेन विनापीति, भावग्रहे प्रतियोगिज्ञानानुपयोगादितिभावः । 'इतरेति आकाशेतरेत्यर्थः, तादात्म्यसम्बन्धेनेति भावः । 'इतरान्योन्याभावः' आकाशेतरान्योन्याभावः, पृथिवीत्वादिहेतुस्थले प्रत्यक्षेणापि साध्यप्रसिद्धिसम्भवादाकाशत्वेनेत्युक्तं, 'प्रामाण्य-

ज्ञाने प्रामाण्यमित्यनुमित्यनन्तरं तेनैव हेतुना तत्रैव प्रामाण्यविशिष्टानुमितिः अभावविशेष्यकप्रतीत्यनन्तरमभाववद्भूतलमिति ज्ञानवत् । एवञ्चेदं वह्नित्वप्रकारकज्ञानं तद्वति तदभाववति वेति संशयानन्तरं तदभाववति तत्प्रकारकत्वव्यतिरेकः सिध्यन् तद्वति तत्प्रकारकतामादाय सिध्यति, तृतीयप्रकाराभावेन तेन विना साध्यस्योपसंहर्त्तुमशक्यत्वात् ज्ञाननित्यत्ववत् ।

विशिष्टानुमितिः' अप्रामाण्याभावविशिष्टानुमितिः, 'न कथञ्चित् प्रथममित्यनन्तरं छेदः, 'प्रामाण्यं' अप्रामाण्याभावः, 'अनुमित्यनन्तरं' साध्यविशेष्यकानुमित्यनन्तरं, 'तेनैव हेतुनेति पूर्व्वोक्तेनैव हेतुनेत्यर्थः, 'तत्रैव' ज्ञाने, 'प्रामाण्यविशिष्टेति अप्रामाण्याभावविशिष्टानुमितिरित्यर्थः, समानप्रकारकसिद्धेरजातत्वात् न सिद्धसाधनमिति भावः । 'तदेव वा सिद्धेरित्युक्तमुपपादयति, 'एवञ्चेति, 'तद्वतीति तद्वद्विशेष्यकं तदभाववद्विशेष्यकं वेत्यर्थः, 'उपसंहर्त्तुं' ज्ञातुं, 'ज्ञाननित्यत्ववदिति यथा क्षितिर्ज्ञानजन्या कार्य्यत्वादितीश्वरानुमानेऽनित्यज्ञानबाधेन ज्ञानस्य नित्यत्वसिद्धिवदित्यर्थः ।

नन्विदमयुक्तं इदं वह्नित्वप्रकारकज्ञानं न वह्नित्वाभाववति वह्नित्वप्रकारकमित्यनुमितेर्वह्नित्ववति वह्नित्वप्रकारकत्वमविषयीकृत्यापि सम्भवति, किञ्च पक्षधर्म्मताबलादपि व्यापकतावच्छेदकावच्छिन्नं पूर्व्वोपस्थितमेव सिद्ध्यति तद्वतीत्यादिप्रामाण्यन्तु नाप्रामाण्याभावत्वावच्छिन्नं न वा तेन रूपेण पूर्व्वोपस्थितमित्यस्वरसादाह, 'यद्वेति, 'दृढ' दाह-

यद्वा इदं वह्नित्वप्रकारकज्ञानं वह्नित्ववद्विषयकं वह्नित्वाभाववद्विषयकत्वे सति सविषयकत्वात् यन्नैवं तन्नैवं यथा वह्न्यप्रमेति व्यतिरेक्यन्तरात्तत्सिद्धिः(१)। अतिरिक्तविषयतापक्षे अयं वह्नित्वेनानुभवोऽवह्निरत्ति-

---

समर्थविशेष्यकं, 'वह्नित्ववद्विषयकं' वह्नित्ववद्विशेष्यकं, 'वह्नित्वाभाववदिति, वह्नित्वाभाववदविशेष्यकत्वे सति सविशेष्यकत्वादित्यर्थः, तेन वह्नित्वाभाववतो वह्नित्वादेर्व्विषयत्वेपि नासिद्धिः, न वा निर्व्विकल्पके व्यभिचारः। नचात्र सत्यन्तदलमेवासिद्धं पूर्व्वोक्तानुमानाद्वह्नित्वाभाववति वह्नित्वप्रकारकत्वाभावरूपस्य विशिष्टाभावस्य सिद्धावपि वह्नित्वाभाववद्विशेष्यकत्वाभावासिद्धिरिति वाच्यम्। पूर्व्वोक्तविशिष्टाभावानुमानानन्तरं वह्नित्वप्रकारकत्वे सतीति सत्यन्तदलसहकृतेन तेनैव हेतुना वह्नित्वाभाववद्विशेष्यकत्वाभावस्यापि सिद्धेः। सविशेष्यकत्वस्यानुव्यवसायादेव सिद्धं विशेष्यत्वादेरनुपस्थितस्यापि प्रकारतया प्रथमानुव्यवसायेपि तज्ज्ञाने बाधकाभावात् प्रथमानुव्यवसाये सविशेष्यकत्वस्य निर्व्विकल्पकोपस्थित्या द्वितीयानुव्यवसाये तस्य प्रकारतया भानसम्भवाच्च। न च तथापि वह्नित्ववद्विशेष्यकत्वं साध्यमप्रसिद्धमिति वाच्यं। विशिष्टप्रामाण्यस्यैवानुव्यवसायाग्राह्यतया केवलवह्नित्ववद्विशेष्यकत्वस्याप्यनुव्यवसायेन ग्रहे बाधकाभावात्। नचैवमनुमानवैयर्थ्यमिति वाच्यं। वह्नित्वप्रकारकत्वावच्छिन्नवह्नित्ववद्विशेष्यकत्वरूपविशिष्टप्रामाण्यसिद्ध्यर्थमनुमानस्यावश्यकत्वात्। नचैतदनुमानादपि न विशिष्ट-

---

(१) व्यतिरेक्यन्तरेण तत्सिद्धिरिति ग०।

वह्नित्वप्रकारकविषयताको न, वह्नित्वासमानाधिकरणवह्नित्वप्रकारकविषयताको न, विषयताश्रयावृत्तिप्रकारको न वेति साध्यं, वह्निवृत्तिवह्नित्वप्रकारकविषयताकत्वं विषयताश्रयवृत्तिप्रकारकत्वं वा अर्थात् सिध्यति न तु प्रथमं, साध्याप्रसिद्धेः वह्निभ्रमे च विषयताश्रयो न वह्निः विषयताया विशेष्यवृत्तित्वादिति भ्रमत्वेन न सिद्धसाधनम्।

अन्ये तु वह्निभ्रमे[१] या विशेषणवृत्तिर्विषयता सा

प्रामाण्यसिद्धिः वह्नित्ववद्विशेष्यकत्वस्यैव साध्यत्वादिति वाच्यम्। वह्नित्वप्रकारकत्वस्य पक्षतावच्छेदकतया तदवच्छिन्नतया वह्नित्ववद्विशेष्यकत्वसिद्ध्या वह्नित्वप्रकारकत्वावच्छिन्नवह्नित्ववद्विशेष्यकत्वरूपप्रामाण्यसिद्धेः। न च पक्षतावच्छेदकस्य स्वरूपसम्बन्धरूपावच्छेदकताया अनुमितिविषयत्वे मानाभावः व्यापकत्वरूपस्यैवावच्छेदकत्वस्य तद्विषयत्वोपगमादिति वाच्यम्। अस्ति बाधनिश्चये स्वरूपसम्बन्धरूपावच्छिन्नतासम्बन्धेन पक्षतावच्छेदकस्यापि साध्ये प्रकारीभूय भानाभ्युपगमात्। अन्यथा मूलावच्छिन्नो वृक्षः कपिसंयोगी गन्धप्रागभावकालावच्छिन्नो घटो गन्धवानित्याद्यनुमितेर्भ्रमत्वानुपपत्तेरिति भावः।

अन्ये तु वह्नित्वप्रकारकत्वमेव पक्षीकृत्यावच्छिन्नतासम्बन्धेन

---

(१) वह्नित्वभ्रम इति ख० ग० च।

विशेष्यवृत्तिविषयताया अभिन्नेति न सा वह्नित्वास-मानाधिकरणधर्म्मानवच्छिन्नेति न सिद्धसाधनमिति।

वह्नित्ववद्विशेष्यकत्वं साधनीयं हेतुश्च दाहसमर्थविशेष्यकत्वावच्छिन्न-वह्नित्वप्रकारितात्वं, वह्नित्वभ्रमस्य वह्नित्वप्रकारित्वं व्यतिरेके दृष्टान्तः, तदनन्तरञ्च इदं वह्निज्ञानं वह्नित्ववद्विशेष्यकत्वावच्छिन्न-वह्नित्व-प्रकारकत्ववत् दाहसमर्थवह्नित्वप्रकारकत्वात् यन्नैवं तन्नैवं यथा वह्नित्वभ्रम इति ज्ञानविशेष्यकप्रामाण्यज्ञानमित्याहुः।

'अतिरिक्तविषयतापक्ष' इति विषयता विशेष्यवृत्तिरतिरिक्तः पदार्थः सैव च सप्रकारिका सविशेष्यिका च न तु ज्ञानं सविशेष्यकं सप्रकारकं वेति मत इत्यर्थः। 'अयमिति दाहसमर्थवृत्तिर्या वह्नि-त्वप्रकारकविषयता तन्निरूपकोऽनुभव इत्यर्थः, वह्नित्वभ्रमेऽंशतो बाधवारणाय वृत्त्यन्तं विषयताविशेषणं, वह्न्यावह्निभ्रमे भागासिद्धि-वारणाय 'वह्नित्वप्रकारकेति तद्विशेषणमिति भावः। 'अवह्नीति, वह्नि-भिन्नवृत्तिर्या वह्नित्वप्रकारकविषयता तन्निरूपकेणेत्यर्थः, वह्नि-गुञ्जे इति प्रमायां व्यभिचारवारणाय 'वह्नित्वप्रकारकेति विषयताविशेषणं, हेतुश्च दाहसमर्थवृत्तिवह्नित्वप्रकारकविषयताकनिश्चयत्वं निश्चयत्वञ्च दाहसमर्थासमर्थोभयवृत्तिवह्नित्वप्रकारकविषयताकान्यत्वं तेन वह्न्य-वह्न्योर्व्वह्नित्वज्ञाने न व्यभिचारः। पक्षेप्यनुभवपदमेतादृशनिश्चयपरं तेन तादृशवह्नित्वज्ञाने न भागासिद्धि-बाधौ।

केचित्तु दाहासमर्थवृत्तिवह्नित्वप्रकारकविषयताकान्यत्वं हेतुरि-त्याहुः। तदसत् पक्षे वह्नित्वप्रकारत्वपदवैयर्थ्यापत्तेः।

द्वितीयसाध्यमाह, 'वह्नित्वासमानाधिकरणेति वह्न्यवृत्तीत्यर्थः, हेतुस्तूक्त एव। तृतीयसाध्यमाह, 'विषयताश्रयेति स्वाधिकरणावृत्तिवह्नित्वप्रकारकविषयताको नेत्यर्थः, बाधवारणाय स्वाधिकरणावृत्तीति वह्नित्वविशेषणं स्वं विषयता, हेतुस्तु पूर्व्ववत्। नन्वेतावता भ्रमत्वाभावसिद्धावपि न भावरूपप्रामाण्यसिद्धिरित्यत आह, 'वह्नि-वृत्तीति, 'विषयताश्रयेति स्वाधिकरणवृत्तिप्रकारकविषयताकत्वमित्यर्थः, 'अर्थादिति, इयं वह्नित्वप्रकारकविषयता वह्निवृत्तिः दाहसमर्थविशेष्यकवह्नित्वप्रकारकविषयतात्वात् इयं विषयता स्वाधिकरणवृत्तिप्रकारिका दाहसमर्थविशेष्यकवह्नित्वप्रकारकविषयतात्वात् यन्नैवं तन्नैवं यथा वह्नित्वभ्रमे वह्नित्वप्रकारकविषयतेति क्रमेण खण्डशः प्रसिद्ध्या व्यतिरेक्यनन्तरमिदं ज्ञानं वह्निवृत्तिवह्नित्वप्रकारकविषयताकं स्वाधिकरणवृत्तिप्रकारकविषयताकं वा दाहसमर्थवृत्तिवह्नित्वप्रकारकविषयताकत्वात् यन्नैवं तन्नैवं यथा वह्नित्वभ्रम इति व्यतिरेक्यन्तरादित्यर्थः, 'साध्याप्रसिद्धेरिति विशिष्टस्य प्रामाण्यस्याप्रसिद्धेरित्यर्थः। ननु यथोक्तपक्षतावच्छेदकस्य वह्नेस्तादात्म्यारोपसाधारणत्वात् तन्नाभावसाध्यकानुमाने द्वितीयसाध्ये अंशतः सिद्धसाधनं तत्र वह्नित्वप्रकारकविषयताया विशेषणीभूतवह्निवृत्तित्वेन वह्नित्वसमानाधिकरणत्वात् प्राचीननये पक्षतावच्छेदकावच्छेदेन साध्यसिद्धेरुद्देश्यत्वेऽप्यंशतः सिद्धसाधनस्य दोषत्वादित्यत आह, 'वह्नित्वभ्रमे चेति वह्नेस्तादात्म्यारोपे चेत्यर्थः, 'विशेष्यवृत्तित्वादिति, मुख्यविशेष्यमात्रवृत्तित्वादित्यर्थः, 'भ्रमत्वेनेति वैशिष्ट्यं तृतीयार्थः, न भ्रमत्वविशिष्टे सिद्धसाधनमित्यर्थः, तस्य यथोक्तपक्षतावच्छेदकाना-

न च मणिज्ञानस्य प्रामाण्यानुमाने मणिप्रभायां मणिभ्रमेण प्रवृत्तस्य मणिप्राप्तौ मणिगोचरप्रयत्नजनकमणित्वप्रकारकनिश्चयत्वमनैकान्तिकमिति वाच्यम्। मणिप्रभाविषयज्ञानेन भिन्नविषयतया मणिगोचरप्रयत्नानुत्पादात्। मणिप्राप्तिस्तु नान्तरीयकत्वात्। ज्ञान-

---

कान्तत्वादिति भावः। इदमुपलक्षणं अप्रसिद्धसाध्यकत्वादेव नांशतः सिद्धसाधनावकाश इत्यपि बोध्यम्।

केचित्तु[१] विशेष्यताया मुख्यविशेष्यमात्रवृत्तित्वेन साध्याभावसत्त्वान्नांशतः सिद्धसाधनमिति मणिकृतो निगर्व इत्याहुः। तदसत् विशेषणे तादृशविषयताविरहे तदंश एव तादृशविषयताकत्वविरहसत्त्वेन साध्यसत्त्वसम्भवात्।

'वह्निभ्रम इति वह्नितादात्म्यारोपे इत्यर्थः, 'अभिप्रैतीति मतेपीति शेषः। 'न चेति, तथा च वह्नित्वासमानाधिकरणधर्म्मावच्छिन्नवह्नित्वप्रकारकविषयताको नेत्येव साध्यमितिभावः। अवच्छिन्नत्वञ्च सामानाधिकरण्यं। अत्रेदमस्वरसवीजं, एवं सति बाधः स्यात् वह्नित्वप्रमायामपि तादृशविषयताया वह्नित्ववृत्तितया वह्नित्वसमानाधिकरणवह्नित्वत्वावच्छिन्नत्वात्। 'न च मणिज्ञानस्येति, 'प्रामाण्यानुमाने' मणिगोचरप्रयत्नजनकत्वे सति मणित्वप्रकारकनिश्चयत्वेन हेतुना प्रामाण्यानुमाने, 'मणिप्राप्तौ' मणिप्राप्तिस्थले, 'अनैकान्तिकमिति मणिप्रभायां मणित्वभ्रमेऽनैकान्तिकमित्यर्थः। 'नान्तरीयकत्वादिति

---

(१) केचित्त्वित्यादिपाठः ख-ग-पुस्तके नास्ति।

प्रयत्नयोरसमानकालत्वेप्यनुभवस्मरणयोरिव मनसा कार्य्यकारणभावग्रह इति नासिद्धिः। अभावसाध्यके च निर्व्विकल्पकस्य प्रथमं सपक्षत्वेनानिश्चयान्नासाधारण्यं। तथायं पृथिवीत्यनुभवः पृथिवीत्वाभाववति

मणिप्रभाधिकरणे देशे मणेरप्यवश्यं सत्त्वादित्यर्थः। यद्यप्येवमपि मणिर्मणिजनक इति मणित्वप्रकारकप्रभाजनकताज्ञानाद्यत्र मणौ प्रवृत्तिस्तत्र तज्ज्ञाने व्यभिचारः। तथापि निश्चयपदेन मण्यमण्युभय-विशेष्यकमणित्वप्रकारकज्ञानान्यज्ञानस्य विवक्षितत्वादेव न तत्र व्यभि-चार इति भावः। ननु ज्ञान-प्रयत्नयोर्युगपदनवस्थानाद्युगपत् सन्नि-कर्षासम्भवेन तयोः कार्य्य-कारणभावग्रहासम्भवादज्ञानासिद्धो हेतु-रित्यत आह,'ज्ञान-प्रयत्नयोरिति, 'मनसेति, ज्ञान-प्रयत्नयोरुपनय-लक्षणसन्निकर्षसहकारादिति शेषः। न च प्रयत्नोपधायकज्ञानव्यक्तेः कदाचिदप्यग्रहात् कथं तदुपनय इति वाच्यं। ज्ञानत्वसामान्यलक्षण-प्रत्यासत्त्या अनुमानेन वा फलोपधायकज्ञानव्यक्तेरपि ग्रहसम्भवात् फलोपधायकव्यक्तेर्ज्ञानाभावेपि क्षतिविरहाच्च। सर्व्वत्रानुपधायकज्ञानं स्मारं स्मारमेव कार्य्य-कारणभावग्रहसम्भवात्तस्यापि स्वरूपयोग्य-त्वात् स्वरूपयोग्यतायास्च ग्राह्यत्वादिति भावः। 'अभावसाध्यके चेति अप्रामाण्याभावरूपप्रामाण्यसाध्यके चेत्यर्थः। 'निर्व्विकल्पकस्य' सप्र-कारकभिन्नस्य निष्प्रकारकज्ञान-घटादेरिति यावत्, 'सपक्षत्वेना-निश्चयादिति साध्याप्रसिद्धा साध्यवत्त्वेनानिश्चयादित्यर्थः। वह्नि-ज्ञानस्य प्रामाण्यानुमानप्रकारमभिधाय पृथिवीज्ञानस्य प्रामाण्यानु-

पृथिवीत्वप्रकारको न, अपृथिवीवृत्तिप्रकारको न, विशे-ष्यावृत्तिप्रकारको न, पृथिवीत्वप्रकारकत्वे सति पृथिव्य-विशेष्यको न, पृथिवीत्वव्यधिकरणप्रकारावच्छिन्नो न, पृथिव्यवृत्तिप्रकारको न वा[१] गन्धवद्विशेष्यकपृथिवी-त्वप्रकारकनिश्चयत्वादिति व्यतिरेकी। पृथिवीत्वभ्रमः पृथिवीत्वाभाववति पृथिवीत्वप्रकारक इति न भ्रमत्वेन सिद्धसाधनं, न वा गन्धवद्विशेष्यक इति न व्यभि-चारः। पृथिवीत्ववति पृथिवीत्वप्रकारकत्वादिकम-

---

मानप्रकारमाह, 'तथेति, 'अयमिति गन्धवद्विशेष्यक इत्यर्थः, प्रत्ये-कदलप्रयोजनन्तु पूर्ववत्। 'अपृथिवीवृत्तीति अपृथिवीवृत्तिर्या पृथि-वीत्वप्रकारकता तदाश्रयो न वृत्तित्वावच्छेदकतासम्बन्धेन पृथिव्यन्या-वच्छिन्नपृथिवीत्वप्रकारकताश्रयो नेति यावत्। 'विशेष्यावृत्तीति पृथिव्यवृत्तिर्या पृथिवीत्वप्रकारकता तद्वानित्यर्थः, पृथिव्यवृत्तित्वं पृथिव्यनवच्छिन्नत्वं। 'पृथिव्यविशेष्यक इति पृथिवीभिन्नविशेष्यक इत्यर्थः, विशेषण-विशेष्यभावभेदेन प्रथमतो भेदः। 'पृथिवीत्वव्यधि-करणेति पृथिवीत्वानधिकरणे पृथिवीत्वप्रकारको नेत्यर्थः, अधि-करणत्वाभावप्रवेशान्न प्रथमाभेदः। 'पृथिव्यवृत्तीति पृथिव्यवृत्तिर्या पृथिवीत्वप्रकारकता तद्वानित्यर्थः, पृथिव्यवृत्तित्वं पृथिव्यनवच्छिन्नत्वं।

---

(१) पृथिवीत्वाभाववति न पृथिवीत्वप्रकारकः, नापृथिवीवृत्तिप्रकारकः, न विशेष्यावृत्तिप्रकारकः, न पृथिवीत्वप्रकारकत्वे सति पृथिव्य-विशेष्यकः, न पृथिवीत्वव्यधिकरणप्रकारावच्छिन्नः, न पृथिव्यवृत्ति-प्रकारको वेति ग०।

र्थात् सिध्यति। विषयतापक्षे[१] अयं पृथिवीत्वेनानुभवः अपृथिवीवृत्तिपृथिवीत्वप्रकारकविषयताको न, पृथिव्यवृत्तिपृथिवीत्वप्रकारकविषयताको न, पृथिवीत्वासमानाधिकरणपृथिवीत्वप्रकारकविषयताको न, विषयताश्रयावृत्ति प्रकारको न वेति साध्यं। पृथिवीत्वसमानाधिकरणपृथिवीत्वप्रकारकविषयताकत्वादिकं[२] अर्थात् सिध्यति।

न च तृतीयाभेदः, अवच्छिन्नत्वात्यन्ताभाव-तद्वदन्योन्याभावभेदाभ्यां भेदादिति दिक्। व्याख्याबीजन्तु वह्निज्ञानप्रामाण्यानुमानवद्बोध्यं। ननु पृथिवीत्वाभाववति पृथिवीत्वप्रकारकत्वाभावस्य साध्यस्य पृथिवीत्वभ्रमेपि सत्त्वात् कुतः प्रामाण्यरूपत्वमित्यत आह, 'पृथिवीत्वभ्रम इति, 'भ्रमत्वेनेति वैशिष्ट्यं तृतीयार्थः पृथिवीत्वभ्रमत्वविशिष्ट इत्यर्थः, 'सिद्धसाधनं' साध्यसत्त्वं। नन्वेवं तत्रैव व्यभिचारः इत्यत आह, 'न वेति, पृथिवीत्वभ्रम इत्यनुषज्यते, 'अर्थादिति अयं पृथिवीत्वप्रकारकोऽनुभवः पृथिवीत्ववद्विशेष्यकः पृथिवीत्वाभाववदविशेष्यकत्वे सति सविशेष्यकत्वात् यन्नैवं तन्नैवं यथा पृथिवीत्वाप्रमेति व्यतिरेक्यन्तरादित्यर्थः। 'विषयतापक्षे इति अतिरिक्तविषयताया एव सप्रकारकत्वादिमत इत्यर्थः, 'अयं पृथिवीत्वेनेत्यादिसर्व्वं, पूर्व्वोक्तक्रमेण वह्निज्ञानत्ववद्बोध्यं, हेतुश्चात्र गन्धवद्वृत्तिपृथिवीत्वप्रकारकविषयताकनिश्चयत्वं।

---

(१) अतिरिक्तविषयतापक्षे इति ग०।
(२) पृथिवीवृत्तिपृथिवीत्वप्रकारकविषयताकत्वमिति ख०।

अन्ये तु पृथिवीत्वासमानाधिकरणप्रकारावच्छिन्न-विषयताकत्वाभावः साध्यः गन्धासमानाधिकरणप्रकारकगन्धसमानाधिकरणप्रकारकविषयताप्रतियोगिज्ञानत्वात् । तेन संशयव्यवच्छेदः । निश्चयत्वं वा विवक्षितमित्याहुः ।

शीता पृथिवीत्यनुभवः पृथिव्यंशे प्रमैव, भ्रम-प्रमारूपे च समूहालम्बने न व्यभिचारः अंशे तस्यापि प्रमात्वात् विशेष्यभेदेन विषयताभेदाच्च । न च प्रकारभेदेन विषयताभेदः, मानाभावात् ।

'अन्ये त्विति, 'पृथिवीत्वासमानाधिकरणः' पृथिव्यवृत्तिः, यः 'प्रकारः' योधर्म्मः, तदवच्छिन्नविषयताकान्यत्वमित्यर्थः, तदवच्छिन्नत्वञ्च न तत्प्रकारकत्वं प्रमुष्टतत्ताकभ्रमसाधारण्यप्रसङ्गात् प्रमामात्रवृत्ति-धर्म्मस्यैव बाधे सिषाधयिषितत्वात् हेतौ गन्धसमानाधिकरणपदवैयर्थ्य-प्रसङ्गाच्च, अपि तु तत्सामानाधिकरण्यं, तथा च पृथिव्यवृत्तिधर्म्म-समानाधिकरणविषयताकान्यत्वं साध्यं पर्य्यवसितं । न चैवं पृथिवीत्व-प्रमायां बाधः विशेषणेऽपि विषयताङ्गीकारात् तद्विषयताया अपि पृथिव्यवृत्तिपृथिवीत्वत्वसमानाधिकरणत्वादिति वाच्यं । विशेष्यताया मुख्यविशेष्यमात्रवृत्तित्वात् अस्यैव वाच्यात्पृथिवीजलत्वात् । हेतौ च इदन्त्वावच्छेदेन पृथिवीत्वभ्रमे जलादिधर्म्मिकपृथिवीत्वसंशये च व्यभिचारवारणाय 'गन्धासमानाधिकरणप्रकारके'ति तदर्थश्च गन्धवदवृत्त्यप्रकारकत्वं, तेन गगने गगनत्वमित्याद्यवृत्तिप्रकारकज्ञाने न

यत्त्वियं पृथिवीत्यनुभवः पृथिवीत्वसमानाधिकरण-धर्म्मावच्छिन्नपृथिवीविशेष्यकविषयताकः[(१)], पृथिवीत्व-व्यधिकरणधर्म्मानवच्छिन्नपृथिवीविशेष्यकविषयताकः, पृथिव्यवृत्तिधर्म्मानवच्छिन्नपृथिवीवृत्तिविषयताको वा, गन्धासमानाधिकरणधर्म्माप्रकारकविषयताप्रतियोगि-ज्ञानत्वात्, अगन्धवदवृत्ति पृथिवीत्वप्रकारकविषय-ताकत्वात्, गन्धसमानाधिकरणविषयताप्रतियोगिज्ञा-नत्वाद्वेति। तन्न। साध्याप्रसिद्धेः। किन्त्वर्थादेव तत् सिध्यति। एवं यत्प्रकारव्याप्यतया यद्गन्धस्तेष्टसमर्थ-प्रवृत्तिजनकत्वकरचरणादिकमवगतं तद्वति तत्प्रकारक-

---

व्यभिचारः, जलादिनिर्व्विकल्पके प्रमुष्टतत्ताकपृथिवीत्वभ्रमे च व्यभि-चारवारणाय 'गन्धसमानाधिकरणप्रकारकेति सविधेयकार्थकं, प्रमुष्ट-तत्ताकभ्रमे च पृथिवीत्वं न विधेयं, विषयता च स्वातिरिक्तवृत्ति-धर्म्मानवच्छिन्नविशेष्यताकत्वेन स्वातिरिक्तवृत्तिधर्म्मानवच्छिन्नत्वेन वा विशेषणीया तेन द्रव्यं पृथिवी गन्धवती पृथिवीत्यादौ द्रव्यत्व-गन्ध-वत्त्वरूपेण जलादौ पृथिवीत्वभ्रमे न व्यभिचारः। गन्धवन्मात्रविशेष्यक-ज्ञानस्य पक्षत्वाभ्युपगमे तो बाध-भागासिद्धी इति भावः। 'तेनेति गन्धासमानाधिकरणाप्रकारकत्वविशेषणेनेत्यर्थः, 'संशयव्यवच्छेद इति जलादिधर्म्मिकपृथिवीत्वसंशयव्यवच्छेद इत्यर्थः। इदमुपलक्षणं इदं

---

(१) पृथिवीत्वसमानाधिकरणधर्म्मप्रकारकपृथिवीविशेष्यकविषयिताक इति ख०, ग०।

ज्ञानत्वमेव प्रामाण्ये लिङ्गम्। ननु वह्निज्ञानस्य दाहसमर्थंपिषयत्वं न दाहसमर्थोऽयमितिव्यवसायगम्यं ज्ञानविषयतयोस्तदविषयत्वात्। नापि तदनुव्यवसायगम्यं पुरोवर्त्तिदाहसामर्थ्यस्य तदगोचरत्वात्। व्यवसायोपनीतदाहसामर्थ्यस्य च भाने तदसामर्थ्यात्। अन्यथा व्यवसायोपनीतस्य पुरोवर्त्तिनि वह्नित्वस्य अनुव्यवसायविषयत्वे स्वतः प्रामाण्यग्रहापत्तेः। एवं पृथिवी-

---

पृथिवीति भ्रमे च न व्यभिचार इत्यपि बोध्यं। लाघवादाह, 'निश्चयत्वं वेति अप्रकारान्तं विशेषणं विहाय निश्चयत्वं वा विवक्षितमित्यर्थः। निश्चयत्वञ्च पृथिवीत्वविरुद्धाप्रकारकत्वं पृथिव्यवृत्त्यप्रकारकत्वमिति यावत्, तेनेदं जलमित्यादिप्रमायामिदन्त्वावच्छेदेन पृथिवीत्वभ्रमे च न व्यभिचारः। विषयता च पूर्व्वोक्तविशेषणेन विशेषणीया तेन गन्धवत्त्वादिरूपेण जलादौ पृथिवीत्वभ्रमे न व्यभिचार इति भावः।

ननु भवन्मते पृथिवीभिन्नवृत्तिपृथिवीत्वप्रकारकविषयताकत्वाभावस्य प्रथमसाध्यस्य प्रमात्वरूपत्वे शीता पृथिवीतिभ्रमस्यापि प्रमात्वापत्तिरित्यत आह, 'शीतेति। नन्वेकदेशिप्रयोगे पाथः-पृथिव्योः पाथसि प्रमुष्टतत्ताकं पृथिव्यंशे च इदन्त्वावच्छेदेन पृथिवीत्वप्रकारकं यज्ज्ञानं प्रमा-भ्रमरूपं तत्र व्यभिचारइत्यत आह, 'प्रमा-भ्रमेति, 'अंशे' पृथिव्यंशे, 'प्रमात्वादिति पृथिव्यवृत्तिधर्म्मासमानाधिकरणत्व-

जलज्ञानयोर्गन्ध-स्नेहवद्विषयकत्वग्रहोऽप्यनुपपन्न इति। उच्यते। वह्नित्वप्रकारकानुव्यवसाये सति तत्र विषये दाहसामर्थ्यज्ञानानन्तरं स्मृत्युपनीते वह्निव्यवसाये स्मृत्युपनीतदाहसमर्थ्यविषयकत्वम्। एवं जल-पृथिवी-ज्ञानयोः स्मृत्युपनीतयोः ज्ञानोपनीत-स्नेहगन्धवद्विषयकत्वं

षयताकत्वाभावादित्यर्थः। ननु तादृशसमूहालम्बनभ्रमस्य पृथिवी-जलवृत्तिरेकैव विषयता प्रकारभेदेनैव विषयताभेदात् तथा च कथं पृथिव्यंशे तादृशविषयताभाववत्त्वमित्यत आह, 'विशेष्यभेदेनेति, अग्रिमचकारोऽत्र योजनीयः स च अप्यर्थः, तथा च विशेष्यभेदेनापि विषयताभेदादित्यर्थः, 'न च' न तु, 'प्रकारभेदेन' प्रकारभेदेनैव, 'मानाभावात्' विनिगमकाभावात्।

'पृथिवीत्वसमानाधिकरणेति पृथिवीवृत्तिधर्मप्रकारकत्वमवच्छिन्नान्तार्थः, पृथिवीविशेष्यकत्वं पृथिवीवृत्तित्वं, एवमग्रेऽपि, 'पृथिवीत्वव्यधिकरणेति पृथिव्यवृत्तिधर्मप्रकारकेत्यर्थः, 'पृथिव्यवृत्तीति पृथिव्यवृत्तिधर्मासमानाधिकरणेत्यर्थः, 'पृथिवीवृत्तीति पृथिवीत्वप्रकारकेत्यर्थः, 'गन्धासमानाधिकरणेति, अनेदं जलमित्यादिज्ञाने व्यभिचारवारणायाप्रकारकान्तं विषयताविशेषणं, तदर्थश्च गन्धवदवृत्तिधर्मप्रकारकत्व-गन्धवदवृत्तिधर्मसमानाधिकरणत्वान्यतरशून्यत्वं, तेन पृथिव्यां जलभ्रमे जले प्रमुष्टतत्ताकपृथिवीत्वभ्रमे च न व्यभिचारः, अयञ्च द्वितीयसाध्ये हेतुः न तु प्रथम-तृतीययोः पृथिवीत्वनिर्विकल्पके व्यभिचारापत्तेः। त्रितयसाधारणं हेतुमाह, 'अगन्धेति पृथिवीत्व-

मनसा परिच्छिद्यते। गन्धादिमत्येव मम पृथिवीत्वाद्यनुभव इति तच्च गन्धादिमत्त्वपरिच्छेदानन्तरमनुभवात्। स्मृत्युपनीते धूमादौ व्याप्तिपरिच्छेदवत् चक्षुषा चन्दने-सौरभज्ञानवच्च। तर्हि पृथिवीत्वज्ञाने गन्धवद्विशेष्यकत्ववत् चक्षुषा गन्धवति पृथिवीत्वोपनयानन्तरमियं पृथिवीति पृथिवीत्वप्रकारकानुभवे उपनीते पृथिवी-

---

प्रकारकभ्रमे व्यभिचारवारणायावृत्त्यन्तं विषयताविशेषणं, तदर्थश्च गन्धवद्भिन्नावृत्तित्वं, पृथिवीत्वप्रकारकेत्यनुक्तौ प्रथमतृतीयसाध्ये पृथिव्यां प्रमुष्टतत्ताकजलभ्रमे पृथिवीत्वनिर्विकल्पके च व्यभिचारः, द्वितीयसाध्ये पृथिव्यां जलभ्रममात्रे व्यभिचार इति तदुपादानं। त्रितयसाधारणं हेत्वन्तरमाह. 'गन्धेति, अत्रापि विषयता पृथिवीत्वप्रकारकत्वेन विशेषणीया क्वचित्तथैव पाठः। 'साध्याप्रसिद्धेरिति प्रथमं विशिष्टसाधने साध्याप्रसिद्धेरित्यर्थः। इदमुपलक्षणं प्रथम-द्वितीयसाध्ययोः पृथिवीविशेष्यकगन्धादिप्रकारकज्ञानेपि सत्त्वेन पृथिवीत्वप्रमात्मकतया तत्सिद्धावपि पृथिवीत्वांशे प्रमात्वस्यासिद्धेरित्यपि बोध्यं। 'किन्त्वर्थादेवेति इयं पृथिवीवृत्तिधर्म्मप्रकारिका पृथिव्यवृत्तिधर्म्माप्रकारिका वा विषयता पृथिवीवृत्तिः गन्धवद्वृत्तित्वात्, इयं पृथिवीत्वप्रकारकविषयता पृथिव्यवृत्तिधर्म्मासमानाधिकरणा गन्धवद्वृत्तित्वात् यन्नैवं तन्नैवं यथा पृथिवीत्वभ्रमस्य विषयतेति क्रमेण खण्डशः प्रसिद्ध्या व्यतिरेक्यनन्तरमेवैतदनुमानात् तत्सिद्ध्यतीत्यर्थः। 'समर्थप्रवृत्तिजनकत्वेति दाहसमर्थेत्यर्थः, प्रामाण्यज्ञान-

त्ववति पृथिवीत्वप्रकारकत्वं तथा तत्रैव ज्ञाने घटत्व-प्रकारकताविरहवत् पृथिव्यवृत्तिप्रकाराभाववत्त्वं विशेष्यावृत्तिप्रकाराभाववत्त्वं वा प्रामाण्यं मनसैव परिच्छिद्यतामिति स्वतएव प्रामाण्यग्रह इति चेत् । न ।

प्रामाण्यानुमानाभिप्रायेणेदमित्यपि केचित्। 'दाहसमर्थविषयत्वं' दाहसमर्थविषयकत्वं, 'तदसामार्थ्यादिति मनसोऽसामर्थ्यादित्यर्थः, 'स्वतः प्रामाण्येति प्रामाण्यस्यानुव्यवसायग्राह्यत्वापत्तेरित्यर्थः। 'वह्नित्वप्रकारकेति वह्नित्वप्रकारकप्रमाया अनुव्यवसाये सतीत्यर्थः । 'तत्र विषय इति मानान्तरादितिशेषः । 'ज्ञानानन्तरमिति तज्ज्ञाननाशे सतीत्यर्थः, 'वह्निव्यवसाये' पुरोवर्त्तिविशेष्यकवह्नित्वप्रकारकप्रमायां, 'स्मृत्युपनीतेति उच्छृङ्खलस्मृत्युपनीतदाहसमर्थत्वरूपेण स्मृत्युपनीतं पुरोवर्तिविशेष्यकत्वं 'मनसा परिच्छिद्यत इति योजना । न चैतावता दाहसमर्थविशेष्यकत्वग्रहेऽपि तदवच्छिन्नवह्नित्वप्रकारकत्वस्य विशिष्टस्याग्रहात् हेतुसिद्धिरिति वाच्यं । तदानीमुपनीते वह्नित्वप्रकारकत्वे अवच्छिन्नतासम्बन्धेन दाहसमर्थविशेष्यकत्वप्रकारकत्वग्रहेऽपि बाधकाभावादिति भावः। 'ज्ञानोपनीतेति उच्छृङ्खलस्मृत्युपनीतगन्ध-स्नेहादिमत्त्वरूपेण स्मृत्युपनीतं पुरोवर्त्तिविशेष्यकत्वं मनसा परिच्छिद्यत इत्यर्थः। शङ्कते, 'तर्हीति, 'पृथिवीत्वोपनयानन्तरमिति पृथिवीत्वप्रकारकव्यवसायानन्तरमित्यर्थः, 'उपनीत इति पुरोवर्त्तिविशेष्यकत्वे सति पृथिवीत्वप्रकारकत्वरूपेणानुव्यवसित इत्यर्थः, व्यवसायनाशे सतीति शेषः । 'पृथिवीत्ववतीति पृथिवीत्व-तद्वद्विशेष्यकत्व-पृथिवी-

ज्ञानान्तरोपस्थापितज्ञानवृत्तिप्रामाण्यग्रहे परतस्त्वानपायात्। यावज्ज्ञानग्राहकसामग्रीग्राह्यत्वं, यावत्स्वाश्रयग्राहकग्राह्यत्वं, तज्ज्ञानविषयकजन्यज्ञानाजन्यजन्यज्ञानग्राह्यत्वं वा स्वतस्त्वं, तदन्यथाग्राह्यत्वन्तु परतस्त्वं. मनसा चैवं प्रामाण्यग्रहस्याभ्युपगमे तज्ज्ञानविषयकजन्यज्ञानजन्यज्ञानग्राह्यत्वान्न परतस्त्वहानिः। व्यतिरेक्यनन्तरं तज्जातीयत्वेनान्वयिना प्रामाण्यानु-

---

स्वप्रकारकत्वव्यवसायानां सर्व्वेषामेवोपनयसत्त्वात् प्रतिबन्धकस्य व्यवसायस्यासत्त्वाच्चेति भावः। 'प्रामाण्यमिति स्वत्वुपनीतमिति शेषः, 'मनसैवेति एवकारोऽप्यर्थे, 'स्वत एव प्रामाण्यग्रह इति न प्रामाण्यस्य परतो ग्रह इत्यर्थः। 'ज्ञानान्तरेति मनसा ज्ञानान्तरोपस्थापिते ज्ञाने क्वचित् प्रामाण्यग्रह इत्यर्थः। तदनपाये हेतुमाह, 'यावज्ज्ञानग्राहकेति, 'यावत्स्वाश्रयग्राहकेति स्वाश्रयविषयकयावद्ग्रहविषयत्वमित्यर्थः, 'तदन्यथेति तादृशस्वतस्त्वाभाववत्त्वे सति ग्राह्यत्वमित्यर्थः, ननु यावज्ज्ञानग्राहकग्राह्यत्वाभावादिरूपस्य परतस्त्वस्याहानावपि तज्ज्ञानविषयकजन्यज्ञानाजन्यजन्यज्ञानविषयत्वाभावरूपस्य परतस्त्वस्य हानिरेवेत्यत आह, 'मनसा चेति, 'तज्ज्ञानविषयकजन्यज्ञानजन्यत्वादिति पाठः, 'तज्ज्ञानविषयकजन्यज्ञानजन्यज्ञानग्राह्यत्वादिति पाठे 'ग्राह्यत्वादित्यस्य रूपत्वादित्यर्थः, 'न परतस्त्वहानिरिति न तज्ज्ञानविषयकेत्यादिरूपस्यापि परतस्त्वस्य हानिरित्यर्थः। न च परतस्त्वानपायेऽपि उत्क्रमेण दाहसमर्थविशेष्यकत्वे सति वह्निमत्प्रकार-

मानं। यथेदं शरीरज्ञानं प्रमा कर-चरणवति शरीर-ज्ञानत्वात् स्वशरीरज्ञानवत्। न च कर-चरणान्तरवति कर-चरणान्तरवत्त्वज्ञाने व्यभिचारः, शरीरांशे तस्य प्रमात्वात्। एतेन कर-चरणवति शरीरज्ञानत्वादित्यत्र कर-चरणवत्त्वं नोपलक्षणं व्यावर्त्त्योपलक्ष्याभावात्। न च विषयतया ज्ञानविशेषणं, कर-चरणवत्त्वप्रकारक-शरीरज्ञानत्वस्य व्यभिचारात् शरीरमिति ज्ञाने तदसि-

---

कत्वस्य स्मृतिकाले वह्नित्ववद्विशेष्यकत्वे सति वह्नित्वप्रकारकत्व-स्यापि ग्रहे बाधकाभावात् सिद्धसाधनं दुर्व्वारमिति वाच्यं। कदाचि-न्मनसा दाहसमर्थविशेष्यकत्वे सति वह्नित्वप्रकारकत्वग्रहे तन्मात्रस्म-रणादेव प्रामाण्यानुमानसम्भवात्। न हि दाहसमर्थविशेष्यकत्वे सति वह्नित्वप्रकारकत्वस्मृतिकालेऽपि वह्नित्ववद्विशेष्यकत्वे सति वह्नित्वप्रका-रकत्वस्य स्मृतिनियमः, येन सिद्धसाधनं स्यादिति भावः। 'व्यतिरे-क्यनन्तरमिति कुत्रचिज्ज्ञाने व्यतिरेकिणा प्रामाण्यानुमानानन्तर-मित्यर्थः, तदुत्तरवर्त्तिषु ज्ञानान्तरेष्विति शेषः। 'अन्वयिनेति अन्वयिनापीत्यर्थः, 'प्रमेति शरीरत्ववति शरीरत्वप्रकारकमित्यर्थः, 'कर-चरणादीति, 'शरीरज्ञानत्वात्' शरीरत्वप्रकारकज्ञानत्वात्, करादिकन्तु प्रत्येकमेव हेतुघटकं न तु मिलितं व्यर्थत्वात्, 'स्वशरी-रज्ञानेति स्वीयपूर्व्वशरीरज्ञानेत्यर्थः, शरीराभेदभ्रमे व्यभिचारमा-शङ्क्य निराकरोति, 'न चेति, 'करचरणान्तरवतीति कर-चरणवद्भिन्ने

हेश्च। विषयविशेषणत्वे कर-चरणवद्विषयकशरीरज्ञानत्वस्य व्यभिचारात् शरीरभ्रमस्यापि वस्तुतः करादिमद्विषयकत्वात्। नापि कर-चरणादिशून्ये यच्छरीरत्वेन ज्ञानं तदन्यत्वे सतीति विवक्षितम्, शून्य इत्यत्र विषयत्वं सप्तम्यर्थ इति कर-चरणशून्यविषयकशरीरज्ञानान्यशरीरज्ञानत्वादित्यर्थः, तथाचासिद्धिः शरीरज्ञानस्य तच्छून्यशरीरत्वादिविषयकत्वनियमात्। न वा कर-चरणशून्ये यच्छरीरत्वेन ज्ञानं न भवतीति विवक्षितं, तृतीयार्थविषयत्वे उक्तदोषादन्यस्यासम्भवादिति निर-

---

इत्यर्थः, 'कर-चरणान्तरवत्त्वज्ञान इति शरीराभेदभ्रम इत्यर्थः, 'शरीरांश इति, मुख्यविशेष्यतापर्य्यन्तस्य साध्ये अविवक्षितत्वादिति भावः। 'एतेनेति वक्ष्यमाणरीत्येत्यर्थः, 'इत्यत्रेति कर-चरणवद्वृत्तिशरीरत्वज्ञानत्वादित्यर्थक इति शेषः, वृत्त्यन्तं ज्ञानत्वविशेषणं, 'कर-चरणवत्त्वमिति कर-चरणवाचकपदमित्यर्थः, 'नोपलक्षणमिति न ज्ञानवृत्तिधर्म्मान्तरं लाक्षणिकमित्यर्थः, 'व्यावृत्तेति लक्षणीयस्य भ्रमव्यावृत्तस्य धर्म्मान्तरस्य तदानीं ज्ञानाभावादित्यर्थः। 'विषयतयेति प्रकारितयेत्यर्थः, तथा च प्रकारितासम्बन्धेन यत् कर-चरणादिमत्त्वज्ञानं तद्वृत्तिशरीरत्वज्ञानत्वादिति हेत्वर्थ इति भावः। 'शरीरज्ञानत्वस्येति शरीरत्वज्ञानत्वस्येत्यर्थः, फलितहेत्वर्थस्येति शेषः, 'व्यभिचारादिति स्वान्वादौ कर-चरणवत्त्व-शरीरत्वोभयप्रकारकभ्रमे व्यभिचा-

त्त्वम्। कर-चरणवद्विशेष्यकशरीरत्वप्रकारकज्ञानत्वस्य हेतुत्वात् शरीरभ्रमे च कर-चरणवतः शरीरस्य विशेषणत्वात्। विषयतापक्षे करचरणादिशून्यनिष्ठशरीरत्वप्रकारकविषयताप्रतियोगित्वशून्यत्वे सति शरीरज्ञानत्वादिति हेतुः।

ननु न गृहीतप्रामाण्यं ज्ञानं परप्रामाण्यनिश्चयरूपं अनवस्थानात्। नापि ज्ञायमानप्रामाण्यं, स्वतः प्रामाण्यग्रहापत्तेः अतोऽगृहीतप्रामाण्यमेव ज्ञानं परप्रामाण्यनिश्चयरूपमास्थेयं। तथा च व्यवसायोऽप्यव-

रादित्यर्थः, 'ज्ञान इति पत्नीभूत इति शेषः। 'विषयविशेषणत्व इति करादिमत्त्वं विषये स च ज्ञाने विशेषणमित्युक्तं इत्यर्थः, 'शरीरज्ञानत्वस्येति 'शरीरत्वज्ञानत्वस्येत्यर्थः, फलितहेत्वर्थस्येति शेषः, 'व्यभिचारादिति स्वाश्रयाभेदसम्बन्धेन शरीरत्वप्रकारकभ्रमे व्यभिचारादित्यर्थः। व्यभिचारमेव विवृणोति, 'शरीरभ्रमस्यापीति शरीरसम्बन्धेन शरीरत्वप्रकारकभ्रमस्यापीत्यर्थः, 'असिद्धिरिति अप्रसिद्धिरित्यर्थः, 'शरीरज्ञानस्य' शरीरत्वज्ञानस्य। इतीयार्थमादाय दूषणदानाय पुनराशङ्कते, 'न वेति, 'कर-चरणादिशून्य इति यच्छरीरत्वेन ज्ञानं कर-चरणशून्ये न भवतीत्यर्थः। 'शरीरभ्रमे चेति शरीरसम्बन्धेन शरीरत्वप्रकारकभ्रमे इत्यर्थः, 'विशेषणत्वादिति अविशेष्यत्वादित्यर्थः। यद्वा विशेषणतावच्छेदकसम्बन्धत्वादित्यर्थः[१]।

(१) विशेषणतावच्छेदकत्वादित्यर्थः इति ग०।

हीतप्रामाण्य एव स्वविषयं निश्चाययतु किं विषयनिश्चयार्थं तत्प्रामाण्यनिश्चयेन[1]। अथ व्यवसायस्याप्रामाण्यदर्शनान्न तन्मात्रादर्थनिश्चयः, तर्हि प्रामाण्यानुमितेरप्यप्रामाण्यदर्शनान्न ततोपि प्रामाण्यनिश्चय इति चेत्। न ब्रूमः ज्ञानप्रामाण्यनिश्चयादेवार्थनिश्चय इति, किन्तु यत्राप्रामाण्यशङ्का नास्ति करतलामलकादिज्ञाने

दीधित्यनुयायिनस्तु 'कर-चरणान्तरवत्त्वज्ञान इति कर-चरणान्तरवत्त्वावच्छेदेन शरीरत्वप्रकारकभ्रम इत्यर्थः[2] 'शरीरांश इति शरीरत्वांश इत्यर्थः, 'एतेनेत्यादिग्रन्थस्तु पूर्ववत्। 'शरीरभ्रमस्यापीति शरीराभेदारोपस्यापीत्यर्थः, 'मुख्यविशेष्यत्वस्य साध्यघटकतया च साध्याभावादिति भावः। 'कर-चरणवद्विशेष्यकेति कर-चरणवन्मुख्यविशेष्यकेत्यर्थः, 'शरीरभ्रमे चेति शरीराभेदारोपे चेत्यर्थः, इत्याहुः।

'विषयतापन्न इति विषयताया एव सविशेष्यकत्व-सप्रकारकत्वमत इत्यर्थः, 'शरीरज्ञानत्वादिति शरीरत्वप्रकारकविषयताप्रतियोगिज्ञानत्वादित्यर्थः, इमे स्थाणु-शरीरे इति समूहालम्बनप्रमायां भागासिद्धिवारणाय प्रतियोगिकोटौ 'शरीरत्वप्रकारकेति, अस्यपक्षाभावतया च न वैयर्थ्यं। इमे शरीरे इति प्रमा-भ्रमसमूहालम्बनस्य न पक्ष इति न तत्र भागासिद्धिः। इदमुपलक्षणं कर-चरणवद्भिन्नशरीरत्वप्रकारकविषयताप्रतियोगिज्ञानत्वादित्यपि हेतुः सम्भवतीति बोध्यं।

---

(१) विषयनिश्चयाय तत्प्रमाण्यग्रहणेनेति क०।

(२) शरीरत्वप्रकारकज्ञाने इत्यर्थ इति ख०।

तत्र व्यवसाय एवार्थनिश्चय इति। तत एव प्रवृत्तिर्निष्कम्पा। यत्रानभ्यासदशायामप्रामाण्यसंशयेनार्थनिश्चयं परिभूयार्थसंशयः तत्र प्रामाण्यनिश्चयाधीनज्ञानादर्थं निश्चित्य निष्कम्पं प्रवर्त्तते नान्यथेति सर्व्वानुभवसिद्धं। अतएवागृहीतप्रामाण्यमेव ज्ञानं परप्रामाण्यं निश्चाययति अप्रामाण्यशङ्काकलङ्कभावात्। यत्र तु प्रामाण्यज्ञाने अप्रामाण्यशङ्कया प्रामाण्यसंशयः तत्र प्रामाण्यज्ञाने प्रामाण्यनिश्चयादेव प्रामाण्यनिश्चयः, एवं यावदप्रामाण्यशङ्कं तज्ज्ञानप्रामाण्यनिश्चयादेव तन्निश्चयः। न चैवमनवस्था, चरमज्ञानप्रामाण्यस्य

'ज्ञायमानप्रामाण्यमिति स्वस्मिन् स्वप्रामाण्यविषयकं ज्ञानमित्यर्थः, 'स्वविषयं निश्चाययत्विति स्वविषयनिश्चयरूपतामामादयत्वित्यर्थः,'विषयनिश्चयार्थं विषयनिश्चयकार्य्यार्थं(१),'अर्थनिश्चय इति अर्थनिश्चयकार्य्यमित्यर्थः, 'प्रामाण्यनिश्चय इति प्रामाण्यनिश्चयकार्य्यमित्यर्थः,'अर्थनिश्चय इति तत्कार्य्यमित्यर्थः, एवमग्रेपि। 'अनभ्यासदशायामिति अप्रामाण्यसंशयप्रतिबन्धकासमवधानदशायामित्यर्थः, 'परिभूयेति निष्कम्पप्रवृत्तिलक्षणस्वकार्य्याक्षमीकृत्येर्थः, 'प्रामाण्यनिश्चयाधीनज्ञानादिति पूर्व्वोत्पन्नार्थनिश्चयविशेष्यकप्रामाण्यनिश्चयोत्तरवर्त्तिज्ञानान्तरादित्यर्थः, पञ्चम्यर्थोऽभेदः अन्वयस्तस्य 'निश्चित्येत्यत्र निश्चयेन। 'अत एवेति निश्चय-

---

(१) विषयनिश्चयत्वार्थमिति क०, ख०, च।

ज्ञानाभावेन कोटिस्मरणाभावेन विषयान्तरसञ्चारेण वा प्रामाण्यसंशयानवश्यम्भावात्। अन्यथा भट्टमते[१] प्रामाण्यस्य ज्ञानानुमितिग्राह्यत्वेनानवस्था स्यात्। गुरु-मते च प्रामाण्यस्य स्वग्राह्यत्वं न स्वग्राह्यं स्वरूप-प्रामाण्याभ्यां वहिर्भूतत्वात्। किन्तु परग्राह्यत्वे अन-वस्थानात् परिशेषानुमानेन प्रमाणान्तरेण वा ग्राह्यं, तथा च तत्प्रामाण्यस्यापि स्वग्राह्यत्वमन्येनैवेत्यनवस्थैव। यत्तु व्यवसायस्य प्रामाण्यनिश्चयादेव प्रवृत्तेर्न तस्यापि प्रामाण्यानुसरणमिति नानवस्थेति। न च प्रामाण्य-

कार्य्यं प्रति सर्व्वत्र निश्चयनिष्ठप्रामाण्ये निश्चयस्यानपेक्षितत्वादित्यर्थः, 'ज्ञानं' प्रामाण्यज्ञानं, 'परप्रामाण्यं निश्चाययति' परप्रामाण्यनिश्चय-कार्य्यं जनयतीत्यर्थः, 'प्रामाण्यनिश्चयादेव' प्रामाण्यज्ञानप्रामाण्यनिश्च-यादेव, 'प्रामाण्यनिश्चयः' प्रामाण्यनिश्चयकार्य्यं, 'ज्ञानप्रामाण्यनिश्चया-देवेति प्रामाण्यज्ञाने प्रामाण्यनिश्चयादेवेत्यर्थः, 'तन्निश्चयः' 'तन्निश्चय-कार्य्यं, 'अन्यथेति सर्व्वत्रैव प्रामाण्यनिश्चये प्रामाण्यनिश्चयस्यापेक्षि-तत्वे इत्यर्थः, 'गुरुमते चेति गुरुमतेपीत्यर्थः, 'प्रामाण्यस्य' स्वनिष्ठप्रा-माण्यस्य, 'स्वग्राह्यत्वं' स्वविषयत्वं, 'स्वरूप-प्रामाण्याभ्यामिति, तन्मत-सिद्धस्वग्राह्यमात्रोपलक्षणं 'परग्राह्यत्वे' परमात्रग्राह्यत्वे, 'परिशेषानु-मानेनेति एतज्ज्ञानप्रामाण्यमेतज्ज्ञानग्राह्यं एतज्ज्ञानभिन्नमात्रा-

(१) भट्टपक्ष इति ख०।

संशयादौचित्यावर्जितो विषयसंशय इति वाच्यं। निश्चिते संशयाभावात्। अन्यथा स्वतोग्रहेऽपि तत्संशयेऽनवस्थेति। तदसत्। यदि प्रामाण्यसंशयान्न विषये संशयो निश्चितत्वात् तदा विषयनिश्चयार्थं प्रामाण्यनिश्चयो व्यर्थः प्राथमिकविषयनिश्चयादेव निष्कम्पप्रवृत्त्युपपत्तेः। न हि विषयसंशयमनाहृत्य प्रामाण्यनिश्चयः प्रवृत्तिहेतुरित्युक्तं। अन्यसंशयादन्यत्र निश्चिते कथं संशय इति चेदनुभवं पृच्छ। येन स्वसाक्षिकमेव प्रामाण्याप्रामाण्यसंशयस्य विषयसंशयहेतुत्वमनुमतं। ज्ञान विषयत्वमपि प्रामाण्यसंशयमासाद्य विषयसंशायकं।

ग्राह्यत्वादित्यनुमानेनेत्यर्थः, 'प्रमाणान्तरेण वेति शब्दादिना वेत्यर्थः, तत्प्रामाण्यस्यापीति स्वग्राह्यत्वज्ञाननिष्ठप्रामाण्यस्यापीत्यर्थः, इदमुपलक्षणं मिश्रमतेप्यनुव्यवसायस्य प्रामाण्यमनुव्यवसायान्तरेण ग्राह्यमेवं तत्प्रामाण्यमप्यनुव्यवसायान्तरेणेत्यनवस्थेत्यपि बोध्यं।

'तस्यापि' प्रामाण्यनिश्चयस्यापि, 'प्रामाण्यं' प्रामाण्यज्ञानं, काप्यपेक्षितमिति शेषः। 'न चेति, प्रामाण्यनिश्चये प्रामाण्यनिश्चयाभावे इति शेषः, 'प्रामाण्यसंशयात्' प्रामाण्यज्ञाने प्रामाण्यसंशयात्, 'औचित्यावर्जित इति व्यवसाये प्रामाण्यसंशयाधीन इत्यर्थः, 'विषयसंशयः व्यवसायस्य विषये संशयः, स्यादिति शेषः, 'निश्चित इति व्यवसायस्य प्रामाण्ये निश्चिते इत्यर्थः, 'संशयाभावादिति व्यवसाये प्रामाण्यसंशयासम्भवादित्यर्थः, 'स्वतोग्रहेऽपि' व्यवसायनिष्ठप्रामाण्यस्यानुव्यवसायादि-

ननु लिङ्ग-पक्ष-व्याप्त्यादीनां ज्ञानस्य प्रामाण्यावधारणेऽनवस्था, अनवधारणे हेत्वसिद्धिः[१]। अथ लिङ्गादिज्ञानं स्वविषयावधारणे कर्त्तव्ये स्वप्रामाण्यज्ञानं नापेक्षते अनुमानमात्रोच्छेदप्रसङ्गात्। लिङ्गादिनिश्चयस्य च स्वकारणाधीनस्य सर्व्वसिद्धत्वादिति चेत्। न। प्रामाण्यसंशयेन लिङ्गसन्देहात्। न हि न लिङ्गज्ञाने प्रामाण्यसंशयः, अविरोधादिति[२]।

मा निश्चयेपि, 'तत्संशये' अनुव्यवसायादौ प्रामाण्यसंशयात् व्यवसायनिष्ठप्रामाण्यसंशये, 'अनवस्थेति मिश्रादिमतेपि अनुव्यवसायादौ प्रामाण्यनिश्चयार्थमनुव्यवसायाद्यन्तरापेक्षायामनवस्थेत्यर्थः। 'प्रामाण्यसंशयादिति निश्चये प्रामाण्यसंशयादित्यर्थः, 'विषये' तद्विषये, 'विषयनिश्चयार्थमिति प्रामाण्यसंशयाधीनविषयसंशयनिवृत्त्यर्थमित्यर्थः, 'प्रामाण्यनिश्चयः' व्यवसायनिष्ठप्रामाण्यनिश्चयः, 'विषयसंशयमिति व्यवसाये प्रामाण्यसंशयाद्विषयसंशयमित्यर्थः, 'अनादृत्य' अनभ्युपगम्य, 'प्रवृत्तिहेतुः' साक्षादेव प्रवृत्तिहेतुः, 'उक्तं' कैश्चिदुक्तं। प्रकृते, 'अन्यसंशयादिति, 'विषयसंशयहेतुत्वमिति निश्चयोत्तरविषयसंशयहेतुत्वमित्यर्थः।

ननु ज्ञानविषयत्वात्समानधर्म्मादपि तादृशविषयसंशयोदयात् कथं

---

(१) ननु लिङ्ग-पक्ष-व्याप्त्यादिज्ञानानां प्रामाण्यानवधारणे हेत्वाद्यसिद्धिः, अवधारणे चानवस्थेति क०।

(२) अनुभवविरोधादितीति ग०।

उच्यते। अप्रामाण्यशङ्काकलङ्काभावे लिङ्गादिज्ञानस्यैवार्थनिश्चायकत्वात्, तत्कलङ्के तूक्तैव गतिः। यत्तु व्यवसाये क्वचिदप्रामाण्यशङ्का भवति क्वचिन्नेति त्वयापि वक्तव्यम्। एवं बहुवित्तव्ययायाससाध्ये स्वर्गसाधनं याग इति ज्ञानं न गृहीतप्रामाण्यं प्रवर्त्तकं प्रामाण्यानुमितेः पूर्व्वमेव तस्य विनाशात्, किन्तु तज्ज्ञानसमानविषयकमप्रामाण्यशङ्काशून्यं ज्ञानान्तरमेव। नन्वेवं बहुवित्तव्ययायाससाध्ये निष्कम्पप्रवृत्तावनुपयोगित्वात्

प्रामाण्यसंशयस्य तद्धेतुत्वमित्यत आह, 'ज्ञानविषयत्वमपीति। 'नन्विति, पर्व्वतो वह्निमान् धूमादित्यादाविति शेषः, 'हेत्वसिद्धिरिति कारणासिद्धिरित्यर्थः, अभिप्रायानभिज्ञः कारणासिद्धिं परिहरति, 'अथेति, 'स्वविषयेति स्वग्राह्येत्यर्थः, 'अनुमानमात्रेति, अनवस्थया प्रामाण्यनिश्चयासम्भवादिति भावः। अभिसन्धिमुद्घाटयति, 'प्रामाण्यसंशयेनेति, 'लिङ्गसन्देहादिति सन्देहपदं अगृहीताप्रामाण्यकनिश्चयाभावपरं, तथाचागृहीताप्रामाण्यकलिङ्गनिश्चयाभावादित्यर्थः, तस्यैवानुमितिहेतुत्वादिति भावः। 'अविरोधादिति बाधकाभावादित्यर्थः। 'लिङ्गादिज्ञानस्यैवेति लिङ्गादिनिश्चयस्यैवेत्यर्थः, एवकारात् प्रामाण्यनिश्चयव्यवच्छेदः, 'तत्कलङ्के तु' तत्सत्त्वे तु, 'उक्तैव' प्रामाण्यनिश्चयरूपैव। ननु प्रामाण्यशङ्काया न सार्व्वत्रिकत्वं किन्तु क्वाचित्कत्वमित्यत्र किं बीजमित्यत आह, 'यत्त्विति यत् पुनरित्यर्थः, 'त्वया

निष्फलं प्रामाण्यज्ञानमिति किं तदुपायानुसरणेनेति चेत्। न। स्वर्गसाधनं याग इति ज्ञानप्रामाण्ये निश्चिते तत्समानविषयकज्ञानान्तरे अप्रामाण्यशङ्का न भवतीति ज्ञानान्तरमगृहीतप्रामाण्यमपि स्वार्थनिश्चयरूपं निष्कम्पप्रवृत्तिं जनयतीत्यप्रामाण्यशङ्काप्रतिबन्धद्वारा निष्कम्पप्रवृत्तावुपयुज्यते प्रामाण्यज्ञानमिति न निष्फलम्। यत्त्वनुमानस्य निरस्तसमस्तविभ्रमाशङ्कस्य स्वत एव प्रामाण्यग्रह इत्युक्तम्। तद्धूमवति वह्निज्ञानत्वमनुमितेः प्रामाण्यनियतमनुव्यवसायेनोप-

---

पीत्यस्य पूर्व्वं तदित्यध्याहार्य्यं, तथाच संशयसामग्र्या असार्व्वत्रिकत्वमुभयानुमतमिति भावः। 'एवमिति यथा निश्चितप्रामाण्यकपरामर्श एवानुमितिहेतुस्तथेत्यर्थः, 'तज्ज्ञानेति निश्चितप्रामाण्यकज्ञानेत्यर्थः, 'ज्ञानान्तरमेवेति उत्तरोत्पन्नज्ञानान्तरमेवेत्यर्थः। 'नन्वेवमिति, 'एवं' ज्ञानान्तरस्यैव प्रवर्त्तकत्वे। 'तत्समानविषयकज्ञानान्तर इति। न चान्यत्र प्रामाण्यनिश्चये कथमन्यत्र नाशङ्केति वाच्यं। तादृशज्ञानत्वावच्छेदेनाप्रामाण्यवत्तानिश्चयाद्द्विती ज्ञानानुव्यवसायेन तादृशज्ञानत्ववत्ताग्रहादेव प्रामाण्यसंशयासम्भवादनुव्यवसायाभावे च धर्म्मिज्ञानाभावादिति भावः। ननु प्रामाण्यस्य स्वतोग्राह्यत्वाभावे टीकाकृतोऽनुमितौ स्वतः प्रामाण्यग्रहाभिधानं विरुद्धमित्यत आह, 'यत्त्विति, 'निरस्तसमस्तेति अप्रामाण्यशङ्कासामग्रीनिरहविशिष्टस्येत्यर्थः,

मीतं अतो विशेषदर्शनाच्च तथाप्रामाण्यशङ्केति, प्रामाण्यनिश्चयादेवाप्रामाण्यशङ्काविरहात् अर्थं निश्चित्य[१] निष्कम्पव्यवहार इत्यभिप्रायः। वस्तुतस्तु परतः पक्षे न क्वचिदपि प्रामाण्यग्रहः प्रवर्त्तक इति। एवमनुव्यवसायस्य प्रामाण्यनियतत्वान्न प्रामाण्यशङ्का। न ह्यजानन् जानामीति प्रत्येति। न वा घट-

---

'उक्तं' टीकाकृद्भिरुक्तं, 'तत्' इति षष्ठ्यन्तमव्ययं तस्येत्यर्थः, 'इत्यभिप्रायः' इत्यग्रेतनेनान्वयः, 'उपनीतमिति यदोपनयमर्य्यादया विषयीकृतमित्यर्थः, तदेति शेषः, 'अत इति अस्मादित्यर्थः, 'तथ' अनुमितौ, 'अर्थं निश्चित्येति अर्थविषयकानुमित्युत्तरमेवेत्यर्थः। न चैवमनुमितिपर्य्यन्तानुधावनवैयर्थ्यमिति वाच्यं। अनुमानपदस्यार्थनिश्चय-सामान्यपरत्वादिति भावः। 'वस्तुतस्त्विति वस्तुगत्या पुनरित्यर्थः, 'परतः पक्षे' न्यायनये, 'प्रामाण्यग्रहः' स्वतः प्रामाण्यग्रहः, 'प्रवर्त्तकः' प्रवृत्तिप्रयोजकः। ननु यदि क्वचिदपि न स्वतः प्रामाण्यग्रहः तदानुव्यवसाये रजतत्वादिप्रकारकत्वांशे ज्ञानांशे च प्रामाण्यसंशयापत्तिरित्यत आह, 'एवमिति, 'अनुव्यवसायस्य' तत्प्रकारकज्ञानानुव्यवसायत्वस्य, 'प्रामाण्यनियतत्वादिति तत्प्रकारकत्वांशे ज्ञानांशे च प्रामाण्यनियतत्वेन गृहीतत्वादित्यर्थः, यदा तु तत्र प्रामाण्यनियतत्वावधारणं नास्ति तदा तादृशशङ्कापीष्यत एवेति भावः। प्रामाण्यनियतत्वमेवोपपादयति, 'न हीति, 'घटज्ञाने' घटत्वप्रकारकज्ञाने, 'पटज्ञानामीति

---

(४) अर्थे निश्चिते इति ख०, ग०, घ।

ज्ञाने पटं जानामीति। भ्रमेप्यनुव्यवसायेन रजतत्वादिकं व्यवसायप्रकारत्वेनोल्लिख्यते तच्च तथैव। यत्त्वभ्यासदशायां झटिति प्रचुरतर-निष्कम्पप्रवृत्तिदर्शनात् प्रामाण्यं स्वतएव गृह्यते अन्यत्र तु परत इति तन्न। विशेष्यनिष्ठात्यन्ताभावप्रतियोगि प्रकारानवच्छिन्नत्वादिकं प्रामाण्यं स्वतो ग्रहीतुमशक्यमिति परत एव गृह्यते। झटितिप्रवृत्तिस्तु कर-चरणादिमति शरीर-ज्ञानत्वादेर्विशेषस्यानुव्यवसायेन ग्रहादप्रामाण्यशङ्का-

---

पटत्वेन जानामीत्यर्थः, 'प्रत्येतीत्यनुषज्यते। ननु रजतत्वादिप्रकारक-प्रमानुव्यवसायस्य रजतत्वादिप्रकारकत्वांशे भ्रमत्वात् कथमनुव्यवसायस्य तदंशे प्रमात्वनियतत्वमित्यत आह, 'भ्रमेपीति भ्रमस्थलेपीत्यर्थः, 'तथैव व्यवसायप्रकार एव, तथा च रजतत्वादिप्रकारकभ्रमानुव्यवसायस्यापि न रजतत्वादिप्रकारकत्वांशे भ्रमत्वमिति। 'अभ्यासदशायामिति पुरोवर्त्तिनि शरीरत्वादिप्रकारकज्ञानदशायामित्यर्थः, 'प्रकारानवच्छिन्नत्वादिकमिति धर्म्यप्रकारकत्वादिकमित्यर्थः, आदिपदात्तद्वति तत्प्रकारकत्वपरिग्रहः 'परत एवेति, अभ्यासदशायामपीत्यादिः, 'विशेषस्य' प्रामाण्यव्याप्यस्य, 'अनुव्यवसायेन ग्रहादिति, प्रामाण्यानुमितेरिति शेषः। प्रकारान्तरमाह, 'प्रामाण्यग्रहेति, 'व्यवसायादेवेति व्यवसायादेव वेत्यर्थः। द्वितीयकल्पमाह, 'प्रामाण्यज्ञानमिति, प्रथमकल्पमभिप्रेत्याह, झटितीति, 'तत्समवधानं' प्रामा-

शून्याद् व्यवसायादेव, न प्रामाण्यज्ञानं प्रवर्त्तकमित्युक्तम्। झटिति तत्समवधानन्तु स्वकारणाधीनं। न हि पिपासूनां झटिति प्रचुरतरा समर्था च प्रवृत्तिरस्मसीति, पिपासोपशमनशक्तिरस्य प्रत्यक्षेति।

इति श्रीमद्गङ्गेशोपाध्यायविरचिते तत्त्वचिन्तामणौ प्रत्यक्षखण्डे प्रामाण्यवादे ज्ञप्तिवादः ॥०॥

ण्यानुमितिसामग्रीसमवधानं, 'पिपासोपशमनशक्तिरिति पिपासाया उपशमनं यस्मादिति व्युत्पत्त्या पिपासोपशमनं पानं तस्य या 'शक्तिः' तस्य या साधनताधीः, सा 'प्रत्यक्षा' सा स्वप्रामाण्यप्रत्यक्षात्मिकेत्यर्थः। अत्र केचित् प्रामाण्यनिश्चयो न साक्षात् प्रवृत्तिहेतुरिति ग्रन्थकृतवोक्तं न वा यथोक्तयुक्त्या द्वितीयज्ञाने प्रामाण्यसंशयनिवृत्तिद्वारा स निष्कम्पप्रवृत्त्युपयोगी, प्रवृत्तिसामग्र्या बुद्धिसामग्रीतो बलवत्तया शङ्काया एवासम्भवात्। न च प्रामाण्यशङ्कासामग्री निष्कम्पप्रवृत्तिसामग्रीतो बलवतीति वाच्यम्। मानाभावादित्याहुः। तदसत्। यत्रोपादानप्रत्यक्षादिविलम्बेन प्रवृत्तिसामग्रीविलम्बस्तत्रैवाप्रामाण्यसंशयासम्भवादिति संक्षेपः॥

इति श्रीमथुरानाथतर्कवागीश-विरचिते प्रामाण्यवादरहस्ये ज्ञप्तिवादरहस्यम्॥०॥

अथ प्रामाण्यवादे उत्पत्तिवादः।

उत्पद्यतेऽपि प्रमा[१] परतो न तु स्वतः ज्ञानसामग्री-मात्रात्। तज्जन्यत्वेनाप्रमापि प्रमा स्यात्। अन्यथा

ननु प्रमात्वस्य परतो ग्राह्यत्वे स्वत उत्पत्तिकत्वानुपपत्तिरपि न स्यात्, परतो ग्राह्यत्वस्य ज्ञानमात्रादिविभाजकोपाधेः स्वत उत्पत्तिकत्वत्त्वा-भावनियमादप्रमात्वे तथा क्लृप्तत्वादित्युपोद्घातसङ्गत्या प्रमायाः परत उत्पत्तिकत्वं व्यवस्थापयति, 'उत्पद्यतेऽपीति, प्रमा परत उत्पद्यते-पीतियोजना, प्रमा परतः प्रामाण्यस्येव परत उत्पत्तिकत्वस्याप्याश्रय इत्यर्थः। एतेन प्रामाण्यस्य परतो ज्ञप्तिर्निरूपिता उत्पत्तिस्च प्रमाया निरूप्यत इत्येकत्र धर्म्मिण्युभयानिरूपणादिति शब्दसमुच्चयानुपपत्ति-रिति निरस्तं। परत उत्पत्तिकत्वञ्च ज्ञानमात्रादिविभाजकोपाध्यवच्छि-न्नकार्य्यताप्रतियोगिककारणतानिरूपितकार्य्यतावत्त्वं, तादृशकार्य्यत्वञ्च भ्रमे प्रसिद्धं भ्रम प्रति दोषहेतुतायाः सर्व्वसिद्धत्वात् स्वमतेनैवायं ग्रन्थ इति परनये तदप्रसिद्धावपि क्षतिविरहाच्च। ज्ञानमात्रादिविभाजको-पाधित्वञ्च ज्ञानविभाजकोपाध्यव्याप्यत्वे सति[२] ज्ञानविभाजकोपाधित्वं तादृशञ्च प्रमात्वमप्रमात्वञ्च, ज्ञानं द्विविधं विद्या अविद्या चेति विभा-गकरणात्। अयञ्च विभागः मिश्रस्य भट्टस्य वा ग्राह्यः न तु वैशेषिकस्य

---

(१) प्रामाण्यमिति क० ग० च।

(२) सत्यन्तदलेन चाक्षुषत्वादिनिरासः।

ज्ञानमपि सा न स्यात्। ज्ञानसामग्र्यां दोषानुप्रवेशाद्प्रमेति चेत्तर्हि ज्ञानविशेषवदप्रमा प्रमाविशेषः स्यात् ज्ञानसामग्रीजन्यत्वात्। तस्मात् प्रमाप्रमयोर्वैचित्र्यात् गुणदोषजन्यत्वम्। अथ यत्र गुण-दोषौ विना तयो-

---

तत्र विद्यात्वस्य निर्विकल्पकसाधारण्यार्थं भ्रमभिन्नज्ञानत्वरूपतया प्रमात्वरूपत्वाभावात्। यद्वा भ्रम-प्रमान्यतरपदप्रवृत्तिनिमित्तत्वं ज्ञानसाक्षाद्विभाजकोपाधित्वमिति भावः। स्वत इत्यस्य विवरणं 'ज्ञानसामग्रीमात्रादिति न तु ज्ञानसामान्यसामग्रीजन्यतामात्राश्रय इत्यर्थः। ज्ञानसामान्यसामग्रीजन्यत्वस्य ज्ञानसाक्षाद्विभाजकोपाध्यनवच्छिन्नज्ञाननिष्ठकार्य्यताप्रतियोगिककारणतानिरूपितजन्यत्वं, अत्र हेतुमाह, 'तज्जन्यत्वेनेति, तथात्व इत्यादिः, प्रमाया ज्ञानसामान्यसामग्रीजन्यतामात्राश्रयत्वे ज्ञानसामान्यसामग्रीजन्यत्वेनाप्रमापि प्रमा स्यादित्यर्थः, सामग्र्यवैचित्र्यादिति भावः। 'अन्यथा' अप्रमाया ज्ञानसामान्यसामग्रीजन्यत्वाभावे, 'सा' अप्रमा। अप्रमायां ज्ञानसामान्यसामग्रीजन्यत्वसत्त्वेऽपि न तज्जन्यतामात्रमित्याशङ्कते, 'ज्ञानसामग्र्यामिति ज्ञानसामान्यसामग्र्यामित्यर्थः, 'दोषानुप्रवेशात्' दोषस्याधिकस्यानुप्रवेशात्, 'तर्हीति तथापीत्यर्थः, 'प्रमाविशेषः स्यादिति प्रमाविशेषः स्यादेवेत्यर्थः, 'ज्ञानसामग्रीति प्रमासामग्रीरूपज्ञानसामान्यसामग्रीजन्यत्वादित्यर्थः, तत्सामग्रीजन्यत्वस्य च तदात्मकत्वव्याप्यत्वादिति भावः। 'वैचित्र्यादिति प्रमात्वाप्रमात्वरूपपरस्परविरुद्धधर्मवत्त्वादित्यर्थः। ननु गुणदोषयोर्व्यतिरेके यदि प्रमाप्रमयोर्व्यतिरेकः स्यात्तदा तयोः

रभावस्तत्र ज्ञानसामग्र्येव नास्ति तत्सत्त्वे ज्ञानमात्रोत्पत्तिप्रसङ्गादिति चेत् । न । विशेषविनाकृतसामान्यकार्य्याभावात् । तत्सामग्रीमादायैव हि सामान्यसामग्री तां विना नास्त्येव वा । अन्यथा कार्य्यविशेषे कारणविशेषोच्छेदः ।

ननु यथैकजातीयसामग्रीसत्त्वेऽपि घटयोर्भेदो यमजयोर्वैधर्म्यञ्च तथा प्रमाप्रमयोर्भेदो वैधर्म्यञ्च(१)

प्रमाप्रमाहेतुत्वं स्यादनन्यथासिद्धान्वयव्यतिरेकस्य कारणताव्यापकत्वात् । न चैवं, तयोर्व्यतिरेके ज्ञानसामान्यसामग्र्या एव विरहादिति तटस्थः शङ्कते, 'अथेति, 'तयोरिति प्रमाप्रमयोरित्यर्थः, 'ज्ञानमात्रेति प्रमाप्रमावहिर्भूतज्ञानसामान्योत्पत्तिप्रसङ्गादित्यर्थः, तथा च ज्ञानसामान्यसामग्रीविरहप्रयुक्त एव तत्र तदुभयाभावः, न तु गुण-दोषाभावप्रयुक्त इति भावः । यद्यपि प्रमास्थले गुणस्य भ्रमस्थले दोषस्य पृथगन्वय-व्यतिरेकोऽस्त्येव तत्र ज्ञानसामान्यसामग्रीविरहस्य वक्तुमशक्यत्वात् तथापि प्रौढ्या समाधानान्तरमाह, 'विशेषेति, 'तत्सामग्रीमादायेति विशेषसामग्रीमादायेत्यर्थः, 'सामान्यसामग्रीति, कार्य्यजनिकेति शेषः । तथा च तत्र ज्ञानसामान्यसामग्री तिष्ठत्येव विशेषसामग्रीविरहाच्च न कार्य्योत्पत्तिरिति न सामान्यसामग्रीविरहप्रयुक्तः प्रमाप्रमोभयाभावः, किन्तु गुण-दोषाभावप्रयुक्त एवेति भावः । वस्तुतस्तु फलाव्यभिचारिकारणसमूहस्यैव सामग्रीत्वाद्विशेषसामग्र्य-

---

(१) वैरूप्यञ्चेति ख०, ग० च ।

भविष्यति[१]। अथानुगतव्यवहारात् प्रमात्वमनुगतमिति प्रमामात्रे अनुगतो हेतुर्वाच्यः अनुगतकार्य्यस्याननुगतादनुत्पत्तेरिति चेत्। न। प्रमात्वस्योपाधित्वेन कार्य्यतावच्छेदकत्वे मानाभावात्। कार्य्यमात्रवृत्तिधर्मत्वस्य नीलघटत्व-घटज्ञानत्वादौ व्यभिचारात्।

तिरिक्तसामान्यसामग्र्येव नास्तीत्याह, 'तां विनेति, तथा च विशेषसामग्र्यतिरिक्ता यदि सामान्यसामग्री तिष्ठति तदा तद्विरहप्रयुक्तस्तत्र कार्य्यविरहः स्यात् न चैवमिति भावः। 'अन्यथेति, त्वदुक्तरीत्या अन्यत्रापि कारणविशेषस्य पृथगन्वय-व्यतिरेकानुविधायित्वाभावादिति भावः।

मीमांसकः शङ्कते, 'नन्विति, 'उच्यते' इत्यन्तमेकः पूर्व्वपक्षः। 'भेदः' व्यक्तिभेदः, 'वैधर्म्यं' वैजात्यं, 'तथेति, 'वैधर्म्यञ्च' प्रमात्वाप्रमात्वरूपपरस्परविरुद्धधर्म्मवत्त्वञ्च, तथा च किं प्रमात्वावच्छिन्ने गुणस्य हेतुत्वेनेति भावः। अत्र प्रमायां गुणजन्यत्वखण्डनमात्रे शङ्कितुस्तात्पर्य्यं न तु अप्रमाया दोषजन्यत्वखण्डने मीमांसकैरप्यप्रमाया दोषजन्यत्वाभ्युपगमात्।

केचित्तु प्रमावदप्रमापि स्वत एवोत्पद्यत इति मन्वानस्य तटस्थस्याशङ्केयं तथाचोभयखण्डने तात्पर्य्येऽपि न क्षतिरित्याहुः। तदसत् तथा सति तं प्रत्येवमप्रमापि स्वत एव स्यादिति सिद्धान्तेऽनिष्टापादनस्यासङ्गतेः।

---

(१) भवतीति ग०।

अथ प्रमा ज्ञानहेत्वतिरिक्तहेतुजन्या जन्यज्ञानत्वात् अप्रमावदिति चेत्। न। प्रमाया ज्ञानत्वे तद्धेतुजन्यतया साध्ये[१] बाधात्। ज्ञानाजनकजन्यत्वे विरोधात्। अप्रमायां तदसिद्धेः। व्यर्थविशेषणत्वात्

अत्र प्रमात्वं कार्य्यतावच्छेदकं न वेति विप्रतिपत्तिः, कार्य्यतावच्छेदकत्वञ्च न तत्पर्य्याप्त्यधिकरणत्वं अपि तु यथा कथञ्चित्कार्य्यतावच्छेदकताश्रयत्वमात्रं तेन प्रमात्वस्य नित्यवृत्तितया तत्पर्य्याप्त्यनधिकरणत्वेऽपि न क्षतिः।

केचित्तु प्रमात्वं कार्य्यतावच्छेदकव्यापकं न वेति विप्रतिपत्तिः, तत्तद्व्यक्तित्वस्य कार्य्यतावच्छेदकत्वे कार्य्यतावच्छेदकमनेकवृत्तित्वेन विशेष्यमित्याहुः।

ननु अनुगतकार्य्यवैचित्र्यं कारणवैचित्र्याधीनं घटयोः स्वरूपभेदस्तु न तथा, यमजयोस्तथात्वञ्चादृष्टवैचित्र्यादित्याशयेनाह, 'अथेति, 'उपाधित्वेनेति, इदमुपलक्षणं नित्यवृत्तित्वेनेत्यपि द्रष्टव्यं। प्रमात्वस्य कार्य्यमात्रवृत्तिजातित्वे हि कार्य्यमात्रवृत्तिजातेः कार्य्यतावच्छेदकत्वनियमस्यैव मानत्वसम्भवादिति भावः।

ननु अनित्यप्रमात्वं कार्य्यतावच्छेदकं कार्य्यमात्रवृत्तित्वादित्यनुमानमेव मानमित्यत आह, 'कार्य्यमात्रेति, 'घटज्ञानत्वेति जन्यघटज्ञानत्वेत्यर्थः, यथाश्रुते कार्य्यमात्रवृत्तित्वाभावेन व्यभिचारासङ्गतेः प्रमाया गुणजन्यत्वसाधकमाचार्य्यानुमानं शङ्कते, 'प्रमेति, अत्र ज्ञान-

---

(१) तदतिरिक्तजन्यत्वे साध्ये इति ख०।

व्यावर्त्त्याप्रसिद्धेः। किञ्च यत्किञ्चिज्ज्ञानहेत्वपेक्षया सर्वतद्धेत्वपेक्षया वा अतिरिक्तत्वे इन्द्रियादिभिः सिद्धसाधनात्। नापि ज्ञानसामान्यसामग्र्यतिरिक्त-सामग्रीजन्येति साध्यम्, पूर्ववत् सिद्धसाधनात् विरो-

---

हेत्वतिरिक्तत्वं सामान्याभावो वा यत्किञ्चिद्विशेषाभावो वा यावत्त्वा-वच्छिन्नाभावो वा आद्ये आह, 'प्रमाया इति, 'तद्धेतुजन्यतया' ज्ञानहेतुमात्रजन्यतया। बाधमुक्त्वा विरोधमाह, 'ज्ञानाजनकजन्यत्व इति, तस्य इति शेषः, 'विरोधात्' अन्यज्ञानत्वरूपहेतोर्विरोधात्। दृष्टान्तस्य साध्यवैकल्यमाह, 'अप्रमायामिति। व्यर्थविशेषणतामप्याह, 'व्यर्थेति, 'विशेषणं' जन्यत्वं। व्यर्थतामेव विवृणोति, 'व्यावर्त्त्येति तद्व्यावर्त्त्यस्य ईश्वरज्ञानस्येदानीमसिद्धेरित्यर्थः। प्रमाया गुणजन्यत्व-सिद्धावेव वैदिकप्रमायां गुणतया भगवज्ज्ञानसिद्धिरिति भावः। द्वितीय-तृतीययोराह, 'किञ्चेति, 'इन्द्रियेति, एकस्य यावद्भि-न्नत्वादिति भावः। ज्ञानसामग्रीभेदः किं विशेषाभावः, यावत्त्वा-वच्छिन्नाभावः, सामान्याभावो वा आद्ययोराह, 'सिद्धसाधनेति, अन्त्ये 'विरोधादिति। ज्ञानसामान्यसामग्र्यन्यसामग्रीजन्यत्वं साध्यं सामान्य-विशेषयोः सामग्रीभेदात् प्रमासामग्री ज्ञानसामान्यसामग्री-भिन्नैवेति न बाध इति निराकुरुते, 'न चेति, 'प्रमाया इति, यत् यत्सामग्रीभिन्नसामग्रीजन्यं तत् ततो भिद्यते इति नियमादिति भावः। 'तस्य' सामग्रीभेदस्य। 'इन्द्रियादिभिरिति, एकस्य यावद्भि-न्नत्वादिति भावः। 'ज्ञानत्वाभिप्राय इति ज्ञानसामान्यपदस्य ज्ञान-

धात्व। न च सामान्य-विशेषयोः सामग्रीद्वयं। प्रमाया ज्ञानभिन्नत्वापत्तेः अन्यथा सामग्रीभेदासिद्धिः तस्य कार्य्यभेदकल्प्यत्वात्। एतेन ज्ञानसामान्यहेत्वतिरिक्तहेतुजन्येति साध्यं प्रत्युक्तं। सकलज्ञानाभिप्राये चेन्द्रियादिभिः सिद्धसाधनं। ज्ञानत्वाभिप्राये हेत्व-

---

त्वपरत्वे इत्यर्थः, 'हेत्वसिद्धिरिति, ज्ञानत्वस्येति शेषः, नित्यत्वात् तथा च तद्घटितसाध्याप्रसिद्धिरिति भावः। 'नित्यवृत्तितयेत्यस्य तव मत इत्यादिः, तथा च तव नये साध्याप्रसिद्धिरस्मन्नये तु इन्द्रियादिभिरेव सिद्धसाधनमिति हृदयं। ज्ञानत्वस्य नित्यवृत्तित्वेऽपि कार्य्यतावच्छेदकत्वं स्यादित्याशङ्कते, 'अथेति, 'यद्धर्म्माश्रयस्येति 'असतः', 'सत्त्वं' उत्पत्तिः आद्यक्षणसम्बन्ध इति यावत्। 'हेत्वधीनं यद्धेत्वधीनं, 'तत्कार्य्यतावच्छेदकं' तस्य हेतोः कार्य्यतावच्छेदकं अत्रामतः सत्त्वं यावत्त्वेन विशेषणीयं नातो दण्डजन्यतावच्छेदकज्ञेयत्वं भवति च कृत्यादिजन्यतावच्छेदकं, बाधकाभावे सतीति विशेषणीयं तेन नीलघटत्वादिवारणं, घटज्ञानत्वादेरपि आत्ममनोयोगादेर्जन्यतावच्छेदकत्वे ज्ञानत्वाद्यपेक्षया गौरवमेव बाधकमिति न तत्रापि व्यभिचारः। एवञ्च यद्धर्म्माश्रयस्य सर्व्वमसतः सत्त्वं सर्व्वा उत्पत्तिः यद्धर्म्माश्रयाधीना बाधकं विना स धर्म्मस्तद्धर्म्माश्रयकार्य्यतावच्छेदक इति पर्य्यवसितं। अधीनत्वञ्च जन्यत्वं अयमस्मादुत्पद्यत इति प्रत्ययादुत्पत्तेरपि दण्डादिजन्यत्वात्। यद्वा तदधिकरणक्षणध्वंसोत्पत्तिव्याप्यत्वं व्याप्यत्वञ्च कालिकं, उत्पत्तिप्रवेशात्

सिद्धिः। नापि ज्ञानत्वावच्छिन्नकार्य्यत्वान्यकार्य्यत्वप्रतियोगिककारणजन्येति साध्यम्। ज्ञानत्वस्य नित्यवृत्तितया कार्य्यत्वानवच्छेदकत्वात्। अथ यद्धर्माश्रयस्यासतः सत्त्वं हेत्वधीनं तत् कार्य्यतावच्छेदकं, ज्ञानत्वञ्च तथा। न चासत इत्यधिकं, व्योमादिसाधारणसत्त्वमात्रस्य हेत्वनियम्यत्वादिति चेत्। न।

व्यभिचारिणो निरासः। बाधकं विनेतिविशेषणाद्देवान्यथासिद्धस्य निरास इति भावः। 'ज्ञानत्वञ्च तथेति ज्ञानत्वाश्रयस्य सर्व्वस्यैवासतः सत्त्वं, ज्ञानसामान्यहेतुमनःप्रवृत्त्यधीनमिति तज्जन्यतावच्छेदकं ज्ञानत्वमित्यर्थः। 'अधिकमिति, तथा च नित्यज्ञानसत्त्वस्य हेत्वनधीनतया ज्ञानत्वस्य न कार्य्यतावच्छेदकत्वमिति भावः, हेत्वधीनत्वस्य अन्वयरूपत्वे यथाश्रुतमेव तदधिकरणक्षणध्वंसोत्पत्तिव्याप्यत्वरूपत्वे तु महाप्रलयीयतत्सत्त्व एव व्यभिचारो बोध्यः। 'व्योमादिसाधारणसत्त्वमात्रस्य' उत्पत्त्यतिरिक्तकालसम्बन्धमात्रस्य, तथा च घटत्वादेरपि दण्डादिजन्यतावच्छेदकत्वं न स्यादिति भावः। 'यदालिङ्गितस्येति, 'स्वरूपं' सर्व्वं स्वरूपं, यदालिङ्गितं सर्व्वमित्यर्थः, 'लाघवादिति, उत्पत्त्यघटितत्वादिति भावः। एवञ्च कृत्यादिजन्यतावच्छेदकन्तु न ज्ञेयत्वं किन्तु कार्य्यत्वमिति हृदयं। 'ज्ञानत्वमिति, नित्यज्ञानस्य कारणानधीनत्वादिति भावः। 'अनित्यज्ञानत्वेति ज्ञानत्वावच्छिन्नेत्यस्य स्थाने अनित्यज्ञानत्वावच्छिन्नेतिकरणे इत्यर्थः, 'इन्द्रियादीति, आदिना व्याप्तिज्ञान-सादृश्यज्ञान-पदज्ञानादिसंग्रहः,

यदालिङ्गितस्य स्वरूपं हेत्वधीनं तत्कार्य्यतावच्छेदकं लाघवात् ज्ञानत्वन्तु न तथा। अनित्यज्ञानत्वेति-

---

इदञ्च स्वमतावष्टम्भेन, परनये तु नित्यज्ञानाप्रसिद्ध्या ज्ञानत्वस्यैवात्ममनःप्रभृतीनां कार्य्यतावच्छेदकत्वेनानित्यज्ञानत्वावच्छिन्नकार्य्यत्वाप्रसिद्ध्या साध्याप्रसिद्धिरेव द्रष्टव्या। 'एतेनेति, 'प्रमात्वं' घटत्ववति घटत्वप्रकारकानुभवत्वादिकमित्यर्थः, 'ज्ञानत्वावच्छिन्नेति जन्यज्ञानत्वावच्छिन्नेत्यर्थः, क्वचित्तथैव पाठः जन्यज्ञानत्वावच्छिन्नत्वन्तु जन्यज्ञाननिष्ठान्योन्याभावप्रतियोगितानवच्छेदकधर्म्मावच्छिन्नत्वं जन्यज्ञानत्वान्यूनवृत्तिधर्म्मावच्छिन्नत्वमिति यावत्। सकलतद्वृत्तित्वस्यात्रत्यत्वप्रत्ययार्थत्वात्तेन परनये व्यावर्त्त्याप्रसिद्ध्या जन्यज्ञानत्वस्य शरीरादेः कार्य्यतावच्छेदकत्वेपि नाप्रसिद्धिः। अत्र कार्य्यतावच्छेदकत्वमात्रे साध्ये ज्ञानसामान्यकारणशरीरादिनिरूपितकारणताप्रतियोगिककार्य्यतावच्छेदकत्वेनार्थान्तरप्रसङ्गः। जन्यत्व-संयोगत्वाभ्यां द्रव्यत्वावच्छिन्नजन्यत्वदर्शनेन सामान्य-विशेषयोरप्येकप्रयोज्यत्वसम्भवादतः प्रतियोगिकान्तं कार्य्यताविशेषणं, 'कारणताभिन्नत्वं तादृशकारणतावच्छेदकानवच्छिन्नत्वं, तेन कार्य्यतावच्छेदकभेदेनैव कारणताभेदान्नार्थान्तरतादवस्थ्यमिति भावः।

भट्टाचार्य्यास्तु कार्य्यतावच्छेदकत्वमत्र कार्य्यतानतिरिक्तवृत्तित्वं न तु स्वरूपसम्बन्धविशेषः, तथा च ज्ञानादिसामान्यकारणजन्यतानतिरिक्तवृत्तित्वेन सिद्धसाधनवारणायैव प्रतियोगिकान्तं कार्य्यताविशेषणं, शेषं पूर्व्ववदित्याहुः। तदसत् अत्रावच्छेदकत्वस्य कार्य्यतावच्छेद-

करणे इन्द्रियादिभिर्यथायथं सिद्धसाधनं तेषां प्रत्येकं ज्ञानमात्राहेतुत्वात्। एतेन प्रमात्वम् ज्ञानत्वावच्छिन्न-

---

कतानतिरिक्तवृत्तित्वरूपत्वे ऽग्निमानुमानेपि तथाशब्देन निरुक्तका-र्य्यतानतिरिक्तवृत्तित्वस्यैव साध्यस्य परामर्शान्नीलघटत्वादौ तत्र व्यभिचाराभिधानस्यासङ्गतत्वापत्तेः, स्वरूपसम्बन्धरूपकार्य्यतावच्छेद-कत्वमात्रपरत्वे च सन्दर्भविरोधापत्तेः तस्य पूर्व्वप्रक्रान्तत्वादिति ध्येयम् ।

'ज्ञानत्वसाक्षाद्व्याप्येति, धर्म्मत्वमात्रं सत्तादौ व्यभिचारीति व्याप्यान्त प्रत्यक्षत्वे व्यभिचारवारणाय साक्षादिति । ननु अनुभवत्वे व्यभिचारः । न च ज्ञानत्वपदमनुभवत्वपरं, प्रत्यक्षत्वे व्यभिचारताद-वस्थ्यात् । किञ्च साक्षाद्व्याप्यत्वं न तद्व्याप्याव्याप्यत्वे सति तद्व्याप्यत्वं, प्रमात्वाप्रमात्वयोर्द्वैत्वसिद्धेः तयोस्तादृशस्य स्वस्यैव व्याप्यत्वात् । नापि तद्व्याप्यान्यूनवृत्तित्वे सति तद्व्याप्यत्वं प्रमाप्रमान्यतरत्वादिव्याप्यतया प्रमात्वाप्रमात्वयोर्द्वैत्वसिद्धितादवस्थ्यात । नापि तद्व्याप्यजात्यन्यून-वृत्तित्वे सतीत्यादिरूपं, प्रमाप्रमान्यतरत्वादौ तत्तज्ज्ञानत्वादौ च व्यभिचारात्। बाधकाभावे सतीति विशेषणान्न दोष इति चेत् । न। तावन्मात्रस्यैव सार्थकत्वात् व्यर्थविशेषणत्वात् तादृशानुभवत्वन्यू-नवृत्तितया स्वरूपासिद्धेश्च । उच्यते । ज्ञानत्वसाक्षाद्व्याप्यधर्म्मत्वं ज्ञानसाक्षाद्विभाजकोपाधित्वं भवति च भ्रमत्वं प्रमात्वञ्च तथा, ज्ञानं द्विविधं विद्या चाविद्या चेति प्रथमं विभागात् । अयञ्च विभागो मिश्रस्य भट्टस्य वा ग्राह्यः, न तु वैशेषिकस्य, तत्र

कार्य्यतानिरूपितकारणताभिन्नकारणताप्रतियोगिककार्य्यतावच्छेदकं ज्ञानत्वमात्रसाक्षाद्व्याप्यधर्म्मत्वात् अप्रमावदिति निरस्तं। प्रमात्वस्य नित्यवृत्तित्वात्। अनित्यप्रमात्वं तथा कार्य्यमात्रवृत्तिधर्म्मत्वादित्यपि नीलघटत्वादिना व्यभिचारि। अनित्यप्रमाप्रमोभयहेतुभिन्नहेतुजन्या अन्यत्वात् अप्रमावदिति चेत्। न। दोषस्य पित्तादेः स्वविषयप्रमाहेतुत्वेनाप्रमायां

निर्व्विकल्पकसाधारण्यार्थं विशिष्टत्वस्य भ्रमभिन्नज्ञानत्वरूपतया प्रमात्वरूपत्वाभावेन स्वरूपासिद्ध्यापत्तेः ।

यद्वा ज्ञानत्वसाक्षाद्व्याप्यधर्म्मत्वं भ्रमत्व-प्रमात्वान्यतरत्वं भ्रम-प्रमान्यतरपदप्रवृत्तिनिमित्तत्वं वा, तेन न काप्यनुपपत्तिः । ‘प्रमात्वस्येति, तथा च बाध इति भावः । ‘तथा’ कार्य्यतावच्छेदकं, सति तात्पर्य्ये तथादिपदानामेकदेशपरामर्शकत्वस्यापि व्युत्पत्तिसिद्धत्वात् । अवच्छेदकत्वञ्च स्वरूपसम्बन्धविशेषः, नातोऽनित्यज्ञानत्वावच्छिन्नकार्य्यतानतिरिक्तवृत्तित्वेन सिद्धसाधनं । ‘नीलघटत्वादिनेति, आदिना अन्यतरत्वादिपरिग्रहः ।

यद्वा ‘तथा’ अनित्यज्ञानत्वावच्छिन्नकार्य्यतानिरूपितकारणताभिन्नकारणतानिरूपितकार्य्यतावच्छेदकमित्यर्थः, पूर्व्वं प्रमात्वं पक्षीकृतमत्र तु अनित्यप्रमात्वमतो न पुनरुक्तिः । ‘नीलघटत्वादिनेति, आदिना अनित्यज्ञानत्वादिपरिग्रहः ।

साध्याप्रसिद्धेः। घटदृष्टान्तत्व तयैव व्यभिचारात्। शङ्खाद्यंशे पीतः शङ्ख इति ज्ञानस्यापि[१] प्रमात्वात् कारणव्यक्तिभेदजन्यत्वेन[२] सिद्धसाधनाच्च।

अथ प्रमा अप्रमाव्यावृत्तधर्म्मावच्छिन्नकार्य्यत्वप्रति-

'प्रमाप्रमोभयेति, प्रमाहेतुभिन्नहेतुजन्यत्वे साध्ये बाधः, अप्रमाहेतुभिन्नहेतुजन्यत्वे साध्ये दृष्टान्तासिद्धिरतः 'उभयेति, इन्द्रियादिकञ्च तदुभयहेतुरेवेति न तेन सिद्धसाधनमिति भावः। 'अप्रमायामिति, तथाच दृष्टान्तासिद्धिरिति भावः। 'घटदृष्टान्तत्व इति। यद्यपि स्वविषयकप्रमाप्रमोभयहेतुदण्डादिहेतुकतया घटोपि न दृष्टान्तः। तथापि द्व्यणुकदृष्टान्तत्वे तात्पर्य्यं। 'तयैव' अप्रमयैव। ननु विषयतातिरिक्तरूपेण हेतुत्वविवक्षणान्नोक्तदोष इत्यरुचेराह, 'शङ्खेति, 'प्रमात्वादिति, तथा च तज्जनकीभूतदोषोऽपि प्रमाप्रमोभयहेतुरेवेति तदुभयहेतुभिन्नहेतुजन्यत्वाभावात् तत्र व्यभिचार इति भावः। व्यभिचारस्तु सर्व्वांशे अलौकिकप्रत्यक्षानुमित्यात्मके शङ्खः पीत इति ज्ञाने एव न तु शङ्खाद्यंशे लौकिकप्रत्यक्षात्मके तत्र व्यभिचारः, तत्र च विषयतातिरिक्तरूपेण प्रमाप्रमोभयहेतुभिन्नो हेतुः शङ्खएव तज्जन्यत्वेन साध्यसत्त्वादित्यमंशतो बाधोऽपि तत्रैव द्रष्टव्यः।

ननु साध्ये प्रमापदेन भ्रमभिन्नज्ञानविवक्षणान्नोक्तदोष इत्यरुचे-

---

(१) पीतशङ्खज्ञानस्यापीति ख० ग० च।

(२) कारणव्यक्तिविशेषजन्यत्वेनेति क०।

योगिककारणजन्या अप्रमाविजातीयकार्य्यत्वात् घट-वत्। यदि प्रमा अप्रमात्वासमानाधिकरणरूपनिरू-पितकार्य्यत्वप्रतियोगिककारणजन्या न स्यात् अप्र-

---

राच, 'कारणेति, 'व्यक्तिभेदेति व्यक्तिविशेषेत्यर्थः,(१) यत्सन्निकर्षव्यक्त्या अप्रमा न जनिता प्रमैव जनिता तज्जन्यत्वेन सिद्धसाधनादित्यर्थः। 'अथ प्रमेति, 'प्रमा' अनित्यप्रमा, 'अप्रमाव्यावृत्तेति, अत्र अप्रमाव्यावृत्तत्वं न भ्रमभिन्नवृत्तित्वं, अन्यथा नत्वाद्यवच्छिन्नकार्य्यतामादाय सिद्धसा-धनापत्तेः तादृशकार्य्यतामादाय भ्रमेपि साध्यसत्त्वेन हेतौ विजा-तीयान्तवैयर्थ्यापत्तेश्च। किन्तु एकमात्रविशेष्यकप्रमावृत्तित्वं, एक-मात्रविशेष्यकेत्युपादानात् अप्रमात्वस्यापि प्रमाप्रमोभयसमूहालम्बन-वृत्तित्वेपि न प्रकृतासिद्धिः। न च तथापि दृष्टकालाद्यवच्छिन्नका-र्य्यताप्रतियोगिककारताश्रयात्मादिजन्यत्वेन संयोगत्वाद्यवच्छिन्नकार्य्यता-प्रतियोगिककारणताश्रयद्रव्यजन्यत्वेन च सिद्धसाधनं तादृशजन्यता-मादायाप्रमायामपि साध्यसत्त्वे 'अप्रमाविजातीयेति विशेषणञ्च हेतौ व्यर्थमिति वाच्यं। कारणजन्येत्यनेन कारणताप्रतियोगिककार्य्य-तावत्त्वविवक्षणात्। 'अप्रमाविजातीयेति भ्रमभिन्नेत्यर्थः, पक्षताव-च्छेदकसामानाधिकरण्येन साध्यसिद्धेरुद्देश्यत्वाच न भागासिद्धिः, भ्रमभिन्नप्रमैव वा पक्षः। अत्रानुमाने तर्कं प्रदर्शयति, 'यदीति, अप्रमाव्यावृत्तधर्मावच्छिन्नेत्यस्य विवरणम् 'अप्रमात्वेति, 'अप्रमा

---

(१) क्वचिन्मूलपुस्तके व्यक्तिविशेषजन्यत्वेनेत्येव पाठो वर्तते।

स्यादिति चेत्। न। अप्रमाव्यावृत्तधर्म्मावच्छिन्नकार्य्यत्वं संयोगस्य तत्प्रतियोगिककारणमिन्द्रियादीति तज्जन्यत्वेन सिद्धसाधनात्। अप्रमासाधारणव्यक्ति-जन्यत्वञ्चाप्रमातादात्म्ये प्रयोजकमिति तर्कोऽप्यप्रयो-

---

स्यादिति। न चेश्वरज्ञाने आकाशादौ व्यभिचार इति वाच्य। जन्यत्वे सतीति आपादके विशेषणात् विपर्य्ययानुमाने जन्यत्वाभावबाधेन पक्षधर्मतावलादनन्तरं वा जन्यत्वविशेषितेनैव विशिष्टाभावेनोक्त-साध्यसिद्धिः।

मिश्रास्तु 'अप्रमा स्यात्' अप्रमाविजातीयकार्य्यं न स्यादि-त्यर्थः। अग्रे चाप्रमातादात्म्ये इत्यस्याप्रमाविजातीयकार्य्यान्यत्व इत्यर्थः, इत्याहुः।

केचित्तु 'अप्रमा स्यात्' जन्यप्रमा न स्यादित्यर्थः। अप्रामाण्या-भाव एव च प्रमात्वं मतः परमते जन्यपदव्यावर्त्त्याप्रसिद्धिः। आका-शादेरेव तादृशत्वात्। अग्रे चाप्रमातादात्म्ये प्रयोजकमित्यस्य जन्य-प्रमाभिन्नत्वे व्याप्यमित्यर्थः, इत्याहुः।

नव्यास्तु 'अप्रमा स्यात' प्रमाभिन्नः स्यात्, रजतमात्रविशेष्य-कत्वे सति रजतत्वप्रकारकत्वाभाववान् स्यादित्यर्थः। ईश्वरज्ञाने च रजतमात्रविशेष्यकत्वाभावेनापाद्यसत्त्वान्न व्यभिचारः। तादृशज्ञानस्यैव पक्षत्वात् पक्षतावच्छेदकसामानाधिकरण्येन विपर्य्ययसिद्धेरुद्देश्यत्वाद्दा न विपर्य्ययानुमाने भागासिद्धिः। अग्रे अप्रमातादात्म्ये प्रयोजक-

जकः। अथानित्यप्रमा प्रमाप्रमान्यतरप्रतिबन्धकजन्या

मित्यस्य रजतमात्रविशेष्यकरजतत्वप्रकारकभिन्नत्वे व्याप्यमित्यर्थः, इत्याहुः।

यथाश्रुतानुमानाभिप्रायेणाह, 'अप्रमेति, संयोगत्वावच्छिन्नं प्रति द्रव्यत्वेन जनकत्वादिन्द्रियमपि द्रव्यं तथेति तज्जन्यत्वेन सिद्धसाधनमित्यर्थः। ननु विवक्षितानुमानमदुष्टमेवेति तत्र दूषणमाह, 'अप्रमासाधारणेति अप्रमासाधारणकारणजन्यत्वमेव, 'अप्रमातादात्म्ये प्रयोजकं' अप्रमातादात्म्ये व्याप्यं, न त्वापादकीभूततादृशजन्यत्वाभाव इति तर्कोऽप्यप्रयोजक इत्यर्थः। तथा च तदुपजीवकमनुमानमपि सुतरामप्रयोजकमित्यपेरर्थः। इदमुपलक्षणं प्रमात्वव्याप्यतत्तद्व्यक्तित्वावच्छिन्नकार्य्यतामादाय सिद्धसाधनमर्थान्तरं वेत्यपि बोध्यम्।

'अनित्यप्रमेति, दृष्टान्ते प्रमाप्रतिबन्धकदोषजन्यतामादाय साध्यसत्त्वं, पक्षे च तद्द्वारा बाधादप्रमाप्रतिबन्धकगुणजन्यत्वमादाय पर्य्यवस्यतीति भावः। अप्रमाप्रतिबन्धकजन्यत्वमात्रे साध्ये अप्रमायां व्यभिचारः, प्रमाप्रतिबन्धकजन्यत्वमात्रे साध्ये बाध इत्यन्यतरोपादानं, 'प्रमाप्रामान्यतरत्वादिति। न चेश्वरज्ञाने व्यभिचार इति वाच्यम्। अनित्यत्वे सतीति विशेषणात्। न च जन्यज्ञानत्वादित्येवास्त्विति वाच्यम्। अखण्डाभावत्वात्(१)। 'चाक्षुषप्रमेति, पक्षे चाक्षुषपदं

---

(१) प्रमाभेदाप्रमाभेदोभयावच्छिन्नप्रतियोगिताकभेदस्य अन्यतरत्वरूपत्वेन तादृशान्यतरत्वस्य जन्यज्ञानत्वाघटितत्वान्न हेतोर्व्यर्थविशेषणघटितत्वमिति भावः।

प्रमाप्रमान्यतरत्वात् अप्रमावत्। चाक्षुषप्रमा चाक्षुषभ्रमाजनकजन्या अनित्यप्रमात्वात् रासनप्रमावदिति चेत्। न। प्रमाजनकासाधारणव्यक्तिभेदस्याप्रमाप्रतिबन्धकत्वेन चाक्षुषभ्रमाजनकत्वेन च

ईश्वरज्ञाने बाधवारणाय, साध्ये च तत् दृष्टान्तलाभाय, हेतौ च प्रमापदं चाक्षुषभ्रमे व्यभिचारवारणाय, अनित्यपदमीश्वरज्ञाने व्यभिचारवारणाय। 'प्रमाजनकेति, 'व्यक्तिभेदस्य' व्यक्तिविशेषस्य, प्रमामात्रं जनयति यत्सन्निकर्षादिव्यक्तिः तस्या अप्रमाप्रतिबन्धकत्वेन चाक्षुषभ्रमाजनकत्वेन च प्रमायां तज्जन्यत्वात् सिद्धसाधनमित्यर्थः। अत्र प्रमाप्रमान्यतरप्रतिबन्धकत्वं न तत्कारणीभूताभावप्रतियोगित्वं, किन्तु प्रमाप्रमान्यतराजनकत्वमित्यभिप्रेत्य 'अप्रमाप्रतिबन्धकत्वेनेत्युक्तं। 'स्वविरोधीति स्वस्य विरोधी प्रतिबन्धको योऽनुभव इत्यर्थः, स च भ्रम एव, प्रमाप्रतिबन्धकज्ञानस्य भ्रमत्वनियमादिति भ्रमप्रतिबन्धकजन्यत्वं प्रमायां सिद्ध्यति। अत्र स्वप्रतिबन्धकग्राह्याभावविषयकस्मृतिप्रतिबन्धकानुभवसामग्रीजन्यतया लौकिकप्रत्यक्षनिश्चयान्यप्रमायामंशतः सिद्धसाधनस्यांशतोऽर्थान्तरस्य च वारणाय साध्ये अनुभवपदं, हेतौ चानुभवपदं स्मृतौ भ्रमप्रतिबन्धकगुणजन्यत्वानभ्युपगमात् स्मृतिसामग्र्या अनुभवाप्रतिबन्धकत्वाच्च स्मृतौ व्यभिचारवारणाय। ननु तथापि स्वप्रतिबन्धकग्राह्याभावविषयकमानसज्ञानप्रतिबन्धकसामग्रीजन्यतया मानसेतरानुभवे अंशतः सिद्धसाधनं। अथ तद्वति तत्प्रकारकानुभवस्य पक्षतया तदवच्छेदेन

सिद्धसाधनात् । एतेन प्रमा स्वविरोध्यनुभवप्रतिबन्धकजन्या अनित्यानुभवत्वात् अप्रमावत् । दूरात्पुरुषस्य स्थाणुतया ज्ञाने सन्निधौ च भूयोऽवयवेन्द्रियसन्निकर्षस्य विरोधिस्थाण्वनुभवप्रतिबन्धकत्वं पुरुषज्ञा-

---

साध्यसिद्धेरुद्देश्यत्वान्नांशतः सिद्धसाधनं दोषाय, अवच्छेदकावच्छेदेन सिद्धसाधनन्तु नास्त्येव, मानसप्रत्यक्षसामग्र्या ज्ञानान्तराप्रतिबन्धकतया मानसप्रमायामेव साध्यसिद्धेः । न च साध्येऽनुभवपदवैयर्थ्यं लौकिकप्रत्यक्षप्रमायां ग्राह्याभावविषयकस्मृतेरप्रतिबन्धकतया स्वविरोधिग्राह्याभावस्मृतिप्रतिबन्धकीभूतानुभवसामग्रीजन्यत्वस्य तत्रैवाभावेन सिद्धसाधनविरहात् अंशतः सिद्धसाधनस्य चादोषत्वादिति वाच्यं । साध्ये स्वविरोधित्वं हि न स्वप्रतिबन्धकत्वं अपि तु स्वविरोधिविषयकत्वं स्वविशेष्ये स्वप्रकाराभावविषयकत्वमिति यावत्, तथा च ग्राह्याभावस्मृतेरपि लौकिकप्रत्यक्षप्रमाविरोधितया तत्रापि स्वविरोधिग्राह्याभावस्मृतिप्रतिबन्धकीभूतानुभवसामग्रीजन्यत्वसत्त्वेन-सिद्धसाधनस्यैव सम्भवतादिति चेत् । न । नव्यनये सामान्यतः प्रत्यक्षसामग्रीत्वेनैवानुमितिप्रतिबन्धकतया मानससामग्र्या अपि अनुमितिप्रतिबन्धकत्वात्, प्रत्यक्षसामग्रीत्वञ्च समानाधिकरणत्वे सति स्वाव्यवहितपूर्ववर्त्तित्वसम्बन्धेन प्रत्यक्षविशिष्टत्वं तेन नातिप्रसङ्गः, अतएवानुमितीच्छादेरपि नोत्तेजकत्वं न वा लौकिकत्व-समानविषयत्वयोः प्रवेशः, सम्प्रदायमतेपि मानसप्रत्यक्षं जायतां चाक्षुषाद्यतिरिक्तं प्रत्यक्षं जायतामित्यादीच्छादशायां मानसप्रत्यक्षसामग्रीसत्त्वे

जनकत्वञ्च दृष्टम्, अप्रमायां पित्तादेर्लिङ्गादिभ्रमस्य च तथात्वमिति निरस्तं। प्रमाजनकव्यक्तिविशेषस्याप्रमाप्रतिबन्धकत्वं प्रमाजनकत्वञ्चास्तीति सिद्धसा-

---

अनुमितेरनुदयात् तत्तदिच्छाभावकूटाभावविशिष्टमानससामग्रीत्वेन मानसेतरज्ञानं प्रति प्रतिबन्धकत्वावच्छेदकत्वाच्च, तथा च ग्राह्याभावविषयकमानसप्रत्यक्षप्रतिबन्धकसामग्रीजन्यतया मानसेतरानुभव इव ग्राह्याभावविषयकानुमितिप्रतिबन्धकसामग्रीजन्यतया मानसप्रमायामपि सिद्धसाधनसम्भवेन पक्षीभूतप्रमामात्र एव सिद्धसाधनस्य दुर्वारत्वात् मानसप्रत्यक्षं प्रति मानसेतरज्ञानसामग्रीत्वेनैव प्रतिबन्धकतया स्मृतिसामग्र्या अपि मानसप्रत्यक्षप्रतिबन्धकत्वेन ग्राह्याभावविषयकमानसप्रतिबन्धकस्मृतिसामग्रीजन्यतामादायैव स्मृतावपि साध्यसम्भवाद्धेतावनुभवपदवैयर्थ्यञ्चेति। मैवं। मानसेतरानुभवेऽतः सिद्धसाधनस्योक्तक्रमेण प्रमामात्र एव सिद्धसाधनस्य वारणाय प्रतिबन्धकपदेन ज्ञानसाक्षात्त्वादिभाजकोपाध्यवच्छिन्नप्रतिबध्यतानिरूपितप्रतिबन्धकताया विवक्षितत्वात्, ज्ञानसाक्षात्त्वादिभाजकोपाधित्वञ्च ज्ञानत्वव्याप्यविभाजकोपाध्यव्याप्यत्वे सति ज्ञानविभाजकोपाधित्वं तादृशञ्च प्रमात्वाप्रमात्वे स्मृतित्वानुभूतित्वे च, न तु अनुमितित्वादिर्मानसत्वादिर्वा, अतो हेतौ नानुभवपदवैयर्थ्यं, स्मृतिसामग्र्या मानसेतरज्ञानसामग्रीत्वेन मानसप्रत्यक्षप्रतिबन्धकत्वेऽपि मानसत्वस्यैव तत्प्रतिबध्यतावच्छेदकतया तादृशविभाजकोपाध्यवच्छिन्नप्रतिबध्यतानवच्छेदकत्वादिति भावः। 'अप्रमावदिति, अप्रमाप्रतिबन्धकज्ञानस्य प्रमात्वनियमेन प्रमाप्रति-

धनादिति न प्रमायामतिरिक्तगुणसिद्धिः। किञ्च प्रत्यक्षप्रमादौ अनुगतस्यार्थान्तरस्य गुणस्याभावः इन्द्रियसन्निकर्षादीनाञ्चाननुगमः। न च जात्यैव गुण-दोषौ।

बन्धकदोषजन्यत्वादेव तत्र साध्यसत्त्वादिति भावः। अप्रयोजकत्वं निरस्यति, 'दूरादिति, 'सन्निधौ चेति, तदज्ञानेन तदभाववत्तया ज्ञानेन चेतिशेषः, 'विरोधि' स्थाणुत्वाभावप्रमाविरोधि, 'पुरुषज्ञान-जनकत्वं' स्थाणुत्वाभावप्रमाजनकत्वं, तथाचान्वय-व्यतिरेकसिद्धमेव प्रमाविशेषे तथात्वमिति भावः।

ननु तथापि साध्यविकलो दृष्टान्त इत्यत आह, 'अप्रमायामिति, 'शङ्खादिभ्रमस्य चेति, स्वविरोधिप्रमाप्रतिबन्धकस्येति शेषः, 'तथात्वं' जनकत्वं। 'प्रमाजनकव्यक्तिविशेषस्येति प्रमोपधायकतत्तज्ज्ञानादि-व्यक्तिविशेषस्येत्यर्थः, 'अप्रमाप्रतिबन्धकत्वं' अप्रमात्वावच्छिन्नप्रतिबन्ध-कत्वं, 'प्रमाजनकत्वं' तत्तत्प्रमाव्यक्तित्वावच्छिन्नजनकत्वं, 'अस्ति' अस्तु, 'सिद्धसाधनात्' प्रमात्वनिष्ठकार्य्यतावच्छेदकत्वस्योद्देश्यस्य सिद्ध्या अर्था-न्तरात्, उपसंहरति, 'इति नेति, 'अतिरिक्तगुणसिद्धिः' प्रमात्वावच्छि-न्नकार्य्यतानिरूपितकारणताकगुणसिद्धिः। ननु प्रमात्वावच्छिन्नस्य पक्ष-त्वात्तदवच्छेदेनैव साध्यसिद्ध्या तादृशगुणसिद्धिरित्यत आह, 'किञ्चेति, 'अर्थान्तरस्य' पदार्थान्तरस्य, 'गुणस्य' गुणपदवाच्यस्य, तथा च प्रमात्वावच्छेदेन साध्यसिद्धौ बाध इति भावः। ननु गुणत्वजात्यैव तेषामनुगमान्न बाध इत्यत आह, 'नचेति, 'गुण-दोषाविति, हेतू इति शेषः, ज्ञानत्वेन सह साङ्कर्य्यादिति भावः। दोषः दृष्टान्तत्वेनोपात्तः।

प्रमाजनकत्वं गुणत्वं भ्रमजनत्वं च दोषत्वमतिप्रसक्तं, तन्मात्रजनकत्वञ्चासिद्धमिति ।

इति श्रीमद्गङ्गेशोपाध्यायविरचिते तत्त्वचिन्तामणौ प्रत्यक्षखण्डे प्रामाण्यवादे उत्पत्तिवादपूर्व्वपक्षः ।

ननु प्रमाजनकत्वादिना तदनुगम इत्यत आह, 'प्रमेति, 'अतिप्रसक्तं' कालात्मादावतिप्रसक्तं, 'तन्मात्रजनकत्वं' तदन्यज्ञानाजनकत्वे सति तज्जनकत्वं, तच्छब्देन यथायथं प्रमाप्रमयोः परामर्शः, 'असिद्धमिति, गुणत्वेनाभिमतस्य सल्लिङ्गपरामर्शादेरपि सन्निकर्षघटकतया विषयविधया च स्वविशेष्यकभ्रमजनकत्वात् दोषत्वेनाभिमतस्यापि पित्तादेः स्वविषयकप्रमाजनकत्वादिति भावः ।

इति श्रीमथुरानाथतर्कवागीश-विरचिते तत्त्वचिन्तामणिरहस्ये प्रत्यक्षखण्डे प्रामाण्यवादरहस्ये उत्पत्तिवादपूर्व्वपक्षरहस्यम् ॥०॥

अथ उत्पत्तिवादसिद्धान्तः ।

उच्यते । एवमप्रमापि स्वत एवस्यान्न तु परतः, प्रमावदसाधारणकारणादेव तदुत्पत्तौ दोषस्य तत्राहेतुत्वात् । अथ ज्ञानसामग्रीसत्त्वेऽपि विशेषादर्शनादिपित्तादेरनुविधानादप्रमायां दोषो हेतुरिति चेत्तर्हि विशेषदर्शन-पित्ताद्यभावादितस्तत्रैव विषये

'एवमप्रमापि स्वतएव स्यादिति प्रमात्ववदप्रमात्वमपि कार्य्यतानवच्छेदकमेव स्यादिति भावः[१]। एवकारार्थमेव विवृणोति, 'न त्विति न तु कार्य्यतावच्छेदकमित्यर्थः, 'असाधारणकारणादेवेति प्रमानुपधायकासाधारणकारणताक्रान्ततत्तद्व्यक्तित एवेत्यर्थः, 'अहेतुत्वात्' अहेतुतायाः सुवचत्वात् । 'आगन्तुकेति भ्रमाजनकेत्यर्थः । नन्वेतावता प्रमाम्प्रति विशेषदर्शन-पित्ताद्यभावानां कारणत्वमस्तु प्रमात्वस्य कथं कार्य्यतावच्छेदकत्वं तत्तद्व्यक्तित्वेनैव कार्य्य-कारणभावसम्भवादित्यत आह, 'अपि चेति, 'नियमस्येति कार्य्य-कारणभावघटको नियमस्येत्यर्थः, 'न व्यक्त्योरेव' न तत्तद्व्यक्त्योरपि न तत्तद्व्यक्तित्वावच्छिन्नप्रतियोगितानुयोगिताकोपीति यावत्, कार्य्य-कारणभावघटकनियमप्रतियोगितावच्छेदकं तदनुयोगितावच्छेदकं वा न तत्तद्व्यक्तित्वमपीति तु फलि-

---

(१) स्यादित्यर्थ इति ख०, ग० च ।

प्रमा तदभावान्नेति प्रमायामागन्तुककारणापेक्षेति कथं न परतस्त्वम्। अपि च नियमगर्भः कार्य्य-कारण-भावः नियमस्य न व्यक्तेरेव व्यभिचारादतिप्रसङ्गाच्चेति नियमनिरूपकमनुगुणमनुगतमास्थेयम्। एवञ्चाप्रमा-यामिव प्रमायामपि तद्व्यावृत्तं कारणमनुगतमास्थेयं। किञ्च यत्कार्य्यं यत्कार्य्यविजातीयं तत्तत्कारणविजाती-यकारणजन्यं यथा घटविजातीयः पटः, अन्यथा कार्य्य-

---

तार्थः। अवच्छेदकत्वञ्च स्वरूपसम्बन्धविशेषः, तद्रूपादिव्यक्तिप्रति-योगिकनियमानुयोगित्व-प्रतियोगित्वयोः तत्तद्व्यक्तित्वेनावच्छिन्नत्वा-द्युपगमाद्घटकान्तं नियमविशेषणं, कारणताघटकनियमातिरिक्त-नियमप्रतियोगित्वानुयोगित्वयोः स्वरूपसम्बन्धविशेषात्मकावच्छेद-कतानभ्युपगमे तु तन्नोपादेयं। तत्तद्व्यक्तित्वं कुतो नावच्छेदकं तदाह, 'व्यभिचारादतिप्रसङ्गाच्चेति। यदि सामान्यरूपेण प्रतियो-गितानुयोगिता च तत्तद्व्यक्तित्वेन तदा व्यभिचारः तद्व्यक्तिमन्तरे-णापि सामान्यधर्म्मावच्छिन्नोत्पत्तेः। यदि च प्रतियोगित्वमनुयोगित्वञ्च द्वयमेव तत्तद्व्यक्तित्वेन, यदि वा प्रतियोगित्वं तद्व्यक्तित्वेन अनुयोगि-त्वञ्च सामान्यरूपेण तदा अप्रसङ्गः, आद्ये तद्घटव्यक्तित्वावच्छिन्नं प्रति तद्रासभव्यक्तित्वेनापि कारणत्वप्रसङ्गात्, अन्त्ये सामान्यधर्म्मावच्छि-न्नव्यक्त्यन्तरोत्पत्तिसमयेऽपि तद्व्यक्तेरुत्पादप्रसङ्गादित्यर्थः। 'इतीति अत इत्यर्थः, 'नियमनिरूपकं' नियतत्वावच्छेदकं कार्य्यतावच्छेदक-मिति यावत्, 'अनुगुणं' अनुगुणत्वावच्छेदकं कारणतावच्छेदकमिति

वैजात्यस्याकस्मिकतापत्तेः, घटज्ञानजातीयमपि कार्य्यं तद्विजातीयकार्य्य-कारणविजातीयघटेन्द्रियसन्निकर्षादिजन्यमिति न व्यभिचारः। एवञ्चानित्यप्रमा अप्रमाकारणविजातीयकारणजन्या[१] अप्रमाविजातीयकार्य्यत्वात् घटवत्। एवञ्चानुगतस्य प्रमाहेतुत्वे प्रमा स्वविरोध्यनुभवप्रतिबन्धकजातीयजन्या जन्यानुभवत्वात्

यावत्, 'आस्थेयं' प्रकृत आस्थेयं,[२] तच्च परिशेषात् प्रमात्वमेवेति भावः। उपसंहरति, 'एवञ्चेति, 'प्रमायामपि' प्रमात्वावच्छिन्नेपि। ननु विशेषदर्शनाद्यभावे प्रमा नेत्युक्तमयुक्तं विशेषदर्शनस्य विपरीतज्ञानोत्तरप्रत्यक्षमात्रे हेतुतया तेन विनापि प्रमोत्पत्तेः, तदुत्तरप्रमायाश्च तत्प्रमाकारणान्तरादन्यथासिद्धिः, एवं पित्ताद्यभावोपि न प्रमाहेतुः शङ्खे श्वैत्यप्रत्यक्षत्वावच्छिन्नं प्रत्येव तस्य हेतुत्वात् पित्तादिसत्त्वेपि शङ्खे श्वैत्यानुमित्युदयात् घटादौ श्वैत्यादिप्रत्यक्षप्रमोत्पादाच्च प्रतिबन्धिस्त्वनुत्तरमित्यरुचेराह, 'किञ्चेति, 'यत्कार्य्यविजातीयं' यत्कार्य्यापेक्षया वैधर्म्यवत्, 'तत्कारणविजातीयेति तद्वृत्तिकार्य्यताप्रतियोगिककारणतान्यकारणताप्रतियोगिककार्य्यताश्रय इत्यर्थः। यद्वा तद्वृत्तिधर्म्मानवच्छिन्नकार्य्यताश्रय इत्यर्थः, यमजयोरपि अदृष्ट-

---

(१) एवं प्रमा अप्रमाकारणविजातीयकारणजन्या इति ग॰।

(२) 'उपस्थेयं' प्रकृते उपस्थेयं इति क॰ पुस्तकपाठेन कस्यचित् मूलपुस्तकस्य तादृशः पाठोऽनुमीयत इति॥

अप्रमावदित्यादावपि न सिद्धसाधनं। अपि चानित्यप्रमात्वं कार्य्यतावच्छेदकं बाधकं विना कार्य्यमात्रवृत्तिधर्म्मत्वात् अप्रमात्ववत्। नीलघटत्वं तु विशिष्टं न कार्य्यतावच्छेदकं, प्रत्येकानुगतप्रयोजकद्वयादेव

विशेषः प्रयोजक इति भावः। 'आकस्मिकतेति निर्निमित्तिकतेत्यर्थः। ननु घटप्रत्यक्षादौ व्यभिचारः तद्धि पटप्रत्यक्षादिविजातीयं न तत्कारणविजातीयकारणजन्यं इन्द्रियसन्निकर्षादीनां पटप्रत्यक्षेऽपि कारणत्वादित्यत आह, 'घटज्ञानेति 'घटज्ञानजातीयं' घटप्रत्यक्षादि, 'तद्विजातीयं कार्य्यं' घटज्ञानविजातीयं कार्य्यं पटप्रत्यक्षादि, 'एवं' एवंरूपेण यत्तद्भ्यां सामान्यतो व्याप्तौ, 'अप्रमाकारणेति अप्रमावृत्तिकार्य्यताप्रतियोगिककारणतान्यकारणताप्रतियोगिककार्य्यताश्रय इत्यर्थः। यद्वा तद्वृत्तिधर्मानवच्छिन्नकार्य्यताश्रय इत्यर्थः। ननु अनेन तत्तत्प्रमां प्रति तत्तत्पित्ताद्यभावानां कारणत्वं सिद्ध्यतु न तु प्रमात्वस्य कार्य्यतावच्छेदकत्वं सिद्धं, किञ्च प्रमामात्रं जनयति यत्सन्निकर्षव्यक्त्यादि तज्जन्यत्वेन सिद्धसाधनञ्च। मैवं प्रमात्वावच्छेदेन साध्यसिद्धेरुद्देश्यत्वात् प्रमात्वे तादृशजन्यतारूपसाध्यस्य स्वरूपसम्बन्धरूपावच्छेदकत्वसिद्धेः, एवञ्च तादृशी सिद्धिरपि न प्रतिबन्धिका पक्षतावच्छेदकावच्छेदेन साध्यानुमितिं प्रति तादृशसिद्धेरेव प्रतिबन्धकत्वादिति भावः। पूर्वोक्तार्थान्तरदोषमुद्धरति, 'एवञ्चेति, 'प्रमाहेतुत्वे' प्रमात्वावच्छिन्नं प्रति हेतुत्वे, आवश्यक इति शेषः। 'न सिद्धसाधनमिति न प्रमात्वनिष्ठकार्य्यतावच्छेदकत्वस्योद्देश्यस्यासिद्धा

विशिष्टसिद्धेरार्थः समाजः। घटज्ञानत्वादौ तु बाधकम्। अस्तु वा तथाप्यनुगतभोजकादृष्टहेतुकत्वम्। अन्यथा कार्य्यमात्रे नादृष्टं हेतुः स्यात्। एवमनित्यप्रमात्वं अनित्यज्ञानत्वावच्छिन्नकार्य्यत्वप्रतियोगिककारणताभिन्नकारणताप्रतियोगिककार्य्यतावच्छेदकम् अनित्यज्ञा-

---

अर्थान्तरमित्यर्थः, प्रमात्वविशिष्टस्य पक्षतया तदवच्छेदेनैव तादृश-जन्यतासिद्ध्या उद्देश्यसिद्धेः तादृशसिद्धौ अनुगतकारणासम्भवस्यैव पूर्वं बाधकत्वेनाभिधानादिति भावः। 'अनित्यप्रमात्वमिति विषय-भेदेनानित्यप्रमात्वस्यैकस्याभावात् अनित्यत्वविशिष्टघटत्ववतिघटत्व-प्रकारकत्वादीत्यर्थः, एवं सर्वत्र,'कार्य्यतावच्छेदकमिति, पक्षधर्मताबलाद् गुणजन्यतावच्छेदकत्वसिद्धिरिति भावः। हेतौ नीलघटत्ववारणाय 'बाधकं विनेति, 'कार्य्यमात्रेति। न च मेयत्वादौ अकार्य्यवृत्तित्वरूप-बाधकसत्त्वेन व्यभिचाराभावात् किं मात्रपदेनेति वाच्यम्। 'बाधकं विनेत्यत्र अकार्य्यवृत्तित्वरूपबाधकाप्रवेशात् मेयत्वे व्यभिचारवारणाय तदुपादानात्। 'कार्य्यमात्रवृत्तिधर्मत्वञ्च' कार्य्यान्यावृत्तिधर्मत्वं, येन सम्बन्धेन कार्य्यतावच्छेदकत्वं तेन कार्य्यान्यावृत्तित्वं वाच्यं तेन महाकालादिवृत्तितया नासिद्धिः। 'प्रत्येकेति नीलसामग्र्या नीलं, घटसामग्र्या च घटस्तयोः समाजादर्थवशसम्पन्नं विशिष्टं न तु विशिष्ट-निर्वाहाय नीलकपालत्वादिना तद्विशिष्टं प्रति हेतुत्वं। अतएव नीलसामग्र्यभावादेव नीलाभावसम्भवेन नीलेतरघटत्वादिकमप्यर्थ-समाजसिद्धमिति भावः। अत्रेदं चिन्त्यं प्रमात्वमपि अर्थसमाजग्रस्तं

मत्वव्याप्यकार्य्यतावच्छेदकधर्म्मत्वात् अप्रमात्ववत् इत्य-
नित्यप्रमायामप्रमाव्यावृत्तानुगतहेतुसिद्धिः। अन्यथा-
नुगतकार्य्यानुपपत्तेः। तथा अनित्यप्रमात्वम् अप्रमाका-
रणतानवच्छेदकरूपावच्छिन्नकारणताप्रतियोगिकका-

तथा हि प्रमात्वं तद्वद्विशेष्यकत्वावच्छिन्नतत्प्रकारकत्वं तथा च तत्प्र-
कारकज्ञानसामग्रीसत्त्वात् तत्प्रकारकत्वं, तद्वदिन्द्रियसन्निकर्षादेस्तद्वति
असंसर्गाग्रहादेश्च सत्त्वात् तद्विशेष्यकत्वावच्छिन्नत्वमिति। अनित्य-
घटज्ञानत्वादौ व्यभिचारमुद्धरति, 'घटेति' अनित्यघटज्ञानत्वादा-
वित्यर्थः, 'बाधकमिति, अस्तीति शेषः, असम्भवं कारणतावच्छेदक-
त्वमेव बाधकमिति भावः। 'तत्रापि' घटज्ञानत्वादावपि, 'अनु-
गतभोजकादृष्टहेतुकत्वं' अनुगतभोजकादृष्टजन्यतावच्छेदकत्वं, प्रकृते
च तादृशादृष्टविशेषसिद्धावपि गुणजन्यत्वसिद्धिरप्रत्यूहैवेति भावः।
'अन्यथेति, घटज्ञानं प्रति भोजकादृष्टस्याकारणत्वे इत्यर्थः। इदमा-
पाततः अदृष्टत्वेन हेतुत्वेपि विशेषरूपेण हेतुत्वे मानाभावादिति
भाव्यं। पूर्वानुमाने आत्म-मनोयोगादिजन्यतावच्छेदकत्वं बाधान्न सिद्धं
पक्षधर्मताबलात् कारणविशेषजन्यतावच्छेदकत्वमेव सिद्धमिदानीं सा-
क्षादेव तत्साधयति, 'एवमिति, यद्यपि अनेनापि साक्षात्कारण-
विशेषजन्यतावच्छेदकत्वं न सिद्ध्यति तादृशकारणताभिन्ना कारणता
अनित्यप्रमात्वावच्छिन्नस्य आत्म-मनोयोगवृत्तिकारणता तत्प्रतियो-
गिककार्य्यतावच्छेदकत्वसम्भवात् तथापि 'कारणताभिन्नेत्यस्य कारण-
तावच्छिन्नवृत्तीत्यर्थः। न च चक्षुरादिनिष्ठकारणताप्रतियोगिककार्य्य-

र्य्यतावच्छेदकं भ्रमावृत्तिकार्य्यतावच्छेदकत्वात् घटत्व-वत्। चाक्षषप्रमात्वं चाक्षुषाप्रमाकारणतानवच्छेदक-रूपावच्छिन्नकारणताप्रतियोगिककार्य्यतावच्छेदकं चा-क्षुषभ्रमावृत्तिकार्य्यतावच्छेदकत्वात् घटत्ववत्। अनित्य-

---

तावच्छेदकत्वेनार्थान्तरं बाधात्। न चैवं प्रतियोग्यन्तमपि हीयतां बाधादेव नार्थान्तरत्वमिति वाच्यं। तथैवोद्देश्यत्वात्। 'अनित्यज्ञान-त्वव्याप्येति, अनित्यज्ञानत्वे व्यभिचारवारणाय व्याप्यान्तं, 'व्याप्यत्वं' न्यूनवृत्तित्वं तत्समानाधिकरणान्योन्याभावप्रतियोगितावच्छेदकत्वमिति यावत्, यथाश्रुते अनित्यज्ञानत्वे व्यभिचारतादवस्थ्यात्। 'अनित्य-ज्ञानत्वव्याप्यत्वं' अनित्यज्ञानत्वान्यत्वं इति केचित्। अनित्यघटज्ञान-त्वादौ व्यभिचारवारणाय 'कार्य्यतावच्छेदकेति, 'अन्यथा' अनुगत-कारणं विना। पूर्वानुमाने दोषजन्यतावच्छेदकत्वं बाधान्न सिद्धमिदानीं साक्षादेव साधयति, 'अनित्येति अनित्यत्वविशिष्टघटत्ववतिघटत्व-प्रकारकत्वादीत्यर्थः, 'अप्रमाकारणतेति अप्रमात्वावच्छिन्नकार्य्यताप्रति-योगिककारणतेत्यर्थः, तेन गुणनिष्ठकारणतायामपि प्रमाप्रमासमूहा-लम्बनमादाय न तादृशकारणतावच्छेदकावच्छिन्नत्वं, अप्रमापदेन एकमात्रविशेष्यकघटत्वाभाववतिघटत्वप्रकारकज्ञानं वा विवक्षितं तथा च यथाश्रुतमेव साधु एवमग्रेपि बोध्यं। भ्रमत्वे व्यभिचारवार-णाय हेतौ 'भ्रमावृत्तीति भ्रमावृत्तित्वं घटत्वांशे या प्रमा तद्भिन्न-ज्ञानावृत्तित्वं भ्रमत्वान्यत्वं वा, तेन न प्रमात्वस्यापि भ्रमवृत्तितया स्वरूपासिद्धिः। 'चाक्षुषप्रमेति घटत्ववतिघटत्वप्रकारकचाक्षुषत्वेत्यर्थः।

रजतप्रमात्वं रजतप्रमाकारणतावच्छेदकरूपानवच्छिन्नकारणताप्रतियोगिककार्य्यतावच्छेदकं रजतभ्रमावृत्तिकार्य्यतावच्छेदकत्वात् घटत्ववत्। अन्यथा नियामकं विना चाक्षुषादिरजतज्ञानं किञ्चिद्रजतवृत्तिप्रकारकं किञ्चिद्रजतावृत्तिप्रकारकमिति नियमो न स्यात्। ज्ञानसामग्र्यास्तुल्यत्वात्। यत्तु प्रमाया असाधारणकारणजन्यत्वे साध्ये प्रमान्यत्वमुपाधिः। न च पक्षेतरत्वम्, तव ईश्वरज्ञानस्य प्रमात्वात्पक्षस्य

ननु यदि प्रमासामान्ये अनुगतो हेतुः सिद्धस्तदा चाक्षुषसामग्री-प्रमासामग्रीभ्यां चाक्षुषप्रमासिद्धौ नीलघटत्ववच्चाक्षुषप्रमात्वस्यापि न कार्य्यतावच्छेदकत्वं अतो बाधः स्वरूपासिद्धिश्च। नैवं प्रमामात्रे साक्षात्कारिप्रमायां वा यदि सामान्येनानुगतो गुणोऽस्तीत्युच्यते परैस्तदर्थमनुमानाङ्गीकारात्। अनतिरिक्तवृत्तित्वमत्रावच्छेदकत्वमिति केचित्। 'चाक्षुषभ्रमेति, चाक्षुषभ्रमत्वे व्यभिचारवारणाय वृत्त्यन्तं घटत्वप्रमाभिन्नचाक्षुषावृत्तित्वं तदर्थः, तेन न स्वरूपासिद्धिः, दृष्टान्तासिद्धिवारणाय चाक्षुषत्वमखण्डाभावघटकं। न च तद्वारणाय ज्ञानत्वेनैव प्रवेशोऽस्त्विति वाच्यं। ज्ञानत्व-चाक्षुषत्वयोस्तुल्यशरीरत्वात्[१]। गगणादौ व्यभिचारवारणाय 'कार्य्यतावच्छेदकेति। इदानीं रजताभेदप्रमात्वस्य विशेषकारणजन्यतावच्छेदकत्वं साधयति, 'अनि-

---

(१) ज्ञानत्व-चाक्षुषत्वयोर्द्वयोरेव जातित्वादिति भावः।

व्यावर्त्त्यत्वात्। उभयसिद्धव्यावर्त्तकत्वं तन्त्रम् न तु व्यावर्त्त्यस्य उभयसिद्धिः गौरवात्। व्यतिरेकेऽसाधारणत्वञ्च पक्षेतरत्वस्यानुपाधित्वे वीजं तच्चात्र नास्ति भगवज्ज्ञानस्य त्वत्सम्मतस्य सपक्षत्वादिति।

त्येति, 'रजतभ्रमावृत्तीति पूर्व्ववत् रजतांशे प्रामाण्यज्ञानान्यज्ञानावृत्तीत्यर्थः, 'रजतवृत्तिप्रकारकं' रजतविशेष्यकत्वावच्छिन्नरजतत्वप्रकारिताकं, 'रजतावृत्तिप्रकारकं' रजतत्वाभाववद्विशेष्यकत्वावच्छिन्नरजतत्वप्रकारिताकं, तादृशप्रामाण्यस्यैव पक्षत्वेन तथैव वक्तुमुचितत्वादितिध्येयं। प्राथमिकानुमाने कश्चिदुपाधिमाह तन्मतमुत्थापयति, 'यत्त्विति, 'प्रमाया असाधारणकारणजन्यत्वे' प्रमाया अप्रमाकारणविजातीयकारणजन्यत्वे, 'साध्ये', 'न च पक्षेतरत्वमिति, अतोनेापाधिरिति शेषः। पक्षेतरत्वस्यानुपाधित्वे वीजद्वयं विपक्षाव्यावर्त्तकत्वविशेषणवत्त्वं व्यतिरेकेऽसाधारणत्वञ्च तचाद्यमत्र नास्तीत्याह, 'तवेति, प्रमान्यत्वोपाधौ प्रमाविशेषस्य भवन्मते ईश्वरज्ञानरूपविपक्षस्य व्यावर्त्तकत्वात् ईश्वरानङ्गीकर्त्तृसम्मते तत्र पक्षस्य प्रमाया एव विपक्षत्वेन तद्व्यावर्त्तकत्वादित्यर्थः। ननु उभयमतसिद्धविपक्षस्य व्यावर्त्तकत्वमुपाधित्वे तन्त्रं तच्चात्र नास्तीत्यतआह, 'उभयसिद्धेति उभयसिद्धं विपक्षव्यावर्त्तकत्वं तन्त्रं तच्चात्रास्त्येव न तूभयसिद्धो यो विपक्षस्तद्व्यावर्त्तकत्वं तन्त्रमित्यर्थः, 'गौरवादिति यत्र व्यावर्त्तकत्वं नेाभयमतसिद्धं विपक्षस्तु उभयमतसिद्धः तत्र त्वन्मतस्यापि नोपाधिरतोऽवश्यं व्यावर्त्तकत्वे उभयमतसिद्धत्वं वाच्यम्। तथाचोभयत्र तत्प्रवेशे गौरवमित्यर्थः

तन्न। विपक्षबाधकबलेन हेतोः साध्यव्याप्यत्वेनोपाधेः साध्याव्यापकत्वात्। नन्वस्तु प्रमायां दोषाभावो हेतुः आगन्तुकभावानपेक्ष्य ज्ञानसामग्रीजन्यत्वं स्वतस्त्वं। यत्त्वभावो न कारणं किन्तु दण्डत्वादिवत्कारणतावच्छेदकत्वेन सामग्रीभेदोपलक्षक इति। तन्न। जपाकुसुमादिसन्निधौ न प्रमा तदसन्निधौ[१] स्फटिकादौ प्रमोत्पत्तेरनन्यथासिद्धत्वेन हेतुत्वादिति चेत्। न। भूयोऽवयवेन्द्रियसन्निकर्षविशेषदर्शनादि समवधाने

मान्यमप्यत्रास्तीत्याह, 'व्यतिरेक इति, 'तच्च' तदपि. 'भगवज्ज्ञानस्येत्यस्य त्वन्मते इत्यादिः, 'त्वन्मतस्येत्यस्य मन्मते इत्यादिः, 'त्वन्मतस्य' भवता पक्षत्वेनाभिमतस्येति यावत्, 'सपक्षत्वात्' व्यतिरेके साध्ये सपक्षत्वात्। ननूक्तानुमानेषु दोषाभावजन्यतावच्छेदकत्वेनैवार्थान्तरमिति न गुणसिद्धिरित्याशङ्कते, 'नन्विति,। ननु तथापि प्रमायाः स्वत उत्पत्तिकत्वव्याघात एव इत्यत आह, 'आगन्तुकेति 'आगन्तुकत्वं' भ्रमाकारणत्वं। अभावः कारणतावच्छेदको न कारणमिति मिश्रमतमुत्थापयति, 'यत्त्विति, तथा च दोषाभावसहितव्यक्तिविशेषत्वमेव कारणतावच्छेदकमिति भावः। 'न प्रमा' न स्वैत्यप्रमा, 'अनन्यथासिद्धत्वेन' अनन्यथासिद्धान्वय-व्यतिरेकित्वेन 'हेतुत्वात्' अभावस्यापि हेतुत्वात्, उपस्थितिगौरवस्य कारणतायां बाधकत्वे कारणतावच्छेदकत्वेपि तस्य बाधकत्वापत्तेरिति भावः। 'भूयोऽवयवेति

---

(२) तदपगमे इति ख०। तदसिद्धौ इति ग०।

प्रमा तदभावे त्वप्रमेति प्रमायाङ्गुणोऽप्रमायान्तद्भावो हेतुरित्येव किं न स्यात्। अथासदर्थविषयकत्वे सदर्थविषयकहेत्वभावो न प्रयोजकः, ज्ञाने सदर्थविषयतानियमेन तदसम्भवात्। सदर्थविषयकत्वेऽसदर्थविषयकारणाभावो हेतुः सम्भवति प्रमायाः सदर्थमात्रविषयत्ववदप्रमायामसदर्थमात्रविषयत्वाभावादिति चेत् तर्ह्यप्रमायाः सदर्थविषयता न स्यात् हेत्व-

---

भूयोऽवयवावच्छेदेन सन्निकर्ष इत्यर्थः, तथा च प्रमायां गुणः दोषाभावश्च कारणं, अप्रमायां दोषो गुणाभावश्च कारणं अन्वयव्यतिरेकानुविधायित्वादिति भावः। अप्रमां प्रति गुणाभावस्य हेतुत्वं न सम्भवतीत्याशङ्कते, 'अथेति, 'असदर्थविषयकत्व इति, असद्विषयकं ज्ञानं भ्रम इत्यभिप्रायेण 'सदर्थविषयकेति सदर्थविषयकज्ञानहेत्वभाव इत्यर्थः, 'नियमेनेति, भ्रमेपि सदुपरागेणैवासद्वैशिष्ट्यभानाङ्गीकरादिति भावः। 'तदसम्भवादिति असद्विषयकत्वरूपभ्रमत्वावच्छिन्नं प्रति सद्विषयकज्ञानहेत्वभावस्य कारणत्वासम्भवादित्यर्थः, भ्रमस्यापि सद्विषयकत्वेन व्यभिचारादिति भावः। प्रमायान्तु दोषाभावस्य हेतुत्वं सम्भवत्येवेत्यत आह, 'सदर्थविषयकत्व इति, 'असदर्थविषयकारणाभावः' असदर्थविषयकत्वावच्छिन्नकार्य्यताप्रतियोगिककारणताश्रयाभावः, 'हेतुः' प्रयोजकः, सदर्थविषयिन्याः प्रमाया असदर्थविषयकत्वाभावादिति भावः। नन्वेवमप्रमायामपि सदर्थविषयकत्वाभावेन सदर्थविषयकज्ञानकारणाभावो हेतुः सम्भवतीत्यत

भावात्। सदर्थमात्रविषयत्वे असदर्थविषयहेत्वभावो हेतुरिति चेत्, तर्हि गुण एव तत्र हेतुः तदभावस्त्वसदर्थविषयत्वे प्रयोजक इत्यस्तु। ननु गुणाभावस्य साधारणत्वात्तदेव सत्यमसत्यञ्च न स्यात् गुण-तदभावयोरेकत्रासत्त्वादिति चेत्। न। दोषाभावेऽपि तुल्यत्वात् क्वचित् कश्चिद्दोष इति गुणेऽपि समानम्[१]। गुणाभावादसन्मात्रविषयकमपि ज्ञानं स्यादिति चेत्।

आह, 'प्रमाया इति, 'तर्हीति सदर्थविषयकज्ञाने असदर्थविषयकज्ञानहेत्वभावस्य हेतुत्वे इत्यर्थः, 'हेत्वभावात्' असदर्थविषयकज्ञानकारणाभावरूपहेत्वभावात्। 'सदर्थमात्रविषयकत्व इति सदर्थमात्रविषयकत्वं सर्वांशे प्रमात्वमेव, 'हेतुः' प्रयोजकः, 'तत्र हेतुः' सदर्थमात्रविषयकज्ञाने हेतुः, धर्म्यांशे प्रमात्मकभ्रमस्थलेऽपि गुणाभावो वर्त्तत एव सर्वांशे प्रमां प्रत्येव गुणस्य कारणत्वादिति भावः। 'इत्यस्त्विति आपादनं, तेन वस्तुत इदं न भवति धर्म्यंशिकप्रमां प्रत्यपि गुणस्य कारणत्वात्, प्रमामात्रं प्रत्येव गुणः कारणं, भ्रमं प्रति गुणाभाव इति हृदयं। ननु यदि प्रमां प्रति गुणः कारणं भ्रमं प्रति गुणाभावः तदा एकमेव ज्ञानं प्रमा अप्रमा च कथं स्यादित्याशङ्कते, 'नन्विति, 'साधारणत्वात्' विषयविशेषनियन्त्रितत्वात्, 'तदेवेति एकमेव ज्ञानमित्यर्थः, 'दोषाभावेऽपीति दोषा-

---

(१) तुल्यमिति ख०, ग० च।

न। दोषादप्यसम्भावविषयकज्ञानापत्तेः । सर्वत्र विषये दोषो न सम्भवतीति गुणाभावेऽपि तुल्यं। अथ विशेषदर्शनादिर्गुणस्तदभावश्चाननुगत इति न तौ प्रमाप्रमाहेतू किन्तु दोष-तदभावाविति चेत् तर्हि पित्तादिर्दोषस्तदभावश्चाननुगत इति तावपि न तत्र हेतू स्वप्रमायां स्वाभावस्य व्यभिचारश्च । अथ दोषत्वं नैकं न हि तत्तद्भ्रमहेतुत्वं तत्, आत्मादौ गतत्वाद-

---

भावस्य प्रमाहेतुत्वस्वीकारेऽपीत्यर्थः, 'क्वचिदिति क्वचिदंशे इत्यर्थः, तथा च तदंशे दोषाभावः तदंशे प्रमाम्प्रति कारणमिति भावः। 'गुणाभावादिति कुत्रचित् सर्व्वांशे गुणाभावात् असम्भावविषयकमपि ज्ञानं स्यादित्यर्थः, 'दोषात्' कुत्रचित् सर्व्वांशे दोषात्, 'सर्व्वत्र विषय इति सर्व्वांशे इत्यर्थः। 'तदभावश्चेति चकारात्तस्यापि समुच्चयः, 'तावपि' दोष-तदभावावपि, 'न तत्र हेतू' न भ्रमत्वावच्छिन्ने प्रमात्वावच्छिन्ने हेतू, 'स्वप्रमायां' दोषप्रमायां, 'स्वाभावव्यभिचारश्च' दोषाभावव्यभिचारश्चेत्यर्थः, दोषाभावस्य इन्द्रियसन्निकृष्टतयैव हेतुत्वाभ्युपगमादिति भावः। दोषाननुगमस्य दोषत्वं स्वप्रमायां व्यभिचारश्च निराकर्त्तुमाशङ्कते, 'अथ दोषत्वं नैकमिति, 'नापीति, मात्रार्थः साकल्यमवधारणं वा, आद्ये आह, 'पित्तादेरिति, 'अननुगतत्वेनेति, व्यभिचारितयेतिशेषः, 'तदभावात्' सकलभ्रमहेतुत्वाभावात्। अन्ये आह, 'असम्भवाच्चेति, स्वप्रमायां स्वध्वंसेऽपि पित्तादेर्जनकत्वादिति भावः। 'नापीति, न च घटाभावस्य स्वप्रमा-

ननुगमाच्च। नापि भ्रममात्रहेतुत्वं, पित्तादेरननुगतत्वेन तदभावादसम्भवाच्च। नापि प्रमाहेत्वभावप्रतियोगित्वं, अन्योन्याश्रयात् पित्तादेः स्वप्रमाहेतुत्वाच्च। नापि स्वप्रमाभिन्नप्रमाप्रतिबन्धकत्वम्, एवं हि प्रत्यक्षप्रतिबन्धकस्य सल्लिङ्गपरामर्शस्य दोषत्वादनुमितिः प्रमा न स्यात् भ्रमश्च स्यात्। तस्मात्

हेतुत्वेन घटस्यापि दोषत्वं स्यात् स्याच्च सिद्ध्यभावस्यानुमितिहेतुतया सिद्धेरपि दोषत्वमिति वाच्यं। सकलप्रमाहेतुत्वस्यैवात्र विवक्षितत्वात्, क्वचित्साकल्यार्थकमात्रपदघटित एव पाठः, 'अन्योन्याश्रयादिति प्रमासामान्यकारणताग्रहे दोषत्वग्रहः, दोषत्वग्रहे च दोषाभावत्वग्रहात् प्रमासामान्यकारणताग्रह इत्यन्योन्याश्रय इत्यर्थः, 'पित्तादेरिति, तथा च पित्ताद्यभावस्य प्रमासामान्याहेतुत्वात् पित्तादौ लक्षणमव्याप्तमिति भावः। 'एवं हीति, 'स्वप्रमाभिन्नप्रमाप्रतिबन्धकत्वं' न तादृशप्रमासामान्यप्रतिबन्धकत्वं, पित्तादेरपि शङ्खत्वादिप्रमायामप्रतिबन्धकत्वेनाव्याप्त्यापत्तेः, परन्तु यत्किञ्चित्तादृशप्रमाप्रतिबन्धकत्वमेव तद्वाच्यं तथाचायं दोष इति भावः। इदमुपलक्षणं यत्किञ्चित्प्रमाप्रतिबन्धकत्वे विवक्षिते स्वप्रमाभिन्नत्वविशेषणवैयर्थ्यञ्च बोध्यं। 'तस्मादिति स्वप्रमायां स्वस्यादोषत्वात्, नोक्तव्यभिचारः, कार्य्यानुगमाच्च कारणाननुगमो न दोषायेति भावः। 'स्यादेतदिति उच्यते इत्यन्तमेकः पूर्व्वपक्षः, 'प्रमामिति, 'प्रमां भ्रमञ्चाकुर्व्वति ज्ञानहेतुस्तोमे' प्रमात्वावच्छिन्नं प्रति भ्रमत्वावच्छिन्नं प्रति चाजनके ज्ञानहेतु-

क्वचित् कश्चिद्दोष इति चेत्, तर्हि गुणेऽपि तुल्यम्। स्यादेतत्। प्रमां भ्रमञ्चाकुर्वति ज्ञानहेतुस्तोमे मण्डूकवसाञ्जनदोषात् वंशोरगविभ्रमः, तदभावे वंशप्रमेति तत्र दोषाभावः प्रमाहेतुरित्यन्यत्रापि तथा क्लृप्तत्वात्। मण्डूकवसा नयन एव दोषः न त्वचीति तत्र दोषाभावात् त्वचा वंशप्रमैव। गौरोऽहमित्यभेदभ्रमहेतुदोषसंस्कारसत्त्वेपि मम शरीरमिति प्रमेति चेत्।

स्तोमे, ज्ञानसामान्यसामग्रीसत्त्व इति यावत्, 'उरगविभ्रमः' उरगत्वभ्रम एव, न तु वंशत्वप्रमेति यावत्, तथा च ज्ञानसामान्यसामग्र्यां सत्यां मण्डूकवसाञ्जनदोषाद् वंशे न वंशत्वप्रमा तदभावात् वंशत्वप्रमा इत्यन्वय-व्यतिरेकाभ्यां वंशत्वप्रमास्थले दोषाभावो हेतुः क्लृप्त इत्यर्थः, 'इतीति अतो हेतोरित्यर्थः, 'तथा' दोषाभावो हेतुः, अत्र हेतुमाह, 'क्लृप्तत्वादिति, न तु गुणः अक्लृप्तत्वादिति भावः। ननु मण्डूकवसाञ्जनदोषाभावः कथं वंशत्वप्रमाहेतुः तस्मिन् सत्यपि त्वचा वंशत्वप्रमोत्पत्तेरित्यत आह, 'मण्डूकेति, मण्डूकवसाञ्जनाभावः चाक्षुषवंशत्वप्रमायामेव हेतुरित्यभिप्रायः। दोषाभावत्वेन कारणता प्रमात्वेन कार्य्यता इत्यस्य व्यभिचारमाशङ्कते, 'गौरोऽहमिति, 'दोषसंस्कारसत्त्वे' दोषरूपमिथ्याज्ञानजन्यसंस्कारसत्त्वे, 'तत्र' गौरोऽहमित्यभेदभ्रमे, 'न तु संस्कारस्य' न तु मिथ्याज्ञानजन्यसंस्कारस्य, तथा च यदा विशेषादर्शनं तदा अभेदभ्रमः, यदा विशेषदर्शनं तदा शरीरभेदप्रमेति भावः। ननु विशेषदर्शनासत्त्वेऽपि

न। विशेषादर्शनस्य तत्र हेतुत्वं न तु संस्कारस्य तद-सत्त्वे[१] तदसिद्धेः। न च दूरे चक्षुषः सन्निकर्षेऽपि केशादौ सजातीयसंयोगे प्रमा, तदभावे नेति[२] तत्र संयोगरूपो गुणः प्रमाहेतुरित्यन्यत्रापि गुणजन्यतेति वाच्यं। तावद्देशवर्त्तिकेशसाक्षात्कारे स हेतुः तेन विना तदभावात्। तत्रापि तावद्दूरप्रमायां स हेतुः सन्नि-

---

गौरोऽहमिति भ्रमोदयात् स न तत्र हेतुरित्यत आह, 'तदसत्त्व इति विशेषादर्शनस्यासत्त्वे, 'तदसिद्धेः' भ्रमासिद्धेरित्यर्थः, क्वचित् 'तत्सत्त्वे इति पाठः तदा विशेषदर्शनसत्त्व इत्यर्थः, गुणस्यापि अन्वय-व्यतिरेकाभ्यां प्रमाकारणत्वेन क्लृप्तत्वमाशङ्कते, 'दूरेत्यादिना, 'सजातीयसंयोगे' स्वसजातीयसंयोगे, 'तदाभावे नेति सूक्ष्मत्वादिति भावः। 'तावदिति तावद्दूरवर्त्तिविशेष्यककेशत्वप्रकारकसाक्षात्कारत्वावच्छिन्नं प्रत्येव बहुतरकेशसंयोगोहेतुः न तु तादृशप्रमात्वावच्छिन्न इत्यर्थः, तथा च भ्रम-प्रमासाधारणकेशसाक्षात्कारहेतुतया न तस्य गुणत्वं प्रमात्वघटितधर्म्मावच्छिन्नकार्य्यताप्रतियोगिककारणस्यैव[३] गुणत्वादिति भावः। 'तदभावात्' केशसाक्षात्कारमात्राभावात्। अथ तावद्दूरवर्त्तिकेशसाक्षात्कारत्वस्य बहुतरकेशसंयोगकार्य्यतावच्छेदकत्वे गौरवमतः केशप्रमात्वान्तर्भावेनैव कार्य्यतेत्यत आह, 'तत्रापीति, 'तावद्दूरप्रमायां' तावद्दूरवर्त्तिविशेष्यकचाक्षुषप्रमात्वावच्छिन्ने, 'स हेतुः'

१। तत्सत्त्वे इति ख०।
२। तदभावान्नेतीति ख०, ग० घ।
३। प्रमाया असाधारणकारणस्यैवेति ख०, ग० घ।

दृष्टकेशप्रमायास्तेन विनापि भावात्। तत्रापि वा दोषाभावः कल्प्यो दोषजन्यत्वे अप्रमात्वापातात्। ननु विशेषदर्शनं प्रमाहेतुः विशेषादर्शनस्य दोषत्वे तद-भावस्य हेतुत्वादिति चेत्, तर्हि दोषाभावत्वेन स हेतुर्न तु गुणत्वेन भावत्वेन वा। किञ्च विशेषदर्शनप्रति-बन्धकाः पित्तादयो दोषाः आवश्यकत्वान्न विशेषादर्शनम्। न च तेषामननुगतत्वेन[१] विशेषदर्शन-

---

बहुतरकेशसंयोगो हेतुः। ननु दूरवर्त्तिकेशप्रमायामेव दोषाभावे व्यभिचारी तत्र दूरत्वलक्षणदोषसत्त्वादित्यत आह, 'तत्रापीति, दूरत्वं तत्र दोष एव न, अन्यत्र क्लृप्तदोषस्य च तत्राभावोऽस्त्येवेति भावः। 'दोषजन्यत्वे' दोषसत्त्वे, 'अप्रमात्वापातात्' प्रमानुदयापा-तात्।

केचित्तु 'दोषजन्यत्व इति सति दोषे तस्यान्यथासिद्धिग्राहका-भावेन तज्जन्यत्वस्यावश्यकत्वादिति भावः। तथा च यथाश्रुतमेव साध्वित्याहुः।

'नन्विति, तथा चागन्तुकविशेषदर्शनरूपभावापेक्षज्ञानसामग्री-जन्यत्वात् प्रमायाः स्वत उत्पत्तिकत्वव्याघात इति भावः। 'तर्हीति विशेषदर्शनाभावाभावस्य विशेषदर्शनरूपत्वं यदि तदेत्यर्थः, यदि चाभावाभावोऽतिरिच्यते तदा नैतद्दोषशङ्कापीति भावः। 'स हेतुः' विशेषादर्शनाभावो हेतुः, 'गुणत्वेन' भ्रमप्रतिबन्धकत्वेन, 'भावत्वेन'

१। तेषां नानात्वेनेति ख०।

प्रतिबन्धकतयानुगमे लाघवात् विशेषादर्शनमेव हेतुरिति वाच्यं। क्वचित् कश्चिद्दोष इत्यनुगमात्। अन्यथा पित्तादितोऽप्यप्रमा न स्यात् अननुगमात् मण्यादेरिवाननुगमेऽप्यदोषत्वाच्च। तदभावकूटस्य हेतुत्वात्।

विशेषदर्शनत्वेन, अभावत्वातिरिक्तरूपेणागन्तुकभावानपेक्ष्य ज्ञानसामग्रीजन्यत्वं स्वतस्त्वमिति भावः। ननु दोषत्वस्य एकस्याभावात् न दोषाभावत्वं कारणतावच्छेदकं न वा विशेषदर्शनाभावाभावत्वेन गौरवात् किन्तु विशेषदर्शनत्वेन लाघवादित्यरुचेराह, 'किञ्चेति, 'पित्तादयः' पित्तादय एव, 'दोषाः' प्रमाकारणीभूताभावप्रतियोगिनः, 'आवश्यकत्वादिति विशेषादर्शनस्य दोषत्वेऽपि विशेषदर्शनमेव भ्रमस्थले कुतो न भवति अतस्तत्र पित्तादय एव प्रतिबन्धका वाच्याः तदा सर्वत्र पित्तादय एव दोषाः सन्तु आवश्यकत्वादित्यर्थः, उद्बुद्धमिथ्याज्ञानवासनाया एव च दोषत्वोपगमान्नोक्तो दोष इति भावः। 'न चेति, पित्तादीनां नानात्वेन व्यभिचाराद्विशेषदर्शनप्रतिबन्धकत्वेनानुगम इत्यर्थः, नानात्वेपि व्यभिचाराभावमुपपादयन्ति, 'क्वचिदिति तत्तदप्रमायां तत्तद्दोषः कारणमित्यर्थः, 'इत्यनुगमात्, इतिव्यभिचाराभावात्। 'अन्यथेति अन्यथा तत्तदप्रमायां तत्तद्दोषस्याकारणत्वे, पित्तादि क्वचिदप्रमायां कारणं न स्यादित्यर्थः, 'अननुगमात' अननुगमेन व्यभिचारात्। यद्यप्यप्रमायां विशेषादर्शनमेव हेतुरितिवादिनाम् अप्रमायां पित्तादि कारणमेव न भवतीति एतद्बाधकमसङ्गतं, तथापि अप्रमासामान्ये विशेषाद-

सर्वत्र विशेषादर्शनमेव हेतुः पित्तादेरननुगमेन तत्रोप-क्षयादिति चेत्। न। पित्ताद्युत्कर्षेण भ्रमोत्कर्षात्। पित्तादेरदोषत्वे च विशेषप्रमैव कुतो न भवति विशेषस्य विशेषान्तरादर्शनादिति यदि तदा अनवस्थैव। किञ्च विशेषदर्शनं न प्रमामात्रे न वा प्रत्यक्षप्रमायां हेतु-र्व्यभिचारात् तत्रैव तद्धेतुत्वेऽनवस्थापाताच्च। अथ

र्शनमेव हेतुः विशेषदर्शनरूपाप्रमायां पित्ताद्यपि कारणमिति मतम-वगम्य एतद्बाधकमुक्तं, तथा च 'पित्तादितोप्यऽप्रमा न स्यात्' विशेषदर्शनरूपाप्यप्रमा न स्यादित्यर्थः, एतद्बाधकमेव पश्चात्परिह-रणीयं 'सर्वत्रेत्यादिना, 'सर्वत्र' विशेषदर्शनरूपाप्रमायां तद्भिन्ना-प्रमायाञ्च। ननु भवतु अननुगत एव दोषः अननुगतानां तत्तद-भावानां कथं प्रमाकारणत्वमित्यत आह, 'मण्यादेरिति, 'अननुगमेपि' पित्तादेरननुगमेपि, 'अदोषत्वादिति तदभावस्य प्रमां प्रति हेतुत्वे व्यभिचारादिदोषविरहादित्यर्थः, दाहप्रतिबन्धकस्य मण्यादेरननुगमेपि तदभावानां कारणत्व इवेति भावः। 'तत्रोपक्षयात्' अप्रमां प्रति अन्यथासिद्धत्वात्। पीतः शङ्ख इतिभ्रमे पीतत्वाभावविशेषादर्शनस्य व्यभिचारं स्फुटत्वादुपेक्ष्याह, 'पित्ताद्युत्कर्षेणेति। युक्त्यन्तरमाह, 'पित्तादेरिति पित्तादेरदोषत्वे प्रमां प्रति तस्याप्रतिबन्धकतया सर्वत्र प्रमारूपविशेषदर्शनमेव कुतो न भवतीत्यर्थः, प्रमारूपविशेष-दर्शनं प्रति प्रमारूपविशेषदर्शनस्य हेतुत्वान्नैतद्दोष इत्यत आह, 'विशेषस्येति। 'व्यभिचारात्' प्रत्यक्षरूपविशेषप्रमायां व्यभिचारात्।

प्रत्यक्षे इन्द्रियसन्निकर्षो गुणः अप्रमांशे तदर्थस्यासत्त्वेन सन्निकर्षाभावात् दोषो हेतुः। न च प्रमांशेऽपि स एव हेतुः, अदोषत्वप्रसङ्गात् प्रमांशस्याप्रमात्वप्रसङ्गाच्च। साक्षात्कारित्वञ्चेन्द्रियसन्निकर्षजन्यत्वादिति चेत्। न। ज्ञाने विषयरूपस्यांशस्येन्द्रिय-तद्दोषाजन्यत्वात् अप्रमांशे चेन्द्रियसन्निकर्षाभावेन साक्षात्कारित्वं न स्यात्। दोषस्य तद्धेतुत्वे अतिप्रसङ्गोऽननुगमश्च। प्रमायां प्र-

---

ननु प्रत्यक्षरूपविशेषप्रमायामपि विशेषदर्शनं हेतुरिति न व्यभिचार इत्यत आह, 'तत्रैवेति, तस्मादनायत्या अननुगतानामेव पित्तादि-तदभावानामननुगततत्तद्भ्रम-प्रमे प्रति हेतुत्वं वाच्यमित्युक्तप्रणाल्या प्रमायाः स्वतस्त्वमिति भावः। 'अथेति तदंशे प्रत्यक्षप्रमायां तदंशे इन्द्रियसन्निकर्षो गुण इत्यर्थः। ननु तदंशे प्रत्यक्षप्रमाया-मपि तदिन्द्रियसन्निकर्षस्य हेतुत्वेन कथं तस्य गुणत्वमित्यत आह, 'अप्रमांश इति यदंशे अप्रमा तदर्थस्य धर्मिणि असत्त्वेन तदंशे इन्द्रियसन्निकर्षाभावाद्दोषो हेतुर्न इन्द्रियसन्निकर्ष इत्यर्थः। अथ रजतत्वादिप्रमायामपि दोषजन्यता किमिति नोच्यत इति तट-स्थजिज्ञासायामाह, 'प्रमांश इति रजतत्वाद्यंशे प्रमायां दोषो हेतुर्न चेत्यर्थः, 'अदोषत्वेति प्रमाया अकारणत्वे सति भ्रमकारणस्य दोषत्वादिति भावः। 'प्रमांशस्येति रजतत्वाद्यंशे प्रमायामपि रजत-त्वाद्यंशे अप्रमात्वप्रसङ्गाच्चेत्यर्थः, तदंशे दोषजन्यत्वस्य तदंशे भ्रमत्व-व्याप्यत्वादिति भावः। नन्वेवं अप्रमायां इन्द्रियासन्निकृष्टस्य दोष-

माप्रमायाञ्च[1] याथार्थ्यप्रयोजकमस्त्यप्रमायां दोषव-दिति चेत्। न। दोषाभावस्य सत्त्वादिति। उच्यते। प्रमामात्रे च नानुगतो गुणः किन्तु तत्तत्प्रमायां भूयोऽवयवेन्द्रियसन्निकर्ष-यथार्थलिङ्ग-सादृश्य-वाक्यार्थज्ञानानां यथायथं प्रत्येकमेव गुणत्वं अन्वय-व्यतिरेकात्। तत्तदप्रमायां पित्तादि-लिङ्गभ्रमादीनां दोषत्ववत्प्रत्यक्षे विशेषदर्शनमपि गुणः तदनुविधानात्। ननु विशेष-दर्शनहेतुरेव तद्धेतुरस्तु तद्व्यतिरेकादेव तदभावोपपत्तेः,

---

वंशाज्ञाने अप्रमायां साक्षात्कारित्वं न स्यादिन्द्रियसन्निकर्षाजन्यत्वादित्यत आह, 'साक्षात्कारित्वञ्चेति धर्म्माद्यंशे इन्द्रियसन्निकर्षजन्यत्वादित्यर्थः। अप्रमांशे दोषो हेतुरित्युक्तं दूषयति, 'ज्ञान इति, 'अंशस्येति अवच्छेदकस्येत्यर्थः। ननु विषयतया तदवच्छिन्नकार्य्यतानिरूपितकारणताश्रयत्वमेव तदंशे हेतुत्वमित्यनुशयादाह, 'अप्रमांशे चेति तदिन्द्रियसन्निकर्षजन्यत्वं तत्साक्षात्कारित्वप्रयोजकं एवञ्च यदंशेऽप्रमा तदंशे इन्द्रियसन्निकर्षश्चेन्नास्ति तदा तदजन्यत्वेन प्रमायाः तदंशे साक्षात्कारित्वं न स्यादित्यर्थः, 'दोषस्य तद्धेतुत्वे' जन्यतासम्बन्धेन दोषस्यापि साक्षात्कारित्वप्रयोजकत्वे, 'अतिप्रसङ्गः' भ्रमानुमित्यादेरपि साक्षात्कारित्वप्रसङ्गः, 'अननुगमश्च' व्यभिचारश्च प्रमानुमित्यादौ[2] इति भावः। ननु प्रमात्वस्यानुगतत्वात्तत्प्रयोजकः कश्चि-

---

१। प्रमाप्रमारूपे चेति ख०, ग० च।

२। भ्रम-प्रमात्मकप्रत्यक्षानुमित्यादाविति ग०।

अन्यथा विशेषदर्शनमेव तत्र कुतो न स्यात्। तत्रापि तदपेक्षायामनवस्थानादिति चेत्। एवं व्याप्यविषयकव्यापकप्रत्यक्षनियमे अनुमिताविव पुरुषप्रत्यक्षे प्रामाण्यसंशयो न स्यात्। करादिमति पुरुषज्ञानत्वस्यानुव्यवसायेन निश्चयात्। तत्रापि विशेषदर्शनं विना कथं व्यापकप्रत्यक्षमिति चेत्। न। संशय-विपर्य्ययोत्तरप्रमायां तस्य हेतुत्वात्। ममापि तद्धेतुस्तत्रैव हेतु-

---

रवश्यं स्वीकरणीयः दोषाभावस्य प्रतियोग्यननुगमेनाननुगतत्वात् स एव च गुण इत्याशयेन शङ्कते, 'प्रमायामिति सर्वांशे प्रमायामित्यर्थः, 'प्रमाप्रमायाश्च' प्रमारूपाप्रमायश्च, आंशिकप्रमायाश्चेति यावत्, 'दोषवदिति अतिरिक्तकारणत्वमात्रे दृष्टान्तः। 'दोषाभावस्य' दोषाणामभावकूटस्येत्यर्थः। तदेवमन्वय-व्यतिरेकात् दोषाभाव एव कारणं न तु गुण इति स्थिते आह, 'उच्यत इति, 'नानुगतोगुण इति। न च प्रमासामान्यं प्रत्येव तद्वन्निष्ठविषयतासम्बन्धेन स्वपरसाधारणस्य ज्ञानसामान्यस्य गुणत्वसम्भवात् प्रमामात्रे नानुगतो गुण इति कथमुच्यत इति वाच्यं। तत्तत्प्रकारघटितत्वेन प्रमात्वस्य एकस्याभावात् घटत्व-पटत्वादिसकलप्रमासाधारणो नानुगतोगुणः सम्भवतीत्यभिप्रायात्, 'भूयोऽवयवेति भूयोऽवयवावच्छेदेनेन्द्रियसन्निकर्ष इत्यर्थः, 'यथार्थेति लिङ्गज्ञानादिषु सर्वत्र सम्बध्यते, 'यथायथं' यथायोग्यं, प्रत्यक्षप्रमायाः भूयोऽवयवेन्द्रियसन्निकर्ष इत्यादिक्रमेणेति यावत्। ननु भूयोऽवयवेन्द्रियसन्निकर्षो न प्रत्यक्षमात्रे गुणः सम्भ-

वति, रूपादिप्रत्यक्षे शब्द-सुखात्मादिप्रत्यक्षे च व्यभिचारात्। नापि सावयवप्रत्यक्षप्रमायां, उपनयादिजन्यतत्प्रमायां व्यभिचारात्। नापि सावयवलौकिकप्रत्यक्षप्रमायां, अनुभूयमानतदारोपस्थले तादृशप्रमोत्पत्त्यापत्तेः, तादृशप्रत्यक्षमात्रे एव तस्य हेतुतायाः सुवचत्वेन प्रमात्वान्तर्भाववैयर्थ्याच्च पटादिपिहितघटादिस्थले निर्विकल्पकस्याप्यनुत्पत्तेः। किञ्च भूयोऽवयवेत्यधिकं। न च किञ्चिदपिहितपटादिपिहितघटादेः प्रमापत्तेस्तदवश्यं वाच्यमिति वाच्यं। प्रत्यक्षमात्रं प्रत्येव प्रतिबन्धकत्वात् अन्यथा निर्विकल्पकोत्पत्त्यापत्तेः। भूयस्त्वमपि दुर्वचनं तथाहि भूयस्त्वं न बहुत्वं द्विकपालारब्धघटे तदभावात्। न चावयवपदं अवयवावयवसाधारणारम्भकपरमिति वाच्यं। सर्वसाधारणारम्भकताया निर्वक्तुमशक्यत्वात् किञ्चिदपिहितपटादिपिहितघटादिप्रमापत्तेश्च। नापि विशेषण-विशेष्योभयसन्निकर्षः जन्यप्रत्यक्षप्रमासामान्ये तथा, भ्रमस्थलेपि उभयसन्निकर्षसत्त्वात्। न च तदुभयप्रतियोगिक एकः सन्निकर्षस्तथा भ्रमस्थले तु विशेषणांशे ज्ञानरूपः सन्निकर्षः विशेष्यांशे संयोगादिरिति नैकः सन्निकर्षः, गृह्यमाणारोपस्थले अन्यधर्मस्यान्यतारोपस्थले च नोभयप्रतियोगिकः कोऽपि सन्निकर्ष इति वाच्यं। प्रमास्थलेऽपि विशेष्यांशे संयोगः विशेषणांशे संयुक्तसमवाय इति विशेषण-विशेष्योभयप्रतियोगिकैकसन्निकर्षस्य क्वचिदप्यभावात्। अथ विशेष्यघटितविशेषणेन्द्रियसन्निकर्षो हेतुरित्याशयः। न च विशेष्यं सामान्यतः, वा प्रमाविशेष्यं, एतज्ज्ञानविशेष्यं वा, नाद्यो भ्रमस्थलातिव्याप्तेः, नहि रजतं न तथा, न वा रजतत्वं तदवृत्ति, नान्त्यः अननुगमादिति वाच्यं। तच्च

तत्प्रत्यक्षप्रमायां तद्घटिततत्सन्निकर्षस्य हेतुत्वेनोक्तत्वादिति चेत्। न। अतीतानागतप्रमायां विशेषणज्ञानस्यैव प्रत्यासत्तित्वेन तत्र व्यभिचारात् सुरभि चन्दनं गुरुत्ववान् घट इत्याद्युपनीतप्रत्यक्षे सामान्यलक्षणाजन्यप्रत्यक्षे च व्यभिचाराच्च अतीतानागतविशेषण-विशेष्ययोर्मानसप्रमायां तदसम्भवाच्च। न च तत्रोभयविषयकमेकं ज्ञानमेव विशेष्यघटितविशेषणेन्द्रियसन्निकर्षरूपमिति वाच्यं। तादृशसन्निकर्षस्य भ्रमस्थलेऽपि सत्वात् विशेषणांशे लौकिकत्वेन विशेषणेऽपि दण्डी पुरुष इत्यादिलौकिकप्रत्यक्षप्रमायां तदसम्भवात्। अथ विशेष्यवृत्तिः विशेषणस्य सन्निकर्षः जन्यप्रत्यक्षप्रमामात्रे तथा तद्धर्मिकतत्प्रत्यक्षप्रमायां तद्धर्मिवृत्तेस्तस्य इन्द्रियसन्निकर्षो हेतुरिति यावत्। यद्वा विशेषणवतो विशेष्यस्येन्द्रियसन्निकर्षस्तथा तद्धर्मिकतद्धर्मप्रत्यक्षप्रमायां तद्धर्मवतस्तद्धर्मिण इन्द्रियसन्निकर्षो हेतुरिति यावत्। न च शुक्तौ इदं रजतमितिभ्रमकाले शुक्तिवृत्तिशुक्तित्वस्य शुक्तित्ववत्याः शुक्तेरिन्द्रियसन्निकर्षसत्वेन शुक्तित्वप्रमापत्तिरिति वाच्यं। शुक्तित्वप्रत्यक्षमात्रप्रतिबन्धकस्य दोषविशेषस्य सत्त्वादिति चेत्। न। 'तद्धर्मिवृत्तेरित्यस्य 'तद्धर्मवत इत्यस्य च वैयर्थ्यापत्तेः। न चैवं रजतत्वसन्निकर्षसत्त्वेन शुक्तिधर्मिकरजतत्वप्रमापत्तिरिति वाच्यं। तस्याप्रसिद्धत्वेनापादनासम्भवात्। न च शुक्तौ रजतत्वप्रमापत्तिरिति वाच्यं। केवलरजतत्वप्रमात्वस्य कार्य्यतानवच्छेदकत्वेनापादनासम्भवात्[१] इति। उच्यते। तद्वत्सन्निकर्ष एव तत्प्रत्यक्षप्रमामात्रे गुणः, तस्य च सामानाधिकरण्यं प्रत्यासत्तिः, तद्घटकस्य सम्बन्धः

(१) कार्य्यतानवच्छेदकत्वेनामापादनादिति ग०।

कारणस्याधिकरणता, कार्य्यस्य विशेष्यतेति क्वचिदेवाधिकरणे प्रमा, नापरत्र, शुक्तौ इदं रजतमित्यादिभ्रमकाले शङ्खे पीतत्वादिभ्रमकाले च शुक्लित्व-श्वैत्यादिप्रमानुत्पादस्य प्रतिबन्धकीभूतपित्तादिदोषविशेषसत्त्वात्। न चैवं तादृशदोषविशेषाभाव एव हेतुरस्तु गुणत्वेपि तस्यावश्यकत्वादिति वाच्यं। तादृशदोषविशेषाभावस्य जन्यश्वैत्यादिप्रत्यक्षत्वावच्छिन्नं प्रत्येव हेतुत्वात् न तु तत्र प्रमात्वान्तर्भावः तत्सत्त्वे श्वैत्यादिनिर्व्विकल्पकस्याप्यनुत्पत्तेः। न च सैव सामान्यसामग्री जनिकास्तु किं विशेषसामग्रीकल्पनेन, अस्तु वा सैव सामान्यसामग्री प्रत्यक्षप्रमात्वावच्छिन्नं प्रत्यपि हेतुः किं सामग्र्यन्तरकल्पनेन, सामान्य-विशेषयोर्नैकसामग्रीप्रयोज्यत्वमिति प्रवादस्य निर्युक्तिकत्वादिति वाच्यं। असत्यपि तादृशे प्रत्यक्षसामान्यप्रतिबन्धकदोषविशेषे शुक्लित्वादिविरहिणि शुक्लित्वादिप्रमानुत्पादेन उक्तरूपगुणहेतुत्वस्यावश्यकत्वात। भ्रमजनकीभूतदोषस्य न प्रमाप्रतिबन्धकः येनावश्यकत्वात् तदभाव एव कारणं स्यात्(१) इति मणिकृतो निगर्व्वः। सन्निकर्षत्वस्यैकस्याभावात् अननुगमः परमत्र विभावनीयः।

केचित्तु। तद्व्याप्यसन्निकर्ष एव तत्प्रत्यक्षप्रमाहेतुः उक्तसामानाधिकरण्यं प्रत्यासत्तिरिति। तदसत्। व्याप्यत्वप्रवेशे गौरवादिति दिक्।

ननु तथापि यथार्थलिङ्गपरामर्शस्य प्रमानुमितौ न गुणत्वसम्भवः, वह्निव्याप्यधूमवान् पर्व्वत इति यथार्थपरामर्शेन बाधानवतारदशायां(२)

(१) कारणीभूताभावप्रतियोगिन एव प्रतिबन्धकत्वादिति भावः।
(२) बाधावतारे तेनैवानुमितिप्रतिबन्धाशापत्तिसम्भावनेति भावः।

लाघवप्रतिसन्धानसहकारेण[१] पर्व्वतो महानसीयवह्निमानित्यनुमिति-जननकाले प्रमानुमितिप्रसङ्गात्। एवं वह्निव्याप्यधूमवान् पर्व्वत इति यथार्थपरामर्शेन पर्व्वतीयवह्निबाधबुद्धिसहकारेण पर्व्वतो-महानसीयवह्निमानित्यनुमितिजननकाले प्रमानुमित्युत्पत्तिप्रस-ङ्गाच्च कूटलिङ्गस्थलीयप्रमानुमि ौ व्यभिचाराच्च। किञ्च गन्ध-प्रागभावकालावच्छिन्नो घटो गन्धवानित्यादावपि प्रमानुमित्युत्पत्त्या-पत्तिः परामर्शस्य यथार्थत्वादिति। मैवं। बाधभ्रमाभाव-लाघव-भ्रमाभावयोरपि पृथक् हेतुत्वेनाद्यदोषद्वयानवकाशात्। न चैतयोर्हेतु-त्वोपगमे कृतं तादृशगुणेनेति वाच्यं। असत्यपि लाघव-बाधभ्रमे[२] साध्यविरहिणि पक्षे परामर्शात् प्रमानुमित्यनुत्पादात् तादृशगुणहेतु-त्वस्यावश्यकत्वात्। न वा तृतीयः, तत्रेश्वरीयतद्व्याप्यप्रमायाः सत्त्वात्, साध्यवद्विशेष्यकत्वस्यैव प्रकृते परामर्शनिष्ठयथार्थतया कूटलिङ्गकपरा-मर्शस्यापि यथार्थत्वाच्च। वस्तुतः वस्तुगत्या यत्तद्व्याप्यं तत्प्रमा तत्प्रमा-नुमितौ गुणः, घटो द्रव्यं सत्त्वादित्यादिकूटलिङ्गस्थलेऽप्यन्ततो घट-त्वादेरेव तादृशज्ञानसत्त्वात्। न च यत्र जलत्वेनैव पर्व्वतं पक्षीकृत्य कूटलिङ्गेन जलं वह्निमदिति वह्निप्रमानुमितिः तत्र का गतिरिति वाच्यं। वह्निसामानाधिकरण्यज्ञाने सामान्यतोऽधिकरणत्वरूपेण पर्व्वते वह्निव्याप्यस्य वह्नेरेव भावात्। कथमिदं ज्ञातमिति चेत् फलबलादेव। न च हेतुभेदेन हेतुतावच्छेदकसम्बन्धभेदेन च व्या-प्तेर्भेदादननुगमः, साध्यतावच्छेदकसम्बन्धेन तद्वदन्यावृत्तित्वस्वरूपाया-

(१) इतरबाधसहकारस्थले लाघवप्रतिसन्धानस्थले च सामान्यपरामर्श-स्यापि विशेषधर्म्मावच्छिन्नानुमितिजनकत्वम्।

(२) लाघवप्रतिसन्धाने बाधभ्रमे इति ग०।

व्याप्तेरत्र प्रवेशात् । न च केवलान्वयिनि तदभावः, तत्र प्रमात्वस्य कार्य्यतानवच्छेदकत्वात् व्यावर्त्तनीयतदप्रमाया अप्रसिद्धेः । अस्तु वा तत्र तत्समानाधिकरणत्वेनैवानुगमः । न वा चतुर्थः, गन्धप्रागभावकालावच्छिन्नो घटो गन्धवानित्यनुमितेरपि प्रमात्वात् गन्धप्रागभावकालावच्छिन्नत्वविशिष्टसमवायसम्बन्धेनेव शुद्धसमवायसम्बन्धेनापि घटे गन्धस्य प्रकारत्वाभ्युपगमादिति दिक् । ननु तथापि यथार्थसादृश्यज्ञानस्य प्रमोपमितौ न गुणत्वसम्भवः, खरविधर्म्मा अश्व इत्यतिदेशवाक्यप्रभववैधर्म्योपमितौ व्यभिचारात् । न च सादृश्यज्ञानजन्यप्रमोपमिताविदं निदानमिति वाच्यं । गोसदृशः खर इत्यतिदेशवाक्यप्रभवप्रमोपमितौ व्यभिचारात् खरे गोसादृश्यप्रमाया अभावात् । न च, गोसमानधर्म्मवत्त्वं येन केनापि धर्म्मेण खरेऽप्यस्तीति वाच्यं । अप्रमासाधारण्यात् । मैवं । तत्प्रकारकप्रमोपमितौ तदव्यभिचारी यो लघुधर्म्म ईश्वरीयसाधारणः तत्प्रमैव गुणः स च क्वचित् सादृश्यं क्वचिदन्यत् ग्रन्थस्तूपलक्षणपरः इति । न चैवं प्रमासामान्यं प्रत्येव ईश्वरीयसाधारणग्राह्यप्रमाया गुणत्वसम्भव इति वाच्यं । ईश्वरीयसाधारणग्राह्यप्रमावदेतस्या अपि तथात्वे क्षतिविरहात् । ननु तथापि यथार्थवाक्यार्थज्ञानस्य शाब्दप्रमायां न गुणत्वसम्भवः, वाक्यपदं हि यत्किञ्चित्परं वा, प्रकृतवाक्यपरं वा, नाद्यः, अतिप्रसङ्गात् । नान्त्यः, अननुगमात् शुक-बालकवाक्यजन्यप्रमायां व्यभिचाराच्च । मैवं वाक्यार्थज्ञानपदेन तदर्थतत्त्वज्ञानस्योक्तत्वात् । तथा च शाब्दप्रमायां यथार्थतदर्थतत्त्वज्ञानमेव गुणः विशेष्यतासम्बन्धेन सामानाधिकरण्यं प्रत्यासत्तिरिति यत्र सा अस्ति तत्रैव शाब्दप्रमा, शुक-बालकादि-

स्थले ईश्वरीयमेव तत् सुलभमिति न काप्यनुपपत्तिः। न चान्योन्याश्रयः शाब्दप्रमाया यथार्थवाक्यार्थज्ञानरूपगुणजन्यत्वे सिद्धे वैदिकप्रमाहेतुवाक्यार्थप्रमारूपगुणाश्रयत्वेनेश्वरसिद्धिः, तत्सिद्धौ च तदीयवाक्यार्थज्ञानजन्यतया शुकादिवाक्ये व्यभिचारज्ञानाभावे शाब्दप्रमायास्तादृशगुणजन्यत्वसिद्धिरिति वाच्यं। प्रकारान्तरेणापि[१] ईश्वरसिद्धेरुक्तत्वात् ज्ञानस्यासार्वदिकत्वेन शुकादिस्थले यथार्थवाक्यार्थज्ञानाभावग्रहासत्त्वदशायां कारणत्वग्रहसम्भवाच्च। अन्यथा पर्वतादौ वह्नेः सन्देहात् धूमकारणत्वग्रहोऽपि तत्र न स्यादिति संक्षेपः।

'विशेषदर्शनं' विशेषप्रमा, तेन पुरुषे स्थाणुत्वव्याप्यवत्ताज्ञानात् तत्र न स्थाणुत्वप्रमा, 'विशेषदर्शनहेतुरेवेति विशेषदर्शनसामग्र्येवेत्यर्थः, तद्धेतोरेवेतिन्यायादिति भावः। नन्वेवं यत्र विशेषदर्शनाभावः तत्र कथं न प्रमेत्यत आह, 'तद्व्यतिरेकेति, 'तद्व्यतिरेकात्' विशेषदर्शनसामग्रीव्यतिरेकात्, 'तदभावः' प्रत्यक्षप्रमाया अभावः, 'अन्यथा' विशेषदर्शनसामग्र्यभावासत्त्वे। ननु विशेषदर्शनमपि विशेषदर्शनहेतुरेवेति विशेषदर्शनस्य हेतुत्वं दुष्परिहरमित्यत आह, 'तत्रापीति विशेषदर्शनेऽपीत्यर्थः, 'तदपेक्षायां, विशेषदर्शनापेक्षायां, 'अनवस्थानादिति। यद्यपि विशेषदर्शनस्य प्रत्यक्षत्वनियमाभावान्नानवस्थाप्रसङ्गः, तथापि तन्मूलीभूतप्रत्यक्षमादाय तत्प्रसङ्ग इति भावः। अथ व्याप्यदर्शनसामग्री चेत् कारणं तदा पूर्वं व्याप्यसामग्रीमत्त्वेन सर्वस्या एव व्यापकप्रत्यक्षप्रमाया व्याप्यवत्त्वविषय-

---

(१) क्षित्यादिः सकर्तृका कार्य्यत्वादित्यनुमानेनापीश्वरसिद्धिरिति भावः।

त्वनियमेन पुरुषत्वप्रत्यक्षप्रमाया अपि पुरुषत्वव्याप्यकरादि-मत्त्वविषयकत्वनियमात् लिङ्गोपहितलैङ्गिकभाननये अनुमिताविव तत्र प्रामाण्यसंशयो न स्यात् प्रामाण्यावच्छेदकत्वेन गृहीतस्य करादिमद्विशेष्यकत्वावच्छिन्नपुरुषत्वप्रकारकत्वस्यानुव्यवसायेन निश्च-यादित्याह, 'एवमिति, 'एवं' व्याप्यदर्शनसामग्र्याः प्रत्यक्षमात्र-कारणत्वे, 'व्याप्यविषयकव्यापकप्रत्यक्षनियमे' व्यापकप्रत्यक्षप्रमाया व्याप्यविषयकत्वनियमे, 'अनुमिताविवेति लिङ्गोपहितलैङ्गिकभाननये अनुमिताविवेत्यर्थः, 'करादिमतीति। यद्यपि अनुव्यवसायेन पुरु-षत्वव्याप्यकरादिमद्विशेष्यकत्वावच्छिन्नपुरुषत्वप्रकारकत्वग्रहे तद्विशे-ष्यकत्वावच्छिन्न-तत्प्रकारकत्वमपि ग्राह्यं तुल्यसामग्रीकत्वादिति प्रामा-ण्यस्य स्वतस्त्वापत्तिः, तथापि अनुव्यवसायेन तद्विशेष्यकत्वावच्छि-न्नत्वं तत्प्रकारकत्वे न गृह्यते प्रामाण्यसंशयानुपपत्तेः, विधेयो-द्देश्यतावच्छेदकत्वेन व्यवसाये भासमानो यो धर्मस्तद्विशेष्यकत्वा-वच्छिन्नत्वं विधेयप्रकारकत्वे गृह्यत एव बाधकाभावात्, अन्यथा अनुव्यवसायानन्तरं प्रामाण्यस्येवास्मिन् रजतत्वप्रकारकं न वेत्यपि संशयः स्यादिति भावः। ननु विशेषदर्शनस्य हेतुत्वेपि पूर्वं व्याप्य-वत्तोपनयसत्त्वात प्रत्यक्षप्रमामात्रस्यैव उपनीतव्याप्यवत्त्वविषयकत्वनिय-मात् कथं कुत्रचित् पुरुषत्वप्रत्यक्षप्रमायां प्रामाण्यसंशय इति उक्त-दोषतादवस्थ्यमिति कुत्रचित् प्रामाण्यसंशयानुरोधात विशेषदर्शनं विनापि प्रत्यक्षप्रमा स्वीकार्य्या तत् कथमित्याशङ्कते, 'तत्रापीति, 'अपिः' भिन्नक्रमे, विशेषदर्शनं विनापीत्यर्थः, 'तस्य हेतुत्वादिति, तत्र च प्रामाण्यसंशय एव न भवतीति भावः। 'ममापीति,

'तद्धेतुः' तत्सामग्री, 'तत्रैव' संशय-विपर्य्ययोत्तरप्रमायामेव, 'तद्धेतूनां' विशेषदर्शनहेतूनां, 'तादृशप्रत्यक्षे' संशयाद्युत्तरप्रत्यक्षे, 'तद्दर्शनेषु च' विशेषदर्शनेषु च, 'व्याप्यदर्शनत्वं' व्याप्यप्रमात्वं, विशेषदर्शनसामग्र्या अपि व्याप्यदर्शनसामग्रीत्वेनानुगमे लाघवाद्विशेषदर्शनत्वेनैव कारणत्वं न तु तत्त्वेन गौरवात् अनुमित्यात्मकव्याप्यदर्शनस्थले तत्सामग्र्या प्रत्यक्षजनकत्वासम्भवाच्च भिन्नविषये अनुमितिसामग्र्या बलवत्त्वेन व्याप्यानुमितेरेव प्रथममुत्पादात् इति भावः। यद्यप्येतद्विशेष्यक-तद्व्याप्यप्रमात्वेन कारणता, तद्विशेष्यक-तद्विपरीतज्ञानोत्तर-तद्विशेष्यकतत्प्रत्यक्षप्रमात्वेन कार्य्यता, समवायघटितसामानाधिकरण्यं प्रत्यासत्तिः, शुक्तिविशेष्यकरजतत्वप्रमात्वादेरप्रसिद्धत्वेन कार्य्यतावच्छेदकत्वासम्भवेपि यावद्विशेषसामग्रीबाधादेव न शुक्त्यादौ रजतत्वप्रमोदय इति क्रमेण कार्य्य-कारणभावो न सम्भवति, संशयोत्तरतत्संशयप्रमायां व्यभिचारात् आलोकाभावाद्यधीनसंशय विपर्य्ययोत्तरमालोकादिसमवधाने सति जायमाने प्रत्यक्षप्रमानिश्चये पुरुषत्वाद्यवच्छेदकीभूतकरादिमत्त्वज्ञानाजायमाने संशय-विपर्य्ययोत्तरपुरुषत्वादिप्रत्यक्षप्रमानिश्चये च व्यभिचाराच्च पुरुषत्वादिव्याप्यत्वेन तत्र ज्ञानाभावात् व्याप्तेरननुगमेमाननुगमाच्च। अथ वस्तुगत्या यत्तद्व्याप्यं स्व-परसाधारणतत्प्रमात्वेनैव कारणता, तद्विपरीतज्ञानोत्तरतत्प्रत्यक्षप्रमात्वेन च कार्य्यता, विशेष्यताघटितसामानाधिकरण्यं प्रत्यासत्तिः, संशयोत्तरसंशयस्थले तत्रापि स्वव्याप्यत्वेन पूर्व्वसंशयस्यैव तद्व्याप्यप्रमात्वात्। अत एव संशयोत्तरमालोकसमवधाने सति जायमाने प्रत्यक्ष-

रिति चेत्। न। कर-चरण-चिवुकादीनां प्रत्येकं विशेषत्वेन तद्धेतूनामननुगततया तादृशप्रत्यक्षे अहेतुत्वात्।

प्रमानिश्चये अवच्छेदकीभूतकरादिमत्त्वज्ञानाज्जायमाने विपरीतज्ञानोत्तरप्रत्यक्षप्रमानिश्चये च न व्यभिचारः, संशयावच्छेदकीभूतकरादिमत्त्वज्ञानयोरेव वस्तुगत्या तद्व्याप्यप्रमारूपत्वात् सर्व्वत्रेश्वरीयतद्व्याप्यप्रमामादायैव विशेष्यतासम्बन्धेन तद्व्याप्यप्रमायाः सुलभत्वाच्च। अतएव तदभावनिश्चयोत्तरमालोकसमवधाने सति जायमाने प्रत्यक्षप्रमानिश्चये तदव्याप्ये तद्व्याप्यताभ्रमाज्जायमाने विपरीतज्ञानोत्तरप्रत्यक्षप्रमानिश्चये च न व्यभिचारः ईश्वरीयतद्व्याप्यप्रमाया एव सुलभत्वात्। न चैवं पुरुषत्वादिविपरीतनिश्चयोत्तरं विनापि व्याप्यदर्शनादिकं पुरुषत्वादिप्रत्यक्षप्रमापत्तिरीश्वरीयतद्व्याप्यप्रमासत्त्वादिति वाच्यं। तद्विपरीतज्ञानोत्तरतत्प्रत्यक्षनिश्चयत्वेन कार्य्यता, तद्विपरीतज्ञानविरोधित्वेन कारणतेति सामान्यकार्य्य-कारणभावान्तरसत्त्वेन सामान्यकारणाभावादेव तदनुत्पत्तेः, तद्विपरीतप्रमोत्तरं विनापि व्याप्यदर्शनादिकं भ्रमात्मकतत्प्रत्यक्षनिश्चयवारणाय तादृशसामान्यकार्य्य-कारणभावस्यावश्यकत्वात्। लाघवात् प्रमात्वनिरूपकसम्बन्धेन तद्वदन्यावृत्तित्वरूपाया एव व्याप्तेरत्र प्रवेशाद्व्याप्यननुगमेऽपि माननुगमः। केवलान्वयिस्थले पूर्व्वोक्तैव गतिरिरितिचेत्। न। तथासति प्रमासामान्यं प्रत्येव एकरूपेण कार्य्य-कारणभावस्य सुवचतया कार्य्यतावच्छेदकदिशि तद्विपरीतज्ञानोत्तरत्वप्रवेशस्य व्यर्थत्वापत्तेः मूले संशय-विपर्य्ययोत्तरप्रमापर्य्यन्तानुधावनस्यासङ्गतत्वापत्तेश्च। तथापि

तद्दर्शनेषु च व्याप्यदर्शनत्वमनुगतमस्ति। नन्वेवं संशयोत्तरं[1] व्याप्यज्ञाने सत्यनुमितिः स्यान्न प्रत्यक्षमनु-

---

तद्विशेष्यक-तद्व्याप्यप्रमात्वेन तद्विषेय्यकतद्विपरीतज्ञानोत्तरतद्विशेष्यक-तत्प्रत्यक्षप्रमात्वेनैव कार्य्य-कारणभावः, उत्तरत्वञ्चालोकाभावाधीन-विपरीतनिश्चयादिव्यावृत्तं संसर्गमर्य्यादया कार्य्यतावच्छेदकघटकं तेनालोकादिसमवधानाधीनतदुत्तरप्रत्यक्षप्रमायां न व्यभिचारः, न वा तदव्याप्ये तद्व्याप्यताभ्रमाज्जायमाने तद्विपरीतनिश्चयोत्तरप्रत्यक्षे च व्यभिचारः तद्व्यावृत्तोत्तरत्वस्यैव संसर्गत्वात्। यद्वा तद्विशेष्यक-तद्व्याप्य-प्रमात्वेन कारणता, तादृशप्रमोत्तरतद्विशेष्यक-तत्प्रत्यक्षप्रमात्वेनैव कार्य्यता, संशय-विपर्य्ययोत्तरप्रमापदञ्च तद्व्याप्यप्रमोत्तरतादृशप्रमा-परमिति मणिकृतां निगर्व्वः।

'नन्विति, 'एवं' संशयाद्युत्तरप्रत्यक्षप्रमायां विशेषदर्शनस्य कारणत्वे, 'तथात्वेपि' अनुमितिसामग्रीसत्त्वेपि,'प्रत्यक्षेति सिषाधयिषाविरहविशिष्टतद्विशेष्यकलौकिकप्रत्यक्षसामग्र्याः तद्विशेष्यक-तद्विधेयकानुमितिप्रतिबन्धकत्वादित्यर्थः, अनुमितिसामग्रीविरहादिति शेषः। तद्विधेयकेत्युपादानात् पर्व्वतो वह्निमानित्यत्र पर्वतप्रत्यक्षसामग्रीसत्त्वेपि न पर्वतस्य प्रत्यक्षं किन्तु अनुमितिरेव, लौकिकेत्युपादानात् पर्वते वह्न्युपनीतभानसामग्रीसत्त्वेपि वह्न्यनुमितिरेव न प्रत्यक्षं।

केचित्तु 'अन्यत्र' भिन्नविषयकप्रत्यक्षे, 'तथात्वेपि' अनुमितिसामग्र्याः प्रतिबन्धकत्वेपि, 'अत्रेति, 'अत्र' समानविषयकानुमितौ,

---

(१) संशय-विपर्य्ययोत्तरमिति ग०।

मितिसामग्र्या बलवत्त्वादिति चेत्। न। अन्यत्र तथात्वे-प्यत्र प्रत्यक्षसामग्र्या बलवत्त्वात्। तत्र पुरुषं पश्यामी-त्यनुव्यवसायात्। अतएव विशेषदर्शनजन्यत्वेन ज्ञातं बाधकं। तद्दर्शनजन्यं बाध्यम्। अन्यथा बाध्य-बाधक-व्यवस्था न स्यात्। न च प्रमा बाधिका, करभ्रमजन्य-पुरुषज्ञानस्यापि स्थाणुज्ञानबाधकत्वात्। नापि विप-

---

प्रत्यक्षसामग्र्याः प्रतिबन्धकत्वादित्यर्थः इति वदन्ति। तत्र भिन्नवि-षयकप्रत्यक्षत्वं नानुमितिसामग्र्याः प्रतिबध्यतावच्छेदकं गौरवात्, अपि तु लाघवात् प्रत्यक्षत्वमेव। समानविषयकानुमितित्वं प्रत्यक्षसामग्री-प्रतिबध्यतावच्छेदकं तेन समानविषयकप्रत्यक्षस्थले प्रत्यक्षसामग्र्यभा-वरूपकारणाभावादनुमितिसामग्रीविरहादेव न व्यभिचार इति ध्येयं।

ननु प्रत्यक्षसामग्र्या अनुमितिप्रतिबन्धकत्वे किं मानमित्यत आह, 'तत्रेति, 'तत्र' संशयोत्तरप्रत्यक्षस्थले, 'इति' इत्येव, नानुमिनो-मीत्यर्थः। 'अतएवेति क्वचित् ज्ञाने विशेषदर्शनजन्यत्वादेवेत्यर्थः। 'ज्ञातमित्यस्य ज्ञानमितिशेषः, 'बाधकं' भ्रमत्वज्ञापकं, 'बाध्यं' भ्रम-त्वेन ज्ञाप्यं। 'अन्यथा' कस्यचिदपि ज्ञानस्य विशेषदर्शनाजन्यत्वे। 'पुरुषज्ञानस्य' पुरुषत्वभ्रमस्य, 'नापीति, तद्विपरीतज्ञानमेव तज्ज्ञा-नबाधकमित्यर्थः। 'अनन्यथासिद्धमिति प्रमात्वेन ज्ञातं बाधकमित्यर्थः, तथा च करभ्रमजन्यपुरुषत्वभ्रमस्यापि प्रमात्वेन ज्ञातत्वेन बाधकत्व-मिति भावः। 'तदर्थत्वात्' तज्ज्ञापकत्वात्, तथा च तदर्थमेव क्वचित् प्रत्यक्षप्रमायां विशेषदर्शनजन्यत्वं स्वीकरणीयमिति भावः।

रीतबोधकत्वेन बाधकत्वं बाध्यतुल्यत्वात्। अनन्यथासिद्धं बाधकमिति चेत्। न। विशेषदर्शनजन्यत्वस्यैव तदर्थत्वात्। न च पीतः शङ्ख इत्यत्र विशेषदर्शनेऽपि श्वैत्यप्रमा नेति न तद्धेतुः, यद्विशेषदर्शनं हि भ्रमविरोधि तद्भावः प्रमाहेतुः, प्रत्यक्षभ्रमे च प्रत्यक्षविशेषदर्शनं विरोधि दिङ्मोहे गौरोऽहमिति भ्रमे च तथा दर्शनात्,

---

भ्रमोत्तरप्रत्यक्षप्रमां प्रति व्याप्यदर्शनस्यान्वयव्यभिचारमाशङ्क्य निराकरोति, 'न चेति, 'विशेषदर्शनेऽपि' श्वैत्यव्याप्यवत्तादर्शनेऽपि, 'तद्भावः' तद्वृत्तिधर्मः, तद्वृत्तिभ्रमविरोधित्वमिति यावत्। 'प्रमाहेतुः' भ्रमोत्तरप्रत्यक्षप्रमायाः कारणतावच्छेदकं, पीतः शङ्ख इत्यत्र यद्विशेषदर्शनं तद्भ्रमविरोध्येव न तत्सत्त्वेपि पीतः शङ्ख इति भ्रमोत्पत्तिरिति भावः। यद्यप्यत्र श्वैत्यविशेषदर्शनमपि भ्रमविरोध्येव दोषविशेषाद्यजन्यभ्रमं प्रत्येव तस्यैव विरोधित्वात्, तथापि यद्विशेषदर्शनं यत्प्रत्यक्षभ्रमविरोधि तद्वृत्ति तत्प्रत्यक्षभ्रमविरोधित्वं तद्भ्रमोत्तरप्रत्यक्षकारणतावच्छेदकमित्यर्थः। तथा च पीतः शङ्ख इत्यत्र यद्विशेषदर्शनं तन्न पीतत्वप्रत्यक्षभ्रमविरोधीति भावः। ननु श्वैत्यविशेषदर्शनं कुतो न पीतत्वप्रत्यक्षभ्रमविरोधि इत्यत आह, 'प्रत्यक्षेति, 'प्रत्यक्षविशेषदर्शनं' प्रत्यक्षविपरीतनिश्चयः, तदेव 'विरोधि', न तु विशेषदर्शनानुमानिकविपरीतनिश्चयादीत्यर्थः[१], 'दिङ्मोह-

---

(१) व्याप्यदर्शनानुमानिकविपरीतनिश्चयादीत्यर्थ इति ख०।

तत्र तत्र दोषान्नास्ति। अपि च लिङ्ग-सादृश्य-वाक्यार्थ-भ्रमदोषाभावमात्रान्नानुमित्यादिरिति सत्यपरामर्शादिगुणसिद्धिः। एवं प्रमाया गुणजन्यत्वेन वेदेऽपि प्रमा वाक्यार्थयथार्थज्ञानगुणजन्येति तदाश्रयेश्वरसिद्धिः। ननु प्रत्यक्षादावस्तु गुणजन्यत्वं, वेदे तु भ्रमाद्यभावचतुष्टयं प्रमा हेतुः। लोके च भ्रमाद्यभाव एव प्रमोत्पत्तेरिति

इति, 'तथादर्शनात्' प्राचीत्वव्याप्यसूर्य्योदयशालित्ववतीयमितिविशेष-दर्शन-अहं न गौर इत्यानुमानिकविपरीतनिश्चययोः प्रतिबन्धकत्व-दर्शनात्। ननु प्रत्यक्षात्मकपीतत्वविपरीतनिश्चय एव कुतो न भवतीत्यत आह, 'तत्रेति, तत्र' प्रत्यक्षात्मकविपरीतनिश्चयस्य, यद्यपि प्रत्यक्षभ्रमे प्रत्यक्षविपरीतनिश्चय एव विरोधीति 'यद्विशेष-दर्शनं भ्रमविरोधि तद्भावः प्रमाहेतुः' इति ग्रन्थोऽसङ्गतः विशेषदर्शनस्य प्रत्यक्षभ्रमाविरोधित्वात्, तथापि यत् यत्प्रत्यक्षभ्रमविरोधि तद्वृत्ति तत्प्रत्यक्षभ्रमविरोधित्वं तद्भ्रमोत्तरप्रत्यक्षप्रमाकारणतावच्छेदकं तच्च प्रकृते विशेषदर्शनं विपरीतनिश्चय एव न विशेषदर्शनमित्यर्थः।

किञ्च[1] 'यद्विशेषदर्शनं भ्रमविरोधि' यत्प्रत्यक्षप्रमानुपधायकं वस्तुतो यदव्यवहितोत्तरं यत्प्रत्यक्षभ्रमो न भवतीति यावत्, 'तद्भावः'

---

(१) किञ्चेत्यादिग्रन्थस्य पूर्वं "ननु विशेषदर्शनं कथं न प्रत्यक्षभ्रमविरोधि इत्यत आह, 'प्रत्यक्षेति, 'प्रत्यक्षविशेषदर्शनं' प्रत्यक्षविपरीतनिश्चयः, तदेव विरोधीत्यर्थः" इत्ययं पाठः आदर्शपुस्तकेषु वर्त्तते, परन्त्वयं न समीचीनः 'प्रत्यक्षविशेषदर्शनं' इति मूलपाठस्य पूर्वमेव धृतत्वात्।

चेत्। न। तत्र लाघवाद्वाक्यार्थयथार्थज्ञानस्य[१] हेतुत्वेन भ्रमाद्यभावानामन्यथासिद्धत्वात्। आप्तस्य भ्रमाद्य-

---

तत्स्वरूपं तद्विशेषदर्शनमिति यावत्, 'प्रमाहेतुः' तद्भ्रमोत्तरप्रत्यक्षप्रमाफलोपघायकं, यद्विशेषदर्शनव्यक्तेरव्यवहितोत्तरं यत्प्रत्यक्षभ्रमो न भवति सैव विशेषदर्शनव्यक्तिः तद्भ्रमोत्तरप्रत्यक्षप्रमाफलोपधायिकेति वस्तुस्थितिरिति समुदायार्थः। प्रकृते श्वैत्यविशेषदर्शनं एवं न भवति तदुत्तरमपि पीतत्वभ्रमस्योत्पत्तेरिति भावः। ननु श्वैत्यविशेषदर्शनो-त्तरं कथं पीतत्वभ्रमः विशेषदर्शनस्य भ्रमप्रतिबन्धकत्वात् इत्यत आह, 'प्रत्यक्षेति, अर्थस्तु पूर्ववत्। अथ पीतत्वविपरीतप्रत्यक्षनिश्चय एव कथं न जायते इत्यत आह, 'तत्रेति। यद्यपि विशेषप्रमात्वेन कारणता, भ्रमोत्तरप्रत्यक्षप्रमात्वेनैव कार्य्यता, तथापि विशेषदर्शने सत्यपि पीतः शङ्ख इत्यनन्तरं न श्वैत्यप्रमा दोषरूपप्रतिबन्धकसत्त्वा-दिति भावः।

'अनुमित्यादिरिति, प्रमेतिशेषः। 'सत्येति यथार्थपरामर्शादि-रूपगुणस्य कारणत्वमित्यर्थः। ननु यत्र एतेषां भ्रमः प्रमा च नास्ति तत्र अनुमित्यादिसामान्यकारणपरामर्शाद्यभावादेव तेषामभावः किं गुणस्य कारणत्वेनेति चेत्। न। अनुमित्यादिभ्रमेऽपि यथार्थपराम-र्शादिरूपगुणाभाव एव कारणमस्तु न दोषः, यत्र तु यथार्थपराम-र्शाद्यभावोऽस्ति अयथार्थपरामर्शादिरूपदोषोऽपि नास्ति तत्रानुमि-त्यादिसामान्यकारणपरामर्शाद्यभावादेव तेषामभावः किं दोषस्य

---

(१) वक्तृवाक्यार्थज्ञानस्येति ग०।

भावमात्रेण वाक्यार्थज्ञानं विना तादृशवाक्याभा-वाच्च। अन्यथा तवापि तत्र वक्तृज्ञानानुमानं न स्यात् तस्याहेतुत्वात्। अस्तु वोभयमपि हेतुः विनिगमका-भावात्। तथापि वेदे गुणसिद्धिः। न च नित्यनिर्दोष-

---

कारणत्वेन द्वयस्यापि सुवचत्वे विनिगमनाविरहादुभयोरपि हेतुत्वात्। 'वेदे तु' वैदिकस्थले तु, 'भ्रमादिः' भ्रमः, प्रमादः, विप्रलिप्सा, करणापाटवं, 'प्रमा' यथार्थशाब्दज्ञानं। 'लोके' लौकिकस्थले, 'भ्रमाद्यभाव एव' भ्रमाद्यभावसत्त्व एव। 'तत्रेति लौकिकस्थले उभयोरेव सत्त्वेन लाघवाद्यथार्थवाक्यार्थज्ञानस्यैव हेतुत्वेन क्लृप्तत्वात् इत्यर्थः। 'तादृशः' यथार्थशाब्दबुद्धिजनकः, 'अन्यथा' यथार्थवा-क्यार्थज्ञानं विना तादृशवाक्यप्रयोगे, 'तत्र' लौकिकस्थले, 'वक्तृज्ञानं' वक्तृयथार्थवाक्यार्थज्ञानं, 'तस्येति, 'तस्य' वाक्यार्थज्ञानस्य, 'अहेतुत्वात्' वाक्याहेतुत्वात्। भ्रमाद्यभावसत्त्वे यथार्थशाब्दबोधोत्पत्तिः, भ्रमा-दिसत्त्वे तदनुत्पत्तिरिति सोऽपि कारणमित्यभिप्रायवानाह, 'अस्तु वेति। 'न चेति, 'नित्यनिर्दोषत्वात्' नित्यत्वात्वाग्रष्टभ्रमादिदोषाजन्या-नुपूर्वीमत्त्वात्, 'प्रामाण्योपपत्तौ' प्रमाजनकत्वोपपत्तौ, 'अपरिदृष्टः' अक्लृप्तः। 'फलमुखेति कार्य्य-कारणभावग्रहोत्तरकालीनप्रमाणवद्दो-रत्नज्ञानस्येत्यर्थः, कथं तस्यादोषत्वमित्यत आह, 'पूर्व्वमिति कारण-तायहपूर्व्वं फलानुपस्थित्या कारणताग्रहसमये गौरवज्ञानाभावादि-त्यर्थः, उक्तकार्य्य-कारणभावस्य व्यभिचारमाशङ्कते, 'लोके इति लौकिकानुपूर्व्यामित्यर्थः।

त्वाददृष्टादेव वेदे प्रामाण्योपपत्तौ नापरिदृष्टनित्यज्ञानादिसर्वज्ञकल्पना गौरवादिति वाच्यं। प्रामाणवतः फलमुखगौरवस्यापि स्वर्गादाविवादोषत्वात् पूर्वं कारणताग्रहसमये फलानुपस्थित्या गौरवाज्ञानात् लोके नित्यत्वाभावाच्च। अथ वेदे कर्त्रस्मरणादेर्बाधकात् लोकेऽपि निर्दोषत्वेनैव प्रमाहेतुत्वं[1] वेदे तु नित्यत्वेनैव वक्तुरभावेऽपि निर्दोषत्वमवधार्य्यत इति चेत्।

ननु लौकिकस्थले लाघवात् शाब्दप्रमात्वेन कार्य्यता, वक्तृयथार्थवाक्यार्थज्ञानत्वेन कारणतेति यदुक्तं तत् वैदिकस्थले व्यभिचारि वक्तुरश्रूयमाणत्वेन प्रमाणाभावात् वेदस्य वक्तुरभावात् अतः लौकिकस्थलेऽपि भ्रमादिदोषाजन्यवाक्यत्वेन कारणता इत्येवाह, 'अथेति, 'कर्त्रस्मरणादेः' अश्रूयमाणकर्तृकत्वादेः, 'बाधकात्' सकर्तृकत्वे बाधकात्, 'निर्द्दोषत्वेन' जन्यतासम्बन्धेन भ्रमादिदोषाभाववत्त्वेन, 'प्रमाहेतुत्वमिति शाब्दप्रमाहेतुत्वमित्यर्थः, न तु शाब्दप्रमात्वेन वक्तृयथार्थवाक्यार्थज्ञानत्वेन वक्तुरश्रूयमाणत्वेन प्रमाणाभावात् वेदस्य वक्तुरभावेन वैदिकस्थले व्यभिचारादिति भावः। अथ वेदस्य दोषाजन्यत्वे किं मानमित्यत आह, 'वेदे त्विति, 'नित्यत्वेनेति नित्यानुपूर्व्वीकत्वेनेत्यर्थः, यथाश्रुतन्तु न सम्यक् केवलनित्यत्वस्य लौकिकसाधारणत्वात्। 'निराकरिष्य...णत्वादिति "प्रतिमचन्तरश्चैषा श्रुति-

---

(१) प्रामाण्यमि..ति ख०, ग०।

न। बाधकस्य बहुशो निराकरिष्यमाणत्वात् भ्रान्त-प्रतारकवाक्ये, घटोऽस्तीति वाच्ये पटोऽस्तीति दोष-जन्यवाक्ये च संवादात् प्रमाणे तदभावाच्च। किञ्च दैववशसम्पन्नं चैत्यं वन्देतेत्यादिकं शुक-बालादिवाक्य-मप्येवं प्रमाणं स्यात् वक्तृदोषाभावात् प्रमाणा-नपेक्षत्वेन वेदतुल्यत्वाच्च। ननु तवापि शुकादि-भ्रान्त-प्रतारकवाक्यं कथं प्रमाणं गुणाजन्यत्वात्(१)। न च

रन्या विधीयते" एवं "यतो वेदाश्च" इत्यादिना वेदस्यापि ब्रह्म-श्रुतेरित्यर्थः। दोषाजन्यवाक्यत्वेन कारणता, शाब्दप्रमात्वेन कार्य्यता एतस्य व्यभिचारमाशङ्कते, 'भ्रान्तेति, 'संवादात्' घटादिरूपविषय-स्याबाधितत्वात्, 'प्रमाणे' शाब्दप्रमाजनके, 'तदभावात्' दोषाजन्यत्वा-भावात्, तथाच तज्जन्यप्रमायां व्यभिचार इति भावः। 'दैवेति चैत्यवन्दनमिष्टसाधनमित्यादिज्ञानं विना प्रयुक्तं चैत्यं वन्देतेत्या-दिकं वाक्यमित्यर्थः, 'शुकेति वह्निना सिञ्चतीत्यादि शुक-बालक-वाक्यमित्यर्थः, 'प्रमाणं स्यात्' शाब्दप्रमाजनकं स्यात्। ननु शब्दानु-पजीविप्रमाणबोधितार्थकेतरवाक्यत्वेन कारणता शाब्दप्रमात्वेन कार्य्यता वाच्या, वेदस्तु एवं भवत्येव, तथाच वह्निना सिञ्चतीत्यादि शुक-बालकादिवाक्यन्तु शब्दानुपजीविप्रमाणं प्रत्यक्षादिप्रमाणमेव तद्बोधितार्थकमेव, न तदितरदिति नान्वयव्यभिचार इत्यत आह,

---

(१) 'गुणाजन्यत्वात्' इत्यत्र गुणजन्यत्वाभावात्' इति मूलप्रतीकस्य टीकाकृतोद्धृतत्वेन कुत्रचिन्मूलपुस्तके तादृशः पाठो विद्यते इत्यनुमीयते।

गुणाजन्यत्वात् वक्तृतात्पर्य्याविषयत्वाच्च तदप्रमाणं, संवादेन साध्ये बाधात्। यत्तु भ्रान्त-प्रतारकवाक्ये योग्यतैव नास्ति, वक्तृज्ञातवाक्यार्थाबाधो हि योग्यता, भ्रमविषयस्य बाधित इति। तन्न। घटवति घटो नास्तीति

'प्रमाणेति, 'प्रमाणानपेक्षत्वेन' प्रमाणबोधितार्थेतरत्वेन, वह्निना सिञ्चतीत्यादिवाक्यार्थस्तु भ्रमजनकबोधित एव न प्रमाणबोधित इति भावः। यथार्थवाक्यार्थज्ञानत्वेन कारणता शाब्द-प्रमात्वेन कार्य्यता वाक्यन्तु व्यापार इति बोध्यं, एतस्यैव व्यभिचारमाह, 'नन्विति, 'वाक्यं' पयसा सिञ्चतीत्यादि वाक्यमित्यर्थः, 'कथं प्रमाणं' कथं प्रमाजनकमित्यर्थः, 'गुणजन्यत्वाभावात्' यथार्थ-वाक्यार्थज्ञानजन्यत्वाभावात्। 'न चेति, 'गुणाजन्यत्वात्' यथार्थ-वाक्यार्थज्ञानाजन्यत्वात्, 'वक्तृतात्पर्य्याविषयत्वाच्च' वक्तुर्यत्किञ्चित्ता-त्पर्य्यकत्वाभावाच्च वक्तुः किञ्चिद्‌बोधेच्छया उच्चरितत्वाभावाच्चेति यावत्। इदन्तु शुकवाक्यस्य प्रमाजनकत्वाभावे हेतुः न तु भ्रान्त-प्रतारकवाक्यस्य, तस्य वक्तुर्यत्किञ्चित्तात्पर्य्यकत्वात्। 'तदिति शुका-दिवाक्यं भ्रान्त-प्रतारकवाक्यञ्च न प्रमाजनकमित्यर्थः, 'संवादेन' अबाधितार्थविषयकशाब्दबोधजनकत्वेन, 'साध्ये बाधादिति प्रमाजन-कत्वाभावस्य बाधितत्वादित्यर्थः। अथ वक्तृज्ञातवाक्यार्थाबाधो न योग्यता कुत्रचिदपि तस्या अभावात्सर्व्वत्रैवावश्यं वक्तृज्ञातयत्किञ्चि-द्वाक्यार्थबाधस्य सत्त्वात्किन्तु प्रकृतवाक्यकारणीभूतवक्तृज्ञानविषय-वाक्यार्थाबाधो योग्यता वाच्या तथासति आह, 'घटवतीति घटवति

भिन्नविषयतया भ्रमस्याहेतुत्वात्। किञ्च वाक्यार्थाबाधो योग्यता लाघवात्, वाक्यार्थश्च तत्राबाधित एव। नच शुक-बालादिवाक्यादर्थबोध एव न भवति किन्त्वेवमयं वदतीत्येवंप्रकारा प्रतीतिरिति वाच्यं। आकाङ्क्षा-

---

घटो नास्तीति भ्रमस्य भिन्नविषयतया घटोऽस्तीति भ्रान्त-प्रतारकवाक्याहेतुत्वादित्यर्थः, तथा च तद्विषयस्य बाधितत्वे का क्षतिरिति भावः। कुत्रचिद् घटवति पटोऽस्तीति पाठः, तदा घटवति पटोऽस्तीतिभ्रमस्य भिन्नविषयतया घटोऽस्तीतिभ्रान्त-प्रतारकवाक्ये अहेतुत्वादित्यर्थः। ननु शुकादिवाक्यस्थले भ्रान्त-प्रतारकवाक्यस्थले च प्रकृतवाक्यकारणीभूतवक्तृज्ञानविषयवाक्यार्थाप्रसिद्धेः तदबाधरूपयोग्यताया अभावादेव न शाब्दप्रमेत्यतआह, 'किञ्चेति, 'वाक्यार्थाबाधः' प्रकृतवाक्यार्थाबाधः, 'लाघवात्', एकपदार्थे अपरपदार्थसंसर्गाबाधमात्रं योग्यता न प्रकृतवाक्यकारणीभूतवक्तृज्ञानविषयत्वमपि विशेषणं गौरवादित्याशयः। 'वाक्यार्थस्त्विति [१]भ्रान्त-प्रतारक-शुकादिवाक्यार्थस्तु, 'तत्र' शुकादिवाक्यस्थले भ्रान्त-प्रतारकवाक्यस्थले च,। ननु शुकादिवाक्याच्छ्रवत्वान्वयबोधः, किन्तु स न प्रमेत्यत आह, 'संवादेनेति अबाधितार्थविषयकत्वेनेत्यर्थः,। यथार्थलिङ्गपरामर्शत्वेन कारणता प्रमानुमितित्वेन कार्य्यता एतस्य व्यभिचारमाशङ्कते, 'एवमिति। 'प्रत्यभिज्ञानात्' यो वह्निरनुमितः स

---

(१) 'वाक्यार्थश्च' इत्यत्र 'वाक्यार्थस्तु' इति कस्यचिन्मूलपुस्तकस्य पाठमनुसृत्य 'वाक्यार्थस्तु' इति पाठः टीकाकारेणाधारि।

देरन्वयबोधसामग्र्याः सत्त्वेऽनुभवानपलापात् संवादेन[१] यथार्थत्वानुभवाच्च। एवं धूमभ्रमाद्वह्निमत्येव वह्न्यनुमितिर्न प्रमा स्यात् यथार्थलिङ्गज्ञानाजन्यत्वात्। न च वह्न्यन्तरमेव तत्र विषयः, प्रत्यभिज्ञानात् गोत्वाद्येकव्यक्तिके तदभावाच्च[२]। नापि तत्रान्यतादात्म्यारोपः,

एवात्र इति प्रत्यभिज्ञानादित्यर्थः, 'गोत्वादीति' गोत्वव्याप्यद्रव्यत्ववती-यमित्यादिभ्रमपरामर्शजन्यगोत्वाद्येकव्यक्तिसाध्यकप्रमानुमितौ, 'तद-सम्भवाच्च' व्यक्त्यन्तरविषयकत्वासम्भवाच्चेत्यर्थः,[३] तथाच एतस्या-मेवानुमितौ व्यभिचार इति भावः। अथ तत्र गोत्वानुमितिरेव न भवति किन्तु अन्यगोतादात्म्यभ्रमानुमितिरेव जायते इति निरा-करोति, 'नापीति', 'संसर्गारोपादिति', 'संसर्गेण' समवायादिना, 'आरोपात्' भानात् गोत्वव्याप्तिभानादित्यर्थः, तथाच यत्सम्बन्धेन व्याप्तिज्ञानं तत्सम्बन्धेन तस्यानुमितिः, प्रकृते तु समवायेन गोत्वव्याप्ति-भानं कथं तादात्म्येन गोरनुमितिरिति भावः।

ननु धूमभ्रमाद्वह्निमति वह्न्यनुमितिर्भ्रम एव वह्निव्याप्यधूम-वत्त्वविषयकत्वात् तथाच कथं व्यभिचार इत्यत आह, 'लिङ्गेति', तथाच प्रमानुमितित्वेन कार्य्यता यथार्थलिङ्गपरामर्शत्वेन कारणता एतस्य तत्र व्यभिचारस्तदवस्थ एवेति भावः। 'भ्रान्तेति', 'आप्तोक्त-त्वात्' यथार्थवाक्यार्थज्ञानजन्यत्वात्, यः प्रमाणशब्दः स यथार्थवा-

(१) संवादादिनेति ख०, ग०।

(२) तदसम्भवाच्चेति ग०।

(३) गोत्वस्य जातित्वेन एकव्यक्तित्वादिति भावः।

संसर्गारोपात् लिङ्गोपधानांशे भ्रमत्वेऽपि साध्यांशे प्रमात्वादिति। उच्यते। भ्रान्त-प्रतारकवाक्ये शुकादिवाक्ये च प्रमाणशब्दत्वेनाप्तोक्तत्वात् वेदवदीश्वरस्यैव यथार्थवाक्यार्थज्ञानं जनकं तस्य कार्यमात्रे कर्तृत्वात्[१]। शुकादिवाक्यस्य च वेदतुल्यता दोषाभाववादिनापि वाच्या। नन्वेवं शब्दाभासोच्छेदः तस्यापीश्वरवक्तृकत्वादिति चेत्। न। तद्वाक्यार्थस्यासत्त्वेन भगवज्ज्ञानागोचरत्वात्।

कार्यंज्ञानजन्य इति नियमात् भ्रान्त-प्रतारक-शुकादिवाक्ये ईश्वरीयवाक्यार्थज्ञानमेव जनकमित्यर्थः। नन्वेवञ्चेत् शुकादिवाक्यं वेदतुल्यमेव जातमित्यत आह, 'शुकादीति, 'दोषाभाववादिना' दोषाभावस्य कारणतावच्छेदकत्ववादिना, तन्मतेऽपि दोषाजन्यत्वेनैव तुल्यत्वादिति भावः। 'शब्दाभासोच्छेदः' भ्रमजनकशब्दोच्छेदः, 'ईश्वरवक्तृकत्वात्' ईश्वरीयवाक्यार्थज्ञानजन्यत्वात्, तस्य कार्य्यमात्र-कारणत्वादिति भावः[२]। 'तद्वाक्यार्थस्येति भ्रमजनकवाक्यार्थस्य, 'असत्त्वेन' बाधितत्वेनेत्यर्थः। 'सम्प्रदायविदः' इत्यस्वरसोद्भावनं, तदीजन्तु यथा शाब्दप्रमात्वेन कार्य्यता यथार्थवाक्यार्थज्ञानत्वेन कारणता इति कार्य्य-कारणभावसत्त्वात् वैदिकस्थले तज्जन्यैव शाब्द-प्रमेति परिशेषात् तदाश्रयेश्वरसिद्धिः, तथा शाब्दभ्रमत्वेन कार्य्यता अयथार्थवाक्यार्थज्ञानत्वेन कारणता इति कार्य्य-कारणभावसत्त्वात्

---

(१) जनकत्वादिति ख०।

(२) ईश्वरीयज्ञानस्य उपादानप्रत्यक्षविधया कार्य्यमात्रं प्रति कारणत्वमिति भावः।

एवं लिङ्गाभासजन्यप्रमायामपि वह्निव्याप्यवत्त्वज्ञानमीश्वरस्यैव जनकमिति सम्प्रदायविदः ।

अत्र ब्रूमः । शाब्दप्रमायां लोके वक्तुर्यथार्थवाक्यार्थज्ञानं न गुणः किन्तु योग्यतादिकं यथार्थतज्ज्ञानं वा लाघवादावश्यकत्वाच्च । भ्रम-प्रमाद-विप्रलिप्साजन्ये वाक्ये विसंवादिनि न यथार्थयोग्यताज्ञानं वाक्यार्थस्य बाधितत्वात् । एवं करणापाटवादन्यस्मिन्वक्तव्येऽन्याभिधाने

विसंवादिशुकादिवाक्यस्थलेऽपि तज्जन्य एव भ्रम इति परिशेषादयथार्थवाक्यार्थज्ञानवान् कश्चन सिद्ध्यतु, शाब्दभ्रमं प्रति एवं कार्य्य-कारणभावे चेन्मानाभावः तदा शाब्दप्रमां प्रत्यपि तत्तत्कार्य्य-कारणभावे मानाभाव इति ।

क्षितेः सकर्त्तृकत्वानुमानेनैव ईश्वरसिद्धिः न तु प्रमाया गुणजन्यत्वेनेत्याह, 'अत्र ब्रूमः' इत्यादिना, योग्यता न एकपदार्थे अपरपदार्थसंसर्गरूपा अतीतानागतसंसर्गस्थले व्यभिचारात्किन्तु एकपदार्थे अपरपदार्थसंसर्गाधिकरणत्वरूपा । 'एवमिति, 'अन्याभिधाने विसंवादिनि' 'एवमित्यन्वयः, 'एवं' योग्यताज्ञानं न यथार्थं वाक्यार्थस्य बाधितत्वात् । 'संवादीति करणापाटवजन्यसंवादिवाक्यस्थले तु योग्यताज्ञानं प्रमैवेत्यर्थः, तत्र वाक्यार्थस्याबाधितत्वादिति भावः । अथ योग्यता चेद्गुणः तदा कश्चित्स्वरूपसती योग्यता वर्त्तते शाब्दप्रमा कथं न जायते इत्यत आह, 'कश्चिदिति, तथाच शाब्दबोधसामान्यकारणयोग्यताज्ञानाभावादेव कार्य्याभाव इति भावः ।

विसंवादिनि। संवादिनि तु प्रमाणमेव। योग्यतादिज्ञानमेव क्वचिन्नास्ति। नन्वेवं नानार्थादन्यपरात्तात्पर्य्यभ्रमे तं विनैव वा यथार्थयोग्यतादिज्ञाने सति संवाद्यपरशक्यज्ञानमपि प्रमेति तत्रापि तद्वाक्यं प्रमाणं स्यादिति चेत्। न। इष्टत्वात्। तात्पर्य्यविषये च तद्वाक्यं न तदा प्रमाजनकमिति न प्रमाणं। एवं वेदेऽपि यथार्थयोग्यताज्ञानमेव गुण इति न वैदिकप्रमाया गुणजन्यत्वेनेश्वरसिद्धिः। स्यादेतत्। वेदे[१] वक्तुर्यथार्थवाक्यार्थज्ञानमपि गुणः लोके प्रमाणशब्दं प्रति तादृशस्य ज्ञानस्य हेतुत्वात्। अत एव तव लोके वक्तृज्ञानानुमानं। एवं

अथ यत्र विष्णुबोधेच्छया हरिरस्तीति वाक्यं प्रयुक्तं तात्पर्य्यभ्रमेण यथार्थयोग्यताज्ञानसत्त्वात् सिंहप्रमा जाता तत्रापि तद्वाक्यं प्रमाणं स्यादित्येवाह, 'नन्विति, 'अन्यपरात्' अन्यतात्पर्य्यकात्, तात्पर्य्यज्ञानस्याकारणत्वपक्षे आह, 'तं विनैवेति तात्पर्य्यभ्रमं विनैवेत्यर्थः, 'संवाद्यपरशक्यं' अबाधितापरशक्यं। एवञ्चेत्तदा तद्वाक्यस्य कथं प्रमाणत्वेन न व्यवहार इत्यत आह, 'तात्पर्य्यविषयेति, 'तात्पर्य्यविषये' वक्तृबोधेच्छाविषये, 'न प्रमाणमिति न प्रमाणत्वेन व्यवह्रियते। ननु शाब्दप्रमायां वक्तृयथार्थवाक्यार्थज्ञानस्य हेतुत्वकल्पने गौरवं यद्यपि तथापि लौकिकस्थले प्रमाणशब्दं प्रति तस्य हेतुत्वं क्लृप्तमिति शाब्दप्रमायामपि तदेव हेतुः अन्यथा प्रमाया अजनकत्वे

---

(१) शब्दे इति ख०, ग०।

च वेदो वाक्यार्थगोचरयथार्थज्ञानवत्स्वतन्त्रप्रणीतः प्रमाणशब्दत्वात् गामानयेति वाक्यवदितीश्वरसिद्धिः। मैवम्। प्रमाणशब्दत्वं हि वाक्यार्थयथार्थज्ञानपूर्वकतां विनापि सम्भवति आवश्यकयोग्यतादिसत्त्वात् यथार्थतज्ज्ञानादहेत्युपपादितमतोऽप्रयोजकमेतदिति। तथापि लोके वाक्यार्थज्ञानं प्रमाणवाक्ये कारणं गृहीतमिति तेन विना कथं तदिति चेत्। न। प्रवृत्त्याद्यर्थं हि प्रयोज्यस्य वाक्यार्थज्ञानमुद्दिश्यैतादृशपदेभ्यो वाक्यार्थं ज्ञास्यतीति बुद्ध्या वाक्यप्रयोग इत्यन्यथासिद्धं प्रथमं वक्तुर्वा-

---

प्रमाणत्वप्रयोजकं न स्यादिति भावः। अथ प्रमाणशब्देऽपि न यथार्थवाक्यार्थज्ञानं हेतुरित्यत आह, 'अत एवेति यत एव प्रमाणशाब्दं प्रति यथार्थवाक्यार्थज्ञानं हेतुरत एवेत्यर्थः, 'वक्तृज्ञानानुमानमिति प्रमाणशब्देन वक्तृयथार्थवाक्यार्थज्ञानानुमानमित्यर्थः। 'एवञ्चेति वेदः स्वतन्त्रवाक्यार्थगोचरयथार्थज्ञानजन्यः प्रमोपधायकशब्दत्वादित्यर्थः। 'स्वतन्त्रत्वं' शब्दाप्रयोज्यत्वं, तेनाध्यापकस्य वेदजन्यवाक्यार्थगोचरयथार्थवाक्यार्थज्ञानजन्यतया न सिद्धसाधनं। न चैवं शाब्दवाक्यार्थज्ञानजन्यप्रमाणशब्दे व्यभिचार इति वाच्यं। तत्रापि परमेश्वरज्ञानमादाय साध्यसत्त्वादिति भावः। 'इतीश्वरसिद्धिः' इत्यनेनापीश्वरसिद्धिः। 'प्रमाणशब्दत्वं हि' शब्दस्य प्रमोपधायकत्वं हि। ननु शब्दस्य प्रमोपधायकत्वं कथं यथार्थवाक्यार्थज्ञानपूर्व्वकतां विना सम्भवति, प्रमां प्रति यथार्थवाक्यार्थज्ञानस्य हेतुत्वात् इत्यत आह, 'आव-

यथार्थज्ञानं। न तु तादृशपदावलीप्रयोगे तस्य हेतुत्वम्। तादृशपदसमूहस्य प्रत्येकपदहेतोरेव शुकादिवदुपपत्तेः। अथ तात्पर्य्यविषये वेदः प्रमाणं तात्पर्य्यञ्च तत्प्रतीतीच्छयोच्चारणं। नचास्मदादेर्वेदं विनातीन्द्रियवेदार्थगोचरज्ञानं येन तत्प्रतीतीच्छयोच्चारणं भवेत्। नच वेदादेव तत्, अन्योन्याश्रयात्। अतः सकलवेदार्थदर्शिना यस्य वेदस्य यदर्थप्रतीतीच्छयोच्चारणं कृतं स तत्र प्रमाणमिति तादृशेच्छैव गुणस्तज्जन्या वेदार्थप्रमेति तदा

यथेति, 'यथार्थेति यथार्थतज्ज्ञानाद्वा प्रमा जायते इत्युपपादितमित्यर्थः। ननु कथमप्रयोजकं प्रमोपधायकशब्दत्वेन कार्य्यता, यथार्थवाक्यार्थज्ञानत्वेन कारणता इति कार्य्य-कारणभावसत्त्वादित्यत आह, 'तथापीति, 'वाक्यार्थज्ञानं' यथार्थवाक्यार्थज्ञानं, 'तेन विना' यथार्थवाक्यार्थज्ञानं विना, 'कथं तदिति, 'तत्' प्रमाणशब्दस्वरूपं। अथ वाक्यमात्रे एव वाक्यार्थज्ञानं न कारणं। न च नियतपूर्व्ववर्त्तितासत्त्वे[१] कथं कारणं नेति वाच्यं। प्रवृत्त्यर्थं प्रयोज्यस्य वाक्यार्थज्ञानं भवत्विति प्रयोक्तुरिच्छानन्तरं वाक्ये एतादृशपदेभ्यो वाक्यार्थं ज्ञास्यतीति इष्टसाधनताज्ञानं जायते ततो वाक्यप्रयोगः क्रियते इति नियतपूर्व्ववर्त्ति वाक्यार्थज्ञानं किन्तु अन्यथासिद्धमित्यत आह, 'प्रवृत्त्यादीति, 'उद्दिश्य' तद्विषयकेच्छाया अनन्तरं, 'इति बुद्ध्या वाक्य-

---

(१) नियतपूर्व्ववर्त्तिभावादिति ख०।

अयस्वतन्त्रपुरुषधौरेयसिद्धिरिति चेत्। नैवं। मीमांसादिसकलाङ्गसाचिव्याद्वेदवाक्यार्थज्ञानवताध्यापकेन तत्तदर्थप्रतीतीच्छया वेदस्योच्चारणमिति वेदार्थयथार्थविदस्तत्तदर्थे तात्पर्य्यमस्त्येव। एवं पूर्वपूर्वतादृशाध्यापकेन तत्तदर्थप्रतीतीच्छयोच्चरितत्वं तत्परत्वमवगम्योत्तरोत्तरेषां वेदार्थप्रत्यय इत्यनादिस्तात्पर्यपरम्परेति कि-

---

प्रयोग इति, 'प्रथमं वक्तृवाक्यार्थज्ञानमित्यन्वयः, 'प्रथमं' पूर्व्ववर्त्ति, 'अन्यथासिद्धं' किन्तु तदन्यथासिद्धं। अथ केन अन्यथासिद्धमित्यत आह, 'तादृशपदसमूहस्येति, 'प्रत्येकपदहेतोरेव' प्रत्येकपदहेतोस्तत्पदज्ञानादेव। 'अथेति यत्तात्पर्य्यको वेदस्तच प्रमाणमित्यर्थः। अथ वेदं विना वेदार्थगोचरज्ञानं न जातमेतावता किं वेदेनैव वेदार्थज्ञानं उत्पत्स्यते तदा तत्प्रतीतीच्छयोच्चारणं भवेदित्यत आह, 'नचेति, वैदिकस्थले वेदादेव वेदार्थज्ञानं तदा तत्प्रतीतीच्छयोच्चारणं भवेदिति नचेत्यर्थः। 'अन्योन्येति, किं परोच्चरितवेदात् वेदार्थज्ञानं भविष्यति तदा तत्प्रतीतीच्छयोच्चारणं भवेत्, किं वा स्वोच्चरितवेदात्स्वस्य वेदार्थज्ञानं भविष्यति तदा तत्प्रतीतीच्छयोच्चारणं भवेत्। नाद्यः, तदा परस्यैव वेदार्थज्ञानं कथं अन्योच्चरितवेदात् तथाचानवस्थानात्। नान्त्यः स्वस्य वेदार्थज्ञाने सति तत्प्रतीतीच्छया वेदोच्चारणं वेदे उच्चरिते तस्माद्वेदार्थज्ञानमित्यन्योन्याश्रयादित्यर्थः। तस्मादनवस्थान्योन्याश्रयभङ्गाय वेदाजन्यवेदार्थप्रतीतीच्छा अवश्यं वेदोच्चारणे हेतुर्वाच्या इति भावः। 'अत इति यतो वेदोच्चारणे वेदा-

मीश्वरेण, तर्हि वेदार्थानभिज्ञापकेनोच्चारितवेदस्य न तदर्थप्रतीतीच्छयोच्चारणमिति तात्पर्य्याभावान्न प्रमाणं न वा ततोऽर्थनिश्चय इति चेत्। न। अनादौ संसारे तस्य वेदस्य कदाचित् केनचित् मीमांसाद्यधीनवेदार्थज्ञानवता तत्प्रतीतीच्छयोच्चारणं कृतं तावतैव तत्परत्वमिति।

जन्यवेदार्थप्रतीतीच्छा हेतुरत इत्यर्थः, 'सकलवेदार्थदर्शिना' वेदाजन्यसकलवेदार्थदर्शिना, 'सः' वेदः, 'तत्र' तस्मिन्नर्थे, 'इतीति, तस्यां प्रमायां तादृशेच्छैव गुण इत्यर्थः, तस्य वेदस्य अस्मदादिवेदार्थप्रतीतीच्छयोच्चरितत्वाभावादिति भावः। 'तादृशेच्छा' वेदाजन्यवेदार्थप्रतीतीच्छा, 'तदाश्रयः' वेदाजन्यवेदार्थप्रतीतीच्छाश्रयः, 'स्वतन्त्रेति शब्दाप्रयोज्यज्ञानवत्पुरुषश्रेष्ठभिद्धिरित्यर्थः। 'मीमांसादीति अस्य वेदस्य अयमेवार्थः अयं नार्थ इति विनिगमकप्रमाणसहकारादित्यर्थः। 'वेदार्थेति वेदार्थयथार्थविदोऽध्यापकस्यैव वेदार्थप्रतीतीच्छास्ति स एव गुण इत्यर्थः। ननु अध्यापकस्यैव वेदार्थप्रतीतिः कथं वेदार्थस्यातीन्द्रियत्वादित्यत आह, 'एवमिति, 'एवं' एवंप्रकारेण विनिगमकप्रमाणसहकारेणेति यावत्, 'तादृशः' वेदार्थज्ञानवान्, तथाच विनिगमकप्रमाणसहकारेण वेदार्थज्ञानवत्पूर्व्वपूर्व्वाध्यापकेनेति प्रतीकसमुदायार्थः। 'अनादीति, तथाचानाद्यनवस्था न दूषणावहेति भावः। 'न वेति, 'ततः' तद्वाक्यात्, 'अर्थनिश्चयः' शाब्दबोधः स्यादित्यर्थः, शाब्दबोधसामान्यकारणता-

प्राभाकरास्तु प्रामाण्यं स्वत एव उत्पद्यते ज्ञायते चेति। तथाहि निष्कम्पप्रवृत्त्यङ्गं स्मृत्यनुभवसाधारणं यथार्थत्वमेव प्रामाण्यं, तच्च ज्ञानमात्रसामग्रीजन्यं न तु गुणं दोषाभावं वापेक्षते। सर्वज्ञानानां यथार्थत्वेनाव्यभिचारात्(१)। अयथार्थस्तु व्यवहारः तस्यैव बाध्यत्वात्। ज्ञानन्तु न बाध्यते बाधकाभिमतज्ञानतुल्यत्वात्(२)। ज्ञाने चायथार्थत्वव्यपदेशो विपरीतव्यवहारजननोपाधिकः। अथ यथार्थत्वस्य प्रामाण्यत्वे रजतज्ञानं शुक्तौ कथमप्रमाणं, अप्रमाण्यञ्च कथं परत उत्पद्यत इति

त्पर्य्यज्ञानाभावादिति भावः। 'तत्परत्वं' तत्प्रतीतीच्छया उच्चरितत्वं, वेदानुपूर्व्या नित्यत्वादिति भावः।

अन्यखण्डे दूषयिष्यमाणत्वात् प्रागुक्तमदूषयित्वैव प्राभाकरमतमाह, 'प्राभाकरास्त्विति, 'प्रामाण्यमिति घटत्वादिप्रामाण्यमित्यर्थः, 'स्वत-एवेति स्वत उत्पत्तिकत्वं स्वतो ग्राह्यत्वञ्चेत्यर्थः, घटत्वप्रकारकज्ञानसामग्रीजन्ययावज्ज्ञानवृत्तित्वं स्वतस्त्वं, घटत्वप्रकारकज्ञानसामग्रीजन्ययावज्ज्ञानविषयत्वञ्च स्वतो ग्राह्यत्वं। ननु प्रामाण्यं अनुभवत्वगर्भं कथं स्वतउत्पत्तिकं स्मृत्यवृत्तेरित्यत आह, 'तथाहीति, 'ज्ञानमात्रसामग्रीजन्यं' ज्ञानसामग्रीजन्यज्ञानमात्रवृत्ति, मात्रपदं साकल्यार्थकं। ननु प्रमाया गुण-दोषाभावजन्यत्वात् प्रामाण्यं कथं ज्ञानसामग्री-

---

(१) यथार्थत्वेन व्यभिचाराभावादिति ख०, ग०।

(२) बाधकत्वाभिमतज्ञानतुल्यत्वादिति क०, ख०।

चेत्। न। अयथार्थत्वं नाप्रामाण्यं सर्वधियां यथार्थत्वात्। किन्तु विपरीतव्यवहारप्रवर्तकत्वम्। तच्च ज्ञानसामग्र्यामधिकदोषानुप्रवेशात् दोषहेतुकासंसर्गाग्रहाद्वा उत्पन्ने ज्ञाने दोषसहकाराद्वा धर्म-धर्मिणोरसंसर्गाग्रहरूपमेकत्वासंसर्गाग्रहसहितं परत उत्पद्यते। न तु ज्ञानमात्रसामाग्रीतः प्रमायामतिप्रसङ्गात्। उक्ती-

अन्ययावज्ज्ञानवृत्ति गुण-दोषाभावाजन्यज्ञानावृत्तित्वात् अत आह, 'न त्विति, 'अपेक्षते,' प्रमेति शेषः। ननु गुणादि चेन्न कारणं तदा तद्भ्रमोत्पत्तिसमये तत्प्रमोत्पत्तिर्नेति ज्ञानसामान्यसामग्र्यां अन्वयव्यभिचार इत्यत आह. 'सर्व्वेति। अथ ज्ञानत्वेनायथार्थं अयथार्थः क इत्यत आह, 'अयथार्थस्त्विति, 'व्यवहारः' प्रवृत्तिः, 'बाध्यत्वात्' भ्रमत्वेन ज्ञातत्वात्। ज्ञानमपि भ्रमत्वेन ज्ञायते तत् कथं नायथार्थमित्यत आह, 'ज्ञानन्त्विति, 'न बाध्यते' न भ्रमत्वेन ज्ञायते, 'बाधकाभिमतेति, 'बाधकाभिमतज्ञानं' प्रमा, तुल्यत्वं प्रमात्वेन रूपेण, तथाच प्रमात्वादिति समुदायार्थः, प्रमा च भ्रमत्वेन न ज्ञायते अन्यथाख्यात्यभावादिति भावः। नन्वेवमिदं ज्ञानमयथार्थमिति कथं व्यवहार इत्यत आह, 'ज्ञाने चेति, 'विपरीतव्यवहारेति अयथार्थप्रवृत्तिजनकत्वनिबन्धन इत्यर्थः, तथाच भाक्तो व्यवहार इति भावः(१)। अयथार्थव्यवहारस्य लक्षणया समर्थनेऽपि

(१) तथाच तादृशव्यवहारो लक्षणया विपरीतव्यवहारजनकत्वं बोधयतीति भाव इति ग०।

यते च विपरीतव्यवहारजनकत्वं बाधकात् । तस्य तेन तदनुव्यवसायेन वा ग्रहीतुमशक्यत्वात् । ज्ञानस्वरूपे च न दोष-तदभावौ हेतू व्यभिचारात् । ज्ञानायथार्थत्वेऽपि यथार्थत्वं ज्ञानसामग्रीजन्यमेव, न तु गुणात् दोषाभावाद्वा, विपर्ययादेरपि धर्म्यंशे यथार्थ-

---

अप्रमात्वव्यवहारस्तच कथं समर्थनीयः सर्व्वधीयाथार्थ्येन ज्ञानाप्रामाण्याभावात् "अप्रामाण्यं परत उत्पद्यते" इति प्राचीनैर्व्वा कथमुच्यते(१) इत्याह, 'अथेति, 'प्रामाण्यत्वे' प्रामाण्यरूपत्वे, एतदनन्तरं तस्य च सर्व्वधीवृत्तित्वादिति पूरणीयं। 'रजतेति शुक्तौ रजतज्ञानं कथमप्रमात्वेन व्यवह्रियत इत्यर्थः, 'परत उत्पद्यत-इति, इति प्राचीनैरुच्यते इति शेषः। 'किन्त्विति अयथार्थ-प्रवृत्तिजनकत्वमित्यर्थः, तथाच नाप्रमात्वव्यवहारानुपपत्तिरिति भावः। अयथार्थप्रवृत्तिजनकत्वं तज्जननयोग्यत्वं, तच्च सहकारियोग्यत्वं, अर्थात् तादृशप्रवृत्तिसहकार्य्येव, स च दोषसहकृतज्ञानसामान्यसामग्रीहेतुकोधर्म्म-धर्म्मिणोरसंसर्गाग्रहः, दोषहेतुकधर्म्म-धर्म्म्यसंसर्गाग्रहाधीनो दोषसहकृतज्ञानसामान्यकारणकलापाधीनो वा धर्म्म-धर्म्मिविषयकज्ञानद्वयैकत्वासंसर्गाग्रहस्येत्यभिप्रायेण "अप्रामाण्यं परत उत्पद्यते" इति प्राचीनप्रवादं सङ्गमयति,(२) 'तचेति, अप्रामाण्यस्येत्यर्थः, एतस्य

---

(१) इति प्राचीनग्रन्थो वा कथं संगच्छते इति ग०।

(२) स च धर्म्म-धर्म्मिणोरसंसर्गाग्रहः ज्ञानद्वयैकत्वासंसर्गाग्रहस्येत्यभिप्रायेण "अप्रामाण्यं परत उत्पद्यते" इति मीमांसकग्रन्थं संगमयतीति ग०।

त्वात् असदर्थविषयता दोषात् इन्द्रियाणामसन्नि-हितेऽसदर्थे सामर्थ्याभावात्। ननु दोषमात्रं न कारणं किन्तु तदपेक्षा ज्ञानसामग्रीति यथार्थत्वे दोषाभाव-

---

'असंसर्गाग्रहरूपमित्यग्रेतनेनान्वयः, 'ज्ञानसामग्र्यां दोषानुप्रवेशादि-त्यनन्तरं जातमिति पूरणीयं, एतस्यापि असंसर्गाग्रहरूपमित्यग्रेत-नेनान्वयः, तथाच ज्ञानसामग्र्यां दोषानुप्रवेशाज्जातं धर्म्म-धर्म्मि-णोरसंसर्गाग्रहरूपमप्रामाण्यमित्यर्थः, 'दोषसहकारादित्येतत्पूर्व्वस्य 'उत्पन्ने ज्ञाने' इति 'दोषहेतुकेत्यस्यादौ बोध्यं, 'दोषसहकारादित्यनन्तरं उत्पन्ने इति पूरणीयं। 'एकत्वासंसर्गाग्रहसहितं' एकत्वासंसर्गाग्रहेणायः तेन सहितं, 'सहितमित्यनन्तरं भवतीति पूरणीयं, तथाच ज्ञानसामग्र्यां दोषानुप्रवेशाज्जातं धर्म्म-धर्म्मिणोरसंसर्गाग्रहरूपमप्रामाण्यञ्च उत्पन्ने ज्ञाने दोषहेतुकासंसर्गाग्रहात् दोषसहकाराद्वा तज्ज्ञानद्वयोरेकत्वा-संसर्गाग्रहसहितं भवतीति योजना। 'सहितमित्यनन्तरं भवती-त्यध्याहारात्। 'दोषानुप्रवेशादित्यत्र अधीनत्वं पञ्चम्यर्थः, अन्वय-श्चास्य 'असंसर्गाग्रहे'। 'परत उत्पद्यते' अतः परत उत्पत्तिकत्वव्य-वहारविषय इति यावत्। तथाच 'अप्रामाण्यं परत 'उत्पद्यते' इत्यस्य एकं अप्रामाण्यं सहितं भवतीत्यर्थः। 'न तु प्रामाण्येति न पुनरप्रमात्वाश्रयज्ञाने अन्यतासम्बन्धेन ज्ञानसामान्यसामग्रीत इत्यर्थः, अप्रमात्वं परत उत्पत्तिकत्वव्यवहार-विषय इति शेषः। 'अतिप्रस-ङ्गादिति अन्यतासम्बन्धेन ज्ञानसामान्यसामग्र्या अतिप्रसक्तत्वादि-त्यर्थः। तथाच अप्रमात्ववत् प्रमात्वेपि स्वत उत्पत्तिकत्वव्यवहारा-

सापेक्षा सा हेतुरिति चेत् । न । सैव सामग्र्यसदर्थांशे दोषसापेक्षेति तदंशे ज्ञानमयथार्थं, सदर्थांशे दोषनिरपेक्षेति तदंशे यथार्थं, न तु सैव तत्रैव ज्ञाने दोष-तद-

---

पत्तिरिति भावः । अथाप्रामाण्यं परतो गृह्यते इति सिद्धान्तः कथं संगच्छते इत्यत आह, 'उन्नीयत इति, 'बाधकात्' व्यापकशून्ये व्याप्यप्रकारकप्रवृत्तिजनकत्वात् । 'तस्य' विपरीतप्रवृत्तिजनकत्वस्य, 'तेन' ज्ञानेन, 'तदनुव्यवसायेन' ज्ञानानुव्यवसायेन । इदानीं नैयायिकोक्तं दोष-तदभावस्य कारणत्वं दूषयति, 'ज्ञानस्वरूप इति । नैयायिकमतेनापि दूषणमाह, 'ज्ञानयथार्थेत्यादिना 'मान्तरीयकावित्यन्तेन, 'यथार्थत्वं' यथार्थत्वविशिष्टं, 'दोषाभावादेति, जायते इति शेषः । नन्वेवं भ्रमोऽपि ज्ञानसामग्रीमात्रात्स्यात् किं दोषस्य कारणत्वेनेत्यत आह, 'असदर्थविषयेति, असदर्थविषयकत्वं विशेष्यावृत्तिप्रकारकत्वं, 'इन्द्रियाणामिति इन्द्रियाणामसदर्थविषयकज्ञानजनने सामर्थ्याभावादित्यर्थः । ननु भ्रमस्य दोषमात्रकारणकत्वे ज्ञानत्वं न स्यादतो दोषसहकृतज्ञानसामान्यसामग्र्या हेतुत्वं वाच्यं, एवञ्चेद्दोषाभावसहकृताया एव तस्याः प्रमाहेतुत्वं वाच्यं अन्यथा ज्ञानसामग्र्येव प्रमासामग्री तज्जन्यत्वे भ्रमस्यापि प्रमात्वप्रसङ्गादित्याशङ्कते, 'नन्विति, 'यथार्थत्वे' यथार्थत्वावच्छिन्ने, अन्यथा ज्ञानसामग्र्येव प्रमासामग्री तज्जन्यत्वेन भ्रमस्यापि प्रमात्वप्रसङ्गादिति भावः । 'सैव सामग्रीति, तथाच दोषनिरपेक्षज्ञानसामग्रीजन्यत्वमेव प्रमात्वव्याप्यमिति भावः । 'सैव' ज्ञानसामान्यसामग्र्येव, 'विरोधात्' दोष-तदभावयोर्विरोधात् । अथ तदंशे दोषाभावः तत्प्रमायां

भावसापेक्षा विरोधात् अयथार्थ-यथार्थत्वे दोष-तद-भावौ नान्तरीयकौ। यथार्थत्वञ्च ज्ञानोल्लिखितप्रकारवत्त्वमर्थस्य, यद्धर्मवत्त्वमर्थस्य तत्प्रकारकज्ञानत्वं वा। इदं रजतमिति ज्ञानमर्थस्य रजतत्वं स्वस्य रजतत्वाश्रयविषयकत्वं यथार्थत्वरूपं प्रामाण्यं स्वप्रकाशत्वेन स्वयमेव परिच्छिन्दत् स्वार्थनिश्चयरूपं। तदतिरिक्तञ्च न प्रामाण्यं मानाभावात्। अस्तु वा[१] तदपि स्वतो ज्ञायतां परतो वा मा वा ज्ञायि[२] किं तन्निरूपणेन

कारणं वाच्यं, तदा यद्यपि इदं रजतमिति भ्रमस्थले रजतत्वांशे दोषोऽस्ति तथापि शुक्तित्वांशे तदभावोऽस्त्येवेत्यत आह, 'अयथार्थ-यथार्थत्वे' इति, 'नान्तरीयकौ' अन्यथासिद्धौ, यथा अस्मन्मते अयथार्थत्वविशिष्टे दोषः अन्यथासिद्धः तथा भवन्मतेऽपि प्रमायां दोषाभावः अन्यथासिद्ध इत्यर्थः। यथाश्रुतन्तु न सम्यक् पूर्व्वं स्वयमेव असदर्थविषयकतत्तद्दोषादित्युक्तत्वात् भ्रमं प्रति इदानीं दोषकारणत्वे विवादाभावात्।

ननु प्रामाण्यस्य स्वतउत्पत्तिकत्वमुपपादितं स्वतोग्राह्यत्वं कथमित्यत आह, 'यथार्थत्वञ्चेति, 'अर्थस्य' विशेष्यस्य, स्वविशेष्ये स्वविषयीकृतप्रकारकत्वमिति निष्कर्षः, इदन्तु विषयतया ज्ञान-

---

(१) अथवेति ग० ।

(२) तदपि ज्ञायतां स्वतः परतो वेति ख०, ग० ।

प्रवृत्तावनुपयोगात्। अर्थं हि निश्चित्य प्रवर्त्तत इत्यावश्यकार्थनिश्चयादेव प्रवृत्त्युपपत्तेः। अथार्थनिश्चयादेव प्रवृत्तिरिति सत्यं, किन्त्वेवंरूपोऽयमर्थ इति निश्चयो ज्ञानप्रामाण्यग्रहाधीन इति चेत्। न। सर्वं हि ज्ञानं रजतरूपोऽयमर्थ इत्याद्याकारं स्वार्थनिश्चयरूपमेवोत्पद्यते, का तत्र परापेक्षा। अतएवार्थतथात्वं स्वयमेव परिच्छिद्यत इति स्वतः प्रामाण्यग्रहः। यदि च तज्ज्ञानं न स्वार्थनिश्चयरूपं तदा प्रामाण्यज्ञानमपि न प्रामाण्यनिश्चयरूपं, न वा तदधीनं ज्ञानान्तरमपि स्वार्थनिश्चयरूपमिति व्यर्थमर्थनिश्चयार्थं प्रामाण्यनिरूपणं, प्रामाण्यज्ञानेऽपि स्वविषयनिश्चयार्थमन्यापे-

---

वृत्ति। 'यद्धर्मवत्त्वमिति, 'अर्थस्य' विशेष्यस्य, तथाच तद्वद्विशेष्यकत्वे सति तत्प्रकारकत्वमिति निष्कर्षः। 'इदमिति, 'इदं रजतमित्यनेन अग्रेतनस्वार्थनिश्चयरूपमित्यस्यान्वयः, तथाच इदं रजतमिति स्वार्थनिश्चयरूपं ज्ञानमित्यर्थः। 'स्वस्येति स्वस्य रजतत्वाश्रयविशेष्यकत्वं रजतत्वप्रकारकत्वञ्चेत्यर्थः, 'परिच्छिन्दत्' परिच्छिन्दत्ति विषयीकरोतीति यावत्। ननु विशेष्यावृत्त्यप्रकारकत्वं प्रामाण्यं तत्कथं स्वतोज्ञेयमित्यत आह, 'तदतिरिक्तञ्चेति ज्ञानोल्लिखितप्रकारकत्वाद्यतिरिक्तं न प्रामाण्यपदवाच्यमित्यर्थः, 'मानाभावात्' प्रामाण्यपदवाच्यत्वे मानाभावात्।

ज्ञायामनवस्था। किञ्च परतः पक्षे गृहीतप्रामाण्यस्य परस्य प्रामाण्यनिश्चायकत्वेऽनवस्था, अतो यथा ज्ञानान्तरमगृहीतप्रामाण्यमेव परप्रामाण्यनिश्चयरूपं यदा तु तत्प्रामाण्यजिज्ञासा तदा तस्यापि प्रामाण्यमगृहीतप्रामाण्येनैव परेण निश्चीयत इति नानवस्था, तथा अर्थज्ञानमपि अनिश्चितप्रामाण्यमेवार्थनिश्चयरूपमविशेषात्। न ह्युत्पन्ने ज्ञाने अर्थसंशयः किमेवमनेवं वेति। अथ ज्ञानमर्थनिश्चयरूपमपि स्वमगृह्णत्कथं स्वप्रामाण्यं गृह्णीयादिति चेत्। तर्हि स्वप्रकाशत्वे विवादः, अर्थस्य तथाभावरूपं प्रामाण्यं स्वत एव गृह्यत इति तवाप्य-

---

'अस्तु वेति, 'तदपि' तद्वद्विशेष्यकत्वे सति तत्प्रकारकत्वरूपप्रामाण्यमपि, 'स्वतोऽज्ञायतां परतो वा मा वा ज्ञायि' इति विचारोऽस्त्वित्यर्थः, 'किन्त्विति किन्तस्य स्वतो ग्राह्यत्वनिरूपणेनेत्यर्थः। ननु प्रामाण्यं स्वतो ग्राह्यं वेति विवादः, तदा तस्यापि प्रामाण्यत्वेन स्वतो ग्राह्यत्वविवादविषयत्वात् कथं तस्य स्वतो ग्राह्यत्वनिरूपणे प्रयोजनाभाव इत्यत आह, 'प्रवृत्ताविति, प्रवृत्त्युपयुक्तं प्रामाण्यं स्वतो ग्राह्यं वा परतो ग्राह्यं वेत्येव विवाद इति भावः। 'किन्त्विति एवंरूपोऽयमर्थ इतिनिश्चयरूपं ज्ञानं तद्वतितत्प्रकारकत्वरूपज्ञानप्रामाण्यनिश्चयाधीनमित्यर्थ, तथा च एतस्यापि परम्परया प्रवृत्त्युपयुक्तत्वमिति भाव.। 'सत्त्व.मति रजतरूपोऽयमित्याकारकं स्वार्थ-

नुमतम्। अथ स्वतः प्रामाण्यग्रहे अनभ्यासदशापन्न-ज्ञाने इदं प्रमा न वेति संशयो न स्यात् निश्चिते तदभावात्। अत एवाप्रमात्वशङ्कया अर्थेऽपि किमेवमनेवं वेति संशयात् न ज्ञानमात्रात्करतलामलकादावप्यर्थनिश्चयो व्यभिचारादिति चेत्। न। न ह्यत्र

निश्चयरूपं सर्व्वं हि ज्ञानं कृत्स्नसामग्रीत एव उत्पद्यते इत्यर्थः, 'परापेक्षेति तदिदिशेष्यकत्वे सति तत्प्रकारकत्वनिश्चयापेक्षेत्यर्थः। 'अत एवेति यत एव प्रवृत्त्युपयुक्तं विशेष्यस्य प्रकारीभूतधर्म्मवत्त्वरूपं प्रामाण्यं अत एवेत्यर्थः, 'अर्थतथात्वमिति विशेष्यस्य प्रकारीभूतधर्म्म-वत्त्वं, 'स्वयमेव परिच्छिद्यत इति भवन्मतेऽपि प्रवृत्त्युपयुक्तप्रा-माण्यस्य स्वतोग्रह इत्यर्थः। 'तज्ज्ञानमिति प्रामाण्यनिश्चयनिरपेक्षं ज्ञानमित्यर्थः, 'स्वार्थनिश्चयरूपमिति, प्रामाण्यनिश्चयस्यैव अर्थनिश्चयं प्रति हेतुत्वादिति भावः। 'व्यर्थमिति अर्थनिश्चयकारणत्वेनाभिमत प्रामाण्यज्ञानं व्यर्थं फलाजनकमित्यर्थः, प्रामाण्यनिश्चयत्वरूपकार-णतावच्छेदकानाक्रान्तत्वादिति भावः। अथ तदा किं प्रामाण्य-ज्ञाने प्रामाण्यनिश्चयो न भवतीत्यत आह, 'यदा त्विति। 'इदं प्रमा न वेति संशयो न स्यात्' प्रवृत्त्युपयुक्तप्रामाण्यसंशयो न स्यादित्यर्थः, प्रवृत्त्युपयुक्तप्रामाण्यसंशयस्यानुभवसाक्षिक इति भावः। 'निश्चित इति, तथाच भवन्मते प्रवृत्त्युपयुक्तं प्रामाण्यं अर्थतथात्वं कथं तत्र संशयः, तेनार्थतथात्वं न प्रवृत्त्युपयुक्तं प्रामाण्यं किन्तु तदति तत्प्रकारकत्वमेव प्रवृत्त्युपयुक्तमिति भावः। अनुभवमनङ्गीकृत्याह,

ज्ञाने सत्यत्वासत्यत्वसंशयः, सर्वज्ञानानां सत्यत्वात्। किन्तु अगृहीतभेदं ज्ञानद्वयमेकं वा ज्ञानमित्याकारो ज्ञानं प्रमा न वेति संशयः, स च कारणदोषसंशयात्, स च ज्ञानान्तरान्निवर्त्तते। नन्वनुभूतित्वं प्रमात्वं तच्च स्मृत्यन्यज्ञानत्वम्। स्मृतित्वञ्च संस्कारासाधारणकारणकत्वमिति स्वतो न गृह्यते संस्कारादेरग्रहात्। अत एव न स्वत एव उत्पद्यते स्मृतिसाधारणत्वादिति चेत्। न। प्रवृत्त्यौपयिकं हि प्रामाण्यमर्थतथात्वनिश्चयत्वम् तच्च स्वत एव गृह्यते उत्पद्यते च न त्वनुभूतित्वसहितं गौरवात्। तवापि संवादादिना प्रवृत्तेः प्रामाण्यं यथार्थत्वमेवानुमीयते, न त्वनुभूतित्वे सति, स्मृतौ व्यभि-

---

'नहीति, 'सत्यत्वासत्यत्वसंशयः' प्रामाण्याप्रामाण्यसंशयः, 'सत्यत्वादिति, तथाच ज्ञानत्वावच्छेदेनैव प्रमाण्यस्य गृहीतत्वात् तद्वत्ताज्ञाने सति कथं प्रामाण्यसंशय इति भावः। 'स चेति असंसर्गाग्रहप्रयोजकदोषसंशयादित्यर्थः। अथ तत्संशयस्य निवर्त्तकः क इत्यत आह, 'स चेति, 'ज्ञानान्तरात्' एककोटिज्ञानात्। 'स्मृतिसाधारणत्वात्' ज्ञानसामग्रीजन्यत्वस्य स्मृतिवृत्तित्वात्। नन्वेवमनुभव एव प्रमात्वव्यवहारः स्मृतौ अप्रमात्वव्यवहारः कथमित्यत आह, 'स्मृत्यनुभवयोरिति, 'सापेक्षत्वं' संस्कारसापेक्षत्वं, 'निरपेक्षत्वं' संस्कारनिरपेक्षत्वं, 'तान्त्रिकाणां', संस्कारसापेक्षे अप्रमापदस्य संके-

चारात्। स्मृत्यनुभवयोरप्रमा-प्रमाव्यपदेशस्तान्त्रिकाणां सापेक्षत्व-निरपेक्षत्वनिबन्धनः, “यथार्थानुभवोमानमनपेक्षतयेष्यते” इति तैरभिधानादिति।

अत्र ब्रूमः। प्रामाण्यनिश्चयो निष्कम्पप्रवृत्तिहेतुः न तत्संशय इत्यनुभवसिद्धम् त्वदनुमतञ्च। तच्च प्रामाण्यं नार्थतथात्वनिश्चयरूपम्। अनभ्यासदशापन्नज्ञानस्य स्वप्रकाशेनानुव्यवसायेन वार्थतथात्वनिश्चयत्वग्रहेऽपि निष्कम्पप्रवृत्त्यभावात् प्रामाण्यसंशयाच्च। सर्वधियां यथार्थत्वनियमेनार्थतथात्वनिश्चयत्वस्य स्वरूपतो विषयतश्चागृहीतभेदज्ञानद्वयरूपभ्रमसाधारणत्वात्। त-

---

तात् संस्कारनिरपेक्षे प्रमापदस्य सङ्केतादित्यभिप्रायः। ‘यथार्थेति, “यथार्थानुभवो मानं” इति व्यवहारस्तु संस्कारनिरपेक्षतया इष्यते इत्यर्थः।

मीमांसकैकदेशिसंवादमाह,(१) ‘अत्र ब्रूम इति। ‘प्रामाण्यसंशयाच्च’ प्रवृत्त्युपयुक्तप्रामाण्यसंशयाच्च। ‘स एव’ विशिष्टज्ञानत्वसंशय एव। ‘ज्ञानान्तरात्’ विशिष्टज्ञानत्वनिश्चयात्। ‘न त्वर्थतथात्वस्येत्यस्य निश्चयत्वस्येति शेषः। ‘तत्संशयाभावसहितस्येति विशिष्टज्ञानत्वसंशयाभावार्थतथात्वनिश्चययोरुभयोः प्रवर्त्तकत्वे गौरवात् लाघवात् एकस्य विशिष्टज्ञानत्वनिश्चयस्य कारणत्वं कल्प्यत इत्यर्थः।

---

(१) मीमांसकैकदेशिमतमाश्रित्याहेति ग०।

स्मान्न भ्रमसमानाकारादिदं रजतमिति ज्ञानान्निष्कम्पप्रवृत्तिः, किन्तु तद्व्यावृत्ताकारात्। अथ तत्र प्रामाण्ये न संशयस्तस्यार्थतथात्वनिश्चयत्वरूपस्य निश्चयात्। किन्त्वगृहीतभेदं ज्ञानद्वयं विशिष्टज्ञानं वेति संशयः, स एव निष्कम्पप्रवृत्तिप्रतिबन्धकोऽपि अतस्तस्य ज्ञानान्तरान्निवृत्तौ निष्कम्पप्रवृत्तिरिति चेत् तर्हि यस्य संशयो व्यतिरेकनिश्चयस्य यत्प्रतिबन्धकस्तन्निश्चयस्तद्धेतुरिति व्याप्तेः भ्रमव्यावृत्तस्य विशिष्टज्ञानत्वस्य निश्चयः प्रवृत्तिहेतुर्न त्वर्थतथात्वस्य, भ्रमसाधारण्यात् तस्मिन् सत्यप्यप्रवृत्तेश्च। तत्संशयाभावसहितस्यार्थतथात्वनिश्चयस्य प्रवर्त्तकत्वे गौरवात्।

ननु प्रामाण्यपदशक्यनिश्चयः प्रवृत्तिं प्रति कारणं तच्च अर्थतथात्वमेव न तु विशिष्टज्ञानत्वमित्यत आह' 'अपि चेति, 'प्रामाण्यं' प्रामाण्यपदशक्यं, 'भ्रमव्यावृत्ते' भ्रमभिन्ने, 'तदतिक्रमे' व्यवहारातिक्रमे। 'अगृहीतासंसर्गेति. 'प्रागनुपस्थितेः' पूर्व्वक्षणे उपस्थितिसामग्रीविरहात्, 'सामग्रीविरहात्' समुदायोपस्थितिसामग्रीविरहात्, तथाचागृहीतासंसर्गादेरेकदेशोपस्थितिसामग्र्या विरहेण समुदायोपस्थितिसामग्रीविरहादित्यर्थः। यथाश्रुतन्तु न सम्यक् परनये विशिष्टज्ञानस्य विशेषणज्ञानाजन्यत्वात् ज्ञानलक्षणानङ्गीकाराच्च। अथ विशिष्टज्ञानजन्यत्वमेव चेत् प्रामाण्यं तदा तत् स्वतो न गृह्यत इति प्रमायाः स्वप्रकाशत्वव्याघातः स्वस्ववृत्तिप्रामाण्यादिविषयकत्वमेव

किञ्च प्रवृत्तिहेतुज्ञानं विघटयत एव ज्ञानस्य तत्र प्रतिबन्धकत्वम्। न चेह तथा, संशये सत्यपि तस्य सत्त्वात्।

अपि च विशिष्टज्ञानत्वमेव प्रामाण्यं भ्रमव्यावृत्तत्वात्। न त्वर्थतथात्वनिश्चयत्वं, भ्रमसाधारणत्वात्। लौकिकपरीक्षकाणां भ्रमव्यावृत्ते प्रामाण्यव्यवहारात् तदतिक्रमे प्रमात्वस्य पारिभाषिकत्वापत्तेः। तस्मात् भ्रमव्यावृत्तत्वात् निष्कम्पप्रवृत्तिहेतुत्वात् प्रामाण्यसंशयनिवर्त्तकत्वाच्च विशिष्टज्ञानत्वमेव प्रामाण्यम्। नन्वस्तु तथा तदेव स्वतोगृह्यते इति चेत्। न। अगृहीतासंसर्गधर्म-धर्मिविषयैकज्ञानत्वं भ्रमव्यावृत्तं विशिष्टज्ञानत्वं तत्तु स्वतो ग्रहीतुं न शक्यते, अगृहीतासंसर्गादेः प्रागनुपस्थितेः सामग्रीविरहात्। स्वप्रकाशता हि स्वभावसाक्षिणी, अन्यथानभ्यासदशापन्नेऽपि तस्य स्वतो ग्रहादप्रामाण्यसंशयो न स्यात्। अत एव न ज्ञानसामग्रीत एव प्रामाण्यमुत्पद्यते, भ्रमस्यापि तथात्वापत्तेः।

स्वप्रकाशत्वमित्यत आह, 'स्वप्रकाशता हीति 'स्वभावसाक्षिणी' स्वविषयकत्वमात्रं स्वप्रकाशकत्वं, न तु स्ववृत्तिप्रामाण्यादिविषयकत्वघटितमिति समुदायार्थनिष्कर्षः। 'अन्यथा' तद्घटितत्वे, 'तस्य' विशिष्टज्ञानत्वरूपप्रामाण्यस्य। 'अत एवेति यतएव ज्ञानसामग्रीजन्यत्वव्यापकं न प्रामाण्यमित्यर्थः, 'तथात्वापत्तेः' प्रामाण्यापत्तेः, व्याप्यवत्त्वादिति भावः॥

नव्यास्तु । अविद्यमानभेदस्याग्रहः प्रामाण्यं, स चात्यन्ताभावः, कदापि तस्य ज्ञानाभावादत्यन्ताभावरूपतया[1] स्वतः सिद्धत्वेन प्रामाण्यं स्वत इत्युच्यते । विद्यमानभेदस्याग्रहोऽप्रामाण्यं स चाग्रहः प्रागभावः अग्रे भेदस्य ग्रहात् । भेदग्रहे प्रसक्ते न स जायते दोषादित्युत्तरकालसंसर्गरूपस्य तत्परिपालनस्य दोषजन्यत्वेनाप्रामाण्यं परत उत्पद्यते । विसंवादि-संवादिविचित्रव्यवहारोऽपि विद्यमानाविद्यमानभेदाग्रहरूपविलक्षणहेतुक एव । व्यवहारोपयुक्तन्तु प्रामाण्यं यथार्थत्वमेव, तच्च ज्ञानहेतुमात्रहेतुकं । अप्रामाण्यं दोषात् । अनभ्यासदशापन्ने प्रामाण्यसंशयोऽपि विद्यमानाविद्यमानभेदाग्रहकोटिद्वयावलम्बी, स एव निष्कम्पप्रवृत्ति-

---

'नव्यास्त्विति, "प्रामाण्यं स्वतः, अप्रामाण्यं परतः" इति प्राचीनमीमांसकग्रन्थः प्राभाकरादिभिः स्वतउत्पत्तिकत्व परतउत्पत्तिकत्वपरतया व्याख्यातः, मीमांसकनव्यैस्तु अन्यथैव व्याख्यायत इत्यर्थः । कथं व्याख्यायते तत्राह, 'अविद्यमानेति, 'प्रामाण्यं' मीमांसकग्रन्थस्थप्रामाण्यपदवाच्यमित्यर्थः । 'स्वतःसिद्धत्वेन' परतोऽनुत्पद्यमानत्वेन, 'उच्यते' इत्यस्य मीमांसकैरिति शेषः । तथाच परतोऽनुत्पन्न-

---

(१) ज्ञानाभावादित्यत्यन्ताभावरूपत । इति ख०, ग० ।

प्रतिबन्धक इति । तन्न । निष्कम्पप्रवृत्तिहेतुर्हि प्रामाण्यं ग्राह्यं न त्वन्यत् निष्प्रयोजनत्वात् । तच्च यद्यपि विद्यमानभेदाग्रहरूपं, तदा तन्न स्वतो ज्ञातुं शक्यते । अविद्यमानभेदग्रहस्य तत्प्रतियोगिनोऽसत्त्वात् प्रागनुपस्थितेश्च । अनभ्यासदशायां ज्ञाने ज्ञातेप्यविद्यमानभेदाग्रहे संशयाच्च । एतेनौत्सर्गिकः संसर्गग्रह एव प्रामाण्यं, संसर्गाग्रह एवाप्रामाण्यमिति निरस्तं । संसर्गग्रहत्वस्य स्वेन ग्रहीतुमशक्यत्वात् । शक्यत्वे वानभ्यासदशायामपि तद्ग्रहे तत्संशयो न स्यात् । तस्मात् भ्रमव्यावृत्तं निष्कम्पप्रवृत्तिहेतुः प्रामाण्यमगृहीतासंसगधर्म-धर्मिविषयैकज्ञानत्वरूपं विशिष्टज्ञानत्वं, संसर्गज्ञानत्वं वा, अविद्यमानभेदाग्रहत्वं वा, स्वतो

मानत्वमेव, स्वतस्त्वमितिभावः । "अप्रामाण्यं परतः" इति मीमांसकग्रन्थमुपपादयति, 'विद्यमानेति, 'भेदग्रहे प्रसक्ते' भेदग्रहस्य सकलकारणसत्त्वे, 'उत्तरकालेति प्रागभावस्य उत्तरकालसम्बन्धरूपप्रागभावपरिपालनस्य दोषजन्यत्वेन, 'अप्रामाण्यं परत उत्पद्यत इति "अप्रामाण्यं परतः" इति मीमांसकग्रन्थस्यार्थ इत्यर्थः । 'ग्राह्यं' स्वतोग्राह्यत्वेनोक्तं । 'प्रागनुपस्थितेः' पूर्व्वक्षणे उपस्थितिसामग्र्या विरहादित्यर्थः । तथाच "प्रामाण्यं स्वतः" इति मीमांसकग्रन्थ उपपा-

ज्ञातुं न शक्यते, किन्तु विशेषदर्शनादिजन्यज्ञानादव-धार्य्यत इति वज्रलेपायितं परतः प्रामाण्यं इत्युत्पत्ति-वादः ।

इति श्रीमद्गङ्गेशोपाध्यायविरचिते तत्त्वचिन्तामणौ प्रत्यक्षखण्डे प्रामाण्यवादे उत्पत्तिवादः ।

दितः । तथापि "प्रामाण्यं स्वतो गृह्यते" इति ग्रन्थस्तु अनुपपन्न एवेति भावः । इत्युत्पत्तिवादरहस्यं ॥

इति श्रीमथुरानाथतर्कवागीश-विरचिते तत्त्वचिन्तामणिरहस्ये प्रत्यक्षखण्डे प्रामाण्यवादरहस्ये उत्पत्तिवादरहस्यम् ॥०॥

अथ प्रमालक्षणपूर्व्वपक्षः ।

अथ किं तत् प्रामाण्यम् । न तावज्जातिः योग्यव्यक्तिवृत्तित्वेन प्रत्यक्षत्वे प्रमात्वसंशयानुपपत्तेः प्रमात्वस्यानुमेयत्वाच्च साक्षात्त्वादिना सङ्करापत्तेश्च । बीजसाम्येन गुणेपि तस्य दोषत्वात् तारत्वादेरुत्कर्षरूपतया

अथ प्रमालक्षणपूर्व्वपक्षरहस्यं ।

प्रमात्वं गुणस्य कार्य्यतावच्छेदकं इत्यभिमानेन पृच्छति[1], 'अथ किमिति यत्प्रमात्वं कार्य्यतावच्छेदकं उच्यते तत् प्रमात्वं किमित्यर्थः ।

मिश्रास्तु । प्रामाण्यमनुमेयमित्यादि स्वतोग्राह्यत्वाभावसाधकानुमानपक्षस्वरूपं पृच्छति, 'अथ किमिति यत्प्रामाण्यं पक्षीकृत्य स्वाश्रयग्राह्यत्वाभावः साध्यते तत्प्रामाण्यं किमित्यर्थं इत्याहुः ।

प्रमात्वं निर्व्विकल्पकादिव्यावृत्तोजातिविशेषः, तच्चाभावत्वादिवत्सप्रतियोगिकं तेनेयं रजतत्वस्य प्रमा रङ्गत्वस्य प्रमेत्यादिव्यवहारोपपत्तिः, समवायवत् तत्तत्प्रतियोगिकमेव लाघवान्न तु प्रतियोगिभेदाद्भिन्नं गौरवात्, इमे रङ्ग-रजते इति समूहालम्बनप्रमायां रङ्गत्वप्रतियोगिकत्वविशिष्टप्रमात्व-रजतत्वप्रतियोगिकत्वविशिष्टप्रमात्वयोः साङ्कर्य्यप्रसङ्गाच्च[2] । तत्तत्प्रतियोगिकत्वविशिष्टनिरूपिताधा-

---

(१) कार्य्यतावच्छेदकस्वरूपं पृच्छतीति ग० ।

(२) समूहालम्बनरङ्ग-रजतप्रमान्तर्भावेन परस्पराभावसामानाधिकरण्यं, समूहालम्बनरङ्ग-रजतप्रमान्तर्भावेन ऐकाधिकरण्यमिति भावः ।

जातित्वनियमे चानन्यगतिकतया च नानात्वात् । प्रमात्वनानात्वे त्वननुगमः । किञ्चैवमप्रमाया अंशे प्रमात्वं न स्यात् जातेर्व्याप्यवृत्तितानियमात् । न चेष्टापत्तिः, अंशे संवादिनि विसंवादिनि च समूहा-

---

लम्बनेऽपि प्रमात्वाप्रमात्वयोः ...

रत्वविरहाच्च नातिप्रसङ्ग इति केषाञ्चिन्मतं निराकरोति[१], 'न तावज्जातिरिति, 'प्रत्यक्षत्वइति ज्ञानत्वविशिष्टप्रत्यक्षोत्पत्तिसमये प्रमात्वस्यापि विशिष्टप्रत्यक्षविषयत्वे तदनन्तरं प्रमात्व-तदभावोपस्थित्या तस्य संशयानुपपत्तेरित्यर्थः । नन्वेवं स्थाणुत्वादेर्योग्यव्यक्तिवृत्तितया स्थाणाविन्द्रियसन्निकर्षेण धर्म्मितावच्छेदकप्रकारकस्थाणुप्रत्यक्षदशायां स्थाणुत्वस्यापि योग्यत्वेन प्रत्यक्षेण ग्रहात् कथं तत्संशयः, दोषप्रतिबन्धकवशात्तदानीं स्थाणुत्वस्य न प्रत्यक्षमिति चेत् प्रमात्वेऽपि तत् तुल्यत्वादित्यत आह, 'प्रमात्वस्येति यच्चेदं ज्ञानं प्रमा न वा अयञ्च घट इति समूहालम्बनप्रामाण्यसंशयात्मको व्यवसायः ततो विशेषदर्शनं तत्र प्रमात्वस्य प्रमात्वसंशयोत्तरमनुमेयत्वाच्च इत्यर्थः, अन्यथा संशयोत्तरं स्थाणुत्वादिबुद्धिवत् तत्र प्रामाण्यबुद्धिरपि प्रत्यक्षा स्यात् नानुमितिः तादृशस्थले प्रत्यक्षसामग्र्याबलवत्त्वात् । न चेष्टापत्तिः, अनुमिनोमीत्यनुव्यवसायादिति भावः । अथ तत्रानुव्यवसायोऽसिद्ध इत्यरुचेराह, 'साक्षात्त्वादिनेति प्रमात्वं विना साक्षात्त्वं निर्व्विकल्पके, साक्षात्त्वं विना च प्रमात्वमनुमित्यादौ, एकस्याञ्च साक्षात्कारिप्रमायां तयोः सङ्कर इत्यर्थः, आदिना चाक्षुषत्वादिपरिग्रहः ।

---

(१) केषाञ्चिन्मतमाशङ्क्य निराकरोतीति ख० ।

लम्बने प्रमात्वाप्रमात्वयोरनुभूयमानत्वेन एकशेषस्य कर्त्तुमशक्यत्वात्। अथ विपर्ययस्यांशे न प्रमात्वं किन्तु स्मृतिवद्यथार्थत्वमेवेति[१] चेत् तर्हि यथार्थानुभवत्वमेव प्रामाण्यमावश्यकत्वात्। न च तदपीति वक्ष्यते। अथ

ननु गुणे जातेः सङ्करो न दोषायेत्यत आह, 'वीजेति, 'तस्य' सङ्करस्य। नन्वेवं कत्वादिना साङ्कर्य्येऽपि कथं तारत्वं मन्दत्वं जातिरित्यत आह, 'तारत्वादेरिति, 'उत्कर्षरूपतयेति, उत्कर्षस्तु जातिं विना अन्यन्निर्वक्तुं न शक्यते इत्यभिप्रायः। 'तन्नानात्वात्' तारत्वादेः ककार-खकारादिभेदेन नानात्वात्। नन्वेवं प्रमात्वान्यपि चाक्षुषत्वादिव्याप्यानि षट्, प्रत्यक्षत्वविरुद्धमनुमित्यादिचयसाधारणञ्चैकमतो न सङ्कर इत्यत आह. 'प्रमात्वेति, 'अननुगमः' अनुगतबुद्ध्यभावः। ननु अनुगतबुद्धिरेवासिद्धेत्यत आह, 'किञ्चेति। वस्तुतस्तु ननु निर्व्विकल्पकेऽपि प्रमात्वाभ्युपगमान्न साङ्कर्य्यं। अथ तथाप्यनुभवत्वेन समव्याप्तिरिक्तवृत्तितया न जातित्वसम्भवः, प्रमुष्टतत्ताकस्मरणात्मकभ्रमस्य सर्व्वांशे भ्रमत्वसम्भवेऽपि सर्व्वांशे भ्रमात्मकानुभवस्याप्रसिद्धेः "धर्म्मिणि सर्वमभ्रान्तं" इति न्यायेन परोक्षानुभवस्य सर्वांशे भ्रमत्वासम्भवात् प्रत्यक्षे चान्ततस्तादात्म्यसम्बन्धेन स्वस्मिन्नपि निर्धर्म्मितावच्छेदककस्वभाने बाधकाभावेन सर्वांशभ्रमत्वासम्भवात् स्मरणेऽपि प्रमात्वाभ्युपगमे च स्मृतित्वेनैव साङ्कर्य्यात् प्रमुष्टतत्ताकस्मरणात्मकभ्रमे प्रमात्वविरहादिति चेत्। न। समनियतयो-

---

(१) यथार्थत्वमात्रमितीति ग०।

यथा भावाऽभावोवा नाव्याप्यवृत्तिरितिनियमन्तिर-स्कृत्याबाधितानुभवबलात् संयोग-तदभावयोरव्याप्य-वृत्तित्वं तथा जातिर्व्याप्यवृत्तिरेवेति व्याप्तिमभिभूया-

---

विभिन्नजातित्वाभावे मानाभावात् अत्र तु रजतत्वस्य प्रमा रङ्गत्वस्य प्रमेति भ्रमव्यावृत्तविलक्षणप्रतीतेरेव मानतया निर्विकल्पकसाधारणप्रमात्वजातेरनुभवत्वसमनियतत्वेऽपि पृथक् जातित्वादित्यत आह, 'किञ्चेति, 'एवं' प्रमात्वस्य जातित्वे, 'अप्रमायामिति रजतत्वप्रतियोगिकत्वविशिष्टप्रमात्वाभाववति ज्ञाने किञ्चिदंशे रजतत्वप्रतियोगिकत्वविशिष्टप्रमात्वं न स्यादित्यर्थः। अथ तत्र रजतत्वप्रतियोगिकत्वविशिष्टप्रमात्वं नास्त्येवेत्यत आह, 'न चेति, संवादित्वं रजतत्ववति रजतत्वप्रकारकत्वं, विसंवादित्वं रजतत्वाभाववति रजतत्वप्रकारकत्वं, 'समूहालम्बने' रजत-रङ्गयोरिदमिदञ्च रजतमिति समूहालम्बने, 'प्रमात्वाप्रमात्वयोरिति रजतत्वप्रतियोगिकत्वविशिष्टप्रमात्व-तदभावयोरित्यर्थः, 'एकशेषस्येति इदं ज्ञानं रजतत्वप्रतियोगिकत्व-विशिष्टप्रमात्वाभाववदेव न तु तादृशप्रमात्ववत्, किं वा रजतत्वप्रतियोगिकत्वविशिष्टप्रमात्ववदेव न तु तादृशप्रमात्वाभाववत् इत्येकशेषस्य कर्त्तुमशक्यत्वादित्यर्थः। शङ्कते, 'विपर्य्ययस्येति, "न प्रमात्वं' न रजतत्वप्रतियोगिकत्वविशिष्टप्रमात्वं। नन्वेवमनुभवस्य का गतिरित्यत आह, 'किन्त्विति, 'यथार्थत्वमात्रमिति[१] रजतत्वयथार्थत्वमात्रमित्यर्थः, अनुभवविषय इति शेषः। रजतत्वप्रमात्वाभावमादाय

---

(१) 'यथार्थत्वमात्रं' इत्यपि कस्यचिन्मूलपुस्तकस्य पाठः।

नुभवबलादेव प्रमात्व-तदभावयोरव्याप्यवृत्तित्वमस्तु। न च यदव्याप्यवृत्ति तन्न व्याप्यवृत्ति, यच्च व्याप्यवृत्ति न तदव्याप्यवृत्तीति व्याप्तेः प्रमात्वस्य नोभयरूपत्वमिति वाच्यं। संयोगात्यन्ताभावे व्यभिचारात्। न च तस्याभावद्वयं, मानाभावात् गुण-दोषयोरेकत्र सत्त्वे अव्याप्यवृत्तित्वं गुणमात्रसत्त्वे व्याप्यवृत्तित्वमित्यन्यथोपपत्तेश्च।

विनिगमनाविरहे सत्येव दूषणान्तरमाह, 'तर्हीति, 'प्रामाण्यं' गुणजन्यतावच्छेदकं, 'आवश्यकत्वात्' तत्र प्रमाव्यवहारप्रयोजकत्वस्यावश्यकत्वात्। ननु लाघवात् प्रमात्वजातिरेव तज्जन्यतावच्छेदकतया कल्प्यत इत्यत आह, 'न चेति न वेत्यर्थः, 'तदपि' यथार्थानुभवत्वमपि, निर्व्वक्तुं शक्यमिति शेषः। यत्र ज्ञाने रजतत्वप्रतियोगिकत्वविशिष्टप्रमात्वं तत्प्रतियोगिकत्वविशिष्टभ्रमत्वञ्च द्वयमेव वर्त्तते तत्र तदुभयमव्याप्यवृत्ति, यत्र चैकैकमात्रं तत्र व्याप्यवृत्त्येव इत्यभिप्रायेणाशङ्कते, 'न च यदव्याप्येति, 'अव्याप्यवृत्तित्वं' अवच्छिन्नवृत्तिमत्त्वं, 'व्याप्यवृत्तित्वं' अनवच्छिन्नवृत्तिमत्त्वं, अत्र शब्द-संयोगादिर्दृष्टान्तः, 'यच्चेत्यादौ घटादिर्दृष्टान्तः। 'प्रमात्वस्य' रजतत्वप्रतियोकत्वविशिष्टप्रमात्वस्य, 'नोभयरूपत्वमिति, इदं रजतमिति प्रमायां तस्य व्याप्यवृत्तित्वादिति भावः। ननु भाव एवायं नियम इत्यत आह।(१) 'गुणेति, तथाच भावत्वे सति यदव्याप्यवृत्ति तन्न व्याप्यवृत्ति इत्या-

---

(१) ननु भाव एवायं नियमः तथाच संयोगाद्यभावे न व्यभिचार इत्यत आहेति क०।

अन्यथा प्रमात्वस्योपाधेरप्यत्यन्ताभावसामानाधिक-रण्यं न स्यात् सामान्यत्वात्, न स्याच्चोभयरूपत्वमिति। मैवं। अवच्छेदकभेदं विना विरुद्धयोरेकत्रासमावेशादप्रतीतेश्च। न च विषय एवांशरूपः प्रमात्ववृत्त्यावच्छेदकः,(१) तद्विषयत्वस्य भ्रमेऽपि सत्त्वात्। ननु

दिव्याप्तिरप्रयोजिकेति भावः। 'अन्यथेति तादृशव्याप्त्यभ्युपगमे, 'उपाधेरपि' उपाधित्वेऽपि, 'अत्यन्ताभावेति अत्यन्ताभावाधिकरणे रजत-रङ्ग्योरिदमिदञ्च रजतमिति समूहालम्बने अवच्छिन्नवृत्तिकत्वमेव न स्यात्। 'न स्याच्चोभयरूपत्वं' न स्यात् व्याप्याव्याप्यवृत्त्युभयरूपत्वं, 'सामान्यत्वादिति योजना, 'सामान्यत्वात्' भावत्वात्। 'विषय एव' विशेष्य एव रजतमेवेति यावत्, 'अंशरूपः' अंशपदवाच्यः, 'प्रमात्ववृत्ताविति विशेष्यतासम्बन्धेन रजतत्वप्रतियोगिकत्वविशिष्टप्रमात्ववृत्त्यावच्छेदक इत्यर्थः। अतिप्रसक्तत्वात् तस्य नावच्छेदकत्वसम्भव इत्याह, 'तद्विषयकत्वस्येति रजतविशेष्यकत्वस्येत्यर्थः, 'भ्रमेऽपि' रजतविशेष्यकरङ्गत्वादिभ्रमेऽपि, भ्रमेत्युपलक्षणं रजतविशेष्यकद्रव्यत्वादिप्रकारकप्रमायामपि बोध्यं। 'विशेष्यावृत्त्यप्रकारकत्वमिति स्वासमानाधिकरणप्रकारानिरूपितरजतत्वनिष्ठप्रकारतानिरूपितानुभवीयविशेष्यताकत्वमित्यर्थः, 'विशेष्यावृत्तिप्रकारकत्वमिति स्वासमानाधिकरणप्रकारनिरूपितानुभवीयविशेष्यताकत्वमित्यर्थः, 'प्रमा-

(१) विषय एव प्रमात्ववृत्तेरंशरूपोऽवच्छेदकभेद इति ग॰।

विशेष्यावृत्त्यप्रकारकत्वं, विशेष्यावृत्तिप्रकारकत्वञ्च प्रमात्वतदभावयोर्वृत्तावच्छेदकमस्तीति चेत् तर्हि तयोरेव प्रमाप्रमाव्यवहारजनकत्वमस्तु आवश्यकत्वात् प्रथमोपस्थितत्वाच्च, किं जात्या । न च तदपीति वक्ष्यते ।

प्रमाव्यवहारेति प्रमा-भ्रमव्यवहारेत्यर्थः, 'आवश्यकत्वात्' प्रमा-भ्रमयोरवश्यं तयोः सत्त्वात् । 'प्रथमेति, अवच्छेद्यज्ञानं प्रति अवच्छेदकज्ञानस्य हेतुत्वादित्यभिमानः । ननु प्रमाव्यवहारप्रयोजकत्वसम्भवेऽपि न गुणजन्यतावच्छेदकत्वसम्भवः गौरवादतः प्रमात्वं जातिरेव तदवच्छेदकतया कल्प्यत इत्यनुशयादाह, 'न चेति न वेत्यर्थः, 'तदपि' विशेष्यावृत्त्यप्रकारकत्व-तत्प्रकारकत्वमपि, रजतत्वप्रतियोगिकत्वविशिष्टप्रमात्व-तदभावयोरवच्छेदकं सर्वत्र सम्भवतीति शेषः । 'इति वक्ष्यते' इति त्वयापि वक्ष्यते, विशेष्यतावच्छेदकाभेदे विशेष्यताया अप्यभिन्नतया द्रव्यं रजतमित्यादिरजतारजतविशेष्यकज्ञाने तदुभयावच्छेदेन रजतत्वप्रतियोगिकत्वविशिष्टप्रमात्व-तदभावयोरसम्भवात् तत्र निरुक्तविशेष्यावृत्तिप्रकारकत्वविरहात् विशेष्यतावच्छेदक-विधेययोरेकैव विशेष्यता इति मते रङ्गत्वरूपेण रजतविशेष्यके रङ्गं सुवर्णञ्च रजतमिति समूहालम्बनेऽपि तदुभयावच्छेदेन तादृशप्रमात्व-तदभावयोरसम्भवाच्च तत्र निरुक्तविशेष्यावृत्त्यप्रकारकत्वविरहात्, एवं संशये कोटिद्वयनिरूपितैकैव विशेष्यतेति मते इदं रजतं न वा सुवर्णञ्च रजतमिति रजतविशेष्यकसमूहालम्बनसंशये तदुभयावच्छेदेन तादृशप्रमात्व-तदभावयोरसम्भवाच्च इति निरूढाभिप्रायः । एतच्चापाततः,

नापि यथार्थागृहीतग्राहित्वं लोकसिद्धप्रमात्वं, धारावाहिकबुद्ध्यव्याप्तेः। न च प्रत्यक्षस्य वर्त्तमानार्थग्राहित्वेन स्वाश्रयक्षणविशिष्टस्तम्भादिग्राहकत्वेनागृहीतग्राहित्वं लोकसिद्धमन्यथैकसमये ज्ञानयौगपद्यप्रसङ्ग·

अन्यत्रातिप्रसक्तधर्मस्यावच्छेदकत्वानभ्युपगमेऽपि रजतत्वप्रतियोगिकत्वविशिष्टप्रमात्वावच्छेदकत्वस्यातिप्रसक्तेऽपि रजतादौ विशेष्यितासम्बन्धेनाभ्युपगमात् अत्र ज्ञाने रजतत्वप्रमात्वमित्यादिप्रत्ययात् रजतत्वनिष्ठप्रकारतानिरूपितत्वविशिष्टविशेष्यतासम्बन्धस्यावच्छेदकतानियामकसम्बन्धत्वाभ्युपगमेनातिप्रसङ्गस्यापि वारणसम्भवाच्च। वस्तुतस्तु प्रमात्वं यदि सर्वप्रतियोगिकमेकमेव वैजात्यं तदा रजतत्वविषयकप्रमायामपीदं ज्ञानं रजतत्वप्रमेति प्रत्ययापत्तिः, तत्र रजतत्वप्रतियोगिकत्वविशिष्टप्रमात्वाधारताविरहान्न तथा प्रत्यय इति चेत्तथापि गुणे गुणान्यत्वविशिष्टसत्तेति प्रतीतिवदत्र ज्ञाने रजतत्वप्रतियोगिकप्रमात्वमित्याधेयतोल्लेखप्रतीतेर्दुर्वारत्वात्। यदि च प्रतियोगिभेदात् प्रमात्वं विभिन्नं तदा इमे रङ्ग-रजते इति समूहालम्बनप्रमायामेव रङ्गत्वप्रतियोगिकप्रमात्व-रजतत्वप्रतियोगिकप्रमात्वयोः साङ्कर्य्यापत्तिः। न च वक्ष्यमाणोपाधिरेव प्रमात्वप्रतीतिनियामकः, गुणजन्यतावच्छेदिका च लाघवाज्जातिः कल्प्यते सा च न प्रमात्वप्रतीतिनियमिकेति वाच्यं। गुणस्य हेतुतायामेव मानाभावादित्येव दूषणं सारं।

यत्तु विनिगमनाविरहात् प्रमात्वमिव भ्रमत्वमपि दोषजन्यतावच्छेदकतया जातिः स्यात्तथाच प्रमात्व-भ्रमत्वयोरेव परस्परं स-

इति वाच्यम्। क्षणानामतीन्द्रियत्वात्, स्थूलोपाधिमादाय वर्त्तमानत्वग्रहात्,[१] स्वरूपसत्त्व भिकक्षणोत्पत्तिकत्वेन ज्ञानायौगपद्यात्। न च स्तम्भादिषु प्रतिक्षणं गुण-कर्माद्युत्पत्तिरस्ति येन तदादायागृहीतग्राहित्वं

ङ्करप्रसङ्गः, प्रमात्वं विनापि प्रमुष्टतत्ताकस्मरणात्मकभ्रमे भ्रमत्वसत्त्वादिति। तन्न। स्मृतित्वानुभवत्वाभ्यां निखिलानुभवव्याप्यजातिभिस्सङ्करापत्त्या भ्रमत्वस्य सर्वसाधारणैकजातित्वासम्भवात्, सर्वानुभवस्य प्रमात्ववत् सर्वज्ञानस्य भ्रमत्वविरहात्। भ्रमत्वस्य चाक्षुषत्वादिव्याप्यनानाजातित्वाभ्युपगमे च प्रमात्वव्याप्यस्यैव सुवचत्वादिति कृतं पल्लवेन। निर्विकल्पकविशेषणज्ञानकारणत्व-ज्ञानलक्षणा-सामान्यलक्षणाद्यनङ्गीकुर्व्वतां प्राभाकराणां लक्षणमाह, 'नापीति यथार्थत्वे सति स्वसमानाधिकरण-स्वाव्यवहितपूर्व्ववर्त्तिस्वसमानाकारनिश्चयाविषयग्राहित्वमित्यर्थः, यथार्थत्वमात्रं लौकिकवाक्यजन्ययथार्थशाब्दज्ञाने, अगृहीतग्राहित्वमात्रञ्च प्रत्यक्षभ्रमे गतमिति विशिष्टं[२]। यथार्थत्वञ्च तन्मते अगृहीतासंसर्गकधर्म्म-धर्म्मिगोचरैकज्ञानत्वं। नन्विदं प्रवृत्त्युपयुक्तं न भवतीत्यत आह, 'लोकसिद्धप्रमात्वमिति व्यवहारोपयुक्तं प्रमात्वमित्यर्थः। 'धारावाहिकेति अयं स्तम्भ इति ज्ञानोत्तरमयं

---

(१) वर्त्तमानव्यवहारादिति ख० ।

(२) 'विशिष्टं' यथार्थत्वविशिष्टागृहीतग्राहित्वं, तच्च लौकिकवाक्यजन्ययथार्थशाब्दज्ञाने प्रत्यक्षभ्रमे च नास्ति अतो न तत्र तत्रातिव्याप्तिरिति भावः ।

स्यात् । वेदात् क्रमोत्पन्नवेदार्थगोचरधारावाहिकबुद्ध्यव्याप्तेश्च । नापि यथार्थानुभवत्वं । ज्ञाने घटत्वादिना यथाशब्दार्थसादृश्याभावात् सादृश्यमात्रस्य भ्रमेऽपि गतत्वात् । न च गुणजन्यानुभवत्वं, दोषाभावजन्या-

---

लक्षणमिति ज्ञाने अव्याप्तेरित्यर्थः । कुत्रचित् 'लोकसिद्धप्रमात्ववद्धारावाहिकबुद्ध्यव्याप्तेः' इति पाठः, तत्र ननु तत्र धारावाहिकबुद्धिः प्रमैव इत्यत उक्तं 'लोकेति, । क्वचिच्च 'लोकसिद्धप्रमात्वधारावाहिकेति मतुप्शून्यः पाठः, तत्रापि लोकसिद्धं प्रमात्वं यत्रेति बहुव्रीहिरिति बोध्यं । अथ प्रत्यक्षस्य स्वोत्पत्तिक्षणवृत्तितया अर्थविषयकत्वनियमेनायं लक्षण इति द्वितीयज्ञानस्य पूर्वज्ञानागृहीतस्वोत्पत्तिक्षणविषयकत्वान्नाव्याप्तिरित्याशङ्क्य निराकरोति, 'नचेति, 'वर्त्तमानार्थग्राहित्वेन' स्वोत्पत्तिक्षणवृत्तितया अर्थविषयकत्वेन, 'स्वाश्रयक्षणेति स्वोत्पत्त्याश्रयक्षणेत्यर्थः, 'अन्यथेति, 'अन्यथा' प्रत्यक्षस्य स्वोत्पत्तिक्षणाविषयकत्वे, 'ज्ञानयौगपद्यप्रसङ्गः' धारावाहिकबुद्धीनां एकदोत्पत्तिप्रसङ्गः, विषयविधयैव क्षणानां प्रतीतिकारणतया धारावाहिकबुद्धीनां स्वोत्पत्तिक्षणाविषयकत्वे तस्य तद्धेतुत्वासम्भवात् क्षणातिरिक्तसकलहेतूनाञ्च तुल्यतया युगपदेव सत्त्वात्, तेषां स्वोत्पत्तिक्षणविषयकत्वे तु एकदा स्वोत्पत्तिक्षणरूपहेत्वभावादेव न युगपदुत्पादः । नचोत्पत्तिक्षणानां पूर्व्ववर्त्तित्वाभावात् कथं कारणत्वमिति वाच्यं । अन्येषां सहवर्त्तित्व-पूर्व्ववर्त्तित्वाभ्यामेव कारणत्वनियमेऽपि क्षणानां सहवर्त्तितामात्रेणैव कारणत्वादिति पराभि-

नुभवत्वं वा, तयोरननुगतत्वात् प्रमाप्रमानिरूप्यत्वाच्च । नाप्यबाधितानुभवत्वं, बाधस्य विपरीतप्रमात्वात् । नापि संवाद्यनुभवत्वं, ज्ञानान्तरेण तथोल्लिख्यमानत्वस्य संवादित्वस्य भ्रमसाधारणत्वात् । नापि

प्रायः । नन्वेवमिदानीं घट इति बुद्धिः कथं स्यात् क्षणानामतीन्द्रियत्वादित्यत आह, 'स्थूलेति । यद्यपि स्थूलकालोपाधेरपि सूर्य्यक्रियारूपत्वेनातीन्द्रियतया कथं तस्य प्रत्यक्षे भानं, उपनीतभानञ्च क्षणस्यापि सुलभमिति स्थूलकालपर्य्यन्तानुधावनमफलं, तथापि जन्यमात्रस्य कालोपाधितया घटादिलक्षणस्थूलकालोपाधेरेव लौकिकप्रत्यक्षं सम्भवतीत्यभिप्रायः । नन्वेवमुक्तज्ञानयौगपद्यप्रसङ्ग इत्यत आह, 'स्वरूपसदिति स्वस्वाविषयीभूतानामपि स्वस्वाव्यवहितपूर्व्वक्षणानां कारणत्वेनेत्यर्थः । 'नचेति, प्रमाणाभावादिति भावः । 'तदादाय' तद्विषयकत्वेन । मास्तु धारावाहिकप्रत्यक्षेऽव्याप्तिस्तथापि अन्यत्र धारावाहिके का गतिरित्याह, 'वेदेति, परमते लौकिकशब्दः प्रमाणमेव नेति 'वेदादित्युक्तं । 'यथार्थानुभवत्वमिति यथा अर्थः तथा अनुभवत्वमिति व्युत्पत्त्या अर्थसदृशानुभवत्वं प्रामाण्यमित्यर्थः, इत्यभिप्रायेण दूषयति, 'ज्ञाने इति 'सादृश्यमात्रस्येति यथाकथञ्चिद्रूपेण सादृश्यस्येत्यर्थः । 'तयोः' गुणत्व-दोषत्वयोः, 'प्रमेति गुणत्व-दोषत्वयोः प्रमाप्रमाघटितत्वाच्चेत्यर्थः, तथा चात्माश्रय इति भावः । यद्यपि अप्रमाजनकत्वं दोषत्वं तदभावजन्यानुभवत्वं प्रामाण्यमित्यर्थः इत्युक्ते नात्माश्रयः, तथापि अप्रमात्वं प्रमाभिन्नत्वमेव, अन्यथाप्रमात्वस्य दुर्व्वचत्वादित्यभिप्रायः । 'अबाधितेति अबाधिते तदनुभवत्वं तत्प्र-

समर्थप्रवृत्तिजनकानुभवत्वं, उपेक्षाप्रमायामव्याप्तेः तद्योग्यतायाः प्रमानिरूप्यत्वात्। नापि तत्त्वानुभवत्वं, अवस्तुनोऽभानात्। भाने वा भ्रमसाधारण्यात्। नापि विशेष्यनिष्ठात्यन्ताभावाप्रतियोगिधर्मप्रकारका-

---

मात्वमित्यर्थः, 'बाधस्य' बाधकस्य, 'प्रमात्वात्' प्रमात्वघटितत्वात्, तदभावप्रमा हि बाधः, तथा च तदभाववत्तया अप्रमिते तदनुभवत्वं तत्प्रमात्वं, तदभावप्रमात्वमपि तद्वत्तया अप्रमिते तदभावानुभवत्वं, एवञ्च तत्प्रमात्वज्ञाने तदभावप्रमात्वग्रहः, तदभावप्रमात्वे ज्ञाते एव तत्प्रमात्वग्रह इत्यन्योन्याश्रय इति भावः। 'ज्ञानान्तरेण तथोल्लिख्यमानत्वस्य' ज्ञानान्तरविषयीकृतार्थविषयकत्वस्य। समर्थप्रवृत्तिजनकत्वं तदुपधायकत्वं, तत्त्वावच्छिन्नस्वरूपयोग्यत्वं वा, आद्ये आह, 'उपेक्षाप्रमायामिति प्रवृत्त्यनुपधायकप्रमायामित्यर्थः। द्वितीये आह, 'तद्योग्यताया इति, प्रमात्वेनैव तादृशप्रवृत्तित्वावच्छिन्नस्वरूपयोग्यत्वादिति भावः। 'तत्त्वानुभवत्वमिति असद्विषयकान्यानुभवत्वमित्यर्थः, 'अवस्तुनः' इति तथा चान्यत्वप्रतियोगिप्रसिद्धिरिति भावः। 'भाने वेति भ्रमे सतोर्विशेषण-विशेष्ययोः सम्बन्धविधया असतो भानाभ्युपगमे वेत्यर्थः, 'भ्रमसाधारण्यादिति तादृशासज्ज्ञानस्य प्रमां भ्रमसाधारणत्वादित्यर्थः, तथा च तत्त्वया स्थितिरिति भावः। इदमुपलक्षणं, सर्वांशभ्रमात्मकस्यानुभवस्याप्रसिद्धतया आंशिकभ्रमस्य च लक्ष्यतया अन्यान्तविशेषणवैयर्थ्यञ्च(१)।

---

(१) 'अन्यान्तविशेषणस्य' असद्विषयकान्येतिविशेषणस्य, अनुभवत्वस्यैव सम्यक्त्वादिति भावः।

नुभवत्वं, संयोगादिप्रमाऽव्याप्तेः, अभावे व्याप्यवृत्ति-त्वविशेषणे संयोगभ्रमेऽतिव्याप्तिः तदत्यन्ताभावस्यैक-त्वात्। नापि विशेष्यवृत्त्यन्योन्याभावप्रतियोगितावा-

---

मिश्रास्तु 'तत्त्वानुभवत्वं' तत्त्वस्यानुभवत्वं, सद्विषयकानुभवत्व-मिति यावत्। 'अवस्तुनोऽभानादिति केवलमवस्तुनः क्वाप्यभाना-दित्यर्थः, तथा च सद्विषयकत्वविशेषणव्यावृत्त्यप्रसिद्धिरिति भावः। 'भाने वेति क्वचिदसन्मात्रस्य भानाभ्युपगमे वेत्यर्थः, 'भ्रमसाधारण-त्वादिति इदं रजतमित्यादिभ्रमेप्युक्तलक्षणसत्त्वादित्यर्थः, तत्रापि शुक्त्यादेः सतो विषयत्वात्तथा चातिव्याप्तिरिति भावः। इति व्याचक्षुः।

'नापीति, यद्यपि विशेष्यत्वं केवलान्वयि विशेष्यपदस्य स्ववि-शेष्यपरत्वेऽपि घट-पटाविति समूहालम्बनप्रमायामव्याप्तिः, तथापि स्वसमानाधिकरणात्यन्ताभावाप्रतियोगित्व-स्वनिरूपकप्रकारताश्रयत्वो-भयवत्तद्व्यक्तिकविशेष्यताप्रतियोग्यनुभवत्वं तद्व्यक्तेः प्रमात्वं, प्रतियो-गिता च स्वनिरूपकसम्बन्धावच्छिन्नत्वेन स्वरूपतोऽधिकरणतावच्छि-न्नत्वेन च विशेषणीया, तेन व्यधिकरणसम्बन्धावच्छिन्नाभावं वैशिष्ट्य-व्यासज्यवृत्तिधर्मावच्छिन्नाभावञ्चादाय नाप्रसिद्धिः। स्वत्रयं विशेष्य-तापरं, रजतत्वादिमात्रवृत्तितत्ताव्याखण्डाधिकरणताव्यक्तेः शुक्त्या-दिनिष्ठाभावप्रतियोगितावच्छेदकत्वादिदं रजतमित्यादि भ्रमे नाति-व्याप्तिः, विशेष्यतावच्छेदकाभेदेऽपि प्रतिविशेष्यं विशेष्यताभेदाभ्युप-गमाच्च प्रमेयं द्रव्यमित्याद्यतिप्रसक्तधर्मावच्छिन्नविशेष्यताकप्रमायां नाव्याप्तिः, गुणाद्यन्यत्वविशिष्टसत्तावान् गुणः, द्रव्यत्व-गुणत्वोभयवान्

च्छेदकधर्माप्रकारकानुभवत्वं, अव्याप्यवृत्तिप्रमानुपग्रहात्। मूले वृक्षः कपिसंयोगाभाववान्नाग्रे इत्यबाधितानुभवात् संयोगवदन्योन्याभावस्याव्याप्यवृत्तित्वात्। भेदाभेद एवं स्यादिति चेत् अनुभवमुपालभस्व यद्बलाद्वच्छेदभेदेनात्यन्ताभाववदन्योन्याभावस्याप्यव्याप्यवृत्तित्वमुपेयं। अतएव पक्के इदानीं न श्याम इति धीः

घट इत्यादिप्रतीतेः सत्त्व-द्रव्यत्वादिव्यक्तिप्रमात्वस्य सर्व्वसम्मततया न तत्रातिव्याप्तिः, विशिष्टसत्तात्व-द्रव्यत्व-गुणत्वोभयत्वादिविशिष्टप्रमा तु सा न भवति स्वसमानाधिकरणात्यन्ताभावीयस्वनिरूपकसम्बन्धावच्छिन्नप्रतियोगितानवच्छेदकत्व—स्वनिरूपकतावच्छेदकत्वोभयवत्तद्धर्मकविशेष्यताप्रतियोग्यनुभवत्वं तद्धर्मविशिष्टस्य प्रमात्वमिति विशिष्टप्रमाया लक्षणत्वात्। विशिष्टस्य वैशिष्ट्यमिति रीत्या गुणान्यत्वविशिष्टसत्तावद्द्रव्यमित्यादि धीरेव तादृशविशिष्टस्य प्रमा, विशेष्ये विशेषणमिति रीत्या तादृशधीस्तु सत्तादिव्यक्तेरेव प्रमा न तु विशिष्टस्येत्यभिप्रायः। अवृत्तिप्रकारकप्रमायामव्याप्तिं सुगमत्वादुपेक्ष्य दूषणान्तरमाह, 'संयोगादीति, 'व्याप्यवृत्तित्वविशेषण इति, 'व्याप्यवृत्तित्वं' अवच्छिन्नवृत्तिकभिन्नत्वं, 'संयोगधर्मेति गुणः संयोगवानित्यादिधर्मेत्यर्थः। ननु व्याप्यवृत्तिरेव संयोगाभावो गुणादौ[१] इत्यत आह, 'तदन्ताभावस्येति[२]। अन्योन्याभावो नाव्याप्यवृत्तिरितिनिय-

---

(१) अधिकरणभेदेनाभावस्य भिन्नत्वमिति नियमादिति भावः।

(२) तादृशनियमे मानाभावादिति भावः।

समयभेदादविरुद्धा, तत्रैव तदन्योन्याभावमवलम्बते। नापि विशेष्यावृत्त्यप्रकारकानुभवत्वं, एकैकविशेष्यावृत्तिनामाप्रकारकसमूहालम्बनाऽव्याप्तेः। न च प्रकारस्यैकविशेष्यवृत्तितया न विशेष्यावृत्तित्वमिति वाच्यं, प्रमाप्रमारूपसमूहालम्बनातिव्याप्तेः। न च यावद्विशेष्यावृत्तित्वं विवक्षितं, एकैकविशेष्यवृत्तेर्यावद्विशेष्यावृत्तित्वेन समूहालम्बनाव्याप्तेः एकविशेष्यके यावदर्था-

---

माभिप्रायेणाशङ्कते, 'नापीति स्वाधिकरणनिष्ठान्योन्याभावप्रतियोगितानवच्छेदकधर्मनिष्ठप्रकारतानिरूपितविशेष्यताप्रतियोग्यनुभवत्वमित्यर्थः[१], स्वं विषयता, तेन घट-पटाविति समूहालम्बनप्रमायां नाव्याप्तिः। प्रमा-भ्रमरूपस्य समूहालम्बनं लक्ष्यमित्यभिमानः। संयोगादिव्यधिकरणसम्बन्धेन रूपादिप्रकारकभ्रमे अतिव्याप्तिसत्त्वेपि उक्तनियमं[२] निराकृत्य दूषयति, 'अव्याप्यवृत्तित्वादिति संयोगवति वृक्षे सत्त्वादित्यर्थः। आशङ्कते, 'एवमिति संयोगवदन्योन्याभावस्यापि संयोगवति वृक्षे सत्त्वे इत्यर्थः, 'भेदाभेद इति वृक्षः संयोगिभेदतदभावोभयवान् स्यादित्यर्थः, संयोगिभेदाभावस्य संयोगानतिरिक्तत्वादिति भावः। 'अव्याप्यवृत्तित्व' संयोगवति सत्त्वं। 'अत एवेति अव्याप्यवृत्तिमतोऽन्योन्याभावस्याव्याप्यवृत्तित्वादेवेत्यर्थः, 'तत्रैव' अस्या-

---

(१) स्वाधिकरणनिष्ठान्योन्याभावप्रतियोगितावच्छेदकधर्मनिष्ठप्रकारतानिरूपितविशेष्यताप्रतियोग्यनुभवत्वमित्यर्थ इति ख०।

(२) अन्योन्याभावमात्रस्य व्याप्यवृत्तितानियमं इत्यर्थः।

भावाच्च । अथ विषयताया आश्रयो विशेष्यः, ज्ञानं तत्प्रतियोगि, भ्रमे च शुक्तिवृत्तिविषयता व्यधिकरणेन रजतत्वेनावच्छिद्यते, रजतवृत्तिस्तु समानाधिकरणेन रजतत्वेन, विषयता च विषये न ज्ञानाहिता ज्ञाततारूपा

महूपवत्त्येव, 'तदन्योन्याभावं' श्यामरूपवदन्योन्याभावं । नन्वत्यन्ताभावलक्षणे प्रतियोग्यनधिकरणत्वेन, अन्योन्याभावलक्षणे च प्रतियोगितावच्छेदकानधिकरणत्वेन स्वाधिकरणं विशेषणीयमित्युभयथापि नोक्तदोष इत्यत आह, 'विशेष्यभेदमादाय समूहालम्बनप्रमायामव्याप्तेश्चेति, 'समूहालम्बनप्रमायां' द्रव्यत्वादिरूपेण रजतारजतविशेष्यकरजतत्वप्रकारकप्रमायां, विशेष्यतावच्छेदकाभेदेन विशेष्यताया अप्रसिद्धत्वादिति भावः । अयन्तु क्वाचित्कः पाठः, क्वचित् 'तदत्यन्ताभावस्यैकत्वादित्यनन्तरं अयं पाठः, स प्रामादिकः 'नापि विशेष्यावृत्तीत्याद्यग्रिमलक्षणेन तद्दोषानुद्धारात् सन्दर्भाशुद्धेः । क्वचिच्च कुत्रापि नायं पाठः । 'विशेष्येति स्वविशेष्यावृत्तिप्रकारकं यद्यत् तदन्यानुभवत्वं इत्यर्थः, स्वं ज्ञानं, येन सम्बन्धेनावृत्तित्वं तेनैव तत्प्रकारकत्वं बोध्यं, तेनावृत्तित्वं यदि वृत्तिनियामकसम्बन्धमात्रेण विवक्षितं तदा गगणे द्रव्यत्वमित्याद्यवृत्तिप्रकारकप्रमायामव्याप्तिः, यदि च सम्बन्धसामान्येन विवक्षितं तदा अप्रसिद्धिः, यदि च यत्किञ्चित्सम्बन्धेन विवक्षितं तदेदं रजतमित्यादि प्रमायामेवासम्भव इति निरस्तं । अत्र स्वविशेष्यावृत्तित्वं यत्किञ्चित्स्वविशेष्यवृत्तिभिन्नत्वं, स्वविशेष्यवृत्तिसामान्यभिन्नत्वं वा, आद्ये आह

विवक्षितताऽपसिद्धान्तादसिद्धेः अतीतानागतप्रमायां तद-
भावाच्च। किन्तु ज्ञानस्य विषये विशेषणता विशेषः कश्चित्। परज्ञानं ज्ञानत्वेन तद्विषयं च घटत्वेन जानतो घटमयं जनाति न वेति संशयाद्विषयज्ञानस्य-

---

'एकेति, 'समूहालम्बने' घट-पटाविति समूहालम्बने। द्वितीय-माशङ्क्य निराकरोति, 'नचेति, 'प्रकारस्य' घटत्व-पटत्वरूपप्रकारस्य, 'न विशेष्यावृत्तित्वं' न स्वविशेष्यवृत्तिसामान्यभिन्नत्वं। आंशिक-प्रमाया लक्ष्यत्वे इदं रजतमिति भ्रमस्यापीदन्त्वांशे प्रमात्वेन लक्ष्य-तया तत्राव्याप्तिरतः सर्वांशप्रमैव लक्ष्येत्यभिप्रायेणाह, 'प्रमाप्रमेति रजत-रङ्गयोरिमे रजते इति समूहालम्बनेत्यर्थः। इदमुपलक्षणं रजतरङ्गयोरिमे रङ्ग-रजते इति विपरीतभ्रमेऽप्यतिव्याप्तिर्बोध्या। 'समूहालम्बनाव्याप्तेः' घट-पटाविति समूहालम्बनाव्याप्तितादवस्थ्यात्। पश्चाद्वक्ष्यमाणं स्वसमानाधिकरणधर्मप्रकारकविषयताप्रतियोग्यनुभवः प्रमेति लक्षणमसङ्गतं विषयत्वाभाव एव विषयत्वस्य प्रतियोगी (१), न तु ज्ञानमित्यप्रसिद्धेः, इदं रजतमिति प्रमायामव्याप्तेश्च। विषय-तायाः प्रकारवृत्तित्वेन विषयतासमानाधिकरणो धर्मः रजतत्वमेव तस्य तत्र विषयतायामप्रकारत्वादतः प्रथमं तद्वारणप्रकारमाह, 'अथेति 'विशेष्य इति, तेनोक्तरीत्या स्वरूपतो रजतत्वादिप्रकारक-प्रमायां न वक्ष्यमाणलक्षणमव्याप्तमितिभावः। 'ज्ञानं तत्प्रतियो-गीति, तेन वक्ष्यमाणलक्षणे नोक्तरीत्या अप्रसिद्धिरिति भावः। अथ-

---

(१) विषयत्वस्य हि विषयत्वाभावाभावरूपत्वादिति भावः।

रूपातिरिक्तस्य स्वाश्रय-स्वाभावादिविशेषणताविशेष-
स्यावश्यं स्वीकारात्, अन्यथा घटत्वेन ज्ञातोऽयमर्थं

च्छिन्नत्वघटितवक्ष्यमाणलक्षणस्य भ्रम-प्रमयोरतिव्याप्त्यव्याप्तिवारणप्रकारमाह, 'भ्रम इति, 'व्यधिकरणेति प्रकारितासम्बन्धेनासमानाधिकरणरजतत्वविशिष्टेत्यर्थः, 'समानाधिकरणेति प्रकारितासम्बन्धेन समानाधिकरणरजतत्वविशिष्टेत्यर्थः। ननु विषयता कः पदार्थ इत्यत आह, 'विषयता चेति, 'ज्ञानाहिता' ज्ञानजन्या। सति प्रमाणे अप्रसिद्धत्वमकिञ्चित्करमित्यत आह, 'असिद्धेरिति प्रमाणस्यासिद्धेरित्यर्थः। ननु बाधकाभाव एव मानमतो बाधकमाह, 'अतीतेति अतीतानागतविशेष्यकप्रमायामित्यर्थः, 'तदभावाच्च' ज्ञाततायाः असम्भवाच्च, ज्ञाततां प्रति विषयस्य समवायिकारणतया अतीतानागतविशेष्ये तदुत्पादासम्भवादिति भावः। प्रमात्वेनोपादानं प्रकृतलक्षणाव्याप्तिप्रदर्शनाय तेन ज्ञाततानिराकरणे अतीतानागतविषयकज्ञानमात्रस्यैवोपयोगित्वेऽपि न क्षतिः। 'विशेषणताविशेषः' ज्ञानविषययोः स्वरूपसम्बन्धविशेषः, 'कश्चित्' क्लृप्तपदार्थातिरिक्तः, स एव सविशेष्यकः सप्रकारकः न तु ज्ञानं सविशेष्यकं सप्रकारकं इति भावः। ननु विषयता नातिरिक्ता किन्तु ज्ञानविषयस्वरूपमेवेत्यत आह, 'परज्ञानमिति अयं पुरुषो ज्ञानवान् अयञ्च घट इति निश्चिन्वत इत्यर्थः, 'घटमयमिति अयं पुरुषो घटविषयकज्ञानवान्न वेत्यर्थः, 'स्वाश्रयस्वाभावेति ज्ञानाश्रय-ज्ञानाभावयोर्या विशेषणता तद्विलक्षणस्येत्यर्थः, 'अन्यथा' ज्ञानस्य विशेष्ये विषयताख्यातिरिक्तपदार्थानभ्युपगमे, 'इतौ-

इति तृतीयार्थासम्भवः, प्रकारत्वमपि विषयस्य ज्ञाने विशेषणताविशेष एव, न तु विषयत्वमतिप्रसङ्गात्। एवञ्च विषयतासमानाधिकरणप्रकारकानुभवः, प्रकारसमाधिकरणविषयताप्रतियोग्यनुभवो वा, स्वसमानाधिकरणधर्मप्रकारकविषयताप्रतियोग्यनुभवो वा, स्वसमानाधिकरणधर्मावच्छिन्नविषयताप्रतियोग्यनुभवो वा

यार्थासम्भव इति तृतीयार्थस्य प्रकारत्वस्य क्तप्रत्ययार्थे विषयत्वे ऽन्वयासम्भव इत्यर्थः, 'प्रकारत्वमपीति, यत इत्यादिः, 'ज्ञाने विशेषणताविशेष एवेति ज्ञानीयविषयताख्यातिरिक्तविशेषणताविशेष एव वर्त्तत इत्यर्थः। ननु ज्ञान-विषयोभयरूपसम्बन्ध एव तदभ्युपगमात्तान्वयासम्भव इत्यत आह, 'न त्विति, 'विषयत्वं' ज्ञान-विषयोभयरूपं विषयत्वं, प्रकारत्वाश्रय इति शेषः। 'अतिप्रसङ्गादिति विषये घटादावपि सप्रकारकव्यवहारप्रसङ्गादित्यर्थः। 'विषयतेति स्वसमानाधिकरणधर्मप्रकारकविषयताश्रयोऽनुभव इत्यर्थः, विषयतारूपो यः समानाधिकरणप्रकारकस्तस्यानुभव इति कर्मधारयोत्तरमाश्रयत्वात्मकषष्ठीतत्पुरुषसमासात्, स्वं विषयता, एवमग्रेऽपि। अथ येन केनचित् सम्बन्धेनाश्रयत्वमादायातिव्याप्तिरतो लक्षणान्तरमाह, 'प्रकारेति स्वप्रकारसमानाधिकरणेत्यर्थः, 'स्वसमानाधिकरणेति, प्रथमे आश्रयमात्रं, अत्र तु प्रतियोगित्वमिति भेदः। 'स्वसमानाधिकरणधर्मावच्छिन्नेति प्रकारितासम्बन्धेन स्वसमाधिकरणधर्मविशिष्टेत्यर्थः, पूर्वत्र प्रकारित्वं विशेषणं, अत्र तु सम्बन्ध इति भेदः, अतस्तस्मा-

प्रमेति चेत्। न। निर्विकल्पकाव्याप्तेः विषयतासमानाधिकरणेदन्त्वप्रकारकभ्रमस्यापि प्रमात्वप्रसङ्गाच्च। भ्रमस्तत्त्वांशे प्रमैवेति चेत् तर्हि अनुभवत्वमेव प्रमात्वं

लाघवमपि। निर्व्विकल्पकस्यासंग्राह्यत्वमतेऽपि दूषणमाह, 'विषयतेति, 'भ्रमस्यापीति इदं रजतमित्यादिभ्रमस्यापीत्यर्थः, 'प्रमात्वापत्तेः' प्रमाव्यवहारविषयत्वापत्तेः। इष्टापत्तिमाह, 'भ्रमेति 'तत्त्वांशे' इदन्त्वांशे, 'प्रमात्वं' प्रमाव्यवहारविषयतावच्छेदकं, अस्त्विति शेषः। 'व्यर्थमधिकमिति, प्रमुष्टतत्ताकस्मरणात्मकस्य सर्व्वांशे भ्रमस्य सत्त्वेऽपि सर्व्वांशभ्रमात्मकस्यानुभवस्याप्रसिद्धेः प्रत्यक्षभ्रमे अन्ततस्तादात्म्यसम्बन्धेन प्रकारीभूतधर्म्मस्य स्वस्मिन्नेव प्रकारतया सर्व्वांशभ्रमत्वासम्भवात्। न च हृदत्वरूपेण पर्वते वह्नित्वरूपेण जलानुमित्यादिरेव सर्व्वांशे भ्रमात्मकोऽनुभवः प्रसिद्ध इति वाच्यं। विशेष्यतावच्छेदकांशे भ्रमात्मकस्य विशेषणतावच्छेदकांशे भ्रमात्मकस्य वा परोक्षानुभवस्यानभ्युपगमात् तन्निराकरणप्रकारस्यास्मत्कृतसिद्धान्तरहस्ये अनुसन्धेयः। अतएव "धर्म्मिणि सर्व्वमभ्रान्तं प्रकारे तु विपर्य्ययः" इति प्रामाणिकप्रवादः, 'सर्व्वं' परोक्षानुभवरूपं ज्ञानं, 'धर्म्मिणि' धर्म्मितावच्छेदकांशे, 'अभ्रान्तं' परोक्षानुभवीयधर्म्मिता न स्वव्यधिकरणधर्म्मावच्छिन्नेति यावत्, 'प्रकारे तु विपर्य्ययः' इति विशेषणतावच्छेदकातिरिक्तप्रकारे एव विपर्य्ययः, विशेषणतावच्छेदकांशे न विपर्य्यय इति यावत् (१), परोक्षानुभवीयप्रकारता न स्वव्यधिकरण-

---

(१) तुशब्दलभ्यस्वार्थात् विशेषणतावच्छेदकांशे न विपर्य्यय इति यावदिति सं।

व्यर्थमधिकं। अनुभव एव क्वचिदंशे भ्रमः प्रमा चेति चेत्। न। उक्तलक्षणे तादृशालाभात्। अथ स्वव्यधिकरणधर्मानवच्छिन्नविषयताप्रतियोग्यनुभवः प्रमा, समूहालम्बने च प्रतिविशेष्यं विषयताभेदादेकवृत्तिर्विषयता नापरवृत्तिनावच्छिद्यते, अतो नाव्याप्तिरिति चेत्[१]। न। भ्रमांशप्रमायामव्याप्तेः। न हि

धर्म्मावच्छिन्नेति तु निष्कर्षः। न च सर्व्वं ज्ञानं धर्म्यंशे अभ्रान्तमिति यथाश्रुत एव तदर्थ इति वाच्यं। तदभाववति तत्प्रकारकत्वरूपस्य भ्रमत्वस्य धर्म्म्यंश एव सत्त्वात्। न च धर्म्मिणीत्यत्र अंशता न सप्तम्यर्थः, किन्तु निरूपितत्वमिति वाच्यं। ह्रदो वह्निमान् ह्रदत्वाभाववांश्च वह्निरिति विशिष्टज्ञाने धर्म्मिनिरूपितभ्रमत्वस्यापि सत्त्वात्। न च तथापि प्रकारे तु विपर्य्यय इत्यस्य प्रकारांशे पुनर्विपर्य्यय इति यथा श्रुत एवार्थ इति वाच्यं। सर्व्वमित्यसङ्गतेः। न च सर्व्वपदं भ्रमात्मकसकलज्ञानपरमिति वाच्यं। तथापि 'प्रकारे तु विपर्य्ययः' इत्यस्य स्वप्रकाराभाववति स्वप्रकारप्रकारक इत्यर्थेबाधः इदं रजतमित्यादिभ्रमस्य स्वप्रकारसामान्याभाववति स्वप्रकाराप्रकारकत्वात्, विशिष्य रजतत्वादिरूपप्रकारोपादाने च सर्व्वमित्यसङ्गतेः, सर्व्वपदस्यापि विशिष्य रजतत्वादिभ्रमपरत्वे साध्याविशेषात्। मध्यांशत्वं सप्तम्यर्थः तथाच प्रकारांशे तु विपर्य्ययः इत्यर्थ इति वाच्यं। तदभाववद्विशेष्यकत्वावच्छिन्नतत्प्रकारकत्वरूपस्य भ्रमत्वस्य विशेष्यांशेऽपि सत्त्वेन व्यवच्छेदार्थकस्य तुशब्दस्यासङ्गतेः।

---

(१) इति नाव्याप्तिरिति चेदिति ख०।

या विषयता व्यधिकरणधर्मेणावच्छिद्यते सा तदनव-च्छिन्ना, विरोधात्। नापि प्रकारव्यधिकरणविषयत्वा-प्रतियोग्यनुभवः प्रमा, प्रकारव्यधिकरणविषयताप्रति-योगिनि तदप्रतियोगित्वस्याभावेन भ्रमांशप्रमाव्याप्तेः। नापि स्वव्यधिकरणधर्मावच्छिन्नविषयत्वाप्रतियोग्यनु-

---

अथ सर्व्वं भ्रमात्मकं ज्ञानं न धर्म्यंशे तत्प्रकारकत्वावच्छिन्नतद-भाववद्विशेष्यकत्वरूपभ्रमत्वविशेषाश्रयः, 'प्रकारे तु विपर्य्ययः' किन्तु प्रकारांश एव तादृशभ्रमत्वविशेषाश्रय इत्यर्थः, तदभाववद्विशेष्यक-त्वावच्छिन्नतत्प्रकारकत्वरूपस्य भ्रमत्वस्य विशेष्यांशे सत्त्वेऽपि ता-दृशभ्रमत्वस्य विशेष्यांशे विरहादिति चेत्। न। तथा सति वि-शेष्यतासामान्यस्यैव विशेष्यावच्छेदेनाभावात् भ्रमत्वपर्य्यन्तानुधावनस्य व्यर्थत्वप्रसङ्गात् तावता प्रामाणिकप्रवादोपपादनेऽपि सर्व्वांशभ्रमात्मक-स्यानुमित्यादेरभ्युपगमे "व्यर्थमधिकं" इति मूलग्रन्थविरोधस्य गौ-रवप्रसङ्गस्य दुर्व्वारत्वाच। गौरवञ्च सिद्धान्तरहस्ये प्रपञ्चितमिति दिक्। 'क्वचिदंश इति तथाच सामान्यतोऽनुभवत्वस्य लक्षणत्वे आंशिकभ्रमत्वस्य व्यावृत्तिर्न सिध्यतीति भावः। 'उक्तलक्षणे' उक्त-लक्षणेष्वपि, 'तादृशालाभादिति आंशिकभ्रमव्यावृत्त्यलाभादित्यर्थः। एतच्चापाततः सामानाधिकरण्य-प्रकारत्वयोः प्रमात्वनिरूपकसम्बन्ध-घटकतया तत्तत्सम्बन्धमन्तर्भाव्य सामान्यतः प्रमाव्यवहारौपयिका-न्येव ह्येतानि लक्षणानि, तच्च च न वैयर्थ्यसम्भावनापि। तत्तत्-सम्बन्धावच्छिन्नप्रकारताकानुभवत्वस्य तत्तत्सम्बन्धेन प्रमाव्यवहारौप-

भवः, स्वाधिकरणावृत्त्यप्रकारकविषयताप्रतियोग्यनुभवो वा प्रमा, तत एव। भ्रमे विषयतायाः स्वव्यधिकरणप्रकारावच्छिन्नत्वात्[१] स्वाधिकरणावृत्तिप्रकारकत्वाच्च। नापि स्वसमानाधिकरणान्योन्याभावप्रतियोगितावच्छेदकधर्मानवच्छिन्नविषयताप्रतियोग्यनु-

---

यिकत्वे तादात्म्य-विषयत्वादिसम्बन्धेन पर्व्वतादिपक्षक-वह्न्यादिविधेयकानुमित्यादावपि तेन सम्बन्धेन सामान्यतः प्रमाव्यवहारापत्तेरिति ध्येयम्।

निर्व्विकल्पकसाधारणमिदं रजतमित्यादिभ्रमव्यावृत्तञ्च लक्षणमाशङ्कते, 'अथेति, 'अनवच्छिन्नत्वं' तदप्रकारकत्वं, 'स्वं' विषयता, 'समूहालम्बने चेति, घट-पटाविति समूहालम्बनप्रमायाञ्चेत्यर्थः, 'विषयताभेदात्' विशेष्यताभेदात्। 'भ्रमांशप्रमायामिति रजत एवेदं रजतं रङ्गञ्चेति रङ्गत्वांशभ्रमात्मकरजतत्वप्रमायामित्यर्थः, 'गृहीति, 'व्यधिकरणधर्म्मेणावच्छिद्यते' स्वव्यधिकरणधर्म्मप्रकारिका, 'तदनवच्छिन्ना' तदप्रकारिका, 'विरोधादिति, प्रकारभेदेन च विषयताभेद इति भावः। 'प्रकारव्यधिकरणेति, स्वप्रकारानधिकरणवृत्तीत्यर्थः, 'स्वं' विषयता। अत्र स्वप्रकारानधिकरणत्वं यदि स्वप्रकाराधिकरणसामान्यभेदः तदेदं रजतमित्यादिभ्रमानुभवमात्रेऽतिव्याप्तिः तद्विषयतायाः स्वप्रकारेदन्त्वाधिकरणमात्रवृत्तित्वादतो यत्किञ्चित्स्वप्रकाराधिकरणभिन्नत्वमेव वक्तव्यं, तथाच पूर्व्वोक्ताव्याप्तिरेव

---

(१) स्वव्यधिकरणधर्म्मावच्छिन्नत्वादिति क०, ख०।

भवः प्रमा, भ्रमांशप्रमाव्याप्तेः अन्योन्याभावस्याव्याप्यवृत्तित्वेनाव्याप्यवृत्तिप्रमायामव्याप्तेश्च। यत्तु प्रमात्वाप्रमात्वयोर्विरोध एवेति भ्रमोन प्रमेति। तन्तुच्छं। अंशभेदमादायोभयस्यानुभवात्। अन्यथा भ्रमस्योभयबहिर्भावापत्तेः। एतेन स्वव्यधिकरणप्रकारकं ज्ञानं भ्रम-

---

तदवस्थेत्याह, 'प्रकारव्यधिकरणेति यत्किञ्चित्स्वप्रकारव्यधिकरणेत्यर्थः, 'भ्रमांशप्रमेति, एतल्लक्षणपक्षे प्रकारभेदेन विषयताभेदोपगमेऽपि न प्रतीकारः इति भावः। 'स्वव्यधिकरणेति, 'अवच्छिन्नत्वं' तत्प्रकारकत्वं। 'तत एवेति भ्रमांशप्रमाव्याप्तेरेवेत्यर्थः। अव्याप्तिमेव विवृणोति, 'भ्रम इति प्रमांशभ्रमेत्यर्थः, 'प्रकारावच्छिन्नत्वादिति, 'प्रकारः' धर्म्मः,। 'धर्म्मानवच्छिन्नेति, 'अनवच्छिन्नत्वं' तदप्रकारकत्वं। भ्रमांशप्रमायामव्याप्तिमुद्धरति, 'यत्त्विति। 'उभयस्यानुभवादिति उभयस्यैव व्यवहारादित्यर्थः, 'अन्यथेति प्रमाव्यवहारस्याप्रमात्वोपगमे इत्यर्थः, 'भ्रमस्येति इदं रजतमित्यादिभ्रमस्येत्यर्थः, धर्म्मितावच्छेदकांशे प्रमाव्यवहारस्येव विनिगमकाभावेन विधेयांशे भ्रमव्यवहारस्याप्यप्रमात्वस्य सुवचत्वादिति भावः। 'एतेनेति भ्रमेऽपि धर्म्मितावच्छेदकांशे प्रामाणिकानां प्रमाव्यवहारसत्त्वेनेत्यर्थः, 'स्वव्यधिकरणेति स्वविशेष्यतानधिकरणवृत्तिधर्म्मेत्यर्थः, स्वपदं ज्ञानपरं। 'प्रकाराधिकरणावृत्तीति यत्किञ्चित्प्रकाराधिकरणावृत्त्यप्रकारकविषयताप्रतियोग्यनुभव इत्यर्थः, स्वपदं विषयतापरम्, इदं रजतमित्यादिभ्रमे अतिव्याप्तिवारणाय यत्किञ्चिदिति स्वप्रकारविशेषणं, धर्म्मितावच्छे-

स्तदन्योऽनुभवः प्रमा भ्रमो धर्म्यंशे न प्रमेति निरस्तं। नापि प्रकाराधिकरणावृत्त्यप्रकारकविषयताप्रतियोग्यनुभवः, प्रकारानधिकरणावृत्तिविषयताप्रतियोग्यनुभवो वा [१] प्रमा। प्रमेयमिदमिति ज्ञाने प्रकारानधिकरणस्याप्रसिद्धेः। किञ्च रजतत्वप्रकारकविषय-

---

दकप्रकारकधर्म्मिज्ञानस्य भ्रमानुभवहेतुतया प्रमुष्टतत्ताकभ्रमानुभवस्याप्रसिद्धत्वाच्च न तत्रातिव्याप्तिरिति भावः। लक्षणान्तरमाह, 'प्रकारानधिकरणावृत्तीति यत्किञ्चित्स्वप्रकारानधिकरणावृत्तिविषयतायाः प्रतियोग्यनुभव इत्यर्थः। इदं रजतमित्यादिभ्रमविषयताया अपि स्वप्रकारेदन्त्वाधिकरणमात्रवृत्तित्वेन प्रकारानधिकरणावृत्तित्वादतिव्याप्तिवारणाय यत्किञ्चिदिति स्वप्रकारविशेषणमिति भावः। द्वितीये दूषणमाह, 'प्रमेयमिदमितीति प्रमेयत्वसामान्यलक्षणादिजन्यप्रमेयमित्यादिप्रमुष्टतत्ताकप्रमायामित्यर्थः। इदमुपलक्षणं लक्षणद्वय एव निर्व्विकल्पकाव्याप्तिः, इदं रजतमित्यादिभ्रमांशप्रमानुपपत्तेश्च दूषणं बोध्यम्। रजततादात्म्यारोपे विषयतात्रयी प्रकाररजतत्वमात्रप्रकारिका रजतमात्रनिष्ठा, अन्या रजतमात्रप्रकारिका शुक्तिमात्रनिष्ठा, अपरा च इदन्त्वमात्रप्रकारिका शुक्तिमात्रनिष्ठा, प्रकारभेदेन विषयताभेदादिति मतमालम्ब्य लक्षणद्वय एव तत्रातिव्याप्तिमाह, 'किञ्चेति, रजततादात्म्यारोप इति शेषः।

---

(१) प्रकारानधिकरणावृत्तिविषयत्वाप्रतियोग्यनुभवो वेति पाठान्तरं कस्मिंश्चित् मूलपुस्तके वर्त्तते परन्तु तन्न टीकाकारसम्मतमिति।

ताया रजतवृत्तित्वनियमात् रजतत्वावच्छिन्नैव रजतभ्रमे रजतवृत्तिविषयता अतो रजतभ्रमोऽपि रजते[१] प्रमा स्यात्। अथ रजत-पुरोवर्त्तिनोरेकैव विषयता सा च प्रकारानधिकरणवृत्तिधर्मावच्छिन्नैवेति चेत् तर्हि धर्म्यंशेऽपि तज्ज्ञानं प्रमा न स्यात्। व्यधिकरणप्रकारक-

---

'रजतवृत्तित्वेति रजतमात्रवृत्तित्वादित्यर्थः, 'रजतत्वावच्छिन्नैव' रजतत्वसमानाधिकरणैव, न त्विदन्त्वसमानाधिकरणा, 'रजतभ्रमे' रजततादात्म्यारोपे, तथाच रजतवृत्तिविषयता स्वप्रकाररजतत्वाधिकरणावृत्त्यप्रकारिका स्वप्रकाररजतत्वानधिकरणावर्त्तमाना चेति भावः। 'रजते प्रमा स्यादिति रजतांशे प्रमा स्यादित्यर्थः। तादृश-विषयताधिकरणस्यैव भवन्मते प्रमात्वव्यक्तावंशत्वादित्यभिमानः।

पूर्व्वोक्तमतमनादृत्य शङ्कते, 'अथेति, 'प्रकारानधिकरणेति यत्किञ्चित् स्वप्रकारानधिकरणवृत्तित्वविशिष्टेत्यर्थः। इदमुपलक्षणं यत्किञ्चित्स्वप्रकाराधिकरणावृत्तिप्रकारिका चेत्यपि बोध्यं। 'धर्म्यंशेऽपीति इदमंशेऽपीत्यर्थः। 'व्यधिकरणेति यत्किञ्चित्स्वप्रकाराधिकरणावृत्तिप्रकारकत्वस्येत्यर्थः, 'तुल्यत्वादिति, रजतत्वप्रकारकविषयतावदिदन्त्वप्रकारकविषयतायामपि तत्त्वात्तयोरभेदादिति भावः। 'धर्म्यंशे त्विति प्रकारभेदेन विषयताभेदमभ्युपेत्य इदन्त्वमात्रप्रकारक-विषयताव्यक्तिमादाय धर्म्यंशे प्रमात्वोपपादन इत्यर्थः, 'रजतेऽपीति रजतत्वमात्रप्रकारकविषयताव्यक्तिमादाय रजतांशेऽपि प्रमा स्यादि-

---

(१) रजतांश इति ख०।

त्वस्य तुल्यत्वात् धर्म्म्यंशे तु प्रमात्वे रजतेऽपि प्रमा स्यात्। अथ रजतांशे धर्म्म्यंशे च तज्ज्ञानं प्रमैव वैशिष्ट्यांशे न प्रमेति चेत्। न। वैशिष्ट्यस्य पूर्वंज्ञानाविषयत्वेनाप्रकारत्वात्। वैशिष्ट्यवृत्तिविषयतायां रजतत्व-पुरोवर्त्तिनोः प्रकारत्वेन भ्रमस्य वैशिष्ट्यांशे प्रमात्वाप्रमात्वापातात्। नापि स्वव्यधिकरणप्रकारानवच्छिन्नविषयताप्रतियो-

---

त्यर्थः। 'प्रमैवेति, रजत-धर्म्मिणोरुभयोरेव निरुक्तविषयताधिकरणत्वादिति भावः। 'वैशिष्ट्यांश इति वैशिष्ट्यमात्रवृत्तिविषयताव्यक्तेः प्रकाराप्रसिद्ध्या वैशिष्ट्यस्य निरुक्तविषयतानधिकरणत्वेन वैशिष्ट्यांश एव प्रमत्वाभावादित्यर्थः। वैशिष्ट्यस्याप्रकारकत्वेन प्रमात्वाभाववृत्तावंशत्वमेव न सम्भवतीत्यभिप्रायेण समाधत्ते, 'वैशिष्ट्यस्येति, 'अप्रकारत्वादिति, स्वप्रकारस्यैव च प्रमात्वाभाव-प्रमात्वयोर्वृत्तावंशत्वादिति भावः। लक्षणे प्रकारपदं न विशेषणपरं परन्तु निरूपकपरं निरूपकभेदेनैव च विषयताभेदः, तथाच तादात्म्यारोपस्य वैशिष्ट्यांशे प्रमात्व-भ्रमत्वोभयप्रसङ्गः भवन्मते प्रकारीभूतधर्म्मस्यैव भ्रमत्ववृत्तावंशत्वमिति नियमादित्यभिप्रायेण दूषणान्तरमाह, 'वैशिष्ट्येति' 'प्रकारत्वेन' निरूपकत्वेन, 'भ्रमस्य' तादात्म्यारोपस्य, 'वैशिष्ट्यांशे' रजततादात्म्यारोपस्य वैशिष्ट्यांशे, 'प्रमात्वाप्रमात्वेति रजतमात्रनिरूपितविषयताव्यक्त्यधिकरणत्वमादाय प्रमात्वप्रसङ्गः तस्याः स्वनिरूपकाधिकरणवृत्तित्वात्, शुक्तिमात्रनिरूपितविषयताव्यक्तिमादायैव च भ्रमत्वप्रसङ्गः तस्याः स्वनिरूपकानधिकरणवृत्तित्वादित्यर्थः। 'स्वव्य-

ताया रजतवृत्तित्वनियमात् रजतत्वावच्छिन्नैव रजतभ्रमे रजतवृत्तिविषयता अतो रजतभ्रमोऽपि रजते[१] प्रमा स्यात्। अथ रजत-पुरोवर्त्तिनोरेकैव विषयता सा च प्रकारानधिकरणवृत्तिधर्मावच्छिन्नैवेति चेत् तर्हि धर्म्यंशेऽपि तज्ज्ञानं प्रमा न स्यात्। व्यधिकरणप्रकारक-

---

'रजतवृत्तित्वे'ति रजतमात्रवृत्तित्वादित्यर्थः, 'रजतत्वावच्छिन्नैव' रजतत्वसमानाधिकरणैव, न त्विदन्त्वसमानाधिकरणा, 'रजतभ्रमे' रजततादात्म्यारोपे, तथाच रजतवृत्तिविषयता स्वप्रकाररजतत्वाधिकरणावृत्त्यप्रकारिका स्वप्रकाररजतत्वानधिकरणावर्त्तमाना चेति भावः। 'रजते प्रमा स्या'दिति रजतांशे प्रमा स्यादित्यर्थः। तादृश-विषयताधिकरणस्यैव भवन्मते प्रमात्वघटकत्वादित्यभिमानः।

पूर्व्वोक्तमतमनादृत्य शङ्कते, 'अथे'ति, 'प्रकारानधिकरणे'ति यत्किञ्चित् स्वप्रकारानधिकरणवृत्तित्वविशिष्टेत्यर्थः। इदमुपलक्षणं यत्किञ्चित्स्वप्रकाराधिकरणावृत्तिप्रकारिका चेत्यपि बोध्यं। 'धर्म्यंशेऽपी'ति इदमंशेऽपीत्यर्थः। 'व्यधिकरणे'ति यत्किञ्चित्स्वप्रकाराधिकरणावृत्तिप्रकारकत्वस्येत्यर्थः, 'तुल्यत्वा'दिति, रजतत्वप्रकारकविषयतावदिदन्त्वप्रकारकविषयतायामपि सत्त्वात्तयोरभेदादिति भावः। 'धर्म्यंशे त्वि'ति प्रकारभेदेन विषयताभेदमभ्युपेत्य इदन्त्वमात्रप्रकारकविषयताव्यक्तिमादाय धर्म्यंशे प्रमात्वोपपादन इत्यर्थः, 'रजतेऽपी'ति रजतत्वमात्रप्रकारकविषयताव्यक्तिमादाय रजतांशेऽपि प्रमा स्यादि-

---

(१) रजतांश इति ख०।

त्वस्य तुल्यत्वात् धर्म्यंशे तु प्रमात्वे रजतेऽपि प्रमा स्यात्। अथ रजतांशे धर्म्यंशे च तज्ज्ञानं प्रमैव वैशिष्ट्यांशे न प्रमेति चेत्। न। वैशिष्ट्यस्य पूर्वज्ञानाविषयत्वेनाप्रकारत्वात्। वैशिष्ट्यवृत्तिविषयतायां रजतत्व-पुरोवर्त्तिनोः प्रकारत्वेन भ्रमस्य वैशिष्ट्यांशे प्रमात्वाप्रमात्वापातात्। नापि स्वव्यधिकरणप्रकारानवच्छिन्नविषयताप्रतियो-

---

त्यर्थः। 'प्रमैवेति, रजत-धर्म्मिणोरुभयोरेव निरुक्तविषयताधिकरणत्वादिति भावः। 'वैशिष्ट्यांश इति वैशिष्ट्यमात्रवृत्तिविषयताव्यक्तेः प्रकाराप्रसिद्ध्या वैशिष्ट्यस्य निरुक्तविषयतानधिकरणत्वेन वैशिष्ट्यांश एव प्रमत्वाभावादित्यर्थः। वैशिष्ट्यस्याप्रकारकत्वेन प्रमात्वाभाववृत्तावंशत्वमेव न सम्भवतीत्यभिप्रायेण समाधत्ते, 'वैशिष्ट्यस्येति, 'अप्रकारत्वादिति, स्वप्रकारस्यैव च प्रमात्वाभाव-प्रमात्वयोर्वृत्तावंशत्वादिति भावः। लक्षणे प्रकारपदं न विशेषणपरं परन्तु निरूपकपरं निरूपकभेदेनैव च विषयताभेदः, तथाच तादात्म्यारोपस्य वैशिष्ट्यांशे प्रमात्व-भ्रमत्वोभयप्रसङ्गः भवन्मते प्रकारीभूतधर्म्मस्यैव भ्रमत्ववृत्त्यावंशत्वमिति नियमादित्यभिप्रायेण दूषणान्तरमाह, 'वैशिष्ट्येति' 'प्रकारत्वेन' निरूपकत्वेन, 'भ्रमस्य' तादात्म्यारोपस्य, 'वैशिष्ट्यांशे' रजततादात्म्यारोपस्य वैशिष्ट्यांशे, 'प्रमात्वाप्रमात्वेति रजतमात्रनिरूपितविषयताव्यक्त्यधिकरणत्वमादाय प्रमात्वप्रसङ्गः तस्याः स्वनिरूपकाधिकरणवृत्तित्वात्, शुक्तिमात्रनिरूपितविषयताव्यक्तिमादायैव च भ्रमत्वप्रसङ्गः तस्याः स्वनिरूपकानधिकरणवृत्तित्वादित्यर्थः। 'स्वव्य-

ण्यनुभवः प्रमा। प्रमेयमिदमिति ज्ञाने प्रमेयत्वप्रकारकविषयतानाश्रयस्याप्रसिद्ध्याव्याप्तेः। न च संयोगित्वादिना प्रमेयत्वप्रकारकविषयताव्यतिरेको घटादौ प्रसिद्ध इति वाच्यं। प्रतियोगितावच्छेदकरूपवत्त्वेन प्रतियोगिज्ञानस्याभावधीहेतुत्वात्। किञ्च यत्किञ्चिद्व्यधिकरणप्रकारानवच्छिन्नत्वं भ्रमसाधारणं, प्रकृतज्ञानव्यधिकरणप्रकारानवच्छिन्नत्वं निर्विकल्पकाव्याप्तं तस्य निष्प्रकारकत्वादिति।

धिकरणेति स्वविषयतानधिकरणवृत्तिधर्म्माप्रकारकोऽनुभव इत्यर्थः। 'संयोगित्वादिनेति संयोगित्वादिना व्यधिकरणधर्म्मेणेत्यर्थः, अप्रकारकत्वमपि व्यधिकरणधर्म्मावच्छिन्नप्रतियोगिताकाभाव एव वाच्यः तेन प्रमामात्रे नासम्भव इति भावः। अत्र भ्रमातिव्याप्तौ सत्यामेव दोषमाह, 'प्रतियोगितावच्छेदकेति, तथाच व्यधिकरणधर्म्मावच्छिन्नाभावे मानाभावादिति भावः। 'यत्किञ्चिदिति यत्किञ्चिज्ज्ञानीयविषयताव्यधिकरणधर्म्माप्रकारकत्वमित्यर्थः,'भ्रमसाधारणमिति, इदं रजतमित्यादिभ्रमेऽपि द्रव्यमित्यादिज्ञानीयविषयताव्यधिकरणधर्म्माप्रकारकत्वस्य सत्त्वादिति भावः। 'प्रकृतज्ञानेति प्रकृतज्ञानीयविषयताव्यधिकरणधर्म्माप्रकारकत्वमित्यर्थः, 'निष्प्रकारकत्वादिति, विषयतायाः विशेष्यमात्रनिष्ठत्वनियमेन निष्प्रकारकज्ञाने विषयताविरहादिति भावः। न च स्वविषयताव्यधिकरणधर्म्मप्रकारकं यद्यत्

इति श्रीमद्गङ्गेशोपाध्यायविरचिते तत्त्वचिन्तामणौ प्रत्यक्षखण्डे प्रमालक्षणपूर्वपक्षः ।

तदन्यत्वं लक्षणमस्तु तथाच न निर्विकल्पकाव्याप्तिरिति वाच्यं तथापि भ्रमांशप्रमानुपपत्त्यापत्तेः (१) इति दिक् ।

इति श्रीमथुरानाथतर्कवागीशविरचिते तत्त्वचिन्तामणिरहस्ये प्रत्यक्षखण्डरहस्ये प्रमालक्षणपूर्वपक्षरहस्यम् ॥

(१) भ्रमांशप्रमानपग्रहापत्तेरिति ख० ।

अथ प्रमालक्षणसिद्धान्तः ।

उच्यते । यत्र यदस्ति तत्र तस्यानुभवः प्रमा । तद्वति तत्प्रकारकानुभवो वा ।

यत्र यन्नास्ति तत्र तस्य ज्ञानं तदभाववति तत्प्रकारकज्ञानं वा अप्रमा । तदन्यत्वे सत्यनुभवत्वमेव वा प्रमात्वं । तत्प्रकारकत्वञ्च तद्वैशिष्ट्यविषयकत्वं,

अथ प्रमालक्षणसिद्धान्तरहस्यं ।

'यत्र यदस्तीति अस्तित्वं सम्बन्धित्वमात्रं न त्वाधेयत्वं तथाच यत् यत्सम्बन्धीति फलितार्थः । तेन गगने शब्द इत्याद्यवृत्ति-प्रमायां नाव्याप्तिः(१) । 'तत्रेति निरूपितत्वं सप्तम्यर्थः, अन्वयश्चास्य 'तस्येतिषष्ठ्यर्थविषयतायां, तन्निरूपित-तन्निष्ठविषयताप्रतियोग्यनुभव इत्यर्थः, तथाच तत्सम्बन्धिनिरूपित-तन्निष्ठविषयताप्रतियोग्यनुभवत्वं तत्र तत्प्रमात्वमिति समुदितार्थः । सम्बन्धिता विषयता च प्रमात्वनियामकसम्बन्धेन ग्राह्या तेन संयोगसम्बन्धेन वह्न्यादिमति पर्वतादौ समवायसम्बन्धेन वह्न्यादिभ्रमे नातिव्याप्तिः, न वा

(१) अस्तित्वस्य अधिकरणत्वरूपत्वे आधेयत्वस्य वृत्त्यनियामकसम्बन्धतया तत्सम्बन्धावच्छिन्नाधिकरणताप्रसिद्ध्या गगने शब्द इत्यादिज्ञानस्य प्रमात्वानुपपत्तिरिति भावः ।

तद्विशेषणज्ञानजन्यत्वं वा । ईश्वरस्य तद्विशिष्टविषयं ज्ञानं न तु तत्प्रकारकं । निर्विकल्पकञ्च प्रमाप्रमा-बहिर्भूतमेव व्यवहारानङ्गत्वात् । अव्यपदेश्यपदेन तदुपग्रहस्य नाम-जात्यादियोजनारहितमपि प्रत्यक्ष-मस्तीत्यत्र तात्पर्य्यं । इदं रजतमिति ज्ञानमिदन्त्ववति

तत्संसर्गकज्ञानस्य तत्प्रमात्वापत्तिः[१] सांसर्गिकविषयतायाः सम्बन्धा-नवच्छिन्नत्वात् । एतेन तत्र प्रमात्वनियामकसम्बन्धेन सम्बन्धित्वं सप्तम्यर्थो विषयत्वं वा, आद्ये यत् यत्सम्बन्धि तत्सम्बन्धिनस्तस्यानुभवः तत्र तस्य प्रमेति पर्य्यवसितं तथाच शुक्ताविदं रजतमिति संसर्गा-रोपस्यापि रजते रजतत्वप्रकारकप्रमात्वापत्तिः तस्यापि रजतसम्बन्धि-रजतत्वविषयत्वात् । द्वितीये यत् यत्सम्बन्धि तद्विषयकस्तदनु-भवस्तत्र तस्य प्रमेति पर्य्यवसितं तथाच रजत-रङ्गयोरिमे रङ्ग-रजते इति विपरीतभ्रमस्यापि रजते रजतत्वप्रमात्वापत्तिः इत्यादिदूषणम् अपास्तम् । अथ यथोक्तनिर्व्विकल्पकेऽव्याप्तिः, जाति-व्यक्तिनिर्व्वि-कल्पकविषयतायाः परस्परं निरूप्य-निरूपकभावे मानाभावात्, परन्तु जाति-व्यक्त्योरुभयनिष्ठा एकैव निर्विकल्पकविषयता लाघवा-दधिकरणस्य चानिरूपकत्वादिति चेत् । न । निर्विकल्पकालक्ष्य-त्वस्यानुपदं ग्रन्थकृतैव वक्ष्यमाणत्वादन्यथा द्वितीयलक्षणेऽपि तत्रा-व्याप्तेर्दुर्वारत्वादिति दिक् ।

---

(१) तत्संसर्गकज्ञानस्य संसर्गांशेऽपि प्रमात्वापत्तिरिति ख० ।

नन्वेवं तद्विशेष्यकज्ञानस्यापि तत्प्रमात्वापत्तिः। न चेष्टापत्तिः, तत्प्रकारकज्ञान एव तत्प्रमाव्यवहारादित्यस्वरसात् लक्षणान्तरमाह, 'तद्वतीति, विशेष्यित्वं सप्तम्यर्थः। न चैवं तद्वद्विशेष्यकत्वे सति तत्प्रकारकत्वं इति फलितं तच्च रजत-रङ्गयोरिमे रङ्ग-रजते इत्यादि-विपरीतसमूहालम्बनभ्रमेऽतिव्याप्तिरिति वाच्यं। विशेष्यित्वस्य सप्तम्यर्थस्य अवच्छिन्नतासम्बन्धेन तत्प्रकारकतायामन्वयात् तथाच तद्वद्विशेष्यकत्वावच्छिन्नतत्प्रकारकताशाल्यनुभवस्तत्प्रमेति फलितं। अवच्छिन्नत्वञ्च इदमेतद्विशेष्यकत्वांशे एतत्प्रकारकमिति प्रतीतिसाक्षिकः स्वरूपसम्बन्धविशेषः, विपरीतभ्रमे च रजतविशेष्यकत्वावच्छिन्नं न रजतत्वप्रकारकत्वं अपि तु रङ्गविशेष्यकत्वावच्छिन्नं। वस्तुतस्तु 'तद्वतीत्यत्र विशेष्यितासम्बन्धेनावच्छिन्नत्वमेव सप्तम्यर्थः, अन्वयश्चास्य तत्प्रकारकत्वे, तथाच विशेष्यितासम्बन्धेन तदवच्छिन्ना या तत्प्रकारिता तच्छाल्यनुभवत्वं तत्प्रमात्वमिति फलितं। इदमंशे एतत्प्रकारकमिति प्रतीत्या विशेष्यस्यापि विशेष्यितासम्बन्धेन तत्प्रकारितायामवच्छेदकत्वात्, विपरीतभ्रमे च रजतावच्छिन्नं न रजतत्वप्रकारकत्वमपि तु रङ्गावच्छिन्नं। न चैवमिदमंशांशे एतद्विशेष्यकमिति प्रतीत्या प्रकारितासम्बन्धेन प्रकारस्यापि विशेष्यितायामवच्छेदकतया प्रकारितासम्बन्धेन तदवच्छिन्ना या तद्विशेष्यिता तच्छाल्यनुभवत्वं तत्प्रमात्वं इत्यपि लक्षणमस्त्विति वाच्यं। विनिगमकाभावेन तयोरेव लक्षणत्वस्येष्टत्वात्। सर्वत्र तद्वत्ताप्रकारिता च प्रमात्वनियामकसम्बन्धेन ग्राह्या तेन संयोगादिसम्बन्धेन वह्न्यादिमति पर्व्वतादौ समवायादिना तद्बुद्धौ नातिव्याप्तिः।

प्रकारभेदेनेव सम्बन्धभेदेनापि प्रमालक्षणभेदस्येष्टत्वात्। तदत्ता च तन्निरूपितसम्बन्धिता, न तु तन्निरूपिताधारतामात्रं, तेन स्वत्व-नियामकसम्बन्धेन प्रमायां नाव्याप्तिः। समवायस्यैकत्वेऽपि समवाय-सम्बन्धावच्छिन्नरूपनिरूपितसम्बन्धितायाः वायावभावात् न वायू रूपवानित्यादिसमवायसंसर्गकरूपादिभ्रमेऽतिव्याप्तिः[१]। सम्बन्धिता च धर्मितापरनाम्नी आधाराधारसाधारणः सम्बन्धिमात्रसाधा-रणः स्वरूपसम्बन्धविशेषः। न चैवं गुण-कर्मान्यत्वविशिष्टसत्ता-वान् गुण इत्यादिसमवायसंसर्गकज्ञानस्यापि सत्तायाः प्रमात्वापत्तिः गुणादावपि समवायसम्बन्धेन सत्तानिरूपितसम्बन्धित्वसत्त्वादिति वाच्यं। शुद्धसत्तायाः समवायसम्बन्धेन प्रमात्वस्य तत्रेष्टत्वात्, विशिष्टसत्ता-त्वावच्छिन्नसत्तायाः समवायसम्बन्धेन प्रमात्वस्यैव तत्रानभ्युपगमात्, तत्सम्बन्धेन तद्धर्मविशिष्टतन्निरूपितसम्बन्धितावति तत्सम्बन्धेन तद्ध-र्मविशिष्टतत्प्रकारकोऽनुभवः[२] तत्सम्बन्धेन तद्धर्मविशिष्टतत्प्रमेति विशिष्टप्रमाया लक्षणत्वात्। अतएव विशिष्टवैशिष्ट्यमितिरीत्या गुणा-द्यन्यत्वविशिष्टसत्तावत्द्रव्यमिति धीरेव विशिष्टसत्तात्वविशिष्टस्य प्रमा, न तु विशेष्ये विशेषणमिति रीत्या गुणाद्यन्यत्वविशिष्टसत्तावत् द्रव्य-मितिधीर्विशिष्टसत्तात्वविशिष्टप्रमा, किन्तु सत्ताव्यक्तेरेव प्रमा। न चेदमेव सर्व्वसाधारणं लक्षणमस्तु किं विशिष्टाविशिष्टभेदात्लक्षणद्वयेनेति वाच्यं। अयं घट इत्यादौ स्वरूपतो घटत्वादिप्रमायामव्याप्त्यापत्तेः,

---

(१) तथाच सम्बन्धिसत्त्वं प्रति सम्बन्धि-सम्बन्धोभयसत्त्वं नियामकमिति भावः।

(२) तद्धर्म्मविशिष्टतन्निरूपितवैशिष्ट्यविषयताशाल्यनुभव इति सं।

तत्र घटत्वादौ धर्मान्तरवैशिष्ट्याभानादिति भावः । 'तत्र तस्येति तन्निरूपिततन्निष्ठविषयताप्रतियोगिज्ञानं तत्र तद्भ्रम इत्यर्थः, तथाच तदभाववन्निरूपिततन्निष्ठविषयताप्रतियोगिज्ञानत्वं तद्भ्रमत्वमिति समुदितार्थः । स्मृतेरपि भ्रमतया अनुभवत्वमपहाय ज्ञानत्वप्रवेशः । नन्वेवमत्र रजतत्वमित्यादिरजतत्वविशेष्यकभ्रमस्यापि रजतत्वभ्रमत्वापत्तिः। न चेष्टापत्तिः, प्रकारीभूतधर्मांश एव भ्रमव्यवहारादित्यत आह, 'तदभाववतीति, विशेष्यत्वं सप्तम्यर्थः । न चैवं तदभाववद्विशेष्यकत्वे सति तत्प्रकारकं ज्ञानं तद्भ्रम इति फलितं, तच्च रजतरङ्गे इति समूहालम्बनप्रमायामतिव्याप्तमिति वाच्यं । सप्तम्यर्थस्य विशेष्यित्वस्यावच्छिन्नतासम्बन्धेन तत्प्रकारकतायामन्वयात्, तथा च तद्व्यक्तित्वावच्छिन्नप्रतियोगिताकाभाववद्विशेष्यकत्वावच्छिन्नतद्व्यक्तिप्रकारिताशालिज्ञानं तद्व्यक्तेर्भ्रम इति फलितं । यद्वा 'तदभाववतीत्यत्र विशेष्यितासम्बन्धेनावच्छिन्नत्वमेव सप्तम्यर्थः, तथा च विशेष्यितासम्बन्धेन तद्व्यक्तित्वावच्छिन्नप्रतियोगिताकाभाववदवच्छिन्ना या तद्व्यक्तिप्रकारिता तच्छालि ज्ञानं तद्व्यक्तेर्भ्रम इति फलितं । शेषं पूर्वोक्तदिशावसेयं । अभावः, प्रकारिता च भ्रमत्वनियामकसम्बन्धेन ग्राह्या तेन समवायादिसम्बन्धेन वह्न्याद्यभाववति पर्वतादौ संयोगादिना तद्बुद्धौ नातिव्याप्तिः । प्रतियोगिताकान्तोपादानात् न वैशिष्ट्यव्यासज्यवृत्तिधर्मावच्छिन्नप्रतियोगिताकाभावमादाय प्रमामात्रे नातिप्रसङ्गः[१] । न चैवं गुण-कर्मान्यत्वविशिष्टसत्तावान् गुण इत्यादि-

---

(१) द्रव्यत्ववत्यपि घटे पटवृत्तित्वविशिष्टद्रव्यत्वाभावस्य द्रव्यत्व-गुणत्वोभयाभावस्य च सत्त्वात द्रव्यं घट इत्यादि प्रमायामतिव्याप्त्यापत्तेरिति भावः।

समवायसंसर्गकज्ञानस्य सत्ताधमत्वं न स्यात् तद्व्यक्तित्वावच्छिन्नप्रतियोगिताकसत्ताव्यक्त्यभावस्य गुणादावभावादिति वाच्यं। समवायसम्बन्धेन स्वरूपतः सत्ताव्यक्तेर्भ्रमत्वाभावस्य तत्रेष्टत्वात्, विशिष्टसत्तात्वावच्छिन्नसत्तायाः समवायसम्बन्धेन भ्रमत्वस्यैव तत्राभ्युपगमात्, तत्सम्बन्धावच्छिन्न-तद्धर्म्मावच्छिन्नप्रतियोगिताकतदभाववति तत्सम्बन्धेन तद्धर्म्मविशिष्ट-तत्प्रकारकज्ञानं(१) तद्धर्म्मरूपेण तद्भ्रम इति विशिष्टभ्रमस्य लक्षणत्वात्। न चेदमेव सर्व्वसाधारणं लक्षणमस्तु किं विशिष्टाविशिष्टभेदात् लक्षणद्वयेन इति वाच्यं। इदं रजतमित्यादौ स्वरूपतोरजतत्वादिभ्रमे अव्याप्त्यापत्तेः, तत्र रजतत्वादौ धर्म्मान्तरवैशिष्ट्याभानात्। अतएव वह्नित्वरूपेण वह्निसामान्यप्रकारकस्य पर्व्वतो वह्निमानिति ज्ञानस्य वह्नित्वरूपेण महानसीयवह्न्यादेर्भ्रमत्वाभावेऽपि स्वरूपतो महानसीयवह्न्यादेर्भ्रमत्वं सर्व्वसिद्धं। अतएव च विशेष्ये विशेषणमिति रीत्या समवायसम्बन्धेन गुणाद्यन्यत्वविशिष्टसत्तावान् गुण इति धीर्न भ्रमस्तत्र विशिष्टनिरूपितप्रकारिताविरहेण विशिष्टभ्रमत्वाभावात् सत्ताव्यक्तित्वावच्छिन्नाभाववति सत्ताव्यक्तिप्रकारकत्वाभावेन तद्व्यक्तिभ्रमत्वाभावाच्च, तादृशमेव ज्ञानं उपलक्षणविधया गुणाद्यन्यत्वप्रकारकमिति गीयते, विशिष्टस्य वैशिष्ट्यमिति रीत्या तादृशज्ञानन्तु विशेषणविधया गुणाद्यन्यत्वप्रकारकं ज्ञानं तच्च विशिष्टस्य भ्रमः, न तु सत्ताव्यक्तेरिति विषयविभागः। ननु तथापि सत्ता गुणवृत्तिरितिप्रतीतेर्भ्रमत्वं दुर्व्वारं विशिष्टसत्तायां गुणवृत्तित्वा-

(१) तत्सम्बन्धावच्छिन्न-तद्धर्म्मावच्छिन्नप्रतियोगिताकतदभाववति तत्सम्बन्धेन तद्धर्म्मविशिष्टनिरूपितवैशिष्ट्यविषयताशालि ज्ञानं इति ख०, ग०।

भावसत्त्वेन तदनतिरिक्तायां सत्तायामपि गुणवृत्तित्वाभावसत्त्वात्। न च सत्तायां विशिष्टसत्तात्वावच्छेदेन गुणवृत्तित्वाभावेपि सत्तात्वावच्छेदेन गुणवृत्तित्वसत्त्वात् वक्ष्यमाणरीत्या वृक्षः संयोगवानिति ज्ञानस्येव न भ्रमत्वमपि तु प्रमात्वमेवेति वाच्यं। तथा सति गुणकर्म्मान्यत्वविशिष्टसत्ता गुणवृत्तिरिति प्रतीतेरपि स्वरूपसम्बन्धेन गुणवृत्तित्वभ्रमत्वाभाव-तत्प्रमात्वयोरापत्तेः सत्तायां गुणवृत्तित्वस्याव्याप्यवृत्तित्वे गुणवृत्तित्वाभाववती सत्ता गुणवृत्तित्वाभावः सत्तावृत्तिरित्यपि प्रतीत्यापत्तेश्चेति चेत्। न। अतएवानुपपत्त्या गुणादौ विशिष्टसत्तानिरूपिताधारताविरहेऽपि विशिष्टसत्तायां गुणाद्याधेयत्वमस्त्येवेत्यभ्युपगमात्, तथा च सत्ता गुणवृत्तिर्विशिष्टसत्ता गुणवृत्तिरिति प्रतीतिद्वयमेव न भ्रमः, किन्तु प्रमैवेत्ति न काप्यनुपपत्तिः।

नव्यास्तु यावतीस्तद्व्यक्तीः प्रातिस्विकरूपेणोपादाय तत्तद्व्यक्तिविशेष्यक-तत्प्रकारकानुभवस्तत्प्रमेति प्रथमलक्षणार्थः। नन्वेवं विशेष्यव्यक्तिभेदेन प्रमात्वानन्त्यमतो द्वितीयं, भ्रमलक्षणद्वयमप्येवमेव योजनीयं। सर्व्वमन्यत् पूर्व्ववदिति प्राहुः।

'तदन्यत्वे सतीति यावद्भ्रमभिन्नत्वे सति तत्प्रकारकानुभवत्वमित्यर्थः। तद्विशेष्यक-तत्संसर्गकज्ञानयोः निर्विकल्पकस्य च व्युदासाय प्रकारकत्वान्तर्भावः। न चैवं विषयान्तरांशे भ्रमरूपायां प्रमायामव्याप्तिरिति वाच्यं। अतांशिकभ्रमस्यालक्ष्यत्वादिति भावः। वस्तुतस्तु यद्‌यज्ज्ञानं तस्य भ्रम एव न तु तस्य प्रमा तत्तज्ज्ञानव्यक्तिभिन्नत्वे सति तत्प्रकारकानुभवत्वं तस्य प्रमात्वमित्यर्थः। तेनां-

तदनुभवत्वात् प्रमा, रजतत्वाभाववति तत्प्रकारक-
ज्ञानत्वादप्रमा, अंशे समूहालम्बनञ्च नाप्रमा । एक-

त्रिकभ्रमरूपाया अपि प्रमायाः संग्रहः इत्येव तत्त्वं । एतच्चासर्व्वज्ञस्य दुर्ज्ञेयत्वादनादेयं । ननु तत्प्रकारकत्वं तद्धर्म्मकत्वं तथा च रजतत्वादिप्रमा-भ्रमयोरव्याप्तिः प्रमात्व-भ्रमत्वनियामकसम्बन्धेन रजतत्वादेर्ज्ञानाधर्म्मत्वात् साकारवादिभिरेव रजतत्वादेर्ज्ञानधर्म्मत्वाभ्युपगमादित्यत आह, 'तत्प्रकारकत्वञ्चेति, 'तद्वैशिष्ट्यविषयकत्वमिति तद्विशेषणकत्वमित्यर्थः, विशेषणता च विशेष्यतावत् स्वरूपसम्बन्धविशेष इति भावः । एतेन सामान्यतस्तद्वैशिष्ट्यविषयकत्वं यदि तत्प्रकारकत्वं तदा दण्ड-पुरुषसंयोग इति समूहालम्बनस्यापि दण्डादिप्रकारकत्वापत्तिः, यदि च संसर्गमर्य्यादया तद्वैशिष्ट्यावगाहित्वं तदा तद्विशेष्यकज्ञानस्यापि तत्प्रकारकत्वापत्तिरिति दूषणमपास्तं । यदिचेश्वरज्ञानं प्रमाप्रमावहिर्भूतमेवेति पचस्तदाह, 'तद्विशेषणेति 'ज्ञानपदं सम्पातायातं तद्विशेषणकत्वे सति अन्यत्वमित्यर्थः । 'ईश्वरस्येति, अत इत्यादि । ननूक्तलक्षणानां निर्व्विकल्पकेऽव्याप्तिरित्यत आह, 'निर्व्विकल्पकञ्चेति, 'व्यवहारेति प्रवृत्त्यादीत्यर्थः । नन्वेवं "इन्द्रियार्थसन्निकर्षोत्पन्नमव्यपदेश्यमव्यभिचारिव्यवसायात्मकं ज्ञानं प्रत्यक्षं" इति प्रत्यक्षप्रमालक्षणसूत्रे प्रत्यक्षप्रमामध्ये निर्व्विकल्पकस्य गणनमसङ्गतमित्यत आह, 'अव्यपदेश्येति, 'तदुपग्रहस्येति निर्व्विकल्पकाभिधानस्येत्यर्थः, 'नाम-जात्यादीति नाम-जात्यादीनां या 'योजना' वैशिष्ट्यं, तदविषयकमपीत्यर्थः, तथा च तत्सूत्रस्य इन्द्रियार्थसन्निकर्षोत्पन्नमव्यभिचारि ज्ञानं

प्रकाराभाववत्यपि तदप्रतीतेः। नन्वेवमव्याप्यवृत्तिभावाभावयोरेकत्र प्रमाप्रमा च स्यात् तदभाववति तत्प्रकारकज्ञानत्वादिति चेत्। न। भिन्न-भिन्नावच्छेदेन

प्रत्यक्षप्रमा, सा च द्विविधा 'अव्यपदेश्यं' निर्विकल्पकं ज्ञानं, 'व्यवसायात्मकं' विशिष्टज्ञानात्मकं ज्ञानञ्चेति नार्थः अव्यभिचारित्वस्य यथार्थत्वरूपतया लक्षणस्याव्याप्त्यापत्तेः निर्विकल्पकस्य व्यवहारानङ्गत्वाच्च। किन्तु इन्द्रियार्थसन्निकर्षोत्पन्नमव्यभिचारि यथार्थं यज्ज्ञानं तत्प्रत्यक्षप्रमेति प्रत्यक्षप्रमालक्षणं, प्रत्यक्षप्रमाया लक्षणमुक्त्वा परमतनिराकरणाय प्रत्यक्षसामान्यं विभजते, 'अव्यपदेश्यमिति, प्रत्यक्षन्तु द्विविधं अव्यपदेश्यं व्यवसायात्मकञ्चेत्येव तद्व्याख्येयमिति भावः। नन्वेवं शुक्ताविदं रजतमिति ज्ञानमेकस्मिन् विशेष्ये इदन्त्वस्य प्रमा, रजतत्वस्य च भ्रमः स्यादित्यत आह, 'इदमिति, 'अंशे' एकस्मिन्नेव विशेष्यांशे, 'समूहालम्बनञ्चेति घट-पटावित्यादि समूहालम्बनञ्चेत्यर्थः। 'एकप्रकाराभाववत्यपीति घटत्वाभाववति घटत्वप्रकारकत्वस्य पटत्वाभाववति पटत्वप्रकारकत्वस्य च विरहादित्यर्थः। 'भावाभावयोरिति, स्वानवच्छेदकावच्छेदेन ज्ञानमिति शेषः, 'एकत्र' एकस्मिन्नेव विशेष्ये, तथा च मूले वृक्षः कपिसंयोगीति ज्ञानस्य वृत्ते प्रमात्वाप्रमात्वोभयप्रसङ्गः, तथा अग्रे वृक्षः कपिसंयोगाभाववान् इति ज्ञानस्यापीत्यर्थः। लीलावतीकारमते संयोगस्य व्याप्यवृत्तितया तन्मतमाश्रित्यैव समाधत्ते, 'भिन्न-भिन्नेति, 'संयोग-तदभावौ नेति

हि वृक्षे संयोग-तदभावौ न वृक्षमात्रे विरोधादननु-भवाच्च। तथा च यत्र वृक्षे संयोगो न तत्र तदभावः, यदवच्छेदेन यत्र यदस्तीति वा विवक्षितं। गोत्वादेरपि

च्छेदः, भिन्न-भिन्नावच्छेदेन वृक्षे संयोग-तदभावौ न स इत्यर्थः, 'वृक्षमात्रे' सर्व्वस्मिन्नेव वृक्षे, 'विरोधादिति कपिसंयोग-तदभावयोः सत्त्वासम्भवादित्यर्थः, प्रतियोग्यत्यन्ताभावयोः सामान्यत एव विरोधस्य क्लृप्तत्वादिति भावः। 'अननुभवाच्चेति वृक्षे कपिसंयोग-तदभावयोरनुभवविरहाच्चेत्यर्थः। मूले वृक्षे न कपिसंयोग-इति प्रतीतिर्हि घटे वृक्षे न कपिसंयोग-इति प्रतीतिवत् वृक्षवृत्तित्वस्यावच्छेदकतासम्बन्धेनाभावमेव मूले अवगाहते न तु वृक्ष एव कपिसंयोगाभावमिति भावः। 'तथाचेति, 'संयोगः' कपिसंयोगः, एवञ्च वृक्षे कपिसंयोगवत्त्वज्ञानं प्रमैव, तदभाववत्त्वज्ञानञ्च भ्रम एवेति भावः।

संयोगस्याव्याप्यवृत्तित्वमतमाश्रित्य समाधत्ते, 'यदवच्छेदेनेति यदवच्छेदेन यत्र यदस्ति तदवच्छेदेन तत्र तस्यानुभवः तत्प्रमेत्यर्थः, तथाच मूले वृक्षः कपिसंयोगीति ज्ञानं न प्रमा अपि तु भ्रमः, तथा अग्रे वृक्षः कपिसंयोगाभाववान् इति ज्ञानमपीति भावः। एतच्च प्रथमलक्षणाभिप्रायेण, द्वितीयलक्षणे तु यदवच्छेदेन यत्र यदस्ति तदवच्छेदेन तद्वति तत्प्रकारकानुभवस्तत्प्रमेति वक्तव्यमिति भावः।

केचित्तु विशिष्टस्यातिरिक्तत्वमतमाश्रित्य समाधत्ते, 'भिन्न-भिन्नेति अग्र-मूलादिरूपभिन्न-भिन्नावयवविशिष्टे हि वृक्षे कपिसंयोग-

साक्षाद्यवच्छेदेन वृत्तेः। पाकरक्ते श्यामोऽयमिति धीः प्रमैव कदाचित्तत्र तत्सत्त्वात् इदानीं श्याम इति तु

तदभावावित्यर्थः, 'न वृत्तमात्र इति न त्वेकस्मिन्नेव मूलदृक्षे तदुभयमित्यर्थः, 'विरोधादिति प्रतियोगि-तदभावयोर्विरोधादित्यर्थः, 'अननुभवाच' एकस्मिन्नेव मूलवृक्षे तयोरनुभवविरहाच्चेत्यर्थः। 'तथाचेति, इत्यत्र मूले वृत्तः कपिसंयोगीतिज्ञानं भ्रम एव न तु प्रमा मूलविशिष्टे वृत्ते कपिसंयोगवत्त्वविरहात्, तथा अये वृत्तः कपिसंयोगाभाववानिति ज्ञानमपीति भावः। विशिष्टस्यानतिरिक्तत्वमतमाश्रित्य समाधत्ते, 'यदवच्छेदेनेति, इत्याहुः।

नन्वेवं गोत्वादेर्व्याप्यवृत्तिधर्मस्य प्रमायामव्याप्तिस्तस्यावच्छेदकविरहादित्यत आह, 'गोत्वादेरपीति। नन्वेवं पाकरक्ते घटे कालान्तरे अयं श्याम इति धीः प्रमा स्यादित्यत्रेष्टापत्तिमाह, 'पाकेति, 'श्यामोऽयं' कालान्तरे श्यामोऽयं, 'कदाचित्' कालान्तरावच्छेदेन। 'अप्रमैव' न प्रमैव। ननु तदवच्छेदकावच्छेदेन तद्वति तत्प्रकारकानुभवत्वं तत्प्रमात्वं इत्युक्तावच्छेदकतानवगाहिनी धीः प्रमा न स्यात्। न च तदविषयकप्रत्ययोऽसिद्ध एवेति वाच्यम्। व्याप्यवृत्तिधर्मस्यावच्छेदकत्वाविषयिकाया अपि प्रतीतेः सर्व्वसिद्धत्वादव्याप्यवृत्तिधर्मस्यापि लौकिकप्रत्यक्ष एव प्राचीनैर्नियमतोऽवच्छेदकत्वविषयताभ्युपगमेन तदतिरिक्तप्रत्ययस्यावच्छेदकत्वाविषयकस्यापि सत्त्वाच्च। न च तदनवच्छेदकावच्छेदेन तत्र तत्प्रकारकत्वशून्यत्वे सति तद्वति तत्प्रकारकानुभवत्वं तत्र तत्प्रमात्वमिति

अप्रमैव। न च यत्तद्भ्यां लक्षणेऽननुगमः, न हि प्रमा सर्वत्र प्रमा, किन्तु क्वचित्तथाच किं ज्ञानं कुत्र प्रमेति तत्तद्विशेषस्य लक्ष्यत्वेन यत्तद्भ्यामेव लक्षणं युक्तं।

विवक्षितं, तत्रेत्युपादानादधिकरणान्तरे तदनवच्छेदकावच्छेदेन तत्प्रकारिकायां समूहालम्बनप्रमायां नाव्याप्तिरिति वाच्यम्। तथा च मूले अग्रे वृक्षः कपिसंयोगीति प्रमायां तत्तदभावावच्छेदकोभयावच्छेदेन तत्प्रकारिकायामव्याप्तिरिति चेत्। न। तदवच्छेदकावच्छेदेन तत्र तदप्रकारकत्वे सति यत् तदनवच्छेदकावच्छेदेन तत्र तत्प्रकारकत्वं तच्छून्यत्वे सतीति विवक्षितत्वात्। तदनवच्छेदकावच्छेदेन तत्र तत्प्रकारकत्वञ्च तत्र तदनवच्छेदकनिष्ठतद्वृत्तितदधिकरणतावच्छेदकत्वावगाहित्वे सति तत्र तत्प्रकारकत्वं, मूले वृक्षः कपिसंयोगीति ज्ञानञ्च मूले वृक्षवृत्तिकपिसंयोगाधारतावच्छेदकत्वावगाह्येवेति भावः। एतच्चापाततः, तथापि वृक्षः कपिसंयोगी अग्रे वृक्षः कपिसंयोगीति धीरुभयात्मिका स्यात् कपिसंयोगाभाववति कपिसंयोगप्रकारकत्वात्। न च तदवच्छिन्न निरवच्छिन्नतदभावाधिकरणतावति वा तत्प्रकारकज्ञानत्वं भ्रमत्वमिति विवक्षितमिति वाच्यं। मूले वृक्षः कपिसंयोगीत्यत्राव्याप्तेः आद्ये समवायादिसम्बन्धेन गगनादेर्भ्रमे अव्याप्तेश्च। न च तदभावावच्छेदकावच्छेदेन तत्प्रकारकत्वं विवक्षितमिति वाच्यं ; गुणः संयोगवानित्याद्यनवच्छेदकतामवगाहिभ्रमेऽव्याप्तेः। न च तदभावानवच्छेदकावच्छेदेन तत्र तत्प्रकारकत्वशून्यत्वे सति तदभाववति तत्प्रकारकत्वं विवक्षितं,

अन्ये तु अनुभवत्वमेव प्रामाण्यं। भ्रमेऽप्यंशमादाय प्रमाव्यवहारात् रजतादिप्रमाऽप्रमा च विशिष्य लक्ष-

---

वृक्षः संयोगीत्यवच्छेदकतानवगाहिप्रमायामतिव्याप्तेः। न च यथाविवक्षितप्रामाण्यशून्यत्वे सति तदभाववति तत्प्रकारकत्वं विवक्षितं, मूले अग्रे वृक्षः कपिसंयोगीत्यत्राव्याप्तेः। वस्तुतस्तु प्रमालक्षणे अवच्छेदकत्वं न निवेश्यते गौरवात् व्यर्थत्वाच्च, अपि तु तद्वति तत्प्रकारकानुभवत्वमेव प्रमात्वं, मूले वृक्षः कपिसंयोगवान् अग्रे वृक्षः कपिसंयोगाभाववानित्यादि ज्ञानस्य यदि केवलसमवाय-विशेषणताभ्यां वृक्षे संयोग-तदभाववावगाहेते, तदा वृक्षः कपिसंयोगवान् तदभाववांश्चेतिवद्वृक्षे तदुभयोः प्रमैव किन्तु मूलाग्रयोर्वृक्षवृत्तितदुभयाधारतावच्छेदकत्वावगाहित्वांश एव न प्रमा। यदि च मूलाग्रावच्छिन्नत्वविशिष्टसमवाय-विशेषणताभ्यां वृक्षे तावगाहेते तदा तु वृक्षे न तदुभयोः प्रमा तादृशविशिष्टसम्बन्धाभ्यां वृक्षस्य तदुभयवत्त्वविरहात् प्रमालक्षणे सम्बन्धभेदनिवेशस्य प्रागुक्तयुक्त्या आवश्यकत्वात्। एतेन पाकरक्ते घटे इदानीमयं श्यामरूपवान् तदानीमयं श्यामरूपाभाववान् इत्यादि ज्ञानमपि व्याख्यातं। न च तथापि वृक्षादिषु कपिसंयोग-तदभाववत्त्वादिबुद्धेः तत्र तयोर्भ्रमत्वमपि दुर्वारं तदभाववति तत्प्रकारकज्ञानस्यैव भ्रमत्वादिति वाच्यं। भ्रमलक्षणे तदभाववत्पदेन निरवच्छिन्नतदभावाधिकरणताया विवक्षितत्वात्। मूले वृक्षः कपिसंयोगवान् अग्रे वृक्षः कपिसंयोगाभाववान्

णीया रजतत्ववति तदनुभवः तदभाववति तदनुभवो वेत्यादिना[१]। नन्वनुभवत्वस्य प्रमाप्रमासाधारण्येन

इत्यादि ज्ञाने च[२] यदि केवलसमवायादिः सम्बन्धः तदा वृक्षे तदुभयोर्न भ्रमः किन्तु मूलादेर्वृत्त्यवृत्तिकपिसंयोग-तदभावाद्याधारतावच्छेदकत्वावगाहित्वांश एव भ्रमः। यदि च मूलावच्छिन्नत्वविशिष्टसमवायादिसम्बन्धस्तदा वृक्षे कपिसंयोगादेरपि भ्रम एव तादृशविशिष्टसम्बन्धावच्छिन्नकपिसंयोगाद्यभावस्य निरवच्छिन्नाधिकरणत्वस्यैव वृक्षे सत्त्वात्। एतेन पाकरक्तघटे इदानीमयं श्यामरूपवानित्यादि ज्ञानमपि व्याख्यातं। न च निरवच्छिन्नाधिकरणत्वस्य भ्रमलक्षणनिवेशे अन्योन्याभावस्य व्याप्यवृत्तित्वनियमवादिनये वृक्षः कपिसंयोगिभिन्न इति ज्ञानस्य भ्रमतया तत्राव्याप्तिः कपिसंयोगिभेदाभावस्य कपिसंयोगस्य[३] निरवच्छिन्नाधिकरणाप्रसिद्धेरिति वाच्यं। तन्नये[४] कपिसंयोगिभेदाभावो न कपिसंयोगस्वरूपः, किन्तु व्याप्यवृत्तिरतिरिक्त एवाभाव इत्यभ्युपगमात्[५]

---

(१) तज्ज्ञानं वेत्यादिनेति क०।

(२) मूले वृक्षः संयोगवान् अग्रे वृक्षः संयोगाभाववान् इत्यादिज्ञाने चेति क०।

(३) अत्यन्ताभावाभावस्य प्रतियोगिरूपत्वमिव अन्योन्याभावाभावस्य प्रतियोगितावच्छेदकरूपत्वमिति नियमात् इति भावः।

(४) अन्योन्याभावस्य व्याप्यवृत्तितानियमवादिनये इत्यर्थः।

(५) तथा च व्याप्यवृत्तिमद्भेदाभावस्यैव प्रतियोगितावच्छेदकरूपत्वं न त्वव्याप्यवृत्तिमद्भेदाभावस्य इति नियम इति भावः।

तज्ज्ञानस्य न निष्कम्पप्रवृत्त्यङ्गत्वमिति चेत् । सत्यं । विशेषविषयप्रमाया एव प्रवर्त्तकत्वात् । अतिरिक्तविष-

---

इत्यंव तत्त्वमिति समास' । 'सर्व्वत्र प्रमेति सर्व्वत्र सर्व्वस्य प्रमेत्यर्थः, 'किन्तु क्वचित्' किन्तु क्वचित् कस्यचित्, 'कुत्र प्रमेतीति कुत्र कस्य प्रमेत्यर्थः, जिज्ञासायामिति शेषः, 'लक्ष्यत्वेन' लक्षयितुमुचितत्वेन ।

नन्वेवं भ्रमेऽतिव्याप्तिरित्यतो लक्ष्यत्वेन परिहरति, 'भ्रमेऽपीति । 'विषयतेति विषयताश्रयावृत्त्यप्रकारकविषयताप्रतियोग्यनुभव इत्यर्थः, विषयताश्रयावृत्त्यप्रकारकस्यानुभव इति प्रतियोगित्वार्थक-षष्ठ्या समासात्, विषयताश्रयावृत्त्यप्रकारकोऽनुभवः प्रमेत्यसमस्त-पाठस्तु प्रामादिकः । यद्यपि 'विषयताश्रयावृत्तीत्यत्र विषयतापदं न विषयतासामान्यपरं रजतत्वादिभ्रमातिव्याप्तेः, समवायादि-सम्बन्धेनावृत्तेरेव समवायादिसम्बन्धेन विषयताश्रयावृत्तित्वात् तस्य धर्म्मितावच्छेदकांशे प्रमात्वेन लक्ष्यत्वाभ्युपगमे अनुभवत्वमात्र-स्यैव सम्यक्त्वेन प्रतियोग्यन्तविशेषणवैयर्थ्यात् । नापि स्वविषयतापरं स्वमनुभवः, रजत-रङ्गयोरिमे रङ्ग-रजते इति विपरीभ्रमेऽति-व्याप्तेः तद्विषयतायाः तदीयविषयताश्रयावृत्त्यप्रकारकत्वात् । तथापि स्वाश्रयावृत्तिप्रकारकान्यविषयताप्रतियोग्यनुभवत्वं विवक्षितं, स्वं विषयता, धर्म्मितावच्छेदकमात्रांशे प्रमारूपोभ्रमस्तु न लक्ष्यः तेन शुक्ताविदं रजतमित्यादिभ्रमे नाव्याप्तिः, धर्म्मितावच्छेदकातिरिक्तांशे प्रमारूपो भ्रमस्तु लक्ष्य एव तेन रङ्ग-रजतयोरिदमिदञ्च रजत-मित्यादिसमूहालम्बने विशेष्यतावच्छेदकभेदेन विषयताभेदेऽपि

यत्तापक्षे विषयताश्रयावृत्त्यप्रकारकानुभवः[१] प्रमा। केवलान्वयिनि विषयताश्रयावृत्तिरवृत्तिरेव प्रसिद्धः।

नातिव्याप्तिः, न वा रजतारजतयोर्द्वयं रजतमित्यादिज्ञाने अतिव्याप्तिः तत्रापि सत्त्वात्। नन्वेवं रजत एवेदं रजतं रङ्गञ्चेति भ्रमांश-प्रमायामव्याप्तिः तद्विषयतायाः स्वाश्रयावृत्तिरङ्गत्वप्रकारकतया तद-प्रकारकत्वाभावादिति वाच्यं। विशेष्यतावच्छेदकतातिरिक्तप्रकारता-भेदेनापि विषयताभेदाभ्युपगमात्। एतच्च ग्रन्थकृदेवाग्रे वक्ष्यति। विषयताया विशेष्यमात्रनिष्ठत्वोपगमात् निर्व्विकल्पके निर्विशेष्यके विषयताविरहान्न तत्रातिव्याप्तिः, सप्रकारकत्वेन वा अनुभवो वि-शेष्यः। 'स्वाश्रयावृत्तीत्यत्र च वृत्तित्वं स्वनिरूपकसम्बन्धेन सम्बन्धित्वं न तु सामान्यतो वृत्तित्वं घटे घटत्वमित्यादिप्रमायामव्याप्तेः। न हि घटत्वे घटो वर्त्तते, न च वृत्तित्वं सम्बन्धित्वमात्रं, स्वाश्रया-सम्बन्धिप्रकारकत्वस्याप्रसिद्धेः अवृत्तेरपि येन केनचित् सम्बन्धेन सम्बन्धित्वात्। स्वपदद्वयञ्च भेदप्रतियोगिविषयतापरं न तु प्रकृत-विषयतापरं, सर्व्वं प्रमेयं इति तादात्म्यसम्बन्धसंसर्गकप्रमायां भग-वज्ज्ञानं घटवदित्यादि विषयितासम्बन्धसंसर्गकप्रमायाञ्चाव्याप्तेः, तत्र स्वनिरूपकतादात्म्य-विषयितादिसम्बन्धेन स्वाश्रयासम्बन्धिनो-ऽप्रसिद्धेः। न च स्वपदद्वयस्य भेदप्रतियोगिपरत्वे संयोगादिव्यधि-करणसम्बन्धेन गुणादिविशेष्यक-घटादिभ्रमेऽतिव्याप्तेः तद्विषयताया

---

(१) विषयताश्रयावृत्त्यप्रकारकोऽनुभवः इति ख०।

यद्वा यत्प्रकारिका या विषयता तत्प्रकारसमानाधिकरणविषयताकः, स्वप्रकारसमानाधिकरणविषयताको वानुभवः प्रमा। यत्प्रकारिका या विषयता

अपि स्वनिरूपकसम्बन्धेन स्वाश्रये गुणे वर्त्तमानस्याप्रसिद्ध्या तादृशभेदकूटवत्त्वादिति वाच्यं। स्वनिरूपकसम्बन्धेन कस्यचिदधिकरणे वर्त्तमानत्वेन चरमविषयताविशेषणात्। ननु प्रमेयं रजतमित्यादिनिखिलप्रमेयविशेष्यकरजतत्वादिप्रकारकांशिकप्रमायामव्याप्तिः तद्विषयतायाः स्वनिरूपकसम्बन्धेन यत्किञ्चित्स्वाश्रयव्यक्तिवृत्तिप्रकारकतया तादृशभेदकूटवत्त्वविरहादित्यत आह, 'केवलान्वयिनीति व्यापकत्वरूपमवच्छिन्नत्वं सप्तम्यर्थः, अन्वयश्चास्य विषयतायां, केवलान्वयिधर्म्मावच्छिन्नविषयतायाः स्वनिरूपकसम्बन्धेन स्वाश्रयवृत्तिसामान्यभिन्न इत्यर्थः, 'अवृत्तिरेव प्रसिद्ध' इति स्वनिरूपकसम्बन्धेन अवृत्तिरेव प्रसिद्धः न तु प्रकारीभूतो रजतत्वादिरित्यर्थः, तथाच 'स्वाश्रयावृत्तिपदेन स्वाश्रयवृत्तिसमान्यभिन्नस्य विवक्षणान्नाव्याप्तिरिति भावः। ननु तथापि प्रकारतावच्छेदकैक्ये प्रकारभेदेन विषयताभेदाभावात् घटो रूपवानित्यादिनिखिलरूपादिप्रकारकप्रमायामव्याप्तिस्तद्विषयतायाः स्वाश्रयावृत्तिजलादिनिष्ठरूपादिप्रकारकतया तत्प्रकारकान्यत्वविरहात् इति चेदेतदस्वरसेनैव 'यद्वेत्यादिना लक्षणान्तरप्रणयनात्। वस्तुतस्तु 'स्वाश्रयावृत्तिप्रकारकपदेन स्वाश्रयवृत्तिनिष्ठत्वाभाववत्प्रकारताकं विवक्षितं तदन्यत्वमर्थः, इदं

तत्प्रकारव्यधिकरणविषयताकं, स्वप्रकारव्यधिकरणविषयताकं वा ज्ञानं[१] भ्रमः । प्रकारभेदेनैकत्र विषयताभेद इतिलक्षणद्वयसमावेशात् प्रमा-भ्रमसङ्करः ।

रजतमित्यादिभ्रमीयविषयतायाः रजतत्वादिनिष्ठप्रकारताव्यक्तेरेव तादृशनिष्ठत्वाभाववत्त्वान्नातिव्याप्तिः, रजत एवेदं रजतं रङ्गञ्चेति भ्रमांशप्रमीयविषयतायाः रङ्गत्वनिष्ठप्रकारताव्यक्तेस्तादृशनिष्ठत्वाभाववत्त्वेऽपि प्रकारताभेदेन विषयताभेदात् रजतत्वनिष्ठप्रकारताकविषयताव्यक्तिमादायैव लक्षणसमन्वयः, एवञ्चात्र निषेधद्वयप्रवेशाद्गौरवं प्रकारताभेदेन विषयताभेदाभावे रजत एवेदं रजतं रङ्गञ्चेति भ्रमांशप्रमाया असङ्ग्रहश्चेत्यस्वरसाद् 'यद्वेत्यादिना लक्षणान्तरप्रणयनमित्येव तत्त्वं ।

केचित्तु ननु निखिलप्रमेयविशेष्यक-संयोगादिसम्बन्धेन रजतत्वप्रकारकभ्रमे अतिव्याप्तिः तद्विषयतायाः केवलान्वयित्वेन स्वाश्रयावृत्तेरप्रसिद्धतया तत्प्रकारकान्यत्वादित्यत आह, 'केवलान्वयिनीति केवलान्वयिधर्मावच्छिन्नव्यधिकरणप्रकारकविषयतायाः स्वनिरूपकसम्बन्धेन स्वाश्रयावृत्तिरित्यर्थः, 'अवृत्तिरेव प्रसिद्ध इति स्वनिरूपकसम्बन्धेनावृत्तिः स्वप्रकारीभूतधर्म्म एव प्रसिद्ध इत्यर्थः, इत्याहुः ।

प्राञ्चस्तु ननु निखिलप्रमेयविशेष्यक-प्रमेयमित्यादिसामान्यप्रत्यासत्तिजप्रत्यक्षे अव्याप्तिः तत्र विषयताश्रयावृत्तेरप्रसिद्धेरित्यत

---

(१) यत्प्रकारिका या विषयता तत्प्रकारव्यधिकरणविषयताकः स्वप्रकारव्यधिकरणविषयताको वानुभव इति ख० ग० ।

यद्वा विशेष्यनिष्ठात्यन्ताभावाप्रतियोगिप्रकारक-विषयताप्रतियोगी, विशेष्यनिष्ठात्यन्ताभावप्रतियोगि-प्रकारानवच्छिन्नविषयत्वप्रतियोगी वा, विषयतासमा-नाधिकरणात्यन्ताभावप्रतियोगिप्रकारकविषयत्वाप्रति-

---

आह, 'केवलान्वयिनीति निरूपितत्वं सप्तम्यर्थः, केवलान्वयिधर्म-निरूपितविषयतायाः स्वनिरूपकसम्बन्धेन स्वाश्रयावृत्तिरित्यर्थः, 'अवृत्तिरेव प्रसिद्ध इति स्वनिरूपकविशेषणताविशेषसम्बन्धेनावृत्तिरेव प्रसिद्ध इत्यर्थः, इति व्याचख्युः। तदसत्प्रागुक्तयुक्त्या स्वपदस्य भेद-प्रतियोगिपरत्वावश्यकतया विषयताश्रयावृत्तेरप्रसिद्धावपि अव्याप्ति-विरहादिति दिक्।

'तत्प्रकारसमानाधिकरणेति प्रकारपदं धर्मपरं, तद्धर्मसमाना-धिकरण-तद्विषयताक इत्यर्थः, 'अनुभवः प्रमा' इत्यग्रेतनमत्रापि सम्बध्यते, 'प्रमा' तद्धर्मस्य प्रमा। यत्तद्भ्यां विषयताया उभयथा प्रवेशे गौरवादाह, 'स्वप्रकारेति, 'स्वं' विषयता, प्रकारता च धर्मितावच्छेदकतातिरिक्ता ग्राह्या, तेनेदं रजतमित्यादिभ्रमे नाति-व्याप्तिः, तस्यापि लक्ष्यत्वे अनुभवत्वमात्रस्यैव सम्यक्त्वात्। एतल्ल-क्षणद्वये इदं रजतं रङ्गञ्चेत्यादौ प्रकारभेदेन विषयताभेदाभावेऽपि न क्षतिरिति ध्येयं। अतिरिक्तविषयतापक्षे प्रमां लक्षयित्वा भ्रमं लक्षयति, 'यत्प्रकारिकेति, 'तत्प्रकारव्यधिकरणविषयताक इति 'प्रकारः' धर्मः, तद्धर्माधिकरणावृत्तितद्विषयताकं ज्ञानं भ्रम इत्यर्थः, अत्रेऽपि 'स्वप्रकारव्यधिकरणत्वं' स्वप्रकाराधिकरणावृत्तित्वं,

योगी वा, विषयतासमानाधिकरणात्यन्ताभावप्रतियोगिप्रकारानवच्छिन्नविषयताप्रतियोगी वानुभवः प्रमा। स्वसमानाधिकरणप्रकारानवच्छिन्नविषयताप्रतियोगि ज्ञानं, स्वव्यधिकरणप्रकारावच्छिन्नविषयताप्रतियोगि

रजतारजतसाधारणधर्म्मद्रव्यविशेष्यकं द्रव्यं रजतमित्यादि ज्ञानन्तु न रजतत्वादिभ्रमः (१)।

मिश्रास्तु 'तत्प्रकारव्यधिकरणत्वं' तत्प्रकारानधिकरणवृत्तित्वं, अग्रेऽपि 'स्वप्रकारव्यधिकरणत्वं' स्वप्रकारानधिकरणवृत्तित्वं, तथाच द्रव्यं रजतमित्यादि ज्ञानमपि रजतत्वस्य भ्रमः इत्याहुः।

प्राथमिकप्रमालक्षणं द्वितीयभ्रमलक्षणञ्चाभिप्रेत्याह, 'प्रकारभेदेनेति विशेष्यतावच्छेदकतातिरिक्तप्रकारताभेदेनेत्यर्थः, 'प्रमाभ्रमसङ्कर इति रजत एवेदं रजतं रङ्गञ्च इत्यादि समूहालम्बने प्रमा-भ्रमयोः 'सङ्करः' अभेद इत्यर्थः। सामान्यतः प्रकारताभेदेनैव विषयताभेदाभ्युपगमे इदं रजतमित्यादि भ्रमेऽपि धर्म्मितावच्छेदकनिरूपितविषयताव्यक्तिमादायैवातिव्याप्तिरतोऽतिरिक्तान्तं प्रकारताविशेषणं। एकधर्म्मावच्छिन्नतत्तदभावोभयवन्निष्ठविशेष्यताकं द्रव्यं रजतमित्यादि ज्ञानं न लक्ष्यमितिमते लक्षणान्याह, 'विशेष्यनिष्ठेति स्वाश्रयनिष्ठेत्यर्थः, 'स्वं' विषयता, प्रतियोगिता च स्वरूपतो व्यक्तिद्वयावृत्त्यधिकरणत्वावच्छिन्नत्वेन स्वनिरूपकसम्बन्धावच्छिन्नत्वेन च विशेषणीया, तेन नैयायिक-व्यासज्यवृत्तिधर्म्मावच्छिन्नाभावं

---

(१) न रजतमित्यादि भ्रम इति क०।

ज्ञानं वा भ्रमः(१) इदं रजतमितिभ्रमे च विषयताद्वये व्यधिकरणप्रकारावच्छिन्नत्व-तदनवच्छिन्नत्वयोः विषयत्वप्रतियोगित्व-तदप्रतियोगित्वयोरविरोधात् समूहा-

---

व्यधिकरणसम्बन्धावच्छिन्नाभावत्वमादाय नाप्रसिद्धिः, प्रकारता च विशेष्यतावच्छेदकतातिरिक्ता ग्राह्या तेनेदं रजतमित्यादि भ्रमे नातिव्याप्तिः, तस्यापि लक्ष्यत्वे अनुभवत्वमात्रस्यैव सम्यक्त्वात्। एवमग्रेऽपि वृत्तः संयोगवानित्याद्यव्याप्यवृत्तिसंयोगादिप्रमायां संयोगत्वादिनिरूपितविषयतामादाय लक्षणसम्भवेऽपि कालिकादिसम्बन्धेन स्वरूपतो गोत्वादिप्रमायामव्याप्तिरतो निरवच्छिन्ननिष्ठतालाभार्थं 'अत्यन्तपदं, एवमग्रेऽपि। अत्र विषयितादिसम्बन्धेन भगवज्ज्ञानादिविशेष्यकप्रमायामव्याप्तिस्तत्र तादृशप्रतियोगिनोऽप्रसिद्धेरतो लक्षणान्तरमाह, 'विशेष्यनिष्ठेति स्वाश्रयनिष्ठेत्यर्थः, 'प्रतियोगिप्रकारानवच्छिन्नेति प्रतियोगिप्रकारकं यद्यत् तत्त्वाभावकूटवदित्यर्थः। प्रतियोगिप्रकारकत्वञ्च तादृशप्रतियोगिनिष्ठत्वाभाववत्प्रकारताकत्वं, तेनेदं रूपवदित्यादि निखिलरूपादिप्रकारकप्रमायां नाव्याप्तिः। 'विषयतासमानाधिकरणेति स्वसमानाधिकरणाभावप्रतियोगिप्रकारकविषयताप्रतियोगि यद्यत् तत्तदन्यानुभव इत्यर्थः। अत्र सर्व्वांशप्रमैव लक्ष्या तेनांशिकप्रमायां नाव्याप्तिरिति भावः। 'विषयतासमानाधिकरणेति स्वाधिकरणनिष्ठेत्यर्थः, 'प्रतियोगिप्रका

---

(१) स्वव्यधिकरणप्रकारावच्छिन्नविषयत्वप्रतियोगिज्ञानं भ्रमः, स्वसमानाधिकरणप्रकारकविषयत्वाप्रतियोगि ज्ञानं भ्रम इति ख०।

सम्बन्धे च विषयताभेदान्न प्रमाप्रमालक्षणेऽव्याप्त्यति-व्याप्ती । वस्तुतस्तु विशेषणताविशेषो नास्त्येव माना-भावात् । सामान्यतो ज्ञाने ज्ञाते तस्य क्वचिद्विशेषणतेति

रामवच्छिन्नेति प्रतियोगिप्रकारकं यद् यत् तदन्येत्यर्थः, प्रति-योगिप्रकारकत्वञ्च तादृशप्रतियोगिनिष्ठत्वाभाववत्प्रकारताकत्वं । न चैवं द्वितीयाभेदः, अत्यन्तान्योन्याभावभेदेन भेदात् ।

केचित्तु द्वितीये विशेष्यनिष्ठेत्यस्य स्ववन्निष्ठेत्यर्थः, स्वं विषता, तथाचात्र विषयताधिकरणत्वं प्रकारतया घटकं, तत्र तु संसर्गतयेति भेदः इत्याहुः ।

'स्वव्यधिकरणेति स्वाश्रयावृत्तिधर्म्मप्रकारकेत्यर्थः । लक्षणान्तर-माह, 'स्वसमानाधिकरणेति स्वसमानाधिकरणधर्म्मप्रकारकेत्यर्थः, प्रकारता च विशेष्यतावच्छेदकतातिरिक्ता ग्राह्या, तेनेदं रज-तमिति शुक्तिमात्रविशेष्यकभ्रमे नाव्याप्तिः, विशेष्यतावच्छेदकांशे भ्रमरूपं विधेयांशे च प्रमारूपं ज्ञानं न लक्ष्यमिति न तत्राव्या-प्तिरिति भावः । अयञ्च क्वाचित्कः पाठः । स्वाश्रया वृत्त्य-प्रकारकविषयताप्रतियोग्यनुभवः प्रमेति प्राथमिकप्रमालक्षणं स्व-व्यधिकरणधर्म्मप्रकारकविषयताप्रतियोगि ज्ञानं भ्रम इति द्वती-यभ्रमलक्षणञ्च सङ्ग्रामयति, 'इदं रजतमिति, चकारोभिन्नक्रमे, इदं रजतमिति तादात्म्यारोपे तदीयरजतत्व-पुरोवर्त्तिनिष्ठवि-षयताद्वये चेत्यर्थः । व्युत्क्रमेणाह, 'व्यधिकरणप्रकारावच्छिन्नेति 'स्वाश्रयावृत्तिप्रकारकत्व-स्वाश्रयावृत्त्यप्रकारकत्वयोरित्यर्थः, इदञ्च

सामान्यतो विशेषणताज्ञानेऽपि घटमयं जानाति न वेति सन्देहतादवस्थ्यात् । तस्माद्घट-तज्ज्ञानयोः स्वरूपग्रहेऽपि तदीयत्वं तद्विषयत्वं न गृहीतमिति तद्विषयत्वे

विषयताद्वये, 'विषयत्वप्रतियोगित्व-तदप्रतियोगित्वयोरिति स्वाश्रयवृत्तिप्रकारकविषयताप्रतियोगित्वस्वाश्रयावृत्त्यप्रकारकविषयताप्रतियोगित्वयोरित्यर्थः । यथाश्रुते भावाभावरूपतया विरोधस्य दुर्व्वारत्वात् । 'अविरोधात्' सत्त्वे बाधकाभावात्, प्राथमिकप्रमालक्षण-तृतीयप्रथमलक्षणयोः समन्वय इति शेषः । 'समूहालम्बने चेति इमौ घट-पटाविति समूहालम्बनप्रमायाञ्चेत्यर्थः, 'प्रमाप्रमालक्षण इति समाहारः(१) । 'विशेषणतेति क्लृप्तपदार्थातिरिक्तविषयताख्यविशेषणताविशेषो नास्त्येवेत्यर्थः, किन्तु ज्ञानविषयस्वरूपमेव विषयत्वमिति भावः । नन्वेवमयं पुरुषो ज्ञानवान् अयञ्च घट इति निश्चिन्वतोऽयं पुरुषो घटविषयकज्ञानवान्नवेति संशयो न स्यादतो विशेषणताविशेष आवश्यक इत्यत आह, 'सामान्येति, तथाचातिरिक्तविषयताभ्युपगमेऽपि सन्देहो दुरुपपद इति भावः । स्वमते संशयमुपपादयति, 'तस्मादिति, 'स्वरूपग्रहेऽपीति घटत्वज्ञानत्वाभ्यां निश्चयेऽपीत्यर्थः, 'तदीयत्वं तद्विषयत्वमिति घटीयत्वरूपं घटविषयत्वमित्यर्थः, 'न गृहीतमिति पुरुषविशेषणीभूतज्ञाने प्रकारतया न निश्चितमित्यर्थः, 'इतीति, समानप्रकारक-समान-

---

(१) समाहारादेकवचनान्ततानिर्वाहः, अन्यथा 'प्रमाप्रमालक्षणयोः' इति द्विवचनान्तप्रयोगः स्यात् ।

सन्देहः। तदीयत्वञ्च सम्बन्धं विना तत्सम्बन्धस्वभावत्वं[१]। तदुक्तं। "प्रकाशस्य सतस्तदीयतामात्रनिबन्धनः स्वभावविशेषस्तद्विषयत्वं" इति। सम्बन्धं विना कथं

विशेष्यकनिश्चयस्यैव संशयविरोधित्वादितिभावः। 'तदीयत्वञ्चेति ज्ञाननिष्ठघटीयत्वञ्चेत्यर्थः, 'सम्बन्धं विना' ज्ञानघटातिरिक्तसम्बन्धं विना, 'तत्सम्बन्धस्वभावत्वं' घटसम्बन्धस्वरूपत्वं, घटसम्बन्धाश्रयत्वमिति यावत् तदीयत्वस्य तद्विषयत्वरूपत्वे आचार्य्यसंवादमाह, 'तदुक्तमिति, बौद्धाधिकारे आचार्य्यचरणैरिति शेषः। 'प्रकाशस्य सत इति ज्ञानाभिन्नस्य सतस्तदीयताव्यवहारमात्रप्रयोजक इत्यर्थः, 'स्वभावविशेषः' धर्म्मविशेषः, मात्रपदादिच्छादिषु तदीयताव्यवहारप्रयोजकस्य तद्विषयतारूपत्वव्यवच्छेदः। न चैवमिच्छादिषु कथं तद्विषयताव्यवहार इति वाच्यं। तद्विषयताव्यवहारस्यौपचारिकत्वात्। उपचर्य्यतावच्छेदकधर्म्मस्य व्यापार्य्यनुबन्धिविषयितानामकं तज्ज्ञानजन्यत्वमेव, तत्र तदीयताव्यवहारप्रयोजकमपि तदेव। तज्ज्ञानजन्यत्वञ्च इच्छास्थले स्वसमानाधिकरणज्ञानाधिकरणक्षणध्वंसोत्पत्तिक्षणवृत्तित्वं, तेन भगवदिच्छाया नित्यत्वेऽपि न घटादिविषयकत्वव्यवहारोऽनुपपन्नः। कृतिस्थले च तादृशक्षणवृत्तीच्छाधिकरणक्षणध्वंसोत्पत्तिक्षणवृत्तित्वं, तेन भगवत्कृतेर्नित्यत्वेऽपि नासङ्गहः। न वा तज्ज्ञाननाशानन्तरोत्पन्नकृतिव्यक्तेरसंग्रहः। घटमिच्छामि घटं करो-

---

(१) सम्बन्धान्तरमनपेक्ष्य स्वसम्बन्धस्वभावत्वमिति ख०। सम्बन्धान्तरं विना तत्सम्बन्धस्वभावत्वमिति ग०।

तद्दीयत्वं, सम्बन्धस्यैव स्वभावत्वात्। यथा तत्रैव विशेषणतायां, अन्यथानवस्थानात्। अन्यथापि स्वरूपसम्बन्धे एषैव गतिः अन्यथा सामान्येनाभाव-समवाययोर्ज्ञानेऽधिकरणे ज्ञाते तयोः संशयो न स्यात्। अधि-

---

मीत्याद्यनुव्यवसायविषयोऽपीदमेव। अतएवेच्छादीनां याचितमण्डनन्यायेनैव विषयित्वमिति प्राचीनप्रवादः। यथा दरिद्रपत्नीनां याचितपरकीयालङ्काराधीनं स्वस्य भूषणं न स्वस्यालङ्कारोऽस्ति तथेच्छादीनामपि परकीयविषयित्वोपाधिको विषयित्वव्यवहार इति तत्प्रवादार्थः। न चेच्छादिष्वेव तद्विषयित्वव्यवहारो मुख्यः, ज्ञाने तद्व्यवहारस्य तदिच्छादिजनकत्वनिबन्धनो लाक्षणिक इत्येव किं न स्याद्विनिगमकाभावादिति वाच्यं। इच्छाद्यनुत्पादस्थलेऽपि ज्ञाने तद्विषयिताव्यवहारात्। न च तथापीच्छादिषु तद्विषयिताव्यवहारस्य मुख्यत्वाभ्युपगमे किं बीजमिति वाच्यं। ज्ञानविषयरूपस्य विषयसम्बन्धस्य विषयिपदमुख्यार्थत्वात् लाघवादिच्छाद्यनुत्पादस्थले तस्य तद्विषयिताव्यवहारप्रयोजकत्वावश्यकत्वाच्च इच्छादेश्च विषयसम्बन्धत्वे मानाभावात् तस्य तत्सम्बन्धत्वकल्पने गौरवाच्च। यद्यप्येवं कारणीभूतज्ञानविषयत्वस्य घटादाविष्टसाधनत्वादावपि सत्त्वाद्घटमिच्छामीत्यनुव्यवसायवदिष्टसाधनत्वमिच्छामीत्याद्यनुव्यवसायोऽपि स्यात्, किञ्चैवं ज्ञानेच्छादीनां कार्य्यकारणभावे सर्वत्र निरूपकजन्यत्वरूपमव्यवहितोत्तरत्वमेव कार्य्यता-

करण-तदुभयस्वरूपाणां ज्ञातत्वात्। तत्राप्यभाव-सम-वाययोर्विशेषणताविशेषो न गृहीत इति चेत्। न। सामान्यतस्तद्ग्रहेऽपि संशयात्।

वच्छेदकघटकं स्यात् तथा च महद्गौरवं। तथापि अयमेव तन्मते दोष इति स्मर्त्तव्यं। शङ्कते, 'सम्बन्धं विनेति ज्ञाने तस्य सम्बन्धं विनेत्यर्थः, 'तदीयत्वं' तदीयताव्यवहारप्रयोजकं तत्सम्बन्धाश्रयत्वं। उत्तरयति, 'सम्बन्धस्यैवेति विषय-स्वात्मकस्य विषयत्वस्य सम्बन्धस्यैव स्वस्मिन् भावादित्यर्थः, स्वं ज्ञानं, 'विशेषणतायां' अतिरिक्तविषयतायां, स्वात्मकसत्सम्बन्धस्तदीयताव्यवहारप्रयोजक इति शेषः। 'अन्यथा' सम्बन्धान्तरस्य तत्र तदीयताव्यवहार-प्रयोजकत्वे, तथाच ज्ञाने घटादिरूपः सम्बन्ध एव ज्ञाने घटादि-विषयित्वं घटादौ ज्ञानविषयत्वञ्चेति भावः। 'अन्यथापीति घटा-भाववद्भूतलं घटसमवायवत्कपालमित्यादिप्रतीतावपीत्यर्थः, 'स्वरू-पसम्बन्धे' घटाभाववद्भूतल-घटसमवायवत्कपालादिरूपस्य सम्बन्धत्वे, 'एषैव गतिरिति भूतलं घटाभाववन्नवा कपालं घटसमवायवन्नवे-त्यादिसंशयप्रतिबन्धकतानुपपत्तिरेव विद्धूपाय इत्यर्थः। 'अन्यथा' घटाभाववद्भूतलादिविषयकज्ञानत्वेनैव तत्प्रतीतेस्तादृशसंशयप्रति-बन्धकत्वे, 'सामान्येन' घटाभावत्व-घटसमवायत्वाभ्यां, 'अधिकरणे ज्ञाते' भूतल-कपालादिरूपे अधिकरणे उदासीनतयाभाते। शङ्कते, 'तत्रेति उदासीनतया अधिकरणविषयके घटाभाव-घटसमवाययोर्वै

यत्तु समूहालम्बन-विशिष्टज्ञानयोर्विशेषानुभवाद्वि-शिष्टज्ञाने विशेषणताविशेषोविषय इति। तन्न। विशे-षणतामादायापि समूहालम्बनसम्भवात्। तत्रापि विशेषणतान्तरस्वीकारेऽनवस्था। समूहालम्बनात्तु

इत्यर्थः, 'विशेषणताविशेषः' क्लृप्तपदार्थातिरिक्तोऽधिकरणनिष्ठो विशेषणताविशेषः, तथाच घटाभावादिनिरूपिततादृशपदार्थविष-यकघटाभाववद्भूतलादिज्ञानमेव तादृशसंशयप्रतिबन्धकमिति भावः। 'सामान्यत इति विशेषणतात्वरूपेणेत्यर्थः, 'तत्संशयात्' तत्संशयस्य त्वयाभ्युपगमात्। क्लृप्तपदार्थेनैवोपपत्तावतिरिक्तपदार्थकल्पने गौर-वाच्चेत्यपि बोध्यं।

'समूहालम्बनेति घटाभावोभूतलञ्चेत्यादिसमूहालम्बन-घटाभा-ववद्भूतलमित्यादिविशिष्टज्ञानयोरित्यर्थः, 'विशेषानुभवात्' वैलक्षण्या-नुभवात्, 'विशिष्टज्ञाने' घटाभाववद्भूतलमित्यादिविशिष्टज्ञाने, 'विशे-षणताविशेष इति क्लृप्तपदार्थातिरिक्तो घटाभावादिनिरूपितविशेष-णताविशेषः सम्बन्धमर्य्यादया विषय इत्यर्थः, अन्यथा विषयाधि-क्याभावाद्वैलक्षण्यं न स्यादिति भावः॥ ननु घटाभावादिविशिष्टबुद्धौ विशेषणताया अपि विशेषणता भासते विशेषणतामादाय समूहा-लम्बने च न भासते अतो विषयाधिक्याद्वैलक्षण्यमित्यत आह, 'तत्रापीति। नन्वेवं कथं वैलक्षण्यमित्यत आह, 'समूहेति घटाभावो भूतलञ्चेत्यादिसमूहालम्बनादित्यर्थः, 'विशिष्टज्ञानस्य'

विशिष्टज्ञानस्य विशेषः कारणत्वतः कार्यत्वतः प्रकारत्वतो वा । प्रकारोऽपि विशेषणताविशेषः स च धर्मिण्येवास्त्विति चेत् । न । तमादायाऽपि समूहालम्बनसम्भवात् ।

घटाभाववद्भूतलमित्यादिविशिष्टज्ञानस्य, 'कारणेति अन्यताविशेषसम्बन्धेन घटाभावादिज्ञानरूपकारणवत्त्वत इत्यर्थः, घटाभावादिविशिष्टबुद्धौ घटाभावादिज्ञानस्य हेतुत्वादिति भावः । 'कार्यत्वत इति जनकताविशेषसम्बन्धेन विशिष्टवैशिष्ट्यबोधादिलक्षणकार्यवत्त्वत इत्यर्थः, घटाभावादिविशिष्टवैशिष्ट्यबोधादौ घटाभावादिविशिष्टज्ञानस्य हेतुत्वादिति भावः । नन्विदं द्वयमपि न युक्तं अन्यता-जनकता-विशेषयोरितरव्यावृत्त-तदवच्छेदकं विना असम्भवादित्यत आह, 'प्रकारत्वतो वेति स्वरूपतः प्रकारितात्वतो वेत्यर्थः, विशिष्टज्ञाने घटाभावादिकं प्रकारः, समूहालम्बने च न तथेत्येव विशेषादिति भावः । इदमुपलक्षणं विशिष्टज्ञाने घटाभावद्भूतलादेः सम्बन्धमर्यादयापि भानं समूहालम्बने च न तथेति संसर्गिताख्यतोऽपि विशेष इति मन्तव्यं । प्रकृते, 'प्रकारोऽपीति घटाभावादिनिरूपिततत्प्रकारितापीत्यर्थः, 'विशेषणताविशेषः' विशेषणता नाम पदार्थविशेषः, 'धर्मिण्येवेति एवकारोऽप्यर्थे भूतलादावधिकरणेऽपि घटाभावादेः सम्बन्धरूपोऽस्त्वित्यर्थः, तथाचाधिकतद्विषयतात्वत एव विशिष्टबुद्धौ विशेष इति भावः । 'तमादायापीति, इदमुपलक्षणं, प्रकारितापि

इति श्रीमद्गङ्गेशोपाध्यायविरचिते तत्त्वचिन्तामणौ प्रत्यक्षखण्डे प्रामाण्यवादे प्रमालक्षणसिद्धान्तः।

समाप्तोऽयं प्रामाण्यवादः।

न पदार्थविशेषः, किन्तु तत्तज्ज्ञानरूपः, पदार्थविशेषत्वेऽपि भूतलादौ तदभ्युपगमे भूतलं घटाभावप्रकारकमिति व्यवहारप्रसङ्ग इत्यपि बोध्यं॥

इति श्रीमथुरानाथतर्कवागीशविरचिते प्रामाण्यवादरहस्ये प्रमालक्षणसिद्धान्तरहस्यं सम्पूर्णं। समाप्तमिदं प्रामाण्यवादरहस्यं॥

अथान्यथाख्यातिवादः ।

ननु सर्वज्ञानानां यथार्थत्वात्प्रमालक्षणे विशेषण-व्यावर्त्त्याप्रसिद्धेर्विशेषणवैयर्थ्यमन्यथाख्यातौ मानाभा-

---

अथान्यथाख्यातिवादरहस्यं ।

प्रमालक्षणोपोद्घातसङ्गत्या अन्यथाख्यातिविचारमवतारयति, 'नन्विति, 'सर्व्वज्ञानानां' तत्प्रकारकसर्व्वज्ञानानां,(१) 'यथार्थत्वात्' तत्तद्विशेष्यकत्वावच्छिन्न-तत्प्रकारकत्वात् ।

केचित्तु 'सर्व्वज्ञानानां' रजतत्वाभाववद्विशेष्यकत्वावच्छिन्नरजत-धर्म्मप्रकारकं यज्ज्ञान तद्भिन्नानां, 'यथार्थत्वात्' रजतत्वाभाववद्वि-शेष्यकत्वावच्छिन्न-रजतत्वप्रकारताशून्यत्वादित्याहुः(२) ।

'विशेषणव्यावर्त्त्येति तद्वद्विशेष्यकत्वावच्छिन्नत्वविशेषणव्यावर्त्तनी-येत्यर्थः, 'विशेषणवैयर्थ्यमिति तद्वद्विशेष्यकत्वावच्छिन्नत्वविशेषणवैयर्थ्य-मित्यर्थः । ननु तदभाववन्मात्रे तत्प्रकारकज्ञानस्यैव तद्वद्विशेष्यकत्वा-वच्छिन्न-तत्प्रकारकत्वविरहात् तदेव व्यावर्त्तनीयमित्यत आह, 'अन्यथाख्याताविति 'ख्यातौ' ज्ञाने, अन्यथात्वसाधकप्रमाणाभावा-

---

(१) 'ज्ञानानां' तत्प्रकारकज्ञानानां, इति क०, ग० ।

(२) केचित्त्वित्यादिपाठः क०, ग० पुस्तकद्वये नास्ति ।

वात्। तथाहि रजतार्थिप्रवृत्तिविषयत्वं रजतत्व-प्रकारकानुभवविषयत्वव्याप्यं रजतार्थिप्रवृत्तिविषय-

---

दित्यर्थः। 'अन्यथात्वं' तदभाववद्विशेष्यकत्वावच्छिन्न-तत्प्रकारकत्वं। यथाश्रुते अन्यथाख्यातिरूपे अधिकरणे प्रमाणसामान्याभावादित्यर्थस्य विवक्षितत्वे प्रमाणसामान्याभावोऽप्रसिद्धः तन्मते अधिकरणाप्रसिद्धेः। यदि सान्यथाख्यातिसाधकप्रमाणाभावादित्यर्थो विवक्षितः तदा तन्मते प्रतियोग्यप्रसिद्ध्या तदभावाप्रसिद्धेरिति ध्येयं। न च तन्मते तदभाववद्विशेष्यकत्वावच्छिन्न-तत्प्रकारत्वमप्यप्रसिद्धमिति वाच्यं। तदभाववति तत्प्रकारकेच्छादौ प्रसिद्धेः तैर्ज्ञान-संस्कारयोरयथार्थत्वानभ्युपगमेऽपि इच्छादीनामयथार्थत्वाभ्युपगमात्। अत्र ज्ञानं रजतत्वाभाववद्विशेष्यकत्वावच्छिन्न-रजतत्वप्रकारकं न वेति विप्रतिपत्तिः, विधिकोटिर्नैयायिकानां, पक्षतावच्छेदकसामानाधिकरण्येन तत्सिद्धेरुद्देश्यत्वात् रजतत्वभ्रमाद्यन्यज्ञानमात्रे नांशतो बाधः। निषेधकोटिस्तु इदं रजतमित्यादिभ्रमस्थले इदन्त्वप्रकारकग्रहणानुभव-रजतस्मरणाद्यात्मकज्ञानद्वयमङ्गीकर्तॄणां गुरूणां, पक्षतावच्छेदकावच्छेदेन तत्सिद्धेरुद्देश्यतया न रजतत्वभ्रमान्यज्ञानमात्रेऽंशतः सिद्धसाधनं। न च रजतत्वाभाववद्विशेष्यकत्वावच्छिन्न-तत्प्रकारकत्वस्य तन्मते इच्छायामेव प्रसिद्धतया ज्ञाने तदभावसाधने नैयायिकानां सिद्धसाधनमिति वाच्यं। नैयायिकनये ज्ञानेच्छादिभेदेन प्रकारिता-विशेष्यितयोर्भेदाभावेन सिद्धसाधनासम्भवात्, तद्भेदेन प्रका-

माथवृत्तिधर्म्मत्वात् रजतमाथवृत्तिधर्म्मवदित्यन्यथा-ख्यातिव्याप्यं सिद्ध्यतीत्यप्राप्तकालत्वं। रजतभाथवृत्तित्व-

---

रिता-विशेष्यितयोर्भेदेऽपि प्रकारितात्व-विशेष्यितात्वयोः सर्व्वसाधारणानुगतधर्म्मयोः सत्त्वेन सामान्याभावस्य साध्यतया सिद्धसाधनासम्भवाच्च। न हीच्छादिवृत्तिरजतत्वाभाववद्विशेष्यकत्वावच्छिन्न-रजतत्वप्रकारकत्वत्वावच्छिन्नाभावत्वेन साध्यत्वं, अपि तु सामान्यतोरजतत्वाभाववद्विशेष्यकत्वावच्छिन्न-रजतत्वप्रकारकत्वत्वावच्छिन्नाभावत्वेन, तादृशाभावस्य न्यायमते ज्ञानसामान्ये अप्रसिद्ध एव। यद्वा 'अन्यथाख्यातौ मानाभावादित्यस्य ख्यातिवृत्तिरजतत्वप्रकारकत्वस्य ख्यातिवृत्तिरजतत्वाभाववद्विशेष्यकत्वावच्छिन्नत्वे, ख्यातिवृत्तिरजतत्वाभाववद्विशेष्यकत्वस्य ख्यातिवृत्तिरजतत्वप्रकारकत्वावच्छिन्नत्वे मानाभावादित्यर्थः, तथा च ज्ञानवृत्तिरजतत्वप्रकारकत्वं ज्ञानवृत्तिरजतत्वाभाववद्विशेष्यकत्वावच्छिन्नं न वा, ज्ञानवृत्तिरजतत्वाभाववद्विशेष्यकत्वं ज्ञानवृत्तिरजतत्वप्रकारकत्वावच्छिन्नं न वेति वा विप्रतिपत्तिः, ज्ञानवृत्तिरजतत्वप्रकारकत्वं रजतत्वप्रमायामेव प्रसिद्धं, तदवच्छिन्नत्वस्य रजतत्वप्रमावृत्तिरजतत्ववद्विशेष्यकत्वे प्रसिद्धं, एवं ज्ञानवृत्तिरजतत्वाभाववद्विशेष्यकत्वं रजतत्वाभावप्रमायामेव प्रसिद्धं, तदवच्छिन्नत्वस्य रजतत्वाभावप्रमावृत्तिरजतत्वाभावप्रकारकत्वे एव प्रसिद्धमिति, ज्ञानेच्छादिभेदेन प्रकरिता-विशेष्यितयोर्भेदेऽपि सर्व्वसाधारणानुगतप्रकारितात्व-विशेष्यितात्वयोरभावेऽपि च न क्षतिः इति संक्षेपः।

प्रमाणाभावमेव नैयायिकाभिमतं प्रमाणमात्रस्य उपपादयति,

स्वोपाधिः। शुक्तिवृत्तिज्ञानविषयता[१] रजतत्वप्रकारिका रजतार्थिताजन्यप्रवृत्तिविषयवृत्तिविषयतात्वात् रजतवृत्तिविषयतावदित्यत्र रजतवृत्तित्वमुपाधिः। रज-

'तथाहीति, 'रजतार्थीति रजतत्वप्रकारकत्वावच्छिन्नप्रवृत्तिविशेष्यत्वमित्यर्थः, रजतत्वप्रकारकानुभवविशेष्यत्वेऽंशतः सिद्धसाधनवारणाय 'प्रवृत्तीति, तादृशप्रवृत्तिविशेष्यत्वस्य च गुरुनये शुक्तावपि सत्त्वान्न सिद्धसाधनमिति भावः। 'रजतत्वप्रकारकेति रजतत्वप्रकारकत्वावच्छिन्नानुभवविशेष्यत्वव्याप्यमित्यर्थः। यथाश्रुते इदं रजतमिदञ्च शुक्तिभिन्नमिति समूहालम्बनप्रत्यक्षविषयतामादायार्थान्तरतापत्तेः व्यापकसामानाधिकरण्यरूपव्याप्तेः स्वत्वाननुगमेनाननुगतत्वात्तदभाववदवृत्तित्वरूपव्याप्तेरेवात्र प्रवेशात् रजतत्वप्रकारकभगवत्साक्षात्कारविशेष्यत्वमादाय न्यायनये तादृशव्याप्यत्वासिद्ध्यापत्तेश्च। अनुभवपदञ्च रजतत्वप्रकारकत्वावच्छिन्नेच्छादिविशेष्यत्वमादाय सिद्धसाधनवारणाय, अनुभवविशेष्यत्वञ्च साक्षात्कारत्वनिरूपितविशेष्यत्वं, अन्यथा उक्तयुक्त्या[२] तदभाववदवृत्तित्वरूपव्याप्तेरेवात्र प्रवेशात् न्यायनये सर्व्वं रजतमिति भ्रमविशेष्यत्वस्य सर्व्वत्र सत्त्वात् तदभावाप्रसिद्ध्यापत्तेः। उपादानत्वाख्यप्रवृत्तिविषयताया एव पक्षत्वान्न बाधः। रजतत्वप्रकारकत्वावच्छिन्न-रजतारजतोभयविशेष्यकप्रवृत्तिविशेष्यत्वस्य रजतमादाय तादृशानुभवविशेष्यत्वसामानाधिकरण्यसत्त्वात् सिद्धसाधन-

(१) शुक्तिनिष्ठा ज्ञानविषयतेति ख०।

(२) तुल्ययुक्त्येति ग०।

सत्त्वं अरजतवृत्तिज्ञानविषयतावच्छेदकं अरजतविषय-प्रवृत्तिहेतुज्ञानप्रकारत्वात् शुक्तित्ववदित्यत्र रजता-

---

वारणाय व्याप्यत्वानुसरणं। व्याप्यत्वन्तु तदभाववदवृत्तित्वमात्रं न तु तदभाववदवृत्तित्वे सति तत्सामानाधिकरण्यं, तत्र सामानाधिकरण्यांशस्य निष्फलत्वात्। ननु तथापि रजतमात्रविशेष्यक-रजतत्वप्रकारकप्रवृत्तिविशेष्यताव्यक्त्यंशतः सिद्धसाधनं तस्या रजतमात्रनिष्ठत्वात् पक्षतावच्छेदकावच्छेदेन साध्यसिद्धेरुद्देश्यत्वे व्याप्यत्वपर्य्यन्तानुसरण-वैयर्थ्यप्रसङ्गाच्च सामानाधिकरण्यमात्रेणैव सामञ्जस्यादिति चेत्। न। निखिलरजतत्वप्रकारकप्रवृत्तेरेकैव विशेष्यता सकलतद्विशेष्यसाधारणीतिमताश्रयणात् समवायादिवदतिप्रसङ्गभङ्गात्।

यद्वा रजतत्वप्रकारकरजतारजतोभयविशेष्यकप्रवृत्तिविशेष्यत्वं पक्षः तस्याः प्रवृत्तेरुभयत्र एकैव विशेष्यता इति रजतमादाय सामानाधिकरण्यसत्त्वात् सिद्धसाधनवारणाय व्याप्यत्वपर्य्यन्तानुधावनमिति-भावः। 'रजतार्थी'ति रजतत्वप्रकारकत्वावच्छिन्नप्रवृत्तिविशेष्यताश्रयातिरिक्तावृत्तिधर्म्मत्वात् इत्यर्थः, विशेषणताविशेषसम्बन्धेनावृत्तित्वलाभाय 'धर्म्मे'ति, तदभाववदवृत्तित्वरूपव्याप्तेरवृत्तावपि सत्त्वेन व्यभिचारविरहाद्धर्म्मपदस्य प्रयोजनान्तरविरहादिति भावः[१]। 'रजतमात्रे'ति विशेषणताविशेषेण रजतत्वप्रकारकप्रवृत्तिविशेष्यरजतमात्रवृत्तिधर्म्मवदित्यर्थः, तेन रजतत्वादिव्युदासः। रजतत्वादेः रजतत्वप्रकारकप्रवृत्त्यविषये रजतेऽपि सत्त्वात् साधनविकलत्वेन दृष्टान्तत्वासम्भवादिति

---

(१) प्रयोजनान्तरविरहादितिध्येयमिति क०, ख०।

वृत्तित्वमुपाधिः । रजतत्वप्रकारिका ज्ञानविषयता अरजतवृत्तिः अरजतनिष्ठात्यन्ताभावाप्रतियोगिनी वा अरजतविषयप्रवृत्तिहेतुज्ञानविषयतात्वात् शुक्तिवृत्ति-

भावः। 'अन्यथाख्यातिव्याप्यमिति अन्यथाख्यातिसाधिका व्याप्तिरित्यर्थः, अनेनानुमानेन रजतत्वप्रकारकप्रवृत्तिविशेष्यत्वस्य तादृशानुभवविशेष्यत्वव्याप्यत्वनिश्चयादनन्तरं शुक्तिः रजतत्वप्रकारकानुभवविशेष्या रजतत्वप्रकारकप्रवृत्तिविशेष्यत्वादित्यनुमानेनान्यथाख्यातिसिद्धिरिति भावः। 'अप्राप्तकालत्वमिति, शुक्तिः रजतत्वप्रकारकानुभवविशेष्या रजतत्वप्रकारकप्रवृत्तिविशेष्यत्वादित्यनुमानोद्भावनानन्तरमेव[१] तादृशप्रवृत्तिविशेष्यत्वव्याप्यत्वे जिज्ञासोत्पत्तेः प्रथमं तत्र तद्व्याप्यत्वे आकाङ्क्षाविरहादिति भावः। ननु तदनुमानोद्भावनानन्तरमेव एतदनुमानमुद्भावनीयं तथा च नाप्राप्तकालत्वमतो दूषणान्तरमाह, 'रजतमात्रेति रजतवृत्तित्वस्यावृत्तौ शुद्धसाध्याव्यापकत्वान्मात्रपदोपादानं रजतान्यावृत्तित्वमर्थः। 'शुक्तिवृत्तिज्ञानविषयतेति, रजतवृत्तिज्ञानविषयतायामंशतः सिद्धसाधनवारणाय 'वृत्त्यन्तं, दुःखादिनिरूपितविषयतायामंशतः सिद्धसाधनवारणाय 'ज्ञानपदं, 'रजतत्वप्रकारिकेति, इदञ्च विषयतातिरिक्तपदार्थः सा च ज्ञानादिवत्सविशेष्यिका सप्रकारिका चेत्यभिमानेन। पक्षतावच्छेदकसामानाधिकरण्येन साध्यसिद्धेरुद्देश्यत्वाच्च नांशतोबाधः। 'रजतार्थितेति रजतत्वप्रकारकप्रवृत्तिमात्रजनकज्ञानविषयतात्वादि-

(१) शुक्तिः रजतत्वप्रकारकेत्याद्युपदर्शितानुमानोद्भावनानन्तरमेवेति ग०।

विषयतावदित्यत्र रजतावृत्तित्वमुपाधिः। विषयताया निरस्तत्वाच्च(१) विवादपदं रजतज्ञानं शुक्तिविषयकं शुक्तौ प्रवर्त्तकज्ञानत्वात् शुक्तिज्ञानवदित्यत्र ज्ञायमानेष्टभेदा-

---

त्यर्थः। अन्यथा शुक्तिवृत्तिशुक्तित्वादिप्रकारकज्ञानविषयतायां व्यभिचारापत्तेः। 'रजतवृत्तीति प्रवृत्तिविषयरजतनिष्ठरजतत्व-प्रकारकज्ञानविषयतावदित्यर्थः। तेन रजतवृत्तिद्रव्यत्वादिप्रकारक-ज्ञानविषयतायाः प्रवृत्त्यविषयरजतनिष्ठरजतत्वप्रकारकज्ञानविषय-तायाश्च व्युदासः, तयोः साध्य-साधनविकलत्वेन दृष्टान्तत्वासम्भवा-दिति ध्येयं। 'रजतवृत्तित्वमिति तस्य ज्ञानविषयतारूपपक्षधर्म्मा-वच्छिन्नसाध्यव्यापकत्वादिति भावः। रजतत्वप्रकारकशुक्तीच्छादि-विषयतायां व्यभिचारेण शुद्धसाध्यव्यापकत्वासम्भवादिति ध्येयं। 'अरजतवृत्तिज्ञानविषयतावच्छेदकमिति अरजतवृत्तिर्या ज्ञानविष-यता तदवच्छेदकमित्यर्थः, अवच्छेदकत्वं प्रकारत्वं, अन्यथा अरजत-वृत्तित्वस्य ज्ञानविशेषणत्वे शुक्ति-रजते इति समूहालम्बनमादाय सिद्धसाधनापत्ते हेतौ प्रकारत्वमात्रस्यैव गमकत्वेन शेषवैयर्थ्यप्रसङ्गा-च्चेति ध्येयं। अरजतेति अरजतविशेष्यकप्रवृत्तिहेतुज्ञानप्रकारत्वा-दित्यर्थः। न चेदं सर्व्ववदित्यरजतविशेष्यकभ्रममादाय साध्यस्य केवलान्वयितया प्रकारत्वादित्येवास्त्विति वाच्यं। साध्ये अवच्छेदक-पदेन निरवच्छिन्नप्रकारताया विवक्षणात् यस्य जातिविशेषस्य स्वरूपतो नारजते भानं तत्र व्यभिचारापत्तेः। न चेदं सर्व्ववदित्य-

---

(१) निराकृतत्वाच्चेति ग०।

ग्रहे कारणतावच्छेदकं रजतज्ञानं न प्रवर्त्तकमित्य-सिद्धिः । शुक्तिः रजतज्ञानविषयताश्रयः[१] रजतार्थिप्र-

रजतविशेष्यकभ्रममादाय विवक्षितहेतोरपि तत्र सत्त्वाद्व्यभि-चारतादवस्थ्यमिति वाच्यं ! हेतोरपि निरवच्छिन्नप्रकारतया विवक्षणात् । न च तथापि रजतारजतोभयगोचरसमूहालम्बन-ज्ञानप्रकारीभूते तादृशजातिविशेषे व्यभिचार इति वाच्यम् । अर-जतविशेष्यकप्रवृत्तिमात्रहेतुज्ञानप्रकारत्वस्य विवक्षितत्वात् । 'रज-तावृत्तित्वमिति अरजतवृत्तित्वमित्यर्थः, यथाश्रुते द्रव्यत्वादौ सा-ध्याव्यापकत्वादिति[२] ध्येयम् । 'रजतत्वप्रकारिका ज्ञानविषयतेति, अत्र शुक्तित्वप्रकारकज्ञानविषयतायामंशतः सिद्धसाधनवारणाय 'रजतत्वप्रकारिकेति, रजतत्वप्रकारकशुक्तीच्छादिविषयतायामंशतः सिद्धसाधनवारणाय 'ज्ञानेति, पक्षतावच्छेदकसामानाधिकरण्येन साध्यसिद्धेरुद्देश्यत्वाच्च न सत्यरजतज्ञानविषयतायामंशतोबाध इति भावः । 'अरजतनिष्ठेति अरजतत्वव्यापकत्वं तादात्म्यसम्बन्धेनारजत-व्यापकत्वं वा अरजतनिष्ठत्वं, तेन रजतत्वप्रकारकभ्रमाविषयारजत-व्यक्तिमादाय न दोषः[३] । 'अरजतविषयकप्रवृत्तिहेत्विति अरज-तविशेष्यकप्रवृत्तिमात्रहेत्वित्यर्थः, तेन रजतवृत्तिरजतारजतोभय-विषयकसमूहालम्बनविषयतायां न व्यभिचारः । 'ज्ञानेति स्वरूप-

(१) रजतत्वप्रकारकज्ञानविषयताश्रय इति ख० ।

(२) साध्याव्यापकत्वे उपाधित्वव्याघातः साध्यव्यापकत्वे सति साधनाव्याप-कत्वस्य उपाधिलक्षणत्वादिति भावः ।

(३) न बाधः इति क०, ख० ।

वृत्तिविषयत्वात् रजतवदित्यत्र रजतत्वमुपाधिः। शुक्तौ रजतार्थिप्रवृत्तिः[१] स्वधर्मिधर्मिकरजतत्वप्रकारकज्ञान-साध्या रजतार्थिप्रवृत्तित्वात् रजतप्रवृत्तिवदित्यत्र रज-

---

कथनं, 'रजतावृत्तित्वमिति। यद्यपि द्रव्यत्वप्रकारकप्रमाविशेष्यत्वा-दाविदं साध्याव्यापकं तथापि रजतारजतोभयवृत्तिधर्मान्यप्रकार-कविषयतात्वावच्छिन्नसाध्यव्यापकत्वमत्र बोध्यं। न च तथापि रज-तारजते इति समूहालम्बनज्ञानविषयतायां व्यभिचार इति वाच्यं। अत्र विशेष्यभेदेन विशेष्यताभेदादिति भावः। 'विषयताया इति सविशेष्यक-सप्रकारकातिरिक्तविषयताया निरस्तत्वाच्चेत्यर्थः, तथाच पक्षाप्रसिद्धिः, हेत्वप्रसिद्धिः, दृष्टान्ताप्रसिद्धिः, तृतीयानुमाने साध्या-प्रसिद्धिश्चेति भावः। 'विवादपदं रजतज्ञानमिति शुक्तिविशेष्यक-प्रवृत्तिजनकं रजतत्वप्रकारकज्ञानमित्यर्थः, रजतमात्रविशेष्यकरज-तत्वप्रकारकज्ञाने अंशतो बाधवारणाय अनकान्तं, प्राचीननये पक्षतावच्छेदकावच्छेदेन साध्यसिद्धेरुद्देश्यत्वादंशतः सिद्धसाधनस्य दोषतया शुक्ताविदं शुक्तिरितिज्ञाने अंशतः सिद्धसाधनवारणाय 'रजतत्वप्रकारकेति, शुक्तौ रजतत्वप्रकारकेच्छायामंशतः सिद्धसा-धनवारणाय 'ज्ञानमिति, एकमात्रविशेष्यकत्वेनापि विशेषणीयं, तेन शुक्ति-रजतोभयसमूहालम्बने शुक्ताविदं रजतवदिति ज्ञाने वा नांशतः सिद्धसाधनमिति भावः। 'शुक्तिविषयकमिति शुक्ति-विशेष्यकमित्यर्थः। अग्रावच्छिन्नो वृक्षः कपिसंयोगीत्यादिवत् पक्ष-तावच्छेदकावच्छेदेन साध्यसिद्धावेव रजतत्वप्रकारकत्वावच्छिन्नशु-

---

(१) रजतार्थिताजन्या प्रवृत्तिरिति ग०।

तद्विषयत्वं उपाधिः स्वपदार्थाननुगमश्च। तत्परित्यागे तु रजतार्थिप्रवृत्तिधर्मिधर्मिकरजतत्वप्रकारकज्ञानेनो-भयसिद्धेन रजतस्मरणेनार्थान्तरम्। उच्यते। रजता-

---

क्तिविशेष्यकज्ञानसिद्धिस्तदेवान्यथाख्यातिरिति भावः। 'शुक्तौ प्रवर्त्त-कज्ञानत्वादिति शुक्तिविशेष्यकप्रवृत्तिजनकज्ञानत्वादित्यर्थः, इदं रज-तमित्यादिप्रमायां व्यभिचारवारणाय जनकान्तं, आत्म-शरीरादौ व्यभिचारवारणाय ज्ञानपदं, फलज्ञानस्य प्रवृत्त्यहेतुत्वान्न तत्र व्यभि-चारः[१]। 'ज्ञायमानेति इष्टतावच्छेदकज्ञानविशिष्टेष्टभेदाग्रहनिष्ठ-प्रवृत्तिकारणतायामवच्छेदकं रजतत्वप्रकारकं ज्ञानमित्यर्थः, 'न प्रव-र्त्तकं' न प्रवृत्तिजनकं, 'असिद्धिरिति आश्रयासिद्धिरित्यर्थः, रज-तत्वप्रकारकज्ञाने शुक्तिविशेष्यकप्रवृत्तिजनकत्वस्य पक्षतावच्छेदक-स्याभावादिति भावः।

यद्वा 'असिद्धिः' स्वरूपासिद्धिः। न च हेतुतावच्छेदकावच्छिन्न-हेत्वभाववत्पक्षतावच्छेदकविशिष्टपक्ष एव स्वरूपासिद्धिः स च प्रकृते नास्ति पक्षतावच्छेदकविशिष्टपक्षाप्रसिद्धेरिति वाच्यं। काञ्चनमयपर्व्वतो वह्निमान् जलत्वादित्यादौ जलत्वाभाववत्पर्व्वतस्य स्वरूपासिद्धित्व-वदत्रापि शुक्तिविशेष्यकप्रवृत्तिजनकज्ञानत्वाभाववद्रजतत्वप्रकारकज्ञा-नस्यैव स्वरूपासिद्धित्वादिति ध्येयं।

'रजतज्ञानेति रजतत्वप्रकारकत्वावच्छिन्नज्ञानविशेष्यताश्रयेत्यर्थः, तेन शुक्ति-रजते इति समूहालम्बनमादाय न सिद्धसाधनं, तादृ-

---

(१) न तत्र व्यभिचार इति भाव इति क॰, ख॰।

र्थिताजन्या मुक्तौ प्रवृत्तिरिष्टप्रवृत्तिविषयविशिष्टज्ञानसाध्या प्रवृत्तित्वात् मुक्तौ मुक्त्यर्थिप्रवृत्तिवत्। न चेष्टविषयप्रवृत्तित्वमुपाधिः, साधनविशेषितत्वात्।

शेच्छादिविशेष्यत्वमादाय सिद्धसाधनवारणाय ज्ञानप्रवेशः। 'रजतार्थीति रजतत्वप्रकारकत्वावच्छिन्नप्रवृत्तिविशेष्यत्वादित्यर्थः, तेन समूहालम्बनप्रवृत्तिविशेष्यतामादायारजतप्रमाविषये[१] अरजते न व्यभिचारः। 'रजतवदिति रजतत्वप्रकारकप्रवृत्तिविशेष्यरजतवदित्यर्थः, तेन तादृशप्रवृत्त्यविषयरजतस्य साधनविकलत्वेऽपि न क्षतिः। 'शुक्ताविति शुक्तिविशेष्यिका रजतत्वप्रकारिका प्रवृत्तिरित्यर्थः, अत्र शुक्तिविशेष्यकशुक्तित्वप्रकारकप्रवृत्तावंशतो बाधवारणाय रजतत्वप्रकारिकेति, प्राचीननये पक्षतावच्छेदकावच्छेदेन साध्यसिद्धेरुद्देश्यत्वेऽप्यंशतः सिद्धसाधनस्य दोषत्वात् रजतप्रवृत्तावंशतः सिद्धसाधनवारणाय शुक्तिविशेष्यिकेतीति भावः। 'स्वधर्म्मिधर्म्मिकेति स्वविशेष्यविशेष्यकेत्यर्थः। 'स्वं' प्रवृत्तिः, 'रजतार्थीति रजतत्वप्रकारकप्रवृत्तित्वादित्यर्थः। 'रजतप्रवृत्तिवदिति रजतविशेष्यकरजतत्वप्रकारकप्रवृत्तिवदित्यर्थः, 'स्वपदार्थेति, तथाच स्वपदस्य प्रकृतपक्षव्यक्तिपरत्वे साध्याप्रसिद्धिः दृष्टान्ताप्रसिद्धिश्च, दृष्टान्तपरत्वे च रजतस्मरणजन्यत्वेन सिद्धसाधनमिति भावः। 'तत्परित्यागेति स्वपदं परित्यज्य रजतत्वप्रकारकप्रवृत्तिधर्म्मिधर्म्मिकरजतत्वप्रकारकज्ञानसाध्येत्यभिमाने त्वित्यर्थः, 'रजतार्थिप्रवृत्तीति रजतत्वप्रकारकप्रवृत्तीत्यर्थः। 'रज-

---

(१) रजतत्वभ्रमाविषये इति ख०।

तार्थितेति समवायसम्बन्धेन रजतत्वप्रकारिका शुक्तिविशेष्यिका प्रवृत्तिरित्यर्थः, अत्र शुक्तिविशेष्यक-शुक्तित्वप्रकारकप्रवृत्तावंशतः सिद्धसाधनवारणाय रजतत्वप्रकारिकेति, रजतविशेष्यक-रजतत्वप्रकारकप्रवृत्तावंशतः सिद्धसाधनवारणाय शुक्तिविशेष्यिकेतीति भावः। 'इष्टप्रवृत्तिविषयेति समवायसम्बन्धेनेष्टप्रकारकप्रवृत्तिविषयविशेष्यकज्ञानसाध्येत्यर्थः। अत्रेष्टत्वं न स्वजनकेच्छाविशेष्यत्वं, शुक्तिविशेष्यकरजतत्वप्रकारकप्रवृत्तिस्थले शुक्तेरेव स्वजनकेच्छाविशेष्यतया तत्प्रकारकज्ञानस्य चाहेतुत्वाद्‌बाधापत्तेः, किन्तु इष्टतावच्छेदकत्वं स्वजनकेच्छाप्रकारत्वमिति यावत् स्वप्रकारत्वमिति तु निष्कर्षः। प्रवृत्तिविषयत्वञ्च प्रवृत्तिविशेष्यत्वं स्वविशेष्यत्वमिति यावत्। तथा च समवायसम्बन्धेन स्वप्रकारप्रकारक-स्वविशेष्यविशेष्यकज्ञानसाध्येति साध्यं, समवायसम्बन्धेनेति साक्षाद्धधिकरणप्रकारकत्वसिद्धये। प्राचीननये स्वत्वस्याननुगतत्वात् न साध्याप्रसिद्धिः संवादिप्रवृत्तावेव तत्प्रसिद्धेः, अत एव न दृष्टान्तासिद्धिः। समवायसम्बन्धेन रजतत्वमात्रप्रकारक-शुक्तिमात्रविशेष्यकप्रवृत्तेः पक्षत्वान्न समूहालम्बनप्रवृत्तावंशतः सिद्धसाधनमिति भावः। 'प्रवृत्तित्वात्' समवायसंसर्गकप्रवृत्तित्वात्, तेन तादात्म्यसम्बन्धेन रजतादिप्रकारकप्रवृत्तौ न व्यभिचारः। न चेश्वरप्रयत्ने व्यभिचार इति वाच्यं। प्रवृत्तित्वस्य इच्छाजन्यतावच्छेदकजातिविशेषरूपतया भगवत्प्रयत्ने तदभावादिति भावः। 'शुक्ताविति शुक्तिविशेष्यकसमवायसम्बन्धेन शुक्तित्वप्रकारकप्रवृत्तिवदित्यर्थः।

केचित्तु तादात्म्यसम्बन्धेन रजतप्रकारिका शुक्तिविशेष्यिका प्रवृ-

त्तिरिति पञ्चार्थः, तादात्म्यसम्बन्धेनेष्टप्रकारकप्रवृत्तिविषयविशेष्यक-ज्ञानसाध्येति साध्यार्थः, इष्टत्वादिकञ्च पूर्ववत्, अन्यथा शुक्तिविशेष्यकरजतप्रकारकप्रवृत्तिस्थले शुक्तेरेव स्वजनकेच्छाविशेष्यतया तद्भेदज्ञानस्य चाहेतुत्वाद्बाधापत्तेः, तादात्म्यसंसर्गकप्रवृत्तित्वादिति हेत्वर्थः, तेन समवायसम्बन्धेन रजतत्वादिप्रकारकप्रवृत्तौ न व्यभिचारः, तादात्म्यसम्बन्धेन शुक्तिप्रकारक-शुक्तिविशेष्यकप्रवृत्तिवदिति दृष्टान्तार्थः इत्याहुः। तदसत्। 'समवायातीन्द्रियत्ववादिनं प्रतीत्याद्यग्रिमग्रन्थासङ्गतेः तच्च तत्रैव स्फुटीभविष्यति इति दिक्।

'इष्टविषयप्रवृत्तित्वमिति इष्टविशेष्यकप्रवृत्तित्वमित्यर्थः, अत्रेष्टत्वं इष्टतावच्छेदकाश्रयत्वं, स्वजनकेच्छाप्रकाराश्रयत्वमिति यावत् स्वप्रकाराश्रयत्वमिति तु निष्कर्षः। स्वजनकेच्छाविशेष्यत्वरूपे यथाश्रुतेऽर्थे रजतत्वेन शुक्तेरेव स्वजनकेच्छाविशेष्यतया साधनव्यापकत्वापत्तेः। 'साधनविशेषितत्वादिति प्रवृत्तित्वघटितत्वादित्यर्थः, विषयविशेषितेच्छानुव्यवसायादौ आहार्य्यधारावाहिकज्ञानादौ च साध्यवति प्रवृत्तित्वघटितत्वस्याभावेन साध्याव्यापकत्वात् स्वविशेष्यविशेष्यक-स्वप्रकारप्रकारकज्ञानसाध्यत्वस्य साध्यत्वे अनुमित्यादावपि साध्याव्यापकत्वाच्चेति भावः। यद्यपि प्रवृत्तित्वरूपसाधनावच्छिन्नसाध्यव्यापकत्वमस्त्येव तथापि शुद्धसाध्यव्यापक एवोपाधिरिति मतेनेदमभिहितं।

वस्तुतस्तु अस्योपाधित्वज्ञानसत्त्वात् कथं व्याप्तिग्रह इति पूर्व्वपक्षिणोऽभिमतं,[१] किं वा वस्तुगत्या अनेनोपाधिना सोपाधितया

(१) पूर्व्वपक्षिणाभिहितमिति ग०।

यद्वा रजतेच्छाजन्यशुक्तिविषयप्रवृत्तिजनकरजतत्वप्रकारकं ज्ञानं शुक्तिविशेष्यकं शुक्तिप्रवृत्तिप्रयोजकज्ञानत्वात् शुक्तौ शुक्त्यर्थिप्रवृत्तिजनकज्ञानवत्। अव-

---

अयं हेतुर्दुष्ट इत्यभिमतं,[१] नाद्यः उपाधिज्ञानस्य कादाचित्कतया तद्विरहदशायामेव व्याप्तिग्रहसम्भवात् अन्यथा अनुमानमात्रोच्छेदात् सर्व्वत्रैव कस्यचिदुपाधिलभ्रमसम्भवात्। नान्त्यः लाघवेन तद्विशेष्यक-तत्प्रकारकप्रवृत्तिं प्रति तद्विशेष्यक-तत्प्रकारकप्रत्ययत्वेन हेतुत्वात् पक्ष एव साध्याव्यापकतया अस्य वस्तुगत्या उपाधित्वविरहादित्येव दूषणं सारं। एतेन प्रवृत्तित्वाविशेषितं स्वजनकेच्छाप्रकाराश्रयविशेष्यकत्वं स्वप्रकाराश्रयविशेष्यकत्वस्य शुद्धसाध्यव्यापकतया उपाधिरित्यपि निरस्तं।

नवीननये स्वत्वस्य तत्तद्व्यक्तिविश्रान्ततया स्वपदस्य प्रकृतपक्षपरत्वे अपसिद्धिः, दृष्टान्तपरत्वे बाध इत्यतोऽनुमानान्तरमाह, 'यद्वेति रजतेच्छाजन्या या शुक्तिविशेष्यिका प्रवृत्तिः तत्प्रयोजकं रजतत्वप्रकारकज्ञानमित्यर्थः, अत्र 'रजतेच्छाजन्येति स्वरूपकथनं, अन्यत्सर्व्वं पूर्व्वोक्तदिशावसेयं। 'शुक्तिविशेष्यकमिति अग्रावच्छिन्नो वृक्षः संयोगीत्यादिवत् पक्षतावच्छेदकरजतत्वप्रकारकत्वावच्छेदेन शुक्तिविशेष्यकत्वसिद्ध्या अन्यथाख्यातिसिद्धिरित्यर्थः, 'शुक्तिप्रवृत्तीति शुक्तिविशेष्यकप्रवृत्तिप्रयोजकज्ञानत्वादित्यर्थः। पूर्व्वोक्तासिद्धिमुद्धरति, 'अवच्छेदकत्वेऽपीति अवच्छेदकव्यावृत्तान्यथासिद्धिचतुष्टयराहित्ये सति

---

(२) इत्यभिहितमिति ग०।

च्छेदकत्वेऽपि प्रयोजकत्वाभ्नासिद्धिः। हेतुत्वमपि तस्य साधयिष्यामः। तथाविधमिदं ज्ञानं वा रजतत्वप्रकारकं रजतेच्छाजन्यप्रवृत्तिहेतुज्ञानत्वात् सत्यरजतज्ञान-

---

नियतपूर्ववर्त्तित्वरूपस्यात्र प्रयोजकत्वरूपत्वादितिभावः[१]। 'हेतुत्व-मपीति, इष्टतावच्छेदकज्ञान-इष्टभेदाग्रहयोर्विशेष्य-विशेषणभावे विनिगमकाभावात् कार्य्य-कारणभावद्वयस्यावश्यकतया उभयोरस्वातन्त्र्येण हेतुत्वादिति भावः। 'तथाविधमिति रजतत्वप्रकारकप्रवृत्तिजनकमित्यर्थः, 'इदं ज्ञानं' शुक्तिविशेष्यकं ज्ञानं, अत्र शुक्तावियं शुक्तिरिति ज्ञानेऽंशतो बाधवारणाय जनकान्तं। प्राचीनमते पक्षतावच्छेदकावच्छेदेन साध्यसिद्धेरुद्देश्यत्वादंशतः सिद्धसाधनस्य दोषत्वात् रजतमात्रविशेष्यक-रजतत्वप्रकारकज्ञानेऽंशतः सिद्धसाधनवारणाय 'शुक्तिविशेष्यकेति, शुक्तौ रजतत्वप्रकारकेच्छायामंशतः सिद्धसाधनवारणाय 'ज्ञानमिति। एकमात्रविशेष्यकत्वेन ज्ञानं विशेषणीयं, तेन शुक्तिरजतोभयसमूहालम्बने नांशतः सिद्धसाधनमिति भावः। 'रजतत्वप्रकारकमिति अत्राप्यव्याप्यावच्छिन्नोवृत्तः कपिसंयोगीत्यादिवत् पक्षतावच्छेदकावच्छेदेन साध्यसिद्धौ शुक्तिविशेष्यकत्वावच्छिन्नरजतत्वप्रकारिताकज्ञानसिद्धिः तदेव चान्यथाख्यातिसिद्धिरित्यर्थः, 'रजतेच्छा-

---

(१) अनुगतान्यथासिद्धित्वस्य निर्वक्तुमशक्यत्वात् कारणतावच्छेदकघटितान्यथासिद्धिसामान्याभावनिवेशासम्भवादुक्तं अन्यथासिद्धिचतुष्टयराहित्ये सतीति, तथा च तत्तदन्यथासिद्ध्यभावघटितकूटस्यैव प्रयोजकत्वशरीरेऽन्तर्भाव इति भावः।

वत्। न च ग्रहण-स्मरणयोर्विशिष्टस्य ज्ञानस्य वा पक्षत्वे बाध आश्रयासिद्धिर्वा, उभयसिद्धेन शुक्तिनिष्ठ-प्रवृत्तिहेतुत्वेन पक्षत्वात्। अन्यथा साध्य-तदभाववतः

जन्येति रजतत्वप्रकारकप्रवृत्तिहेतुज्ञानत्वादित्यर्थः। तेनेश्वरीयरजतेच्छाजन्यशुक्तिविशेष्यकशुक्तित्वादिप्रकारकप्रवृत्त्यादिजनके इयं शुक्तिरिति ज्ञाने न व्यभिचार इति ध्येयं। 'यद्देत्याद्यनुमानद्वये शङ्कते, 'नचेति, 'ग्रहण-स्मरणयोरिति 'तथाविधमित्यादिद्वितीयानुमाने ग्रहणस्य केवलेदन्त्वप्रकारकानुभवस्य पक्षत्वे बाधः, 'रजतेच्छाजन्येत्यादिप्रथमानुमाने स्मरणस्य रजतमात्रविशेष्यकस्मरणस्य पक्षत्वे बाधः, उभयत्रैव शुक्तिविशेष्यकरजतत्वप्रकारकज्ञानस्य पक्षत्वे आश्रयस्य पक्षस्याज्ञानरूपासिद्धिरित्यर्थः। 'शुक्तिनिष्ठेति शुक्तिविशेष्यकप्रवृत्तिप्रयोजकज्ञानत्वेनेत्यर्थः, इदञ्च प्रथमाभिप्रायेण, द्वितीये तु रजतत्वप्रकारकप्रवृत्तिजनकज्ञानत्वेनेति बोध्यं। 'पक्षत्वादिति अतिरिक्तविशिष्टभ्रमव्यक्तेरेव पक्षत्वादित्यर्थः। न च तज्ज्ञानासिद्धिरिति वाच्यं। तव नये पक्षधर्मताबललभ्यसाध्यव्यक्तेरिव पक्षधर्मताबललभ्यपक्षव्यक्तेरपि ज्ञानस्याहेतुतया पक्षतावच्छेदकरूपेण प्रसिद्धपक्षकपरामर्शादेव पक्षधर्मताबलादप्रसिद्धपक्षव्यक्तिभानसम्भवेन तदप्रसिद्धावपि क्षतिविरहात्, मम तु शुक्तिविशेष्यकप्रवृत्तिप्रयोजकज्ञानत्वादिरूपेण तस्यापि ज्ञानसत्त्वादिति भावः। 'अन्यथा' पक्षधर्मताबललभ्यपक्षव्यक्तेर्विशेषतो ज्ञानस्यापेक्षितत्वे, 'साध्य-तदभाववतः पक्षत्वेनेति 'साध्यः' साधनीयो यो धर्मी, यस्य 'तदभाववान्' साधनी-

पक्षत्वेनानुमानोच्छेदः। समवायातीन्द्रियत्ववादिनं प्रति अगृहीतासंसर्गकधर्मधर्मिविषयकमेकं ज्ञानमेव विशिष्टज्ञानं सिद्ध्यति। नचैवमुभयख्यातिः नान्यथाख्या-

---

यान्योन्याभाववान् धर्मी प्रसिद्धो धर्मीति यावत्, तयोः पक्षत्ववि-कल्पेनेत्यर्थः, 'अनुमानोच्छेदः' पक्षधर्मताबलेन पक्षविधया अपूर्व्व-व्यक्तिसाध्यकानुमानमात्रोच्छेदः। ननु तन्मते समवायसम्बन्धेन स्वजनकेच्छाप्रकारप्रकारक-स्वविशेष्य-विशेष्यकज्ञानजन्यत्वं साध्यमप्रसिद्धं तन्मते समवायस्यातीन्द्रियतया सत्यस्थलेऽपि समवायस्य संसर्गमर्य्या-दया अभानात् उपादानगोचरप्रत्यक्षस्यैव हेतुतया आनुमानिकादि-ज्ञानस्याहेतुत्वादित्यत आह, 'समवायेति समवायस्यातीन्द्रियतया संसर्गमर्य्यादयाप्यभानवादिनं प्रतीत्यर्थः, 'अगृहीतासंसर्गकधर्म-धर्मिविषयकमिति समवायसम्बन्धावच्छिन्नधर्म-धर्मिभावाख्यस्वरूप-सम्बन्धविशेषसंसर्गकमित्यर्थः, 'एकं ज्ञानमिति स्वजनकेच्छाप्रकार-प्रकारक-स्वविशेष्यविशेष्यकज्ञानमित्यर्थः, तैः समवायस्य संसर्गमर्य्या-दया भानानभ्युपगमेऽपि समवायसम्बन्धावच्छिन्नधर्म-धर्मिभावात्मक-स्वरूपसम्बन्धविशेषस्य संसर्गमर्य्यादया भानाभ्युपगमात् तज्जन्यत्वस्यैव साध्यत्वात्। न चैवं न्यायनये अप्रसिद्धिरिति वाच्यं। नैयायिकैरपि इदं रजतमित्यत्र समवायवत् तदवच्छिन्नधर्म-धर्मिभावस्यापि संस-र्गत्वाभ्युपगमादिति भावः। 'उभयख्यातिरिति शुक्तिविशेष्यक-रज-तत्वप्रकारकख्यातिरित्यर्थः, सिद्धान्तीति शेषः, 'नान्यथाख्यातिरिति न तु रजतत्वाभाववद्विशेष्यकत्वावच्छिन्न-रजतत्वप्रकारकत्वविशिष्टख्याति-

तिरिति वाच्यं। व्यधिकरणप्रकारकज्ञानस्य तत्त्वात्। न च विसंवादिप्रवृत्त्यजनकत्वमुपाधिः, तथाविधे इदं-ज्ञाने रजतज्ञाने च[१] त्वन्मते साध्याव्यापकत्वात्।

रित्यर्थः, शुक्तौ रजतत्वाभाववत्त्वभासकाभावादिति भावः। 'व्यधि-करणप्रकारकज्ञानस्येति रजतत्वाभाववद्विशेष्यकत्वावच्छिन्नरजतत्व-प्रकारकत्वाश्रयज्ञानस्यैवेत्यर्थः, 'तत्त्वादिति शुक्तिविशेष्यक-रजतत्व-प्रकारकत्वसम्भवादित्यर्थः, तथा च शुक्तिविशेष्यक-रजतत्वप्रकारकत्वे सिद्धे तेन हेतुना पश्चात्तदनुमेयमिति हृदयं। 'यद्वेत्याद्यनुमानद्वये उपाधिमाशङ्कते, 'न चेति, पक्षधर्मज्ञानत्वावच्छिन्नसाध्यव्यापकत्वा-दित्यभिमानः। अभिमानं निराकरोति, 'तथाविध इति विसंवा-दिप्रवृत्तिजनक इत्यर्थः, 'इदंज्ञाने' इदन्त्वरूपेण शुक्त्यनुभवे, एतच्च शुक्तिविषयकत्वे साध्ये बोध्यं। रजतत्वप्रकारकत्वे साध्ये त्वाह, 'रज-तज्ञाने चेति रजतस्मरणेचेत्यर्थः, 'त्वन्मत इति, मन्मते तु शुक्तिविशे-ष्यक-रजतत्वप्रकारकज्ञाने च साध्याव्यापकमिति भावः। 'परस्येति, तथाच साधनव्यापकत्वमिति भावः। 'तथात्वात्' दोषाजन्यत्वात्। अस्मन्मते तु शुक्तिविशेष्यक-रजतत्वप्रकारकज्ञाने एव साध्याव्याप-कत्वमिति हृदयं। 'अन्यथा' विसंवादिप्रवृत्तिजनकज्ञानस्य दोष-जन्यत्वाभ्युपगमे, 'तयोरेवेति शुक्तिविषयकत्वे साध्ये इदन्त्वरूपेण शुक्त्यनुभव एव साध्याव्यापकत्वं, रजतत्वप्रकारकत्वे साध्ये रजतस्मरण-

---

(१) रजतस्मरणे चेति ग।

नापि दोषाजन्यत्वं, परस्य ज्ञानमात्रे तथात्वात्। अन्यथा तयोरेव साध्याव्यापकत्वात्। न चाप्रयोजकत्वं, इष्टपुरोवर्त्तिविशिष्टज्ञानस्य प्रवृत्तिहेतुत्वात्।

अत्र प्राभाकराः। अप्रयोजकमिदं स्वतन्त्रोपस्थितेष्टभेदाग्रहादेव प्रवृत्त्युपपत्तेः किं विशिष्टज्ञानेन। परेणाप्यारोपनियमार्थं तदभ्युपगमात्। न च रजते प्रवृ-

---

एव साध्याव्यापकत्वमित्यर्थः। 'इष्टपुरोवर्त्तीति पुरोवर्त्तिविशेष्यकेष्टतावच्छेदकप्रकारकज्ञानस्येत्यर्थः, 'प्रवृत्तिहेतुत्वादिति पुरोवर्त्तिविशेष्यकेष्टतावच्छेदकप्रकारकप्रवृत्तिं प्रति हेतुत्वादित्यर्थः।

'स्वतन्त्रोपस्थितेति स्वातन्त्र्येणाभावाविशेषणत्वेनोपस्थितयोः रजतत्वावच्छिन्नेदन्त्वावच्छिन्नयोर्भेदाग्रहादेवेत्यर्थः, 'प्रवृत्त्युपपत्तेरिति शुक्तौ रजतत्वादिप्रकारकप्रवृत्त्युपपत्तेरित्यर्थः, 'किं विशिष्टज्ञानेनेति किं शुक्तौ रजतत्वादिप्रकारकज्ञानेनेत्यर्थः, तथा च स्वातन्त्र्येणेदन्त्वावच्छिन्न-रजतत्वावच्छिन्नयोरुपस्थितिरिदन्त्वावच्छिन्न-रजतत्वावच्छिन्नयोर्भेदाग्रहश्च रजतत्वप्रकारकप्रवृत्तिहेतुरिति भावः। अत्रेदं-रजतयोरनुपस्थितिदशायामपि तयोर्भेदाग्रहस्य सत्त्वात्तदानीं प्रवृत्तिवारणाय उपस्थितेरादरः, रजते नेदं रजतमिति ज्ञानस्याप्यन्यथाख्यात्यापत्त्या ज्ञानद्वयात्मकत्वेनेदन्त्वरूपेण रजते रजतभेदाविषयकत्वात्ततोऽपि प्रवृत्तिप्रसङ्गवारणाय स्वातन्त्र्येणेति रजतत्वावच्छिन्नोपस्थितिविशेषणं, यत्र चात्र भेद इत्यनुभवो रजतस्मरणञ्चेति क्रमेण रजते नेदं रजतमिति भ्रमस्तत्र प्रवृत्तिवारणाय स्वातन्त्र्ये-

त्तिं प्रति विशिष्टज्ञानस्य हेतुत्वादिहापि तत्सिद्धिः, प्रवृत्तिमात्रे भेदाग्रहे सतीष्ट-पुरोवर्त्तिज्ञानस्य लाघवेन हेतुत्वान्न तु सदपि विशिष्टज्ञानं तन्त्रं गौरवात्। न च

णेति इदन्त्वावच्छिन्नोपस्थितेरपि विशेषणं। प्रतियोगितावच्छेदकप्रकारकप्रतियोगिज्ञानस्याभावलौकिकप्रत्यक्षहेतुतया शुक्तौ नेदं रजतमिति भेदलौकिकप्रत्यक्षदशायामपि स्मरणादिलक्षणस्वतन्त्ररजतत्वावच्छिन्नोपस्थितिसत्त्वादेवं रजत-शुक्त्योरिमे रजत-रजतभिन्ने इति समूहालम्बनदशायामपि इदन्त्व-रजतत्वरूपेण शुक्ति-रजतयोः स्वतन्त्रोपस्थितिसत्त्वाच्च तदानीं शुक्तौ रजतत्वप्रकारकप्रवृत्तिवारणाय भेदाग्रहादरः। भेदपदस्योपलक्षणं रजतत्वात्यन्ताभावोऽपि द्रष्टव्यः, नातो रजतमिति स्मरणदशायामिदं रजतत्वात्यन्ताभाववदिति ज्ञानात् शुक्तौ रजतत्वप्रकारकप्रवृत्तिः, न वा रजत-शुक्त्योरिमे रजतत्व-तदत्यन्ताभाववती इति समूहालम्बनदशायामपीदन्त्व-रजतत्वरूपेण शुक्ति-रजतयोः स्वतन्त्रोपस्थितिसत्त्वेऽपि शुक्तौ रजतत्वप्रकारकप्रवृत्तिः। न चैवं प्रतियोगितावच्छेदकविशिष्टप्रतियोगिज्ञानमादाय रजते नेदं रजतमिति ज्ञानस्थले प्रवृत्त्यतिप्रसङ्गो दुर्वार इति वाच्यं। अभावलौकिकप्रत्यक्षं प्रति प्रतियोगितावच्छेदकविशिष्टप्रतियोगिज्ञानस्य हेतुत्वात् रजते नेदं रजतमिति ज्ञानस्य च भ्रमरूपतया तन्मते अभावांशे लौकिकप्रत्यक्षानात्मकत्वात् तन्मते रजते नेदं रजतमिति भ्रमस्य ज्ञानद्वयतया तज्जनकीभूतप्रतियोगितावच्छेदकविशिष्टप्रतियोगिज्ञानस्य प्रवृत्तिपूर्व्वमनवस्थानाच्च युग-

रजते इष्ट-पुरोवर्त्तिभेदग्रहस्याप्रसिद्धा कथन्तदभाव इति वाच्यं। पुरोवर्त्तिनिष्ठे भेदे रजतप्रतियोगित्वज्ञानविषयत्वाभावस्य पुरोवर्त्तिनीष्टभिन्नत्वप्रकारकज्ञान-

---

पजज्ञानद्वयानुपस्थितेः। न चैवं घटं रजतवत् इदञ्च तद्रजतमित्यादि समूहालम्बनादपि प्रवृत्तिप्रसङ्गः स्वतन्त्ररजतत्वावच्छिन्नेदन्त्वावच्छिन्नोपस्थिति-भेदाग्रहयोः सत्त्वादिति वाच्यं। इष्टत्वात्। तथापि तदनन्तरं इदं रजतमिति विशिष्टज्ञानसम्भवेन तृतीयक्षणे तत्र प्रवृत्तेरभ्युपगमादिति भावः। इदमापाततः रजतमिदं गेहे नास्ति रजतवन्निष्ठभेदप्रतियोगि भूतलमित्यादिज्ञानादप्रवृत्त्यापत्तेः अभावाविशेषणत्वेनेदन्त्वावच्छिन्न-रजतत्वावच्छिन्नयोरुपस्थितिविरहात्। यत्र च भेदप्रकारेणेदमनुभवो रजतस्मरणञ्चेतिक्रमेण रजते नेदं रजतमिति भ्रमस्तत्र, यत्र वा घटं रजतवदिदञ्च न रजतमिति समूहालम्बनात्मा रजते रजतभेदवत्ताभ्रमस्तत्र च प्रवृत्त्यापत्तेः। किञ्च यन्मते ग्रहण-स्मरणात्मकमेकमेव ज्ञानं भ्रमस्तन्मते रजतमिति स्मरणदशायां रजते नेदं रजतमितिज्ञानात् प्रवृत्त्यतिप्रसङ्गोदुर्व्वारः। न च भ्रमस्यैव ज्ञानत्वाभ्युपगमे धर्म्म-धर्म्मिविषयकैकज्ञानत्वेन विशिष्टधीत्वादन्यथाख्यातित्वापत्तिरिति वाच्यं। समूहालम्बनवत् प्रकारप्रकारीभावविरहादिति दिक्।

ननु यत्र भेदाग्रहो नास्ति तत्र प्रवृत्तिः कथं स्यादित्यत आह, 'परेणापीति, 'नियमार्थं' उत्पादार्थं, 'तदभ्यूपगमात्' प्रवृत्तिपूर्व्वं भेदाग्रहस्यावश्यमभ्युपगमात्।'रजते प्रवृत्तिं प्रतीति रजतविशेष्यक-रज-

विषयत्वाभावस्य वा हेतुत्वात्। न चाभेदव्यवहारो व्यवहर्त्तव्यधीसाध्यो न तु तदभावाग्रहात् अन्यथा-भेदाग्रहाद्भेदव्यवहारापत्तिरिति वाच्यं। इच्छादीनां

तत्वप्रकारकप्रवृत्तिं प्रतीत्यर्थः, 'विशिष्टज्ञानस्येति इदन्त्वधर्म्मितावच्छे-दककरजतविशेष्यक-रजतत्वप्रकारकज्ञानस्येत्यर्थः, 'इहापि' शुक्तिवि-ष्यक-रजतत्वप्रकारकप्रवृत्तिस्थलेऽपि, 'तत्सिद्धिरिति इदन्त्वधर्म्मिताव-च्छेदकक-शुक्तिविशेष्यक-रजतत्वप्रकारकज्ञानसिद्धिरित्यर्थः,तत्रेदन्त्वध-र्म्मितावच्छेदकक-रजतविशेष्यक-रजतत्वप्रकारकज्ञानस्य हेतुत्वे कल्प्य-माने सामान्यतस्तद्विशेष्यक-रजतत्वप्रकारकप्रवृत्तित्वेन कार्य्यता इदन्त्व-धर्म्मितावच्छेदकक-तद्विशेष्यक-रजतत्वप्रकारकज्ञानत्वेन कारणतेति-क्रमेण कल्पनादिति भावः। इदञ्च तत्त्वेदन्त्वयोरनुगतत्वमभिप्रेत्य।

नन्वास्तु तत्पुरुषीयरजतत्वप्रकारकप्रवृत्तित्वेन तत्पुरुषीयरजतत्व-प्रकारकज्ञानत्वेन हेतु-हेतुमद्भावः, यत्र विशेष्यतासम्बन्धेन तत्पु-रुषीयरजतत्वप्रकारकप्रवृत्तिः तत्र व्यक्तिद्वयावृत्तिधर्म्मविशिष्टविशेष्य-तासम्बन्धेन तत्पुरुषीयरजतत्वप्रकारकज्ञानमिति विशेष्यताघटित-सामानाधिकरण्यं प्रत्यासत्तिरित्यभिप्रायेणायं ग्रन्थः, प्रवृत्तित्वञ्चा-भावीयविशेषणतया विवक्षितं, तादृशधर्म्मः तत्तद्विशेष्यव्यक्तिमात्र-वृत्तिविशेष्यताव्यक्त्यात्मकं तादृशविशेष्यताव्यक्त्यात्मकं वा इदन्त्वमेव। तद्विशिष्टत्वञ्च स्व(१) सामानाधिकरण्य-स्वावच्छिन्नावच्छेदकतानिरूप-

---

(१) स्वं तादृशधर्म्मः।

ज्ञातपुरोवर्त्तिमात्रविषयत्वात्। अभेदाभिलापोऽपि ज्ञाताभेदस्यासंसर्गाग्रहादिति नाज्ञाते व्यवहारः। ननु

कत्वोभयसम्बन्धेन ग्राह्यं, तेन शुक्तिवृत्ति[१]तादृशेदन्त्वधर्म्मितावच्छेदककादभावीयविशेषणताविशेषसम्बन्धेन[२] द्रव्यत्वादिधर्म्मितावच्छेदककाद्वा रजतविशेष्यक-रजतत्वप्रकारकज्ञानान्न रजते रजतत्वप्रकारिका प्रवृत्तिः सर्व्वत्र स्वरूपतस्तत्तदधिकरणताव्यक्त्यात्मकेदन्त्वधर्म्मितावच्छेदककं स्वरूपतस्तत्तद्विशेष्यताव्यक्त्यात्मकेदन्त्वधर्म्मितावच्छेदककं वा ज्ञानमेव प्रवर्त्तकं न त्विदन्त्वान्तरधर्म्मितावच्छेदककमिति न व्यभिचार इति प्राञ्चः।

'प्रवृत्तिमात्रे' सत्यासत्यस्थलीयरजतत्वप्रकारकप्रवृत्तिमात्रे, 'भेदाग्रहे सति' इदन्त्वरूपेण प्रवृत्तिविशेष्ये रजतभेदाग्रहे सति, 'इष्टपुरोवर्त्तिज्ञानस्येति रजतत्वावच्छिन्नरजतेदन्त्वावच्छिन्नप्रवृत्तिविशेष्ययोर्ज्ञानस्येत्यर्थः, 'लाघवेन' अनन्यथासिद्धत्वमात्रकल्पनालाघवेन। 'सदपीति सत्यस्थलीयरजतत्वप्रकारकप्रवृत्तिस्थले सदपीत्यर्थः, 'विशिष्टज्ञानमिति इदन्त्वधर्म्मितावच्छेदकक-प्रवृत्तिविशेष्यविशेष्यक-रजतत्वप्रकारकज्ञानमित्यर्थः, 'तन्त्रमिति तद्विशेष्यक-रजतत्वप्रकारकप्रवृत्तित्वावच्छिन्नं प्रति इदन्त्वधर्म्मितावच्छेदकक-तद्विशेष्यकरजतत्वप्रकारकज्ञानत्वेन तन्त्रमित्यर्थः, 'गौरवादिति अनन्यथासिद्धत्व-नियतपूर्व्ववर्त्तित्वोभयकल्पनागौरवादित्यर्थः। 'रजत इति रजतविशेष्यक-रजतत्वप्रकारकप्रवृत्तिस्थल इत्यर्थः, 'इष्ट-पुरोवर्त्तीति इदन्त्वरूपेण प्रवृत्ति-

(१) स्वसामानाधिकरण्येत्यादिसम्बन्धनिवेशप्रयोजनमाह शुक्तीति।
(२) इदन्तु व्यक्तिद्वयावृत्तीत्यस्य प्रयोजनं।

पीतः शङ्खो न श्वेत इति भेदज्ञानेऽपि श्वेताभेदानुमित्या श्वेतार्थिप्रवृत्तेरभेदधीस्तद्धेतुरिति चेत् । न । तवापि

विशेष्ये रजतत्वावच्छिन्नभेदग्रहस्येत्यर्थः, अन्यथाख्यात्यनभ्युपगमादिति भावः । 'कथं तदभाव इति, कारणमिति शेषः । 'पुरोवर्त्तिनिष्ठेति इदन्त्वावच्छिन्ननिष्ठभेदत्वावच्छिन्ने इत्यर्थः, 'रजतप्रतियोगित्वेति रजतत्वावच्छिन्नप्रतियोगिताकत्वप्रकारकज्ञानविशेष्यत्वाभावस्येत्यर्थः, एतन्निष्ठभेदोरजतत्वावच्छिन्नप्रतियोगिताक इति ज्ञाने प्रवृत्त्यनुदयादिति भावः । अत्र तत्तत्पुरुषीयत्वेन ज्ञानं विशेषणीयं, तेन पुरुषान्तरीयतादृशज्ञानविशेष्यत्वसत्त्वेऽपि न प्रवृत्त्यनुपपत्तिः । कालान्तरे तत्पुरुषस्य तादृशज्ञानसत्त्वेपि प्रवृत्त्यव्यवहितपूर्व्वकाले तदभावसत्त्वान्न यदाकदाचित् तत्पुरुषीयतादृशज्ञानमादायातिप्रसङ्गः, एवमग्रेऽपीति ध्येयं । 'पुरोवर्त्तिनीति इदन्त्वावच्छिन्ने प्रवृत्तिविशेष्ये इत्यर्थः, 'इष्टभिन्नत्वेति रजतभिन्नत्वेत्यर्थः, इदं रजतभिन्नमिति ज्ञानेऽपि प्रवृत्त्यनुदयादिति भावः । 'वाशब्दस्समुच्चयार्थे, न तु विकल्पे, उभयोरेव ज्ञानयोः प्रतिबन्धकतया अभावद्वयस्यैव हेतुत्वात् । न च रजत एव नेदं रजतमिति ज्ञानात् प्रवृत्त्यापत्तिः भ्रमानङ्गीकारेण तत्रापि इदन्त्वावच्छिन्ने रजते च रजतभिन्नत्वप्रकारकज्ञानविषयत्वाभावसत्त्वादिति वाच्यं । तत्र निरुक्तभेदाग्रहसत्त्वेऽपि निरुक्तस्वतन्त्ररजतत्वोपस्थितिविरहादप्रवृत्तेरिति भावः । 'अभेदव्यवहार इति, शुक्तिविशेष्यक-रजताभेदप्रकारकेच्छादिरित्यर्थः, 'व्यवहर्त्तव्यधीसाध्य इति स्वविशेष्यविशेष्यक-रजताभेदप्रकारकज्ञानसाध्य इत्यर्थः, यो रजताभेदप्रकारकव्यवहारः

पीतः शङ्ख इत्यभेदज्ञानात् पीतार्थी न प्रवर्त्तते भेदानुमितेरिति भेदाग्रह एव तद्धेतुः स्यात् । भ्रमत्वेन ज्ञातम-

---

स स्वविशेष्यकतादृशज्ञानसाध्यः रजताभेदप्रकारकव्यवहारवदिति व्याप्तेरिति भावः । 'न तु तदभावाग्रहादिति न तु शुक्तौ रजताभेदाभावाग्रहमात्रादित्यर्थः । 'अन्यथा' तदभावाग्रहमात्रादेव तत्प्रकारकव्यवहाराभ्युपगमे, 'अभेदाग्रहादिति यदा भेदोऽभेदश्च न गृहीतस्तदाप्यभेदाग्रहसत्त्वात् भेदव्यवहारापत्तिरित्यर्थः । ज्ञानवदिच्छादेरपि व्यधिकरणप्रकारकत्वमनभ्युपेत्य समाधत्ते, 'इच्छादीनामिति, 'ज्ञातपुरोवर्त्तिमात्रेति खण्डशो रजताभेद-शुक्तिविषयकत्वादित्यर्थः, तथाच शुक्तिविशेष्यक-रजताभेदप्रकारकव्यवहारत्वमेवासिद्धमिति भावः । नन्विच्छादीनां व्यधिकरणप्रकारकत्वानभ्युपगमे तवापसिद्धान्त इत्यस्वरसादाह, 'अभेदाभिलापोऽपीति प्रवृत्तिवदिदं रजताभिन्नमित्यभिलापादिरपीत्यर्थः, आदिपदादिच्छादिपरिग्रहः, तथाचाप्रयोजकत्वमितिभावः । 'ननु पीतः शङ्ख इति 'पीत इति स्वरूपकथनं, अयं न श्वेत इतिदोषविशेषजन्यभेदज्ञानेऽपीत्यर्थः, 'श्वेताभेदानुमित्येति अयं श्वेत इतिविशेषदर्शनजन्यभ्रमोत्तरप्रत्यक्षेणेत्यर्थः, यथाश्रुते उपादानगोचरप्रत्यक्षस्यैव प्रवृत्तिहेतुत्वादानुमानिकज्ञानात् प्रवृत्त्यसम्भवादसङ्गतेः । 'अभेदधीस्तद्धेतुरिति अभेदधीरेव प्रवृत्तिहेतुरित्यर्थः, अन्यथा भेदाग्रहस्य प्रवर्त्तकत्वे तत्र भेदग्रहसत्त्वात् प्रवृत्त्यनुपपत्तेः । न च तत्र विशेषदर्शनेनाभेदप्रत्यक्षोत्पत्तिसमये श्वेतभेदज्ञानमावश्यकं प्रवृत्त्यनुपपत्तिरिति वाच्यं । यत्र श्वेताभेदव्याप्य-

भेदज्ञानमकिञ्चित्करमिति यदि तदा भ्रमत्वेन ज्ञातं भेदज्ञानमपि तथा।

वत्तापरामर्शरूपविशेषदर्शनात्मकमेव भेदज्ञानं तच्च प्रवृत्त्यनुपपत्ते-रिति भावः। यद्यपि शङ्खे श्वेतभेदग्रहे अन्यथाख्यात्यापत्त्या तत्रापि तन्मते भेदाग्रहोऽस्त्येवेति न प्रवृत्त्यनुपपत्तिः, तथापि स्फुटतरत्वा-दुपेत्य समाधानान्तरमाह, 'तत्रापीति, 'अभेदज्ञानात्' दोषविशेष-जन्याभेदप्रत्यक्षात्। कुतो न प्रवर्त्तते तदेवाह, 'भेदानुमितेरिति शङ्खत्वहेतुकपीतभेदानुमितेरित्यर्थः। 'अभेदज्ञानं' पीतः शङ्ख इति दोषविशेषजन्यमभेदज्ञानं, 'अकिञ्चित्करं' प्रवृत्त्यजनकं, अगृहीत-भ्रमत्वकाभेदज्ञानस्यैव प्रवृत्तिहेतुत्वादिति भावः। 'भेदज्ञानमपि' दोषविशेषजन्यश्वेतभेदज्ञानमपि, 'तथा' प्रवृत्त्यप्रतिबन्धकं। समाप्य-गृहीतभ्रमत्वकभेदग्रहाभावस्यैव प्रवृत्तिहेतुत्वादिति भावः। भ्रम-त्वन्तु इच्छादिप्रसिद्धव्यधिकरणप्रकारकत्वं ज्ञानद्वयत्वं वा तज्ज्ञानमपि स्वतन्त्रोपस्थितस्यासंसर्गाग्रहो विशिष्टज्ञानं वेत्यन्यदेतत्।

ननु तन्मते[१] अभावस्याकारणत्वाद्भेदाग्रहस्य न हेतुत्व-सम्भव इत्यस्वरसादाह, 'यद्वेति, 'इष्टभेदाविषयकमिति, 'इष्टः' स्वजनकेच्छाप्रकाराश्रयो रजतादिः, तद्भेदाविषयकं रजतत्वावच्छिन्न-स्येदन्त्वावच्छिन्नस्य च स्वातन्त्र्येण ज्ञानमित्यर्थः, एवञ्च शङ्खो न श्वेत इत्यत्र पूर्व्वं श्वेतभेदप्रत्ययेऽपि तदुत्तरं श्वेताभेदप्रत्यक्षस्यैव

---

(१) ननु भवन्मते इति ख०।

यद्वा इष्टभेदाविषयकं ज्ञानं प्रवर्त्तकं। न चाभेदानुमिताविष्टभेदोविषयः। अत एव पूर्वं भेदप्रत्ययेऽपि स प्रत्ययो न भेदग्राहीतिदिङ्मोह-प्रतिविम्बादिप्रत्ययाः।

तादृशज्ञानस्य सत्त्वान्न प्रवृत्त्यनुपपत्तिरिति भावः। नन्वेवं रङ्गं न रजतमिदञ्च रजतमित्यादिसमूहालम्बनादप्रवृत्त्यापत्तिस्तस्येष्टभेदविषयकत्वात्। न चेष्टभेदाविषयकत्वपदेन स्वसमानकालीनस्वसमानाधिकरणोपस्थितिविषयेष्टभेदाग्रहीतासंसर्गकपुरोवर्त्तिविषयकं यद्यत् तदन्यत्वं विवक्षितं, भवति च उक्तसमूहालम्बनमपि तथा तेन पुरोवर्त्तिनि रजते तादृशरजतभेदासंसर्गस्य रजतत्वस्य ग्रहादिति वाच्यं। घटो न रजतमिति समूहालम्बनात्मकाच्छुक्तौ रजतत्वभ्रमादिदं न रजतभिन्नं किन्तु रजतमितिभ्रमाच्च शुक्तावप्रवृत्त्यापत्तेः तत्र ज्ञानद्वयतया पुरोवर्त्तिन्यां शुक्तौ रजतभेदासंसर्गस्य रजतत्वस्याग्रहात् रजतस्यानुपस्थितत्वाच्च इति चेत्। न। इष्टभेदाविषयकत्वपदेन इदन्त्वावच्छिन्नपुरोवर्त्तिनिष्ठेष्टभेदाविषयकत्वस्य विवक्षितत्वात्। यत्रेदन्त्वावच्छिन्नेदमनुभवो रजतभेदस्मरणञ्चेति क्रमेण रजते नेदं रजतमिति भ्रमस्तत्र, यत्र वा अत्र भेद इत्यनुभवो रजतस्मरणञ्चेति क्रमेण तादृशभ्रमस्तत्र च प्रवृत्त्यापत्तिः तयोरप्यन्यथाख्यात्यापत्त्या पुरोवर्त्तिनि रजते रजतभेदाविषयकत्वादतः स्वातन्त्र्येणेति ज्ञानविशेषणं, 'स्वातन्त्र्य' अभावाविशेषणत्वं। न चैवमयं न पीत इत्यनुमितिसत्त्वेऽपि चाक्षुषपीतत्वज्ञानात् पीतार्थिप्रवृत्त्यापत्तिरिति वाच्यं। अगृहीताप्रामाण्यकत्वेन ज्ञानविशेषणात्

नन्वेवं रजतेऽपि विशिष्टज्ञानं न सिद्ध्येत्प्रवृत्तेर्भेदाग्रहादेवोपपत्तेः। इदं रजततया जानामि रजततया ज्ञातमित्यनुभवः शुक्तावपि तुल्यः। न च शुक्तौ रजतत्वबाधात् सोऽप्यसंसर्गाग्रहः, बाधस्यापि विशिष्टज्ञानत्वे मानाभावादिति चेत्। न। तत्र हि रजतस्य न स्मृतिः प्रागननुभवात्, ग्रहणञ्च तस्य धर्मिविषयकं योग्यधर्मियोगेन रजतत्वजातिग्रहादित्यर्थसिद्धं धर्म-

---

अप्रामाण्यज्ञानदशायां न्यायनयेऽपि तत्र प्रवृत्तेर्दुर्वारत्वादिति निगर्वः। इदञ्चापाततः पूर्व्वकल्पोक्तदूषणस्यात्रनाप्यविशेषात् नेदं रजतमिति भेदग्रहदशायामपि रजतं द्रव्यं इदञ्च प्रमेयमित्यादिसमूहालम्बनात् प्रवृत्त्यापत्तेश्चेति ध्येयं।

नव्यास्तु 'इष्टभेदाविषयकं ज्ञानमित्यस्य इष्टभेदविषयतासाका-ङ्क्षपुरोवर्त्तिविषयतातिरिक्ता या इष्टतावच्छेदकविषयतासाकाङ्क्षेदन्त्वा-वच्छिन्नपुरोवर्त्तिविषयता तदाश्रयीभूतं ज्ञानमित्यर्थः, भेदेत्युप-लक्षणं अत्यन्ताभावोऽपि द्रष्टव्यः, तेनेदं रजतात्यन्ताभाववदित्यादि-ज्ञानादपि न प्रवृत्तिः। अगृहीताप्रामाण्यकत्वेनापि ज्ञानं विशेष-णीयं, नातः 'न चैवमित्याद्युक्तदोषस्यावकाश इति प्राहुः।

केचित्तु ननु पीतः शङ्ख इति पूर्व्वपक्षे समाधानान्तरमाह, 'यद्वेति, न तु पूर्वकल्पापेक्षया कल्पान्तरमिदं, तथाचेष्टभेदाविषय-कमित्यस्य श्वेतभेदविषयकज्ञानानुपरक्त-श्वेताभेदानुमित्यन्तरमेव तत्र प्रवृत्तिजनकं न तु प्राथमिकमित्यर्थः। न च पित्तदोषसत्त्वात्

धर्मिविषयकमेकं ज्ञानं। न च रजतत्वस्य शुक्त्यनुभवविषयत्वे हेतुरस्ति। न च प्रत्यभिज्ञानवत् संस्कारेन्द्रिये हेतू, तयोरत्र भिन्नविषयकत्वात्। एकदा स्वतन्त्रो-

---

कथमनुमित्यन्तरमिति वाच्यं। गुरुमते सिद्धेरप्रतिबन्धकत्वात्(१) अनुमितिपदस्य प्रकृते विशेषदर्शनजन्यभ्रमोत्तरप्रत्यक्षपरत्वाच्च। यद्वा 'इष्टभेदाविषयकं ज्ञानं' श्वेतभेदाविषयकं श्वेताभेदानुमानं, 'प्रवर्त्तकं' तत्र तृतीयक्षणे एव प्रवृत्तिजनकं न तु द्वितीयक्षणे क्षणविलम्बस्य अपक्षनिर्णेयत्वात् इत्यर्थः, इत्याहुः।

ननु प्रत्यक्षेण श्वेतभिन्नतया गृह्यमाणशङ्खे श्वेताभेदानुमितिर्भवतीति तत्र श्वेतभेदमपि विषयीकरोति तस्य पूर्व्वोपस्थितत्वेन उपनीतभाने बाधकाभावात्तथा चेष्टभेदाविषयकज्ञानमपि तत्र नास्तीत्यत आह, 'न चेति, 'अभेदानुमितौ' श्वेताभेदानुमितौ, 'इष्टभेदः' श्वेतभेदः, विरोधिनोरेकनिश्चयप्रकारत्वासम्भवादिति भावः। 'अत एवेति विरोधिनोरेकनिश्चयप्रकारत्वासम्भवादेवेत्यर्थः, 'भेदप्रत्ययेऽपीति प्राच्यां प्रतीचीभेदप्रत्यये जले चन्द्रवद्भेदप्रत्ययेऽनुमितिरूपे विद्यमानेऽपीत्यर्थः, 'स प्रत्ययः' तदनन्तरभावी दोषविशेषजन्यः प्राच्यां प्रतीच्यभेदप्रत्ययः जले चन्द्रवदभेदप्रत्यय इत्यर्थः, 'न भेदग्राही' न प्रतीचीभेद-चन्द्रवद्भेदविषयकः, 'दिङ्मोहेति तदनन्तरभाविप्राचीविशेष्यक-प्रतीच्यभेदभ्रम-जलविशेष्यक-चन्द्रवदभे-

---

(१) धारावाहिकप्रत्यक्षमिव धारावाहिकानुमितिरपि गुरुभिरङ्गीक्रियत इति भावः।

पस्थितविरुद्धानेकभेदाग्रहे संशयः। न च क्रमेणोपस्थितानेकभेदाग्रहो येन स क्रमिकविपर्य्ययद्वयरूपः स्यात्, अन्यथा तवाप्यप्रतीकारात्। न च संशयानन्तरं विपर्य्ययदशायामुभयभेदाग्रहे संशयः एक भेदाग्रहे अन्यथाख्यातिः। दोषमहिम्ना ह्येकस्य न स्यातन्त्र्येणोपस्थितिः,

---

दभ्रमादिरूपाः प्रत्यया इत्यर्थः, निश्चयात्मका इति शेषः। अन्यथा तत्र भेदाभेदयोरुभयोर्भानात् संशयत्वापत्तेरिति भावः। 'रजतत्वबाधादिति कदाचिद्रजतत्वस्य बाधादित्यर्थः, 'सोऽपि' अनुव्यवसायोऽपि, 'असंसर्गाग्रह इति इदन्त्वावच्छिन्नपुरोवर्त्तिज्ञाने रजतत्वप्रकारकत्वस्य रजतत्वप्रकारकज्ञाने इदन्त्वावच्छिन्नपुरोवर्त्तिविशेष्यकत्वस्यासंसर्गाग्रह इत्यर्थः। 'बाधस्यापीति, असंसर्गाग्रहरूपोबाधः कदाचिद्रजतेऽपि तुल्य इति भावः। सत्यस्थले ज्ञानद्वयेन विशिष्टज्ञानस्य नान्यथासिद्धिसम्भव इति समाधत्ते, 'तत्रेति सत्यरजतानुभवस्थले इत्यर्थः(१), 'रजतस्य' रजतत्वावच्छिन्नस्य, 'प्रागिति, एतज्जन्मनीति शेषः। न च जन्मान्तरानुभूतस्य स्मरणं, तस्य तदानीमुद्‌बोधके मानाभावात् अपूर्वचैत्रादिस्थले तदभावाच्च इति भावः। ननु मास्तु स्मरणं तथापि रजत-रजतत्वयोः साक्षात्कारात्मकज्ञानद्वयेनैवान्यथासिद्धिरित्यत आह, 'ग्रहणञ्चेति साक्षात्कारश्चेत्यर्थः, 'तस्य' रजतत्वस्य, 'धर्म्मिविषयकं' इदन्त्वावच्छिन्नरजतविषयकं। धर्म्मिविषयकत्वे हेतुमाह, 'योग्येति, 'अर्थसिद्धं' सामग्रीबलसिद्धं, 'धर्म्म-धर्म्मीति।

---

(२) सत्ये रजतानुभवे इत्यर्थं इति ग०।

किन्त्वभावविशेषणतयेति तद्भेदाग्रहोऽप्यकिञ्चित्करः। न च संशयानन्तरन्धूमभ्रमादस्ति क्वचिदवह्न्यर्थिप्रवृत्तिर्न तु तेन विना। न च तस्य स्वतन्त्रोपस्थितवह्न्यसंसर्गाग्रहो द्वारं संशयानुरोधेन तस्य प्रागपि सत्त्वादवह्न्यनुमितिर्द्वारमिति वाच्यं। लिङ्गभ्रमस्य हि निर्वह्नित्वस्य

न चैतावता समूहालम्बनादेकप्रत्ययगोचरत्वसिद्धावपि विशिष्टज्ञानत्वनियामकधर्म-धर्मिभावविषयकत्वासिद्ध्या न तत्सिद्धिरिति वाच्यं। कारणबाधाभावेनैकानुभवगोचरत्वेन द्वयोः सिद्धेः इदं रजततया जानामीत्यनुव्यवसायस्यैव धर्म्म-धर्म्मिविषयकत्वे प्रमाणीकर्त्तुं शक्यत्वात् प्रकृते तु कारणबाधादेकानुभवगोचरत्वासम्भवेनानुव्यवसायस्यातथात्वादित्यत्र तात्पर्य्यात्। सत्यरजतस्थले सामग्रीबलाद्विशिष्टज्ञानसिद्धिर्न तु प्रकृते सोऽस्तीत्याह, 'न चेति, रजतत्वेन समं सन्निकर्षाभावादिति भावः। 'संस्कारेन्द्रिये इति रजतत्वविषयकसंस्कार-शुक्तीन्द्रियसन्निकर्षावित्यर्थः, 'तयोः' संस्कार-शुक्तीन्द्रियसन्निकर्षयोः, 'भिन्नविषयकत्वादिति एकधर्मिविषयकत्वाभावादित्यर्थः, प्रत्यभिज्ञानस्थले तु तत्ताविशिष्टेदन्त्वविशिष्टयोरभेदादेकधर्मिविषयकत्वमेव तयोरिति भावः। मिथ्याज्ञानाभावे संशयस्य व्यवहारं समर्थयति, 'एकदेति एककालोत्पन्ना या स्वातन्त्र्येणोपस्थितिस्तद्विषयकेत्यर्थः, 'भेदाग्रहे' भेदाग्रहसत्त्वे, धर्मिज्ञानमिति शेषः, नातः सप्तम्यनन्वयः। रजत एव नेदं रजतं किन्तु शुक्तिरिति विपर्य्ययवारणाय 'स्वातन्त्र्येणेति, 'स्वातन्त्र्यं' अभावाविशेषणत्वं। 'एकदेत्यस्य व्यावृत्तिमाह,

स्वातन्त्र्येणोपस्थितिप्रतिबन्धकत्वेन नियमतः स्वतन्त्रव-ह्निस्मृतिर्द्वारमिति न संशयान्यथाख्याती। न च पर्वतस्य प्रत्यक्षत्वे वह्नेश्च स्मरणे प्रत्यक्षभ्रमान्न विशेष इति साक्षात्करोमीति स्यान्न त्वनुमिनोमीति वाच्यं। लिङ्ग-ज्ञानानन्तरभावित्वप्रतिसन्धानाप्रतिसन्धानाभ्यामुभय-

---

'न चेति न लित्यर्थः, 'अनेकभेदाग्रहः' विरुद्धानेकभेदाग्रहः, 'संशय-इत्यनुषज्यते, 'क्रमिकविपर्य्ययद्वयेति एकधर्म्मिक-क्रमिकगोलाश्वत्वा-दिभ्रमरूपः स्यादित्यर्थः। नन्वेकदा विरुद्धोभयस्मृतेः सर्व्वथासिद्धा प्रत्येकानुभवजसंस्कारस्य प्रत्येकमात्रस्मारकत्वनियमादित्यत आह, 'अन्यथेति युगपदुभयस्मृत्यनभ्युपगमे इत्यर्थः, 'अप्रतीकारादिति संशयासम्भवादित्यर्थः, क्रमिकप्रत्येककोटिद्वयोपस्थिति-धर्म्मिज्ञानानां युगपदनवस्थानादिति भावः। 'संशयानन्तरमिति स्थाणौ स्थाणु-पु-रुषसंशयोत्तरमयं पुरुष इति भ्रमदशायामित्यर्थः, 'उभयभेदाग्रहे' स्थाणु-पुरुषोभयभेदाग्रहे। ननु भ्रमानुरोधात् पुरुषभेदग्रह एव तत्र नास्ति स्थाणुभेदग्रहस्तु तत्र वर्त्तत एवेत्यत आह, 'एकभेदाग्रह-इति पुरुषभेदाग्रहमात्राभ्युपगमे इत्यर्थः, स्थाणौ स्थाणुभेदाग्रहाभ्यु-पगम इति यावत्। 'एकभेदग्रह इत्येव क्वचित्पाठः, तत्र 'एकभेद-ग्रहे' स्थाणुभेदग्रहे। समाधत्ते, 'दोषमहिम्नेति दोषप्राधान्येन संश-योत्तरं पुरुष एवायं न तु स्थाणुरित्येव तत्र भ्रमस्तथा च स्थाणुत्वको-टेर्न स्वातन्त्र्येणोपस्थितत्वमित्यर्थः, संशयात्मकस्वतन्त्रोपस्थितेर्विशेषद-र्शनेन नाशादिति भावः। 'तद्भेदाग्रहेऽपि' स्थाणौ स्थाणुभेदाग्रहो-

सम्भवात्। एवं स्वतन्त्रोपस्थितानिष्टभेदाग्रहोऽपि निवर्त्तकः। तेनेदं रजतं न शुक्तिरित्यभावप्रतियोगित्वेनानिष्टोपस्थितेस्तद्भेदाग्रहेण निवर्त्तकः, शुक्त्यभावासंसर्गाग्रहस्य नकारस्यार्थ इति नान्यथाख्यातिः। अनिष्टाभेदग्रहस्य निवर्त्तकत्वे च रजत एव नेदं रजतमिति

ऽपि, 'अकिञ्चित्करः' न संशयापादकः। अनुमितिरूपामन्यथाख्यातिमाशङ्कते, 'न चेति, 'संशयानन्तरमिति जलह्रदादौ वह्निसंशयानन्तरमित्यर्थः, 'धूमभ्रमात्' उपस्थितधूमासंसर्गाग्रहात्, 'वह्न्यर्थिप्रवृत्तिः' वह्न्यर्थिनिष्कम्पप्रवृत्तिः, 'तेन' धूमभ्रमेण। 'तस्य' धूमस्य, 'वह्न्यसंसर्गाग्रहः' ह्रदादौ वह्न्यसंसर्गाग्रहः, 'तस्य' ह्रदादौ वह्न्यसंसर्गाग्रहस्य, 'वह्न्यनुमितिरिति अत इत्यादिः अतोह्रदादिविशेष्यकवह्न्यनुमितिरेव द्वारमित्यर्थः, ह्रदविशेष्यक-वह्न्यनुमितिरेव चान्यथाख्यातिरिति भावः। स्वतन्त्रनिर्वह्नित्वस्मृत्यसमवहिता स्वतन्त्रवह्निस्मृतिरेव द्वारमित्याह, 'लिङ्गभ्रमस्येति। न चैवं ह्रदादौ धूमभ्रमे सति महानसादावपि निर्वह्नित्वभ्रमो न स्यात् तस्य तदुपस्थितिप्रतिबन्धकत्वादिति वाच्यं। यत्र लिङ्गभ्रमस्तत्र तदभावव्यवहारकैककोट्युपस्थितेरेव फलबलेन प्रतिबन्धकत्वकल्पनादिति भावः। 'नियमतः' व्याप्तिज्ञानसहभावेन[१], 'संशयान्यथाख्याती' इति लिङ्गभ्रमस्य वह्न्यनुमितिजनकत्वे अन्यथाख्यातिः, तदजनकत्वे प्रागेव लिङ्गभ्रमानन्तरमपि संशय इत्यर्थः। 'न विशेष इति धूमभ्रमाधीनवह्न्यर्थि-

---

(१) व्याप्तिज्ञानसहकारेणेति म०।

कृत्वा न निवर्त्तेत, अन्यथान्यथाख्यात्यापत्तेः। अत एव रजत एव नेदं रजतमिति ज्ञानेऽपि न प्रवृत्त्यन्यथाख्याती रजतभेदासंसर्गाग्रहात्। ननु रजत-रङ्गयोरिमे रङ्ग-रजते इत्यत्र प्रत्येकमुभयभेदाग्रहे युगपत्प्रवृत्ति-निवृत्ती स्यातामिति चेत्। न। एवंविधभ्रमे माना-

---

प्रवृत्तिहेतुज्ञानस्य(१) न विशेष इत्यर्थः। 'लिङ्गज्ञानेति, स्वतन्त्रवह्नि-स्मृतेरुद्बोधकविधया लिङ्गज्ञानजन्यत्वेऽपि पर्व्वतानुभवस्य लिङ्गज्ञानाजन्यत्वमतोऽजन्यत्वं विहाय 'अनन्तरभावित्वमात्रमुक्तं। न चैवं यदानुमितौ न तत्प्रतिसन्धानं तत्रानुमिनोमीत्यनुव्यवसायो न स्यात् संशयानुत्तरप्रत्यक्षेऽपि लिङ्गज्ञानजन्यत्वप्रतिसन्धानादनुमिनोमीत्यनुव्यवसायापत्तिश्चेति वाच्यं। तन्मते अनुमितित्वजातेरभावेन लिङ्गज्ञानजन्यत्वस्यैव तादृशानुव्यवसायविषयत्वात् तदप्रतिसन्धाने तादृशानुव्यवसायस्येष्टत्वात् एवं संशयोत्तरप्रत्यक्षेऽपि तत्प्रतिसन्धानदशायां तादृशानुव्यवसायस्येष्टत्वादिति भावः। 'उभयसम्भवादिति अत्रानुमिनोमीत्यनुव्यवसायस्य प्रत्यक्षभ्रमे तादृशानुव्यवसायाभावस्य च सम्भवादित्यर्थः। प्रवृत्तिवन्निवृत्तिमपि अन्यथोपपादयति, 'एव-मिति, 'स्वतन्त्रोपस्थितेति 'स्वातन्त्र्येण' अभावाविशेषणत्वेन, या अनिष्टस्य इदन्त्वावच्छिन्ननिवृत्तिविशेष्यस्य चोपस्थितिः तत्सहकृतः इदन्त्वावच्छिन्ननिवृत्तिविशेष्यानिष्टयोर्भेदाग्रह इत्यर्थः। 'अनिष्टं'

---

(२) धूमभ्रमाधीनवह्निज्ञानस्येति ग०।

भावात्। कार्य्यौन्नेयधर्म्माणां यथाकार्य्यमुन्नयनात् क्रमो-त्पन्नज्ञानयोर्भेदाग्रहादेकत्वाभिमानः। अन्यथा तवापि स्वतन्त्रोभयभेदाग्रहात्प्रत्येकं रजतं रङ्गं वेति[१] संशयः स्यात्। यदेव वा तत्र विपर्य्ययनियामकन्तत एव प्रवृत्ति-निवृत्ती स्यातां, तद्धेतोरेवेतिन्यायात्।

स्वजनकद्वेषप्रकारीभूतधर्म्माश्रयः शुक्त्यादिः, तदुपस्थितिश्च शुक्तित्वा-दिरूपेण। स्वातन्त्र्यविशेषणप्रयोजनमाह, 'तेनेति, शुक्ताविति शेषः, 'अनिष्टोपस्थितेः' शुक्त्युपस्थितेः। यद्यपि धर्म्मिज्ञानरूपा स्वातन्त्र्येण शुक्त्युपस्थितिः तत्राप्यस्ति तथाप्यनिष्टतावच्छेदकशुक्तित्वप्रकारेण स्वातन्त्र्येणोपस्थितिर्नास्तीति भावः। अन्यत्सर्व्वं पूर्व्ववत्।

ननु न शुक्तिरित्यत्र शुक्तिभेदस्य नञर्थतया शुक्तौ शुक्तिभेदज्ञा-नाभ्युपगमे अन्यथाख्यात्यापत्तिः, तदनभ्युपगमे इदं न शुक्तिरिति वाक्यप्रयोगानुपपत्तिः तादृशवाक्यप्रयोगं प्रति इदन्त्वावच्छिन्नशुक्तिवि-शेष्यक-शुक्तिभेदप्रकारकज्ञानस्य हेतुत्वादित्यत आह, 'शुक्त्यभावेति इदन्त्वावच्छिन्नशुक्तावुपस्थितशुक्तिभेदासंसर्गाग्रहस्येत्यर्थः, 'नञ्स्यार्थइति[२] इदं न शुक्तिरितिनञ्शब्दघटितवाक्यप्रयोगकारणमित्यर्थः. शुक्तित्वा-प्रतियोगिताकभेदस्यैवात्र नञर्थतया यथाश्रुतासङ्गतेरिति ध्येयं।

---

(१) रङ्गं वा रजतं वेतीति ख०।

(२) 'नञ्स्यार्थं इतीत्यनेन पाठधारणं कस्यचित् मूलपुस्तकस्य तादृशपाठ-मनुसृत्य इत्यनुमीयते, अस्मल्लब्धमूलपुस्तकेषु सर्व्वत्रैव 'नकारस्यार्थः' इत्येव पाठो वर्त्तते।

यत्तु "प्रसक्तप्रतिषेधात्मा बाधोऽख्यातौ न युज्यते।
साधयत्यन्यथाख्यातिं बाध एव हि नः स्फुटं" ॥
इति तद्विपरीतं, परस्परविरुद्धत्वाविशेषेण बाध्यत्वा-

नन्विदन्त्वावच्छिन्ननिवृत्तिविशेष्ये अनिष्टाभेदग्रह एव गुरूणां कथं निवर्त्तक इति सत्यां जिज्ञासायामाह, 'अनिष्टाभेदेति, 'कृत्वेति ज्ञात्वेत्यर्थः, 'न निवर्त्तेतेति इदन्त्वावच्छिन्नतद्रजत-विशेष्यक-रजतभिन्नत्वप्रकारकनिवृत्तिर्न जायेतेत्यर्थः, इदन्त्वावच्छिन्ने रजते रजतभिन्नाभेदज्ञानविरहादित्यर्थः, 'अन्यथा' इदन्त्वावच्छिन्ने रजते रजतभिन्नाभेदग्रहे। प्रवर्त्तकस्वातन्त्र्यविशेषणव्यावृत्तिमाह, 'अत एवेति स्वातन्त्र्यविशेषणादेवेत्यर्थः, 'न प्रवर्त्त्येति रजते रजतभेदाग्रहे प्रवृत्त्यापत्तिः तद्भेदग्रहे अन्यथाख्यात्यापत्तिरित्यर्थः, 'रजतभेदेति, 'असंसर्गाग्रहः' संसर्गाग्रहाभावः संसर्गग्रह इति यावत् भेदे रजतस्य संसर्गग्रहादिति फलितार्थः, तथाचाभावाविशेषणत्वरूपस्वातन्त्र्येण रजतस्य उपस्थितिर्नास्तीति भावः। 'इमे रङ्ग-रजते इति रजते रङ्गत्वभ्रमे रङ्गे च रजतत्वभ्रमे इत्यर्थः, 'उभयभेदाग्रहे' रजत रङ्गोभयभेदाग्रहे, 'युगपत्प्रवृत्ति-निवृत्ती इति एकस्मिन्नेव रजते धर्म्मिणि रजतत्वप्रकारकप्रवृत्ति-रङ्गत्वप्रकारकनिवृत्त्योर्युगपदुत्पत्त्यापत्तिरेवं रङ्गेऽपीत्यर्थः, रजतभेदाग्रह-रङ्गभेदाग्रहयोः रजत-रङ्गयोः स्वतन्त्रोपस्थितेश्च सत्त्वादिति भावः। 'एवंविधभ्रम इति युगपद्रजत-रङ्गयोः स्वतन्त्रोपस्थितौ इदन्त्वरूपेण रजत-रङ्गयोर्युगपदनुभवे च मानाभाव इत्यर्थः। तत्र हि कार्य्यं मानं प्रत्यक्षं वा आद्ये 'कार्य्येति,

व्यवस्थितेः। विरुद्धार्थकतयोत्पन्नत्वञ्च तुल्यं। पूर्वेणापि क्वचित्परस्य बाधात्। तस्माद्भेदाग्रहात् प्रसञ्जितो व्यवहारो भेदग्रहाद्बाध्यत इति युक्तं। उपेक्षाभ्रमे

प्रकृते युगपत्प्रवृत्ति-निवृत्तिलक्षणकार्य्यस्याननुभवादिति भावः। अन्ये 'क्रमेति, यद्यपि ज्ञानचतुष्टयमेव तदभ्युपगतं तथापि ग्रहणत्व-स्मरणत्वाभ्यामैक्यविवक्षया द्विवचनं। न च तथापि ज्ञानचतुष्टयस्य एकदा असत्त्वात् कथं तेष्वेकत्वाभिमान इति वाच्यं। स्मरणोपनीतानां ज्ञानचतुष्टयानां भेदाग्रहादभेदाभिमान इत्यभिप्रायात्। 'अन्यथेति यद्येकदैव स्वातन्त्र्येणोभयोपस्थितिरित्यर्थः, 'स्वतन्त्रोभयेति प्रत्येकं स्वतन्त्रोपस्थितयोः रजत-रङ्गयोर्भेदाग्रहादित्यर्थः। ननु मम प्रत्येकं स्वतन्त्रोपस्थितरजत-रङ्गोभयभेदाग्रहसत्त्वेऽपि रजते रङ्गत्व-भ्रमजनकदोषेण रजतत्वविशिष्टज्ञानप्रतिबन्धाद्रङ्गे रजतत्वभ्रमजनक-दोषेण रङ्गत्वविशिष्टज्ञानप्रतिबन्धान्न तत्र संशय इत्यत आह, 'यदेव-वेति, 'विपर्य्ययनियामकं' एकैकविशिष्टबुद्धिमात्रोत्पादनियामकं अपर-कोटिविशिष्टबुद्धिप्रतिबन्धकमिति यावत्, 'प्रवृत्ति-निवृत्ती इति रङ्गे रजतत्वप्रकारकप्रवृत्तिमात्रं रजते रङ्गत्वप्रकारकनिवृत्तिमात्रमास्ता-मित्यर्थः, तथाच ममापि रङ्गे रजतत्वभ्रमजनकदोषो रङ्गत्वप्रकारक-निवृत्तिप्रतिबन्धकः रजते च रङ्गत्वभ्रमजनकदोषो रजतत्वप्रकारक-प्रवृत्तिप्रतिबन्धक इति भावः। 'तद्धेतोरेवेति रजतविशेष्यक-रजतत्व-विशिष्टज्ञानाभाव-रङ्गविशेष्यक-रङ्गत्वप्रकारकज्ञानाभावयोः प्रयोजका-द्दोषादेव रजतविशेष्यक-रजतत्वप्रकारकप्रवृत्त्यभावोरङ्गविशेष्यक-रङ्गत्व-

च शब्दप्रयोगो बाध्यः। तदीयतामात्रस्वभावत्वात् तद्विषयत्वस्य कथं रजतीयमात्रज्ञानमरजतीयं स्वभावव्याघातात्। न चोभयीयं, समूहालम्बनापत्तेः। तदुक्तं।

प्रकारकनिवृत्त्यभावश्चास्तु किं रजतविशेष्यक-रजतत्वविशिष्टज्ञानाभाव-रङ्गविशेष्यक-रङ्गत्वविशिष्टज्ञानाभावयोस्तत्प्रयोजकत्वेनेत्यर्थः। 'प्रसक्तप्रतिषेधात्मेति प्रसक्तस्य तत्रारोपितस्य प्रामाण्यस्य तत्राभावनिश्चयरूप इत्यर्थः, 'बाधः' बाधशब्दार्थः, 'अख्याताविति तत्र प्रामाण्यस्यारोपं विनेत्यर्थः, 'साधयतीति, अत इत्यादिः, 'बाध एवेति विशेषदर्शनजन्यज्ञाने बाधकव्यवहारान्तर्गतबाधशब्दार्थएवेत्यर्थः। 'विपरीतं' सद्विपरीतं असदिति यावत्, 'परस्परेति यदि तत्रारोपितस्य प्रामाण्यस्य तत्राभावनिश्चयजनकत्वं तद्बाधकत्वं स्वनिष्ठारोपितस्य प्रामाण्यस्याभाववत्तया तज्ज्ञाप्यत्वमेव च तद्बाध्यत्वं तदा पूर्व्वोत्तरज्ञानयोः प्रामाण्याभाववत्ताज्ञापकताप्रयोजकस्य परस्परविरुद्धार्थकत्वस्याविशेषेण बाध्यपदप्रयोगनियमभङ्गापत्तेरित्यर्थः, बाधकेऽपि बाध्यपदप्रयोगापत्तेरिति भावः। ननु तद्विरुद्धार्थकत्वे सति तदुत्तरोत्पन्नत्वं तन्निष्ठप्रामाण्याभाववत्ताज्ञापकतायां प्रयोजकं न तु तद्विरुद्धार्थकत्वमात्रमित्यत आह, 'विरुद्धार्थकतयेति तद्विरुद्धार्थकत्वे सति तदुत्तरोत्पन्नत्वञ्चेत्यर्थः, 'तुल्यं' बाधतुल्यं, बाध्येऽपि तद्विरुद्धार्थकत्वे सति तदुत्तरोत्पन्नत्वमस्तीत्यर्थः। एतदेवोपपादयति, 'पूर्व्वेणापीति, 'बाधात्' प्रामाण्याभावज्ञापनात्।

मिश्रास्तु 'तुल्यं' तद्विरुद्धार्थकत्वमात्रस्य तुल्यं, यथा तद्विरु-

"अन्यस्य ह्यन्यथा भानं प्रतीत्यैव पराहतं। परस्मिन् भासमाने तु न परम्भासते यतः" इति। विषयं विनैव तदाकारं ज्ञानमिति साकारवादः। ज्ञानायथार्थत्वे

द्धार्थकत्वमात्रं न तन्निष्ठप्रामाण्याभावज्ञापकतायां प्रयोजकं, तथा तद्विरुद्धार्थकत्वे सति तदुत्तरोत्पन्नत्वमपि न तत्र प्रयोजकमिति यावत्, अत्र हेतुमाह, 'पूर्व्वेणापीति, तथाच व्यभिचारान्न प्रयोजकमिति भावः इति व्याचख्युः।

नन्वेवं कस्तावत् तत्र बाधकशब्दार्थ इत्यत आह, 'तस्मादिति, 'भेदाग्रहात्' अगृहीतभेदकज्ञानद्वयरूपादिदं रजतमितिपूर्व्वोत्पन्नज्ञानात्, 'प्रसञ्जितः' प्रसक्तः, 'व्यवहारः' प्रवृत्त्यादिः, 'भेदग्रहात्' उत्तरोत्पन्नेदं न रजतमिति शुक्तिविशेष्यक-रजतभेदज्ञानात्, 'बाध्यते' प्रतिबध्यते, 'इतियुक्तमिति इत्यस्यैव बाधकशब्दार्थत्वं युक्तमित्यर्थः। तथाच तत्रारोपितस्य प्रामाण्याभावनिश्चायकत्वं न तद्बाधकत्वं अपि तु तज्जन्यप्रवृत्त्यादिरूपव्यवहारप्रतिबन्धकत्वमेव तद्बाधकत्वं, पूर्व्वोत्पन्नज्ञानस्य नोत्तरज्ञानजन्यप्रवृत्त्यादिप्रतिबन्धकमसत्त्वाद्विशेषदर्शनाद्यभावविशिष्टस्यैव विरोधिविषयकज्ञानस्य प्रतिबन्धकत्वाच्चेति भावः। नन्वेवमुपेक्षाभ्रमेण प्रवृत्ति-निवृत्त्योरजननात् तदुत्तरोत्पन्नविरोधिविषयकज्ञाने तद्बाधकव्यवहारो न स्यादित्यत आह, 'उपेक्षेति प्रवृत्ति-निवृत्त्याद्यजनकभ्रमे चेत्यर्थः,' 'शब्दप्रयोगः' तज्जन्यशब्दप्रयोगरूपव्यवहारः, 'बाध्यः' प्रतिबध्यः।

अन्यथाख्यातौ दूषणान्तरमाह, 'तदीयतेति तादात्म्यसम्बन्धेन

च ज्ञानमात्रस्य तच्छङ्कया न निष्कम्पप्रवृत्तिः। न च दोषाजन्यत्वादिना विश्वासः, भ्रमादविश्वासे प्रवृत्त्यभावापत्तेः। नापि तज्ज्ञानात्, ज्ञानत्वेन तत्राप्य-

---

तद्वन्मात्रवृत्तित्वव्याप्यत्वादित्यर्थः, 'तद्विषयत्वस्य' तन्निरूपितज्ञान-विशेष्यत्वस्य, तत्प्रकारकत्वावच्छिन्नज्ञानविशेष्यत्वस्येति यावत्। 'रजतीयमात्रज्ञानमिति रजतमात्रीयस्य रजतत्वस्य ज्ञानमित्यर्थः, 'अरजतीयमिति अरजतविशेष्यकमित्यर्थः, ज्ञानजिष्ठरजतत्वप्रकारकत्वं कथमरजतविशेष्यकत्वावच्छिन्नमिति तु समुदितार्थः। 'स्वभावव्याघातादिति यथोक्तव्याप्तिव्याघातप्रसङ्गादित्यर्थः। 'उभयीयमिति तत्प्रकारकत्वावच्छिन्नज्ञानविशेष्यत्वं तद्वत्तदभाववदेतदुभयवृत्तित्वव्याप्यमित्यर्थः, 'समूहालम्बनेति निखिलरजतत्वप्रकारकज्ञानानामरजतविशेष्यकत्वापत्तेरित्यर्थः। 'तदुक्तमिति प्राभाकरैरित्यर्थः। 'अन्यस्येति तदनाश्रयस्य तत्प्रकारेण भानमित्यर्थः, 'प्रतीत्यैव प्रतीतिविशेष्यत्वस्वभावाद्वैव, तत्प्रकारकत्वावच्छिन्नज्ञानविशेष्यत्वस्य तद्वन्मात्रवृत्तित्वनियमादेवेति यावत्। ननु तत्प्रकारकत्वावच्छिन्नज्ञानविशेष्यत्वं न तद्वन्मात्रवृत्तित्वव्याप्यं अपि तु तद्वत्तदभाववदुभयवृत्तित्वस्यैव व्याप्यमित्यत आह, 'परस्मिन्निति तदाश्रय इत्यर्थः, 'भासमाने' तत्प्रकारेण-भासमाने, 'न परं भासते' यत इति न तदनधिकरणं नियमतो भासते यत इत्यर्थः। तथाच निखिलरजतत्वादिप्रकारकज्ञानानां तदनधिकरण-विशेष्यकत्वापत्त्या न तथा नियम इति भावः।

अन्यथाख्यातौ दूषणान्तरमाह, 'विषयं विनैवेति विना सन्निकर्षं

विश्वासात्। तदुच्यते। "अहोवत महानेष प्रमादो-धीमतामपि। ज्ञानस्य व्यभिचारित्वे विश्वासः किंनिबन्धनः" इति॥ भ्रमस्य च सन्मात्रविषयकत्वेनायथार्थता,

---

रजतत्वभानासम्भवात् रजतत्वरूपं विषयं विनैव सन्निकर्षस्यासम्भवाद्-तत्तदाकारमेव ज्ञानं वाच्यं इत्यथ स्वप्रकाशमर्य्यादया स्वनिष्ठरजत-त्वमादाय रजतत्वप्रकारकं शुक्काविदं रजतमिति ज्ञानं तथाच साकारत्वापत्तिरित्यर्थः। साकारत्वं ज्ञानस्य रजतत्वादिधर्म्माश्रयत्वं।

अन्यथाख्यातौ दूषणान्तरमप्याह, 'ज्ञानायथार्थत्व इति, 'तच्छ-ङ्कया'. ज्ञानत्वरूपसाधारणधर्म्मदर्शनेन सर्व्वत्र ज्ञाने अयथार्थत्वशङ्कया। 'विश्वासः' प्रामाण्यनिश्चयः, दोषाजन्यत्वं ज्ञातं स्वरूपसत्त्वाविश्वासहेतुः, अन्त्ये 'भ्रमादिति, भ्रमादप्रवृत्त्यापत्तेरिति[१] योजना, 'अविश्वासे' विश्वासाभावे, तत्र दोषाजन्यत्वाभावर्वादात भावः। आद्ये 'नापीति, 'तत्रापि' दोषाजन्यत्वज्ञानेऽपि। 'अहोवतेति, 'वत' खेदे, 'महानेषः प्रमादः' एषा महती अनवधानता, 'धीमतामपि' धीमतां नैया-यिकानामपि, 'व्यभिचारित्वे' व्यधिकरणप्रकारकत्वे, 'विश्वासः' अयथार्थत्वशङ्कानिवृत्तिः।

अन्यथाख्यातौ दूषणान्तरमप्याह,[२] 'भ्रमस्य चेति, 'नायथा-र्थतेति तथाच भ्रमस्य सन्मात्रविषयकत्वे कथमयथार्थत्वमित्यर्थः, सन्मात्रविषयकत्वमेव यथार्थत्वमिति भावः। 'असद्विषयकत्व इति

---

(१) 'प्रवृत्त्यभावापत्तेः' इत्यत्र 'अप्रवृत्त्यापत्तेः' इति कस्यचिन्मूलपुस्त-कस्य पाठमनुसृत्येदं।

(२) अन्यथाख्यातौ बाधकान्तरमाहेति ग०।

असद्विषयकत्वेऽसत्ख्यातिः। न च तत्र हेतुरस्ति, शब्दस्याप्तोक्तस्य निर्दोषस्य लिङ्गस्य चाहेतुत्वात्। न च शब्दानुमानाभासात्सा। योग्यतादिमत्तया शब्दस्य

सदुपरागेणासद्वैशिष्ट्यविषयकत्व इत्यर्थः, 'असत्ख्यातिः' असत्ख्यात्यापत्तिः, तस्याश्च नैयायिकैरनभ्युपगमादिति भावः। अन्यथाख्यातौ हेत्वभावरूपं बाधकमाह, 'नचेति नवेत्यर्थः, 'तत्र' अन्यथाख्यातौ। ननु शब्दादेवान्यथाख्यातिरुत्पत्स्यतीत्यत आह, 'शब्देति, 'आप्तोक्तस्य' प्रकृतवाक्यार्थयथार्थज्ञानवदुक्तस्य, 'निर्दोषस्य' दोषाजन्यस्य, 'अहेतुत्वात्' अन्यथाख्यातावहेतुत्वात्। 'सा' अन्यथाख्यातिः, 'योग्यतादीत्यादिपदात् यथार्थतात्पर्य्यकत्वस्य परिग्रहः। 'न वाभास इति। न च तत्रापि लिङ्गाद्यसंसर्गाग्रहस्य हेतुत्वमिति वाच्यं। लाघवेन विशिष्टज्ञानस्यानुमित्यादिहेतुत्वादिति भावः। न च प्रत्यक्षत एव तदुत्पत्तिरित्याह, 'इन्द्रियस्येति, 'सम्बद्धग्राहकत्वात्' सम्बद्धमात्रग्राहकत्वात्। ननु प्रत्यभिज्ञायां तत्ताया इव संस्कारोपनीतरजतत्वस्य चक्षुषा शुक्तौ ग्रहः स्यादित्यत आह, 'न चेति, 'उक्तेति, संस्कार-चक्षुषोरचैकविषयत्वाभावादिति भावः। 'दोषवशात्' दोषसहकारात्, इन्द्रियेणेति शेषः, 'असम्बन्धेऽपि' असन्निकृष्टेऽपि रजतत्वे, 'विजातीयकार्य्यं' साक्षात्काराभिन्नमन्यथाख्यातिरूपं ज्ञानं, 'अजनकत्वात्' भ्रमाजनकत्वात्, दोषस्य शुक्तित्वग्रहप्रतिबन्धमात्रप्रयोजकत्वाभ्युपगमादिति भावः। 'न हीति न वेत्यर्थः। ननु यथा-भस्मकरूपदोषसहकारात् उदर्य्यानलस्य आहारभस्मलक्षणविजाती-

लिङ्गवत्तया पक्षस्य ज्ञानाच्छाब्दानुमिती। न चाभासे तज्ज्ञानमस्ति हेत्वभावादेव, किन्त्वगृहीतासंसर्गज्ञानद्वयं तत्र इन्द्रियस्य सम्बद्धग्राहकत्वात्। न च प्रत्य-

यकार्य्यजनकत्वं, तथाचापि दोषसहकारादिन्द्रियस्य विजातीयज्ञानजनकत्वमित्यत-आह, 'भस्मकश्चेति, 'उद्भवः' उद्भूतस्पर्शविशेषः, 'रसार्जनमिति, 'रसः' बल-पुष्ट्यादि। ननु यथादवदहनरूपदोषविशेषसहकृतं वेत्रबीजं कदलीत्वरूपविजातीयकार्य्यजनकं तथेहापि स्यादित्यत आह 'दवेति। नन्वेवं कथं कदलीत्व इत्यत आह, 'भस्मन इति। अन्यथाख्यातावुक्तदोषेषु प्राचीनसम्मतिं[१] आह, 'तदुक्तमिति, 'साकारेति ज्ञानस्य साकारत्वप्रसङ्गादित्यर्थः, 'असतो न भानादिति असत्ख्यात्यनभ्युपगमादित्यर्थः, 'संविद्विरोधादिति प्रतीतिविशेष्यत्वस्वाभाव्यव्याघातात्, तत्प्रकारकत्वावच्छिन्नज्ञानविशेष्यत्वस्य तद्वन्मात्रवृत्तित्वनियमव्याघातादिति यावत्। 'धियामनाश्वासेति ज्ञानत्वरूपसाधारणधर्म्मदर्शनेन सर्व्वत्र ज्ञाने अयथार्थत्वप्रसङ्गादित्यर्थः, 'यत इति, 'यतः ख्यातिः', 'अन्यथा' व्यधिकरणप्रकारिका, 'नेष्टा', अतः 'सा यथार्थेति योजना। 'विवादपदं ज्ञानमिति शुक्तिविशेष्यक-रजतत्वप्रकारकप्रवृत्तिजनकं ज्ञानमित्यर्थः, 'न व्यधिकरणेति न रजतत्वाभाववति रजतत्वप्रकारकमित्यर्थः। 'स्वव्यधिकरणेति स्वव्यधिकरणधर्म्मप्रकारत्वावच्छिन्नविशेष्यतेत्यर्थः, 'स्वं'

(१) प्राचीनसंवादमिति ख०।

भिन्नानलवत्, उक्तोत्तरत्वात्। न च दोषवशादसम्बद्धे-ऽपि विजातीयं कार्य्यं, दोषस्याजनकत्वात्। नहि दुष्टात्[१] कुटजवीजाद्यवाङ्कुरः। भस्मकञ्च न दोषः, किन्तु वह्नेरुद्भवः, तस्य च दाहसामर्थ्यं दृष्टमेव। रसा-र्जनन्तु न भवति, भक्ष्यदाहात्। दवदहनदग्धवेत्र-वीजञ्च नष्टमेव। तद्भस्मानः कदलीजनकत्वं। तदुक्तं।

विशेष्यता। नच सर्व्वं प्रमेयमिति ज्ञानत्वे व्यभिचारः तद्विषयता-व्यधिकरणप्रकाराप्रसिद्धेरिति वाच्यं। तादृशप्रतियोगि यद्यत् तद-न्यत्वस्य साध्यस्य तत्रापि सत्त्वादिति भावः। 'ज्ञानमात्रेति, गुणत्वे व्यभिचारवारणाय 'मात्रपदं ज्ञानान्यव्यावृत्त्यर्थकं, 'धर्म्मेति वृत्तेः समवायतालाभाय, तेन ज्ञानान्यासमवेतत्वादिति फलितं। 'प्रमा-त्ववदिति सर्व्वांशे प्रमामात्रवृत्तित्तत्प्रमात्ववदित्यर्थः, तेन न भ्रमे-ऽप्यंशतः प्रमात्वसत्त्वात् साध्यविकल्यमिति ध्येयं। 'इति प्रतिरोध इति इतिप्रतिबन्धिः, पूर्व्वानुमानात् ख्यातावन्यथात्वाभावसिद्धिवत् एतद-नुमानात्पक्षधर्म्मताबलेन ख्यातेरन्यथात्वस्यापि सिद्ध्यापत्तिरिति यावत्। यथाश्रुतन्तु न सङ्गच्छते भिन्नपक्षकतया प्रकृतसाध्याभावासाधकतया च सत्प्रतिपक्षत्वासम्भवात्। अत्र चाक्षुषपदेन तन्मते अप्रसिद्धेः सत्य-पदेन बाधस्य द्वितीयज्ञानपदेन संयोगादिमादाय सिद्धसाधनस्य निरासः। प्रथमं ज्ञानपदञ्च सम्पातायातं। सत्यत्वञ्च रजतत्वाभाववति

---

(१) भ्रष्टादिति ग०।

"साकारपातादसतोन भानात्संविद्विरोधादथ हेत्वभावात्। धियामनाश्वासभयाच्च नेष्टा यतोऽन्यथाख्यातिरतो यथार्था" इति ॥ तस्माद्विवादपदं ज्ञानं न व्यधिकरणप्रकारकं ज्ञानत्वात् सत्यज्ञानवत्। भेदाग्रहजन्यरजतत्वप्राकारकशुक्तीच्छायां प्रतियोगिप्रसिद्धिः। ज्ञानत्वं स्वव्यधिकरणप्रकारावच्छिन्नविषयता-

---

रजतत्वप्रकारकत्वाभाववत्त्वं, न तु रजतत्ववति रजतत्वप्रकारकत्वं घटादिधी-रजतत्वनिर्व्विकल्पकाभ्यां सिद्धसाधनापत्तेः। न च द्वितीयज्ञानं रजतत्वप्रकारकत्वेन विशेषणीयं, चाक्षुषरजतत्ववद्विशेष्यक-रजतत्वप्रकारकातिरिक्तरजतत्वप्रकारकज्ञानस्य रजतत्वप्रकारक-लाचादिकमेव प्रसिद्धमिति वाच्यं। दृष्टान्तस्य साधनविकलत्वापत्तेः, रसनस्य द्रव्याग्राहकत्वात् अलौकिकप्रत्यक्षस्य च परैरनभ्युपगमात्।

केचित्तु सत्यत्वं गुणत्ववति गुणत्वप्रकारकत्वं, द्वितीयज्ञानस्य गुणत्वप्रकारकत्वेन विशेषणीयं, रसनाया अपि गुणत्वग्राहकत्वाच्च न न दृष्टान्तस्य साध्यवैकल्यं, परैरपि अखण्डोपाधिरूपस्य गुणत्वस्याभ्युपगमाच्च न साध्याप्रसिद्धिरित्याहुः।

'इन्द्रियत्वादिति। नच रजतत्वप्रमाजनकखण्डचक्षुर्व्यक्तौ व्यभिचार इति वाच्यं। तादृशजनकवृत्तीन्द्रियत्वव्याप्यजातिमत्त्वस्य साध्यत्वादिति भावः। अतएव च इन्द्रियत्वविवेचने न वैयर्थ्यसम्भावनेति ध्येयं। ननु निरुपाधित्वमेवानुकूलतर्कः स्यादित्याशङ्कायामुपाधिमाह, 'चाक्षुषेति, 'जनकत्वं' स्वरूपयोग्यत्वं, नातो ज्ञानानुपस्थिते साध्या-

प्रतियोगिवृत्ति न भवति ज्ञानमात्रवृत्तिधर्म्मत्वात् प्रमात्ववत्। न च चक्षुश्चाक्षुषसत्यज्ञानातिरिक्तज्ञान-जनकं इन्द्रियत्वाद्रसनवदिति प्रतिरोधः, अप्रयोजक-त्वात् चाक्षुषज्ञानातिरिक्तज्ञानजनकत्वोपाधेः अन्यथा-ख्यातेरपि धर्म्म्यंशे सत्यत्वात्तुल्यन्यायतया व्यापकेऽपि व्यर्थविशेषणत्वाच्च। एवं स्वरूपतो विषयतश्चागृहीत-भेदं ज्ञानद्वयमेव विसंवादिप्रवृत्तिहेतुः। तदुक्तं। "सन्निहितरजतशकले रजतमतिर्भवति यादृशी सत्या।

व्यापकत्वमिति भावः। बाधमाह, 'अन्यथेति, 'धर्म्म्यंशे' धर्म्मिताव-च्छेदकांशे, इदमुपलक्षणं रजतांशे चेत्यपि बोध्यं। 'सत्यत्वादिति रजतत्वाभाववति रजतत्वप्रकारकत्वाभाववत्त्वादित्यर्थः, रजतत्वप्रका-रकत्वस्याव्याप्यवृत्तित्वादिति भावः। ननु सत्यत्वं रजतत्वाभाववति रजतत्वप्रकारकेतरत्वं अन्योन्याभावस्य नाव्याप्यवृत्तिरित्यत आह, 'तुल्येति, ज्ञानजनकत्वमात्रस्यैव साध्यत्वमभ्युपगमादिति भावः। उपसं-हरति, 'एवमिति, स्वरूपतोऽगृहीतभेदत्वं भ्रमत्वेनाज्ञातत्वलाभाय। 'सन्निहितेति सन्निकृष्टरजतखण्डे, 'सत्या रजतमतिः', 'यादृशी' यथा प्रवृत्तिजनिका, 'भेदानध्यवसायात्' स्वरूपतो भेदाग्रहात्, 'द्वयमपि' अगृहीतासंसर्गक-शुक्ति-रजतधीरपि, 'तादृक्' तथा प्रवृत्तिजनिका भवतीत्यर्थः। नन्वेवं विसंवादिप्रवृत्तिस्थलीये इदं रजतमिति ज्ञाने कथमयथार्थत्वव्यपदेशः इत्यत आह, 'व्यवहार-

भेदानध्यवसायादियमपि तादृक्परिस्फुरति" इति ॥ व्यवहारमात्रस्य भेदाग्रहजन्यत्वेऽपि तस्य संवाद-तद्भावाभ्यां ज्ञाने यथार्थत्वायथार्थत्वव्यपदेशः। अत एव लोके उष्णञ्जलमिति ज्ञाने नायथार्थत्वव्यपदेशः। उपेक्षाज्ञाने तु तद्व्यपदेशस्तद्‌योग्यत्वात्।

इति श्रीमद्गङ्गेशोपाध्यायविरचिते तत्त्वचिन्तामणौ प्रत्यक्षखण्डे अन्यथाख्यातिवादपूर्व्वपक्षः।

मात्रस्येति, 'भेदाग्रहजन्यत्वेऽपि' स्वरूपतोऽगृहीतभेदकप्रमाजन्यत्वेऽपि, 'स्वरूपतोऽगृहीतभेदेति भ्रमत्वेनाज्ञातत्वलाभार्थं स्वरूपकथनं, 'तस्य' व्यवहारस्य। 'अतएव' विसंवादिप्रवृत्तिजनकत्वस्यायथार्थत्वव्यपदेश-नियामकत्वादेव, 'उष्णं जलमितीति जले परम्परासम्बन्धेन उष्णत्व-प्रकारकज्ञान इत्यर्थः। तस्य विसंवादिप्रवृत्त्यजनकत्वादिति भावः। 'तद्योग्यत्वात्' विसंवादिप्रवृत्तिस्वरूपयोग्यत्वात्।

इति श्रीमथुरानाथतर्कवागीशविरचिते प्रत्यक्षखण्डरहस्ये अन्यथा-ख्यातिपूर्व्वपक्षरहस्यं।

अथान्यथाख्यातिवादसिद्धान्तः ।

सिद्धान्तस्तु[१] । सत्यस्थले प्रवृत्तिमात्रं प्रतीष्ट-पुरोवर्त्तिज्ञाने हेतुतया व्यवस्थितेऽतिप्रसङ्गवारणार्थं विषयतया वैशिष्ट्यमेव[२] कारणतावच्छेदकं कल्प्यते लाघवात् । कारणताग्रहसमये ज्ञान-वित्तिवेद्यतया शीघ्रो-

---

अथान्यथाख्यातिसिद्धान्तरहस्यं ।

रजतत्वादिप्रकारेण शुक्त्युपादानकविसंवादिप्रवृत्तिकारणतया लाघवादन्यथाख्यातिः सिद्धतीत्याह, 'सत्यस्थले प्रवृत्तिमात्रं प्रतीति सत्यस्थलोपादानकप्रवृत्तिमात्रं प्रतीत्यर्थः, उपादानत्वस्य सप्तम्यर्थत्वात् । सत्यस्थलोपादानकत्वञ्च रजतत्वादिप्रकारेण वस्तुगत्या रजतत्वाद्यधिकरणोपादानकत्वं, तथाच रजतत्वादिप्रकारेण रजताद्युपादानकसंवादिप्रवृत्तिमात्रं प्रतीति समुदितार्थः, 'इष्ट-पुरोवर्त्तिज्ञान इति सावधारणं, पुरोवर्त्तित्वावच्छिन्ने इष्टतावच्छेदकधर्म्मवैशिष्ट्यावगाहिप्रत्यक्ष एवेत्यर्थः, पुरोवर्त्तित्वं इदन्त्वं, इष्टतावच्छेदकधर्म्मः उपादानेच्छाविषयतावच्छेदको धर्म्मः उपादानतानिरूपकप्रकारताश्रयधर्म्म इति यावत्, स च रजतत्वादिः, एवं सर्व्वत्र । एवकारात् स्वतन्त्रताद्रुग्र-

---

(१) राद्धान्तस्त्विति ख० ।

(२) विशिष्टत्वमेवेति क० ।

पस्थितिकत्वात्(१) बाधकाभावाच्च । ननु स्वतन्त्रोपस्थितेष्टभेदाग्रहः(२) कारणं, तादृशभेदाग्रहत्वञ्च कारणतावच्छेदकं(३) गौरवात् कल्प्यनीयोपस्थितिकत्वाच्च ।

धर्म्मप्रत्यक्षकालीनपुरोवर्त्तित्वप्रकारकोपादानप्रत्यक्षमात्रस्य व्यवच्छेदः । 'हेतुतया व्यवस्थिते' कारणतावच्छेदकशरीरलाघवेन कारणतयोभयवादिसिद्धे, रजतत्वादिप्रकारेण शुक्त्यांद्युपादानकविसंवादिप्रवृत्तावपीति शेषः । 'अतिप्रसङ्गवारणार्थं' पुरोवर्त्तित्वावच्छिन्ने इदं रजतमित्युपादानतानिरूपकप्रकारताश्रयधर्म्मावच्छिन्नभेदग्रहदशायामपि तदुत्पत्तिवारणार्थं, 'विषयतया वैशिष्ट्यमेवेति पुरोवर्त्तित्वावच्छिन्ने उपादानतानिरूपकधर्म्मवैशिष्ट्यविषयकत्वमेवेत्यर्थः, एवकारात् स्वतन्त्रोपस्थिततादृशधर्म्मावच्छिन्नभेदाग्रहत्वव्यवच्छेदः । 'लाघवादिति कारणतावच्छेदकशरीरलाघवादित्यर्थः, परेणापि शरीरलाघवस्य हेतुत्वासिद्धेरिति भावः । हेत्वन्तरमाह, 'कारणताग्रहसमय इति प्रवृत्त्युत्पादानन्तरमेव उपादानप्रत्यक्षप्रवृत्तेः प्रत्यक्षतः कारणताग्रहसमय इत्यर्थः, 'ज्ञानवित्तीति उपादानप्रत्यक्षानुव्यवसायवेद्यतयेत्यर्थः । एतच्च इच्छादिज्ञानानुव्यवसायस्य यौगपद्याभ्युपगमेन । 'शीघ्रोपस्थितिकत्वादिति अवश्योपस्थितिकत्वादित्यर्थः । 'अवश्यं शीघ्रोपस्थितिकत्वात्' इति पाठस्तु प्रामादिकः । न च पुरोवर्त्तित्वावच्छिन्ने उपादानतानिरूपकधर्म्मवैशिष्ट्यविषयकत्वस्यानुव्यवसायग्राह्यत्वे स्वतः प्रामाण्यापत्ति-

---

(१) अवश्यं शीघ्रोपस्थितिकत्वादिति क० ।

(२) स्वतन्त्रोपस्थितेष्टभेदग्रहस्याभावः इति ख०, ग० ।

(३) हेतुतावच्छेदकमिति ख०, ग० ।

विशिष्टज्ञानेऽपि हेतुत्वेनावश्यककत्वाद्भेदाग्रह एव हेतुरिति चेत्। न। विशिष्टज्ञाने तद्धेतुत्वस्य तत्कल्पनोत्तरकल्प्यत्वेन प्रवृत्तिकारणताग्रहसमये तदनुप-

---

रिति वाच्यं। तद्वति तद्वैशिष्ट्यावगाहित्वस्य तद्वति तत्प्रकारकत्वस्य वा प्रामाण्यतया तस्य प्रामाण्यत्वाभावादिति भावः। एतत्स्वमतेनाभिहितं, परनये विसंवादिप्रवृत्तौ विशिष्टप्रत्यक्षस्य भ्रमरूपस्याप्रसिद्धत्वेनाहेतुतया कारणताग्रहसमये अनुव्यवसायात् ताद्रूप्येणानुपस्थितेरिति मन्तव्यं। सति बाधके उपस्थितत्वमप्रयोजकमत आह, 'बाधकाभावाच्चेति। 'इष्टभेदाग्रहः' उपादानतानिरूपकधर्मावच्छिन्नभेदाग्रहः, इदन्त्वरूपेणोपादानव्यक्तिप्रत्यक्षसहकृत इति शेषः। 'गौरवादिति कारणतावच्छेदकशरीरगौरवादित्यर्थः। 'कल्पनीयेति उपादानव्यक्तिप्रत्यक्ष-प्रवृत्त्योः कारणताग्रहदशायामनियतोपस्थितिकत्वाच्चेत्यर्थः।

मिश्रानुयायिनस्तु 'सत्यस्थल इति संवादिप्रवृत्तावित्यर्थः, विशिष्टज्ञानस्यान्वय-व्यतिरेकसहचारज्ञानाभ्यामिति शेषः। 'कल्प्यत इति अग्रेतनेन चास्यान्वयः। 'इष्ट-पुरोवर्त्तिज्ञाने' इष्टतावच्छेदकधर्मप्रत्यक्षसमकालीनपुरोवर्त्तिप्रत्यक्षे, इष्टतावच्छेदकधर्मः पूर्ववदुपादानतानिरूपकप्रकारताश्रयोधर्मः, पुरोवर्त्ती च इदन्त्वविशिष्टोपादानव्यक्तिः, 'हेतुतया व्यवस्थिते' हेतुतया निश्चिते, 'अतिप्रसङ्गवारणार्थं' नेदं रजतमिति भेदग्रहदशायामप्युक्तप्रत्यक्षात् प्रवृत्त्यापत्तिवारणाय, 'विषयतया वैशिष्ट्यमेवेति इदन्त्वविशिष्टे उपादानतानिरूपकप्रकार-

स्थितेः। न चैवं मिथ्याज्ञानकल्पने गौरवं, प्रमाण-प्रवृत्तिसमये सिद्धासिद्धिपराहतत्वेन फलमुखगौरव-स्यादोषत्वात्। प्रमाणवतस्तस्य न्याय्यत्वात्। एवञ्च

ताश्रयधर्म्मप्रकारकत्वमेवेत्यर्थः, तथाच तन्निष्ठप्रकारतानिरूपित-तद्व्यक्त्युपादानकप्रवृत्तित्वेन इदन्त्वधर्म्मितावच्छेदकक-तद्व्यक्तिविशेष्यक-तत्प्रकारकप्रत्ययत्वेन सामान्यकार्य्य-कारणभाव इति भावः, शेषं पूर्व्ववत्। न च कारणतानिश्चयोत्तरमवच्छेदककल्पने प्रथमं कारणतानिश्चय एव कथं स्यादिति वाच्यं। विशेषणतावच्छेदकीभूतधर्म्मस्य तन्निष्ठावच्छेदकत्वस्य वा ग्रहं विनाप्यन्यथासिद्धनिरूपकनियतपूर्व्व-वर्त्तितावच्छेदकधर्म्मवत्त्वरूपेण सामान्यतः कारणतानिश्चयसम्भवा-दन्यथा कारणतावच्छेदकतया धर्म्मसिद्धिः क्वापि न स्यादन्योन्याश्रय-ग्रासात्। अस्तु वा 'व्यवस्थित इत्यस्य व्यवस्थाप्यमान इत्यर्थः, तथाच नायं दोषः। न चैवं सत्यस्थल इत्यस्य सत्यप्रवृत्त्युत्पादानन्तरमित्ये-वार्थोऽस्तु अन्वयस्तस्य व्यवस्थित इत्यनेन किमन्वय-व्यतिरेकसहचार-ज्ञानाभ्यां इति पूरणेनेति वाच्यं। प्रवृत्तौ सत्यत्वविशेषणोपादाना-सङ्गतेः प्रवृत्त्युत्पादानन्तरमित्यस्यैव सम्यक्त्वादित्याहुः। तदसत्। तद्भेदत्वादेरननुगततया विशेष्यभेदेनैव ज्ञान-प्रवृत्त्योः कार्य्य-कारण-भावभेदाद्विसंवादि-संवाद्युभयप्रवृत्तिं प्रति एकरूपेण उपादान-प्रत्ययस्य हेतुत्वासम्भवात्। न च रजतत्वादिप्रकारकप्रत्ययत्वेन कार-णता रजतत्वादिनिष्ठप्रकारतानिरूपितोपादानताकप्रवृत्तित्वेन कार्य्यता विशेष्यत्वोपादानत्वघटितसामानाधिकरण्यस्य प्रत्यासत्तिरिति वाच्यं।

तथासति नेदं रजतमिति भेदग्रहदशायामपि निधर्म्मितावच्छेदकात् द्रव्यत्वादिसामान्यधर्म्मधर्म्मितावच्छेदकाच्च रजतत्वप्रकारकप्रत्ययाद्रजतत्वप्रकारक-तद्दृत्युपादानकप्रवृत्तिप्रसङ्गस्य दुर्व्वारत्वात्। न च विशेष्यतावच्छेदकत्वोपादानतावच्छेदकत्वोभयघटितसामानाधिकरण्यं प्रत्यासत्तिरिति वाच्यं। उपादानप्रत्यक्षस्येदन्त्वधर्म्मितावच्छेदककस्यैव सर्व्वत्र प्रवृत्तिहेतुतया तस्य तेन रूपेण कार्य्य-कारणत्वासम्भवात्। अन्यथा नेदं रजतमिति पुरोवर्त्तिव्यक्तौ भेदग्रहदशायामपि द्रव्यत्वादिधर्म्मितावच्छेदककतद्व्यक्तिविशेष्यक-रजतत्वादिप्रकारकप्रत्यक्षात द्रव्यत्वाद्युपादानतावच्छेदकक-रजतत्वप्रकारक-तद्व्यक्त्युपादानक-प्रवृत्तिप्रसङ्गात् रजताद्युपादानकप्रवृत्तेः रजतमित्याद्याकारकतया निधर्म्मितावच्छेदकत्वेन प्रवृत्तेः उपादानतावच्छेदकविरहाच्च इत्यन्यत्र विस्तरः।

कारणतावच्छेदकशरीरगौरवेऽपि कल्पनालाघवात् भेदाग्रह एव संवादिन्यां विसंवादिन्याञ्च प्रवृत्तौ हेतुरित्याशङ्कते 'विशिष्ट ज्ञानेऽपीति इदं रजतमिति भ्रम-प्रमासाधारणविशिष्टप्रत्यक्षसामान्यं प्रति भेदाग्रहस्य हेतुत्वेनेत्यर्थः, 'आवश्यकत्वादिति प्रवृत्तिं प्रत्यनन्यथासिद्धनियतपूर्व्ववर्त्तिताकत्वादित्यर्थः, 'हेतुरिति संवादिन्यां विसंवादिन्याञ्च प्रवृत्तौ हेतुरित्यर्थः, विशिष्टज्ञानस्य नियतपूर्व्ववर्त्तित्वानन्यथासिद्धत्वोभयकल्पनामपेक्ष्य सिद्धनियतपूर्व्ववर्त्तिताकस्य भेदाग्रहस्यानन्यथासिद्धत्वमात्रकल्पनाया लघुत्वादिति भावः। भ्रम-प्रमासाधारण-विशिष्टप्रत्यक्षकारणत्वेन सिद्धनियतपूर्व्ववर्त्तिताकतया भेदाग्रहस्यैव संवादिविसंवादिसाधारणप्रवृत्तिसामान्यहेतुत्वाभ्युपगमेऽप्यन्यथाख्यातिसिद्धिरप्रत्यूहा। विशिष्टोभयसिद्धिं विना भेदाग्रहे विशिष्टभ्रमहेतुत्वसिद्धु-

रसम्भवादित्यभिप्रायेण समाधत्ते, 'विशिष्टज्ञाने तद्धेतुत्वस्येति विशिष्टभ्रमं प्रति भेदाग्रहहेतुत्वस्येत्यर्थः, 'तत्कल्पनेति विशिष्टभ्रमसिद्ध्यधीनसिद्धिकत्वेनेत्यर्थः, 'प्रवृत्तिकारणताग्रहसमये' विशिष्टभ्रमे विसंवादिप्रवृत्तिकारणताया विसंवादिप्रवृत्तिनियतपूर्व्ववर्त्तितया ग्रहसमये विसंवादिप्रवृत्तिपूर्व्वं विशिष्टभ्रमस्यासिद्धाविति यावत्, विसंवादिप्रवृत्तिपूर्व्वमिति स्वरूपकथनं, 'तदनुपस्थितेरिति भेदाग्रहस्य विशिष्टभ्रमहेतुत्वासिद्धेरित्यर्थः, विशिष्टभ्रमसिद्धौ च सिद्धं नः समीहितमिति भावः। इदमुपलक्षणं, अन्यथाख्यातिसिद्धिं विना रजतत्वप्रकारक-रजतोपादानकसंवादिप्रवृत्तिं प्रत्यपि रजतनिष्ठरजतभेदग्रहाभावरूपस्य भेदाग्रहस्य हेतुत्वं न सम्भवति रजतव्यक्तौ रजतभेदग्रहस्य भ्रमत्वनियमेन तदप्रसिद्धौ तदभावस्याप्रसिद्धेः। नचान्यथाख्यातिसिद्धिं विनापीदन्त्वनिष्ठरजतभिन्नत्वप्रकारक-ज्ञानविशेष्यतावच्छेदकत्वाभावरूपस्य भेदाग्रहस्य तत्र हेतुत्वं सम्भवतीति वाच्यं। अन्यथाख्यात्यनभ्युपगमे रजतवृत्तीदन्त्वावां तादृशाभावस्य सर्व्वदैव वर्त्तमानत्वेनाव्यावर्त्तकतया कारणत्वे मानाभावात्तद्व्यतिरेकेण केवलव्यतिरेकविरहादेवमन्यथाख्यात्यनभ्युपगमे भ्रमात्मकविशिष्टज्ञानं प्रत्यपि भेदग्रहस्य प्रतिबन्धकत्वं न सम्भवति तत्र विशेष्ये विशेषणवद्भेदग्रहस्य भ्रमत्वनियमात् भेदग्रहादेः समानविशेष्यतावच्छेदकताप्रत्यासत्त्या प्रतिबन्धकत्वासम्भवस्यान्यत्र प्रतिपादितत्वादित्यपि बोध्यं। न च मास्त्वन्यथाख्यातिः तथाच प्रवृत्तिं प्रति विशिष्टप्रत्यक्षहेतुत्वे मानाभावः कल्पनालाघवेन स्वतन्त्रोपस्थितोपादानतानिरूपकप्रकारताश्रयधर्म्मावच्छिन्नप्रतियोगिताकभेदाग्रहस्यैव

इदन्त्वप्रकारकोपादानव्यक्तिप्रत्यक्षसहकृतस्य हेतुत्वौचित्यादिति वाच्यं। कारणतावच्छेदकशरीरगौरवे कल्पनालाघवस्याकिञ्चित्करत्वात् प्रागुक्तरीत्या स्वातन्त्र्यस्य दुर्व्वचत्वाच्च तादृशभेद-तद्व्याप्यादिग्रहाभावानां स्वतन्त्रोपस्थिततादृशधर्म्मात्यन्ताभाव-तद्व्याप्यादिग्रहाभावानाञ्च वह्नामनन्यथासिद्धत्वकल्पनामपेक्ष्य विशिष्टप्रत्यक्षस्य नियमानन्यथासिद्धत्वोभयकल्पनाया एव लघुतया कल्पनालाघवविरहाच्च।

मिश्रानुयायिनस्तु विशिष्टज्ञानस्य प्रवृत्तिसामान्यनियतपूर्व्ववर्त्तितासाधकत्वमेव न सम्भवति अप्रयोजकत्वात्, तन्नियतपूर्व्ववर्त्तिनोऽनियपूर्व्ववर्त्तिनस्तन्नियतपूर्व्ववर्त्तित्वावश्यकत्वस्यैव तत्तद्विपक्षबाधकत्वात् तथाच विशिष्टज्ञानस्य यदि प्रवृत्तिनियतपूर्ववर्त्तित्वं न सिद्धं तदा द्वयमेवासिद्धनियतपूर्व्ववर्त्तिताकं, यदि च तस्य नियतपूर्व्ववर्त्तित्वं सिद्धं तदा द्वयमेव सिद्धनियतपूर्व्ववर्त्तिताकमिति न कल्पनालाघवं, द्वितीये सिद्धञ्च नः समीहितमित्यभिप्रायेण समाधत्ते, 'विशिष्टज्ञानइति, 'तद्धेतुत्वस्य' भेदाग्रहप्रवृत्तिनियतपूर्व्ववर्त्तित्वस्य, 'विशिष्टज्ञाने तत्कल्पनोत्तरकल्प्यत्वेन' विशिष्टज्ञाने प्रवृत्तिनियतपूर्व्ववर्त्तित्वसिद्ध्यधीनसिद्धिकत्वेनेति योजना, 'प्रवृत्तिकारणताग्रहसमये' विशिष्टज्ञाने प्रवृत्तिकारणताया अग्रहदशायां, 'तदनुपस्थितेरिति भेदाग्रहनिष्ठप्रवृत्तिनियतपूर्व्ववर्त्तित्वासिद्धेरिति प्राञ्चः।

'नचैवमिति, 'एवं' विसंवादिप्रवृत्तिं प्रत्यपि विशिष्टप्रत्यक्षत्वेन कारणत्वे, 'मिथ्याज्ञानेति सर्व्वत्र विसंवादिप्रवृत्तिपूर्व्वं मिथ्याज्ञानव्यक्तीनां कल्पनागौरवमित्यर्थः। अतो विसंवादिप्रवृत्तौ भेदाग्रहादेरहेतुत्वं युक्तमिति भावः। गौरवं न स्वरूपसत् कारणत्वादिग्रह-

विसंवादिप्रवृत्तिरपि विशिष्टज्ञानसाध्या प्रवृत्तित्वात्

प्रतिबन्धकं, नापि तत्संशयः तत्र प्रतिबन्धकः, किन्तु तन्निर्णय एव प्रतिबन्धकः स च प्रकृतकारणताग्रहपूर्वं न सम्भवति, तत्तत्क्षणो-मिथ्याज्ञानवान् विसंवादिप्रवृत्त्यव्यवहितपूर्वत्वात् इत्यनुमानेनानन्त-मिथ्याज्ञानव्यक्त्यात्मकगौरवनिर्णये अनुकूलतर्कविधया विशिष्टज्ञान-विसंवादिप्रवृत्त्योः कार्य्य-कारणभावग्रहस्योपजीव्यत्वेन तत्पूर्वं तद-सम्भवादतो विशिष्टप्रत्ययत्वेन कारणत्वमेव युक्तं इत्यभिप्रायेण समा-धत्ते, 'प्रमाणेति, 'प्रमाणप्रवृत्तिसमयः' कारणताग्राहकप्रमाणप्रवृ-त्तिसमयः कारणताग्रहपूर्ववर्त्तिसमय इति यावत्, 'सिद्ध्यसिद्धिप-राहतत्वेनेति 'सिद्धेः' अनन्तमिथ्याज्ञानव्यक्त्यात्मकगौरवसिद्धेः, 'असि-द्धा' कारणत्वासिद्धा, 'पराहतत्वेन' असम्भवित्वेन इत्यर्थः, 'सिद्धिः' निर्णयः, 'असिद्धिः' तदभावः, 'फलमुखगौरवस्येति 'फलं' मिथ्या-ज्ञान-विसंवादिप्रवृत्तिकारणत्वावधारणं, तदेव मुखं निर्णयवीजं यस्य एवम्भूतस्यानन्तमिथ्याज्ञानव्यक्त्यात्मकगौरवस्येत्यर्थः, 'अदोषत्वात्' कार-णताग्रहाविघटकत्वात्, एतच्च 'न्याय्यत्वादित्यत्र हेतुः, 'तस्य' तस्यैव विशिष्टप्रत्ययत्वेन विसंवादिप्रवृत्तौ कारणत्वस्यैवेति यावत्। 'विसंवा-दिप्रवृत्तिरपीति शुक्त्यादिमात्रविशेष्यक-रजतत्वादिप्रकारिका प्रवृ-त्तिरपीत्यर्थः, 'विशिष्टज्ञानसाध्येति रजतत्वादिप्रकारक-ज्ञानविशेष्य-विधेयिकेत्यर्थः, 'प्रवृत्तित्वादिति रजतत्वादिप्रकारकप्रवृत्तित्वादि-त्यर्थः, 'सत्यप्रवृत्तिवदिति, रजतादिविशेष्यक-रजतत्वादिप्रकारक-प्रवृत्तिः दृष्टान्त इति भावः। ननु यत्र रजतत्वप्रकारक-रजत-

सत्यप्रवृत्तिवत्। भ्रमकारणं विनानुपपत्तेः अनन्यथा-सिद्धतया प्रवृत्त्या समानीतविशिष्टज्ञानबलात् तत्कारणं

विशेष्यकप्रवृत्तिविशेष्यव्यक्तिविशेष्यकरजतत्वप्रकारकज्ञानं न कस्याप्यसिद्धमिति तत्रैव व्यभिचार इत्यत आह, 'भ्रमेति रजतत्वप्रकारक-रजतोपादानकप्रवृत्तिं प्रति रजतत्वप्रकारक-रजतविशेष्यकप्रत्यक्षस्य हेतुतया तेन विना तदुत्पत्तेरसम्भवादित्यर्थः। इदमुपलक्षणं अन्ततो भगवतो योगिनां वा ज्ञानमादायैव सर्व्वत्र साध्यसत्त्वाच्चेत्यपि बोध्यं।

प्राञ्चस्तु 'विशिष्टज्ञानसाध्येति शुक्त्यादिविशेष्यक-रजतत्वादिप्रकारकज्ञानजन्येत्यर्थः, 'प्रवृत्तित्वादिति शुक्त्यादिविशेष्यक-रजतत्वादिप्रकारकप्रवृत्तित्वादित्यर्थः। या यद्विशेष्यक-यत्प्रकारिका प्रवृत्तिः सा तत्प्रकारक-तद्विशेष्यकज्ञानजन्या रजतविशेष्यक-रजतत्वप्रकारकप्रवृत्तिवदिति यत्तद्भ्यां सामान्यमुखी च व्याप्तिरतः साध्याप्रसिद्धावपि न क्षतिर्न वा दृष्टान्तासिद्धिरिति भावः। ननु या रजतविशेष्यक-रजतत्वप्रकारकप्रवृत्तिः तादृशज्ञानं विनैव उत्पन्ना तत्र व्यभिचार इत्यत आह, 'भ्रमेति, अर्थस्तु पूर्व्ववदित्याहुः।

ननु तथापि विसंवादिप्रवृत्तिकारणीभूतं मिथ्याज्ञानमकारणकं सकारणकं वा, नाद्यः सदातनत्वापत्तेः। नान्यः तत्कारणस्य दुर्व्वचत्वादित्यत आह, 'अनन्यथासिद्धतयेति विसंवादिप्रवृत्तेः विशिष्टभ्रमव्यतिरेकानुपपन्नतयेत्यर्थः, 'प्रवृत्त्या समानीतेति विसंवादिप्रवृत्तिसिद्धविशिष्टभ्रमात्मकात् प्रमाणादित्यर्थः, 'इन्द्रियाद्येवेति, सिद्ध्यतीति शेषः। आदिपदादिन्द्रियसन्निकर्षपरिग्रहः। ननु दोषस्य

सदोषमिन्द्रियाद्येव। सर्वतो बलवती ह्यन्यथानुपपत्तिः। न च भेदाग्रहात् प्रवृत्त्युपपत्तिरपि। विपरीतचतुष्के

ज्ञानजनकत्वमदृष्टचरमित्यत आह, 'सर्व्वत इति, तथाच कार्य्यान्यथानुपपत्त्या ज्ञानान्तरं प्रत्यदृष्टमपि दोषस्य जनकत्वमत्र कल्प्यत इति भावः। संवाद्यसंवादिसाधारणप्रवृत्ति-निवृत्तिसामान्यं प्रत्येव भेदाग्रहस्य कारणत्वे बाधकान्तरमाह, 'न चेति न वेत्यर्थः, 'विपरीतचतुष्क इति इमे रङ्ग-रजते इत्याकारकमिदन्त्वरूपेण रजते रङ्गत्वप्रकारकं रङ्गे च रजतत्वप्रकारकं विपरीतं नैकमेवात्र पारिभाषिकं विपरीतचतुष्के तादृशप्रत्यक्षस्थले युगपद्रजत-रङ्गयोरुभयत्रैव रजतत्वप्रकारकप्रवृत्ति-रङ्गत्वप्रकारकनिवृत्त्योरापत्तेरिदन्त्वरूपेण रजत-रङ्गव्यक्तिप्रत्यक्ष-स्वतन्त्ररजत-रङ्गत्वसाक्षात्कार-रजत-रङ्गभेदाग्रहाणां सत्त्वादित्यर्थः। इदमुपलक्षणं रजत-रङ्गयोरिमे रङ्ग-रजते इति प्रमात्मकप्रत्यक्षादपि तन्मते युगपद्रङ्ग-रजतयोरुभयत्रैव रङ्गत्वप्रकारकनिवृत्ति-रजतत्वप्रकारकप्रवृत्त्योरापत्तिः, तथा यत्र रजते रजतत्वप्रमा सुवर्णे च सुवर्णत्वप्रमा तत्र रजत-सुवर्णयोरुभयोरेव रजतत्व-सुवर्णत्वोभयप्रकारकप्रवृत्त्यापत्तिः, रजतत्व-सुवर्णत्वयोः स्वतन्त्रानुपस्थितौ रजतेऽपि रजतत्वप्रकारकप्रवृत्तेः सुवर्णेऽपि सुवर्णत्वप्रकारकप्रवृत्तेरनुपपत्त्या तथोपस्थितेरावश्यकत्वमित्यादिकमपि बोध्यं।

भट्टाचार्य्यानुयायिनस्तु 'विपरीतचतुष्क इति इमे रङ्ग-रजते नेमे रजत-रङ्गे इति समूहालम्बनप्रत्यक्ष इत्यर्थः। न च तत्र रजत-

युगपत् प्रवृत्तिनिवृत्त्यापत्तेः। न च तत्र मानाभावः, इमे-रङ्ग-रजते इति सत्यज्ञानवत् रजत-रङ्गयोः प्रत्येकभ्रम-

---

रङ्गयोः रजत-रङ्गभेदाग्रहस्यैवासत्त्वात् कथं तयोरुभयोरुपादानमिति वाच्यं। मीमांसकनये रजते रजतभेदस्य रङ्गे रङ्गभेदस्य ग्रहाभ्युपगमे अन्यथाख्यात्यापत्त्या तदसत्त्वात्। न च तथापि भेदज्ञानपर्य्यन्तानुधावनं व्यर्थं रङ्ग-रजतयोरिमे रङ्ग-रजते इति विपरीतद्विकेऽपि उक्तरीत्या अतिप्रसङ्गसाम्राज्यादिति वाच्यं। तत्र कदाचिदिष्टापत्तेः सम्भवात्। न चात्रापीष्टापत्तेः सम्भवः, अगृहीतासंसर्गकभेदग्रहसत्त्वेऽपि इष्टापत्तावत्यन्तानुभवविरोधादिति मणिकृतो निगर्व्वः। अतएव रङ्ग-रजतयोरिमे रङ्ग-रजते इति भ्रमात्मकप्रत्यक्षादेरपि परित्यागः तत्रापि कदाचिदिष्टापत्तिसम्भवात्। न च तथाप्यरजत-रजतयोरिमे रजतारजत इति विपरीतद्विकस्य कुतः परित्यागः तत्राप्यगृहीतासंसर्गकस्य रजतभेदस्य अगृहीतासंसर्गकस्यारजतभेदस्य रजतत्वस्य ग्रहसत्त्वेन इष्टापत्तेरसम्भवादिति वाच्यं। 'विपरीतचतुष्कपदस्य तादृशविपरीतद्विकस्याप्युपलक्षकत्वात्। एवं यत्र रजतारजतयोरेकत्र रजतत्वप्रमा अन्यत्र चारजतत्वभ्रमस्तत्र रजतत्वप्रमाविषय इवारजतत्वभ्रमविषयेऽपि रजतत्वप्रकारकप्रवृत्तिप्रसङ्गः, रजतत्वस्य स्वतन्त्रानुपस्थितौ रजतत्वप्रमाविषयेऽपि तत्प्रकारकप्रमानुपपत्त्या तथोपस्थितेरावश्यकत्वात् रजते रजतभेदस्य ग्रहे 'अन्यथाख्यात्यापत्त्या तदभावस्य स्फुटत्वादिति प्राहुः।

सामग्र्या रेकदा सत्त्वेन तादृशभ्रमोत्पत्तेरानुभविकत्वात्। अन्यथा समूहालम्बनोच्छेदे द्वित्वाद्यप्रत्यक्षतापत्तेः।

यद्यपि न्यायनयेऽपि विपरीतद्विकाद्विपरीतचतुष्काद्वा युगपद्रजते रङ्गत्वप्रकारिका निवृत्तिः रङ्गे रजतत्वप्रकारिका प्रवृत्तिः कुतो नोत्पद्यते, एवं यत्रैकस्यामेव व्यक्ताविदं रजतं रङ्गञ्चेति समुच्चयात्मकं प्रत्यक्षं तत्रापि एकस्यां व्यक्तौ रजतत्वप्रकारकप्रवृत्ति-रङ्गत्वप्रकारकनिवृत्त्योः कुतो युगपदनुत्पत्तिः तद्वारणाय परस्परसामग्र्या-विरोधित्वाभ्युपगमे च मीमांसकनयेऽपि तस्य सुवचत्वात्, तथापि न्यायनये विपरीतद्विकादितोयुगपत् रजते रङ्गत्वप्रकारकनिवृत्तेः रङ्गे च रजतत्वप्रकारकप्रवृत्तेरुत्पत्तिरुक्तस्थले एकस्यामेव व्यक्तौ रजतत्वप्रकारक-प्रवृत्ति-रङ्गत्वप्रकारक-निवृत्त्योर्युगपदुत्पत्तिस्त्वेवं ज्ञानद्वयोरेव यौगपद्यानभ्युपगमात् विप्रत्यङ्गुल्यवच्छेदेन परस्परविलक्षणानां विप्रतिप्रयत्नानां युगपदेवोत्पादात् मीमांसकनये च विपरीतद्विकादितो रजत-रङ्गयोरुभयत्रैव युगपद्रजतत्वप्रकारकप्रवृत्ति-रङ्गत्वप्रकारकनिवृत्त्योरापत्तिरित्येव विशेषात्तत्रापीष्टापत्तौ चानुभवविरोधादिति भावः। एतेन उपादानप्रत्यक्षवदुपादानगोचरराग-द्वेषयोरपि प्रवृत्ति-निवृत्तिहेतुतया क्रमोत्पन्नज्ञानाद्य तत्त्रयाणां एकदानवस्थानात् कथं युगपत् प्रवृत्ति-निवृत्त्यापादनं मीमांसकैरपेक्षाबुद्धेरपि क्षणत्रयमात्रावस्थायित्वाभ्युपगमात्। न च प्रवृत्ति-निवृत्तिपदं तत्कारणीभूतराग-द्वेषपरमिति वाच्यं। फलगोचरचिकीर्षा-द्वेषयो-

इमे रङ्ग-रजते इति शब्दाभासादेवंविधभ्रमसम्भवाच्च। मम दोषमहिम्ना रजत-रङ्गयोः रजत-रङ्गभेदग्रहान्न संशयः तव चैकत्र स्वतन्त्रोभयभेदाग्रहात् प्रत्येकं रङ्गं रजतं वेति संशयः स्यात्। अथ यद्धर्म्मज्ञानाद्यदुप-

---

दुपादानगोचरराग-द्वेषजनकतया फलगोचरराग-द्वेषोपादानगोचर-ज्ञानानाञ्च त्रयाणामेकदानवस्थित्या तयोरपि युगपदुत्पत्त्यसम्भवादित्यपि निरस्तं। ज्ञानेतरात्मविशेषगुणद्वयोर्यौगपद्याभ्युपगन्तृनये इष्टानिष्टफलसाधनताविषयकविपरीतचतुष्कस्य पूर्व्वक्षणे युगपत् फलगोरविकीर्षा-द्वेषयोस्तद्द्वितीयक्षणे चोपादानगोचर-रागद्वेषयोः सम्भवेन तत्तृतीयक्षणे प्रवृत्ति-विवृत्त्यापत्तेर्दुर्व्वारत्वात्। फलचिकीर्षादेरुपादानेच्छाद्वारैव प्रवृत्त्यादौ हेतुतया प्रवृत्त्यादिपूर्व्वं तन्नाशेऽपि क्षतिविरहात्। यदि च उपादानप्रत्यक्षमुपादानेच्छाद्वारैव प्रवृत्तिहेतुः न तु साक्षात् तदा तादृशविपरीतचतुष्कानन्तरं फलचिकीर्षाभ्युपगमेऽपि न क्षतिः।

नव्यास्तु 'युगपत् प्रवृत्ति-निवृत्त्यापत्तेः' इत्यत्र प्रवृत्ति-निवृत्त्योर्यौगपद्यं नार्थः, किन्तु विपरीतद्विकादितो रङ्गे रजतत्वप्रकारकप्रवृत्त्युत्पत्तिदशायां रजतेऽपि रजतत्वप्रकारकप्रवृत्त्यापत्तिः, रजते रङ्गत्वप्रकारकनिवृत्त्युत्पत्तिदशायां रङ्गेऽपि रङ्गत्वप्रकारकनिवृत्त्यापत्तिरित्येवार्थः, रङ्गे रजतत्वप्रकारकरागोत्पत्तिदशायां रजतेऽपि रजतत्वप्रकारकरागस्य समूहालम्बनरूपस्य, रजते रङ्गत्वप्रकारकद्वेषोत्पत्तिदशायां रङ्गेऽपि रङ्गत्वप्रकारकद्वेषस्य समूहालम्बनरूपस्य

स्थितिस्तत्र तद्भेदाग्रहात् प्रवृत्ति-निवृत्ती। रङ्ग-रजत-धर्मेण रजत-रङ्गे स्मारिते न तु रङ्ग-रजते, माष-राशिस्थमसीविषये माषार्थिप्रवृत्तिः मसीनीलिमस्मा-

---

सम्भवात् राग-द्वेषौ प्रत्यपि तन्नये भेदाग्रहादेर्हेतुत्वादिति भावः। एवञ्च योग्यात्मविशेषगुणमात्रस्य यौगपद्यविरहेऽपि न यन्थासङ्गति-रिति प्राञ्चः।

'न चेति, 'तत्र' तादृशसमूहालम्बनप्रत्यक्षे, 'प्रत्येकभ्रमसामग्र्यो-रिति रजतादिप्रत्यक्षसामग्री-रङ्गादिप्रत्यक्षसामग्र्योरित्यर्थः। प्रथमा-दिपदाद्रङ्गत्वस्य, द्वितीयादिपदाद्रजतत्वस्य परिग्रहः। भट्टाचार्य्यमते प्रथमादिपदाद्रङ्गत्व-रजतभिन्नत्वयोः, द्वितीयादिपदाच्च रजतत्व-रङ्गभिन्नत्वयोः परिग्रहः। 'तादृशभ्रमेति तादृशसमूहालम्बनप्रत्य-क्षेत्यर्थः, 'आनुभविकत्वात्' प्रामाणिकत्वात्। नन्वेवमेकमुख्यविशेष्यक-धीसामग्री नापरमुख्यविशेष्यिकां धियमर्जयतीति नियमव्याघात इत्यत आह, 'अन्यथेति तादृशनियमानुपगम इत्यर्थः, 'समूहालम्बनं' नानामुख्यविशेष्यकं ज्ञानं, 'द्वित्वाद्यप्रत्यक्षतेति, तन्नये द्वित्वादेरपेक्षा-बुद्धिव्यङ्ग्यत्वात्तस्य च समूहालम्बनरूपत्वनियमादिति भावः। एतच्च न्यायनये अयमेकोऽयञ्चैक इति समूहालम्बनापेक्षाबुद्धेरेव द्वित्वादि-जनकत्ववत् परनयेऽपि तादृशसमूहालम्बनापेक्षाबुद्धिरेव द्वित्वादि-व्यञ्जिका अन्यथा क्रमिकापेक्षाज्ञानस्थले द्वित्वानुत्पत्त्या द्वावितिप्रत्य-क्षस्य नैयायिकैरभ्युपगमेनानुभवकलहापत्तेः व्यङ्ग्य-व्यञ्जकभावे गौरवापत्तेश्च इत्यभिप्रायेणाभिहितं। विवेचितञ्चेदं सिद्धान्तरहस्ये।

रितमात्रभेदाग्रहात्। अनुभूयमानारोपोऽसिद्ध एव। अन्यथा तवापि प्रत्येकमुभयज्ञानं स्यादिति चेत्। मैवं। शब्दाभासात् प्रत्यक्षाद्वा इष्टानिष्टोपस्थितौ तदभावात्।

केचित्तु 'द्वित्वादीत्यतद्गुणसंविज्ञानबहुव्रीहिणा त्रित्वादिपरं क्रमिकापेक्षाबुद्धित्रयाणां एकदावस्थानासम्भवात् समूहालम्बनोच्छेदे तदप्रत्यक्षतापत्तेरित्यभिप्राय इत्याहुः।

अन्ये तु न्यायनयेनैवेदं बाधकं, न्यायनये क्रमिकापेक्षाज्ञानाभ्यामेव द्वित्वोत्पत्तौ प्राथमिकापेक्षाबुद्धिनाशस्य द्वित्वोत्पत्तिक्षणोत्पत्तौ बाधकाभावेन तन्नाशादेव द्वित्वनाशे तस्य क्षणिकतया तदप्रत्यक्षतापत्तेरित्यभिप्रायादित्याहुः।

केचित्तु 'द्वित्वाद्यप्रत्यक्षतापत्तेरिति पर्य्याप्त्याख्यसम्बन्धेन द्वित्वादिप्रकारकप्रत्यक्षाभावापत्तेरित्यर्थः, तादृशप्रत्यक्षस्य नानामुख्यविशेष्यकत्वनियमाभावात् इत्याहुः।

उक्तनियमे व्यभिचारमप्याह, 'इमे' इति, 'एवंविधभ्रमेणि भवन्मतेऽपि नानापदार्थमुख्यविशेष्यकसमूहालम्बनस्मरणसम्भवाच्च इत्यर्थः, अत्र शब्दाभासपदं भ्रमपदस्योपलक्षणं तादृशशब्दजन्यप्रमायामपि व्यभिचारो बोध्यः। वस्तुतस्तु 'शब्दाभासात्' शब्दज्ञानात्, 'एवंविधभ्रमेत्यत्र च 'भ्रमः' विशिष्टानुभवः, नानापदार्थमुख्यविशेष्यकविशिष्टानुभवसम्भवाच्चेत्यर्थः, इत्येव तत्त्वं। नन्वेवं भवन्मते विपरीतद्विकादिपरीतचतुष्काद्वा रजते रङ्गत्वप्रकारिका निष्कम्पनिवृत्तिः, रङ्गे च रजतत्वप्रकारिका निष्कम्पप्रवृत्तिः न स्यात् रजत-रङ्गात्मक-धर्मि-

मम त्वेकधर्मादुभयोपस्थितावपि रजत-रङ्गयोस्तत्तया न ज्ञानं दोषादित्युभयसिद्धं विपरीतज्ञानञ्च दोषात्।

द्वयज्ञान-रजतत्व-रङ्गत्वात्मककोटिद्वयोपस्थित्यादिरूपायाः संशयसामग्र्याः सत्त्वेन तस्य संशयरूपत्वादित्यत आह, 'ममेति, 'रजत-रङ्गयोरिति, 'रजत-रङ्गभेदाग्रहादित्यत्र यथाक्रममन्वितं, 'रजत-रङ्गभेदग्रहात्' रजत-रङ्गभेदस्यैव ग्रहात् रजतत्व-रङ्गभेदयोः रङ्गत्व-रजतभेदयोरग्रहादिति यावत्, प्रत्युत तत्रैव तस्य संशयत्वापत्त्या ततो रजते रङ्गत्वप्रकारकनिष्कम्पनिवृत्तिः, रङ्गे च रजतत्वप्रकारकनिष्कम्प-प्रवृत्तिर्न स्यादित्याह, 'तत्रेति तत्रैवेत्यर्थः, 'एकत्र स्वतन्त्रोभय-भेदाग्रहादिति स्वतन्त्रोपस्थितरजतत्व-रङ्गत्वावच्छिन्न-प्रतियोगिताक-भेदाग्रहादित्यर्थः, रजते अन्यथाख्यात्यापत्त्या रजतभेदस्य दोषप्रति-बन्धवशाच्च रङ्गभेदस्याग्रहादेवं रङ्गे अन्यथाख्यात्यापत्त्या रङ्गभेदस्य दोषप्रतिबन्धवशाच्च रजतभेदस्याग्रहादिति भावः। 'प्रत्येकमिति, भवन्मये अगृहीतभेदधर्म्मिज्ञानसहितस्वतन्त्रविरुद्धकोटिद्वयज्ञानस्यैव संशयत्वादिति भावः। युगपत् प्रवृत्ति-निवृत्त्यापत्तौ समाधानं प्रकृते, 'अथेति रजतवृत्तिवाचकपदेन रङ्गमेव स्मारितं न तु रजतं तादृश-वाचकपदस्य विशेषस्य तेन पुंसा रङ्गवृत्तितयैव पूर्व्वं ग्रहात् एवं रङ्ग-वृत्तिवाचकपदेन रजतमेव स्मारितं न तु रङ्गमतः प्रवृत्ति-निवृत्ति-विषयवृत्तिधर्म्मोपस्थितेष्टानिष्टभेदाग्रहयोरेव प्रवृत्ति-निवृत्तिहेतुतया रङ्गरजतयोः रजतत्व-रङ्गत्वप्रकारकप्रवृत्ति-निवृत्ती एव न तु वैपरी-त्यमित्यर्थः। नन्वेवं माषभेदाग्रहात् मस्यां माषत्वप्रकारकप्रवृत्तिः

न चैवमावश्यकदोषादेव प्रवृत्ति-निवृत्ती, सत्यस्थले तदभावात्। न च विसंवादिनी दोषात्, इन्द्रिय-लिङ्ग-

कथं स्यादित्यत आह, 'माषेति। नन्वेवमनुभूयमानारोपात् प्रवृत्ति-निवृत्ती न स्यातां तत्रारोप्यस्यानुभूयमानत्वेन प्रवृत्तिविशेष्यवृत्ति-धर्म्मान्यथानुपस्थितेरित्यत आह, 'अनुभूयमानारोप इति अनुभूय-मानरजतत्वादेः पुरोवर्त्तिन्यसंसर्गाग्रहात् क्वचित् प्रवृत्ति-निवृत्त्युत्पा-दोऽसिद्ध एवेत्यर्थः। नन्वेक एव धर्म्मो रजत-रङ्गयोरुभयोरपि स्मारक इति नोक्तं समाधानमित्यत आह, 'अन्यथेति एकस्यैवोभय-स्मारकत्वे इत्यर्थः, 'उभयज्ञानं स्यादिति रङ्गं रजतं वेति संशयः स्या-दित्यर्थः, साधारणधर्म्मवद्धर्म्मिज्ञानजन्यकोटिद्वयस्मृतेः सत्त्वादित्यभि-मानः। एतच्च पूर्व्वोक्तरीत्यैवाग्रे स्वयमेव निवारयिष्यत इति मास-ङ्गतिः। यत्र शब्दात् प्रत्यक्षाद्वा रङ्ग-रजतयोरुपस्थितिः ततो रज-तत्व-रङ्गत्वप्रकारकप्रत्यक्षात् प्रवृत्ति-निवृत्तिः तत्र रजत-रङ्गोपस्थितौ प्रवृत्ति-निवृत्त्यभावादुक्तकारणं व्यभिचारीत्यभिप्रायेण समाधत्ते, 'शब्दाभावादिति शब्दज्ञानादित्यर्थः, यथाश्रुते आभासपर्य्यन्तानु-धावनस्य व्यर्थत्वात्, 'इष्टानिष्टेति रजत-रङ्गोपस्थितावित्यर्थः, 'तद-भावात्' इति प्रवृत्ति-निवृत्तिविशेष्यवृत्तिधर्म्मजन्यत्वाभावादित्यर्थः। नचानुभूयमानारोपात् प्रवृत्त्यादिकमेवासिद्धमिति प्रागेवाभिहित-मिति वाच्यम्। तत्रापि प्रवृत्त्यादेरनुभवसिद्धत्वादिति भावः। 'अन्यथेत्यादिकमपि पूर्व्वोक्तदोषेणैव दुष्टमित्याह, 'मम त्विति, 'तत्तया।' रजतत्व-रङ्गत्वप्रकारेण, 'इत्युभयसिद्धमिति इदञ्चोभयसिद्ध-

शब्दादिदोषाणामननुगतत्वात्। तज्जन्यज्ञाने च जाति-
भेदात्।

नव्यास्तु रङ्गवृत्तितया ज्ञातधर्मस्य रजते उत्कटा-

मित्यर्थः। नन्वेवं दोषस्य रजतादौ रजतत्वाद्यग्रहं प्रत्येव प्रयोजकतया रजतादौ रङ्गत्वादिग्रहः कथं स्यादित्यत आह, 'विपरीतज्ञानञ्चेति विपरीतज्ञानमपीत्यर्थः, 'विपरीतज्ञानं' रजते रङ्गत्वज्ञानं रङ्गे रजतत्व-ज्ञानञ्च, 'आवश्यकत्वादिति, आवश्यकत्वं रजतत्वाद्यग्रहप्रयोजकतया रङ्गत्वादिभ्रमजनकतया च, 'तदभावात्' दोषाभावात्। स्वेष्टा-साधने स्वेष्टसाधनताभ्रमादुक्तप्रवृत्तिस्तत्रापि तज्जनकीभूतदोषा एव हेतवो वाच्या अन्यथा तत्र स्वेष्टसाधनताविशिष्टज्ञानस्य हेतुत्वाभ्यु-पगमे तत एवान्यथाख्यातिसिद्ध्यापत्तेरित्यभिप्रेत्य दूषणमाह, 'दुष्टेन्द्रि-येति प्रात्यक्षिकेष्टसाधनत्वादिभ्रमानुमानिकेष्टसाधनत्वादिभ्रम-शाब्देष्ट-साधनत्वादिभ्रमजनकीभूतानां दोषाणामननुगतत्वादित्यर्थः। एते-नोपादानप्रत्यक्षकारणताविचारकोऽयं ग्रन्थस्तत्र लिङ्ग-शब्दयोः प्रसङ्ग इति पूर्व्वपक्षो निरस्तः। नन्वेवमिष्टसाधनत्वादिभ्रमं प्रत्येव कथं दोषाणां हेतुत्वमननुगमादित्यत आह, 'तज्जन्येति तथा च प्रात्य-क्षिकभ्रमत्वादिकं तत्कार्य्यतावच्छेदकमित्यर्थः, प्रवृत्त्यादौ च वैजा-त्यस्यानुपलम्भबाधितत्वात् लाघवेन प्रवृत्तिमात्रे विशिष्टधिय एव हेतुतायाः क्लृप्तत्वाच्चेति भावः।

'नव्याः' प्राभाकरनव्याः, 'ज्ञातधर्म्मस्येति ज्ञातस्य चाकचक्य-विशेषस्येत्यर्थः, 'रजते' रजतत्वोपस्थितौ, 'उत्कटाकाङ्क्षेति, आकाङ्क्षा

काङ्क्षा तेन सह भूयःसहचारदर्शनात्। न रङ्गे अल्पतयात्वादिति तत्रानुत्कटा सा। एवं रजतवृत्तितया ज्ञातधर्मस्यापि, अत उत्कटाकाङ्क्षयानुत्कटाकाङ्क्षाप्रतिबन्धान्न रङ्गे निवृत्तिः। एवं रजते न प्रवृत्तिरिति

घोपस्थितिनिष्ठपदार्थान्तरं, 'तेन सह' रजतत्वेन सह, 'न रङ्गे' न रङ्गत्वोपस्थितौ, 'अल्पतयात्वात्' अल्पसहचारज्ञानात्, 'रजतवृत्तितया ज्ञातधर्मस्यापीति, रङ्गत्वोपस्थितावुत्कटाकाङ्क्षा रजतत्वोपस्थितावनुत्कटा चेति शेषः। 'उत्कटाकाङ्क्षयेति रङ्गादिवृत्तितया ज्ञातधर्मोत्कटाकाङ्क्षाविशिष्टरजतत्वाद्युपस्थित्येत्यर्थः, 'अनुत्कटाकाङ्क्षाप्रतिबन्धादिति रङ्गादिवृत्तितया ज्ञातधर्मानुत्कटाकाङ्क्षाविशिष्टरङ्गत्वानुपस्थितिजन्यरङ्गादिविशेष्यक-रङ्गत्वादिप्रकारकप्रयत्नस्य प्रतिबन्धादित्यर्थः, 'निवृत्तिः' रङ्गत्वप्रकारिका निवृत्तिः, 'न प्रवृत्तिः' न रजतत्वप्रकारकप्रवृत्तिः। 'शब्दाभावादिति तादृशशब्दाभावजन्यरङ्गत्वरजतत्वोपस्थितिसहकृतादिदन्त्वरूपेण रजत-रङ्गप्रत्ययादित्यर्थः, 'प्रवृत्तिनिवृत्तीति रजत-रङ्गयोरुभयोरेव प्रवृत्ति-निवृत्तिप्रसङ्गादित्यर्थः, 'शब्दादुपस्थिताविति तत्रापि केनापि समं भूयः सहचाराध्यवसायाभावेन कुत्राप्युत्कटाकाङ्क्षाविरहादिति भावः। 'धर्मयोर्द्वयोरिति रजतत्व-रङ्गत्वरूपयोर्धर्मद्वयोरित्यर्थः, 'अल्पाधिकसहचारावगमादिति[१] रङ्गादिवृत्तिधर्मेण सममल्पाधिकसहचारावगमादित्यर्थः,

---

(१) 'किञ्चैवंधर्मयोर्द्वयोरल्पाधिकसहचारावगमात्' इति कस्यचिन्मूलपुस्तकस्य पाठः इति टीकाकारप्रतीकधारणेनानुमीयत इति।

तन्न। इमे रज्जु-रजते इति शब्दाभासाद्युगपत्प्रवृत्ति-निवृत्तिप्रसङ्गात् शब्दादुपस्थितौ आकाङ्क्षायास्तुल्यत्वात्। किञ्चैवं धर्म्मयोर्भूयोऽल्पसहचारावगमादुत्कटानुत्कटकोटिको रज्जुं रजतं वेति संशयः स्यात्।

भूयःसहचरितधर्म्मवद्धर्म्मिज्ञानाल्पसहचरितधर्म्मवद्धर्म्मिज्ञानयोरेवोत्कटानुत्कटकोटिकसंशयनियामकत्वात्, भवन्मये अगृहीतासंसर्गकधर्म्मिज्ञानसहितस्वतन्त्रविरुद्धकोटिद्वयज्ञानस्यैव संशयतया दोषाद्रजत-रज्ज्वोः रज्जुत्व-रजतत्ववत्ताज्ञानासम्भवेऽपि संशयत्वे बाधकाभावादिति भावः। मूलदोषमाह, 'उत्कटेति, 'उत्कटत्वेति, जातिव्यञ्जकत्वाभावात् तन्मते न तस्य जातित्वं पदार्थान्तरकल्पने च गौरवमिति भावः।

ननु यदि संवाद्यसंवादिसाधारणप्रवृत्तिसामान्यं प्रत्येव भेदाग्रहोहेतुरुपेयते तदैव विपरीतचतुष्के रजत-रज्ज्वोरुभयत्रैव युगपत्प्रवृत्ति-निवृत्त्यापत्तिर्यदि पुनः संवादिप्रवृत्तिं प्रति विशिष्टज्ञानमेव हेतुर्विसंवादिप्रवृत्तौ च भेदाग्रह इत्युपेयते तदा तु नेत्यभिप्रेत्य ब्रूते, 'स्यादेतदिति, 'प्रवृत्त्योर्वैचित्र्ये' तद्रूपविचित्रप्रवृत्त्योः, 'क्लृप्तत्वादिति भेदाग्रहस्य विसंवादिप्रवृत्तिं प्रति क्लृप्तनियतपूर्व्ववर्त्तिताकत्वादित्यर्थः। न च विसंवादिप्रवृत्तिनियतपूर्व्ववर्त्तिनो विशिष्टभ्रमस्य नियतपूर्व्ववर्त्तित्वादेव भेदाग्रहे विसंवादिप्रवृत्ति-नियतपूर्व्ववर्त्तित्वकल्पनाद्विशिष्टज्ञानमपि क्लृप्तनियतपूर्व्ववर्त्तिताकं सिद्धमन्यथाख्यात्या विशिष्टभ्रमसिद्धिं विना भेदाग्रहे विशिष्ट-

उत्कटानुत्कटाकाङ्क्षाकल्पने मानाभावात् उत्कटत्वानिरुक्तेश्च।

स्यादेतत्। संवादि-विसंवादिप्रवृत्त्योर्वैचित्र्ये विशिष्टज्ञान-भेदाग्रहौ हेतू क्लृप्तत्वात् न तु विशिष्टज्ञान-सत्यत्वासत्यत्वे गौरवादसिद्धेश्च। प्रवृत्ति-निवृत्तिमात्रे

भ्रमपूर्ववर्त्तित्वसिद्धेरसम्भवादिति वाच्यं। भेदग्रहो विसंवादिप्रवृत्ति-नियतपूर्ववृत्त्यभावप्रतियोगी तत्पूर्ववर्त्तित्वे मानाभावादित्यादिना प्रकारान्तरेणापि तत्सिद्धिसम्भवादिति भावः। 'विशिष्टज्ञानसत्यत्वा-सत्यत्वे' सत्यासत्यविशिष्टज्ञाने, प्रथमे हेतुमाह, 'गौरवादिति संवादि-प्रवृत्तौ विशिष्टधीत्वापेक्षया सत्यविशिष्टधीत्वेन हेतुत्वे गौरवादित्यर्थः। इदमुपलक्षणं अयथार्थज्ञानासिद्धिदशायां सत्यत्वस्योपरञ्जकतया अव्यावर्त्तकत्वेन कारणतानवच्छेदकत्वाच्चेत्यपि बोध्यं। द्वितीये हेतु-माह, 'असिद्धेरिति ज्ञाने असत्यत्वस्यासिद्धेरित्यर्थः, इति सम्प्रदायः।

वस्तुतस्तु विसंवादिप्रवृत्तावसत्यविशिष्टज्ञानस्य हेतुत्वे एव हेतु-द्वयमाह, 'गौरवादसिद्धेश्चेति, 'गौरवात्' सर्व्वत्र विसंवादिप्रवृत्ति-पूर्व्वमनन्तादिविशिष्टज्ञानव्यक्तिकल्पने गौरवात्, 'असिद्धेः' विशिष्टज्ञाने विसंवादिप्रवृत्तिनियतपूर्व्ववर्त्तित्वासिद्धेश्चेत्यर्थः। न च फलमुखगौरव-स्यादोषतया प्रथमो हेतुरसङ्गत इति वाच्यं। एतदस्वरसेनैव द्वितीयहेतुप्रणयनात् संशय-निश्चयसाधारणगौरवज्ञानत्वेनैव लाघ-वेन प्रतिबन्धकतया फलमुखगौरवस्यापि संशयात्मकज्ञानस्य कारण-तायहपूर्व्वं सम्भवात् ज्ञातेरपि कारणताग्रहे तदुत्तरोत्पन्नतज्ज्ञानेन

चेष्टानिष्टपुरोवर्त्तिज्ञानं हेतुरिति नाननुगमः, न तु विशिष्टज्ञानं गौरवात्। न च भेदाग्रहेऽतिप्रसङ्गः, विशिष्टज्ञानं भेदाग्रहश्च विशेषद्वयहेतुं विना सामान्यहेतोः कार्य्यानुत्पादात्। न हि निर्विशेषं सामान्यं नाम। अन्यथा अन्धस्य त्वक्सम्बन्धे महत्युद्भूतरूपवति चन्द्र-

---

तथाप्रामाण्यकल्पनाच्च। तादृशगौरवमपि न दोषायेत्यभिप्रायाद्वा। 'प्रवृत्ति-निवृत्तिमात्र' इति तत्प्रकारकप्रवृत्ति-निवृत्तिसामान्य इत्यर्थः, 'इष्टानिष्टपुरोवर्त्तिज्ञानमिति इष्टानिष्टतावच्छेदकतज्ज्ञानमित्यर्थः, अवच्छेदकान्तं स्वरूपकथनं, तज्ज्ञानत्वमात्रं कारणतावच्छेदकमित्यर्थः, 'न तु विशिष्टज्ञानमिति समानविशेष्यताप्रत्यासत्त्या तत्प्रकारकं ज्ञानमित्यर्थः। 'अतिप्रसङ्ग' इति सामान्यसामग्रीतः सामान्यकार्य्यप्रसङ्ग इत्यर्थः। 'अन्यथेति सामान्यसामग्रीसत्त्वेऽपि विशेषहेतुं विना कार्य्यानुदयानभ्युपगम इत्यर्थः, 'त्वक्सम्बन्ध' इति जन्यज्ञानसामान्यहेतोस्त्वङ्मनःसम्बन्धस्य सत्त्व इत्यर्थः, 'चन्द्रमहसि' चन्द्रप्रभायां, 'प्रत्यक्षतापत्तिरिति बहिरिन्द्रियजन्यद्रव्यसाक्षात्कारसामान्यापत्तिरित्यर्थः, 'द्रव्यसाक्षात्कारेति त्वाचप्रत्यक्षकारणस्योद्भूतस्पर्शस्य चाक्षुषप्रत्यक्षकारणस्य चक्षुःसंयोगस्याभावेऽपि बहिरिन्द्रियजन्यद्रव्यसाक्षात्कारसामान्यकारणस्य महत्त्वसमानाधिकरणोद्भूतरूपस्य सत्त्वादित्यर्थः।

प्राञ्चस्तु 'त्वक्सम्बन्धे'- त्वक्चन्द्रप्रभयोः संयोगे, महत्त्वोद्भूतरूप-

महसि प्रत्यक्षतापत्तिः द्रव्यसाक्षात्कारहेतोः सत्त्वात्। एवं रङ्गे रजते च विसंवादिन्यौ भवतः भेदाग्रहात् न च संवादिन्यौ, विशिष्टज्ञानाभावात्। अथ रजत-रङ्गयोः रजत-रङ्गभेदाग्रहात् विसंवादिन्यौ बलात्स्यातां तत्सामग्रीसत्त्वात्। विसंवादिनी तत्र सत्यरजते न सम्भवतीति चेत्। अत एव भेदाग्रहो न तद्धेतुः तत्-

---

वत्याः चन्द्रप्रभायाः बहिरिन्द्रियजद्रव्यसाक्षात्कारसामान्यापत्तिः बहिरिन्द्रियजद्रव्यसाक्षात्कारसामान्यहेतोर्बहिरिन्द्रियसंयोगस्य महत्त्वसमानाधिकरणोद्भूतरूपस्य च सत्त्वादित्यर्थः इत्याहुः।

एवञ्च विपरीतचतुष्कादयुगपत्प्रवृत्ति-निवृत्ती न सम्भवत इत्याह, 'एवमिति, विपरीतचतुष्कादिति शेषः, 'विसंवादिन्याविति, रजतत्वप्रकारकप्रवृत्ति-रङ्गत्वप्रकारकनिवृत्ती इति शेषः, 'संवादिन्याविति, रङ्गत्वप्रकारकप्रवृत्ति-रजतत्वप्रकारकनिवृत्ती इति शेषः। रजतत्वाभाववद्वृत्तिविशेष्यतासम्बन्धेन रजतत्वप्रकारकप्रवृत्त्युत्पत्तिं प्रति स्वरूपसम्बन्धेन विशेष्यतासम्बन्धावच्छिन्नप्रतियोगिताकरजतभेदग्रहाभावो रङ्गत्वाभाववद्वृत्तिविशेष्यतासम्बन्धेन रङ्गत्वप्रकारकनिवृत्त्युत्पत्तिं प्रति च स्वरूपसम्बन्धेन विशेष्यतासम्बन्धावच्छिन्नप्रतियोगिताकरङ्गभेदग्रहाभावो हेतुरिति क्रमेण भेदाग्रह-विसंवादिप्रवृत्ति-निवृत्तीनां कार्य्य-कारणभाव इत्यभिप्रायेणाशङ्कते, 'अथेति, 'रजत-रङ्गभेदाग्रहादिति विशेष्यतासम्बन्धावच्छिन्नप्रतियोगिताकरजत-रङ्गभेदग्रहाभावसत्त्वादित्यर्थः,

सत्त्वेऽपि तदभावात्। न च प्रवृत्ति-निवृत्तिगतं विसंवादित्वं संवादित्वमपेक्ष्य तद्धेतुना ते जन्येते, कारणस्य कार्य्यानपेक्षणादिति। मैवं। प्रवृत्तेरनिष्टविषयत्वं निवृत्तेरिष्टविषयत्वं विसंवादः, तथाचानिष्टविषयप्रवृत्ताववि-

---

'विसंवादिन्याविति विसंवादित्वसम्बन्धेन रजते रजतत्वप्रकारकप्रवृत्तिः रङ्गे रङ्गत्वप्रकारकनिवृत्तिः स्यातामित्यर्थः। विसंवादित्वञ्च रजतत्व-रङ्गत्वाभाववद्वृत्तिविशेष्यत्वमिति शङ्कते, 'विसंवादिनीति रजते विसंवादित्वसम्बन्धे रजतत्वप्रकारकप्रवृत्तिः रङ्गे विसंवादित्वसम्बन्धेन रङ्गत्वप्रकारकनिवृत्तिर्न सम्भवतीत्यर्थः, रजत-रङ्गयोर्वस्तुगत्या रजतत्व-रङ्गत्वाधिकरणत्वादिति भावः। 'अतएवेति रजतत्वादिमति रजतत्वाभाववद्वृत्तिविशेष्यत्वादिसम्बन्धेन प्रवृत्त्यादेरसम्भवादेवेत्यर्थः, 'तत्सत्त्वेऽपीति, तथात्वापत्तौ बाधस्यानुगुणतया तस्य तद्धेतुत्वे आपत्तिर्दुर्व्वारेति भावः। 'न चेति न हीत्यर्थः, 'प्रवृत्ति-निवृत्तिगतं विसंवादित्वमिति रजतत्वप्रकारकप्रवृत्ति-रजतत्वप्रकारकनिवृत्त्योर्विसंवादित्वसम्बन्धेन विशेष्यसत्त्वमित्यर्थः, 'कार्य्यानपेक्षणादिति कार्य्योत्पत्त्यधिकरणे कार्य्यतावच्छेदकसम्बन्धेन सत्तासहकारेण कार्य्याजनकत्वादित्यर्थः। यथोक्तरीत्या भेदाग्रहस्य न प्रवृत्त्यादिहेतुत्वं तथासति निर्द्धर्म्मितावच्छेदककस्य प्रमेयत्वादिसामान्यधर्म्मधर्म्मितावच्छेदककस्य वा रजतत्वादिप्रकारकभेदग्रहस्य सत्त्वेऽपि रजतत्वादिप्रकारकप्रवृत्त्यादेरनुत्पादापत्तेरपि तु उपादानव्यक्तिभेदेनैव भेदाग्रहस्य विसंवादि-

ष्टविषयनिवृत्तौ च भेदाग्रहो हेतुरिति कथन्तत इष्टानि-ष्टविषयप्रवृत्ति-निवृत्ती स्यातां, तच्च तस्यासामर्थ्यादिति। अत्र ब्रूमः। ज्ञानं स्वविषये प्रवर्त्तकमित्याद्यप्रवृत्तौ

प्रवृत्त्यादिकं प्रति कार्य्य-कारणभावभेदाभ्युपगमात् वस्तुगत्या रजतत्वाभाववती या या व्यक्तिः तत्तद्व्यक्त्युपादानकरजतत्वप्रकारकप्रवृत्तिं प्रति इदन्त्वधर्म्मितावच्छेदककतत्तद्व्यक्तिविशेष्यक-रजतभेदग्रहाभावः पुरुषनिष्ठो हेतुरेवं वस्तुतो रङ्गत्वाभाववती या या व्यक्तिः तत्तद्व्यक्त्युपादानकरङ्गत्वप्रकारकनिवृत्तिं प्रति इदन्त्वधर्म्मितावच्छेदककतत्तद्व्यक्तिविशेष्यक-रङ्गभेदग्रहाभावः पुरुषनिष्ठो हेतुः रजतव्यक्त्युपादानक-रजतत्वादिप्रकारकप्रवृत्त्यादिकं प्रति तु नेदन्त्वधर्म्मितावच्छेदकक-तत्तद्रजतव्यक्तिविशेष्यक-रजतभेदग्रहाभावो हेतुः तादृशप्रवृत्त्यादेः संवादित्वनियमात् तादृशभेदाग्रहस्य परनये अप्रसिद्धत्वाच्च अतो-नोक्तापत्तिसम्भव इत्यभिप्रायेण भ्रमं निराकृत्य दूषयति, 'नैव-मिति, 'प्रवृत्तेः' रजतत्वप्रकारकप्रवृत्तेः, 'अनिष्टविषयत्वं' रजतत्वा-भाववत्तत्तद्व्यक्त्युपादानकत्वं, 'निवृत्तेः' रङ्गत्वप्रकारकनिवृत्तेः, 'इष्ट-विषयत्वं' रङ्गत्वाभाववत्तत्तद्व्यक्त्युपादानकत्वं, 'अनिष्टविषयप्रवृत्ताविति रजतत्वाभाववत्तत्तद्व्यक्त्युपादानकरजतत्वप्रकारकप्रवृत्तावित्यर्थः, 'इष्ट-विषयनिवृत्तौ चेति रङ्गत्वाभाववत्तत्तद्व्यक्त्युपादानकरङ्गत्वप्रकारकनि-वृत्तौ चेत्यर्थः, 'भेदाग्रहो हेतुरिति इदन्त्वधर्म्मितावच्छेदकक-तत्त-द्रजतव्यक्तिविशेष्यक-रजतभेदाग्रहः इदन्त्वधर्म्मितावच्छेदकक-तत्त-द्रङ्गविशेष्यक-रङ्गभेदाग्रहः यथाक्रमं हेतुरित्यर्थः। 'कथं तत इति

संवादिप्रवृत्तौ च सर्व्वैरवधारितं लाघवाद्बाधकाभा-
वाच्च। तत इष्टज्ञानं मुक्तौ प्रवर्त्तकं तद्विषयकं तद्व्यव-
हारहेतुत्वात् स्वाविषये तस्यासामर्थ्यात्। अथ भेदाग्र-
हात् ग्रहण-स्मरणाच्चावश्यकाद्विसंवादिप्रवृत्त्युपपत्तेर्वि-

कथं विशेष्यतासम्बन्धावच्छिन्नप्रतियोगिताकरजत-रङ्गभेदग्रहाभावाभ्यां रजतोपादानकरजतत्वप्रकारकप्रवृत्ति-रङ्गोपादानक-रङ्गत्वप्रकारकनिवृत्ती स्यातामित्यर्थः, 'तत्र तथेति तादृशरजतभेदग्रहाद्यभावस्य प्रवृत्तादावहेतुत्वादित्यर्थः।

केचित्तु यथोक्तसम्बन्धेन रजतत्व-रङ्गत्वप्रकारकप्रवृत्ति-निवृत्त्युत्पत्तिं प्रति विशेष्यतासम्बन्धावच्छिन्नरजत-रङ्गभेदग्रहाभावयोः विशेषणतासामान्यसम्बन्धेन न हेतुत्वमपि तु रजतत्व-रङ्गत्वाभाववद्वृत्तिविशेषणतासम्बन्धाभ्यामिति नोक्तापत्तिसम्भव इत्यभिप्रेत्य भ्रममभ्युपेत्यैव दूषयति, 'नैवमिति, 'प्रवृत्तेः' रजतत्वादिप्रकारकप्रवृत्तेः, 'अनिष्टविषयत्वं' इष्टतावच्छेदकरजतत्वाद्यभाववद्विशेष्यकत्वं, 'निवृत्तेः' रङ्गत्वादिप्रकारकनिवृत्तेः, 'इष्टविषयत्वं' इष्टतावच्छेदकरङ्गत्वाद्यभाववद्विशेष्यकत्वं, 'अनिष्टविषयप्रवृत्ताविति रजतत्वाभाववद्वृत्तिविशेष्यतासम्बन्धेन रजतत्वप्रकारकनिवृत्त्युत्पत्तावित्यर्थः, 'इष्टविषयनिवृत्तौ चेति रङ्गत्वाभाववद्वृत्तिविशेष्यतासम्बन्धेन रङ्गत्वप्रकारकनिवृत्त्युत्पत्तौ चेत्यर्थः, 'भेदाग्रहो हेतुरिति रजतभेदवद्वृत्तिविशेषणतासम्बन्धेन विशेष्यतासम्बन्धावच्छिन्नरजतभेदग्रहाभावो रङ्गभेदवद्वृत्तिविशेषणतासम्बन्धेन विशेष्यतासम्बन्धावच्छिन्नरङ्गभेदग्रहाभावः

शिष्टज्ञानकल्पने गौरवाच्च स्वाविषयेऽपि ज्ञानं प्रवर्त्तकमिति कल्पनात्। सर्वैः प्रथममवधारितमपि त्यज्यतामिति चेत्। न। प्रथमप्रवृत्तप्रमाणबलेन तत्रापि विशि-

---

यथाक्रमं हेतुरित्यर्थः, 'तत इति विशेष्यतासम्बन्धावच्छिन्नरजतभेदग्रहाभावादित्यर्थः, 'इष्टानिष्टेति रजत-रङ्गविशेष्यक-रजतत्व-रङ्गत्वप्रकारक-प्रवृत्ति-निवृत्ती स्यातामित्यर्थः, 'तत्र तथासामर्थ्यादिति रजत-रङ्गयोः रजत-रङ्गभेदग्रहाभावस्य कारणताघटकसम्बन्धविरहादित्यर्थः।

यद्वा रजतत्वाभाववद्वृत्तिविशेष्यतासम्बन्धेन रजतत्वप्रकारकप्रवृत्त्युत्पत्तौ रजतभेदस्य रङ्गत्वाभाववद्वृत्तिविशेष्यतासम्बन्धेन रङ्गत्वप्रकारकनिवृत्त्युत्पत्तौ रङ्गभेदस्य च सहकार्य्यन्तरान्नोक्तापत्तिसम्भव इत्यभिप्रेत्य भ्रममभ्युपेत्यैव दूषयति, 'नैवमिति, 'प्रवृत्तेरित्यादेरर्थस्तु पूर्व्ववत्। 'भेदाग्रहो हेतुरिति स्वरूपसम्बन्धेन यथोक्तरजत-रङ्गभेदाग्रहोहेतुरित्यर्थः, 'ततः' तन्मात्रात्, 'तत्र तथासामर्थ्यादिति रजत-रङ्गयोः रङ्ग-रजतभेदाग्रहस्य रजत-रङ्गभेदात्मकसहकारिविरहादित्यर्थः, इत्याहुः।

'स्यादेतदितिपूर्व्वपक्षे समाधत्ते, 'अत्र ब्रूम इति, यद्यपि सत्यंवच्छेदकशरीरलाघवे प्रकृते कार्य्यं प्रति कार्य्य-कारणभावह्रासे च व्यक्तिकल्पनागौरवं कल्पनागौरवञ्चाकिञ्चित्करमित्येव समाधानं युक्तं तथापि स्फुटत्वादुपेक्षितं। 'ज्ञानं स्वविषये प्रवर्त्तकमितीति, 'स्वविषये' स्वविषय एव स्वविशेष्य एवेति यावत्, तथा च यज्ज्ञानं

ष्टज्ञानकल्पनात् तच्च बाधकं विना तद्विरोधेन कल्प-
नान्तरानुदयाच्च फलमुखगौरवस्यादोषत्वात्। अन्यथा
प्रथमं सर्व्वैर्गृहीतापि कार्य्यान्विते शक्तिः सिद्धार्थदर्श-

---

यत्प्रकारकत्वे सति यदुपादानकप्रवृत्तिजनककं भवति तत् तन्निष्ठ-
विशेष्यतानिरूपित-तत्प्रकारताकं भवतीति यत्तज्ज्ञ्यां सामान्यतो
नियम इत्यर्थः, 'आद्यप्रवृत्तौ' स्तनोपादानकाद्यप्रवृत्तिजनकप्रत्यक्षे,
'संवादिप्रवृत्तौ च' संवाद्याद्यप्रवृत्त्यन्तरजनकप्रत्यक्षे, 'सर्व्वैरिति,
बालैरिति शेषः, अवधारणे हेतुमाह, 'लाघवादिति कारणतावच्छे-
दकशरीरलाघवादित्यर्थः, 'बाधकाभावाच्चेति कल्पनागौरवादि-
स्वरूपबाधकास्फुरणाच्चेत्यर्थः। अत्र विशेषणता-विशेष्यतावच्छेदकत्वा-
घटकत्वेन प्रकारकत्वं हेतौ निविष्टमतो नेष्टसाधनत्वादिघटकपदार्थ-
मादाय तज्ज्ञाने व्यभिचारः। न च तथापि-उदासीनपदार्थमादाय
तद्विषयकसमूहालम्बन-प्रवर्त्तकज्ञाने हविराद्युपादानकप्रवृत्तिजनके
यागादिनिष्ठे साधनत्वादिज्ञाने च व्यभिचार इति वाच्यं। तदु-
पादानकत्वघटितधर्म्मावच्छिन्नकार्य्यताप्रतियोगिक-कारणतावच्छेदकं
यत्प्रकारकं भवतीति विवक्षितत्वादित्यादि स्वयमूह्यमिति भावः।
'इष्टज्ञानं शुक्तौ प्रवर्त्तकमिति शुक्तौ प्रवर्त्तकमिष्टज्ञानमिति योजना,
शुक्त्युपादानकप्रवृत्तिजनकं रजतत्वप्रकारकं ज्ञानमित्यर्थः, 'तद्वि-
षयकमिति शुक्तिनिष्ठविशेष्यतानिरूपितरजतत्वप्रकारताकमित्यर्थः,
'तद्व्यवहारहेतुत्वादिति रजतप्रकारकत्वे सति शुक्त्युपादानकप्रवृत्ति-
हेतुत्वादित्यर्थः. 'स्वाविषये इति शुक्त्यविशेष्यके ज्ञाने इत्यर्थः, 'तच्च'

नात् गौरवाच्च परित्यज्येतेति साधु समर्थितङ्गुरुमतं। ननु स्वविषये ज्ञानं प्रवर्त्तकमिति सत्यं किन्तु विसंवादिप्रवृत्ताविदं ज्ञानमेव प्रवर्त्तकं[१] न त्विष्टज्ञानमपि, तद्धि ज्ञायमानेष्टभेदाग्रहे कारणतावच्छेदकं लाघवादिति दण्डत्ववदन्यथासिद्धं[२]। एवं हि तत्प्रतिबद्धव्यवहारा-

---

शुक्त्युपादानकप्रवृत्तिजनकत्वस्य, 'असामर्थ्यात्' असत्त्वात्। 'अथेति, 'ग्रहणं' इदन्त्वरूपेणोपादानप्रत्यक्षं, 'स्मरणं' उपादानेच्छाविषयतावच्छेदकधर्म्मप्रकारकस्मरणं, 'आवश्यकादिति अवश्यक्लृप्तनियतपूर्व्ववर्त्तिताकादित्यर्थः, 'विशिष्टज्ञानेति विशिष्टप्रत्यक्षेत्यर्थः, 'स्वाविषयेऽपि ज्ञानमिति स्वोपादानाविशेष्यकमपि प्रत्यक्षमित्यर्थः, 'स्वं' विसंवादिप्रवृत्तिः, 'प्रवर्त्तकं' विसंवादिप्रवृत्तिजनकं, 'अवधारितमपीति, व्याप्यत्वमिति शेषः। 'प्रथमप्रवृत्तेति प्रथमोत्पन्नव्याप्तिनिश्चयबलेनेत्यर्थः, 'तत्रापि' विसंवादिप्रवृत्तिपूर्व्वमपि, 'तत्र बाधकं विनेति प्रथमं व्याप्तिनिश्चयोत्पत्तौ प्रतिबन्धकं विनेत्यर्थः, 'तद्विरोधेनेति तद्विरोधिविषयककल्पनान्तरासम्भवाच्चेत्यर्थः। ननु सर्व्वत्र विसंवादिप्रवृत्तिपूर्व्वं विशिष्टज्ञानकल्पनमपि कथं गौरवज्ञानमेव तत्र प्रतिबन्धकं इत्यत आह, 'फलमुखेति फलान्तरवर्त्तिगौरवस्येत्यर्थः, तथाच बालस्य प्रथमं तादृशगौरवस्फूर्त्तिरेव नास्तीतिभावः।

---

(१) 'ज्ञानमेव प्रवर्त्तकं' इत्यत्र 'ज्ञानं प्रवर्त्तकमेव' इत्ययं पाठः टीकाकारसम्मतः।

(२) लाघवात् दण्डत्ववदित्यन्यथासिद्धमिति क०।

नुकूलत्वं तद्विषयत्वं रजतज्ञानस्य शुक्तौ नास्ति। अन्यथा रजतज्ञानस्य शुक्तिविषयत्वापत्तेः। संवादिप्रवृत्तौ[१]

'अन्यथेति सर्व्वैः प्रथमावधारितस्यापि परित्यागे इत्यर्थः, 'कार्य्यान्विते शक्तिरिति पदत्वावच्छेदेन कार्य्यविषयकशाब्दबोधजनकतेत्यर्थः, 'सिद्धार्थदर्शनादिति सिद्धार्थकवाक्यादप्यन्वयबोधानुरोधादित्यर्थः। 'साधु समर्थितमिति, यद्यपि प्रथमगृहीतापरित्यागे सिद्धार्थकस्याप्रामाण्यापत्त्या साधु न्यायमतसमर्थनमिति तैरपि वक्तुं शक्यं, तथापि नच प्रथमगृहीतपरित्यागे अनुभवविरोधो वीजं, सिद्धार्थकादप्यन्वयानुभवस्यानुभवसिद्धत्वात् अत्र तु न सोऽस्तीति भावः। 'स्वविषय इति पूर्व्ववत् सावधारणं, यज्ज्ञानं यत्प्रकारकज्ञानत्वे सति यदुपादानकप्रवृत्तिजनकं भवति तदवश्यं तन्निष्ठविशेष्यतानिरूपिततत्प्रकारताकं भवतीति सत्यमित्यर्थः, 'प्रवर्त्तकमेवेति एवकारोभिन्नक्रमे इदन्त्वरूपेणोपादानप्रत्यक्षमेव जनकमित्यर्थः,'न लिङ्गज्ञानमपीति न तु उपादानेच्छाविषयतावच्छेदकरजतत्वादिप्रकारकज्ञानमपीत्यर्थः, 'इष्टभेदाग्रह इति उपादानेच्छाविषयतावच्छेदकावच्छिन्नभेदाग्रह इत्यर्थः, 'लाघवादिति उपादानप्रत्यक्ष-भेदाग्रहेष्टतावच्छेदकप्रकारकज्ञानानां त्रयाणां हेतुत्वापेक्षया लाघवादित्यर्थः।

केचित्तु 'लाघवादिति मिथ्याज्ञानकल्पनामपेक्ष्य लाघवात् कल्पनालाघवाच्चेत्यर्थः, इत्याहुः। तदसत्। सिद्धान्ते अन्यथेत्यादिना विनिगमनाविरहाभिधानासङ्गतेः।

(१) अविसंवादिप्रवृत्ताविति ख०।

चेष्टज्ञानं प्रवर्त्तकं तस्य विशिष्टज्ञानत्वात्। अभेदेनाव-च्छेदकत्वाभावादिति मम सिद्धान्तसार इति चेत्। उच्यते। स्वतन्त्रान्वय-व्यतिरेकादिष्टज्ञानं हेतुरेव न त्वितरहेतुतावच्छेदकमन्यथासिद्धं वा। न हीष्टज्ञान-मादायैवेष्टभेदाग्रहस्यान्वय-व्यतिरेकौ येन दण्डत्व-वत्तदवच्छेदकं(१) नापीष्टज्ञानस्य भेदाग्रहगर्भत्वेनान्वय-व्यतिरेकौ येन दण्डरूपवत्तदन्यथासिद्धं। अन्यथा अगृहीतभेदेष्टज्ञानं हेतुरवच्छेदको भेदाग्रह इत्येव किं न स्यात् तस्मात्स्वतन्त्रान्वय-व्यतिरेकात् उभयो-रपि हेतुत्वं। किञ्चेष्टविषयप्रवृत्तिस्थले प्रवृत्तिमात्रं

उपसंहरति, 'एवं हीति, 'तत्प्रतिबद्धेति रजतत्वप्रकारकज्ञान-जन्यप्रवृत्त्युपादानत्वमित्यर्थः, 'विषयत्वं' उक्तनियमबलाद्विशेष्यत्वसाधकं, 'रजतज्ञानस्य' रजतत्वप्रकारकज्ञानस्य। 'अन्यथेति विशेष्यतासाधकं विनापि विशेष्यतासत्त्वे इत्यर्थः, 'रजतज्ञानस्य' रजतज्ञानमात्रस्य सत्य-रजतज्ञानस्यापीति यावत्। नन्वेवं संवादिप्रवृत्तावपि उपादानेच्छा-विषयतावच्छेदकधर्म्मप्रकारकज्ञानं न हेतुः स्यात् तस्यापि विशिष्टज्ञा-ननिष्ठकारणतायामवच्छेदकत्वेनान्यथासिद्धत्वादित्यत आह, 'संवा-दीति, 'इष्टज्ञानं' उपादानेच्छाविषयतावच्छेदकधर्म्मप्रकारकं ज्ञानं, एवमग्रेऽपि, सर्व्वत्र 'प्रवर्त्तकं' जनकं, 'तस्य' तस्यैव। 'अन्यथासिद्धं

---

(१) दण्डत्ववदवच्छेदकमिति ख०।

प्रतीष्टज्ञानस्य हेतुत्वादियमपि प्रवृत्तिस्तज्जन्या क्लृप्त-हेतुं विना कार्य्यानुत्पत्तेः। न चेष्टज्ञानजन्यत्वे इष्ट-विषयप्रवृत्तित्वमवच्छेदकं गौरवात्। बाधकं विना सामान्ययोः कार्य्य-कारणभावनियमात्। अत एव तन्नोपाधिरपि। अथ तत्रापीदं ज्ञानं प्रवर्त्तकं दैवा-धीनं तस्येष्टविषयत्वमपीति चेत्। तर्हि इष्टे इदमिति-ज्ञानादेव प्रवृत्तिः स्यात्। न ह्यत्रेव तत्रापि ज्ञायमाने-ष्टभेदाग्रहः प्रवर्त्तकः। एतेन न रजतज्ञानं शुक्तिविष-यकं तत्प्रतिबद्धव्यवहाराहेतुत्वादिति निरस्तं। असि-द्धेः। ननु ज्ञानं यथार्थमेवेति व्याप्तिरेव तद्बाधिका,

---

वेति तत एवान्यथासिद्धं वेत्यर्थः। 'इष्टज्ञानमादायैवेति इष्टज्ञान-विशिष्टत्वेनैवेत्यर्थः, किन्तु भेदाग्रहत्वेनैवेति भावः। 'भेदाग्रहगर्भ-त्वेनेति भेदाग्रहगर्भेष्टज्ञानत्वेनैवेत्यर्थः, 'दण्डरूपवदिति यथा लाघवज्ञानात् दण्डत्वेनैव हेतुता दण्डरूपत्वेन दण्डरूपमन्यथासिद्धं, तथा लाघवाद्भेदाग्रहत्वेनैव हेतुतया तदन्यथासिद्धं स्यादित्यर्थः। 'अन्यथा' स्वातन्त्र्येणान्वय-व्यतिरेकसत्त्वेऽप्यन्यनिष्ठहेतुतावच्छेदकत्वे इत्यर्थः, 'उभयोरपीति, तन्मये इति शेषः। 'इष्टविषयप्रवृत्तित्वेन-इति रजतोपादानक-रजतत्वप्रकारकप्रवृत्तावित्यर्थः, अन्वय-व्यतिरेक-ज्ञानादिति शेषः, 'प्रवृत्तिमात्रं प्रति' रजतत्वप्रकारकप्रवृत्तिमात्रं प्रति, 'इष्टज्ञानस्य' रजतत्वप्रकारकज्ञानस्य, 'हेतुत्वादिति वक्ष्यमाणयुक्त्या

अतएव प्रवृत्तिमात्रे विशिष्टज्ञानमिष्टज्ञानञ्च हेतुर्लाघवात् स्वविषये ज्ञानं प्रवर्त्तकं सर्वैरेवाद्यप्रवृत्तौ तथावगमात् असत्यस्थले इष्टज्ञानमपि प्रवर्त्तकं न तु भेदाग्रहे हेतुतावच्छेदकमित्यन्यथाख्यातिसाधनं न भवतीति चेत्। न। तेषामन्यथासिद्धान्वय-व्यतिरेकावधारितकारणतामूलकत्वेन तैरेव व्याप्तिबाधात्। क्लृप्तहेतुं विना

समानविशेष्यताप्रत्यासत्त्या सामान्यतो हेतुत्वादित्यर्थः 'इयमपीति शुक्त्युपादानक रजतत्वप्रकारिकापीत्यर्थः, 'तज्जन्या' समानविशेष्यताप्रत्यासत्त्या रजतत्वप्रकारकज्ञानजन्या, 'क्लृप्तहेतुं विनेति क्लृप्तसामान्यहेतुं विनेत्यर्थः। 'इष्टज्ञानजन्यत्व इति सामान्यतो रजतत्वप्रकारकज्ञानजन्यत्वइत्यर्थः, 'इष्टविषयकेति रजतत्ववद्विशेष्यकप्रवृत्तित्वमित्यर्थः। ननु तथापि तादृशसामान्यकार्य्य-कारणभावे मानाभाव इत्यत आह, 'साधकं विनेति, 'सामान्ययोरिति यद्विशेषयोः कार्य्यकारणभावस्तत्सामान्ययोरपीत्यर्थः। 'अत एवेति गौरवेण रजतत्ववद्विशेष्यक-प्रवृत्तित्वस्य कार्य्यतानवच्छेदकत्वादेवेत्यर्थः, 'तन्नोपाधिरिति रजतत्वप्रकारकप्रवृत्तिहेतुकोक्तानुमाने रजतवद्विशेष्यकत्वं नोपाधिरित्यर्थः, साध्यव्यापकताग्राहकानुकूलतर्काभावादिति भावः।

केचित्तु 'अत एवेति यद्विशेषयोरितिन्यायेन सामान्यतः कार्य्यकारणभावग्रहादेवेत्यर्थः, तेनैवानुकूलतर्केण हेतोः साध्यव्याप्यत्वनिश्चयादिति भावः इत्याहुः।

कार्य्यानुत्पत्तेः विपक्षे बाधकाभावाच्च ज्ञानायथार्थत्वेऽपि निष्कम्पप्रवृत्त्याद्युपायस्य वक्ष्यमाणत्वात्। एतेन संस्कारेन्द्रियाभ्यां प्रत्यभिज्ञानवच्छब्दाभासादितो वा

उक्तानुमाने दृष्टान्तासिद्धिमाशङ्कते, 'अथेति, 'तचापि' संवादिप्रवृत्तावपि, 'दैवाधीनं' सामग्र्यधीनं, 'इष्टविषयकत्वं' क्वचिद्रजतत्वप्रकारकत्वं। 'इष्ट इति वस्तुगत्या रजतविशेष्यकादित्यर्थः, 'ज्ञानादेवेत्येवकारेण रजतत्वप्रकारकज्ञानस्य व्यवच्छेदः। 'अत्रेव' विसंवादिप्रवृत्ताविव, 'तचापि' संवादिप्रवृत्तावपि, 'ज्ञायमानेष्टेति स्वतन्त्रोपस्थितरजतत्वावच्छिन्नप्रतियोगिताकभेदाग्रह इत्यर्थः। 'रजतज्ञानमिति विसंवादिप्रवृत्त्यव्यवहितप्राक्कालिकं रजतज्ञानमित्यर्थः, 'तत्प्रतिबद्धेति तदुपादानकेत्यर्थः, 'असिद्धेः' स्वरूपासिद्धेः। 'तद्बाधिकेति अन्यथाख्यातौ बाधिकेत्यर्थः। 'अत एव' उक्तव्याप्तेर्बाधकत्वादेव, 'अन्यथाख्यातिसाधनं न भवतीत्यग्रेतनेनान्वयः, 'प्रवृत्तिमात्रे' रजतत्वप्रकारकप्रवृत्तिमात्रे, "यद्विशेषयोरितिन्यायेनेतिशेषः। 'विशिष्टज्ञानं' रजतत्ववैशिष्ट्यावगाहिज्ञानं, 'इष्टज्ञानं' रजतत्वप्रकारकं ज्ञानं, 'चकारो वार्थे, 'हेतुरिति समानविशेष्यताप्रत्यासत्त्या हेतुरित्यर्थः। 'स्वविषय इति सावधारणं, यद्यज्ज्ञानं यत्प्रकारकत्वे सति यदुपादनकप्रवृत्तिजनकं भवति तत्तन्निष्ठविशेष्यतानिरूपित-तत्प्रकारताकं भवतीति सर्वैराद्यप्रवृत्ताववधारितायामित्यर्थः, अत इति शेषः। 'असत्यस्थल इति 'इष्टज्ञानमपीत्यपिरत्र योज्यः, तेनासत्यस्थलेऽपी-

परस्परं सम्बन्धविरहिणि एकं ज्ञानं न भवतीति ज्ञानं यथार्थमेवेति व्याप्तिरिति निरस्तं। व्याप्त्याद्यसिद्धेः सामग्रीसत्त्वे कार्य्यावश्यकत्वाच्च।

त्यर्थः, अयथार्थत्वं शुक्त्यादिकं, 'इष्टज्ञानं प्रवर्त्तकमिति प्रवर्त्तकं रजतत्वप्रकारकं ज्ञानमित्यर्थः, शुक्त्यादिविषयकमिति शेषः, 'न त्विति न चेत्यर्थः, तदिति शेषः, 'इत्यन्यथाख्यातिसाधनमिति इत्युक्तद्वयमन्यथाख्यातिसाधनमित्यर्थः। 'तेषामिति शुक्तिविशेष्यक-रजतत्वप्रकारकप्रवृत्तिः समानविशेष्यताप्रत्यासत्त्या रजतत्वप्रकारकज्ञानजन्या रजतत्वप्रकारकप्रवृत्तित्वात् शुक्तौ प्रवर्त्तकं रजतत्वप्रकारकज्ञानं शुक्तिविशेष्यकं रजतत्वप्रकारकत्वे सति शुक्त्युपादानकप्रवृत्तिहेतुत्वादित्यन्यथाख्यातिसाधनानुमानानामित्यर्थः, 'व्याप्तिबाधादिति ज्ञानं यथार्थमेवेति व्याप्तिबाधादित्यर्थः। 'क्लृप्तहेतुं विनेति क्लृप्तसामान्यकारणं विनेत्यर्थः, 'कार्य्यानुत्पत्तेरिति विसंवादिप्रवृत्तिलक्षणकार्य्योत्पत्तेरसम्भवादित्यर्थः, 'विपक्षे बाधकाभावात्' तत्र ज्ञानं यथार्थमेवेति व्याप्तिपक्षे विपक्षे बाधकाभावाच्चेत्यर्थः। ननु ज्ञानायथार्थत्वे ज्ञानत्वसमानाधिकरणधर्मादर्शनात् सर्व्वत्रैव ज्ञाने तच्छङ्कया निष्कम्पप्रवृत्तिर्न स्यादित्येव विपक्षे बाधकमित्यत आह, 'ज्ञानेति। 'प्रत्यभिज्ञानवदिति, 'प्रत्यभिज्ञानवत् संस्कारेन्द्रियाभ्यामिति योजना। 'सामग्रीसत्त्व इति, न हि व्याप्तिभङ्गभियैव सामग्री कार्य्यं नार्जयिष्यति, इति भावः।

एकदेशिनस्तु। रजत-रङ्गयोः रजत-रङ्गभेदग्रहान्न युगपत्प्रवृत्ति-निवृत्ती। न चान्यथाख्यातिः, दोषवशा-त्पुरोवर्त्तिनं विहाय स्मृतरजत-रङ्गाभ्यां पुरोवर्त्तिनि भेदग्रहात्। न च रजतत्वेन स्मृतिः संस्कारगोचर-

---

'एकदेशिनस्त्विति प्राभाकरैकदेशिनस्त्वित्यर्थः, 'नेति, विपरीत-चतुष्कादिति शेषः। 'नचान्यथाख्यातिरिति रजते रजतभेदस्य रङ्गे-रङ्गभेदस्य च ग्रहे अन्यथाख्यात्यापत्तिरित्यर्थः, 'पुरोवर्त्तिनं विहाय स्मृतेति पुरोवर्त्त्यविषयकस्मृतिविषयेत्यर्थः, 'दोषवशादिति च पुरो-वर्त्त्यविषयकत्वे हेतुः। यद्यपि यत्किञ्चिद्रजतादिव्यक्तिभेदग्रहमात्रं न प्रवृत्त्यादिप्रतिबन्धकं इदं रजतं ग्रथितरजतभिन्नमिति ज्ञाने-ऽपि प्रवृत्तिप्रतिबन्धापत्तेः किन्तु रजतत्वावच्छिन्नप्रतियोगिताक-भेदग्रह एव प्रतिबन्धकः स च प्रकृते नास्त्येवान्यथाख्यात्यापत्तेः तथापि प्रतियोग्यंशे रजतत्वस्य शुद्धस्य यत्र प्रकारतया भानं तादृशभेदग्रहः प्रतिबन्धकः तत्र रजतत्वस्य प्रतियोगितावच्छेदक-तया भानमावश्यकं तथा च पुरोवर्त्तिनि रजते शुद्धरजतत्वेन रजतान्तरभेदग्रहस्य प्रतिबन्धकत्वान्न प्रवृत्तिः एवं रङ्गेऽपि न प्रवृत्ति-रित्यभिमानेनेदं। 'सामान्यप्रत्यासत्तेरिति रजतत्वात्रिविषयकनिर्वि-कल्पकस्मरणरूपस्य संस्कारव्यापारस्येत्यर्थः, "तुल्यत्वात्' विषयता-सम्बन्धेन सर्व्वरजत एव तुल्यत्वात्। यद्यपि सर्व्वरजतविषयकस्मरणे-ऽपि प्रकृते न कापि क्षतिः तथापि समाधिसौकर्य्यादाह, 'तत्तांश इति, 'प्रत्यासत्तावपि' निर्व्विकल्पकरूपस्य व्यापारस्य सत्त्वेऽपि, यथा

सर्वरजतविषया स्यात् सामान्यप्रत्यासत्तेस्तुल्यत्वादिति वाच्यं। तत्तांशे रजतत्वे च प्रत्यासत्तावपि दोषात् स्मृत्यनुभवप्रतिबन्धवदुपपत्तेः। किञ्च प्रत्यक्षे सामान्यं प्रत्यासत्तिः, स्मरणे तु मनः करणं संस्कारः प्रत्यासत्तिः, न तु तस्य सामान्यं प्रत्यासत्तिरकरणत्वात्। तन्न। एकरङ्ग-रजतमात्रज्ञानानन्तरन्तयोरेव यमजयोर्व्वा विपरीतचतुष्केऽतिप्रसङ्गादन्यथाख्यातेर्व्वा।

प्रमुष्टतत्ताकस्मरणस्थले तत्तांशे निर्व्विकल्पकस्मरणरूपस्य संस्कारव्यापारस्य सत्त्वेऽपि सा न स्मर्य्यते दोषात् किन्तु रजतमात्रं, यथा वा रजते शुक्त्यादिभ्रमकाले रजत-रजतत्वे इति निर्व्विकल्पकरूपस्य इन्द्रियव्यापारस्य सत्त्वेऽपि तत्सत्ता नानुभूयते दोषात् तथात्रापि दोषात् पुरोवर्त्ति रङ्गं रजते न स्मर्य्यते इत्यर्थः। 'प्रत्यक्षे' विशिष्टप्रत्यक्षे एव, 'सामान्यं' सामान्यनिर्व्विकल्पकं, 'प्रत्यासत्तिः' इन्द्रियस्य व्यापारः, 'प्रत्यासत्तिः' मनसो व्यापारः, 'तस्य' संस्कारस्य, 'सामान्यं प्रत्यासत्तिः' सामान्यनिर्व्विकल्पकं व्यापारः, 'अकरणत्वादित्युपलक्षणं निर्व्विकल्पकात्मकस्मरणे मानाभावाच्चेत्यपि बोध्यं। यद्येवमपि भेदानुपस्थितिदशायां रङ्ग-रजते इत्यादिविपरीतात्मकादतिप्रसङ्गो दुर्व्वारस्तथापि स्फुटत्वादुपेक्ष्य दोषान्तरमाह, एकेति एकरङ्ग-रजतत्वप्रकारकज्ञानानन्तरमित्यर्थः, तत्र रङ्गाद्यन्तरस्यानुपस्थितत्वेन पुरोवर्त्तिनि तद्भेदग्रहासम्भवादिति भावः। ननु तथापि पूर्व्वजन्मानु-

अन्ये तु रजते नेदं रजतमिति ज्ञानं रजतत्वासंसर्गासंसर्गाग्रहरूपं रजतभेदासंसर्गाग्रहरूपं प्रवृत्तिप्रतिबन्धकमिति। तन्न। अन्यवृत्तितयोपस्थितस्य रजतत्वासंसर्गस्य रजतभेदस्य च रङ्गे असंसगाग्रहान्निवृत्ति-

---

भूतरङ्गाद्यन्तरस्मरणं कल्प्यते बलवत्त्वादित्यत आह, 'यमजयोरिति, 'अतिप्रसङ्गादन्यथाख्यातेरिति तत्रैव तद्भेदग्रहे अन्यथाख्यात्यापत्तेरित्यर्थः।

'रजतत्वासंसर्गासंसर्गाग्रहरूपमिति रजतत्वात्यन्ताभावसंसर्गविषयकमित्यर्थः, एवमग्रेऽपि, 'प्रतिबन्धकं' विपरीतात्मकादितो रजते रजतत्वप्रकारकप्रवृत्त्युत्पत्तौ प्रतिबन्धकं। नचैवं इदं रजतमिति भ्रमादपि रङ्गे रजतत्वप्रवृत्तिर्न स्यात् रजतत्वासंसर्गादेरसंसर्गस्य रजतत्वरूपस्य रङ्गे ग्रहाभ्युपगमे अन्यथाख्यात्यापत्त्या ततस्तद्ग्रहसत्त्वादिति वाच्यं। उपस्थितस्य रजतत्वासंसर्गादेरसंसर्गाग्रहस्यैव प्रतिबन्धकत्वात् संसर्गादिकं नोपस्थितमिति भावः। अत एव वा दूषणात् 'अन्यवृत्तितया उपस्थितस्येति वक्ष्यति। यद्यप्येवमपि रजतत्वासंसर्गादेरनुपस्थितिदशायां इमे रङ्ग-रजते इति विपरीतदिकात् रजते रजतत्वप्रकारकप्रवृत्तिर्दुर्व्वारा उपस्थितस्य रजतत्वासंसर्गादेरसंसर्गाग्रहस्यैव प्रतिबन्धकत्वात् तथापि तद्दोषे सत्येव दोषान्तरमाह. 'अन्यवृत्तितयोपस्थितस्येति, निरधिकरणकोपस्थितस्येत्यपि बोध्यं, 'असंसर्गाग्रहात्' असंसर्गाग्रहसत्त्वात्, 'निवृत्तिप्रस-

प्रसङ्गात् रङ्गे च तयोरसंसर्गग्रहेऽन्यथाख्यातिः। रजते रजतभेदासंसर्गासंसर्गस्यासंसर्गाग्रहान्निवृत्तिरिति चेत्। न। भेदासंसर्गासंसगस्य भेदसंसर्गरूपत्वेन रजतभेद-संसर्गासंसर्गाग्रहाद्रङ्गे निवृत्तिप्रसङ्गात्। रजतभेदसंस-र्गासंसर्गग्रहे चान्यथाख्यातिः। रजतवृत्तितयोपस्थिते भेदे रजतभेदेन सह भेदाग्रहः प्रवृत्तिप्रतिबन्धकः, एवं

ङ्गादिति अन्यवृत्तित्वेनाधिकरणान्तर्भावे रजतत्वासंसर्गादेरुपस्थिति-दशायां रङ्गे इदं रजतमिति भ्रमाद्रजतत्वप्रकारकप्रवृत्त्यनुत्पाद-प्रसङ्गादित्यर्थः, 'तयोः' रजतत्वासंसर्ग-रजतभेदयोः। पदार्थाविवे-चनेन भ्रान्तः शङ्कते, 'रजत इति, 'रजतभेदासंसर्गासंसर्गस्य' रजतभेदासंसर्गसम्बन्धव्यतिरेकस्य, 'निवृत्तिः' विपरीतद्विकादितो रजते रजतभेदप्रवृत्त्यनुत्पाद इत्यर्थः। भ्रमं निराकृत्य समा-धत्ते, 'भेदासंसर्गासंसर्गस्येति रजतभेदासंसर्गसम्बन्धव्यतिरेकस्येत्यर्थः, 'निवृत्तिप्रसङ्गादिति इदं रजतमिति भ्रमाद्रजतत्वप्रकारकप्रवृत्त्यनु-त्पादप्रसङ्गादित्यर्थः। मतान्तरं शङ्कते, 'रजतवृत्तितयेति, 'भेदे' घटादिप्रतियोगिकभेदे, 'भेदाग्रहः' सतोऽपि भेदस्य दोषादग्रहः, 'प्रवृत्तिप्रतिबन्धक इति विपरीतद्विकादितो रजते रजतत्वप्रकारक-प्रवृत्त्यनुत्पत्तौ प्रतिबन्धक इत्यर्थः। 'निवृत्तावपीति, रङ्गवृत्तितया ज्ञाते भेदे रङ्गभेदेन सह भेदाग्रहः प्रतिबन्धक इति शेषः। न च रजतादिनिष्ठभेदे इत्येवास्तु किमुपस्थितिगर्भतयेति वाच्यं। एवं सति रजतमिदमिति ज्ञानादप्रवृत्त्यापत्तेः तत्र रजतवृत्तितादृशभेदे

रङ्गे निवृत्तावपीति चेत्। न। एवमपि शब्दाभासात् युगपत्प्रवृत्ति-निवृत्त्यापत्तेः प्रवृत्ति-निवृत्तिविषयनिष्ठ-भेदयोः रजत-रङ्ग-भेदयोश्च[१] शब्दादनुपस्थित्या प्रति-बन्धकत्वाभावात्।

अपरे तु पुरोवर्त्तिनिष्ठतया ज्ञाते भेदे इष्टानिष्ट-प्रतियोगित्वाभावग्रहात् प्रवृत्ति-निवृत्ती। तथा हि रङ्गे रजतभेदः सन्नपि दोषान्न भासतेऽन्यस्माद्भासत

रजतभेदेन सह भेदाग्रहस्य सत्त्वात्। एवं रजतादिभेदेऽप्युपस्थितत्वं विवक्षणीयं अन्यथा घटभिन्नमिदं रजतमिति ज्ञानादप्यप्रवृत्ति-प्रसङ्गादिति भावः। 'शब्दाभासादिति इमे रङ्ग-रजते इति शब्दा-भासजन्यरङ्ग-रजतोपस्थितिसहकृततादिदन्त्वरूपेण रङ्ग-रजतप्रत्ययत्वा-दित्यर्थः। 'प्रवृत्ति-निवृत्तिविषयेति प्रवृत्ति-निवृत्तिविषयनिष्ठे-त्यर्थः, 'रजत-रङ्गभेदयोः' रजत-रङ्गप्रतियोगिकभेदयोः।

'पुरोवर्त्तिनिष्ठतयेति, 'भेदे' भेदसामान्ये. अन्यथा तद्वृत्ति-घटभेदो न रजतप्रतियोगिक इति ज्ञानकाले रजतभिन्नमिति ज्ञाना-दपि प्रवृत्त्यापत्तेः, अतएव ज्ञातमित्युक्तं, अन्यथा शुक्तिनिष्ठे यावति भेदे रजतप्रतियोगिकत्वाभावग्रहे अन्यथाख्यात्यापत्तेरिति ध्येयं। 'अन्यस्मादिति घट-पटादित इत्यर्थः, 'भेदे' भेदसामान्ये,

---

(१) रङ्ग-रजतभेदयोरित्ययं क० पुस्तके पाठः परन्त्वयं न टीका-कारसम्मतः।

एव। तथाच रङ्गवृत्तितया ज्ञाते भेदे रजतप्रतियोगित्वाभावग्रहाद्यथार्थादेव रङ्गे प्रवृत्तिः, रङ्गप्रतियोगित्वाभावः सन्नपि दोषान्न भासते इति तत्र न निवर्त्तते। एवं रजतनिष्ठतयोपस्थिते भेदे रङ्गप्रतियोगित्वाभावग्रहा-

'रङ्गे प्रवृत्तिरिति रङ्गे रजतत्वप्रकारकप्रवृत्तिरित्यर्थः। नन्वत्र रङ्गप्रतियोगिकत्वाभावोऽप्यस्तीति तद्ग्रहाद्रङ्गे रङ्गत्वप्रकारकनिवृत्तिरपि स्यादित्यत आह, 'रङ्गेति, 'न निवर्त्तते' न रङ्गत्वप्रकारकनिवृत्तिः, रङ्गत्वप्रकारकप्रवृत्तिर्भवतीति। 'न युगपत्प्रवृत्ति-निवृत्ती इति न विपरीतद्विकादितो युगपद्रङ्ग-रजतयोः रजतत्वप्रकारकप्रवृत्ति-रङ्गत्वप्रकारकनिवृत्तिरेवेत्यर्थः। लौकिकप्रत्यक्षं प्रत्येव दोषः प्रतिबन्धको न तु सामान्यलक्षणादिजन्यालौकिकप्रत्यक्षे इत्यभिमानेनाशङ्कते, 'न च रङ्गेति, यथाश्रुते रङ्गे रजतभेदः सन्नपि दोषान्न भासते इति पूर्व्वमेवाभिधानात् पुनराशङ्कासङ्गतेः। 'सामान्यबुद्धेः' सामान्यज्ञानात्मकप्रत्यासत्तेः, 'सर्व्वविषयत्वादिति सकलसामान्याश्रयविषयकप्रत्यक्षजनकत्वादित्यर्थः, 'रजतभेदेऽपीति, सामान्यत इति शेषः। अभिमानं निराकृत्य समाधत्ते, 'प्रत्यासत्त्तावपीति, तथाच सामान्यलक्षणादिजन्यालौकिकप्रत्यक्षेऽपि दोषः प्रतिबन्धक इति भावः।

अपरेषां मतं दूषयति, 'मैवमिति, 'इदं रजतमितीति, तथा च तन्मते केवलादिदं रजतमितिज्ञानात् प्रवृत्तिर्न स्यात् तदानीं पुरोवर्त्तिवृत्तितया उपस्थितस्य भेदस्य रजतप्रतियोगिकत्वाभावाग्रहादिति भावः। नन्विदं रजतमिति ज्ञानं प्रवृत्तिजनकमेव

द्रजते निवर्त्तते, रजतप्रतियोगित्वाभावः सन्नपि दोषान्न गृह्यते इति न युगपत्प्रवृत्ति-निवृत्ती। न च रङ्गवृत्तिभेदत्वं रजतभेदेऽप्यस्तीति तेन रूपेण से ऽपि भासते सामान्यबुद्धेः सर्वविशेषविषयत्वात्[१] तथा च रजतभेदेऽपि तत्प्रतियोगित्वाभावग्रहेऽन्यथाख्यातिरिति वाच्यं। प्रत्यासत्तावपि रङ्गवृत्तिभेदत्वेन रजतभेदस्य दोषेणाग्रहादिति। मैवं। इदं रजतमिति ज्ञानमन्वय-व्यतिरेकाभ्यां प्रवर्त्तकमित्यनुभवसिद्धं। तत्र सत्यस्थले विशिष्ट-

---

नेत्यत आह, 'तत्रेति प्रवृत्तावित्यर्थः, 'तज्ज्ञानं' इदं रजतमिति ज्ञानं।

केचित्तु 'तत्र' विवादे, विषयर्त्ते सप्तम्यर्थः, अन्वयश्चास्य 'तज्ज्ञानमित्यनेन, तथाच विवादविषयीभूतमिदं रजतमिति ज्ञानं प्रवृत्तौ कारणमित्यनुभवबाधितमित्यर्थ इत्याहुः।

'न प्रवर्त्तकं' न जनकं, 'तत्र तज्ज्ञानं प्रवर्त्तकमिति ग्रन्थपाठे तु तत्र पुरोवर्त्तिनिष्ठतया ज्ञाते भेदे इष्टप्रतियोगिकत्वाभावज्ञानमेव सर्व्वत्र प्रवर्त्तकमित्यनुभवबाधितमित्यर्थः। 'तदपि हेतुरिति इदं रजतमिति ज्ञानं उक्ताभावज्ञानञ्च द्वयमेव हेतुरित्यर्थः। उभयं किं प्रवृत्तिमात्रे हेतुः विसंवादिप्रवृत्तौ वा आद्ये आह, 'सत्यस्थल इति, 'तत्र' पुरोवर्त्तिनिष्ठतया ज्ञाते भेदे इष्टप्रतियोगि-

---

(१) सर्व्वविशेषविषयत्वनियमादिति ख०।

ज्ञानमन्यच्च ज्ञानद्वयमेकं वा ज्ञानमिति विवादः, तच्च तज्ज्ञानं न प्रवर्त्तकमित्यनुभवबाधितं। तदपि हेतुरित्यपि न। तस्य सत्यस्थलेऽसिद्धत्वात्[१] विशिष्टज्ञाना-

---

कत्वाभावज्ञानस्य, 'अप्रसिद्धत्वादिति नियमतः पूर्व्वसिद्धत्वाभावादित्यर्थः। नियमांशाभावमुक्त्वा अन्यथासिद्धिमाह, 'विशिष्टेति, तथाच यथा प्रत्यक्षे महत्त्वं कारणं अनेकद्रव्यवत्त्वं अन्यथासिद्धं तथा तादृशस्वरूपमन्यथासिद्धमिति भावः। अन्ये आह, 'शब्दाभावादिति इदं रजतमितिशब्दाभावअन्यरजतोपस्थितिसहकृतात् इदन्त्वरूपेण शुक्तिप्रत्यक्षादित्यर्थः, तच्च भेदाद्युपस्थापकशब्दाभावादिति भावः। 'एवं निरुक्तावपीति, कश्चिदिदं रजतमिति ज्ञानमपि केवलं जनकमित्यनुभवसिद्धमिति शेषः। तच्च अपरेषां मते न स्यादिति भावः। इदमुपलक्षणं, पुरोवर्त्तिवृत्तितया ज्ञाते भेदसामान्ये केन रूपेण इष्टानिष्टप्रतियोगिकत्वाभावस्य ग्रहो हेतुः, किं प्रातिस्विकं तत्तद्व्यक्तित्वेन, तत्पुरोवर्त्तिनिष्ठभेदत्वावच्छेदेन, सामानाधिकरण्येन वा, नाद्यः दुर्ग्रहत्वात्, न द्वितीयः रङ्गवृत्तिभेदत्वावच्छेदेन रजतप्रतियोगिकत्वाभावग्रहे अन्यथाख्यात्यापत्तेः, न तृतीयः तद्वृत्तिघटभेदो न रजतप्रतियोगिक इतिज्ञानकाले न रजतभिन्नमिदमिति ज्ञानादपि प्रवृत्तिप्रसङ्गात्। नापि पुरोवर्त्तिवृत्तितया ज्ञातभेदत्वावच्छेदेन तज्ज्ञानं, ज्ञानाविषयकस्य एतद्वृत्तिभेदसामान्यं न रजतप्रतियोगिकमिति ज्ञानस्याकारणत्वापत्तेः। नापि पुरोवर्त्ति-

---

(१) सत्यस्थले तस्यासिद्धत्वादिति ख॰ ।

पेक्षया गुरुत्वात् शब्दाभासात्प्रवृत्तौ भेदादिज्ञानाभावाच्च । एवं निवृत्तावपि ।

अन्ये तु इष्टवृत्तितया गृह्यमाणोऽनिष्टवृत्तितया चागृह्यमाणो धर्मः स्वाश्रये प्रवर्त्तक इति स च धर्मो रजते रजतत्वं रङ्गे रजतसादृश्यं । एवं निवृत्तावपीति न

निष्ठतया ज्ञातयावच्छेदान् किञ्चिद्रूपेणानुगतीकृत्य तदवच्छेदेन रजतज्ञानं, रजतभेदातिरिक्तपुरोवर्त्तिनिष्ठभेदो न रजतप्रतियोगिक इति ग्रहादपि नेदं रजतमिति ज्ञानकाले प्रवृत्त्यापत्तेः इत्यपि दूषणं द्रष्टव्यं ।

'इष्टवृत्तितयेति उपादानेच्छाविषयतावच्छेदकरजतत्वादिरूपधर्म्मसमानाधिकरणतयेत्यर्थः, 'अनिष्टवृत्तितया' तादृशधर्म्माभावसमानाधिकरणतया, 'स्वाश्रये' स्वप्रकारकज्ञानविषये, तथा च तादृशधर्म्मप्रकारकं ज्ञानं प्रवृत्तौ कारणमिति फलितं । 'रजते' इति सत्यरजतगोचररजतत्वप्रकारकप्रवृत्तावित्यर्थः, 'रङ्गे' रङ्गगोचररजतत्वप्रकारकप्रवृत्तौ, 'रजतसादृश्यमिति । यद्यपि रजतसादृश्यं न रजतत्वसमानाधिकरणतया गृह्यमाणं, तन्मये सादृश्यस्यातिरिक्तपदार्थत्वेऽपि तस्य भेदनियततद्रजतत्वसामानाधिकरण्यग्रहे अन्यथाख्यात्यापत्तेः । नापि रजतसादृश्यं रङ्गवृत्तिसाकचक्यं तस्यापि रङ्गवृत्तिरूपविशेषणात्मकतया तत्रापि रजतत्वसमानाधिकरणत्वेन ग्रहे अन्यथाख्यात्यापत्तेः, तथापि रजतपदं यत्किञ्चिद्रजतपरं, तत्सादृश्यमतिरिक्तपदार्थरूपं रजतत्वसमानाधिकरणमपि । स च रजतत्वा-

युगपत्प्रवृत्ति-निवृत्ती इति। तन्न। एवं हि इमे रङ्ग-रजते इति शब्दाभासाद्रङ्ग-रजतयोः प्रवृत्ति-निवृत्ती न स्यातां रजतवृत्तिधर्म्मस्य च रङ्गे रङ्गवृत्तिधर्म्मस्य रजते[१] शब्दादनुपस्थितेः। न च शब्दानन्तरं प्रत्यक्षेण तयोरुपस्थितिः तत्र हेतुर्न शब्द इति वाच्यं। अन-न्यथासिद्धशब्दानुविधानात् इमे रजत-रङ्गे इति स्वकीयं

भावसमानाधिकरणमपि भवतीति वाच्यं। वस्तुगत्या तथात्वेऽपि दोषात्तथात्वेनाग्रहसम्भवादित्यदोषः।

'रजतसादृश्यं' रङ्गनिष्ठचाकचक्यविशेषः। नच स न रजतत्वसमानाधिरणतया गृह्यमाण इति वा[illegible]। 'इष्टवृत्तितया गृह्यमाणेत्यस्य उपादानेच्छाविषयतावच्छेदकधर्म्मसमानाधिकरणता-तीयतया गृह्यमाणेत्यर्थात् रङ्गवृत्तिचाकचक्यविशेषोऽपि तथा गृह्य-माणः सम्भवतीत्याहुः।

'एवं निवृत्तावपीति उपादानद्वेषविषयतावच्छेदकधर्म्मसमाना-धिकरणत्वेन गृह्यमाणो योधर्म्मः तत्प्रकारकज्ञानं कारणमित्यर्थः, स च धर्म्मोरङ्गे रङ्गत्वप्रकारकनिवृत्तौ रङ्गत्वं, रजतत्वप्रकारकनिवृत्तौ च यत्किञ्चिद्रङ्गसादृश्यमिति भावः। 'न युगपदिति न विपरीत-द्विकादितो युगपद्रङ्ग-रजतयोरुभयोरेव रजतत्वप्रकारकप्रवृत्तिः रङ्गत्वप्रकारकनिवृत्तिर्व्वा इत्यर्थः। रजते रङ्गसमानाधिकरणतया गृह्यमाणस्य रजतत्वस्य यत्किञ्चिद्रजतसादृश्यस्य च दोषादग्रहादेवं

---

(१) रङ्गे रजतवृत्तिधर्म्मस्य रजते रङ्गवृत्तिधर्म्मस्य चेति ख०।

यथार्थज्ञानमनादृत्य[१] तत्रैवेमे रङ्ग-रजते इति प्रतारकवाक्ये विश्वासेन प्रवृत्ति-निवृत्तिदर्शनाच्च ।

इतरे तु रजते रजतत्वं न गृह्यते दोषात् तथा च रजतवृत्तितया यावदुपस्थितधर्म्मस्य रजतत्वेन भेदाग्रहान्न प्रवर्त्तते रङ्गवृत्तितयोपस्थितस्य च कस्यचिद्धर्म्मस्य रजतत्वेन भेदाग्रहाद्रङ्गे प्रवर्त्तते, एवं निवृत्ता-

---

रङ्गे रङ्गत्वसमानाधिकरणतया गृह्यमाणस्य रङ्गत्वादेरपि दोषादग्रहाच्चेति भावः। 'भ्रमाभावादिति, इदन्त्वरूपेण रङ्ग-रजतप्रत्यक्षस्य सत्यत्वादितिशेषः। 'प्रवृत्ति-निवृत्ती इति रजतत्वप्रकारकप्रवृत्ति-रङ्गत्वप्रकारकनिवृत्ती इत्यर्थः, 'रजतवृत्तिधर्म्मस्येति रजतत्वसमानाधिकरणतया गृह्यमाणधर्म्मस्य रजतसादृश्यादेरित्यर्थः, 'रङ्गवृत्तिधर्म्मस्येति रङ्गत्वसमानाधिकरणतया गृह्यमाणधर्म्मस्य रङ्गसादृश्यादेरित्यर्थः। 'तयोः' रङ्ग-रजतसादृश्ययोः, 'तत्र' भ्रमाभासस्थलीयविसंवादिप्रवृत्ति-निवृत्त्योः। नन्विष्टतावच्छेदकधर्म्मसमानाधिकरणत्वेन तद्धर्म्मज्ञानार्थमिष्टतावच्छेदकोपस्थितिरपेक्षिता इदन्तु भ्रमानुभवविधानत्यित आह, 'इमे इति।

'न प्रवर्त्तते' इति विपरीतदिकादितो न रजते रजतत्वप्रकारेण प्रवर्त्तत इत्यर्थः। 'कस्यचित्' कस्यचिदपि, 'रङ्गे प्रवर्त्तते' इति विपरीतदिकादितो रङ्ग एव रजतत्वप्रकारेण प्रवर्त्तते इत्यर्थः, 'एवं

---

(१) खज्ञानं यथार्थमनादृत्येति ख०।

वपि। यथा तवाभेदग्रहेऽपि मानान्तरात् भेदग्रहः प्रवृत्तिप्रतिबन्धकः तथा रजते रजतभेदाग्रहेऽपि रजतवृत्तितया यावदुपस्थितस्य रजतत्वेन मम भेदग्रहः प्रवृत्तिप्रतिबन्धक इति। तन्न। एतदपेक्षया विशिष्टज्ञानस्य लघुत्वेनान्वय-व्यतिरेकाभ्याञ्च हेतुत्वात्। न च हेत्वभावः, प्रत्यभिज्ञानवत् संस्कारेन्द्रियाभ्यां विशि-

---

निवृत्तावपीति विपरीतदिक्कादितो रङ्गत्वप्रकारकनिवृत्त्युत्पत्तावपि, रङ्गवृत्तितयोपस्थितयावद्धर्म्माणां रङ्गत्वेन मम भेदग्रहः प्रतिबन्धक इत्यर्थः। रजतवृत्तितयोपस्थितस्य च कस्यचिद्धर्मस्य न तदानीं रङ्गत्वेन मम भेदग्रह इति रजत एव रङ्गत्वप्रकारेण निवर्त्तत इति भावः। ननु सतीष्टपुरोवर्त्तिभेदाग्रहे तादृशभेदग्रहोऽकिञ्चित्कर इत्यत आह, 'यथेति यथा तव पीतः शङ्ख इति पीताभेदग्रहेऽपि न शङ्खे पीतत्वप्रकारकप्रवृत्तिः पीतभेदानुमित्या प्रतिबन्धादित्यर्थः। एतच्चापाततः शङ्खः पीत इत्यभेदज्ञानस्य भ्रमत्वेनाज्ञायमानत्वाभावादेव न प्रवर्त्तकता न तु भेदग्रहस्य प्रतिबन्धकता इत्युक्तत्वादिति ध्येयं। 'एतदपेक्षयेति, इदमुपलक्षणं तथापि तादृशभेदविरहदशायां विपरीतदिक्कादितो युगपत् प्रवृत्ति-निवृत्त्यापत्तेर्दुर्वारत्वाश्चेत्यपि द्रष्टव्यं। 'हेत्वभाव इति इदं रजतमिति विशिष्टप्रमोत्पत्तौ हेत्वभाव इत्यर्थः। न हि बौद्धानामिव तवापि प्रत्यभिज्ञानद्वयमित्यत आह, 'तस्येति, 'अभेदोच्छेदः' पूर्व्वकालवर्त्तिनां समनन्तरकालवर्त्तिनोऽभेदस्याप्रामाणिकत्वप्रसङ्गः। 'तस्य तदेकेति, अभेदानुमानादेरपि प्रत्य-

ष्टधीसम्भवात्[१]। तस्य ज्ञानद्वयत्वेऽभेदोच्छेदः तस्य तदेकमानत्वात्। नचैकविषयत्वेन तयोः परस्परसह-करिता, नामविशिष्टनामिप्रत्यक्षे तत्तांशे च तद-भावात् गौरवाच्च। न चातिप्रसङ्गः, भेदाग्रहस्यापि तद्धेतुत्वात्। अथ प्रत्यभिज्ञाया एकत्वेऽपि तत्तां-

---

भिज्ञानोपजीवकत्वादिति भावः। 'न चेति, 'तयोः' संस्कारेन्द्रिययोः, तद्विशेष्यक-तत्प्रकारकसंस्कारसहकारेणैव इन्द्रियं तद्विशेष्यक-तत्प्र-कारकप्रत्यक्षं जनयतीत्यर्थः, प्रकृते तु रजतविशेष्यक-रजतत्वप्रकार-कसंस्कारात् कथं शुक्तिविशेष्यक-रजतत्वप्रकारकप्रत्यक्षमित्यर्थः। 'नामिप्रत्यक्ष इति, नामांशे इति शेषः। 'तत्तांशे' तत्ताप्रत्यभि-ज्ञाने, 'तदभावात्' समानविशेष्यकसंस्कारविरहात्, 'गौरवाच्चेति' तद्विषयकसंस्कारत्वमपेक्ष्य तद्विशेष्यक-तत्प्रकारकसंस्कारत्वेन कार-णत्वे गौरवाच्चेत्यर्थः। 'अतिप्रसङ्ग इति सत्यपि भेदग्रहे प्रत्यक्षे संस्कारेन्द्रियाभ्यां विशिष्टभ्रमोदयप्रसङ्ग इत्यर्थः। 'तद्धेतुत्वात्' विशिष्टज्ञानहेतुत्वात् संस्कारद्वारा सविकल्पकजन्यस्यैव साक्षात्त्वादिति भावः। 'पुरोवर्त्त्यभेदांशे चेति पुरोवर्त्त्यंशे अभेदांशे चेत्यर्थः। सम्बन्धांशे सन्निकर्षस्याहेतुत्वमिति भावः। जातिसाङ्कर्य्यमाशङ्क्याह, 'स्मृतित्वमिति, 'अनुभूतित्वञ्चेति अनुभूतित्वादिकञ्चेत्यर्थः। आदि-पदात्साक्षात्कारत्वादिपरिग्रहः 'अव्याप्यवृत्तिर्वेत्यादि, तथा च साङ्क-र्य्यस्य एकावच्छेदेन सामानाधिकरण्यगर्भतया न साङ्कर्य्यमित्याशयः।

---

(१) विशिष्टज्ञानस्य सम्भवादिति ख०।

शे न साक्षात्कारित्वं तच्चेन्द्रियासंन्निकर्षात् तज्ज्ञानजन्यत्वाच्च। किन्तु स्मृतित्वं। पुरोवर्त्त्यंशेदांशे च साक्षात्त्वं स्मृतित्वमनुभूतित्वञ्च न जातिरव्याप्यवृत्तिर्वेति चेत्। तर्हि संस्कारादसन्निकृष्टमपि भासत इति तवाप्यनुमतं। तथा च तवैव रीत्या प्रत्यभिज्ञानवदिदं रजतमित्येकं ज्ञानमस्तु तत्सामग्रीसत्त्वात्। मम त्विन्द्रियजन्यत्वात् जात्यसंस्कराच्च साक्षात्कारित्वमेवेभयत्र। ननु यो यत्साक्षात्कारः स तदिन्द्रियसन्निकर्षजन्यः। न च रजते स इहास्ति इति चेत्। न। प्रत्यभिज्ञाया इन्द्रियजन्यतया साक्षात्कारित्वेन तत्तायां(१) नाम्नि च

'एकं ज्ञानमिति इदमंशे अनुभवरूपं रजतत्वांशे च स्मृतिरूपमित्यर्थः, 'जात्यसङ्करश्चेति परस्पराभावसमानाधिकरणयोर्जात्योरेकाधिकरणावृत्तित्वस्वभावाच्चेत्यर्थः। 'रजते' रजतत्वे वा, 'सः' इन्द्रियसन्निकर्षः, 'इह' स्मर्य्यमाणारोपस्थले। स्वमते दूषयति, 'प्रत्यभिज्ञाया इति, 'संस्कारस्येति, इदमपि स्वमतेन। 'तदिति रजतत्वप्रकारकप्रत्यक्षमित्यर्थः, 'तस्य' विशेषणलौकिकसन्निकर्षस्य। 'किञ्चेति किन्त्वित्यर्थः, 'तयोरसंसर्गाग्रहः', विशिष्टप्रत्यक्षहेतुरिति शेषः। 'किञ्चेत्यस्य मतान्तरत्वे पूर्व्वेण सह पौनरुक्त्यापत्तेः, भ्रमेण हेत्वभाव इति शेषः। ननु मास्तु रजतत्वलौकिकसन्निकर्षो हेतु-

---

(१) तत्तांशे इति ख०।

व्यभिचारात् संस्कारस्य स्मृतेर्वा सन्निकर्षत्वाच्च। न च रजतत्वप्रत्यक्षे संयुक्तसमवायस्य प्रत्यासत्तित्वेन हेतुत्वात्तं विना न तदिति वाच्यं। तद्विशिष्टज्ञाने विशेषणज्ञानोपक्षीणत्वेन तस्याहेतुत्वात्। न हि विशिष्टधीसामग्रीसत्त्वे तेन विना तद्विलम्बः। किञ्च विशेषणज्ञानं विशेष्यसम्बन्धस्तयोरसंसर्गाग्रह इति प्रत्यभिज्ञासत्यप्रत्यक्षसाधारणस्य विशिष्टप्रत्यक्षहेतोर्भ्रमेऽपि सम्भवात्। रजतसाक्षात्कारे रजतसंयोगस्य हेतुत्वेऽपि विशेष्यसन्निकर्षत्वेन हेतुता न तु रजतसंयोगत्वेन। यत्सामान्ये यत्सामान्यं हेतुस्तद्विशेषे तद्विशेषस्य हेतुत्व-

---

ननु तथापि रजतसंयोगस्य रजतत्वविशिष्टसाक्षात्कारहेतुतया तदजन्यत्वान्नासौ तथेत्यत आह, 'रजतसाक्षात्कार इति रजतत्वविशिष्टसाक्षात्कार इत्यर्थः, 'हेतुत्वेऽपि' क्वचित् फलोपधायकत्वेऽपि, 'विशेष्यसन्निकर्षत्वेनेति रजतविशेष्यकप्रत्यक्षं प्रति रजतसंयोगहेतुत्वावश्यकत्वादित्यर्थः। ननु संयोगो रजतविशेष्यकप्रत्यक्षवत् रजतत्वविशिष्टसाक्षात्कारं प्रत्यपि हेतुः सत्यरजतत्वविशिष्टप्रत्यक्षे तदन्वय-व्यतिरेकानुविधानदर्शनादित्यत आह,'संयोगस्येति रजतसंयोगस्येत्यर्थः, 'विशेष्यभानसामग्र्यन्तरितत्वेनेति रजतविशेष्यक-प्रत्यक्षत्वावच्छिन्नं प्रति कारणत्वेनेत्यर्थः,'अन्यथासिद्धतयेति सत्यरजतत्वविशिष्टप्रत्यक्षे तदन्वय-व्यतिरेकानुविधानस्यान्यथासिद्धतयेत्यर्थः, 'विशेषसामग्र्यन्तरेति रजतसंयोगत्वेन रजत-

नियमात्[१]। संयोगस्य विशेष्यभानसामग्र्यन्तरितत्वेना-न्यथासिद्धतया विशेषसामग्र्यन्तराकल्पनात् गौरवाच्च। प्रत्यक्षहेतुत्वेन क्लृप्तविशेष्यसम्बन्धादेव तदुपपत्तेः। अपिच प्रवृत्तौ स्वतन्त्रोपस्थितेष्टभेदाग्रहकारणत्वापेक्षया रजतसाक्षात्कारे विशेष्यसन्निकर्षत्वेन हेतुत्वस्य लघुत्वात्। वस्तुतस्तु दोषाद्भ्रम इत्युभयसिद्धं, तच्च भ्रमो नासंसर्गाग्रहाभावः, तस्याधिकरणरूपत्वे असाध्यत्वात्, तज्ज्ञानरूपत्वे च तस्य प्रमात्वेन दोषाजन्यत्वात्। भ्रमस्थानाभिषिक्तप्रमा दोषजन्यैवेति[२]

त्वविशिष्टसाक्षात्कारत्वेन विशेषकार्य्य-कारणभावान्तरकल्पनादित्यर्थः। 'प्रत्यक्षहेतुत्वेन' शुक्तिविशेष्यक-प्रत्यक्षसामान्यहेतुत्वेन, 'विशेष्यसम्बन्धादेवेति शुक्तीन्द्रियसन्निकर्षादेवेत्यर्थः, 'तदुपपत्तेरिति शुक्तौ रजतत्वविशिष्टसाक्षात्कारोपपत्तेरित्यर्थः। ननु लाघवात्सामान्यतो रजतविषयक-प्रत्यक्षत्वावच्छिन्नं प्रति रजतसंयोगत्वेन हेतुत्वं रजतविशेष्यकप्रत्यक्षत्वस्य कार्य्यतावच्छेदकत्वे गौरवात् निर्व्विकल्पकसंग्रहार्थं प्रकारता-संसर्गतातिरिक्तविषयताया एवात्र विशेष्यतात्वात् तथा च रजत-चक्षुरादिसंयोगं विना कथं शुक्त्यादौ रजतभेदविशिष्टधीरित्यत आह, 'अपिचेति, 'रजत-साक्षात्कार इति रजतविशेष्यक-साक्षात्कारे रजतसंयोगत्वेन हेतुत्वस्येत्यर्थः,एतच्च समाधिसौकार्य्यादुक्तं। वस्तुतस्तु रजतविषयकप्रत्यक्षत्वमुपेक्ष्य

---

(१) तद्विशेषस्य तद्विशेषहेतुत्वनियमादिति क०।

(२) दोषाभिषिक्ता प्रमैव दोषजन्येतीति ख०।

चेत्। न। तस्याः क्लृप्तसामग्र्यन्तरजन्यत्वादिति भ्रमोऽसत्यज्ञानमित्यसन्निकृष्टमपि दोषाद्भासत इत्युपेयं। अपि च दोषस्य विशिष्टमेव ज्ञानं व्यापारः प्रवृत्तौ तद्धेतुत्वस्य क्लृप्तत्वात्। न च भेदाग्रहः, कल्पनीयकारणभावत्वात्।

रजतविशेष्यकप्रत्यक्षत्वमेव लघुशरीरमगृह्यमाणव्यतिरेकञ्च तत्र विशेषणतारूपविषयत्वस्याधिकस्य प्रवेशेन गुरुत्वात् सन्दिग्धव्यतिरेकाच्च। न च निर्व्विकल्पकसंग्रहार्थं विशेषणतातिरिक्तविषयताया एवात्र विशेष्यतापदार्थत्वात् लघुशरीरत्वं, अतएव सन्दिग्धव्यतिरेकमप्यकिञ्चित्करं समशरीरार्थमेव तस्य कारणतायां विनिगमकत्वादिति वाच्यं। निर्व्विकल्पकविषयता-विशेष्यतासम्बन्धेन तद्विशिष्टप्रत्यक्षत्वस्यैव तद्विशेष्यकप्रत्यक्षत्वरूपत्वात् सम्बन्धाननुगमस्यादोषत्वादिति ध्येयं। 'दोषाद्भ्रम इति दोषमध्ये भ्रम इत्यर्थः, 'उभयसिद्धः' उभयवादिसिद्धः सिद्धान्तः, तदनभ्युपगमे चापसिद्धान्त इति भावः। 'अधिकरणरूपत्वे इति अतिरिक्तत्वेऽपि नित्यत्वादित्यपि बोध्यं। 'तज्ज्ञानेति अधिकरणज्ञानेत्यर्थः, 'तस्याः' प्रमायाः, 'क्लृप्तसामग्र्यन्तरेति दोषाघटितक्लृप्तसामग्रीत्यर्थः, 'असत्यज्ञानं' असत्यविशिष्टज्ञानं, 'इतीति, अनायत्येति शेषः। ननु 'दोषाद्भ्रम इत्यत्र भ्रमपदं भ्रमजन्यविसंवादिव्यवहारपरं अतो नोक्तदोष इत्यत आह, 'अपिचेति, 'विशिष्टज्ञानमेव' विशिष्टभ्रम एव, 'व्यापारः' विसंवादिप्रवृत्तिजनने व्यापारः, 'प्रवृत्तौ' विसंवादिप्रवृत्तौ, 'तद्धेतुत्वस्य' तेन रूपेण

यत्तु दुष्टात्कार्य्यन्नेति, तन्न वीजेन्द्रियसाधारणं न दुष्टत्वमेकमस्ति। एवं प्रत्यक्षमप्यन्यथाख्यातौ मानं कारणबाधाभावात्(१)। तथाहि इदं रजततया जानामीत्यनुव्यवसायसाक्षिकमेवान्यस्यान्यथा भानं। नहि विषयत्वेऽनुव्यवसायादन्यत्प्रमाणं। न ह्यतद्विषयस्तज्ज्ञानविषयत्वेन, न वा तदविषयकं तद्विषयकत्वेनानुव्यवसीयते। अनुव्यवसायस्य प्रमात्वनियमात्। अन्यथा घटज्ञानेऽपि कदाचित् पटज्ञानामीति स्यात्।

दोषाणां हेतुत्वस्य, भ्रमजनकत्वेनैव रूपेण दोषाणां हेतुत्वस्येति यावत्। अन्यथा दोषाणां नानाविधतया अननुगमापत्तेः इति भावः। इदमुपलक्षणं दोषस्य साक्षात्संवादिप्रवृत्तिहेतुत्वे विनश्यदवस्थदोषाव्यवहितोत्तरक्षणोत्पन्नज्ञानात्तादृशप्रवृत्त्यभावाच्चेत्यपि द्रष्टव्यं। 'कल्पनीयकारणभावत्वात् कल्पनीयकारणसत्ताकत्वात्, नित्यत्वादिति यावत्। 'दुष्टादिति, दुष्टे वीजे तथा दर्शनादिति भावः। 'नैकमस्तीति, तथा च दुष्टवीजात् कार्य्यानुदयेऽपि दुष्टादिन्द्रियात् कार्य्यं स्यादिति भावः।'एवमिति उक्तरीत्या कारणबाधनिरास इत्यर्थः,'अन्यथाख्यातौ' ख्यातेर्व्यधिकरणप्रकारकत्वे, ख्यातेः शुक्त्यादिविशेष्यकत्वावच्छिन्न-रजतत्वप्रकारकत्वे इति यावत्। 'अनुव्यवसायेति भ्रमानुव्यवसायेत्यर्थः,'अन्यस्यान्यथा भानमिति शुक्त्यादिविशेष्यकत्वावच्छिन्न-रजतत्वप्रकारकमि-

---

(१) कारणसद्भावादिति ख०।

न च भेदाग्रहदशायां रजतज्ञानविषयत्वासंसर्गाग्रहः, शुक्तौ भेदग्रहेऽपि शुक्तीरजतत्वेन मया ज्ञाता शुक्तौ रजतज्ञानं मे वृत्तमित्यनुव्यवसायात्। अथ विचारसाध्यासंसर्गग्रहबाध्योऽयमसंसर्गाग्रहस्तेन विचारं विना भेदग्रहेऽप्यवतिष्ठत इति चेत्। न। इदं रजततया जानामीत्यत्र शुक्तिकर्मकरजतत्वप्रकारकज्ञानासंसर्गाग्रहस्यात्मन्यसम्भवात् तादृशज्ञानाप्रसिद्धेः। नचेदं

त्यर्थः। ननु तावदेव यद्यनुव्यवसायो विषयतां गृह्णीयात् न त्वेवमित्यत आह, 'न हीति, विषयानुवसायस्य तत्तदर्थविषयत्वेन तदनुव्यवसायो भ्रम इत्यत आह, 'न हीति। ननु मास्तु अनुव्यवसाये विशिष्टभ्रमः किन्तु भेदाग्रहसहितः शुक्तौ रजतत्वप्रकारत्वावच्छिन्नविशेष्यत्वासंसर्गाग्रह एव स इत्यभिप्रायेणाशङ्कते, 'न चेति, 'भेदग्रहेऽपीति शुक्ति-रजतयोर्भेदग्रहेऽपीत्यर्थः। ननु भेदग्रहे सतीति सत्यन्तं नोपादेयमित्यभिप्रायेण शङ्कते, 'अथेति, 'विचारः' शुक्तिर्न रजतत्वप्रकारकधीविशेष्यः रजतभिन्नत्वादित्यनुमानरूपः, 'तत्साध्यः' तज्जन्यः, यः 'असंसर्गग्रहः' शुक्तौ रजतत्वप्रकारकत्वावच्छिन्नज्ञानविशेष्यत्वासंसर्गग्रह इति यावत्, 'तद्बाध्यः' तदभावरूपः, यः 'असंसर्गाग्रहः' शुक्तौनिरुक्तविशेष्यत्वासंसर्गाग्रह इति यावत्। स एवायमिति योजना, 'अयं' अनुव्यवसायः, 'विचारं विना' तादृशविचारसाध्यासंसर्गाग्रहं विनेत्यर्थः, भेदग्रहेऽपि शुक्ति-रजतयोर्भेदग्रहसत्त्वेऽपि, 'इदं रजत-

जानामीति रजतं जानामीति तदाकारः, तृतीयार्थस्य प्रकारत्वेन प्रकारिणोऽभानेऽभानप्रसङ्गात्। विशिष्ट-ज्ञानञ्च सर्वञ्च विशेषण-विशेष्यीयमित्यन्यथा भानमपि

तया जानामीत्यनुव्यवसायाभिलापः, तच्च च भवन्मते शुक्तिविशेष्यक-रजतत्वप्रकारकज्ञानासंसर्गाग्रह एवात्मनिष्ठो हेतुर्न तु निरुक्तासंसर्गाग्रहः। न च सम्भवति, तादृशज्ञानाप्रसिद्धेः इत्यभिप्रायेण दूषयति, 'इदमिति इत्यभिलापे, भवन्मते जनकीभूतस्येति शेषः। 'रजतं जानामि' रजतत्वेन जानामि, यथाश्रुते 'तृतीयार्थस्येत्यग्रिमग्रन्थासङ्गतेः। 'तदाकार इति अनुव्यवसायाभिलाप इत्यर्थः, तच्च शुक्ति-कर्मकरजतत्वप्रकारकज्ञानयोरुभयोरात्मन्यसंसर्गाग्रह एव हेतुस्तच्च च नाप्रसिद्ध इति भावः। एतच्चापाततः दोषात् प्रकारिणोऽभानेऽपि प्रकारताभानस्य सुवचत्वात्। एवमिदं रजततया जानामीत्यनुव्यव-सायादिकमप्येवमुक्तं तादृशानुव्यवसायेऽपि शुक्तौ रजतत्वप्रकारत्वाव-च्छिन्न-विशेष्यत्वासंसर्गाग्रहादेरेव हेतुत्वस्य सुवचत्वात्। वस्तुतस्तु संसर्गग्रहे बाधकाभावान्नासंसर्गाग्रहः, अन्यथा रजतेऽपि तथा ज्ञानं न सिद्ध्येदित्येव तत्त्वं। ननु सिद्ध्यति तदभाववति तद्वैशिष्ट्याव-गाहि ज्ञानं, तथापि तस्य विशेषणविशेष्यकत्वे मानाभावः इत्यत आह, 'विशिष्टज्ञानञ्चेति, 'विशेषण-विशेष्यीयमिति विषयितासम्बन्धेन विशेष्यसम्बन्धीत्यर्थः, सांसर्गिकविषयितायाः समानाधिकरणप्रका-रिता-विशेष्यितानिरूपितत्वनियमादिति भावः। नन्वेवं ज्ञानस्य रज-तत्वसम्बन्धित्वाभ्युपगमे भवतामपि सप्रकारत्वापत्तिरित्यत आह,

तथा। ज्ञाने रजतत्वानभ्युपगमाद्विशेषण-विशेष्य-विषयकत्वाच्च न साकारवादः।

यत्तु ज्ञानमिथ्यात्वे बाध्य-बाधकव्यवस्था न स्यादविशेषादिति। तन्न। अनन्यथासिद्धाया धियोबाधकत्वात्। तथाहि यत्र दुष्टादुष्टेन्द्रियजन्यं परस्परनिरपेक्ष्यमेकत्र विरुद्धं ज्ञानद्वयमुत्पद्यते, तत्र प्रथममनुपजातविरोधित्वान्नानागतं बाधते तस्याप्राप्तत्वात्। उत्तरन्तु स्वकारणादुत्पद्यमानमुपजातविरोधितया नानुपमृद्य पूर्वमुत्पत्तुमर्हतीति पूर्वं बाधात्मकमुत्पद्यते, अन्यथा नोत्पद्येतैव। नचैवमेवेति वाच्यं। अनुभवविरोधात्। यदाहुः। "पूर्वात्परबलीयस्त्वं तत्र नाम प्रतीयते। अन्योन्यनिरपेक्षाणां यत्र जन्मधियां भवेत्"। इति। यत्र पूर्वापेक्षमुत्तरं ज्ञानमुत्पत्तुमुन्मुखं तत्रोपजीव्यपूर्वविरोधेनोत्तरं नोत्पद्यते, अतोऽजातं सत्पूर्वं कथं

'ज्ञान इति, 'रजतत्वानभ्युपगमात्' समवायसम्बन्धेन रजतत्वानभ्युपगमात्, 'विशेषण-विशेष्यविषयकत्वाच्चेति तदनभ्युपगमाच्चेत्यर्थः, 'न साकारवादः' न साकारवादित्वं, साकारवादिना सौगतेन सौत्रान्तिकापरनाम्ना रजतज्ञानेऽपि समवायसम्बन्धेन रजतत्वाभ्युपगमात् विषयितायाः अनभ्युपगमाच्चेति भावः।

बाधतां[१] । यथा प्रत्यक्षादिविरुद्धानुमितिः । ननु भ्रमस्य किं बाध्यते। न स्वरूपं तस्य सत्त्वात्। नापि रजतत्वप्रकारकत्वं, शुक्तिविषयकत्वं वा तयोरपनेतुमशक्यत्वात् । जातं हि तद्रजतत्वेन शुक्तिं विषयीकृत्य नापि व्यवहारः, प्रवृत्त्यादेर्वृत्तत्वात् । नाप्यनागतव्यवहारजनकत्वं, तस्य कारणाभावादेवासम्भवात् । उच्यते । बाधकेन भ्रमस्य भ्रमत्वबुद्धिरेव बाधः ।

यत्तु धियामयथार्थत्वे कथमाश्वास इति । तन्न । प्रामाण्यग्रहोपायस्य दर्शितत्वात । सत्यत्वनियमेऽपि सदसंसर्गाग्रहस्यागृहीतासंसर्गस्य ज्ञानद्वयस्य च बहुषु दर्शनात् कथमाश्वासः । अथ सदसंसर्गाग्रहस्य प्रतिसन्धानं विलम्बितं सद्विषयत्वञ्च शीघ्रोपस्थितमित्यौ-

केचित्तु शुक्ताविदं रजतमितिभ्रमस्य शुक्तिविशेष्यकत्वावच्छिन्नरजतत्वप्रकारकत्वेऽपि शुक्तौ रजतत्ववैशिष्ट्यावगाहित्वे मानाभावः, तथासति तादृशज्ञानस्य बाध्यत्वं तदुत्तरोत्पन्नस्य नेदं रजतमिति विशेषदर्शनजन्यज्ञानस्य च बाधकत्वमिति न स्यात् परस्परविरुद्धार्थवैशिष्ट्यावगाहित्वस्याविशेषादिविषयिताविशेषरूपयोर्विशेष्यत्व-प्रकारित्वयोर्वैशिष्ट्यावगाहित्वं विनापि सम्भवादित्याहुः, तन्मतं निराकरोति, 'यत्त्विति मित्याशुक्त्यादिविशेष्यक-रजतत्वादिप्रकारकधियां शुक्त्यादौ

(१) कथं पूर्वं बाधकमिति ख० ।

त्सर्गिकसद्विषयत्वज्ञानाद्विश्वासः। यत्र तु कदाचित् संशयस्तत्र ज्ञानान्तरादेव संशयनिवृत्तिरिति चेत्। ममाप्यौत्सर्गिकन्धियां सत्यत्वं बाधकेनापनोद्यत इति तदनवतारात्सत्यत्वविश्वासः। किञ्च तव ज्ञानान्तरेऽप्यविश्वासः। विशेषदर्शनाद्विश्वासस्तुल्य एव। यथा च तत्रापि न सन्देहस्तथोक्तं परतः प्रामाण्ये।

अन्ये तु स्मृतयोग्यवैधर्म्याभावोऽधिकरणं तज्ज्ञानं वा तच्च प्रत्यक्षत एव गृहीतं(१) इति युक्तोविश्वासः।

रजतत्ववैशिष्ट्यावगाहित्वे इत्यर्थः, 'बाध्य-बाधकव्यवस्थेति तादृशधियां बाध्यत्वं तदुत्तरोत्पन्नस्य नेदं रजतमित्यादिविशेषदर्शनजन्यज्ञानस्य बाधकत्वमिति न स्यादित्यर्थः, बाध्य-बाधकत्वञ्च स्वयमेवाग्रे निर्वक्ष्यते, 'अविशेषादिति परस्परविरुद्धार्थवैशिष्ट्यावगाहित्वं स्यादित्यर्थः। 'अनन्यथासिद्धायाः' पूर्वोत्पन्नज्ञाने उत्तेजकवैशिष्ट्यं विनानुत्पद्यमानायाः पूर्वोत्पन्नज्ञाने उत्तेजकवैशिष्ट्याधीनाया इति यावत्, उत्तेजकञ्च विशेषदर्शनं, भ्रमत्वज्ञानादिनेत्यर्थः। तदेव विवरयति, 'तथाहीति, 'एकत्र' एकस्मिन् धर्म्मिणि, 'विरुद्धज्ञानद्वयमिति परस्परविरुद्धार्थ-विषयकज्ञानद्वयमित्यर्थः, 'अनुपजातविरोधित्वादिति विरोधिविषयकज्ञानाव्यवहितपूर्ववर्त्तिकालानुत्पत्तिकत्वेन उत्तेजकाधीनत्वादित्यर्थः। ननु नात्र ज्ञानमेव तस्य विरुद्धार्थविषयकमित्यत आह,

---

(१) गृह्यते इति ख०।

अयोग्ये भेदकेऽधिकरणे च भेदसंशये ज्ञानान्तराद्विश्वास इति। तन्न। उभयत्रापि ज्ञानान्तराद्विश्वासतुल्यत्वेन शिष्यधन्धनमात्रत्वात्। वस्तुतस्तु भेदाग्रहादेवाभेदव्यवहारोपपत्तावभेदविषयत्वं क्वापि न सिद्धमस्तीति कथं सद्विषयत्वसिद्धिः।

यत्तु दोषो न हेतुरिति। तन्न। फलबलेन[१] तथात्वात्।

अथेदं रजतमिति ज्ञानद्वयमयथार्थं इदं-रजतयोः सत्त्वात्। नच तदुभयतादात्म्यमसत उभयस्तादात्म्य-

'तस्येति अनागतज्ञानस्येत्यर्थः, 'अप्राप्तत्वादिति अव्यवहितप्राक्कालाप्राप्तत्वादित्यर्थः, 'उत्तरन्त्विति, उत्तरन्तु 'उपजातविरोधितया' विरोधिविषयकज्ञानाव्यवहितपूर्ववर्त्तिकालोत्पत्तिकतया, 'स्वकारणात्' विशेषदर्शनाद्युत्तेजकघटितात्, 'उत्पद्यमानं पूर्वमनुपमृद्य' पूर्वज्ञानस्याबाधकीभूय, 'नोत्पत्तुमर्हतीति, ज्ञानस्य पूर्वज्ञानबाधकत्वनियमादिति भावः। ननु विशेषदर्शनादेरुत्तेजकत्वे मानाभाव इत्यत आह, 'अन्यथेति। तटस्थः शङ्कते, 'न चेति, 'एवमेव' नोत्पद्यत एव। अनुभवमेव दृढयति, 'यदाऽऽऊरिति यस्मादाऽऽऊरित्यर्थः।

'तथात्वादिति दोषस्यापि ज्ञानहेतुत्वादित्यर्थः, तथाचोक्तयुक्त्या भ्रमे सिद्धे तदन्यथापत्तिरेव दोषाणां हेतुत्वे मानमिति भावः।

(१) फलवत्त्वेनेति ख०।

श्चेति, अतोऽधिकस्याभावात् । तयोश्च सत्त्वात् । असत्त्वे वा असत्ख्यातिः, एवं संसर्गारोपोऽपीति । उच्यते । सन्मात्रविषयत्वेऽपि तदभाववति तत्प्रकारकत्वं प्रकारव्यधिकरणविषयताकत्वं वा अयथार्थत्वं ।

प्राञ्चस्तु । तादात्म्य-संसर्गयोरसतोरेव मन्यन्ते विषयत्वं । नचैवमसत्ख्यातिः, सदुपरक्तस्यात्यन्तासतः

श्रमद्विषयकत्वव्याप्यमयथार्थत्वमित्यभिमानेन शङ्कते, 'अथेति इत्ये-ताभ्यामतिरिक्तस्य तदुभयतादात्म्यस्य इदं रजतमिति भ्रमे भाना-दित्यर्थः, 'अभावादिति आरोपिताभावादित्यर्थः, 'असत्त्वे वा' असत एव तदुभयतादात्म्यस्य विषयत्वे वा, 'संसर्गारोपोऽपीति, कथमयथार्थ-इति शेषः । अभिमानं निराकृत्य समाधत्ते 'सन्मात्रविषयत्वेऽपीति इदं रजतमितिभ्रमस्य सन्मात्रविषयत्वेऽपीत्यर्थः, 'प्रकारव्यधिकरणेति स्वव्यधिकरणधर्मनिरूपितविशेष्यताकत्वमित्यर्थः, स्वं विशेष्यता, तथा च यथार्थत्वं सद्विषयकत्वव्याप्यमिति भावः ।

'तादात्म्य-संसर्गयोः' तादात्म्य-तदतिरिक्त-संसर्गयोः, 'विषयत्वं' संसर्गमर्य्यादया विषयत्वं, 'सदुपरक्तस्येति सतोर्विशेषण-विशेष्ययोः संसर्गमर्य्यादयेत्यर्थः, 'सदनुपरक्तस्येति संसर्गत्वेनेत्यर्थः, 'कारणाभावा-दिति व्याप्तिज्ञान-शक्तिज्ञान-सादृश्यज्ञान-सन्निकर्षरूपकारणाभावा-दित्यर्थः । शङ्कते, 'तदनुपपत्तिरिति संसर्गमर्य्यादया ज्ञानेऽपि कारणानुपपत्तिरित्यर्थः, स्वोक्तमतद्वये टीकाकारसंवादमाह, 'तदुक्त-मिति, 'यज्ज्ञानमन्यथा सन्तमिति तत्सम्बन्धावच्छिन्नतदभाववन्तमि-

ख्यात्यभ्युपगमात् । सदनुपरक्तस्याखण्डस्यात्यन्तासतः ख्यातिरसत्ख्यातिर्नाभ्युपेयते कारणाभावात् । तदनुपपत्तिस्तुल्यैवेति चेत् । न । अत्र विशिष्टज्ञानसामग्र्या दर्शितत्वात् । तदुक्तं वाचस्पतिमिश्रैः "तस्माद्यदन्यथा सन्तमन्यथा प्रतिपद्यते । तन्निरालम्बनं ज्ञानमसदालम्बनञ्च तत्" ॥ इति ।

इति श्रीमद्गङ्गेशोपाध्याय-विरचिते तत्त्वचिन्तामणौ प्रत्यक्षखण्डे अन्यथाख्यातिवादः ।

त्यर्थः, 'अन्यथा प्रतिपद्यते' तत्सम्बन्धेन त॰ ‌ यात्विषयीकरोति, 'निरालम्बनं' निरालम्बनव्यवहारविषयः, अयथार्थव्यवहारविषय इति यावत्, 'असदालम्बनञ्च' संसर्गमर्य्यादया असद्वैशिष्ट्यविषयकञ्च, अत्र 'प्राञ्च इत्यस्वरसोद्भावनं, तद्बीजन्तु भ्रमे संसर्गमर्य्यादया असतोभाने मानाभावः ।

केचित्तु संसर्गमर्य्यादया असतोभाने तदुत्तरं विशेषणत्व-विशेष्यत्वेनापि तज्ज्ञानं स्यात् संसर्गमर्य्यादया तज्ज्ञानस्यैव विशेषणज्ञानत्वात् सन्निकर्षत्वादित्यस्वरसबीजमाहुः । तदसत् । सांसर्गिकातिरिक्ततद्विषयताशालिज्ञानस्यैव तद्विशिष्टबुद्धौ तदुपनीतभाने च हेतुत्वादन्यथा सार्व्वज्ञ्यापत्तेरित्यन्यत्र विस्तरः ॥

इति श्रीमथुरानाथतर्कवागीशविरचिते तत्त्वचिन्तामणिरहस्ये प्रत्यक्षखण्डरहस्ये अन्यथाख्यातिवादरहस्यं ।

अथ सन्निकर्षवादः।

सा च प्रमा चतुर्विधा प्रत्यक्षानुमित्युपमिति-शाब्दी-भेदात्। एवञ्चतस्याः करणन्तासाङ्करणं प्रमाणमपि चतुर्विधं प्रत्यक्षानुमानोपमान-शब्दभेदात्। अन्येषां यथायथमेष्वेवान्तर्भावात्। तथाच वक्ष्यामः। ननु न

अथ सन्निकर्षवादरहस्यं।

लक्षितां तां विभजते, 'सा च प्रमेति तद्वति तत्प्रकारकानुभवरूपा च प्रमेत्यर्थः, 'चतुर्विधा' अनुभवत्वसाक्षाद्व्याप्यजातिचतुष्टयवतीत्यर्थः, अनुभवत्वसाक्षाद्व्याप्यजातिचतुष्टयं तादृशप्रमावृत्ति इति तु समुदितार्थः। तेन कस्याश्चिदपि प्रमाव्यक्तेः तादृशजातिचतुष्टयवत्त्वविरहेऽपि न क्षतिः। तादृशजातिचतुष्टयस्य परस्परं व्याप्य-व्यापकभावानापन्नस्य एकप्रमाव्यक्तिवृत्तित्वे भूतल-मूर्त्तत्ववत् साङ्कर्य्यं स्यादित्यत आह, 'प्रत्यक्षेति प्रत्यक्षानुमित्युपमिति-शाब्दात्मकप्रमाव्यक्तीनां परस्परं भेदादित्यर्थः। तथाचाधिकरणीभूतप्रमाव्यक्तिभेदान्न साङ्कर्य्यमिति भावः। प्रमां विभज्य प्रमाणमपि विभजते, 'एवमिति, 'चतुर्विधं' प्रमाणविभाजकोपाधिचतुष्टयवत्, प्रमाणविभाजकोपाधिचतुष्टयं प्रमाकरणवृत्तीति तु समुदितार्थः। ननु विभाजकोपाधीनां परस्परं भेदविरहेण चतुष्टयत्वमेवासिद्धमित्यत

प्रत्यक्षन्तावदिन्द्रियार्थसन्निकर्षोत्पन्नं ज्ञानमव्यभिचारि। आत्मानुमिति-स्मृत्योर्ज्ञानमात्रे चातिव्याप्तेः आत्मनोऽर्थस्य मनसेन्द्रियेण संयोगादुत्पत्तेः। ईश्वरप्रत्य-

---

आह, 'प्रत्यक्षानुमानेति प्रत्यक्षत्वानुमानत्वोपमानत्व शब्दत्वरूपाणां विभाजकोपाधीनां परस्परं भेदसत्त्वादित्यर्थः। ननु विभागन्यूनत्वमत आह, 'अन्येषामिति अनुपलब्ध्यर्थापत्त्यादीनामित्यर्थः। ननु प्रत्यक्षप्रमात्वं दुर्वचमिति ज्ञानेनाशङ्कते, 'नन्विति, 'प्रत्यक्षं' प्रत्यक्षप्रमा, 'ज्ञानमव्यभिचारीति अव्यभिचारि ज्ञानमिति योजना, यथार्थज्ञानमित्यर्थः, तथाचेन्द्रियार्थसन्निकर्षजन्ययथार्थज्ञानत्वं प्रत्यक्षप्रमात्वमिति भावः। अत्र 'अर्थपदं स्वविषयपरं, स्वं लक्ष्यत्वेनाभिमतं, विषयमात्रपरं वा आद्ये आह, 'आत्मानुमितीति, 'अनुमितिपदमत्र परोक्षानुभवमात्रपरं, तेन नात्मशाब्दोपमित्योरव्याप्तिः। द्वितीये त्वाह, 'ज्ञानमात्रे चेति लक्ष्यभिन्नज्ञानमात्रे चेत्यर्थः। ननु जन्यज्ञानत्वावच्छिन्ना समवायसम्बन्धावच्छिन्ना वा लौकिकविषयतासम्बन्धावच्छिन्ना वा जन्यता निवेशिता(१) अतोनातिव्याप्तिरित्यत आह, 'ईश्वरेति। ननु जन्यप्रत्यक्षमेव लक्ष्यमतो नाव्याप्तिरित्यत आह, 'सन्निकर्षस्य चेति। नन्विन्द्रियार्थसंयोगाद्यन्यतमत्वेनानुगम इत्यत आह, 'संयोगाद्यन्यतमस्येति संयोगाद्यन्य-

---

(२) आत्म-मनःसंयोगस्य कार्यतावच्छेदकं जन्यज्ञानत्वं कार्यतावच्छेदकसम्बन्धश्च समवायः न तु लौकिकविषयतासम्बन्धो नातिव्याप्तिरिति भावः।

ह्याव्याप्तेश्च। सन्निकर्षस्य च संयोगादिरूपत्वेनाननुगमाच्च। संयोगाद्यन्यतमस्य चानिर्द्धारितैकपरत्वे भागासिद्धिरितरभेदसाधने, व्यर्थविशेषणत्वञ्च। इन्द्रियार्थयोरेकजन्यत्वस्य लक्षणत्वे व्यर्थविशेषणत्वं। न च तयोरेकैकजन्यत्वमेव लक्षणं, आत्म-मनोजन्य-

---

तमपदस्य चेत्यर्थः, 'अनिर्द्धारितैकेति संयोगादीनां मध्ये यत्किञ्चिद्व्यक्तिपरत्वे इत्यर्थः, 'भागासिद्धिरितरभेदसाधने' इति च्छेदः, इतरभेदसाधने भागासिद्धिरित्यर्थः, परस्परमव्याप्तत्वादिति भावः। नन्वन्यतमपदं तत्तद्भेदकूटावच्छिन्नप्रतियोगिताकभेदवत्परमतो नाव्याप्तिरित्यत आह, 'व्यर्थविशेषणत्वञ्चेति संयोगादियत्किञ्चिद्व्यक्तिभेदावच्छिन्नप्रतियोगिताकभेदवज्जन्यत्वस्यैव सम्यक्त्वेन तावद्भेदकूटरूपविशेषणानां भागासिद्धिवारणमात्रप्रयोजकानां वैयर्थ्यमित्यर्थः[१]। सन्निकर्षविशेषणमपि व्यर्थमित्याह, 'इन्द्रियेति, 'एकजन्यत्वस्य' एकैकजन्यत्वस्य, 'लक्षणत्वे' लक्षणत्वसम्भवे, 'व्यर्थविशेषणत्वमिति जन्यतांशे विशेषणस्य सन्निकर्षभागस्य व्यर्थत्वमित्यर्थः। एतद्व्यर्थविशेषणतादयोद्भावनमापाततः, यथासन्निवेशे वैयर्थ्याभावादिति ध्येयं[२]। 'तयोः' अर्थयोर्मध्ये, 'आत्मेति आत्मजन्यत्वेन मनोजन्यत्वेन

---

(१) व्यभिचारावारकविशेषणस्य व्यर्थत्वमिति मतेनेदं।

(२) यत्किञ्चिद्व्यक्तिभेदावच्छिन्नप्रतियोगिताकभेदवज्जन्यत्वस्य तत्तद्भेदकूटावच्छिन्नप्रतियोगिताकभेदवज्जन्यत्वाघटकतया, एकैकजन्यत्वस्य इन्द्रियार्थसन्निकर्षजन्यत्वाघटकतया च स्वसमानाधिकरणव्याप्यतावच्छेदकधर्मान्तरघटितलक्षणवर्थविशेषणत्वस्यासम्भवादिति भावः।

त्वेन ज्ञानमात्रे गतत्वात्। इन्द्रियस्य प्रत्यक्षनिरूप्यत्वाच्च। नापि ज्ञातकरणाजन्यत्वे सति सत्योऽनुभवः प्रत्यक्षं, लिङ्गादेरजनकतया ज्ञानस्याज्ञातस्य करणत्वे अनुमित्यादौ गतत्वात्। ज्ञानाजन्योऽनुभवः सत्य-

---

चेत्यर्थः, 'ज्ञानमात्रे' अन्यज्ञानमात्रे। ननु जन्यताविशेषस्य प्रवेशान्नायं दोष इत्यत आह, 'इन्द्रियस्येति इन्द्रियत्वस्येत्यर्थः, साक्षात्प्रतीतिसाधनशरीरसंयोगवदतीन्द्रियत्वमिति तल्लक्षणात्। न च तथाप्यर्थजन्यत्वं लक्षणं सम्यगेवेति वाच्यं। तत्रापि सर्वांशालौकिकप्रत्यक्षाभ्युपगमे तदव्याप्तेरिति भावः। अत्र साक्षात्प्रतीतिसाधनत्वे सत्यतीन्द्रियत्वमात्रोक्तौ कालादावतिप्रसङ्गः स्यादतः शरीरसंयोगपदं; काल-शरीरसंयोगस्य न प्रत्यक्षहेतुः क्रियैव कालोपाधिरिति मतेन लक्षणकरणान्महाकालसंयोगस्यापि न कालत्वेन प्रत्यक्षहेतुत्वं। स्वीयस्पर्शसाक्षात्कारकारणेन्द्रियसंयोगमादायातिव्याप्तिवारणाय शरीरपदं स्वेतरशरीरपरं, स्वं लक्ष्यत्वेनाभिमतं, शरीरसंयोगपदं वा शरीरानिरूपितसंयोगपरं तेन न वायवीयशरीरनिष्ठस्पर्शसाक्षात्कारकारणेन्द्रियसंयोगमादाय वायवीयशरीरेऽतिव्याप्तिः, न वा घटादिविषयकपिशाचादिकर्त्तृकसाक्षात्कारकारणपिशाचादिशरीरेन्द्रियसंयोगमादाय पिशाचादिशरीरेऽतिव्याप्तिः। आत्म-शरीरसंयोगस्यापि प्रत्यक्षहेतुतया आत्मन्यतिव्याप्तिवारणाय अतीन्द्रियेति। ज्ञायमानलिङ्गस्य अनुमितिकरण-

इत्यपि न, विशिष्टप्रत्यक्षाव्याप्तेः तस्य विशेषणज्ञान-जन्यत्वात्। नापि सत्यत्वे सति साक्षात्कारित्वं, नियत-व्यञ्जकाभावेन ग्रहीतुमशक्यतया तस्य जातित्वा-

---

तानये शरीराकाशादिसंयोगमादायातिव्याप्तिवारणाय साक्षात्त्व-प्रवेशः(१)। वस्तुतः(२) अखण्डजातेः प्रवेशान्न वैयर्थ्यशङ्कापि(३)। इन्द्रियावयवशरीरसंयोगस्य न प्रत्यक्षहेतुरतो नेन्द्रियावयवेऽतिव्याप्तिः। अन्त्यावयवित्वेन न विशेषणीयं, चक्षुरादि मान्त्यावयव्येवेति मन्तव्यं। 'नापीति, 'प्रत्यक्षं' प्रत्यक्षप्रमा, 'ज्ञानाजन्य इति, 'अनुभवपदं स्वरूप-कथनं सत्यस्मरणस्य ज्ञानजन्यत्वेनैवातिप्रसङ्गविरहात्। 'साक्षात्कारित्वं' साक्षात्कारित्वरूपजातिविशेषः। 'नियतव्यञ्जकेति अनुगतानति-प्रसक्तव्यञ्जकेत्यर्थः। 'सत्त्वे वा' अनुगतानतिप्रसक्तव्यञ्जकस्य सत्त्वे वा, 'लक्षणं' इतरभेदकं, 'व्यवहारनिमित्तं' साक्षात्कारपदप्रवृत्तिनिमित्तञ्च, 'किं जात्येति, साक्षात्कारित्वरूपयेति शेषः। 'साक्षात्कारित्वमिति, जातिविशेष इति शेषः। ननु तादृशजातौ मानाभाव इत्यत आह, 'चाक्षुषादिज्ञान इति। यद्यपि साक्षात्करोमीत्यनुव्यवसायस्य

---

(१) यत्र शरीराकाशसंयोगरूपलिङ्गेनानुमानं तत्र शरीराकाशसंयोगस्य प्रतीतिसाधनत्वमस्त्येवेति भावः।

(२) ज्ञायमानलिङ्गस्याहेतुत्वनयेऽपि साक्षात्पदस्य सांगत्यमाह वस्तुत इति।

(३) साक्षात्कारत्वस्य साक्षात्करोमीत्यनुव्यवसायसिद्धजातित्वात् साक्षात्कारसाधनशरीरसंयोगवदतीन्द्रियत्वमिन्द्रियत्वमिव व्यावर्तकत्वात् न साक्षात्पदस्य वैयर्थ्यशङ्केति भावः।

सिद्धेः । सत्त्वे वा तदेव लक्षणं व्यवहारनिमित्तञ्चास्तु किं जात्या । उच्यते । प्रत्यक्षस्य साक्षात्कारित्वं लक्षणं, चाक्षुषादिज्ञाने साक्षात्करोमीत्यनुगतबुद्धेर्बाधकं विना जातिविषयत्वात् । नचेन्द्रियजन्यत्वं तथा, अन्योन्याश्रयात् इन्द्रियस्यातीन्द्रियत्वाच्च । नच नियतव्य-

---

विषयिताविशेष एव विषयोऽस्तु किं जात्या, सुरभि चन्दनमित्यत्र सौरभं साक्षात्करोमीत्यनुव्यवसायवारणाय विषयिताविशेषस्यावश्यकत्वात् । नचैवमनुमितित्वस्याप्यसिद्ध्यापत्तिः अनुमिनोमीत्यनुव्यवसायस्य विधेयताख्यविषयिताविशेषविषयकत्वेनैवोपपत्तेर्वह्निमनुमिनोमीत्यनुव्यवसायवारणाय विषयिताविशेषस्यावश्यकत्वादिति वाच्यं । तादृशविषयिताविशेषस्य शाब्दबोधेऽप्यनुभवसिद्धतया अनुमितित्वरूपत्वासम्भवात् । तथाप्यनुव्यवसायसिद्धं साक्षात्कारत्वं लाघवाज्जातिरूपमेव न तु विषयिताविशेषः । तस्यैव जातिविशेषस्य यदंशे लौकिकसन्निकर्षजन्यत्वं ज्ञानस्य तदेव निरूपकं न त्वन्यदतो न सौरभं साक्षात्करोमीत्यनुव्यवसायः, विषयिताविशेषाभ्युपगमेऽपि कस्यचिदेव तादृशविषयितानिरूपकत्वं न तु सर्व्वस्येत्यवश्यं वाच्यत्वादिति भावः । 'तथा' अनुव्यवसायविषयः, 'अन्योन्याश्रयादिति. साक्षात्कारत्वस्य जातिरूपस्यानभ्युपगमे पूर्व्वोक्तेन्द्रियलक्षणघटकसाक्षात्कारत्वस्यापीन्द्रियजन्यज्ञानत्वरूपतया इन्द्रियजन्यज्ञानत्वज्ञानेऽन्योन्याश्रयादित्यर्थः । इन्द्रियज्ञानादेव इन्द्रियजन्यज्ञानत्वज्ञानं, तज्ज्ञाने च तद्घटितेन्द्रियत्वज्ञानमिति भावः । ननु स्यादेव इन्द्रियत्वमेतद्घटकं

ञ्जकाभावान्न जातिः, गोत्वादौ सास्नादेरिवाननुगतस्यापि चक्षुःकरणकानुभवत्वादेर्व्यञ्जकत्वात्। न च जातावनुगतव्यञ्जकनियमः, ज्ञानेच्छा-प्रयत्न-सुख-दुःखादेस्तदभावात्। प्रत्युत नियतव्यञ्जकसत्त्वे जात्यसिद्धिरेव। तत एवानुगतबुद्ध्युपपत्तेः। निर्विकल्प-

---

वाच्यमतमाह, 'इन्द्रियस्येति, तथाच व्यवसायानुपनीतस्य तस्यानुव्यवसायविषयता न स्यादिति भावः। 'नियतेति अनुगतानतिप्रसक्तेत्यर्थः, 'न जातिः' निरुक्तानुव्यवसायप्रकारीभूतो न जातिः, 'चक्षुःकरणकानुभवत्वादेरिति चाक्षुषत्वादिजातेरित्यर्थः। आदिपदाद्वाच्यत्वादिपरिग्रहः। एतेन तद्व्यञ्जकत्वं तल्लौकिकसाक्षात्कारजनकज्ञानविषयत्वं स्वविषययावल्लौकिकसाक्षात्कारविषयताकत्वं वा, आद्ये लाघवाच्चाक्षुषत्वादिविषयकज्ञानस्यैव साक्षात्त्वविषयकलौकिकसाक्षात्कारजनकतया चक्षुःकरणकानुभवत्वे तदसिद्धिः, द्वितीये चक्षुष्ट्वादेरतीन्द्रियतया तद्विषयकेलौकिकप्रत्यक्षाप्रसिद्धिरिति परास्तं। ननु सास्नादिकमपि सास्नात्वादिना अनुगतमेवेत्यत आह, 'नचेति न वेत्यर्थः, 'ज्ञानेच्छेति, तच्च निर्विकल्पकादिव्यावृत्त-तत्तज्ज्ञानादिव्यक्तेरेव व्यञ्जकत्वादिति भावः। 'तत एव' अनुगतव्यञ्जकत्वादेव। नन्वेवं साक्षात्करोमीत्यनुव्यवसायस्य साक्षात्त्वजातिव्यवस्थापकत्वे अतीन्द्रिये निर्विकल्पकादौ तन्न सिध्येत तच्चोक्तानुगतजात्यभावादित्याशङ्क्याह, 'निर्विकल्पकेति घट-घटत्वादिनिर्विकल्पकेत्यर्थः, 'योगिप्रत्यक्षं योगिनां मोक्षसाधनीभूतपरमतत्त्वसाक्षात्कारः, 'धर्मिग्राहकेति,

केश्वर-योगिप्रत्यक्षे च प्रत्यक्षत्वं धर्मिग्राहकमानसिद्धं। योगजधर्माजन्यजन्यस्वविषयकसविकल्पकाजन्यसामा-

---

इयं विशिष्टधीः विशेषणज्ञानजन्या विशिष्टधीत्वादनुमित्यादिवदि-त्याद्यविशिष्टप्रत्यक्षपक्षकानुमानान्निर्विकल्पकसाधकादेवानुमित्यादिवैधर्म्यसहकारेण निर्विकल्पकस्य साक्षात्कारत्वसिद्धिः। तथा क्षिति उपादानगोचरसाक्षात्कारजन्या कार्य्यत्वादित्यनुमानादीश्वरज्ञानसाधकादेव साक्षात्कारत्वरूपेण तत्सिद्धिः। तथा इयं मुक्तिस्तत्त्वसाक्षात्कारजन्या मुक्तित्वादित्यनुमानात्तत्त्वज्ञानसाधकात् साक्षात्कारत्वरूपेणैव तत्सिद्धिरिति भावः। नच साक्षात्कारत्वं न जातिः अनुमितित्वेन समं साङ्कर्य्यात् आंशिकत्वाच्च, पर्व्वतो वह्निमानित्यनुमित्यनन्तरं पर्व्वतः साक्षात्कृतो वह्निश्चानुमित इत्यनुभवात्तच पर्व्वतांशे साक्षात्त्वस्य वह्न्यंशे चानुमितित्वस्य सत्त्वात्तस्माद्विनिगमकाभावात् साक्षात्त्वमनुमितित्वमुभयमेवाखण्डविषयिताविशेष इति वाच्यं। धर्मिग्राहक-प्रमाणेन साक्षात्त्वानुमितित्वयोर्लाघवात् जातिरूपत्वे सिद्धे परामर्शमादाय तत्र पर्व्वतः साक्षात्कृत इत्यनुभव इतिकल्पनात्, यौगपद्यप्रत्ययस्यापि स्थूलकालमादाय सम्भवात्। नचैवं पर्व्वतमनुमिनोमीत्यनुव्यवसायापत्तिः, पर्व्वतोवह्निमान् इत्यनुमितौ पर्व्वतस्याविधेयतया तादृशानुव्यवसायविरहात् विधेयताख्यविषयताविशेषस्यैव तादृशानुव्यावसायविषयत्वात्। अनुमितित्वस्य विषयिताविशेषत्वाभ्युपगमेऽपि तस्यांशांशिभावत्वलक्षणस्वरूपसम्बन्धविशेषस्य वह्न्यादौ स्वीकर्त्तव्यत्वादिति दिक्। सोऽयं साक्षात्कारो द्विविधः लौकिकस्तदन्यश्च. तत्राद्यस्य

न्यलक्षणप्रत्यासत्त्यजन्य-जन्यप्रत्यक्षस्य लक्षणमनागतगोचरसाक्षात्कारहेतुप्रत्यासत्त्यजन्यजन्यसाक्षात्कारत्वं ।

लक्ष्यतावच्छेदकं लक्षणमाह, 'योगजेत्यादिना, 'स्वपदं यदीयलौकिकप्रत्यक्षं लक्षणीयं तत्परं, तथाच योगजधर्म्माजन्य-जन्यतत्तद्विषयकसविकल्पकाजन्यतत्तदीयसामान्यप्रत्यासत्त्यजन्य-जन्यतत्तत्साक्षात्कारत्वं लक्ष्यतावच्छेदकमितिभावः। अत्र योगजन्यात्मातततत्प्रत्यक्षेऽतिव्याप्तिवारणाय 'योगजधर्म्माजन्येति। प्राचां नये साक्षात्कारत्वनिरूपितविषयिताव्याप्तिप्रत्यक्षसामग्र्या योगजधर्म्मजन्यप्रत्यक्षप्रतिबन्धकतया तज्जन्यप्रत्यक्षस्य सर्व्वांश एवालौकिकत्वनियमाद्योगजधर्म्म-तल्लौकिकसन्निकर्षोभयजन्यतल्लौकिकप्रत्यक्षे नाव्याप्तिः। ज्ञानलक्षणसन्निकर्षजन्य-तदलौकिकप्रत्यक्षेऽतिव्याप्तिवारणाय 'जन्यतत्तद्विषयकसविकल्पकाजन्येति, सुरभि चन्दनमित्याद्युपनीतभानस्य चन्दनाद्यंशे लौकिकप्रत्यक्षत्वसम्पादनाय तत्तद्विषयकत्वं सविकल्पकविशेषणं, जन्यतत्तद्विषयकसविकल्पकजन्यत्वञ्च जन्यतत्तद्विषयकसविकल्पकत्वावच्छिन्नकारणताप्रतियोगिक-कार्य्यताव्याप्तित्वं, तेन विशिष्टवैशिष्टबुद्धौ विशेषणतावच्छेदकप्रकारकज्ञानत्वेन हेतुत्वेऽपि तादृशतल्लौकिकप्रत्यक्षे नाव्याप्तिः, न वा धारावाहिकतल्लौकिकप्रत्यक्षे विशेषणज्ञानविधया पूर्व्वविशिष्टज्ञानजन्ये प्रमेयत्वसामान्यलक्षणाजन्य-वस्तुमात्रविषयकज्ञानानुव्यवसाये विषयविधया सर्व्वविषयसविकल्पकात्मकव्यवसायजन्ये चातिव्याप्तिः, तत्र तद्विषयकसविकल्पकत्वेनाहेतुत्वात्। तद्विषयकसविकल्पकत्वञ्च सांसर्गिकविषयितानिरूपकविषयितासम्बन्धेन तद्वज्ज्ञानत्वं, तादृशी च विष-

अन्ये तु सामान्यज्ञान-प्रत्यासत्त्योरिन्द्रियसम्बद्धविशेषणतान्तर्भावात् तज्जन्यं प्रत्यक्षं संग्राह्यमेवेति। यद्वा विषयत्वेन स्वविशेष्यजन्यं ज्ञानं जन्यप्रत्यक्षं। आत्म-

---

यिता प्रकारिता विशेष्यिता च, ज्ञानलक्षणप्रत्यासत्तेः तादृशसविकल्पकत्वेनैव हेतुत्वात् "नित्यस्य स्वरूपयोग्यस्येति नियमात्। फलानुपहितभगवज्ज्ञानवारणाय जन्यत्वस्य कारणतावच्छेदके प्रवेशस्यावश्यकत्वादप्रसिद्धिवारणाय 'जन्यपदं, तत्रालौकिकप्रत्यक्षसामग्र्याः प्रतिबन्धकतया न तत्रालौकिकसन्निकर्ष-तत्सविकल्पकोभयाभ्यां लौकिकालौकिकोभयरूपमेकन्तत्प्रत्यक्षं जन्यत इति न तत्राव्याप्तिः। ननु तथापि विनश्यदवस्थेन्द्रियालोकसंयोगजन्य-घट-घटत्वादिनिर्विकल्पकानन्तरजातजातित्वादिप्रकारकघटत्वाद्युपस्थितितो विशेष्ये विशेषणमिति न्यायेन स्वरूपतो घटत्वविशिष्टघटविशेषणकभूतलादिप्रत्यक्षवारणाय स्वरूपतो जात्युपनीतभाने स्वरूपतस्तत्प्रकारकज्ञानत्वेनैव प्रत्यासत्तित्वमित्युपेयते तदा स्वरूपतो घटत्वादिप्रकारकोपनीतभाने अतिव्याप्तिरेव यथोक्तसविकल्पकत्वेनाहेतुत्वादिति चेत्, तर्हि संसर्गविशेषावच्छिन्नत्वाविशेषितसांसर्गिकविषयितानिरूपितविषयिताभावसम्बन्धेन तदवच्छिन्ना या ज्ञाननिष्ठकारणता तन्निरूपितजन्यत्वं तद्विषयकसविकल्पकजन्यपदेन विवक्षणीयं, स्वरूपतो घटत्वादिप्रकारकोपनीतभाने च निरवच्छिन्नप्रकारितासम्बन्धेन घटत्वादिमज्ज्ञानत्वेन हेतुतया तत्रापि तादृशकारणतानिरूपितजन्यताश्रयत्वात् विशिष्टवैशिष्ट्यज्ञाने च यादृशसम्बन्धेन विशेषणतावच्छेद-

विशेष्यकानुमिति-शाब्द-स्मृतिषु विशेष्यत्वेन तस्य न हेतुत्वं। विशेष्यं विनापि तासामुत्पत्तेः। किन्तु समवायित्वेन। यद्वा इन्द्रियजन्यं ज्ञानं जन्यप्रत्यक्षं,

---

कीभूय भासते तत्सम्बन्धावच्छिन्नप्रकारितासम्बन्धेन तद्वज्ज्ञानत्वेनैव हेतुत्वं, उपनीतभाने तु नायं नियमः। अवधारणार्थकमात्रपदोपादानाद्विशेषणज्ञानविधया कारणत्वस्य व्यवच्छेदः, तत्र निर्विकल्पकविषयिताया अपि सम्बन्धविधया कारणतावच्छेदके प्रवेशः, सामान्यप्रत्यासत्तिजन्यतन्मुख्यविशेष्यकप्रत्यक्षेऽतिव्याप्तिवारणाय 'सामान्यप्रत्यासत्त्यजन्येति, तदीयसामान्यप्रत्यासत्तिजन्यत्वञ्च तद्वृत्तिधर्मप्रकारकज्ञानत्वावच्छिन्नकारणतानिरूपितकार्य्यताशालित्वं, तेन धारावाहिकघटत्वादिविशिष्टघटादिलौकिकप्रत्यक्षे विशेषणज्ञानविधया घटत्वादिसामान्यज्ञानजन्ये नाव्याप्तिः। सामान्यलक्षणप्रत्यासत्तेश्च तेनैव रूपेण हेतुत्वं, तदलौकिकमुख्यविशेष्यताशालिप्रत्यक्षे तद्वृत्तिधर्मप्रकारकज्ञानत्वेनैव हेतुत्वोपगमात् । तदलौकिकप्रत्यक्षं प्रति तल्लौकिकप्रत्यक्षसामग्र्याः प्रतिबन्धकतया तल्लौकिकसन्निकर्ष-तदीयसामान्यलक्षणसन्निकर्षोभयाभ्यां लौकिकालौकिकोभयरूपमेकं प्रत्यक्षं न जन्यत इति न तत्राव्याप्तिः। फलीभूतप्रत्यक्षस्यैव लक्ष्यतया भगवतः प्रत्यक्षेऽतिव्याप्तिवारणाय जन्यत्वं तत्तद्विषयकप्रत्यक्षविशेषणं। तत्तद्विषयकत्वञ्च सांसर्गिकविषयतातिरिक्ततत्तद्विषयिताशालित्वं, तेन वैशिष्ट्यांशे लौकिकालौकिकबहिर्भूतत्वेऽपि न क्षतिः। नच्वेवं यत्र संसर्गेन समं लौकिक सन्निकर्षो वर्त्तते तत्रापि संसर्गांशे लौकिकप्रत्यक्षत्व

इन्द्रियत्वेन जनकत्वं विवक्षितं। अन्यप्रत्यक्षमात्रे इन्द्रियत्वेन चक्षुरादीनां कारणता, अनुगतहेतुं विना

न स्यादिति वाच्यं। सांसर्गिकविषयतातिरिक्तविषयताया लौकिकसन्निकर्षजन्यताघटकतया तत्र संसर्गस्य विधिविषयत्वाभ्युपगमात्। वक्ष्यमाणलौकिकत्वं तत्रापीष्यत एवेत्यन्ये। न चाभावलौकिकप्रत्यक्षे प्रतियोगित्वमनुपस्थितमेव प्रतियोग्यंशे प्रकारीभूय भासत इति मये तदंशे तस्य लौकिकप्रत्यक्षत्वापत्तिरिति वाच्यं। प्रतियोगित्वस्याभावात्मकत्वे पदार्थान्तररूपत्वे वा तदंशे लौकिकत्वस्य तत्रेष्टापत्तेः। अतिरिक्तत्वमयेऽपि निरूपकतासम्बन्धेन तस्याभावनिष्ठतया अभावमादायैव तत्रेन्द्रियसम्बद्धविशेषणतात्मकलौकिकसन्निकर्षसम्भवात्। प्रतियोग्यात्मकत्वे तु प्रतियोग्यंश इव तत्राप्यलौकिकत्वमेव प्रतियोग्युपनयस्यैव तद्विषयकसविकल्पकत्वादिति न काप्यनुपपत्तिः। 'अनागतेति, 'अन्यसाक्षात्कारत्वमिति, अत्र योगजधर्म्मादिजन्य-तदलौकिकप्रत्यक्षे अतिव्याप्तिवारणाय 'अजन्यान्तं, अनागतत्वञ्च स्वफलीभूतज्ञानकालीनप्रागभावप्रतियोगित्वं, तथाच स्वफलकालीनप्रागभावप्रतियोगिविषयकसाक्षात्कारस्वरूपयोग्यप्रत्यासत्त्यजन्यत्वे सति अन्यतत्तद्विषयकसाक्षात्कारत्वं लक्षणमिति फलितं। तादृशप्रत्यासत्त्यजन्यत्वञ्च तत्तद्विषयत्वांशे तादृशप्रत्यासत्त्यजन्यत्वं तादृशप्रत्यासत्तिनिरूपिततत्तद्विषयत्वातिरिक्तविषयत्वानवच्छिन्न-प्रत्यक्षमात्रवृत्तिजन्यतानाश्रयत्वमिति यावत्, तेनांशिकालौकिकप्रत्यक्षात्मके तल्लौकिकप्रत्यक्षे नाव्याप्तिः, योगजधर्म्मनिरूपितजन्यतायाः संप्रदाय

अनुगतकार्य्यस्याकस्मिकतापत्तेः। स्मृत्यनुमित्यादौ च मनसो नेन्द्रियत्वेन हेतुत्वं किन्तु मनस्त्वेन। अन्यथा स्मृत्यादेः साक्षात्कारत्वापत्तेः। इन्द्रियत्वञ्च स्मृत्यज-

---

निषेधद्वयगर्भता, जातिविशेषस्यैव तज्जन्यतावच्छेदकत्वात् अदृष्टत्वावच्छिन्नकारणताप्रतियोगिक-कार्य्यत्वावच्छिन्नजन्यतायाः तज्ज्ञानस्य विशेषणज्ञानविधया जन्यतायाश्च वारणाय प्रत्यक्षमात्रवृत्तित्वं जन्यताविशेषणं। न च तथापि परमाण्वादिनित्यगोचरोपनीतभानेऽतिव्याप्तिः तदुपनयस्यानागतगोचरसाक्षात्कारस्वरूपायोग्यत्वात्, जातित्वादिनित्यमात्रवृत्तिसामान्यप्रत्यासत्तिजन्यप्रत्यक्षेऽतिव्याप्तिश्च तदलौकिकमुख्यविशेष्यताशालिप्रत्यक्षे तद्वृत्तिधर्म्मप्रकारज्ञानत्वेन हेतुतया तत्रापि तादृशसाक्षात्कारस्वरूपयोग्यत्वविरहादिति वाच्यं। तादृशसाक्षात्कारस्वरूपयोग्यप्रत्यासत्तिपदेन तादृशसाक्षात्कारस्वरूपयोग्यवृत्तिप्रत्यासत्तिविभाजकोपाध्याश्रयस्य विवक्षितत्वात्, ज्ञानप्रत्यासत्तित्वादिकञ्च तथैति दिक्।

'इन्द्रियसम्बद्धविशेषणतान्तर्भावादिति, स्वजन्यज्ञानप्रकारत्वरूपेन्द्रियसम्बन्धाश्रयस्य सामान्यस्य धर्म्मिताख्यविशेषणतायास्तदाश्रयनिष्ठायाः सामान्यप्रत्यासत्तित्वेन सामान्यलक्षणायास्तदन्तर्भावः, मनःसंयुक्तसमवेतत्वरूपेन्द्रियसम्बन्धाश्रयस्य ज्ञानस्य विषयतारूपविशेषणताया ज्ञानप्रत्यासत्तित्वाज्ज्ञानलक्षणायास्तदन्तर्भाव इति भावः। 'संग्राह्यमेवेति, तथा च योगजधर्म्माजन्यत्वमात्रं लक्ष्यतावच्छेदके प्रवेशनीयमिति भावः।

नकज्ञानहेतुमनःसंयोगाश्रयत्वं, प्राण-शरीरात्मानश्च स्मृतिजनकमनःसंयोगवन्तः। शब्देतरोद्भूतविशेषगुणानाश्रयत्वे सति ज्ञानहेतुमनःसंयोगाश्रयत्वं वा।

लौकिकप्रत्यक्षस्य लक्षणान्तरमाह, 'यद्वेति, विशेष्यपदं विषयमात्रपरं, स्वपदस्थानादेयं, तथाच विषयत्वेन विषयजन्यं ज्ञानं लौकिकप्रत्यक्षमित्यर्थः। एतेन लौकिकप्रत्यक्षे विशेष्यत्वेन न हेतुता योग्यवस्तुमात्रस्यैव लौकिकप्रत्यक्षविशेष्यत्वे मानाभावात् तथाचासम्भवः स्वत्वघटितत्वादननुगमश्चेति निरस्तं। अत्रात्मविषयकानुमित्यादावतिव्याप्तिवारणाय 'विषयत्वेनेति, विषयत्वञ्च लौकिकविषयतासम्बन्धेन साक्षात्कारवत्त्वं, तेन गुरुत्वादेरयोग्यस्य न लौकिकप्रत्यक्षमिति भावः।

केचित्तु तज्जन्यप्रत्यक्षसामान्यमेव प्रत्यक्षं तथाच विषयत्वेन विषयजन्यं ज्ञानं जन्यप्रत्यक्षमित्यर्थः। नचैवं सर्व्वांशे अलौकिकप्रत्यक्षस्य विषयाजन्यत्वात् तत्राव्याप्तिरिति वाच्यं। तस्याप्यात्मांशे लौकिकत्वे बाधकाभावेन विषयजन्यत्वात् प्रत्यक्षमात्रस्यैव यत्किञ्चिद्विषयांशे लौकिकत्वनियमात्। अस्तु वा विषयत्वेन विषयजन्यज्ञानवृत्त्यनुभवत्वाव्यापकजातिमत्त्वे सति जन्यत्वं लक्षणार्थ इत्याहुः।

'विषयत्वेनेत्यस्य प्रयोजनं दर्शयति, 'आत्मविशेष्यकेति आत्मविषयकेत्यर्थः, 'विशेष्यत्वेन' विषयत्वेन, 'तस्य' आत्मनः, 'विशेष्यं विनापि' विषयविरहेऽपि, अतीतानागतविषयस्थल इति शेषः। 'तासां' अनुमित्यादीनां, 'समवायित्वेन' जन्यज्ञानत्वावच्छिन्नं प्रति समवायिकारणतावच्छेदको योधर्म्मस्तेन आत्मत्वेनेति यावत्।

ज्ञानाकरणकं ज्ञानमिति तु वयं। विशिष्टप्रत्यक्षे च विशेषणज्ञानं न करणं व्यापाराभावात्। विशिष्टवै-

---

जन्यप्रत्यक्षसामान्यस्य लक्षणमाह, 'यद्वेति, अनुमित्यादेरपि मनोरूपेन्द्रियजन्यत्वादतिव्याप्तेराह, 'इन्द्रियत्वेनेति, 'अन्यथेति स्मृत्यादावपि इन्द्रियत्वेन मनसो हेतुत्व इत्यर्थः, इन्द्रियत्वेनेन्द्रियजन्यस्य साक्षात्कारत्वनियामकत्वादिति भावः। ननु इन्द्रियत्वं जन्यसाक्षात्कारत्वावच्छिन्नकार्य्यता-प्रतियोगिक-कारणताश्रयत्वं, कालादिवारणायावच्छिन्नान्तं, तच्च न जन्यसाक्षात्कारजनकतावच्छेदकमात्माश्रयादित्यत आह, 'इन्द्रियत्वञ्चेति, 'स्मृत्यजनकेति संयोगविशेषणं, तथाच स्मृत्यजनको यो ज्ञानहेतुमनःसंयोगस्तदाश्रयत्वमित्यर्थः। आत्म-मनःसंयोगवच्चक्षुरादि-मनःसंयोगस्यापि चाक्षुषादिप्रत्यक्षहेतुत्वाच्चक्षुरादौ लक्षणसमन्वयः। शरीर-मनःसंयोगमादाय शरीरे आत्म-मनःसंयोगमादायात्मन्यतिव्याप्तिवारणाय स्मृत्यजनकत्वं संयोगविशेषणं, शरीरात्म-मनःसंयोगस्य न स्मृत्यजनकः तस्य ज्ञानमात्रजनकत्वात्। स्मृत्यजनकत्वञ्च स्मृतिस्वरूपायोग्यत्वं, तेनानुभवमात्रोपधायकात्म-मनोयोगव्यक्तिमादाय नात्मन्यतिव्याप्तिताद्वस्थ्यं। यद्यपि चक्षुरादि-मनःसंयोगमादायैव लक्षणसमन्वयः संयोगस्य द्विष्ठत्वात्। मनोघटसंयोगादिमादाय घटादावतिव्याप्तिवारणाय 'ज्ञानहेत्विति संयोगविशेषणं, मनोघटादिसंयोगस्यापि विभागादिहेतुत्वाज्ज्ञानपदं। चक्षुरादिसंयोगमादाय विषये घटादावतिव्याप्तिवारणाय मनःपदं। मनःसमवेततावृत्तिद्रव्यत्वादिकमादाय घटादावतिप्रसङ्ग-

शिष्टप्रत्यक्षे च विशेषणज्ञानं हेतुर्न तु विशेषणविशेषणधीरपि विशेषणधीद्वारा करणं मानाभावात्।

वारणाय संयोगत्वेन प्रवेशः। न च यत्र चक्षुषि मनःसंयोगो न जातस्तत्राव्याप्तिरिति वाच्यं। तस्यालक्ष्यत्वात्। न च स्वप्नवहनाड़ी-मनःसंयोगमादाय स्वप्नवहनाड्यामतिप्रसङ्गः तस्यापि स्वप्नजनकत्वेन ज्ञानहेतुत्वादिति वाच्यं। तस्य स्वप्नानुभववत् स्वप्नकालीनस्मृतावपि जनकत्वात्। गोलक-मनःसंयोगस्य न ज्ञानहेतुर्मानाभावादतो गोलके नातिव्याप्तिः। यदि च गोलकावच्छेदेनेन्द्रिय-मनःसंयोगवदिन्द्रियावच्छेदेन गोलक-मनःसंयोगोऽपि ज्ञानहेतुर्विनिगमकाभावादिति विभाव्यते तदापि शरीर-मनःसंयोगत्वेन गोलक-मनःसंयोगस्यापि, स्मृतिस्वरूपयोग्यत्वादेव नातिव्याप्तिः स्वाश्रयत्वरूपस्य शरीरत्वस्य गोलकेऽपि सत्त्वात्, इन्द्रियावयव-मनःसंयोगस्य न ज्ञानजनकत्वेनेन्द्रियावयवे नातिव्याप्तिः। नच तथापि स्वसमवेतज्ञानाद्यभावसाक्षात्कारजनकघट-मनःसंयोगवति कालादावतिप्रसङ्ग इति वाच्यं। तस्य सन्निकर्षघटकतया कारणतावच्छेदकत्वेऽपि कारणत्वे मानाभावात्, भावमात्रविषयकत्वेन वा ज्ञानं विशेषणीयं। ननु तथापि त्वच्यव्याप्तिः त्वङ्मनोयोगस्यापि ज्ञानमात्रहेतुतया स्मृत्यजनकत्वविरहात्। न च त्वङ्मनोयोगस्य जन्यज्ञानमात्रहेतुत्वे मानाभाव इति वाच्यं। तस्य जन्यज्ञानमात्राहेतुत्वे सुष्वापोत्पादद्वितीयादिक्षणेऽपि ज्ञानोत्पत्त्यापत्तेः आत्मनोविभुतया पुरीतति-मनःसंयोगात्मकसुषुप्त्यापत्तिसमये पुरीतत्यवच्छेदेनात्ममनोयोगे तादृशवैजात्याभा-

प्रत्यभिज्ञायान्तु तत्तास्मृतिः कारणं न तु संस्कारद्वारा अनुभवः कारणं, तस्याः संस्कारजन्यत्वे स्मृतित्वापत्तेः

वाच ज्ञानोत्पत्तिरित्यपि निरस्तं। आत्म-मनःसंयोगस्यासमवायिकारणस्य कार्य्यतावच्छेदके न जन्यज्ञानत्वं, किन्तु लाघवात् ज्ञानेच्छादिकफलसाधारणं जन्यात्मविशेषगुणत्वं तथाच सुषुप्तिकालेऽपि श्वासप्रश्वासहेतुजीवनयोनियत्नान्यथानुपपत्त्या विजातीयात्म-मनःसंयोगस्यावश्यकत्वात् त्वङ्मनःसंयोगस्य तदा नास्ति। यदा मनस्त्वचमपि परिहृत्य पुरीततिमनुविशते तदा सुषुप्तिरित्यभिधानात्। न च सुष्वापदशायां ज्ञानोत्पादवारणाय प्राण-मनःसंयोग एव हेतुरुपेयते न तु त्वङ्मनःसंयोग इति वाच्यं। त्वक्त्व-प्राणत्वयोरुभयोरेव जातिरूपतया विनिगमनाविरहेण त्वङ्मनोयोगस्यापि हेतुत्वस्य दुर्वारत्वादिति चेत्। न। सुष्वापदशायां हि कीदृशं ज्ञानमापाद्यते, न तावत् चाक्षुषादि चक्षुरादिमनःसंयोगविरहादेव तदानीं तदनुत्पत्तेः। नाप्यनुमित्यादि परामर्शादीनामभावात्। नापि स्मृतिरुद्बोधकस्य फलबलकल्प्यत्वात्। न चात्म-मनःसंयोगसत्त्वादात्मादिमानसापत्तिरिति वाच्यं। ज्ञानाद्यात्मकविशेषगुणाविषयकात्मादिमानसस्यालीकतया सुष्वापोत्पादकाले ज्ञानादिप्रत्यक्षसामग्रीविरहादेव सुष्वापानन्तरमात्मादिमानसानुत्पत्तेः, सुष्वापप्रयोजकमनःक्रियोत्पत्तिकाले तादृशमनःपूर्व्वदेशविभागोत्पत्तिकाले वा जातस्य ज्ञानादेः सुष्वापोत्पादकाले अवस्थानासम्भवात्। न च मनःपूर्व्वदेशे विभागकालोत्पन्नस्यापेक्षाबुद्ध्यात्मकज्ञानस्य सुष्वापोत्पादकाले अवस्थान-

स्मृतित्वे लाघवेन संस्कारजन्यत्वस्य तन्त्रत्वात् तद्धेतुत्वेनैव तत्सिद्धेश्च।

सम्भव इति वाच्यं। तदानीमपेक्षाबुद्ध्यात्मकज्ञानोत्पादे मानाभावात् अपेक्षाबुद्धेरपि क्षणत्रयावस्थायित्वे मानाभावाच्च। न च सुषुप्तिप्रयोजकमनःपूर्व्वसंयोगनाशकालोत्पन्नज्ञानादेः सुषुप्त्युत्पादक्षणावस्थानसम्भव इति वाच्यं। असमवायिकारणस्य कार्य्यसहभावेन हेतुतया मनःपूर्व्वसंयोगनाशदशायां ज्ञानाद्युत्पादासम्भवात्। न च यत्रासमवायिकारणस्य नाशात् कार्य्यविनाशस्तत्रैव कार्य्यसहभावेन हेतुतया आत्म-मनःसंयोगस्य कार्य्यसहभावेन हेतुत्वे मानाभाव इति वाच्यं। लक्षणोयोगस्यातिरिक्तकारणत्वकल्पनापेक्षया आत्म-मनःसंयोगस्यैव आत्म-मनोयोगत्वेन कार्य्यसहवर्त्तितया हेतुत्वमात्रकल्पनाया लघुत्वात्। न चात्म-मनोयोगत्वेन कार्य्यसहवर्त्तितया हेतुत्वेऽपि यत्र मनःक्रियया न पुरीतति-मनःसंयोगात्मकसुषुप्त्युत्पादः किन्तु पूर्व्वदेशसंयुक्त एव मनसि पुरीततिसंयोगरूपः सुषुप्तिस्तत्र सुषुप्त्युत्पत्तिप्राक्काले ज्ञानाद्युत्पत्तिसम्भव इति वाच्यं। पुरीततिक्रियामात्राधीनपुरीतति-मनःसंयोगस्य सुषुप्तित्वविरहात्। यदा त्वचमपि परित्यज्य मनः पुरीततिमनुविशते तदा सुषुप्तिरित्यभिधानात्।

केचित्तु स्मृत्यजनकत्वं समवायघटितसामानाधिकरण्यप्रत्यासत्त्या स्मृतिजनकं यत्तदन्यत्वं स्मृत्यसमानाधिकरणत्वमिति यावत्। तथाच स्मृत्यसमानाधिकरणज्ञानजनकमनःसंयोगाश्रयत्वं फलितमतो नाव्याप्तिः। शरीर-मनःसंयोगादिस्तु न ज्ञानजनक इति शरीरे नातिव्याप्तिरित्याहुः। तदसत्। आत्म-शरीरेत्याद्युपिमग्रन्थासङ्गतेः।

प्राभाकरास्तु साक्षात्त्वीः प्रत्यक्षं, साक्षात्त्वञ्च न जातिः नियतव्यञ्जकाभावात्। नापि सविकल्पका-

---

अन्ये तु सुषुप्त्यापानन्तरं ज्ञानोत्पादवारणाय अन्यज्ञानत्वावच्छिन्नं प्रत्यात्म-मनःसंयोगस्यैव सुषुप्तिकालीनमनःसंयोगव्यावृत्तवैजात्येन हेतुत्वमुपेयते न तु त्वङ्मनोयोगस्य। न च विनिगमकाभावात् त्वङ्मनोयोगस्यापि वैजात्येन हेतुत्वं दुर्वारं ज्ञानेच्छादिसाधारणजन्यत्वे विशेषगुणत्वावच्छिन्नं प्रत्यात्म-मनःसंयोगस्य पृथक् समवायादिसम्बन्धेन कारणतायास्तवाप्यावश्यकत्वादिति वाच्य। आत्म-मनःसंयोगस्य वैजात्येन हेतुत्वे समवायस्य प्रत्यासत्तितया प्रत्यासत्तिलाघवात् त्वङ्मनोयोगस्य हेतुत्वे अवच्छेदकत्वस्यैव प्रत्यासत्तितया गौरवात् चर्ममनःसंयोगजन्यतावच्छेदकवैजात्यद्वयस्याधिकस्य कल्पनापत्त्या गौरवापत्तेश्चेत्याहुः।

मिश्रास्तु सुषुप्त्यापोत्तरं ज्ञानोत्पत्तिवारणाय चर्म-मनःसंयोग एव अन्यज्ञानसामान्ये हेतुरुपेयते न तु त्वङ्मनःसंयोगः। न च विनिगमनाविरहः, अन्यज्ञानसामान्ये त्वङ्मनोयोगस्य हेतुत्वे रसादिसाक्षात्कारकाले त्वचा द्रव्यसाक्षात्कारापत्तेः सामान्यसामग्रीतया त्वङ्मनोयोगस्यावश्यकत्वात्, रसादिसाक्षात्कारसामग्र्याः प्रतिबन्धकत्वोपगमे च गौरवादित्याहुः। तदसत्। रसादिसाक्षात्कारकाले द्रव्येण समं त्वक्सन्निकर्षे मानाभावेन तदभावादेव त्वचा द्रव्यसाक्षात्कारानुपपत्तेः। उक्तक्रमेणैव सुषुप्तिकाले ज्ञानानुत्पादसम्भवेन चर्म-मनःसंयोगस्यापि अन्यज्ञानमात्रहेतुत्वे मानाभावाच्च।

नपेक्ष्यज्ञानत्वं, प्रत्यभिज्ञा-सादृश्य-द्वित्वादिप्रत्यक्षाव्यापनात्। किन्तु यज्ज्ञानं यद्विषयत्वे सविकल्पकाजन्यं

केचित्तु सुषुप्त्युत्तरं ज्ञानोत्पत्तिवारणाय शरीर-मनःसंयोग एव जन्यज्ञानसामान्यहेतुरुपेयते न तु त्वङ्मनःसंयोगः शरीरस्य त्वग्व्याप्यतया सुषुप्तिदशायां त्वङ्मनःसंयोगस्यावश्यसत्त्वात्। न च शरीरत्वमपेक्ष्य(१) त्वक्त्वस्य जातिरूपतया लाघवेन त्वङ्मनः-संयोग एव हेतुरुचित इति वाच्यं। शरीर-मनःसंयोगस्य हि न शरीर-मनः-संयोगत्वेन हेतुत्वं येन शरीरस्य प्रवेशः, अपि तु शरीरनिष्ठतया मनः-संयोगत्वेन समवायावच्छेदकत्वघटितसामानाधिकरण्यं प्रत्यासत्तिः कारणदिशि समवायः, कार्य्यदिश्यवच्छेदकत्वं। यद्वा संयोगसम्बन्धेन शरीरनिष्ठतया मनस्त्वेनैव हेतुत्वं कार्य्यतावच्छेदकसम्बन्धस्यावच्छेदकत्वं त्वङ्मनःसंयोगस्य हेतुत्वे च त्वक्त्व-संयोगत्वयोरवच्छेदककोटौ प्रवेशावश्यकतया गौरवादित्याहुः। तदसत्। मनःसंयोगत्वेन शरीर-मनःसंयोगस्य जन्यज्ञानसामान्यहेतुत्वे चक्षुरादि-मनःसंयोगस्यापि स्मृतिरूपयोग्यत्वादिन्द्रियव्यवस्थाया अभावापत्तेः। सुषुप्त्युत्तरं ज्ञानोत्पादप्रसङ्गस्योपक्रमेणैव वारणसम्भवादतिरिक्तज्ञानोत्पादस्य चोपक्रमेणापादयितुमशक्यत्वात् तथा च त्वङ्मनःसंयोगस्य स्वत्वजनकत्वमस्त्येव क्व त्वचव्याप्तिरिति प्राहुः। तदप्यसत्। आत्मादिमानसस्याप्युपक्रमेणापादयितुमशक्यतया मानसत्वावच्छिन्नं प्रत्यपि त्वङ्मनोयोगस्य हेतुत्वे मानाभावादिति दिक्।

---

(१) शरीरत्वस्य पृथिवीत्वादिना साङ्कर्य्यात् न जातित्वमपि तु चेष्टाश्रयत्वरूपत्वमेव।

तत् तत्र साक्षात्कारः, मिति-मातृप्रकाशे च सर्वमेव ज्ञानं प्रत्यक्षं ज्ञानाजन्यत्वात्। जातावनुगतधीरपि

स्मृत्यजनकत्वविशेषणस्य व्यावृत्तिं फलतो दर्शयति, 'प्राणेति, अत्र प्राणेत्यभ्युपगमवादेन, स्वीयप्राण-मनः-संयोगकारणताया अन्यत्र निराकृतत्वात्। 'शब्देतरेति शब्देतरो य उद्भूतविशेषगुणस्तदनाश्रयत्वे सति ज्ञानहेतुमनःसंयोगाश्रयत्वमित्यर्थः। शरीरात्मादिवारणाय सत्यन्तं, चक्षुरादेरप्यनुद्भूतरूपादिमत्त्वादव्याप्तिवारणाय 'उद्भूतेति, उद्भूतत्वं रूप-रस-गन्ध-स्पर्शमात्रवृत्त्यनुद्भूतत्वाख्यजात्यभावकूटः, तद्वांश्च ज्ञानादिरपीति नात्मन्यतिव्याप्तिः। अतएव तादृशोद्भूतत्ववान् परिमाणादिरपीत्यसम्भववारणाय विशेषपदं। तादृशोद्भूतत्वं शब्देऽपीत्यतः शब्दमादाय श्रोत्रेऽव्याप्तिवारणाय 'शब्देतरेति। कालादावतिव्याप्तिवारणाय विशेष्यदलं। इन्द्रियावयवार्थसन्निकर्षोऽपि प्रत्यक्षहेतुरिति इन्द्रियावयवेऽतिव्याप्तिवारणाय 'मनःपदं, इन्द्रियावयव-मनःसंयोगस्य न ज्ञानहेतुर्मानाभावात्। दिक्कालनिष्ठोद्भूतरूपाभावप्रत्यक्षहेतुचक्षुःसंयोगवतोस्तयोर्वारणाय मनःपदमित्यपि कश्चित्। न चानुद्भूतस्पर्शवति वायवीयशरीरे शरीर-मनःसंयोगमादायातिव्याप्तिरिति वाच्यं। तादृशवायवीयशरीरे मानाभावादिति भावः।

केचित्तु प्रत्यक्षत्वसाक्षात्त्वाख्यजात्यवच्छिन्नकार्य्यताप्रतियोगिककारणताश्रयत्वमिन्द्रियत्वं चाक्षुषत्वाद्यवच्छिन्नं प्रति चक्षुरादिना हेतुत्वात् सर्व्वंच लक्षणमसम्भव इत्याहुः। तदसत्। मनस्त्वव्याप्तैः मानसज्ञानत्वावच्छिन्नं प्रत्येव मनसो हेतुतया मानसत्वस्य तत्कार्य्य-

प्रत्यक्षा जाति-व्यक्तिनिर्विकल्पकजन्यत्वात्। साहश्यादिविशिष्टवैशिष्ट्यप्रत्यक्षे च न विशेषणज्ञानं हेतुः

तावच्छेदकत्वे मानाभावात्। न च मानसत्वस्य कार्य्यमात्रवृत्तिजातितया कार्य्यतावच्छेदकत्वावश्यकतया मनस एव तदवच्छिन्नं प्रति हेतुत्वमिति वाच्यं। तथा सति विनिगमनाविरहेणात्मत्वेनापि हेतुतया आत्मन्यतिव्याप्तेरिति दिक्।

नित्यानित्यसकलप्रत्यक्षसाधारणलक्षणमाह, 'ज्ञानेति, प्रत्यक्षे चक्षुरादिकमेव करणं न तु ज्ञानं अनुमित्यादौ च लिङ्गादिज्ञानमेव करणमिति भावः। कारणत्वमपहाय करणत्वपर्य्यन्तानुधावनस्य प्रयोजनं फलतोदर्शयति, 'विशिष्टप्रत्यक्षे चेति, तथाच करणत्वपर्य्यन्तस्याप्रवेशे विशिष्टप्रत्यक्षेऽव्याप्तिः स्यादिति हृदयं। ननु किमिदं ज्ञानाकरणकत्वं, न तावज्ज्ञानजन्यत्वे सति ज्ञानजन्यजन्यो यस्तद्भिन्नत्वं, अन्यप्रत्यक्षमात्रस्यैव भगवज्ज्ञानजन्यतया तज्जन्यसन्निकर्षादिजन्यतया चाव्याप्तेः धारावाहिकविशिष्टप्रत्यक्षे क्रमोत्पन्नसौरभज्ञानदयानन्तरोत्पन्नसुरभिचन्दनमित्युपनीतप्रत्यक्षे चाव्याप्तेस्तत्र विशेषणज्ञानविधया उपनयविधया च प्रथम-द्वितीयज्ञानयोरुभयोरेव जनकत्वादिति। मैवं। स्वावच्छिन्नकार्य्यताप्रतियोगिक-कारणताश्रयज्ञानजन्यमात्रवृत्तिधर्मावच्छिन्नकारणताप्रतियोगिक-कार्य्यतावच्छेदकं यत्तद्भिन्नत्वस्य तत्त्वात्। तादृशकार्य्यतावच्छेदकञ्च धूमलिङ्गक-वह्न्यनुमितित्वादिकमेव प्रसिद्धं, तस्य स्वावच्छिन्नकार्य्यताप्रतियोगिक-कारणताश्रयव्याप्तिज्ञानादिजन्यपरामर्षमात्रवृत्तिधर्मावच्छि-

तेन विनापि युगपदिन्द्रियसन्निकृष्टे विशिष्टप्रत्ययोदयात्। दीर्घादिप्रत्यक्षे च न ह्रस्वादिज्ञानापेक्षा, किन्तु

सकारणता-प्रतियोगिककार्य्यतावच्छेदकत्वात्। कार्य्यतावच्छेदकत्वञ्च तत्कोटिप्रविष्टं, तेन व्याप्तिज्ञानस्य कार्य्यतावच्छेदकं धूमलिङ्गकवह्न्यनुमितित्वं न परामर्षकार्य्यतावच्छेदकं, धूमलिङ्गकपर्व्वतपक्षकवह्न्यनुमितित्वस्यैव परामर्षकार्य्यतावच्छेदकत्वादित्यनुमितावधिव्याप्तिरिति निरस्तं। न च तथापि परामर्षत्वस्य भगवज्ज्ञानवृत्तितया तादृशव्याप्तिज्ञानजन्यमात्रवृत्तित्वादतिव्याप्तितादवस्थ्यमिति वाच्यं। तादृशकारणताश्रयजन्यवृत्तित्वं हि तादृशकारणताश्रयज्ञानाजन्य-जन्यज्ञानावृत्तित्वे सति तादृशकारणताश्रयजन्यवृत्तित्वं, सत्यन्ते च तादृशकारणताश्रयज्ञानं अन्यत्वेन विशेषणीयं अन्यथा अन्यज्ञानमात्रस्यैव तादृशकारणताश्रयपरमेश्वरज्ञानजन्यतया तादृशकारणताश्रयज्ञानाजन्य-जन्यज्ञानाप्रसिद्धेः। संशयोत्तरप्रत्यक्षे च व्याप्तिज्ञानस्याकारणत्वात्। विशेषदर्शनहेतुत्वस्य निरस्तत्वाच्च नाव्याप्तिः। न च तथाप्यात्मसाक्षात्कारेऽव्याप्तिः आत्मसाक्षात्कारत्वस्य स्वावच्छिन्नकार्य्यताप्रतियोगिक-कारणताश्रयश्रवणजन्यमननमात्रवृत्तिधर्म्मावच्छिन्न-कारणताप्रतियोगिक-कार्य्यतावच्छेदकत्वादिति वाच्यं। स्वावच्छिन्न-कार्य्यताप्रतियोगिक-कारणताया ज्ञानत्वघटितधर्म्मावच्छिन्नत्वेन विशेषणीयत्वात्। आत्मसाक्षात्कारं प्रति च श्रवणस्य श्रुतिवाक्यजन्यशाब्दत्वेन हेतुत्वात्। असति बाधके श्रौतधर्म्मावच्छेदेनैव कारणतायाः कल्पयितुमुचितत्वात्। यद्वा स्वावच्छिन्नकार्य्यताप्रतियोगिक-

तद्व्यवहारे। अनुमित्यादेर्मेयांशे प्रत्यभिज्ञायाश्च तत्तांशे ज्ञानजन्यत्वान्न प्रत्यक्षत्वं किन्तु परोक्षत्वमेव, मितिमात्रंशे इदन्तांशे च द्वयोरेव प्रत्यक्षत्वं।

कारणता ज्ञानत्वन्युनवृत्तिजात्यनियतत्वेन विशेषणीया, श्रवणनिष्ठकारणता च श्रुतिजन्यज्ञानत्वावच्छिन्नापि शाब्दत्वनियतैव।

केचित्तु श्रवणं मनने, मननं निदिध्यासने, निदिध्यासनं साक्षात्कारे, साक्षात्कारश्च मुक्तौ, न तु साक्षात्कारे श्रवणादेर्हेतुत्वं माना-भावादिति नाव्याप्तिरित्याहुः।

केचित्तु ज्ञानाकरणकज्ञानमात्रवृत्त्यनुभवत्वसाक्षाद्व्याप्यजातिरहितज्ञानत्वमुक्तलक्षणार्थः। मोक्षजनकतावच्छेदकात्मतत्त्वसाक्षात्कारमात्रवृत्तिजातिमादायात्मतत्त्वसाक्षात्कारेऽव्याप्तिवारणाय व्याप्यान्तं जातिविशेषणं। यद्वा ज्ञानाजन्यज्ञानवृत्त्यनुभवत्वाव्यापकजातिमात्रेतात्पर्य्यं, निर्विकल्पकं ज्ञानं आदाय सर्व्वत्र लक्षणसङ्गतिः। अत्र लक्षणाभावतया ज्ञानाजन्येत्यत्र न ज्ञानपदवैयर्थ्यं। 'विशिष्टप्रत्यक्षे'त्यादिवक्ष्यमाणग्रन्थस्तु यथाश्रुताभिप्रायेणेत्याहुः।

ननु विशिष्टवैशिष्ट्यबोधत्वावच्छिन्नं प्रति विशेषणतावच्छेदकज्ञानत्वेन विशेषणतावच्छेदकप्रकारकज्ञानत्वेन च हेतुता एवञ्च विशिष्टवैशिष्ट्यबोधत्वस्य स्वावच्छिन्नकार्य्यताप्रतियोगिक-कारणताश्रयो विशेषणतावच्छेदकज्ञानं तज्जन्यमात्रवृत्तिधर्म्मो विशेषणतावच्छेदकप्रकारकज्ञानत्वं तदवच्छिन्नकारणताप्रतियोगिक-कार्य्यतावच्छेदकत्वा-

यत्तु तत्ताप्रकाशे न तत्तासविकल्पकत्वेन कारणता किन्तु तत्ताज्ञानत्वेन। तन्न। अनुमित्यादावपि लिङ्गादिज्ञानत्वेनानुमेयादितुल्यत्वादिति। अत्रोच्यते। यदि तत्तायां प्रत्यभिज्ञा परोक्षानुभवरूपा तदा नोत्पद्येत तद्धेतुलिङ्गादेरभावात्। तत्ताज्ञानसहितं

तदाऽत्र प्रत्यक्षेऽव्याप्तिरित्यत आह, 'विशिष्टवैशिष्ट्यप्रत्यक्ष इति विशिष्टवैशिष्ट्यबुद्धित्वावच्छिन्ने प्रत्यक्षे इत्यर्थः, 'विशेषणज्ञानं' विशेषणतावच्छेदकप्रकारक-विशेषणज्ञानं, 'विशेषणविशेषणधीः' विशेषणतावच्छेदकधीः, 'विशेषणधीद्वारा', तथाच विशिष्टवैशिष्ट्यबोधत्वस्य स्वावच्छिन्नकार्य्यताप्रतियोगिक-कारणताश्रयो न विशेषणतावच्छेदकज्ञानमिति नाव्याप्तिरिति भावः। ननु संयोगाद्यजन्यतत्तत्प्रत्यक्षत्वेन कार्य्यता तत्ताज्ञानत्वेन तत्तासंस्कारत्वेन च हेतुता एवञ्च तत्ताप्रत्यभिज्ञायामव्याप्तिरित्यत आह, 'प्रत्यभिज्ञायामिति, 'लाघवेनेति अनुभवसामग्य्रसमवहितसंस्कारजन्यत्वमपेक्ष्य लाघवेनेत्यर्थः। ननु तत्त्वत्वं कारणत्वञ्चेदसम्भवः, व्यापकत्वञ्चेत् न क्षतिः, व्याप्यत्वञ्चेदिष्टस्याप्यसिद्धिरिति किन्तत्र गौरवेणेत्यस्वरसादाह, 'तद्धेतुत्वेनैवेति स्मृतिहेतुत्वेनैव, 'तत्सिद्धेश्च' संस्कारज्ञानाच्चेत्यर्थः, तथाच स्मृतिं प्रति पूर्व्ववर्त्तित्वे गृहीत एव प्रत्यभिज्ञां प्रति पूर्व्ववर्त्तित्वग्रहो भविष्यतीति "अन्यं प्रति" इत्याद्यन्यथासिद्धिरिति भावः। इदमुपलक्षणं व्यभिचारादपि संस्कारो न हेतुरित्यपि बोध्यं।

इन्द्रियं जनकमिति चेत् । तर्हि इन्द्रियजन्यत्वात् तत्र साक्षात्कारीरेव स्यात् । न च ज्ञानानपेक्षेन्द्रियजन्यत्वं तत्र तन्त्रं, गौरवात् ज्ञानसहितेन्द्रियजन्यत्वेनेदन्तांशे-ऽप्यप्रत्यक्षत्वप्रसङ्गाच्च । न ह्येकस्मिन् ज्ञाने जनयितव्ये तदपेक्षा तदनपेक्षा च सम्भवति । अंशे तदुभयमपीति

ज्ञानाकरणकं ज्ञानं प्रत्यक्षमिति लक्षणं प्राभाकरमते न सम्भ-वति, अनुमित्यादेरपि मात्राद्यंशे प्रत्यक्षतया तत्राव्याप्तेरतस्तन्मते लक्षणमाह, 'प्राभाकरास्त्विति, 'नियतेति अनुगतानतिप्रसक्तेत्यर्थः, 'सविकल्पकानपेक्षज्ञानत्वमिति, साक्षात्त्वमिति शेषः । सविकल्पकत्वं सप्रकारकज्ञानत्वं । यद्यपि तन्मते निर्व्विकल्पकाप्रसिद्ध्या सप्रकारक-पदस्याव्यावर्त्तकत्वं, तथापि तन्मते विशिष्टबुद्धौ विशेषणज्ञानस्याहेतु-त्वेऽपि विशिष्टबुद्धौ विशेषणतावच्छेदकविषयकज्ञानमात्रस्य विशेषण-तावच्छेदकविशेष्यकज्ञानसाधारणस्य हेतुतया विशिष्टवैशिष्ट्यप्रत्यक्षे-ऽव्याप्तिवारणाय सविकल्पकत्वेन प्रवेशः । न च तथापि तद्दोषतादव-स्थ्यमिति वाच्यं । सविकल्पकत्वघटितधर्म्मावच्छिन्नकारणताप्रति-योगिककार्य्यतानाश्रयत्वस्य विवक्षितत्वात् । सविकल्पकत्वघटितत्वं प्रकारिताघटितत्वं । विशिष्टबुद्धौ च विशेषणतावच्छेदकविषयक-ज्ञानत्वेनैव हेतुत्वं न तु विशेषणतावच्छेदकप्रकारकज्ञानत्वेनेति भावः । 'प्रत्यभिज्ञेति अभेदप्रत्यभिज्ञेत्यर्थः । तत्र तत्ताप्रकारकज्ञानत्वेन, प्रति-योगितावच्छेदकप्रकारकप्रतियोगिज्ञानत्वेन, एकत्वत्वप्रकारक-नामे-

चेत्। न। ज्ञाने अंशस्य विषयत्वेन तदजन्यत्वात्। एवं मिति-मात्रंशे च सर्वं ज्ञानं न प्रत्यक्षं इन्द्रिया-जन्यत्वात् साक्षात्कारे तस्य कारणत्वात्। मनोजन्यत्वे अनुमेयांशेऽपि तत्त्वप्रसङ्गः। न च मानमात्र-

---

त्वगोचरज्ञानत्वेन च हेतुत्वादिति भावः[१]। इदमुपलक्षणमनुमित्यादेरपि मिति-मात्रंशे प्रत्यक्षरूपतया तत्राव्याप्तेश्चेत्यपि बोध्यं। 'किञ्चिति, 'यद्विषयत्वे' यद्विषयत्वांशे, प्रत्यभिज्ञायास्तेदंशे तत्तायाः सविकल्पकाजन्यत्वान्नाव्याप्तिः। सविकल्पकाजन्यत्वञ्च सविकल्पकत्वघटितधर्म्मावच्छिन्नकारणताप्रतियोगिक-कार्य्यतानाश्रयत्वं, तेन विशिष्टवैशिष्ट्यप्रत्यक्षे विशेषणतावच्छेदकप्रकारकादिज्ञानजन्ये नाव्याप्तितादवस्थ्यं। तथाच सविकल्पकत्वघटितधर्म्मावच्छिन्नकारणतानिरूपित-यन्निष्ठकार्य्यताया विषयतया तदनवच्छेदकं तद्धीत्वं प्रत्यक्षमिति फलितं। न च तथापि सादृश्य-द्वित्वादिप्रत्यक्षेऽव्याप्तिः तदवस्थेति वाच्यं। सादृश्य-द्वित्वादिव्यवहार एव प्रतियोगिज्ञानापेक्षाबुद्ध्यपेक्षा न तु तत्प्रत्यक्षे इत्यभ्युपगमादिति भावः। 'मिति-मात्रप्रकाशे चेति मिति-मात्रंशे चेत्यर्थः, 'ज्ञानाजन्यत्वादिति तदंशे

---

(१) तत्ताप्रकारकज्ञानत्वेन हेतुत्वात् प्रत्यभिज्ञायां, प्रतियोगितावच्छेदकप्रकारकप्रतियोगिज्ञानत्वेन हेतुत्वात् सादृश्यप्रत्यक्षे, एकत्वत्वप्रकारकमानैकत्वज्ञानत्वेन हेतुत्वात् द्वित्वप्रत्यक्षे सविकल्पकानपेक्षत्वरूपं लक्षणमव्याप्तमिति भावः।

सामग्रीजन्यत्वं प्रत्यक्षत्वे तन्त्रं, गौरवात् ज्ञानमात्रस्य न ज्ञानत्वं तस्याजन्यत्वात्। नापि सर्वं ज्ञानं प्रत्यक्षज्ञाने, प्रत्येकं सर्वज्ञानसामग्र्यजन्यत्वात् सर्वज्ञानसामग्र्यप्रसिद्धेश्च। अपि च ज्ञाने अवयवाभावेनांशो

ज्ञानमात्रस्यैवाजन्यत्वादित्यर्थः, तथाच सुतरां सविकल्पकाजन्यत्वमिति भावः। इदमापाततः तथापि स्वात्मविषयकानुमित्यादेस्तदंशे प्रत्यक्षत्वानुपपत्तेर्दुर्वारत्वादिति ध्येयं। नन्वेतस्य लक्षणत्वे विशिष्टबुद्धौ विशेषणधियो हेतुत्वसत्त्वे अयं गौरयं गौरित्यादिधारावाहिकविशिष्टप्रत्यक्षेऽव्याप्तिरित्यत आह, 'जातावनुगतधीरिति जातिधारावाहिकविशिष्टधीरपीत्यर्थः, विशिष्टबुद्धौ विशेषणधियो हेतुत्वसत्त्वेपीति शेषः। 'जाति-व्यक्तीति विशिष्टबुद्धौ विशेषणधियो हेतुत्वनये आद्यविशिष्टप्रत्यक्षस्य जाति-व्यक्तिनिर्विकल्पकजन्यत्वादित्यर्थः, तथाच व्यभिचारेण सविकल्पकत्वघटितधर्म्मेण कारणत्वाभावान्नाव्याप्तिरिति भावः। नन्वन्यच्च विशिष्टवैशिष्ट्यबुद्धौ सामान्यतोविशेषणतावच्छेदकविषयकज्ञानत्वेन हेतुत्वेऽपि सादृश्यत्वादिविशिष्टवैशिष्ट्यबुद्धौ विशेषणतावच्छेदकप्रकारकज्ञानत्वेनैव हेतुत्वात् सदृशोऽयमित्यादिसादृश्यत्वविशिष्टसादृश्यादिवैशिष्ट्यप्रत्यक्षेऽव्याप्तिरित्यत आह, 'सादृश्यादिविशिष्टवैशिष्ट्यप्रत्यक्षे चेति सादृश्यादि यद्विशिष्टं तद्वैशिष्ट्यप्रत्यक्षेऽपीत्यर्थः, तेन सादृश्यत्वादिविशिष्ट-वैशिष्ट्यप्रत्यक्षलाभः। सादृश्यादिपदं सादृश्यत्वादिपरमित्यपि केचित्। 'न विशेषणज्ञानं हेतुरिति न

विषय एव विषये च ज्ञानं न कारणं अतोऽनुमिति-प्रत्यभिज्ञयोः स्वविषयेऽनुमेये तत्तायाश्च प्रत्यक्षत्वं स्यात् विषयस्य सविकल्पकाजन्यत्वात्। अथ प्रत्यभिज्ञायां

सादृश्यत्वप्रकारकसादृश्यज्ञानं सादृश्यत्वप्रकारकज्ञानत्वेन हेतुरित्यर्थः, 'तेन विनापीति सादृश्यत्वप्रकारक-सादृश्यज्ञानं विनापीत्यर्थः, 'युगपदिन्द्रियसन्निकृष्ट इति सादृश्यत्वे सादृश्ये च युगपदिन्द्रिय-सन्निकृष्टे सति तयोः खण्डशो ज्ञाने च सतीत्यर्थः, 'विशिष्ट-प्रत्ययोदयादिति सदृशोऽयमित्याकारकप्रत्यक्षोदयादित्यर्थः। 'दीर्घा-दीति दीर्घत्वादीत्यर्थः, आदिपदेन सादृश्य-द्वित्वादिपरिग्रहः, 'ह्रस्वादिज्ञानं' ह्रस्वत्वादिप्रकारकज्ञानं, आदिना प्रतियोगि-ज्ञाने-कत्वादिपरिग्रहः। ननु तथापि अनुमित्यादेः साध्यांशे प्रत्यभि-ज्ञायास्तत्तांशे प्रत्यक्षव्यवहारो न स्यादित्यत इष्टापत्तिमाह, 'अनुमि-त्यादेरिति, 'मेयांशे' साध्याद्यंशे, 'ज्ञानजन्यत्वात्' सविकल्पकत्वघटित-धर्मेण तज्जन्यत्वात्, 'प्रत्यक्षत्वं' प्रत्यक्षव्यवहारविषयत्वं, 'परोक्षत्वं' परोक्षव्यवहारविषयत्वं, 'द्वयोरेवेति, एवकारो भिन्नक्रमे तथाच-मिति-मात्रांशे इदन्त्वांश एव चेत्यर्थः, 'प्रत्यक्षत्वं' प्रत्यक्षव्यवहार-विषयत्वं।

तत्तांशेऽपि प्रत्यभिज्ञायाः प्रत्यक्षव्यवहारविषयत्वमेवेति मीमां-सकैकदेशिमतमपाकर्त्तुं शङ्कते, 'यत्त्विति, 'तत्ताप्रकाशे' तत्ता-विशिष्टाभेदप्रत्यभिज्ञायां, 'तत्तासविकल्पकत्वेन' तत्ताप्रकारकज्ञानत्वेन,

तत्ताविषयत्वेन तज्ज्ञानं कारणं, एवमनुमित्यादौ मेयविषयत्वेऽपि। मिति-मात्रिदन्ता-धर्म्मिविषयत्वे च न ज्ञानं कारणं किन्तु ज्ञानसामग्रीति चेत्। न। त-

---

'किञ्चिति, तथाच तत्तांशेऽपि प्रत्यक्षव्यवहारविषयत्वमेवेति भावः। प्रतिबन्दिमुखेन दूषयति, 'अनुमित्यादावपीति तत्ताशविकल्पकादेव तत्ताप्रकाशो न तु तत्ताज्ञानमात्रात्तथापि यदि तत्ताज्ञानत्वेन हेतुत्वन्तदा अनुमित्यादावपि लिङ्गादिज्ञानत्वेन हेतुत्वेन तुल्यत्वादिति व्याप्तिरित्यर्थः, तत्र यदि लिङ्गादिज्ञानमात्रादनुमित्यनुत्पत्तेर्न लिङ्गादिज्ञानत्वेन हेतुत्वं किन्तु व्याप्यत्वादिप्रकारकज्ञानत्वेन तदाऽत्रापि तथेति भावः। प्राभाकरमतं दूषयति, 'अत्रोच्यत इति, 'परोक्षानुभवरूपा' परोक्षानुभवव्यवहारविषया, 'तदेति, यावद्विशेषकारणबाधेन सामान्यकार्य्यानुत्पत्तेरिति भावः। इन्द्रियजन्यत्वात्' इन्द्रियत्वेनेन्द्रियजन्यत्वात्, 'साक्षाद्वौरेवेति साक्षात्कारव्यवहारएवेत्यर्थः। 'ज्ञानानपेक्षेति सविकल्पकत्वघटितधर्म्मेण ज्ञानानपेक्षेत्यर्थः तेन विशिष्टवैशिष्ट्यप्रत्यक्षे नाव्याप्तिः, 'तत्र' साक्षात्कारव्यवहारे। तन्त्रत्वं कारणत्वं व्याप्यत्वं वा आद्य आह, 'गौरवादिति, अन्त्य आह, 'ज्ञानसहितेन्द्रियजन्यत्वेनेति ज्ञानानपेक्षेन्द्रियजन्यत्वाभावादिति शेषः। 'अप्रत्यक्षत्वं' प्रत्यक्षव्यवहाराविषयत्वं, 'चकारेण गौरवमपि समुच्चितं। ननु ज्ञानानपेक्षेन्द्रियजन्यत्वाभावोनास्ति किन्तु ज्ञानसापेक्षेन्द्रियजन्यत्व-ज्ञाननिरपेक्षेन्द्रियजन्यत्वोभयमेवास्तीत्यत आह, 'न हीति।

द्विषयत्वं हि ज्ञाने स्वकारणाधीनतदीयस्वभावत्वं स्वरूपविशेषः स च ज्ञानाजन्य एव[१]। इच्छिज्ञानादौ चाव्याप्तिः तस्यानुमित्यादिवद्विशिष्टज्ञानत्वेन विशेषण-

---

'न प्रत्यक्षं' न प्रत्यक्षव्यवहारविषयः। ननु मानोरूपेन्द्रियजन्यत्व-मस्त्येवेत्यत आह, 'मनोजन्यत्वे इति, साक्षात्कारत्वव्यवहारप्रयोजक इति शेषः। 'अनुमेयांशेऽपि साध्यांशेऽपि। ननु सर्व्वस्यैव ज्ञानस्य मिति-मात्रांशे प्रत्यक्षत्वात् ज्ञानमात्रसामग्रीजन्यत्वमप्यपरं मिति-मात्रांशे प्रत्यक्षव्यवहारप्रयोजकं व्याप्यमित्याशङ्कते, 'न च ज्ञानमात्र-सामग्रीजन्यत्वमिति, 'प्रत्यक्षत्वे' मिति-मात्रांशे प्रत्यक्षव्यवहारे, यथा-श्रुते अनुमयांशेऽपि प्रत्यक्षव्यवहारापत्तेस्तादवस्थ्यात्। अत एव 'गौरवादित्यपि सङ्गच्छते, एतस्यापि प्रत्यक्षव्यवहारप्रयोजकत्वे गौर-वादित्यर्थः, अन्यथा इन्द्रिय-शरीरनिर्व्वचने इन्द्रियजन्यत्वस्यैव गुरु-त्वात्। यद्यपि ज्ञानत्वावच्छिन्नकार्य्यतानिरूपितकारणताश्रयसामग्री-जन्यत्वमेव ज्ञानमात्रसामग्रीजन्यत्वं सुवचं तथाप्याशयमविज्ञा स दूषणान्तरमाह, 'ज्ञानमात्रस्येति। 'अनुमिति-प्रत्यभिज्ञयोरिति, 'अनुमितिपदं परोक्षज्ञानमात्रोपलक्षणं। 'अथेति, 'तज्ज्ञानं' तत्ता-प्रकारकज्ञानजन्यं, तथाच यज्ज्ञानस्य यद्विषयत्वं सविकल्पकत्व-घटितधर्म्मेण तदजन्यं तज्ज्ञानं तस्य प्रत्यक्षमिति लक्षणं वाच्यमि-

---

(१) ज्ञानजन्य एवेति ख०।

ज्ञानजन्यत्वात्। न च परोक्षत्वमुपाधिः, प्रत्यभिज्ञायां प्रथमोत्पन्नजाति-व्यक्तिज्ञाने जन्ये जातेरनुगत-प्रत्यक्षे च साध्याव्यापकत्वात्। पूर्व्वव्यक्तिवृत्तित्वे सत्ये-तद्व्यक्तिवृत्तित्वमनुगतत्वमिति तत्र पूर्व्वानुभूतव्यक्ते-र्विशेषणत्वेन तत्र ज्ञानस्यानुगतत्वप्रत्यक्षे कारणत्वात्।

ति भावः। 'स्वकारणाधीनं' स्वाश्रयकारणस्य कार्य्यतावच्छेदकमिति यावत्, 'तदीयस्वभावत्वं' स्वरूपसम्बन्धेन ज्ञाननिष्ठमिति यावत्, 'स्वरूपविशेषः स चेति स्वरूपसम्बन्धेन वर्त्तमानः स च धर्म्म-इत्यर्थः, 'ज्ञानाजन्य एव' तत्त्वादिज्ञानाजन्य एव, तथाच तत्त्वाद्यंशेऽपि प्रत्यक्षत्वं स्यादिति भावः।

यद्वा 'स्वकारणाधीनं' स्वकारणजन्यं, 'तदीयस्वभावत्वं' ज्ञानीय-विषयस्वरूपः, 'स्वरूपविशेषः स चेति विषयस्वरूपः स च धर्म्म इत्यर्थः। क्वचित्तु 'ज्ञानजन्य एवेति पाठः, तत्र 'स्वकारणाधीनं' ज्ञानकारणजन्यं, 'तदीयस्वभावत्वं' ज्ञानस्वरूपं, 'स्वरूपविशेषः स च' ज्ञानस्वरूपः स च धर्म्मः, 'ज्ञानजन्य एव' तत्त्वादिज्ञानजन्य एव, तथाचेदन्त्वाद्यंशेऽपि प्रत्यक्षत्वं न स्यादिति भावः। ननु यज्ज्ञाननिष्ठं यद्विषयकत्वं सविकल्पकत्वघटितधर्म्मावच्छिन्नकारणताप्रतियोगिक-कार्य्यतानवच्छेदकं तत्तस्य प्रत्यक्षमिति विवक्षितं सविकल्पकत्वघटितध-र्म्मावच्छिन्नकारणताप्रतियोगिक-कार्य्यतानवच्छेदकतद्विषयिताशालि-ज्ञानत्वं तस्य प्रत्यक्षत्वमिति तु निष्कर्षः। अनवच्छेदकान्तं विष-

अन्यथा प्रथममप्यनुगतधीप्रसङ्गः । अत एव ज्ञानसाक्षाद्जन्यं ज्ञानं प्रत्यक्षं प्रत्यभिज्ञायां संस्कार एव साक्षाज्जनकः, जातावनुगतधीरपि संस्कारजन्या, एवं सादृश्यादिप्रत्यक्षेऽपि प्रतियोगिसंस्कार एव कारणमिति निरस्तं । दण्डानुभवजन्यदण्डिप्रत्यक्षे धारावाहिकप्रत्यक्षे चाव्यापनात् । उत्तरविशिष्टज्ञाने पूर्वविशिष्टानुभवस्यैव विशेषणज्ञानत्वेन हेतुत्वात् संस्का-

---

यिताविशेषणमतो न कोऽपिदोष इत्यस्वरसादाह, 'दण्डीत्यादिज्ञाने चेति दण्डत्वादिविशिष्टवैशिष्ट्यप्रत्यक्षे चेत्यर्थः । 'विशिष्टज्ञानत्वेनेति विशिष्टवैशिष्ट्यज्ञानत्वेन हेतुनेत्यर्थः, विशेषणज्ञानजन्यत्वादिति विशेषणतावच्छेदकप्रकारकज्ञानत्वेन विशेषणज्ञानजन्यत्वसाधनादित्यर्थः । 'परोक्षत्वमिति साक्षात्कारभिन्नत्वमित्यर्थः, 'प्रत्यभिज्ञायामिति सोऽयमित्यभेदप्रत्यभिज्ञायामित्यर्थः । 'तत्र ज्ञानस्य' तत्र तत्ताप्रकारकज्ञानस्य, 'प्रथममपि' पूर्व्वव्यक्तिज्ञानं विनापि । न च तथाप्यप्रयोजकमिति वाच्यं । सामान्यतो विशेषणतावच्छेदकज्ञानत्वेन हेतुत्वे विशेष्ये विशेषणमितिन्यायात् अन्यज्ञानमात्रस्यैव तादृशविलक्षणविषयत्वापत्तेरिति भावः । 'अतएवेति विशिष्टप्रत्यक्षेऽव्याप्तत्वादेवेत्यर्थः, 'ज्ञानेति, प्रथमज्ञानपदं सविकल्पकपरं तेनाद्यविशिष्टप्रत्यक्षे नाव्याप्तिः, चरमज्ञानपदमनुभवपरं तेन स्मरणव्यवच्छेदः, 'संस्कार एव' तत्ताप्रकारकसंस्कार एव, क्षणविलम्बस्तु अन्यथानुपपत्त्या कुत्रचित्

संयुक्तसमवेतसमवायेन रूपत्वादेः, समवायेन शब्दस्य,

व्यापारिणा व्यापारस्य नान्यथासिद्धिरिति चेत्। न। व्यापार-व्यापारि-भावस्यैवासिद्धेरसम्भवात्। संयोगसन्निकर्षस्य कारणत्वानुरोधेन सामान्यतः संयोगत्वेनैव द्रव्यविशिष्टत्वावच्छिन्नं प्रति तस्य कारणत्वं द्रव्य-विशिष्टत्वञ्च लौकिकविषयत्वावच्छिन्नाधेयतासम्बन्धेन द्रव्यविशिष्टत्वं न तु चक्षुःसंयोगत्वादिनेत्याहुः।

'संयुक्तसमवायेनेति चक्षुरादिसंयुक्तसमवायेनेत्यर्थः, 'रूप-कर्म्म-णोरिति, 'रूप-कर्म्मपदं सामान्यतो द्रव्यसमवेतपरं, तेन संख्यादेः द्रव्यवृत्तिजातेस्च परिग्रहः, 'ग्रहणं' चाक्षुषादि, तथा च चक्षुःसंयुक्त-समवायत्व-त्वक्संयुक्तसमवायत्व-मनःसंयुक्तसमवायत्व-घ्राणसंयुक्तसम-वायत्व-रसनसंयुक्तसमवायत्वेन कारणत्वं, यथाक्रमं द्रव्यसमवे-तचाक्षुषत्व-द्रव्यसमवेतत्वाचत्व-द्रव्यसमवेतमानसत्व-गन्धघ्राणजत्व-रस-रासनत्वेन च कार्य्यत्वं, कार्य्यदिशि विषयत्वं कारणदिशि विशेषण-ताविशेषः प्रत्यासत्तिः। द्रव्यसमवेतचाक्षुषत्वञ्च लौकिकविषयता-सम्बन्धावच्छिन्नाधेयतासम्बन्धेन द्रव्यसमवेतविशिष्टचाक्षुषत्वं तेन रूपा-दिचाक्षुषस्य रूपत्वादिविषयकस्य रूपत्वादौ विषयतासम्बन्धेनोत्पा-देऽपि न व्यभिचारः विशिष्टस्य द्रव्यसमवेतमात्रवृत्तित्वात्। द्रव्य-समवेतविशिष्टालौकिकचाक्षुषमादायातीतानागतादिषु द्रव्यसमवेतेषु व्यभिचारवारणाय लौकिकात्मकविषयताविशेषानुधावनं। न च तथापि संयुक्तसमवेतसमवायसन्निकर्षेण रूपादौ सत्ताचाक्षुषमादाय सत्तायां व्यभिचार इति वाच्यं। रूपादौ चक्षुःसन्निकर्षदशायां तदा-

समवेतसमवायेन शब्दत्वादेः, विशेषणतया शब्दाभा-

अयद्रव्येऽपि चक्षुःसंयोगस्यावश्यकतया द्रव्यमादायैव चक्षुःसंयुक्तसमवायस्य सत्तायां सत्त्वान्न व्यभिचारः। अतएव संयोगसन्निकर्षेण घटादिचाक्षुषेऽपि न व्यभिचारः घट-चक्षुःसंयोगदशायां कपाल-चक्षुः-संयोगस्यावश्यकतया तदादायैव संयुक्तसमवायस्य तत्र सत्त्वात् त्रसरेणुप्रत्यक्षे च द्व्यणुकमादायैव तत्सम्भवः। न चैवं द्व्यणुकरूपादेरपि चाक्षुषापत्तिरिति वाच्यं। घटादिवृत्तिगुरुत्वादिवदयोग्यत्वेनैव तत्प्रत्यक्षासम्भवात्। एवं द्रव्यसमवेतत्वाचत्वं द्रव्यसमवेतमानसत्वं गन्धघ्राणजत्वं रसरासनत्वञ्च निर्व्वाच्यं। वस्तुतस्तु लाघवादत्रापि सामान्यतः चाक्षुषत्व-त्वाचत्व-मानसत्व-घ्राणजत्व-रासनत्वमेव कार्य्यतावच्छेदकं न तु द्रव्यसमवेतविशिष्टत्व-गन्धविशिष्टत्वादिप्रवेशः, द्रव्यसमवेतत्वविशिष्टस्य वस्तुगत्या द्रव्यसमवेतनिरूपितस्य वा लौकिकविषयत्वस्य गन्धत्वविशिष्टस्य वस्तुगत्या गन्धनिरूपितस्य वा लौकिकविषयत्वस्य रसत्वविशिष्टस्य वस्तुगत्या रसनिरूपितस्य वा लौकिकविषयत्वस्य कार्य्यतावच्छेदकसम्बन्धत्वान्न व्यभिचारः, कारणतावच्छेदकमपि चक्षुःसंयोगत्व-त्वक्संयोगत्व-मनःसंयोगत्व-रसनसंयोगत्वमेव न तु समवायत्वादिप्रवेशः, स्वसमवायिसमवेतत्वञ्च कारणतावच्छेदकसम्बन्धः तेन गुणादौ न व्यभिचार इति मणिकृतो निगर्भः(१)।

स्वतन्त्रास्तु चक्षुःसंयुक्तसमवायत्वादिना न कारणत्वं गौरवात् अपि तु स्वसंयुक्तसमवेतत्वसम्बन्धेन चक्षुष्ट्वादिनैव हेतुत्वं लाघवात्

---

(१) अत्रापि 'निगर्भः' इत्यत्र 'निगर्व्वः' इति पाठान्तरम्।

रस्य स्मरणेतराजनकत्वाच्च । अन्यथा प्रत्यभिज्ञादेः संस्कारजन्यत्वेन स्मृतित्वं स्यादित्युक्तत्वात् । इतिप्रत्यक्षलक्षणं ।

स्वीकार्य्यं इति भावः । हेत्वन्तरमाह, 'दण्डानुभवेति, 'दण्डिप्रत्यक्षे' दण्डविशिष्टप्रत्यक्षे, धारावाहिकप्रत्यक्षेऽव्याप्तिमुपपादयति, 'उक्तरेति । 'संस्कारस्येति, 'स्मरणेतराजनकत्वात्' इति स्मरणेतरज्ञानाजनकत्वात् । इति प्रत्यक्षपरिच्छेदरहस्ये प्रत्यक्षलक्षणरहस्यं ।

इन्द्रियसन्निकर्षजन्यत्वं प्रत्यक्षत्वमिति सौत्रलक्षणं तच्च न सम्भवति सन्निकर्षाणामननुगततया परस्परव्यभिचारेण प्रत्यक्षहेतुत्वासम्भवा-दिति पूर्व्वमुक्तं तत्राह, 'प्रत्यक्षविशेष इति, 'अनुगत एव' अव्यभि-चार्य्येव, तथाच सौत्रमपि लक्षणं प्रत्यक्षस्य सम्भवतीति भावः । इत्यञ्च सौत्रलक्षणोपोद्घातसङ्गत्या सन्निकर्षनिरूपणमिति मन्तव्यं।

केचित्तु ननु सन्निकर्षाणां परस्परव्यभिचारेण प्रत्यक्षहेतुत्वा-सम्भवात् तद्द्वारकमिन्द्रियाणामपि प्रत्यक्षहेतुत्वमसम्भवि तत्कथमि-न्द्रियजन्यत्वं प्रत्यक्षलक्षणमिति सौत्रलक्षणोपोद्घातसङ्गत्याह, 'प्रत्यक्ष-विशेष इतीत्याहुः ।

ननु कोऽसौ विशेष इत्यत आह, 'संयोगेनेति चक्षुरादिसंयोगे-नेत्यर्थः, 'द्रव्यग्रहः' द्रव्यचाक्षुषादिः, तथाच चक्षुःसंयोगत्वं त्वक्संयो-गत्वं मनःसंयोगत्वञ्च कारणतावच्छेदकं, द्रव्यचाक्षुषत्वं द्रव्यत्वाचत्वं द्रव्यमानसत्वञ्च यथाक्रमं कार्य्यतावच्छेदकं कार्य्यदिशि विषयत्वं कारणदिशि समवायः प्रत्यासत्तिः, द्रव्यचाक्षुषत्वञ्च लौकिकविषयता-

प्रत्यक्षविशेषे सन्निकर्षविशेषो हेतुरनुगत एव। संयोगेन द्रव्यग्रहः, संयुक्तसमवायेन रूप-कर्मणोर्ग्रहणं[१],

वच्छिन्नाधेयतासम्बन्धेन द्रव्यविशिष्टचाक्षुषत्वं तेन चक्षुःसंयोगं विनापि द्रव्यचाक्षुषस्य गुणादिविषयकस्य विषयतासम्बन्धेन गुणादावप्युत्पादेऽपि न व्यभिचारः विशिष्टस्य द्रव्यमात्रवृत्तित्वात्। सामान्यतो विषयत्वावच्छिन्नाधेयतासम्बन्धेन द्रव्यविशिष्टत्वाभिधाने चक्षुःसंयोगं विनाप्यतीतानागतद्रव्ये द्रव्यविशिष्टालौकिकचाक्षुषोदयाद्व्यभिचारापत्तिरतो लौकिकत्वरूपविषयताविशेषणानुधावनं। नचेदं रजतमिति स्मर्य्यमाणभेदारोपस्यापि रजतांशे तादृशविषयताया अनुभवसिद्धतया व्यभिचार इति वाच्यं। तादृशविषयकानुभवस्यापि तत्र भ्रमत्वात् एवं द्रव्यमानसत्वमपि निर्वाच्यं। वस्तुतस्तु चाक्षुषत्व-त्वाचत्व-मानसत्वमेव सामान्यतः कार्य्यतावच्छेदकं न तु द्रव्यविशिष्टत्वप्रवेशः, द्रव्यविशिष्टस्य वस्तुगत्या द्रव्यनिरूपितस्य वा लौकिकविषयत्वस्य कार्य्यतावच्छेदकसम्बन्धतया च न समूहालम्बनमादाय गुणादौ अलौकिकचाक्षुषमादायातीतादिद्रव्ये व्यभिचार इति मणिकृतोऽभिगर्भः[२]।

स्वतन्त्रास्तु चक्षुःसंयोगत्वादिना हेतुत्वे गौरवात् संयोगसम्बन्धेन चक्षुष्ट्वादिनैव हेतुत्वं लाघवात् चक्षुषा घटं पश्यामीत्यादिप्रत्ययबलेन चक्षुरादेः कारणत्वस्यावश्यकत्वाच्च। कार्य्यतावच्छेदकञ्च पूर्व्ववदेव। न चैवं संयोगसन्निकर्षस्य कारणत्वविलोप इति वाच्यं। इष्टत्वात्।

(१) रूप-कर्म्म-गोत्वादेर्ग्रहणमिति क०-ख०-चिह्नितपुस्तकद्वयपाठः, परन्त्वयं टीकाकृदसम्मतत्वात् न समीचीनः।

(२) निगर्व्व इत्यपि पाठान्तरम्।

वस्य, इन्द्रियसम्बद्धविशेषणतया समवाय-घटाभावादे-

चक्षुषा रूपं पश्यामीत्यादिप्रत्ययबलेन चक्षुरादेः कारणत्वस्यावश्यकत्वात्। कार्य्यतावच्छेदकन्तु यथोक्तमेव। न चैवं चक्षुरादिसन्निकर्षस्य हेतुत्वविलोपः मम तु संयोगरूपसन्निकर्षस्यैव सम्बन्धभेदेन सर्व्वत्र हेतुत्वमिति वाच्यं। इष्टत्वात्। अस्तु वा सन्निकर्षकारणत्वानुरोधेन सामान्यतः समवायत्वेनैव द्रव्यसमवेतविशिष्टत्वावच्छिन्नं प्रति तस्य हेतुत्वं न तु चक्षुःसंयुक्तसमवायत्वादिनेत्याहुः।

'संयुक्तसमवेतसमवायेनेति चक्षुरादिसंयुक्तसमवेतसमवायेनेत्यर्थः। 'रूपत्वादेरिति, 'ग्रहणमित्यनुषज्यते, आदिपदाद्द्रव्यसमवेतसमवेतमात्रपरिग्रहः, तथाच चक्षुःसंयुक्तसमवेतसमवायत्व-त्वक्संयुक्तसमवेतसमवायत्व-मनःसंयुक्तसमवेतसमवायत्व-घ्राणसंयुक्तसमवेतसमवायत्व-रसनसंयुक्तसमवेतसमवायत्वेन कारणत्वं, यथाक्रमं समवेतचाक्षुषत्व-समवेतत्वाचत्व-द्रव्यसमवेतसमवेतमानसत्व-समवेतघ्राणजत्व-समवेतरासनत्वेन च कार्य्यत्वं, विषयत्व-विशेषणत्वाभ्यां सामानाधिकरण्यं प्रत्यासत्तिः। त्रसरेण्वादिसमवेतद्रव्यचाक्षुषादावपि परमाण्वाद्यन्त्यावयवचक्षुःसंयोगादिमादायैव तत्सम्भवः। नचैवं द्व्यणुकनिष्ठरूपादेरपि प्रत्यक्षापत्तिः परमाणुमादायैव चक्षुरादिसंयुक्तसमवेतसमवायस्य तत्र विद्यमानत्वादिति वाच्यं। गुरुत्वादिवदयोग्यत्वादेव तदप्रत्यक्षतोपपत्तेः। द्रव्यसमवेतगुणादिचाक्षुषादावपि द्रव्यावयवमादायैव तत्सम्भवः। समवेतचाक्षुषत्वस्य लौकिकविषयतासम्बन्धावच्छिन्नाधेयतासम्बन्धेन समवेत-

यौग्यसन्निकर्षादेव ग्रहो न सन्निकर्षमात्रात् ।

विशिष्टचाक्षुषत्वं तेन रूपत्वादिचाक्षुषस्याभावादिलौकिकचाक्षुषात्मकस्य विषयतासम्बन्धेनाभावादावुत्पादेऽपि न व्यभिचारः विशिष्टस्य समवेतमात्रवृत्तित्वात् । अलौकिकचाक्षुषमादायातीतानागतेषु घटादिसमवेतरूपादिषु व्यभिचारवारणाय लौकिकात्मकविषयताविशेषानुधावनं, त्रसरेणुघटितसन्निकर्षेण सत्ताचाक्षुषत्वेऽपि द्व्यणुकमादाय त्रसरेणुनिष्ठरूपादिमादाय वा चक्षुःसंयुक्तसमवेतसमवायस्य विद्यमानत्वान्न व्यभिचारः । एवं समवेतविशिष्टत्वाचत्व-द्रव्यसमवेतसमवेतविशिष्टमानसत्व-समवेतविशिष्टघ्राणजत्व-समवेतविशिष्टरासनत्वमपि निर्वाच्यं। वस्तुतस्तु लाघवादत्रापि चाक्षुषत्व-त्वाचत्व-मानसत्व-घ्राणजत्व-रासनत्वमेव कार्य्यतावच्छेदकं न तु समवेतविशिष्टत्व-द्रव्यसमवेतसमवेतविशिष्टत्वप्रवेशः, समवेतत्वविशिष्टस्य वस्तुगत्या समवेतनिरूपितस्य वा लौकिकविषयत्वस्य द्रव्यसमवेतसमवेतत्वविशिष्टस्य वस्तुगत्या द्रव्यसमवेतसमवेतनिरूपितस्य वा लौकिकविषयत्वस्य कार्य्यतावच्छेदकसम्बन्धत्वान्न व्यभिचारः । कारणतावच्छेदकमपि चक्षुःसंयोगत्व-त्वक्संयोगत्व-मनःसंयोगत्व-घ्राणसंयोगत्व-रसनसंयोगत्वमेव न तु समवेतसमवायत्वादिप्रवेशः । स्वसमवायिसमवेतत्वञ्च कारणतावच्छेदकसम्बन्धः तेन रूपत्वादौ न व्यभिचार इति मणिकृतोनिगर्भः ।

अत्रापि स्वतन्त्राः चक्षुःसंयुक्तसमवेतसमवायत्वादिना स्वसमवायिसमवेतसमवेतत्वसम्बन्धेन चक्षुःसंयोगत्वादिना वा न हेतुत्वं गौरवादपि तु स्वसंयुक्तसमवेतसमवायसम्बन्धेन चक्षुष्ट्वादिनैव हेतुत्वं

कार्य्यतावच्छेदकस्य यथोक्तत्वेन । न चैवं चक्षुरादिसन्निकर्षस्य हेतुत्व-विलोप इति वाच्यं । इष्टत्वादित्याहुः ।

'शब्दस्येति ग्रहणमित्यनुषज्यते, तथाच श्रोत्रसमवायत्वेन कारणता शब्दश्रावणत्वेन कार्य्यता, कार्य्यदिशि विषयत्वं कारणदिशि च विशेषणताविशेषः प्रत्यासत्तिः, पुरुषान्तरीयकर्णस्थशब्दस्य प्रत्यक्षवारणाय कारणतावच्छेदके श्रोत्रप्रवेशः, श्रोत्रत्वं तत्तत्पुरुषीयकर्णावच्छिन्नं, शब्दश्रावणत्वञ्च लौकिकविषयत्वावच्छिन्नाधेयतासम्बन्धेन शब्दविशिष्टं श्रावणत्वं, तेन शब्दलौकिकप्रत्यक्षस्य शब्दाभावांशेऽपि लौकिकप्रत्यक्षात्मकस्य(१) विषयतासम्बन्धेन शब्दाभावे उत्पादेऽपि न व्यभिचारः विशिष्टस्य शब्दमात्रवृत्तित्वात् । अलौकिकप्रत्यक्षमादायातीतानागतादिशब्दे व्यभिचारवारणाय लौकिकत्वानुधावनं । वस्तुतस्तु श्रावणत्वमेव कार्य्यतावच्छेदकं शब्दत्वविशिष्टं वस्तुगत्या शब्दनिरूपितं वा लौकिकविषयत्वं कार्य्यदिशि प्रत्यासत्तिरिति निगर्भः ।

स्वतन्त्रास्तु श्रोत्रसमवायत्वेन न हेतुत्वं गौरवादपि तु स्वसमवायसम्बन्धेन श्रोत्रत्वेनैव हेतुत्वं, कार्य्यतावच्छेदकञ्च यथोक्तमेव । न चैवमिन्द्रियसन्निकर्षस्य न हेतुत्वमिति वाच्यं । इष्टत्वादित्याहुः ।

'शब्दत्वादेरिति 'ग्रहणमित्यनुषज्यते, आदिपदाच्छब्दसमवेतमात्रपरिग्रहः, तथाच श्रोत्रसमवेतसमवायत्वेन कारणता शब्दसमवेत-

---

(१) अत्र शब्दाभावपदेन शब्दविशेषाभावपरिग्रहः, अन्यथा शब्दे श्रोत्रसन्निकर्षदशायां शब्दसामान्याभावे श्रोत्रसन्निकर्षो न सम्भवति, स्वसमयेऽपीति ध्येयम् ।

श्रावणत्वेन कार्य्यता कार्य्यदिशि विषयत्वं कारणदिशि च विशेषणता-विशेषः प्रत्यासत्तिः, शब्दसमवेतश्रावणत्वञ्च लौकिकविषयत्वावच्छिन्ना-धेयतासम्बन्धेन शब्दसमवेतविशिष्टश्रावणत्वं तेन शब्दत्वलौकिकप्रत्य-क्षस्य शब्दाभावांशेऽपि लौकिकप्रत्यक्षात्मकस्य विषयतासम्बन्धेन शब्दा-भावेऽप्युत्पादेऽपि न व्यभिचारः। विशिष्टस्य शब्दसमवेतमात्रवृत्ति-त्वात्। अलौकिकप्रत्यक्षमादायातीतानागतादिशब्दे व्यभिचारवार-णाय लौकिकत्वरूपविषयताविशेषणानुसरणं। वस्तुतस्तु श्रावणत्वमेव कार्य्यतावच्छेदकं शब्दसमवेतत्वविशिष्टं वस्तुगत्या शब्दसमवेतनिरूपितं वा लौकिकविषयत्वं कार्य्यदिशि प्रत्यासत्तिरिति मणिकृतोनिगर्भः।

स्वतन्त्रास्तु अत्रापि श्रोत्रसमवेतसमवायत्वं न कारणतावच्छेदकं अपि तु श्रोत्रत्वमेव स्वाश्रयसमवेतत्वं कारणदिशि प्रत्यासत्तिः कार्य्य-तावच्छेदकञ्च यथोक्तमेवेत्याहुः।

'शब्दाभावस्येति शब्दसमवायस्याप्युपलक्षकं, तथाच नभोवृत्ति-श्रावणत्वेन श्रोत्रविशिष्टविशेषणतात्वेन हेतु-हेतुमद्भावः, विषयत्व-स्वरूपसम्बन्धघटितसामानाधिकरण्यं प्रत्यासत्तिः, नभोवृत्तित्वञ्च स्वरूपसम्बन्धेन नभोवृत्तित्वं, तच्छ्रावणत्वञ्च लौकिकविषयितासम्बन्धेन तद्विशिष्टश्रावणत्वं, तेनातीतानागतयोः शब्दप्रागभाव-प्रध्वंसयो-र्लौकिकश्रावणप्रत्यक्षमादाय न व्यभिचारः। वस्तुतस्तु श्रावणत्व-मेव कार्य्यतावच्छेदकं नभोवृत्तिनिरूपितलौकिकविषयत्वं कार्य्यदिशि प्रत्यासत्तिः देशान्तरवृत्तिशब्दप्रागभावादौ श्रोत्रवृत्तित्वप्रत्ययाभावेन श्रोत्रविशिष्टविशेषणत्वाभावान्न साक्षात्कार इति भावः।

केचित्तु विशेषणताया विशेषणतात्वेनैव हेतुत्वं तादृशविषय-

तासम्बन्धेन तत्तत्पुरुषायश्रावणोत्पत्तौ तत्तत्पुरुषीयकर्णविवरस्यापि विशेषणतासम्बन्धावच्छिन्नाधेयतासम्बन्धेन हेतुतया न देशान्तरवृत्ति-शब्दप्रागभावादेर्ग्रहणमित्याहुः।

'इन्द्रियसम्बद्धविशेषणतयेति, इन्द्रियसम्बन्धः संयोगादिसन्निकर्ष-रूपो ग्राह्यः अन्यथा यथाकथञ्चित्सम्बन्धेनेन्द्रियसम्बद्धत्वाभिधाने देश-मात्रवृत्तिप्रागभावादेरपि प्रत्यक्षापत्तेः, तथाच इन्द्रियसंयुक्तविशेषणता, इन्द्रियसंयुक्तसमवेतविशेषणता, इन्द्रियसंयुक्तसमवेतसमवेतविशेषणता, इन्द्रियसमवेतविशेषणता, इन्द्रियसमवेतसमवेतविशेषणता, इन्द्रियवि-शेषणविशेषणता, इन्द्रियसंयुक्तविशेषणविशेषणतादिभेदे इन्द्रियसम्बद्ध-विशेषणतैव नानाविधा, उदाहरणन्तु भूतलादिघटितसन्निकर्षेण घटाभावादिप्रत्यक्षमिन्द्रियसंयुक्तविशेषणतायाः, रूपादिघटितसन्नि-कर्षेण नीलत्वादिभेदप्रत्यक्षमिन्द्रियसंयुक्तसमवेतविशेषणतायाः, रूप-त्वादिघटितसन्निकर्षेण नीलत्वादिभेदप्रत्यक्षमिन्द्रियसंयुक्तसमवेतसम-वेतविशेषणतायाः, शब्दघटितसन्निकर्षेण ककारादिभेदप्रत्यक्षमिन्द्रि-यसमवेतविशेषणतायाः, शब्दत्वादिघटितसन्निकर्षेण कत्वादिभेदप्रत्यक्ष-मिन्द्रियसमवेतसमवेतविशेषणतायाः, शब्दप्रागभाव-शब्दसमवायादि-घटितसन्निकर्षेण शब्दादिभेदप्रत्यक्षमिन्द्रियविशेषणविशेषणतायाः, भूतलादिनिष्ठघटाभावादिघटितसन्निकर्षेण घटत्वाद्यभावप्रत्यक्षमि-न्द्रियसंयुक्तविशेषणविशेषणतायाः, अभावेप्यतिरिक्ताभावस्वीकारात् रूपादिनिष्ठघटाभावादिघटितसन्निकर्षेण घटत्वाद्यभावप्रत्यक्षमिन्द्रि-यसंयुक्तसमवेतविशेषणविशेषणतायाः, इत्यादि। एतासामसङ्करस्त त्तद्व्यक्तिभिन्नमेदस्यातिरिक्तत्वे तत्रैव ध्येयः। कार्य्यतावच्छेदकश्च

एतासां तत्तत्प्रत्यासत्तिमत्प्रत्यक्षत्वं मतुबर्थोऽव्यवहितोत्तरत्वं अन्वय दुर्वचं एकस्यैवाभावस्य एकेनैवेन्द्रियेण कदाचित् कयाचिदितरप्रत्यासत्त्या ग्रहेण परस्परं व्यभिचारात्। सामान्यलक्षणा-ज्ञानलक्षणयोर्हेतुहेतुमद्भावश्चानुमानदीधितावेव विवेचितः। योगजधर्मस्य तु ज्ञानलक्षणव्याप्यजातिविशेष एव जन्यतावच्छेदकः, अध्यानेन शृणोतीत्यादौ श्रुवादिधातूनां साक्षात्कारमात्रे शक्तता, चाक्षुषत्वादिव्याप्या नानाजातय एव वा जन्यतावच्छेदिकाः, इति च लौकिकसन्निकर्षे आर्थः समाज इति बोध्यं। नन्वेवं घटत्वादिवद्घटादिनिष्ठगुरुत्वादेरपि लौकिकप्रत्यक्षापत्तिः संयुक्तसमवायादेः सन्निकर्षस्य तेन सम्बन्धेन चक्षुरादेस्तत्रापि विद्यमानत्वादित्यत आह, 'योग्यसन्निकर्षादिति योग्यविषयनिष्ठसन्निकर्षादित्यर्थः। तथाच लौकिकप्रत्यक्षं प्रति योग्यत्वेन गुरुत्वादिव्यावृत्तधर्मेण विषयस्यापि तादात्म्यसम्बन्धेन विषयनिष्ठकारणतया गुरुत्वादौ तादात्म्यसम्बन्धेन तादृशविषयाभावादेव न प्रत्यक्षत्वं, योग्यत्वञ्च लौकिकविषयतासम्बन्धेन साक्षात्कारवत्त्वं। न चैतावता अतीन्द्रियव्यावृत्तावपि चक्षुषा स्पर्शादेः, घ्राणेन रसादेः, रसनेन गन्धादेः कुतो न लौकिकप्रत्यक्षं तेषां योग्यत्वादिति वाच्यं। चाक्षुषादिप्रत्यक्षं प्रति विषयस्य चक्षुरादियोग्यत्वेन हेतुत्वात् चक्षुरादियोग्यत्वञ्च लौकिकविषयतासम्बन्धेन चाक्षुषादिमत्त्वमिति भावः।

केचित्तु लौकिकप्रत्यक्षसामान्ये तादात्म्यसम्बन्धेन गुरुत्वादेः प्रतिबन्धकत्वान्न गुरुत्वादेरतीन्द्रियस्य लौकिकप्रत्यक्षं, एवं लौकिकचाक्षुषादिसामान्ये स्पर्शादेरपि तादात्म्यसम्बन्धेन प्रतिबन्धकतया न तेषामपि चक्षुरादिना लौकिकप्रत्यक्षमित्याहुः।

अथ सूक्ष्मावयवावच्छेदेनावयविसंयोगेऽपि न तद्ग्रह इति महावयवावच्छेदेन संयोगो हेतुः तथा चावयवे-

---

'सूक्ष्मावयवावच्छेदेनेति परमाण्वाद्यवच्छेदेनेत्यर्थः, 'अवयविसंयोगेऽपि' अवयवि-चक्षुरादिसंयोगेऽपि, 'संयोगः' स्वनिष्ठचक्षुरादिसंयोगः, 'हेतुः' अवयविचाक्षुषादौ हेतुः, त्वया वाच्य इति शेषः। 'अवयवेन्द्रियसंयोग एवेति महावयवेन्द्रियसंयोग एवावयविचाक्षुषादौ हेतुरस्त्वित्यर्थः, महावयवावच्छिन्नस्वनिष्ठचक्षुरादिसंयोगापेक्षया महावयवचक्षुरादिसंयोगस्य लघुत्वादिति भावः। महावयवसंयोगानामतिप्रसक्ततया स्वनिष्ठसंयोगाधारतावच्छेदकमहत्त्वसंयोगो हेतुर्वाच्यस्तथा च गौरवं तदपेक्ष्य स्वनिष्ठसंयोगस्य लघुत्वादित्याशङ्कते 'न चेति ग्राह्यसंयोगावच्छेदकेति स्वनिष्ठसंयोगाधारतावच्छेदकमहत्त्वसंयोगापेक्षयेत्यर्थः, 'ग्राह्यसंयोगस्य' स्वनिष्ठसंयोगस्य, 'तस्येति स्वनिष्ठसंयोगमात्रस्य, 'स्वावयवसंयोगापेक्षयेति स्वसमवायिमहत्त्वसंयोगापेक्षयेत्यर्थः, पूर्व्वं स्वनिष्ठसंयोगावच्छेदकत्वेन प्रवेशोऽत्र तु स्वसमवायित्वेनेति भेदः। आशयमविद्वानाशङ्कते, 'नापीति, 'तच्चापि' महावयवसंयोगेऽपि, अत्र स्वनिष्ठसंयोगाधारतावच्छेदकमहदवच्छिन्नसंयोगत्वेनैव त्वयापि हेतुत्वं वाच्यं, तथा च तदपेक्ष्य स्वनिष्ठसंयोगाधारतावच्छेदकमहत्त्वसंयोगत्वमेव लघु। 'हेतुरेव न स्यादिति, स्वतोग्राह्यनिष्ठसंयोगहेतुरिति शेषः। आशयमुद्घाटयति, 'अन्यतरत्वेनेति, 'संयोगस्य' ग्राह्यनिष्ठसंयोगस्य, तथा चावच्छेदकसंयोगेनान्यथासिद्ध्या ग्राह्यनिष्ठसंयोगो न हेतुरिति न पूर्व्वपक्षि-

न्द्रियसंयोग एव हेतुः। न च ग्राह्यसंयोगावच्छेदकाव यवसंयोगापेक्षया ग्राह्यसंयोगस्य लघुत्वात्स एव हेतुः, तस्यातिप्रसक्तत्वात्। एतेन स्वावयवसंयोगापेक्षया स्वसं-

---

णामाशयः, अपि तु ग्राह्यनिष्ठसंयोगमात्रस्य हेतुत्वे अतिप्रसङ्गात्तद्वा-रणाय स्वीयमहावयवावच्छिन्नसंयोग एव हेतुर्वाच्यः, तथाच लाघ-वात् स्वीयमहावयवसंयोग एव हेतुरस्त्वित्येव तस्याशय इति भावः। यद्यपि पूर्व्वपक्षिणापि स्वल्पावयवावच्छेदेनोत्पन्नमहावयवसंयोगस्या-ग्राहकतया स्वीयमहावयवसंयोग एव हेतुर्वाच्यः, प्रथमस्वपदं महा-वयवपरं, द्वितीयस्वपदं ग्राह्यव्यक्तिपरं, तथाच तदपेक्षया लाघ-वात् स्वीयमहावयवावच्छिन्नसंयोग एव हेतुरित्येव समाधानं सुकरं तथापि स्फुटतरं दोषमाह, 'मैवमिति, 'द्रव्यग्रहे' द्रव्यमात्रग्रहे, 'स्थूलावयवावच्छेदेन संयोग इति स्थूलविषयकनिष्ठः संयोग इत्यर्थः, 'त्रसरेणुसूक्ष्मभागग्रह इति त्रसरेणुसूक्ष्मावयवकद्रव्यग्रह इत्यर्थः, 'स हेतुरिति तदभिमत इति शेषः। 'आत्मादीत्यादिना द्रव्यत्वक्-परिग्रहः, 'स्वग्राह्यसंयोगजन्य इति स्वग्राह्यनिष्ठसंयोगजन्य इत्यर्थः। लाघवादिविषयत्व-समवायघटितसामानाधिकरण्यप्रत्यासत्त्या सामान्यत एव द्रव्यलौकिकप्रत्यक्षत्वावच्छिन्नं प्रति इन्द्रियसंयोगत्वेन हेतुत्व-कल्पनादिति भावः। 'तस्मिन् सत्यपीति परमाण्वादिसूक्ष्मावयवा-वच्छेदेनेन्द्रियसंयोगे सत्यपीत्यर्थः,। वस्तुतस्तत्रापि घटादिग्रहोभवत्येव किन्तु सूक्ष्मावयवाच्छिन्नेन्द्रियसंयोगाद्यात्मकदोषवशात् उत्पन्नेऽपि तज्ज्ञानेऽप्रामाण्यसंशयात् कदाचित् कस्यचिद्विषयसंशयः। न चैवं

योगस्य लघुत्वात् स एव हेतुरिति निरस्तं। नाप्यवच्छेदक-संयोगेनान्यथासिद्धौ तच्चाप्यवच्छेदकान्तरसंयोगेनान्यथासिद्धिरिति संयोगो हेतुरेव न स्यादिति वाच्यं। अल्पतरतमभागावच्छेदेन संयोगस्य हेतुत्वे अतिप्रसङ्गा-

---

परमाण्वाद्यवच्छेदेन चक्षुरादिसंयोगेऽपि घटादिसाक्षात्कारापत्तिरिति वाच्यम। महावयवावच्छेदेनेन्द्रियसंयोगाभावदशायां केवलपरमाण्वाद्यवच्छेदेनैन्द्रियसंयोगे मानाभावादित्यभिप्रायो यदित्यादिना सूचितः। 'स्थूलावयवसंयोगेति। यद्यपि घटादिचाक्षुषत्वाद्यवच्छेदेन चतुरणुकाद्यवच्छेदेन वा चक्षुरादिसंयोगेऽपि घटादिप्रत्यक्षापत्तिर्दुर्वारा तथापि यादृशयादृशापकर्षाश्रयपरिमाणकावयवावच्छेदेन चक्षुरादिसंयोगे सत्यपि यादृशजन्यग्रहो न भवति तादृशद्रव्यचाक्षुषादौ तादृशापकर्षाश्रयेतरपरिमाणकावयवावच्छिन्नाधारतासम्बन्धेन चक्षुरादिसंयोगः तादृशावयवावच्छिन्नसंयोगसम्बन्धावच्छिन्नाधारतासम्बन्धेन चक्षुरादिर्वा हेतुरित्यननुगत एव कार्य्य-कारणभावः। न च तथापि त्रसरेण्वादिसूक्ष्मभागावच्छिन्नघटादिनिष्ठसंयोगस्य त्रसरेण्वादिसमवेतमहावयवेनाप्यवच्छिन्नत्वादतिप्रसङ्गतादवस्थ्यमिति वाच्यं। तद्देशव्यापकसंयोगस्यैव तद्देशावच्छिन्नत्वनियमेन सूक्ष्मभागावच्छिन्नसंयोगस्य स्थूलावच्छेद्यत्वाभावात्। न चैवंरूपेण विशेषतो हेतुत्वे यत्रावयवनाशदशायां घटादौ चक्षुःसंयोगस्तदनन्तरमवयवसंयोगनाशाद्घटनाशः तत्र घटनाशक्षणेऽवयवसंयोगनाशक्षणे च घटप्रत्यक्षं न स्यात् विनश्यतोऽवयवस्यावच्छेदकत्वासम्भवादिति

दिति। मैवं। द्रव्यग्रहे अवयवविभागग्रहे वा स्थूलावयवावच्छेदेन संयोगो न हेतुः आत्म-त्रसरेणुसूक्ष्मभागग्रहे व्यभिचारात्। किन्तु घटादिग्रहे स हेतुः। एवञ्चात्मादिद्रव्यग्रहोऽग्राह्यसंयोगजन्य इति घटादिग्रहोऽ-

---

वाच्यं। तदाऽवयवरूपादिवद्घटस्याप्यप्रत्यक्षत्वस्येष्टत्वादिति भावः। 'तत्संयोगोऽपि वेति स्थूलावयवसंयोगोऽपि वेत्यर्थः, 'हेतुः' घटादिचाक्षुषत्वावच्छिन्नं प्रति हेतुः। न चैवं घटस्योत्पत्तिप्राक्क्षणे कपाले न चक्षुःसंयोगस्तत्र घटोत्पत्त्यनन्तरं घट-चक्षुःसंयोगोत्पत्तिकालेऽपि घटप्रत्यक्षं स्यादिति वाच्यं। ग्राह्यनिष्ठसंयोगस्यापि सामान्यसामग्रीतया तदभावादेव तदानीं प्रत्यक्षानुत्पादादिति भावः। अत्र वाशब्दोऽस्वरससूचनाय, तद्बीजन्तु स्थूलावयवसंयोगस्य हेतुत्वे कारणतावच्छेदकगौरवं स्वसमवायिसमवेतत्वस्य प्रत्यासत्तितया प्रत्यासत्तिगौरवञ्च सूक्ष्मविभागावच्छेदेन स्थूलावयवसंयोगेऽपि साक्षात्कारप्रसङ्गश्च। न च सूक्ष्मभागावच्छिन्नस्थूलावयवाधारताकसंयोगो हेतुरिति वाच्यं। तथासति स्थूलावयवावच्छिन्नाधारतासम्बन्धेनैव चक्षुरादिसंयोगस्य हेतुताया लाघवेनोचितत्वादिति बोध्यं।

अत्र स्वतन्त्राः स्थूलावयवावच्छिन्नसंयोगत्वेनावयवविभेदेन विभेदतः प्रयोजकत्वेऽनन्तकार्य्य-कारणभावापत्तिः सूक्ष्मभागावच्छेदेन चक्षुरादिसंयोगादपि कदाचित् घटादिप्रत्यक्षोदयेन व्यभिचारश्च। तस्माच्चक्षुरादिसंयोगस्य साक्षात्कारानुपधायकसंयोगव्यावृत्तवैजात्येन सामान्यतो द्रव्यचाक्षुषत्वावच्छिन्नं प्रत्येव हेतुत्वं तेन सूक्ष्मभागा-

वच्छेदेन चक्षुरादिसंयोगान्न कदाचित् पटादिग्रहः वैजात्यस्य फल-बलकल्प्यत्वात्। नचैवं सूक्ष्मभागावच्छिन्नचक्षुरादिसंयोगः कदाचित्फलोपधायकः कदाचिच्च नेति वाच्यं। तत्र फलबलेन संयोग-भेदकल्पनात्। इत्यत्रापरमपि लाघवं, चक्षुरादिसंयोगस्य वैजात्येनाहेतुत्वे आलोकसंयोगावच्छिन्नत्वं एकावच्छिन्नत्वसम्बन्धेनालोक-संयोगविशिष्टत्वं वा चक्षुःसंयोगस्य चक्षुषो वा विशेषणमावश्यकमन्यथा आलोकसंयुक्त एव पटे अन्धकारावच्छेदेनैव चक्षुःसंयोगेऽपि प्रत्यक्षा-पत्तेः, वैजात्येन हेतुत्वे च तस्याप्यनुपादेयत्वात् वैजात्यस्य फलबल-कल्प्यत्वात्। एवं चक्षुरादिसंयोगस्य वैजात्येनाहेतुत्वे त्रसरेणुचाक्षुषं प्रति गवाक्षविवरवर्त्यालोकसंयोगावच्छिन्नचक्षुःसंयोगत्वेन हेतुत्वं वाच्यं। आलोकान्तरसंयोगावच्छिन्नचक्षुःसंयोगे त्रसरेणुचाक्षुषानुदयात्, वैजात्येन हेतुत्वे तस्याप्यकल्पनात् वैजात्यस्य फलबलकल्प्यत्वात्। तच्च वैजात्यं सर्व्वपुरुषसाधारणमेकमेव, तत्तत्पुरुषीयचक्षुःप्रतियो-गिकत्वविशिष्टत्वस्य वैजात्यविशेषणतया कारणतावच्छेदककोटिप्रवेशा-देवातिप्रसङ्गभङ्गात्। विशिष्टत्वञ्च सामानाधिकरण्येन। वस्तुतस्तु तद्वैजात्यं प्रतिपुरुषं विभिन्नमेव, अन्यथा तत्तत्पुरुषीयचक्षुरादिप्रति-योगिकत्वविशिष्टत्वस्यावच्छेदककोटिप्रवेशे गौरवात् तत्तत्पुरुषीयचक्षुः-प्रतियोगिकत्वविशिष्टत्व-वैजात्ययोर्विशेष्य-विशेषणभावे विनिगमका-भावेन प्रतिपुरुषं कार्य्य-कारणभावद्वयप्रसङ्गाच्च। कार्य्यतावच्छेदकन्तु तत्तत्पुरुषीयचाक्षुषत्वादिकमेव तत्तत्पुरुषीयचाक्षुषादिमात्रवृत्ति वैजात्यमेव वा। एतेन चक्षुःसंयोगस्य वैजात्येन हेतुत्वे आलोक-संयोगस्यापि हेतुत्वे मानाभावः वैजात्यस्य फलबलकल्प्यतया अन्ध-

कारे विजातीयचक्षुःसंयोगविरहादेव घटादेरप्रत्यक्षतोपपत्तेः, आलोकसंयोगावच्छिन्नचक्षुःसंयोगत्वेन हेतुत्वे विनिगमकाभावाच्चक्षुःसंयोगावच्छिन्नालोकसंयोगत्वेनापि हेतुत्वं। नचैकस्यैव चक्षुःसंयोगस्य आलोकसमवधानासमवधानाभ्यां ज्ञापकत्वाज्ञापकत्वसत्त्वादालोकसंयोगस्य हेतुत्वमावश्यकमिति वाच्यं। तत्र फलबलेन संयोगभेदस्य सुवचत्वात्। नच जनकतावच्छेदकवैजात्यमालोकसंयोगावच्छिन्नचक्षुःसंयोगे चक्षुःसंयोगावच्छिन्नालोकसंयोगे वा कल्प्यत इत्यत्र विनिगमकाभावादुभयोरेव हेतुत्वमिति वाच्यं। आलोकसंयोगनिष्ठवैजात्यकल्पने एकस्य पुरुषस्य चक्षुःसंयोगावच्छिन्नालोकसंयोगवति पटे तत्पुरुषीयचाक्षुषवदन्धकारावच्छिन्नतच्चक्षुःसंयोगवतः पुरुषान्तरस्यापि चाक्षुषापत्तेः। न हि चक्षुरिवालोकोऽपि पुरुषभेदेन विभिन्नो येन तत्तत्पुरुषीयालोकप्रतियोगिकत्वविशिष्टत्वविशेषणदानादतिप्रसङ्गभङ्गः स्यादिति कस्यचिद्दूषणमपि परास्तं। उक्तयुक्त्या चक्षुःसंयोगेऽपि वैजात्यस्य प्रतिपुरुषं विभिन्नतया आलोकसंयोगेऽपि पुरुषभेदेन वैजात्यभेदस्य सुवचत्वाद्विनिगमकाभावेनालोकसंयोगस्यापि हेतुत्वात् एकस्यैवालोकसंयोगस्य नानापुरुषीयचाक्षुषजनकत्वस्यासिद्धेः फलबलेन संयोगभेदकल्पनात्। नचैवमालोकसंयोगचक्षुःसंयोगयोरेकरूपेण हेतुत्वेप्यालोकसंयोगस्य पृथक् हेतुत्वं भग्नमेवेति वाच्यं। इष्टत्वात्। न हि पार्थक्येनापि तद्धेतुताऽनुभवसिद्धा। नचैवं विनिगमकाभावाद्वाय्वादिसंयोगस्यापि हेतुत्वापत्तिरिति वाच्यं। वाय्वादिसंयोगसाधारणधर्मेण चक्षुःसंयोगस्य हेतुत्वेऽपि क्षतिविरहात्। नच कर्म्मादिजन्यतावच्छेदकवैजात्येन

साङ्कर्य्यान्न चक्षुरादिसंयोगनिष्ठवैजात्यसम्भव इति वाच्यं। कपालादि-जन्यतावच्छेदकवैजात्यस्य नानात्वात् कार्य्यतावच्छेदकाननुगमस्या-दोषत्वात्। नच तथाप्यभिघातत्वादिना साङ्कर्य्यमिति वाच्यं। तत्राभिघातत्वादिसत्त्वे मानाभावेन तस्याभिघातत्वादिविरुद्धत्वात्। ननु तथापि चक्षुःसंयोगस्य फलबलकल्प्यवैजात्येन हेतुत्वे उद्भूत-रूप-महत्त्वयोः कारणत्वे मानाभावः पिशाच-परमाण्वादेर्विजाती-यचक्षुःसंयोगविरहादेवाचाक्षुषतोपपत्तेः। नच पिशाचनिष्ठचक्षुः-संयोगे वैजात्यानभ्युपगमे पिशाचे उद्भूतरूपाभावचाक्षुषं न स्यात् विजातीयचक्षुःसंयोगाश्रयविशेषणताश्रयताया एवाभावग्राहकत्वात्। एवं परमाणुनिष्ठचक्षुःसंयोगे वैजात्यानभ्युपगमे परमाणौ महत्त्वा-भावचाक्षुषं न स्यादिति वाच्यं। पिशाचघटितसन्निकर्ष-परमाणुघ-टितसन्निकर्षयोस्तत्राहेतुत्वेऽपि क्षतिविरहात् तदानीं आलोक-त्रस-रेण्वादियत्किञ्चिन्महत्त्वोद्भूतरूपवच्चक्षुःसंयोगस्यावश्यकतया तद्वृत्तिरू-पादिघटितसन्निकर्षेणैव पिशाचे उद्भूतरूपं नास्ति परमाणौ महत्त्वं नास्तीति चाक्षुषोपपत्तिरिति चेत्। न। वैजात्येन हेतुत्वेऽपि संयोगस्य द्विष्ठतया चक्षुषश्चाक्षुषतावारणाय उद्भूतरूपहेतुत्वस्यावश्य-कत्वात्। वस्तुतस्तु वैजात्येन संयोगस्य हेतुत्वे संयोगस्य द्विष्ठतया चक्षुषः चाक्षुषतावारणाय उद्भूतरूपस्य हेतुत्वावश्यकत्वेऽपि विजा-तीयसंयोगसम्बन्धेन चक्षुर्विशिष्टत्वेन हेतुत्वे उद्भूतरूपहेतुत्वं विनापि चक्षुषश्चाक्षुषतावारणसम्भवादुक्तयुक्तेरकिञ्चित्करतया महत्त्वोद्भूतरूपयो-रुभयोरेव प्रामाणिकव्यवहारबलात् कारणत्वसिद्धिः, तदनादरे चाकारणत्वमिष्टमेव, अन्यथा सामान्यतश्चक्षुःसंयोगत्वादिना हेतुत्वे-

पि तद्वदेव स्वग्राह्यसंयोगजन्य इति। तस्मिन् सत्यपि घटादिग्रहो नास्तीति यदि तदा स्थूलावयवसंयोगावच्छेदकोऽस्तु तत्संयोगोऽपि वा हेतुः, न तु क्लृप्तहेतुपरित्यागः। ननु संयुक्तसमवायेनावयविग्रहोऽस्तु न तु संयोगादिस्तत्र हेतुः तस्य रूपादिग्रहे क्लृप्तत्वात्। न च लाघवात्संयोग एव तथा, तस्य कल्पनीयकारणत्वात्(१)

ऽप्युद्भूतरूप-महत्त्वयोः कारणत्वे मानाभावः लौकिकप्रत्यक्षं प्रति विषयस्य योग्यत्वेन हेतुत्वादेव परमाणु-पिशाचादेरप्रत्यक्षतोपपत्तेः। 'क्लृप्तत्वादिति द्रव्यसमवेतचाक्षुषत्वावच्छिन्नं प्रति कारणत्वेन क्लृप्तत्वादित्यर्थः। 'न चेति, 'लाघवादिति संयुक्तसमवायत्वमपेक्ष्य संयोगत्वस्य कारणतावच्छेदकस्य लघुत्वादित्यर्थः, 'तथा' अवयविग्रहे हेतुः, 'तस्य' संयोगस्य। 'इन्द्रियसंयोगस्य' इन्द्रियसंयोगत्वावच्छिन्नस्य, 'कारणत्वादिति द्रव्यसाक्षात्कारत्वावच्छिन्नं प्रति कारणत्वादित्यर्थः, 'अन्यत्रापि' अवयविसाक्षात्कारेऽपि। 'न चेति, आत्ममानसस्यैव मनःसंयोगकार्यतावच्छेदकत्वादिति शेषः। 'बहिरिन्द्रियजद्रव्यग्रह इति मानसेतरद्रव्यसाक्षात्कारे इत्यर्थः, 'अवयविग्रहे' अवयविसाक्षात्कारे, 'संयुक्तसमवाय इति, क्लृप्तत्वादिति शेषः, 'लाघवेन' सामान्यरूपतालाघवेन, 'संयोगस्य' मनःसंयोगस्य, एवकारपूर्वं

---

(१) कल्पनीयकारणभावादिति भ०।

इति चेत्। न। आत्मग्रहे इन्द्रियसंयोगस्य कारणत्वादन्यत्रापि द्रव्यसाक्षात्कारत्वेन तथा कल्पनात्। न च बहिरिन्द्रियजद्रव्यग्रहे अवयविग्रहे वा संयुक्तसमवायः कारणं, लाघवेन संयोगस्यैव कारणत्वेन कल्पनात्। ननु संयुक्तसमवायो न गन्धग्राहकः

द्रव्यसाक्षात्कारत्वावच्छिन्नं प्रतीति पूरणीयं, 'कारणत्वेन कल्पनादिति इन्द्रियसंयोगत्वेन कारणत्वेन कल्पनादित्यर्थः।

अत्र केचित् गुणादिसाक्षात्कारानुरोधेन द्रव्यसमवेतचाक्षुषत्व-द्रव्यसमवेतत्वाचत्वावच्छिन्नं प्रति चक्षुस्त्वक्संयुक्तसमवाययोः स्वसमवायिसमवेतत्वसम्बन्धेन चक्षुस्त्वक्संयोगयोर्वा स्वसंयुक्तसमवेतत्वसम्बन्धेन चक्षुस्त्वचोर्वा हेतुत्वावश्यकत्वात्तत एव घटादेरपि चाक्षुष-त्वाचोपपत्तेः किं समवायसम्बन्धेन चक्षुःसंयोग-त्वक्संयोगयोः संयोगसम्बन्धेन चक्षुस्त्वचोर्वा द्रव्यचाक्षुषत्व-द्रव्यत्वाचत्वावच्छिन्नं प्रति हेतुत्वेन। यथात्मप्रत्यक्षे समवायसम्बन्धेन मनःसंयोगस्य इन्द्रियसंयोगत्वेन, संयोगसम्बन्धेन मनसो वा इन्द्रियत्वेन द्रव्यसाक्षात्कारत्वावच्छिन्नं प्रति हेतुत्वात् द्रव्यचाक्षुषादावपि समवायसम्बन्धेन चक्षुःसंयोगादेः, संयोगसम्बन्धेन चक्षुरादेर्वा हेतुत्वमावश्यकमिति वाच्यं। तथापि द्रव्यचाक्षुषत्वाद्यवच्छिन्नं प्रति तेषां हेतुत्वे मानाभावात् आत्मप्रत्यक्षस्थाने लाघवान्मानसत्वावच्छिन्नं प्रत्येव मनःसंयोगत्वादिना हेतुत्वकल्पनाच। शरीरचाम्म एव सामान्यरूपतालाघवाभ्युपगमात्।

किन्त्वाश्रयसंयोगः। एवं गन्धत्वग्रहोऽप्याश्रयाश्रयसंयोगादिति संयुक्तसमवेतसमवायोऽपि न हेतुः। न च गन्धे सति गन्धसमवायं विना गन्धाग्रहोऽस्ति। न चैवं संयुक्तघटे भाविगन्धग्रहः स्यात्, गन्धस्यापि स्वग्रहे

न च द्रव्यचाक्षुषादिकं प्रति चक्षुःसंयोगादेरहेतुत्वे यत्र पटस्योत्पत्तिप्राक्क्षणे तन्तुना चक्षुःसंयोगस्तत्र पटोत्पत्त्यनन्तरं पटचक्षुःसंयोगस्योत्पत्तिकालेऽपि पटप्रत्यक्षं स्यादिति वाच्यं। इष्टत्वात्। क्षणविलम्बस्य ज्ञपथनिर्णेयत्वात्। अथ चक्षुःसंयुक्तसमवायमात्रस्य ग्राहकत्वे द्व्यणुकादेरपि रूपप्रत्यक्षप्रसङ्गात् चक्षुःसंयुक्तमहत्त्वोद्भूतरूपवत्समवाय एव तथा वाच्यः, कार्य्यतावच्छेदकमपि महत्समवेतविशिष्टचाक्षुषत्वमन्यथा विषयत्व-विशेषणताभ्यां सामानाधिकरण्यस्य प्रत्यासत्तितया त्रसरेणौ व्यभिचारापत्तेः, महच्चाक्षुषत्वमेव वा कार्य्यतावच्छेदकं महत्समवेतत्वविशिष्टं वस्तुगत्या महत्समवेतनिरूपितं वा लौकिकविषयत्वं कार्य्यदिशि प्रत्यासत्तिः। इत्यञ्च त्रसरेणुचाक्षुषानुरोधेन चक्षुःसंयोगस्य सन्निकर्षत्वमावश्यकं तत्कार्य्यतावच्छेदकञ्च द्रव्यविशिष्टचाक्षुषत्वं विषयत्वं कार्य्यदिशि प्रत्यासत्तिः। चाक्षुषत्वमेव वा कार्य्यतावच्छेदकं द्रव्यत्वविशिष्टं वस्तुगत्या द्रव्यनिरूपितं वा लौकिकविषयत्वं प्रत्यासत्तिः, न त्रसरेणुविशिष्टचाक्षुषत्वं कार्य्यतावच्छेदकं न वा चाक्षुषत्वमेव कार्य्यतावच्छेदकं त्रसरेणुत्वविशिष्टं वस्तुगत्या त्रसरेणुनिरूपितं वा लौकिकविषयत्वं प्रत्यासत्तिः गौरवात् घटादावपि त्रसरेणुविशिष्टचाक्षुषस्य त्रसरेणुत्वविशिष्टविषयतासम्बन्धेन चाक्षु-

हेतुत्वात्। न च गन्धस्य प्रत्यक्षत्वेनेन्द्रियसन्निकर्षा-श्रयत्वमनुमेयं शब्दप्रत्यक्षहेतोः समवायस्य गन्धेऽपि सत्त्वात्, गन्धेन्द्रियसन्निकर्षसाधने साध्याप्रसिद्धेः। मैवं। गन्धसमवायिसंयोगस्य हेतुत्वे हि यदि गन्ध-

---

षस्य वा उत्पादप्रसङ्गाच्च। अत एव चाक्षुषत्वमेव कार्य्यतावच्छेदकं वस्तुगत्या त्रसरेणुनिरूपितं लौकिकविषयत्वं प्रत्यासत्ति-रित्यपि न तेन सम्बन्धेन घटादावपि चाक्षुषापत्तेः त्रसरेणुत्वविशिष्टसमवायस्य कारणतावच्छेदकसम्बन्धत्वे च गौरवात्। एवन्त्वक्-संयुक्तसमवायमात्रस्य प्रत्यासत्तित्वे द्व्यणुकस्पर्शादेः त्रसरेण्वादेश्च त्वाचप्रसङ्गात् त्वक्संयुक्तप्रकृष्टमहत्त्वाश्रयसमवाय एव तथा वाच्यः, कार्य्यतावच्छेदकमपि प्रकृष्टमहत्त्ववत्समवेतविशिष्टत्वाचत्वं अन्यथा विषयत्व-विशेषणताभ्यां सामान्याधिकरण्यस्य प्रत्यासत्तितया चतुरणुके व्यभिचारापत्तेः। यद्वा त्वाचत्वमेव कार्य्यतावच्छेदकं प्रकृष्टमहत्समवेतत्वविशिष्टं वस्तुगत्या तत्समवेतनिरूपितं वा लौकिकविषयत्वं प्रत्यासत्तिः, इत्यञ्च चतुरणुकत्वाचानुरोधेन त्वक्संयोगस्य सन्निकर्षत्वमावश्यकं तत्कार्य्यतावच्छेदकञ्च द्रव्यविशिष्टत्वाचत्वं विषयत्वं प्रत्यासत्तिः, त्वाचत्वमेव वा कार्य्यतावच्छेदकं द्रव्यत्वविशिष्टं वस्तुगत्या द्रव्यनिरूपितं वा लौकिकविषयत्वं प्रत्यासत्तिः, न तु चतुरणुकविशिष्टत्वाचत्वादिकमुक्तयुक्तेः। न च सामान्यतश्चक्षुःसंयुक्त-समवाय—त्वक्संयुक्तसमवाययोरेव सन्निकर्षत्वमेकार्थसमवायसम्बन्धेन

समवायस्य विशेषणता तदा स हेतुरेव। उपलक्षणत्वे च संयुक्तद्रव्यमात्रमुपलक्ष्यं तथा च घटसंयोगात्पटगन्धग्रहप्रसङ्गः। अथ स्वसमवायिसंयोगो हेतुः तच्च

महत्त्वस्य द्रव्यान्यद्रव्यसमवेतचाक्षुषं प्रति, प्रकृष्टमहत्त्वस्य तादृशत्वाचं प्रति पृथक्हेतुतया न द्व्यणुकरूपादेः न त्रसरेणुस्पर्शादेश्च ग्रह इति वाच्यं। पृथक्कारणतान्तरकल्पने गौरवात् परमाण्वादिघटितसन्निकर्षेण पृथिवीत्वादिग्रहप्रसङ्गाच्च पृथिवीत्वादेर्घटादौ महत्यपि सत्त्वेन तदानीमपि पृथिवीत्वादौ सत्त्वात्। एतेन सामान्यतः चक्षुःसंयुक्तसमवाय एव सन्निकर्षः न तु तत्र महत्त्वस्य प्रवेशः। नचैवं द्व्यणुकरूपादेरपि चाक्षुषापत्तिरिति वाच्यं। द्रव्यान्यचाक्षुषत्वावच्छिन्नं प्रति स्वाश्रयसमवेतत्वसम्बन्धेन चाक्षुषवत्त्वेदस्य निरवच्छिन्नस्वाधिकरणताश्रयसमवेतत्वसम्बन्धेन चाक्षुषात्यन्ताभावस्य वा प्रतिबन्धकत्वादेव द्व्यणुकरूपादेरचाक्षुषतोपपत्तेः, गगनादिमादाय स्वाश्रयसमवेतत्वसम्बन्धेन चाक्षुषवत्त्वेदादेः सर्व्वदैव सत्ता-द्रव्यत्वादौ सत्त्वात्तदप्रत्यक्षतापत्तिवारणाय प्रतिबध्यतावच्छेदककोटौ समवेतत्वमपहाय सत्त्वेन प्रवेशः, पूर्व्वं घटादिचाक्षुषं विनापि तद्वृत्तिरूपादेश्चाक्षुषोदयान्निरवच्छिन्नेति स्वाधिकरणतर्म्मविशेषणं। न चातिरिक्तप्रतिबध्य-प्रतिबन्धकभावकल्पनामपेक्ष्य सन्निकर्षमध्ये महत्त्वप्रवेश एव लघीयानिति वाच्यं। परमाणु-घटवृत्तिद्वित्व-गगन-घटवृत्तिद्वित्वादेः चाक्षुषतावारणाय व्यासज्यवृत्तिधर्म्मचाक्षुषं प्रति तादृशप्र-

समवायोऽवच्छेदक इति चेत्। तर्हि संयोगिसमवायस्य हेतुत्वे संयोगोऽवच्छेदकः समवायो हेतुरिति

तिबन्धकताकल्पनस्य तवाप्यावश्यकत्वात् । न च पटासन्निकर्षदशायामपि घटसन्निकर्षमात्राद् घट-पटवृत्तिद्वित्वादेश्चाक्षुषवारणाय व्यासज्यवृत्तिधर्मचाक्षुषं प्रति यावदाश्रयलौकिकसन्निकर्षस्य हेतुत्वावश्यकत्वात्तद्विरहादेव परमाणु-घटद्वित्वादेर्न चाक्षुषमिति वाच्यं । चक्षुःसंयोगलक्षणस्य लौकिकसन्निकर्षस्य परमाण्वादावपि सम्भवादिति केषाञ्चित् प्रलपितमप्यपास्तं । परमाण्वादिघटितसन्निकर्षेण पृथिवीत्वादिग्रहवारणाय चक्षुःसंयुक्तमहत्समवायस्यैव प्रत्यासत्तित्वावश्यकत्वात् विजातीयचक्षुःसंयोगस्यैव लौकिकसन्निकर्षतया यावदाश्रयलौकिकसन्निकर्षविरहादेव परमाणु-घटवृत्तिद्वित्वादेरचाक्षुषतोपपत्तेस्तादृशातिरिक्तप्रतिबध्य-प्रतिबन्धकभावकल्पने गौरवाच्च । अपिच परमाणुघटवृत्तिद्वित्वादेश्चाक्षुषवारणाय द्रव्यान्यचाक्षुषं प्रति स्वाश्रयसमवेतत्वसम्बन्धेन चाक्षुषत्वावच्छेदादेः प्रतिबन्धकत्वं, एकाश्रयमात्रसन्निकर्षाद्घट-पटद्वित्वादेश्चाक्षुषवारणाय व्यासज्यवृत्तिधर्मचाक्षुषं प्रति यावदाश्रयसन्निकर्षस्य च यावत्स्वाश्रयसन्निकर्षत्वेन हेतुत्वकल्पनामपेक्ष्य लाघवादनुगतत्वाच्च व्यासज्यवृत्तिधर्मचाक्षुषं प्रति सामान्यतः स्वाश्रयसमवेतत्वसम्बन्धेन चाक्षुषात्यन्ताभावस्यैव प्रतिबन्धकत्वं कल्प्यते यावदाश्रयप्रत्यक्षं विना व्यासज्यवृत्तिधर्मप्रत्यक्षाभ्युपगमात् । न च तस्यैव प्रतिबध्यतावच्छेदकं द्रव्यान्यचाक्षुषत्वमिति वाच्यं। तथासति पूर्वं घटादिचाक्षुषं विना तद्वृत्तिद्वित्वादेरिव तद्वृत्ति-

तुल्यं। तदेतत्परिवर्त्त्य क्षौमपरिधानमित्युच्यते। ननु संयुक्तसमवायो न संयोगः, न वा समवायः, न उभौ वा गन्धे इन्द्रिये चावृत्तेः। न चेन्द्रियेण गन्धस्य पर-

---

रूपादेरप्यप्रत्यक्षत्वापत्तेः किन्तु उभयसमवेतगुणचाक्षुषत्वं तत्प्रतिबध्यतावच्छेदकं तथाच द्व्यणुकरूपादेः प्रत्यक्षवारणाय सन्निकर्षे महत्त्वप्रवेश आवश्यक इति चेत्। न। द्व्यणुकरूपादेः त्रसरेणुस्पर्शादेश्चायोग्यत्वादेव घटादिवृत्तिगुरुत्वादिवदप्रत्यक्षतोपपत्तेः महत्त्वस्य तत्रानन्तर्भावात्। न चैवं द्रव्यचाक्षुषादिकं प्रत्यपि महत्त्वादेर्हेतुत्वं विनापि नाति प्रसङ्गः अयोग्यत्वादेव परमाण्वादेरप्रत्यक्षोपपत्तेरिति वाच्यं। प्रामाणिकव्यवहारानादरे तत्र तदहेतुत्वस्यापीष्टत्वात्। न च महत्त्वस्य तत्रानन्तर्भावे परमाण्वादिघटितसन्निकर्षेण पृथिवीत्वादिप्रत्यक्षापत्तिरिति वाच्यं। परमाणुसन्निकर्षदशायां महदवयविसन्निकर्षस्याप्यावश्यकत्वेनेष्टापत्तेः। अपिच त्रसरेणुचाक्षुषस्थले त्रसरेणुनिरूपितेन लौकिकविषयतासम्बन्धेन चाक्षुषत्वावच्छिन्नोत्पत्तौ त्रसरेणुत्वविशिष्टसमवायसम्बन्धेन गवाक्षविवरावच्छिन्नालोकसंयोगावच्छिन्नचक्षुःसंयोगत्वेन विशेषतो हेतुत्वमावश्यकं आलोकान्तरसंयोगावच्छिन्नचक्षुःसंयोगात् त्रसरेणोरग्रहात् तथाच सामान्यतो द्रव्यचाक्षुषत्वावच्छिन्नं प्रति चक्षुःसंयोगस्य हेतुत्वे मानाभावः। अथ चक्षुःसंयुक्तसमवायादेर्द्रव्येतरद्रव्यसमवेतचाक्षुषत्वादिकमेव कार्य्यतावच्छेदकं न तु सामान्यतो द्रव्यसमवेतचाक्षुषत्वादिकं, यत्रावयवनाशदशायां

म्परासम्बन्धः, परम्परा हि संयोग-समवायावेव तत्र विरोध एव नाधिकोऽपसिद्धान्तादिति चेत्। न। इन्द्रिय-तत्संयोग-तदाश्रयसमवायानामेव परम्परास-

---

घटे न चक्षुरादिसंयोगस्तदनन्तरमवयवसंयोगनाशाद्घटनाशस्तत्र घटनाशक्षणोत्पन्ने अवयवसंयोगनाशक्षणोत्पन्ने वा घटप्रत्यक्षे व्यभिचारापत्तेः तत्रावयवेन्द्रियसंयोगाभावेन संयुक्तसमवायाभावादिति चेत्। न। तदावयवरूपादिवद्घटस्यापि प्रत्यक्षानभ्युपगमात्। अन्यथा प्रागुक्तस्थूलावयवावच्छिन्नसंयोगकारणतायामपि तत्र व्यभिचारापत्तेः। अथ चक्षुरादिसंयुक्तसमवायस्य द्रव्यग्राहकत्वे यदवच्छेदेन द्रव्यारम्भकसंयोगो नास्ति तदवच्छेदेनावयवेन समं चक्षुरादिसंयोगेऽपि च द्रव्यचाक्षुषादिप्रसङ्गः। न चेष्टापत्तिः, दशाद्यवच्छेदेन तन्तुना चक्षुरादिसंयोगे पटाप्रत्यक्षत्वात्। तथाच द्रव्यचाक्षुषादौ आरम्भकसंयोगावच्छेदेन चक्षुरादिसंयोगस्य विशेषतो हेतुत्वमावश्यकं। न च तदनुरोधादारम्भकसंयोगावच्छेदेन यत्र चक्षुरादिसंयोगस्तद्वत्समवाय एव विशिष्टद्रव्यचाक्षुषादौ हेतुरस्त्विति वाच्यं। तदपेक्षया तदवच्छेदेन चक्षुरादिसंयोगस्यैव लघुत्वादिति चेत्। न। व्याप्यवृत्तिगुण-कर्मप्रत्यक्षानुरोधेन चक्षुरादिसंयोगावच्छेदकावच्छिन्नानुयोगितासम्बन्धेन चक्षुरादिसंयुक्तविशिष्टस्य समवायस्यैव द्रव्यसमवेतचाक्षुषादिकं प्रति हेतुतया आरम्भकसंयोगानवच्छेदकावच्छेदेनावयवसंयोगाद्द्रव्याग्रहात्। यदवच्छेदेनारम्भकसंयोगो नास्ति तदवच्छेदेन द्रव्यस्य वृत्तौ मानाभावेन द्रव्यस्यापि समवायसम्बन्धेनाव्याप्यवृत्ति-

म्बन्धत्वात्। अन्यथा नीलत्वजातेः परम्परासम्बन्धेन वस्त्र-चर्म-कम्बलेष्वनुगतव्यवहारोच्छेदः। ननु संयुक्तसमवेतसमवायान्न रूपत्वादिग्रहः तदभावादिति चेत्। न। तदनभ्युपगमेऽपि रूपादिसाहचर्य्यस्य ततो ग्रहात्।

त्वात्। न चैतादृशसंयुक्तसमवायस्य हेतुत्वे द्रव्यसमवेतजात्यादेः प्रत्यक्षे व्यभिचारः व्याप्यवृत्तेरवच्छेदकविरहादिति वाच्यं। प्रत्ययबलेन व्याप्यवृत्तेरप्यवच्छेदकाभ्युपगमात् द्रव्यसमवेताव्याप्यवृत्तिचाक्षुषत्वादेर्वा तादृशसंयुक्तसमवायस्य कार्य्यतावच्छेदकत्वात्। द्रव्यसमवेताव्याप्यवृत्तित्वञ्च द्रव्ये समवायसम्बन्धेन किञ्चिदवच्छिन्नवृत्तिमत्त्वं, तस्माच्चक्षुःसंयोग-त्वक्संयोगयोः प्रत्यासत्तित्वे मानाभावः। वस्तुतस्तु चक्षुःसंयुक्तसमवाय-त्वक्संयुक्तसमवाययोरपि सन्निकर्षत्वे मानाभावः, एवं घ्राणसंयुक्तसमवाय-रसनसंयुक्तसमवाययोरपि न सन्निकर्षत्वं, गुण-कर्मवृत्तिजातिप्रत्यक्षानुरोधेन चक्षुःसंयुक्तसमवेतसमवायादेः प्रत्यासत्तित्वावश्यकतया तत एव गुणादिप्रत्यक्षोपपत्तेरिति। अथोच्यते त्रसरेणोर्नित्यत्वे तत्प्रत्यक्षानुरोधेन चक्षुःसंयोगस्य, तद्वृत्तिरूपादिप्रत्यक्षानुरोधेन चक्षुःसंयुक्तसमवायस्य च प्रत्यासत्तित्वावश्यकत्वात्। 'न गन्धग्रह' इति न गन्धादिग्राहक इत्यर्थः, 'आश्रयसंयोग' इति स्वसमवायिसंयोग इत्यर्थः, 'गन्धत्वग्रहः' गन्धत्वादिग्रहः, 'आश्रयाश्रयसंयोगा'दिति स्वसमवायिसमवायिसंयोगादित्यर्थः, 'अन्वय-व्यतिरेकरूपग्राहकाभावमाह, 'न चेति महीत्यर्थः, 'गन्धे सतीत्यस्य सति

न च द्रव्यसादृश्यादेव तद्व्यवहारः, बाधकं विना प्रतीत्यविशेषाद्वैपरीत्यापत्तेः। आश्रयवैसादृश्येऽपि रूप-

स्वाश्रयसंयोग इति शेषः। 'न चैवमिति, अंशत्रये सामानाधिकरण्य-प्रत्ययशक्तिनिर्वाहकतयैव गन्धस्य तदानीमावश्यकत्वादेवेति भावः। 'इन्द्रियसन्निकर्षाश्रयत्वमिति साक्षात्कारकारणेन्द्रियसन्निकर्षाश्रयत्व-मित्यर्थः, यथाश्रुते घ्राणसंयुक्तसमवायमादायैव सिद्धसाधनापत्तेरिति ध्येयं। 'शब्दप्रत्यक्षेति समवायस्य लभ्यते ऐक्यादिति भावः। नन्वयं गन्धः साक्षात्कारकारणेन्द्रियसन्निकर्षाश्रयः प्रत्यक्षगन्धत्वादिति व्यति-रेक्यस्त्वित्यत आह, 'गन्धेन्द्रियसन्निकर्षसाधने चेति गन्धसाक्षात्कार-कारणेन्द्रियसन्निकर्षाश्रयत्वसाधने चेत्यर्थः, 'साध्याप्रसिद्धिरिति, आश्र-यत्वं हि न यथाकथञ्चित्सम्बन्धेन, स्वाश्रयसंयोगमादायैव सिद्धसा-धनापत्तेः। नापि समवायेन, बाधात्। किन्तु समवायनिरूपित-विशेषणताविशेषेण, तथाच साध्याप्रसिद्धिरित्यर्थः। न च यत्प्रत्यक्षवि-षयो यो भवति स तत्प्रत्यक्षकारणेन्द्रियसन्निकर्षाश्रयो भवति शब्दवदिति यत्तद्भ्यां सामान्यतोव्याप्तिरस्तु तथाच साध्याप्रसिद्धावपि न क्षतिरिति वाच्यं। यत्तदर्थयोरननुगमात। न च समवायनि-रूपितविशेषणताविशेषेण सम्बन्धेन तादृशेन्द्रियसन्निकर्ष एव साध्योऽस्तु तथाच न साध्याप्रसिद्धिरिति वाच्यं। तथाप्यप्रयोजकत्वादिति भावः।

केचित्तु ननु गन्धप्रत्यक्षं गन्धेन्द्रियसन्निकर्षजन्यं गन्धप्रत्यक्षत्वादिति व्यतिरेक्यस्त्वित्यत आह, 'गन्धेन्द्रियेति गन्धेन्द्रियसन्निकर्षजन्यत्वसाधने चेत्यर्थ इत्याहुः।

रसादेः साक्षात्कारानुभवाच्च। रसत्व-मधुरत्व-गन्धत्व-सुरभित्वादिश्च जातिः अनुगतप्रत्ययात्। रूपे च

'गन्धसमवायिसंयोगस्येति स्वसमवायिसंयोगस्येत्यर्थः, 'हेतुत्वेऽपि' हेतुत्वाभ्युपगमेऽपि, 'गन्धसमवायस्य' स्वसमवायस्य, 'विशेषणता' विशेषणीभूयावच्छेदकता, 'तदेति, विशेष्यान्वयिनोऽन्वयिन एव विशेषणत्वादिति भावः। 'उपलक्षणत्वे चेति अवच्छेदकाघटकत्वे चेत्यर्थः, 'संयुक्तद्रव्यमात्रं' द्रव्यमात्रस्य संयोगत्वं, 'उपलक्ष्यं' कारणत्वेनाभिमतं। 'अवच्छेदक इति दण्डत्वादिवद्विशेषणतया अवच्छेदक इत्यर्थः 'इतितुल्यमिति इत्यपि सुवचमित्यर्थः, तथाच विनिगमकाभावादुभयोरेव हेतुत्वमिति भावः। एतच्चापाततः स्वसमवायिसंयोगस्य हेतुत्वे स्वत्वस्य तत्तद्व्यक्तिविश्रान्ततया अनन्तकार्य्य-कारणभावापत्तेः। न च तवापि घ्राणादिसंयुक्तस्वसमवायस्य हेतुतया स्वत्वघटितत्वेनानन्तकार्य्य-कारणभाव इति वाच्यं। मम घ्राणादिसंयुक्तसमवायमात्रस्य हेतुत्वात् न तु स्वत्वप्रवेशः, गन्धनिरूपितलौकिकविषयत्व-विशेषणताभ्यां सामानाधिकरण्यस्य प्रत्यासत्तितया चातिप्रसङ्गविरहादिति ध्येयं।

अत्र केचित्संयुक्तसमवायस्य हेतुत्वे कालान्तरीनचक्षुःसंयोगवत्यपि घटे घटरूपादिप्रत्यक्षप्रसङ्गः। न च तत्तत्कालीनसंयोगवत्समवायस्तत्तत्कालाव्यवहितोत्तरकालीनप्रत्यक्षे हेतुरिति वाच्यं। कालभेदेनानन्तकार्य्य-कारणभावप्रसङ्गात्तस्मात् संयुक्तसमवायो न हेतुः किन्तु तन्मात्रसमवेतचाक्षुषं प्रति तच्चक्षुःसंयोगो हेतुः तद्व्यक्तिचक्षुः-

यद्यपीदं नीलमित्यनुभवो न त्विदं रूपमिदं रूपमिति तथापि पीतो वर्णः नीलो वर्ण इति वर्णाकारानुगत-

---

संयोगं विनापि व्यक्त्यन्तरसंयोगेन तद्व्यक्तिसमवेतजाति-द्रव्ययोश्चाक्षुषोत्पत्तेर्मात्रपदं, सत्त्वादिजातिचाक्षुषे च तच्चाक्षुषं प्रति तदाश्रयसंयोगत्वेन हेतुत्वं, द्रव्यचाक्षुषे च लाघवात् सामान्यतो द्रव्यचाक्षुषं प्रति चक्षुःसंयोगत्वेनैव हेतुत्वं, त्वाच-मानसयोरप्येवमेव, रासनादौ च तत्समवेतरसप्रत्यक्षं प्रति तद्रसनसंयोगः, तत्समवेतगन्धप्रत्यक्षं प्रति तद्घ्राणसंयोगो हेतुः, एवं दण्डादिगतजातिप्रत्यक्षेऽपि संयुक्तसमवेतसमवायो न हेतुः यदाकदाचिच्चक्षुरादिसंयोगमादायातिप्रसङ्गात् किन्तु तत्तद्विषयकचाक्षुषादिकं प्रति तत्तत्समवायिसमवायिसंयोगो हेतुरित्याहुः । तदसत् व्यक्तिभेदेनानन्तकार्य्य-कारणभावापत्त्या चक्षुःसंयुक्तसमवायत्वादिनैव हेतुत्वात् । न च यदाकदाचिच्चक्षुरादिसंयोगमादायातिप्रसङ्ग इति वाच्यं । अन्यत्र कारणतावच्छेदकावलीढमात्रस्य पूर्व्वसत्ताया अपेक्षितत्वेऽप्यत्र कारणतावच्छेदकविशिष्टस्य पूर्व्वसत्ताया अपेक्षितत्वादेव चक्षुरादिसंयोग-तदाश्रययोः कारणतावच्छेदकयोः पूर्व्वकाले सत्त्वं विना कार्य्योत्पत्तेरसम्भवात् । न च तथापि समवायस्यैक्याद्घटचक्षुःसंयोगेऽपि पटवृत्तिरूपादिप्रत्यक्षप्रसङ्ग इति वाच्यं । चक्षुःसंयुक्तविशिष्टसमवायत्वादिना हेतुत्वात् पटवृत्तिरूपं घटसमवेतमित्यादिप्रत्ययाभावेन घटविशिष्टसमवायस्य च पटवृत्तिरूपादावभावात् । वस्तुतस्तु चक्षुरादिसंयुक्तसमवायत्वे तत्समवेतसमवायत्वेऽपि च लाघवात् चक्षुःसंयोगत्वादिनैव

बुद्धिरस्ति[१] रूपत्वे मानं। न च चक्षुराद्येकैकमात्रग्राह्यत्वं रूपत्वादिकं, बाधकं विनानुगतबुद्धेर्जातिविषय-

---

हेतुत्वं स्वसमवायिसमवेतत्वं स्वसमवायिसमवायिसमवेतत्वञ्च कारणतावच्छेदकप्रत्यासत्तिः तेन यदाकदाचिच्चक्षुरादिसंयोगमादायापि नातिप्रसङ्ग इति तत्त्वं ॥

केचित्तु घ्राणसंयुक्तसमवाय-रसनसंयुक्तसमवायत्वे समवायसम्बन्धेनैव घ्राणादिसंयोगत्वेन हेतुत्वं, कार्य्यतावच्छेदकप्रत्यासत्तिश्च स्वीयलौकिकविषयताश्रयगन्धवत्त्वं तादृशविषयताश्रयरसवत्त्वञ्चेत्याहुः।

'नन्विति, 'संयोगः' चक्षुरादिना संयोगः, 'समवायः' यत्रेन्द्रियस्य संयोगस्तत्समवायः। 'गन्ध इति चक्षुरादिसंयोगो न गन्धे यच्च चक्षुरादिसंयोगस्तन्निरूपितसमवायो नेन्द्रिय इत्यर्थः। 'परम्परासम्बन्धत्वादिति संयुक्तसमवायरूपपरम्परासम्बन्धघटकत्वादित्यर्थः, 'परम्परासम्बन्धेनेति स्वसमवायिसमवायिसमवेतत्वरूपपरम्परासम्बन्धेनेत्यर्थः, तत्राप्युक्तत्रिकस्यैव परम्परासम्बन्धत्वासम्भवादिति भावः। 'रूपत्वादिग्रहः' रूपादिपदप्रवृत्तिनिमित्तस्य ग्रहः, 'तदभावादिति तन्मते रूपादिपदप्रवृत्तिनिमित्तस्योपाधिरूपतया समवेतत्वाभावादित्यर्थः। 'तदनभ्युपगमेऽपि' तस्य समवेतत्वानभ्युपगमेऽपि, 'रूपादिसादृश्यस्येति रूपादिनिष्ठसादृश्यस्येत्यर्थः, सादृश्यस्य तन्मते समवेतपदार्थान्तरत्वादिति भावः। 'तद्व्यवहारः' परम्परासम्बन्धेन रूपादिषु सादृश्यव्यवहारः, 'प्रतीत्यविशेषादिति साक्षात्सम्बन्धेन प्रतीत्योः

---

(१) इत्यनुगताकारा बुद्धिरस्तीति ख०।

प्रमात्वाविशेषादित्यर्थः, 'वैपरीत्येति गुणादिसादृश्यादेव तदाश्रये परम्परया सादृश्यव्यवहार इत्येव किन्न स्यादित्यर्थः। न चाश्रितानामनेकत्वान्न वैपरीत्यमिति वाच्यं। पूर्व्वापरकालोत्पन्नघटत्रादिसङ्ख्यायाः सादृश्यस्य चाश्रयवृत्तित्व एव गौरवात् आश्रयाणामनेकत्वादिति भावः। ननु ग्राहकान्तरकल्पनाभिया आश्रयवृत्तित्वं कल्प्यत इत्यत आह, 'आश्रयेति। ननु परनये सादृश्यवैरूप्यादेव न प्रत्यक्षमित्यत आह, 'रसत्वेति। रूपत्वस्यापि जातित्वं बाधयति, 'रूपे चेति, 'इत्येवानुभव इति द्रव्यनिष्ठेदन्त्वस्य नीलरूपाद्यधिकरणतावच्छेदकावगाह्येवानुभव इत्यर्थः, 'न त्विदं रूपं नीलमिति रूपपदप्रवृत्तिनिमित्तनिष्ठनीलरूपाद्यधिकरणतावच्छेदकत्वावगाह्यनुभव इत्यर्थः, बाधादिति भावः। 'वर्णाकारानुगतबुद्धिरिति रूपपदप्रवृत्तिनिमित्तस्य नीलत्वादिजात्यधिकरणतावच्छेदकत्वावगाहिनी बुद्धिरित्यर्थः, 'रूपत्वे मानं' रूपपदप्रवृत्तिनिमित्तस्य जातित्वे मानं, यथाश्रुतन्तु न सङ्गच्छते। 'चक्षुराद्येकेति 'चक्षुर्मात्रग्राह्यगुणत्वादिकमित्यर्थः, रूपादिपदप्रवृत्तिनिमित्तं तदेव च 'रूपत्वादिकं', आदिपदात्त्वङ्मात्रग्राह्यगुणत्व-रसनग्राह्यगुणत्व-घ्राणग्राह्यगुणत्वादीनां स्पर्श-रस-गन्धादिपदप्रवृत्तिनिमित्तानां परिग्रहः, नीलोवर्णः पीतोवर्ण इत्याद्यनुगतबुद्धिविशेष्यतावच्छेदकमिति शेषः। अत्र चक्षुस्त्वगुभयग्राह्येषु सङ्ख्या-परिमाणादिषु तादृशसंख्यादिषु द्रव्यत्वादिषु अतिव्याप्तिवारणाय मात्रपदं, तद्व्यवच्छेद्यञ्च त्वगिन्द्रियं, तेन त्वगग्राह्यत्वे सति चक्षुर्ग्राह्यगुणत्वमिति फलितं। ज्ञानादावतिव्याप्तिवारणाय विशेष्यदले चक्षुःपदं, त्रसरेणु-तत्कर्मादीनां

त्वात्। इन्द्रियातीन्द्रियत्वेन चक्षुराद्यग्रहेऽपि रूपत्वादिप्रतीतेः। न ह्यननुसंहितोपाधेरुपहितप्रत्ययः। अतीन्द्रियरूप-रस-गन्धाननुमानापत्तेश्च। योग्यताया रूपत्वादिजातिनिरूप्यत्वात्। यद्यपि तन्मते नील-पी-

---

वारणाय गुणपदं, गुणत्वस्य शक्तिविशेषसम्बन्धेन गुणपदवत्त्वं न तु जातिः, तेन तद्ग्रहार्थमपि न संयुक्तसमवेतसमवायस्य प्रत्यासत्तितावश्यकीति भावः। 'अनुगतबुद्धेः' नीलो वर्णः पीतो वर्ण इत्यनुगतबुद्धेः, 'रूपत्वादिप्रतीतेरिति रूपादिपदप्रवृत्तिनिमित्तप्रकारकप्रतीतेरित्यर्थः, अतीन्द्रियरूपादावव्याप्तिमप्याह, 'अतीन्द्रियेति अतीन्द्रियरूप-रस-गन्धेषु रूपादिपदप्रवृत्तिनिमित्तेन हेतुना रूपादिपदवाच्यत्वानुमानानुपपत्तेश्चेत्यर्थः, ग्राह्यत्वघटितस्य प्रवृत्तिनिमित्तस्य तत्र विरहादिति भावः। ननु ग्राह्यत्वं ग्रहणयोग्यत्वं वाच्यमित्यत आह, 'योग्यतायाश्चेति, 'रूपत्वादिजातिनिरूप्यत्वादिति चक्षुर्ग्राह्यवृत्तिगुणत्वव्याप्यधर्मसमवायित्वस्य चक्षुर्ग्राह्यो यो गुणत्वव्याप्यो धर्मस्तत्समवायित्वस्य वा योग्यतात्वादिति भावः। गुणत्वविशिष्टनीलादिभेदस्य वारणाय समवायित्वप्रवेशः। इदमुपलक्षणं त्रसरेणुपरिमाणादौ देवाचक्षुर्मात्रग्राह्यस्नेह-द्रवत्व-संयोगादौ चातिव्याप्तिः। न च त्वग्ग्राह्यत्वं त्वग्ग्रहणायोग्यत्वं तच्च त्वग्ग्राह्यगुणत्वव्याप्यधर्मशून्यत्वं परिमाण-स्नेहादौ परिमाणत्व-स्नेहत्वादेस्तादृशधर्मस्य सत्त्वान्नातिव्याप्तिः, तैः रूपत्व-रसत्वादेरनभ्युपगमेऽपि परिमाणत्व-स्नेहत्वा-

ताद्यकैकमेव नित्यं नातीन्द्रियं, तथापि चक्षुर्घ्राणादिरूपस्यालोक-पृथिव्यादिरूपाभिन्नत्वेन प्रत्यक्षत्वप्रसङ्गः। नचैकमेव रूपमुद्भूतमनुद्भूतञ्चेति, विरोधात्। रूपत्वादिना परस्परव्यावृत्ततया ज्ञातस्य रूपादेरुपलब्ध्या

देरखण्डोपाधिरूपस्याभ्युपगमादिति वाच्यं। गुणत्वविशिष्टनीतादिभेदस्य तादृशधर्मस्य नीलादावपि सत्त्वेनासम्भवापत्तेः, समवायसम्बन्धेन तादृशधर्मशून्यत्वाभिधाने चोक्तातिव्याप्तितादवस्थ्यात् परिमाणत्वादेरखण्डोपाधिरूपतया समवेतत्वाभावादन्यथा तद्ग्रहार्थमेव संयुक्तसमवेतसमवायस्य प्रत्यासत्तित्वावश्यकत्वादित्यपि बोध्यं। अतीन्द्रियरूपे अव्याप्तिमुद्धरति, 'यद्यपीति, 'प्रत्यक्षत्वप्रसङ्ग इति चक्षुरादेरपि प्रत्यक्षत्वप्रसङ्ग इत्यर्थः, उद्भूतरूप-रसत्वादिति भावः। ननु तन्नये अनुद्भूतरूपत्वादौ मानाभावेन चक्षुरादेर्नीरूपत्वान्न प्रत्यक्षत्वं। अस्तु वा अनुद्भूतरूपादिर्व्यक्त्यन्तरमित्यस्वरसादाह, 'रूपत्वेति, 'परस्परव्यावृत्तचक्षुराद्यनुमितिरिति चक्षुरादौ घ्राणादिभिन्नत्वानुमितिरित्यर्थः। अन्यथा रूपादि-गन्धाद्योरभेदज्ञानाद्घ्राणादावेव व्यभिचारज्ञानापत्तेरिति भावः। 'परस्परव्यावृत्तचक्षुराद्यनुमिताविति चक्षुरादेर्घ्राणादिभिन्नत्वानुमितावित्यर्थः। 'रूपादिपरस्परव्यावृत्तधीरिति रूपादौ गन्धादिभिन्नत्वधीरित्यर्थः। अन्यथा चक्षुरादि-घ्राणाद्योरभेदभ्रमाद्गन्धादावेव व्याभिचारज्ञानापत्तेरिति भावः। ननु नीलोपलब्धिः सकारका कार्य्यत्वाद्घटवदित्याद्यनुमित्या नील-पीताद्युपलब्धीनां

तत्करणत्वेन परस्परव्यावृत्तचक्षुराद्यनुमितिः, परस्परव्यावृत्तचक्षुराद्यनुमितौ च चक्षुर्ग्राह्यत्वादिना रूपादिपरस्परव्यावृत्तधीरित्यन्योन्याश्रयाच्च। नील-पीतादिप्रतीतौ भिन्न-भिन्नकरणत्वसिद्धावपि तत्तत्करण-

---

घ्राणाद्यकरणकत्वेन विलक्षणकरणसिद्धौ तत्करणग्राह्यत्वं रूपत्वं वाच्यमतो नान्योन्याश्रय इत्यत आह. 'नीलेति। 'गन्ध-रसेति, गन्धादीनां प्रत्येकमेव प्रवेशो न तु मिलितानां, तथाच गन्धाव्यञ्जकत्वे सति नीलव्यञ्जकत्वादित्यादिहेतुत्रये तात्पर्य्यं, नातो निष्प्रयोजनत्वं। आत्म-मनःप्रभृतिषु व्यभिचारवारणाय सत्यन्तं, पार्थिवादिपरमाण्वादौ व्यभिचारवारणाय विशेष्यदलं। न चालोकस्यापि विषयविधया स्वविषयकसमूहालम्बनगन्धप्रत्यक्षजनकतया दृष्टान्तासिद्धिरिति वाच्यं। गन्धाव्यञ्जकत्वपदेन गन्धविषयकलौकिकप्रत्यक्षाजनकत्वस्य विषयतातिरिक्तरूपेण गन्धव्यञ्जकत्वाभावस्य वा विवक्षितत्वात्। न चैवं नीलत्रसरेणौ नीलघटादौ च व्यभिचारः तस्य विषयविधया स्वीयनीलव्यञ्जकत्वादिति वाच्यं। नीलव्यञ्जकताया अपि विषयतातिरिक्तरूपेण विवक्षितत्वात्। न च तथापि नीलत्रसरेणौ व्यभिचारस्तत्र सन्निकर्षघटकतया स्वीयव्यञ्जकत्वसत्त्वात् गन्धाव्यञ्जकत्वसत्त्वाच्चेति वाच्यं। सन्निकर्षस्य जनकत्वे मानाभावात् द्रव्यत्वेन विशेषणाच्च सन्निकर्षे न व्यभिचारः, गोलकस्य प्रत्यक्षजनकत्वे मानाभावान्न चक्षुःगोलके व्यभिचारः। न च तथापि लुप्ताचरमषीनीलिमाभिव्यञ्जकजले व्यभिचार इति वाच्यं। तस्य नवशरावग-

ग्राह्यत्वस्य सर्वरूपेष्वसिद्धिः। ननु नील-पीताद्युपल-
ब्धिकरणेषु गन्ध-रस-स्पर्शाव्यञ्जकत्वे सति नीलादि-
व्यञ्जकत्वादालोकवदिति तैजसत्वं प्रसाध्य तैजसेन्द्रि-
यग्राह्यत्वेन नीलादौ(१) रूपाकारानुगतधीरेवं गन्धादा-

न्धाभिव्यक्तिस्वरूपयोग्यत्वात्। न च तथापि पीतव्यञ्जकत्वगर्भहेतौ सुवर्णपीतरूपव्यञ्जके निकषोपले व्यभिचार इति वाच्यं। तस्य न सुवर्णपीताभिव्यञ्जकत्वं तेन विनापि सुवर्णपीतिमोपलब्धेः, किन्तु पीतद्वारा गुरुवैलक्षण्यव्यञ्जकत्वमेव तस्य तच्च वैलक्षण्यं परनयेऽखण्डोपाधिरूपमिति भावः। 'तैजसेन्द्रियग्राह्यत्वेन' तैजसेन्द्रियमात्रग्राह्यगुणत्वेन, वायवीयेन्द्रियाग्राह्यत्वे सति तैजसेन्द्रियग्राह्यगुणत्वेनेति यावत्। 'एवं गन्धादावपीति तत्रापि सौरभाद्युपलब्धिकरणेषु रसाव्यञ्जकत्वे सति सौरभादिव्यञ्जकत्वात् कुङ्कुमगन्धाभिव्यञ्जकतैलवदित्यनुमानेन पार्थिवत्वं प्रसाध्य पार्थिवेन्द्रियग्राह्यगुणत्वेन गन्धाकारानुगतधीरित्यर्थः। 'एवंप्रणालीज्ञानाभावेऽपीति एवं प्रणाल्या ज्ञानाभावेऽपीत्यर्थः, तथाच नीलं रूपं पीतं रूपमित्याद्यनुगतप्रत्ययबलादेव रूपत्वजातिसिद्धिः। न च रूपत्वमखण्डोपाधिरेव तस्य विषय इति वाच्यं। समवायसम्बन्धविषयकत्वे बाधके सत्येव सम्बन्धान्तरविषयकत्वकल्पनादिति मणिकृतो निष्कर्षः।

मिश्रास्तु चाक्षुषजनकतावच्छेदकतया रूपत्वजातिसिद्धिः। न च

(१) नील-पीतादाविति ख०।

वपीति चेत्। न। एवं प्रणालीज्ञानाभावेऽपि रूपरसादावनुगतप्रत्ययात् नीलाकारानुगतबुद्धेश्च नीलत्वं जातिः। न च चक्षुर्ग्राह्यत्वं तत्, पीतादौ गतत्वात्। नन्वेकैका एव नीलारुणादिव्यक्तयः, नानामसीनी-

---

तावता रूपत्वजातिसिद्धावपि तस्य नीलादिवृत्तित्वे मानाभावः एकत्वादिवृत्तित्वेऽप्युपपत्तेरिति वाच्यं। रूपत्वजातिसिद्धौ लाघवात्तस्यैव रूपपदप्रवृत्तिनिमित्तत्वादन्यत्र रूपव्यवहाराभावादेव नीलादिवृत्तित्वसिद्धेः। एवं लाघवसाक्षात्कारजनकतावच्छेदकतया स्पर्शत्वादिसिद्धिरित्याहुः।

'नीलाकारेति, नीलत्वं नीलपदप्रवृत्तिनिमित्तं, तथाच नीलत्वग्राहकतयैव संयुक्तसमवेतसमवायसिद्धिरिति भावः। 'यद्यपीत्यादिना पूर्व्वं दूषितमपि दूषणान्तरदानाय पुनः शङ्कते, 'नन्विति, तथाचैकव्यक्तिवृत्तित्वान्नीलत्वं न जातिरिति भावः। 'मसीभेदग्रहेऽपीति, एतेनाश्रयाभेदनिबन्धनाभेदभ्रमो निराकृतः। 'तत्त्वेन प्रत्यभिज्ञानादिति तदेवेदं नीलं रूपमिति तद्व्यक्तित्वेनाभेदप्रत्यभिज्ञानादित्यर्थः, 'अनेकव्यक्तिवृत्तित्वेनेति एकस्या एव नीलरूपव्यक्तेः सकलनीलद्रव्यवृत्तित्वेनेत्यर्थः, 'नित्यत्वे इति, अनित्यत्वे तन्नाशवक्तत्समवेतनाशं प्रति तन्नाशस्य हेतुतया घटादिनाशादेव तद्वृत्तिनीलनाशावश्यक एवानीलत्वापातादेकनीलरूपव्यक्तेः सकलवृत्तित्वं न सम्भवतीति भावः। 'जातित्वापत्तिः' जातिव्यवहारविषयत्वापत्तिः द्रव्या-

लिम्नि समीभेदग्रहेऽपि तत्त्वेन प्रत्यभिज्ञानात्। न चानेकव्यक्तिवृत्तित्वे नित्यत्वे जातित्वापत्तिः, जातेः संस्थानमात्रव्यङ्ग्यत्वात् अवयवावयविवृत्तित्वात् गोत्वादिना परापरभावानुपपत्तेश्च । नीलतरादिप्रतीतिश्च

दिपञ्चकान्यभावत्वापत्तिर्वा[१]। यथाश्रुते आपाद्यापादकयोरविशेषप्रसङ्गात् । स्वमते संस्थानव्यङ्ग्यत्वं अवयवावयविवृत्त्यन्यत्वञ्च उपाधिमाह, 'जातेरिति जातिव्यवहारविषयस्य द्रव्यादिपञ्चकान्यभावस्येति वार्थः। एतेन साध्यव्यापकता दर्शिता, साधनाव्यपकत्वञ्च पक्ष एवेति भावः। 'अवयवावयविवृत्तित्वादिति नीलादेरवयवावयविवृत्तित्वादित्यर्थः। एतेनावयवावयविवृत्त्यन्यत्वस्योपाधेः पक्षे साधनाव्यापकता दर्शिता, साध्यव्यापकत्वञ्च घटत्वादावेव। अवयवावयविवृत्त्यन्यत्वञ्च यस्यैवावयवे वर्त्तते तस्मिन्नेवावयविनि यद्वर्त्तते तदन्यत्वं, स्वसमवायिसमवायिवृत्त्यन्यत्वमिति यावत्। तेन कपालत्व-तन्तुत्वादौ न साध्याव्यापकता, पृथिवीत्व-द्रव्यत्वसत्त्वादिकमपि तन्मते जातिरेवं मृत्तिकात्व-पाषाणत्व-दण्डत्वादेः संस्थानव्यङ्ग्यस्यापि न जातित्वं तन्मते संस्थानव्यङ्ग्यस्याप्यवयवावयव्यवृत्तेरेव जातित्वादिति न तत्रापि साध्याव्यापकता। जातिलक्षणञ्च गुणान्यत्वेन विशेषणीयं, तेन नीलादौ नातिव्याप्तिरिति भावः। स्वमतेनोपाधिमभिधाय उभयमतेनासङ्कीर्णत्वमुपाधिमाह, 'गोत्वादिनेति नीलादेरित्यादि, 'गो-

---

(१) नित्यत्वे सति अनेकसमवेतत्वस्यैव जातित्वरूपत्वादिति भावः।

तदन्यरूपासम्भेदादिति चेत् । न । पाकेन श्यामनष्टं रक्तमुत्पन्नमिति प्रत्ययात्[१] । न चासौभ्रमः, बाधकाभावात् । न चोत्पाद-विनाशप्रत्ययस्य समवायो विषयः,

---

त्वादिना' स्वसमानाधिकरणगोत्वादिजात्या, 'परापरभावानुपपत्तेः' व्याप्य-व्यापकभावविरहात् । एतेन स्वसमानाधिकरणजातिव्याप्य-व्यापकभावविरहात्तदर्थेतरत्वरूपासङ्कीर्णत्वस्य पक्षे बाधमाव्यापता दर्शिता । ननु नीलादिव्यक्तीनां नानात्वविरहात् अयं घटो नीलतरः अयं घटो नीलतम इत्यादिप्रत्ययः कथं स्यादित्यत आह, 'नीलतरादीति, 'असम्भेदात्' स्वसामानाधिकरण्यात् । यद्यप्युत्कृष्टा नीलव्यक्तिरेकापकृष्टा चापरेति स्वीकारेऽपि तारतम्यधीरुपपद्यते एव तथाप्युत्कृष्टापकृष्टनीलरूपव्यक्तेर्भेदे तदधिकरणयोर्द्वयोरेव घटो नीलोऽयञ्च घटो नील इत्यनुगतप्रतीत्यनुरोधादेव नीलत्वजातिसिद्धिप्रसङ्ग इति तदुपेक्षितं । 'बाधकाभावादिति । न च गौरवमेव बाधकं, तथासति सुखादेरपि नित्यत्वापत्तेः । न च प्रत्यभिज्ञैव बाधिका, तज्जातीयत्वावगाहित्वेनैव तदुपपत्तेरिति भावः । समवायस्य प्रत्यक्षत्वमभ्युपेत्याह, 'न चेति, 'समवायोविषय इति नीलादिसमवाय एव उत्पत्ति-विनाशांशे विशेष्य इत्यर्थः, नीलादेर्नित्यत्वेऽपि तत्समवायस्यानित्यत्वात् । न च तत्समवेतनाशं प्रत्येव तन्नाशस्य हेतुत्वात् कथमाश्रयनाशानन्तरं तद्वृत्तिनीलादिसमवा-

---

(१) इत्यनुभवादिति ख० ।

तदनुल्लेखात्। एवञ्च मधुरादिरसानां[१] सौरभासौरभाणाञ्च गन्धानामेकैकत्वं स्यात् नीलादितुल्यत्वात्। एवमस्त्विति चेत्। न। तेषामुत्पादविनाशानुभवात्।

यनाशः समवायस्यासमवेतत्वादिति वाच्यं। समवायस्यापि स्वात्मकसम्बन्धेन वर्त्तमानतया समवेतत्वात्। एतेन भावकार्य्यस्य समवायिकारणत्वनियमात् समवायस्यासमवेतत्वेन समवायिकारणाभावात् कथमुत्पाद इत्यपि निरस्तं। नीलादिसमवायिन एव तत्समवायस्य समवायिकारणत्वात्। न च तथापि जात्यादेराश्रयनाशान्नाशवारणाय ध्वंसत्वावच्छिन्नं प्रति सत्त्वेन हेतुत्वस्यावश्यकत्वात् कथं समवायस्य नाश इति वाच्यं। प्रागभावव्यावृत्तस्यैव प्रतियोगित्वस्य काय्यतावच्छेदकत्वेन सुवचत्वात् सत्त्वस्याकृत्यव्यङ्गतयाऽवयवावयविवृत्तितया च तन्मते जातित्वासम्भवात्समवायसाधारणस्यापि तस्य सुवचत्वाच्चेति भावः। 'तदनुल्लेखादिति प्रतियोगित्वेन नीलादेरेवावगाहनान्न तु तत्समवायस्येत्यर्थः, प्रतिबन्धिमप्याह, 'एवञ्चेति, प्रत्यभिज्ञायास्तत्रापि सत्त्वादिति भावः। 'एवमस्त्विति, अन्यथाऽनुगतप्रत्ययानुरोधे तत्रैव जातिस्वीकारे तद्ग्रहार्थमेव संयुक्तसमवेतसमवायस्य प्रत्यासत्तितास्वीकारापत्तेरिति भावः।

केचित्तु तन्नाशत्वेन तत्समवेतनाशत्वेन नाश्य-नाशकभावाद्घटादिनाशेन नीलादिनाशस्य दुर्वारत्वात्तद्वृत्तिनीलादेर्नित्यत्वासम्भवः। न च

---

(१) मधुराम्ल-लवण-कटु-तिक्त-कषायाणामिति ख०।

एकैकत्वे मधुरतरत्वाद्यनुपपत्तेश्च। ननु श्रोत्रेण समवायेन शब्दग्रहे सर्वशब्दोपलब्धिः स्यात्। न च कर्णशष्कुल्यवच्छेदेनोत्पन्नो गृह्यते, अवच्छेदस्याकाशत्वेनाविशेषात्। तदन्यत्वे शब्दस्य तत्रासमवायात्। तस्माद्यः शब्दो यं प्रति योग्यः स तेन गृह्यते

जात्यादेर्नाशवारणाय स्वप्रतियोगिजन्यत्वस्यैव नाशकतावच्छेदकसम्बन्धत्वेन नीलादेर्नित्यत्वे स्वप्रतियोगिजन्यत्वविरहादेव न नाश इति वाच्यं। लाघवेन स्वप्रतियोगिसमवेतत्वस्यैव नाशकतावच्छेदकसम्बन्धत्वात् अनन्तनीलादिव्यक्तिकल्पनायाश्च फलमुखत्वात् सत्त्वेन ध्वंसत्वेन नाश्य-नाशकभावान्तरादेव नाशोपपत्तेः, अनन्तस्थले स्वप्रतियोगिजन्यत्वस्य नाशकतावच्छेदकसम्बन्धत्वकल्पनामपेक्ष्यातिरिक्तैकव्यक्तिनाश्यनाशकभावकल्पनाया लघुत्वादित्याहुः।

'समवायेन शब्दग्रह' इति यत्पूर्व्वमुक्तं तच्च शङ्कते, 'नन्विति, 'सर्व्वत्रेति सर्व्वस्मिन् पुरुष इत्यर्थः, आकाशात्मकश्रोत्रसमवायस्याविशेषादिति भावः। 'कर्णशस्कुल्यवच्छेदेनेति कर्णशस्कुल्यवच्छिन्न इत्यर्थः, 'तस्मादिति, तथाच तद्ग्रहार्थं न समवायप्रत्यासत्तिरपेक्षेति भावः। 'न चेति 'वाच्यमित्यग्रेतनेनान्वितं। 'न स्वरूपमिति न तु तद्व्यक्तिस्वरूपमित्यर्थः, 'न च जातिरिति। न च पुरुषद्वयसंश्लेषेकशब्दे जातिद्वयसङ्कर इति वाच्यं। स-स्वकर्णावच्छेदेनोत्पन्नस्यैव शब्दस्य ग्रह इत्यभ्युपगमादुभाभ्यामेकशब्दाग्रहादिति भावः। 'तस्मा:'

नान्यः। न च पुरुषविशेषं प्रति योग्यत्वं न स्वरूपं, अननुगमात्। न च जातिः, तस्याः निष्प्रतियोगिकत्वात्। न हि गौः कश्चित्प्रत्यगौरिति वाच्यं। सप्रतियोगिकत्वं हि न सावधित्वं दीर्घत्वादिवत्। नापीतरधीनिरूप्यत्वमभाववत्। किन्तु शब्दग्रहे सा जातिः कारणं तदवच्छेदिका वा। अत एव न कुर्व्वद्रूपत्वप्रवेशः सहकारितास्वीकारात्। सर्व्वसा-

---

जातेः, 'निष्प्रतियोगिकत्वादिति, तथाच सा जातिर्यत्पुरुषप्रतियोगिका तस्य साक्षात्कारं जनयतीति न वक्तुं शक्यमित्यर्थः। 'दीर्घत्वादिवदिति, व्यतिरेके दृष्टान्तः, एवं 'अभाववदित्यपि। 'शब्दग्रह इति पुरुषविशेषस्य ककारादिग्रह इत्यर्थः, 'कारणमिति, यच कत्वादिविशिष्टेन वस्तुगत्या कादिनिष्ठानुगतेन वा लौकिकविषयत्वेन तत्पुरुषीयश्रावणं तत्र समवायेन सा जातिसामानाधिकरण्यप्रत्यासत्तिरिति भावः। जातेः कारणत्वे तज्जातित्वस्य कारणतावच्छेदकतया गौरवापत्तिरत आह, 'तदवच्छेदिका वेति कारणतावच्छेदिका वेत्यर्थः, इत्यञ्च तादात्म्यं कारणतावच्छेदकप्रत्यासत्तिरिति भावः। एतेन प्रत्यासत्त्यादिनियामकं विनापि कश्चिदेव शब्दः कस्यचिद्विषयविधया प्रत्यक्षजनक इति स्वीकारे कुर्व्वद्रूपत्वस्वीकार इति परास्तमित्याह, 'अत एवेति, 'सहकारितास्वीकारादिति जातिविशेषस्य नियामकतास्वीकारादित्यर्थः। ननु तत्तत्पुरुषीयशब्दप्रत्य-

धारणत्वमिष्टमेव सर्व्वैस्तथा व्यवह्रियमाणत्वात्। गोत्वेऽपि तदेव तत्। शब्दमात्रस्य योग्यत्वमननुगतमेव गुणयोग्यत्ववदिति। मैवं। शब्दस्य प्रत्यक्षत्वेन प्रत्यासत्तिसाधनात्। न च समवायोऽतिप्रसक्तोऽन्यो-

---

नियामकस्य तस्य जातिरूपत्वे सर्व्वसाधारण्यापत्तिरित्यत आह, 'सर्व्वेति, 'सर्व्वैः' बहुभिः पुरुषैः, 'तथा' तज्जातिप्रकारेण, 'तदेव' बहुतरपुरुषव्यवहारविषयतावच्छेदकत्वमेव, 'तत्' सर्व्वसाधारणत्वं। ननु तज्जातीनां ककारादिभेदेन नानात्वाच्छब्दमात्रनिष्ठमेकं योग्यत्वमनुगतं दुर्निरूपमेवेत्यत्रेष्टापत्तिमाह, 'शब्दमात्रस्येति. 'अननुगतमेवेति। 'शब्दस्येति शब्दः साक्षात्कारजनकतावच्छेदकावच्छिन्नेन्द्रियनिरूपितधर्माश्रयः प्रत्यक्षत्वादित्यनुमानेन श्रोत्रप्रत्यासत्तेः शब्दसाक्षात्कारजनकत्वसाधनादित्यर्थः, तथाच श्रोत्रसन्निकर्षस्यैव शब्दग्राहकत्वं न तु जातेरिति भावः। अत्र प्रत्यक्षजनकत्वं विषयतातिरिक्तरूपेण विवक्षितं तेन पिशाचभेदवदिन्द्रियान्योन्याभावस्यापि प्रत्यक्षतया न तमादायार्थान्तरं। नच तथापि मनःसंयुक्तसमवायेन सिद्धसाधनं गगनस्यापि मनःसंयुक्तत्वादिति वाच्यं। मनःसंयुक्तात्मसमवायत्वेन हेतुत्वात्। मानसेतरत्वेन वा साक्षात्कारस्य विशेषणीयत्वादतो न कोऽपि दोषः।

केचित्तु 'प्रत्यक्षत्वेन' प्रत्यक्षगुणत्वेन, 'प्रत्यासत्तिसाधनात्' समवायजन्यप्रत्यक्षविषयत्वसाधनादित्यर्थः, संयुक्तसमवायस्यापि समवायानतिरेकादिति भावः इति प्राहुः।

ऽनभ्युपगत इति वाच्यं। कर्णसंयोगावच्छिन्नसमवायस्य प्रत्यासत्तित्वात्। कर्णसंयोगो हि समवायवृत्त्या शब्दाधारतायां परिचायकः एवञ्चेह शब्दो नेह शब्द इत्यनुभवात् शब्दस्याव्याप्यवृत्तित्वे सिद्ध

'अतिप्रसङ्ग इति देशान्तरवृत्तिशब्दे अतिप्रसङ्ग इत्यर्थः 'कर्णसंयोगावच्छिन्नेति, तत्तत्पुरुषीयकर्णसंयोगावच्छिन्नत्वं कर्णसंयोगविशिष्टत्वं तच्च समवायसम्बन्धेन विवक्षितं यथाकथञ्चित् सम्बन्धेन वा आद्ये बाधः समवायसम्बन्धेन संयोगस्यावृत्तेः, अन्त्ये स एवातिप्रसङ्ग इत्यत आह, 'कर्णसंयोगो हीति, 'परिचायकः' स्वरूपसम्बन्धविशेषात्मकावच्छेदकताश्रयः, तथाचावच्छिन्नत्वमात्रस्वरूपसम्बन्धविशेषः कपिसंयोगे शाखावच्छिन्नत्ववदिति भावः।

केचित्तु ननु कर्णसंयोगविशिष्टाकाशनिष्ठाधारत्वमप्यतिप्रसक्तं विशिष्टस्याकाशस्यानतिरिक्तत्वादित्यत आह, 'कर्णसंयोगो हीति, 'शब्दाधारतायां' शब्दसमवेततायामेव, 'परिचायकः' स्वरूपसम्बन्धविशेषात्मकावच्छिन्नतासम्बन्धेन विशेषणीभूतः, न तु कर्णसंयोगावच्छिन्नत्वमाकाशस्य विशेषणमित्यर्थः, तथाच 'कर्णसंयोगावच्छिन्नसमवायेत्यत्र कर्मधारयसमास इति भाव इत्याहुः।

उपसंहरति, 'एवञ्चेति, 'कर्णसंयोगेन' यत्पुरुषीयकर्णसंयोगेन, 'स गृह्यते' स तेन गृह्यते, 'स न गृह्यते' स तेन न गृह्यते, 'संयोगस्येति शरीरसंयोगस्येत्यर्थः, 'समवायेनाधारतेति वृक्षादिनिष्ठा

यस्य शब्दस्य समवायवृत्त्या आधारता कर्णसंयोगेनावच्छिद्यते स गृह्यते, यस्य तु तदत्यन्ताभावेनावच्छिद्यते स न गृह्यते तथा संयोगस्य समवायेनाधारता हस्तसंयोगेनावच्छिद्यते न तदभावेनेति हस्तसंयो-

---

समवायेनाधारतेत्यर्थः, 'गृह्यते' शरीरसंयोगो गृह्यते, 'नान्यत्र' नान्यावच्छेदेन, 'सर्व्वमिदमिति हस्त-चरणादिविशिष्टसर्व्वं शरीरमित्यर्थः, 'तुल्यं'(१) अभिन्नं, 'संयोगस्यापि' शरीरसंयोगस्यापि,'सर्व्वत्रेति चरणावच्छेदेन संयुक्तसमवायेनापीत्यर्थः । ननु समवायवृत्त्या शब्दाधारत्वस्याव्याप्यवृत्तित्वे तद्वत्समवायोऽप्यव्याप्यवृत्तिरस्त्वित्याशङ्कते, 'न चैवमिति, 'एवं' समवायवृत्त्या शब्दाधारत्वस्याव्याप्यवृत्तित्वे,'अव्याप्यवृत्तिरित्यस्यास्त्विति शेषः । 'तस्य' समवायस्य । न च तथापि विशेषणतया तस्याव्याप्यवृत्तित्वमस्त्विति वाच्यं । विशेषणतया तस्य स्वाधिकरणे अभावविरहेण तस्याप्यव्याप्यवृत्तित्वविरहादिति भावः । ननु समवायस्य समवायसम्बन्धेनावृत्तित्वे तेन सम्बन्धेन तदभावस्य व्याप्यवृत्तित्वं स्यादित्यत्रेष्टापत्तिमाह, 'अभावस्त्विति समवायसम्बन्धावच्छिन्नसमवायाभावस्त्वित्यर्थः । भावार्थोपरि शङ्कते, 'न चैवमिति, 'एवं' विशेषणतया यदि शब्दसमवायो व्याप्यवृत्तिः, 'सर्व्वत्रेति सर्व्वस्य पुरुषस्येत्यर्थः, 'सर्व्वशब्दोपलब्धिः' सर्व्वशब्दोपलब्धिप्रसङ्गः, समवायसम्ब-

---

(१) इदं 'समानमित्यत्र 'तुल्यमिति कस्यचिन्मूलपुस्तकस्य पाठमनुसृत्येति बोध्यम् ।

गावच्छेदेन गृह्यते नान्यत्र अन्यथा हस्तसंयोगस्या-
नवच्छेदकत्वे सर्व्वमिदं समानमिति संयोगस्यापि सर्व-
त्रोपलब्धिः स्यात्। न चैवं समवायोऽप्यव्याप्यवृत्तिः, स-
मवायेन वृत्त्या तस्याधारावृत्तित्वात्। अभावस्तु विशे-

न्धावच्छिन्नाधारत्वस्य समवायसम्बन्धानतिरिक्तत्वादिति भावः। 'शब्द-
समवायस्य सत्त्वेऽपीति सर्व्वस्मिन्नेव कर्णे सर्व्वेषां शब्दानां समवायस्य
सत्त्वेऽपीत्यर्थः, 'अन्यत्रेति यत्र शब्दोत्पत्तिस्तद्भिन्नकर्णे इत्यर्थः, 'शब्दा-
त्यन्ताभावेति शब्दाधारत्वात्यन्ताभावेत्यर्थः, तथाचाधारत्वमति-
रिक्तमिति भावः। यद्वा शब्दात्यन्ताभावेति समवायसम्बन्धावच्छि-
न्नशब्दात्यन्ताभावेत्यर्थः, तथाच शब्दाधारत्वं शब्दस्वरूपमिति
भावः। इत्यञ्च तत्तत्पुरुषीयकर्णसंयोगावच्छिन्नाधारत्वं शब्दग्रहे
सन्निकर्ष इति मणिकृतोनिष्कर्षः। स च न सद्युक्तः कर्णसंयोगस्य
शब्दाधारत्वावच्छेदकत्वे मानाभावात् कर्णे शब्द इत्येव हि प्रत्ययो
न तु कर्णसंयोगे इति, तावता आधारत्वस्य प्रत्यासत्तित्वेऽपि समवा-
यस्य प्रत्यासत्तित्वानिर्वाहाच्च। वस्तुतस्तु तत्तत्पुरुषीयकर्णविवरावच्छि-
न्ननभोविशिष्टः समवायः प्रत्यासत्तिः तेन न देशान्तरवृत्तिशब्दग्रहः।
यथा समवायस्यैकत्वेऽपि रूपं वायुसमवेतमिति प्रत्ययाभावाद्वायु-
विशिष्टसमवायो न रूपे तथा देशान्तरस्थशब्दे तत्तत्पुरुषीयश्रोत्र-
समवेतत्वप्रत्ययाभावात्तादृशनभोविशिष्टसमवायोऽपि न देशान्तर-
वृत्तिशब्दे।

प्रत्यक्षतया व्याप्यवृत्तिरेव। न चैवं सर्वत्र सर्वशब्दोपलब्धिः स्यात्, शब्दसमवायस्य सत्त्वेऽपि अन्यत्र शब्दा-

---

केचित्तु तत्तत्पुरुषीयकर्णावच्छिन्नत्वविशिष्टः समवायः प्रत्यासत्तिः तेन न देशान्तरवृत्तिशब्दग्रहः। यथाहि पुरुषस्यैकत्वेऽपि दण्डापनयनदशायां तदधिकरणे देशे दण्डिमानिति प्रत्ययाभावान्न दण्डविशिष्टपुरुषवत्त्वं तथा समवायस्यैकत्वेऽपि देशान्तरस्थशब्दे तत्तत्पुरुषीयकर्णावच्छेदेन समवेत इति प्रत्ययाभावेन तादृशसमवायस्यापि तत्र विरहात्। नच समवायस्य व्याप्यवृत्तितया कथं कर्णावच्छिन्नत्वमिति वाच्यं। समवायस्य स्वरूपतोऽव्याप्यवृत्तितया कर्णावच्छिन्नत्वसम्भवादित्याहुः।

स्वतन्त्रास्तु तत्तत्पुरुषीयकर्णसंयोगावच्छिन्नाधारत्वस्य, तादृशकर्णावच्छिन्ननभोविशिष्टसमवायस्य, तादृशकर्णावच्छिन्नत्वविशिष्टसमवायस्य वा न हेतुत्वं गौरवात् किन्तु तत्तत्पुरुषीयकर्णविवर एवावच्छिन्नतासम्बन्धेन शब्दनिष्ठतया शब्दप्रत्यक्षे हेतुर्लाघवात्। नचोक्तानुमानेन श्रोत्रसन्निकर्षस्य शब्दनिष्ठस्य शब्दप्रत्यक्षजनकत्वसाधनात्तेषां कारणत्वमावश्यकं तदनुरोधेन श्रोत्रसमवायस्यापि सामान्यतः समवायत्वेन हेतुत्वाभ्युपगमे तु कारणान्तरकल्पनमपेक्ष्य यथोक्तगुरुरूपेण समवायस्य कारणत्वकल्पनाया एव लघुत्वादिति वाच्यं। कर्णेन शब्दं शृणोमीतिप्रत्ययबलेन तवापि कर्णस्य पृथक् हेतुताया आवश्यकत्वात्तदनुमानस्याप्रयोजकत्वाच्च। न हीन्द्रियसन्निकर्षत्वेन प्रत्यक्षत्वेन सामान्यतो हेतु-हेतुमद्भावोऽस्तीति प्राहुः।

त्यन्ताभावसत्त्वात् । अथ वीणादौ शब्द इत्यबाधितानुभवबलात् तदवच्छिन्नं नभः श्रोत्रं न तु कर्णावच्छिन्नमेव, कर्णे न शब्दः किन्तु वीणायामित्यनुभवात् । अन्य-

---

केचित्तु अवच्छिन्नतासम्बन्धेन तत्तत्पुरुषीयकर्णोऽपि न हेतुः पुरुषभेदेनानन्तकार्य्यकारणभावापत्तेः, किन्तु तत्तद्विलक्षणशब्दोत्पत्तिनिमित्तस्य तत्तद्विलक्षणवायुसंयोगस्यैव तत्तद्विलक्षणशब्दप्रतीतावपि कर्णावच्छेदेन शरीरनिष्ठतया हेतुत्वं नातो व्यवहितशब्दग्रहः तदुत्पादकविलक्षणवायुसंयोगस्य कर्णावच्छेदेनाभावात् । तत्सत्त्वे शब्दस्यैव कर्णावच्छेदेनोत्पत्त्यापत्तेरित्याहुः । तदसत् तत्तत्पुरुषप्रयोजकत्वादिव्याप्यनानाजात्यवच्छिन्नप्रत्यक्षं प्रतितदुत्पादकतत्तद्विलक्षणवायुसंयोगानां प्रत्येकहेतुत्वे प्रतिपुरुषमनन्तकार्य्य-कारणभावापत्त्या तदपेक्ष्य तत्तत्पुरुषीयकर्णत्वेन हेतुत्वस्यैव लघुत्वात् । कदम्बगोलकन्यायेन शब्दोत्पत्तिनये यत्रैकजातीयमेव शब्दद्वयं चैत्र-मैत्रयोरुभयोः कर्णे उत्पद्यते तत्र तदुत्पादकवायुसंयोगस्याविशिष्टतया परस्परं तदुभयोरुभयकर्णावच्छिन्नशब्देऽयं शब्द इति प्रत्यक्षापत्तेश्चेति दिक् ।

प्रसङ्गात श्रोत्रपदार्थं विवेचयितुं शङ्कते, 'अथे'ति, 'तदवच्छिन्नं' तदवच्छिन्नमपि, शब्दजनकीभूतवीणाद्यवच्छिन्नमपीति यावत्, 'श्रोत्रं' श्रोत्रपदशक्यं, यद्यदवच्छेदेन तत्तत्पुरुषगृह्यमाणशब्दाधारता तदवच्छिन्ननभस्त्वस्यैव श्रोत्रपदशक्यतावच्छेदकत्वात् तथाच तत्तत्पुरुषीयकर्णशष्कुल्यवच्छिन्नाकाशमेव श्रोत्रमिति सिद्धान्तव्याघात इति

था कर्णे शब्द इति धीः स्यात्। न चानन्तवीणाद्यव-च्छेदकत्वेनानन्तश्रोत्रस्वीकारे गौरवं शब्ददेशत्वेनैक-त्वे चातिप्रसङ्गः सर्व्वदेशानां शब्दावच्छेदकत्वादिति

भावः। ननु 'वीणादावित्यत्र अन्यत्वं न सप्तम्यर्थः, अपि तु अवच्छेदकत्वं, अवच्छेदकस्तु तत्रापि कर्ण एवेत्यत आह, 'कर्णे न शब्द इति, 'कर्णे' कर्णावच्छेदेन, 'न शब्दः' नायं शब्दः, 'वीणायां' वीणावच्छेदेन, 'इत्यनुभवादिति वीणावच्छेदेन गृह्यमाणशब्दाऽनुभवात्, 'अन्यथेति तत्रापि कर्णस्यावच्छेदकत्वे इत्यर्थः, 'इति धीः स्यात्' इत्येव तादृशशब्दधीः स्यात्। 'नचेति 'वाच्यमित्यग्रेतनेनान्वयः, 'अनन्तवीणाद्येति अनन्तानां वीणादीनां गृह्यमाणशब्दाधारतावच्छेदकत्वेनेत्यर्थः, 'अनन्तश्रोत्रस्वीकार इति अनन्तानां श्रोत्रपदशक्यतावच्छेदकत्वस्वीकार इत्यर्थः, 'शब्ददेशत्वेनेति शब्दावच्छेदकत्वेनेत्यर्थः, 'एकत्वे' अनुगमे, 'अतिप्रसङ्ग इति शब्दजनकीभूतवीणादिभिन्नस्यापि देशस्य श्रोत्रपदशक्यतावच्छेदकत्वप्रसङ्ग इत्यर्थः। 'शब्दावच्छेदकत्वादिति शब्दजशब्दावच्छेदकत्वादित्यर्थः, एतच्च स्वमतेन, पूर्व्वपक्षिणा शब्दजशब्दानभ्युपगमात्। 'देशतायग्रहस्येति वीणादौ शब्द इत्यवच्छेदकतायग्रहस्येत्यर्थः, 'प्रमाणत्वेन' अवच्छेदकतांशे प्रमात्वेन, 'गौरवस्य' शक्यतावच्छेदकानन्त्यगौरवस्य, 'अन्याय्यत्वादिति, एतच्च समाधिसौकर्य्यादुक्तं। वस्तुतस्तु तत्तत्पुरुषगृह्यमाणशब्दावच्छेदकत्वेन वीणादीनामननुगमान्न शक्यतावच्छेदकानन्त्यं। सामान्यतः शब्दावच्छेदकत्वेनाननुगमे चैत्रस्य श्रोत्रमित्यादावनन्वयापत्तेः, गृह्यमाणत्वस्य षष्ठ्यर्थत्वस-

वाच्यम्। वीणादिदेशताग्रहस्य बाधकं विना प्रमाणत्वे गौरवस्य न्याय्यत्वात्। प्रत्युत सर्व्वतो दिक्ष्वनन्तशब्द-सन्तानोत्पादक्रमेण कर्णोत्पादे कल्पनागौरवं माना-

---

भावेऽपि एकदेशान्वयस्याव्युत्पन्नत्वात्। अत एव सिद्धान्तिमतेऽपि तत्तत्पुरुषीयत्वं कर्णविशेषणं, श्रोत्रपदस्य नानार्थत्वञ्च इष्टमेवेति ध्येयं। ननु वीणादेर्गृह्यमाणशब्दावच्छेदकत्वेऽपि न तद्विशिष्टनभसः श्रोत्रपदशक्यत्वं, तत्तत्पुरुषगृह्यमाणशब्दावच्छेदकविशिष्टनभस्त्वापेक्षया लाघवात् तत्तत्पुरुषीयकर्णविशिष्टनभस्त्वस्यैव श्रोत्रपदशक्यतावच्छेद-कत्वात् कर्णेन समं तत्तत्पुरुषस्य सम्बन्धः न समवायः कर्णस्य साक्षाच्छरीरावयवत्वाभावादपि तु तत्तत्पुरुषनिष्ठसमवायसम्बन्धाव-च्छिन्नाधारतावच्छेदकत्वमेव सम्बन्धः, तस्यावयव-तदवयवादिसाधार-णत्वादवयव-तदवयवादेरेवावयविनिष्ठसंयोगाद्याधारतावच्छेदकत्वादि-त्यस्वरसादाह, 'प्रत्युतेति, कर्णावच्छिन्ननभस एव श्रोत्रत्वे इति शेषः। 'सर्व्वतोदिक्ष्वेति वीणाद्यभिघातजन्यशब्दस्थलेऽपि सर्व्वदिग्वृत्तिशब्द-असन्तानोत्पादक्रमेण कर्णे शब्दोत्पादकल्पनायां गौरवमित्यर्थः। तदकल्पने वीणादिप्रभवविलक्षणशब्दस्य प्रत्यक्षानुपपत्तेः, भवन्मये यद्देशविशिष्टस्य नभसः श्रोत्रत्वं तद्देशावच्छिन्नाधारत्वादावेव प्रत्या-सत्तित्वात् अवच्छिन्नतासम्बन्धेन तद्देशस्यैव वा शब्दनिष्ठतया शब्दग्राह-कत्वाच्चेति भावः। ननु प्रामाणिकत्वाद्गौरवं न दोषायेत्यत आह, 'मानाभावादिति। न चैवं कर्णावच्छिन्ननभसोऽपि कथं श्रोत्रत्वं कर्णस्य शब्दाधारतानवच्छेदकत्वादिति वाच्यं। तत्र कर्णस्यावच्छेदक-

भावात्। न च दूर-सन्निधानयोः शब्दानामबाधिततार-मन्दत्वादिवैधर्म्यप्रतीत्या भेदसिद्धेः सन्तानसिद्धिः, दूरत्वादिदोषात्तारत्वाग्रहे[१] मन्दत्वारोपात्त-

---

त्वादिति भावः। शब्दजशब्दे युक्तिमाह, 'दूर-सन्निधानयोरिति दूरस्थ-समीपस्थपुरुषयोरित्यर्थः, 'शब्दानां' वीणादिशब्दानां। नन्वेवं समीपस्थवीणादिशब्दव्यवहितवीणादिशब्दस्याप्युपलम्भ इत्यत आह, 'व्यवहितकर्ण इति, भवन्मत इति शेषः। 'शब्दानुत्पादवत्' वीणादिशब्दानुत्पादवत्, 'व्यवहितशब्दस्य व्यवहितवीणादिशब्दस्य, 'निमित्तवायुसंयोगाभावादिति विलक्षणवायूनां संयोगाभावादित्यर्थः, तथाच तत्तद्विलक्षणशब्दप्रत्यक्षं प्रति तत्तद्विलक्षणवायुसंयोगस्य संयोगसम्बन्धेन तत्तद्विलक्षणवायोर्वा शरीरनिष्ठतया हेतुत्वं, त्वथाप्यवच्छेदकतासम्बन्धेन तत्तद्विलक्षणशब्दोत्पत्ताववच्छेकनिष्ठतया तस्य हेतुत्वाभ्युपगमात्। न च शरीरनिष्ठतया हेतुत्वे हस्ताद्यवच्छेदेन शरीरे तादृशवायोः संयोगेऽपि शब्दोपलम्भापत्तिः कर्णनिष्ठतया हेतुत्वे च कार्य्यतावच्छेदकसम्बन्धस्य दुर्वचत्वं कर्णस्य ज्ञानानवच्छेदकत्वादिति वाच्यं। कर्णावच्छिन्नसमवायस्य कारणतावच्छेदकत्वात् तादृशवायोः संयोगस्य फलबलकल्प्यतया शब्दानुपलम्भदशायां हस्ताद्यवच्छेदेन तादृशवायोः संयोगे मानाभावाच्चेति भावः। कस्यचित्समाधानं दूषयति, 'नन्विति,

---

(१) तदग्रहे इति ख०।

दुपपत्तेः। व्यवहितकर्णे शब्दानुत्पादवद्व्यवहितशब्दानु-पलब्धिः निमित्तवायुसंयोगाभावात्। ननु व्यवधाना-भावस्य हेतुत्वात् तस्य सन्निध्युपक्षीणत्वात् कर्णानु-

---

'तस्य' व्यवधानाभावस्य, 'सन्निध्युपक्षीणत्वादिति इन्द्रियसन्निकर्ष-रूपत्वादित्यर्थः, तस्य च समवायरूपस्य व्यवहितशब्देऽप्यविशेषादिति भावः। 'कर्णानुपघातोऽपीति कर्णनिष्ठदोषाभावोऽपीत्यर्थः, 'तदुप-घाते' कर्णस्य दुष्टत्वे, एतच्च प्रौढिवादमात्रं, वस्तुतस्तु व्यवहितकर्णे विलक्षणवायोः संयोगस्य फलबलकल्प्यस्याभावादेव न शब्दग्रहः, अत एव शब्दोत्पत्तिं प्रत्येव विलक्षणवायुसंयोगस्य हेतुत्ववादिनः सिद्धा-न्तिनो नयेऽपि कर्णानुपघातो न शब्दग्रहे हेतुः। उपहतकर्णे तत्तद्विलक्षणवायुसंयोगाभाववच्छिन्नस्यैवानुत्पत्तेः। न चैतावद्विशिष्ट-कर्णस्य हेतुत्वे वीणाद्यभिघातजन्यशब्दप्रत्यक्षोपपादनेऽपि कर्णाभिघा-तजन्यविलक्षणाद्यशब्दस्याप्रत्यक्षतानुपपत्त्या सिद्धान्तिनये कर्णानुपघा-तस्य हेतुत्वमावश्यकं पुरुषान्तरेण तच्छब्दजशब्दग्रहणात्तत्र शब्दानु-त्पादस्य वक्तुमशक्यत्वात् इति वाच्यं। सिद्धान्तिनये आद्यशब्दस्य गुरुत्वादिवदयोग्यत्वस्य सुवचत्वादित्येव तत्त्वं। 'आवश्यकत्वादिति उभयवादिसिद्धत्वादित्यर्थः। ननूभयवादिसिद्धत्वेऽपि तत्तत्पुरुषगृह्य-माणशब्दावच्छेदकविशिष्टनभस्त्वस्य शक्यतावच्छेदकस्य वीणाद्यवच्छि-न्नःसाधारणतया तन्मात्रस्य शक्यत्वमसङ्गतमित्यत आह, 'लाघवा-दिति तत्तत्पुरुषगृह्यमाणशब्दावच्छेदकविशिष्टनभस्त्वापेक्षया तत्तत्पु-रुषीयकर्णविशिष्टनभस्त्वस्य शक्यतावच्छेदकस्य लघुत्वादित्यर्थः। हेत्व-

पघातोऽपि हेतुरिति न तदुपघाते शब्दग्रह इति। मैवम्। कर्णावच्छेदेनापि शब्दग्रहात्। कर्णशष्कुल्यप्यवच्छेदिकेति कर्णावच्छिन्नमेव नभः श्रोत्रं श्राव-

---

न्तरमाह, 'शब्दमात्रग्रह इति, 'तदनुविधानादिति कर्णपिधानाभावस्यानुविधानादित्यर्थः, कर्णावच्छिन्ननभस एव श्रोत्रत्वे यद्देशावच्छिन्ननभसः श्रोत्रत्वं तद्देशावच्छिन्नाधारत्वादेः सन्निकर्षतया सर्व्वत्र कर्णावच्छिन्नाधारत्वादेरसन्निकर्षत्वेन तन्निर्वाहार्थमेव नियमतः तदनुविधानात् पिहितकर्णे निमित्तवायुसंयोगासम्भवेन शब्दोत्पत्तेरसम्भवात्ताद‍ृशाधारत्वानिर्व्वाहादिति भावः। ननु तावता कर्णावच्छिन्नाधारत्वादेरेव सन्निकर्षत्वसिद्धावपि तदवच्छिन्नस्यैव नभसः श्रोत्रपदशक्यत्वे मानाभावः। न हि यदवच्छिन्नाधारत्वं सन्निकर्षस्तदवच्छिन्नमेव नभः श्रोत्रपदशक्यमिति नियमः, मानाभावादित्यत आह, 'शरीरसंयुक्तस्येति साक्षात्प्रतीतिसाधनशरीरसंयोगविशिष्टस्यैव इन्द्रियपदशक्यत्वादित्यर्थः, तथाच वीणादिसंयोगविशिष्टस्य कथमिन्द्रियपदशक्यत्वमिति भावः। अत्र शरीरत्वं शरीर-तदवयवसाधारणं, तेन कर्णसंयोगविशिष्टस्यापि नेन्द्रियपदशक्यत्वासम्भव इति ध्येयं। ननु वीणादिसंयोगविशिष्टस्येन्द्रियपदाशक्यत्वेऽपि श्रोत्रपदशक्यत्वे न बाधकं, न हि यत्संयोगविशिष्टस्येन्द्रियपदशक्यत्वं तत्संयोगविशिष्टस्यैव श्रोत्रादिपदशक्यत्वमिति नियमः, घ्राणादिपदे व्यभिचारात् मानाभावाच्चेत्यत आह, 'कर्णेनेति, 'तत्करणत्वेनेति कर्ण-

शब्दकत्वात् लाघवाच्च। शब्दमात्रग्रहे तदनुविधानात्। शरीरसंयुक्तस्य सतः साक्षात्प्रतीतिसाधनस्येन्द्रियत्वात्[१] कर्णेन वीणाशब्दं शृणोमीति तत्करणत्वेना-

स्यैवावच्छिन्नतासम्बन्धेन शब्दनिष्ठतया शब्दप्रत्यक्षकरणत्वेनेत्यर्थः। यद्यप्येतावता कर्णस्यैव शब्दप्रत्यक्षहेतुत्वसिद्धावपि तत्संयोगविशिष्टस्यैव श्रोत्रेपदशक्यत्वं नायाति, तथापि वीणाद्यवच्छिन्ननभसोऽपि श्रोत्रत्वविशिष्टकारणताग्राहकप्रमाणेन विशेषणीभूतस्य वीणादेरपि कारणताग्रहात्तादृशानुभवापत्तेरिति भावः। उक्तहेतूनां व्यतिरेकं वीणादौ दर्शयति, 'न त्विति' न तत्तत्पुरुषगृह्यमाणशब्दावच्छेदकत्वेन वीणादिकं शक्यतावच्छेदकमित्यर्थः, 'अनन्तत्वादिति'। न च तथापि प्रत्येकमादाय विनिगमकाभावाद्वीणात्वादिरूपेण वीणादेः शक्यतावच्छेदकत्वं दुर्वारमिति वाच्यं। चैत्रस्य श्रोत्रमित्यादावनन्वयापत्तेः, अवच्छेदकतासम्बन्धेन प्रयोजकतासम्बन्धेन वा वीणादावन्वितस्य गृह्यमाणशब्दस्य षष्ठ्यर्थत्वसम्भवेऽप्येकदेशान्वयस्याव्युत्पन्नत्वात् तत्तत्पुरुषगृह्यमाणशब्दावच्छेदकवीणात्वादिना तादृशशब्दप्रयोजकवीणात्वादिना वा शक्यतावच्छेदकत्वे च गौरवात्। किञ्च एकदेशान्वयस्वीकारेऽपि कर्णावच्छिन्ननभस्त्वमेव शक्यतावच्छेदकं न तु वीणाद्यवच्छिन्ननभस्त्वं, खण्डशक्तिस्वीकारेऽपि कर्णत्वं नभस्त्वमेव शक्यतावच्छेदकं न तु वीणात्वादिकं, येन पुरुषेण वीणाशब्दो न श्रुतः तस्य श्रोत्रव्यवहारानुरोधेन कर्णविवरावच्छिन्ननभस्त्वस्य

(१) साक्षात्प्रतीतिसाधनस्य शरीरसंयुक्तस्य सत इन्द्रियत्वादिति ख॰।

बाधितानुभवाच्च। न तु वीणादिकमनन्तत्वात् शब्दमात्रग्रहे तदननुविधानात्। वीणाद्यवच्छिन्नस्य नभसः शरीरासंयुक्तत्वेनानिन्द्रियत्वात् वीणया शब्दं शृणोमीत्यननुभवाच्च। कथन्तर्हि वीणायां शब्द इति ज्ञानं श्रूयमाणस्य शब्दस्य तदनधिकरणत्वादिति चेत्। न।

कर्णत्व-नभस्त्वयोर्वा शक्यतावच्छेदकत्वावश्यकतया प्रत्येकमादाय विनिगमनाविरहादिति भावः। 'शब्दमात्रग्रह इति क्वचिदपि शब्दग्रहे इत्यर्थः। 'वीणयेति, वीणावच्छिन्ननभसः श्रोत्रत्वे विशिष्टकारणताग्रहात्तादृशानुभवापत्तेरिति भावः।

अत्र नव्याः श्रोत्रपदस्य सामान्यतो नभस्त्वमेव शक्यतावच्छेदकं लाघवान्न तु कर्णावच्छिन्नत्वस्य प्रवेशः, श्रोत्रपदात्कर्णावच्छिन्नत्वप्रकारेण स्वारसिकबोधस्यासिद्धत्वात्। न चैवं चैत्रस्य श्रोत्रमिति कथं व्यवहारः यथाकथञ्चित् संयोगेनैव तादृशव्यवहारे घटस्य श्रोत्रमित्यपि व्यवहारापत्तिरिति वाच्यं। कर्णावच्छिन्नत्वस्यावच्छिन्नतासम्बन्धेन कर्णस्य वा वाक्यार्थत्वात्। कारणत्वमपि तस्य नभस्त्वेन न तु कर्णावच्छिन्ननभस्त्वेन गौरवात्। अकारणत्वमेव वा उक्तरूपेण सन्निकर्षाणां, कर्णानाञ्च हेतुत्वादेव अतिप्रसङ्गभङ्गात् श्रोत्रेण शब्दं शृणोमीतिप्रत्ययस्य च कर्णविषयत्वात्। न च नभोमात्रस्याश्रोत्रत्वे चाक्षुषादिज्ञानकालेऽपि श्रोत्र-मनःसंयोगसत्त्वाच्छब्दग्रहप्रसङ्ग इति वाच्यं। कर्णशष्कुल्यवच्छेदेनाकाश-मनःसंयोगस्य हेतुत्वात्, विशिष्टस्य श्रोत्रपदशक्यत्वेऽपि तथैव वाच्यत्वात् विशिष्टस्यानतिरिक्तत्वात्। वस्तुतस्तु

न हि सर्व्वत्र शब्दे मृदङ्गाद्यधिकरणग्रहनियमः,(१) अन्यथा क्वचिदपि देशे सन्देह-विपर्य्यय-तदनुल्लेखानामनुपपत्तेः। यत्राप्यस्ति तत्र शरीरे सुखमिति वदुत्पत्तये परम्परया वीणाद्यपेक्षणात् तदधिकरणत्वं। तत्रापि वीणायाः शब्दानाश्रयत्वेन तथैवाधिकरणत्वात्। नन्वेवं

कर्णविवरत्वमेव श्रोत्रपदशक्यतावच्छेदकं कर्णविवरत्वस्यावयवविशेषवृत्तिजातिरूपतया नभस्त्वमपेक्ष्य लघुत्वात्। अत एव तत्तत्पुरुषीयकर्णविवरावच्छिन्ननभसः परस्परं विभिन्नत्वाभावेऽपीदं चैत्रश्रोत्रमिति व्यवहारोऽप्युपपद्यते। न च कर्णशष्कुलीविवरस्येन्द्रियत्वे समवायरूपेन्द्रियसन्निकर्षात् कथं शब्दग्रह इति वाच्यं। संयुक्तसमवायप्रत्यासत्त्या अवच्छिन्नतालक्षणविशेषणताप्रत्यासत्त्या वा शब्दग्रहात् अवच्छिन्नासम्बन्धेन तस्यैव हेतुतया सन्निकर्षस्य शब्दग्राहकत्वे मानाभावाच्च। न चैवं कर्णशष्कुलीविवरत्वस्य पृथिवीत्व-जलत्वादिव्याप्यनानाजातिरूपतया श्रोत्रपदस्य नानार्थत्वापत्तिरतो नभस्त्वमेव शक्यतावच्छेदकमुचितमिति वाच्यं। नभस्त्वस्य शक्यतावच्छेदकत्वेऽपि कत्वत्वादिप्रत्येकमादाय विनिगमनाविरहेणानन्तशक्तेरावश्यकतया तदपेक्ष्य पृथिवीत्वादिव्याप्यजातिचतुष्टयस्यैव शक्यतावच्छेदकतौचित्यात् कर्णशष्कुलीविवरत्वस्य कर्णजन्यतावच्छेदकजातिव्याप्यसंस्थानविशेषवृत्तिजातिरूपतया नानार्थत्वविरहाच्चेति प्राञ्चः॥

---

(१) वीणाद्यधिकरणग्रहनियम इति ख०।

कर्णेऽनेकगकारोत्पादेऽनेकग्रहणप्रसङ्गः। नचैकग्रहेऽन्यग्रहसामग्री प्रतिबन्धिका, कोलाहले तथा अदर्शनादिति चेत्। न। तारेण मन्दाभिभवात्। तुल्यत्वे चानेकग्रहस्येष्टत्वात्। भेदाग्रहस्त्वत्यन्तसारूप्यात्। एवञ्च वीणादेरश्रोत्रत्वे मैवेणाहमनुवाकमध्यापितो यज्ञोत-

---

ननु तथापि तत्तत्पुरुषीयकर्णावच्छिन्नाधारत्वादेः शब्दकर्णत्वेऽवच्छिन्नतासम्बन्धेन शब्दनिष्ठतया शब्दग्राहकत्वे वा वीणायां शब्द इति कथमनुभवः कर्णावच्छेदेन वर्त्तमानस्य शब्दस्य वीणानवच्छिन्नत्वात् वीणावच्छिन्नस्य च कर्णावच्छेदेनावर्त्तमानत्वादित्याशङ्कते, 'कथं तर्हीति कथं तथापीत्यर्थः, 'श्रूयमाणशब्दस्य' कर्णावच्छिन्नशब्दस्य, 'तदनधिकरणत्वात्' तदनवच्छिन्नत्वात्। 'शरीरे सुखमिति वदिति शरीरे सुखमिति यथा मानसज्ञानं तथेदमप्यलौकिकमानसज्ञानमित्यर्थः, तथाच वीणावच्छिन्नशब्द एव तद्विषय इति भावः। ननु वीणायां शब्दं शृणोमीत्यनुव्यवसायान्न तस्य मानसत्वसम्भव इत्यस्वरसात प्रकारान्तरेणेत्यादर्शयति, 'उत्पन्नस्य इति, पक्षान्तरसूचको वाशब्दः पूरणीयः, 'अपेक्षणात्' कर्णावच्छिन्नशब्दापेक्षणात्, तथाच वीणाजन्यजातीयत्वं वीणाप्रयोज्यत्वं वा विषय इति भावः। 'शब्दानाश्रयत्वेन' शब्दासमवायित्वेन, 'तथैवेति परम्परयैवेत्यर्थः। यद्यप्यवच्छेदकत्वं साक्षात्सम्बन्ध एव तथापि संयोग-समवायसम्बन्धभिन्नस्यैव परम्परासम्बन्धत्वाभ्युपगमान्नासङ्गतिः। 'नन्वेवमिति, 'एवं' एवंक्रमेण, शब्दजशब्दसन्तानक्रमेणेतियावत्। यद्वा 'एवं' एवमपि,

न्वया श्रुतन्तन्त्ययापीत्यादिप्रतीतीनां तदुच्चारणादि-प्रयोज्यजातीयत्वं विषयः। शब्दे हि कारणविशेष-प्रयोज्या जातिरवश्यं वाच्या। अन्यथा शब्दविशेषेण पुत्राद्यनुमानं न स्यात् जातिं विना विशेषान्तरा-भावात्। एवञ्च कर्णावच्छिन्नस्य नभसः श्रोत्रत्वे तेन

वीणायां शब्द इत्यस्य प्रयोज्यत्वादिविषयकत्वेनोपपादनेऽपीति यावत्। इयञ्च तटस्थशङ्का न तु 'अथ वीणादावित्युक्तपूर्व्वपक्षिणः, तन्मतेऽपि समानकालीनानेकगकारोच्चारणादेकगकारप्रत्यक्षदशायामनेकगकार-प्रत्यक्षस्य दुर्व्वारत्वात् व्यञ्जकवायुसंयोगसत्त्वादिति ध्येयं। 'तथा अदर्शनात्' प्रतिबन्धकत्वादर्शनात्। 'भेदाग्रहस्त्विति विजातीयतुल्य-मानावर्णोत्पादस्थले भेदाग्रहस्यापीष्टत्वादिति भावः। तत्र नानागका-रोत्पत्तौ मानाभाव इति तु न्यायः। ननु शब्दजनकदेशमात्रस्य श्रोत्रपदशक्यतानवच्छेदकत्वे तदवच्छिन्नाधारत्वमपि न सन्निकर्षः यद्देशविशिष्टनभः श्रोत्रपदशक्यं तदवच्छिन्नाधारत्वस्यैव सन्निकर्षत्वेन तत्तत्पुरुषीयकर्णावच्छिन्नाधारत्वस्यैव तत्तत्पुरुषीयशब्दग्रहे सन्निकर्ष-त्वात्तथा च मैत्रेणाहमनुवाकमध्यापित इत्यादिप्रत्ययः कथं स्यात् मैत्रोदीरितस्यानुवाकस्य शिष्यश्रावणप्रत्यक्षविषयतायामेव तादृशप्र-त्ययनिर्व्वाहात् तस्य मैत्रोदीरितशब्दे मैत्रीयकण्ठाद्यवच्छेदेन वर्त्तमाने शिष्यकर्णावच्छिन्नाधारत्वविरहेणासम्भवादित्यत आह, 'एवमिति, 'वीणादेः' शब्दजनकदेशमात्रस्य, 'अश्रोत्रत्वे' श्रोत्रपदशक्यतानवच्छे-दकत्वे, 'अनुवाकः' वेदभागविशेषः, 'अध्यापित इति तदुदीरितानु-

वीणादिप्रभवशब्दग्रहो न तत्र सन्तानक्रमेणोत्पादं विनेत्यनन्यगतिकतया तत्कल्पनापि प्रामाणिकी। शब्देन चाव्यवहितपरमाणुदेशोत्पादक्रमेण न शब्दारम्भो येन मेघजादिशब्दानां भूलोकप्राप्तिर्युगान्तरेऽपि न स्यात्। किन्तु मेघाद्यभिहतं सर्व्वतोगामि महा-

---

वाकविषयकाद्यप्रत्यक्षवानहमित्यर्थः। 'तदुच्चारणादीति मैत्रोच्चारणादिप्रयोज्यमात्रवृत्तिजातित्वमित्यर्थः, 'मैत्रोच्चारणादीत्यादिपदात् 'गीतमित्यादौ गायकोच्चारणपरिग्रहः, एवञ्च 'मैत्रेणेत्यादेर्मैत्रोच्चारणप्रयोज्यमात्रवृत्तिजातिमदनुवाकविषयकाद्यप्रत्यक्षवानित्यर्थः, 'यद्गीतमित्यादेर्गायकोच्चारणप्रयोज्यमात्रवृत्तिजातिमद्गीतं त्वया श्रुतं, 'तत्' तादृशजातिमद्गीतं मयापीत्यर्थ इति भावः। इदमुपलक्षणं, 'मैत्रेणेत्यादेर्मैत्रप्रयोज्यानुवाकविषयकाद्यप्रत्यक्षवानित्यर्थः, 'यद्गीतमित्यादेर्गायकप्रयोज्यगीतं, तत्प्रयोज्यं मयापीत्यर्थः, इत्यपि सुवचं। ननु मैत्रोच्चारणादिप्रयोज्यमात्रवृत्तिजातौ मानाभावः। न हि मैत्रादिजन्यतावच्छेदकतया तत्सिद्धिः, श्रूयमाणशब्दस्य मैत्राद्यहेतुकतया तत्साधरणानुपपत्तेः। नापि मैत्रादिजन्यशब्दजन्यतावच्छेदकतया, द्वितीयादिशब्देऽपि सत्त्वादित्यत आह, 'शब्दे हीति, 'कारणविशेषप्रयोज्यजातिः' कारणविशेषप्रयोज्यमात्रवृत्तिजातिः, प्रयोज्यत्वञ्च कार्य्य-तत्कार्य्यादिसाधारणं, 'शब्दविशेषेण' शब्दनिष्ठवैलक्षण्येन, 'पुत्राद्यनुमानमिति अयं शब्दो मम पुत्रप्रयोज्यः विलक्षणशब्दत्वादित्यनुमानं न स्यादित्यर्थः, इदमुपलक्षणं, वीणादिकारणविशेषप्रयोज्य-

वायोर्महति देशे संयोगनिमित्तमासाद्याद्यशब्देन सर्व-
दिग्वर्त्ती शब्द एक एव जन्यते निमित्तसंयोगानुरो-
धित्वाद्विभुकार्य्याणां उत्तरोत्तरेणाप्यधिकाधिकदेशतः
सर्व्वत्र एकैक एव शब्दो वीची-तरङ्गवदुत्पाद्यते। अत-
एव सर्व्वैरेकशब्दग्रहः। वायोश्च नयनवन्महावेगतया

शब्दमात्रवृत्तिवैलक्षण्यस्य तत्तत्पुरुषोच्चारणप्रयोज्यशब्दमात्रवृत्तिवैल-
क्षण्यस्य च सर्व्वानुभवसिद्धतया दुरपह्नवत्वाच्चेत्यपि बोध्यं॥

केचित्तु तत्कारणविशेषप्रयोज्यतावच्छेदकतया तादृशजातिसि-
द्धिरित्याहुः। तदसत् कार्य्यतावच्छेदकतया हि जातिसिद्धिर्न तु
प्रयोज्यतावच्छेदकतयापि तथासति पित्रादिप्रयोज्यतावच्छेदकतयापि
पुत्र-पौत्रसाधारणजातिसिद्ध्यापत्तेः॥

ननु तवाप्यनुभवसिद्धा सा जातिः कस्य कार्य्यतावच्छेदिका कार्य्य-
मात्रवृत्तिजातेः कार्य्यतावच्छेदकत्वनियमात्, न हि सा जातिर्वीणा-
दिजन्यतावच्छेदिका, वीणाद्यहेतुकेऽपि शब्दे सत्त्वात् वीणादिनाशे-
ऽपि तादृशशब्दोत्पादाच्चेति चेत्। न। परस्परविलक्षणवायुसंयो-
गानामेवावच्छेदकतासम्बन्धेन तदवच्छिन्नोत्पत्तिं प्रति समवाय-
सम्बन्धेन हेतुत्वात् सैव तज्जातिर्वीणादिशब्दजशब्दं प्रति शब्दनिष्ठस-
मवायिकारणतावच्छेदिका वीणादिजन्याद्यशब्देऽपि तत्सत्त्वात्, अत-
एव वीणादिशब्दजशब्दजनकतावच्छेदकतया तादृशजातिसिद्धिरि-
त्यपि सुवचं॥

शीघ्रगामित्वेनाग्रिमशब्दारम्भादाद्यशब्दानन्तरमचिरेणैव शब्दोपलम्भः। वायोरेव च मन्द-तर-तमादिक्रमेण मन्दादिशब्दोत्पत्तिः। यद्वा आद्यशब्देन कदम्बगोलकवद्दशदिशि दश शब्दा आरभ्यन्ते तैश्च दश शब्दसन्ताना इति। नन्वेकशब्देन कथमनेकशब्दारम्भः

केचित्तु सा जातिः स्वजन्यशब्दसम्बन्धेन वीणादेरेव जन्यतावच्छेदिका, वीणादिजन्याद्यशब्द तत्सत्त्वे मानाभावात्। न चैवं तादृशजात्यवच्छिन्नं वीणादिशब्दजशब्दं प्रति शब्दस्य केन रूपेण समवायिकारणत्वमिति वाच्यं। शब्दत्वेनैव तत्सम्भवात् स्वजन्यशब्दसम्बन्धेन वीणादेः कारणत्वादेवातिप्रसङ्गभङ्गादित्याहुः। तदसत् स्वजन्यशब्दसम्बन्धेन वीणादेः कारणत्वकल्पने गौरवात् अवच्छेदकतासम्बन्धेन तादृशजात्यवच्छिन्नोत्पत्तौ वायुसंयोगहेतुतायास्तत्रावश्यकत्वादिति दिक्।

पूर्व्वोक्तशब्दबाधककल्पनागौरवमुद्धरति, 'एवञ्चेति, यद्देशावच्छिन्नभसः श्रोत्रत्वं तदवच्छिन्नाधारत्वस्यैव शब्दग्रहे सन्निकर्षत्वादिति भावः। 'वीणाप्रभवशब्दग्रह इति वीणाद्यनुमापकवैलक्षण्याश्रयशब्दग्रह इत्यर्थः, 'उत्पादं विना' शब्दजशब्दोत्पादं विना, 'तत्कल्पनापीति धारावाहिकशब्दकल्पनापीत्यर्थः। ननु तादृशाधारत्वं न प्रत्यासत्तिः, किन्तु समवायत्वेन समवायमात्रं प्रत्यासत्तिः, विलक्षणवायुसंयोगस्य व्यञ्जकत्वाभ्युपगमादेवातिप्रसङ्गविरहात्। तथाच वीणावच्छिन्नाद्यशब्दस्यैव श्रोत्रेण ग्रहसम्भवात् किं शब्दजशब्दधाराकल्पनेन। न च वायु-

सामग्रीभेदादिति चेत्। न। सर्व्वतोऽनेकवाय्वादिसह-
कारात् प्रागभावभेदाद्वा। न च तदितरहेतुसाकल्ये
तद्भेदान्न कार्य्यभेदः तथा अदर्शनादिति वाच्यं।
कार्य्यभेदो हि सामग्रीभेदात्। स च हेत्वन्तरभेदादिव

संयोगातिरिक्तकारणत्वकल्पनामपेक्ष्य तादृशाधारत्वस्य सन्निकर्षत्वकल्पनैव लघीयसी शब्दजशब्दधाराकल्पनं शब्दं प्रति शब्दानामसमवायिकारणत्वकल्पनञ्च फलमुखमिति वाच्यं। तवापि शब्दजशब्दाभ्युपगमे तस्य देशविशेषनियमान्यथानुपपत्त्या अवच्छेदकतासम्बन्धेन तत्तद्दिक्क्षणशब्दोत्पत्तिं प्रत्यवच्छेदकनिष्ठतया वायुसंयोगस्य कार्य्यतावच्छेदकगौरवेऽपि तवापि सन्निकर्षकारणतावच्छेदकगौरवेण तुल्यत्वात् शब्दप्रत्यक्षे प्रत्यासत्तिविरहेऽपि क्षतिविरहाच्च वायुसंयोगेनैवातिप्रसङ्गभङ्गादिति चेत्। न। तथापि कर्णे वीणाशब्द इति कर्णेऽपि वीणाप्रभवशब्दावच्छेदकत्वप्रत्ययाच्छब्दजशब्दधाराकल्पनाया आवश्यकत्वादिति भावः।

अत्र केचित् वीणादिजन्याद्यशब्दस्यैव वीणाद्यवच्छेदेनेव कर्णावच्छेदेनाप्युत्पत्तिरस्तु किं शब्दजशब्दधाराकल्पनेन, कर्णावच्छिन्नाधारत्वादिसन्निकर्षेणावच्छिन्नतासम्बन्धेन कर्णेन वा आद्यशब्दस्यैव ग्रहसम्भवात् तव शब्दजशब्दोत्पादे देशनियमस्येव ममापि तदुत्पादे देशविशेषस्य वायुसंयोगादेव सम्भवात्। न च वीणाजन्यतावच्छेदकजात्यवच्छिन्नं प्रति वीणाहेत्वभिघातस्य समवायसम्बन्धेनावच्छेदकनिष्ठतया हेतुत्वात् कर्णावच्छेदेन कथं तदुत्पाद इति वाच्यं। तादृशजात्यवच्छिन्नं प्रति तदनुविधानस्य वायुप्रेरणेनानुपक्षीणत्वे

प्रागभावभेदादपि। अन्यथा समवाय्यादिभेदेऽपि कार्य्यवैजात्यं न स्यात्। घटव्यक्तिषु तथा अदर्शनात्। पाकजे रूपादौ हेत्वन्तराभेदेऽपि प्रागभावपूर्व्वरूपादिध्वंसभेदेन भेदाच्च। अथ रूपाद्येकैकप्रागभावध्वंसयोः सर्व्वत्र तुल्यत्वे किं विनिगमकं, गन्धादिप्राग-

---

कालिकसामानाधिकरण्यमात्रस्य प्रत्यासत्तित्वेन तत्र सुवचत्वात् अवच्छेदकनियमस्य वायुसंयोगादेव सम्भवात्। एतेनाद्यशब्दमात्रवृत्तिवैजात्यावच्छिन्नं प्रति तादात्म्यसम्बन्धेनावच्छेदकनिष्ठतया वीणादिकं हेतुः इत्यपि निरस्तं। वीणादेरन्यथासिद्धत्वात् कालिकसामानाधिकरण्यमात्रस्य प्रत्यासत्तित्वेन सुवचत्वाच्च। न च दूरस्थस्य मन्दत्वेन समीपस्थस्य च तारत्वेनानुभवाच्छब्दभेद आवश्यक इति वाच्यं। 'दूरत्वादिदोषेण मन्दत्वारोप इति मूल एव पूर्व्वमुक्तत्वात्। अथ वीणाद्याकाशाभिघातानन्तरं तन्नाशेन बहुकालव्यापी शब्दः श्रूयते। नचासावेकः, शब्दस्य क्षणद्वयमात्रावस्थायित्वात्। न च नाशैवाभिघातजन्मा, तस्य नाशात् वायुसंयोगस्य च निमित्तकारणत्वादतः शब्दासमवायिकारणिका शब्दधारा कल्प्यते इति चेत्। न। स्वप्रतियोगिजन्यत्वसम्बन्धेन निमित्तवायुसंयोगस्यैव शब्दनाशकतया तस्य च फलबलकल्प्यत्वादभिघातजन्यशब्दस्यैव तावत्कालस्थायित्वात्। न च ज्ञानादिस्थले कृप्तनाश्यनाशकभावादेवोपपत्तावतिरिक्तनाश्य-नाशकभावकल्पने गौरवमिति वाच्यं। शब्दजशब्दं प्रति तत्तादित्वरूपशब्दानामन्त्यानामसमवायि-

भावानां रसादौ व्यभिचारेऽपि गन्धादौ रसादिप्रागभावानामव्यभिचारादिति चेत्। न। वायुस्पर्शे गन्ध-रस-रूपप्रागभाव-प्रध्वंसानान्तेजोरूपे गन्ध-रसा-

---

कारणत्वकल्पनामपेक्ष्यातिरिक्ताया एवं नाश्य-नाशकभावकल्पनाया एव लघुत्वादिति पूर्व्वपक्षयन्ति। तदसत्, दूर-निकटवर्त्तिनोर्मन्द-तारभावप्रत्ययस्य प्रमात्वेनानुभवसिद्धस्य भ्रमत्वकल्पनापत्तेः कर्णे मे वीणाशब्द इतिलौकिकप्रत्यक्षवत् पुरुषान्तरकर्णेष्वपि चैत्रस्य कर्णे वीणाशब्द इतिलौकिकप्रत्यक्षापत्तेश्च शब्दभेदाभावेन सामग्र्यविशेषात्। न च तवापि वीचि-तरङ्गन्यायेन शब्दोत्पादादेष दोषो दुर्वार इति वाच्यं। एतदस्वरसादेव 'यद्वेति कृत्वा कदम्बगोलकन्यायेनैव शब्दोत्पत्तेर्मणिकृता वक्ष्यमाणत्वात्। किञ्च सन्निहितस्य पुंसः शीघ्रं वीणादिशब्दग्रहः, व्यवहितस्य मध्ये शब्दान्तराग्रहेऽपि विलम्बेन वीणादिशब्दग्रह इति शब्दजशब्दधाराकल्पनावश्यकी मध्ये शब्दान्तरग्रहानुरोधेन श्रवण-मनःसंयोगस्यावश्यकतया तद्विलम्बेनापि विलम्बसम्भवात् विलक्षणवायुसंयोगस्य शब्दोत्पत्तावेव हेतुत्वेन व्यञ्जकत्वविरहादन्यथा स्वप्रतियोग्यजन्यत्वसम्बन्धेन तन्नाशस्य शब्दनाशकत्वासम्भवात् उत्पादकत्ववद्व्यञ्जकत्वस्याभ्युपगमेऽपि शब्दोत्पत्त्यनुरोधेन तस्याविशिष्टतया तद्विलक्षणविलम्बासम्भवात् तत्तत्पुरुषीयकर्णानां व्यञ्जकत्वमपेक्ष्य पूर्व्वोक्तक्रमेण गौरवाच्च। एतेन वायुसंयोगसहकृतादीणाद्याकाशाभिघातादाद्यशब्दसमय एव कदम्बगोलकन्यायेन प्रति-

भावयोर्जलरसे गन्धप्रागभावस्य व्यभिचारेणाहेतुत्व स्वप्रागभावहेतुताया आवश्यकत्वात् पाकजेषु रूप-रस-स्पर्शेषु गन्धादिप्रागभावानामन्यथासिद्धत्वाच्च ।

कणं विभिन्नशब्दा जायन्ते तेन दूर-निकटवर्त्तिनोर्मन्द-तारप्रत्ययस्य न भ्रमत्वकल्पनं, न वा पुरुषान्तरीयकर्णान्तर्भावेन शब्दलौकिक-प्रत्यक्षं । न चैवमनन्तशब्दस्वीकारात् किं लाघवमिति वाच्यं । शब्दं प्रति शब्दस्यासमवायिकारणत्वाकल्पनादेव लाघवादित्यपि निरस्तं । तथापि निकटवर्त्त्यपेक्षया दूरवर्त्तिनो विलम्बश्रवणानुपपत्तेः ॥

केचित्तु शब्दजशब्दानभ्युपगमे भेर्य्याद्यभिघातोत्पत्त्यनन्तरं यस्य पुरुषस्य कर्णोत्पत्तिस्तस्य भेर्य्यादिशब्दग्रहो न स्यात् भेर्य्याद्यभिघात-समये तस्य कर्णाभावेन तत्कर्णावच्छेदेन भेर्य्याद्यभिघातात् शब्दोत्पत्ते-रसम्भवात् । न च वायुसंयोगमात्रात् कर्णावच्छेदेनापि शब्दोत्पत्तिरिति वाच्यं । भावकार्य्यस्य समवायिकारणकत्वनियमादित्याहुः । तदसत्, यथाहि पूर्व्वोत्पन्नस्यापि घटस्यानन्तरोत्पन्नदेशे संयोगसम्बन्धेन सत्त्वं, यथा वा पूर्व्वोत्पन्नचक्षुःसंयोगादेरणुत्तरकालोत्पन्नालोकसंयो-गावच्छेदेन सत्त्वं तथा पूर्व्वोत्पन्नस्यैव भेर्य्यादिशब्दस्य तदुत्तरोत्पन्नकर्णे अवच्छेदकतासम्बन्धेन वृत्तौ बाधकाभावात् अवच्छेदकतासम्बन्धे-नोत्पत्तेरेव कारणनियम्यत्वात् । न च तेन सम्बन्धेन स्थितिरपि कारणनियम्या अन्यथापि तत्सत्त्वप्रसङ्गादिति वाच्यं । अन्यत्र तत्सत्त्वे मानाभावादिति दिक् ॥

रूपादिषु तथादर्शनात्। गन्धेऽपि स्वप्रागभावस्यावश्य हेतुत्वादभावान्तराणामन्यथा सिद्धत्वं। यद्वा रूप-रस-स्पर्शतुल्यत्वेऽप्यग्निसंयोगविशेषात् क्वचित्सौरभमसौर-

---

'मेघजादिशब्दानामिति मेघजादिशब्दप्रयोज्यशब्दानामित्यर्थः, 'भूलोकप्राप्तिः' तत्स्थानां साक्षात्कारविषयता। 'सर्व्वदिग्वर्त्तीति, 'विभुकार्य्याणां' विभुसमवेतजन्यविशेषगुणानां, 'वीचि-तरङ्गवदिति यथा एकया रीत्या सकलदिग्वर्त्त्येकमेव मण्डलाकारं तरङ्गान्तर-मुत्पद्यते तथा पूर्व्वशब्देनापि समानदेशावस्थितसकलपुरुषकर्णेष्वेक-एव द्वितीयशब्दः उत्पद्यत इत्यर्थः। 'सर्व्वैः' समानदेशावस्थितैः सर्व्वैः। 'वायोरेवेति परस्परविलक्षणवायुसहकारादेवेत्यर्थः, 'मन्दा-दिशब्दोत्पत्तिरिति मन्दादिशब्दाच्छब्दोत्पत्तिरित्यर्थः। ननु वीचि-तरङ्गन्यायेन नानापुरुषकर्णेष्वेकशब्दोत्पादे कर्णे मे वीणाशब्द इति लौकिकप्रत्यक्षवत् पुरुषान्तरकर्णेऽपि चैत्रस्य कर्णे वीणाशब्द इति लौकिकप्रत्यक्षापत्तिः शब्दभेदाभावेन सामग्र्यविशेषादित्यस्वरसादाह, 'यद्वेति, 'कदम्बगोलकवदिति। 'अनेकवाय्वादीति तत्तद्वाय्वादि-व्यक्तिरूपसहकारिणो भेदादित्यर्थः, तत्तच्छब्दव्यक्तिं प्रति तत्तद्वा-य्वादिव्यक्तीनां विशिष्य हेतुत्वादिति भावः। आदिना वायु-संयोगव्यक्तीनां परिग्रहः। 'तदितरेति अभावेतरसकलकारणाभेदे अभावात्मकहेतुभेदान्न कार्य्यभेद इत्यर्थः, तेन 'पूर्व्वरूपादिध्वंसभेदा-च्चेत्यग्रिमग्रन्थस्य नासङ्गतिरिति ध्येयं। 'अन्यथा' अन्यथासिद्धत्वा-

भस्मोत्पद्यते। नचाग्निसंयोगो रूपादिमात्रे कारणं, व्यभिचारात्। एवं रसादावपि। ननु कार्य्यमात्रे प्रागभावमात्रं न हेतुः तयोर्व्यतिरेककालानवगमात्।

देवाकल्पने इत्यर्थः, 'कार्य्यवैजात्यमिति घट-पटादिलक्षणकार्य्यवैजात्यं न स्यादित्यर्थः। 'घटव्यक्तिष्विति घटव्यक्तिसमवायादिभेदेऽपि वैजात्यादर्शनादित्यर्थः। अन्यत्रादृष्टत्वमपि नास्तीत्याह, 'पाकजरूपादाविति, 'सर्व्वत्रेति पाकजेषु रूप-रस-गन्ध-स्पर्शेषु सर्व्वेष्वित्यर्थः, 'तुल्यत्वे' तुल्यन्यायव्यतिरेकानुविधायित्वे, 'किं विनिगमकमिति स्वप्रागभाव-स्वसमानजातीयध्वंसावेव हेतू न त्वन्यावित्यत्र किं विनिगमकमित्यर्थः।

ननु रूपादिमात्रेषु व्यभिचारेणाहेतुत्वेऽपि पाकजेषु रूपादिषु तत्स्यादित्यत आह, 'पाकजेष्विति। 'रूपादिष्विति अजातीयरूपादिष्वित्यर्थः, 'तथा दर्शनादिति गन्धादिप्रागभावानामहेतुत्वदर्शनादित्यर्थः। ननु व्यभिचाराभावाद्‌गन्धे रूपादिप्रागभावो हेतुरस्त्वित्यत आह, 'गन्ध इति, 'स्वप्रागभावस्येति यत्र कार्य्योत्पत्तिः तत्र प्रागभाव इति सामान्यतः कारणत्वावधारणादित्यर्थः, 'अभावान्तराणां' रूपादिप्रागभावानां। गन्धे रूपादिप्रागभावानां व्यभिचारमप्याह, 'यदेति, 'तुल्यत्वेऽपि' अपराहृत्तावपि। नन्वग्निसंयोगत्वेन रूपादिकं प्रति हेतुत्वात् कथं तत्र रूपाद्यन्तरोत्पत्तिरित्यत आह, 'न चाग्नीति, 'मात्रपदं भिन्नक्रमे, अग्निसंयोगमात्रं रूपादौ कारणमित्यर्थः,

सर्व्वमुक्तावितरहेत्वभावादेव कार्य्यानुत्पादादिति चेत्। न। हेत्वन्तरसत्त्वेऽप्युत्पन्नस्य पुनरनुत्पादेन प्रागभावस्य हेतुत्वात्। एका सामग्र्येकमेव कार्य्यं जनयति स्वभावादिति चेत्। न। कार्य्यानुत्पादस्य सामग्रीविर-

---

'व्यभिचारात्'। न च गन्धनाशकतावच्छेदकस्यैव लाघवात् रूपादिनाशकतावच्छेदकतया गन्धपरावृत्तौ रूपादिपरावृत्तिरप्यावश्यकीति वाच्यं। अनन्तव्यक्तिकल्पनगौरवेण प्रत्यभिज्ञायाः प्रामाण्यानुरोधेन चाग्निसंयोगे तत्तन्नाशकतावच्छेदकजातिचतुष्टयकल्पनाया एव न्याय्यत्वात् अन्यथा प्रतियोगिमात्रस्य लाघवान्नाशकत्वमुपगम्य क्षणिकत्वमेव ततः स्वीक्रियतामिति॥

मिश्रास्तु 'तुल्यत्वेऽपि' पूर्व्वाविलक्षणत्वेऽपि। ननु तवापि पूर्व्वरूपादिपरावृत्त्या सजातीयरूपाद्यन्तरमुत्पद्यते इत्यत आह, 'न चेति, 'रूपादिमात्रे' पूर्व्वविलक्षणेऽपि रूपादौ, 'व्यभिचारात्' अन्वयव्यभिचारात्, अग्निसंयोगे सत्यपि पूर्व्वसजातीयरूपाद्यनुत्पादादिति यावत्। न हि पाके सति पूर्व्वसजातीयं रूपं कुत्राप्युत्पन्नं दृष्टमिति भाव इत्याहुः।

केचित्तु ननु गन्धजनकाग्निसंयोगस्य रूपादिजनकत्वनियमात् रूपादिपरावृत्त्यभावे गन्धोत्पत्तिरसिद्धैवेत्यत आह, 'न चेति, 'अग्निसंयोगः' गन्धजनकाग्निसंयोगः, 'रूपादिमात्रे' रूपादिषु सर्व्वेषु, 'कारणं' नियमतः कारणं, 'व्यभिचारादिति यत्राग्निसंयोगाद्गन्धप-

त्वप्रयोज्यत्वनियमात्। न च कार्य्यसहभावेन कारणत्व, गौरवात्। न च विनश्यदवस्थे समवायिनि कार्य्यानुत्पत्तेस्तथात्वमिति वाच्यं। तावता समवायिकारणस्यैव तथात्वात् कारणमात्रे मानाभावेन तस्याप्रयोजक-

---

रावृत्तावपि मन्त्रादिप्रयोगेन रूपाद्यपरावृत्तिस्तदेवेदं रूपमिति प्रत्यभिज्ञा सिद्धा तत्र तन्नियमस्य व्यभिचारादित्यर्थः, इति प्राहुः॥

'एवं रसादावपीति एवं सत्यामपि रसादिपरावृत्तौ रूपाद्यपरावृत्तेरानुभविकतया रसादावपि प्रागभावः कदापि व्यभिचाराञ्च हेतुरित्यर्थः। नन्वस्तु रूपादौ प्रागभावोऽहेतुर्न तु कार्य्यमात्रे येन शब्देऽपि ततो भेदः स्यादित्याशयेनाशङ्कते, 'नन्विति, 'तयोरिति प्रागभावेतरसकलकारणसत्त्वे प्रागभावव्यतिरेकेण कार्य्यव्यतिरेकादर्शनादित्यर्थः। 'सर्व्वमुक्ताविति, जातायामिति शेषः। 'एकमेवेति एकं कार्य्यं एकदैव जनयतीत्यर्थः, यथाश्रुते तस्यैव कार्य्यस्य पुनर्जननापत्तेरनुद्धारात्। 'कार्य्यसहभावेनेति कार्य्यसहवर्त्तिन एवेत्यर्थः, तथाच प्रागभावस्य कार्य्यासहवर्त्तित्वात् कथं कारणत्वमिति भावः। 'तथात्वं' कार्य्यसहवर्त्तिन एव कारणत्वं। 'तावतेति विनश्यदवस्थे समवायिनि कार्य्यानुत्पत्तेरित्यर्थः, 'समवायिकारणस्यैवेति। न च क्वचिदसमवायिकारण-प्रतिबन्धकाभावयोरपि कार्य्यसहभावेन हेतुत्वादेवकारोऽयमसङ्गत इति वाच्यं। विनश्यदवस्थे समवायिनि कार्य्यानुत्पत्तिबलेन कार्य्यसहवर्त्तितया हेतुत्वं समवायिकारणस्यैव

त्वात्। ननु समवेतसमवायो न ग्राहकः शब्दत्वादिजातेरभावादिति चेत्। न। रूपत्वादिन्यायेन तत्साधनात्॥

इति श्रीमद्गङ्गेशोपाध्याय-विरचिते तत्त्वचिन्तामणौ प्रत्यक्षखण्डे सन्निकर्षवादः।

न त्वन्यस्येति तत्स्वकृतेः। 'रूपत्वादिन्यायेनेति अनुगतप्रत्ययनादित्यर्थः। अत्र नव्याः तत्तत्पुरुषीयकर्णावच्छिन्ननभःसमवायविशिष्टसमवायत्वेन कारणत्वकल्पनामपेक्ष्य लाघवात् स्वावच्छिन्नशब्दसमवायेन तत्तत्पुरुषीयकर्ण एव शब्दसमवेतश्रावणे हेतुः। वस्तुतस्तु एतदपि न, शब्दाविषयकशब्दसमवेतश्रावणस्यालीकतया शब्दप्रत्यक्षसामग्रीविरहादेव श्रोत्रे शब्दविरहदशायां शब्दसमवेतश्रावणानुत्पादसम्भवादिति प्राहुः।

इति श्रीमथुरानाथ-तर्कवागीशविरचिते प्रत्यक्षखण्डरहस्ये सन्निकर्षवादरहस्यं॥

अथ समवायवादः ।

ननु[१] समवायासिद्धेर्न सा प्रत्त्यासत्तिः । विप्रतिपत्तिश्च शुक्लः पट इति प्रतीतिः विशेषण-विशेष्यसम्बन्धविषया न वेति । अथ जाति-गुण-क्रिया-तद्वन्तौ मिथः सम्बद्धावनुभूयेते । न ह्यसम्बद्धस्वरूपद्वये विशिष्टधीव्यपदेशाविति चेत् । न । सम्बद्धानुभवेन हि सम्बन्धो न विशेषणं भासते तस्य प्रथममज्ञानात् संयोगिनाविमावितिवत् समवायिनावित्यननुभवाच्च । नापि विशेष्यः, अनयोः समवाय इत्यननुभवात् । नापि स्वरूपेण भासते, समवायं जानामीति विषयताननुभवात् । ननु नीलोघट इत्याद्यनुभवो विशेषण-

---

अथ समवायवादालोकः ।

'नन्विति शब्द-रूपादेराश्रयसम्बन्धाभावान्न तत्साक्षात्कारः प्रत्यासत्तिजन्य इत्यर्थः । यथाश्रुते सिद्धसिद्धिव्याघातादिति । 'विशेष-

---

(१) परिच्छेदचतुष्टयात्मकतत्त्वचिन्तामण्यन्तर्गतप्रत्यक्षपरिच्छेदस्य सन्निकर्षवादान्तोभागः मथुरानाथतर्कवागीशविरचितरहस्यनामकव्याख्यया सह मुद्रितः, अवशिष्टभागस्य वक्ष्यायासेनापि तादृशव्याख्यापुस्तकस्य दुष्प्राप्यत्वेन तत्त्वचिन्तामण्यभिधानमूलग्रन्थस्य व्याख्यासाहाय्यं विना दुर्बोधत्वेन चागत्यातिप्रामाणिकजयदेवमिश्रविरचितालोकनामकव्याख्यया सह मुद्रणे प्रवृत्तमस्माभिरित्यलं पल्लवितेन ।

विशेष्यसम्बन्धविषयः विशिष्टप्रतीतित्वात् दण्डिज्ञानवदिति[१] चेत् । न । अघटं भूतलं ज्ञातमिष्टं कृतञ्चेत्यत्र व्यभिचारात् । सम्बन्धविषयत्वे बाधकं विनेति विशेषणमिति चेत् । न । बाधकाभावस्यैव समर्थत्वे शेषवैयर्थ्यात् साधकाभावेन सत्प्रतिपक्षाच्च । बाधकाभावस्य साधकत्ववत् साधकाभावस्य बाधकत्वात् । तस्मादुभयाभावे संशयः स्यात् । न च प्रतीतिरेव समवायसाधिका, तस्यास्तद्विषयत्वासिद्धेः अन्यथान्योन्याश्र-

---

णेति, सम्बन्धविषयत्वे सिद्धसाधनं प्रतियोग्यनुयोगिभावसम्बन्धविषयत्वस्य समूहालम्बनवारणाय दण्ड-पुरुषयोरेव विशेषणत्व-विशेष्यत्वप्रतीतिनियमाय च सर्व्वसम्मतत्वात्, अत उक्तं 'विशेषण-विशेष्येति । न च प्रतियोगित्वादेरुभयनिरूप्यत्वं, विशेषणे प्रतियोगित्वस्य विशेष्ये चानुयोगित्वस्य भानात्, संयोगादेस्तूभयनिरूप्यत्वमिति भावः । प्रत्यक्ष एवोपोद्बलकन्तर्कमाह, 'न हीति । 'समवायिनाविति नीलोघट इत्यादिप्रतीतौ तथाकारानुभवादित्यर्थः । एवमग्रेऽपि, स्वातन्त्र्येण तादृशानुभवौ नोभयसम्मतौ येन तौ प्रमाणीक्रियेतामिति भावः । 'स्वरूपेणेति, स्वरूपेण वैशिष्ट्यविधया न विशेषणत्वेन न वा विशेष्यत्वेनेत्यस्मदभिमतं, तत्तु न सम्भवत्येव, उभयथैव ज्ञानेन विषयीकरणादिति स्वाभिसन्धिना स्वरूपेणेति

---

(१) विशिष्टप्रत्ययत्वात् दण्डीतिप्रत्ययवदितीति ख० ।

यात्। अथाघटं भूतलं ज्ञातमित्याद्यपि विशिष्टधीः सम्बन्धविषया, किन्तु भ्रान्ताबाधकसत्त्वादिति चेत्। तर्हि भूतलेऽघटत्वस्य ज्ञातत्वादेस्त्वाभावः स्यात्। तथाच व्यवहारविलोपः। सम्बन्धश्च न संयोगः समवायो वान्यतरो वा बाधादसिद्धेर्वा। नापि सम्बन्धमात्रं, ज्ञापकत्वादिना सिद्धसाधनात्। नाप्यविशिष्टव्यावृत्त-विशिष्टज्ञाननियामकः, अभावज्ञानादाविव स्वरूप-सम्बन्धेनार्थान्तरत्वात्। न च सम्बन्धिभिन्नत्वं साध्ये

अस्मदाक्षेपस्य स्वरूपेण विशेषणाद्यनुपधानेनेत्यर्थं कल्पयित्वा दूषयति, 'समवायमिति, 'स्वरूपेणेत्यस्यार्थान्तरासम्भवादित्यभिमानः परस्येति। 'विशिष्टबुद्धित्वादिति[१] विशेषणधीजन्यबुद्धित्वात् अतज्ज्ञावृत्तधीजनकबुद्धित्वादेत्यर्थः, वस्तुतो विशेषणत्वगोचरबुद्धित्वादिति हेत्वर्थः। प्रतियोगित्वलक्षणस्य विशेषणत्वस्य समूहालम्बनभेदाय विशिष्टज्ञानविषयत्वस्वीकारात्। इयांस्तु परं विशेषः, सम्बन्धविषयत्वेऽपि तत्प्रतियोगित्वं तदवच्छिन्नविशेष्यनिरूपितमेव। अत एव वायौ समवायसत्त्वेऽपि न रूपवानिति धीस्तन्निरूपित-विशेषणत्वस्य रूपे तन्निरूपितविशेष्यत्वस्य च वायावभावादेतदभावे विवक्षितहेत्वोरप्यवच्छेदकाज्ञानादज्ञानापत्तेरिति भावः। अतद्व्यावृ-

---

(१) 'विशिष्टप्रतीतित्वादित्यत्र 'विशिष्टबुद्धित्वादिति पाठधारणं कस्यचिद् मूलपुस्तकस्य तादृशपाठमनुसृत्येति ध्येयं।

विशेषणम्, अभावज्ञानादिना व्यभिचारात्। बाधकाभावस्य च विशेषणत्वं हेतौ निरस्तमेव विनापि भिन्नसम्बन्धमभावज्ञानादाविव विशिष्टधीसम्भवेनाप्रयोजकत्वाच्च। विशेषणताविशेषरूपः प्रकारादिकृतो वा विशेषः सम्बन्धाविषयत्वेऽपि तुल्यः। स्यादेतदवयवगुण-क्रिया-जाति-तद्वतामिह तन्तुषु घट इह पटे शौक्ल्यमिह चलनं पटत्वञ्चेतीहप्रत्यय आधाराधेय-

---

त्तधीजनकत्वमुक्तावच्छेदेन, हेतुस्तु तदेव, तत्रैव तर्कसम्भवेन व्याप्तिग्रहात् तथाहि अतद्व्यावृत्तिः संसर्गविशेषावच्छिन्नविशेषणाभाववद्व्यावृत्तिः, सा च तदा विशिष्टज्ञानेन जन्येत यदि विशिष्टधीस्तत्संसर्गगोचरा स्यात्[१], तत्संसर्गविषया धीस्तद्विशेषणसंसर्गाभाववद्व्यावृत्तिबुद्धिं जनयतीत्येवमतिप्रसक्तस्य नियामकस्य सम्भवादिति सारम्[२]। 'दण्डिज्ञानवदिति, यद्यपि दण्डो नेह विशेषणं, किन्तु मतुवर्थसम्बन्धः, स च संयोगरूप इति तद्विशिष्टबुद्धिः पक्षसमा न दृष्टान्त इति, तथाप्येतच्छब्दाभिलप्यमाना प्रत्यक्षप्रतीतिर्दृष्टप्रकारिका दृष्टान्तो द्रष्टव्या अस्या अन्यथा प्रतिपादनासम्भवेनोक्तवाक्येनैव प्रतिपादनात्। यद्वा उपलक्षणतया द्रव्यविशेषणिका पश्वादिशब्दकृता धीर्दृष्टान्ततया विवक्षिता, तत्र लाङ्गूलादेः प्रवृत्तिनिमित्तत्वं न तत्सम्बन्धस्य गौरवादिति गोपदाद्गोत्वस्यैव प्रकारत्वादिति द्रष्टव्यं

---

(१) तत्संसर्गविषया स्यादिति ख०।

(२) इति ध्येयमिति ख०।

सम्बन्धनिमित्तकः यथार्थेहप्रत्ययत्वात् इह कुण्डे बदरमिति प्रत्ययवदिति चेत् । न । इह भूतले घटाभावो मानञ्चेत्यादौ व्यभिचारात् बाधकं विनेत्यस्य निरस्तत्वात् तथैवाधाराधेयभावादेवोपपत्तेश्च । उत्पत्तये स्थितये ज्ञप्तये चापेक्षणीयस्याधारत्वात् ।

अन्ये तु शब्द-जाति-रूपादिरिन्द्रियसम्बद्धः प्रत्यक्षत्वात् घटवदित्यनुमानात् संयोगबाधे इन्द्रियसम्बन्ध-

---

'तद्विषयकत्वासिद्धेरिति परेण तथात्वासिद्धेः तं प्रति तस्याः प्रमाणीकरणाक्षमत्वादित्यर्थः । 'अन्यथेति अन्यतरासिद्धविषयिताकायाः प्रसाध्याङ्गिकायास्तस्या एव तत्र मानत्व इत्यर्थः, 'अन्योन्येति तस्याः समवायविषयत्वसाधनं समवायसिद्धधीमन्तत्साधने च सिद्धे तस्यास्तद्विषयत्वे ततः समवायसिद्धौ साध्यप्रसिद्धिरित्यन्योन्याश्रय इत्यर्थः । यथाश्रुते क्वाप्येवं प्रत्यक्षं नार्थं साधयेदित्यन्योन्याश्रयानवकाशादिति । 'सम्बन्धमात्रं' उभयनिरूप्यधर्ममात्रम् । 'नाप्यविशिष्टेति, 'अविशिष्टपदं अविशिष्टधीपरं, अविशिष्टस्यासम्बद्धवचनस्य यथाश्रुतस्यान्योन्याश्रयप्रसंगात् अविशिष्टधियस्तु विशेषणत्वागोचरबुद्धित्वेन(१) निर्व्वचनात्, तथा च तद्व्यावृत्तत्वं तदजनकत्वं तद्विषयकत्वे साध्ये नीलविषयकत्वेनैव सिद्धसाधनं नीलस्य नीलाविशिष्टधीरूपनीलाभावज्ञाने अजनकस्य नीलविशिष्टज्ञाने विषयत्वात्, एवञ्च तदजनकं

---

(१) विशेषणत्वागो।चरार्थत्वेनेति क० ।

घटकतया समवायसिद्धिः इन्द्रियस्य सम्बद्धग्राहकत्वात्। अत एव समवायो न प्रत्यक्ष इन्द्रियेणासम्बन्धात्। न च सम्बन्धत्वेन तत्सिद्धिः, अनवस्थानात् स्वभावादेव ज्ञानवत् स्वसम्बद्धव्यवहारकारित्वाच्च। समवायो हि सम्बन्धं विनैव स्वभावादेव कस्यचित्। न च जात्यादेरपि स्वभावादेव स्वसम्बद्धव्यवहारकारित्वे समवायविलोपः, जात्यादेरिन्द्रियासम्बन्धे समवायवदप्रत्यक्ष-

---

तद्विशिष्टधीनियामकं यत् तद्विषयकत्वं साध्यमिति साध्यतावच्छेदकनिरुक्तिरियं द्रष्टव्या न तु सम्बन्धनिरुक्तिः, येनातीन्द्रियसम्बन्धाव्याप्त्यादिदूषणावसरः। तथाच प्रत्यक्षनीलादिविशिष्टबुद्धिं पक्षयित्वा तादृशदण्ड्यादिबुद्धिं दृष्टान्तयित्वा समवाये साधिते विशेषणविशेष्यान्यविशिष्टधीविषयत्वेन सम्बन्धसामान्यं निर्व्वाच्यमिति नैतत् सम्बन्धनिर्वचनक्षमम्निबन्धनं सामानाधिकरण्यप्रविष्टसम्बन्धगर्भतया व्याप्त्यादिलक्षणे चक्रकप्रसञ्जनमित्यवधेयं। नियामकत्वन्तु जनकत्वमेव तेनाविशिष्टज्ञानाजनकं तद्विशिष्टधीजनकं तदसाधारणकारणमुच्यत इति तद्विषयत्वं साध्यं। न चात्र 'सम्बन्धनिमित्तकः' इति साध्ये विशिष्टज्ञानासाधारणकारणनिमित्तकः इति पर्य्यवसितोऽर्थः स्यात् तथाच सिद्धसाधनमिति वाच्यम्। विषयत्वे साध्ये निमित्तत्वस्य, निमित्तत्वे साध्ये विषयत्वस्य नियामकपदेन विवक्षितत्वात्। यद्वा व्यापकत्वमेव नियामकत्वं यथाश्रुते स्वविशिष्टत्वस्यासम्बद्धपर्य्यावसतयान्योन्याश्रयादित्युक्तम्। ननु सम्बन्धाविषयत्वे समूहालम्बनावि-

त्वापातादिति । तन्न । समवायस्वीकारेऽपि स्वरूपसम्बन्धस्यावश्यकत्वात् । घट-ज्ञानयोर्भूतलाभावयोरिव वा द्रव्येण गुण-जात्यादिभिः स्वरूपमेव सम्बन्धोऽस्तु, तथा च शब्दस्येन्द्रियविशेषणतया, शब्दत्वस्य विशेषणविशेषणतया, रूपादि-जात्यादेरिन्द्रियसम्बद्धविशेषणतया, रूपत्वादेरिन्द्रियसम्बद्ध-विशेषण-विशेषणतया स्वभावसम्बन्धरूपया ग्रहणसम्भवे किं समवायेन । द्रव्ये स्वभावसम्बन्धान्नेन्द्रियेण ग्रहणमिति कथं गुणादेस्तेन

शेषापातो विशिष्टज्ञानस्येत्यत आह, 'विशेषणतेति सम्बन्धविषयकसमूहालम्बनवारणाय सम्बन्धविषयत्वे विशिष्टज्ञानस्य स्वीकृतेऽपि विशेषणतादिकृत एव विशेषो वाच्य इत्यर्थः । 'अत एवेति, यद्यपि प्रत्यक्षत्वेनेन्द्रियसम्बन्धसाधने सम्बन्धाभावादप्रत्यक्षत्वसाधनमशक्यमन्योन्याश्रयात् तथाप्यतिरिक्तसम्बन्धाभावे समवाये सर्वथा प्रमिते स एवाप्रत्यक्षत्वे तन्त्रं । अत एव सम्बन्धत्वेनातिरिक्तसम्बन्धसाधनमेवाशङ्क्यानवस्थया परिजहार । न चैवमभावस्याप्रत्यक्षत्वम्, भावविशेषणतायाः सम्बन्धान्तरनियतत्वात् अभावे तु तदभावेऽपि विशेषणतायाः सत्त्वादिति तेषामभिसन्धिः । ननु प्रामाणिक्यनवस्थेत्यत आह, 'स्वभावादिति, अन्यथोपपत्त्या प्रामाणिकत्वाभावादिति भावः । ननु सम्बन्धाव्यवहारकारित्वं स्वभावादसम्भवि सम्बन्धान्तरमन्तरेण रूपाद्यसम्बन्धेतस्य रूपादीयत्वेनानुपस्थित्या केवलस्य च कदाचिदग्रहेण

ग्रह इति चेत्, समवायेनापि न द्रव्यग्रहणमिति तुल्यम् ।

अपरे त्वेकत्र घटे आमपाकदशायां क्रमेण श्याम-रक्तरूपोपलम्भोऽस्ति, स च न तदुभयनिबन्धनः, रूपस्य नित्यत्वेनैकदोपलम्भापत्तेः । नित्यत्वादेव च न तयो-रुत्पाद-विनाशौ, तस्मात्तयोः सम्बन्धस्य तौ स्यातां, स एव समवाय इति । तन्न । श्याममनष्टं रक्तमुत्पन्नमि-त्याद्यबाधितानुभवात् समवायस्योत्पाद-विनाशानुक्ते-

---

रूपादिसमवायीतिप्रतीत्यभावादित्यत आह, 'समवायोऽपीति, यथा स्वभावादाश्रये सम्बन्धस्तथा स्वभावादेव रूपादीयोऽपि इति प्रतियो-गिन्यनुयोगिनि च स्वभाव एव शरणमिति भावः । अत्र भावानामि-त्यादिनियमस्याप्रयोजकत्वाद्व्यभिचाराच्च नैतदित्यभिमन्धायाभाववद्वि-शेषणतयैवोपपत्तेरनुमाने सिद्धसाधनमित्याह, 'समवायेति । अत एव 'घट-ज्ञानयोरिवेतिव्यभिचारस्थानमेव दृष्टान्तत्वेनादावुदाजहार । ननु घट-ज्ञानयोर्न विशेषणतेन्द्रियप्रत्यासत्तिरसन्निकृष्टस्यैव घटादेर्ज्ञानेन-सा ग्रहादविशेषणसन्निधेरहेतुत्वादित्यस्वरसादाह, 'भूतलेति यथा तत्रेन्द्रियसम्बद्धविशेषणता तथाऽत्रापीत्यर्थः । 'समवायेनापीति, समा-धिसौकर्य्यादिदमुक्तम् । वस्तुतः प्रमाणसिद्धतया तत्र संयोगाभ्युपगमो न सा प्रत्यासत्तिः, क्लृप्तविशेषणताया एव सर्व्वत्र प्रत्यासत्तित्वमित्यभ्युप-गमेऽपि तस्य त्वत्यभावादिति । 'अनुक्तेखादित्युपलक्षणमसम्भवाश्चेत्य-पि द्रष्टव्यम् । समवाय्यसमवाय्यादिभावानुत्पत्तेः विनाशकाभावाच

वाच। त्वन्मते तस्यातीन्द्रियत्वात्। अन्यथावयविनाशान-गन्ध-रसादेरपि नित्यत्वं समवायस्योत्पाद-विनाशाविति किन्न रोचयेत्। न ह्युत्पाद-विनाशप्रतीतिरप्रामाणिकी बाधकं विनेति।

उच्यते। गुण-क्रिया-जातिविशिष्टबुद्धयो विशेषण-सम्बन्धविषयाः विशिष्टबुद्धित्वात् दण्डीतिबुद्धिवत्। न च व्यभिचारः, अभावादिविशिष्टबुद्धेरपि स्वरूपसम्बन्धविषयत्वात्। न चैवमन्यापि तेनैवार्थान्तरं, यतो गुण-

---

नाशानुत्पत्तेः(१) इत्युक्तत्वादिति। 'लाघवादिति, ननु यत्रैव माने लघु-गुरुविषयता सम्भवति तत्रैव लाघवं सहकारि, इह तु न तथा, तथा हि तावतीर्बुद्धीः पक्षयित्वैव समवायसाधनानियमात्(२) गुणादि-विशिष्टबुद्धिमात्रपक्षतायामुक्तलाघवानवतारात् तथाभावे वा द्रव्यविशिष्टबुद्धिमपि पक्षयित्वा तदन्तर्भावेनापि समवायसिद्ध्यापत्तेः। न च तत्र बाधः, उक्तलाघवसहकृतोक्तानुमानात्समवायस्य तत्र स्यात् संयोगस्येत्यत्राविरोधात्, तथाच पक्षवाऽऽख्यावाऽऽख्यघटितं लाघवमनादेयमनियतत्वात् नियतसिद्धिहेतौ नियतलाघवस्यैव सहकारित्वात्। लाघवप्रतिसन्धानश्चैवं यथा नानाकार्य्ये कर्त्रैक्यं कर्तृनानात्वञ्च दृष्टमित्युभयोरुपस्थितौ कर्त्रैक्ये लाघवादेकः कर्त्ता, तथा नानावि-

---

(१) नाशाभावादिति क०।

(२) समवायसाधनानावश्यकत्वादिति ख०।

क्रिया-जातिविशिष्टबुद्धीनां पक्षधर्मताबलेन विषयः सम्बन्धः सिध्यन् लाघवादेक एव सिध्यति, स एव समवायः, न तु स्वरूपसम्बन्धः, तत्तत्स्वरूपाणामनन्तत्वात् सम्बन्धत्वेनाक्लृप्तत्वाच्च। अथवा विशेषणसम्बन्धनिमित्तका इति साध्यं हेतौ तु सत्यन्तं विशेषणं, विशे-

---

शेषणसम्बन्धे एकत्वानेकत्वदर्शनादेकत्वे लाघवमिति । न चैतत् क्वापि दृष्टम्, विशेषणभेदेन सम्बन्धभेदादिति कुतो लाघवावतार इति । अत्राहुः प्रत्येकविशिष्टबुद्धेरेव पक्षभूतायाः सम्बन्धविषयत्वे साध्यमाने सम्बन्धत्वावच्छिन्नस्यानेकत्वे गौरवादेक एव तथा सिद्ध्यति, स्वरूपसम्बन्धस्य सम्बन्धिद्वयात्मकत्वेन गौरवादिति तदुक्तं। 'तत्तत्स्वरूपाणां' सम्बन्धिद्वयस्वरूपाणामित्यर्थः, न त्वन्यविशिष्टबुद्धिविषयीभूतस्वरूपाणामिति, तत्पक्षानुपस्थितौ समवायासिद्धिप्रसङ्गादिति । नन्वभावस्थले सम्बन्धिद्वयात्मनः स्वरूपसम्बन्धस्य कल्पनाद्विपरीतं लाघवमत आह, 'सम्बन्धत्वेनेति, अभावस्य सम्बन्धत्वं क्लृप्तमन्यस्य गुण-गुण्यात्मकस्वरूपस्य सम्बन्धत्वेनाकल्पनात् इहैव तत्कल्पनायां धर्मीकल्पनालाघवमपि नादरणीयम्, उभयत्र सम्बन्धत्वधर्मकल्पनस्योभयकल्पनात्वेन तदवच्छिन्नैककल्पन एव लाघवादिति भावः। ननु प्रतीतेर्विषयनियमोऽनुभवाद्वा सामग्रीभेदाद्वा व्यवस्थाप्यते न लाघवात् अन्यथा विशेषण-विशेष्यमात्रविषयत्वे लाघवात् सविषयत्वानुमानात् सम्बन्धाविषयत्वमेव स्यादिति विपरीतमेव लाघवमाप-

षणसम्बन्धस्य कारणत्वेनैक एव सिध्यति लाघवात् अनुगतकार्यस्यानुगतकारणनियम्यत्वाच्च। न तु स्वरूपसम्बन्धः, तेषामननुगतत्वादनन्तत्वाच्च। न चोभयमप्यप्रयोजकं, विशिष्टसाक्षात्कारस्य सम्बन्धाविषयत्वे तदजन्यत्वे वा गवाश्वादावपि विशिष्टबुद्धिप्रसङ्गात्।

तितमित्यस्वरसात् साध्यान्तरमाश्रित्य तत्साधनमाह, 'अथवेति, अत्र पक्ष-हेतु-दृष्टान्तेषु बुद्धिपदं प्रत्यक्षपरतया द्रष्टव्यम्, अन्यथा व्यभिचाराद्यापत्तेः। नन्वेवं लाघवानुरोधाद्यद्येकत्वं तर्हि संयोगिन्यपि समवायापत्तिः। न चानुभवसिद्धसंयोगाद्बाधः, प्रमाणसमाहारे प्रमेयसमाहाराविरोधादिति। मैवम्। अनुगतसंयोगत्वावच्छेदेन सम्बन्धत्वस्य क्लृप्तत्वादन्यसम्बन्धकल्पने लाघववैपरीत्यात्। न च गुण-गुण्यादिद्वयेष्वप्येवमनुगतमस्ति धर्मान्तरम्, येन क्लृप्तत्वा-लाघववैपरीत्यं स्यादिति भावः। ननु माभूल्लाघवमितोऽप्यनुगततत्सिद्धिरित्याह, 'अनुगतेति, गुण-कर्मादिविशिष्टबुद्धीनामन्तेन तेन विषयेणानुगतानां विशेषणसमवायमन्तरेणानुगतस्य नियामकस्याभावात्। न च विशेषणसम्बन्धत्वेनैवानुगमः, सम्बन्धत्वस्य विषयत्वादिगर्भस्य जनकतानवच्छेदकत्वेन द्रव्यविशिष्टप्रत्यक्षे संयोगत्वेनानुगतस्येव गुणादिविशिष्टप्रत्यक्षे समवायस्यैव नियामकत्वात्(१)।

---

(१) सम्बन्धत्वस्य विषयत्वादिगर्भस्य जनकतानवच्छेदकत्वेन संयोग-समवायत्वादिनैव तत्तद्विशिष्टबुद्ध्यनुगतहेतुत्वादिति ख०।

नव्यास्तु गुण-क्रिया-जातिविशिष्टबुद्धिः सम्बन्धि-भिन्नविशेषणसम्बन्धविषया निर्विषयकभावविशेषणक-विशिष्टबुद्धित्वात् इतरानिरूपणानिरूप्यविशेषणकविशि-ष्टबुद्धित्वाद्वा अतोऽभावादिविशिष्टबुद्धौ न व्यभिचारः ।

अभावविशिष्टप्रत्यक्षे त्वभावत्वेनानुगतस्य तस्यैव[१] स्वरूपसम्बन्धरूपत्वात् गुणादौ च तथानुगतस्याप्येकस्याभावादिति भावः ।

अन्ये तु अनुगतस्य भावकार्य्यादेरनुगतसमवायिकारणादिहेतु-कत्वादपि समवायसिद्धेः अभिमतसमवाये मानान्तरमनेन सूचितं, स्वरूपसम्बन्धेन चान्यथासिद्धौ ध्वंसस्थलेऽपि भावोत्पत्तेराश्रयनाशे ध्वंसनाशादिरापद्येतेति वदन्ति ।

गुणादिविशिष्टबुद्ध्यो विशेषणसम्बन्धविषया इत्येव साध्यं हेतुस्तु विशिष्टज्ञानत्वादित्येव । न चाभावज्ञानादौ व्यभिचारः, तदा तत्पक्षत्वेऽपि तत्प्रतिसन्धानानियमेन[२] तत्साधारणसमवायसिद्धौ क्रमेण बाधाव-तारात्तदंशे समवायबाधात् स्वरूपसम्बन्धकल्पनात् । अत एव न तेन तदार्थान्तरं समवायबाधोत्तरकालकल्प्यस्य स्वरूपसम्बन्धस्य तदानीमक्लृप्तत्वात् । न च व्यभिचारिलिङ्गजन्यत्वादनुमितेर्भ्रमत्वापत्तिः, साध्यवति कूटलिङ्गकानुमितेरपि प्रमात्वात् । वस्तुतो व्यभिचारो

---

(१) अभावविशिष्टबुद्धेरभावत्वेनैवानुगतस्य तस्येति ख० ।

(२) तदप्रतिसन्धाननियमेनेति ख० ।

न चाप्रयोजकं, निरुपाधिसम्बन्धशालित्वात्। सम्बन्धस्या-विशिष्टव्यावृत्तविशिष्टधीनियामकः। यद्वेन्द्रियप्रत्यासत्तित्वेन समवायसिद्धिः। तथाहि गुण-क्रिया-जाति-साक्षात्कार इन्द्रियसम्बन्धसाध्यः जन्यप्रत्यक्षत्वाद्घटज्ञानवदित्यतः साक्षात्सम्बन्धबाधकारणत्वेनेन्द्रियसंयुक्ते सम्बन्धः सिध्यन् पक्षधर्मताबलाल्लाघवेनानुगतः समवाय एक एव सिध्यति अनुगतकार्य्यस्यानुगतकारण-

---

नास्त्येव सम्बन्धविषयत्वस्य सत्त्वात् तदानीं स्वरूपसम्बन्धमादाय सम्बन्धविषयत्वाग्रहेऽपि साध्यसत्त्वात् इति समवायसाधनमिष्प्रत्यूहमिति ध्येयम्। 'नव्यास्त्वित्यस्वरसोद्भावनं(१); तद्बीजन्तु उक्तलाघवादरे वृथा विशेषणोपादानप्रयासः, तदनादरे विशेषणोपादानेऽपि न फलसिद्धिरप्रयोजकत्वात् समवायसिद्ध्यनन्तरं तेनैव हेतुना तदतिरिक्तसम्बन्धसाधनस्य स्यादिति प्रतिकूलतर्कपराहतत्वाच्चेति। 'निर्विषयेति निर्विषयकभावमात्रविषयकविशिष्टबुद्धित्वात्, एवं उक्तरचापि, यथाश्रुते भूतले घटाभाव इत्यादिबुद्धौ व्यभिचारात्, ज्ञानादिविशिष्टबुद्धेस्च पक्षे नान्तर्भावो येनैवं भागासिद्ध्यापत्तिः। वने सिंहनाद इत्यादिबुद्धेर्वनावच्छिन्नस्यातिरिक्तस्य नभोभागस्यापि विषयत्वान्न व्यभिचारः, तदविषयत्वे भ्रान्तित्वमेव बुद्धित्वेन प्रमात्वस्यैव हेतौ विवक्षणादिति सर्व्वं सुस्थम्।

---

(१) 'नव्यास्त्वित्यस्वरसाविष्कार इति ख०।

जन्यत्वात् । न तु संयुक्तविशेषणतारूपस्वरूपसम्बन्धः, तस्य च तत्तद्रूपादिरूपत्वेनाननुगतत्वात् । एवं रूपत्वरसत्वसाक्षात्कारेऽपि कारणत्वेनेन्द्रियसम्बन्धः समवाय एवानुगतः सिध्यति लाघवात्, न त्विन्द्रियसम्बद्धविशेषणता तस्या रूपत्वादिस्वरूपत्वेनाननुगतत्वात् । अत एव संयोगो विशेषणता च प्रत्यासत्तिरस्तु न तु समवायादिचतुष्टयमिति निरस्तम् । तस्यास्तत्तत्स्वरूपत्वेनाननुगतत्वात् । प्रत्यासत्तित्वेनाभ्युपगते च समवाये प्रत्यक्षता सम्बन्धिद्वयप्रत्यक्षत्वात् । नन्वेवमभावविशिष्टप्रत्यक्षेऽपि विशिष्टबुद्धित्वात् संयोग-समवायबाधेऽनुगतं वैशिष्ट्यं सम्बन्धो विषयः निमित्तञ्च भवेदिति चेत् । न । तस्य हि समवायवदेकत्वे घटाभाववति पटवति पटाभावधीप्रसङ्गः घटाभाववैशिष्ट्यमेव हि पटाभाववैशिष्ट्यं । पटाभाववैशिष्ट्यसत्त्वेऽपि पटाभावो नास्ति ततः तस्य भिन्नत्वादिति चेत् । न । पटाभावाभावस्याभावत्वे सोऽपि वैशिष्ट्येन सम्बन्धेन तत्रास्ति वैशिष्ट्यस्यैकत्वात्, पटाभावाभावस्य भावत्वे

उक्ततर्कसहकारपुरस्कारेण वैशेषिकानुमानमपि सम्यगिति मत्वा तदुपन्यस्यति, 'यद्वे'ति, 'पटाभावस्ये'ति प्रतिबन्धकाभावमात्रहेतुत्वेऽतिप्रसङ्गात्तत्सम्बन्ध एव हेतुर्वाच्यः, स चास्त्येव, तथासत्यपि कार्य्याभावे

च पट एव प्रतिबन्धको वाच्यः। एवं पटाभावः पटाभावधीहेतुः स्यात्। पटाभावस्य वैशिष्ट्येन सम्बन्धेन तत्रास्त्येव। वैशिष्ट्यस्य प्रत्यभावव्यक्तिनानात्वे चाभावविशिष्टबुद्धौ नैकः सम्बन्धः कारणं विषयो वेति तदभावप्रत्यक्षेऽननुगतमेव वैशिष्ट्यं विषयः कारणञ्च वाच्यं तथा चाननुगततत्तत्स्वरूपरूपा विशेषणतैवास्तु क्लृप्तत्वात् किमनन्तवैशिष्ट्येन, समवायस्य वैशिष्ट्यस्य च प्रत्यक्षत्वे त्वयापीन्द्रियसम्बद्धविशेषणताखीकारात्। ननु समवायस्यैकत्वे कथं रूपि-नीरूपव्यवस्था। घटेन सह रूपसम्बन्धरूपत्वं समवायस्य न वायुनेति चेत्। न। रूपसम्बन्धरूपत्वं हि समवायस्य स्वरूपमेव यदि तदा रससम्बन्धरूपत्वं न स्यात् तयोर्विरोधात् अन्यच्च दुर्वचमिति चेत्। उच्यते। वायौ रूपसमवायसत्त्वेऽपि रूपा-

न पटस्य प्रतिबन्धकतैव नैकवैशिष्ट्यपक्षे, सा हि तदा भवति यदि पटवति देशे[१] पटाभावसम्बन्धो न स्यादित्यर्थः। समवायस्यातीन्द्रियत्वपक्षमाश्रित्य 'वैशिष्ट्यस्य चेत्युक्तं। प्रतिबन्धिमाशङ्कते, 'समवायेति, 'रूपसम्बन्धरूपत्वमित्यत्र विशेषणत्वपक्षे दोषमाह, 'रूपेति, प्रकारान्तरेण विशेषणत्वं दुर्वचं। उपलक्षणत्वपक्षे स एवातिप्रसङ्ग इत्याह,

(१) यदि घटाभाववति पटवति देशे इति ख०।

त्यन्ताभावोऽस्ति न घटे। कथमेवं, अधिकरणस्वभावात् अबाधितरूपि-नीरूपप्रतीतेश्च। नन्वेवं ज्ञातो घट इति प्रतीतेर्ज्ञाततापि स्यात् वर्त्तमाने बाधकाभावात्, अतीतानागतयोश्च तद्धीर्भ्रान्तेति चेत्। न। अतीतानागतयोर्ज्ञातताया अभावे व्यवहाराभावापत्तेः तस्य ज्ञाततासाध्यत्वात्। न च ज्ञातताज्ञानमेव व्यवहारहेतुः, गौरवात् अतीतादौ ज्ञान-तद्विषयावेव ज्ञातताधीगोचराविति चेत्, तर्हि वर्त्तमाने तावेव तद्विषयौ। न ह्यतीत-वर्त्तमानयोर्ज्ञातताप्रतीत्योर्विषयवैलक्षण्य-

'अन्यस्येति। 'अधिकरणेति, न चाभावेऽप्येवं वक्तुं शक्यं। स्वभावो हि वस्तूनां यावद्द्रव्यभावी, तथाच यदि भूतलस्य घटाभावाद्यधिकरणत्वं रूप-तदभावाधिकरणत्ववत्स्वभावः स्यात्तदा सदा तथाभावापत्तिरित्येकमधिकरणं कालभेदेनाप्युभयाधिकरणं न स्यात्। न ह्यभावाधिकरणवदुभयोरप्यधिकरणे द्विरूपतास्ति येनाधिकरणस्वाभाव्यं न व्यवस्थाप्येत। नन्वेवं पाकरक्ते घटे श्यामाधिकरणताप्रत्यय-प्रसङ्गस्तस्य श्यामाधिकरणस्वभावत्वाद्रक्ताधिकरणत्वाप्रत्ययश्चैकस्य विरुद्धानधिकरणस्वभावत्वादिति[१] चेत्। न। तादृशोपनीतभानस्येष्टत्वात्। अतादृशप्रत्ययस्य तदधिकरणत्वेऽपि तदभावादेवाभावात्तत्र विषयस्यापि हेतुत्वात्। अभावस्थले तु घटाभावस्य स्थानान्तरे तस्यैव

(१) एकस्य विरुद्धद्वयाधिकरणस्वभावत्वविरोधादितीति ख॰।

मीक्षामहे[१]। ननु रूप-घटयोर्न समवायः किन्त्वभेदः, दण्डी पुरुष इत्यत्र दण्डि-पुरुषयोरिव नीलो घट इत्यत्रापि नील-घटयोरबाधिताभेदानुभवात्। नीलो घटो दण्डी पुरुष इति बुद्ध्योर्विशेषणसम्बन्धमात्रगोचरत्वे नीलो घटइतिवद्दण्डः पुरुषः, दण्डी पुरुष इतिवत् नीली घट इत्यपि स्यात्। तस्मादेकत्राभेदो विषयः, अपरत्र विशेषणसम्बन्धः, विषयेणैव धियां विशेषात्।

सत्त्वेन विषयाभावस्यात्रैव वक्तुमशक्यत्वात्। उभयाधिकरणतायास्यैकत्राविरोधात् श्याम-रक्तयोरेव तथा विरोधात्। नन्वयं स्वभाव एव कथं अवधारित इत्यत आह, 'अबाधितेति, तस्मात्त्वं प्रतिबन्धिर्यत्समवायसत्त्वादेव रूपप्रतीतिरिति। वस्तुतस्तु परन्ते दण्डीत्यादावपि दण्डवैशिष्ट्यं विषयो न तु दण्डादिरपि, अत एव क्षणानामनाकलनेऽपि तदाहितवैशिष्ट्यमादायागृहीतग्राहित्वं धारावहनबुद्धीनां तैरेवाशङ्कितं कुसुमाञ्जलौ। समूहालम्बनव्यावृत्तये विशिष्टज्ञानस्याक्लृप्तवैशिष्ट्यं धर्मिग्राहकमानाद्विशिष्टज्ञानमात्रगोचरस्तस्य च विशेषणं न विषय[१] एवेति लीलावतीप्रकाशे स्फुटं। अतस्त्वं प्रति प्रतिबन्धिः पटाभावाभावेऽपि पटाभाववैशिष्ट्यगोचरात्मनः पटाभावविशिष्टज्ञानस्यापत्तिः। अस्माकन्तु सत्यपि समवाये रूपाभावेन रूपविशिष्टज्ञानस्यानुत्पत्तिरिति[२] वैधर्म्येण प्रतिबन्ध्युद्धारात्। अत्र

---

(१) विषयवैलक्षण्यमेवमीक्षामहे इति ख०।

(२) रूपविशिष्टप्रत्ययस्यानुपपत्तिरितीति ख०।

अथवा विशेषणता-विशेष्यतावच्छेदकयोर्नीलत्व-घटत्वयोरेकवृत्तित्वं भासते, दण्डित्व-पुरुषत्वयोरिव पुरुषे। एवं नील-घटपदयोः शाब्दमपि सामानाधिकरण्यं युज्यते, नीलत्व-घटत्वाभ्यां भिन्नप्रवृत्तिनिमित्ताभ्यां तयोरेकप्रवृत्तेः। न च मतुपो लोपाद्भेदोपचाराद्वा नीलपदं नीलवत्परमिति वाच्यं। न हि प्रयोगं साधकं ब्रूमः, किन्तु नील-घटयोरभेदप्रतीतिं। पदेऽपि नोपचारादिकल्पना गौरवात् मुख्ये बाधकाभावाच्चेति। उच्यते। शुक्ल-पटशब्दयोरेकार्थत्वे घटः कुम्भ इतिवत् शुक्लः पट इति सहप्रयोगो न स्यात्। अन्धस्य पटग्रहवत् रूपग्रहः, रूपाग्रहवत् पटाग्रहोऽपि

वयम् रूपसमवायसत्त्वे कथं रूपाभावः संसर्गावच्छिन्नप्रतियोगिताकस्य तस्य सति संसर्गेऽसम्भवात्। अन्यथा घटवति भूतले संयोगावच्छिन्नघटाभावापत्तेः। न च तथा प्रत्ययाभावात् मास्तु घटाभाव इह तु प्रतीत्यनुरोधाद्रूपसमवाये सत्यपि रूपाभावः स्यादिति वाच्यम्। इह रूपमिति प्रतीतेः। न चेदमसिद्धं, अभावप्रत्ययानुरोधेन त्वयापि तादृशप्रतीतेर्बाध्यत्वात्। न च सारोपरूपेति वाच्यम्। अभावप्रतीतेः सत्यत्वे तस्यास्तथात्वस्य वक्तव्यत्वात्तथाच तत्प्रमात्वेन वैपरीत्यस्यापत्तेः। प्रत्युत येन सम्बन्धेन यद्यत्रास्ति तत्सम्बन्धपुरस्कारेण तत्र तज्ज्ञानं प्रमेति रूपवत्त्वधीरेव प्रमा स्यात्, यत्संसर्गाव-

वा स्यात्। महारजतरक्ते पटग्रहवत् शुक्लग्रहः शुक्लाग्रह-वत् पटाग्रहोऽपि भवेत्। पटमानयेत्युक्ते यत्किञ्चिच्छु-क्लमानयेत्। अपटः पट इति वदशुक्लः पट इति विरु-ध्येत, पट-शुक्लयोरभेदात्। अग्निसंयोगादेकत्र श्याम-रक्तयोर्विनाशोत्पादे घटस्य तौ स्यातां। घटसत्त्वे वा तयोरपि[१] न स्यातां। अथ शुक्लत्वादीनां द्रव्यभेदात् तद्बोधार्थं सह प्रयोगः। अन्धादिना शुक्लादिग्रहे शुक्ल-त्वादीनामग्रह उपपद्यते। शुक्लत्वादिजातेश्च द्रव्येणा-भेदो न समवायः, किन्तु स्वरूपसम्बन्ध इति चेत्। न। शुक्लत्व-मधुरत्व-सुरभित्वोष्णत्वादीनां द्रव्यवृत्तित्वे द्रव्यग्राहकत्वगादिभिर्ग्रहणप्रसङ्गात्। रूपत्वादीनां प्रतिनियतेन्द्रियग्राह्यत्वनियमान्नैवमिति चेत्, रूपत्वा-दीनां द्रव्यवृत्तित्वे प्रतिनियतेन्द्रियग्राह्यतैव न स्यात् योग्यवृत्तित्वेन जातेर्ग्रहणयोग्यत्वात्। तत्तज्जातित्वे-

---

च्छिन्नो योऽभावः स तत्संसर्गाविरहवत्येवेति सोऽभावप्रत्यय एव च भ्रमः स्यात्तस्मादविद्यमानसंसर्गावच्छिन्न एव संसर्गाभाव इति रूपाभावोऽप्येवं, न तु समवायावच्छिन्नः। किन्तु तद्धर्मतालक्षण-

---

(१) अनयोरपीति ख०।

न योग्यत्वेऽननुगमात्। तस्मात् रूपत्वादीनां प्रतिनियतेन्द्रियग्राह्यतापि गुण-गुणिभेदे मानं। अभेदे च कथं पटस्य शुक्लं रूपमिति भेदबुद्धिः। पटो नीलिमेति बुद्धिप्रसङ्गश्च। नन्वेकान्ताभेदे सर्वमिदन्दूषणं, वयन्तु भेदाभेदवादिनः। तथाच भेदमादायापीनरक्तादि, भेदाभेदे चोक्तमेव प्रमाणं प्रत्यक्षम्। अथवोभयसिद्ध-भेदे सामानाधिकरण्यधीरभेदे प्रमाणम्। यद्वा अत्यन्तमभेदे भेदे च न सामानाधिकरण्यमिति तत एव भेदाभेदसिद्धिः। न च भेदाभेदयोः परस्परविरहरूपतया विरुद्धयोः कथमेकत्र समावेश इति वाच्यं। संयोगतदभावयोरिवाविरोधात्। पाकानन्तरं रक्तोऽयं न श्याम इत्यबाधितानुभवबलात्त्वैव तदन्योन्याभावसिद्धेस्त्वयापि भेदाभेदस्वीकारात्। अन्योन्याभावत्व-

---

स्वरूपसम्बन्धावच्छिन्नः[१] स तु वायौ रूपसमवायसत्त्वेऽपि नास्ति विशिष्टज्ञाने तदेव हि तन्त्रं तद्विषयत्वादेव समूहालम्बनाद्विशिष्टज्ञानम्भिद्यत इत्युक्तम्। एवं सति समवायसिद्धेः कारणतामात्रेण विशिष्टबुद्धिव्यापकतया परैरप्यवश्याभ्युपेयत्वात्। अन्यथा समूहालम्बनाद्विशिष्टज्ञानस्य विशेषो न स्यादिति धर्म्मसाकाङ्क्षधर्म्मीत्यादितद्विशिष्ट-

---

(१) स्वरूपसम्बन्धविशेषावच्छिन्न इति ख०

मव्याप्यवृत्तिर्वृत्ति नित्याभाववृत्त्यभावत्वसाक्षाद्व्याप्यधर्मत्वात् अत्यन्ताभावत्ववत्, नित्येति वा न विशेषणं अव्याप्यवृत्तिप्रतियोगिकप्रागभाव-प्रध्वंसयोरप्यव्याप्यवृत्तित्वात्। इत्यतोऽपि भेदाभेदसिद्धिः। उच्यते। तस्यैव तथाभावोऽवच्छेदभेदेन वर्त्तते ज्ञायते च यथा संयोगाद्यभावः, श्यामावच्छिन्नस्य तस्यैवान्योन्याभावस्तथैव रक्तावच्छिन्ने, तदन्योन्याभावाभावश्च श्यामावच्छेदेन। तदिहापि नीलस्यान्योन्याभावो घटत्वावच्छेदेनेति नीलात् घटस्य भेदोऽस्तु, अभेदस्तु नीलान्योन्याभावाभावरूपो न घटे घटत्वावच्छेदेनैव विरोधात्। एकावच्छेदेन भावाभावयोरेकत्रावृत्तेरज्ञानाच्च। नाप्यवच्छेदकान्तरेण, घटत्वावच्छिन्ने घटे तदभावात् तद-

---

ज्ञानलक्षणविवरणे प्रामाण्यवादे एव व्यक्तमुक्तम्। सर्वाणि लक्षणानि अतिव्यापकानि इत्याक्षेपप्रकरणे द्रव्यप्रकाशेऽप्ययमर्थः कण्ठरवेण स्फुटीकृतोऽस्ति। तथाच समवायवद्व्यापकत्वेनाभावविशिष्टबुद्धीनां वैशिष्ट्यं सिद्ध्यतु पटाभाववैशिष्ट्यसत्त्वेऽपि तद्धर्मतावच्छिन्नपटाभावाभावसत्त्वाच्च पटाभावविशिष्टबुद्धिः। तथाभावविशिष्टबुद्धौ व्यापकवैशिष्ट्यमात्रस्य समवायवदतन्त्रत्वादिति प्रतिबन्धौ सुदृढायामंशे वाच्यम् ध्वंसनाशे घटोन्मज्जनमेवोत्तरं द्रष्टव्यम्। न च समवायस्वीकारे तदापादनं समवायिनाशस्य समवेतनाशहेतुत्वादिति

ज्ञानेऽपि नीलो घट इत्यनुभवाच्च। न चान्योऽन्याभावरूपो भेदोऽस्तु, अभेदस्तु न भेदाभावः किन्त्वन्य एवेति वाच्यम्। अभेदव्यवहारे तस्याहेतुत्वात्। तस्मान्नीलो घट इत्यत्र नीलसम्बन्ध एव भासते। तथा सति नीली घट इति धीः स्यादित्युक्तमिति चेत्। नीली घट इत्यत्र बुद्धौ यदि सम्बन्धविषयत्वमापद्यते तदिष्यत एव। अथ नीलो घट इतिप्रयोगे सम्बन्धवाचकपदवत्त्वं, तदपीष्यत एव मतुपो लोपादभेदोपचाराद्वा नीलपदमेव नीलवत्परमिति। ननु शब्द-रूपादिषु विशेषणता इन्द्रियसम्बद्धविशेषणता वा ग्राहिकास्तु किं समवायादिना।

वाच्यम्। लाघवेन नित्यसम्बन्धिकारणतात्वेन तद्धेतुत्वकल्पनात् न तु तद्विशेषसमवायिकारणतात्वेन। किञ्च समवायत्वं न जातिरिति वैशिष्ट्यान्यनित्यसम्बन्धत्वेनैव तन्निर्वाच्यम्। तथाच सुतरां तथा कारणत्वे गौरवमिति व्यापकत्वेनापि नाभाववैशिष्ट्यसिद्धिरिति सङ्क्षेपः। 'उक्तमेव प्रमाणं प्रत्यक्षमिति पटस्य शुक्लं रूपं शुक्लः पट इत्युभयमित्यर्थः। नन्वत्यन्तभिन्नाभिन्नाभ्यां व्यावृत्तं सदर्थापत्तिविधया भेदं साधयेत्तच्च भेदाभेदरूपं वा साध्यं साधयेत् प्रत्येकं वा, आद्ये अप्रसिद्धिः, अन्त्येऽसाधारण्यम्। न चासाधारण्यं सत्प्रतिपक्षविधया दोषः स च साध्ययोर्विरोधे, इह च रक्तोऽयं श्याम इति दर्शनाद्विरोध एव नासीति वाच्यम्। भिन्नकालावच्छेदेना-

अथ विशेषणतायां समवायः, इन्द्रियसम्बद्धविशेषणतायाञ्च संयुक्तसमवायादिरुपजीव्यः तैर्विना तयोरभावादिति चेत्। विशेषणतास्वरूपे तेषामुपजीव्यत्वं न तु तस्याः प्रत्यासत्तित्वेऽपि। तैर्विनापि समवायाभावयोर्विशेषणतासत्त्वात्। संयुक्तसमवायादिरपि तत्रास्तीति चेत्, आस्तां न तु प्रत्यासत्तिः, किन्तु विशेषणतैव क्लृप्तत्वात्। संयुक्तसमवायादिकं विना विशेषणता रूपादौ न ज्ञायत इति चेत्, माज्ञायि। न हि सा प्रत्यासत्ति-

---

विरोधदर्शनेऽपि प्रकारान्तरेणापि विरोधदर्शनादिति। तत्र मानान्तरमाह, 'अन्योन्याभावत्वमिति, 'अव्याप्येति स्वकालावच्छिन्नस्वात्यन्ताभावसमानाधिकरणवृत्तीत्यर्थः, तेन नोक्तस्थलमादाय सिद्धसाधनम्। 'साक्षादिति अभावविभाजकोपाधित्वादित्यर्थः, चतुर्द्धैवाभावविभजनात्, अन्यथा यथाश्रुतेऽत्यन्ताभावत्वे दृष्टान्ते साधनवैकल्यं स्यादिति भावः(१)। अत्र सिद्धसाधनमाह, 'तस्यैवेति। यद्वा पृथगवच्छेदकावच्छिन्नमात्रवृत्तिवृत्तित्वमुपाधिमाह, 'तस्यैवेति, भेदाभेदवादिमते भेदस्य विरोध एव नास्ति क्वचिदप्य-

---

(१) यदि अभावविभाजकं संसर्गाभावत्वं अन्योन्याभावत्वञ्च, न त्वत्यन्ताभावत्वं तस्य संसर्गाभावविभाजकत्वात् तदा अत्यन्ताभावत्वरूपदृष्टान्तं अभावविभाजकोपाधित्वरूपसाधनविरहितं स्यादिति भावः।

ज्ञाता, अपि तु स्वरूपसती । मैवम् । शब्दादीनां साक्षात्कारविषयत्वेनेन्द्रियसम्बन्धानुमितौ शब्दादौ समवायादिकं ज्ञात्वैव विशेषणताग्रह इत्यवश्यं प्रथमोपस्थितत्वात् समवायादिरेव विषयो न विशेषणता चरमोपस्थितत्वात् । ननु अभावग्रहे नेन्द्रियसम्बद्धविशेषणता प्रत्यासत्तिः चक्षुषा संयुक्ते परमाण्वादौ योग्यस्य जलत्वा-

---

समावेशाभावादिति नाशङ्कनीयं, गवाश्वादेर्भेद-तदभेदासमावेशस्य तैरपि स्वीकारात् । न चोभयोर्गोत्वाभिन्नत्वेन तदभिन्नाभिन्नतया अभेदसत्त्वात्तत्राप्युभयसमावेश इति वाच्यम् । तैरपि गोत्वादिना भेदो ब्रह्मत्वेनाभेद इत्यवच्छेदकभेदेनैव तदुभयसमावेशस्वीकारात्, तदुक्तं 'अवच्छेदभेदेनेतीति भावः । 'नीलो घट इति । न च यदि सम्बन्धप्रकारिका धीस्तदा तद्वाचकमतुप्प्रयोगापत्तिः, इह च नीलप्रकारेण वैशिष्ट्यविधया सम्बन्धो विषय इति कथं मतुप्प्रयोगापादनमिति[१] वाच्यम् । प्रातिपदिकार्थयोरभेदान्वयस्यैव व्युत्पत्तिसिद्धत्वात् । अन्यथा दण्डः पुरुष इत्यपि दण्डप्रकारकं संयोगवैशिष्ट्यविषयकं प्रत्ययमादध्यात् । अत एव घटः कर्मत्वमानयनं कृतिरित्यादिक्रिया-कर्मभावेन नान्वयं बोधयति, अभेदे चायोग्यमात वक्ष्यामः । 'विशेषणतासम्बन्धादिति विशेषणताप्रत्यासत्तिमत्त्वादित्यर्थः ।

---

(१) मतुप्प्रयोगापादनमिवीति ख० ।

देरभावग्रहप्रसङ्गात्, किन्तु स्वग्राह्यसम्बद्धविशेषणता, महति वायावुद्भूतरूपाभावस्य, कुसुमे सौरभाभावस्य, गुडे तिक्तत्वाभावस्य वा न चक्षुरादिना ग्रहोऽपि तु योग्यानुपलब्ध्या सोऽनुमीयते। इन्द्रियविशेषणतापि न प्रत्यासत्तिः, चक्षुरादिना स्वविशेषणजलत्वाद्यभावग्रहप्रसङ्गात्। यदि शब्दाभावः प्रत्यक्षः तदा प्रत्यासत्त्यन्तरं

'शब्दादीनामिति, कर्मसम्बद्धस्यैव करणस्य क्रियाजनकत्वदर्शनादिति सामान्यतो हेतुत्वग्रहोऽत्र मूलम्। इन्द्रियविशेषे संयोगादिसम्बन्धग्रहस्य व्यापारतयापि सम्भवादिति भावः। 'शब्दत्वेनेति वस्तुगतिमनुरुध्योक्तं। वस्तुतः पूर्वाभ्यानेऽपि लाघवादनुगमादपि तदानीं तद्विषय एवानुमानप्रवृत्तेरित्युक्तम्। 'चरमेति, तथा प्रथमोपस्थितावपि गौरवेणैव तन्निरसनसम्भवात्। न च क्लृप्तत्वेन लाघवम्, विशेषणतायाः प्रतिस्वरूपात्वेन समवायादिविशेषणतायाः प्रत्यासत्तित्वकल्पनेऽप्येतद्विशेषणतायास्तत्त्वाकल्पनादित्युक्तप्रायम्। 'अपि त्विति[१], रूपाभावो वायुवृत्तिर्योग्यप्रतियोगिकत्वे सति वायुवृत्तित्वेनानुपलभ्यमानप्रतियोगिकत्वादित्यनुमानं द्रष्टव्यम्। अन्यथाऽनुमानेन वायौ रूपाभाव इति वायुविशेषणकरूपाभावविशेष्यकबुद्धेरसिद्धेरिति। 'तदभाव इति शब्दाभाव इत्यर्थः। क्वचित् 'तदभावे' इति पाठस्तस्य 'तद-

---

(१) किञ्चितीति ख०।

कल्प्यं। तदभावे प्रत्यक्ष एव न भवतीति चेत्। मैवं। लाघवादिन्द्रियसम्बद्धविशेषणतैव प्रत्यासत्तिः। न चैवं परमाणौ जलत्वाद्यभावग्रहप्रसङ्गः, यत्र हि यत्सत्त्व-

भावे' प्रत्यासत्त्यन्तराभाव इत्यर्थः। 'लाघवादिति। न च लाघवादनुपलम्भमात्रं ग्राहकं, अतिप्रसङ्गस्य स्वग्राह्यसम्बद्धविशेषणताप्रत्यासत्तित्वेनैव निवार्य्यतामिति वैपरीत्यमेवास्त्विति वाच्यम्। विशुद्धमातापितृयोनित्वादिव्यञ्जकधीविरहकाले ब्राह्मणत्वाद्यभावग्रहप्रसङ्गेन तादृशयोग्यानुपलम्भस्यावश्यंवाच्यत्वात् स्वग्राह्येत्यादिना तदतिप्रसङ्गावारणादिति। अत एव सम्बद्धत्वं प्रत्यासन्नत्वं तच्चाननुगतमिति तदपेक्षयेन्द्रियग्राह्यत्वमेव लघु इति तद्विशेषणतैव प्रत्यासत्तिरिति अपास्तं। ब्राह्मणाद्यभावग्रहानुरोधेन[१] तादृशयोग्यानुपलम्भेरवश्य वाच्यतया वायौ रूपाभावप्रत्यक्षतानुरोधेनेन्द्रियसम्बद्धविशेषणता[...]: एव प्रत्यासत्तित्वौचित्यात् योग्यानुपलब्धिविषयत्वेनैवाभावस्य योग्यत्वमिति अनुपदमेव वक्ष्यमाणत्वादिति भावः। 'यत्र हीति। ननु वैपरीत्यमेवास्तु, प्रतियोग्युपलम्भविरोधिनी अभावविशेषणता अभावग्राहिका, एवं तादृशविशेषणतास्वीकारे अनुपलब्धिहेतुत्वमेव दुर्लभङ्कुतो वैपरीत्यमिति यदि तदान्यदपि महदननुकूलं लाघवातिरेकात्, अपिचेत्थं विशेषणतास्वीकारेऽनुगमोऽपि, अन्यथा क्वचित् सम्बद्धविशेषणता, क्वचिदिन्द्रियविशेषणतेत्यननुगमेन तत्तदभावप्रत्यक्षं

(१) ब्राह्मणाद्यभावग्रहप्रसङ्गेनेति ख०।

मनुपलब्धिविरोधि तच्च तस्याभाव इन्द्रियसन्निकर्षेण गृह्यते। न च परमाण्वादौ जलत्वादिसत्त्वमनुपलब्धिविरोधि, योग्यसंयुक्तसमवायाभावेन पृथिवीत्ववदनुप-

प्रत्येव तथात्मत्या हेतुत्वं स्वीकरणीयम्। षोढा विभागश्च प्रत्यासत्तेः कथञ्चित्पारिभाषिकोपाधिना निर्व्वाह्य इति महान् प्रयास इति।

अत्राहुः यथाश्रुतविशेषणतायाः पृथिवीपरमाणौ जलत्वाभावेऽपि गतत्वेन यावत्प्रतियोगिग्राहकसत्त्वेऽपि यस्यां विशेषणतायां सत्याञ्च प्रतियोग्युपलम्भ इति प्रतियोग्युपलम्भविरोधित्वं निर्व्वाच्यम्। तथाचाचार्य्ययोग्यानुपलब्धिरेव पर्य्यवसितेत्यनुपलब्धेः प्रकारान्तरनिर्व्वचनं न विशेषणतायाः। न च तदपि निर्व्वहतीति वाच्यते। प्रतियोगिसत्त्वविरोधित्वमनुपलम्भस्य तत्प्रसञ्जितप्रतियोगिकत्वं तेन यत्रैव प्रतियोगिसत्त्वेनापादकेन प्रतियोग्युपलम्भापादनं तत्रैव तदभावः प्रत्यक्षः(१)। अत एव प्रतियोगिसत्त्वं तर्कितमिति वक्ष्यति, तेन यादृशप्रतियोगिसत्त्वेन देशावच्छिन्नेन कालावच्छिन्नेन वा तदुपलम्भापादनं तदवच्छिन्नस्तदभावः प्रत्यक्ष इत्यनुगमोऽपि। यद्वा प्रतियोगिसत्त्वविरोधीति यथाश्रुतमेव, तेनान्धकारस्थघटानुपलम्भेऽपि न तदभावग्रहस्तत्र घटसत्त्वस्यानुपलब्धिसहचरितत्वेनाविरोधात्। न च घटवति दोषाद्घटवत्त्वाज्ञानेऽपि घटाभावभ्रमो न स्यात् प्रतियोगिसत्त्वविरोध्यनुपलम्भाभावादिति वाच्यम्। इन्द्रियसम्बद्धविशेषणतासहकारिण्या उक्तानुपलब्धेः प्रमाजनिकाया एव

(१) तदभावो गृह्यत इति ख०।

लब्धिसम्भवात्। महति वाय्वादौ उद्भूतरूपाद्यभावश्चक्षु-
रादिग्राह्य एव, तत्रोद्भूतरूपादिसत्त्वेऽनुपलब्ध्यनुपपत्तेः।
अत एव स्तम्भे पिशाचतादात्म्याभावः प्रत्यक्षः स्तम्भता-

निर्व्वचनादभावभ्रमस्य रजतभ्रमसामान्यसामग्र्यैवोपपत्तेः। नन्वेवं विशिष्टज्ञानसामान्यसामग्र्यैवाभावज्ञानमस्तु किमनुपलम्भेन। न च सापि विशेषणासंसर्गाग्रहगर्भेति तावताप्यनुपलम्भस्य हेतुतासिद्धि-रिति वाच्यम्। एवम्भूतले घटाभाव इति बुद्धौ भूतलासंसर्गा-ग्रहहेतुतालाभेऽपि घटानुपलम्भस्य हेतुत्वालाभात् वक्ष्यमाणक्रमेण सामान्यसामग्र्यां घटाग्रहाप्रवेशाच्च। न चाभावेन्द्रियसम्बन्धादि-सामान्यसामग्रीसत्त्वेऽपि घटोपलम्भे नाभावधीरित्यनुपलम्भो हेतुरिति वाच्यम्। घटाभाववति घटोपलम्भस्य भ्रमतया तज्जनकदोषस्या-भावप्रमाप्रतिबन्धकत्वात् तदभावे भ्रमस्यैवासम्भवात्। मैवम्। अभावभ्रमस्थले प्रतियोग्युपलम्भे सति नाभावज्ञानमित्यनुपलम्भहेतुत्वे कल्प्यमाने लाघवेनाभावज्ञानत्वावच्छिन्नं प्रति हेतुता कल्प्यते न तु विशिष्य गौरवात्। न च तत्र प्रमासामग्र्येव प्रतिबन्धिका, दोषाभावाद्वा नारोपोत्पत्तिरिति वाच्यम्। विवक्षितविवेकेनान्येषां व्यभिचारेणोक्तानुपलम्भरूपाया एव प्रमासामग्र्या अभावस्यैव दोषत्व-पर्य्यवसानात्। न च प्रतियोगिसत्त्वविरोधेनानुपलम्भस्तत्र हेतुत्वेन क्लृप्तो येन प्रमायां तद्धेतुत्वं लभ्येतेति वाच्यम्। अत एव प्रतियोगि-सत्त्वापादितप्रतियोगिकानुपलम्भहेतुत्वाभ्युपगमात् सामान्यतोऽनु-पलम्भमात्रहेतुत्वकल्पनानन्तरं विशेषद्वये विशेषाभ्यामनुपलम्भसम्भा-

दाव्ये च तस्य स्तम्भस्यैवानुपलम्भासम्भवात्। एवं शब्दस्याप्यभावः प्रत्यक्षः तदा तत्र शब्दसत्त्वस्यानुपलब्धिविरोधित्वादिति तत्रेन्द्रियविशेषणतैव प्रत्यासत्तिः चक्षुषि जलत्वादिसत्त्वञ्च नानुपलब्धिविरोधीति चक्षुषा न

वात्। अत एव सामान्यसामग्र्यामप्यसंसर्गाग्रहप्रवेशो बोद्धव्य इति। यद्यपि य एव भ्रमस्थले प्रतियोग्युपलम्भप्रतिबन्धकः स एव हेतुः स चात्र नेति नातिप्रसङ्गः, तथापि तेषामननुगमादनुगतस्यास्यैव हेतुत्वमिति तु तत्त्वं, चक्षुषि पृथिवीत्वाभावाप्रत्यक्षत्वानुरोधेन योग्ययोग्यानुपलम्भः सर्व्वथा हेतुरिति तत्त्वं। 'महतीति, न चैवमुद्भूतरूपे परमाणौ महत्त्वाभावप्रत्यक्षताप्रसङ्गः(१), इष्टत्वात्। यत्रैवोपलम्भो यस्य प्रतियोगिसत्त्वेनापाद्यते तत्रैव तदभावप्रत्यक्षतास्वीकारात्। एवं मनस्त्वाभावोऽपि घटादौ, उद्भूतरूपवदन्योन्याभावोऽपि वाय्वादौ सुग्रहः। न च प्रतियोगियोग्यत्वं संसर्गाभावे, अधिकरणयोग्यत्वं अन्योन्याभावे योग्यतेति कथमेतदिति वाच्यम्। अनभ्युपगमात् उक्तानुपलम्भविषयत्वेनैवोभयत्र योग्यत्वादिति। अत एवाये तादात्म्याभाव इत्युभयाभाववाचिना पदेन साधारण्येन श्लिष्टनिर्द्देशः। 'स्तम्भेति, यद्ययं पिशाचतदात्मा पिशाचत्वजातिमान्वा स्यात्तदा तत्प्रकारकोपलम्भविषयः स्यादित्यापादनसम्भवात्। न चैवं पिशाचे स्तम्भत्वसत्त्वेऽपि तदुपलम्भापादनं, अयोग्यवृत्तित्वेन पिशाचत्ववदनुपलम्भसम्भवादिति भावः। अत्रोपलम्भाभावः प्रत्यक्षाभावो वाच्यः। न

---

(१) महत्त्वाभावप्रत्यक्षत्वापत्तिरिति ख०।

तद्ग्रहः। नन्वभावे न विशेषणता प्रत्यासत्तिः, किन्तु समवाय एव समवायसाधकविशिष्टप्रतीतेरविशेषात्। न च समवेतत्वे तस्य भावत्वापत्तिः, भावस्य तत्त्वे अभावत्वापत्तिरिति वैपरीत्यसम्भवात्। रूपादौ प्रत्यासत्तित्वेन समवायकल्पनमभावेऽपि तुल्यं, विशेषणतापि तुल्या, प्रागभाव-प्रध्वंसौ प्रतियोग्याश्रये समवेतौ, प्रतियोग्याश्रयनाशजन्यध्वंसो देशे समये वा सम-

---

च पिशाचप्रत्यक्षाप्रसिद्धौ तदभावः सम्भवतीति नाशङ्कनीयम्, प्रत्यक्षेऽधिकरणे प्रतियोगिसंसर्गविषयत्वाभावस्य हेतुत्वात्। वस्तुतस्तु प्रतियोगिसत्त्वेनापादितप्रतियोगिकत्वेनानुगमेन यदि पिशाचत्वं स्तम्भवृत्ति स्यात्तदा स्तम्भवृत्तित्वेनोपलभ्येतेत्यापादने स्तम्भवृत्तित्वोपलम्भाभाव एव तथा, यदि वायौ रूपं स्यात्तदा रूपवत्त्वेनोपलभ्येतेत्यत्र रूपवत्त्वोपलम्भाभावस्तथा इत्युभयत्र प्रतियोगिसत्त्वस्यापादकत्वादापादनमापाद्यप्रसिद्ध्यनुरोधेन द्विरूपमेवेत्युक्तक्रमेणैवानुगम इति सङ्क्षेपः। 'घटत्वाभावादेरिति, न चैवं द्रव्य-गुणान्यान्यत्वादीनां जातित्वं प्रसञ्जितमनुभूतमेवेति वाच्यम्। उक्तरूपपरापरभावाभावेन जातिभेदे सिद्धेऽपि घटत्वाभावादौ नित्यानेकसमवेतत्वेन(१) तावन्मात्रस्य जातित्वे अप्रयोजकत्वमित्यन्यत्र ग्रन्थस्य तात्पर्यादिति। 'समवेतत्व इति, ननु समवायिकारणनाशस्य कारणतासमवायकल्पनोत्तरकल्प्या समवायकल्पनमेव प्राथमिकमुपजीव्यञ्च।

---

(१) नित्यानेकसमवेतत्वसत्त्वेनेति ख०।

वैति तत्रैव निरूपणात्। न च समवायिनाशे ध्वंस-नाशः, घटोन्मज्जनप्रसङ्गात् भावत्वस्योपाधित्वाच्च। अन्यथा तवापि तस्य जन्यत्वेन नाशापत्तिः। अथैव-मन्योन्यात्यन्ताभावयोर्नित्यत्वेऽनेकसमवेतत्वे च जा-तित्वप्रसङ्गः। न च तत्र भावत्वं तन्त्रं, गौरवात्। न चाभावानां विशिष्टप्रतीतौ विशेषो येनात्र समवाय-परित्यागः, इति चेत्। न। घटत्वाभावादेर्जातित्वे सत्त्व-द्रव्यत्व-पृथिवीत्वादिना परापरभावानुपपत्तेः। तेषां व्याप्यत्वे घटे तदभावप्रसङ्गः, व्यापकत्वे सामा-न्यादौ घटत्वाभावो न स्यादिति। उच्यते। समवेतत्वे ध्वंसस्य समवायिकारणनाशान्नाशः स्यात्। न च

गुणादिन्यायेनाभावमपि विषयीकृत्योत्पन्नत्वोपजीव्यविरोधेन न तत्र समवायाभावकल्पनम् प्रत्युत तद्विरोधेन समवायिनाशेन समवेतनाशं प्रति भावत्वं तन्त्रमङ्गीक्रियतां गौरवस्य प्रामाणिकत्वादिति।

अत्राहुः। अभावे समवायकल्पनं नोक्तकारणतायामुपजीव्यं अभावमविषयीकृत्य गुणादिमात्रविषयीकरणे सिद्धेऽपि समवाये समवायिकारणनाशस्य हेतुताग्रहसम्भवात्। दैवात्तु तदानीमभावे बाधकानवतारेण तस्य अभावविषयत्वात् तस्मात् प्रथमतो बाधका-नवतारेणाभावसाधारणसमवायानुमितावपि अनन्तरमुक्तबाधकाव-तारेऽस्य परित्यागः कार्य्यान्वितशक्तिवत्। वस्तुतस्तु समवायकल्प-नमन्तरेणापि घटादिनाशदर्शनेन ध्वंसाद्यनाशदर्शनेनापि साभाव-

नाश्यत्वे भावत्वन्तन्त्रं, गौरवात् प्रागभावेऽभावाच्च। असमवेतत्वे तद्ध्वंसस्य जन्यत्वेऽपि न नाशः आश्रयनाशादेरभावात्। घटोन्मज्जनापत्तेः[१] न नश्यतीति चेत्। न। न हि प्रयोजनक्षतिभयेन सामग्री न कार्य्यमर्जयति, तस्मादुन्मज्जनाभावनिर्वाहकं ध्वंसस्यासमवेतत्वं कल्प्यतां। स्वसमवायिनाशात् ध्वंसपरम्पराकल्पने च घट-कपालादेरापरमाणुनाशे घटादि-तद्ध्वंसविरोधी चरमो ध्वंसः परमाणुवृत्तिः स्यात्। तथा च न प्रत्यक्षः।

सम्बन्धान्यसम्बन्धिकारणनाशत्वेन हेतुतायां क्लृप्तायामग्रे नोक्तानुमानेन तत्साधारणैकसम्बन्धसिद्धिर्विरोधात्, किन्त्वभावव्यावृत्तत्वेन ज्ञातः सम्बन्धः समवायसिद्ध्यनन्तरं तादृप्ये पर्य्यवस्यति, तस्मादुभययापि नाभावसमवायः। न च भिन्नसम्बन्धसिद्धौ भाव एव विशेषणता, अभाव एव समवायः, स्वरूपसम्बन्धिनाश एव कार्य्यनाशहेतुः, समवायिकारणनाशो न समवेतनाशे हेतुरिति वैपरीत्यमेवास्त्विति वाच्यम्। अभावस्वरूपाणामभावत्वेनानुगतानां स्वरूपसम्बन्धत्वकल्पनात् न त्वननुगतावयवि-गुण-कर्म्म-जात्यादीनामित्युक्तप्रायम्। अत एवाभावत्वेन तत्कल्पनात् अत्यन्तान्योन्याभावयोरपि स्वरूपसम्बन्धस्य क्लृप्तत्वेन लघुत्वात् स एव कल्प्यते न समवायः कल्पनीयत्वात्। ध्वंसे समवायबाधकाले कल्प्यमानः स्वरूपसम्बन्धो

---

(१) घटोन्मज्जनप्रसङ्गादिति ख०।

घटध्वंसस्य कपालसमवेतत्वे च न भूतले निरूपणं स्यात्। उभयवृत्तित्वे च व्यासज्यवृत्तित्वेन कपालं विना न निरूप्येत।

इति श्रीमद्गङ्गेशोपाध्यायविरचिते तत्त्वचिन्तामणौ प्रत्यक्षखण्डे समवायवादः।

ध्वंसत्वविशेषमनादाया भावत्वे सामान्ये पर्य्यवस्यति, अन्यथोक्त-बाधकस्यात्यन्ताभावादावसम्भवेन तत्र समवायकल्पनाया वज्रलेपत्वापातादिति दिक्।

इति श्रीजयदेवमिश्रविरचिते तत्त्वचिन्तामण्यालोके प्रत्यक्षखण्डालोके समवायवादालोकः।

अथानुपलब्धिप्रामाण्यवादः ।

नन्वभावग्रहो नेन्द्रियात्, किन्तु योग्यानुपलब्धेः तदुपलम्भे तदभावाग्रहात्[१] । नचैवं भावबुद्धिरप्यभावानुपलब्धेरेव नेन्द्रियादिति[२] वाच्यम् । भावग्रहे इन्द्रियानुविधानात् । अन्यथा निमीलिताक्षस्यापि घटाभावानुपलब्ध्या घटग्रहप्रसङ्गः । अत एव भावग्रहे अभावानुपलब्धिः पृष्ठलग्नापि न हेतुः इन्द्रियेणान्यथासिद्धत्वात् । न हीन्द्रियार्थसन्निकर्षे सति तां विना भावधीविलम्बः । अभावग्रहेऽपीन्द्रियं हेतुः तद-

---

अथानुपलब्धिप्रामाण्यवादालोकः ।

'किन्त्विति, तथाच न विशेषणता प्रत्यासत्तिरिति भावः । ननु ग्राहकत्वे तस्याः सिद्धे करणत्वं कस्यमतस्तदेव व्यतिरेकेण दर्शयति, 'तदिति । अनुविधानमेवाह, 'अन्यथेति । 'अत एवेति इन्द्रियानुविधानादित्यर्थः, 'पृष्ठेति भावग्रहे नियमतोऽन्वयाद्यनुविधानवत्यर्थः । ननु तयैवेन्द्रियमन्यथासिद्धमस्तु । न च निमीलिताक्षस्थले तस्यां सत्यामपि फलाभावादिन्द्रियहेतुत्वनिर्णयः, तर्हि तद्वदेवाभावज्ञानेऽपि इन्द्रियहेतुतासम्भवात् । न च तदानीमधिकरणग्रहाभावान्नाभावधीर्भ

---

(१) तदनुपलम्भे तदभावग्रहादिति क० ।

(२) न त्विन्द्रियादिनेति ख० ।

नुविधानादिति चेत्। न। अभावेन चक्षुरादेः प्राप्त्य-भावेनाश्रयग्रहे तदुपक्षयात्। अथाधिकरणधीरिन्द्रि-यव्यापारः, न च तया तदन्यथा सिद्ध, अन्यथा सन्नि-कर्षोपक्षीणतया इन्द्रियं न हेतुः स्यादिति चेत्। न। हेतुत्वे सिद्धे तद्व्यापारत्वं, तदेव नास्ति प्राप्त्यभावात्। एतेनाधिकरणग्रहेन्द्रिययोः पृथगन्वय-व्यतिरेकग्रहात् दण्ड-चक्रयोरिव हेतुत्वं द्वयोरिति निरस्तं। प्राप्त्य-भावेनाभावाग्राहकत्वात्। न चेन्द्रियं प्राप्तविशेषण-

---

त्विन्द्रियसन्निकर्षाभावादिति वाच्यम्। अधिकरणज्ञानमात्रस्य तत्रापि सत्त्वेन प्रतियोगिग्राहकेन्द्रियजन्याधिकरणज्ञानाभावो वाच्यः, तथाच तस्यापि कल्पनीयत्वादिन्द्रियसन्निकर्ष एव कल्प्यतां। किञ्च योग्या-भावग्रहस्य सामान्यत एव प्रतिबन्धकतया अभावानुपलम्भस्याहेतु-त्वमसङ्गतम्[१]।

यत्तु परिशिष्टप्रकाशे महामहोपाध्यायचरणाः। अभावानुपल-म्भोऽभावोपलम्भप्रागभावो वाच्यः, तथाच भावोपलम्भे तत्प्रागभाव-हेतुतावश्यकतया गन्धादौ रूपादिप्रागभावादीनामिव भावानुपलम्भेन स्वप्रागभावेन सोऽप्यन्यथासिद्ध एवेति, तत्तु भावानुपलम्भसमान-युक्तिकत्वात् न बुध्यामहे।

---

(१) अभावानुपलब्धिरहेतुरित्यसङ्गतमिति ख०। प्रतिबन्धकाभावस्य हेतुत्वात् अभावानुपलम्भस्य अभावोपलम्भरूपप्रतिबन्धकाभावतया हेतुत्वं सिद्धमेवेति भावः।

मप्राप्तमपि गृह्णाति, संयुक्तसमवायाद्युच्छेदप्रसङ्गात् प्राप्तचैत्रगताप्राप्तदण्डस्यापि ग्रहप्रसङ्गात् इन्द्रियस्य प्राप्तग्राहकत्वाच्च। न च विशेषणता प्राप्तिः, अन्यत्र तदकल्पनात्। न च समवाये तत्कल्पनं, तस्यानभ्युपगमात् तत एवातीन्द्रियत्वाद्वा। अथाभावस्येन्द्रिययग्राह्यत्वेन संयोगादिबाधे इहैव सा कल्प्यते रूपादौ तद्बाधे संयुक्तसमवायादिरिवेति चेत्, तत्रानुपक्षीणेन्द्रियानुविधानात्तथैव। इह त्वाश्रयग्रह एव तदुप-

---

किञ्चाधिकरणे प्रतियोगिसंसृष्टत्वोपलम्भविषयत्वाभावरूपानुपलब्धिर्वाच्या, सा च न प्रागभाव एव, स्वप्रागभावेन वा यद्यन्यथासिद्धा तदेन्द्रियेणेत्याद्यपि विरुद्धं। न चाभावानुपलब्धिरपि योग्यताविशेषिता वाच्या सा च यावदभावग्राहिकेत्यादिगर्भा प्रकृते वाच्या, तथाचाभावग्राहकप्रतियोग्यादिस्मरणादेर्भावाग्राहकत्वादभावानुपलब्धिर्न भावग्राहिकेति वाच्यं। एतावता व्यभिचारेणाहेतुत्वं प्राप्तं न त्वन्यथासिद्धेरिति प्रकृतग्रन्थविरोधात्। किञ्च प्रतियोगिस्मरणादि न योग्यताशरीरप्रविष्टं प्रतियोगि-तद्व्याप्येतरपदेन हि असाधारणतदुपलम्भकान्यद्वक्तव्यम्, यथाश्रुते घटोपलम्भप्रागभावस्य घटाभावग्राहकत्वेनासम्भवात्। न हि स प्रतियोगी तद्व्याप्यो वा, तथा च प्रतियोगिस्मृत्यादयोऽभावासाधारणोपलम्भका इति तदन्ययावत्समवधानमस्त्येवेति नोक्तव्यभिचारोऽपीति। न चैवं संयोगिनाशजन्यसंयोगनाशस्थले

क्षीणं लाघवात्, न तु प्राप्यन्तरकल्पना, गौरवात्। अन्यथा त्वगनुविधानाद्रूपं विनापि वायुधीः प्रत्यक्षेति न सा स्पर्शलिङ्गग्रहे उपक्षीयेत। किञ्च विशेषणतायामिन्द्रियग्राह्यत्वं तेन सेत्यन्योन्याश्रयत्वं। अपि च विशेषणता ग्राह्यस्वरूपमेव। न च त्वगादौ स्वरूपसम्बन्धो हेतुः, किन्तु यथायथं संयोग-समवायौ। न च तयोरन्योन्यव्यभिचारादिन्द्रियं सम्बद्धं गृह्णातीत्येव व्याप्तिरिति वाच्यं। दृष्टान्ते हि सम्बन्धिगतः सम्बन्धो

एवं व्यभिचारोद्धारेण यावत्तदुपलम्भकेत्यादिगर्भैवानुपलब्धिर्हेतुः स्यादिति वाच्यम्। एककारणपरिशेषापातादिन्द्रियादेरप्यहेतुतापत्तेर्वक्ष्यमाणत्वात्। अत एव प्रतियोगिसत्त्वप्रसञ्जितप्रतियोगिकानुपलब्धिर्हेतुर्व्वाच्या तेन तादृशापादनस्थल एवाभावधीः, भावग्रहे च प्राथमिकेऽभावस्य तदानीमनुपस्थितत्वेन तथा प्रसञ्जनाभावान्नानुपलब्धिर्हेतुरित्यपास्तम्। एवमपि व्यभिचारप्रदर्शनादिन्द्रियेणान्यथासिद्धप्रदर्शमात्। अथ ग्राह्याभावग्रहाभावो हेतुरित्यभावानुपलम्भोऽपि कारणमेव येन प्रकारेण भावानुपलम्भः कारणन्तेनाभावानुपलम्भोऽन्यथासिद्धः, तथाहि घटतादात्म्यग्रहे तदत्यन्ताभाव-तदाश्रयान्योन्याभावयोर्द्वयोरपि न ग्रह इति वस्तुगतिः, एवञ्च तदुभयग्रहे न घटतादात्म्यग्रह इत्यपि, तथाचाभावग्रहे ग्राह्याभावानुपलम्भो ग्राहको घटतादात्म्यस्य तदुभयस्वरूपग्राह्यविरहरूपत्वात् तद्ग्रहे तेनैव रूपेण तदुभयाग्रहो

हेतुर्गृहीतः चक्षुष्यन्यत्रापि तथा, न तु ग्राह्यस्वरूपं, सम्बन्धस्य सम्बन्धिभिन्नत्वनियमात् । न हि स एव तद्वांस्तेनैव भवति । स्वरूपसम्बन्धस्य हेतुत्वे च रूपादिग्रहेऽपि तत एवास्तु किं समवायादिना, अतः संयोगविशेषणते एव प्रत्यासत्ती इति षोढ़ा कीर्त्तनमपि विफलं । एतेनालोकापेक्षणे चक्षुरपेक्षा तस्य तदेकसहकारित्वादिति निरस्तं । प्राप्तिं विना चक्षुषोऽहेतुत्वात् आलोकस्य च प्रतियोगिग्राहकत्वेन योग्यता-

---

घटतादात्म्यग्रहेऽपि कारणम् तदा घटान्योन्याभावग्रहे सत्यपि तत्तादात्म्यग्रहापत्तिः अन्योन्याभावस्य तदभावत्वाभावात् । न हि यथा तादात्म्यमन्योन्याभावाभावस्तथान्योन्याभावोऽपि तदभावरूपः, घटाप्रतियोगिकत्वापातात् संसर्गाभावत्वापाताच्च । यथाच नेयमिष्टापत्तिस्तथा व्यतिरेकिणि वक्ष्यामः । एवञ्च सानुपलब्धिर्भावग्रहे ग्राह्याभावानुपलम्भतया हेतुर्न त्वभाववद्ग्राह्याभावानुपलम्भत्वेन ताद्रूप्येणान्यथासिद्धेरिति नैवम् । एवमपीन्द्रियेणेत्यादिविरोधात् तस्या एव मानत्वप्रसङ्गनवक्लृप्तत्वाच्च । उच्यते । भावानुपलम्भवदभावानुपलब्धिर्हेतुरविशेषात् ग्राह्यज्ञानविरोधितायाः ग्राह्याभावज्ञानस्य सर्व्वसिद्धत्वात् । न च करणविरोधः, करणतायामन्यथासिद्ध्यभिधानात् प्रमाणत्वापेक्षितस्यैव समाधानस्यौचित्यात् । न च यादृगनुपलब्धिर्हेतुर्भवन्मते तादृशी निमीलिताक्षस्य नास्ती-

घटकतया अभावग्राहकत्वात्। न चैवं प्रतियोग्युपलम्भकत्वेन चक्षुरपि हेतुः, एवं हि तत्तद्व्याप्येतरतदुपलम्भकसाकल्ये अनुपलब्धिर्ग्राहिका भवतीति वाच्यं। प्राप्तिं विना तस्याहेतुत्वेनाश्रयग्रहोपक्षयात्। नन्वेवमन्धस्य त्वगिन्द्रियोपनीते नीले स्मृतपीतस्यानुपलब्ध्या अभावग्रहप्रसङ्गः, प्रतियोगिग्राहकेन्द्रियग्राह्यत्वे त्वभावस्य नायन्दोषोऽन्धस्य चक्षुरभावादिति चेत्। न। अभावग्राहकत्वेनाभिमतमिन्द्रियमाश्रयग्रहोपक्षीणं,

---

त्वन्वयाद्यननुविधानात् इन्द्रियं हेतुरेव न कुतस्तेनान्यथासिद्धिरिति वाच्यम्। अभावानुपलम्भोऽपि न भावमात्रग्रहे कारणं व्यभिचारात् घटाभावग्रहेऽपि घटादिनिर्व्विकल्पकसम्भवात् समानप्रकारकत्वेन ज्ञानयोर्व्विरोधात्। किञ्च सविकल्पकमपि स्यादेव घटाभावस्य क्वचिदधिकरणे ग्रहेऽपि निरधिकरणस्य घटस्य प्रतीतेः, तथाच तदधिकरणनिष्ठभावग्रहे एव तन्निष्ठाभावानुपलम्भो हेतुर्वाच्यः, न तु सामान्यतः, तथाच सामान्यत इन्द्रियस्य प्रामाण्यकल्पनात् तद्धेतुरप्यनुपलब्धिर्न्न प्रमाणं अन्यथासिद्धत्वात् अभावधीस्तु निरधिकरणा नास्त्येव। नापि निर्व्विकल्पकेत्यभावप्रत्यचत्वावच्छिन्नं प्रत्येवानुपलब्धिः कारणं करणञ्च केनाप्यनन्यथासिद्धेरिति दिक्।

यत्तु अभावधीः सकरणिकेति कल्प्यमानं करणमिन्द्रियमेव(१)

---

(१) मानमिन्द्रियमेवेति ख०।

तथाच प्रतियोगिग्राहकेणेन्द्रियेण आश्रयग्रहे अनुपलब्ध्याऽभावग्रहणात्। अन्यथा चक्षुःसंयुक्ते परमाणौ जलत्वाभावग्रहप्रसङ्गः। अथैवं वायौ रूपाभावो जले तिक्ताभावः[१] पाषाणे सौरभाभावश्च न गृह्येत वाय्वादीनां प्रतियोगिग्राहकैश्चक्षुरादिभिरग्रहणात्[२]। न च तथापि ते अभावाः कथं प्रत्यक्षाः वाय्वादीनां तदिन्द्रियायोग्यत्वादिति वाच्यं। लिङ्गेन त्वगादिना वोपनीते

कल्प्यते क्लृप्तत्वात् नानुपलब्धिः, तथात्वेन क्वचिदप्यकल्पनात्। न च सन्निकर्षाभावान्न तथा अनुपलब्धावपि अन्वयव्यभिचारेणातथात्वात्। न च प्रतियोगिग्राहकेन्द्रियजन्याधिकरणज्ञानसहकारित्वकल्पनात्तु नेति वाच्यम्। तस्य सहकारित्वमपि कल्प्यमिति सन्निकर्षकल्पनस्यैव तदपेक्षयोचितत्वात् इति तन्न। धर्मीतिन्यायात् क्लृप्ताधिकरणज्ञानस्य ज्ञानविशेषे उक्तरूपज्ञानत्वेन जनकतौचित्यात् न तु धर्मान्तरस्य सन्निकर्षस्येत्युक्तप्रायत्वादिति।

'तामिति, करणीभूतामिति शेषः। 'प्राप्तविशेषणं' प्राप्ताश्रयकमित्यर्थः। नन्वाश्रयप्राप्तेर्ग्राहकत्वमुक्तं अतो रूपत्वादिग्रहानुरोधेन रूपप्राप्त्यर्थं संयुक्तसमवायः स्यादित्येतावन्मात्राक्षरमादाह, 'प्राप्तेति। नन्वत्रापि धर्म-धर्मिभावग्रहः संयोगविषयक इति दण्डज्ञानादेव न प्रसङ्गोऽन्यादृक्प्रत्यक्षे नोक्तं नियामकमत एव च 'प्राप्तविशेषणेत्युक्तमतो

---

(१) गुडे तिक्ताभाव इति ख०।
(२) प्रतियोगिग्राहकैरिन्द्रियैश्चक्षुरादिभिरग्रहणादिति ख०।

वाय्वादौ योग्यरूपाद्यभावविशेष्यकं प्रत्यक्षं चक्षुरादिनैव न वाय्वादिविशेष्यकं प्रत्यक्षे योग्यविशेष्यस्य हेतुत्वादिति चेत्। न। वाय्वादौ रूपाद्यभावप्रतीतीनामनुपलब्धिलिङ्गकत्वात्। तत्र नीरूपो वायुरिति वायुविशेष्याभावप्रतीतिवत्। अथ भूतले अभावधीरिन्द्रियजन्या साक्षात्कारित्वात्, तत एव विशेषणताकल्पनमपि। न च साक्षात्कारित्वमसिद्धं, परोक्षत्वे अभा-

---

दोषान्तरमाह, 'इन्द्रियस्येति, अत्राप्ययोग्यतयैव न ग्रह इत्यरुचेराह, 'इन्द्रियेति, करणव्यापारविषयतयैव कर्मत्वादिति भावः। 'किञ्चेति, रूपादावीन्द्रियग्राह्यत्वस्य सर्व्वसिद्धत्वादिह त्वन्यतरासिद्धिरिति भावः। ननु 'दृष्टान्ते हीत्युत्कर्षसमा घटादौ शरीरिकर्तृकत्वदर्शनवत्[१] अतोऽत्र व्याप्तिमाह, 'सम्बन्धस्येति। 'न हीति, तदुक्तं "न हि सुशिक्षितोऽपि नटवटुः स्वं स्कन्धमारुह्य नृत्यति"। अत्र यद्यपीन्द्रियेण समं स्वरूपसम्बन्धो नोच्यत एव किन्त्विन्द्रियसम्बद्धेन स च त्वयापि वाच्योऽन्यथाधिकरणग्रहनियामकताभिधानमपि विरुध्येत तत्सम्बन्धं विना तदधिकरणत्वाभावात्, तथापि यद्विशेषणकमभावज्ञानं तज्ज्ञानमेवाधिकरणज्ञानं द्रष्टव्यम्। तद्विशेषणत्वञ्च सम्बन्धं विनैव क्वचित् तत्र रूपसमवायवदिति तदाशयः। 'उपमान इति, यद्यप्यभावपदसङ्केतग्राहकोपमानसत्त्वात् नैतत्, तथापि सिद्धसाधनभिया मानान्तरा-

---

(१) शरीरजन्यत्वदर्शनवदिति ख०।

तकरणकत्वानुपपत्तेः। तथाहि मन्दिरोदरे चैत्रो निपुणमनुसृतोऽपि[१] न चोपलब्ध इत्याप्तवाक्यावगतानुपलब्ध्या श्रोतानुमिनोति नासीत्तत्र चैत्र इति। एवमभावधीः परोक्षा चेत्तदा नाज्ञातकरणिका परोक्षत्वजातेर्ज्ञातकरणप्रयोज्यत्वात्। ज्ञातकरणत्वञ्च ज्ञानकरणत्वं लिङ्गादेरजनकत्वात्। तस्मात् साक्षात्कारित्वमज्ञातकरणत्वात्। न चेन्द्रियजन्यत्वमुपाधिः, तत एव तत्साधनादिति चेत्। मैवं। परोक्षत्वं हि न जातिः अनुभवत्वेन सङ्करप्रसङ्गात्। किन्तु साक्षात्कारिभिन्नज्ञानत्वं, एवञ्चाभावज्ञानं परोक्षमेव स्मृतिवत्। यथा च ज्ञातकरणत्वेऽपि शाब्दादिर्नानुमितिरेवमज्ञातकरणत्वेऽपि इन्द्रियजन्यं साक्षात्कार्य्यनुपलब्धिजन्यं तद्विजातीयमनुपलब्धं। यदि चाज्ञातकरणत्वेन साक्षा-

---

प्रवृत्तिपूर्व्वकं ग्रहणमत्र विवक्षितं इत्ययं व्यभिचारो द्रष्टव्यः। 'उपमानत्वन्त्विति, तद्धि सादृश्यज्ञानत्वन्तच्च साक्षात्त्वादिना परापरभावानुपपत्त्या न जातिरित्यपव्याख्यानम्, एवं प्रत्यक्षरूपसादृश्यज्ञानवृत्तौ साक्षात्त्वे व्यभिचारतादवस्थ्यात्। न हि सा जातिर्ग्राहकतावच्छेदकत्वेन विशेषणीया येन साक्षात्त्वादिर्व्यावर्त्त्येत, तथा-

---

(१) निपुणतरतयानुसृतोऽपीति ख०।

त्कारित्वं तदा ज्ञातकरणत्वेन शाब्दादेरनुमितित्वापत्तिः। ज्ञातकरणत्वेऽपि लिङ्गादिकरणभेदादनुमित्यादिफलभेद इति चेत्, अज्ञातानुपलब्धीन्द्रियकरणभेदात् फलभेद इहापि। एवञ्च साक्षात्कारित्वे इन्द्रियजन्यत्वं परोक्षत्वे च तदजन्यत्वं प्रयोजकं, न तु ज्ञाताज्ञातकरणजन्यत्वं गौरवात् स्मृतावभावाच्च। नन्वनुपलब्धिर्न मानं भावभूतमानसहकृतस्यैव मनसो बाह्यानुभवजनकत्वादिति चेत्। न। भावत्वस्य गुरुत्वेनाप्रयोजकत्वात्। अन्यथेन्द्रियसहकृतस्यैव मनसो बाह्यानुभवजनकत्वमित्यनुमानादि न मानं स्यात्। न चेदमभावज्ञानं भावमानसहकृतमनःसाध्यं बाह्याभावज्ञानत्वाल्लिङ्गादिजन्याभावज्ञानवदिति वाच्यं। अयमभावो नेन्द्रियग्राह्योऽभावत्वादयोग्याभाववत्।

सति शब्दत्वस्य साधनवैकल्यापातात्। न हि शब्दत्व ग्राहकतावच्छेदकं, अपि तु तज्ज्ञानत्वं, तस्मात् ज्ञायमानकरणाभिप्रायेणेदमनुमानमुक्तं, तेन शब्दत्वं जातिरस्ति तथेति भवति दृष्टान्तः। न चोपमानत्वे व्यभिचारस्तस्य ज्ञायमानकरणतापक्षे सादृश्यत्वपर्य्यवसितस्य जातित्वाभावात् "सामान्यान्येव भूयांसि" इति मते सादृश्यस्य जातिरूपतया तद्वृत्तिधर्म्मे जातित्वाभावात् जातौ जातिमत्त्वाभावात्(१) इति फक्कि-

(१) जातौ जात्यन्तराभावादिति ख०।

इयमभावबुद्धिर्नेन्द्रियजन्या अभावबुद्धित्वाल्लिङ्गादिजन्याभावबुद्धिवदिति सत्प्रतिपक्षात् । अथ प्रतियोगिग्राहकं मानं तदभावमपि गृह्णाति यथानुमानादि, प्रतियोगिग्राहकञ्चेन्द्रियमतोऽभावग्राहकमिति चेत् । न । भावग्राहकयोरेव लिङ्ग-शब्दयोस्तदभावाग्राहकत्वात् । प्रतियोगिग्राहकजातीयं मानं तथेति चेत् । न । उपमाने व्यभिचारात् । न च चक्षुष्ट्वादिकं अभावग्राहकवृत्ति जातित्वात्, उपमानत्वञ्च न जातिरिति वाच्यं । प्राप्तिं विना चक्षुरादेरभावाग्राहकत्वसाधनात् । अथ भाववत्यभावभ्रमः स च करणदोषात् । न च प्रतियोगिस्मृत्याश्रयग्रहानुपलब्धयः स्वरूपतो दुष्टाः, किन्त्विन्द्रियं पित्तादिना दुष्टमिति, तदेव च भ्रमहेतुरित्यभावप्रमायामपि तदेव मानमिति चेत् । न । इन्द्रियस्यापि दुष्टत्वं दोषसाहित्यमात्रं न

कार्य्योद्रष्टव्य इति । 'अत, इति, अत्र दोषसहितभ्रमहेतुत्वादिति विशिष्यैव हेतुः कर्त्तव्यो न तु भ्रमहेतुत्वमात्रं, दोष एव व्यभिचारादित्यवधेयम् । ननु प्राप्तिरपेक्ष्यते व्यापारत्वेनान्यत्र, व्यापारस्यात्राधिकरणज्ञानमेवेति कथमन्यथाऽप्राप्ते भ्रमोऽपीत्यत आह, 'किञ्चेति कर्म्मप्राप्तिनियमात्करणस्य प्रमायामिन्द्रियेण प्राप्तिरपेक्ष्यते न तु व्यापारतया, भ्रमे तु विषयः कर्म्मैव न अकारकत्वादतोऽप्राप्ते भ्रमो-

त्वन्यत्, तच्चानुपलब्धावपि तुल्यं। न च ज्ञातकरणा-जन्यभ्रमत्वेनेन्द्रियजन्यत्वं। एवं ह्यभावप्रमाकरण-त्वमपीन्द्रियस्य तत एवास्तु किमनया कुसृष्ट्या। एव-मस्त्विति चेत्। न। प्राप्त्यभावेनोक्तोत्तरत्वात्। किञ्चा-सन्निकृष्टेऽपि दोषादुपनीतेऽभावे भ्रम इन्द्रियेण सम्भ-वति चक्षुषो पाषाणः सुरभिरिति भ्रमवत्। अभाव-प्रमा न सम्भवति प्राप्त्यभावादित्युक्तं। नन्वधिकरणा-भावयोर्व्विशिष्टबुद्धिरस्ति, सा नेन्द्रियजन्या अभा-वबुद्धित्वात्, नानुपलब्धिजन्या भावबुद्धित्वात्, नोभ-यजन्या जातिसङ्करप्रसङ्गात् अत उभयग्राहकमिन्द्रि-यमभ्युपेयमिति चेत्, अभाववद्भूतलमित्यनुपलब्ध्यु-पनीताभावविशिष्टबुद्धिरिन्द्रियेणैव चक्षुषा चन्दनं सुरभीतिवत्, भूतले घटो नास्तीति च चक्षुरुपनीत-भूतलेऽभावबुद्धिरनुपलब्ध्यैव घ्राणेन चन्दने सौरभमि-तिवत्।

जायते इत्यर्थः। 'अत इति, अनुपलम्भस्योभयग्राहकत्वासम्भवादिति भावः। 'लाघवेनेति, अस्माकन्तु तत्रानुमानस्वीकारेण कार्य्यवैजात्यात् वैजात्य एव व्यभिचारस्य कारणताविरोधित्वादिति भावः। व्यभि-चारोदाहरणान्तरमाह, 'वाय्वादाविति। 'अपसिद्धान्तादिति। ननु

यत्तु व्यापाराभावान्नानुपलब्धिः प्रमाणं व्यापारवत एव करणत्वादिति। तन्न। क्रियया ह्ययोगव्यवच्छेदेन सम्बन्धि करणं, न तु व्यापारवदित्यपि विशेषणं गौरवादिति।

अत्रोच्यते। प्रतियोगिग्राहकेन्द्रियेणाश्रयग्रहो न हेतुः प्राङ्नास्तिताग्रहे त्वन्वयेन व्यभिचारात्। वाय्वादौ च रूपाद्यभावधीरिन्द्रियजन्यैव नानुपलब्धिलिङ्गजन्या अनुपलब्धेरज्ञानात्। आप्तवाक्यस्यैव तज्ज्ञापकस्याभावात्। अथाज्ञातैव रूपाद्युपलम्भस्यानुपलब्धीरूपाद्यनुपलब्धिं गृह्णाति भुतले घटाभावमिवेति चेत्, त्वन्मते उपलम्भस्यातीन्द्रियत्वेन योग्यानुपलब्ध्या उपलम्भाभावस्य ग्रहीतुमशक्यत्वात् अनुपलब्धिमात्र-

---

नायं वस्तुदोषः किन्तु पूर्व्वापराभ्युपगमविरोधेन[१] वादिदोषः तथाच योग्योपलम्भत्वादिनामनुपलम्भो मानान्तरं स्यादेव बाधकाभावात् अतो दोषान्तरमाह, 'योग्यत्वेऽपीति, 'मानान्तरेणेति, घटाभावादिग्राहकेणेति शेषः, अन्यथोपलम्भानुपलम्भस्यैवानुपलम्भत्वस्वीकारेण विरोधापत्तेरिति। नन्वेतावतापि भवतु पटाद्यभावे ज्ञातानुपलब्धिर्ग्राहिका, न चैवमनुपलब्धेर्मानान्तरस्य निरासः, उपलम्भानुपलब्धेरभ्युपगमादित्यरुचेराह, 'अपिचेति। नन्विदमपि न सम्यक्, अन्यस्य

---

(१) पूर्व्वाभ्युपगमबाधातेनेति ख०।

स्याभावाग्राहकत्वात्। अस्तु तर्हि ज्ञानं योग्यमिति चेत्। न। अपसिद्धान्तात्। योग्यत्वेऽपि भूतलीय-घटाभावेऽपि ज्ञानैव योग्यानुपलब्धिर्लिङ्गमस्तु योग्य-घटोपलम्भस्यानुपलब्ध्या ग्रहसम्भवात् ज्ञातमनुपलब्ध्या मानान्तरेण। घटाभावधीरज्ञातकरणिका लिङ्गाद्यनु-सन्धानं(१) विना जायमानत्वादिति चेत्। न। वाय्वादौ रूपाद्यभावप्रतीतिरपि तथा। अथ रूपादिमत्तया ज्ञातत्वाभावस्तदनुमितरूपवत्तानुपलब्धिर्वा लिङ्गमिति चेत्। न। वाय्वादौ ज्ञातत्वाभावस्यापि रूपाद्यभावतुल्यतया ग्रहीतुमशक्यत्वात्। वाय्वादौ तस्य प्रत्यक्षत्वे रूपाद्यभावोऽपि तथास्तु। नापि काय-वाग्व्यवहाराभावेनानुपलब्धिरनुमीयते उपेक्षाज्ञान-मूकस्व-

---

त्वगिन्द्रियोपनीतनीले पीताभावाग्रहादेव प्रतियोगिग्राहकेन्द्रिय-जाधिकरणग्रहणस्य कारणत्वात्। न च प्रतियोगिग्राहकेन्द्रिय-विलम्बादेव तत्र विलम्ब इति, इन्द्रियविलम्बो हि ग्राह्येन्द्रिय-विलम्बः। न च ततस्तत्र तदभावः, घटाभावस्थलेऽपि तादृश-तद्विलम्बादित्यस्वरसादाह(२) 'किञ्चेति। नन्विदमपि न युक्तम्, रूपाभावो वायुवृत्तिः योग्यप्रतियोगिकत्वे सति तद्वृत्तित्वेनानुपलभ्य-

---

(१) लिङ्गाद्यनुविधानमिति क०।

(२) तादृशविलम्बादित्यरुचेराहेति ख०।

प्रयोर्दर्शनेन व्यभिचारात्। न च व्यवहाराभावमात्र लिङ्गं, कस्यचिद्व्यवहाराभावस्य व्यभिचारात् सर्व्वव्यवहाराभावस्य ग्रहीतुमशक्यत्वात्। किञ्च घटवत्तया ज्ञातत्वाभावेन तदनुमितानुपलब्ध्या वा लिङ्गेन भूतलादावभावानुमितिरस्तु किं मानान्तरेणानुपलब्ध्या। अपि च प्रतियोगिग्राह्यकेन्द्रियजन्यमधिकरणज्ञानमनुपलब्धिसहकारि तदा स्याद्यदि तेन विना सा नाभावं बोधयेत्। न चैतद्दृष्टं, वाय्वादौ रूपाद्यभावे तथा दृष्टमिति चेत्। न। असिद्धेः। न च व्याप्तिबलात्सहकारित्वं, एवं हि वाय्वादौ रूपाद्यभावप्रत्ययोऽनुपलब्धेर्भवंस्तादृशाश्रयमाक्षिपेत्। अनाक्षेपे वाऽनुपलब्धेर्न भवेत्। ततो न भवति किन्तु लिङ्गादिति चेत्, लिङ्गमपि सैव, तच्च दूषितमेव। किञ्च नानुपलब्धिर्लिङ्गं ततो हि नीरूपो वायुरित्यनुमितिः स्यात्, न तु वायौ रूपाभाव इति। अपि च घटवत्युपलम्भ-

---

मानयोग्यप्रतियोगिकत्वादित्यनुमानसम्भवात् इत्यरुचेराह, 'अपि चेति। नन्विदमप्यनुपपन्नं, यावत्तदुपलम्भकसाकल्ये सति अनुपलब्धिर्ग्राहिका उक्तस्थले यावत्तत्सत्त्वे उपलम्भप्रागभावात् अव्यवहितक्षणे घटोपलम्भस्यैव चोत्पत्त्या कथमभावधीरुत्पद्यतां। न चोभयसामग्रीसत्त्वे उभयोपल-

प्राक्कालेऽनुपलब्ध्या घटस्मृतिमतः कुतो नाभावधीः
घटाभावादिति चेत्, तर्ह्यभावरूपार्थजन्याभावबुद्धि-
रर्थजन्यत्वेन साक्षात्कारिणी इन्द्रियजन्या च स्यात्।
तदा घट एव प्रतिबन्धक इति चेत्, तथापि तद-
भावोऽभावबुद्धौ जनक एव स्यात्। स्यादेतत्।
गृहमुपलभ्य निर्गतश्चैत्रो यत्र केनचित्पृष्टस्तत्र मैत्र-
आसीदिति, स च क्षणं ध्यात्वाऽनुपलब्ध्या तत्र
मैत्राभावमवगम्याह नासीत्तत्र मैत्र इति, सेयं
प्राङ्नास्तिताधीर्न स्मृतिः पुरा गेहेऽनुभूयमाने मै-
त्रास्मरणेन तदभावाननुभवात्। एवञ्च तत्रैवेन्द्रिय-
व्यापारं विनैवानुपलब्ध्या अभावानुभवादन्यत्रापि
सैव हेतुः क्लृप्तत्वात्। तदाहुः। "स्वरूपमात्रं दृष्टं
हि वेश्माद्यर्थं स्मरन्नथ। तत्रान्येनास्तितां पृष्ट-
स्तदैव प्रतिपद्यते" इति। मैवं। प्राङ्नास्तितायां

भयोरन्यतरोत्पत्तौ विनिगमकाभावः, प्रतिबन्धकाभावस्य कार्य्यसह-
भावेन जनकतया तत्रोत्तरकाले उपलम्भस्योत्पत्त्या तादृशानुपलम्भस्या-
भावाग्राहकत्वात्। किञ्च घटवति घटाभावधीर्भ्रम इति तत्र दोषा-
भावादेवाभावप्रत्ययो न विषयाभावादिति। अत्र ब्रूमः। सत्यनु-
पलब्धिहेतुत्वे सर्व्वमिदमनुपपद्यते तदेव तु नास्ति इत्यत्र तात्पर्य्यं,

हि न तावदज्ञातानुपलब्धिर्भूतले घटाभावस्येवाऽभाव-ग्राहिका तदानीं(१) गेहस्य विप्रकृष्टत्वेन योग्यानुपलब्धेरभावात् । नापि ज्ञाता, अनवस्थाप्रसङ्गात् । अनुपलब्धेरप्यभावरूपतयाऽनुपलब्ध्यन्तरेण ग्राह्यत्वात् । उपलम्भस्यानुपलब्धिरज्ञातैव स्वरूपसती मैत्रानुपलब्धिं गृह्णाति चेत्, त्वन्नये उपलम्भस्यातीन्द्रियत्वेन तदभावस्य योग्यानुपलब्ध्यग्राह्यत्वात् । अथ गेहस्य योग्यमैत्रवत्तया स्मरणार्हस्य स्मरणाभावस्तत्राज्ञात एव गेहे मैत्राभावग्राहक इति चेत् । न । स्वरूपसतः स्मरणाभावस्य ग्राहकत्वे तस्मिन् सत्यभावसंशय-विपर्य्ययाभावप्रसङ्गात् । भवति च कदाचित् तत्रासीदिति विपर्य्ययस्तत्रासीन्न वेति संशयश्च । अथ दोषात्संशय-

घटस्थलेऽभावानुपलम्भस्य विषयाभावेनैवोपपत्तेः । विषयकारणत्वस्य क्लृप्तत्वात् अनुपलम्भकारणस्य कल्पनीयत्वात् । न च घटाभावे सति घटोपलम्भवतो घटाभावानुपलम्भेन तद्धेतुत्वनिश्चयः, तत्र घटोपलम्भकदोषस्यैव प्रतिबन्धकत्वात् । तस्माद्विषयाभावेनैवान्यथासिद्धिसम्भवात् । अनुपलब्ध्यभावात् क्वचित् कार्य्याभावादर्शनेन न साभावधीहेतुः

(१) इदानीमिति ख० ।

विपर्य्ययौ। न चासाधारणं प्रमाकरणं दूषयन्त एव दोषाः संशयादिहेतवो भवन्ति। न चाच स्वरससिद्धस्य योग्यास्मरणस्य किञ्चिद्दूषितमिति वाच्यं। दोषसाहित्यमेव हि करणानां दुष्टता। न हि दूरत्वादिना चक्षुषः किञ्चिदपक्रियते, किन्तु मण्यादेर्दाह इव स्वरूपसतामेव प्रतिबन्धकत्वमिति चेत्। न। अज्ञाताद्योग्यास्मरणात् तथाभावधीरित्यसिद्धेः। किन्तु मनसा ज्ञाताद्योग्यास्मरणाल्लिङ्गात् प्रमाणत्वेन क्लृप्तात्तत्राभावप्रतीत्युपपत्तौ नानुपलब्धिः प्रमाणान्तरं कल्प्यते। योग्यस्मरणाभावो न मनोग्राह्यः प्रत्यासत्त्यभावात् ज्ञानस्यायोग्यत्वाद्वेति[१] चेत्। न। वाय्वादौ रूपाद्यभावप्रतीतेरलैङ्गिकत्वेनेन्द्रियानुविधानेन तज्ज-

कुतः करणमिति सर्व्वत्र तात्पर्य्यम्। न च ग्रन्थेऽन्वय-व्यभिचारदर्शनादिदमसङ्गतम्, तद्व्यतिरेकेण फलव्यतिरेकस्य बीजत्वादिति। 'वाय्वादाविति, घटाभावस्थले तेनानुपलब्धेर्मानान्तरत्वाभ्युपगमादुदाहृतं। 'इन्द्रियेति, इन्द्रियसम्बद्धविशेषणताचेन्द्रियसंयुक्तात्मसमवेतविशेषणविशेषणता द्रष्टव्या, गेहे मनःसंयुक्तात्मसमवेतज्ञानविषयीभूते मैत्रत्वप्रकारकस्मरणविषयत्वाभावस्य विशेषणतासम्भवादिति। 'तत्तुल्य-

(२) ज्ञानस्यायोग्यत्वाच्चेति ख०।

न्यत्वे सिद्धे इन्द्रियसम्बद्धविशेषणतायाः प्रत्यासत्तित्वकल्पनात् । तज्ज्ञानं प्रत्यक्षं जानामीत्यनुभवस्य लिङ्गाद्यजन्यत्वात् । न च ज्ञातता लिङ्गं, निराकृतत्वात् । तवापि कथमभावे संशय-विपर्य्ययाविति चेत् । न । लिङ्गसंशय-विपर्य्ययाभ्यां लैङ्गिकसंशय-विपर्य्ययदर्शनात् । यदा तु सुनिपुणेनैकज्ञानविषयतायोग्यस्य मैत्रस्यानुभवे सति स्मरणार्हस्यास्मरणमवधार्य्यते तदानुमितिः प्रमा । अत एवास्मरणमात्रस्य व्यभिचारमुपलभ्य तदुपेक्ष्य विशिष्टास्मरणं ज्ञातुकामस्य प्रणिधानमुपयुज्यते । अन्यथा ध्यानमनुपपन्नं स्वरूपसत एवास्मरणस्याभावग्राहकत्वात् । तस्माद्योग्यास्मरणं लिङ्गत्वेनैवोपयुज्यते । प्रयोगस्तु तत्रेदं तदा मैत्राभाववत् तत्तुल्यपरि-

---

परिमाणेति, मया मैत्रवत्त्वेनास्मर्य्यमाणत्वादिति विशिष्यैव हेतुर्द्रष्टव्यः, तेन तत्तुल्यपरिमाणवत्तया अस्मर्य्यमाणे नायं हेतुरस्तीति तत्र हेत्वभावादस्मरणं न पृथक् प्रमाणं प्रसज्येत । मयेति च विशेषणाद्यस्य मैत्रे न तादृशप्रत्ययः तत्र संस्कारानुत्पाद-विलोपादिसम्भवादस्मरणस्य सम्भवेन व्यभिचारोऽपि न भवति, यस्य यत्रानुभवे सति स्मरणनियमस्तद्वत्तया अस्मर्य्यमाणत्वस्य अव्यभिचारात् स तु कोऽपि कस्यापि तादृशो भवतीति मयेत्युक्तं विशेषणमिति, तत्सूचनायैव 'तत्तुल्यपरिमाणेत्यादिविशेषणमिति ।

माणादियोगितया स्मरणेऽपि तद्वत्तया अस्मर्य्यमाण-
त्वात् यदेवं तदेवं यथा घटाभाववद्भूतलमिति ।

इतिश्रीमद्गङ्गेशोपाध्यायविरचिते तत्त्वचिन्तामणौ
प्रत्यक्षखण्डे अनुपलब्ध्यप्रामाण्यवादः ।

इति श्रीजयदेवमिश्रविरचिते तत्त्वचिन्तामण्यालोके प्रत्यक्ष-
खण्डालोके अनुपलब्ध्यप्रामाण्यवादालोकः ।

अथाभाववादः ।

नन्वभावो भावात्मैव ततस्तत्र संयोगादिरेव ग्राहक इति न तत्र विशेषणता प्रत्यासत्तिः । तत्र प्राह्वः । अस्ति तावदिह भूतले घटो नास्तीत्यबाधिता बुद्धिः सा चेयं न भूतलालम्बना घटवत्यपि प्रसङ्गात् । नापि केवलतदालम्बना अतिरिक्तकैवल्यानभ्युपगमात् । भूतलमेव कैवल्यमिति चेत्, तर्हि पौनरुक्त्यमधिकं, अभेदे आधाराधेयभावानुपपत्तिश्च । अथाधिकाभाववादिनापि अभावः साश्रयो वाच्यः देशादिनियमेन व्यवहारात् । तथाचास्ति भूतले विशेषो योऽभावाश्रयः स न भूतल-

---

अथाभाववादालोकः ।

'विशेषणतेति, समवायस्यातीन्द्रिय एवेति भावः । 'अधिकमिति, अत्र घटवत्यप्यतिप्रसङ्गस्तदवस्थ एवेति भावः । नन्वग्नीषोमावपि न प्रत्येकभिन्नौ मेलकस्यातिरिक्तस्यानभ्युपगमादित्यन्यतरासम्बन्धितयैव तन्मात्रपदार्थनिर्व्वचनम् तथाचाभावाभ्युपगम इति दोषमग्रे वक्ष्यमाणत्वेनोपेक्ष्यान्यदाह, 'ततो भूतलेति । ननु प्रतियोग्यविषयाधिकरणबुद्धिरेव तन्मात्रबुद्धिः । न चाभावा-

मात्रं घटवत्यपि प्रसङ्गात्। नाभावयुक्तमन्योन्याश्रयात्। न च घटवत्, विरोधादिति चेत्। न। विशेषस्यैव[१] अभावाश्रयत्वात् स चाननुगत एव। एकाश्रयता त्वननुगतस्यापि घटाश्रयतेव भवति। किञ्च कुत्राभाव इति, यत्र प्रतीयेत इत्येवोत्तरं, क्व प्रतीयेत इत्यत्र यत्रास्तीत्येव। अन्यथा गोत्वादिकमपि न स्वीक्रियेत तदाश्रयविशेषादेव व्यवहारसम्भवात्। तथापि कीदृशि भूतले अभाव इति चेत्, अभावपूर्व्वसमये कीदृशं भूतलमिति प्रश्ने घटवदित्युत्तरं, अभावसमयेऽभाववदिति, मध्यसमयस्तु नास्त्येव, इह भूतले घटोनास्तीत्याधाराधेयभावप्रतीतेश्च। अभावाधारत्वं भूतलस्य न प्रतीयते किन्तु तन्मात्रबुद्धिविषयत्वमिति चेत्, अहो व्याख्याकौशलमनुभवोऽपि व्याख्याय कथ्यते तन्मात्र-

---

भ्युपगमदोषः, तत्रापीत्थमेव तन्मात्रबुद्धिः रूपाभावस्वीकारात् एवं तत्रापीति धारायामविश्रान्तिः प्रमाणिकत्वेवेत्यरुचेराह, 'कित्वेति, 'व्यवहारस्येति। न चोत्कर्षरूपाया जातेः व्यक्तिवित्तिवेद्यायास्तारशब्दाभिलापात्मनि व्यवहारे व्यवहर्त्तव्याधिकस्यावधेर्ज्ञानं हेतुर्द्रष्टव्य इति वाच्यम्। तत्रापि सजातीयसाक्षात्कारप्रतिबन्धकशब्दत्वेनानुगतीकृततारत्वरूपप्रवृत्तिनिमित्तज्ञानस्य हेतुत्वात् तस्य चाव-

---

(१) भूतलविशेषस्यैवेति ख०।

पदार्थानिर्वचनञ्च । न हि भूतलबुद्धिस्तन्मात्रबुद्धिः, घटवद्भूतलबुद्धेरपि भूतलबुद्धित्वात्। सा बुद्धिर्न भूतलस्य किन्तु घट-भूतलयोरग्नीषोमयोरिव देवतात्वमिति चेत्। न। ततो भूतलाव्यवहारप्रसङ्गात् भूतलस्याविषयत्वात् । आशुभाविभूतलविषयकज्ञानान्तरादिति चेत् तर्हि सैव भूतलबुद्धिस्तन्मात्रबुद्धिरिति तद्देशे घटाभावस्य व्यवहारप्रसङ्गः। एतेन भूतलेन्द्रियसन्निकर्षज-घटवद्भूतलेन्द्रियसन्निकर्षजज्ञानयोर्विशेषोऽङ्गीकरणीयः सामग्रीभेदस्य कार्यभेदनियतत्वात्। तथाच स एव तन्मात्रपदार्थ इति निरस्तं। ततोऽपि भूतलव्यवहारात् । प्रतियोगि-तद्व्याप्येतरजनिता भूतलबुद्धिरभाव इति चेत्। न। घटवति तज्जनितायाः अपीतरजनितत्वात्। तन्मात्रजनिता सेति चेत्। न। मात्रार्थस्याभावत्वात् तस्य चापरिज्ञानात्। घटाविषया सती भूतलविषयेति चेत् । न । उक्तोत्तरत्वात्। किञ्च प्रतियोगिनिरूपणाधीननिरूपणोऽभावो बुद्धि-

---

धिगर्भतयाऽवधेरपि व्यवहर्त्तव्यत्वादिति शब्दानित्यतायां वाच्यत्वादिति भावः। 'तथाचेति, नन्वन्धकारे कण्टकाभावो मास्तु कण्टकाभावाभावोऽस्तीत्यपि न, तस्यापि बुद्धिरूपत्वात् भावे वा वेधः कुतस्तस्य कण्टकबाध्यत्वात् तस्य च कण्टकाभावाभावादन्यत्वात्, निर्जने इत्या-

स्तु न तथा प्रतियोगिप्रकाशं विनापि बुद्धिनिरूपणात्। व्यवहारार्थं दृश्यप्रतियोगिज्ञानापेक्षा अभावो ज्ञात एवेति चेत्। न। व्यवहारस्य व्यवहर्त्तव्योपलम्भनिबन्धनत्वेन तथा अदृष्टचरत्वात्। यदि च प्रतियोगिस्मरणसापेक्षा तन्मात्रधीरभावपदार्थः तदान्धकारादौ या तन्मात्रधीः सा अभावो न स्यात्। तथा च तत्र विचरन् कण्टकैर्विध्येत कण्टकस्मरणं विना कण्टकाभावाभावात्। निर्जने बन्धविच्छेदेऽपि जलनिःसरणं न स्यात् तदानीं तन्मात्रबुद्धेः सर्वथाऽभावात्। किञ्च तन्मात्रधीनाशे घटोन्मज्जनप्रसङ्गः घटाभावाभावस्य घटत्वात्। यदि चाभावो नातिरिक्तस्तदा यत्र घटसंसृष्टत्वबुद्धिरासीत् कुतस्तत्र तन्मात्रधीः मुद्गरपातजन्यातिरिक्तविषयानङ्गीकारात्। अतिरिक्ताभावे किं मानमिति चेत्, नास्तीति बुद्धिरेव। नन्वभावव्यवहारानुपपत्तिरन्योन्याश्रयादिति। अत्र प्राभाकराः। घटवद्भूतलबुद्धिभिन्ना भूतलबुद्धिरभावव्यव-

---

स्यापि सावद्यं, तथाहि प्रतिबन्धकाभावस्य हेतुभावोऽन्वय-व्यतिरेकगम्यः, स च प्रतिबन्धकाभावे कार्य्यम् तदभावे नेत्यात्मको न तु प्रतिबन्धके न कार्य्यमित्याद्यात्मकः, प्रतिबन्धकाभावाभावो न प्रतिबन्धकः किन्त्वन्य इति भ्राम्यतः पूर्व्वपक्षिणो मते तादृशव्यतिरेकग्रहस्य

हारकारणं। न च दोषात् घटवति घटवत्त्वाज्ञाने भूतलज्ञानमभावः स्यादिति वाच्यं। घटवतो भूतलस्य ज्ञानाद्भिन्नस्य भूतलज्ञानस्याभावत्वात् तद्भ्रमाद्वा-भावभ्रमः। वस्तुतोऽत्यन्ताभावे प्रतियोगिमदधिकरण-ज्ञानस्याप्रसिद्धेः प्रतियोगिमज्ज्ञानभिन्नमधिकरण-ज्ञानं व्यधिकरणाभावव्यवहारे कारणं, समानाधि-करणनिषेधप्रतीतिश्च प्रतियोग्यधिकरणयोः स्वरूपभेद-

---

प्रतिबन्धकाभावहेतुत्वग्रहानुपयोगित्वात् तथाच बन्धाभावाभावे जल-निःसरणाभावोभवतीह तु तन्मात्रबुद्धिरूपतया बन्धाभावाभावोना-स्तीति कथं जलनिःसरणाभावः। न चैवं बन्धाभावो बन्धाभावाभावो वा द्वयमपि नास्तीति विरुद्धं[१] बुद्ध्यात्मनोर्द्वयोरपि अभावे तदभावा-दित्यपरितुष्यन्नाह, 'किञ्चेति। 'नास्तीति, तत्र विषयान्तरासम्भवा-दिति भावः। 'न त्विति, इदं तु स्वम्प्रति द्रष्टव्यम्, स्वस्मिन्नेवाभा-वज्ञाने तद्व्यवहारस्तदनुपपत्त्या तद्धीरित्यात्माश्रयात्[२] परम्प्रति तु सा प्रमाणमेवेति भावः। ननु तद्भ्रमादित्याद्यसङ्गतम्, प्रतियोगि-ज्ञानादेरभावव्यवहारार्थमेवापेक्षणादिति सिद्धान्तात्, आकाशादेरत्य-न्तेरभावस्य केवलान्वयिनः स्वीकारपक्षे प्रतियोगिमदधिकरणस्या-

---

(१) विप्रतिषिद्धमिति ख०।

(२) तत्रैवाभावज्ञाने तद्व्यवहारः तदनुपपत्त्या तद्धीरित्यन्योन्याश्रयसम्भ-वादिति ख०।

मालम्बते। तेन घटवत्त्वेन ज्ञायमानेऽपि भूतले भूतलं घटो नेति प्रतीतिः। तथाच यस्याभावज्ञानकारणत्वं परेषान्तदेवाभावव्यवहृतिकारणमस्तु। न ह्यधिकरणबुद्धिं विना तद्बुद्धिः। न च भूतलबुद्धिस्तथा, घटवत्यपि प्रसङ्गात्। न चाभावाधिकरणभूतलविषयत्वाद्बुद्धेर्विशेषः, प्रतियोगिसत्त्वेऽपि प्राङ्नासीदिदमत्रेति प्रतीतेः। किञ्च ज्ञानविषयभूतलस्याभावो यदि विशेषणं तदा अभावज्ञानमेव तज्ज्ञानकारणं, उपलक्षणं चेत्, न कश्चिद्विशेषः। प्रतियोगिमत्तयानुपलब्धिरपि कारणमिति चेत्। न। प्रतियोगिमत्तयोपलम्भेऽपि प्राङ्नासीदिदमत्रेति प्रतीतेः, बुद्धोश्च विशेषः(१) स्वरूपविशे-

---

प्रसिद्धिरित्यस्वरसादाह, 'वस्तुत इति, 'अत्यन्ताभावे' आकाशादिप्रतियोगिके, 'प्रतियोगिमदिति। न च घटवति घटाज्ञानदशायामभावापत्तिरभावो नाम शून्यो नास्त्येवेति, अभावव्यवहारापादनन्तु नानिष्टम् प्रतियोगिस्मृतौ यावत्तदुपलम्भकसत्त्वेऽधिकरणज्ञाने चाभावव्यवहारात्। न चोत्तरकाले बाधावतारेऽपि तदापत्तिः, प्रतियोगिसत्त्वज्ञानस्य बाधकत्वेनाभावव्यवहारस्य तदानीमभावात्। न च बाधानवतारकालीनाभावव्यवहारस्यापि संवादापत्तिः, बाधितत्वेनासंवादादिति भावः। 'समानेति प्रतियोगिसमानाधिकरणेत्यर्थः। न

---

(१) भेद इति क०।

षावेव नान्योन्याभावोऽनवस्थानादात्माश्रयाद्वा। भूतलज्ञानापेक्षया घटवद्भूतलज्ञानत्वमेव वा वैधर्म्यभेदः। न चातिरिक्ताभावपक्षेऽप्यन्योन्याभावेऽत्यन्ताभावे च नित्ये मानमस्ति, प्रतियोगिनि बुद्धिस्थेऽधिकरणस्वरूपस्यैवानतिप्रसञ्जकत्वात्। न हि तत्राधिकरणस्य प्रतियोगितादात्म्यं प्रतियोगिमत्त्वं वा सम्भवति। अतएवाभावे ऽभावान्तरं त्वया न स्वीक्रियते[१] अधिकरणस्य तद्वैरूप्याभावात्। नन्वर्थेनैव विशेषो बुद्धेः, न चा-

---

चैवमननुगम इत्याह, तथाचेति। ननु यत्कालीनोऽभावो बुध्यते तदातनाभावाधिकरणत्वं बुद्धेर्विशेष उच्यत इत्यरुचेराह, 'किञ्चेति। नन्वभावोऽधिकरणे विशेषणमेव तद्बुद्धौ तूपलक्षणम्, प्रतियोगिसत्त्वानुपलम्भोऽपि ग्राह्याभावकालीनप्रतियोगिसत्त्वानुपलम्भ इत्येतन्नियामकमभावपक्षे घटते केवलाधिकरणाभावपक्षेऽधिकरणस्यैकरूपत्वात्कथं तत्रैव कदाचिद्घटवदिति कदाचिद्घटाभाववदिति व्यवहारवैचित्र्यमित्यत आह, 'न चेति एवमधिकरणद्वैरूप्यात्प्रागभावध्वंसातिरेकेऽपि अन्योन्याभावादेरतिरिक्तत्वे मानं नास्तीत्यर्थः। एवं तदुभयोराधारात्मकत्वे[२] प्रागभावादेरपि तथात्वमनुमेयमिति भावः। 'अतएव' अनतिप्रसङ्गादेव, 'धारेति, एतच्च प्रतियोगिमद्भिन्नत्वानव-

---

(१) अभावे नाभावान्तरं स्वीकुरुते इति ख०।

(२) तदुभयोरनतिरिक्तत्वे इति ख०।

चार्थभेदोऽस्ति। मैवं। न हि तावदर्थो ज्ञानकारणमवश्यं, किन्तु सामग्रीविशेषाद्बुद्धिविशेषो जायते धारावाहिकबुद्धिवत्। यद्वा घटवद्भूतलभिन्नं भूतलमभावः यच्च परेषामभावः भेदश्च स्वरूपमेव। तादात्म्येनाप्रतीतौ प्रतीतिरिति तवापि स्वरूपभेदलक्षणं इदानीमिदं भूतलं घटवद्भूतलं न भवतीति प्रतीतेः। एतावांस्तु विशेषो यत् तव समानाधिकरणनिषेधप्रतीतिरियमन्योन्याभावभेदमवगाहते, मम तु स्वरूपं[१]। ननु यदेव भूतलं घटवद्भूतलाभिन्नमासीत्तदेव कथन्तद्-

---

गाहित्वे बुद्धेर्द्रष्टव्यम्, तद्भिन्नत्वप्रकारकबुद्ध्यभ्युपगमे चार्थभेद एवेत्यनुपदमेव स्फुटमिति। ननु प्रतियोगिमदधिकरणबुद्धिभिन्नमित्यत्र प्रतियोगिमत्त्वं यद्यधिकरणविशेषणं न किन्तु धीविशेषणं[२] तदा घटवत्यपि घटाभावापत्तिः, अथाधिकरणविशेषणम् तर्हि तावदेवास्तु कृतं बुद्ध्यन्तर्भावेण। न चाधाराधेयभावानुपपत्तिः, घटाभावे घटात्यन्ताभाववदुपपत्तेरिति पूर्व्वाक्षरसादाशङ्किते सम्प्रतिपत्तिमाह, 'यदेति। न चाकाशाभावादौ प्रतियोगिमदधिकरणप्रसिद्धिः, तदनभ्युपगमात्, अभ्युपगमे वा प्रतियोगिप्रतियोगिकभिन्नोऽधिकरणनिष्ठसम्बन्ध उक्तस्यार्थो द्रष्टव्यः। अस्ति चाकाशादिप्रतियोगिकभिन्नः

---

(१) स्वरूपभेदमिति ख०।

(२) यद्यधिकरणबुद्धिविशेषणमिति ख०।

भिन्नमिति चेत्। न। तवाप्यबाधितसमानाधिकरण-निषेधप्रतीतिबलेनान्योन्याभावसिद्धौ तथात्वस्य दुर्वारत्वात्। समयभेदेनैव भेदाभेदौ न विरुध्येते इति तु समं। यदि च घटवद्भूतलाभिन्नं तदिदानीं स्यात् तदा घटवद्भूतलव्यवहारस्तच्च स्यात् घट-तदभावावच्छेदभेदेनान्योन्याभाव-तदभावौ भूतले वर्त्तेते इति चेत्, ममापि भूतलबुद्धिर्घटवद्भूतलबुद्ध्यवच्छेदेन स्वरूपभेद-तदभावौ[१] वर्त्तेते इति गृहाण। ननु भूतले घटोऽस्ति न वेति संशयो घटो नास्तीति विपर्य्ययो वा कथम्भवेत् प्रतियोगिनि बुद्धिस्थेऽधिकरणस्य तज्ज्ञानस्य चाभावस्योपलम्भादिति चेत्। न। भूतले तज्ज्ञाने वा घटवद्भिन्नत्वस्य घटवद्भूतलज्ञानभिन्नत्वस्य

सर्व्वनिष्ठः सम्बन्धः, न तु घटप्रतियोगिकभिन्नो घटवति सम्बन्धः, तस्य घटप्रतियोगिकत्वात् आधाराधेयत्वप्रतितीरप्यत एवोत्पद्यते, तादृशसम्बन्धस्य भूतलादिवृत्तित्वादिति भावः। 'भेदश्चेति कश्चित्स्वरूपभेदः कुतोऽपि भेद इत्यर्थः। स्वरूपस्यैव भेदत्वे संवादमाह, 'तादात्म्येनेति तदात्मत्वेनाप्रतीयमानत्वे सति प्रतीयमानत्वस्यैव तद्भेदरूपत्वादित्यर्थः। 'तवापीत्युक्त्या स्वमतेऽप्रतीयमानत्वेन प्रतीयमानत्वाभावेन भेदलक्षणं भेदेन वा प्रतीयमानत्वनिर्व्वचनम्। भिन्नाधिकरणस्यैव तन्मतेऽभावत्वेने-

---

(१) स्वरूप एव भेदाभेदौ इति ख०।

च दोषवशेनानिश्चयात्। भूतल-तज्ज्ञानस्वरूपाणामननुगमात् कथमनुगतव्यवहार इति चेत्। न। अभावेऽपि तुल्यत्वात्। न ह्यभावत्वं सामान्यं, अभावत्वगतान्योन्याभावाव्यापकत्वात्। न च भावविरोधित्वं, विरोधस्याभावनिरूप्यत्वात् भावाभावयोः सहावस्थानाभावस्य स्वरूपानतिरेकाच्च। नापि भावप्रतियोगित्वं प्रतियोगित्वस्याभावविरहरूपत्वात् अभावाभावस्य भावाप्रतियोगिकत्वाच्च[१]। नापि सप्रतियोगिकत्वं, समवाय-सादृश्यादीनामपि तथात्वात्। नापि परकीयस्वभावत्वं, ज्ञानादिगतत्वात् स्वभावशब्दस्य

त्यन्योन्याश्रयान्नेदं लक्षणमिति सूचितम्। तन्मतेऽभावस्यातिरिक्तत्वेन न तस्य भेदलक्षणत्वविरोध इति भावः। तादात्म्येनाप्रतीयमानत्वं रजतत्वभ्रमविषयशुक्तावपीति तस्यामपि शुक्तिभेदापत्त्या भगवज्ज्ञानमादाय तादात्म्येनाप्रतीयमानत्वस्यासिद्धिर्व्वाच्या। न च तन्मते भगवान्नास्तीति, तवापीत्युक्तं इत्यन्ये।

ऋजवस्तु न ममैवेदं लक्षणं किन्तु तवापीति यथाश्रुतमेवार्थमाहुः। 'भूतलबुद्धी'त्युपलक्षणं समयभेदोऽपि द्रष्टव्यः। 'भूतल इति, ननु वस्तुतो घटवतो भूतलाद्भिन्नस्याधिकरणस्याभावतया तन्मात्रगोचरैव धीरभावधीः, घटादिप्रतियोगिनापेक्षा चाभावशब्दाभिलापादौ

---

(१) अभावप्रतियोगिकत्वाच्चेति ख०।

स्वरूपार्थेऽननुगमाच्च । नापि सत्ताशून्यत्वं, सत्तायामेव गतत्वात् शून्यत्वस्याभावरूपत्वाच्च । सत्तात्यन्ताभाववत्त्वमभावत्वं अत्यन्ताभावस्याभावत्वानवगतावप्यवगतइति चेत् । न । अभावे अभावानभ्युपगमात् तथात्वेऽपि तत्रैव तदभ्युपगमात् । सत्ताबोधविधुरत्वमभावत्वं, सामान्यादौ सत्तावगमेऽपि बाधात् सा त्यज्यते अभावस्य तद्विरुद्धतयैव प्रतीतेरिति चेत् । न । विरोधित्वस्य स्वरूपानतिरेकात् । सहानवस्थाननियमो विरोध इति चेत् । न । अनवस्थानस्यावस्थानाभावत्वेनात्माश्रयात् । भावभिन्नत्वमिति चेत् । न । भेदस्य

व्यवहारे इति यदि पक्षस्तदा कथं उक्तक्रमेण संशयसमर्थनमिति । मैवम् । तदाप्यभावसंशयस्योक्तरीत्यैव निर्व्वाहात् घटवत्त्वकोटेस्सन्निधत्वकोटिविरोधित्वेनाधिकरणरूपघटाभावनिश्चयस्य घटवत्त्वनिश्चयतत्संशयादावकिञ्चित्करत्वात् इति । इयांस्तु विशेषो यदेकत्र प्रतियोगिसन्निधत्वमभावत्वं तत्कोटिकः संशयोऽपरत्राधिकरणत्वमभावत्वं तत्र संशय एव न किन्तूक्तसंशयोऽभावसंशयत्वेनाभिलप्यते इति संशयस्योक्तविषयत्वमुभयकल्पेऽपीति । 'अभावेऽपीति अतिरिक्ताभावेऽप्यनुगमाभावस्य तुल्यत्वात् इत्यर्थः । तथाच व्यवहारोऽप्यननुगत एव व्यवहर्त्तव्याननुगमेनैव व्यवहारानुगमात्, तथाचाननुगते किमनुगतेन निमित्तेनेति भावः । 'तुल्यत्वादित्यस्य तवाप्यननुगतेनैवानु-

स्वरूपान्योन्याभावरूपत्वे उक्तदोषात् वैधर्म्यस्य चिन्त्यमानत्वात् प्रागभावत्वादेरभावनिरूप्यत्वात्। एवञ्चेदभावेऽपि नानुगमस्तदा किमधिकेन। स्वरूपविशेषादेव घटव्यवहारोऽप्यस्त्विति चेत्। न। भूतलविलक्षणघटानुभवात्। एक एवाभावोऽनुगत इति चेत्। न। तस्य नित्यत्वेन प्रतियोगिकालेऽप्यभावव्यवहारप्रसङ्गात् प्रागभावादिव्युत्पादनविरोधाच्च। यद्वा अभाववादिनाप्यभावज्ञानकारणमनुगतो भूत-

---

गतव्यवहार इत्यपव्याख्यानम् असम्भवादपसिद्धान्ताच्चेति। न ह्यभावत्वं सामान्यमिति, सामान्योक्त्यानुगतं पदार्थान्तरमभावत्वमित्यपि च प्रत्युक्तं वेदितव्यम्। 'अभावाभावेति, न च तत्साधारणाभावत्वानिर्व्वचनम्। तथामति तत्राभावव्यवहारस्यान्यनिबन्धनत्वेनाननुगतादेव व्यवहार इत्यागतमिति भावः। सप्रतियोगिकत्वं तन्निरूपणाधीननिरूपणत्वं, परकीयत्वं परवित्तिवेद्यत्वमिति भेदः। आशङ्कितस्यैव सत्ताशून्यत्वस्यार्थं विविच्य परीहारमुद्धरति, 'सत्तेति, 'अभाव इति, द्रव्यत्वाज्ञाने घटव्यक्तिवदभावत्वेनानवगततया सत्तात्यन्ताभावव्यक्त्यनुगमस्तदा स्याद्यद्यभावेषु सैका व्यक्तिर्भवेत्, न त्वेवम्। अभावेऽभावाभावात् किन्तु तत्तद्व्यक्तिस्वरूपं, तच्च चानुगतधर्म्मान्तराभावेऽननुगमः। अभावत्वेन चानुगमे 'आत्माश्रय एवेति भावः। 'तथात्वेऽपि' अभावेऽप्यत्यन्ताभावाभ्युपगमेऽपि(१)। 'तच्चैवेति, आत्माश्रयादिति

---

(१) अभावत्वस्याभावान्तराभ्युपगमेऽपीति ख०।

त्वबुद्धिविशेषः स्वीकार्य्यः तद्वरं स एवास्तु प्रमेयं प्रमाणञ्च स्वप्रकाशत्वाद्बुद्धीनां । ननु तन्मात्रबुद्धेरभावत्वे तस्याः स्वप्रकाशत्वेन प्रतियोगिज्ञानापेक्षा न स्यादिति चेत् । न । न ग्रहणाय तदपेक्षा किन्तु व्यवहाराय । ज्ञानस्य सत्यामिच्छायां व्यवहारार्थमधिकापेक्षेति चेत् । न । दृष्टा हि व्यवहारार्थमधिकापेक्षा यथा परिमाणस्य दीर्घत्वव्यवहारे । तथाह्यधिकसङ्ख्यावच्छिन्नहस्तवितस्त्याद्यवच्छेदः परिमाणस्य दीर्घत्वं तद्विपरीतन्तु ह्रस्वत्वं तादृशपरिमाणञ्चावयवि-

---

भावः । इदञ्चापाततः, परमार्थतस्तु तथानुगतस्य ज्ञातस्यानुगमकत्वं वाच्यं तज्ज्ञानं न प्रतियोगिज्ञाननिरपेक्षं, न वा निर्व्विकल्पकरूपमिति तदभावत्वेन ज्ञातमनुगमयेत् तथाचात्माश्रयः । किञ्च सत्तापदं सत्तादिवारणाय द्रव्यत्वादिषट्कपरं भावत्वपरं वोभयथापि सामान्यत्वादेर्भावत्वस्य च ज्ञानेऽभावत्वस्य ज्ञानादात्माश्रय इति द्रष्टव्यम् । ननु सत्ताबोधविरहः कदाचित्सत्तावत्यपीति तद्विरोधितावच्छेदकत्वमस्यार्थः । तदुक्तमभावस्येत्यादि तथासत्याह, 'विरोधित्वस्येति । ननु , अनुगतघटाभावव्यवहारोऽनुगतेन घटात्यन्ताभावेनेति कथमननुगतसाम्यमुभयोरित्यस्वरसादाह, 'यद्वेति अतिरिक्ताभाववादिनापि तत्तदभावज्ञाने स्वाधिकरणज्ञानत्वेनानुगतो बुद्धिविशेषोऽङ्गीकर्त्तव्यः, तद्वरं तत्तदधिकरणज्ञानत्वेन तत्तदभावव्यवहारजनकत्वमस्तु इत्यर्थः ।

ग्रहणसमकालमेवानुभूतं दीर्घत्वव्यपदेशस्त्वल्पसङ्ख्याद्यवच्छिन्नहस्ताद्यवच्छेद्यपरिमाणज्ञानमपेक्षते, तन्मात्रबुद्धेरभावत्वे दृश्यप्रतियोगिज्ञानापेक्षतया दृश्यतासम्पत्त्यर्थं केश-कीटादिसूक्ष्मजिज्ञासाऽप्यर्थवती। न च तन्मात्रबुद्धेरभावत्वे तद्विनाशे अभावाभावे भावोन्मज्जनप्रसङ्ग इति वाच्यं। यथा घटाभावो बुद्धिस्तथा बुद्ध्यभावस्यापि बुद्ध्यन्तरत्वात्। निर्जने बन्धविच्छेदे च जलनिःसरणं नानुपपन्नं मनुष्याभावेऽपि पक्षि-कीटादिबुद्धिविशेषसम्भवात्। मोक्षे पुरुषान्तरस्य नियमे प्रमाणं नास्तीति चेत्। न। कार्य्यात् कारणकल्पनात्।

'म ग्रहणायेति, एतच्च स्वरूपज्ञातबुद्धिविशेषस्यैवाभावव्यवहारकत्वमिति मते, यदा तु प्रतियोगिमदधिकरणज्ञानभिन्नत्वेन ज्ञातं ज्ञानं व्यवहारकं तदा ग्रहणायैव प्रतियोगिज्ञानापेक्षेति द्रष्टव्यम्। 'हस्तवितस्त्याद्यवच्छेद इति, यद्यप्येतत्परिमाणस्य दीर्घत्वं धर्मस्तथाच तद्ग्रहे एवावधिज्ञानापेक्षा न तु दीर्घत्वव्यवहारमात्रे, तथापि तदवच्छेदोऽपि परिमाणस्वरूपमात्रमिति दीर्घत्वव्यवहार एवावधिज्ञानापेक्षा परिमाणस्वरूपस्य ज्ञातत्वादिति भावः[१]। ननु तन्मात्रबुद्धेरभावत्वे तण्डुलादौ केशादिजिज्ञासाऽनुपपन्ना तण्डुलरूपाधिकरणबुद्धिरूपस्य केशाद्यभावस्य निश्चयादित्यत आह, 'तन्मात्रेति,

---

(१) ज्ञातत्वादित्याशय इति ख०।

न चैवं बुद्धिनाशे पुनः संसारिता, बुद्धिधारासत्त्वात् । न च सर्वमुक्तिः, प्रमाणाभावात् । प्रतियोगिमदधिकरणभिन्नाधिकरणस्वरूपस्याभावत्वे सर्वं समञ्जसमेवेति पूर्वपक्षः ।

सिद्धान्तस्तु सप्रतियोगिकोऽभावोऽनुभूयते घटो न पटो नेत्यनुभवात्, न तु तन्मात्रं । अतोऽभाववित्ति-

---

'दृश्यता' प्रतियोगिग्राहकयावत्सम्पत्तिः, तथाच केशादेः सूक्ष्मस्य प्रतियोगिनो जिज्ञासापि ग्राहिकेति दृश्यतासम्पत्तये जिज्ञासापेक्ष्यते तेन जिज्ञासायां सत्यां तन्मात्रधीरेव व्यवहारं करोतीत्यर्थः । 'कार्य्यादिति, तद्धेतोरितिन्यायेनाधिकरणज्ञानस्यैवाभावव्यवहारजनकत्वप्रतीतेरिति भावः । ननु बुद्धिधारा परात्मीया, न च परात्मा प्रत्यक्षः, इत्यनुमित्यादिरूपा बुद्धिधारा वाच्या, न चानुमित्यादयो धारावाहिन्यः, स्मृतेरपि संस्कारोद्बोधकज्ञानसान्तरत्वेन सान्तरत्वादिति तदा तदन्यपुरुषीया तथा धीर्व्वाच्या, तस्यापि तथा बुद्धिविच्छेदे तदन्यपुरुषीया तथा धीर्व्वाच्या, एवञ्चात्मकोटीनामामानन्त्यमेव परापरतादृशबुद्धिकल्पनमप्रामाणिकं गुरु चेत्यरुचेराह, 'प्रतियोगिमदिति ।

'प्रतियोगीति, यद्यप्येतन्नानुभवसाक्षिकं, तथाप्यनुभवसाक्षिके तद्वित्तिवेद्यत्वे पूर्व्वाप्रतीतस्य विशेषणतया विशेषणत्वानुभवेनैव तदाक्षिप्तमिति परम्परया तत्राप्यनुभवः साक्षीत्येतदपास्तं । 'न च

वेद्यत्वं प्रतियोगिनः, प्रतियोगिज्ञानाधीनज्ञानत्वञ्चा-भावस्यानुभवसाक्षिकं गोसादृश्यवत्। न च केवलमधिकरणं तज्ज्ञानं वा अभावः, प्रतियोगिज्ञानं विनापि तद्वित्तेः तद्वित्तौ प्रतियोगिनोऽविषयत्वाच्च। सप्रतियोगिकत्वाभावे च कस्य प्रतियोगी घटः। अथ केवलमधिकरणं तज्ज्ञानं वा अभावः स चाप्रतियोगिक एव, अभावव्यवहारस्तु प्रतियोगिज्ञानमपेक्षते इति तस्य प्रतियोगी घटः घट-तदभावव्यवहारयोर्विरोधादिति चेत्। न। इह घटो नेति नञर्थस्य प्रतियोगी घटोऽनुभूयते न त्वभावज्ञानानन्तरभाविनोऽभावव्य-

---

केवलमिति। न च त्वन्मतेऽप्यभावो न सप्रतियोगिकः इदन्त्वेन तदनुभवस्य प्रतियोगिनिरपेक्षत्वात् किन्तु अभावत्वं, तच्च ममापि तथैव घटवच्छिन्नत्वरूपस्य तस्य घटधीसापेक्षत्वादिति वाच्यम्। तच्छिन्नत्वस्यापि तस्य स्वरूपातिरिक्तस्याभावेन सप्रतियोगिकत्वानुपपत्तेः अभावज्ञानं विना प्रतियोगिमच्छिन्नत्वानवगमाच्च। प्रतियोगयवृत्त्यनुयोगिवृत्तिधर्मज्ञानाधीनत्वाद्भेदग्रहस्य। न चेदमसिद्धं प्रतियोग्यवृत्तित्वेन धर्मग्रहस्य भेदग्राहकत्वे सति प्रतियोगिवृत्तित्वं धर्मस्य घटत्वादेर्घटत्वत्वाद्युपस्थितिसाध्यम्, तच्चेह घटेतरत्वगर्भतया भेदधीसापेक्षमित्यन्योन्याश्रयादिति वाच्यम्। वस्तुतः प्रतियोग्यवृत्तिना स्वरूपतो ज्ञातेन धर्मेण भेदग्रहात्। न च भेदभ्रमासम्भवः, प्रमाया-

वहारस्य, तस्याभावानुभवसमयेऽप्रतीतेः। व्यवह्रियते-ऽसौ न त्वनुभूयते इति चेत्। न। तादृशानुभवं विना तथा व्यवहाराभावात्। व्यवहारे प्रतियोगिज्ञाना-पेक्षेत्यपि न युक्तं व्यवहर्त्तव्यज्ञानस्य सत्यामिच्छायां व्यवहारेऽधिकापेक्षाया, अदृष्टचरत्वात्। लघवादिष्व तथा कल्प्यते न त्वभाव इति चेत्। न। व्यवहार-मात्रे तथा कारणत्वानवधारणात् व्यवहारविशेष-स्याननुगतत्वात्। ह्रस्वत्व-दीर्घत्वे च परिमाणान्तरे एव। तवाप्यल्याधिकसङ्ख्यावच्छिन्नहस्ताद्यवच्छेद्यत्वं परिमाणस्य ह्रस्वत्वं दीर्घत्वञ्चाल्याधिकावधिज्ञाना-धीनज्ञातं अतो द्रव्यसमकालं परिमाणानुभवेऽपि नानुभूतमिति न तदा तद्व्यवहारः। गोसादृश्यं यद्यपि

मभावग्राहकसामग्री वेषणात्। भ्रमस्य तु भावभ्रमवदारोप्यस्मृति-विशेषादर्शनदोषादिघटितया सामान्यसामग्र्यैव निर्व्वाहात्। प्रतियोगि-स्मृत्तित्वेनाज्ञातधर्म्मग्रहो वा हेतुर्व्वाच्य इत्यन्यत्र विस्तरः। 'तवाप्यल्पेति त्वन्मते गुणगतजात्यभावादवच्छेद्यत्वं स्वरूपं, मम त्ववच्छेद्यतावच्छेदक-जातिमत्त्वं तत्, तथाच परिमाणग्रहेऽपि व्यञ्जकाभावात्तन्न गृहीतं स्वरूपत्वेऽपि तस्य तेन रूपेण ज्ञानं तथा व्यवहारे निदानमिति तत्प्रकारकज्ञानार्थमेवावध्यपेक्षेत्यर्थः।

गवयगतानि सामान्यानि तज्ज्ञानसमकालमेवानुभूतानि, तथापि गोवृत्तित्वे सति गवयवृत्तित्वं गोसादृश्यत्वं गोज्ञानाधीनज्ञातमिति न तदा सादृश्यव्यवहारः। स्यादेतत् अस्ति तावत्कस्यचिज्ज्ञानात् क्वचिदभावपदप्रयोगः सर्वसिद्धः, तच्च प्रयोगालम्बनं भूतलाद्येव घटवदतिरिक्ताप्रकाशात्, ततश्च यदपेक्षं यस्याभावपदप्रयोगविषयत्वं तत्तस्याभाव इत्युपेयते, तद्बुद्धिजनिताभावपदप्रयोगविषयत्वमेव घट-भूतलयोः प्रतियोग्यनुयोगिरूपः सम्बन्धः। अत एव भूतलस्य सप्रतियोगिकत्वं तद्बुद्धिजनिताभावपदप्रयोगविषयत्वेन तद्बुद्धिं विना अभावपदप्रयोगाविषयत्वात्। अनेनैवो-

केचित्तु तादृशपरिमाणग्रह एवावधिसापेक्ष इति द्रव्यग्रहसमकालं महत्त्वरूपपरिमाणग्रहेऽपि व्यञ्जकावधिज्ञानाभावान्न दीर्घत्वादिपरिमाणग्रह इति व्याचक्षत इति । तन्न। परिमाणस्य सावधित्वे मानाभावात्। किन्तूत्कर्षेणैतद्वृत्तिधर्म्मविशेषस्यैव तथात्वात्(१)। न चैवं धर्म्मस्यापि जातिरूपस्य सावधित्वे मानाभावः, स्वरूपेणेष्टापत्तेः। उत्कर्षधर्म्मावच्छेदेन गृहीतायाः जातेः प्रवृत्तिनिमित्तत्वात् तारत्वादिवत् तस्याश्च तद्वदेव सावधित्वादिति दिक्। अत्र यद्यपि यावदुक्तं

(१) तथा भावादिति ख० ।

पाधिना घटाभावादिपदव्युत्पत्तिग्रह इति चेत् । न । अभावप्रयोगालम्बनं[१] न भूतलं न हि भूतलं घटाभाव इति प्रतीति-प्रयोगौ, अपि तु भूतले घटाभाव इति भूतले घट इति वत् । भूतले घटो नास्तीति भूतलाधिकरणातिरिक्तमर्थप्रकाशात् । अपि च घटबुद्धिजनिताभावपदप्रयोगविषयत्वं भूतलस्य घटाभावत्वं तथाच घटाभावत्वे तस्यावगते घटाभावपदप्रयोगविषयत्वं, घटाभावपदप्रयोगविषयत्वे च ज्ञाते तस्य घटाभावत्वमित्यन्योन्याश्रयः पदप्रवृत्तिनिमित्तेऽवगते पदप्रयोगनियमात् । घटाभावत्वञ्च घटाभावपदे प्रवृत्तिनिमित्तं । यदि च भूतलं सप्रतियोगिकं तदा प्रतियोगिनं विना केवलं न भासेत साहश्यादिवत् । घटाभावपदप्रयोगदशायां तत् सप्रतियोपिकं नान्यदेति चेत्, तर्हि घटप्रतियोगिकत्वे

घटाभावो न पटाभाव इत्यादि प्रतीत्या घटाभावे पटस्याभाव इत्यादि प्रतीत्या च तस्यापि सप्रतियोगिकत्वानुभवादप्रतियोगिकाधिकरणरूपत्वाभ्युपगमाच्च प्रतिबन्धिकवलितं, तथाप्यभावसिद्धिदशायामेतादृशप्रतिबन्ध्यनवतारेणाप्रतिबन्धिमोक्तयुक्तिदार्ढ्येनाभाव-

---

(१) अभावपदप्रयोगालम्बनमिति ख० ।

तस्य घटबुद्धिजनिताभावपदप्रयोगविषयत्वं, सति च तस्मिन् घटप्रतियोगिकत्वमित्यन्योन्याश्रयः केवलस्याप्रतियोगिकत्वात्। एवञ्च गोबुद्धिजनितसदृशपदप्रयोगविषयत्वं गवयस्य गोसादृश्यमस्तु कृतमतिरिक्तसादृश्येनेति सप्रतियोगिकपदार्थापलापः। अपि च न केवलं भूतलमभावः भूतलाभावयोराधाराधेयभावानुभवात्, अभेदे तदनुपपत्तेः। दुःखवदात्मभिन्नस्य च आत्मनो दुःखाभावत्वे मोक्षस्यापुरुषार्थत्वप्रसङ्गः आत्मनोऽसाध्यत्वात्। अथ घटवद्भूतलज्ञानभिन्नं भूतलज्ञानमभावः तस्य च भूतलाधारता स्वरूपसम्बन्धेनानुभूयत इति चेत्। न। तस्य निष्प्रतियोगिकत्वेनाभावत्वानुपपत्तेः[१] इत्युक्तत्वात्। अपि च तज्ज्ञानं किं स्वरूपसदेवाभावव्यवहारकारणं, भूत-

---

सिद्धौ तदुत्तरकालेऽनवस्थाभयादिना अभावाधाराभावप्रतियोगिकाभावान्तराप्रमितौ तयोर्भावैकपर्य्यवसानेऽप्यवतीर्णा सा प्रतिबन्धिर्नाभावग्राहकं प्रमाणं बाधते उपजीव्यत्वात् फलमुखगौरवादित्याखण्डलकस्यैव मूलावष्टम्भयुक्तिर्धारणीयेति सर्व्वतात्पर्य्यसंक्षेपः। 'यथेति येन प्रकारेण यथा युक्त्येति यावत्, सा च प्रतीतिः प्रयो-

---

(१) ज्ञानस्याप्रतियोगिकत्वेनाभावत्वानुपपत्तेरिति ख०।

त्ताधिकरणकनिषेधरूपतयानुभूयमानं वा, नाद्यः स्वरूपसतो भूतलाधेयतया प्रतीत्यनुपपत्तेः । न द्वितीयः घटवद्भूतलज्ञानस्य तदानीमनुपस्थितेः तद्भिन्नज्ञानस्य प्रत्येतुमशक्यत्वात् । किञ्च यदि घटवद्भूतलज्ञानाद्भिन्नभूतलज्ञानमभावः तदा घटवति दोषात् घटवत्त्वाज्ञाने भूतलज्ञानमभावो भवेत्, तथाच तदेव तदैव घटवत् घटाभाववच्च स्यात्, न स्याताञ्च घटाभावज्ञान-तद्व्यवहारौ विसंवादिनौ विषयाबाधात्[१] । अथ वस्तुतोघटवतो भूतलस्य ज्ञानाद्भिन्नं भूतलज्ञानमभावः । न च घटवति भूतलज्ञानं तथा व्यवहारस्तु विसंवादी, तथाविधभ्रमादर्शनादिति चेत्, तर्हि घटवतो भूतलस्य ज्ञानाद्भिन्नत्वेन ज्ञानं

गानुगम एवेत्यर्थः । यद्वा येन धर्म्मेणैकपदार्थत्वमिति स्फुट एवार्थो ग्राह्यः । न चाग्रे तदप्रदर्शनाद्विरोधः, समयविशेषस्य निष्प्रतियोगिकत्वेनेति ब्रुवता अर्थात्सप्रतियोगिकत्वमभावत्वमित्युक्तत्वात् । न च समवायाद्यतिव्याप्तिः, सप्रतियोगिकत्वेन प्रतियोग्यविशेषणकप्रत्ययाविषयत्वस्योक्तत्वात् । समवाय-संयोगयोस्तादृशप्रतीतिविषयत्वात् नीलोघट इति प्रत्ययात् संयोगे निर्व्विकल्पकसम्भवाच्च । न च

---

(१) विषयबाधाभावादिति ख० ।

भूतलज्ञानं अभावव्यवहृतिहेतुः। न च तत्सम्भवति, स्वप्रकाशेनानुव्यवसायेन वाधिकरणज्ञाने तदप्रकाशात् भेदप्रतियोगिनोऽनुपस्थितेः। न च ज्ञानान्तरेण तथानुभवः, योग्यानुपलब्ध्या तत्र घटाभावनिश्चयं विना तथा निश्चेतुमशक्यत्वात्। अपिचाधिकरणतज्ज्ञानानामननुगतत्वेनानुगताभावव्यवहारानुपपत्तिः। न चातिरिक्ताभावपक्षेऽपि तथा अभावत्वस्यानुगतस्याभावादिति वाच्यं। अनुगताभावत्वं विनापि घटादिर्न पट इति समानाधिकरणनिषेधादनुगतव्यवहारः पटान्योन्याभावेनैकेन, एवं घटादौ न गोत्वमित्यनुगतव्यवहार एकेनात्यन्ताभावेन, कपालेषु भूतलेषु इदानीं घटो विनष्ट इत्यनुगतव्यवहारो ध्वंसेनैकेन, घटानुत्पाददशायामेतेषु घटो नास्तीत्यनुगतव्यवहार एकेन प्रागभावेन, एवं चत्वारोऽनुग-

---

ज्ञानादावतिप्रसङ्गः, विषयातिरिक्तप्रतियोगिज्ञानजन्यज्ञानविषयत्वस्यापि विशेषणत्वात्। एतच्चाभावविभाजकोपाधिरूपं द्रष्टव्यम्, प्रतीतिविषयस्वभावत्वमभावस्वरूपमेवेत्युक्तं प्रामाण्ये। 'सम्बन्धान्तरमिति विशिष्टप्रत्ययजननयोग्यतालिङ्गितस्वरूपस्य सम्बन्धत्वादित्यर्थः। यथाश्रुते योग्यत्वस्यैव सम्बन्धत्वप्राप्तेः। न च तथैव किं न स्यादिति वाच्यम्। विशिष्टधीविषयस्य सम्बन्धित्वात्। विशिष्टबुद्धेश्च विशिष्ट-

तन्निषेधव्यवहाराश्चतसृभिरेव व्यक्तिभिः क्रियन्ते। तच त्वभावचतुष्टयं तत्तदधिकरण-तत्तद्घटोनामननुगतत्वान्न सम्भवति अनुगताभावचतुष्टयव्यवहारस्य प्रत्येकाभावेनोपपादयितुमशक्यत्वादित्यतिरिक्ताभावव्यक्तिचतुष्टयसिद्धिः। तस्य च यथा अभावत्वेनैकेनैकपदार्थत्वं तथानुपदमेव वक्ष्यामः। स्यादेतत् यस्मिन् समयविशेषे यत्र भूतले अभावः परैः स्वीक्रियते तत्समयविशेषयोग एव भूतलस्य घटाभावः, एवञ्चेह भूतले घटो नास्तीत्याधाराधेयभावप्रतीतिरप्युपपद्यते, समयविशेषयोगस्य भूतलवृत्तित्वात्। न च समयविशेषयोगस्याभावत्वे अननुगमो दोषः, अतिरिक्ताभावपक्षेऽपि तुल्यत्वात् अभावत्वस्य जातेरुपाधेर्वा असत्त्वात्। यदि चाभावप्रतीतिप्रयोगानुगमार्थं तत्र धर्मा-

---

बुद्धिविषयत्वात्। अतएव सम्बन्धस्य सम्बन्धिभिन्नत्वनियमेन स्वरूपसम्बन्धं परे दूषयन्तीति भावः। अत्र वदन्ति। एवं सति घटाभावभ्रमानुपपत्तिस्तद्योग्यतायाः फलदर्शनगम्यतया तत्र विशिष्टज्ञानोत्पत्त्या योग्यतावश्यकत्वात्। न च प्रमायोग्यता सम्बन्धः, सम्बन्धघटकत्वेन तस्यापि प्रमात्वात्। अन्यथा तस्याप्रमात्वे तत्र सम्बन्धाभावः, तस्मिंश्च तस्याप्रमात्वमित्यन्योन्याश्रयः। किञ्च यो-

न्तरं स्वीक्रियते तदा समयविशेषयोगवृत्त्येव तदस्तु लाघवादिति। तन्न। समयविशेषयोगस्य निष्प्रति-योगिकत्वेनाभावव्यवहारासामर्थ्यात्। किञ्च भूतल-वत् समयविशेषोऽपि अभावाधारतयानुभूयते इदानीं भूतले घटो नास्तीति प्रतीतेः। न च तत्समयविशेषे तत्समयविशेषयोगः, अभेदे सम्बन्धानुपपत्तौ आधा-राधेयभावाभावात्। अपिच समये किमभावाश्रयतैव विशेषः, तत्तत्समयस्वरूपं वा, आद्ये अभावस्वीकारः, द्वितीये अननुगमः। मम त्वेकाभावव्यक्तेरेव तथा नानासमयवृत्तित्वात्। किञ्च समयविशेषयोगादि-दानीं भूतलमिति प्रतीति-प्रयोगौ स्यातां विशेषणस्य स्वप्रकारकविशिष्टप्रत्ययजनकत्वात्, न तु भूतले घटा-भाव इति। यदि च तत्तत्समयविशेषयोगाद्भूतले

ग्यतायाः प्रत्ययाविषयत्वे धर्मिद्वयमात्रविषयतायां कथं काचित्प्रमा काचिन्नेति प्रतीतिविभागः विशिष्टधीयोग्यतासत्त्वासत्त्वस्य प्रत्ययावि-षयत्वेनानियामकत्वात्। किञ्चातीन्द्रियाभावस्वरूपसम्बन्धाव्यापकमिदं तच्च स्वरूपद्वयस्य विशिष्टज्ञानाजनकत्वादिति। मैवम्। एतेन विशिष्टधीजननयोग्यतावच्छेदकावच्छिन्नस्वरूपद्वयस्य सम्बन्धत्वाभि-मानात् तदभावे किञ्चिद्योग्यं किञ्चिन्नेति विभागासम्भवात्।

घटाभावव्यवहारस्तदा याद्दशसंस्थानविशेषविशिष्टे कपाले घटो वर्त्तते ताद्दशकपालादिकमेव तत्तत्समयविशेषयोगाद्घटादिव्यवहारजनकमस्तु किं घटादिना प्रतीतिश्च तुल्या। एतेन "द्दष्टस्तावदयं घटोऽत्र च पतन् द्दष्टस्तथा मुद्गरः द्दष्टा खर्परसंहतिः परमितोऽभावो न द्दष्टोऽपरः। तेनाभाव इति श्रुतिः क्व निहिता किञ्चात्र तत्कारणं स्वाधीना कलशस्य केवलमियं द्दष्टा कपालावली" इति निरस्तं। मुद्गरपाताद्विनष्टो घट इति प्रतीत्यातिरिक्तविनाशानुभवात्। न च केवलभूतलं तद्बुद्धिर्वा तज्जन्या, तेन विनापि तयोः सत्त्वात्। त्वन्मते च तयोरभावमात्रत्वेन विनाशत्वायोगात्। योगे वा अभावमात्रस्य विनाशित्वापत्तिः। अथ त्वन्मते यद्विनाशकं तदेव तत्सहितं भूतलं ज्ञानं वा विनाश इति चेत्। न। मुद्गरपातजन्यो हि विनाशो-

---

योग्यतावच्छेदकं क्वचित् प्रतियोगिदेशान्यदेशत्वं, क्वचित् प्रतियोगिदेशत्वे सति प्रतियोगिकालान्यकालत्वं, क्वचित् प्रतियोगितावच्छेदकाभाववद्वृत्तित्वं। न च भेदवत्त्वादावपि[१] मतुवर्थः सम्बन्धानुयोग:, तत्रापि तत्प्रतियोगि-तदवच्छेदकदेशान्यदेशभेदेन भेद-तदत्यन्ताभाव-

---

(१) भेदवत्त्वाभाववत्त्वादावपीति ख० ।

ऽनुभूयते। न च तस्यैव तज्जनकत्वं, सप्रतियोगिकस्य विनाशोऽनुभूयते, न च मुद्गरपातस्तथा। नन्वभावेन समं भूतलस्य सम्बन्धाभावात् कथं भूतले घटाभाव-प्रत्ययः। स्वरूपसम्बन्धादिति चेत्, तर्हि घटवद्भूतल-स्यापि चत्वरीयाभावेन स्वरूपसम्बन्धोऽस्ति भूतलम-भावश्चेत्यतोऽधिकस्य स्वरूपसम्बन्धस्याभावात्। प्रति-योग्यारोप एव स्वरूपसम्बन्धः,[१] अत एवारोप्य निषिध्यत इत्युच्यत इति चेत्। न। तत्राभावसम्बन्धे सत्यारोपः स एव चाभावसम्बन्ध इत्यन्योन्याश्रय इति चेत्। न। सम्बन्धान्तरमन्तरेण विशिष्टप्रत्ययजननयो-ग्यत्वस्य स्वरूपसम्बन्धत्वात्। न च घटवद्भूतल-चत्व-रीयाभावयोः परस्परं विशिष्टप्रत्ययः। ज्ञान-विषययोः समवाय-समवायिनोरिव सम्बन्धान्तराभ्युपगमे ज्ञान-

---

सम्भवात्। न चानवस्था, वस्तुगत्याऽसत्वात्। प्रत्ययानवस्था तु नास्त्येव ज्ञानावच्छेदकवत्तया स्वरूपपरिचायकत्वात्[२] अत एवातीन्द्रियाव्याप्ति-रप्यपास्ता। एवञ्च तादृशस्वरूपाभावे यत्राभावधीस्तत्रैव भ्रम इति किमनुपपन्नम्। न च विषये विशेषाभावात् कथं भ्रमत्वं, एकघट-

---

(१) स्वभावसम्बन्ध इति क०।

(२) स्वरूपविशेषणत्वादिति ख०।

वस्थाभिया तत्सम्बन्ध-सम्बन्धिनोरपि तादृशसम्बन्ध-स्वीकारादिति सिद्धोऽतिरिक्तोऽभाव इति[१] तद्ग्राहिका विशेषणतेति सिद्धमेतत्।

इति श्रीमद्गङ्गेशोपाध्यायविरचिते तत्त्वचिन्तामणौ प्रत्यक्षखण्डे अभाववादः।

वत्यभावस्य प्रकारत्वात्। अन्यत्र तद्देशान्यदेश इति विशेषस्य स्फुटत्वात् प्रकारत्वस्य च स्वरूपसम्बन्धविशेषत्वात्तद्विशेषस्यावश्य वाच्यत्वात्। अन्यथा अन्यत्रापि प्रत्ययवैचित्र्यानुपपत्तेरिति दिक्।

इति श्रीजयदेवमिश्रविरचिते तत्त्वचिन्तामण्यालोके प्रत्यक्षखण्डालोके अभाववादालोकः।

---

(१) सिद्धोऽधिकोऽभाव इतीति ख॰।

अथ प्रत्यक्षकारणवादः ।

षोढा सन्निकर्षः प्रत्यक्षविशेषे कारणं, विषयेणालोकसंयोगविशेषश्च तत्र कारणं, न तु चक्षुषा, प्रकाशस्थेन चक्षुषान्धकारस्थस्याग्रहणात् वैपरीत्ये च ग्रहणात् । नन्वेवं परभागावच्छेदेनालोकसंयुक्तोऽपि घटो गृह्येत । न चावयविग्रहसामग्र्याः स्वावयवग्रहसामग्रीनियमात् परभागावच्छिन्नो न गृह्यत इति वाच्यं । त्र्यणुके व्यभिचारात् प्रत्यक्षावयवे च सामग्रीभेदकल्पने मानाभावात् । अथाभिमुखावयवावच्छेदेन घटालोकसंयोगः कारणं, तर्ह्यभिमुखावयवावच्छेदेन चक्षुरालोकसंयोगोऽपि हेतुरस्तु । यदि चालोकसंयोगावच्छिन्ने चक्षुःसंयोगस्तथा समानदेशताविरोधश्च नि-

---

अथ प्रत्यक्षकारणवादालोकः ।

'अन्वय-व्यतिरेकाभ्यामिति अन्वय-व्यतिरेकसहकारिप्रत्यक्षगम्यतया प्रथमोपस्थितविषयालोकसंयोगेनातीन्द्रियतया अनुमानगम्यहेतुताकश्चक्षुरालोकसंयोगोऽन्यथासिद्ध इत्यर्थः । अतएव कल्पान्तरेऽपि अक्षरयोज्ञावनं । 'अन्ये त्विति, 'उद्भूतरूपेति । न चैवं दण्डदृढ़त्वमपि घटहेतुः स्यादिति वाच्यम् । तत्र चक्रभ्रमिव्यापार-

विडयोरेव, अन्यथा पट-महारजतयोः पटोदक-योश्चाग्रहप्रसङ्गः, तर्हि घटसंयोगावच्छिन्ने चक्षुरा-लोकसंयोगः कारणमस्तु। अथ चालनीन्यायेन आलोकसंयोगसन्निहिते चक्षुर्घटसंयोगः कारणं, तदा घटचक्षुःसंयोगसन्निहिते चक्षुरालोकसंयोगो हेतुरस्त्विति चेत्। नैवं। अन्वय-व्यतिरेकाभ्यां विषया-लोकसंयोगस्य कारणत्वे निश्चिते तेनैवोपपत्तौ न चक्षुरालोकसंयोगः कारणं कल्प्यते।

अन्ये तु द्वयोरप्यालोकसंयोगयोः कारणत्वे विष-यालोकसंयोगः कारणमेवेति। नन्वभिमुखावयवाव-च्छेदेन विषयालोकसंयोगयोः कारणत्वे विषयालोक-संयोगः कारणमेवेति।

कतया दण्डहेतुत्वकल्पने दृढ़त्वस्यान्यथासिद्धेः। न च तत्रापि दृढ़त्वं हेतुरिति वाच्यम्। तत्र चक्रभ्रमिजनकत्वे चक्रभ्रमिजनक-त्वस्याभावात् दार्ढ्यस्य तत्रैव विश्रामात् भ्रमिं प्रति दण्डसंयोगहे-तुताग्राहके सति विशेषणीभूतदण्डस्यापि कारणताग्रहाचेति वैषम्यात्। वस्तुतस्तूद्भूतरूपोत्कर्षेण प्रत्यक्षोत्कर्षात् तस्य हेतुता न हि दृढ़त्वे-ऽप्येवमिति भावः। अथ सगुणानामिन्द्रियभाव इति सिद्धान्तं साधयति, 'चक्षुरिति, 'रूपस्येति रूपत्वपक्षधर्म्मावच्छिन्नसाध्य-व्यापकमुद्भूतरूपत्वं तेजोरूपत्वपक्षधर्म्मावच्छिन्नसाध्यव्यापकं तेजो-

नन्वभिमुखावयवावच्छेदेन विषयालोकसंयोगस्य कारणत्वे आवश्यकत्वादवयवालोकसंयोग एव हेतुरस्त्विति[१] चेत्। न। अवयवसंयोगमात्रस्यातिप्रसक्तेः स्वावयवसंयोगो वक्तव्यः तथा च स्वसंयोग एव लाघवात्। अवयवसंयोगेन चान्यथासिद्धौ कारणतैव न स्यात् संयोगस्येत्युक्तं[२]। आलोकस्योद्भूतरूपमपि व्यञ्जकं अन्वय-व्यतिरेकित्वात्। ननु तेजःकारणतावच्छेदकं तत् उष्मादीनां चाक्षुषत्वाभावात्। न च स्वातन्त्र्येणान्वय-व्यतिरेकित्वात् द्वयोरपि हेतुत्वं अन्यथा दण्डादेरपि चक्रावच्छेदकत्वं स्यादिति[३] वाच्यं। उद्भूतरूप-तेजोमात्रयोः समवधाने कार्य्यानुदयादिति

गतोद्भूतरूपत्वं वा नोपाधिरित्यर्थः। उद्भूतत्वमात्रे वक्तव्ये रूपत्वघटणमुद्भूतत्वस्य तत्तद्व्याप्यस्य नानात्वेन रूपत्वव्याप्योद्भूतत्वविशेषलाभायेति द्रष्टव्यम्। उपाधेः साध्यव्यापकताग्राहकाभावमाह, 'व्यभिचारेणेति, उक्तोपाधेः साध्यव्यापकता तदा स्याद्यद्युपाधितावच्छेदकोद्भूतरूपत्वेन व्यञ्जकतेजोगतोद्भुतरूपत्वेन वा व्यञ्जकत्वव्याप्यत्वमवच्छिद्येत, समव्याप्तोपाधिपक्षे साध्यव्याप्यतावच्छेदकरूपेणैव साध्य-

---

(१) कारणमस्त्वितीति ख॰।
(२) संयोगस्य कारणतैव न स्यादित्युक्तमिति ख॰।
(३) चक्रावच्छेदादितीति ख॰।

चेत्। नैवं। उद्भूतरूपतेजस्त्वं तेजसश्च उद्भूतरूपत्वं वावच्छेदकमिति विनिगमकाभावादुभयोरपि हेतुत्वात् दण्ड-चक्रयोरिवैकैकं विहायापरस्यान्वय-व्यतिरेकाभावात्। एवं चक्षुषो रूपमपि व्यञ्जकं व्यञ्जकतेजोरूपत्वात् आलोकरूपवत्। रूपस्य व्यञ्जकत्वे उद्भूतरूपत्वन्तेजोगतोद्भूतरूपत्वं वा नोपाधिः व्यभिचारेण गौरवेण चाप्रयोजकत्वात्। किन्तु व्यञ्जकरूपमेव तथा लाघवात्। विषयस्थमपि रूपमुद्भूतं सहकारि तदुद्भवे च मानं। इन्द्रियालोकादिप्रत्यासन्नं महदवयविवायूपनीतसुरभिशीतोष्णचक्षुरादिकं साक्षात्कारकारणकिञ्चित्समवधानशून्यं अप्रत्यक्षत्वादन्धकारस्थघटवदिति। तत्र कारणं लाघवादनुगतं

व्यापकतावच्छेदात्। न चैव ताभ्यां व्यञ्जकत्वव्याप्यत्वच्छेदः, प्रथमे व्यभिचारात् अन्वयव्यभिचारात् विषयाद्युद्भूतरूपे सत्यपि नभसि तदग्रहात्, द्वितीये गौरवं उद्भूतत्वस्य व्यर्थत्वात्, तथाच न तदुभयं साध्यव्यापकमिति भावः। अत एवोक्तं 'किन्त्वित्यादि, न हि व्यञ्जकतेजोरूपत्वं हेतुतावच्छेदकं, अपि तु व्यापकतावच्छेदकमेव। न च तत्कारणतावच्छेदकमेव कुतो न स्यात् लाघवादिति वाच्यम्। एवं सति व्यञ्जकगुणत्वे लाघवाद्गुणमात्रस्यैव हेतुतापत्तेः। तस्मात्तद-भावात् कार्य्याभावस्यैव कारणत्वं। तथाच यथा आलोकोद्भूतरू-

सामान्यं रूपादिवृत्ति न द्रव्यगतं उष्मादौ स्पर्शग्रहे रूपस्य, प्रभादौ रूपग्रहे स्पर्शस्य ग्रहप्रसङ्गात् उद्भवत्वैकार्थसमवायाविशेषात्। अन्यथा स्पर्श-रूपयोरग्रहप्रसङ्गात्। नाप्युभयवृत्ति, रूपादिवृत्तित्वेनैवोपपत्तेः रूप-स्पर्शयोस्तु तन्नाना एकग्रहेऽप्यपरस्याग्रहात्। न च रूपत्वादिना परापरभावानुपपत्तिः, तारत्वादिवन्नानात्वात्। रूपादिप्रत्यक्षे एकैकोद्भवस्यैव प्रयोजकत्वात्। ननु महत्त्वे एवोद्भवत्वमस्तु तदेव प्रत्यक्षत्वे तन्त्रं लाघवात्। न च रूपेऽपि, गौरवादिति चेत्। न। आश्रयमहत्त्वोद्भवाभावेऽपि गन्ध-स्पर्शयोः प्रत्यक्षत्वेनोद्भवत्वमिति प्रत्यक्षमूर्त्तविशेषगुणत्वेन रूपेऽप्युद्भवत्वात् न महत्त्वे सामान्यगुणत्वात्। अथानुद्भवत्व-

---

पाभावे कार्य्याभाव इति तस्य हेतुत्वं तथा ग्राह्यजातीयगुणवदिन्द्रियव्यतिरेकेण रूपादिग्राह्यविषयाग्रहात तच ग्राह्यजातीयगुणस्यापि हेतुत्वं। न चैवं हेतुतावच्छेदकं तन्न हेतुरिति वाच्यम्। ग्राह्यजातीयगुणवदिन्द्रियत्वं वा इन्द्रियनिष्ठग्राह्यजातीयगुणत्वं वा अवच्छेदकं न च विनिगमकं[१] इत्युभयोरपि हेतुत्वादिति, तच तेजोमतोद्भूतरूपेत्यादिनोक्तप्रायमिति नाचरेणोक्तं। तथाच तयोर्व्यञ्जक-

---

(१) अवच्छेदकमित्यत्र किं विनिगमकमिति ख०।

मेव जातिः अप्रत्यक्षत्वप्रयोजकत्वेन साक्षादेव तत्कल्पनात् तदभावात् प्रत्यक्षत्वमिति चेत्। न। अप्रत्यक्षतायाः प्रत्यक्षकारणविरहप्रयोज्यत्वेन प्रत्यक्षकारणस्य लाघवेन जातेः कल्पनात्। न तु प्रतिबन्धकत्वेनानुद्भवत्वं कल्पयित्वा तदभावः कारणं गौरवादिति संप्रदायविदः।

वयन्तु ब्रूमः। शुक्लत्वादिना कारणरूपाग्निसंयोगप्रयोज्याभ्यां जातिभ्यां परापरभावानुपपत्त्या रूपवृत्त्युद्भवत्वमनेकं वाच्यं, तथाचोद्भूतत्वेन कारणत्वे अननुगमः। तस्मादनुद्भवत्वं शुक्लत्वादिव्याप्यं नानाजातिस्तदभावकूटस्तु प्रत्यक्षत्वे प्रयोजकः। अन्यथानुगतप्रत्यक्षानुपपत्तेः। एवं स्पर्शादावपि। अथ वोद्भूतत्वमनुद्भूतत्वं वा न जातिः किन्तु रूपत्वव्याप्यजाति-

---

तेजोरूपयोर्ग्राहकत्वे(१) व्यञ्जकतेजोरूपत्वमेव व्यञ्जकत्वव्याप्यतावच्छेदकं लाघवादिति तद्व्याप्यत्वे उपाध्योः साध्याव्यापकत्वमर्थसिद्धमिति सर्व्वनिगर्भः। साक्षात्कारत्वसमवधानशून्यत्वं साक्षात्कारप्रयोजकसमवधानशून्यत्वमिति कारण-तदवच्छेदकसाधारणेनानुमानमन्यथा द्रव्यवृत्त्येव तदास्तामिति शङ्कानुत्थानात् 'न त्वित्यादिग्रन्थविरोधः। तद्वृत्तित्वेन तदाश्रयद्रव्यस्य हेतुत्वे तस्या जातेरवच्छेदकत्वपर्य्यवसा-

---

(१) यद्धेतुत्वे इति ख०।

मत्त्वमेवोद्भूतत्वं तदभावोऽनुद्भवत्वं प्रत्यक्षे रूपे शुक्लतर-तमत्वादिजातिमत्त्वात्, उष्ण-चक्षुरादिरूपे तु शुक्लत्वमात्रमेव तद्व्याप्यजातौ मानाभावादुत्कर्षाभावात्। न च रूपत्वमेव मानं, लाघवेन तस्य प्रयोजकत्वे प्रत्यक्षत्वप्रसङ्गात्। एवं स्पर्शादावपीति। इतोऽपि महत्त्वेनोद्भवत्वं प्रयोजकं वाय्वादौ महत्त्वोत्कर्षेऽप्यप्रत्यक्षत्वात्। ननु भर्जनकपालगतो वह्निर्वारिस्थघटव्यञ्जकद्रव्यतेजश्च गृह्येत वारि-कपालयोः प्रत्यक्षत्वेनोद्भूतरूपवत्त्वात्। तयोः संयोगविशेष एव प्रतिबन्धक इति चेत्। न। जल-कपालादीनामालोकव्यञ्जकतया तद्ग्रहे प्रतिबन्धकत्वाभावात्[१]। प्रतिबन्धकत्वे वा भर्जनकपाल-वारिसंयोगिवह्नि-सौरालोकयोरग्रहप्रसङ्गः संयोगे च न विशेषो जातिकृतः अन्यतरकर्मजत्वादिना

मादिति। 'एकपद' इत्युपलक्षणं रूपत्वादिना परापरभावानुपपत्तेश्चेति द्रष्टव्यम्। 'रूपत्वादिनेत्यतद्गुणसंविज्ञानबहुव्रीहिणा नीलत्वादीति द्रष्टव्यम्। रूपादिवृत्तितन्नानात्वस्यानुपदमेवोक्तत्वेन तादृशप्रश्नानवतारादिति द्रष्टव्यम्। 'प्रत्यक्षेति, न च विशेषपदवैयर्थ्यमिति वाच्यम्। महत्त्वस्यैवोद्भूतत्वं महत्त्वस्यापीति वा आद्ये तदेकार्थसमवा-

---

(१) प्रतिबन्धाभावादिति ख०।

सङ्करप्रसङ्गात् । तारत्वनानात्वे गौरवात् । नापि तत्संयोगभेदः, अननुगमादिति । मैवं । जलस्थन्तु तेजो गृह्यत एव । उभयोः स्वच्छतया विविच्य ग्रहो न भवति । भर्जनकपाले चानुद्भूतरूपमुद्भूतस्पर्शमन्यदेव तेजः तादृशैरवयवैर्वह्निसहचरितैरारभ्यते, अतितप्ततैलादौ कदाचिदुद्भूतरूपावयवप्रवेशाद्यङ्गारारम्भोऽपि । न चैवं दुग्धसहचरितदधिपरमाणुभिरेव दध्यारम्भः, दुग्धध्वंसजन्यद्रव्यत्वेन खण्डदुग्धवद्दध्नो दुग्धोपादानोपादेयत्वात्[१] । नन्वेवमुद्भूतरूपवह्न्यादावनुद्भूतस्पर्शो नास्ति तत्सहचरिततेजोऽन्तरनियमेन तत्रोष्णबुद्धेरुपपत्तेः[२] उद्भूतरूपोद्भूतस्पर्शसामग्र्योरूष्मणि प्रभादौ विरोधावधारणादिति चेत् । न । यं

यद्य प्रत्यक्षत्वप्रयोजकत्वे रूप-स्पर्शयोरन्यतरप्रत्यक्षतायामन्यतरप्रत्यक्षत्वापातात्, द्वितीये रूपमात्रवृत्तित्वेनोपपत्तौ महत्त्वे तद्वृत्तौ मानाभावादिति विशेषान्तर्भावेणैव व्याप्तेरिति । 'अप्रत्यक्षत्वे'ति अप्रत्यक्षताप्रयोजकवदित्येवानुमानादित्यर्थः । 'अप्रत्यक्षताया' इति, भवत्वक्रमेणानुमानं, तथापि कार्य्यं प्रत्यभावकारणत्वकल्पनापेक्षया

---

(१) यत् द्रव्यं यद्द्रव्यध्वंसजन्यं तत् तदुपादानोपादेयमिति नियमादिति भावः ।

(२) तत्सहचरिततेजोऽन्तरसम्बन्धनियमेन तत्रोष्णत्वबुद्धेरुपपत्तेरिति ख० ।

वह्निमद्राक्षं तं स्पृशामीत्यबाधितप्रत्यभिज्ञानवशात् दर्शन-स्पर्शनाभ्यां वह्नौ रूप-स्पर्शयोरुपलम्भात्। न च तेजस्त्वम्बाधकं, उद्भवानुद्भवयोर्निमित्तभेदसंसर्ग-प्रयोज्यत्वात् तेजस्त्वस्य रूपवद्वृत्तिद्रव्यत्वसाक्षाद्व्याप्य-जातित्वेनोद्भूतरूप-स्पर्शवद्वृत्तित्वात्। न चोद्भूतरूप-स्पर्शयोर्विरोधः, जल-पृथिव्योरुभयसत्त्वात्। तेजसि विरोधस्य निमित्तभेदोपाधिकत्वादिति उद्भूतरूपसह-चरितयोर्महत्त्वानेकद्रव्यवत्त्वयोर्युगपद्भवाहितया अन्व-य-व्यतिरेकतुल्यत्वेऽपि द्रव्यचाक्षुषत्वे नानेकद्रव्यवत्त्व-मुभयं वा तन्त्रं किन्तु महत्त्वमेव लाघवात् अनेकद्र-व्योत्कर्षं विनापि तूलकादौ प्रचयजन्योत्कृष्टपरिमा-णात् प्रत्यक्षोत्कर्षदर्शनाच्च। दूरस्थकेशराशौ द्रव्यानु-त्पादेन महत्त्वाभावेऽप्येककेशस्य सजातीयसंयोगेना-

---

भावकारणत्वे लाघवात् अप्रत्यक्षत्वप्रयोजकोऽप्युद्भूतत्वजात्यभाव एव सिद्ध्यति न तु अनुद्भूतत्वं। अनुद्भूतत्वाभावहेतुत्वापेक्षया उद्भू-तत्वजातिहेतुत्वे लाघवादिति भावः। ननु लाघवाद्भावहेतुत्वमनुमन्यते, तदेवात्मसुगमेन तत्तत्कार्य्यं प्रति तत्तत्कारणत्वेन विपरीतमतोनो-द्भूतत्वं प्रत्यक्षत्वप्रयोजकं, न तूद्भवत्वं जातिरेव नास्तीति, एकत्र कोटावनुद्भूतत्वे तदितरद्विषि तद्विरुद्धजातिनियमादिति खण्डिद्धा-न्तमाह, 'वयन्त्विति, 'न जातिः' नातिरिक्तजातिः, 'किन्त्विति।

नेकद्रव्यवत्त्वात् द्रव्यप्रत्यक्षतेत्यनेकद्रव्यवत्त्वं तत्र तन्त्रमिति चेत्। न। अनेकद्रव्यसम्बन्धित्वस्य समवायेन प्रयोजकत्वात्। न तु संयोगेन, अतिप्रसङ्गात्। तथाच दूरग्रहणे सजातीयसंयोगस्य अनेकद्रव्यवत्त्वे सहकारिता वाच्या, सा महत्त्व एवास्तु। ननु यद्युद्भूतरूपवत्त्वं महत्त्वञ्च द्रव्यप्रत्यक्षतायां स्वरूपयोग्यता तदा दण्डत्ववत्तयोः कारणता न स्यादिति चेत्। न। तदुत्कर्षात् प्रत्यक्षोत्कर्षेण तयोः कारणत्वात्। न ह्यकारणोत्कर्षमकार्य्यमनुविधत्ते। दण्डत्वादौ नैवं, प्रकार-

---

ननु चक्षुषोऽपि रूपे रूपत्वव्याप्यशुक्लत्वव्याप्यं भास्वरत्वं जातिरस्तीति(१) तस्यापि प्रत्यक्षतापत्तिः। किञ्च प्रत्यक्षरूपे उत्कर्षरूपजातिमत्त्वे अप्रत्यक्षे तत्राप्यनुत्कर्षरूपा रूपत्वव्याप्यव्याप्या जातिरस्तीति तस्यापि तदापत्तिः। न चोत्कर्षरूपा जातिस्तथेति वाच्यम्। उत्कर्षाणामननुगमेनोत्कर्षेणैवानुगमादिति। मैवम्। व्याप्यजातेरुत्कर्षरूपाया विवक्षितत्वेन रूपत्वव्याप्योत्कर्षवत्त्वस्य प्रत्यक्षताप्रयोजकत्वात् उत्कर्षाणाञ्चोत्कृष्टपदप्रवृत्तिनिमित्तत्वेनानुगमात्। यद्वा नानाजातिव्यापकत्वेन सा जातिर्व्विवक्षिता अतो नोक्तदोषः। 'लाघवादिति, इदञ्चोपलक्षणं आत्मनि क्लृप्तत्वादित्यपि द्रष्टव्यम्। 'अनेकेति, इदञ्च

---

(१) रूपत्वव्याप्यव्याप्यजातिरस्तीतीति ख०।

भेदेनोभयरूपत्वाच्च चाक्षुषद्रव्यज्ञाने विषयत्वेन तयोः कारणत्वं, द्रव्ये अनुगतत्वेन कारणतावच्छेदकत्वमिति।

ननु नोद्भूतरूपवत्त्वं तच्च तन्त्रं वायोः प्रत्यक्षत्वात्। तथाहि वायुः प्रत्यक्षः प्रत्यक्षस्पर्शाश्रयत्वात् महत्त्वे सत्युद्भूतस्पर्शवत्त्वाद्वा घटवत्। उष्मादौ प्रत्यक्षत्वान्न व्यभिचारः। न चाप्रयोजकं, स्पार्शनप्रत्यक्षत्वे महत्त्वे सत्युद्भूतस्पर्शवत्त्वं प्रयोजकं, नोद्भूतरूपवत्त्वमपि गौरवात्। न च पक्षधर्मावच्छिन्नसाध्यव्यापकः साधनावच्छिन्नसाध्यव्यापकश्चोद्भूतरूपवत्त्वमुपाधिः, स्पार्शनप्रत्यक्षत्वे तस्याप्रयोजकत्वात् त्वगिन्द्रियव्यापारानन्तरं वायुर्वातीति प्रतीतेश्च। न च स्पर्शलिङ्गाग्रहे तदुपक्षयः, घटेऽपि तथात्वापत्तेः। लैङ्गिकत्वे च स्पर्शो वायुवृत्तिरिति धीः स्यात्, न त्वनुष्णाशीतस्पर्शो वायुरिति, स्पर्शाग्रहेऽपि शीतो वायुरिति प्रतीतेश्च।

यद्युत्कर्षरूपा जातिस्तदा द्रष्टव्यं। वस्तुतस्तु उत्कृष्टपरिमाणविषयत्वमेव तत्र प्रत्यक्षस्योत्कर्ष इति पूर्वोक्तैव मूलयुक्तिरनुसन्धेयेति, अत एवाग्रेऽपि तदुत्कर्षेणेत्यादिहेतुमुक्त्वा तथास्वरसेन हेत्वन्तरं वक्ष्यति, 'प्रकारेति।

'वायुरिति प्रत्यक्षस्पर्शाश्रयो वायुरित्यर्थः। यथाश्रुते भाग-

न च शीतद्रव्योपनायकत्वेनानुमिते वायौ तथा धीः, बाधकाभावात् विशेषदर्शने सत्यारोपाभावाच्च। अथाचाक्षुषत्वं स्पार्शनत्वे बाधकं चक्षुषानुपलभ्यमानस्य त्वचानुपलम्भादिति चेत्, तर्हि चक्षुरेव द्रव्यग्राहकन्त्वचा स्पर्शमात्रं प्रतीयेत वायाविव प्रत्यभिज्ञापि तद्वदेव। अथानुभवस्य दुरपह्नवत्वात् त्वचाश्रयसहित एव स्पर्श उपलभ्यते, तदा वायावपि तुल्यं। अथ दोषाभावे सति द्रव्यग्रहे तद्गतसङ्ख्यादिग्रहनियमात् वायौ सर्वथा तदग्रहान्न स प्रत्यक्ष इति चेत्। न। न च तावदयं व्यक्तौ नियमः, पृष्ठलग्नवस्त्रादेः सङ्ख्या-परिमाणाग्रहे त्वचा ग्रहणात्। तज्जातीये तु फूत्कारादौ सङ्ख्या-परिमाणादीनां वाय्वभिघातस्य च शरीरे प्रत्यक्षत्वात्। स्यादेतत् बहिरिन्द्रियजद्रव्यसाक्षात्कारे महत्त्वे सत्युद्भूतरूपवत्त्वं प्रयोजकं सति

बाधाविरहयोः प्रसङ्गात्। न च पक्षतावच्छेदकभेद एव ते समानप्रकारकविरोधिज्ञानस्यैव प्रतिबन्धकतया वायुपरमाणुत्वाद्यवच्छेदेन तदुभयाभावनिश्चयेऽपि वायुत्वाद्यवच्छेदेनोभयज्ञानादिति वाच्यम्। एवमपि तत्र तज्ज्ञानस्य भ्रमत्वेन तत्त्वनिर्णयाभावेन वादकथायामतत्त्वनिर्णयाय तद्धारकविशेषणोपादानस्य सर्व्वसिद्ध-

सम्भवे त्यागायोगात्। न तु अन्येन्द्रियग्राह्यविशेषगुणवत्त्वं कार्यमहत्त्वसमानाधिकरणविशेषगुणवत्त्वं वा, रसनगतपित्तद्रव्यस्योद्भूततिक्तरसस्य वायूपनीतसुरभिद्रव्यस्य च प्रत्यक्षतापत्तेः। मैवं। नोद्भूतरूपवत्वं तथा नयनगतपित्तद्रव्यस्य च प्रत्यक्षतापत्तेः। अस्तु वोद्भूतस्पर्शवत्त्वं तत्र तन्त्रं। न चैवं प्रभायामप्रत्यक्षत्वं, प्रभा हि तेजसो रूपं न द्रव्यं तदाश्रयतेजःप्रतीतिः प्रत्यक्षरूपलिङ्गाधीनैव यथा तवोष्मादिप्रतीतिः। तत्र संयोग-कर्मादि कथं प्रत्यक्षमिति चेत्, चान्द्र-सौर-दीपप्रभादौ तु न कथञ्चित्। इन्द्रनीलादिप्रभाया रूपस्य पूर्वदेशानुपलम्भेन उत्तरदेशोपलम्भेन लिङ्गेन तदाश्रयतेजःसंयोग-विभागाद्यनुमानमिति। त्वन्मये यथा त्वचा स्पर्शमात्रग्रहानन्तरं फूत्कारे संयोगा-

---

त्वादिति भावः। 'प्रत्यक्ष' इति स्वविशेष्यकप्रत्यक्षजनक इत्यर्थः, न तु विषयतया प्रत्यक्षजनक इत्यर्थः, विषयत्वस्य ज्ञानसमानकालीनत्वेन तज्जनकतानवच्छेदकतया तादृशसाध्यस्याप्रसिद्धेः। न च तत्रापि विशेष्यत्वपर्य्यन्तमधिकं, वायौ स्पर्श इत्यादिप्रतीतीनामपि सन्निकर्षप्रविष्टत्वेन वायुजन्यत्वात्। एवं विवक्षिते सामान्यलक्षणादिजन्यप्रत्यक्षविषयतया सिद्धसाधनं लौकिकत्वविशेषणे च तत्रागागत-

दीनां । एतेन धूम-वाष्पयोरस्पार्शनत्वेनोद्भूतस्पर्शा-
भावेऽपि[१] चाक्षुषत्वं अन्यथा तद्गतसंयोग-विभाग-
कर्मणां प्रत्यक्षता न स्यात् लिङ्गाभावादिति निरस्तं ।
न च वहिरिन्द्रिययोग्यानेकविशेषगुणवत्त्वं तन्त्रं, तत्र
त्रसरेणु-प्रभयोरप्रत्यक्षतापत्तेः गौरवाच्च । नन्वेवं विनि-
गमकाभावादुभयोरपि तथात्वमस्तु तथापि वायुर-
प्रत्यक्ष इति चेत्, एवं वहिरिन्द्रियजद्रव्यसाक्षात्कारे
चाक्षुषत्वे स्पार्शनप्रत्यक्षत्वे च प्रत्येकमुद्भूतरूपवत्त्वे
सत्युद्भूतस्पर्शवत्त्वं प्रयोजकं पर्य्यवस्यतीति गौरवं ।
मम तु चाक्षुषत्वे उद्भूतरूपवत्त्वं स्पर्शनत्वे उद्भूत-
स्पर्शवत्त्वं, यस्य विशेषे प्रयोजकत्वं तस्यानुगतेन रूपेण

गोचरसाक्षात्कारहेतुसन्निकर्षाजन्यत्वपरत्वेऽप्रसिद्धिः । चोद्भावसन्नि-
कर्षजन्यत्वपरत्वे च विशेषणव्यावृत्त्या प्रसिद्धिरित्यादिदोषानवकाश
इति भावः । 'प्रत्यक्षेति, प्रत्यक्षस्वरूपयोग्यस्पर्शाश्रयत्वादिति भावः ।
फलोपधानपरे प्रत्यक्षपदे अप्रयोजकता तस्य प्रत्यक्षजनकतानव-
च्छेदकत्वात् समानकालीनस्यातथात्वात् । तद्योग्यता तु महत्त्व-
समानाधिकरणोद्भूतस्पर्शाश्रयत्वेनेत्यतोऽप्ये तमेव हेतुमाह, 'महत्त्व-
इति । न चैवमुभयोरेकार्थत्वेन पौनरुक्त्यम्, उपाधिभेदेन भेदात् ।

---

(१) चानुद्भूतस्पर्शवत्त्वेऽपीति क० ।

सामान्यप्रयोजकत्वमिति द्रव्यग्राहकबहिरिन्द्रियव्यवस्थापकोद्भूतविशेषगुणवत्त्वं सामान्यप्रयोजकमिति लाघवं। विशेषस्य सामान्यस्य च भिन्नप्रयोज्यत्वनियमात् नैकं प्रयोजकं। अथ वायुर्यदि बहिरिन्द्रियजन्यसाक्षात्कारविषयद्रव्यं स्पार्शनसाक्षात्कारविषयद्रव्यं वा स्यात् उद्भूतरूपः स्यात्। न चैवं तस्मात् तथा, तादृशसाक्षात्कारविषयद्रव्यस्य रूपजनकत्वनियमादिति चेत्। न। रूपवत्समवेतत्वेन हि द्रव्यस्य रूपजनकत्वं न तु तादृशसाक्षात्कारविषयद्रव्यत्वेन तस्य रूप-

---

न च वायुत्र्यणुके व्यभिचारः, उद्भूतत्वस्य फलबलकल्प्यत्वेन निमित्तभेदनिबन्धनत्वेन च तथोद्भूतस्पर्शाभावात्। न चाश्रयत्वप्रवेशवैयर्थ्यं, एकाधिकरणकावच्छेदकद्वयसम्भव एव तदवतारात्। अत एव यन्निष्ठेत्यादि सार्थकताबीजं वक्ष्यति। न चैवं धूमवत्त्वादित्यपि कथायां प्रयुज्येत, धूमवत्त्वहेतुत्वे तस्येष्टत्वात् इति वक्ष्यते इति भावः। 'साधनेति साधनैकदेशेत्यर्थः, स्पर्शवत्त्वमात्रेणैव व्यभिचारवारणे शेषवैयर्थ्यादिति[२]। अथ यद्यपि रूपवत्त्वमेवोपाधिरुद्भूतत्ववैयर्थ्यात्[३]। तथापि तस्याप्रयोजकतायामुद्भूतरूपत्वावच्छेदेन जन-

---

(१) यन्निष्ठेत्यादि सार्थकतानियामकमिति ख०।

(२) स्पर्शवत्त्वमात्रेणैव व्यभिचारवारणादिति क०।

(३) उद्भूतत्वे वैयर्थ्यापातादिति ख०।

जननोत्तरकालीनत्वात् । घटो यदि चक्षुरितरेन्द्रियग्राह्यद्रव्यं स्यात् अरूपमस्पर्शमचाक्षुषादि स्यात्, त्वगिन्द्रियं यदि द्रव्यग्राहकवहिरिन्द्रियं स्यात् रूपवत् स्यात् स्पर्शग्राहकं वा न स्यात् रूपग्राहि वा स्यात् चक्षुर्वत् । न चैवं तस्मान्न तथेति, घटोपि न त्वगिन्द्रियग्राह्यः स्यात् तद्गतसङ्ख्यादिज्ञानं फूत्कारादाविवेति स्यात् स्पृशामीत्यनुव्यवसायश्च घटवद्वायावपि । अथ स्पार्शनत्वे उद्भूतस्पर्शवदुद्भूतं रूपमपि तन्त्रं उद्भूतरूपवत्त्वे चाक्षुषत्ववत् स्पार्शनत्वदर्शनादिति चेत् । न । उद्भूतरूपवत्त्वे सत्यपि प्रभायां न स्पार्शनत्वमिति उद्भूतस्पर्शस्यावश्यकत्वेनोद्भूतरूपस्यान्यथा-

---

कत्वात् । कार्य्य-कारणभाव एव तर्कः प्रतीकार इत्युपजीव्यत्वात् प्रथमोपस्थितत्वाच्च स एवोपाधिरुपन्यस्तः । अत एव व्यर्थविशेषणतापि नेति भावः ।

उद्भूतपदं प्रत्यक्षपरं तथाच समव्याप्तोपाध्यभिप्रायेणेदमित्यन्ये ।

'स्पार्शनेति, स्वव्यवस्थापकगुणपुरस्कारेणैव द्रव्ये चक्षुरादीनां प्रवृत्तिरिति स्वव्यवस्थापकगुणयोग्यतायास्तन्त्रत्वमिति चाक्षुषत्वे रूपमस्तु तन्त्रं कुतस्पार्शनत्वेऽपीति भावः । ननु स्वव्यवस्थापकगुणमादायैव प्रवर्त्ततां, न चैतावता अयोग्ये स्वव्यवस्थापकविशेषगुणयोग्यता तत्प्रवृत्तिहेतुः, इत्यतः अन्वय-व्यतिरेकमेव मानमाह, 'त्वगिति ।

सिद्धत्वात्। न ह्युद्भूतस्पर्शे सत्युद्भूतरूपाभावात् स्पार्शनत्वाभावः। नन्वेवं स्पर्शगत उद्भवः कारणमस्तु न तु रूपमकारणमिति चेत्, तथापि स्पर्शस्तदुद्भवश्च कारणं न तु रूपमपि तस्मिन् द्वये सति तदभावेन तदभावादर्शनात्। वस्तुतो रूप-स्पर्शगते उद्भवत्वजाती कारणतावच्छेदिके न तु कारणे इति। उच्यते। द्रव्यस्य स्पार्शनत्वे उद्भूतस्पर्शमात्रं न तन्त्रं निदाघोष्मणि वायू-

---

नन्विन्द्रियजद्रव्यसाक्षात्कार इव बहिरिन्द्रियजद्रव्यसाक्षात्कारेऽपि नैकं किञ्चिदनुगतं कारणं भवेत् अतआह, 'सतीति, तत्रासम्भवात्तदभाव इह तु सम्भवतोऽपि त्यागो नोचित इति भावः। ननु सम्भवमात्रेणैवात्यागे अन्येन्द्रियेत्यादिद्वयमप्यस्तु नियामकमत आह, 'न त्विति, तथा च तयोरसम्भव एवेति भावः। इह प्रथमे विशेषपदोपादानस्वरमे समानाधिकरणेत्यादिपदोपादानस्य प्रयोजकत्वाभाय। न हि स्वव्यवस्थापकगुणयोगित्वं तादृशगुणवत्त्वं वा तत्तदिन्द्रियप्रवृत्तौ तन्त्रं, अतो अन्येन्द्रिय ग्राह्यस्वव्यवस्थापकगुणवत्त्वं कार्य्यमहत्त्वसमानाधिकरणतादृशगुणवत्त्वस्योपात्तं, विशेषगुणपदस्य अन्येन्द्रियव्यवस्थापकगुणपरमिति[१] बोद्धव्यम्। 'प्रत्यक्षतापत्तेरिति, न चेष्टापत्तिः, महत्तमसङ्ख्यादेः प्रत्यक्षत्वापातात्[२]। 'अस्तु वेति वस्तुतोबहिरिन्द्रियज-

---

(१) स्वव्यवस्थापकगुणपरमितीति ख०।

(२) महत्तमसङ्ख्यादिप्रत्यक्षतापत्तेरित्यर्थं इति ख०।

पनीतशीतोष्णद्रव्ये च प्रत्यक्षत्वेन तद्गतसङ्ख्या-परिमाण-संयोग-विभाग-कर्मणां प्रत्यक्षत्वप्रसङ्गात्। योग्यव्यक्तिवृत्तित्वेन तेषां योग्यतया द्रव्यग्राहकसामग्रीग्राह्यत्वावधारणात्। न चोष्मादिजातीये दोषाभावेऽपि घटादाविव करपरामर्शे कदाचित् केनापि सङ्ख्या गृह्यते, तथोद्भूतरूपवत्त्वमात्रस्य तथात्वे

द्रव्यप्रत्यक्षेऽनुगतं रूपं नास्त्येव यदि च सति सम्भव इत्यादिन्यायात् स्वीक्रियेत तदोद्भूतस्पर्शवत्त्वमेवास्त्वित्यर्थः। 'यथेति, लभ्यत इति शेषः। 'एतेन' प्रभाप्रत्यक्षत्वेनेत्यर्थः, 'पर्य्यवस्यतीति विशेषौ प्रति रूप-स्पर्शयोः सामान्यसामग्र्यपेक्षणात् त्रिष्वप्युभयोर्व्रजस्य प्रयोजकत्वं पर्य्यवसितं न तूभयत्वेन विशेषयोरपि प्रयोजकत्वमित्यर्थः। ननु ममैकमेव त्रिषु प्रयोजकत्वमिति लाघवं तव तु त्रिषु त्रीणि प्रयोजकानीति गौरवमत आह, 'विशेषस्येति तथाच तल्लाघवं विरोधाद्धेयमित्यर्थः।

'स्पार्शनत्व इति, यद्यपि वहिरिन्द्रियजन्यद्रव्यसाक्षात्कारविषयत्वे तत्तत्त्वं स्पार्शनत्वे तूद्भूतस्पर्शवत्त्वमेव, तथापि सामान्यसामग्रीसापेक्षा विशेषसामग्रीति स्पार्शनत्वेऽपि तत्प्रयोजकत्वमुक्तं। वस्तुतस्तु स्पार्शनपदं वहिरिन्द्रियजन्यद्रव्यप्रत्यक्षपरमेव(१) मन्तव्यम्। 'दोषाभाव इति, पृष्ठलग्नवस्त्रादौ(२) दोष एव प्रतिबन्धकोऽत एवाभिमुख्ये पुनस्तत्रैव

---

(१) स्पार्शनत्वपदं वहिरिन्द्रियजन्यप्रत्यक्षविषयत्वपरमेवेति ख०।

(२) पृष्ठनिष्ठवस्त्रादाविति ख०।

चान्द्राद्युद्योतस्य नयनगतपित्तद्रव्यस्य च प्रत्यक्षत्वे तद्गतसङ्ख्याग्रहोऽपि स्यात्। न च घटादाविव निपुणं निभालयन्तोऽपि तद्गतसङ्ख्याद्वित्वादि हस्तवितस्त्यादि-परिमाणं कर्म वा वीक्षामहे, इत्येकैकव्यभिचारादिविनिगमकाभावादुभयमपि बहिरिन्द्रियद्रव्यप्रत्यक्षत्वे प्रयोजकमिति वायुरप्रत्यक्षः। न चैवमपसिद्धान्तः, पीतः शङ्ख इत्यादौ नयनपित्तपीतिमैव गृह्यते न तु पित्तद्रव्यं विभक्तावयवत्वात् प्रभायामिव तेजस इति टीकाकृतामभिधानादिति नवीनाः।

सङ्ख्याद्यग्रहात् दोषः प्रतिबन्धकोऽपि कल्पनीय इति भावः। 'नवीना इत्यस्वरसोद्भावनन्तदीजन्तूभयप्रयोजकतायां गौरवमेव द्रष्टव्यम्। 'तस्मादिति, नन्वेवं चन्द्र-तारादौ(१) सङ्ख्योपलम्भापत्तिः, किञ्च रूपवत्त्वस्य बहिरिन्द्रियजद्रव्यप्रत्यक्षप्रयोजकत्वे तस्यैव तथात्वचाक्षुषत्वप्रयोजकत्वे सामान्य-विशेषयोर्भिन्नप्रयोजकतानियमो भज्येतेति। मैवं पश्चिकाष्ठादिगतिप्रत्यक्षान्यथानुपपत्त्योद्भूतस्य(२) प्रत्यक्षताप्रयोजकत्वे सङ्ख्याद्यग्रहस्य दोषनिबन्धनत्वस्थितौ विष्वग्विसारिजातीयसमुदायादेरेव(३) दोषत्वव्यवस्थितेः सामान्य-विशेषयोः प्रयोजकभेद एव

---

(१) चन्द्रप्रभादाविति ख०।
(२) उद्भूतरूपस्येति ख०।
(३) विष्वग्विसारिस्वरूपजातीयसमवायादेरेवेति ख०।

सम्प्रदायविदस्तु चलति पक्षिकाण्डादौ पूर्वदेश-विभागोत्तरदेशसंयोगयोः प्रत्यक्षता न स्यात् पूर्वोत्तर-देशस्य प्रभामण्डलस्यानुद्भूतस्पर्शत्वेनाप्रत्यक्षत्वात्। तथाच परेषां चलतीतिप्रतीतिरपि तल्लिङ्गिका न स्यात्। अस्माकमपि चन्द्र-तारादौ संयोग-विभाग-लिङ्गकगत्यनुमानं न स्यात्। न च पूर्वोत्तरदेशे उप-लम्भानुपलम्भाभ्यां संयोग-विभागावनुमाय ताभ्यामेव गत्यनुमानं, पूर्वोत्तरदेशयोरप्रत्यक्षत्वेन लिङ्गासिद्धेः। तस्मादुद्भूतरूपवत्त्वं तत्र प्रयोजकमिति वायुर-प्रत्यक्षः। ननु शीतो वायुरित्यारोपो न स्यार्शनः विशेष्यस्यायोग्यत्वात्। न च प्रमायान्तथा, सामान्ये बाधकाभावात्। नाप्यनुमानोपनीते वायौ त्वगिन्द्रि-योपनीतः शीतारोपः शीतद्रव्याभेदारोपो वा, मनसा

सामान्ये उद्भूतरूपवत्त्वस्य चाक्षुषत्वे रूपग्राहकसामग्रीसमावेशस्य प्रयोजकत्वात् । अत एव न तमसि सुवर्णं प्रत्यक्षं ।

द्रव्यत्वेनैव गुणं प्रति, संयोगादिकस्य विशेषं प्रति प्रयोजकत्वदर्श-नात् भिन्नप्रयोजकतानियम एव[१] नास्तीत्यन्ये ।

---

(१) गुणत्वसामान्यधर्मावच्छिन्नं प्रति द्रव्यत्वेन प्रयोजकत्वमिव संयोग-त्वादिविशेषधर्मावच्छिन्नं प्रत्यपि तेनैव रूपेण प्रयोजकत्वात् सामान्य-विशेषधर्मावच्छिन्नं प्रति विभिन्नधर्मावच्छिन्नप्रयोजकतानियमो न प्रामा-णिक इति भावः ॥

तल्लिङ्गस्पर्शादिचतुष्कस्याग्रहणात् शीतस्पर्शस्यातल्लिङ्गत्वात्। न च शीतद्रव्योपनायकत्वेनानुमिते वायौ मनसा शीतारोपः, शीतानाश्रयत्वेनानुमिते वायौ तदनारोपात्। नापि पीतः शङ्ख इति वद्बहिरिन्द्रियजन्योऽयं भ्रमः, येनानुमानिकविशेषग्रहेऽपि[१] दोषमाहात्म्याद्भवेत् शीतद्रव्योपनयनजनकप्रश्वासीमविदुषोऽपि शीतो वायुरिति प्रत्ययाच्च। नापि लिङ्गाभासजन्यानुमितिरूपोभ्रमः, तदप्रतीतेः शीतस्पर्शस्य वायुलिङ्गत्वेन भ्रमाविषयत्वात्। न च शीतस्पर्शानुमिते द्रव्ये स्मृतवाय्वभेदारोपः, वायुविशेष्यकशीतप्रत्ययात्। अत एव शीतस्पर्शोऽयं वायोरिति भ्रमशरीर-

---

यत्तु स्वव्यवस्थापकयोग्यगुणवत्त्वं प्रयोजकमित्युक्तं, तद्गौरवादेव न सम्भवतीत्युक्तरूपस्य लाघवाभिधानादेवार्थतः प्रत्युक्तम्।

'वायुलिङ्गत्वेति, एतच्च प्रकारान्तरानवतारेण प्राथमिकप्रत्ययमभिप्रेत्य, तदानीं वायोरनुपस्थित्या वायवीयत्वारोपस्यान्यथा असम्भवात्। यदा तु कुतश्चिल्लिङ्गात्कदाचिद्वायूपस्थितौ शीतो वायुरिति धीस्तदा तल्लिङ्गत्वारोपं विनैव शीतस्पर्शे वायवीयत्वमारोप्यते। न च वायोरन्यतोऽनुपस्थितिदशायां शीतस्पर्शस्य जलवृत्तितया गृहीतस्य व्यभिचारे स्फुरति कथं वायुलिङ्गत्वारोपोऽपीति वाच्यम्।

---

(१) आनुमानिकविशेषदर्शनेऽपीति ख०।

मपास्तं। न च स्वप्नविभ्रमवत् स्वोत्प्रेक्षितपदार्थसंसर्गारोपवच्च मानसोऽयं, त्वगिन्द्रियव्यापारानुविधानादिति। उच्यते। यथा वायुवैधर्म्येण जलवृत्तितया गृहीतस्य शीतस्पर्शस्य वायावारोपो दिङ्मोहवद्दोषमाहात्म्यात् तथा शीतस्पर्शे वायुलिङ्गत्वारोपाद्वायवीयत्वानुमानं। न चैवं शीतो वायुरिति प्रतीतिः[१] न स्यादिति वाच्यं। शीतोऽयं वायवीय इति ज्ञानानन्तरं शीतोऽयं वायुरिति च मनसारोपात् अनुष्णो वायुरिति वत्। अथ त्वग्व्यापारानन्तरं कथं वायुर्वातीति प्रतीतिः तल्लिङ्गसंयोग-विभागयोरप्रत्यक्षत्वात्। न च शरीरे वाय्वभिघात एव तल्लिङ्गं, अभिघातस्य संयोगत्वेनाप्रत्यक्षत्वादिति चेत्। न।

तदानीं जलस्यानुपस्थितत्वेन[२] शीतोऽयं पृथिव्यादित्रयान्यवृत्ति तदवृत्तित्वे सति वृत्तिमत्त्वात् इत्यनुमानाभासस्यैव तल्लिङ्गत्वारोपपदेन विवक्षितत्वादिति दिक्। 'ज्ञानेनेति ज्ञानं पृथिव्याद्यष्टद्रव्यान्यद्रव्यवृत्तीत्येवं प्रकारेणेत्यर्थः। ज्ञाने आत्मीयत्वं स्वात्मीयत्वं एतच्छरीरावच्छिन्नात्मवृत्तित्वमिति यावत्। 'एवमिति, न चानुभवकस्वरः, स्वशरीरावच्छिन्नात्मवृत्तितानुमानं हि शरीरान्तरावच्छेदे-

---

(१) इति धीरिति ख०।

(२) अनुपलम्भबाधेनेति ख०।

अभिघातजन्यसुख-दुःखविशेषेणाभिघातमुन्नीय तस्य स्पर्शवद्वेगवज्जन्यत्वमनुमाय वेगेन कर्मानुमानात्। एवं प्रणालीमविदुषस्तत्प्रत्ययासिद्धेः। अथ वायुः शीतो वातीति कथं विशिष्टवैशिष्ट्यप्रतीतिरेका शीतविशिष्ट-प्रतीतेर्मानसत्वेन कर्मप्रतीतेः[१] आनुमानिकत्वेन जातिसङ्करप्रसङ्गादिति चेत्। न। शीतविशिष्टत्वेन स्मृते वायौ कर्मानुमानाद्विशिष्टवैशिष्ट्यं न तूभयं विशेषणमेकदा भासते। न चैवं कल्पनागौरवं दोषाय, प्रत्यक्षत्वे बलवद्बाधकसत्त्वात्[२]। एवं बहिरिन्द्रिय-जद्रव्यप्रत्यक्षत्वे उद्भूतरूपवत्त्वस्य प्रयोजकत्वे व्यव-

---

मानुपलभ्यमानतया ग्राह्यम्। न च योऽहं सोऽहमिति प्रत्यभिज्ञान-काले शरीरान्तरोपस्थितिनियमः, येन लिङ्गज्ञानादौ दृष्टप्रणालीनि-यमः स्यादिति न किञ्चिदेतत्। 'न च साधनेति, अस्मन्मते उभयो-रुद्भूतसाध्यव्यभिचारादिदमुदाहृतम्, न तु पार्थिवादिपरमाणुषु व्यभिचारवारणाय, उद्भूतपदेन प्रत्यक्षयोग्यत्वेन परमाणुषु तदस-त्त्वात् अन्यथा साधनावच्छिन्नत्वेऽपि वायुपरमाणौ व्यभिचारतादव-स्थ्यात् इति दिक्। 'किञ्चेति, यद्यप्युद्भूतस्पर्शवत्त्वमतैः स्पार्शनत्वे तन्त्रमुच्यते न वाह्येन्द्रियग्राह्यत्वे[१] इत्यनुक्तोपालम्भः, तथापि रूप-

---

(१) कर्मविशेषप्रतीतेरिति ख०।

(२) बलवद्विरोधादिति ख०।

(१) वाह्यप्रत्यक्षत्व इति ख०।

स्थिते प्रत्यक्षत्वसाध्यकानुमाने पक्षधर्मावच्छिन्नस्य साध्यस्य साधनावच्छिन्नस्य वा व्यापकमुद्भूतरूपवत्त्वमुपाधिः। न च विशिष्टस्य व्यभिचार-व्यतिरेकयोः साधनेऽर्थान्तरं, विशेष्यव्यभिचार-व्यतिरेकसिद्धिपर्य्यवसानादित्युपाधौ वक्ष्यामः। अथ वायुवदात्मापि न प्रत्यक्षः द्रव्यप्रत्यक्षत्वे उद्‌भूतरूपवत्त्वस्य तन्त्रत्वात्[१]। न च लिङ्गज्ञानं विनैवाहं जानामीति प्रत्ययात् न लैङ्गिकत्वं, ज्ञानमविदुषो जानामीति विशिष्टप्रत्ययाभावेन ज्ञानस्य लिङ्गत्वात्। न च घटमहं जानामीति वर्त्तमानप्रत्ययो न स्यात् घटज्ञानस्यानुमितिपूर्वतृतीयक्षणे विनाशादिति वाच्यं। स्थूलसमयो-

---

वत्त्वस्य तन्त्रतायां सम्भव इत्येव न्यायः स च सर्व्वसाधारण इति नियामकत्वकल्पनायां विनिगमकाभावोऽनियामकत्वे सर्व्वत्वे गमना-द्व्यभिचारी वा न्यायः स्यादिति तस्यागमनव्युत्पादनमिदं न तु तदुक्तपरिहार इति भावः। 'प्रभावत्' मण्यादिप्रभावत। ननु वस्तु-वत्सजातीयग्रहणकृतमग्रहणं खल्वभिभव इत्यन्धकारे सजातीयग्रहण-च्छायायान्तदुपलभ्येतेत्यत आह, 'अभिभवस्येति, लाघवादिति भावः। ननु प्रभारूपतेजोऽन्तरकल्पने गौरवं तदीयालोकव्यभानापत्तेश्चेत्यस्व-रसादाह, 'यदेति, यद्यपि भास्वरत्वेऽनभिभवाभिधानमप्रसक्तप्रति-

---

(१) प्रयोजकत्वादिति ख० ।

पाणिमादाय वर्त्तमानप्रत्ययात्, यथा कुलाले चेष्टादर्शनेन करोतीत्यनुमितिरिति उच्यते। योऽहं घटमद्राक्षं सोऽहं घटं स्पृशामीत्यभेदप्रत्यभिज्ञानादात्मा प्रत्यक्षः। न चैतत्स्पर्शनेन्द्रियजन्यज्ञानाश्रयोऽहं तद्दर्शनज्ञानाश्रयाभिन्नः मदीयाहंप्रत्ययविषयत्वात् तद्दर्शनज्ञानाश्रयवदित्यात्माभेदप्रत्यय इति वाच्यं। मद्दंशस्याप्रत्यक्षत्वेनानुमानलिङ्गासिद्धेः। न च ज्ञानेनात्मानुमानं ततस्तत्र ज्ञाने आत्मीयत्वानुमानं ततो मदीयाहंप्रत्ययविषयत्वज्ञानमात्मनीति वाच्यं। एवं प्रणालीमविदुषोऽपि योऽहं सोऽहमिति प्रत्ययात्। न च वायौ प्रत्यभिज्ञानमस्ति, सदागतिमत्त्वेन गतस्य पुनरज्ञानात्। स एव पुनः पुरोवात इति प्रतीतेः तज्जातीयानुमितिरूपत्वात्। तस्माद्वायुर्बहिरिन्द्रियाप्रत्यक्षः नीरूपद्रव्यत्वात् आकाशवत्। न च साधनाव-

---

षेधः परप्रकाशकत्वव्यञ्जकस्य तस्य तदन्वय-परव्यतिरेकानुविधायित्वाग्रहस्याग्रहायाभिभवाकल्पनात् कारणाभावेन कार्य्याभावे प्रतिबन्धकाकल्पनादिति तथापि शुक्लत्वसहचारितामात्रेण प्रसज्यप्रतिषेधो द्रष्टव्यः। व्यञ्जग्रहादिदमुपलक्षणं परप्रकाशकत्वव्यञ्जकाग्रहादित्यपि द्रष्टव्यं। एतत्सर्व्वमग्रहणपर्य्यन्तमभिभवपदार्थमुपेत्य समाहितम्। वस्तुतस्तु बलवत्सजातीयसम्बन्ध एवाभिभव इति तदसम्बन्ध एवान-

च्छिन्नसाध्यव्यापकमुद्भूतस्पर्शानाश्रयत्वमुपाधिः, उद्भूतस्पर्शस्य तत्राहेतुत्वेनोपाधेः साध्याव्यापकत्वात् । किञ्चोद्भूतस्पर्शवत्त्वस्य वहिरिन्द्रियजन्यद्रव्यसाक्षात्कारप्रयोजकत्वे सुवर्णरूपन्तेजोद्रव्यं प्रत्यक्षं न स्यात् प्रभावत् तस्यानुद्भूतस्पर्शवत्त्वात् रूपन्तु तस्योद्भूतमेव । किन्तु उपष्टम्भकपीतरूपाभिभूतं । अभिभवश्च बलवत्सजातीयसम्बन्धः । एवमन्धकारे पीताग्रहणेऽप्यभिभवः । न चैवमन्धकारे सुवर्णोपलम्भापत्तिरभिभूतस्यापि तैजसेा ग्रहात्, न च तेजसि तेजोऽन्तरं व्यञ्जकं, इति वाच्यं । रूपे गृह्यमाण एव चक्षुषा द्रव्यग्रहात्, सुवर्णरूपमभिभवादेव नोपलभ्यते, उपष्टम्भकरूपञ्चालोकाभावात् । अथ यथा अरुण-कपिलादिरूपाभिभूतमपि वह्निरूपं परं आत्मानञ्च प्रका-

---

भिभवः, अतस्तादृशस्यैव व्यञ्जकत्वम्, तथाच तत्सम्बन्धः प्रतिबन्धकस्तदभावः कारणमिति पर्य्यवसितोऽर्थः । तथाचारुण-कपिलाद्यभिभूतस्य वह्निरूपस्य ग्राहकत्वेन सुवर्णरूपस्याग्राहकत्वेन च किञ्चित्सजातीयसम्बन्धः प्रतिबन्धकः किञ्चित्सम्बन्धोनेति कल्प्यते(१) । अग्रहणगर्भे ह्यभिभवे न अभिभवो ग्रहणं वाच्यम् । तथाचानभिभू-

---

(१) किञ्चित्सम्बन्धो न तथेत्येव फलबलात् कल्प्यत इति ख० ।

श्यति तथा कनकमपि प्रकाशेत प्रकाशयेच्चेति चेत्। न। तत्र ह्यभिभूतरूपवह्निसम्बद्धानभिभूतरूपा वह्निमध्याद्व्यापिनी[१] प्रभैव व्यञ्जिका। यद्वा वह्नौ रूपभास्वरत्वे नाभिभूते किन्तु शुक्लत्वमात्रं, सुवर्णे तु रूपमभिभूतन्तेन तद्गतशुक्लत्व-भास्वरत्वे अनभिभूते अपि व्यक्त्यग्रहान्न गृह्येते इति फलबलात्कल्प्यते। न च पीतिमगुरुत्वाश्रयातिरिक्तं तदसिद्धं, अस्ति हि सुवर्णस्यात्यन्तानलसंयोगेऽपि पीतं रूपं न तद्विजातीयं, तदनुपपन्नमसति द्रवद्रव्यसम्बन्धे, पार्थिवेऽत्यन्ताग्निसंयोगस्य पूर्वरूपविजातीयरूपजनकत्वनियमात्। जलसम्बन्धे तदपगमे च पटादौ दाहादाहदर्शनात्।

तद्रूपं तेजोग्राहकं गृह्यमाणरूपन्तेजोग्राहकमिति पर्य्यवस्येत्। न चैतत् सम्भवति, तेजोरूपस्य रूपाग्राहकत्वात् गौरवाद्विषय-तेजसोर्युगपदेव रूपग्रहाच्च। किन्तु योग्यमस्तीति गृह्यते न तु ग्रहणस्यापि विषयग्रहणे विनियोगः। किञ्चैवं उद्भूतरूपमप्यधिकं स्यात् अनुद्भूतस्य ग्रहासम्भवादिति वयम्। ननु यत्रात्यन्ताग्निसंयोगेन समानजातीयमेव रूपमारभ्यते भस्मादौ तत्र व्यभिचारः स्यादिति पीतरूपान्तर्भावेण विशिष्यैव हेत्वन्तरमाह, 'यद्वे'ति, पीते ह्यग्निसंयो-

---

(१) वह्न्यादिमध्यपातिनीति ख॰।

तदिदं ध्मायमानं कनकं यद्यत्यन्ताग्निसंयोगि-पार्थिवत्वे सति विजातीयरूपप्रतिबन्धकद्रवद्रव्यसंयुक्तं न स्यात् पूर्वरूपविजातीयरूपवत्स्यात् वह्निसम्बद्धघटवत्। अन्यथा पार्थिवं न स्यात् जलं वा स्यात् अग्निसंयोगि वा न स्यात्। तदयं प्रयोगः। अत्यन्ताग्निसंयोगि पीतं विजातीयरूपप्रतिबन्धकद्रवद्रव्यसंयुक्तं अत्यन्ताग्निसंयोगित्वे सति पूर्वरूपविजातीयरूपानधिकरणपार्थिवत्वात् जलमध्यस्थिताग्निसंयुक्तपीतपटवत्। यद्वा पीतं सुवर्णं पीतरूपातिरिक्तरूपोत्पत्तिप्रतिबन्धकद्रवद्रव्यसंयुक्तं नक्तन्दिवमग्निसंयोगेऽपि पीतरूपातिरिक्तरूपानाश्रय-

---

गात् विजातीयमेव रूपमुत्पद्यत इति नियमादेवमुक्तं, आत्यन्तिकत्वं सावधितया अननुगतमतस्तदनुगमार्थं नक्तन्दिवेत्युक्तं। पार्थिवत्वस्याप्य हेतावनुषञ्जनीयम्[1] ननु करकावत्सहजमेव द्रवत्वं[2] स्यादत आह, 'नैमित्तिके'ति, तथासत्यग्निसंयोगान्वय-व्यतिरेकानुविधानानुपपत्तिरिति भावः। 'तत्रापि' उपष्टम्भकरूपप्रतिबन्धकेऽपीत्यर्थः। एतस्यानुद्भूतगुणस्य पाके सत्युद्भूतगुणत्वनियमात् व्यञ्जनादौ पाक-

---

(१) एतेन 'पीतरूपातिरिक्तरूपानाश्रयपार्थिवत्वात्' इत्ययं क्वचिल्लिखित-मूलपुस्तकपाठो न समीचीनः।

(२) करकावत् प्रतिबद्धसहजद्रवत्वमिति ख०।

त्वात् तावत्पर्यन्तमग्निसंयुक्तजलमध्यस्थपीतपटवत्। न चाप्रयोजकत्वं, विरोधिद्रवद्रव्यसम्बन्धं विना पार्थिवेऽत्यन्ताग्निसंयोगस्य विजातीयरूपजनकत्वात्। तच्च द्रवद्रव्यं न जलं स्वाभाविकद्रवत्वानाश्रयत्वात्। न चानुद्भूतं तत्, शीतलशिलातले अग्निसंयोगाद्दाहदर्शनेनानुद्भूतद्रवत्वस्य दाहाविरोधित्वात् नैमित्तिकद्रवत्वाच्च। नापि तत एव पार्थिवत्वं, द्रुतपार्थिवस्य विजातीयरूपप्रतिबन्धकत्वे घृतादावपि तथात्वापत्तेः तथापि रूपपरावृत्तिप्रसङ्गाच्च। उपष्टम्भकस्यापि पार्थिवत्वेन विजातीयरूपाप्रतिबन्धकत्वात्। यद्यपि तेजोऽन्तरं न नैमित्तिकद्रवत्वाधिकरणं, नापि विजातीयरूपप्रतिबन्धकं, किन्तु तज्जनकं, तथापि प्रत्यक्षद्रव्यत्वेन तस्य रूपवत्त्वे पृथिवी-जलान्यत्वेन तैजसत्वात् धर्मिग्राहकमानसिद्धं तथात्वं, पीतभागद्रवत्वमप्यग्निसंयोगे न नश्यति द्रुततेजःप्रतिबन्धादेव जलमध्यस्थाग्निसंयुक्तघृतवदिति। अथ यदि द्रुततेजसो विजा-

---

जोद्भूतरसवति पाषाणादिभस्मनि पाकजगन्धस्य दर्शनेन निश्चितादृष्टत्वमेयं। अन्यथा तस्यानुद्भूतरूपस्य अनुद्भूतरूपपरावृत्तौ दृष्टापादानस्यापि सम्भवादित्यवधेयं। ननूपष्टम्भकेनैव तद्विजातीयं

तीयरूपप्रतिबन्धकत्वं तदा जलस्थपटवत् द्रुतसुवर्ण-मध्यस्थितपटादेरपि रूपपरावृत्तिर्न स्यादिति चेत् । न । लोके सुवर्णत्वेनानुभूयमाने पीतद्रव्ये अविनि-र्भागवर्त्तिन्युपष्टम्भके द्रुतन्तेजो विजातीयं रूपं प्रति-बध्नाति नान्यच्च तथैवान्वय-व्यतिरेकात् । तर्ह्युपष्टम्भक-त्वमनुभवसिद्धं सुवर्णस्येत्यावश्यकत्वात् । तस्यैव स्वरूप-परावृत्तौ प्रतिबन्धकत्वमस्तु कृतन्दृष्टविजातीयतेजः-कल्पनयेति चेत् । न । उपष्टम्भकमात्रे हि विजातीय-रूपप्रतिबन्धकस्वभावत्वं द्रुततेजसो धर्म्मिग्राहकमान-सिद्धत्वात् तस्य तेनैव रूपेण सिद्धेः । यदि द्रुतन्तेजो रूपपरावृत्तिप्रतिबन्धकं स्यात् पटादिरूपपरावृत्तिमपि प्रतिबध्नीयादिति तर्कस्य तद्विपर्य्ययस्य च सिद्ध्यसिद्धि-व्याहतत्वात्[१] । अनुभूयमानसुवर्णस्य च उपष्टम्भक-रूपपरावृत्तिप्रतिबन्धकस्वभावत्वं[२] न धर्म्मिग्राहक-मानादन्यतो वा सिद्धं येन पार्थिवे असति विरोधिद्र-

---

रूपं प्रतिबध्यतामत आह, 'उपष्टम्भकस्येति, 'तथापीति। ननु पृथि-व्यन्यत्ववत् तेजोऽन्यत्वस्यापि सम्भवः। न च पार्थिवरूपप्रतिबन्धकत्व-

---

(१) सिद्ध्यसिद्धिपराहतत्वादिति ख० ।

(२) स्वरूपपरावृत्तिप्रतिबन्धकस्वभावत्वमिति ख० ।

वद्द्रव्यसम्बन्धे अग्निसंयोगस्य रूपपरावर्त्तकत्वमन्वय-व्यतिरेकसिद्धं परिभूयेतेत्याचार्य्याः ।

नवीनास्तु अत्यन्ताग्निसंयोगेनानुच्छिद्यमानप्रत्यक्ष-द्रवत्वाधिकरणं तैजसं जल-पृथिवीभ्यामन्यत्वे सति रूपवत्त्वात् वह्निवत् । न चासिद्धिः, प्रत्यक्षद्रव्यत्वाधि-करणत्वेन[१] तस्य रूपित्वात्[२] । न च तज्जलं, सांसिद्धिक-द्रवत्वानाश्रयत्वात्[३] नैमित्तिकद्रवत्वाधारत्वात् स्नेह-शून्यत्वाद्वा लाक्षावत् । स्नेहे सति स्नेह-द्रवत्वाधीनसंग्र-हप्रसङ्गात् । न च[४] पार्थिवं, अत्यन्ताग्निसंयोगेऽप्यनुच्छि-द्यमानं यद्द्रवत्वं तदधिकरणत्वात् जलपरमाणुवत् । अस-ति विरोधिद्रवद्द्रव्यसम्बन्धे इति विशेषणान्तेन कथ्यमान-

---

रूपमेवापार्थिवत्वे मानं, तेजोऽन्यत्वेऽपि तत्सम्भवात् । पृथिव्यन्तरे प्रतिबन्धकत्वादर्शनवत् तद्दर्शनस्यासत्त्वात् । अत्रैव तथात्वकल्पनं विशेषे यदि तदा पार्थिवविशेषतयैव तत् कल्प्यतामिति । मैवम् । उपष्टम्भ-कसुवर्णादिरूपं प्रति तेजोद्रवत्वेन प्रतिबन्धकत्वस्य लघुत्वात् तत्पा-र्थिवद्रवत्वेनोपष्टम्भकद्रवत्वेन च तत्तद्रूपं प्रति प्रतिबन्धकत्वे गौरवात्

---

(१) प्रत्यक्षद्रव्यत्वाधारत्वेनेति ख० ।

(२) रूपवत्त्वादिति ख० ।

(३) सांसिद्धिकद्रवत्वानाधारत्वादिति ख० ।

(४) चापीति ख० ।

जलस्थघृतेन न व्यभिचारः। न चाप्रयोजकत्वं, अत्यन्तानलसंयोगेन लाक्षादि-घृतादि-पृथिवीद्रवत्वोच्छेदे पृथिवीद्रवत्वत्वमेव प्रयोजकं असति बाधके अनुगतस्य प्रयोजकत्वे सम्भवति त्यागायोगात्। न च घृतद्रवत्वत्वादिकं, अननुगमात्। नापि नैमित्तिकद्रवत्वत्वं, द्रवत्वत्वमेववा, सुवर्णे द्रवत्वोच्छेदप्रसङ्गात्। अथापार्थिवमपि सांसिद्धिकद्रवत्वं तैले जन्यजलान्तरे चात्यन्ताग्निसंयोगादुच्छिद्यते अतोऽनुगतमेव तृणारणि-मणिन्यायेन द्रवत्वोच्छेदप्रयोजकमिति चेत्। न। पृथिवीद्रवत्वोच्छेदे पृथिवीद्रवत्वत्वं, जलद्रवत्वोच्छेदे जन्यजलद्रवत्वत्वं, द्रवत्वमात्रोच्छेदे च जन्यरसवद्द्रवत्वत्वं प्रयोजकं लाघवात्। एतेन विवादविषयः पृथिवी

प्रथमस्य प्रमाणसिद्धत्वादित्युक्तप्रायत्वात् इति भावः। 'द्रुततेजस इति, द्रवद्रव्यसम्बन्धत्वेन रूपपरावृत्तिप्रतिबन्धकत्वकल्पनात्, न तु स्वगुणप्रतिबन्धकत्वं गुणिनोविरोधादिति भावः। 'प्रत्यक्षद्रव्यत्वेति, न च प्रत्यक्षपदोपादानमधिकं, जलपरमाणौ भाग-बाधवारणात्[१] इति भावः। असतीत्यादिविशेषणमप्यत्र प्रयोज्यमनेन

---

(१) भाग-बाधवायकत्वादिति ख०।

नैमित्तिकद्रवत्वाश्रयत्वात् घृतवदिति सत्प्रतिपक्षत्वमपास्तं। अनुकूलतर्काभावेन अग्निसंयोगाद्द्रवत्वोच्छेदप्रसङ्गलक्षणप्रतिकूलतर्केण च हीनबलत्वात्। अथ नैमित्तिकद्रवत्वे पृथिवीत्वं समवायिकारणतावच्छेदकं असति बाधके त्यागायोगादिति चेत्। न। घटादावपि नैमित्तिकद्रवत्वप्रसङ्गात्[१]। न च घृतलाक्षादिषु पृथिवीत्वावान्तरं किञ्चिदेकमनुगतं नैमित्तिकद्रवत्वसमवायिकारणतावच्छेदकमस्ति। पृथिवीनियतनैमित्तिकद्रवत्वं कथमपृथिव्यामिति चेत्। न। तावत्तिर्य्यग्गमनोर्द्ध्वज्वलनवत्तज्जातिनियतं[२] घटादावभावात्। नापि पृथिवीत्वावान्तरजातिविशेषनियतं, घृतं विहाय लाक्षादिष्वपि भावात्। अथोपष्टम्भके पीतिमगुरुत्वाश्रये पार्थिवेऽत्यन्ताग्निसंयोगेनानुच्छि-

जलम्ब्रक्कथ्यमानघृते न बाध इत्यवधेयं। 'नवीनास्त्विति, अत्र नवीनत्वोपान्यासेऽस्वरसबीजं पीतिमगुरुत्वाश्रयस्य प्रत्यक्षसिद्धद्रवत्वापक्षव एव द्रष्टव्यमित्येके, अपरस्त्वाग्निसंयोगस्य नैमित्तिकद्रवत्वावच्छेदेनैव नाशकत्वं लाघवात् न तु पार्थिवद्रवत्वेनैव गौरवात् सुवर्णादावतिप्रसङ्गस्यासतौत्यादविशेषणेन स्वयमेव निरासादिति।

(१) तत्प्रसङ्गादिति ख०।
(२) तिर्य्यग्गमनोर्द्ध्वज्वलनवज्जातिनियतं तदिति ख०।

यमानद्रवत्वाधारत्वमनैकान्तिकं, न हि तेजोद्रवत्व-दशायान्तदद्रवमेवास्ते, पीतं द्रुतमिति प्रतीतेरिति चेत्। न। तत्र द्रवत्वाभावात्। पार्थिवद्रवत्वस्यात्यन्ताग्निसंयोगेनोच्छित्त्यापत्त्या बाधकेन द्रुतप्रतीतेर्भ्रमत्वात्। तर्हि तदा पीतं कठिनमेवोपलभ्येतेति चेत्। न। जलमध्यस्थितमसीक्षोदादेरिव तदवयवानां द्रवद्रव्यसम्बन्धेन प्रशिथिलसंयोगाश्रयत्वात्। न तु तेषां द्रवत्वं। न चैवं घृतादावपि तथा, द्रवत्वे तत्र बाधकाभावात्।

अन्ये तु उपष्टम्भके द्रवत्वमप्युत्पद्यत एव अनुभ

अत एवाचार्य्यमतेन न पौनरुक्त्यं। 'अन्ये त्वित्यादेरपि न पौनरुक्त्येनापि पार्थिवद्रवत्वावच्छेदेनोच्छेदाभ्युपगमात्। आचार्य्याणान्तु नैमित्तिकद्रवत्वावच्छेदेनैव तथाभ्युपगमः। नन्वाचार्य्यमतेऽप्येतस्य शेषे उपसंहारात् कथं ततोऽस्य भेदः, कथं वा अस्वरसः 'नवीना इति[१]। नैवम्। आचार्य्या हि नोपष्टम्भकद्रवत्वोच्छेदप्रतिबन्धकतयैव तेजोरूपं सुवर्णं साधयन्ति, किन्तु रूपादिप्रतिबन्धकत्वेन सिद्धे द्रुते तेजसि तस्यैव द्रवत्वोच्छेदप्रतिबन्धकत्वमपि कल्पयन्ति लाघवात्।

अन्ये तु[२] द्रवत्वोच्छेदप्रतिबन्धकतयैव द्रवद्रव्यं साधयन्तीति

---

(१) नव्यास्त्विति ख०।
(२) अपरे इति क०।

वस्य दुरपह्नवत्वात्। अत्यन्ताग्निसंयोगेन तदुच्छेदस्तु न भवति द्रवद्रव्यस्य तेजसः प्रतिबन्धकत्वात्। न चैवं द्रुततेजसि मानाभावः। तथाहि पीतन्द्रवत्वाधिकरणं द्रवत्वोच्छेदप्रतिबन्धकद्रवद्रव्यसंयुक्तं अत्यन्ताग्निसंयोगेऽप्यनुच्छिद्यमानद्रवत्वाधारपार्थिवत्वात् क्वथ्यमानजलमध्यस्थितघृतवत्। न चाप्रयोजककत्वं, अत्यन्ताग्निसंयोगेन विरोधिद्रवद्रव्यसम्बन्धासम्बन्धे पार्थिवद्रवत्वोच्छेदानुच्छेददर्शनात्। अथवा रूपवत्त्वे जलान्यत्वे च सति तैजसत्व-पार्थिवत्वसन्देहे विवादाध्यासितं द्रवत्वाधिकरणं तैजसं असति द्रवद्रव्यसंयोगे[१] अत्यन्ताग्निसंयोगेऽप्यनुच्छिन्नानित्यद्रवत्वाधारत्वात्[२] यन्नैवं तन्नैवं यथा जलं घृतं वेति व्यतिरेकी। न चासा-

---

भेदः, इदमेवास्वरसबीजम्। न हि पार्थिवरूपवत्त्वेनाग्निसंयोगनाश्यत्वं तावत् पार्थिवद्रवत्वेनापि तथा नाश्यत्वं शक्यकल्पनं, येनाप्रयोजकता न स्यादपार्थिवरूपवदपार्थिवद्रवत्वस्य तदानीमनुपस्थित्या पार्थिवत्वविशेषणायोगात्। न च जले द्रवत्वदर्शनाद्विशेषणोपादानं, तावता तस्याप्यग्निसंयोगनाश्यत्वदर्शनात्तत्साधारणजन्यद्रवत्वेनैवावच्छेदकेन तथा

---

(१) द्रवद्रव्यसम्बन्धे इति ख०।

(२) अनुच्छिद्यमानानित्यद्रवत्वाधिकरणत्वादिति ख०।

धारणं, अगृह्यमाणविशेषदशायां तस्य दोषत्वात्। तथाहि यथा साध्याभाववद्व्यावृत्तत्वेन पक्षे तस्य साध्यसाधकत्वं, तथा साध्यवद्व्यावृत्तत्वेन साध्याभावसाधकतापि स्यादिति सत्प्रतिपक्षोत्थापकतया तस्य दोषत्वं। न च साध्याभावसाधकस्य पृथिवीत्वसिद्धिपर्य्यवसायिनस्तुल्यबलत्वं, अनुकूलतर्काभावेन हीनबलत्वात्। यदीदं पार्थिवं स्यादसति विरोधिद्रवद्रव्यसम्बन्धे अत्यन्ताग्निसंयोगेनोच्छिद्यमानद्रवत्वाधिकरणं स्यात् तैलवदिति प्रतिकूलतर्केण हीनबलत्वात्। यदीदं असाधारणरूपवत्त्वे सति तैजसं न स्यात् पार्थिवं स्यात् यदि च पार्थिवं स्यादत्यन्ताग्निसंयोगेनोच्छिद्य-

---

कल्पनौचित्यात्, न तु तत्रापि रसवत्त्वविशेषणप्रवेशः[१]। तथाच सिद्धे द्रुततैजसे तादृशविशेषणान्तर्भावः, तदन्तर्भावेण गृहीते च कारणत्वे अप्रयोजकतापरीहार इत्यन्योन्याश्रयः। आचार्य्यमते तु मानान्तरसिद्धे द्रुततैजसे तद्वारकविशेषणान्तर्भावेण कारणताग्रहादुपष्टम्भकद्रवत्वोच्छेदापत्त्या तत्प्रतिबन्धकं तदेव कल्प्यत इति, इदमेव च 'नवीना इत्यचार्य्यरसवीजम्। अत्राप्युपष्टम्भके द्रवत्वाभ्युपगममात्रमत्तो भेद इति तत्त्वम्।

---

(१) रसवत्त्वविशेषणप्रक्षेप इति ख०।

मानद्रवत्वाधिकरणं स्यादित्यनुकूलतर्कसद्भावेन प्रतिकूलतर्काभावेन च तैजसत्वसाधकस्याधिकबलत्वात्। यदि चासाधारणस्य साध्य-तदभाववद्व्यावृत्तत्वेन तदुभयसंशयजनकतया दोषत्वं तथापि विशेषादर्शनसहितस्य संशायकत्वं, प्रकृते चानुकूलतर्क-विशेषदर्शनसहकृतस्य व्यतिरेकिभावेन साधकत्वं[1]। तस्मात् यदा साध्य-तदभावकोटौ न विशेषदर्शनं तदा असाधारण्यस्य दोषत्वं। न चैवं शब्दोऽनित्यः शब्दत्वादित्यादिकमपि[2] हेतुः स्यात्, विशेषदर्शनदशायामिष्टत्वात्।

'पार्थिवद्रवत्वस्येति, न च विरोधिद्रवद्रव्यसम्बन्धादेवानुच्छेद इति वाच्यम्। जलद्रवत्वस्यैव विरोधित्वेन तदभावे सत्येवोच्छेदापत्तेरिति भावः। 'द्रवद्रव्यस्येति, अपार्थिवद्रवत्वमेव विरोधितावच्छेदकं लाघवात् न तु तद्विशेषजलद्रवत्वमिति भावः। 'प्रतिकूलतर्केणेति, इदमुपलक्षणं, व्यर्थविशेषणत्वेनेत्यपि द्रष्टव्यम्, अतैजसत्वाभावेन समन्द्रवत्वाभावस्यैव व्याप्तेः। न च विशिष्टाभावतया प्रतीकारः, विशिष्टस्यातैजसत्वाप्रयोजकत्वे तदभावस्य तदभावेऽप्रयोजकत्वादिति भावः।

---

(१) साध्यसाधकत्वमिति क०।
(२) कृतकत्वादित्यादिकमपीति क०।

अन्ये तु तेजस्त्वं नाद्रववरूपवन्मात्रवृत्ति रूपवद्वृत्तिद्रव्यत्वसाक्षाद्व्याप्यजातित्वात् पृथिवीत्ववत्। यद्वा तेजस्त्वं द्रुतवृत्ति रूपवद्वृत्तिद्रव्यत्वसाक्षाद्व्याप्यजातित्वात् जलत्ववत्। न च रसवद्वृत्तित्वमुपाधिः, रसवत्त्वं द्रवत्वसमानाधिकरणात्यन्ताभावप्रतियोगि अद्रुतवृत्तिद्रव्यत्वव्याप्यधर्म्मत्वात् पटत्ववदिति[१] द्रुततेजःसिद्धौ साध्याव्यापकत्वादिति सामान्यतोदृष्टेन तेजसि द्रवत्वं प्रसाध्य विवादाध्यासितं द्रुतं तैजसं अत्यन्ताग्निसंयोगेनानुच्छिद्यमानानित्यद्रवत्वाधिकरणत्वात् न यदेवं न तदेवं यथा जलमिति वदन्ति।

'अन्ये त्विति, विपक्षबाधकेन बलवत्त्वे तैजसत्वमेव साध्यमास्तां किमसाधारण्यपरीहारार्थकेनायासेन, तदनपेक्षायां तेजोमात्रावृत्तित्वोपाधिविरहेणैव सत्प्रतिपक्षत्वमस्तु, असाधारणरूपः सत्प्रतिपक्षोऽस्त्वन्यथा वेत्यत्राविशेषादित्यत्रास्वरसबीजम्। 'नाद्रवेति, नाद्रवमात्रवृत्तीत्येव साध्यं, रूपवत्पदस्य स्वरूपोत्कीर्त्तनं न तु साध्यप्रविष्टम्। अन्यथा मनस्त्वादावपि साध्यसत्त्वेन तत्र व्यभिचारवारणाय रूपवद्वृत्तिपदानुपादानापत्तेरिति भावः। 'अद्रुतवृत्तीति, ननु यद्यपि द्रुतत्वे अद्रुतवृत्तित्वेन, रूपित्वे रूपित्वव्याप्यत्वेन, द्रुतघटान्यान्यत्वे भावत्वपरेण धर्म्मपदेन व्यभिचारो वार्य्यताम्द्रुत-घटाविति समूहालम्बनविशेष्यत्वे कथं

(१) घटत्ववदितीति ख०।

अथ प्रथमानुमाने तेजोमात्रावृत्तित्वमुपाधिः। न च पक्षेतरत्वं, प्रदीपत्वादेरपि व्यावर्त्त्यत्वादिति चेत्। न। बलवद्विपक्षबाधकेन विवादविषये द्रुततैजसत्वसिद्धावुपाधेः साध्याव्यापकत्वात्। एवञ्च विवादाध्यासिते पार्थिवत्व-तैजसत्वसाधकानि यद्यपि बहून्यनुमानानि सन्ति तथापि विपक्षबाधकतर्कात् तैजसत्वसाधकस्य बलवत्त्वमिति ध्येयम्।

अथ द्रुत-द्रुततरादेः क्रमशः प्रतीतेः प्रबलानलसंयोगेन सुवर्णनाशात्तद्द्रवत्वं नश्यतीति असिद्धो हेतुः। न च द्रवत्वप्रागभावासमानाधिकरणद्रवत्व-

व्यभिचारवारणम्। नैवम्। धर्म्मपदेन समवेतत्वस्याभिधानात्। न चासिद्धिः, रसवत्त्वपदेनापि रसवत्त्वावच्छिन्नस्यैवोक्तत्वात्। 'द्रुततेज इत्यत्र तेजःपदं वास्तवाभिप्रायेण प्रकृते द्रुतनीरसमेवेत्यर्थः।

'प्रथमेति[१] व्यतिरेक्यपेक्षया प्रथमे द्रुतत्वसाधकानुमानद्वय इत्यर्थः। 'अग्निसंयोग इति, आश्रयनाशाधीन घृते द्रवत्वनाशस्य च व्यभिचारवारणाय सत्यन्तं, तेन सत्यग्निसंयोगे तद्धेतुकनाशाप्रतियोगिद्रवत्वमसम्भवि द्वयोरवष्टम्भसामर्थ्यादित्यर्थः। ननु कश्चिद्द्रवत्वान्तरोत्पत्तिर्द्रवत्वनाशानन्तरं कश्चिन्नेति आश्रयवैजात्यकृतमेव वैलक्षण्यमुचितं न तूच्छेदकत्वं अतः स्वरूपासिद्धोऽयं हेतुरित्यत आह, 'अथवेति, 'द्रवत्वोच्छेदसमये' अग्निसंयोगजद्रवत्वोच्छेदसमये इत्यर्थः,

(१) 'आद्येतीति क०।

ध्वंसस्वरूप उच्छेदो न सुवर्णे द्रवत्वनाशेऽप्यग्निमद्रवत्वेनोत्पादात् घृते च तथेति वाच्यम् । सुवर्णे द्रवत्वनाशे सति विनष्टाश्रये द्रवत्वान्तरस्यानुत्पादेन द्रवत्वप्रागभावासमानाधिकरणद्रवत्वध्वंसस्य सत्त्वादिति चेत् । न । सुवर्णद्रवत्वं ह्याश्रयनाशाद्विनश्यति न त्वग्निसंयोगात् । यदि चाग्निसंयोगाद्विनश्येत् तदा घृतवन्न द्रवत्वान्तरमुत्पद्येत द्रवत्वोच्छेदकाग्निसंयोगस्य द्रवत्वान्तरप्रतिबन्धकत्वात् । तथा चाग्निसंयोगित्वे सति तद्धेतुकनाशप्रतियोगिकद्रवत्वाधिकरणत्वादिति हेत्वर्थः । अथवा घृते द्रवत्वोच्छेदसमये समानाधिकरणद्रवत्वसामग्रीसमवधानं नास्ति सुवर्णे त्वस्ति । एवञ्च समानाधिकरणद्रवत्वसामग्रीसमवहिताग्निसंयोगजन्यध्वंसप्रतियोग्यवृत्तिद्रवत्वावान्तरसामान्यवद्द्रवत्वं हेत्वर्थः ।

अन्यथा सुवर्णे जलसंयोगादिना तदुच्छेदेन तादृशसामग्र्यसमवधानात् तदपेक्षयेदं घृतस्य वैलक्षण्यं न स्यादिति भावः । 'समवधानेति समवधाननियम इत्यर्थः, अन्यथा घृते द्रुततरत्वादिप्रतीतेर्द्रवत्वान्तरोत्पत्तिसिद्धौ बाधापत्तेः । नियमस्तु नास्ति भस्मप्राक्कालोच्छेदसमय एव व्यभिचारादिति भावः । 'सुवर्णे त्विति अग्निसंयोगाद्द्रवत्वनाशे तादृशसामग्रीसमवधाननियम इत्यर्थः । 'एवञ्चेति, न च नञ्द्वयगर्भत्वं द्रवत्वावान्तरेत्यादिगर्भत्वञ्च व्यर्थं द्रवत्वोच्छेदसमानाधिकरणद्रवत्व-

यद्वा घृतपरमाणावग्निसंयोगदशायां द्रवत्वनाशे सति[१] द्रवत्वान्तरं नोत्पद्यते तदारब्धभस्मनि द्रवत्वाभावात्। एवं सुवर्णपरमाणुद्रवत्वम् अग्निसंयोगाद्य यदि विनश्येत् तदा तदारब्धसुवर्णमद्रवं स्यात्। तथा सुवर्णारम्भकाः परमाणवो न पार्थिवाः अत्यन्ताग्निसंयोगेनानुच्छिद्यमानद्रवत्वाधिकरणत्वात् जलपरमाणुवत्। तैजसा वा तत एव यन्नैवं[२] तन्नैवं यथा घृतपरमाणुरिति व्यतिरेकी। एवमपार्थिवारब्धं तैजसारब्धं वा सुवर्णमपार्थिवं तैजसं वा अत्यन्तानलसंयोगेऽप्यनुच्छिद्यमानद्रवत्वाधिकरणपरमाण्वारब्धत्वादित्यन्वयिव्यतिरेकी चेति।

सामग्रीसमवहिताग्निसंयोगजन्यध्वंसप्रतियोगिद्रवत्ववत्त्वादित्यस्यैव सम्यक्त्वादिति वाच्यम्। द्रुततरत्वादिप्रतीत्या घृतेऽपि तादृशद्रवत्वसत्त्वेन व्यभिचारात् घृतद्रवत्ववृत्तिजातेः भस्मप्राक्कालिकोच्छिन्नद्रवत्वेऽपि सत्त्वादुक्तहेतुस्तत्र नास्तीति तत्राव्यभिचारात्[३]। न चैवं सुवर्णे द्रवत्वोत्पत्त्यनन्तरं तदुच्छेदो न स्यात्, अग्निसंयोगादन्येन जलसम्पर्कादिनैव द्रवत्वनाशे तदुच्छेदात्। न च द्रवत्वावान्तरपदं व्यर्थं तादृशध्वंसप्रतियोगिवृत्तिसामान्यवद्द्रवत्वस्यैव हेतुत्वादिति वाच्यम्।

---

(१) द्रवत्वनाशादिति ख०।
(२) न यदेवं न तदेवमिति ख०।
(३) नास्तीति व्यभिचाराभावादिति ख०।

एकदेशी तु द्रवत्वाधिकरणं न तेजः पीतत्वात् । न चासिद्धिः, पीतं द्रुतमिति प्रतीतेः[1] । पीतत्वे पार्थिवत्वापत्त्या बाधकेन पीतप्रतीतिर्भ्रम इति चेत् । न । शुक्लत्वेऽप्यपार्थिवत्ववत् पीतत्वेऽप्यपार्थिवत्वे बाधकाभावात् । यथा नैमित्तिकद्रवत्वे पृथिवीत्वं न तन्त्रमतिप्रसङ्गात् तथा पीतत्वेऽपि गन्धनियतत्वमपि नैमित्तिकद्रवत्ववदेव । पृथिवी-जलान्यत्वे सति रूपित्वेन तेज इति चेत् । न । अप्रयोजकत्वात् । अन्यथा जलतेजोऽन्यत्वे सति स्पर्शवत्त्वेन वायोरपि पृथिवीत्वापत्तेः । अथ रूप-रस-गन्धानामभावान्न तथात्वं तेषामनुद्भवे च

विवक्षाभेदेन हेतुत्वात् तादृशध्वंसप्रतियोगिवृत्तिद्रवत्वावान्तरसामान्यवत्त्वस्य तादृशध्वंसप्रतियोगिवृत्तिसामान्यवद्द्रवत्वस्य च समर्थत्वात् । नन्वेवं विवक्षितहेतोर्जलमध्यस्थघृतादावभावेनासतीत्यादिविशेषणप्रक्षेपो नित्यपदप्रक्षेपस्य प्राच्यो विरुद्धोतेति चेत् । न । अग्निसंयोगित्वे सति इत्यादिविवक्षायां तद्विशेषणोपादानात् उपष्टम्भके द्रवत्वोत्पत्तिपक्षे तत्र व्यभिचारवारणायाचैव तदुपादानाद्वा । अतएव तत्र द्रवत्वानुत्पत्तिपक्षे अस्यां विवक्षायाञ्च विशेषणवैयर्थ्यं मत्वा द्वितीयतैजसत्वव्यतिरेकिणि तदुभयविशेषणमनुपादायैव हेतुनिर्देशः कृत इति दिक् ।

---

(१) प्रत्ययादिति ख० ।

पृथिवी उद्भूतरूप-रस-गन्धाद्यन्यतमवतीत्यादिबहुविध-व्याप्तिविरोध इति चेत् । न। तेजोऽद्रवमेव प्रत्यक्षं तेजः प्रत्यक्षरूप-स्पर्शाद्यन्यतरवदेव स्व-परप्रकाशकमेवेत्यादिव्याप्तिविरोधस्य तेजस्यपि सत्त्वात् । द्रवत्वाधिकरणञ्च न पृथिवीति त्वयैव साधितं अतो नैमित्तिकद्रवत्वाधिकरणं पीतं सुवर्णं द्रव्यान्तरमेवेत्याह ।

इति श्रीमद्गङ्गेशोपाध्यायविरचिते तत्त्वचिन्तामणौ प्रत्यक्षखण्डे प्रत्यक्षकारणवादः ।

यदा तु न पिठरेषु पाकाद्रूपलनाशः किन्त्वाश्रयनाशादेव तदा परमाणुपक्षकानुमानमाह, 'यद्वेति । 'एकदेशीत्यस्वरसाविष्कारः । तद्वीजन्तु धर्म्मिकल्पनात इत्यादिकमेव । तेनातिरेक्यबाधे धर्म्मकल्पनाप्रसक्तौ पृथिवी-तेजोधर्म्मकल्पने च कथितमेव विपक्षबाधकं विनिगमकमिति ।

इति श्रीजयदेवमिश्रविरचिते तत्त्वचिन्तामण्यालोके प्रत्यक्षखण्डालोके प्रत्यक्षकारणवादालोकः ।

अथ मनोऽणुत्ववादः।

नन्विन्द्रियजन्यत्वं सुखादिप्रत्यक्षाव्यापकं प्रत्यक्षलक्षणमिति चेत्। न। ज्ञातकरणाजन्यः सुखाद्यनुभवः इन्द्रियजन्यः जन्यप्रत्यक्षत्वात् रूपप्रत्यक्षवत्, जन्यसाक्षात्कारस्येन्द्रियजन्यत्वादिति तत्रापि तल्लक्षणसत्त्वात्। स्पर्शाद्यविषयत्वेन त्वगादिना नार्थान्तरं, गन्ध-रस-रूप-स्पर्शेष्वेकैकमात्रसाक्षात्काराजनकत्वेन पृथिव्यादिभेदसिद्धौ निःस्पर्शं लाघवान्निरवयवञ्च मनः। तच्च विभु ज्ञानासमवायिकारणसंयोगाधारत्वात् नित्येन्द्रियत्वात् नित्यत्वे सति द्रव्यानारम्भकद्रव्यत्वात् आत्मादिवत्, न च महत्त्वमुपाधिः, साधनव्यापकत्वादिति।

अथ मनोऽणुत्ववादालोकः।

उपोद्घातसङ्गतिमाह, 'नन्विति, 'प्रत्यक्षलक्षणं' इन्द्रियजन्यत्वरूपप्रत्यक्षलक्षणमित्यर्थः। 'ज्ञातेति नञ्व्यत्यासेनाज्ञातकरणजन्य इत्यर्थः, तेन भगवत्प्रत्यक्षे नांशतो बाधः। 'इन्द्रियजन्यः' विषयप्रत्यासन्नसंयोगिकरणजन्यः। अन्यथेन्द्रियत्वस्य मनोगर्भतया मनोऽसिद्धिदशायां साध्याप्रसिद्ध्यापत्तेरित्यर्थः। अत एव स्मृतावंशतो बाधवारणायानुभवेति

ननु सुखादिकं मूर्त्तसंयोगासमवायिकारणकगुणवृत्तिगुणत्वावान्तरजातियोगि नित्यवृत्त्यनित्यविशेषगुणत्वात् शब्दवत् पाकजरूपवच्चेति चेत्। न। अनात्मवृत्तित्वस्य शब्दभिन्नविशेषगुणग्राहकेन्द्रियाजन्यत्वस्य शब्दस्य द्रव्यत्वेन मूर्त्तवृत्तिगुणत्वस्य चोपाधित्वात् अप्रयोजकत्वाच्च। कारणे मूर्त्तत्वस्य गुरुत्वात्। अस्तु वा शरीरात्मसंयोगजन्यत्वेनार्थान्तरं। अथासमवाय्यधीनो विभुकार्य्याणां प्रादेशिकत्वनियम इति विभु-मनोयोगादात्ममात्रे सुखादेरुत्पत्तौ नियतदेशता न स्यात् अतोऽणु मन इति। मैवम्। किमसमवायिकारणं स्वावच्छिन्ने विभुकार्य्यं जनयतीति नियमः। स्वावच्छिन्ने जनयत्येवेति वा। स्वावच्छिन्ने एव जनयतीति वा। आद्ये सुखादेरधिकदेशत्वे आपादकाभावः। द्वितीये

पक्षविशेषणम्। अन्यथा स्मृतेरपि इन्द्रियजन्यतया तत्र बाधाभावात्। न चेन्द्रियत्वेन तज्जन्यत्वं विवक्षित्वा तत्र बाधाद्यासञ्जनम्, तत्र हि जनकतावच्छेदकमिन्द्रियत्वमपि यथा विवक्षितमेवेत्युक्तम् प्रत्यक्षलक्षणे। 'स्पर्शादीति, त्वगादीनां स्वव्यञ्जकापकगुणपुरस्कारेण प्रवृत्तिनियमादिति भावः। ननु त्वगन्यद्वायवीयं, चक्षुरन्यत्तैजसमपीन्द्रियं स्यादित्यत आह, 'रूपेति। 'निस्पर्शमित्यनन्तरमत इति पूरणीयमन्तेन निस्पर्शत्वाल्लाघवाच्चेत्यर्थः। 'नित्यत्वे इति। अनारम्भक-

अणुमनःसंयोगेऽपि स्वावच्छिन्ने अधिकदेशे च जनयेन्नियामकाभावात्। अन्ये तत्रापि सुखादेरणुमात्रदेशतापत्तिः। मनोवैभवेऽप्यविरोधश्च। अथ निमित्तचन्दनाद्यनुरोधेन सुखादौ न्यूनाधिकदेशता निमित्तवायुसंयोगादिव शब्दे न त्वसमवाय्यनुरोधात्। तथा च सुखादिकं तदवच्छिन्न एवोत्पद्यत इति चेत्। हन्त तर्हि वैभवेऽपि तथास्तु। न च विभुकार्य्यासमवायी स्वावच्छिन्ने कार्य्यं जनयत्येव भेर्य्याकाशसंयोग इव शब्दमिति चन्दनाद्यनवच्छिन्नेऽपि सुखादिकमुत्पद्येतेति वाच्यम्। तद्देशीयचन्दनसुखे हि तद्देशीयचन्दनसम्बन्ध-

---

द्रव्यत्वमप्रसिद्धमतः 'द्रव्यानारम्भकेति, द्रव्यपदञ्चाग्रेतनन्नित्यगुणे, सत्यन्तं चान्त्यावयविनि व्यभिचारवारणाय। 'विशेषेति खसमानाधिकरणद्रव्यत्वसाक्षाद्व्याप्यजात्यवच्छिन्नव्यावृत्त्यौपयिकावान्तरसामान्यवद्गुणशून्यद्रव्यत्वादित्यर्थः। 'आत्मादीति, आदिपदादाकाश-दिशोः परिग्रहः। 'महत्त्वमिति महत्त्वं परिमाणभेदः। 'वैभवञ्च सकलमूर्त्तसंयोगित्वमिति उपाधौ साध्यभेदो द्रष्टव्यः। 'नन्विति, न च गुणवृत्तीत्यादि व्यर्थम्[१], शब्दजशब्दे व्यभिचारवारणार्थत्वात्। 'नित्येति, जलावयवि-तत्परमाणुस्नेहयोर्व्यभिचारवारणाय प्रथमविशेषणद्वयम्। विशेषगुणपदन्नित्यवृत्तिद्वित्वे व्यभिचारवारणाय। 'पाकजवदिति

---

(१) गुणवृत्तीत्याद्यधिकमिति ख०।

सापेक्षोऽसमवायी हेतुरिति कथं तन्निरपेक्षस्तत्कुर्य्यात्। चन्दनञ्च स्वावच्छिन्ने सुखजनकं कथं स्वानवच्छिन्नेऽपि तदुत्पादयेत् कथं वा तद्देशीयचन्दनसुखं तद्देशचन्दन-सम्बन्धजन्यं तेन विनैवोत्पद्येत। अथ मनोवैभवे सुखाद्युत्पत्तौ नियत उपाधिर्वाच्यः तेन नानानिमित्त-समवधानेऽपि तदवच्छेदेनैकदा सुख-दुःखादिष्वेकमेवो-त्पद्यते, न नाना। एकावच्छेदेनैकदा एक एव विभु-विशेषगुण उत्पद्यत इति नियमात्। निमित्तस्य त्ववच्छेदकत्वे नानासुखादिकमुत्पद्येत शब्दवदिति चेत्। न। श्रोत्रे कर्णशष्कुल्यवच्छेदेन नानानिमित्तादनेक-

---

परमाणुवृत्तिरूपवदित्यर्थः, अन्यथा घटाद्यवयवरूपे साधनवैकल्यम्। 'अनात्मेति, साधनावच्छिन्नसाध्यव्यापकावेतावुपाधी। शुद्धसाध्य-व्यापकत्वे च प्रथमस्य प्रचयजन्यपरिमाणवृत्तिजातियोगिन्यात्मपरि-माणे, द्वितीयस्य चक्षुरादिसंयोगे व्यभिचारादिति। 'गुरुत्वादिति, तथाच व्यर्थविशेषणत्वमपीति भावः। अत्यन्तायोगव्यवच्छेदादि-भेदेन नियमं विकल्पयति, 'किमिति। 'अन्यत्रेति, तथाचैकावच्छेदे-मेत्यादिनियमे एकनिमित्तमात्रसमावेश उपाधिरिति बोध्यम्। 'युगपदुत्पन्नेति युगपद्विद्यमानेत्यर्थः। 'अबाधितेति, तथाचेदमप्य-परं वैभवे मानमिति भावः। 'शरीरावच्छिन्नेति। ननु विशेष-व्याप्त्यावप्रसिद्धिः शरीरावच्छिन्नासमवायिकारणत्वाप्रसिद्धेः। न च

शब्दोत्पादात्। अन्यथा कोलाहलग्रहो न स्यात्। नानावच्छेदेनैकदा चन्दन-दहनादिसम्बन्धे सुख-दुःखयोश्चैकदा अनुभवसिद्धत्वे नेष्टापादनात्। न च तद्यौगपद्यप्रत्ययो भ्रमः, बाधकाभावात्। न चान्यत्र क्रमादत्रापि क्रमानुमानं, अन्यत्र क्रमस्य निमित्तक्रमाधीनत्वात्। एवञ्च विवादविषयसुख-दुःखानि(१) युगपदुत्पन्नासमवायिकारणकानि युगपदुत्पद्यमानत्वात् युगपदुत्पन्नघटादिवत्। अबाधितानुभवाच्च नासिद्धिः। एतेन चरणदुःखं यदि शरीरावच्छिन्नासमवायिहेतुकं स्यात् शरीरव्यापकं स्यादिति निरस्तं। निमित्त-

---

यद्यदवच्छिन्नासमवायिकारणकं तत्तदवच्छिन्नमिति सामान्यव्याप्तेरेवोक्ततर्कप्रवृत्तिः, अङ्गुल्यवच्छिन्नकरतलसंयोगासमवायिकारणकस्य(२) भुज-वृक्षसंयोगस्याङ्गुल्यव्यापकत्वेन व्यभिचारादिति। मैवम्। विभुविशेषगुणत्वावच्छेदेन सामान्यतो व्याप्तेः, एवं विपर्य्ययोऽपि, सुखं न शरीरावच्छिन्नासमवायिकारणकविभुविशेषगुणः शरीराव्यापकत्वादिति प्रयोज्यम्। अन्यथा सामान्यव्याप्तावुक्तविशेषणादाने व्यभिचारादिति ध्येयम्। न चैवमणुमनःपक्षेऽपि बाधः अतिप्रसक्तस्यानवच्छेदकत्वात्। न च वैभवेऽपि साध्यमस्ति चरणावच्छिन्नसुखं प्रति मनो-

---

(१) विवादाध्यासितानि सुख-दुःखानीति ख० ।

(२) अङ्गुल्यवच्छिन्नकर-वृक्षसंयोगासमवायिकारणकस्येति ख० ।

समवधानस्य तन्त्रत्वे अस्याप्रयोजकत्वात्। अन्यथा-णुत्वपक्षे शरीरव्यापकं सुखादि न स्यात्। आभिमानि-काभ्यासिक-मानोरथिकसुखेषु ज्ञानेच्छा-प्रयत्न-द्वेषेषु च देशानियमः। शरीरावयवेषु यत्क्रियायामिच्छा तदवच्छेदेन प्रयत्न इति तत्रैव चेष्टा आवश्यकत्वात् अनियतदेशज्ञानेच्छादौ लघुत्वाच्च। अन्यथाणुत्वपक्षे प्रयत्नस्याणुदेशत्वं शरीरमात्रदेशत्वं वा स्यात्।

अन्ये तु सुखादौ तन्निमित्तावच्छेदेनात्म-मनःसं-योगोऽसमवायी तन्मात्रसुखाद्युपलम्भात्। न त्वात्म-मनःसंयोगमात्रमतिप्रसङ्गादित्याहुः।

योगस्य शरीरावच्छिन्नमनोयोगत्वेनाजनकत्वादिति वाच्यम्। तत्त-दवच्छिन्नमनोयोगत्वेन तत्सुखं प्रति अजनकत्वात् किन्तु चेष्टाश्रया-वच्छिन्नमनोयोगत्वेन जन्यात्मविशेषगुणत्वावच्छिन्नं प्रतीति वस्तु-गतेरिति भावः। 'अन्यथेति यदि यदवच्छिन्नासमवायिकारणक-मिति व्याप्तिरित्यर्थः। ननु यद्यसमवायिकृतो न प्रादेशिकतानि-यमस्तदा वैषयिकसुखादौ निमित्तवदन्यत्र नियामकाभावात् प्रादे-शिकता कथं स्यादत आह, 'मानोरथिकेति, तत्र न शरीरैक-देशतानियमः सुखादिवदिति फलबलाच्छरीरमेव नियामकं कल्प्यत इति भावः। एवमन्यत्रापि नियामकान्तरमाह, 'शरीरेति, 'अनियत-देशज्ञानेच्छादौ' शरीरव्यापकज्ञानोत्पत्तौ। 'न त्वात्म-मनःसंयोगमात्र'

यावति यत्सुखादिप्रागभावः तावत्येव तत्सुखादिक-मुत्पद्यत इत्यपरे।

यत्तु तदितरहेतुसाकल्ये तद्व्यापकत्वेन प्रागभावस्यावश्यकत्वमिति। तन्न। प्रागभावस्याहेतुत्वापत्तेः। तदितरहेतुसाकल्ये तदभावेन कार्य्याभावाभावात्। एतेन व्यापकमनवच्छिन्नं नेन्द्रियमतिप्रसङ्गादित्याकाशे कर्णशष्कुलीवन्नियत उपाधिर्वाच्यः, स च न शरीरं, तदवयवमात्रं वा, नियतस्तदवयवी वा, चेष्टाश्रयमात्रं वा, नानावयवावच्छेदेनाव्याप्यवृत्तिसुखाद्युपलब्धेः, एवञ्च सूक्ष्ममिन्द्रियमुपाधित्वेन कल्पनीयं, तथाच

न शरीरावच्छिन्नात्म-मनःसंयोगमात्रं, क्वचित्तु 'आवश्यकत्वादित्यनन्तरं 'अन्यथाणुत्वपक्षे प्रयत्नस्याणुदेशत्वं शरीरमात्रदेशत्वं वा स्यात् अन्ये तु तन्निमित्तावच्छेदेनात्म-मनःसंयोगोऽसमवायी तस्मात्रसुखाद्युपलम्भात् न तु' इतिपर्य्यन्तं ग्रन्थलिखनं, अग्रे 'लघुत्वाच्चेत्यनन्तरं नाशव्र-णोपस्य दृश्यते तत्तु कल्पितमसाम्प्रदायिकमित्युपेक्षितं। 'चाक्षुषेति चाक्षुषद्रव्यज्ञानवत इत्यर्थः। तेन हेतौ 'तदानीमित्यनेन तस्यैव परामर्शात् अन्धकारस्य काले स्वविषयसाक्षात्काराजनके सुवर्णे[१] न व्यभिचारः। न हि तत्रापि तेजःसंयोगाभावादग्रहो येन तेजः-संयोगः स्वविषयसाक्षात्कारे हेतुः स्यात्तेजसि तेजोऽन्तरस्याग्राहक-

(१) सुवर्णरूपतेजसीति ख०।

तदेव मनः किमुपधेयेन विभुना, तत्र च सर्व एव हेतवो धर्मिग्राहकमानबाधिता इति निरस्तं। इन्द्रियत्वेन तस्य शरीरमात्रस्योपाधित्वेऽपि निमित्तवशात् सुखादेर्नियतदेशतोपपत्तेः। न चैकदानेकविषयेन्द्रियसम्बन्धे युगपज्ज्ञानानुत्पत्त्या इन्द्रियसहकारितयानुमितं मनोऽणु तदेव सुखग्राहकमिन्द्रियं लाघवादिति तद्वैभवहेतवो बाधिता इति वाच्यं। बुभुत्सावशात् करणधर्मत्वाद्वा अणुत्वपक्षे श्रोत्रे अनेकशब्दसमवायेऽपि बुभुत्सितमात्रशब्दग्रहवत् व्यासङ्गदशायां युगपज्ज्ञानानुत्पत्तेरुपपत्तेः अन्यच्च दीर्घशष्कुलीभक्षणादौ

त्वाद्रूपाग्रहेण तत्र सुवर्णाग्रहादिति भावः। विषयेन्द्रियसंयोगशून्यत्वेनार्थान्तरवारणाय 'स्वविषयसम्बद्धानीति पक्षविशेषणं, साक्षात्कारहेतुसंयोगशून्यत्वं तदसमवहितत्वं तत्समवधानस्य कार्य्यप्रयोजकत्वेन तदसमवधानस्य प्रत्यक्षाप्रयोजकत्वेन साधनौचित्यात्। तथाच चाक्षुषसाक्षात्कारहेतुसंयोगसमवधानत्वेन बाधो माभूदतः 'स्वविषयेति साक्षात्कारविशेषणं। 'तदानीमिति चाक्षुषद्रव्यज्ञानकालीनस्व-स्वविषयसाक्षात्काराहेतुत्वादित्यर्थः। अत्र स्वविषयत्वं स्वजन्यसाक्षात्कारविषयत्वं इन्द्रियस्य व्यापारानुबन्धेनैव सविषयत्वात् तथाच दृष्टान्ते घटेऽपि स्वविषयत्वं स्वस्मिन्नस्तीति घटे न दृष्टान्तासिद्धिः न वा परमाण्वादावयोग्ये व्यभिचारः। तत्र स्वविषया-

युगपज्ज्ञानोत्पत्तेरिष्टत्वादिति। अत्रोच्यते। व्यासङ्गदशायामिन्द्रियाणां स्व-स्वविषयसम्बन्धेऽप्येकस्मात् ज्ञानं नान्यस्मादित्यनुभवसिद्धमतो यस्यासम्बन्धान्न युगपज्ज्ञानानि तदिन्द्रियसहकारिक्रमेण तदधिष्ठायकं मनस्तदेव सुखादिग्राहकमिति तस्य धर्म्मिग्राहकमानबाधितं विभुत्वं। तथाहि चाक्षुषज्ञानवतो मैत्रस्य स्व-स्वविषयसम्बद्धानि घ्राण-रसन-त्वक्श्रोत्राणि स्व-स्वविषयसाक्षात्कारहेतुसंयोगशून्यानि तदानीं स्वविषयसाक्षात्काराजनकत्वात् इन्द्रियासम्बद्धघटवत्[१]। एकैकं वा पक्षः अन्यथा हेतुसाकल्ये युगपज्ज्ञानोत्पत्तिप्रसङ्गः। न च वैभवेऽप्यदृष्टविलम्बाद्विलम्बः, तदितर-

प्रसिद्धा हेत्वभावात् द्रव्यपदमधिकं हेतौ प्रवेश्यं, अन्यथा योग्यानुपलम्भाभावादभावे स्वविषयसाक्षात्काराजनके व्यभिचारः। न च स्वविषयाभावादनुत्पन्नशब्दादिसाक्षात्काराजनके श्रोत्रादौ व्यभिचारः, विद्यमानत्वेनापि स्वविषयविशेषणादिति भावः। अत्र प्रयोजकत्वमाशङ्क्य निषेधति, 'न चेति, एवमग्रेऽपि। ननु घटबुभुत्सायामपि पटज्ञानोदयवन्नृत्यदर्शनवतः इच्छाद्यन्वयानुविधानमप्यस्ति तथा-चोभयोरन्यतरस्याप्यबाधे[२] विषयभेदो गतिरिति स चात्र स्फुट एव

(१) घटवदिति ख०।
(२) उभयोरप्यबाधे इति ख०।

हेतुसाकल्ये तस्यापि सत्त्वात् इन्द्रियान्तरविलोपप्रसङ्गाच्च। न च बुभुत्सावशात् क्रमो दृश्यते हि नृत्यदर्शनवतो बुभुत्सातोऽभिमतविषयान्तरज्ञानमिति वाच्यं। सा हि न स्वविषयज्ञाने हेतुः अबुभुत्सितेऽपि[१] ज्ञानोदयात्। नाप्यन्यज्ञानप्रतिबन्धिका, घटबुभुत्सायामपि पटज्ञानोदयात्। बुभुत्सा च क्रियाहेतुमनोगोचरप्रयत्नद्वारेन्द्रियान्तरादाकृष्य अभिमतार्थग्राहिणीन्द्रियान्तरे मनो निवेशयन्ती बुभुत्सितग्रहे हेतुरन्यग्रहे प्रतिबन्धिका च न तु साक्षात्। अत एव बुभुत्सासत्त्वेऽपि मनोगोचरप्रणिधानाभावे[२] सा न किञ्चित्करी। नन्विन्द्रिय-मनःसंयोगविशेष एव विषयविशेषग्रहे हेतुः कल्प्यताम्। न चैवं सिद्धकारणभावस्य विशेषकल्पने हेत्व-

---

स्वविरोधिसामग्र्याः प्रतिबन्धकत्वदर्शनेन स्वविरोधिज्ञानेच्छा प्रतिबन्धिका। न च घटज्ञानस्य पटज्ञानं विरोधि, उभयगोचरसमूहालम्बनसम्भवात्। किन्तु चाक्षुषज्ञानस्य रासनादिज्ञानं तथा। तथाच तदिच्छैव प्रतिबन्धिका तदनुविधानमेव नृत्यदर्शनवत इत्यादिनोक्तं, अतस्तदनुविधानमप्युपाधिना अन्यथासिद्धयति, 'बुभुत्सा चेति, 'तस्यापीति हेत्वन्तरस्यापीत्यर्थः। तथाच यच्चैव हेत्वन्तरमन्वय-व्यतिरेकि

---

(१) अबुभुत्सतेऽपीति ख०।

(२) मनोगोचरप्रयत्नाभावे इति ख०।

न्तरोच्छेदः, तस्याप्यन्वय-व्यतिरेकित्वादिति चेत् । न । इन्द्रिय-मनःसंयोगे हि विशेषो न जातिरूपोऽनुगत-हेत्वभावात् जातिसङ्करप्रसङ्गाच्च । नापि सहकारि-रूपः, तस्यैव हेतुतापत्तेः । अथास्तु करणधर्म्मत्वेन क्रियाक्रमः, एकङ्करणमेकचैकदैकावच्छेदेन तुल्यदेशे वा एकजातीयामनेकां क्रियां न करोति, किन्त्वेका-मेव । एकचेत्यादिविशेषणात्कुठाराग्निसंयोग-शब्देषु न व्यभिचार इति चेत्, तर्हि चक्षुराद्यवच्छेदेन भिन्न-देशीयशब्दवत् परमाणाविव विजातीयामग्निसंयोगव-दनेकां क्रियां कुर्य्यादेव । अथ ज्ञानकरणमेकचात्मन्येक-दैकमेव ज्ञानं करोति समूहालम्बनकरणवत्, कथम-न्यथा नानासामग्रीसत्त्वे[1] समूहालम्बनमेकम् । यत्त्व-परज्ञानसामग्री यदि तदा कार्य्यावश्यम्भावः[2] तदसत्त्वे

तत्रैव सिद्धकारणभावस्य विशेषाकल्पनं, यत्र तु न तथा तत्र धर्म्मी-तिन्यायात्सिद्धकारणभाव एव विशेषकल्पनमिति भावः । 'जाति-सङ्करेति । अन्यतरकर्मजत्वादिनेत्यर्थः[3] । 'तस्यैवेति तथाच किमनेन

(१) नानासामग्रीत इति ख० ।

(२) अपरज्ञानसामग्रीसत्त्वे ज्ञानावश्यम्भाव इति ख० ।

(३) अन्यतरकर्म्मजत्वादिनेति शेषः इति ख० ।

किं कारणधर्मत्वेन तस्य सहकार्य्यन्तरपर्य्यवसायित्वादिति। तन्न। समूहालम्बनसाम्यात्। करणस्यैकदैकमात्रजनकत्वेनापराजनकतया तत्र कारणाभावेनैव सामाग्र्यसत्त्वादिति चेत्, तर्हि पञ्चसु यदेकं जनयति नापराणि तत्र नियामकमास्थेयम्। अन्यथा ज्ञानजनने तेषां कलहङ्कः समादध्यात्। किञ्चैवं युगपज्ज्ञानानि माभूवन् युगपज्ज्ञानन्तु केन वार्य्यते एकजन्यसमूहालम्बनवत्। न च चाक्षुषत्वादिजातिसङ्करापत्तेर्नैकज्ञानमिति वाच्यम्। एवं हि फलविरोधेनैकमपि ज्ञानं न जनयेदविशेषात्। उत्पद्यतां वा चाक्षुषादिविजातीयं ज्ञानं सामग्रीसत्त्वात् चित्ररूपवत्। फलबलात्तत्र तथेति चेत्, तर्ह्यत्र फलाभावे हेतुः कल्पयतां अन्योन्यप्रतिबन्धकस्य तत्त्वे वा ज्ञानमेव

विभुना मनसेत्यर्थः। 'एकङ्करणमिति, न चैकावच्छेदेनेति विशेषणे दत्ते एकत्रेत्यधिकं, एकस्य श्येनकर्म्मणस्मरणावच्छेदेन युगपच्छाखा-श्येनसंयोगद्वयस्यैव जनकत्वेन व्यभिचारात्। अत एवोभयं सकलमप्याह,'तुल्यदेशे चेति। 'अथ ज्ञानकरणमिति, न चैकत्रात्मनीत्यधिकं, ज्ञायमानकरणपक्षे लिङ्गशब्दादौ[१] तदनभ्युपगमेऽपि आलोकादौ व्यभिचारवार-

---

(१) शब्दलिङ्गादाविति क०।

न स्यात् न त्वेकज्ञानमित्युक्तम् । ननु चक्षुरादि न सम्भूय जनकं अन्यविषयेऽन्यस्यासामर्थ्यात् शीतं सुरभि शुभ्रं चन्दनमित्यत्रैव कारणान्तरानुपनयाच्च । न च स्व-स्वविषयज्ञानायोद्यतमिन्द्रियं कारणान्तरसहकारात् तत्तद्विषयमादायैव स्व-स्वविषयं ज्ञापयेदिति वाच्यं । भिन्नविषयप्रमाणानां सम्भूयाजनकत्वनियमात् । तत्तदिन्द्रियन्तत्तज्ज्ञानांशे जनकमित्यपि न विषयस्यांशत्वादिति चेत् । मैवं । न ह्रीन्द्रियाणां सम्भूय कारित्वं, किन्त्वार्थः समाजः, प्रत्येकज्ञानसामग्रीसत्त्वादेकदा नानाज्ञानप्रसक्तौ करणधर्मत्वेन मनस्तावद्गोचरामेकामेव ज्ञानक्रियामुत्पादयेत् समूहालम्बनवत् । न चैकक्रियाजननदशायामपरविषयक्रियायां मनो न समर्थमिति कथं तां जनयेदिति वाच्यम् । भिन्नक्रियायामसामर्थ्येऽप्येकक्रियायां सामर्थ्यात् ।

कत्वादिति भावः । ननु गो-गोत्वयोरालोचनानन्तरं[१] अन्यतरविषयकज्ञानोत्पत्तिवददृष्टमेव नियामकं स्यादित्यरुचेराह, 'किन्त्विति, करणधर्मबलादेकोत्पत्तिमात्रं सिद्ध्यति सा च सर्वगोचरैकज्ञानेऽपि सम्भवतीति भावः ।

(१) गो-गोत्वयोर्निर्विकल्पकज्ञानानन्तरमित्यर्थः ।

वस्तुतस्तु विशेषाभावादेकामिवापरामपि बुद्धिं जनयेदविशेषात्। न चैकामपीत्यनेकज्ञानोत्पत्तिर्ज्ञानानुत्पत्तिर्वा न त्वेकविषयज्ञानोत्पत्तिरिति नियामकमास्थेयं। समूहालम्बने फलबलेन परस्परापेक्षितत्वेनैकैव सामग्री। ननु मनोऽणुत्वे कथं मन्दोऽपि बुभुत्सितः शब्दो गृह्यते नान्यः। अथ शब्दे बुभुत्सैवेतरग्रहप्रतिबन्धिका ग्रहस्य तदनुविधानात् अनन्यगतिककार्य्यदर्शनात् बुभुत्सितशब्दग्रहसामग्र्येव वा बलवतीति यदि मन्यसे, तदा वैभवेऽपि तत एव युगपज्ज्ञानानुत्पत्तिरिति चेत्। मैवम। बुभूत्सा न रूपादिग्रहे हेतुर्न वेतरग्रहे प्रतिबन्धिकेत्युक्तत्वात्। किञ्च रूपादिसकलबुभुत्सायां परस्परप्रतिबन्धादज्ञानम्बुभुत्साधीनसामग्रीबलवत्त्वाद्वा सर्व्वेषां ज्ञानं स्यात् न त्वेकस्य पश्चावधानस्य सर्व्वेषां ज्ञानं भवत्येवेति चेत्। न। तत्रापि क्रमानुमानात्।

ननु चित्रज्ञानमसम्भवि रूपादिषु मध्ये रूपादिमात्रग्रह एव चक्षुरादिसामर्थ्येन स्व-स्वाविषयगुणादिग्रहे तदसामर्थ्यादित्यस्वरसादाह, 'वस्तुतस्त्विति, न चादृष्टमेव नियामकमित्युक्तमेवेति वाच्यम्। अणुना मनसा दृष्टेनैवोपपत्तौ अदृष्टकल्पनानवकाशात्। अन्यथा मन एव कुतो न कल्प्येत, कुतो वैभवाविभवचिन्ता, उदाहृते तु गत्यन्तराभावादिति भावः। 'बुभुत्सितेति, बुभुत्सितशब्दग्रहसामग्र्याः प्रतिबन्ध-

अन्यथा सर्व्वबुभुत्साधीनप्रणिधानेऽप्यन्येषां कथं न स्यात्[१] । नन्वणुत्वेऽपि दशभिः पठ्यमानासु गाथासु तावद्गोचरबुभुत्सायां प्रणिधाने चोक्तरीत्या सर्व्वेषां ज्ञानमज्ञानं वा न त्वेकज्ञानमिति चेत् । अत्र कश्चित् । श्रोत्र-मनःसंयोगे आत्म-मनःसंयोगे वा कश्चिद्विशेषः कार्य्योन्नेयः किञ्चिच्छब्दग्रहे हेतुः, तदन्यग्रहे प्रतिबन्धक इति । तन्न । वैभवेऽपीन्द्रिय-मनःसंयोगविशेषस्य तथात्वे व्यासङ्गोपपत्तेः । अनुगतरूपाभावेन प्रतिव्यक्ति प्रतिबन्धकत्वे हेतुत्वे च व्यभिचारात् । संयोगे च विशेषस्य जातित्वे जातिसङ्करः । उपाधित्वे स एव हेतुर्न मनः ।

अपरे तु प्रत्यक्षानुकूलेन्द्रिय-मनःसंयोगद्वारा बुभुत्सा प्रणिधानञ्च प्रत्यक्षहेतुरिति[२] चाक्षुषादिबुभुत्सितग्रहे क्लृप्तत्वात् ताभ्यां श्रोत्रे बुभुत्सितशब्दावच्छे-

---

कत्वे बुभुत्सानवच्छेदिकेति भेदः[३] इति भावः । 'जातिसङ्कर इति कग्रहजनिका गग्रहप्रतिबन्धिका जातिरेका अपरा च विपरीता तयोरुभयगोचरसमूहालम्बनदर्शनेन तज्जनकमनोयोगे सत्त्वेन सङ्कर-

---

(१) कुतो न स्यादिति ख० ।
(२) बुभुत्सा-प्रणिधानयोः प्रत्यक्षहेतुत्वमितीति ख० ।
(३) विशेष इति ख० ।

देन मनः संयुज्यत इति स गृह्यते नान्यः, क्वचित्प्रणिधानं विनैव तथा। अन्यत्र प्रणिधानाधीनक्रियया अश्रूयमाणशब्दावच्छिन्नात्मनो विभज्य बुभुत्सितशब्दावच्छेदेन मनः संयुज्यते इति तद्ग्रहो न सर्व्वस्येति। तत्तुच्छम्। युगपत्पठ्यमानासु विंशतौ गाथासु तावद्गोचरबुभुत्सायां प्रणिधाने च तावद्गाथावच्छेदेन मनःसंयोगाद्युगपत्तासामुपलम्भप्रसङ्गात् प्रत्येकसामग्रीसत्त्वात् निकटाहन्यमानढक्कादिशब्दानां श्रोत्रव्यापकत्वनियमाच्च।

अथ यत्र कोलाहले श्रूयमाणएव बुभुत्सितशब्दग्रहः तत्रोभयशब्दावच्छेदेन मनःसंयोगादुभयग्रहः कोलाहले तूपेक्षाज्ञानन्तदिति तथात्रापीति चेत्, तर्हि कृतमनया कुसृष्ट्या। अबुभुत्सिते उपेक्षाज्ञानमेवास्तु, न च तदपि, इतो न शब्दान्तरमश्रौषमित्यनुभवात्। अन्यथा वैभवेऽपि व्यासङ्गदशायामितरेषामुपेक्षाज्ञानमेवेति। अत्रोच्यते। यद्यपि बुभुत्सा-प्रणिधाने न शब्दग्रहमात्रे सहकारिणी न वेतरग्रहप्रतिबन्धके, तथापि नानाशब्दसमवायदशायां

इत्यर्थः। 'हेतुरित्यनन्तरं अस्त्विति, 'न मन इत्यनन्तरञ्च कल्प्यमिति शेषः।

यः शब्दग्रहः तच्च तयोस्तथाभावः तथैवत योरन्वय-व्यतिरेकानियमात्।

यदा कोलाहले श्रूयमाण एव बुभुत्सितग्रह इत्य-न्येऽपि कोलाहलत्वेन तद्विषया एव बहूनाञ्चैकदा समवाये युगपत्सन्निधाने वा व्यक्तिग्रहे तद्गतगत्व-कत्वादिग्रहो न भवति। अगृहीतकत्वादिनानाशब्दस्य कोलाहलबुद्धिविषयत्वात्। तस्यां दशायाम्बुभुत्सित-शब्दकत्वादिजातिग्रहे बुभुत्सैव शरणं एककालीन-बहुशब्दबुभुत्सा च न हेतुः व्यभिचारात्।

यत्तु कोलाहलादन्यच्चैकदा नानाशब्दग्रहे श्रोत्रन्न समर्थं किन्त्वेकशब्दग्रहे विनिगमिका बुभुत्सैवेति। तन्न। एकगीयमानापेक्षयैकदा नानागीयमानस-जातीयगीतादिषु सुखादिवैलक्षण्यानुभवात्।

अथ दीर्घशष्कुलीभक्षणे कथं पञ्च ज्ञानानि। क्रमस्तत्रेति चेत्। न। ज्ञानानां यौगपद्यप्रत्ययस्य बाधकं विना प्रमात्वात्। व्यासङ्गोबाधक इति चेत्, तर्हि मनोऽवयव्यस्तु तेन सङ्कोच-विकाशाभ्यामुभयमुप-

---

नानाशब्दसमवायकालीनैकतरबुभुत्सा यद्यपरग्रहप्रतिबन्धिका तदैकबुभुत्सायाङ्कोलाहलधीर्न स्यादित्यस्वरसाद्बुभुत्सायाः शब्दग्रहे न हेतुत्वं अन्यग्रहे वा न प्रतिबन्धकत्वमपि तु तज्जातिग्रहे हेतुत्वं

पद्यते इति केचित्। तन्न। यदि हि सङ्कोच-विकाश-हेतुरदृष्टन्तर्हि तत एव तदुभयमस्तु कृतं मनसा। नाप्येक-पञ्चबुभुत्सया तौ भवतः तस्या अहेतुत्वात्। हेतुत्वे वा अस्तु विभु मनः अवयविनो लघुत्वात्।

अथ यथा क्वचित् बुभुत्सया क्वचित्तीव्रविषयेन्द्रिय-सन्निकर्षादिन्द्रिय-मनःसंयोगः, एवं मनःसङ्कोच-विकाशयोर्बुभुत्सादिकं हेतुरिति चेत्, तर्हि पञ्चबुभुत्सायां प्रणिधाने च सर्व्वदा सर्व्वेषां पञ्च ज्ञानानि जायेरन् पञ्चावधानस्थाने क्रम एव। एतेनाणुमनः-पञ्चतयमस्तु अवयविनो लघुत्वात् बुभुत्सादिवशात्तेषामेक-पञ्चेन्द्रियसम्बन्धादुभयमुपपद्यत इति निरस्तम्। पञ्चबुभुत्सायां सर्व्वेषां पञ्चेन्द्रियसम्बन्धे व्यासङ्गानुपपत्तेः। कथं तर्हि दीर्घशष्कुलीभक्षणे गन्ध-रस-रूप-स्पर्श-शब्दान् प्रत्येमीत्यनुव्यवसायः क्रमिकज्ञानपञ्चतयेन युगपन्मनःसन्निकर्षाभावादिति चेत्।

तादृश्येव प्रतिबन्धकत्वञ्चेत्याह, 'यद्येति, न चैवमेकदा स्वस्वविषय-सम्बद्धेन्द्रियदशायां रूपाद्यन्यतरबुभुत्सा तद्ग्राहिका अन्यग्रहप्रतिबन्धिका चास्त्विति समः समाधिरिति(१) वाच्यम्। तादृशबुभुत्सायामपि

---

(१) परीहार इतीति ख०।

न। अनुव्यवसायस्यैकत्वासिद्धेः, अनुव्यवसायाः पञ्चैव समयसौक्ष्म्यात्तेषां क्रमो न गृह्यते(१)।

अथवा क्रमिकानुव्यवसायाहितसंस्कारात् पञ्च-ज्ञानविषयस्मृतावनुभवत्वारोपात् युगपत्प्रत्येमीत्यनु-व्यवसायः। विभुत्वे हेत्वभावादात्म-मनःसंयोगाभा-वाच्चात्मसुखाद्युपलम्भः स्यात्। द्रव्यत्वेनात्मसंयोगि-त्वसाधने त्वजसंयोगसिद्धौ तत एव तद्विभागित्वेऽपि सर्व्वदा तयोः परस्परविरुद्धसंयोग-विभागप्रसङ्गः। ननु अणुत्वे असमवाय्यनुरोधात् चेष्टाहेतुप्रयत्नस्याणुदेशत्वं शरीरदेशमात्रत्वं वा(२) स्यात्। न तु शरीर-तदवयवदे-शत्वं, येन क्रियानियमो भवेत् नियमकाभावात्। न च नोदनाभिघातादिवाव्यापिनोऽपि प्रयत्नात् शरीरादि-क्रिया, अतिप्रसङ्गात्। एवमेकदा विंशतिप्रयत्नाभावात् कथमङ्गुलीषु विंशतिः क्रियाः। न च यौगपद्यभ्रमः, बाधकाभावात्। युगपत्सन्निकर्षाभावेनाङ्गुल्यस्खलन्तीति

सूची-सर्पादिवेधानुभवेन तादृश्या अपि व्यभिचारादिति भावः।

विभुत्वे बाधकान्तरमाह, 'विभुत्व इति, 'विभागप्रसङ्ग इत्यापा-ततः, परमार्थतस्तत्प्रयोजकमात्मसंयोगित्वे द्रव्यत्वं, मूर्त्तत्वे च सामग्र्येन

---

(१) न लक्ष्यते इति ख०।

(२) शरीरमात्रदेशत्वं वेति ख०।

समूहालम्बनानुपपत्तेः विंशतिज्ञानानामेकदानुव्यवसायासम्भवात् अग्र-पश्चाद्भावे विनिगमकाभावाच्च। क्रमोत्पादे च भ्रू-नयन-कर-चरणादिसकलशरीरावयवानां युगपद्विचित्रनानाकर्मसमूहरूपं नृत्यं न प्रत्यक्षं स्यात्। तथाच प्रत्येककर्मजन्यसुखाद्विलक्षणसुखविशेषो नानुभूयेतेति। अत्र ब्रूमः। सुखे चन्दनादिवत् चिकीर्षैव नियामिका यत्क्रियायां चिकीर्षा सा क्रिया तच्चिकीर्षाजन्यात् प्रयत्नाद्भवति। तत्र शरीरक्रियापि तच्चिकीर्षाजन्यादणुमात्रदेशादपि प्रयत्नाद्भवति। अथवा यस्य क्रियायां चिकीर्षा तदवच्छेदेन प्रयत्न उत्पद्यते तेन शरीरावच्छेदेनोत्पन्नप्रयत्नादेव शरीरक्रिया। एवं विंशतिक्रिया चिकीर्षाजन्यादणुमात्रदेशादपि प्रयत्नाद्विंशतिक्रिया युगपदुत्पद्यन्ते। अथवा अङ्गुलीविंशतिक्रियायां चिकीर्षेति

विपक्षबाधिका, आत्मविभागित्वे तु मूर्त्तत्वमेव न कुतो द्रव्यत्वं, कपालद्वयसंयोगेन घटोत्पत्तिकाले आत्मविभागस्यावाच्छिन्नत्वेनाग्रिमसमये संयोगादिवद्विभागोत्पत्तिसामग्र्यभावेनात्मविभागानुत्पत्तौ व्यभिचारात्। न चाग्रिमकाले तदुत्पादः, तदुत्तरकाले घटनाशस्यापि सम्भवात्। ननु सुखे चन्दनादिवच्चिकीर्षा प्रयत्नोत्पत्तौ नियामिका न तु चेष्टो-

विंशत्यवच्छेदेन विंशतिप्रयत्नाद्विंशतिक्रियाहेतव उत्पद्यन्ते, एवं नृत्यादावपि। एतच्चिकीर्षानुविधानात् क्रिया-प्रयत्नयोरध्यवसेयं। तदेवमणुमनःसिद्धौ तद्ग्राह्या आत्मविशेषगुणाः बुद्धि-सुख-दुःखादय इति नाव्यापकं प्रत्यक्षलक्षणं।

इति श्रीमद्गङ्गेशोपाध्यायविरचिते तत्त्वचिन्तामणौ प्रत्यक्षखण्डे मनोऽणुत्ववादः ।

त्पत्तौ तत्र चिकीर्षाया अनिमित्तत्वात् विभुकार्य्याणामेव निमित्तानुरोधाच्चेत्यतस्तदेव सिद्धान्तयति(१) 'अथ वेति ।

इति श्रीजयदेवमिश्रविरचिते तत्त्वचिन्तामण्यालोके प्रत्यक्षखण्डालोके मनोऽणुत्ववादालोकः ।

---

(१) सिद्धान्तमाहेति ख० ।

अथानुव्यवसायवादः ।

ननु वर्त्तमानं ज्ञानं न मानसं किन्तु स्वयमेव स्वव्यवहारहेतुः, स्वस्मिन् सत्येव स्वव्यवहारात्, न तु ज्ञानान्तरमपेक्षते तदन्वय-व्यतिरेकाननुविधानात् ज्ञानान्तरविरहदशायां स्वविरहादेव स्वव्यवहारविरहात् स्वत एव स्वव्यवहारोपपत्तौ ज्ञानान्तरकल्पने गौरवाच्च । घटादिव्यवहारे ज्ञानान्वय-व्यतिरेकादस्तु तदपेक्षा । स्वीयमतीतमनागतं परकीयञ्च ज्ञानं स्वव्यवहारे ज्ञानान्तरमपेक्षत एव व्यवहारकाले तदभावात्

अथानुव्यवसायवादालोकः ।

'नन्विति, तथाच ज्ञानगोचरप्रत्यक्ष एवाव्याप्तम् प्रत्यक्षलक्षणमिति पूर्वाक्षेपस्तदवस्थ एवेति भावः । नन्वेवं परकीयज्ञानादौ न व्यवहारकालासत्त्वं अतो हेत्वन्तरमाह, 'ज्ञानेति । 'व्यवहारस्येति, इदञ्च समाधिसौकार्य्यादुक्तं यतो व्यवहारानुरोधं विनापीच्छामीति इच्छाविषयकानुभवादेवेच्छाविषयकं ज्ञानं सिध्यति । न चैवं ज्ञाने, तत्र जानामीत्यनुभवस्य स्वप्रकाशतया अन्यथासिद्धौ व्यवहारबलादेव ज्ञानानुव्यवसायस्य वाच्यत्वात् । न चैवं व्यवहारानुरोधं विनापि योग्यत्वादेव ज्ञानानुव्यवसायोऽस्तु लाघवादनुगमाच्च क्षणिकात्मविशेषगुण-

ज्ञानान्तरान्वय-व्यतिरेकानुविधानाच्च। नन्वेवमिच्छादिकमपि स्वव्यवहारज्ञानं नापेक्षेत ज्ञानतुल्यतया स्वयमेव स्वव्यवहारशक्तत्वादिति चेत्। न। व्यवहारस्य ज्ञानजन्यत्वनियमेनेच्छादिव्यवहारे ज्ञानापेक्षणात्। अथ ज्ञानमात्रं न व्यवहारहेतुरतिप्रसङ्गात् किन्तु व्यवहर्त्तव्यविषयमिति ज्ञानव्यवहारोऽपि तद्विषयज्ञानान्तराद्भवेदिति चेत्। सत्यं। स्वस्यैव स्वविषयकत्वात्। यद्व्यवहारानुकूलशक्तियोगि यज्ज्ञानं तस्यैव तद्विषयकत्वात्। शक्तिश्च पदार्थान्तरं न कारणतेति नान्योन्याश्रयः। स्वव्यवहारे ज्ञानं शक्तमिति स्वविषयकं। व्यवहारशक्ति-समवायादयश्च स्वभावत एव तदीयाः सम्बन्धान्तरेऽप्यनवस्थानात् स्वभाव एव शरणं। एतेन भेदनियतो विषय-विषयिभावः कथ-

---

त्वेनैव योग्यत्वात् न तु तेन तेनेच्छात्वादिनेति वाच्यम्। निर्व्विकल्पकजीवनयोनियत्नसाधारण्येनाननुगतस्यैव योग्यतावच्छेदकत्वात्, तथाच फलबलाद्योग्यतावच्छेदककल्पना ज्ञाने तु फलं न निश्चितं येन ज्ञानविशेषत्वं तथा कल्प्येत तन्निश्चायकयोर्व्यवहारानुभवयोरन्यथासिद्धत्वादित्यवधेयम्। 'व्यवहारानुकूलेति, न च ज्ञानेत्यधिकं, ज्ञानं विना तदनुकूलशक्तिमता केवलमात्मना व्यवहाराजननादिति भावः। 'नान्योन्येति, यद्यपि व्यवहारानुकूलका-

मभेद इति निरस्तं। स्वव्यवहारशक्तत्वस्य स्वविषयत्वस्याभेदेऽपि[१] सम्भवात्। अस्तु वा ज्ञानस्य स्वभावविशेष एव स्वविषयत्वं सम्बन्धं विनैव स्वभावविशेषाद्यथा ज्ञानं घटीयं घटव्यवहारजननयोग्यं स्वीयमपि तथा[२]। कोऽसौ स्वभावविशेष इति चेत्। न। आख्यातुमशक्यत्वेऽप्यनुभवसिद्धस्य स्वभावविशेषस्य माधुर्य्यादिविशेषवत् प्रत्याख्यातुमशक्यत्वात्। यद्यपि स्वभावविशेष इति वाक्येनाख्यायत एव, तथापि पदेनाख्यातुमशक्यत्वात्। अथ व्यवहारो व्यवहर्त्तव्यभिन्नज्ञानसाध्यः कथन्तेन विना स्यादिति चेत्। न। व्यवहारं प्रति व्यवहर्त्तव्यज्ञानत्वेन हेतुत्वात्, न तु व्यवहर्त्तव्यभिन्नज्ञानत्वेन गौरवात्। समूहालम्बनञ्चे-

---

रणता व्यवहारकारणतावच्छेदिकेत्यात्माश्रयः, तथापि व्यवहारकारणतावच्छेदकावच्छिन्नत्वज्ञाने सति व्यवहारकारणताज्ञानमवच्छेदकावच्छिन्नत्वज्ञाने सत्येवावच्छेद्यग्रहात् तज्ज्ञाने सति तदवच्छिन्नत्वज्ञानं विशेषणज्ञानसाध्यत्वात् विशिष्टज्ञानस्येत्यन्योन्याश्रयो द्रष्टव्यः। ननु 'स्वव्यवहारः' स्वविषयकव्यवहारः, शक्तेरपि तदीयायास्तत्र समवायः,

---

(२) स्वविषयत्वस्याभिन्नत्वेऽपीति ख०।

(३) तथा स्वीयमपीति ख०।

कैकव्यवहारजनकत्वादेकैकविषयकमपि न तु समूह-विषयकमेव अतिरिक्तस्य तस्यासत्त्वेन सन्निकर्षाभा-वात्। भ्रमस्थले रजतव्यवहारानुकूलशक्तिरस्त्येव रज-तज्ञाने, किन्तु दोषादभिभूतैव सा जायत इति न तया रजते व्यवहारः, रजतज्ञानं न शुक्तौ प्रवर्त्तकं किन्त्विन्द्रियजन्यमिदं ज्ञानमेव, रजतार्थिप्रवृत्त्यर्थन्तू-पस्थितरजतभेदाग्रहमपेक्षत इति रजतज्ञानं कारणता-वच्छेदकम्। एवञ्च स्वविषयत्वं स्वप्रकाशत्वं न तु स्वव्यवहारे ज्ञानान्तरानपेक्षत्वं गौरवात्। अन्यथा ज्ञानस्य स्वाविषयत्वेन संस्काराभावात् स्मरणं न स्यात्।

समवायित्वञ्च समवायसम्बन्धः, तान्येतानि सम्बन्धं विना न सम्भवन्ति, स्वरूपसम्बन्धो नेष्यत एवान्यथा ज्ञानविषयत्वेऽपि तथात्वापत्तेः, तथाच सम्बन्धान्तरमभ्युपेयतामित्यत आह, 'व्यवहारेति, सर्वत्र स्वरू-पसम्बन्धं नापजानीमः किन्तु ज्ञानविषयत्व एवेतिभावः। ननु कारणतायां गृहीतायां शक्तिकल्पनं तस्मिंश्च तदवच्छेदेन हेतुताधी-रित्यन्योन्याश्रयः, किञ्च ज्ञानस्यापि स्वरूपव्यवहारतया तेन सह स्वरूपसम्बन्धाभ्युपगमे ज्ञानेनापि तथाभ्युपगम इत्यरुचेः स्वभा-वमेव विषयतामाह, 'अस्तु वेति। ननु समूहालम्बनं प्रत्येकविषयं न स्यात् समूहेन्द्रियसन्निकर्षजत्वेन प्रत्येकविषयकव्यवहाराजननादि-

यत्तु स्वव्यवहारे ज्ञानान्तरानपेक्षत्वमुक्तं तत् स्वप्रकाशत्वनिर्व्वाहकतया, प्रमाणञ्च स्वप्रकाशे प्रत्यक्षमेव, सर्वाः प्रतीतय इदमहं जानामीत्येवमाकारा- ज्ञातारं ज्ञानं ज्ञेयञ्चोल्लिखन्त्यो जायन्ते, तत्रात्मा[१] कर्तृत्वेन, ज्ञेयं कर्मतया ज्ञानं क्रियात्वेन भासते अतो ज्ञातृ-ज्ञेय-स्वविषयं ज्ञानमनुभूयत इति त्रिपुटीप्रत्यक्षवादिनः।

त्यतआह, 'समूहेति, तस्यातिरिक्तस्याभावेन तत्तदात्मकस्य समूहस्य यः सन्निधिः स प्रत्येकस्यापीति उक्तदोषाभावादिति भावः। ननु व्यवहारजनकत्वं[२] यदि तद्विषयकत्वं तदा रजतज्ञानमपि शुक्तिगोचरमित्यन्यथाख्यातिरतआह[३], 'रजतज्ञानमिति। स्वैकदेशिमतं निरस्यति 'न त्विति।

स्वमते स्वोपजीव्यमविरोधयितुमाह, 'यत्त्विति, 'प्रत्यक्षमेवेति। यद्यपि ज्ञानगोचरतायां प्रत्यक्षं प्रमाणं सम्भवति न तु स्वविषयतायां व्यवसायोत्तरत्वेऽपि तथैवानुव्यवसायाकारात्[४], तथापि ज्ञानान्तरकल्पने गौरवाल्लाघवसहकृतमिदमेव प्रत्यक्षं ज्ञानगोचरत्वेनानुभूयमानं स्वविषयत्वे पर्य्यवस्यतीति हृदयम्। 'कर्तृत्वेन' आश्रयत्वेन,

---

(१) तत्र आतेति ख०।

(२) तद्व्यवहारप्रकत्वमिति ख०।

(३) अन्यथाख्यात्यापत्तिरित्यत आहेति ख०।

(४) अनुव्यवसायस्य तथैवाकारादिति ख०।

नन्विदमिति व्यवसायः तदुत्तरमिदमहं जाना-मीत्यनुव्यवसायो मानस इति चेत्। न। स्वप्रकाशत्वे-नोपपत्तौ ज्ञानान्तरकल्पने गौरवात्[१] परिशेषाच्च स्वप्रकाशत्वं परप्रकाशकत्वे हि न ज्ञानमेव सिद्ध्येत् मानाभावात्। न हि तत्र ज्ञातता लिङ्गं, अतीतानागतयोस्तदभावात्। नापि मानसं प्रत्यक्षं, अजिज्ञासि-

---

'कर्मतया' विषयतया, 'क्रियात्वेन' विशेषणतया, 'अनुभूयत इति ज्ञेय-ज्ञातृ-स्वविषयकत्वानुभवस्वरूपमुत्पद्यत इत्यर्थः। यद्वा ज्ञातृ-ज्ञेय-स्वविषयकानुभवोऽपि स एवानुभव इति तत् सिद्धान्तोऽन्यथा ज्ञानान्तरेण तद्ग्रहाभ्युपगमे तज्ज्ञानगोचरज्ञानान्तराभ्युपगमापत्तावनुव्यवसायस्वीकारापत्तिरिति भावः।

पूर्व्वोक्तप्रमाणे तर्कापेक्षागौरवान्मानान्तरमाह, 'परिशेषादिति। 'अनवस्थानादिति तथाचैतद्भयेनायोग्यमेव ज्ञानमभ्युपगन्तुमर्हं तथाच न मानसप्रत्यक्षमित्यर्थः। न च विषयान्तरसञ्चारः प्रतिबन्धकः, वैपरीत्येन तस्यैवानुत्पत्त्यापत्तेरित्याह, 'विषयान्तरेति। 'जिज्ञासेति अजिज्ञासाग्राह्यभिन्नात्मधर्म्मत्वादित्यर्थः, अजिज्ञासाग्राह्यत्वस्य जिज्ञासानपेक्षप्रत्यक्षविषयत्वम्, यथाश्रुते ग्रहपदस्य प्रत्यक्षपरत्वे दृष्टान्तासिद्धिः। पक्षताकाङ्क्षाघटकजिज्ञासाजन्यं ज्ञानमनुमितिः शाब्दश्च, तद्विषयता

---

(१) ज्ञानान्तरे कल्पनागौरवादिति क०।

तस्य मानसत्वे ज्ञानाविरामादनवस्थानात् विषयान्तरासञ्चाराच्च। जिज्ञासितस्य ग्राह्यत्वे ज्ञानं न मानसं जिज्ञासाग्राह्यात्मधर्मत्वात् संस्कारवदित्यनुमानप्रतिरोधः। अतएव जिज्ञासां विनैव सुखादीनां मानसत्वं, जिज्ञासापि ज्ञानसाध्येत्यनवस्था, धर्मिज्ञानेच्छादिभिर्ज्ञानस्य नाशाच्च न प्रत्यक्षत्वम्। अथ ज्ञानं मानस-

---

संस्कारेऽस्त्येव ग्रहपदस्य ज्ञानमात्रपरत्वादिति यदि तदा सुखादावेव व्यभिचारः। न च सावधारणतया जिज्ञासाजन्यग्रहमात्रगोचरत्वं, तथा च सति मात्रपदार्थप्रविष्टस्य विवक्षितैकदेशस्य समर्थत्वेन हेतुत्वौचित्यात्। न चात्मेत्यधिकं, आत्मन्येव व्यभिचारवारकत्वात्। न चातीन्द्रियत्वमुपाधिः, विपक्षबाधकाभावेन तुल्यबलतया तस्यापि प्रतिरोधपर्य्यवसायित्वादिति भावः। 'अत इति यतोऽजिज्ञासाग्राह्यात्मधर्म्मत्वं मानसत्वे तन्त्रं अतएव सुखादीनां जिज्ञासां विनाऽमानसत्वमित्यर्थः, तथा च मानसत्वव्यापकजिज्ञासाविरहस्याभावाद्व्याप्यस्य मानसत्वस्याभावः साध्यत इति भावः। अतोऽपि विवक्षितो हेतुरुचित इत्यवधेयम्। ननु चाक्षुषत्वाविशेषेऽपि केशादौ जिज्ञासापेक्षा न वृक्षादाविति वदिहापि कश्चिदेव जिज्ञासा कश्चिन्नेति स्यादित्यप्रयोजकत्वं मत्वा दोषान्तरमाह, 'जिज्ञासापीति जिज्ञासा धर्म्मिज्ञानसापेक्षा तच्च जिज्ञासापेक्षमित्यनवस्थानादित्यर्थः। ननु सामान्यतो धर्म्मिज्ञानं जिज्ञासानपेक्षं हेतुः सा च विशेषतो ज्ञानग्रहे कारणमतोऽनवस्था न सम्भवतीति दोषान्तरमाह,

प्रत्यक्षं प्रत्यक्षात्मगुणत्वात्, आत्मविशेषगुणत्वे सति क्षणमात्रस्थायित्वात् सुखवत्, ज्ञानं प्रत्यक्षजनकेन्द्रियसन्निकर्षाश्रयः प्रत्यक्षत्वात् सुखवदिति चेन् । न । मानसत्वेऽनवस्थानात् । अतएव चक्षुर्जन्यं ज्ञानं न चक्षुर्जन्यज्ञानविषयः प्रत्यक्षत्वात् रासनवत्, नैतज्ज्ञानविषयो वा एतज्जनकेन्द्रियसन्निकर्षानाश्रयत्वात् गगनवत्, चक्षुर्न चाक्षुषज्ञानग्राहकं वहिरिन्द्रियत्वात् रसनवदिति प्रतिपक्षानुमानमपास्तं । परप्रकाशत्वे अनवस्थया ज्ञानासिद्धावाश्रयासिद्धेः । स्वप्रकाशत्वेन तत्सिद्धौ

'धर्म्मी'ति, 'प्रत्यक्ष'ेति, मनोयोग्यतावच्छेदकं लाघवात्प्रत्यक्षगोचरात्मगुणत्वमेव न लिङ्गत्वादि गौरवादिति ज्ञानस्य मनोयोग्यत्वस्थितौ योग्यसन्निधेः प्रत्यक्षजनकत्वनियमात् जानामीत्येतदधिकज्ञानान्तराननुभवेन तदेव ज्ञानं मानसं कल्प्यतेऽतस्तदनुरोधादेवानुव्यवसायोऽधिकोऽस्तीति निर्गलितार्थः । अन्यथा तद्गोचरमानसज्ञानान्तरोत्पत्त्यापि साध्यपर्य्यवसानेनास्मादनुमानात्स्वप्रकाशताबाधः स्यादित्यवधेयमम् । तथाचान्यज्ञानासम्भवरूपतर्कसहकारादिदमनुमानं सम्यगिति । मानसप्रत्यक्षत्वम् मानसप्रत्यक्षविषयगुणत्वव्याप्यजातिमत्त्वम् तेनाग्निसंयोगेनाविनाशलोचन-जीवनयोनियत्नयोर्न व्यभिचारः । जातिप्रत्यक्षता व्यक्तिप्रत्यक्षतां विना नेति तावद्दूरमनुमानान्निर्वहतीति ध्येयम् । 'क्षणे'ति चतुर्थक्षणवृत्तिध्वंसप्रतियोगित्वादित्यर्थः, 'आत्मविशेष-

धर्मिग्राहकमानबाधात्। किञ्च स्वव्यवहारशक्तत्वं स्वविषयत्वं, तच्च स्वसन्निकर्षाजन्यत्वे स्वाजन्यत्वे च न विरुद्धम्। न च स्वव्यवहारे शक्तत्वस्याभाव एव साध्यः, अप्रयोजकत्वात् स्वसन्निकर्षाजन्ये स्वाजन्ये व्यवहारशक्ते घटादौ व्यभिचाराच्च। अतएव स्वप्रकाशत्वेन पूर्वानुभवविषयता तत्तानुभूतमात्रविषये स्मरणे उत्सर्गतो भासते ज्ञानान्तरस्यानावश्यकत्वात्। स्वस्य स्वाजन्यत्वे कथं स्वकर्मतेति चेत्। न। अतीतानागतयोरिव स्वविषयत्वं न तु कर्मत्वं, विषयत्वञ्चाभेदेऽपि स्वव्यवहारशक्तत्वस्य ज्ञानस्वभावविशेषस्य वा विषयत्वात्।

गुणत्वम् अत्राप्यनुषञ्जनीयम्, अन्यथा शब्दादौ व्यभिचारप्रसङ्गादिति। 'प्रत्यक्षजनकेति स्वप्रत्यक्षजनकेत्यर्थः, तेन यत्र यत्प्रत्यक्षविषयता तत्र तज्जनकेन्द्रियसन्निकर्षाश्रयत्वमिति व्याप्तिपर्य्यवसाने यथाश्रुतसाध्यमादाय न सिद्धसाधनावकाशः सुखप्रत्यक्षजनकसंयुक्तसमवायस्य ज्ञानेऽपि सत्त्वादिति[१], 'प्रत्यक्षत्वात्' जन्यप्रत्यक्षविषयत्वात्। 'चक्षुरिति न स्वसमानाधिकरण-समानकालीनचाक्षुषधीविषय इत्यर्थः, तेन यथाश्रुते न चाक्षुषोऽयमित्युपनीतधीदर्शनात्स्वमते बाधः न चाक्षुषधीर्विशेष्य इतिसाध्ये परमते सिद्धसाधनं जानामीति ज्ञाने ज्ञानस्य विशेषणत्वात् इति दूषणं न लगति। 'प्रत्यक्षत्वात्'

---

(१) सिद्धत्वादितीति ख०।

न चाधीकर्मतया शशशृङ्गवदसत्त्वं, तस्य कदाप्यप्रकाशात्, धीजन्यव्यवहारभागित्वं कर्म्मत्वं स्वप्रकाशेऽपि तदन्यफलभागित्वञ्च घटेऽप्यसिद्धं ज्ञाततानिषेधात्। ज्ञानानपेक्षेन्द्रियसन्निकर्षजं ज्ञानं प्रत्यक्षमतः सर्व्वं ज्ञानं ज्ञानानपेक्षात्म-मनःसन्निकर्षजन्यत्वेन स्वात्मनि प्रत्यक्षं, विशिष्टप्रत्यक्षञ्च न विशेषणज्ञानजन्यं निर्व्विकल्पकनिषेधात् । सविकल्पकत्वेन ज्ञानाजन्यज्ञानं वा प्रत्यक्षं तेन निर्व्विकल्पकजन्यं जातिविशिष्टज्ञानं प्रत्यक्षं, न त्वसाधारणेन्द्रियादिकरणकं तेन विनाप्यनुमित्यादौ स्वात्मप्रकाशात् । इन्द्रियादिकन्त्वर्थप्रकाश एव हेतुः तस्यैव तत्प्रतिबद्धहेतुजन्यत्वादिति ।

अत्रोच्यते। प्रत्यक्षं न स्वप्रकाशे प्रमाणं व्यवसाया-

साक्षात्त्वात्, यद्यपि ज्ञानत्वादित्येवोचितं तथापि व्यर्थविशेषणत्वाभावेन हेत्वन्तरस्यापि सम्यक्त्वात् इदमुक्तं। 'गगनवदिति, सन्निहितमिन्द्रियमपहाय दृष्टान्तान्तरमुपाददता एतदजनकत्वादिति हेत्वन्तरं सूचितं, तच्च हेताविन्द्रियस्य साधनविकलत्वात् गगनस्य शब्दादन्यत्र ज्ञानादावन्यथासिद्धत्वेनोदाहृतत्वात् अतो न 'स्वसन्निकर्षाजन्यत्वे स्वाजन्यत्वे च' इत्यनेन स्वजन्यत्वहेतोः(१) अप्रयोजकत्वाभिधानमसङ्कप्रतिषेधो भवतीति ध्येयम् ।

---

(१) वाद्यनुक्तहेतोरिति क० ।

नामिदमहं जानामीत्याकारासिद्धेः। न चैवमनुभवविरोधः, अर्थनिश्चयेन प्रवृत्त्यादिदर्शनात्। व्यवसायस्य अर्थविषयत्वमात्रमनुभूयते न तु स्वविषयत्वमपि गौरवेण तस्य स्वविषयभानतया प्रवृत्त्यहेतुत्वात्[१]। अनुभवोऽपीदं रजतमित्याद्येव। न चैवमिदमहं जानामीत्यनुभवापलापे उपेक्षणीयता, व्यवसायोत्तरकालं तदुपगमात् इदं रजतमित्यादिलौकिकानुभवात् व्यवसायस्य तदाकारतां निषेधामो न त्वनुव्यवसायस्य। ननु भिन्नानुव्यवसाये अनवस्थानात् व्यवसाय एवानुव्यवसाय इति चेत्, तर्हि परप्रकाशे बाधकात् स्वप्रकाशत्वसिद्धौ सर्व्वप्रतीतीनामिदमहं जानामीत्या-

ननु स्वप्रकाशत्व-परप्रकाशत्वसंन्देहेऽपि ज्ञानगोचरज्ञानसत्त्वादाश्रयासिद्धिर्न भवतीत्यरुचेराह, 'किञ्चेति, घटादावित्यतद्गुणसंविज्ञानबहुव्रीहिणात्मादेरभिधानं घटस्य व्यवहारजनकत्वाभावादित्यवधेयम्। 'तस्येति प्रत्यक्षस्यासत्त्वे अधीकर्मत्वं न प्रयोजकं किन्तु प्रकाशाविषयत्वं अतः प्रकाशविषयतासत्त्वादधीकर्मत्वेऽपि नासत्त्वमित्यर्थः। अधीकर्मत्वन्तु न ज्ञानासत्त्वसाधकं अतीन्द्रिये व्यभिचारादिति वस्तुस्थितिः। यदि वा ततोऽसत्त्वसाधनं तदा स्वरूपासिद्धिरित्याह, 'धीजन्येति, परसमवेतक्रियाफलशालित्वस्य कर्म्मतात्वादित्यभिप्रेत्य

(१) प्रवृत्त्याद्यहेतुत्वादिति ख०।

कारतासिद्धिः, तथाच स्वप्रकाशत्वासिद्धौ सर्व्वप्रतीतीनामिदमहं जानामीत्याकारत्वमसिद्धमिति न सा प्रतीतिः स्वप्रकाशत्वे प्रमाणं।

अपिच क्रियायाः कृतेर्वा समवायित्वं कर्त्तृत्वं, परसमवेतक्रियाफलशालित्वं करणव्यापारविषयत्वं वा कर्म्मत्वं, धात्वर्थत्वमन्यद्वा क्रियात्वम् इदमहं जानामीति व्यवसाये न भासते तद्बोधकेन्द्रियसन्निकर्षाभावात् किन्त्विदंविषयकज्ञानत्वविशिष्टस्य ज्ञानस्य वैशिष्ट्यमात्मनि भासते। न च स्वप्रकाशे व्यवसाये तादृशं स्वस्य वैशिष्ट्यं भासितुमर्हति, पूर्व्वं विशेषणस्य तस्याज्ञानात्। तस्मा-

---

त्वयानुमानप्रयोगादिति भावः। ननु भवतु स्वप्रकाशपक्षस्तथापि तदंशे प्रत्यक्षं भवितुमर्हति तत्सन्निकर्षजन्यत्वादित्याह, 'ज्ञानेति। ननु यदीन्द्रियनिबन्धनं न प्रत्यक्षत्वं तर्हीन्द्रियानुविधानानुपपत्तिरित्याह, 'इन्द्रियादिकमिति, तस्य ज्ञानोत्पत्तावेव सामर्थ्यात् प्रत्यक्षत्वे तु तस्यातन्त्रत्वादिति भावः[१]। 'तस्यैवेति अर्थप्रकाशमात्रस्यैवेन्द्रियादिसहकृतकारणजन्यत्वादित्यर्थः।

'व्यवसायामामिति, व्यवसायस्य नायमाकारः, किन्तु अनुव्यवसायस्य, तथाच तदाकारकस्य तस्य वस्तुतो ज्ञानविषयस्यार्थगोचरत्वं ज्ञानीयं विषयो न तु स्वस्य ज्ञानव्यवसायीयं विषयत्वमपि

---

(२) तस्यातन्त्रत्वादित्यर्थ इति ख०।

दिदमहं जानामीति न व्यवसायः किन्त्वनुव्यवसायः। स्यादेतत्। कर्तृत्वादिज्ञानवैशिष्ट्यमात्मनि मा ज्ञायि व्यवहारस्य स्वविषयकज्ञानसाध्यत्वसिद्धौ तदेव ज्ञानं स्वविषयकं कल्प्यते लाघवात्। ज्ञानवित्तिवेद्य आत्मापि तद्विषय इत्यात्मविषयत्वं सर्व्ववित्तीनामिति चेत्। न। स्वजनकेन्द्रियसन्निकर्षानाश्रयत्वेन स्वस्य स्वाविषयत्वात्। विषयत्वनियामकेन्द्रियसन्निकर्षादेरभावे स्वविषयत्वानुपपत्तेः, कारणं विना कार्य्यानुत्पादनात् प्रत्यक्षाजनकस्य प्रत्यक्षविषयत्वानुपपत्तेश्च। आत्मधर्म्मप्रत्यासत्त्यनाश्रये प्रत्यक्षविषताया जनकत्व-

---

येन ज्ञानान्तरकल्पनागौरवसहकृतं सत्प्रतिपक्षम् प्रमाणं स्वप्रकाशं निर्व्वहेत् स्वस्य स्वाविषयत्वेन स्वविषयाविषयत्वात्, न च स्वमपि स्वगोचरः, तथासत्यन्योन्याश्रयः, स्वविषयत्वे सिद्धे गौरवसहकृतं ज्ञानगोचरताग्राहकं स्वप्रकाशतायां प्रत्यक्षं प्रमाणीभवेत् तेन च मानेन स्वविषयतासिद्धिरित्यर्थः। तदिदमाह, व्यवसायस्यार्थविषयत्वं अनुभूयते अनुव्यवसायेन न तु स्वविषयत्वमपि उक्तदोषात् न वयमुक्तक्रमेण स्वविषयतां ब्रूमो येन परस्पराश्रयः, किन्तु व्यवहारानुरोधेनैव स्वविषयतेत्यत आह, 'गौरवेणेति'। नन्वर्थमात्रगोचरानुभवाभावादस्त्वनुभवविरोध इत्यत आह, 'अनुभवोऽपीति तथैव तस्यानुव्यवसायेनानुभवादित्यर्थः। 'तदुपगमादिति, व्यवसायविषयत्वेनैव तस्य ज्ञानान्तरेण ग्रहणादिति भावः।

श्यामत्वात्। ज्ञानस्य प्रत्यक्षत्वेनेन्द्रियसन्निकर्षाश्रयत्वात् मनःसन्निकर्षजन्यत्वेन मानसत्वं। तदयं प्रयोगः। विवादाध्यासितं[1] इन्द्रियजन्यं ज्ञानं नैतज्ज्ञानविषयाश्रयः[2] एतज्जनकेन्द्रियसन्निकर्षानाश्रयत्वात् एतदजनकत्वाद्वा असन्निकृष्टवत्। नैतज्ज्ञानविषयकं वा आत्मधर्मप्रत्यासत्त्यनाश्रयत्वे सति एतदजन्यत्वे च सति साक्षात्कारित्वात्। प्रत्यक्षविषयो ज्ञानं स्वप्रत्यक्षजनकेन्द्रियसन्निकर्षाश्रयः प्रत्यक्षविषयत्वादिति मनः-

---

ननु जानामीति ज्ञानं सार्व्वलौकिकं तदेव पूर्व्वापरज्ञानकल्पनागौरवसहकारेण स्वविषयं पर्य्यवस्यतीति सिद्धं प्रत्यक्षप्रमाणात् स्वप्रकाशत्वमित्यरुचेराह, 'अपिचेति, 'क्रियायाः' धात्वर्थस्येत्यर्थः। एतच्च घटोभवतीत्यादिप्रयोगादचेतनस्यापि कर्तृत्वमिति वैयाकरणमते[3]। 'परेति धात्वर्थानधिकरणत्वे सति धात्वर्थतावच्छेदकफलशालित्वमित्यर्थः। आत्मानं जानामीत्यात्मनि अकर्म्मत्वं मा प्रसाङ्क्षीदिति लक्षणान्तरमाह, 'करणेति। 'अन्यदेति कृतित्वं वेत्यर्थः। सर्व्वंच धात्वर्थे कृतिप्रवेशादिति भावः। ननु विषयत्वं घटादेराश्रयत्वमात्मनोविशेषणत्वं ज्ञानस्येत्येव कर्म्मत्व-कर्तृत्व-क्रियात्वादिभानमित्युक्तोपालम्भतया अपरितुष्यन्नाह, 'न चेति, विशेषणत्वमपि तादृशस्य

---

(१) विवादपदमिति ख०।

(२) नैतज्ज्ञानविषयमिति ख०।

(३) वैयाकरणादिमते इति ख०।

सन्निकर्षग्राह्यं। चाक्षुषज्ञानं न चक्षुर्जन्यज्ञानविषयः चक्षुरसन्निकृष्टत्वात् घटवत्। ज्ञानं प्रमेयमेवेतिव्याप्तिज्ञानं ज्ञानत्वप्रत्यासत्त्या स्वविषयं, ईश्वरज्ञानमहेतुकत्वेन सर्व्वविषयत्वात् स्वप्रकाशं। ननु परप्रकाशकत्वे ज्ञानमेव न सिध्येदनवस्थानादिति धर्म्मिग्राहकमानात् स्वप्रकाशत्वसिद्धावनन्यगतिकतया स्वस्यासन्निकृष्टस्यापि प्रत्यक्षविषयत्वमतो धर्म्मिग्राहकमानबाधितास्त्वदीयहेतव इति चेत्। न। वित्तेरवश्यवेद्यत्वाभावेनानवस्थाविगमात्। संयुक्तसमवायेन मनोवेद्यत्वादपेक्षणीयान्तराभावाच्चोत्पन्नैव कुतो नावश्य-

---

व्यवसायस्य तदा यदि तत्पूर्व्वभानं, न च स्वप्रकाशे तथा सम्भवति, इति भावः[१]। यद्यप्यभावत्वविशिष्टबोधस्तद्धियं विनापीति व्यभिचारस्तथापि यथैनं विना न भासते तद्धीहेतुरेव तद्धीहेतुरिति तज्ज्ञानं विनापि तद्विशिष्टबोधः, अतथाभूते तु तद्विशिष्टबुद्धिस्तद्बुद्धिसाध्येति नियम एव। न चाभावत्वाभाने अभावाभानवत् ज्ञानाभाने आत्माभानमस्ति येनेहापि तद्बोधकमेव तद्बोधकमस्तीति विशेषणज्ञानानपेक्षा विशिष्टबुद्धिरभ्युपगम्येत, तथा सति ज्ञानाभाने सुखादिविशिष्टोऽप्यात्मा न भासते इति यत्किञ्चिदेतत्। ननु विशिष्टबुद्धौ विशेषणज्ञानापेक्षेति तव सिद्धान्तो

---

(१) इत्यर्थ इति ख०।

वेद्येति चेत्। न। सुखादि-तद्बुद्ध्यादिसामग्र्या प्रतिबन्धात् विषयान्तरसंचारदर्शनेन तस्या बलवत्त्वात् अनुद्भवादिति केचित्।

योग्यात्मविशेषगुणत्वात् ज्ञानत्वात् ज्ञानं प्रत्यक्षमेवेति व्याप्तेर्व्वित्तेरवश्यवेद्यत्वेन स्वप्रकाशत्वमिति चेत्। न। व्याप्तेरसिद्धेः परप्रकाशकत्वेऽनवस्थानात्। स्वप्रकाशे कारणानुपपत्तेः सन्निकृष्टमेव प्रत्यक्षं तद्विषयजन्यमेव प्रत्यक्षमिति व्याप्तेश्च। अन्यथा कारणं विना कार्य्यानुत्पत्ति-व्याप्तोर्विनिगमकं कारणसत्त्वेपि प्रतिबन्धात् कार्य्यानुत्पादे कारणत्वमप्रत्यूहम् क्लृप्तकारणं विना कार्य्योत्पादे कारणताभङ्गः कार्य्यानुत्पादश्च। अपिच परप्रकाशे अनवस्थानात् परिशेषानुमानेन ज्ञानस्य स्वप्रकाशत्वं, तथाच स्वप्रकाशत्वानुमितेरपि

मम तु साकाङ्क्षविशेष्य-विशेषणोभयविषयकं विशेषणबुद्ध्यनपेक्षमेव विशिष्टज्ञानमित्यभिप्रेत्य शङ्कते, 'स्यादेतदिति। 'स्वजनकसन्निकर्षानाश्रयत्वेन' स्वजनकसन्निकर्षाद्यनाश्रयत्वेनेत्यर्थः। ननु सन्निकर्षादिवत्तदभेदोऽपि विषयतानियामकोऽस्तु अनुगमाभावस्य तुल्यत्वादित्यत आह, 'प्रत्यक्षेति, सत्यपि विशेषेऽनुगतस्यैव सम्भवेनाऽनुगताभ्युपगमानुपपत्तेः, अभेदस्य विषयतानियतत्वे नियामकस्य हेतोरवश्यानुसन्धानादभेदस्य च हेतुत्वादिति भावः। ननु प्रत्यक्षविषयता न

स्वप्रकाशत्वमनुमित्यन्तरगम्यमेवं तस्यापीत्यनवस्था स्वप्रकाशत्वानुमितिपरम्पराद्वारा तवापि स्यात् विषयान्तरसञ्चारस्य प्रतिबन्धकत्वं, यावज्जिज्ञासं वा स्वप्रकाशत्वानुमितिरिति यदि तुल्यं परप्रकाशत्वेऽपि। न च ज्ञानं स्वप्रकाशमित्यनुमित्या स्वप्राशत्वमपि सामान्यप्रत्यासत्त्या विषयीकृतमिति वाच्यम्। परतः पक्षेऽपि तुल्यत्वात् त्वया तदनभ्युपगमाच्च। किञ्चानुमित्यादौ जातिसङ्करान्न प्रत्यक्षत्वम्। न च ज्ञानसापेक्षं मनोजनकमित्यनुमितिविषयवदात्मनि न तत्प्रत्यक्षम्। तस्य स्वविषयत्वे ज्ञानानपेक्षेति चेत्। न। ज्ञानं ज्ञानजन्यं तच्च स्वविषये स्वात्मन्येकमेवेति कथं तदपेक्षं तदनपेक्षञ्च विरुद्धत्वात्। न च ज्ञानभिन्नविषयत्वं सापेक्षं, तथात्वे वह्निज्ञानं प्रत्यक्षं न

जनकत्वव्याप्ता संस्कार-स्मृत्युपनीततत्तादौ व्यभिचारादतो व्याप्तिशरीरमाह, 'आत्मेति। नन्विदमप्यसत् यथाश्रुते सामान्यलक्षणप्रत्यासत्तिजन्यप्रत्यक्षविषये व्यभिचारेणानागतविषयसाक्षात्कारहेतुप्रत्यासत्त्यनाश्रयत्वं तदर्थोवाच्यः सोऽपि विद्यमानत्वसामान्यजन्यप्रत्यक्षविषये व्यभिचारावारकतया अजनकविषयसाक्षात्कारेत्यादिना विशेषणीयः[१] तथाच व्यर्थतया प्रत्यासत्तिभागमपहायाजनकविषय-

---

(१) विवक्षणीय इति ख०।

स्यात्[१]। अथान्यस्यान्यविषयत्वे सन्निकर्षादिर्नियामकः स्वविषयत्वे किन्तेन अनतिप्रसङ्गात् सन्निकर्षस्याननुगमाच्च व्यवहारे शक्तत्वं विषयत्वमभेदे सन्निकर्षं विनापीति चेत्। न। अन्यच्च प्रत्यक्षमात्रे[२] सन्निकर्षस्य हेतुत्वात् अन्यथाननुगमापत्तिः। अथ या वित्तिर्न वेद्या[३] सा प्रमाणाभावादसतीति तदधीनसत्त्वस्य विषयपर्य्यन्तस्यासत्त्वं स्यादिति चेत्। न। अविरलग्नतद्वित्तिवित्तिधारा[४] नाभ्युपेयते किन्नाम केनचित्कदाचित्काचिद्वित्तिर्व्यवहारस्मरणलिङ्गादिना प्रतीयत इति सर्व्वा प्रमाणसिद्धैवेत्यभ्युपगमात्। अथ स्यादेवं यदि घटोऽयं घटमहं जानामीत्यतोऽधिका

साक्षात्कारान्यप्रत्यक्षविषयताया जनकत्वव्याप्यत्वं वाच्यम्, एवञ्च स्वस्याजनकत्वेन स्वविषयतायां जनकत्वस्यानियामकत्वे स्वविषयता न बाधितेत्यरुचेर्मूलयुक्तिमाह,'ज्ञानस्येति, इच्छात्व-रूपत्वादीनां[५] अननुगमेन प्रत्यक्षत्वमेवेन्द्रिययोग्यतावच्छेदकं लाघवात् अनुगमाच्चेति सामान्यतः सिद्धे परिशेषान्मनःसंयोगजन्यत्वान्मानसत्वमिति न प्रागा-

(१) तथात्वेऽपि ज्ञानं प्रत्यक्षं न स्यादिति ख०।

(२) प्रत्यक्षविषयमात्र इति ख०।

(३) वेद्या न भवतीति ख०।

(४) अविरलवित्ति-तद्वित्तिधारेति ख०।

(५) द्रव्यत्व-रूपत्वादीनामिति ख०।

घट-तद्वित्तिधारावाहिविषयशतभारमन्थरा काचिद्वित्तिरस्मदादेरुत्पद्यमानानुभूयेत, नचैवमिति चेत्। न। अनुव्यवसायो विषयमात्रनिरूप्यो न तु तद्विषयपरम्परानिरूप्यो गौरवात्। तथाच ज्ञानज्ञानत्वेन सर्व्वा वित्तिरस्मदादेरुत्पद्यमानानुभूयत एव। न चैवमनिर्मोक्षः, योगजधर्म्मप्रत्यासत्त्या सामान्यलक्षणया वा व्याप्तिज्ञानरूपस्याननुव्यवसायस्यापि स्वविषयत्वाभ्युपगमात्। न च तद्व्यवहारशक्तत्वं तद्विषयत्वं, तद्विषयत्वेन तद्व्यवहारकारणत्वग्रहे सति तच्छक्तत्वज्ञानं तच्छक्तत्वञ्च तद्विषयत्वमित्यन्योन्याश्रयात् कारणत्वग्रहं विना शक्तेरग्रहात् त्वन्मतेऽपि रजतज्ञानस्य शुक्तिविषयत्वापत्तेश्च।

शङ्किताव्याप्तिलेशोऽपीति भावः। 'आत्मेति एतद्विषयकालौकिकप्रत्यासत्त्यजन्यत्व इत्यर्थः। अतएव ज्ञानमित्यत्र हेत्वभावान्न व्यभिचार इति वक्ष्यति, 'साक्षात्कारित्वादिति इन्द्रियजन्यत्वादित्यर्थः। अतएवेश्वरज्ञाने व्यभिचारवारणाय अहेतुकत्वेन हेत्वभावं वक्ष्यति। 'ज्ञानमिति अत्रालौकिकप्रत्यासत्तेः सामान्यस्यैव सत्त्वेन हेत्वभावादेव न व्यभिचार इत्यर्थः। क्लृप्तहेत्वभावेन फलाभावे सत्ययोग्यतया तदभावकल्पनमप्रामाणिकमित्यस्वरसात् केचिदित्युक्तं।

नन कारणताभङ्गः[१] इष्टापत्तिः स्वप्रकाशवादिना प्रत्यक्षविषय-

---

(१) कारणतानभ्युपगमस्येवीति ख०।

रजतार्थिप्रवृत्तौ रजतज्ञानं हेतुः न तु तदवच्छेदक-मित्युक्तत्वात्। लाघवेन स्वविषये ज्ञानस्य प्रवर्त्तकत्वं सर्व्वैरेवाद्यप्रवृत्तौ तथावगमादिति चेत्, हन्तैवमन्यथा-ख्यातिरस्तु न त्वन्यथासिद्धरजतज्ञानस्याप्रवर्त्तकत्व-मिति। एतेन यथा तद्गुणसंविज्ञानबहुव्रीहिसिद्धं कुटा-दिपदमशक्यमपि कुटं गणमादायैव प्रधानमन्यपदार्थं बोधयति तथा ज्ञानमविषयमप्यात्मानमादायैव स्ववि-षये व्यवहारं करोति संस्कारञ्च। स्वजन्यव्यवहार-विषये ज्ञानस्य संस्कारजनकत्वात्। स्वजन्यव्यवहार-विषयः स्वात्मा विषयश्चेति प्राचीनं गुरुमतमपास्तम्। अन्यच्च लाघवेन ज्ञानस्य स्वविषये व्यवहार-संस्कार-

---

तामात्रेण तत्कारणतानभ्युपगमादित्यत उक्तं 'कार्य्यानुत्पादस्येति, कारणान्तरस्याभावादिति भावः। ननु स्वविषयत्वे ज्ञानसामान्य-सामग्रीमात्रं तन्त्रम्, घटादिविषयत्वे क्वचिदिन्द्रियसन्निकर्षः, क्वचि-ल्लिङ्गादिः, परप्रकाशेऽनवस्थानात्. स्वप्रकाशतानिर्व्वाहककल्पनायां गौरवस्य प्रामाणिकत्वादित्यस्वरसादाह, 'अपिचेति अनवस्थैव नास्त्यवश्यवेद्यत्वाभावादनावश्यकत्वेऽप्यनवस्थायान्तवापि साम्यादित्यर्थः। नन्वस्मन्मते नानवस्था स्वप्रकाशत्वानुमितेः स्वप्रकाशत्वानुमितावपि क्षतेरभावात् वस्तुतस्तु स्वप्रकाशत्वपक्षे सानुमितिरिति स्वमिव स्वविषयत्वमपि विषयीकरोत्येवेति तस्य स्वप्रकाशत्वं तद्दोषर एवेति

जनकत्वकल्पनात्। स्वविषये स्वात्मनि व्यवहार-संस्काराजनकत्वात्। व्यवहार-संस्कारयोः स्वविषयज्ञान-साध्यत्वेन स्वाविषयकज्ञानासाध्यत्वात्। ननु ज्ञानस्य मानसत्वे कथं जानामीति विशिष्टबुद्धिः ज्ञानत्वनिर्व्विकल्पकजन्यज्ञानक्षणे विशेष्याभावेन प्रत्यक्षानुत्पत्तेरिति[१] चेत्। न। ज्ञाननाशक्षण एव ज्ञाने ज्ञानत्वविशिष्टबुद्धिः विशेष्यस्य पूर्व्वक्षणसत्त्वात्। प्रत्यक्षे स्वसम-

---

कथं तदर्थं ज्ञानान्तरापेक्षेत्यस्वरसादाह, 'किञ्चेति, नन्वसम्मते साक्षात्त्वं न जातिरपि तु ज्ञानानपेक्षेन्द्रियजन्यत्वमुपाधिरिति क सङ्कर इत्यत आह, 'तवेति। 'विरुद्धत्वादिति, यद्यपि यद्विषयत्वावच्छेदेन ज्ञानाजन्यत्वमित्युक्तौ न कश्चिद्दोषप्रसङ्गः, तथापि स्वविषयत्वेन न प्रत्यक्षत्वं तस्य सकलसाधारण्येनाव्यावर्त्तकतया क्वचिदपि जन्यज्ञानवच्छेदकत्वात् सामान्यसामग्र्यां ज्ञानत्वस्यैवावच्छेदकत्वात् विशेषसामग्र्यां स्वविषयत्वस्य सर्व्वज्ञानसाधारण्येनातिप्रसक्ततयैवानवच्छेदकत्वादिति भावः। 'प्रत्यक्षं न स्यादिति विषयत्वे ज्ञानभिन्ने परज्ञानानपेक्षत्वं ज्ञाने धर्म्मिणि तदपेक्षत्वमिति प्रत्यक्षत्वं न स्यात् इत्यर्थः। नन्ववश्यवेद्यत्वाभावेनानवस्थोद्धृता तदेव तु दुर्लभमित्याह, 'अथेति। 'तथाच ज्ञानज्ञानत्वेनेति, न च घटत्वेन जानामीत्यनुव्यवसायो घटत्वप्रकारकत्वं व्यवसायस्य यथा गृह्णाति न तथा तदीयघटत्व-

---

(१) विशेष्यस्याभावेन प्रत्यक्षानुपपत्तेरिवीवि ख०।

यवर्त्तितया गौरवेण विशेष्यस्याहेतुत्वात्। जानामीति वर्त्तमानत्वेन स्थूल उपाधिर्भासते, न तु क्षणः, तस्यातीन्द्रियत्वात्। ततो ज्ञानविशिष्टबुद्धिरात्मनि विशेषणज्ञानस्य पूर्व्वंसत्त्वात्। विशेषणञ्च न विशिष्टप्रत्ययहेतुर्गौरवात्। किन्तु तज्ज्ञानमावश्यकत्वात्। अतएव तत्तां विनापि तद्बुद्धेः प्रत्यभिज्ञा।

यत्तु व्यवसायनाशक्षणोत्पन्नव्यवसायान्तरे ज्ञानत्व-

प्रकारकत्वं तदनुव्यवसाय इति कथं सर्व्वास्तुल्याकारा इति वाच्यम्। घटत्वप्रकारकमाद्यं ज्ञानं तदनुव्यवसायस्तु घटत्वप्रकारकज्ञानज्ञानं यथा तथा तदनुव्यवसायादेरपि(१) घटत्वप्रकारकज्ञानज्ञानज्ञानतया शेषपर्य्यन्तमेवानुव्यवसायसम्भवात् इति भावः। इदञ्चाभ्युपेत्य, वस्तुतो घटत्वप्रकारकत्वप्रकारकत्वप्रकारकमपि ज्ञानमुत्पद्यत एव नियमस्तु नास्त्येव तथेति द्रष्टव्यम्। ननु ज्ञानसिद्ध्यर्थं ज्ञानान्तरानुसरणे नाशेषविशेषगुणोच्छित्तिलक्षणमोक्ष इत्यत आह, 'न चेति।

'व्यवसायनाशेति, अत्र व्यवसायनाशक्षणोत्पन्नव्यवसायान्तरे ज्ञानत्वविशिष्टधीस्तदुत्पत्त्यग्रिमक्षणे तदा तस्य सत्त्वे विशेष्यवर्त्तमानातः प्रत्ययोभवतीत्यभिसन्धिः। 'तद्धेतोरिति, घटत्वादिज्ञानघटादीन्द्रि-

---

(१) द्वितीयादेरपीति ख०।

विशिष्टबुद्धिरिति। तन्न। तद्धेतोरभावात् अनुमिनोमीत्यादौ अनुव्यवसाये अनुमितित्वाभावाच्च।

यद्वा ज्ञानं ज्ञानत्वञ्च निर्व्विकल्पके भासते, ततो ज्ञानत्ववैशिष्ट्यं ज्ञाने ज्ञानवैशिष्ट्यञ्चात्मनि भासते। विशेष्ये विशेषणं विशेषणे विशेषणान्तरञ्च भासत इत्येव हि विशिष्टवैशिष्ट्यार्थः।

वस्तुतस्तु ज्ञानमभाववद्व विशिष्टज्ञानविषय एवानु-

यसन्निकर्षादेरित्यर्थः। 'अनुव्यवसाये' अनुव्यवसायस्थले, यद्वा 'अनुव्यवसाये' व्यवसायपाश्चात्ये, तन्नाशक्षणोत्पन्नव्यवसायान्तर इत्यर्थः। एतच्च दोषद्वयं नियमपक्षे अनियमपक्षे[१] त्वयमपि कल्पः सम्यक्। व्यवसायानन्तरं ज्ञानत्वनिर्व्विकल्पकेन तन्नाशे तत्क्षणे व्यवसायान्तरोत्पत्तौ बाधकाभावादित्यवधेयम्।

'यद्वेति, न विशिष्टवैशिष्ट्यभाने विशिष्टबुद्ध्यपेक्षानियम इत्युभयथापि विशिष्टवैशिष्ट्यधीरिति तत्सामग्रीद्वैविध्यात् क्वचित्तया क्वचिदेतया च सामग्र्या विशिष्टवैशिष्ट्यधीरिति व्यवस्थितो विकल्पो ग्राह्यः।

'वस्तुतस्त्विति, ज्ञानांशे निर्व्विकल्पकं न सम्भवति विशिष्टज्ञानसामग्रीसत्त्वादिति पूर्व्वास्वरसः। ज्ञानत्वविशिष्टबुद्धौ प्राचीनप्रका-

---

(१) सम्भवपक्षे इति ख०।

व्यवसायस्य विषयरूपविशेषणविषयकव्यवसायसाध्यत्वेन विशिष्टज्ञानसामग्रीसत्त्वात् । ज्ञानत्वमपि तत्र भासते तज्ज्ञानसामग्रीसत्त्वात् । अंशे तत्सप्रकारकं निष्प्रकारकञ्चेति नरसिंहाकारं तत्रैव विशिष्टज्ञाने

रेणास्वरसोऽग्रेऽनुमिनोमीत्यभिधाने ततप्रकारानुसरणस्यैर्थ्यात् जानामीत्यत्र कदाचिदन्योऽपि प्रकारः सम्भवतीत्याह, 'तत्रैवेति, न च निर्विकल्पकतया तदयोग्यमतः कथमेतत्, अंशे तदस्तीत्यंशमात्रं योग्यमिति तु मन्दमेव एकस्य योग्यायोग्योभयरूपतापत्तेरिति वाच्यम् । ज्ञानमात्रस्यैव योग्यत्वात् सम्बन्धितावच्छेदकरूपेण सम्बन्धिनिरूपणं विना न ससम्बन्धिकनिरूपणमिति तद्विरहादेव योग्यस्यापि तद्विषयत्वेनाज्ञानात् । न च नरसिंहाकारज्ञाने घटत्वप्रकारकत्वाभावात्तत्र ज्ञानत्ववैशिष्ट्यबोधेऽपि घटत्वेन जानामीति ज्ञानत्वविशिष्टघटत्वप्रकारकज्ञानवानहमिति धीर्न स्यादिति[1] वाच्यम् । विषयनिरूप्यं हि ज्ञानं न तु यावद्विषयनिरूप्यं[2] गौरवादित्युक्तं । तथाच नरसिंहाकारस्य सत्यपि घटत्वप्रकारकत्ववैशिष्ट्यविषयत्वे घटत्ववैशिष्ट्यविषयत्वमस्त्येवेति तदुत्पत्त्यग्रिमक्षणे तत्र ज्ञानत्वविशिष्टबुद्धौ तदग्रिमक्षणे घटत्ववैशिष्ट्यावगाहिज्ञानवानहमित्येवं रूपो जानामी-

---

(१) प्रतीतिर्न स्यादितीति ख० ।

(२) विषयपरम्परानिरूप्यमिति ख० ।

ज्ञानत्ववैशिष्ट्यं भासते, अनुमीनोमीत्यादौ तु न तथा अनुव्यवसाये अनुमितित्वाभावादिति।

इति श्रीमद्गङ्गेशोपाध्यायविरचिते तत्त्वचिन्तामणौ प्रत्यक्षखण्डे अनुव्यवसायवादः।

त्यनुव्यवसायः सम्भवत्येवेति कदाचिदप्येवमप्यनुव्यवसायः सम्भवतीति न काप्यनुपपत्तिरिति भावः।

इति श्रीजयदेवमिश्रविरचिते तत्त्वचिन्तामण्यालोके प्रत्यक्षखण्डालोके अनुव्यवसायवादालोकः।

अथ निर्व्विकल्पकवादः ।

तच्च प्रत्यक्षं द्विविधं निर्विकल्पकं सविकल्पकञ्चेति। तत्र नाम जात्यादियोजनारहितं वैशिष्ट्यानवगाहि निष्प्रकारकं निर्विकल्पकं। ननु ज्ञानत्वं सविकल्पकभिन्नवृत्ति इत्यत्र किं मानं न प्रत्यक्षमसिद्धेः अतीन्द्रियत्वाभ्युपगमाच्च। न च व्यवहारः, तस्य सविकल्पकसाध्यत्वात्। नापीदं न विवेचितं पूर्वमधुना विवेचयामीत्यनुभवप्रमाणकावालोचन-विकल्पौ, बहुविशेषणज्ञानाज्ञानाभ्यां तदुपपत्तेः। ननु गौरितिप्रत्यक्षं विशेषणज्ञानजन्यं विशिष्टज्ञानत्वादनुमितिवदिति। अथ

अथ निर्व्विकल्पकवादालोकः।

ननु नरसिंहाकारं ज्ञानमित्यसिद्धं[१] सविकल्पकस्य प्रत्यक्षधीजन्यत्वाद्विलक्षणविषयस्य निर्व्विकल्पकस्यैव प्रत्यक्षत्वादित्यत आह, 'तच्चेति, जात्यादेरपि तात्त्विकतया पारमार्थिकविषययोरुभयोरपि प्रत्यक्षत्वादिति भावः[२]। ननु तथापि तथाविधज्ञानानुपपत्तिः

---

(१) ज्ञानमित्यसङ्गतमिति ख०।

(२) प्रत्यक्षत्वादित्यर्थ इति ख०।

विशेषण-विशेष्यज्ञानसामग्रीतः साकाङ्क्षोभयविषयमेकं विशिष्टज्ञानं तत्र प्रत्यक्षे योग्येन्द्रियसन्निकर्षादनुमितौ पक्षधर्म्मताबलात् व्यापकत्वावच्छेदकप्रकारेण शाब्दे योग्यतादिवशात्पदार्थतावच्छेदकरूपेणापूर्वमेव विशेषणं भासते, उपमितावप्येवमेवेति न क्वापि विशेषण-ज्ञानं जनकं[१]। न च प्रत्यभिज्ञायान्तत्तानुभवस्तथा, तत्तानुभवेऽपि संस्कारस्यानुद्बोधात्, विलोपाद्वा प्रत्य-भिज्ञानानुत्पादेनोद्बुद्धः संस्कार एव प्रत्यासत्तितया विशेषणज्ञानार्थमिन्द्रियसहकारी, सुरभिचन्दनमित्या-दावपि विशेषणज्ञानार्थं तज्ज्ञानं प्रत्यासत्तिस्था नीय-

निर्व्विकल्पकत्व-सविकल्पकत्वयोर्विरुद्धजात्योरेकत्रासमवायादत आह, 'नचेति विषयगर्भावुभावुपाधी निर्व्विकल्पकत्व-सविकल्पकत्वे न तु जाती इत्यर्थः, 'असिद्धेः' निर्व्विकल्पकविषयप्रत्ययचासिद्धेः। न च प्रतीतिकत्वह इत्याह, 'अतीन्द्रियेति। 'साकाङ्क्षेति, यदि वैशिष्ट्य-गोचरं विशिष्टज्ञानं भवेत् तदा वैशिष्ट्यज्ञानीयसम्बन्धिनो विशेष-णस्य पूर्व्वं ज्ञानमङ्गीक्रियेतेति भावः। 'संस्कार इत्युपलक्षणम्, स्मृतिरपि यदि हेतुः सापि प्रत्यासत्तितयैव सुरभीत्यादिवत् इति ध्येयम्। 'भ्रम इत्यपि स्वमते वस्तुगतिमनुरुध्योक्तं यतो विशि-

(१) हेतुरिति ख०।

मिन्द्रियसहकारि, भ्रमो विशिष्टज्ञानमेव नास्तीति चेत् । उच्यते । साध्यप्रसिद्धिपदार्थोपस्थिति-वाच्यत्वज्ञानतत्तानुभवानामनुमित्यादिहेतुत्वम् । साध्यप्रसिद्ध्यादिकं विनानुमित्यादेरसम्भवात्(१) । साध्यादिकञ्च विशेषणमिति तज्ज्ञानमनुमित्यादिहेतुः । यद्यप्यनुमित्यादिप्रत्येकं प्रति साध्यादिविशेषणज्ञानत्वेन न कारणता । तथापि विशिष्टज्ञानमात्रं प्रति विशेषणज्ञानत्वेन कारणता बाधकाभावात् । स्यादेतद्वह्निमानित्यादिज्ञानं प्रति वह्निज्ञानस्य न विशेषणज्ञानत्वेन कारणता द्रव्यत्वेन वह्निज्ञानेऽपि वह्निमानितिज्ञानाभावात् । किन्तु विशेषणतावच्छेदकप्रकारकज्ञानत्वेनातो न विशिष्टज्ञाने विशेषणज्ञानं हेतुः । विशेषणज्ञानत्वमपि तत्रास्तीति चेत् । न । तस्यातिप्रसक्तत्वात् अन्यथासिद्धेश्च । न

ष्टज्ञानत्वपक्षेऽपि तत्रापि ज्ञानस्य प्रत्यासत्तित्वमिति सुवचं । 'साध्यप्रसिद्धीति, ननु साध्यप्रसिद्ध्यादिर्न हेतुरावश्यकव्याप्तिज्ञानसत्त्वे तद्विलम्बेन विलम्बाभावात् व्याप्तिधीरेव न तां विनेत्यतो हेतुहेतुत्वमायाति न तु हेतुत्वमिति चेत् । मैवं । व्याप्तिज्ञानादीनामेव साध्यप्रसिद्ध्यादित्वात् न तु तदन्या साध्यादिप्रसिद्धिर्हेतुः येनान्यथा-

---

(१) तदभावात् इति ख० ।

च तादृशविशेषणज्ञानजन्यत्वं साध्यं, बाधादिति। तन्न। विशिष्टवैशिष्ट्यज्ञानं प्रति हि विशेषणतावच्छेदकप्रकारकं ज्ञानं कारणमुभयसिद्धमतो विशिष्टज्ञानमात्रं प्रति विशेषणज्ञानं हेतुः यद्विशेषयोः कार्य्यकारणभावस्तत्सामान्ययोरपि बाधकं विना कार्य्यकारणभावनियमात्[१] अन्यथा सामान्यकार्य्योच्छेदः। न चातिप्रसङ्गः, विशेषसामग्रीविरहेण तत्तत्कार्य्यविशेषानुदयात्। न च परोक्षत्वमुपाधिः, प्रत्यभिज्ञायां साध्याव्यापकत्वात्। नापि विशिष्टविशेषणकत्वं, पक्षेतरत्वादिति। मैवं। तथापि स्मृतिवत्पूर्वानुभवस्य संस्कारद्वारा जनकत्वात् सिद्धसाधनात्। न चाव्यवहितविशेषणज्ञानजन्यत्वं साध्यं, अप्रयोजकत्वात् प्रत्यभिज्ञावत्

सिद्धिर्भवेत्। ननु तथापि क्लृप्तव्याप्तिज्ञानत्वमेव तद्धेतुतावच्छेदकं न तु विशेषणज्ञानत्वं साध्यप्रसिद्धित्वञ्चेति चेत्। न। द्वितीये दृष्टापत्तेः, प्रथमे विशिष्टज्ञानलक्षणकार्य्यस्याकस्मिकतापत्त्या अनुगतहेतुगवेषणायामुक्त एव पर्य्यवसानात्। किञ्च विशिष्टज्ञानं वैशिष्ट्यगोचरज्ञानं तथाच वैशिष्ट्यस्य सम्बन्धरूपतया अवश्यं सम्बन्धीभूतविशेषणधीर्व्यञ्जिका वाच्या। न हि तन्मते इवास्माकमपि धर्म्म-धर्म्मिगोचरमेव

---

(१) तथात्वनियमादिति ख०।

स्मृत्यैवोपपत्तेर्वा । नापि तत एवाव्यवहितविशेषणानुभवजन्यत्वं साध्यं, अप्रसिद्धेः प्रत्यभिज्ञानादौ व्यभिचाराच्च । अथ तत्कालोत्पन्नरूपादिविशिष्टप्रत्यक्षे संस्काराभावेन स्मरणाभावात् पक्षधर्म्मताबलेन निर्विकल्पकसिद्धावन्यत्रापि सामग्रीतौल्यात्तत्सिद्धिरिति चेत् । न । प्रत्युत्पन्नविशेषणस्थले हि शुक्लत्वादिविशिष्टशुक्लवैशिष्ट्यबोधो वा अविशिष्टतद्विशिष्टबोधो वा, आद्ये शुक्लत्वादिजातिस्मरणं प्रथमं, ततः प्रत्यक्षेण तद्विशिष्टशुक्लबोधः, ततः शुक्लत्वादिविशिष्टशुक्लादिवैशिष्ट्यबोधः(१) द्रव्य इति किमनुपपन्नं, शुक्लत्वादिजातिस्मरणमेव वा सामान्यलक्षणया सकलरूपादिविषयमस्तु । द्वितीये अननुभवः, न हि शुक्लत्वादिप्रत्ययविलक्षणं(२) शुक्लरूपादिविशिष्टबोधं कश्चिदनुभवति ।

ज्ञानं विशिष्टज्ञानं येन समूहालम्बनवदुभयग्राहकसामग्रीमात्रादुपपद्येत, न तु विशेषणधियः पूर्वसत्त्वमनुमन्येत । ननु सम्बन्धस्योभयसम्बन्धिनिरूप्यत्वाद्विशेष्यधीरपि विशिष्टधीकारणं भवेदिति चेत् । न । सम्बन्धो हि प्रतियोगिनिरूप्यो न त्वनुयोगिनिरूप्योऽपि तथैवान्वयाद्यनुविधानात्, रूपवानित्यत्र रूपप्रतियोगिकः समवायो भासते

---

(१) शुक्लत्वादिविशिष्टशुक्लवैशिष्ट्यप्रत्यय इति ख० ।

(२) शुक्लत्वादिप्रत्ययविलक्षणमिति ख० ।

अथ जागरादिविशिष्टानुभवो विशेषणज्ञानजन्यो विशिष्टज्ञानत्वात्। न च तत्र संस्कारद्वारा पूर्वविशेषणानुभवः तज्जन्यविशेषणस्मरणं वा तत्र सम्भवति, उद्बोधकं विना संस्कारस्य स्मरणे विशिष्टबोधे वा सामर्थ्याभावादित्युद्बोधकं वक्तव्यं, उद्बोधकश्चान्यत्र ज्ञानं दृष्टमिति तदेव वाच्यं। न च तद्विशिष्टज्ञानमेव, तथापि विशेषणज्ञानापेक्षायामनवस्थापत्तेरित्यालोचनसिद्धिरिति। तन्न। सत्यपि ज्ञाने संस्कारानुद्बोधात्। यस्मात् फलं भवति स ज्ञानविशेषस्तथेति चेत्। न। अननुगतत्वात्। यदनन्तरं फलं दृश्यते तदेवाननुगतमप्युद्बोधकं कल्प्यते फलबलादिति चेत्, तर्हि जागरकारणानन्तरं संस्कारोद्बोधोऽस्तीति तदेव कारणमस्तु क्लृप्तत्वात्। अत एव संस्कारोद्बोधे न नियतो

न द्रव्यप्रतियोगिकः तथा सति कदाचिद्द्रव्यवद्रूपमित्यपि प्रतीतिः स्यात्[१]। न चैवं संयोगोऽप्यन्यतरसंयोगिमात्रनिरूप्यः स्यादिति वाच्यम्। परोक्षे ज्ञाने पक्षज्ञानादिसापेक्षतयैवापरसंयोगिज्ञाननियमात्[२], प्रत्यक्षे स्वाश्रयघटितसन्निकर्षापेक्षणात् उभयसंयोगिग्रहा-

---

(१) धीः स्यादिति ख०।

(२) अपरसंयोगिमानमिवमादिति ख०।

हेतुरिति, "सदृशादृष्टचिन्ताद्याः स्मृतिबीजस्य बोधकाः" इत्याहुः । एवञ्च(१) प्रणिधानादिहेतुत्वमपि सङ्गच्छते । अपिच विशिष्टज्ञानत्वादित्यत्र व्यवच्छेद्यमविशिष्टज्ञानं तच्चाप्रसिद्धं सिद्धौ वा व्यर्थमनुमानं । ज्ञानत्वञ्च स्वतोऽसिद्धव्याप्तिकं निर्विकल्पके व्यभिचारात् अनवस्थापाताच्च । किञ्च विशिष्टज्ञानत्वं न तावद्वस्तुगत्या विशेषण-विशेष्यविषयकज्ञानत्वं आलोचनेन व्यभिचारात् । नापि विशेषणत्वविषयकत्वं, अतद्व्यावृत्तिबोधजनकज्ञानविषयत्वस्य विशेषणत्वस्य तत्राप्रकाशात् । नापि वैशिष्ट्यविषयकज्ञानत्वं, तथा सति गौरितिविकल्पे वैशिष्ट्यं विशेषणमित्यालोचनस्यापि तद्विषयत्वेन विशिष्टज्ञानत्वे अनवस्थापातादिति । नापि सप्रकारकज्ञानत्वं प्रकारश्च विषयताविशेष इति

पेक्षा, व्यासज्यवृत्तित्वेन प्रत्येकपरिसमाप्ताश्रयत्वाभावेन मिलित एवाश्रयत्वपर्य्याप्तेः व्यासज्यवृत्तौ विशेषे उभयाश्रयज्ञानानुविधानाच्च । न हि द्वित्वेऽप्युभयाश्रयप्रत्यक्षापेक्षा, सम्बन्धस्य सम्बन्ध्यपेक्षत्वदृष्टान्तेन द्वित्वस्य संयोगसमवायवदसम्बन्धरूपत्वादिति दिक् । 'यद्विशेषयोरिति, इदमपि समाधिसौकर्य्यादुक्तं, वस्तुतो वैशिष्ट्यस्य

---

(१) अत एवेति ख० ।

वाच्यं। ज्ञानविषयस्वरूपातिरिक्ताया विषयताया अभावात्। न च विशेषणज्ञानजन्यत्वं सप्रकारत्वं, यद्विशेषणज्ञानजन्यं यत् स एव तत्र प्रकार इति गौरितिविकल्पे तस्यैव साध्यत्वात् ईश्वरज्ञानस्य निष्प्रकारकत्वापाताच्च। नाप्यतद्व्यावृत्तिविषयत्वं विशिष्टज्ञानत्वं, अपोहवादनिरासेन गौरितिविकल्पे तथात्वासिद्धेः। नाप्यतद्व्यावृत्तिबोधजनकत्वं तत्, आलोचनव्यावृत्तानुगतरूपमन्तरेण अतद्व्यावृत्तबोधजनकत्वस्य ग्रहीतुमशक्यत्वात्। न च गौरितिज्ञानमेतदन्यसविकल्पकान्यज्ञानभिन्नं प्रमेयत्वात्, यद्वा चक्षुः चाक्षुषसविकल्पकज्ञानातिरिक्तज्ञानजनकं(१) इन्द्रियत्वादिति

प्रतियोगिनिरूप्यत्वादेव विशिष्टबुद्धौ विशेषणधीः कारणमित्युक्तं। अन्यथा विशिष्टज्ञानत्वादित्यप्रयोजकमेव स्यात्, प्रत्युत विशिष्टवैशिष्ट्यावगाहिज्ञाने विशेषणतावच्छेदकप्रकारकधीर्हेतुरित्येव न विशिष्टज्ञाने विशेषणज्ञानं कारणमिति सामान्यसामग्र्यैव निर्वाहे विशेषसामग्र्यकल्पनात्। न च द्रव्यत्वेन वह्निज्ञाने वह्निमानिति धीः स्यादित्यतिप्रसङ्गः, वह्निमानिति वह्नित्वविशिष्टज्ञानं वह्नौ, वह्निविशिष्टधीः पर्व्वते, तथाच यथा वह्निज्ञानात्तद्विशिष्टज्ञानं, तथा

---

(१) चाक्षुषविशिष्टज्ञानातिरिक्तज्ञानजनकमिति ख०।

तत्सिद्धिः, अप्रयोजकत्वात् उभयत्र सविकल्पकपदानन्तरं निर्विकल्पकादिपदप्रक्षेपेण तृतीयादिज्ञानसिद्धिप्रसङ्गाच्चेति[१]।

अत्रोच्यते। प्राथमिकं गौरिति प्रत्यक्षं ज्ञानं जन्यविशेषणज्ञानजन्यं जन्यविशिष्टज्ञानत्वात् अनुमितिवत्। न च स्मरणं तत्र सम्भवति, तज्जन्मनि तेन गोत्वस्याननुभवात्। अथ यथा बालस्याद्यप्रवृत्तिबलात्

वह्निलज्ञानात्तद्विशिष्टज्ञानं भवेत्। न च द्रव्यत्वेन ज्ञाने तदस्ति, तस्माद्यद्यद्विशिष्टज्ञानं तत्तद्विशेषणज्ञानजन्यमिति सामान्यसामग्रीतएव तत्तद्विशिष्टज्ञानं, न तु विशिष्टवैशिष्ट्यज्ञानत्वावच्छेदेन कार्य्यत्वं विशेषणतावच्छेदकप्रकारकज्ञानत्वेन हेतुत्वं नीलघटवदर्थसमाजग्रस्तत्वादित्युक्तं। सम्बन्धितावच्छेदकप्रकारकमेव सम्बन्धिज्ञानमपरसम्बन्धिस्मारकं अन्यथातिप्रसङ्गादिति दोषं स्फुटत्वादुपेक्ष्य दोषान्तरमाह, 'सत्यपीति। ननु यदि जागराद्यज्ञाने संस्कारोपनीतं गोत्वादिविषयस्तदा प्रत्यभिज्ञानवत्तत्तोल्लेखापत्तिः तत्तोल्लेखे संस्कारजन्यत्वस्य नियामकत्वकल्पनादित्यरुचेराह, 'अपिचेति, सत इत्यनन्तरमपीति शेषः। 'अनवस्थानादिति। न च कार्य्यं कारणजन्यमितिवदनवस्था प्रामाणिकीति वाच्यम्। तत्र हि कार्य्यकादाचित्कत्वं कारणकादा-

---

(१) तृतीयादिज्ञानप्रसङ्गाच्चेतीति ख०।

प्रागभवीयसंस्काराद्व्याप्तिस्मरणं तथेहापि जन्मान्तरीयसंस्काराद्गोत्वस्मरणमस्तु प्राथमिकविशिष्टज्ञानबलादिति चेत्। न। जीवनादृष्टेन तत्र संस्कारोद्बोधात्तथास्तु, इह तु न विलक्षणमुद्बोधकमस्ति अतो गोत्वासन्निकर्षेऽपि-गोत्वस्मरणप्रसङ्गः[१]। य एव गोत्वेन्द्रियसन्निकर्षस्तत्र निर्विकल्पके हेतुः स एव संस्कारोद्बोधक इति चेत्, तर्हि च क्लृप्तकारणभावाद्गोत्वेन्द्रियसन्निकर्षाद्गोत्वानुभव एव स्यात् स्मरणसामग्रीतोऽनुभवसामग्र्या बलवत्त्वात्। न च तत् विशिष्टज्ञानं,

---

चित्कत्वं विना नेति कादाचित्कत्वेन हेतुत्वं सिद्ध्यत् कादाचित्कपरम्पराया एव सहेतुकत्वं विषयीकरोतीति युगपत्कारणपरम्परासिद्धेः प्रामाणिकता, इह तु ज्ञानजन्यज्ञानमिति सर्वज्ञानानां ज्ञानजन्यत्वे ज्ञानाविरामे प्रापणाद्यनुपपत्तेर्ज्ञानानवस्था प्रामाणिकीति वा प्रतिकूलतर्करूपतया व्याप्तिधीविरोधिन्येव। अत एव केवलज्ञानत्वे प्रतिकूलतर्केण न व्याप्तिग्रह इति व्याप्तिग्रहौपयिकत्वेन विशिष्टपदं सार्थकमेवेति मत्वा अत्र दूषणे अपरितुष्यन् दोषान्तरमाह, 'किञ्चेति, 'तथाचतीति, विशेषणं विशेष्यञ्च विशिष्टधीविषयो नान्यदित्यभिमानादिदमुक्तम्। 'प्रकार इत्यन्तं 'न चेति सम्बध्यते, तत्र हेतुर्गौ-

---

(१) गोत्वासन्निकर्षेऽपि प्रथमं गोत्वस्मरणप्रसङ्ग इति ख०।

पूर्वं विशेषणज्ञानाभावादित्यर्थान्निर्विकल्पकं। अतएव न तत्र ज्ञानत्वेन विशिष्टज्ञानत्वानुमानं कारणबाधेन बाधात्। यदि चानुभवसामग्रीतः स्मरणं तदा नित्यानां वैदिकार्थानाञ्च स्मरणं स्यान्न त्वनुभवः। न च गोत्वज्ञानं गोत्वज्ञानजन्यं अन्यज्ञानजन्यं अन्यविशेषणज्ञानजन्यञ्चेत्यन्यत्र दर्शनात् प्रथमं न गोत्वानुभव इति वाच्यं। एकस्यैव जन्य-जनकत्वानवच्छेदकत्वात् अनवस्थापाताच्च। ननु गौरित्यत्र गोत्ववैशिष्ट्यमपि भासते तथाच तद्विषयकं ज्ञानं स्यात्, तच्च निर्विकल्पकमिति चेत्। न। गोत्वं हि तत्र विशेषणं, न तु तद्वैशिष्ट्यं। ननु तथाभूतविशेषणधीजन्यविशिष्टज्ञाने विशेषणं स्वधर्मविशिष्टं कथं भासेत पूर्वं तस्यानवगमात्, अव-

रित्यादि, 'अपोहेति, यद्यपगोव्यावृत्तिर्गोत्वमिति निरासेऽपि गोत्वं विशेषणं गौर्विशेष्यः, 'अतद्व्यावृत्तिर्वैशिष्ट्यमिति न निरस्तं तदभिप्रायेणेदं निरस्तं। न चाभावस्य प्रतियोग्यनुयोगिधीघटितत्वेन कथमपोहतिरस्कारोऽपीति वाच्यम्। स्वरूपेण समवायो वैशिष्ट्यमितिवदतद्व्यावृत्तिर्वैशिष्ट्यमिति सम्भवात् समवायवत्तत्तज्ज्ञानविशेषेऽभावे(१) प्रतियोगिज्ञानाद्यपेक्षणात्। तथापि प्रमेयत्वविशिष्टबोधे

(१) समवायवत् ज्ञानविशेष एवाभावे इति।

गमे वा तस्यापि विशेषणान्तरवतो विशेषणमित्यनवस्थेति चेत्। न। गौरिति विशिष्टज्ञाने विशिष्टस्य गोत्वस्याभानात्(१)। अथ सर्वं विशेषणं विशेषणवदेव गोत्वादावपि व्यक्त्यादेर्विशेषणत्वादिति चेत्, अस्तु तथा किन्तु विशेषणं विशेषणवदेव भासेत इति न नियमः। अन्यथा गौरिति ज्ञाने विशेषण-तद्विशेषणानन्तपरम्पराविषयत्वे विषयापर्य्यवसानप्रसङ्गः। क्वचिन्निर्विशेषणस्यापि भाने प्रथमतोऽपि तथा स्यादविशेषात्। न च विशिष्टज्ञानत्वादित्यत्र हेतोर्व्यर्थविशेषणत्वं येन विशेषणेन विना व्याप्तिर्ग्रहीतुं न शक्यते तस्यैव सार्थकत्वात् व्यभिचारवारकस्यापि सार्थकत्वे एतदेव मूलं, इहापि ज्ञानत्व-विशेषणज्ञानजन्यत्वयो-

---

तत्र वैशिष्ट्यं सम्भवतीति वैशिष्ट्यविधया अतद्व्यावृत्तिवैशिष्ट्यविषयत्वमसम्भावितं अतो विशेषणत्वेनैव तज्ज्ञानं वाच्यमिति पराभिसन्धानमदार्ढ्येन तदेव दूषितमिति बोध्यम्। 'स्मरणेति, यत्रैवोभयसामग्री एका तत्र तस्यानुभवजनकत्वमेव न स्मरणजनकत्वं, तथाच सामग्रीत्वे बलाधिक्यपर्य्यवसानम् न तु सामग्र्यामभेदेन न्यूनाधिकब-

---

(१) अविशिष्टस्य गोत्वस्य भानादिति ख०।

विशेषणं विना व्याप्तिर्ग्रहीतुं न शक्यते अनवस्थानात् सामान्यतोऽव्यभिचारावगमात्[1] । अतएव चक्षुस्तैजसत्वादिसाधने रूपादिषु मध्ये रूपस्यैव व्यञ्जकत्वादित्यादावसिद्धिवारकमपि विशेषणं सार्थकं तेन विना रूपस्यैव व्यञ्जकत्वादित्यस्याप्रसिद्धेर्व्याप्त्यग्रहात् । विशेषणं विनापि यत्र व्याप्तिग्रहस्तत्र व्यर्थविशेषणत्वं यथा नीलधूमत्वशरीराजन्यत्वादौ । यस्य यत्र यः सम्बन्धः स एव तत्र तस्य वैशिष्ट्यन्तेन हि स्वासम्बद्धेभ्यो व्यावृत्तो बोध्यते । यथा दण्डी पुरुष इति ज्ञाने दण्डसम्बन्धः पुरुषेऽवगत इति तेनायमदण्डव्यावृत्तो बोध्यते तथा गौरिति विकल्पेऽपि, तथाच विशेषणवद्विशेष्यज्ञानत्वं विशिष्टज्ञानत्वं एतदेवातद्व्यावृत्तबोधजनकतावच्छेदकं । ननु दण्ड-पुरुष-सम्बन्धा इत्यत्रापि दण्डसम्बन्धः पुरु-

---

त्ववत्त्वानुपपत्तेरिति । 'अनवस्थानादिति, अत्र प्रामाणिकतया प्रतिकूलतर्कविधया व्याप्तिधीविरोधित्वं अनवस्थायाः । यदि च तद्भिया क्वचिदपि विश्रान्तिर्वक्तव्या[2] तदाह, 'सामान्यत इति, व्यभिचारावारकमपि विशेषणं सार्थकमित्यत्रोपष्टम्भकमाह, 'अतएवेति,

---

(१) व्यभिचारादिति ख० ।
(२) मन्तव्येति ख० ।

षेऽवगत इति ततोऽप्यदण्डव्यावृत्तपुरुषबोधः स्यादिति चेत्, भवत्येव दण्डसम्बन्ध एव पुरुषे दण्डज्ञानं विना न ज्ञायते इति ब्रूमः। यत्र विशिष्टज्ञानसामग्री नास्ति तत्र निर्विकल्पकं, ज्ञानकरणजन्ये सर्वत्र विशेषणज्ञान-जन्यत्वाच्च तदिति प्रत्यक्षमेवैतदिति। अतएवाभावे न निर्विकल्पकं तद्बुद्धौ प्रतियोग्यधिकरणज्ञानयोः कार-णत्वेन तदुभयविशिष्टज्ञानसामग्रीनियमात्। यद्यभावे न निर्विकल्पकं तदा घटाभाववद्भूतलमिति ज्ञानन्न स्यात् विशेषणज्ञानं विना तदभावात्। भावे वा न निर्विकल्पकसिद्धिः विशिष्टज्ञानत्वस्य तत्रैव व्यभिचा-रादिति चेत्। न। प्रथमम्भूतले घटोनास्तीति बुद्धिः तत्र भूतलं विशेषणं अभावोविशेष्यः विशेष्यज्ञानञ्च न कारणं, पश्चाद्भूतलविशेष्यकं घटाभाववदिति ज्ञानं। नन्विन्द्रियसम्बद्धविशेषणतया अभावो गृह्यत इत्युक्तं

यद्यपि रूपस्यैव व्यञ्जकत्वादित्यत्र व्यञ्जकद्रव्यत्वं हेतुः पर्य्यवसितः, अन्यथा सन्निकर्षे व्यभिचारात्, तथाच रूपादिषु मध्ये इत्यस्ते अप्रसिद्धतया व्यभिचार एव नास्ति कस्य वारणं द्रव्येत्वेन विशेष-णेनेति, प्रसिद्धिद्वारा व्यभिचारधियमुत्पाद्य द्रव्यत्वविशेषणेन स वार्य्यते रूपादिषु मध्य इत्यनेन परम्परया व्यभिचारवारकत्वम-

अतः कथं स विशेष्य इति चेत्, भूतलविशेषणतया स्वभावप्रत्यासत्त्या गृह्यत इति तदर्थः, न त्वभावस्य विशेषणतया भानमिति। अतएव वायौ रूपाभाव इति प्रतीतेश्चाक्षुषत्वमुक्तमाचार्य्यैः। अयोग्यविशेष्ये इन्द्रियस्यासामर्थ्यात्। ज्ञानत्वे च निर्विकल्पकं विषयविशिष्टत्वांशे सविकल्पकमपि, अनुव्यवसायस्य व्यवसायजन्यत्वेन नियमतः पूर्वं विषयरूपविशेषणभानात् तत्रैव ज्ञाने तदेव ज्ञानं निष्प्रकारकं सप्रकारकञ्चेति न विरुद्धं अंशभेदमादायाविरोधात्। अतएव निर्विकल्पकत्वसविकल्पकत्वे न जाती चाक्षुषत्वादिना सङ्करापत्तेः। गौरिति सविकल्पकमपि गोत्वांशे निर्व्विकल्पकमेव तत्र प्रकाराभानात् भाने वानवस्था निर्विकल्पका-

---

स्यापि, तथापि तद्वारकस्य सार्थकतया व्याप्तिग्रहौपयिकत्वं तस्येति ज्ञातमनया कुदृष्ट्या। न हि व्यभिचारवारकस्यापूर्वोऽस्ति शक्तिविशेषो यदित्थमपि तद्वारकं व्यवस्थाप्येत। अत एवास्य हेतोः रसाव्यञ्जकत्वे सति रूपव्यञ्जकत्वमर्थ एवेति कल्पनमपास्तम्। तस्य हेत्वन्तरत्वेऽपि प्रकृतहेत्वर्थत्वे मानाभावात् अस्यैव समर्थत्वादिति। ननु विशिष्टज्ञानत्वादित्यत्र विशिष्टज्ञानत्वं वैशिष्ट्यगोचरज्ञानत्वं तथाचाप्रसिद्धो हेतुः वैशिष्ट्यस्य पदार्थान्तरस्यानभिरनभ्युपगमादित्यतआह, 'यः सम्बन्ध इति, तदेव कथमतआह, 'तेन

सिद्धिश्च। प्रकारश्च द्विविधः विशेषणोपलक्षणभेदात्। ननु व्यावर्त्तकत्वाविशेषे कथन्तयोर्भेदः व्यावर्त्तकत्वे सति सद्विशेषणमसदुपलक्षणं यथा दण्डी पुरुषः कुण्डला श्लेषमिति चेत्। न। काकवद्देवदत्तगृहं जटाभिस्तापस इत्यादावुपरिभ्राम्यतः काकस्य जटादेरसत्त्वेऽप्यविशेषणत्वादुपलक्षणत्वाच्च। एतेन व्यावृत्तिबोधकाले व्यावर्त्तकं सद्विशेषणमसदुपलक्षणं, तेन काकादीनां व्यावृत्तिबोधसमये सतां विशेषणत्वमेव व्यावृत्तिबोधसमये असतामुपलक्षणत्वं। अतएव काकैर्जटाभिः कुण्डेत्यादावित्थम्भूतलक्षणे तृतीयेतिनिरस्तं। व्यावृत्तिबोधसमये सतोऽप्युपरिभ्रमतः काकादेरविशेषणत्वात् उपलक्षणत्वाच्च। नापि विशेष्यवृत्तित्वे सति प्रत्याय्यव्यावृत्तिसमानाधिकरणत्वे सति व्यावर्त्तकं विशेषणं, यदा

हीति(१) ज्ञानाश्रयव्यावृत्तबुद्धिजनकत्वस्यैव वैशिष्ट्यत्वादित्यर्थः। 'भवत्येवेति, एतच्च यदि दण्डप्रतियोगित्वं पुरुषनिष्ठत्वस्य सम्बन्धस्य तद्धीविषयस्तदा। वस्तुतस्तादृशसमूहालम्बने तथात्वानियमः, 'दण्डेति, अयमपि न नियमः, अंशेन सम्बन्धोपस्थापनेऽन्यथापि तथा समूहालम्बनसम्भवादिति प्रतियोग्यधिकरणज्ञानयोरित्युपलक्षणं। 'अभाव-

---

(१) येन हीतीति क०।

यत्र विशेष्यत्वावच्छेदेन व्यावृत्त्या वा यत्समानाधिकरणत्वेन प्रतीयते तत्र तद्विशेषणं विशेष्यत्वञ्च प्रत्याय्यव्यावृत्त्यधिकरणत्वमिति जटाभिस्तापस इत्यादौ जटादावतिप्रसङ्गात्। न हि तापसे न जटा वर्त्तते। नापि विशेष्यसमानविभक्तिकत्वं विशेषणत्वं, काकवद्देवदत्तगृहमित्यादावुपलक्षणेऽपि गतत्वात् अनभिधानदशायामविशेषणत्वापाताच्च। अथ व्यावर्त्तकत्वे सति विशिष्टधीविषयत्वं विशेषणत्वं, विशिष्टबुद्धिश्च न विशेषणत्वगोचरा गौरवात्, किन्तु विशेषणविषया विशेषणोपलक्षणसन्देहानुपपत्तेः। अत एव चाक्षुषत्वादिविरोधः,

---

तस्याभावबुद्धिवेद्यतया(१) अभावत्वविशिष्टज्ञानसामग्र्याः सत्त्वादपि नाभावे निर्विकल्पकमिति मन्तव्यम्, 'प्रकारः' व्यावर्त्तकप्रकारः, 'अत एवेति 'इत्थम्भूतइत्यनेनातीतार्थकक्तप्रत्ययेनासत्त्वस्य बोधनादित्यर्थः। ननु विशेषणवत्त्वात्मकमेव विशेष्यत्वमित्यात्माश्रयशङ्कायां तमेवार्थमन्येन लक्षणेनाह, 'प्रत्याय्येति। नन्विदमपि लोहितः स्फटिक इत्यत्र लौहित्ये विशेषणे अव्याप्तमित्यरुचेः प्रतीतिगर्भं लक्षणमाह,(२) 'यद्वेति, 'वदिति(३), व्यावर्त्तकमिति शेषः। उक्तात्माश्रयभयाद्विशेष्यत्वं निर्वक्ति,

---

(१) अभावत्वस्याभावविशिष्टवेद्यतयेति ख०।
(२) प्रतीतिगर्भं लक्षणद्वयमाहेति ख०।
(३) तद्वतीति ख०।

उपलक्षणत्वे तूपलक्षितं संस्थानादि विशिष्टधीविषयो न काकवत्त्वं तदभावेऽपि तद्गृहप्रतीतेस्ताद्रूप्यात्। अन्यथा भ्रमत्वापत्तेः। न च शब्दोपस्थापितस्य कथं शाब्दज्ञानबहिर्भाव इति वाच्यं। तथैव व्युत्पत्तेः। न हि गङ्गायां घोष इत्यत्र प्रवाहोऽपि तीरावच्छेदकतया भासते, किन्तु तीरत्वेन तीरविशेष एव अन्यथा अजहत्स्वार्थासाम्यात्। न चैवमुपलक्षणपदस्य लाक्षणिकत्वं अशक्यस्य संस्थानादेरुपस्थापनादिति[१] वाच्यं। उपलक्षणबुद्ध्युपस्थापितकारणान्तरजन्यसंस्थानोपस्थित्या तदन्वये तात्पर्य्यादिति। मैवं। तथा व्युत्पत्तेरसिद्धेः। न ह्युपलक्षणपदातिरिक्तमुपलक्ष्योपस्थापकमस्तीत्युपलक्षणपदं स्वार्थमुप-

---

विशेष्यलक्षणेति। 'नापीति, पूर्वस्मिन् सति इदं लक्षणं द्रष्टव्यम्। अन्यथा घटः पट इत्यादौ उदासीनद्वयेऽप्यन्योन्यविशेषणतापातादिति भावः। 'व्यावर्त्तकत्व इति व्यावृत्तिबोधजनकज्ञानप्रकारकत्व इत्यर्थः, अतो न वैशिष्ट्यविषयतामात्रमादायातिव्याप्तिरित्यर्थः। नन्विदं यदि विशेषणत्वं तदा बुद्धिविषयो न स्यात् बुद्धेर्बुद्ध्यविषयतानियमादत आह, 'विशिष्टेति, 'ताद्रूप्यात्' काकवत्त्वाद्याकारत्वात्, 'लक्षणेति, तथापि गङ्गापदस्योपस्थापकं किन्तु तत्तद्बुद्ध्युपस्थापितमन्यदेव तथा स्यादि-

---

(१) अप्रशक्यसंस्थानादेरुपसंस्थानादितीति ख०।

स्थाप्योपलक्ष्यमुपस्थापयतीति लक्षणैव स्यात् । अन्यथा लक्षणोच्छेदः घटो नास्तीत्यत्रोपलक्षणस्य प्रतियोगिनोऽभावधीविषयत्वात् नियतोपलक्ष्याभावाच्च । नापि व्यावर्त्तकत्वे सति क्रियान्वयि विशेषणमन्यदुपलक्षणं । क्रियाहीने सुभगोऽयं दण्डी महाबाहुरित्यादौ[१] दण्डादेरविशेषणत्वापातात् परम्परयोपलक्षणेऽपि क्रियान्वयित्वाच्च ।

त्यस्य सुवचत्वादिति भावः । ननूपलक्षणे भवतु लक्षणैव कोदोष इत्यस्वरसादाह[२], 'घट इति, केवलविशेष्यावगाहिविशिष्टज्ञानासम्भवादिति भावः । ननु तत्रापि तदुपलक्षितविषयत्वमेवास्तामित्यत आह, 'नियतेति, वस्तुतो लक्षणापत्तिरेव दोषः । न चेष्टापत्तिः, शाब्दत्वमेवमिष्टापादनेऽपि प्रत्यक्षादौ तदतिरिक्तविषयत्वस्यानुक्तिसम्भवादिति । 'क्रियेति विशेष्यान्वयिक्रियेत्यर्थः । अत एव विशेष्येऽतिव्याप्तिवारणाय व्यावर्त्तकत्वे सतीति विशेषणमिति । ननु सुभगोऽयमित्यादावप्यस्ति क्रियान्वयित्वं यत्रान्यत् क्रियापदं नास्ति तत्रास्तिभवतिपदं प्रयोज्यमिति[३] वैयाकरणसिद्धान्तादित्यरुचेराह, 'परम्परयेति अवच्छेदकतयेत्यर्थः ।

---

(१) सुभगो हि महाबाहुर्दण्डीत्यादाविति ख॰ ।

(२) इत्यरुचेराहेति ख॰ ।

(३) अस्ति-भवतिपदप्रयोग इतीति ख॰ ।

अथातद्व्यावृत्तिर्वैशिष्ट्यं तथाच विशिष्टज्ञाने अतद्व्यावृत्तिर्विषयो न विशेषणमुपलक्षणं वा तथाच विशिष्टधीकारणज्ञानविषयत्वे सति प्रत्याय्यव्यावृत्तिसमानाधिकरणं विशेषणमिति। तन्न। नीलमुत्पलमित्यादावनीलानुल्लेखे अतद्व्यावृत्त्यनुल्लेखात् नीलञ्जानामीत्यनुव्यवसायविरोधात् अपोहापाताच्च।

'प्रत्याय्येति विशिष्टज्ञानविशेषणीभूतेत्यर्थः। अत एवातद्व्यावृत्तिवैशिष्ट्यमित्यादिग्रन्थमवतार्यैव लक्षणं निरस्तं। न च विशिष्टज्ञानकारणेत्यादिविशेषणं व्यर्थम्, गौरित्यादौ सास्नादेर्विशेषणत्ववारणार्थत्वात्। प्रकारस्य द्वेधेत्युपक्रमेणैव तत्तत्प्रतीतिविशेषणस्यैव लक्ष्यत्वात्। न च काकादेरपि प्रत्याय्यव्यावृत्तिसमानाधिकरणत्वादतिव्याप्तिः, समानाधिकरणत्वेन सामानाधिकरण्यनियमस्य विवक्षणात्। न च प्रतीयमाना देवदत्तगृहव्यावृत्तिसामानाधिकरण्यनियताः काकादयः, अकाकेऽपि गृहे तद्व्यावृत्तिसत्त्वादिति। असम्भवेन दूषयति, 'नीलमिति, प्रतियोग्यप्रतीत्या व्यावृत्तेर्विशिष्टज्ञानागोचरत्वादिति भावः। ननु व्यावृत्तित्वेन तत्तज्ज्ञाने प्रतियोगिज्ञानापेक्षा अन्यथा समवायस्यापि प्रतियोगिज्ञानापेक्षित्वेन समवायात्मनोऽपि वैशिष्ट्यस्य प्रमेयत्वेनापि अभानप्रसङ्गादित्यस्वरसादाह, 'नीलमिति। नन्वनुव्यवसायोऽप्यनीलव्यावृत्तं जानामीत्येवमाकार इत्यस्वरसादाह, 'अपोहेति, तथाच नीलप्रतीत्यभावे अनीलव्यावृत्तेरेव नीलत्वापत्तेरिति भावः।

अथ व्यावर्त्तकं साक्षात्सम्बद्धं नीलादि[1], परम्परासम्बद्धं गृहोपरि भ्रमत्काकादि, तत्र व्यावर्त्तनीयमधितिष्ठति, यदि साक्षादेव तद्विशेषणमतो विपरीतमन्यत्। दण्डी पुमानिति विशेषणमत्र दण्डः पुंसो न जातिरनुदण्ड-मसौ च तस्येति सम्बन्धिद्वयातिरिक्तसम्बन्धघटकाभावे सति सम्बन्ध एव साक्षात्सम्बन्धः। स च संयोग-समवाय-स्वरूपसम्बन्धसाधारणो ज्ञाने विषयस्याधिकरणे अभा-वस्य सम्बन्धिनि समवायस्यास्तीति तेषामपि विशेषण-

---

‘नीलादि’ नीलमश्वीत्यादौ। नन्वेवं साक्षात्सम्बद्धं विशेषण-मित्युक्तलक्षणं प्रतियोगिनि गतमतो निर्गलितमाह[2], ‘तच्चेति, ‘साक्षात्’ सम्बन्धिमध्ये असाक्षात्सम्बन्धेनाधेयं, ‘तद्विशेषणं’ इति, नातिव्याप्ति-रिति भावः[3]। ‘पुंस इति पुंसो विशेषणं दण्डः न तु दण्डत्व-जातिरित्यर्थः, ‘असौ अनुदण्डं’ दण्डे वर्त्तमाना जातिर्दण्डत्वमिति यावत्। ‘तस्य’ दण्डस्य, असत्साक्षात्सम्बन्धस्यापि यतः काकादे-रुपलक्षणत्वमेव न यदि ब्रूते तदाव्याप्त्यतिव्याप्ती लक्षणयोर्न वक्तुं शक्येते इति निःसन्दिग्धे ते दर्शयति, ‘गौरिति, गौरनित्यो गौः रूपवानित्युदाहरणद्वयं द्रष्टव्यं। एकोदाहरणत्वे अन्यतरानुपादानापत्ते-रिति मन्तव्यं। ‘लोहित इति, परम्परासम्बन्धेन लौहित्यादिप्रकारिका

---

(१) दण्डादीति क०।

(२) लक्षणार्थं निर्गलितार्थमाहेति ख०।

(३) नातिव्याप्तिरित्यर्थ इति ख०।

त्वमिति शिवादित्यमिश्राः। तन्न। गौरनित्योरूपवांश्चलति रूपवति रस इत्यादौ जाते रूपस्य च साक्षात्सम्बन्धेऽप्युपलक्षणत्वात्। लोहितः स्फटिक इत्यादौ परम्परासम्बन्धेऽपि लोहितत्वस्य विशेषणत्वात्। अथान्वयप्रतियोग्युपस्थापकतया अन्वितमुपलक्षणं, साक्षादन्वितं विशेषणं, काकादेः संस्थानाद्युपस्थापकतयोपयोगात् अतथात्वे दण्डादिवद्विशेषणत्वमेवेति चेत्। न। उपलक्षणपदस्य लाक्षणिकत्वापत्तेः, प्रतियोगिनोऽभावे धर्मान्तरानुपनयाच्च।

धीर्यथा प्रमा तथोक्तं। अन्यथा शुक्ति-रजतवदवच्छिन्नतायामस्यास्तुपदर्शनविरोधात्। 'प्रतियोग्युपस्थापकतया' तदुपस्थापकज्ञानविषयतया, अर्थस्य ग्राह्यस्यातथात्वात्। ननु काकपदं संस्थानोपस्थापकं न ब्रूमः अपि तु काकपदोपस्थाप्यः काक एव, तत्सम्बन्धश्च मतुपा बोधितः काकस्थारितस्य संस्थानविशेष इति तत्सिद्धान्ते नेदं दूषणं घटते इति दूषणान्तरमाह[१], 'प्रतियोगी'ति। यद्यपि प्रतियोगिनोऽभावग्राहकतया अभावस्य चान्वयप्रतियोगित्वात् अन्वयप्रतियोग्युपस्थापकतया चान्वितत्वेन नोपलक्षणत्वं[२] इत्यव्यापकं, न वा साक्षादन्वितत्वं

---

(१) इत्यस्वरसाद्दोषान्तरमाहेति ख०।
(२) नोपलक्षणलक्षणमिति ख०।

अथ व्यावृत्तिबुद्धिसमये विशेष्यसम्बद्धं व्यावर्त्तकं विशेषणं, तदानीं विशेष्यासम्बद्धं व्यावर्त्तकमुपलक्षणं । न च जटा यदा यत्रास्ति तदा तत्र उपलक्षणं अत एव तत्रैव तदेव सम्बन्धसमये विशेषणमसम्बन्धसमये उप-

---

विशेषणत्वं[1] अतिव्यापकं, तथापि विशेष्यस्यान्वयप्रतियोगिन उपस्थापकत्वं वाच्यम् इन्द्रियसंयोगादौ इन्द्रियस्य संयोगग्राहकस्याप्यनुपलक्षणत्वात् इत्यभिप्रायेणेयं अव्याप्तिर्बोध्या ।

'दण्ड्यासीदिति, स दण्डीत्यतीतदण्डस्मरणस्थलमुदाहरणीयम्, उदाहृते तु दण्डध्वंसवानयमित्यर्थपर्य्यवसानाद्दण्डस्याभावं प्रति उपलक्षणत्वमेव पुरुषं प्रति तु दण्डसम्बन्धो न भासते किन्तु तद्ध्वंसस्य हि सम्बन्धो भासते स च विशेषणमेवेति परेणाभिहिते दोषान्वयकतापातादिति। 'समानाधिकरणत्वेनेति साक्षात्सम्बन्धेन समानाधिकरणत्वमत्र लक्षणार्थः[2], तेन न पूर्व्वेण पौनरुक्त्यमिति।

'दण्डी पुरुष इति, अत्र[3] यद्यपि व्यावृत्तिः कचिदस्ति कचिन्नेति स्वरूपविशेष एव प्रयोजकः, स्वरूपद्वयमात्रस्य स्वरूपसम्बन्धत्वेऽतिप्रसङ्गात् स्वरूपविशेषस्य विशिष्टबुद्धिजनकत्वस्यानुगतेन रूपेणेति अत्यन्ताभावे[4] प्रतियोगिदेशान्यदेशत्ववत्तथापि

---

(१) विशेषणलक्षणमिति ख० ।

(२) लक्षणार्थो द्रष्टव्य इति ख० ।

(३) अत इति ख० ।

(४) संसर्गाभाव इति ख० ।

लक्षणमिति । तन्न । रूपवति घटे रस इत्यादौ रूपस्य विशेषणत्वप्रसङ्गात् । दण्ड्यासीदित्यादावतीते दण्डस्याविशेषणत्वापाताच्च[१] । एतेन यत्र यद्विशेष्यावच्छेदकधर्मेण व्यावृत्त्या वा समानाधिकरणत्वेन प्रतीयते तत्र तद्विशेषणमित्यपि प्रत्युक्तं ।

प्रतियोगितावच्छेदकाभाववत्त्वमेव व्यावृत्त्यधिकरणतावच्छेदकं इत्यभ्युपगमः अनभ्युपगमे अन्यथाभ्युपगमे वा कथितदोषात् तथाच दण्डवत्यदण्डव्यावृत्तिरस्ति इत्येव वस्तुस्थितिः वक्तुमुचिता तस्या एव चावच्छेदककल्पनार्हत्वात् । तथापि तत्सत्त्व एव किं प्रमाणं येन तदनुरोधादवच्छेदकत्वं दण्डादेः कल्पनीयमिति तत्स्थापनाय तथा प्रतीतिरुपन्यस्तेति न कश्चिद्दोषः[२] एवमग्रेऽपि । यद्यपि तदभाववत्यपि तत्सत्त्वात् इत्येव वक्तुमुचितं, तथापि तत्सत्त्वार्थमेव तत्प्रतीतिरिति वक्ष्यते । 'प्रत्याय्येति, तद्व्यावृत्त्यधिकरणत्वलाभाय, तेन यद्व्यावृत्त्यधिकरणतावच्छेदकं तदेव तत्र विशेषणमित्यर्थो लभ्यते । अन्यथा कथंचिद्विशेषणस्य यत्किञ्चिद्व्यावृत्त्यधिकरणतावच्छेदकत्वेऽपि यत्र यद्व्यावृत्त्यधिकरणतानवच्छेदकं तत्रापि तद्विशेषणतापत्तेः । न ह्युपलक्षणं व्यावृत्त्यधिकरणतावच्छेदकमेव न भवति, काकादेरपि अकाकव्यावृत्त्यधिकरणतावच्छेदकस्यायङ्काकवानित्यादौ विशेषणत्वादित्यर्थः ।

---

(१) दण्डविशिष्टव्यवहाराभावप्रसङ्गाच्चेति ख० ।
(२) कश्चिद्विरोध इति ख० ।

अथोच्यते। दण्डी पुरुष इतिज्ञानानन्तरं दण्डवत्यदण्डव्यावृत्तिरवगम्यत इति प्रत्याय्यव्यावृत्त्यधिकरणता पुरुषस्य दण्डेनावच्छिद्यते न पुरुषत्वेनातिव्याप्तेः। उपलक्षणे तु गृहस्थ-तापसादिनिष्ठप्रत्याय्यव्यावृत्त्यधिकरणता न काक-जटादिभिरवच्छिद्यते तदभाववत्यपि व्यावृत्तिप्रतीतेः, किन्तु संस्थानविशेषवत्त्वादिना।

'एवञ्चेति, न च प्रमेयत्वादेः पूर्व्वप्रतीकेन वारणाद्व्यावर्त्तकपदव्यर्थता, अर्थगर्भस्य पूर्व्वप्रतीकस्य तदधिकरणमात्रवृत्तौदन्त्वादौ गतत्वात्, तदवच्छेदकत्वं संयोगादाविव तेन समं स्वरूपसम्बन्धविशेषः, स चानतिप्रसक्तधर्म्ममात्रे। न चेदन्त्वमपि तद्व्यावर्त्तकमेकमेव, तेन रूपेणोपस्थितात्तद्दण्डव्यावृत्त्यप्रतीतेरयमनयन्न भवतीत्यादाविदग्धत्वेन लक्षणगमनं नानिष्टम् संग्राह्यत्वादत एव प्रतियोगी नाभावविशेषणं प्रत्याय्यव्यावृत्तेरभावनिष्ठायास्तदसमानाधिकरणत्वेन प्रतियोग्यनवच्छेद्यत्वात् उक्तयुक्त्या स्वानधिकरणप्रतियोगिकव्यावृत्तेरेव स्वावच्छेद्यत्वेन काक-जटादेरप्यकाकाजटाव्यावृत्तिबोधे विशेषणत्वात् अदेवदत्तव्यावृत्तेस्तूक्तयुक्त्या तदनवच्छेद्यत्वेनाप्रसङ्गादिति सर्व्वं सुस्थम्। व्यावृत्तिरन्योन्याभावो नाभावे तत्र स्वरूपभेदाभ्युपगमादित्यभावे नोक्तरूपं विशेषणं किन्तूपलक्षणमेव प्रतियोग्यादीत्यपि वदन्ति। वस्तुतस्तु प्रत्याय्यव्यावृत्त्यधिकरणतावच्छेदकत्वग्रहे यथा व्याप्यवच्छेदकसंयोगावच्छेदकत्वग्रहो व्याप्तिसंयोगग्राहकतया विषयत्वानियतस्तथा व्यावृत्तिविषयत्वानियत इति यत्र तथावच्छेदकत्वग्रहस्तत्र व्यावृत्त्यबोध-

एवञ्च प्रत्याय्यव्यावृत्त्यधिकरणतावच्छेदकत्वे सति व्यावर्त्तकं विशेषणं तदन्यव्यावर्त्तकमुपलक्षणं व्यावृत्त्युल्लेखानन्तरमेव विशेषणत्वबुद्धिः। तदाहुराचार्य्याः "सदसद्वा समानाधिकरणं व्यवच्छेदकं विशेषणं व्यधिकरणमुपलक्षणम्" इति। अस्यार्थः। स्वाधिकरणमात्रवृत्तिव्यावृत्तिबोधकत्वं स्वावच्छिन्नाधिकरणताक-

---

कालेऽपि विशेषणत्वबुद्धिर्म्मा प्रसाङ्क्षीदिति व्यावर्त्तकत्वं विशेषणत्वं, अत एवाह, 'व्यावृत्त्युल्लेखानन्तरमेव विशेषणत्वबुद्धिरिति। न चावच्छेदकाग्रहे अवच्छेद्याग्रह इति सत्यं न त्ववच्छेदकत्वग्रहे अननुसंहितोपाधेरित्यादेरपीति वाच्यम्। अदण्डव्यावृत्त्यधिकरणतावच्छेदको दण्ड इति शब्दादवगमेऽपि तद्वृत्त्यदण्डव्यावृत्तेरप्रतीतेः सर्व्वसिद्धत्वादिन्द्रियासन्निकर्षादिना प्रत्यक्षसामग्र्यभावात् तस्मादुक्तमेव विशेषणपदप्रवृत्तिनिमित्तं, विशिष्टधीविषयस्तु विशेषणत्वमेव न, यदि विषयस्तदा वैशिष्ट्यप्रतियोगित्वरूपं तदित्यवधेयम्। नन्वेवं व्यावर्त्तकमित्येवास्तु, प्रतियोग्यवृत्तिधर्म्मज्ञानस्य भेदधीहेतुतया प्रतियोगितावच्छेदकभावस्यैव व्यावर्त्तकत्वं न तु काकादेरप्यदेवदत्तगृहव्यावृत्तिबोधकत्वं मानाभावात् स्वयमेव व्यभिचारस्य प्रदर्शनाच्चेति चेत्। न। व्यावृत्तिधीप्रयोजकस्यैव व्यावर्त्तकत्वेनोक्तत्वात्। न हि दण्डधीरपि साक्षाद् दण्डव्यावृत्तिबोधे कारणं। अधिकरणज्ञानानुपलब्ध्यादितद्धीसामग्रीसत्त्वे प्रतियोग्यवृत्तिधर्म्मग्रहं विना तद्धीविलम्बाभावात् अपि तु प्रतियोगितावच्छेदकानुपलम्भसम्पादकतया पर-

व्यावृत्तिबोधकत्वं स्वानधिकरणाधिकरणकव्यावृत्त्यबोधकत्वे सति व्यावृत्तिबोधकत्वं वेति, उपलक्षणन्तु स्वानधिकरणेऽपि व्यावृत्तिं बोधयति। अथ वा विवक्षितान्वयप्रतियोगितावच्छेदकं विशेषणं दण्डिनमानयेत्यादौ दण्डस्तथा, तदनवच्छेदकं उपलक्षणं, काकेन देव

न्यथा दण्डवत्त्वेनोपलम्भे अदण्डवत्त्वोपलम्भासम्भवात्[१]। तथाच तथा व्यावर्त्तकत्वमुपलक्षणस्यापीति सुष्ठूक्तम् विशेषणं विशेषणपरिचायकत्वात्तस्य। अत एव व्यावर्त्तकत्वविशेषे किञ्चित्स्वाकालेन तथा किञ्चित्तदापीति कथमिति पूर्व्वपक्षः, एकमात्यन्तायोगव्यवच्छेदो धर्म्मस्य विषयः अपरत्वायोगव्यवच्छेदः[२] इति समाधानमपि ज्ञेयम्। अयोगव्यवच्छेदादेर्व्विशिष्टज्ञानागोचरत्वात्। एतेन स्वानाधारव्यावृत्तिबोधकत्वं स्वाधारवृत्तिप्रतियोगितावच्छेदकाभावत्वञ्च विशेषणत्वं तदन्यदुपलक्षणत्वञ्चेत्यपि द्रष्टव्यम्। 'तदिति तादृशावच्छेदकत्वशून्यमित्यर्थः। अवच्छेदकत्वमुक्तमेवेति नातिप्रसङ्गस्तन्नियतत्वमवच्छेदकत्वमादायेति भावः। स्वानधिकरणेति स्वानधिकरणनिष्ठव्यावृत्तिबोधकतावच्छेदकतावच्छेदकधर्म्मशून्यत्वे सतीत्यर्थः। तदवच्छेदकत्वन्तु प्रत्याय्यव्यावृत्तिप्रतियोगितावच्छेदकविरहरूपत्वं तेन गुरुत्ववति रस-

---

(१) अदण्डत्वेनोपलम्भासम्भवादिति ख०।

(२) एकत्रायोगव्यवच्छेदो धर्म्मस्य विषयोऽन्यत्रात्यन्तायोगव्यवच्छेद-इति ख०।

दत्तस्य गृहा इत्यादौ काको न गृहस्य देवदत्तान्वय-
प्रतियोगितावच्छेदकः तद्विरहदशायामपि देवदत्तान्व-
यावगमात्, किन्तु गृहविशेष एव उपलक्षणपरिचितः।
अत एवान्वयाप्रतियोगित्वेऽपि नोपलक्षणवैयर्थ्यं। यद्वा
यदन्वितत्तया ज्ञात एव विशेष्ये तात्पर्य्यविषयेतरान्वयधी-
स्तद्यवच्छेदकं विशेषणं अनेवम्भूतं तदुपलक्षणं उपल-
क्षणानच्छिन्नेऽप्युपलक्ष्ये तात्पर्यविषयीभूतान्वयबोधात्,

इत्यादौ विशेषणसमनियते उपलक्षणे न प्रसङ्ग इति भावः। नन्व-
दण्डरूपादौ विधेयान्वयनियमेन विशेषणत्वविचारः, प्रकृतलक्षित-
विशेषणत्वन्तु कोपयुज्यत इति तत्प्रयोजकं सन्दर्भविशेषणत्वमाह, 'अथ-
वेति, विवक्षितत्वाविशेषणे पुरुषभागान्वयतात्पर्य्यपरिचायकतयोपा-
त्तदण्डादिकेऽपि वाक्ये दण्डादेर्विशेषणत्वापातः। त्रिशेषणे च
तादृशानयनस्य दण्डाभावेऽपि सम्भवान्नातिव्याप्तिः। तत्सहितान-
यनविवक्षायान्तु न व्यभिचार एवेति भवत्यवच्छेदकत्वमिति भावः।
'किञ्चिति, गृहस्य विशेषणमुक्तृणत्वादि, न तु धर्म्म्यैव तस्य व्यावर्त्त्य-
त्वात् तु व्यावर्त्तकत्वात्। ननु व्यावृत्त्यधिकरणतावच्छेदकत्वं दण्डस्य
सम्भवति व्यावृत्तेः स्वरूपसम्बन्धात् आनयनस्य तु समवायादिः सम्बन्ध-
इति न तत्र दण्डादेः पूर्व्वोक्तमवच्छेदकत्वं अतो ज्ञानगर्भं तन्मनसिकृत्य
लक्षणान्तरमाह, 'यदन्वितेति, 'प्रतियोग्यभावबुद्धिविषय इति, 'मत-
इति, उपनीत इन्द्रियासन्निकर्षात् विशिष्टधीविषय इति प्राचीनमते

अयमेव कार्य्यान्वयि विशेषणं तदनन्वय्युपलक्षणमित्य-स्यार्थः, न तु तात्पर्य्यविषयीभूतविशेष्यान्वयबोधविष-यत्वं विशिष्टज्ञानविषयत्वं वा, प्रतियोग्यभावबुद्धिवि-षय इति मते तदभावात्। यद्वा विशेष्यान्वयिना यस्या-वश्यमन्वयस्तदवच्छेदकं विशेषणं तदन्यदुपलक्षणमिति तथोपलक्ष्यविशेष्यमात्रान्वयात् यद्व्यावर्त्तकं विशेष्या-

---

नेयमतिव्याप्तिरिति मतभेदाश्रयणमिति भावः। ननु यदन्वितत्वे-त्याद्यनुद्देश्यतावच्छिन्नव्यावृत्तौ गतम् इतरव्यवच्छिन्न एवानयनाद्यन्व-यात्, न च सा न व्यावर्त्तिकेति, अदण्डान्योन्याभाववानयमिति बुद्धौ व्यावृत्तेरेव विशेषणत्वेन तस्या एव व्यावर्त्तकत्वात् अदण्डव्यावृत्ति-शून्यव्यावृत्तेस्तदेकविषयत्वादित्यरुचेराह, 'यद्वेति, अत्राप्यवश्यमित्य-धिकं मत्वा लक्षणान्तरमाह, 'यद्वेति, 'तात्पर्य्येत्यादि, धर्म्मपदञ्च विशेष्य एवातिव्याप्तिवारणाय। न चाव्यावर्त्तकमेयत्वाद्यतिव्याप्तिः, उक्तविशेषणत्वस्य तत्रेष्टत्वात्। न हि प्रमेयत्वविशिष्टं प्रमेयपदशक्य-मित्यत्र प्रमेयत्वं न विशेषणं प्रमेयत्वस्याशक्यतापत्तेरित्यन्यत्र तद्वारणे-ऽप्यत्र सङ्ग्राह्यत्वमेवेति। 'अलं विस्तरेणेति, न हि लौकिकविचारे विशेषणोपलक्षणविचारोऽर्थवान्, वेदार्थविचारे शास्त्रान्तरे तद्विचारो घटत इति शिष्यजिज्ञासायां याचितकन्यायेनेदं विवेचितं न त्वेतद्वि-चारव्यावृत्त्यैव कर्त्तव्यो विचारो व्यासञ्जनीयो भवतीति भावः। ननु सर्व्वलक्षणेन दण्डादि सङ्गृह्यते तत्रासङ्गतं दण्डिनोऽप्यदण्डतया भेदा-

न्वयिनान्वीयते तद्विशेषणं तदन्यदुपलक्षणमिति वा । यद्वा तात्पर्य्यविषयान्वयप्रतियोगी उद्देश्यान्वयप्रतियोगी वा धर्मो विशेषणन्तदन्यदुपलक्षणमित्यलं विस्तरेण ।

इति श्रीगङ्गेशोपाध्यायविरचिते तत्त्वचिन्तामणौ प्रत्यक्षखण्डे निर्व्विकल्पकवादः ।

भेदानङ्गीकारे अतद्व्यावृत्तेः तत्त्वाभावेन तस्यैव तद्बोधकत्वादिति चेत् सत्यं, दण्डात्यन्ताभाववतोऽन्यस्माद्व्यावृत्तेस्तेन बोधनादत एवासत्यपि दण्डे पाकरक्ते श्याम इतिधीवत् दण्डीतिधीर्य्यथार्था अदण्डिव्यावर्त्तिका च पाकरक्ते श्यामबुद्धेरप्येवमेवान्यव्यावर्त्तकतया विशेषणत्वमिति ॥

इति महामहोपाध्याय-पक्षधरमिश्र-श्रीजयदेवविरचिते तत्त्वचिन्तामण्यालोके निर्व्विकल्पकवादालोकः ॥

समाप्तः प्रत्यक्षपरिच्छेदालोकः ।

समाप्तश्च प्रथमखण्डालोकः ।

अथ सविकल्पकवादः ।

सविकल्पकञ्च[१] विशिष्टज्ञानं यथा गौरयमिति, तच्च सामान्यादीनां परमार्थसत्त्वेनार्थजत्वादिन्द्रियजत्वाच्च प्रत्यक्षं क्वचित् संस्कारसहकारिवशेन तत्ताविशिष्टस्येदन्ताविशिष्टाभेदोल्लेख्यैन्द्रियकोविकल्पः । नन्वेककार्य्यसहकारित्वमन्यच्च प्रत्यभिज्ञानन्तु नैकं ज्ञानं तदंशे पारोक्ष्यस्येदमंशे चापारोक्ष्यास्यानुभवेन विरुद्धधर्म्मसंसर्गात् । न चेदं यथार्थं, अनेकदेश-कालसम्बन्धस्यैकत्र बाधात् । एककालादिसंसर्ग-तदभावव्यवच्छेदवत् तदविनाभूतकालान्तरादिसम्बन्धव्यवच्छेदात्, तदयथार्थत्वे वहु विप्लवेतेति चेत् । न । पारोक्ष्यापारोक्ष्ययोरिच्छासिद्धेः इन्द्रियजन्यत्वेनापरोक्षत्वनियमात्, तत्तांशस्य च स्मृत्युपनीतत्वात् इन्द्रियसम्बद्धविशेषणताप्रत्यासत्तेः । न चैककालसम्बन्धः कालान्तरसम्बन्धाभावाविनाभूतः, एकस्मिन्नानादिक्सम्बन्धस्य ज्ञाने अनेकविषयत्वस्य च व्याघातापत्तेः साक्षात्करोमीत्यनुव्यवसाये बाधकाभा-

(१) सविकल्पकवादस्य स्वप्रकाशत्वादालोकक्षता पुनरालोकेन न प्रकाशितत्वमिति ।

वाच्च। ननु केयन्तत्ता न तावदतीतसमयसम्बन्धः, अनागतगोचरस्मृति-प्रत्यभिज्ञयोस्तत्तोल्लेखात् प्रत्यक्षानुभूयमानघटादौ[१] अतीतसमयावच्छेदानुमाने तत्ताधी-व्यपदेशयोरभावात्। अतीतसमयसम्बन्धावगमेऽपि सोऽयं न वेति संशयात् स नायमिति विपर्य्ययात् तदभावावगमेऽपि सोऽयमिति प्रतीतेः अतीतसमयविशिष्टः स इति सद्दप्रयोगात् काले तदभावाच्च। एतेन ज्ञातधर्मान्तरवैशिष्ट्यन्तत्तेति निरस्तम्। न च तद्वृत्ति गुणादिकमेव तत्ता, तदवगमेऽपि तदनवगमात् तदनवगमेऽपि तदवगमाच्च। नाप्यतीतज्ञानवैशिष्ट्यं, परेण ज्ञात इति ज्ञानेऽपि स इति प्रयोगाभावात्। नाप्येतज्जन्मातीतस्वज्ञानवैशिष्ट्यं, तदवगमेऽपि तत्तासंशय-विपर्य्ययदर्शनात् अतीतज्ञानविशिष्टः स इति सद्दप्रयोगात् अतीतानुभवविषयत्वस्यानुभवाविषयत्वेन स्मृत्या तदुल्लेखानुपपत्तेश्च।

यत्त्वतीतानुभवविषयत्वन्तत्ता तच्चानुभवाविषयत्वेन यदा ज्ञानान्तरेण गृह्यते तदा स घट इति स्मरणं नोचेत् प्रमुष्टतत्ताकं[२] घटइति। तन्न। अतीतानु-

(१) प्रत्यक्षानुभूतघटादाविति ख०।

(२) प्रमुष्टतत्तांशमिति ख०।

भवविषयत्वस्यानुमितौ भानेऽपि स इति धी-व्यपदेश-
योरभावात्। अतीतानुभवविषयत्वनिश्चयेऽपि तत्ता-
संशय-विपर्य्ययदर्शनात् सहप्रयोगानुपपत्तेः ज्ञाना-
न्तरेणातीतानुभवविषयत्वग्रहे तत्तोल्लेखापत्तेश्च। अ-
थातीतधर्म्मवैशिष्ट्यं तत्ता स धर्म्मः क्वचित् समयः
क्वचित् ज्ञानादिः। न चातीतधर्म्मविशिष्टः स इति
सहप्रयोगानुपपत्तिः, धर्म्मविशेषमादाय तदुपपत्तेस्त-
दप्रतीतावपि स इति प्रतीतिरसिद्धैव। न चातीतधर्म्म-
विशिष्टप्रतीतावपि स न वेति संशयात् स नाय-
मिति विपर्य्ययाच्च नैवमिति वाच्यं। निश्चितधर्मेतर-
धर्म्मविशेषविषयत्वेन तयोरुपपत्तेरिति चेत्। मैवम्। यदि
वस्तुगत्या योऽतीतोधर्म्मस्तद्वैशिष्ट्यन्तत्ता तदानुभवेऽपि
तद्विषयत्वात्तत्तोल्लेखापत्तिः। नाप्यतीतत्वेन यो भासते
धर्म्मस्तद्वैशिष्ट्यं, भासमानधर्म्मस्यातीतत्वेनानुभवावि-
षयत्वात् प्रत्युत वर्त्तमानत्वेनानुभवात् स्मृतौ तदु-
ल्लेखानुपपत्तेश्च। न चानुभवानन्तरं यदा ज्ञानान्तरेणा-
तीतधर्म्मवैशिष्ट्यभानन्तदा स्मृतौ तत्तोल्लेखो नान्यदेति
वाच्यं। अतीतधर्म्मस्यानुमितौ(१) तत्तोल्लेखापत्तेः। इद-

(१) अतीतधर्म्मवैशिष्ट्यस्यानुमितावित्ति ख०।

न्तापि न तन्मात्रवृत्ति गुणादिकं अनुमानादिना तदवगमेऽपि अयमितिव्यपदेशाभावात्। प्रत्यक्षेण तदवगमे अयमिति व्यपदेश इति चेत्। न। वाच्यस्य प्रमाणगोचरतया व्यपदेशस्य नियन्तुमशक्य-त्वात्। गुणादावपि तन्निर्वचने अननुगमात्। न चैतद्व्य-क्त्याश्रयत्वं, इदमेतदोः पर्य्यायत्वात्। नापि प्रत्यक्षप्रमा-नगोचरत्वं, अचाक्षुषत्वापत्तेः अतीते तदनुमानेऽय-मितिबुद्धिव्यवदेशाभावात् स्मृत्यापि तदुल्लेखापत्तेश्च।

अत्र केचिदाहुः। तत्तेदन्ते स्मृत्यनुभवभासिन्यौ अखण्डे एवोपाधी कृतधर्म्मातिरेकिणौ, एवञ्चेदन्ता-संस्कारेणेदन्तैव तत्तया स्मर्य्यते। न च तत्तायाः क्वचिदनारोपे कथमारोप इति वाच्यं। प्रत्यभिज्ञाया-न्तत्तांशे यथार्थत्वात्। इदन्तानुल्लेख्यनुभवप्रभवस्मरणे धर्म्मान्तरमेव तत्तया भासते। अत एवायं घट इति न स्मरणमतः सर्वा स्मृतिरयथार्था अयथार्थानुभवा च। हरि-हराद्यनुचिन्तनञ्च कविकाव्यमूलज्ञानवन्म-नोरथज्ञानवच्च साकाङ्क्षपदार्थज्ञानप्रभवमनुभवरूपमे-वेति। तन्न। स्मृतेः पूर्वमिदन्तोपस्थितिं विना तत्र तत्तारोपासम्भवात्। किञ्च तत्तांशेऽननुभूतगोचरत्वेन स्मृतेः संस्कारसीमालङ्घने इदन्ता तत्तया स्मर्य्यत इत्यत्र

मानाभावात्। घट एव तत्तया स्मर्य्यते इत्यस्तु लाघवादिति[१]।

अत्रोच्यते। अनुभवे कालो धर्म्मान्तरं वा यो वर्त्तमानत्वेन विषयः स एव स्मरणस्य, अनुभव-स्मरणयोरेकविषयत्वेऽपि स्मरणे तत्र तच्छब्दप्रयोगः संस्कारजन्यज्ञानस्यैव तच्छब्दप्रयोगहेतुत्वात्। अत एव प्रत्यभिज्ञाने तत्र तच्छब्दप्रयोगः प्रत्यक्षानुभवे तत्रैव इदम्शब्दप्रयोगः, न तु विषयकृतोऽनुभव-स्मरणयोर्विशेषः। अत एवायं घट इत्यनुभवादयं घट इति न स्मरणं, स घट इति स्मरणकारणं स घट इति नानुभवः। यद्वा अयं घट इत्यत्र यद्धर्म्मवैशिष्ट्यं भासते तस्यातीतत्वं तत्ता तद्वैशिष्ट्यमननुभूतमपि स्मृतिविषयः। इदन्ताविशिष्टगोचरसंस्कारात् कथन्तत्तास्मृतिरिति चेत्। न। स घट इति स्मृतिं प्रत्यनुभवस्य हेतुत्वनिर्वाहकतया संस्कारस्य तथैव कल्पनात् अयं घट इति स्मृतेः स घट इत्यनुभवस्यादर्शनाच्च। समानविषयत्वेन स्मृतेरयं घट इति स्मृतिर्न स घट इति नानुभवश्च स्यात्। न चैवं स्मृतिरननुभूततत्तांशे अनुभवः स्यात्, संस्कारासाधारणकारणकत्वेन स्मृतित्वात्। सहप्रयोगश्च धर्म्मवि-

(१) इत्याहुस्तन्न लाघवादितीति ख०।

शेषमादाय प्रतिविधेयः। अत एव संस्कारहेत्वनुभव-प्रामाण्यपारतन्त्र्येण यथार्थत्वेऽपि स्मृतिरप्रमेति सर्व-तन्त्रसिद्धान्तः। यद्वा नेयं यथार्था तथाहि स्मृतिः स्वबि-षयवर्त्तमानत्वविषया अतीतानागतागोचरप्रतीतित्वात् प्रत्यभिज्ञावत्। प्रतीतित्वाद्वा घटोऽस्तीति प्रतीतिवत्। प्रतीतेः समयविशेषविषयत्वनियमात्। ज्ञानसामग्री-महिम्ना चाननुभूतेऽपि समयांशे स्मृतिर्न तत्र संस्कार-व्यापारोऽन्यथासिद्धत्वात्। अत एव पाकरक्ते श्यामो-ऽयमितिधियोऽयथार्थत्वव्यवहारः लौकिकानां श्याम-त्वस्य वर्त्तमानत्वेनावगमात्। एतेन श्यामधीस्तत्र यथा-र्थैव घटे कदाचित्तत्सत्त्वात् इदानीमयं श्याम इतिप्रती-तेराकार एव नेत्यपास्तं। अत एवातीतानागतवह्न्यगो-चरत्वे विद्यमानधूमेन पर्व्वते वह्निरित्यनुमितेर्वर्त्तमा-नवह्निविषयत्वादिदानीं वह्निनिश्चयेन वह्न्यर्थिप्रवृत्तिः अन्यथेदानीं तत्सन्देहे प्रवृत्तिर्न स्यात्। यदा धूमस्तदा वह्निरिति व्याप्तावपि तदज्ञानदशायां प्रवृत्तेरन्यथानु-पपत्तेः। यद्वा स घट इतिस्मृतौ तत्ताविशिष्टस्य वर्त्त-मानता भासते संस्कारस्य वर्त्तमानज्ञानसामग्रीसहि-तस्यैव हेतुत्वात् सोऽयमिदानीमित्यादौ तथा कल्पनात् गेहे स घट इति स्मरणान्निःशङ्कप्रवृत्तेश्च। अन्यथा